AMERICAN SOCIETY
AND POLITICS

Institutional, Historical, and Theoretical Perspectives

AMERICAN SOCIETY AND POLITICS

Institutional, Historical, and Theoretical Perspectives

A READER EDITED BY

Theda Skocpol and John L. Campbell

Harvard University

CONSULTING EDITOR
Craig Calhoun
University of North Carolina at Chapel Hill

McGraw-Hill, Inc.
New York St. Louis San Francisco Auckland Bogotá
Caracas Lisbon London Madrid Mexico City Milan
Montreal New Delhi San Juan Singapore
Sydney Tokyo Toronto

This book was set in Times Roman by Better Graphics, Inc.
The editors were Jill S. Gordon and Katherine Blake;
the production supervisor was Paula Keller.
The cover was designed by John Hite.
Project supervision was done by Hockett Editorial Service.
R. R. Donnelley & Sons Company was printer and binder.

AMERICAN SOCIETY AND POLITICS

Institutional, Historical, and Theoretical Perspectives

This book is printed on acid-free paper.

2 3 4 5 6 7 8 9 0   DOC/DOC   9 9 8 7 6 5

ISBN 0-07-057915-6

Library of Congress Cataloging-in-Publication Data

American society and politics: institutional, historical, and
    theoretical perspectives   a reader / edited by Theda Skocpol and
    John L. Campbell.—1st ed.
        p.   cm.
    Includes bibliographical references.
    ISBN 0-07-057915-6
    1. United States—Social policy.   2. United States—Politics and
government—1980-   3. United States—Social conditions—1980-
I. Skocpol, Theda.   II. Campbell, John L.
HN57.A596   1995
306.2'0973—dc20   94-21293

ABOUT THE EDITORS

THEDA SKOCPOL currently teaches at Harvard University; she was previously Professor of Sociology and Political Science at the University of Chicago. Her first book, *States and Social Revolutions: A Comparative Analysis of France, Russia, and China* (Cambridge University Press, 1979), won the 1979 C. Wright Mills Award and the 1980 American Sociological Association Award for a Distinguished Contribution to Scholarship. Skocpol has served as the co-chair of the States and Social Structures Committee, originally organized under the auspices of the Social Science Research Council and now located at the Russell Sage Foundation. For the past decade, Skocpol has been doing research on U.S. politics and public policies in comparative and historical perspective. In 1988, she published a co-edited collection on *The Politics of Social Policy in the United States* (Princeton University Press). Skocpol was a founding member and the 1991–92 president of the Politics and History Section of the American Political Science Association. Her latest book is *Protecting Soldiers and Mothers: The Political Origins of Social Policy in the United States*, published in 1992 by the Belknap Press of Harvard University Press. This book has recently received five scholarly awards: the J. David Greenstone Award of the Politics and History Section of the American Political Science Association; the Best Book Award of the Political Sociology Section of the American Sociological Association; the 1993 Woodrow Wilson Foundation Award of the American Political Science Association, given annually for "the best book published in the United States during the prior year on government, politics or international affairs"; the 1993 Allan Sharlin Memorial Award of the Social Science History Association; and the 1993 Ralph Waldo Emerson Award of Phi

Beta Kappa, given to honor a comprehensive study that contributes significantly to "historical, philosophical, or religious interpretations of the human condition."

JOHN L. CAMPBELL is the John and Ruth Hazel Associate Professor of Social Science in the Department of Sociology at Harvard University. He taught previously at Washington State University and the University of Wisconsin-Parkside. He received his Ph.D in Sociology from the University of Wisconsin-Madison. Campbell is author of *Collapse of an Industry: Nuclear Power and the Contradictions of U.S. Policy* (Cornell University Press, 1988), which examines how political and economic institutions affected policy-making and industrial performance in the U.S., French, Swedish, and West German commercial nuclear energy industries. He is also co-editor of *Governance of the American Economy* (Cambridge University Press, 1991), an historical analysis of the development of economic institutions in the United States. In addition, he has published articles on institutional political economy, property rights, and the transformations in postcommunist Europe. He is currently studying the political economy of tax policy in the United States and fiscal reform in postcommunist societies.

CONTENTS

INTRODUCTION: WHAT THIS READER DOES

American Society and Politics is an edited collection of readings that offers a unique combination of comparative, historical, and theoretical perspectives on U.S. political institutions and public policy-making. It also examines the social groups and movements that have participated in American national politics from the nineteenth century to the present. Cutting across disciplinary boundaries, this volume brings together important articles by prominent political scientists, political sociologists, and some historians. Articles are arranged into four parts:

1. Thinking about Politics in the United States and Beyond
2. The Development of the National Polity
3. Contemporary Movements for Social and Political Change
4. The Politics of Public Policy-Making

American Society and Politics can be used as the basis for an entire, semester-long course; or it can be used as a supplementary text in a wide array of college or university courses for advanced undergraduates or entry-level graduate students. The editors, Theda Skocpol and John L. Campbell, have prepared thoughtful essays to introduce each group of readings in the volume. These introductory essays describe prominent features of U.S. political development, social movements, and contemporary patterns of politics. They also alert students to the issues and debates found in each set of articles, and are further intended to suggest additional topics for discussion and investigation by teachers and students alike. At a number of relevant points in the volume, convenient lists of "dates to remember" also appear, to help students grasp the chronological sequences of important events in American politics.

Part 1 of *American Society and Politics* introduces students to ongoing theoretical debates about the nature and roots of political power, about the interface of business and the capitalist economy with the U.S. state, and about institutions and the goals of political actors. The selections are clearly written discussions of sharply contrasting theoretical and analytical perspectives, including pluralism, neo-Marxist theories, institutional approaches, and public choice (or rational choice) theory. Each author illustrates his or her arguments with references to U.S. politics, and many offer methodological suggestions about how to explore hypotheses through empirical research. The theoretical perspectives introduced in this part reappear in later sections of the Reader.

Part 2 includes major statements about the historical roots of U.S. political institutions, and about both regularities and change in those institutions and in patterns of social participation in politics from the origins of the nation onward. Students gain an overview of what makes U.S. administrative, representative, and electoral arrangements internationally distinctive, and how they have changed over time. They also have the opportunity to consider which social groups have gained political influence in the United States, and when and how. The social groups discussed in Part 2 include industrial wage earners, urban ethnic groups, business groups, and those involved in the women's movements of the late nineteenth and early twentieth centuries. (Other parts of the Reader include further readings about business in U.S. political history and about contemporary liberation movements of African-Americans and women.)

Part 3 of *American Society and Politics* offers a comprehensive introduction to the study of movements for social and political change, bringing together theoretical statements and vivid contemporary examples. The first section (Chapter 6), on perspectives includes clear statements of resource mobilization theory, rational choice theory, cultural identity theory, and analyses that focus on the impact of "political opportunity structures" on the development of social movements. By reading these selections along with the introductory essay, students can gain a comprehensive overview of current social–scientific debates about the causes and course of social movements. Students can then use these theoretical tools to think about the black and women's liberation movements covered in the next two sections of Part 3, Chapters 7 and 8. These sections focus, respectively, on the civil rights and black power movements and their reverberations in U.S. politics from the 1960s to the 1990s; and on the feminist movement of the 1960s and 1970s and the antifeminist efforts that have arisen to challenge such feminist goals as freely available abortion and passage of the Equal Rights Amendment to the U.S. Constitution. Both sections encourage students to analyze how the black and women's movements grew out of long-term societal transformations, and to consider how various movements and countermovements have fared in relation to U.S. governmental institutions and electoral politics.

Part 4, finally, shows students how insights gained form the previous parts of the Reader can be used to understand what happens—and does not happen—in major areas of national public policy-making in the United States. Some readings illuminate the institutional contexts within which U.S. policies have been made and remade historically, comparing American taxation and social programs with those of other democratic–industrial nations. Other readings offer perspectives on current politics and on contemporary public policy choices. Students are encouraged to draw upon the volume as a whole to illuminate such current issues as the politics of health care and welfare reform, the strategic options available to political leaders during the 1990s, and the challenges faced by the United States in a world of ever-intensifying international economic competition.

ACKNOWLEDGMENTS

During the course of preparing this Reader, the editors benefitted from the suggestions and comments of many colleagues, in addition to those of the reviewers. Because of constraints of space especially, they could not always take the excellent advice they were given. But they are very grateful to all those who took time to comment, among them, Ronald Aminzade, Brian Balogh, Craig Calhoun, Christopher Howard, Jane Mansbridge, Gary Marks, Stephen Skowronek, and William G. Roy.

McGraw-Hill and the editors would like to thank the following reviewers for their many helpful comments and suggestions: Alan Brinkley, Columbia University; Craig Jenkins, Ohio State University; Gwen Moore, State University of New York–Albany; Jill Quadagno, Florida State University; and Gretchen Ritter, University of Texas–Austin.

AMERICAN SOCIETY AND POLITICS

Institutional, Historical, and Theoretical Perspectives

PART ONE

THINKING ABOUT POLITICS IN THE UNITED STATES AND BEYOND

Americans live in a political system that is based on the democratic principles of majority rule and government "by the people." Yet most Americans recognize that politics—the art of discussing civic concerns and influencing government policy—is far more complicated. Indeed, people in the United States increasingly feel that government has become unresponsive to their needs, and suspect that some Americans have far more political clout than do others (Teixeira, 1992, p. 32). They may be right, at least to the extent that policies emanating from Washington do not always reflect those that are favored by the public at large (Ferguson & Rogers, 1986). But why is this the case?

Sociologists and political scientists have spent a great deal of time studying how politics operates in the United States, as well as in other industrial democracies. Although there have been profound disagreements among them, most scholars agree that in order to understand politics, we must have a clear idea about what political power is, how it operates, which political actors (including individuals, groups, and organizations) tend to enjoy more power than others, and why these actors exercise their power as they do.

After World War II, many social scientists believed that U.S. politics was becoming increasingly open to a wide variety of groups, and that political power was becoming more diffuse as a result. They argued that, in an increasingly "pluralist system," no one social class or group of political actors could dominate politics at the expense of others. Instead, many groups enjoyed influence, depending on the resources at their disposal and the efficiency and cleverness with which they used them. Pluralist theorists, moreover, viewed the state as a neutral arena in which the conflicts between groups are played out and where policymakers, bureaucrats, and other state actors simply craft policy in response to the balance of interest group pressures. Some proponents of this "liberal" view of politics went so far as to argue that as societies industrialized and, in turn, as the opportunities for social mobility increased, politics in all the industrial democracies would converge toward the pluralist ideal (Goldthorpe, 1984).

Of course, there were critics who maintained that political power was concentrated in the hands of small groups of elites who controlled the large bureaucracies that had become so prevalent in American society, such as business corporations, the military, and the national government (Galbraith, 1967; Mills, 1956). These theorists agreed that the state was basically a neutral ensemble of organizations and procedures, but argued that elites often used it to advance their own interests. Nevertheless, this was clearly the minority view until the 1960s and 1970s, when the United States was disrupted, sometimes violently, by a series of civil rights, antiwar, and other grassroots challenges to the political status quo (see the readings in Part 4).

Many scholars who were students or were just beginning their careers in the 1960s believed that the disruptive challenges of that time proved the pluralists wrong. Political power was not diffuse, after all: many groups, including African-Americans, workers, women, and the poor, had been systematically excluded from politics all along. In an effort to explain how this had happened, the younger scholars developed alternative theories that explored how a privileged "ruling class" of wealthy Americans dominated politics. Such theories flourished during the 1970s, and were often derived in part from the ideas of Karl Marx and his followers (Block, 1987; Domhoff, 1986–1987). In contrast to both pluralist and elite theories, Marxist-inspired theorists argued that the U.S. state and its policies were, for a variety of reasons, systematically biased in favor of the ruling class.

During the 1980s, the appeal of Marxism receded as scholars began to develop theories about how politicians, bureaucrats, and other political actors *inside* the state could act with considerable autonomy from the pressures of interest groups, classes, socioeconomic elites, and other forces *outside* the state when devising and implementing public policy (Evans, Rueschemeyer, & Skocpol, 1985). Although earlier elite theory was influential here, these scholars emphasized how the activities of political elites, classes, and interest groups were embedded within political institutions that had their own independent effects on politics. Institutionalists argued, for example, that workers in the United States had difficulty influencing politics because elections and politics were organized in ways that made it hard for them to create their own national political party (see the readings in Chapter 5). Moreover, these scholars recognized that the organization and accessibility of the state varied across different branches, agencies, and levels of government. Institutionalists also pointed out that the political influence of different actors has been historically contingent, changing over time, just as institutions themselves change. Historical studies are, therefore, essential to the understanding of American politics.

The readings in Chapter 1 represent the debate between pluralists and their

TABLE 1
A Comparison of Pluralist, Elite, Class, and Institutional Theories of the State and Politics

	Pluralist	Elite	Class	Institutional
Who or what determines state action?	Citizens and groups in society organized through interest groups and political parties	Political elites, often unified, who occupy key positions within the state on their own behalf	"Power elite" representing ruling class interests Class struggle Economic and political constraints of capitalist democracy	Elites inside the state operating within the constraints imposed by political institutions
What is the content of state policy?	Reflects the relative balance of interest group forces	Reflects the interests of the political elites	Reproduces capitalist class relations Reflects the balance of class forces Reproduces conditions necessary for capitalism	Reflects the balance of power among politically organized classes and interest groups outside the state and state elites and politicians inside the state as influenced by political institutions
What are the key sources of political conflict?	Conflicts among interest groups	Conflicts among fractions of the power elite Conflicts among elites and their staff	Conflicts among social classes Conflicts among different factions within social classes	Conflicts among actors inside the state Conflicts between actors inside and outside of the state
What are the key sources of political stability?	Overlapping interests of members from different interest groups temper individual group demands. Institutionalized rules of the game	Consensus among political elites about how to use and protect their power Rules of legal and bureaucratic procedure Monopoly of the legitimate use of violence	State repression Material payoffs to subordinate classes, such as minimal welfare programs Control of institutions that shape political consciousness, such as public schools	Policy legacies embedded in already existing political institutions Relatively stable institutions that structure politics
Is the state autonomous from forces in society?	The state is not autonomous because state actors generally respond to the demands of interest groups.	The state is very autonomous because political elites are insulated inside state bureaucracies from social pressures.	The state enjoys only "relative autonomy," which varies according to economic and geopolitical conditions and the degree to which social classes are organized or not.	The state is "potentially autonomous," depending on the institutional structure and capacities of the state.
Is the state biased in favor of certain interests?	The state is a neutral arena in which interest group struggles occur. The state is an umpire regulating interest group struggles.	The state is systematically biased toward the interests of the political elites who control it.	The state is systematically biased toward the interests of the capitalist class unless the working class can gain enough power to transform the state and state policy.	The role and structure of the state are historically contingent. State policies and structures help shape the interests, organization, and influence of social and political actors.

critics about the general nature of political power. These essays discuss how to define and think about political power and the mechanisms through which it operates. Each selection also addresses issues of methodology, suggesting *how* social scientists ought to study political power and shifts in power over time among major actors. Although the readings in Chapter 1 focus on power at the community level, they offer thoughts about politics at the national level as well. Thus ideas from these selections can be used to think about empirical and theoretical issues that come up in the other parts of the Reader.

Chapter 2 asks whether business interests, the capitalist class, and the imperatives of the capitalist system are the most important determinants of public policy in the United States. Does business have predominant weight, or is it one of a multifaceted array of actors? Is capitalism the dominant set of institutional relationships in politics, or do other sorts of social relationships also matter? The readings of Chapter 2 also examine how state policies influence the organization and activity of the business community itself. Thus this part of the Reader begins to explore the reciprocal influences that link the state to its socioeconomic environment at the national level.

The readings in Chapter 3 show how the struggles over public policy among social classes, interest groups, and other political actors unfold within a larger institutional context, consisting of political parties, government bureaucracies and legislatures, the legal system, and shared beliefs about how politics ought to operate. In one way or another, each article demonstrates how political institutions constrain and shape the political choices and strategies that are available to political actors. Institutions also encourage some alliances among politically active groups, and discourage others.

Taken together, the readings in Part 1 frame many of the theoretical and conceptual issues that recur throughout the volume. By reviewing some of the most important debates in political sociology and political science, we gain an overview of the recent development of scholarly thinking about power, political actors, political institutions, and the U.S. state. Table 1 summarizes and compares some of the most important arguments about power, politics, and the state that are discussed in these selections.

REFERENCES

Block, Fred. 1987. "State Theory in Context." In *Revising State Theory: Essays on Politics and Postindustrialism,* 3–35. Philadelphia: Temple University Press.

Domhoff, G. William. 1986–1987. "Corporate Liberal Theory and the Social Security Act: A Chapter in the Sociology of Knowledge." *Politics and Society* 15: 297–330.

Evans, Peter, Dietrich Rueschemeyer, and Theda Skocpol, editors. 1985. *Bringing the State Back In.* New York: Cambridge University Press.

Ferguson, Thomas, and Joel Rogers. 1986. *Right Turn: The Decline of the Democrats and the Future of American Politics.* New York: Hill and Wang.

Galbraith, John Kenneth. 1967. *The New Industrial State.* Boston: Houghton Mifflin.

Goldthorpe, John. 1984. "The End of Convergence: Corporatist and Dualist Tendencies in Modern Western Societies." In *Order and Conflict in Contemporary Capitalism: Studies in the Political Economy of Western European Nations,* John Goldthorpe, 315–43. New York: Oxford University Press.
Mills, C. Wright. 1956. *The Power Elite.* New York: Oxford University Press.
Teixeira, Ruy A. 1992. *The Disappearing American Voter.* Washington, D.C.: Brookings Institution.

CHAPTER 1

POWER AND DEMOCRACY

What is political power? How does it operate in democratic societies? And how should social scientists go about studying it? These are among the most central questions we can ask about politics. Much research on political power has looked for answers to these questions by studying politics in cities around the United States (Crenson, 1971; Trounstine & Christensen, 1982; Whitt, 1982). A classic study was Robert Dahl's (1961) analysis of political power in New Haven, Connecticut. Dahl sought to test the hypothesis that power often lies in the hands of a small group of social and economic elites—an argument that had been advanced by Floyd Hunter (1953) in an earlier study of politics in Atlanta, Georgia. Dahl found that in New Haven political influence was not highly concentrated, but was dispersed among various interest groups depending on the issue area in question. Although business elites historically were key players in New Haven politics, Dahl argued, their influence had waned as the city and local governments expanded. By the mid-twentieth century, they were no longer the dominant political force, even in important areas that directly affected their interests, such as urban development. Dahl felt that he used empirical research to question any presumption of business dominance in American politics.

In another classic statement of this pluralist view of community power, Nelson Polsby, a colleague of Dahl, argues that in America in recent times it is unlikely that a small group of elites or members of a particular social class can dominate community politics at the expense of other groups. According to Polsby (see Reading 1), this is so because people from different groups develop interests that often overlap with those of other groups. Thus different political coalitions emerge around particular political issues. No single group is always in control. For example, two groups may struggle against each other over whether to raise local property taxes, but join forces to oppose school closings. Methodologically, Polsby maintains, we can only determine which groups have power in a given situation by studying clearly observable conflicts. We might focus, for example, on an electoral campaign or on a policy debate, in which there are visible actors taking different positions on an issue and clear winners and losers. Only in this way, Polsby argues, can we see who has best been able to mobilize political resources to get what they want. Any other approach to the study of power, according to Polsby, is not empirically testable.

In a well-known article, Peter Bachrach and Morton Baratz (1962) argued that there is an

6

additional "face" to power that pluralists like Polsby and Dahl neglect. A lot of politics occurs behind the scenes, concealed from public view in places where small groups of elites make decisions that set the political agendas for larger, more visible pluralist contests. For instance, although Dahl may have been correct to say that business leaders were not directly involved in the campaign for urban renewal in New Haven, they earlier played a pivotal role at the national level by persuading the U.S. Congress to pass legislation that would encourage the kind of urban renewal that they preferred—lucrative commercial development rather than the construction of less profitable low-income housing. Once this national legislation had been passed, local elites from New Haven used their connections in Washington, D.C., to ensure that substantial federal funds were channeled to their city to support many of their pet urban renewal projects. Thus the most important struggle over urban development in New Haven was actually waged behind the scenes in Washington, where local elites helped to establish the political agenda for urban development in New Haven (Domhoff, 1978). Bachrach and Baratz (1962) referred to this sort of agenda setting as the "mobilization of bias." In this case, the possibilities for urban renewal, as defined by national legislation and funding, were biased in favor of local business elites rather than the poor.

Bachrach and Baratz (1962) argued that the ability to limit access to agenda-setting forums and other political arenas is an important part of mobilizing bias. For example, the use of poll taxes, literacy tests, intimidation, violence, and other means that prevented African-Americans from voting was an important source of political power for whites during much of U.S. history because it prevented blacks from participating in politics in the first place. Similarly, the costs of mounting national political campaigns and organizing third parties limited the ability of workers, farmers, and other groups to engage effectively in national politics (see the readings in Chapter 5). According to Bachrach and Baratz, the ability to set agendas and limit group access to politics constitutes a "second face" of power generally overlooked by pluralists. They argue that empirical research should include both faces of power.

Despite their differences, Polsby and Bachrach and Baratz agree that, regardless of the forums in which politics occurs, we can only study political power by observing the conflicts that emerge over specific policy issues. In contrast, John Gaventa (see Reading 2) explains that power may still operate, although in very subtle ways, even when there is no conflict to observe! For one thing, Gaventa suggests, elites can often manipulate symbols, rituals, political socialization, and other factors in ways that make it difficult for subordinate groups to recognize that their interests are at odds with those of the dominant elite (see also Lukes, 1974). Thus workers may not struggle for stricter workplace health and safety regulations if they have been convinced that this might jeopardize company profits and, as a result, their jobs. For another thing, even when subordinate groups recognize that their interests clash with those of the dominant elite, they may feel that it is simply impossible to advance their interests, perhaps because they have lost so many times before when they have tried to do so. In either case, Gaventa insists that the *absence* of conflict often indicates that power has been operating, but at a much deeper level that can be revealed only through a careful historical analysis of the long-term interactions among dominant and subordinate groups.

Gaventa and other like-minded scholars have recognized that power operates at three levels, and have developed theories and research strategies based on this presumption (Alford & Friedland, 1985; Lukes, 1974). In order to get at all three levels, such scholars have studied power by making comparisons across time and across communities or nations (for examples, see Crenson, 1971; Whitt, 1982), rather than focusing only on a particular policy battle at one time and place, as did most previous students of power. For instance, some researchers have found that the ability of citizen groups to influence city hall and overcome the resistance of political and business elites is enhanced if city officials are chosen through ward-based rather than at-large elections; popular influence is also enhanced when local business leaders are concerned less with local than with regional or national economic problems (Trounstine &

Christensen, 1982). Others have found that the presence of nationally powerful corporations and labor unions enhances the ability of communities to obtain federal funding for local programs (Friedland, 1976). In any event, the issues raised in these readings continue to stimulate research and to provoke intense debate among social scientists. Sometimes separately, sometimes together, all three types of power are foci for research and theorizing in political sociology and political science.

REFERENCES

Alford, Robert, and Roger Friedland. 1985. *Powers of Theory: Capitalism, the State, and Democracy.* New York: Cambridge University Press.

Bachrach, Peter, and Morton S. Baratz. 1962. "Two Faces of Power." *American Political Science Review* 56: 947–52.

Crenson, Matthew A. 1971. *The Un-Politics of Air Pollution.* Baltimore: Johns Hopkins University Press.

Dahl, Robert A. 1961. *Who Governs?* New Haven, Conn.: Yale University Press.

Domhoff, G. William. 1978. *Who Really Rules?* Santa Monica, Calif.: Goodyear.

Friedland, Roger. 1976. "Class Power and Social Control: The War on Poverty." *Politics and Society* 6(4): 459–89.

Hunter, Floyd. 1953. *Community Power Structure.* Chapel Hill: University of North Carolina Press.

Lukes, Steven. 1974. *Power: A Radical View.* London: Macmillan.

Trounstine, Philip J., and Terry Christensen. 1982. *Movers and Shakers: The Study of Community Power.* New York: St. Martin's.

Whitt, J. Allen. 1982. *Urban Elites and Mass Transportation: The Dialectics of Power.* Princeton, N.J.: Princeton University Press.

HOW TO STUDY COMMUNITY POWER: THE PLURALIST ALTERNATIVE

Nelson W. Polsby

In criticizing the stratification approach to the study of community power, I have suggested, among other things, that this approach encourages research designs which generate self-fulfilling prophecies, that it leads to the systematic misreporting of facts and to the formulation of vague, ambiguous, unrealistic, and unprovable assertions about community power. I now want to discuss an alternative method of studying community power which appears to have successfully avoided these undesirable by-products in a number of community studies.

This alternative research strategy can be called the "pluralist" approach. Old, familiar pluralistic presumptions[1] about the nature of American politics seem to have given researchers strategies for the study of community power which are both feasible to execute and comparatively faithful to conditions in the real world.[2] What follows is an attempt to explain why this seems to be the case for pluralist studies, but not for stratification studies.

The first and perhaps most basic presupposition of the pluralist approach is that nothing categorical can be assumed about power in any community. It rejects the stratification thesis that *some* group necessarily dominates a community. If anything, there seems to be an unspoken notion among pluralist researchers that at bottom *nobody* dominates in a town, so that their first question to a local informant is likely to be not "Who runs this community?" but rather "Does anyone at all run this community?" It is instructive to examine the range of possible answers to each of these questions. The first query is somewhat like "Have you stopped beating your wife?" in that virtually any response short of total unwillingness to answer will supply the researcher with a "power elite" along the lines presupposed by stratification theory.[3] On the other hand, the second question is capable of eliciting a response which *could* lead to the discovery of a power elite (i.e., "Yes"), or any of an infinite number of stable, but nonelitist patterns of decision-making (i.e., "No, but . . . ," "Yes, but . . .") or total fragmentation, or disorganization (i.e., "No").

What sort of question is likely to follow "Who runs the community?" in a questionnaire? Obviously, something like "*How* do the people named in the above response run the community?" This entirely probable pattern of investigation begs the question whether or not those said to rule actually do rule. In the pluralist approach, on the other hand, an attempt is made to study specific outcomes in order to determine who actually prevails in community decision-making. Because the study of actual outcomes requires arduous and expensive field work, outcomes in a few (but for reasons of expense usually only a few) issue-areas are studied closely. More than a single issue-area is always chosen, however, because of the presumption among

From *Journal of Politics* 22(3). (August 1960). Reprinted with the permission of the author and the University of Texas Press.

[1] I am well aware that for other purposes the "pluralist" approach can be divided into several schools of thought. However, all variations of pluralist theory contrast effectively with stratification theory. Pluralist presumptions can be found, for example, in the writings of Tocqueville and Madison and in Arthur Bentley, *The Process of Government* (Chicago, Univ. of Chicago Press, 1908); Pendleton Herring, *The Politics of Democracy* (New York, Rinehart, 1940); David B. Truman, *The Governmental Process* (New York, Knopf, 1953); V. O. Key, Jr., *Politics, Parties and Pressure Groups* (New York, Crowell, 1942 and 1959). More formal treatments of propositions contained in many of these works can be found in Anthony Downs, *An Economic Theory of Democracy* (New York, Harper, 1957); David Braybrooke, "Some Steps toward a Formal System of Political Science," a report prepared for the Committee on Political Behavior of the Social Science Research Council, Sept. 1957; James S. Coleman, "An Examination of Arthur F. Bentley's Theory of Government," ibid., July 1957; and Robert A. Dahl, *A Preface to Democratic Theory* (Chicago, Univ. of Chicago Press, 1956).

2. Among the researchers who have found pluralist presumptions about the nature of the political system useful are Robert A. Dahl (see his "The New Haven Community Leadership Study," Working Paper Number One, Dec. 1957, mimeo.; and *Who Governs?);* Harry Scoble ("Yankeetown"); and George Belknap

and Norton E. Long (see Long, "The Local Community as an Ecology of Games," *Am. J. Soc.,* 64 [Nov. 1958], 251–61; Long and Belknap, "A Research Program on Leadership and Decision-making in Metropolitan Areas" [mimeo., New York, Governmental Affairs Institute, Aug. 1956]; Belknap and John H. Bunzel, "The Trade Union in the Political Community," *PROD,* 2 [Sept. 1958], 3–6; Belknap, "A Plan for Research on the Sociopolitical Dynamics of Metropolitan Areas," presented before a seminar on urban leadership of the Social Science Research Council, New York, Aug. 1957). See also a paper presented to this seminar by Peter H. Rossi, "The Study of Decision-making in the Local Community."

[3] See Herbert Kaufman and Victor Jones, "The Mystery of Power," *Public Administration Review,* 14 (Summer 1954), 205–12.

pluralist researchers that the same pattern of decision-making is highly unlikely to reproduce itself in more than one issue-area. In this expectation, pluralist researchers have seldom been disappointed.[4] They recognize, however, the possibility that the same pattern *could* reproduce itself in more than one issue-area. Since actual behavior is observed or reconstructed from documents, witnesses, and so on, it is possible to determine empirically whether or not the same group rules in two or more issue-areas. The presumption that a power elite is unlikely does not, in other words, prevent finding one.

A superficially persuasive objection to this approach might be phrased as follows: "Suppose research in a community discloses different patterns of decision-making in each of three issue-areas. This does not rule out the possibility that all other issue-areas in the community are dominated by a single power elite." How can pluralists meet this objection? First, it is necessary to acknowledge the *possibility* that this is the case. However, pluralists can (and do) protect themselves in part by studying significant issues. In New Haven, for example, Dahl, Wolfinger, and I studied nominations by the two political parties (which determined who held public office), the urban redevelopment program (the largest in the country, measured by past and present outlays per capita), public education (the most costly item in the city's budget), and a campaign to revise the city charter. In Bennington, Scoble studied political nominations and elections, the issue of consolidation of various municipal governments, the formation of a union high school district, and the construction of a new high school building.[5] A Long and Belknap pilot study of a large eastern city embraced the problems of transportation, race relations, traffic, urban redevelopment, and recreation,[6] and Belknap studied the issues of urban redevelopment, transportation, and race relations in the San Francisco Bay area.[7]

None of these issues is trivial, and a case can be made for the proposition that they were in fact the most important issues before these communities during the time the studies were being carried out. What sort of power elite asserts itself in relatively trivial matters, but

is inactive or ineffective in the most significant areas of community policy-making?

Stratification theory holds that power elites fail to prevail only on trivial issues.[8] By preselecting issues generally agreed to be significant, pluralist researchers can test stratification theory without searching endlessly in issue-area after issue-area in order to discover some semblance of a power elite. After all, we cannot reasonably require of researchers that they validate someone else's preconceived notion of community power distributions. If the researcher's design is such that any power distribution has an equal chance of appearing in his result, we may not properly criticize his result on the ground that it did not conform to expectations. The burden of proof is clearly on the challenger in such a case to make good his assertion that power is actually distributed otherwise.[9]

Another presumption of the pluralist approach runs directly counter to stratification theory's presumption that power distributions are a more or less permanent aspect of social structure. Pluralists hold that power may be tied to issues, and issues can be fleeting or persistent, provoking coalitions among interested groups and citizens ranging in their duration from momentary to semi-permanent. There is a clear gain in descriptive accuracy in formulating power distributions so as to take account of the dimension of time, as pluralists do.[10] For it is easily demonstrated that coalitions *do*

---

[4] Raymond E. Wolfinger, "Reputation and Reality in The Study of 'Community Power,'" *Am. Soc. Rev.,* 25 (Oct. 1960), pp. 636–44, has summarized findings on this point. See also below, Chap. 7.

[5] "Yankeetown."

[6] "A Research Program."

[7] "A Plan for Research."

[8] See, for example, Roland J. Pellegrin and Charles H. Coates, "Absentee-owned Corporations and Community Power Structure," *Am. J. Soc.,* 61 (March 1956), 413–19; and Lynd, *MIT,* p. 89.

[9] See Dahl, "Critique."

[10] See, for example, Belknap ("A Plan for Research"), who discusses this explicitly. One stratification writer who has attempted to take account of the time factor is Jerome K. Myers, "Assimilation in the Political Community," *Sociology and Social Research,* 35 (Jan.–Feb. 1951), 175–82. Myers plots a secular trend which indicates slow increases in the number of Italians and Italian-descended employed by New Haven municipal government over a 50-year period ending in 1940. He claims to have discovered "discrimination" against Italians, because they did not participate in city government to an extent proportional with their representation in the total population of the city. His conclusion in 1951 was that "the early or quick assimilation of New Haven Italians in the political system does not seem very probable. . . . All indications are that political assimilation is inevitable, although it is at least several generations away." By taking account of shorter-term cyclical movements within the allegedly "basic" structure, we may be able to explain the delay in the political assimilation of Italians. As I have mentioned, New Haven Italians were and are predominantly Republican in local politics. From 1920 to 1940, years in which the Italians would "normally" have been expected to come into their own as a politically significant minority group, the city government was in

vary in their permanency, and to presume that the set of coalitions which exists in the community at any given time is a timelessly stable aspect of social structure is to introduce systematic inaccuracies into one's description of social reality.

Why do pluralists reject the idea that some group necessarily dominates every community? The presumption that communities are likely to be less rather than more permanent in their patterns of decision-making is no doubt part of the answer, but another part is an even more fundamental presumption that human behavior is governed in large part by inertia. This notion leads pluralists to look upon overt activity as a more valid indication of involvement in issues than mere reputations for leadership.[11]

Pluralists refuse to regard particular groups as necessarily implicated in decisions when the groups themselves reject such involvement.[12] For pluralists, the imputation of "false class consciousness" suggests that the values of analysts are being imposed arbitrarily on groups in the community. They reject the idea that there is any particular issue or any particular point in the determination of an issue when a group *must* assert itself in order to follow its expressed values. Rather, the pluralist assumes that there are many issues and many points at which group values can be realized. Further, pluralists presume that there are certain costs in taking any action at all. This refers not simply to the possibility of losing, of making political enemies, and so on, but also to the costs in personal time and effort involved in political mobilization, in becoming informed, in lobbying or campaigning, and in taking the trouble to vote.[13]

It is a demonstrated fact that public activity of all kinds is a habit of the middle and upper classes.[14] Vidich and Bensman, in their community study, depicted the life of the lowest-class groups in the community sufficiently well so that the personally functional aspects of withdrawal from the community were revealed.[15] The presumption of inertia permits the researcher to regard the public sector of activity as but one facet of behavior capable of giving people satisfaction and discourages the inappropriate and arbitrary assignment of upper- and middle-class values to all actors in the community.

The presumption of inertia also helps put economic and social notables into perspective. If a man's major life work is banking, the pluralist presumes he will spend his time at the bank, and not in manipulating community decisions. This presumption holds until the banker's activities and participations indicate otherwise. Once again, it is very important to make the point that this assumption is not scientifically equivalent to its opposite. If we presume that the banker is really engaged in running the community, there is practically no way of disproving this notion even if it is totally erroneous. On the other hand, it is easy to spot the banker who really *does* run community affairs when we presume he does not, because his activities will make this fact apparent. In the absence of the requisite activities, we have no grounds for asserting that the banker in fact does run the community.[16]

The pluralist emphasis on the time-bounded nature of coalitions and on the voluntary aspect of political participation leads to a further contrast with stratification theory, since pluralists hold that the "interest group" and the "public" are the social collectives most

---

Democratic hands twice as much as Republican, and this would lead one to expect Italians to be less well represented among office-holders than if this situation were reversed. However, in 1945, when William Celentano, a Republican of Italian descent, was elected mayor, Italians entered the top echelons of city government in large numbers. There is, of course, no sure way of telling what a "normal" rate of absorption into political positions would be. More or less comparable data indicate that in New Haven Italians were perhaps a bit swifter in their rise to political leadership than in Providence, Rhode Island. See Elmer E. Cornwell, Jr., "Party Absorption of Ethnic Groups: The Case of Providence, Rhode Island," *Social Forces,* 38 (March 1960), 205–10.
[11] See the previous critique of Hunter in Chap. 3, and Wolfinger, "Reputation and Reality."
[12] See C. Wright Mills, "The Middle Classes in Middle-sized Cities," *Am. Soc. Rev.,* 11 (Oct. 1946), 520–29, for the stratification theory view.
[13] See Downs, *Economic Theory of Democracy;* see also Samuel Stouffer, *Communism, Conformity and Civil Liberties* (Garden City, Doubleday, 1955), pp. 58 ff.

[14] Robert E. Lane, *Political Life: How People Get Involved in Politics* (Glencoe, Free Press, 1959), pp. 220–34; Angus Campbell, Gerald Gurin, and Warren E. Miller, *The Voter Decides* (Evanston, Row, Peterson, 1954), pp. 70–75.
[15] Arthur J. Vidich and Joseph Bensman, *Small Town in Mass Society* (Princeton, Princeton Univ. Press, 1958), pp. 69–70, 290–91. Studies of social status have been hampered by a similar problem of upper-class-centeredness. See the criticism of Warner on this point by Seymour Martin Lipset and Reinhard Bendix, "Social Status and Social Structure," *British Journal of Sociology,* 2 (June 1951), esp. 163 ff.
[16] See Bentley, *Process of Government,* pp. 175–222, and note at p. 202: "If we can get our social life stated in terms of activity and of nothing else, we have not indeed succeeded in measuring it, but we have at least reached a foundation upon which a coherent system of measurements can be built up. . . . We shall cease to be blocked by the intervention of unmeasurable elements, which claim to be themselves the real causes of all that is happening, and which by their spook-like arbitrariness make impossible any progress toward dependable knowledge."

relevant to the analysis of political processes. In the sociologist's patois, politically important groups would be called phenomena of "collective behavior" rather than of "social structure."[17] Social classes in stratification theory are populations differentially ranked according to economic or status criteria, which embrace the entire community. Everyone in a community is a member of at least one but no more than one class at any given moment, and no one in the community falls outside the system. This is a legitimate heuristic construction; however, it is a mistake to impute to the apparently inescapable fact of class membership any sort of class consciousness. This sociologists have long recognized.[18] But they seem less willing to grant that it is equally incorrect to presume that those sharing similar market or status positions are also equidistant from all the bases of political power, or in fact share class interests. American society has never been noted for its interclass warfare, a fact often reported with great surprise in stratification studies of American communities.[19]

Pluralists, who see American society as fractured into a congeries of hundreds of small special interest groups, with incompletely overlapping memberships, widely differing power bases, and a multitude of techniques for exercising influence on decisions salient to them,[20] are not surprised at the low priority Americans give to their class memberships as bases of social action. In the decision-making of fragmented government—and American national, state, and local governments are nothing if not fragmented—the claims of small, intense minorities are usually attended to.[21] Hence it is not only inefficient but usually unnecessary for entire classes to mobilize when the preferences of class members are pressed and often satisfied in piecemeal fashion. The empirical evidence supporting this pluralist doctrine is overwhelming,[22] however stratification theorists may have missed its significance for them; the fragmentation of American governmental decision-making and of American society makes class consciousness inefficient and, in most cases, makes the political interests of members of the same class different.

Pluralist research is not interested in ascertaining an actor's ranking in a system presumed to operate hierarchically. Rather, pluralists want to find out about leadership *roles,* which are presumed to be diverse and fluid, both within a single issue-area over time and between issue-areas. Long and Belknap, for example, identify the following leadership roles in community decision-making: initiation, staffing and planning, communication and publicity, intra-elite organizing, financing, and public sanctioning.[23]

By describing and specifying leadership roles in concrete situations, pluralists are in a position to determine the extent to which a power structure exists. High degrees of overlap in decision-making personnel among issue-areas, or high degrees of institutionalization in the bases of power in specified issue-areas, or high degrees of regularity in the procedures of decision-making—any one of these situations, if found to exist, could conceivably justify an empirical conclusion that some kind of power structure exists. By specifying leadership roles and activities, the pluralist research strategy makes possible an empirical determination and description of the bounds and durability of a community power structure—if there is one, and the stratification theory presumption that community power is necessarily general and relatively immutable can be discarded as arbitrary.

The final contrast I want to make between the plu-

[17] Only one sociologist seems to have realized what this implies for the methods and conclusions of political analysis. See Rudolf Heberle, *Social Movements* (New York, Appleton, 1951). The relevant theory is compactly expounded by Herbert Blumer in "Collective Behavior," which appears in Alfred M. Lee, ed., *Principles of Sociology* (New York, Barnes and Noble, 1953), pp. 167–220.

[18] Indeed, Max Weber, the most important founding father of modern stratification analysis, makes just this point. See Weber's "Class, Status, Party," in H. H. Gerth and C. W. Mills, ed., *From Max Weber: Essays in Sociology* (New York, Oxford Univ. Press, 1946), pp. 180–95, esp. p. 184.

[19] See, for example, Lynd, *MIT,* pp. 454–55, 509; Alfred Winslow Jones, *Life, Liberty and Property* (Philadelphia, Lippincott, 1941), pp. 336–54; Warner, *Jonesville,* p. 27; C. Wright Mills, "The Middle Classes." Cf. also Richard Centers, *The Psychology of Social Classes* (Princeton, Princeton Univ. Press, 1949), and note the extent to which his conclusions outrun his data.

[20] See, for example, Truman, passim; Alexis de Tocqueville, *Democracy in America* (New York, Vintage, 1952), esp. *1:* 181–205, 281–342; *2:* 114–35.

[21] See Dahl, *Preface to Democratic Theory.*

[22] Truman (*Governmental Process*) summarizes a tremendous amount of this material. For a recent treatment of the same theme in a case study, see Aaron B. Wildavsky, *Dixon-Yates: A Study in Power Politics* (New Haven, Yale Univ. Press, 1962).

[23] Long and Belknap, "A Research Program," 9–11; see Polsby, "The Sociology of Community Power: A Reassessment," *Social Forces,* 37 (March 1959), 232–36; and Edward C. Banfield, "The Concept 'Leadership' in Community Research, delivered at the meetings of the American Political Science Association, 1958, for similar lists.

ralist and stratification methods has to do with their differing conceptions of what is meant by "power." As we have seen, stratification theorists emphasize the cataloguing of power bases, or resources available to actors for the exercise of power.[24] Pluralists, on the other hand, concentrate on power exercise itself. This leads to two subsidiary discoveries. First, there are a great many different kinds of resources which can be put to use in the process of community decision-making—many more resources, in fact, than stratification theorists customarily take into account. One list, for example, might include:

1. Money and credit
2. Control over jobs
3. Control over the information of others
4. Social standing
5. Knowledge and expertness
6. Popularity, esteem, charisma
7. Legality, constitutionality, officiality, legitimacy
8. Ethnic solidarity
9. The right to vote
10. Time
11. Personal (human) energy[25]

Secondly, resources can be employed with greater or less skill. The elaboration of the ways in which resources are employed enables the pluralist researcher to pay attention to what practical politicians customarily see as the heart of their own craft: the processes of bargaining, negotiation, salesmanship and broker-age, and of leadership in mobilizing resources of all kinds. It is also possible using this approach to make a more realistic evaluation of the actual disposable resources of actors. A corporation may be worth millions, but its policies and liquidity position may be such that it cannot possibly bring these millions into play to influence the outcome of a community decision—even one in which the corporation is vitally interested. And interest itself, as noted above, is differentially distributed in a pattern which pluralists assume is rational for most actors most of the time. For example, Long and Belknap observe:

Just as business organizations may be disinterested in community affairs because of the national scope of [their] operations, individual businessmen who move or are shifted from city to city may have little opportunity or incentive to participate in community affairs. Some businesses have strong pressures on them to give attention to community and metropolitan problems. Large department stores are particularly tied up with the destiny of the city and must decide whether to keep to the central city or decentralize in suburban shopping centers. Businessmen with a "metropolitan view" would thus be expected to be found here rather than in the branch office of a national corporation.[26]

What are the practical recommendations which emerge from this comparison of stratification and pluralist approaches to the study of community power?[27] First, the researcher should pick issue-areas as the focus of his study of community power. Secondly, he should be able to defend these issue-areas as very important in the life of the community. Thirdly, he should study actual behavior, either at first hand or by reconstructing behavior from documents, informants, newspapers, and other appropriate sources. There is no harm in starting with a list of people whose behavior the researcher wishes to study vis-à-vis an issue-area. The harm comes, rather, in attributing some mystic significance to the list, so that the examination of activity and of actual participation in decision-making becomes superfluous. This recommendation is not meant to discourage the researcher from collecting information about the reputations of actors, or their intentions with respect to community issues, or their evaluations about the meanings of community incidents. All of these kinds of data are of immeasurable value in tracing patterns of decision-making. However, they must be accompanied by information about behavior so that the researcher has some way of distinguishing between myths and facts.

The final recommendation is of the same order: researchers should study the outcomes of actual decisions within the community. It is important, but insufficient, to know what leaders want to do, intend to do, and think they can do. The researcher still has to decide on the basis of his own examination of the facts what

[24] See above, Chap. 5.
[25] See Robert A. Dahl, "The Analysis of Influence in Local Communities" (mimeo., May 1959), 10; Dahl, "Leadership in a Fragmented Political System: Notes for a Theory," presented to the Social Science Research Council Conference on Metropolitan Leadership, Evanston, Ill., April 1–3, 1960, p. 7.

[26] Long and Belknap, "A Research Program," 13–14. This corresponds to the findings—but not the interpretations—of Robert O. Schulze, "The Role of Economic Dominants in Community Power Structure," *Am. Soc. Rev.,* 23 (Feb. 1958), 3–9.
[27] This presumes that the researcher wants to make some generalization about the "normal" distributions of power in community decision-making.

the actual upshot is of these various intentions, and not conclude prematurely that intentions plus resources inflexibly predetermine outcomes.

READING 2

POWER AND PARTICIPATION

John Gaventa

This is a study about quiescence and rebellion in a situation of glaring inequality. Why, in a social relationship involving the domination of a non-elite by an elite, does challenge to that domination not occur? What is there in certain situations of social deprivation that prevents issues from arising, grievances from being voiced, or interests from being recognized? Why, in an oppressed community where one might intuitively expect upheaval, does one instead find, or appear to find, quiescence? Under what conditions and against what obstacles does rebellion begin to emerge?

The problem is significant to classical democratic and Marxist theories alike, for, in a broad sense, both share the notion that the action of the dispossessed will serve to counter social inequities. Yet, as these views move from political theory to political sociology, so, too, do they appear to move—particularly with reference to the United States—from discussing the necessities of widespread participation and challenge to considering the reasons for their non-occurrence.[1] In their wake, other more conservative theories of democracy present the appearance of quiescence in the midst of inequality as evidence of the legitimacy of an existing order, or as an argument for decision-making by the few, or at least as a phenomenon functional to social stability.[2] More recently, these "neo-elitists"

have in turn been challenged by others who, with C. Wright Mills, argue that the appearance of quiescence need neither suggest consent nor refute the classical ideals.[3] Rather, it may reflect the use or misuse of modern-day power.

While the theories of democracy turn, at least to a degree, upon disputes as to the significance of quiescence, the sociological literature of industrial societies offers an array of explanations for its roots: embourgeoisement, hegemony, no real inequality, low rank on a socio-economic status scale, cultural deficiencies of the deprived, or simply the innate apathy of the human race—to name but a few. Rather than deal with these directly, this study will explore another explanation: in situations of inequality, the political response of the deprived group or class may be seen as a function of power relationships, such that power serves for the development and maintenance of the quiescence of the non-elite. The emergence of rebellion, as a corollary, may be understood as the process by which the relationships of power are altered.

The argument itself immediately introduces a further set of questions to be explored: What is the nature of power? How do power and powerlessness affect the political actions and conceptions of a non-elite?

In his recent book, *Power: A Radical View,* Lukes has summarized what has been an extended debate since C. Wright Mills, especially in American political science, about the concept and appropriate methods for its study.[4] Power, he suggests, may be understood as having three dimensions, the first of which is based upon the traditional pluralists' approach, the second of which is essentially that put forward by Bachrach and Baratz in their consideration of power's second face,[5] and the third of which Lukes develops. In this chapter, I shall examine the dimensions briefly, arguing that each carries with it, implicitly or explicitly, differing assumptions about the nature and roots of participation and non-participation. I shall argue further that together the dimensions of power (and powerlessness) may be developed into a tentative model for more usefully understanding the generation of quiescence, as well as the process by which challenge may emerge. Finally, I shall sketch in general terms a methodology by which the notions may be considered empirically.

From *Power and Powerlessness: Quiescence and Rebellion in an Appalachian Valley* (Urbana, Ill: University of Illinois Press, 1980), 3–32. Reprinted with permission of the University of Illinois Press.

[1] See, for instance, Sidney Verba and Norman H. Nie, *Participation in America: Political Democracy and Social Equality* (Harper and Row, New York, 1972); Anthony Giddens, *The Class Structure of the Advanced Societies* (Hutchinson University Library, London, 1973).
[2] i.e. the so-called "neo-elitists" such as Schumpeter (*Capitalism, Socialism and Democracy,* 1942), Berelson (*Voting,* 1954), Dahl (*A Preface to Democratic Theory,* 1956). The views are neatly summarized and contrasted with classical theories of participation in Carole Pateman, *Participation and Democratic Theory* (Cambridge University Press, 1970).
[3] See, for example, Peter Bachrach, *The Theory of Democratic Elitism: A Critique* (University of London Press, 1969); Jack E. Walker, "A Critique of the Elitist Theory of Democracy," *American Political Science Review,* 60 (1966), 285–95.
4. Steven Lukes, *Power: A Radical View* (Macmillan, London, 1974).

Then, in Chapter 2, I shall begin to specify how the notions might apply to the study of the politics of inequality in a Central Appalachian Valley.

THE NATURE OF POWER AND ROOTS OF QUIESCENCE

The One-Dimensional Approach.   The one-dimensional approach to power is essentially that of the pluralists, developed in American political science most particularly by Robert Dahl and Nelson Polsby. "My intuitive idea of power," Dahl wrote in an early essay, "is something like this: A has power over B to the extent that he can get B to do something that B would not otherwise do."[6] In the politics of a community, Polsby later added, power may be studied by examining "who participates, who gains and loses, and who prevails in decision-making."[7]

The key to the definition is a focus on behaviour—doing, participating—about which several assumptions are made, to be questioned later in this book. First, grievances are assumed to be recognized and acted upon. Polsby writes, for instance, that "presumably people participate in those areas they care about the most. Their values, eloquently expressed by their participation, cannot, it seems to me, be more effectively objectified."[8] Secondly, participation is assumed to occur within decision-making arenas, which are in turn assumed to be open to virtually any organized group. Again, Polsby writes, "in the decision-making of fragmented government—and American national, state and local government are nothing if not fragmented—the claims of small intense minorities are usually attended to."[9] In his study of New Haven Dahl takes a similar view:

In the United States the political system does not constitute a homogeneous class with well-defined class interests. In New Haven, in fact, the political system is easily penetrated by anyone whose interests and concerns attract him to the distinctive political culture of the stratum. . . .

The independence, penetrability and heterogeneity of the various segments of the political stratum all but guarantee that any dissatisfied group will find a spokesman . . . .[10]

Thirdly, because of the openness of the decision-making process, leaders may be studied, not as elites, but as representative spokesmen for a mass. Polsby writes, "the pluralists want to find about leadership's role, presumed to be diverse and fluid."[11] Indeed, it is the conflict amongst various leaders that ensures the essential responsiveness of the political game to all groups or classes. As Dahl puts it, "To a remarkable degree, the existence of democratic ceremonials that give rise to the rules of combat has insured that few social elements have been neglected for long by one party or the other."[12]

Within the one-dimensional approach, because a) people act upon recognized grievances, b) in an open system, c) for themselves or through leaders, then *non-participation* or *inaction* is not a political problem. For Polsby it may be explained away with "the fundamental presumption that human behaviour is governed in large part by inertia."[13] Dahl distinguishes between the activist, *homo politicus,* and the non-activist, *homo civicus,* for whom "political action will seem considerably less efficient than working at his job, earning more money, taking out insurance, joining a club, planning a vacation, moving to another neighbourhood or city, or coping with an uncertain future in manifold other ways. . . ."[14] The pluralists argue that by assuming political action rather than inaction to be the problem to be explained, their methodology avoids the "inappropriate and arbitrary assignment of upper and middle class values to all actors in the community"[15]—i.e., the value of participation. Yet, the assumption itself allows class-bound conclusions. Dahl's characterization of *homo civicus* is certainly one of a citizen for whom there are comfortable alternatives to participation and relatively low costs to inaction. And for Polsby, the assumption of inertia combines with the assumption of an open system to allow the conclusion, without further proof, that class consciousness has not developed in America because it would be "inefficient" or "unnecessary."[16]

[5] Peter Bachrach and Morton S. Baratz, "The Two Faces of Power," *American Political Science Review,* 56 (1962), 947–52; and Bachrach and Baratz, *Power and Poverty: Theory and Practice* (Oxford University Press, New York, 1970).
[6] Robert A. Dahl, "The Concept of Power," in Roderick Bell, David M. Edwards, R. Harrison Wagner, eds., *Political Power: A Reader in Theory and Research* (Free Press, New York, 1969), p. 80, reprinted from *Behavioral Science,* 2 (1957), 201–5.
[7] Nelson W. Polsby, *Community Power and Political Theory* (Yale University Press, New Haven, 1963), p. 55.
[8] Nelson W. Polsby, "The Sociology of Community Power; A Reassessment," *Social Forces,* 37 (1959), 235.
[9] Polsby (1963), op. cit., p. 118.

[10] Robert A. Dahl, *Who Governs? Democracy and Power in an American City* (Yale University Press, New Haven, 1961), pp. 91, 93.
[11] Polsby (1963), op. cit., p. 119.
[12] Dahl (1961), op. cit., p. 114.
[13] Polsby (1963), op. cit., p. 116.
[14] Dahl (1961), op. cit., p. 221.
[15] Polsby (1963), op. cit., p. 116.
[16] ibid., p. 118.

The biases of these assumptions might appear all the more readily were this approach strictly applied to the quiescence of obviously deprived groups. Political silence, or inaction, would have to be taken to reflect "consensus," despite the extent of the deprivation. Yet, rarely is the methodology thus applied, even by the pluralists themselves. To make plausible inaction among those for whom the status quo is not comfortable, other explanations are provided for what appears "irrational" or "inefficient" behaviour. And, because the study of non-participation in this approach is sequestered by definition from the study of power, the explanations must generally be placed within the circumstance or culture of the non-participants themselves. The empirical relationship of low socio-economic status to low participation gets explained away as the apathy, political inefficacy, cynicism or alienation of the impoverished.[17] Or other factors—often thought of as deficiencies—are put forward in the non-political culture of the deprived group, such as in the "amoral familism" argument of Banfield in reference to Southern Italy.[18] Rather than examining the possibility that power may be involved, this approach "blames the victim" for his non-participation.[19] And it also follows that by changing the victim—e.g., through remedial education or cultural integration—patterns of non-participation will also be changed. Increased participation, it is assumed, will not meet power constraints.

Even within its own assumptions, of course, this understanding of the political behaviour of deprived groups is inadequate. What is there inherent in low income, education or status, or in rural or traditional cultures that itself explains quiescence? If these are sufficient components of explanation, how are variations in behaviour amongst such groups to be explained? Why, for instance, do welfare action groups spring up in some cities but not in others? Why are the peasantry of southern Italy quiescent (if they are), while the *ujamaa* villagers of Tanzania are not? Why do rural farmers of Saskatchewan form a socialist party while those in the rural areas of the southern United States remain "backward"?[20] If most blacks are of a relatively low socio-economic status, why did a highly organized civil rights movement develop, and itself alter patterns of political participation?

In short, as operationalized within this view, the power of A is thought to affect the action of B, but it is not considered a factor relevant to why B does not act in a manner that B otherwise might, were he not powerless relative to A. That point, among others, is well made by those who put forward the two-dimensional view of power.

The Two-Dimensional Approach. "It is profoundly characteristic," wrote Schattschneider, that "responsibility for widespread nonparticipation is attributed wholly to the ignorance, indifference and shiftlessness of the people." But, he continued:

There is a better explanation: absenteeism reflects the suppression of the options and alternatives that reflect the needs of the nonparticipants. It is not necessarily true that people with the greatest needs participate in politics most actively—whoever decides what the game is about also decides who gets in the game.[21]

In so writing, Schattschneider introduced a concept later to be developed by Bachrach and Baratz as power's "second face," by which power is exercised not just upon participants within the decision-making process but also towards the exclusion of certain participants and issues altogether.[22] Political organizations, like all organizations, develop a "mobilization of bias . . . in favour of the exploitation of certain kinds of conflict and the suppression of others. . . . Some issues are organized into politics while others are organized out."[23] And, if issues are prevented from arising, so too

[17] For examples of this approach see Gabriel Almond and Sidney Verba, *The Civic Culture* (Princeton University Press, 1963), especially Chaps. 7–8; Lester W. Milbraith, *Political Participation* (Rand, McNally and Co., Chicago, 1965); Stein Rokkan, *Approaches to the Study of Political Participation* (The Christian Michelson Institute for Science and Intellectual Freedom, Bergen, 1962); Peter H. Rossi and Zahava D. Blum, "Class, Status and Poverty," in Daniel P. Moynihan, ed., *On Understanding Poverty* (Basic Books, New York, 1968), pp. 36–63. For more general discussions of this literature see S.M. Lipset, *Political Man* (William Heinemann, London, 1959), especially pp. 170–219; or, more recently, Verba and Nie, op. cit.
[18] Edward C. Banfield, *The Moral Basis of Backward Society* (Free Press, Glencoe, Illinois, 1958).
19. See William Ryan, *Blaming the Victim* (Pantheon Books, New York, 1971).

[20] Contrast Lipset's earlier work, *Agrarian Socialism* (University of California Press, Berkeley, 1950) with his later work, *Political Man,* op. cit., pp. 258–9.
[21] E.E. Schattschneider, *The Semi-Sovereign People: A Realist's View of Democracy in America* (Holt, Rinehart and Winston, New York, 1960), p. 105.
[22] Bachrach and Baratz (1962) and (1970), op. cit. See, too, the same authors', "Decisions and Nondecisions: An Analytical Framework," *American Political Science Review,* 57 (1963), 641–51.
[23] Ibid., p. 8, quoting Schattschneider, op. cit., p. 71.

may actors be prevented from acting. The study of politics must focus "both on who gets what, when and how and who gets left out and how"[24]—and how the two are interrelated.

When this view has been applied (explicitly or implicitly) to the political behaviour of deprived groups, explanations for quiescence in the face of inequalities have emerged, which are quite different from those of the one-dimensional view. For instance, Matthew Crenson, in his extended empirical application of the "non-issues" approach, *The Un-Politics of Air Pollution,* states that "while very few investigators have found it worthwhile to inquire about the political origins of inaction . . . ," in Gary, Indiana, "the reputation for power may have been more important than its exercise. It could have enabled U.S. Steel to prevent political action without taking action itself, and may have been responsible for the political retardation of Gary's air pollution issue."[25] Or, Parenti, in his study of urban blacks in Newark, found that in city hall the "plurality of actors and interests . . . displayed remarkable capacity to move against some rather modest lower-class claims." "One of the most important aspects of power," he adds, is "not to prevail in a struggle but to pre-determine the agenda of struggle—to determine whether certain questions ever reach the competition stage."[26] Salamon and Van Evera, in their work on voting in Mississippi, found patterns of participation and non-participation not to be related to apathy amongst low status blacks as much as to "fear" and "vulnerability" of these blacks to local power elites.[27] Similarly, in his extensive study, *Peasant Wars,* Wolf found acquiescence or rebellion not to be inherent in the traditional values or isolation of the peasantry, but to vary "in the relation of the peasantry to the field of power which surrounds it."[28]

In this view, then, apparent inaction within the political process by deprived groups may be related to power, which in turn is revealed in participation and non-participation, upon issues and non-issues, which arise or are prevented from arising in decision-making arenas. But though the second view goes beyond the first, it still leaves much undone.

Empirically, while the major application of the approach, that by Crenson, recognizes that "perceived industrial influence, industrial inaction, and the neglect of the dirty air issue go together," it still adds "though it is difficult to say how."[29]

Even conceptually, though, this second approach stops short of considering the full range of the possibilities by which power may intervene in the issue-raising process. While Bachrach and Baratz insist that the study of power must include consideration of the barriers to action upon grievances, they equally maintain that it does not go so far as to include how power may affect conceptions of grievances themselves. If "the observer can uncover no grievances," if "in other words, there appears to be universal acquiescence in the status quo," then, they argue, it is not "possible, in such circumstances, to determine empirically whether the consensus is genuine or instead has been enforced."[30]

However difficult the empirical task, though, their assumption must be faulted on two counts. First, as Lukes points out, "to assume the absence of grievance equals genuine consensus is simply to rule out the possibility of false or manipulated consensus by definitional fiat."[31] Secondly, though, the position presents an inconsistency even within their own work. They write further:

For the purposes of analysis, a power struggle exists, overtly or covertly, either when both sets of contestants are aware of its existence *or when only the less powerful party is aware* of it. The latter case is relevant where the domination of status quo defenders is so secure and pervasive that they are oblivious of any persons or groups desirous of challenging their preeminence.[32]

But, if the power of the "defenders of the *status quo*" serves to affect their awareness that they are being challenged, why cannot the powerlessness of potential

[24] ibid., p. 105.

[25] Matthew A. Crenson, *The Un-Politics of Air Pollution: A Study of Non-Decision-Making in the Cities* (Johns Hopkins Press, Baltimore, 1971), pp. 130, 80.

[26] Michael Parenti, "Power and Pluralism: A View From the Bottom," *Journal of Politics,* 32 (1970), 501–30.

[27] Lester Salamon and Stephen Van Evera, "Fear, Apathy and Discrimination: A Test of Three Explanations of Political Participation," *American Political Science Review,* 67 (1973), 1288–1306.

[28] Eric Wolf, *Peasant Wars of the Twentieth Century* (Faber and Faber, London, 1969), pp. 276–302 generally, and especially p. 290.

[29] Crenson, op. cit., p. 124. Also, Crenson's study is more one of inaction amongst decision-makers on a single issue rather than of passivity amongst non-elites who may be outside the decision-making process altogether. See critique by Edward Greer, "Air Pollution and Corporate Power: Municipal Reform Limits in a Black Community," *Politics and Society,* 4 (1974), 483–510.

[30] Bachrach and Baratz (1970), op. cit., pp. 49–50.

[31] Lukes, op. cit., p. 24.

[32] Bachrach and Baratz (1970) op. cit., p. 50 (emphasis supplied).

challengers similarly serve to affect their awareness of interests and conflict within a power situation? That is, just as the dominant may become so "secure" with their position as to become "oblivious," so, too, may such things as routines, internalization of roles or false consensus lead to acceptance of the *status quo* by the dominated. In short, I shall agree with Lukes that the emphasis of this approach upon observable conflict may lead it to neglect what may be the "crucial point": "the most effective and insidious use of power is to prevent such conflict from arising in the first place."[33]

The Three-Dimensional Approach.   In putting forward a further conception of power, Lukes argues that "A exercises power over B when A affects B in a manner contrary to B's interests."[34] The means by which A may do so go significantly beyond, those allowed within the first two approaches.

First, "A may exercise power over B by getting him to do what he does not want to do, but *he also exercises power over him by influencing, shaping or determining his very wants.*"[35] Not only might A exercise power over B by prevailing in the resolution of key issues or by preventing B from effectively raising those issues, but also through affecting B's conceptions of the issues altogether. Secondly, "this may happen in the absence of observable conflict, which may have been successfully averted," though there must be latent conflict, which consists, Lukes argues, "in a contradiction between the interests of those exercising power and the *real interests* of those they exclude."[36] Thirdly, the analysis of power must avoid the individualistic, behavioural confines of the one- and to some extent the two-dimensional approaches. It must allow "for consideration of the many ways in which *potential issues* are kept out of politics, whether through the operation of social forces and institutional practices or through individuals' decisions."[37] In so extending the concept of power, Lukes suggests, "the three-dimensional view . . . offers the prospect of a serious sociological and not merely personalized explanation of how political systems prevent demands from becoming political issues or even from being made."[38]

Though the prospect has been offered, the task has

yet to have been carried out. To do so, though, might bring together usefully approaches often considered separately of the relationship of political conceptions to the social order. For instance, following in a line of American political scientists (beginning perhaps with Lasswell), the emphasis upon consciousness allows consideration of the subjective effects of power, including Edelman's notion that "political actions chiefly arouse or satisfy people not by granting or withholding their stable, substantive demands but rather by changing their demands and expectations."[39] At the same time, by not restricting power to individuals' actions, the three-dimensional definition allows consideration of the social forces and historical patterns involved in Gramsci's concept of hegemony, or what Milliband develops as the use of ideological predominance for the "engineering of consent" amongst the subordinate classes.[40]

Perhaps more significant, however, are the implications of this three-dimensional approach for an understanding of how power shapes participation patterns of the relatively powerless. In a sense, the separation by the pluralists of the notion of power from the phenomenon of quiescence has indicated the need for such a theory, while in the second and third approaches are its beginnings. In the two-dimensional approach is the suggestion of barriers that prevent issues from emerging into political arenas—i.e. that constrain conflict. In the three-dimensional approach is the suggestion of the use of power to pre-empt manifest conflict at all, through the shaping of patterns or conceptions of non-conflict. Yet, the two-dimensional approach may still need development and the three-dimensional prospect has yet to be put to empirical test.

This book therefore will pick up the challenge of attempting to relate the three dimensions of power to an understanding of quiescence and rebellion of a relatively powerless group in a social situation of high inequality. Through the empirical application further refinements of the notion of power may develop, but, of equal importance, more insights may be gleaned as

[33] Lukes, op. cit., pp. 20, 23.
[34] ibid., p. 34.
[35] ibid., p. 23 (emphasis supplied).
[36] ibid., pp. 24–5.
[37] ibid., p. 24.
[38] ibid., p. 38.

[39] Murray Edelman, *Politics as Symbolic Action: Mass Arousal and Quiescence* (Markham Publishing Co., Chicago, 1971), p. 8.
[40] Antonio Gramsci, *Selections from the Prison Notebooks of . . .* ed. and trans., by Quinton Hare and Geoffrey Nowell-Smith (Lawrence and Wishart, London, 1971), see especially selections of "State and Civil Society," in pp. 206–78. Ralph Milliband, *The State in Capitalist Society: An Analysis of the Western Systems of Power* (Weidenfeld and Nicolson, London, 1969), pp. 180–2.

to why non-elites in such situations act and believe as they do.

THE MECHANISMS OF POWER

What are the mechanisms of power? How might its components be wielded in the shaping or containment of conflict?

First Dimension. In the first-dimensional approach to power, with its emphasis on observable conflict in decision-making arenas, power may be understood primarily by looking at who prevails in bargaining over the resolution of key issues. The mechanisms of power are important, but relatively straightforward and widely understood: they involve the political resources—votes, jobs, influence—that can be brought by political actors to the bargaining game and how well those resources can be wielded in each particular play—through personal efficacy, political experience, organizational strength, and so on.

Second Dimension. The second-dimensional approach adds to these resources those of a "mobilization of bias,"

A set of predominant values, beliefs, rituals, and institutional procedures ("rules of the game") that operate systematically and consistently to the benefit of certain persons and groups at the expense of others. Those who benefit are placed in a preferred position to defend and promote their vested interests.[41]

Bachrach and Baratz argue in *Power and Poverty* that the mobilization of bias not only may be wielded upon decision-making in political arenas, but it in turn is sustained primarily through "non-decision," defined as:

A decision that results in suppression or thwarting of a latent or manifest challenge to the values or interests of the decision maker. To be more nearly explicit, nondecision-making is a means by which demands for change in the existing allocation of benefits and privileges in the community can be suffocated before they are voiced, or kept covert; or killed before they gain access to the relevant decision-making arena; or, failing all of these things, maimed or destroyed in the decision-implementing stage of the policy process.[42]

One form of non-decision-making, they suggest, may be force. A second may be the threat of sanctions, "negative or positive," "ranging from intimidation . . . to co-optation." A third may be the "invocation of an existing bias of the political system—a norm, precedent, rule or procedure—to squelch a threatening demand or incipient issue." This may include the manipulation of symbols, such as, in certain political cultures, "communist" or "troublemaker." A fourth process which they cite "involves reshaping or strengthening the mobilization of bias" through the establishment of new barriers or new symbols "against the challengers' efforts to widen the scope of conflict."

While the above mechanisms of power involve identifiable actions which prevent issues from entering the decision-making arenas, there may be other processes of non-decision-making power, which are not so explicitly observable. The first of these, "decisionless decisions," grows from institutional inaction, or the unforeseen sum effect of incremental decisions. A second process has to do with the "rule of anticipated reactions," "situations where B, confronted by A who has greater power resources decides not to make a demand upon A, for fear that the latter will invoke sanctions against him."[43] In both cases, the power process involves a non-event rather than an observable non-decision.

Third Dimension. By far the least developed and least understood mechanisms of power—at least within the field of political science—are those of the third dimension. Their identification, one suspects, involves specifying the means through which power influences, shapes or determines conceptions of the necessities, possibilities, and strategies of challenge in situations of latent conflict. This may include the study of social myths, language, and symbols, and how they are shaped or manipulated in power processes.[44] It may involve the study of communication of information—both of what is communicated and how it is done.[45] It may involve a focus upon the means by which social legitimations are developed around the dominant, and

---

[41] Bachrach and Baratz (1970), op. cit., p. 43.
[42] ibid., p. 44.

[43] ibid., pp. 42–6.
[44] See, for instance, Edelman, op. cit.; Edelman, *The Symbolic Uses of Politics* (University of Illinois Press, Urbana, 1967); and Edelman, "Symbols and Political Quiescence," *American Political Science Review,* 54 (1960), 695–704.
[45] For example, as developed by Claus Mueller, *The Politics of Communication: A Study in the Political Sociology of Language, Socialization and Legitimation* (Oxford University Press, New York, 1973).

instilled as beliefs or roles in the dominated.[46] It may involve, in short, locating the power processes behind the social construction of meanings and patterns[47] that serve to get B to act and believe in a manner in which B otherwise might not, to A's benefit and B's detriment.

Such processes may take direct observable forms, as Lukes suggests. "One does not have to go to the lengths of talking about Brave New World, or the world of B.F. Skinner to see this: thought control takes many less total and more mundane forms, through the control of information, through the mass media, and through the process of socialization."[48] His assertions are supported in various branches of contemporary social science. For instance, Deutsch and Rieselbach, in writing of new developments in the field, say that communications theory "permits us to conceive of such elusive notions as consciousness and the political will as observable processes."[49] Similarly, the study of socialization, enlightened by learning theory, may help to uncover the means by which dominance is maintained or legitimacy instilled, as Mann or Frey, among others, argue.[50]

In addition to these processes of information control or socialization, there may be other more indirect means by which power alters political conceptions. They involve psychological adaptations to the state of being without power. They may be viewed as third-dimensional effects of power, growing from the powerlessness experienced in the first two dimensions. Especially for highly deprived or vulnerable groups, three examples might be given of what shall be called the *indirect* mechanisms of power's third dimension.

In the first instance, the conceptions of the powerless may alter as an adaptive response to continual defeat. If the victories of A over B in the first dimension of power lead to non-challenge of B due to the anticipation of the reactions of A, as in the second-dimensional case, then, over time, the calculated withdrawal by B may lead to an unconscious pattern of withdrawal, maintained not by fear of power of A but by a sense of powerlessness within B, regardless of A's condition. A sense of powerlessness may manifest itself as extensive fatalism, self-deprecation, or undue apathy about one's situation. Katznelson has argued, for instance, in *Black Men, White Cities* that "given the onus of choice, the powerless internalize their impossible situation and internalize their guilt . . . The slave often identified with his master and accepted society's estimate of himself as being without worth . . . The less complete but nonetheless pervasive powerlessness of blacks in America's northern ghettos . . . has had similar effects."[51] Or, the powerless may act, but owing to the sense of their powerlessness, they may alter the level of their demands.[52] The sense of powerlessness may also lead to a greater susceptibility to the internalization of the values, beliefs, or rules of the game of the powerful as a further adaptive response—i.e. as a means of escaping the subjective sense of powerlessness, if not its objective condition.[53]

The sense of powerlessness may often be found with, though it is conceptually distinct from, a second example of the indirect mechanisms of power's third dimension. It has to do with the interrelationship of participation and consciousness. As has been seen in the pluralists' literature, it is sometimes argued that participation is a consequence of a high level of political awareness or knowledge, most often associated with those of a favourable socio-economic status. However, it might also be the case, as is argued by the classical democratic theorists, that it is participation itself which increases political consciousness—a reverse argument from the one given above.[54] Social

[46] ibid.; see, too, Milliband, op. cit., pp. 179–264; and C. Wright Mills, *The Sociological Imagination* (Oxford University Press, New York, 1956), pp. 36–40.

[47] This is to suggest that processes may be similar to those suggested by Berger and Luckmann but that the processes are not random. They occur in a power field and to the advantage of power interests. See Peter L. Berger and Thomas Luckmann, *The Social Construction of Reality* (Doubleday and Co., New York, 1966); and critique by Richard Lichtmann, "Symbolic Interaction and Social Reality: Some Marxist Queries," *Berkeley Journal of Sociology,* 15 (1970), 75–94.

[48] Lukes, op. cit., p. 23.

[49] Karl W. Deutsch and Leroy Rieselbach, "Recent Trends in Political Theory and Political Philosophy," *The Annals of the American Political and Social Science,* 360 (1965), 151.

[50] Michael Mann, "The Social Cohesion of Liberal Democracy," *American Sociological Review,* 35 (1970). Frederick W. Frey, "Comment: On Issues and Non-Issues in the Study of Power," *American Political Science Review,* 65 (1971), 1081–1101.

[51] Ira Katznelson, *Black Men, White Cities* (Oxford University Press, 1973), p. 198.

[52] Walter Korpi, "Conflict, Power and Relative Deprivation," *American Political Science Review,* 68 (1974). Korpi writes, "in the long run the weaker actor will, through internal psychological processes, tend to adjust his aspiration level towards the going rates of exchange in the relationship" (p. 1571).

[53] See discussion by Paulo Freire, *The Pedagogy of the Oppressed* (Penguin Books, Harmondsworth, Middx, 1972), pp. 1–39.

[54] e.g. Rousseau, John Stuart Mill, G.D.H. Cole. See discussion of this theme in Pateman, op. cit., Chap. 3.

psychology studies, for instance, have found that political learning is dependent at least to some degree of political participation within and mastery upon one's environment.[55] And, as Pizzorno points out, there is a "singular relationship, well known by all organizers of parties and political movements: class consciousness promotes political participation, and in its turn, political participation increases class consciousness."[56] If this second understanding of the relationship to participation and consciousness is the case, then it should also be the case that those denied participation—unable to engage actively with others in the determination of their own affairs—also might not develop political consciousness of their own situation or of broader political inequalities.

This relationship of non-participation to non-consciousness of deprived groups is developed by Paulo Freire, one of the few writers to have considered the topic in depth. "Consciousness," he writes, "is constituted in the dialectic of man's *objectification* and *action* upon the world."[57] In situations of highly unequal power relationships, which he terms "closed societies," the powerless are highly dependent. They are prevented from either self-determined action or reflection upon their actions. Denied this dialectic process, and denied the democratic experience out of which the "critical consciousness" grows, they develop a "culture of silence." "The dependent society is by definition a silent society." The culture of silence may preclude the development of consciousness amongst the powerless thus lending to the dominant order an air of legitimacy. As in the sense of powerlessness, it may also encourage a susceptibility among the dependent society to internalization of the values of the dominant themselves. "Its voice is not an authentic voice, but merely an echo of the metropolis. In every way the metropolis speaks, the dependent society listens."[58] Mueller similarly writes about groups which "cannot articulate their interests or perceive social conflict. Since they have been socialized into compliance, so to speak, they accept the definitions of political reality as offered by dominant groups, classes or government institutions."[59]

Even as the "silence" is broken, the initial demands of the dominated may be vague, ambiguous, partially developed. This might help to explain the phenomenon of the "multiple" or "split" consciousness[60] often cited in the literature for poor or working-class groups. As long as elements of the sense of powerlessness or the assuming consciousness that grow from non-participation can be maintained, then although there may be a multitude of grievances, the "unified" or "critical" consciousness will likely remain precluded. And, in turn, the inconsistencies themselves may re-enforce the pattern of non-challenge. In Gramsci's terms, "it can reach the point where the contradiction of conscience will not permit any decision, any choice, and produce a state of moral and political passivity."[61]

This understanding gives rise to a final indirect means through which power's third dimension may work. Garson has described the "multiple consciousness" as being characterized by "ambiguity and overlays of consciousness; different and seemingly contradictory orientations will be evoked *depending upon the context.*"[62] If such is the case, then the consciousness of the relatively powerless, even as it emerges, may be malleable, i.e. especially vulnerable to the manipulation of the power field around it. Through the invocation of myths or symbols, the use of threat or rumours, or other mechanisms of power, the powerful may be able to ensure that certain beliefs and actions emerge in one context while apparently contradictory grievances may be expressed in others. From this perspective, a consistently expressed consensus is not required for the maintenance of dominant interests, only a consistency that certain potentially key issues remain latent issues and that certain interests remain unrecognized—at certain times more than at others.

These direct and indirect mechanisms of power's third dimension combine to suggest numerous possibilities of the means through which power may serve to shape conceptions of the necessities, possibilities, or strategies of conflict. Not only, as in the two-dimensional approach, might grievances be excluded from entering the political process, but they might be precluded from consideration altogether. Or, B, the relatively powerless, may recognize grievances against A, the relatively powerful, but desist from challenge because B's conceptions of self, group, or class may be

[55] Melvin Seeman, "Alienation, Membership, and Political Knowledge: A Comparative Study," *Public Opinion Quarterly,* 30 (1966), 353–67.

[56] Allesandro Pizzorno, "An Introduction to the Theory of Political Participation," *Social Science Information,* 9 (1970), 45.

[57] Paulo Freire, *Cultural Action for Freedom* (Penguin Books, Harmondsworth, Middx, 1972), p. 52.

[58] ibid., pp. 58–9.

[59] Mueller, op. cit., p. 9.

[60] David Garson, "Automobile Workers and the American Dream," *Politics and Society,* 3 (1973), 163–79; Antonio Gramsci, trans. by Lewis Marks, *The Modern Prince and Other Writings* (International Publishers, New York, 1957), p. 66.

[61] Gramsci (1957), op. cit., p. 67.

[62] Garson, op. cit., p. 163.

such as to make actions against A seem inappropriate. Or, B may recognize grievances, be willing to act upon them, but not recognize A as the responsible agent towards which action should be directed—e.g. because of the mystifications or legitimations which surround A. Or, B may recognize grievances against A and be willing to act, but may not through viewing the order as immutable or through lacking conceptions of possible alternatives. Or, B may act, but do so on the basis of misconceived grievances, against the wrong target, or through an ineffective strategy. Any or all of these possibilities may serve the same purpose of protecting A's interests owing to B's shaped conceptions of potential conflict, to B's detriment.

But the indirect mechanisms of power's third dimension, seen as a consequence of the powerlessness experienced in the first two, have suggested yet a further consideration: the dimensions of power, each with its sundry mechanisms, must be seen as interrelated in the totality of their impact. In that simple idea lies the basis for developing a more coherent theory about the effects of power and powerlessness upon quiescence and rebellion in situations of great inequality.

POWER AND POWERLESSNESS: QUIESCENCE AND REBELLION— A TENTATIVE RELATIONSHIP

Power, it has been suggested, involves the capacity of A to prevail over B both in resolution of manifest conflict and through affecting B's actions and conceptions about conflict or potential conflict. Intuitively, if the interests of A and B are contrary, and if A (individual, group, class) exercises power for the protection of its interests, then it will also be to A's advantage if the power can be used to generate and maintain quiescence of B (individual, group, class) upon B's interests. In that process, the dimensions of power and powerlessness may be viewed as interrelated and accumulative in nature, such that each dimension serves to re-enforce the strength of the other. The relationships may be schematized, as in Figure 1, and described as follows[63]:

As A develops power, A prevails over B in decision-making arenas in the allocation of resources and values within the political system [1]. If A prevails consistently, then A may accumulate surplus resources and

values which may be allocated towards the construction of barriers around the decision-making arenas— i.e. towards the development of a mobilization of bias, as in the second dimension of power [2]. The consistent prevalence of A in the decision-making arenas plus the thwarting of challenges to that prevalence may allow A further power to invest in the development of dominant images, legitimations, or beliefs about A's power through control, for instance, of the media or other socialization institutions [3]. The power of A to prevail in the first dimension increases the power to affect B's actions in the second dimension, and increases the power to affect B's conceptions in the third.

The power of A is also strengthened by the fact that the powerlessness of B is similarly accumulative, and that power and powerlessness may each re-enforce the other towards the generation of B's quiescence. In the decision-making arena, B suffers continual defeat at the hands of A [4]. Over time, B may cease to challenge A owing to the anticipation that A will prevail [5]. But B's non-challenge allows A more opportunity to devote power to creating barriers to exclude participation in the future [2, 5]. The inaction of B in the second-dimensional sense becomes a sum of the anticipation by B of defeat and the barriers maintained by A over B's entering the decision-making arena anyway, and the re-enforcing effect of one upon the other.

In turn, the second-dimensional relationship may re-enforce the sense of powerlessness, the maintained non-participation, the ambiguous consciousness, or other factors which comprise the indirect mechanisms of power's third dimension [5, 6]. Further withdrawal of B though, in turn, allows more security for A to develop further legitimations or ideologies which may be used indirectly to affect the conceptions of B [3, 6]. And, as has been seen, the powerlessness of B may also increase the susceptibility of B to introjection of A's values. In the third-dimensional sense, then, B's response becomes understood as the sum of B's powerlessness and A's power, and the re-enforcing effects of the one upon the other.

Once such power relationships are developed, their maintenance is self-propelled and attempts at their alteration are inevitably difficult. In order to remedy the inequalities, B must act, but to do so B must overcome A's power, and the accumulating effects of B's powerlessness. In order to benefit from the inequalities, A need not act, or if acting, may devote energies to strengthening the power relationships. Indeed, to the extent that A can maintain conflict within the second-

---

[63] This is not meant to imply that in an empirical situation the relationships develop in this sequence, or in a linear fashion at all. However, it is analytically useful to describe them in this manner.

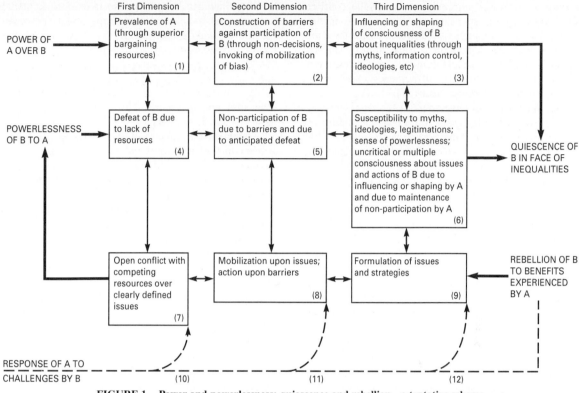

FIGURE 1   Power and powerlessness: quiescence and rebellion—a tentative scheme.

or third-dimensional arenas, then A will continue to prevail simply through the inertia of the situation. Pocock describes what may have been such a relationship with reference to the maintenance of power by Ancient Chinese rulers:

Where A has the power and B has not, it is a sign of weakness for either to take initiative, but B must take it and A need not . . . Once acquired, it (power) is maintained not by exertion but by inaction; not by imposing norms, but by being prerequisite to their imposition; not by the display of virtue, but by the characterless force of its own necessity. The ruler rules not by solving other's problems, but by having none of his own; others have problems—i.e. they desire the power he has—and by keeping these unsolved he retains the power over them.[64]

In such a situation, power relationships can be understood only with reference to their prior development

and their impact comprehended only in the light of their own momentum.

Challenge, or rebellion, may develop if there is a shift in the power relationships—either owing to loss in the power of A or gain in the power of B. (The two need not be the same owing to the possibility of intervention by other actors, technological changes, external structural factors, etc.) But even as challenge emerges, several steps in overcoming powerlessness by B must occur before the conflict is on competitive ground.[65] B must go through a process of *issue and action formulation* by which B develops consciousness of the needs, possibilities, and strategies of challenge. That is, B must counter both the direct and indirect effects of power's third dimension [9]. And, B must carry out the process of *mobilization of action upon issues* to overcome the mobilization of bias of A against B's actions. B must develop its own

---

[64] J.G.A. Pocock, "Ritual, Language and Power," in Pocock, *Politics, Language, and Time: Essays on Political Thought and History* (Methuen, London, 1970), p. 69.

[65] Parenti, op. cit., calls this the problem of political capital accumulation: "just as one needs capital to make capital, so one needs power to use power" (p. 527).

resources—real and symbolic—to wage the conflict [8]. Only as the obstacles to challenge by B in the second and third dimensions are overcome can the conflict which emerges in the first dimension be said to reflect B's genuine participation—i.e. self-determined action with others similarly affected upon clearly conceived and articulated grievances [7].

This formulation of the steps in the emergence of effective challenge provides further understanding of the means by which A may prevail over the outcome of any latent or manifest conflict. In the first instance, A may simply remain aloof from B, for to intervene in a situation of potential conflict may be to introduce the notion of conflict itself. But, if conceptions or actions of challenge do arise on the part of B, A may respond at any point along the process of issue-emergence. That is, the powerless may face barriers to effective challenge in the processes of the formulation of issues, of the mobilization of action upon issues, or in the decision-making about issues—any or all of which may affect the outcome of the conflict [10, 11, 12 . . .]. What are for B barriers to change are for A options for the maintenance of the status quo.

But, by the same token, as the barriers are overcome, so, too, do A's options for control lessen. And, just as the dimensions of power are accumulative and re-enforcing for the maintenance of quiescence, so, too, does the emergence of challenge in one area of a power relationship weaken the power of the total to withstand further challenges by more than the loss of a single component. For example, the development of consciousness of an issue re-enforces the likelihood of attempted action upon it, in turn re-enforcing consciousness. A single victory helps to alter inaction owing to the anticipation of defeat, leading to more action, and so on. Once patterns of quiescence are broken upon one set of grievances, the accumulating resources of challenge—e.g. organization, momentum, consciousness—may become transferable to other issues and other targets.

For this reason, the development and maintenance of a generalized pattern of quiescence of B by A in situations of latent conflict will always be in A's interests. A will act to thwart challenges by B regardless of whether they appear, in the immediate sense, to be directed against A; for once the patterns are broken, the likelihood of further action by B increases and the options for control wielded by A decrease. For this reason, too, A will support A' on matters of common interest *vis-à-vis* the behaviour and conceptions of B; and B must ally with B' for the emergence of effective

challenge against A—giving rise over time to social grouping and social classes of the relatively powerful and the relatively powerless.

METHODOLOGICAL CONSIDERATIONS

What may appear conceptually useful may not correspond to actual circumstance. That which is analytically distinct may in fact occur simultaneously. Thus, a primary task of this study is to consider whether this model of power and participation can be applied to an empirical situation and whether that process in turn can lend further understanding to the relationships so far put forward. That there are methodological difficulties to the task is recognized from the outset. The suggestion of Bachrach and Baratz of even a "second face" of power met vocal challenge on procedural grounds: how can one find the "hidden" aspects of power? How can a non-decision be observed? Which non-events are relevant?[66] The presentation of a "third face" of power poses yet further problems: How can one study what does not happen? What about the problem of imputing interests and values? This book argues that these problems are surmountable. Broad guidelines used for the empirical study are presented here. Then, the telling test for the method, as for the model, will be the extent to which it helps to illuminate the empirical case itself.

In the first instance, the methodology assumes Frey's suggestion that "we can expect non-issues when: 1) glaring inequalities occur in the distribution of things avowedly valued by actors in the system, and 2) those inequalities do not seem to occasion ameliorative influence attempts by those getting less of those values."[67] Secondly, rather than assuming the inaction or inertia to be "natural" in the mass and activism as the phenomenon to be explained (as is done in the pluralist methodology), this approach initially assumes that remedial action upon inequalities by those affected would occur were it not for power relationships. The

---

[66] For example, Raymond E. Wolfinger, "Nondecisions and the Study of Local Politics," *American Political Science Review,* 65 (1971), 1063–80; also, "Rejoinder to Frey's Comment," *American Political Science Review,* 65 (1971), 1102–4; Richard M. Merelman, "On the Neo-Elitist Critiques of Community Power," *American Political Science Review,* 62 (1968), 451–60; Polsby (1963), op. cit.

[67] Frey, op. cit., p. 1097. This is essentially the approach used by Crenson, who objectively identifies varying levels in air pollution, assumes that people generally do not want to be poisoned, and asks why action upon pollution does not occur.

study of quiescence in a situation of potential conflict becomes the task, rather than the study of manifest conflict in a situation otherwise assumed to be conflict-free.

It is not adequate, however, merely to observe that inequalities exist and that such inequalities are met only by quiescence, to conclude that non-challenge is a product of power. As Lukes questions, "Can we always assume that the victims of injustice and inequality would, but for the exercise of power, strive for justice and equality?"[68] On the contrary, he writes, "we need to justify our expectation that B would have thought and acted differently, and we need to specify the means or mechanisms by which A has prevented, or else acted (or abstained from acting) in a manner sufficient to prevent B from doing so."[69] From the model put forward, I suggest there are several means in an empirical study through which "relevant counterfactuals" can be demonstrated to substantiate the expectation that B would have thought and acted differently, were it not for A's power.

In general, to do so requires going outside the decision-making arenas and carrying on extensive, time-consuming research in the community in question. There, non-actors and non-leaders become important, not as objects of scrutiny in themselves but to discover through their experiences, lives, conditions, and attitudes, whether and by what means power processes may serve to maintain non-conflict.

In pursuing the answer to the question more specifically, it may be necessary, first to look at the historical development of an apparent "consensus." In so doing, it may be possible to determine whether that situation has been arrived at by "choice" or whether it has been shaped by power relations. And, the background study may help to identify certain key symbols, cues, or routines that affect the maintenance of quiescence in a given situation but which may not be identifiable as part of the "language of power" without knowledge of their antecedents.

Secondly, within a given situation of apparent non-challenge, processes of communication, socialization, acculturation, etc., can be studied to determine whether there is a specific relationship between the actions or ideologies of the powerholders and the action, inaction or beliefs of the powerless. In addition, it might be possible to determine whether the conditions do exist under which the actions and consciousness of B could

develop, or whether identifiable power barriers serve to preclude their development, as in the indirect mechanisms of power.

Thirdly, it might be possible in a given or changing situation to posit or participate in ideas or actions which speculate about or attempt to develop challenges. The response of the quiescent population to such possibilities, and the response of the power-holders to the beginning formulation or raising of issues may help to show whether power mechanisms are at work to preclude challenge from emerging.

Even if the identification of specific processes of power is successful, it still does not satisfy the requirement of justifying the "expectation that B would have thought and acted differently." Several more types of evidence must be gathered. First, as Lukes suggests, it may be possible to observe what occurs on the part of B when the power of A over B weakens, i.e. in "abnormal times . . . when the apparatus of power is removed or relaxed."[70] Secondly, it may be possible to observe what occurs when alternative opportunities for action develop within B's field—through the intervention of third parties or new resources. If action or conceptions of action emerge upon previously existing conditions—whether due to alteration in the power of A or the powerlessness of B—then it may be possible to argue that the prior inaction or apparent consensus did not reflect real consensus. Finally, it may be possible to develop a comparative approach to the study of the problem: if similarly deprived groups are faced with observably differing degrees of power, and if one rebels while the other does not, then it should be possible to argue that the differing responses are related to differences in the power relationships.

If, after following such guidelines, no mechanisms of power can be identified and no relevant counterfactuals can be found, then the researcher must conclude that the quiescence of a given deprived group is, in fact, based upon consensus of that group to their condition, owing for instance, to differing values from those initially posited by the observer. In this sense, this approach allows the falsifiability of the hypothetical relationships being explored.[71] Moreover, the "third-dimensional methodology" provides the possibility of reaching conclusions that power in a given situation is either three- or two- or one-dimensional in nature—a possibility not provided for in the other two approaches. Thus, the conclusions of this approach are

---

[68] Lukes, op. cit., p. 46.
[69] ibid., pp. 41–2.

[70] ibid., p. 47.
[71] See, for instance, critique by Merelman, op. cit.

less dependent upon the methodological assumptions than they might be in the approach of the pluralists' or of Bachrach and Baratz.

However, assumptions must be made in this, as in all studies of power, about the definitions of three key concepts: interests, consciousness and consensus.

For the observer to posit that B would act towards the attainment of a value X or would want X were it not for the power processes of A may involve avowing that X is in B's interest. However, to do so—unlike it is often alleged[72]—is not necessarily to avow that X is in B's real interest, nor to give the observer the right to impose his interpretation of what is B's interest upon B. Rather, the observer's interpretation of what appears in a given context to be in B's interest may be used as a methodological tool for discovering whether power relationships are such as to have precluded the active and conscious choice by B about such interests, regardless of what the outcome of that choice actually would be. What B would choose (were B free from the power of A to do so) would be B's real interests—but they do not require identification for the study of power. That B is prevented from acting upon or conceiving certain posited interests is sufficient to show that the interests that are expressed by B are probably not B's real ones.[73]

The stance has ramifications for the consideration of consciousness. The unfortunate term "false consciousness" must be avoided, for it is analytically confusing. Consciousness refers to a *state,* as in a state of being, and thus can only be falsified through negation of the state itself. If consciousness exists, it is real to its holders, and thus to the power situation. To discount it as "false" may be to discount too simply the complexities or realities of the situation. What is far more accurate (and useful) is to describe the content, source, or nature of the consciousness—whether it reflects awareness of certain interests and not of others, whether it is critical or assuming, whether it has been developed through undue influence of A, and so on.

To argue that existing consciousness cannot be

"false" is not to argue the same for consensus. "Real" consensus implies a prior process of agreement or choice, which in a situation of apparent consensus may or may not have been the case. The process may not have occurred; it could have been shaped or manipulated; the "consensus" could be maintained by power processes, etc. In any event, what may appear consensus may not be what would appear were the real process to take place. The investigation of the possibility that power processes have given rise to a "false" consensus must be carried on to establish more accurately the nature of the first appearance.

Examples: The Closed and Colonial Societies. Even with the help of these methodological guidelines, the identification of power processes may be easier in some situations than in others. For instance, in his pluralist critique of Bachrach and Baratz, Wolfinger readily accepts that power relationships may affect consciousness and action in closed societies, such as the plantation South. He writes, "Some examples of false consciousness are indisputable, e.g. the long period of feeble protest by southern Negroes. Their reticence was due in part to repression, but much of it was based on myths and procedures." Moreover, in making such conclusions, Wolfinger attributes to the Negro certain interests (as goals) assumed to be common: "Almost any social scientist would agree that the blacks have been manipulated, because almost any social scientists' views of rational behaviour, irrespective of their specific character, would attribute certain goals to southern Negroes."[74] What appears to be in question in this and other pluralists' critiques, then, is not whether the hidden faces of power exist, nor whether methodological assumptions can be made in certain situations for their identification, but whether such methods can be applied to consideration of the concepts in other situations—especially those of the more "open" industrial democracies. There, the assumption is made in the pluralists' methodology that non-conflict represents social cohesion or integration, not, as others have argued, social control or hegemony.

It may be possible to develop an explanatory theory further, though, by looking not just at the example of the closed society but at situations where penetration (or integration) have not fully occurred and in which power processes, if they are at work, may be more readily self-evident. One example of such a case might

[72] See, for instance, Polsby (1963), op. cit., p. 96; Wolfinger "Nondecisions and the Study of Local Politics," op. cit., p. 1066.
[73] See discussion by William E. Connolly, "On 'Interests' in Politics," *Politics and Society,* 2 (1972), 459–77. This definition is similar to Connolly's that: "Policy X is more in A's interest than policy Y if A, were he to *experience* the results of both X and Y, would *choose* X as the result he would rather have for himself" (p. 472). However, less emphasis is put on the ability to experience the unforeseen consequences of a given choice; more on the process of making the choice itself.

[74] Wolfinger, "Nondecisions and the Study of Local Politics," op. cit., p. 1077.

be found in the colonial or neo-colonial relationship, involving, as it does, the power of a metropolis or developed industrial society over a less developed, more traditional society.

In the first instance, the development of domination, or *the colonizing process,* involves the prevailing of the colonizer over the allocation of resources in the colony owing to superior resources of the former, such as capital, technology, or force. Secondly, however, the maintenance of that power involves the establishment of certain institutions and organizational forms. As Emerson describes:

Imperialism spread to the world at large the ideas, techniques, and institutions which had emerged from many centuries of European history. By its direct impact . . . it established many of the forms and methods of the West abroad, inevitably disrupting in greater or lesser degree the native societies on which it encroached in the process.[75]

The establishment of dominance includes the development of an administrative relationship by the dominant society over the dominated, either through the direct control of the representatives of the former, or through the development of collaborators or mediating elites amongst the latter. It includes a prevailing ideology through which the values of the metropolis are legitimated as superior and those of the colony as inferior. In short, the colonization process involves the development of a mobilization of bias—a set of predominant values, beliefs and institutional procedures that operate systematically to the benefit of the colonizer at the expense of the colonized. It is the development of a second-dimensional power relationship.

However, writers of and about the Third World insist that there is a further form of power that grows out of the effective colonizing process—one which serves to shape the legitimacy of the colonizers' dominance. Referring to the internalization of alien norms amongst dependent societies, Balandier wrote in 1951 of the *colonial situation* which "not only conditioned the reaction of dependent peoples but is still responsible for certain reactions of people recently emanci-

pated."[76] Others, such as Freire, Fanon, and Memmi have since described further the means by which the consciousness of the colonized is affected by the values of the colonizer, as well as the extent to which the shaping is strengthened because of the sense of inadequacy or submissiveness amongst the dominated. Memmi, for instance, writes that as power develops its justifying ideology, so, too, must powerlessness:

There undoubtedly exists—at some point in its evolution—a certain adherence of the colonized to colonization. However, this adherence is the result of colonization not its cause. It arises after and not before colonial occupation. In order for the colonizer to be complete master, it is not enough for him to be so in actual fact, but he must believe in its legitimacy. In order for the legitimacy to be complete, it is not enough for the colonized to be a slave, he must also accept this role.[77]

In short, the development of the colonial situation involves the shaping of wants, values, roles, and beliefs of the colonized. It is a third-dimensional power relationship.

Do similar processes exist within developed societies? How can one tell? Admittedly, it may be more difficult to observe whether the second and third faces of power are behind apparent quiescence amongst inequalities in more open or homogeneous societies. But the difficulties in observation should not alone refute the possibilities of the occurrence. Rather than avoid the problem, it might be preferable to attempt further to develop a theory of power relationships as well as a method for their study through an intermediary step: a focus upon the perhaps more visible processes that affect a dominated but relatively non-integrated sector within industrial democracy itself. The possibility for such an exploration lies in the study of the impact of power and powerlessness upon the actions and conceptions of the people of an underdeveloped region of the United States known as Central Appalachia.

[75] Rupert Emerson, *From Empire to Nation: The Rise to Self-Assertion of African and Asian Peoples* (Harvard University Press, Cambridge, Mass., 1960), p. 6.

[76] G. Balandier, "The Colonial Situation: A Theoretical Approach," in Immanuel Wallerstein, ed., *Social Change: The Colonial Situation* (John Wiley and Sons, New York, 1966), pp. 34–61.
[77] Albert Memmi, *The Colonizer and the Colonized* (Beacon Press, Boston, 1967), pp. 88–9.

CHAPTER 2

THE STATE AND CAPITALISM

Debates about the nature of political power have often focused on the relationship between business and government in advanced capitalist democracies, particularly on whether the state systematically represents the interests of the business community and the capitalist class over those of other social groups. One of the most influential sociologists in this debate for over two decades has been G. William Domhoff, who argues (as in Reading 3) that a "power elite"—that is, an influential group of leaders representing the interests of the capitalist class—tends to dominate the federal government through three key mechanisms. First, the power elite influences the choice of who can win election to public offices by providing them with money to run expensive electoral campaigns. Second, members of the power elite lobby government in ways that often lead to the formation and implementation of legislation that caters to the short-term interests of different segments of business and the capitalist class. Finally, and perhaps most important, through its network of policy advisors, academic think tanks, and political appointees, the power elite defines the general interests of the capitalist class and influences government to act in accord with these interests. Domhoff acknowledges that nonelites can occasionally influence policymakers, but he insists that the power elite is still generally able to mobilize vast resources to define the political agenda in favor of the capitalist class and business interests.

Domhoff represents an important radical tradition in state theory that was influenced by political theorists like C. Wright Mills (1956), who believed that the state was dominated by a small group of powerful elites. Also influential was the work of revisionist historians, who argued that the creation of government policies and agencies that seem to work against the interests of business, such as the Federal Trade Commission and other regulatory agencies, were actually sponsored by farsighted members of the business community, called "corporate liberals," to stabilize the capitalist system during periods of crisis (Kolko, 1963; Weinstein, 1968). Despite its radical viewpoint, however, a number of Marxists have criticized this tradition for overemphasizing the ability of the capitalist class to manipulate the state by financing elections, occupying key government positions, and the like (Gold, Lo, & Wright, 1975; Jessop, 1977; Poulantzas, 1969). Marxists tend to see politics as more of an ongoing struggle among fractions of capital and between capitalists and workers.

Building on ideas from the Marxian tradition, yet also going beyond them, Fred Block (1977) argued that there is a fundamental division of labor among capitalists, workers, and state managers (i.e., politicians, high-level bureaucrats, and other influential people working in government). Because state managers recognize that their ability to remain in power and keep the state operating depends on their ability to maintain political and economic order, it is in their interests to promulgate policies that sustain a healthy climate for business investment. In other words, state managers must be careful not to do anything that would seriously undermine business confidence, such as imposing heavy taxes on wealth or corporate profits or doing anything that would undermine capitalism. As a result, Block suggested, the state normally acts in the interests of the capitalist class, not because it is dominated by a power elite, but because state managers can only fulfill their own interests if they maintain conditions favorable to capital investment, and thus to the interests of the capitalist class. Periods of crisis—such as the great depression and the New Deal—may intensify class struggles and spur state managers to respond to working-class and popular pressures "from below." Such a crisis situation may give the state managers an opportunity, at least temporarily, to implement policies at odds with what capitalists are demanding from the state.

In Reading 4, Theda Skocpol applies the theories of Domhoff, Block, and various neo-Marxists to the historical example of the U.S. New Deal of the 1930s. The New Deal consisted of a series of federal governmental programs, sponsored by President Franklin Delano Roosevelt and his Democratic administration, to respond to the massive economic depression of the 1930s. There were attempts to promote industrial and agricultural economic growth and new laws were passed that encouraged the formation of industrial labor unions in the United States. Skocpol inquires whether alternative theoretical perspectives emphasizing capitalist class power, the "needs" of the capitalist system, or pressures from class struggles can adequately explain the changing forms of federal governmental intervention in the national economy during the New Deal. She concludes that Fred Block's (1977) theory does the best job, yet also argues that we must pay more attention than even Block does to the effects of historically evolved U.S. governmental institutions and political parties. These institutions shaped and limited demands from business, industrial labor, and other social groups. They also shaped and limited the capacities of elected politicians and government officials to intervene effectively in the economy. (Originally published in 1980, Skocpol's article helped to stimulate much further research and theoretical debate about the U.S. New Deal. To follow up on some of these debates, see Amenta & Parikh, 1991; Domhoff, 1986–1987; Ferguson, 1984; Finegold & Skocpol, 1984; Goldfield, 1989; Gordon, 1991; Jenkins & Brents, 1989; Levine, 1988; Orloff, 1993; Plotke, 1989; Quadagno, 1984; Skocpol & Amenta, 1985; Skocpol & Ikenberry, 1983; Skocpol, Finegold & Goldfield, 1990; and Weir & Skocpol, 1985.)

An important implication of Skocpol's argument (see also Reading 6 in Chapter 3) is that the state may influence the organization and political activity of business just as much as business and other groups influence the state (for other arguments along this line, see Martin, 1989, and the selection by Vogel included as Reading 15 in Chapter 5). Above all, scholars have explored how states affect the activity and organization of the business community, particularly through the allocation of financial and other resources (Zysman, 1983). For instance, defense spending targeted at particular industries, such as aircraft manufacturing and electronics, has been an important stimulus to the development of these industries in the United States since World War II (Hooks, 1990). Taking a cross-national perspective, certain scholars argue (see Katzenstein, 1978) that the U.S. state is rather "weak," because it has fewer financial resources or administrative capacities for economic intervention than do other national states. But in some sectors and at some historical periods, there may be important exceptions, when the U.S. state has had considerable capacity to reshape sectors of the economy (see Skocpol & Finegold, 1982).

In addition to allocating resources, John Campbell and Leon Lindberg explain (in Reading 5) that states affect business by defining and enforcing property rights and other rules that establish the legal conditions under which economic activity occurs. In the United States, the ability to manipulate these rules has provided policymakers with an important source of "strength" in the sense that they have been able to shape the behavior, organization, and balance of power among economic actors. In particular, changes in property rights have transformed the organizational structure of entire industries, often in ways that were unforeseen by policymakers, such as when business cartels were outlawed during the late 1800s—a decision that inadvertently triggered the formation of the huge corporations that dominated the economic landscape in America during the twentieth century. Although Campbell and Lindberg avoid discussing why the state enacts these rules, their analysis confirms that it plays an important role in determining how economic actors are organized and, by extension, how much political power they may enjoy.

REFERENCES

Amenta, Edwin, and Sunita Parikh. 1991. "Capitalists Did Not Want the Social Security Act: A Critique of the 'Capitalist Dominance' Thesis." *American Sociological Review* 56(1): 124–28.

Fred Block. 1987. "Beyond Relative Autonomy: State Managers as Historical Subjects." In *Revising State Theory: Essays on Politics and Postindustrialism,* 81–96. Philadelphia: Temple University Press.

Domhoff, G. William. 1986–1987. "Corporate Liberal Theory and the Social Security Act." *Politics and Society* 15: 297–330.

Ferguson, Thomas. 1984. "From Normalcy to New Deal: Industrial Structure, Party Competition, and American Public Policy in the Great Depression." *International Organization* 38(1): 51–66.

Finegold, Kenneth, and Theda Skocpol. 1984. "State, Party, and Industry: From Business Recovery to the Wagner Act in America's New Deal." In *Statemaking and Social Movements: Essays in Theory and History,* edited by Charles C. Bright and Susan F. Harding, 159–92. Ann Arbor, Mich.: University of Michigan Press.

Gold, David, Clarence Lo, and Erik Olin Wright. 1975. "Recent Developments in Marxist Theories of the Capitalist State." *Monthly Review* 27 (October): 29–43.

Goldfield, Michael. 1989. "Worker Insurgency, Radical Organization, and New Deal Labor Legislation." *American Political Science Review* 83(4) (December): 1257–82.

Gordon, Colin. 1991. "New Deal, Old Deck: Business and the Origins of Social Security, 1920–1935." *Politics and Society* 19(2): 165–207.

Hooks, Gregory. 1990. "The Rise of the Pentagon and U.S. State Building: The Defense Program as Industrial Policy." *American Journal of Sociology* 96(2): 358–404.

Jenkins, J. Craig, and Barbara G. Brents. 1989. "Social Protest, Hegemonic Competition, and Social Reform: A Political Struggle Interpretation of the Origins of the American Welfare State." *American Sociological Review* 54: 891–909.

Jessop, Bob. 1977. "Recent Theories of the Capitalist State." *Cambridge Journal of Economics* 1: 353–73.

Katzenstein, Peter J., editor. 1978. *Between Power and Plenty.* Madison: University of Wisconsin Press.

Kolko, Gabriel. 1963. *The Triumph of Conservatism.* Chicago: Quadrangle.

Levine, Rhonda F. 1988. *Class Struggle and the New Deal: Industrial Labor, Industrial Capital, and the State.* Lawrence: University Press of Kansas.

Martin, Cathie Jo. 1989. "Business Influence and State Power: The Case of U.S. Corporate Tax Policy." *Politics and Society* 17(2): 189–223.

Mills, C. Wright. 1956. *The Power Elite.* New York: Oxford University Press.

Orloff, Ann Shola. 1993. *The Politics of Pensions: A Comparative Analysis of Britain, Canada, and the United States, 1880–1940.* Madison: University of Wisconsin Press.

Plotke, David. 1989. "The Wagner Act, Again: Politics and Labor, 1935–37." *Studies in American Political Development* no. 3: 105–56.

Poulantzas, Nicos. 1969. "The Problem of the Capitalist State." *New Left Review* 58: 67–78.

Quadagno, Jill. 1984. "Welfare Capitalism and the Social Security Act of 1935." *American Sociological Review* 49 (4): 632–47.

Skocpol, Theda, and Edwin Amenta. 1985. "Did Capitalists Shape Social Security?" *American Sociological Review* 50: 572–75.

Skocpol, Theda, and Kenneth Finegold. 1982. "State Capacity and Economic Intervention in the Early New Deal." *Political Science Quarterly* 97: 255–78.

Skocpol, Theda, and John Ikenberry. 1983. "The Political Formation of the American Welfare State in Historical and Comparative Perspective." *Comparative Social Research* 6: 87–148.

Skocpol, Theda, Kenneth Finegold, and Michael Goldfield. 1990. "Explaining New Deal Labor Policy" (a debate). *American Political Science Review* 84(4): 1297–1315.

Weinstein, James. 1968. *The Corporate Ideal in the Liberal State.* Boston: Beacon Press.

Weir, Margaret, and Theda Skocpol. 1985. "State Structures and the Possibilities for 'Keynesian' Responses to the Great Depression in Sweden, Britain, and the United States." Pp. 107–63 in *Bringing the State Back In,* edited by Peter B. Evans, Dietrich Rueschemeyer, and Theda Skocpol. Cambridge, England, and New York: Cambridge University Press.

Zysman, John. 1983. *Governments, Markets, and Growth.* Ithaca, N.Y.: Cornell University Press.

READING 3

WHO RULES AMERICA?

G. William Domhoff

Who has predominant power in the United States? The short answer to this question can be found in a well-known adaptation of the golden rule: Those who have the gold are the rulers. To be exact, the wealthy elites who own income-producing property—corporations, real estate, plantations, and agribusinesses—set the rules by which policy battles are waged in this country.

The reasons why gold rules in the United States are complex and involve an understanding of social classes, the role of experts, the two-party system, and the history of this country, especially southern slavery. Moreover, this simple statement has to be qualified. Domination by the few does not mean complete control but the ability to set the terms under which other groups and classes operate. For example, highly trained professionals with an interest in environmental and consumer issues have been able to couple their technical expertise and understanding of the legislative process with timely publicity to help establish governmental restrictions on certain corporate practices. When workers are organized or disruptive, they can gain concessions on wages, hours, and working conditions. And while the government is not necessarily responsive to the will of the electorate, voters have been able to restrain the actions of wealthy elites and decide which elites will have the greatest influence on policy, especially when there are disagreements within the higher circles of wealth and influence.

The idea that a relatively fixed group of privileged people dominates the economy and government goes against the American grain and the founding principles of this country. "Class" and "power" are terms that make Americans uneasy, and concepts such as the "upper class" and the "power elite" put people on their guard. Americans may differ in social and income levels and some may have more influence than others, but it is felt that there can be no fixed power group when power is constitutionally lodged in all the people, when there is broad political participation through elec-

From *Primis* Sociology database, Craig Calhoun and George Ritzer, eds. (1993). Reprinted with the permission of McGraw-Hill, Inc.

tions and lobbying, and when *social mobility*—the intergenerational rise or fall in income and occupation—is everywhere apparent. Therefore, most power analysts usually conclude that elected officials, along with interest groups such as organized labor and consumers, have enough countervailing power to create a fluid, pluralistic distribution of power rather than one with rich people and corporations at the top.[1]

Contrary to this view, this essay will demonstrate how rule by the wealthy few is possible despite free speech, regular elections, and organized opposition. It will show how "the rich" have coalesced into a social upper class that has developed institutions through which the children of its members are socialized and newly wealthy people are assimilated into an upper-class world view. It will explain how members of the upper class control corporations, and it will describe the network of nonprofit organizations through which members of the upper class and corporate leaders shape policy debates.

POWER AND POWER INDICATORS

"Power" is a word that is easy to understand but hard to define precisely. We know it means clout or juice or muscle or the ability to make things happen. We know it comes from words implying the ability to make things happen. We know it comes from words implying the ability to act in a strong, compelling, and direct way, but we also know that power can be projected in a quiet and indirect manner.

For the purposes of this essay, *power* means "the capacity of some persons to produce intended and foreseen effects on others."[2] This is a very general definition that allows for many forms of power, such as economic, political, military, and intellectual (knowledge and expertise) power. It leaves open the question of whether force or coercion is a necessary aspect of the exercise of power. However, to define power in this manner does not mean that it is a simple matter to study the power of a group or social class. For one thing, a formal definition does not explain how a concept can be measured. Also, it is seldom possible to observe interactions that reveal the operation of power even in a small group, let alone to see one social class producing effects on another. It is therefore necessary to develop indicators of power.

For research purposes, power can be thought of as an underlying trait or property of a social group or social class. It can be measured by a series of signs, or *indicators,* that bear a probabilistic relationship to it. In other words, all the indicators do not necessarily appear every time power manifests itself. Research proceeds through a series of "if-then" statements: *If* a group or class is powerful, *then* it should be expected that certain indicators of that power will be present. It is important to have more than one indicator. Ideally, these indicators will be of very different types so that any irrelevant components will cancel each other out. When these multiple indicators point to the same group or class, we can be confident that the underlying concept has been measured correctly.

The three primary indicators of power can be summarized as follows: (1) Who benefits? (2) Who governs? and (3) Who wins? In every society certain experiences and material objects are highly valued. If it is assumed that everyone in a society wants to have as great a share as possible of these experiences and objects, the distribution of values in that society can be utilized as a power indicator. Thus, those who benefit the most are powerful. In American society, wealth and well-being are highly valued. People seek to own property, earn high incomes, have interesting and safe jobs, and live long and healthy lives. All these values are unequally distributed and may be used as power indicators.

Power also can be inferred from a determination of who occupies important institutional positions and takes part in important decision-making groups. If a group or class is highly overrepresented in relation to its proportion in the population, it can be inferred that it is powerful. For example, if a group makes up 10 percent of the population but has 50 percent of the seats in the main governing institutions, it has five times more governing positions than would be expected, and there is reason to believe that it is a powerful one.

There are many policy issues over which groups or classes disagree. In the United States different policies are suggested by opposing groups in "issue areas" such as foreign policy, taxation, welfare, and the environment. Power can be inferred here by determining who initiates, modifies, or vetoes policy alternatives. By focusing on actions within the decision-making process, this indicator comes closest to approximating the process of power that is contained in the formal definition. However, the decisional (who wins) indicator is the most difficult to use accurately. It is hard to gain access to decision makers for an interview, much less observe them in action. Aspects of a decision-making process may remain hidden, informants may exaggerate or play down their roles, and the people's memories about who did what often become cloudy shortly after the event.

All three of these indicators have strengths and weaknesses, but their weaknesses do not present a serious problem because each indicator involves different kinds of information drawn from different kinds of studies. The case for the power of a group or class should be considered convincing only if all three types of indicators "triangulate" on a particular group or social class.

THE SOCIAL UPPER CLASS

The best starting point for the study of power in the United States is a careful consideration of the small social upper class at the top of the ladders of wealth, income, and status. This social upper class is the most visible and accessible aspect of the power equation and is the best place to get a handle on the overall power structure.

A *social class* is a set of intermarrying and interacting families that see each other as equals, share a common lifestyle, and have a common world view. This general definition is accepted by most social scientists regardless of their views on the distribution of power. By the social upper class, or simply the upper class, we mean the social class that is commonly agreed to be the "top" or "elite" or "exclusive" class. In various times and places Americans have called such people the "high hats," the "country club set," the "snobs," and the "rich." In turn, members of this class recognize themselves as distinctive, calling themselves "old families," "established families," and "community leaders."

The upper class probably makes up only a few tenths of 1 percent of the population. For the purposes of this essay, we estimate that it includes 0.5 percent to 1 percent of the population. Members of the upper class live in exclusive suburban neighborhoods, expensive downtown co-ops, and large country estates. They often have far-away summer and winter homes as well. They attend a system of private schools that extends from preschool to the university level; the best known of these schools are the "day" and "boarding" prep schools that take the place of public high schools for upper-class teenagers (Table 1). Adult members of the upper class socialize in expensive country clubs, downtown luncheon clubs, hunting clubs, and garden clubs. Young women of the upper class are "introduced" to high society each year through an elaborate series of debutante teas, parties, and balls. Upper-class women gain experience as volunteers through a nationwide

TABLE 1

Some Leading Boarding Schools and Men's Clubs

Male and coed boarding schools	Men's clubs
Choate (Wallingford, CT)	Bohemian Club
Deerfield (Deerfield, MA)	(San Francisco)
Groton (Groton, MA)	Brook (New York)
Hill (Pottstown, PA)	California (Los Angeles)
Kent (Kent, CT)	Eagle Lake (Houston)
Lawrenceville	Knickerbocker (New York)
(Lawrenceville, NJ)	Piedmont Driving (Atlanta)
Middlesex (Concord, MA)	Rainier (Seattle)
St. George's (Newport, RI)	Rittenhouse (Philadelphia)
St. Mark's	Rolling Rock (Pittsburgh)
(Southborough, MA)	Saturn (Buffalo)
St. Paul's (Concord, NH)	St. Cecelia
Taft (Watertown, CT)	(Charlestown, SC)
Woodberry Forest	Somerset (Boston)
(Woodberry Forest, VA)	

Source: G. William Domhoff, *Who Rules America Now?* New York, Simon & Schuster, 1983, pp. 44–47.

organization known as the Junior League and then go on to serve as directors of cultural organizations, family service associations, and hospitals.

These social institutions create social cohesion and a sense of in-group "we-ness." This sense of cohesion is heightened by the fact that people can be excluded from these organizations. Through these institutions, young members of the upper class and those who are new to wealth develop a shared understanding of how to be wealthy. Because these social settings are expensive and exclusive, members of the upper class usually think of themselves as special or superior. They think they are better than other people and certainly better able to lead and govern. Their self-confidence and social polish are useful in dealing with people from other social classes, who often admire them and defer to their judgment.

These social institutions provide a starting point for systematic studies of power. For example, class indicators allow us to determine which economic and political leaders are and are not members of the upper class. Put another way, class indicators allow us to trace the paths of members of the upper class into the economic, political, and ideological power systems of this society.

Starting with these class indicators, it can be shown that the upper class is nationwide in scope because there is overlapping membership among the many

social clubs around the country. A person from Chicago, for example, may belong to clubs in New York, Boston, and San Francisco, implying that he or she interacts with upper-class counterparts in all those cities. By comparing dozens of club membership lists, sociologists have been able to establish the "density" of this club network. Similarly, the alumni lists of exclusive private schools reveal that their students come from all over the country. The summer addresses of members of the upper class who are listed in in-group telephone books called blue books and social registers show that people from all parts of the country mingle at secluded summer resorts that have been upper-class watering holes for generations.[3]

But here we must be cautious, because these class indicators are not perfect. Some members of the upper class do not join clubs, list themselves in a social register, or reveal their school affiliations in *Who's Who in America.* We cannot trace such people through the power system; they are counted as not being part of the upper class when they really are. By contrast, local or scholarship children at some prep schools and some honorary members of social clubs are not members of the upper class; they are counted as part of the upper class when they really are not. In large-scale studies, these two kinds of mistakes tend to cancel each other out, and so in general one can obtain an accurate picture. However, class indicators can be wrong in regard to specific individuals.

There can be no doubt that there is a nationwide upper class in the United States with its own distinctive social institutions, lifestyle, and outlook. There also can be no doubt that most of these people are active in business or the professions and that all of them are wealthy. Their great wealth is evident from the large sums it takes to maintain their homes and their style of life, but systematic studies also show that the wealthiest families are part of the social institutions of the upper class. If we combine our studies with findings on wealth and income distributions, it is possible to say that the upper class, which accounts for 0.5 to 1 percent of the population, owns 25 to 30 percent of all privately held wealth in the United States and receives 10 to 13 percent of total yearly income.[4] In short, the upper class scores very high on the "who benefits" power indicator.

The wealth and income of members of the upper class imply that the upper class is powerful, but they do not demonstrate how power operates. It is therefore necessary to turn to studies of the economy to understand the American power structure.

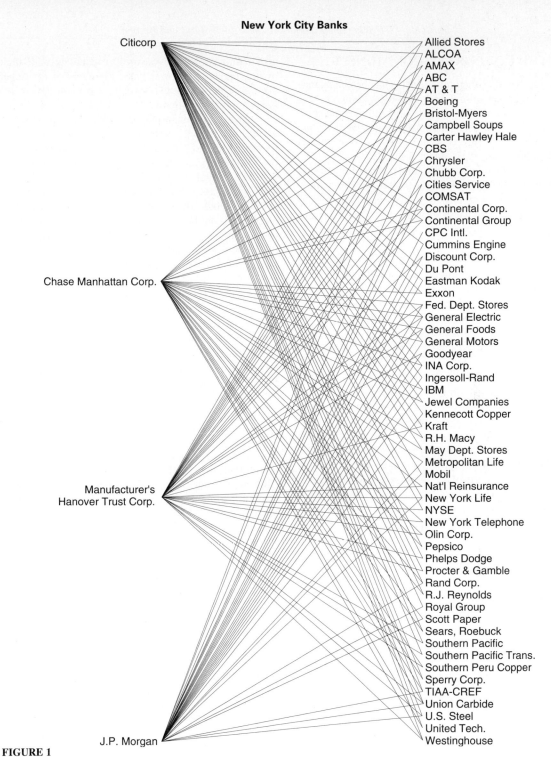

New York City Banks

Citicorp

Chase Manhattan Corp.

Manufacturer's
Hanover Trust Corp.

J.P. Morgan

Allied Stores
ALCOA
AMAX
ABC
AT & T
Boeing
Bristol-Myers
Campbell Soups
Carter Hawley Hale
CBS
Chrysler
Chubb Corp.
Cities Service
COMSAT
Continental Corp.
Continental Group
CPC Intl.
Cummins Engine
Discount Corp.
Du Pont
Eastman Kodak
Exxon
Fed. Dept. Stores
General Electric
General Foods
General Motors
Goodyear
INA Corp.
Ingersoll-Rand
IBM
Jewel Companies
Kennecott Copper
Kraft
R.H. Macy
May Dept. Stores
Metropolitan Life
Mobil
Nat'l Reinsurance
New York Life
NYSE
New York Telephone
Olin Corp.
Pepsico
Phelps Dodge
Procter & Gamble
Rand Corp.
R.J. Reynolds
Royal Group
Scott Paper
Sears, Roebuck
Southern Pacific
Southern Pacific Trans.
Southern Peru Copper
Sperry Corp.
TIAA-CREF
Union Carbide
U.S. Steel
United Tech.
Westinghouse

FIGURE 1

The interlocking directors four large New York City banks have with a sample of large American corporations. (*From U.S. Senate Committee on Governmental Affairs, Structure of Corporate Concentration, 1980.*)

THE CORPORATE COMMUNITY

Economic power in the United States has been concentrated in an organizational and legal form known as the corporation since the last decades of the nineteenth century. Individual corporations have great power in this society. They can hire and fire workers, move their resources, and use their income in a variety of tax-deductible ways to influence schools, charities, and the government. The argument among scholars begins over whether large corporations are united enough to exert a common social power and then moves to the question of whether these corporations are still controlled by members of the upper class.

The unity of corporations can be demonstrated in a number of ways. Corporations share a common interest in making a profit. They are often owned by the same families or financial institutions. Their executives have very similar educational and work experiences. Corporate leaders also see themselves as sharing common opponents in organized labor, environmentalists, consumer advocates, and government officials. A sense of togetherness is created by their use of the same legal, accounting, and consulting firms.

However, the best way to demonstrate unity among corporations is through the study of *interlocking directors*, individuals who sit on two or more of the boards of directors that are in charge of the overall direction of corporations. Boards of directors usually include major owners, top executives from similar corporations, financial and legal advisers, and the three or four officers who run a corporation on a daily basis. Numerous studies show that the 15 to 20 percent of corporate directors who sit on two or more boards, who are called the *inner circle* of the corporate directorate, unite almost every major corporation in the United States into a well-connected corporate community.[5] This network can be said to be very dense in that there are many connections among its members (Figure 1). Corporations with many connections tend to be the most central ones in the corporate community, and they are typically banks or very large manufacturing firms.

Most social scientists agree that corporations have a strong basis for cohesion, but there is disagreement about their relationship to the upper class. Some theorists state that members of the upper class used to dominate corporations but do not do so anymore because of the increase in the size of corporations, the need for highly trained and specialized executives, and the decline in family ownership. Thus, there is an upper class of rich families with one set of interests and a group of professional business executives with their own interests and power base. Members of the upper class have power based on wealth; corporate executives have organizational power.[6]

Contrary to this purported division between owners and managers, there is strong evidence for an overlap in membership and interest between the upper class and the corporate community. The wealthiest and most cohesive upper-class families often have "family offices" through which they can bring to bear the power of their stock ownership, sometimes placing their employees on boards of directors. Members of the upper class also control corporations through financial devices known as *holding companies*, which purchase a controlling interest in operating companies. More generally, members of the upper class own roughly 45 to 50 percent of all corporate stock.[7]

Upper-class control of corporations can be seen in the overrepresentation of this class on boards of directors. Several studies have shown that members of the upper class sit on boards far more than can be accounted for by chance. They are especially likely to be part of the inner circle that has two or more directorships.[8] If we use "who governs" as a power indicator, it is clear that members of the upper class still control the corporate community. Thus, one can conclude that the upper class is rooted in the ownership and control of the corporations that constitute the corporate community. It therefore can be said that members of the upper class are for the most part a corporate rich who are involved in the business world as investors, directors, venture capitalists, bankers, corporate lawyers, and top executives.

Many top corporate executives do not grow up in the upper class. However, they are gradually socialized into that class and its values as they move up the corporate ladder; indeed, they are advanced because of their ability to fulfill upper-class goals of corporate expansion and profitability. In return, these rising managers are given the opportunity to buy corporate stock at below-market prices, are paid very high salaries, and are given other "perks" that allow them to join the upper class economically as well as socially. The end result is a strengthening of the power of the upper class.

SHAPING THE POLITY

The upper class and the corporate community do not stand alone at the top of the power structure. They are supplemented by a wide range of nonprofit organizations that play an important role in framing debates over public policy and shaping public opinion. These organizations are often called nonpartisan or bipartisan because they are not identified with politics or with either of the major political parties. However, they are the real political party of the upper class because they ensure the stability of society and the compliance of the government.

Upper-class and corporate dominance of nonprofit organizations is revealed in the role of wealthy families in their creation of and their reliance on large corporations for funding. However, dominance can be most readily demonstrated through studies of boards of directors, which have the ultimate control of these organizations, including the ability to hire and fire top executives. These studies show that members of the upper class are greatly overrepresented on the boards of these organizations and that non-profit organizations share a large number of directors with the corporate community, particularly directors who are part of the inner circle.[9] In effect, most large nonprofit organizations are part of the corporate community (Tables 2 and 3).

All the organizations in the nonprofit sector have a hand in creating the framework of society and hence in shaping the political climate. Cultural and civic organizations set the standard for what is beautiful, important,

TABLE 2
The 25 Most Central Organizations in the American Corporate Community

	Organization	Size*	Organizational interlocks	Centrality
1.	IBM	18	34	1.00
2.	Conference Board†	31	53	0.87
3.	General Foods	16	24	0.81
4.	Chemical Bank	24	36	0.79
5.	Committee for Economic Development†	200	119	0.78
6.	New York Life	25	36	0.77
7.	Yale University†	18	23	0.66
8.	Morgan Guaranty Trust	24	40	0.65
9.	Consolidated Edison	14	22	0.63
10.	Rockefeller Foundation†	19	25	0.62
11.	Chase Manhattan	24	33	0.62
12.	AT&T	18	35	0.60
13.	U.S. Steel	17	30	0.59
14.	Sloan Foundation†	16	25	0.59
15.	Caterpillar Tractor	11	19	0.59
16.	General Motors	23	31	0.54
17.	Citibank	27	37	0.53
18.	Pan American	23	25	0.52
19.	Council on Foreign Relations†	1,400	154	0.52
20.	Metropolitan Life	29	30	0.51
21.	Metropolitan Museum†	44	37	0.47
22.	Equitable Life	37	42	0.47
23.	Mobil Oil	13	14	0.46
24.	MIT†	74	54	0.45
25.	American Assembly†	19	26	0.44

* The size of an organization is the number of directors or trustees on the controlling board of the organization, except in the cases of the Committee for Economic Development and the Council on Foreign Relations, where all members are included. Organizational interlocks are the number of connections an organization has to other organizations in the corporate community through sharing one or more directors with other organizations. The centrality of an organization is a mathematical expression of both the number of organizational interlocks and the degree to which those interlocks are with other organizations that are highly central to the overall network.
†Nonprofit organization
Source: Harold Salzman and G. William Domhoff, "Nonprofit Organizations and the Corporate Community," *Social Science History* 7:205–216, 1983, p. 210.

TABLE 3
The Centrality Rankings of Prestigious Universities, Foundations, Cultural Groups, and Policy Groups in the Corporate Network*

University	Ranking
Yale	7
MIT	24
Princeton	29
Chicago	41
Columbia	48
Harvard	50
Dartmouth	56
Johns Hopkins	60
Northwestern	63
Stanford	95
Pennsylvania	106
Cornell	145
Cultural and civic group	
Metropolitan Museum	21
Smithsonian Institution	30
American Red Cross	33
Museum of Modern Art	59
National Gallery of Art	90
Metropolitan Opera Association	200
JFK Center for Performing Arts	210
Foundation	
Rockefeller Foundation	10
Sloan Foundation	14
Carnegie Corporation	61
Ford Foundation	69
Hartford Foundation	102
Mellon Foundation	121
Mott Foundation	151
Duke Endowment	172
Lilly Endowment	185
Kellogg Foundation	187
Kresge Foundation	Isolate (no connections to any other organization studied)
Policy group	
Conference Board	2
Committee for Economic Development	5
Council on Foreign Relations	19
American Assembly	25
Brookings Institution	42
National Association of Manufacturers	196

* 256 organizations were studied
Source: Harold Salzman and G. William Domhoff, "Nonprofit Organizations and the Corporate Community," *Social Science History* 7:205–216, 1983, p. 211.

and "classy." They guide our aspirations. Elite universities play a large role in determining what is important to teach, learn, and research, and they train most professionals and experts. However, foundations, think tanks, and policy-discussion organizations have the most direct and important influence. Their ideas, criticisms, and policy suggestions go out to the general public through pamphlets, books, local discussion groups, mass media, and the public relations departments of major corporations. Their materials reach the government through a variety of means. Let us look more closely at foundations, think tanks, and policy-discussion organizations to show how they function as a policy-planning network.

Foundations

Tax-free foundations receive money from wealthy families and corporations. Their primary purpose is to provide money for education, research, and policy discussion. They thus have the power to encourage ideas and researchers compatible with their values and goals. Support by major foundations often has an impact on the direction of research in agriculture, social science, and the health sciences. However, foundations also create policy projects on their own. The Ford foundation's "gray areas" demonstration project in several large cities in the late 1950s and early 1960s was the forerunner of the Johnson Administration's War on Poverty in 1964, for example.

Think Tanks

The role of *think tanks* is to suggest new policies for dealing with the problems that face the economy and the government. Using money from wealthy donors, corporations, and foundations, think tanks hire the experts produced by graduate departments at elite universities. The ideas and proposals developed by these experts are disseminated through pamphlets, books, major magazines and newspapers, and, most important, the participation of these experts in the forums provided by policy-discussion organizations.

Policy-Discussion Organizations

Policy-discussion organizations are the hub of the policy-planning network. They bring together wealthy individuals, corporate executives, experts, and government officials for lectures, forums, meetings, and group discussions of issues ranging from the local to the international and from the economic to the political to the cultural. New ideas are tried out in weekly or monthly discussion groups, and differences of opinion are aired and subjected to compromise. These structured discussion groups usually begin with a presentation by invited experts, followed by questions and discussion involving all the participants. Such groups range in size from ten to fifty, with the usual group having fifteen to twenty-five members.

The many discussion groups within policy-discussion organizations have several functions that are not readily apparent. First, they help familiarize busy corporate leaders with policy options outside their day-to-day business concerns. This allows executives to influence public opinion through the mass media and other outlets, argue with and influence experts, and accept appointments for government service. Second, policy-discussion organizations give members of the upper class and the corporate community an opportunity to determine which of their colleagues are the best natural leaders by watching them in the give-and-take of discussion groups. They can see which of their counterparts understand the issues quickly, offer their own ideas, facilitate discussions, and relate well to experts. These organizations thus serve as sorting and screening

mechanisms for the emergence of new leadership for the corporate rich.

Third, these organizations present their participants to the media and the public as knowledgeable leaders who should be tapped for public service because they have used their free time to acquaint themselves with important issues in nonpartisan forums. These organizations thus help turn wealthy individuals and corporate executives into national leaders and statesmen. Finally, these organizations provide a forum in which members of the upper class and the corporate community can get to know policy experts. This gives them a pool of people from which they can draw advisers if they are asked to serve in government.

These organizations also serve several functions for the experts. First, presenting their ideas and policies to these organizations gives experts an opportunity to gain influence. Second, it gives them a chance to advance their careers.

The policy-planning network is not totally homogeneous. Reflecting differences within the corporate community, it has moderate-conservative and ultraconservative wings (Table 4). Moderate conservatives favor foreign aid, low tariffs, and economic expansion overseas, whereas ultraconservatives tend to see foreign aid

TABLE 4
Moderate-Conservative and Ultraconservative Organizations in the Policy-Planning Network

Moderate conservatives	Ultraconservatives
Foundations	
Ford Foundation	Smith Richardson Foundation
Rockefeller Foundation	Richard K. Mellon Foundation
Rockefeller Brothers Fund	Donner Foundation
Carnegie Corporation	Lilly Endowment
Sloan Foundation	Pew Memorial Trust
Russell Sage Foundation	J.M.F. Foundation
Think tanks	
Brookings Institution	American Enterprise Institute
Urban Institute	Hoover Institution
Aspen Institute	Heritage Foundation
Resources for the Future	Intercollegiate Studies Institute
Overseas Development Council	Institute for Strategic Studies
Policy groups	
Council on Foreign Relations	American Security Council
Committee for Economic Development	National Association of Manufacturers
American Assembly	American Conservative Union
Business Council	Chamber of Commerce of the United States

as a giveaway. Moderate conservatives generally accept the idea that governmental taxation and spending policies can be used to stimulate and stabilize the economy, whereas ultraconservatives insist that taxes should be cut to the minimum and that government spending is basically evil. Moderate conservatives accept some welfare state measures or at least support them in the face of serious social disruption. Ultraconservatives consistently oppose welfare spending, claiming that it destroys moral fiber and saps individual initiative; they prefer to use arrest and detention when there is social unrest.

The reasons for these differences are not well understood. There is a tendency for moderate-conservative organizations to be directed by executives from the largest and most internationally oriented corporations, but there are numerous exceptions. Moreover, there are corporations that support policy organizations within both camps. However, for all their differences, leaders within the two clusters of policy organizations have a tendency to search for compromise because of their common membership in the upper class and the corporate community. There are also powerful lobbying organizations, such as the Business Roundtable, that bring together people and ideas from both wings of the power elite (Figure 2). When compromise is not possible, the final resolution of policy conflicts often takes place in Congress.

The existence of the policy-planning network provides evidence for another form of power possessed by the wealthy few: expertise on social and political issues. This is an important complement to the economic power possessed by corporations.

THE POWER ELITE

The *power elite* can be defined as the leadership group of the upper class. It consists of active working members of the upper class and high-level employees in profit-making and nonprofit institutions controlled by members of the upper class through stock ownership, financial support, and involvement on boards of directors. This does not mean that all members of the upper class are involved in governing. Some are more interested in social life, sports, or culture; their parties may provide a setting where members of the power elite mingle with celebrities, and sometimes they give money to political candidates, but that is as close as

they come to political power. Conversely, not everyone in the power elite is a member of the upper class. Many are top-level employees who started their lives at the middle levels of the social ladder and are never fully assimilated into exclusive social circles.

The idea of the power elite intertwines class theory and organizational theory, which are often thought of as distinctive. The basis for the intertwining of these two theories can be found in the role and composition of the boards of directors that govern every large profit-making and nonprofit organization in the United States. It is on boards of directors that the values and goals of the upper class are integrated with those of the organizational hierarchy. Upper-class directors ensure that their interests are reflected in the organizations they control, but the day-to-day leaders on the board are able to harmonize class interests with organizational principles.

It is important to realize that not all experts are members of the power elite. People have to be high-level employees in institutions controlled by members

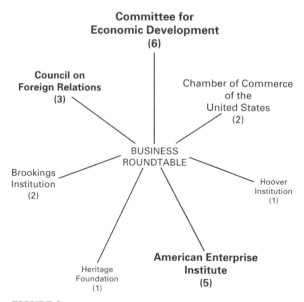

FIGURE 2
The interconnections between the Business Roundtable and important moderate-conservative and ultraconservative think tanks and policy groups (the larger the type and the higher the number, the more interlocks). (*From Val Burris, "Elite Policy-Planning Networks in the United States," paper presented at the 86th annual meeting of the American Sociological Association, Cincinnati, August 23–August 27, 1991.*)

of the upper class to be considered part of the power elite. Receiving a fellowship from a foundation, spending a year at a think tank, or giving advice to a policy-discussion organization does not make a person a member of the power elite. Many experts never go near the policy-planning network. Instead, they concentrate on teaching and research or work for groups that oppose the policies of the power elite. In short, experts and advisers are a separate group just below the power elite in the pecking order.

Let us now discuss how the power elite dominates the federal government in the interest of the upper class and the corporate community.

The Power Elite and Government

Members of the power elite involve themselves in the federal government through three basic processes, each of which has a slightly different role in ensuring access to the White House, Congress, and specific departments in the executive branch. Although some of the same people are involved in all three processes, most leaders specialize in one or two of them. These three processes are

1. The special-interest process, through which specific families, corporations, and industries realize their narrow and short-run interests regarding taxes, subsidies, and regulation in their dealings with congressional committees, regulatory bodies, and executive departments
2. The policy-making process, through which the policies developed in the policy-planning network are brought to the White House and Congress
3. The candidate selection process, through which members of the power elite influence elections through campaign donations to political candidates

Domination of the federal government by the power elite can be seen most directly in the workings of corporate lobbyists, back-room superlawyers, and trade associations that represent the interests of specific corporations or business sectors. This special-interest process is based on varying combinations of information, gifts, friendship, and promises of lucrative private jobs in the future. This is the aspect of business-government relations described by journalists and social scientists in exposés and case studies.[10] While these studies show that the special interests usually get their

way, the conflicts that sometimes erupt within this process, pitting one corporate sector against another, reinforce the image of widely shared and fragmented power, including the image of a divided corporate community. Moreover, the corporate rich suffer some defeats in the special-interest process. For example, laws that improved automobile safety standards were passed over auto industry objections in the 1970s, and higher standards for water cleanliness overcame opposition by the paper and chemical industries.

Policies that concern the corporate community as a whole are not the province of the special-interest process. Instead, such policies come from the network of foundations, think tanks, and policy-discussion organizations discussed earlier. Plans developed in the policy-planning network reach the federal government in a variety of ways (Figure 3). On the most general level, the network's reports, news releases, and interviews are read by elected officials and their staffs either in pamphlet form or in summary articles in the *Washington Post, New York Times,* and *Wall Street Journal.* Members of the policy-planning network also testify before congressional committees and subcommittees that write legislation or prepare budgets. More directly, the leaders of these organizations advise specific departments of the executive branch on general policies, making them in effect unpaid temporary members of the government. They are also very prominent on the presidential commissions that are appointed to make recommendations on issues ranging from foreign policy to highway construction. Finally, they are appointed to government positions with a frequency far beyond what would be expected. Several different studies have shown that top cabinet positions in both Republican and Democratic administrations are held by members of the upper class and corporate executives who are leaders in policy-discussion organizations (Table 5).[11]

The general picture that emerges here is that the highest levels of the executive branch are interlocked with the upper class and the corporate community through the movement of executives and lawyers into and out of the government. Although the same person is not in governmental and corporate positions at the same time, there is enough continuity for the relationship to be described as one of revolving interlocks. Corporate leaders resign their directorships in profit-making and nonprofit organizations to serve in government for two or three years and then return to the corporate commu-

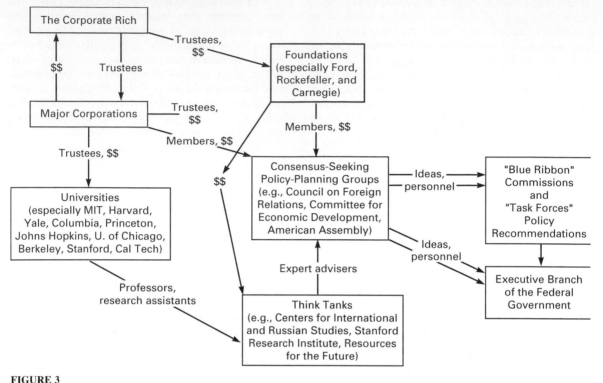

FIGURE 3

The flow of policy from corporations and their owners to government. (*From G. William Domhoff, "How the Power Elite Set National Goals," in Robert Perrucci and Marc Pilisuk [eds.], The Triple Revolution Emerging, Boston, Little, Brown, 1971, p. 213.*)

nity or the policy-planning network. This system gives them temporary independence from the narrow concerns of their organizations and allows them to perform the more general roles they have learned in policy-discussion groups. They return to the private sector with useful personal contacts and information.

As important as the special-interest and policy-planning processes are, they could not operate successfully without sympathetic business-oriented elected officials in the government. That leads to the third process through which members of the power elite dominate the federal government: the candidate selection process that operates through the two major political parties. The two parties play a very small role in political education and policy formation; they have been reduced to the function of filling offices. That is why the American political system can be characterized as a candidate selection process.

The political system focuses on candidate selection to the relative exclusion of political education and policy formulation because there can be only two main parties as a result of the structure of the government and the nature of our electoral system. The fact that Americans select a President instead of a parliament and elect legislators from single-member geographic areas (states for the Senate, districts for the House) leads to a two-party system because in these winner-take-all elections a vote for a third party is a vote for one's least desired choice. A vote for a very liberal party instead of the Democrats, for example, helps the Republicans. Under these rules, the most sensible strategy for both Democrats and Republicans is to blur their policy differences and compete for voters with middle-of-the-road policy views or no policy views at all.

Contrary to what many people believe, American political parties are not very responsive to voter preferences. Their candidates are fairly free to say one thing to get elected and then do another once they are in office. This contributes to confusion and apathy among the electorate and leads to campaigns in which there are no issues except images and personalities even when the polls show that voters are concerned about certain policy issues. You don't raise unnecessary issues during a campaign, President Richard Nixon's communications director said after the 1972 elections.[12]

It is precisely because the candidate selection process is so personalized, and therefore dependent on name recognition, images, and emotional symbolism, that it can be dominated by members of the power elite through large campaign contributions. Playing the role of donors and money raisers, the same people who direct corporations and take part in the policy-planning network have a crucial place in the careers of most politicians who advance beyond the local level. Their

TABLE 5
The Corporate Connections of the Secretary of State, Secretary of the Treasury, and Secretary of Defense in the Carter, Reagan, and Bush Administrations

Carter Administration	Reagan Administration	Bush Administration
Secretary of State		
Cyrus Vance	George P. Schultz	James A. Baker III
Partner, Simpson, Thatcher & Bartlett (Wall Street law firm)	President, Bechtel Construction Company	Partner, Andrews, Kurth, Campell & Jones (Houston law firm)
Director, Council on Foreign Relations	Director, Council on Foreign Relations	Director, Texas Commerce Bank.
Chair, Rockefeller Foundation	Trustee, Sloan Foundation	Director, Herman Brothers, Inc
Member, Trilateral Commission	Director, Morgan Guaranty Trust	
Director, Pan American World Airways	Director, Sears, Roebuck & Company	
Director, New York Times		
Director, IBM		
Director, Aetna Life and Casualty		
Secretary of the Treasury		
W. Michael Blumenthal	Donald Regan	Nicholas F. Brady
Chair, Bendix Corporation	Chairman, Merrill, Lynch	Chair, Dillon-Read (Wall Street investment bank)
Director, Council of Foreign Relations	Member, Council on Foreign Relations	Director, Doubleday & Co.
Trustee, Rockefeller Foundation	Trustee, Committee for Economic Development	Director, H.J. Heinz
Member, Trilateral Commission	Member, Business Roundtable	Director, NCR
Trustee, Committee for Economic Development		Director, Media General, Inc.
Trustee, Princeton University		Director, Purolator Courier Corporation
Secretary of Defense		
Harold Brown	Caspar W. Weinberger	Richard B. Cheney
President, California Institute of Technology	Vice president and general counsel, Bechtel Construction Company	Congressman (R-Wyoming), 1978–1988
Member, Council on Foreign Relations	Member, Trilateral Commission	
Member Trilateral Commission	Director, Quaker Oats	
Director, IBM	Director, Pepsi, Inc.	
Director, Times-Mirror Corporation		
Director, Schroeder Trust		

support is especially important in party primaries, where money is an even larger factor than it is in general elections.

The American two-party system therefore results in elected officials who are willing to go along with the policies advocated by the members of the power elite who work in the special-interest and policy-planning processes. They are motivated by personal ambition far more than by political conviction. Still, some extremely conservative elected Republicans often oppose power elite proposals, claiming that such policies are the work of Communists or pointy-headed intellectuals out to wreck the free enterprise system. Many Democrats from blue-collar and university districts consistently oppose power elite policies as members of the liberal-labor coalition. However, both ultraconservatives and liberals are outnumbered by moderates in both parties, especially in key leadership positions in Congress. After many years in Congress, liberals decide to "go along to get along." "This place has a way of grinding you down," explained Abner Mikvah, a liberal member of Congress in the late 1960s and early 1970s.[13]

Although members of the power elite are the most important financial backers of both parties, there are differences between the parties. The rival leaders have intraclass differences, and the supporters tend to have interclass differences. The Republican party is controlled by the wealthiest families of the upper class and the corporate community, who are largely Protestant. The Democratic party, by contrast, is the party of the "fringes" of the upper class and the power elite. Although often called "the party of the common person," it was in fact the party of the southern segment of the upper class until very recently. The power of southern Democrats in the party and in Congress was secured in a variety of ways, the most important of which was the seniority system for selecting committee chairs in Congress. (By tradition, the person who has been on the committee longest automatically becomes the chair; this avoids conflict among members of the party.) Thus, the one-party system in the south and the exclusion of African-Americans from the voting booth until the mid-1960s gave southern planters and merchants power at the national level out of all proportion to their wealth and numbers. This shows that it is not necessarily the wealthiest people who rule; the nature of the political system also enters into the equation. However, the southern elites are not poor; they are only less rich than many of their northern counterparts.

The southerners dominated the Democratic party in alliance with the "ethnic rich" in the north, meaning wealthy Jews and Catholics who were shunned or mistreated by rich Protestants. The businesses they owned were often local or smaller than those of Republican backers, and they usually were excluded from the social institutions of the upper class. These ethnic rich were the primary financial supporters of the infamous political machines (political organizations made up of government officials and paid precinct workers) that dominated Democratic politics in most large northern cities between 1880 and 1970.

The alliance between the southern segment of the upper class and the northern ethnic rich usually was able to freeze out the policy initiatives of the party's liberal-labor coalition through its control of congressional committees, although there was a time (1940 to 1975) when labor unions had significant influence on the Democrats. When that alliance broke down because the machine Democrats sided with the liberals and labor, southern Democrats joined with northern Republicans to create the *conservative coalition*, in which a majority of southern Democrats and a majority of northern Republicans voted together against the northern Democrats. This conservative coalition usually formed around issues that reflect class conflict in the legislative arena: civil rights, union rights, social welfare, and business regulation. Most legislation involving these issues weakens employers in the face of workers and their unions, and so the conservative coalition is based on the shared interests of northern and southern employers. This alliance won far more often than it lost in the years between 1937, when it was formed, and the early 1980s, when it disappeared for the simple reason that many southerners had become Republicans.

The Democratic party changed in the 1980s. Southern whites started to move into the Republican party once African-Americans had won enforcement of the right to vote, and so the Republican party gradually has become the party of wealthy employers in both the north and the south. Thus, the Democratic party is slowly becoming what many people always thought it to be—the party of liberals, minorities, workers, and the poor.

Why Business Leaders Feel Powerless

Despite the evidence that the power elite has great influence over the federal government, many corporate leaders feel that they are relatively powerless. From their perspective, Congress is more responsive to organized labor, environmentalists, and consumers. They also claim to be harassed by willful and arrogant bureaucrats. These negative feelings toward government are not a recent development, contrary to those who blame the New Deal and the social programs of the 1960s. A study of businesspeople's views in the nineteenth century found that they believed political leaders to be "stupid" and "empty" people who went into politics only to earn a living, and a study of businesspeople's views during their most powerful decade, the 1920s, found the same mistrust of government.[14]

The feelings of business leaders about their supposed lack of power cannot be taken seriously as a power indicator: Feelings are one thing; the effects of one's actions are another. However, it is interesting to speculate why businesspeople complain about a government they dominate. First, complaining about the government puts government officials on the defensive and forces them to keep proving that they are friendly to business. Second, businesspeople complain about government because very few civil servants are part of the upper class and the corporate community. The antigovernment ideology of the United States tends to keep members of the upper class from government careers except in the State Department, and so the main contacts for members of the power elite are at the very top of the government. There is thus uncertainty about how the middle levels will react to new situations and a feeling that it is necessary to ride herd on or rein in potentially troublesome bureaucrats.

There also seems to be an ideological aspect to business leaders' attitudes toward the government: a fear of the populist, democratic ideology that underlies the American political system. Since power is in theory in the hands of all the people, there is always the possibility that someday the majority will turn the government into the pluralist democracy that it is supposed to be. In a real way, then, the great power of the upper class and the corporate community is culturally illegitimate and is therefore vigorously denied: It is all right to be rich, and even to brag about one's wealth a little, but not to be powerful or, worse, to flaunt that power.

Finally, claims of powerlessness by corporate leaders also suggest an explanation that involves the intersection of social psychology and sociology. It is the upper class and the corporate community that have power, not individuals outside this institutional context. As individuals the elite are not always listened to, and they have to convince their peers of the reasonableness of their arguments before anything can get done. Moreover, any policy that is adopted is a group decision, and it is sometimes hard for people to identify with group actions. It is therefore not surprising that specific individuals feel powerless.

The Weaknesses of the Working Class

In many democratic countries, the *working class*, defined as all white-collar and blue-collar workers who earn a salary or a wage, has more social power than it does in the United States. This power is achieved primarily through labor unions and political parties. It is reflected in more egalitarian wealth and income distributions, a more equitable tax structure, more extensive public health services, highly subsidized housing, and higher old-age and unemployment benefits.

How can the American working class be relatively powerless in a country that prides itself on a long-standing history of pluralism and free elections? There are several interacting historical reasons. First, the *primary producers* in the United States—those who work with their hands in factories and fields—were more seriously divided among themselves until the 1930s than was the case in most other countries. The deepest and most important of these divisions was between whites and African-Americans. In the beginning, of course, African-Americans had no social power because of their enslavement, but even after African-Americans gained their freedom, prejudice in the white working class kept the two groups apart.

This black-white split in the working class was reinforced by later conflicts between craft workers—also called skilled workers—and industrial workers—also called mass production or unskilled workers. Craft workers usually tried to keep their wages high by excluding industrial workers from entry into the country. Their sense of superiority as skilled workers was reinforced by the fact that they were of northern European, Protestant origin whereas the industrial workers tended to be Catholics and Jews from eastern and southern Europe. Some African-Americans, along with other racial minorities, were also found in the ranks of the industrial workers.

It would have been difficult to overcome these divisions even if workers could have developed their own political party, but they were unable to do this because the electoral system greatly disadvantages third parties. As a result, workers had no place to go but the Republicans or Democrats. In the late nineteenth and early twentieth centuries, craft workers often supported the Democrats while the immigrant industrial workers tended to support the Republicans. Even when craft and industrial workers moved into the Democratic party en masse in the 1930s, they could not control the party because of the power of wealthy southern planters and merchants.

Nor did workers have much luck organizing themselves through unions. Employers were able to call on the government to crush organizing drives and strikes through both court injunctions and arrests. Not only did employers have great influence with politicians, but the American tradition of law, based on laissez-faire liberalism, was fiercely opposed to any restraint of trade or interference with private property. It was not until the 1930s that the liberal-labor coalition was able to pass legislation guaranteeing workers the right to join a union and engage in collective bargaining. Even this advance was made possible only by excluding the southern work force, that is, agricultural and seasonal labor, from coverage by the new laws. Further, the passage of this legislation had only a limited impact because the industrial unions were defeated almost completely in the south and southwest. Unions thrived in a few major industries in the north after World War II, but their power was eroded beginning in the 1970s as the big corporations moved their factories to other countries or lost market share to European and Japanese companies.

Given this history of internal division, political frustration, and union defeat, it is not surprising that American workers continue to accept the highly individualistic ideology that has characterized the United States since its founding. This acceptance makes it even more difficult to organize workers around bread-and-butter issues. They often vote instead on the basis of social issues or religious convictions. Those who are deeply religious, opposed to affirmative action, or opposed to gun control often vote for the avowedly antiunion Republican party.

Thus, it is important not to confuse freedom with social power. Between 1962 and 1988 there was a great expansion in individual rights as a result of the civil rights, feminist, and lesbian-gay movements, but during that time the ratio of a top business executive's pay to a factory worker's pay increased from 41 to 1 to 93 to 1. American workers can say and do what they want within very broad limits, and their children can study hard in school and then join the well-off professional class as doctors, lawyers, architects, or engineers. However, most Americans have very little social power if they are not part of the power elite.

Community Power

Not all power is wielded at the national level. To gain a full picture of who rules in the United States, it is necessary to understand the power structures that exist at the local level and see how they relate to the national power elite. Power at the local level is based on the ownership and control of land and buildings. A community power structure is essentially an aggregation of land-based interests that profit from increasingly intensive use of land. The typical way of intensifying land use is growth, which usually expresses itself in a constantly rising local population. A successful local elite is able to attract the corporate plants and offices, defense contracts, federal and state buildings, and educational and research establishments that lead to an expanded work force and then to an expansion of retail and other commercial activity, extensive land and housing development, and increased financial activity. Because this chain of events is at the core of every developed locality, power analysts call the city and its local elite a *growth machine*.[15]

Growth machines are local counterparts to the national power elite and have many interests in common with it. However, there also can be tensions between local and national elites. For example, if corporations decide that the local business climate has not be made favorable by a growth machine, they can pull up stakes and leave. There also can be conflicts between rival growth machines as they compete for investment from corporations, universities, and government agencies.

Because so many government decisions can affect land values and growth potential, leaders of the growth machine are prime participants in local government. The growth machine is the most overrepresented group on local city councils and is also well represented on planning commissions, zoning boards, water boards, and downtown parking authorities. However, this direct involvement in government is usually not the first or only contact with government for the members of a growth machine. These individuals often have served on the local chamber of commerce's committees and commissions concerned with growth, planning, roadways, and off-street parking. These committees are the local counterparts of policy-discussion organizations.

A growth machine does not dominate local government without opposition. There is sometimes conflict between the machine and specific neighborhoods. Neighborhoods are something to be used and enjoyed in the eyes of those who live in them, but they are sites of further development for the "highest and best use" of the land in the eyes of those who run the growth machine. This conflict between use value and exchange value is a basic one in most cities where the downtown interests try to expand. Sometimes the neighborhoods win these battles, especially when they are aided by organized environmentalists or supplemented by a university community which can marshal professorial expertise and student votes.

The differentiation between a national corporate community based on the production of goods and services and local growth machines based on land use provides a more subtle, less monolithic picture of power in the United States. At the same time, it shows that politics in this country, at whatever level, is mostly business in one form or another.

CONCLUSION

The argument over the structure and distribution of power in the United States has been going on since the 1950s and has generated many empirical studies. In the final analysis, however, people's conclusions about the American power structure depend on their beliefs concerning power indicators, that is, on their philosophy of political science. If "who benefits" and "who sits" are considered valid indicators of power, the kind of evidence presented in this essay makes a convincing case for the dominant role of the power elite and the growth machines. If "who wins" on a wide range of government decisions is considered the only valid indicator of power and if it is expected that the power elite and the growth machines will win every time, the arguments in this essay will be seen as less impressive. This is the case because it is so difficult to show the full range of power elite and growth machine predominance in regard to policy issues. A good start has been made, but it will take more to convince the skeptics.

Thus, the argument about who rules America is as much philosophical as it is empirical. While the debate continues, however, we should remember that the members of a small upper class own 25 to 30 percent of all privately held wealth and 45 to 50 percent of all corporate stock, are overrepresented in seats of formal power from the corporations to the federal government, and win much more often than they lose on issues ranging from the tax structure to labor policy to foreign policy.

ENDNOTES

1. John K. Galbraith, *American Capitalism*, Boston, Houghton Mifflin, 1956; Arnold Rose, *The Power Structure*, New York, Oxford University Press, 1967; Nelson Polsby, *Community Power and Political Theory*, 2d ed., New Haven, Conn., Yale University Press, 1980.
2. Dennis Wrong, *Power: Its Forms, Bases, and Uses*, Chicago, University of Chicago Press, 1979, p. 2.
3. E. Digby Baltzell, *Philadelphia Gentlemen: The Making of a National Upper Class*, New York, Free Press, 1958; G. William Domhoff, *The Higher Circles*, New York, Random House, 1970; G. William Domhoff, *The Bohemian Grove and Other Retreats*, New York, Harper & Row, 1974.
4. G. William Domhoff, *Who Rules America Now?* New York, Simon & Schuster, 1983, pp. 42–43.
5. Michael Useem, *The Inner Circle*, New York, Oxford University Press, 1984; Beth Mintz and Michael Schwartz, *The Power Structure of American Business*, Chicago, University of Chicago Press, 1985.
6. Daniel Bell, "The Break-up of Family Capitalism," in Daniel Bell (ed.), *The End of Ideology*, New York, Free Press, 1960; A. A. Berle, Jr., and Gardner Means, *The Modern Corporation and Private Property*, New York, Macmillan, 1932; A. A. Berle, Jr., *Power without Property*, New York, Harcourt, Brace, 1959.
7. Domhoff, *Who Rules America Now?*
8. Thomas R. Dye, *Who's Running America?* Englewood Cliffs, N.J., Prentice-Hall, 1976, pp. 151–152; Useem, op. cit., Domhoff, *Who Rules America Now?* pp. 66–72.
9. Dye, op cit., chap. 5; Domhoff, *Who Rules America Now?* chap. 4; Harold Salzman and G. William Domhoff, "Nonprofit Organizations and the Corporate Community," *Social Science History* 7:205–216,1983.
10. Grant McConnell, *Private Power and American Democracy*, New York, Knopf, 1966; Morton Mintz and Jerry Cohen, *Power, Inc.*, New York, Viking, 1976; Mark Green, *Who Runs Congress?* New York, Bantam, 1979.
11. Domhoff, *Who Rules America Now?* pp. 136–143.
12. "Post-Election Candor," *Newsweek*, March 26, 1973, p. 15.
13. Robert Sherrill, "92nd Congress: Eulogies and Evasions," *The Nation*, February 15, 1971, p. 200.
14. James W. Prothro, *The Dollar Decade*, Baton Rouge, Louisiana State University Press, 1954; Leonard Silk and David Vogel, *Ethics and Profits*, New York, Simon & Schuster, 1976.
15. Jonathan Logan and Harvey Molotch, *Urban Fortunes*, Berkeley, University of California Press, 1987.

READING 4

POLITICAL RESPONSE TO CAPITALIST CRISIS: NEO-MARXIST THEORIES OF THE STATE AND THE CASE OF THE NEW DEAL

Theda Skocpol

DESPITE all that has been observed since Marx's time, as to the operations of elites, bureaucracies, etc., Marxists generally seek to reduce political phenomena to their "real" class significance, and often fail, in analysis, to allow sufficient distance between the one and the other. But in fact those moments, in which governing institutions appear as the direct, emphatic, and unmediated organs of a "ruling class," are exceedingly rare, as well as transient. More often these institutions operate with a good deal of autonomy, and sometimes with distinct interests of their own, within a general context of class power which prescribes the limits beyond which this autonomy cannot be safely stretched, and which, very generally, discloses the questions which arise for executive decision. Attempts to short-circuit analysis end up by explaining nothing.
—E. P. Thompson[1].

This essay uses the history of New Deal politics during the Depression of the 1930s in the United States to assess the strengths and limitations of several kinds of neo-Marxist theories of the capitalist state. One purpose of the essay is to compare some alternative neo-Marxist approaches, asking which raises the most fruitful questions and offers the best explanations of New Deal politics. More basically, the essay sketches

From *Politics and Society* 10(2) 1980: 155–201. Reprinted with the permission of Sage Publications.

An earlier version of this article was presented in the session on "Political Systems" of the seventy-fourth Annual Meeting of the American Sociological Association, Boston, August 1979. In gaining historical background and formulating ideas for the paper, I especially benefited from the research assistance of Kenneth Finegold and from individual discussions with him and with Jonathan Zeiltlin. Critical reactions and suggestions for revisions (not all of which I was able or willing to accept) came from Fred Block, William Domhoff, William Hixson, Christopher Jencks, John Mollenkopf, Charles Sabel, David Stark, and Erik Olin Wright.

[1] E. P. Thompson, *The Poverty of Theory and Other Essays* (London: Merlin, Press, 1978), p. 48.

some of the ways U.S. political institutions shaped and limited the accomplishments of the New Deal and argues that neo-Marxists of all varieties have so far given insufficient weight to state and party organizations as independent determinants of political conflicts and outcomes. The formulations here are meant to be suggestive rather than conclusive. Theoretical debates on the state and politics in capitalist societies are still wide open. An exploratory essay that probes the interface between theories and a concrete historical trajectory may help to push discussion away from abstract conceptual disputes toward meeting the challenge of explaining actual historical developments.

EXPLAINING THE NEW DEAL

Recent historiographical disputes have worried about the "conservative" versus "radical" nature of the New Deal, often asking, in effect, whether or not the New Deal was intended to "save capitalism." In truth, U.S. capitalism was not fundamentally challenged—not by the leaders of the New Deal and not by any powerful oppositional political forces. While the question of why there was no such challenge remains an important problem, we need to devote more attention to understanding what actually did change politically and socially during the 1930s and to understanding the limits placed on concretely present tendencies within the New Deal.

The massive Depression of the 1930s not surprisingly stimulated important political transformations in the United States. The Democratic party triumphed electorally and incorporated new popular groups into its coalition. An unprecedented plethora of federal agencies was established to implement new welfare and regulatory policies. Labor militancy spread in the mass production industries. The Congress of Industrial Organizations enrolled millions of workers in industry-wide unions. And the federal government was transformed from a mildly interventionist, business-dominated regime into an active "broker state" that incorporated commercial farmers and organized labor into processes of political bargaining at the national level.

Still, certain changes that were conceivably possible failed to occur in the New Deal. Although urban-liberal elements gained major new ground within the Democratic party, they were not able to implement a truly social-democratic program. And increased state intervention in the economy, however significant as a break with the recent American past, nonetheless failed to achieve its overriding objective of full economic re-covery. Not until after the United States had geared up economically for World War II did extraordinary unemployment disappear and national output fully revive.[2]

How can we account for New Deal transformations in the American state and politics? And how can we explain why full economic recovery was not induced despite the political changes? The orthodox "pluralist" paradigm in political sociology is not well equipped to handle such questions. Pluralism attempts to explain governmental decisions in terms of the conflicting play of organized group interests in society and as such it offers little that would help to explain major institutional transformations in history. To be sure, some classic pluralist works, such as David Truman's *The Governmental Process*,[3] include rich descriptions of U.S. institutional patterns and allude to how they encourage or block governmental access for different kinds of groups and interests. Nevertheless, pluralists fail to offer (or seek) well-developed explanations of how economic and political institutions variously influence group formation and intergroup conflicts. Nor do they feel the need to go beyond vague, evolutionist schemes that posit institutional change in politics as an inevitable progression of ever-increasing democracy, governmental effectiveness, and the specialization of political arrangements, all occurring in smooth, adaptive responses to the "modernization" of the economy and society.[4] Thus, to explain transformations such as those that occurred in the U.S. during the 1930s, a pluralist would either have to refer to broad, amorphous evolutionary trends at one extreme or to immediate maneuverings of interest groups at the other. Explaining an increase in state intervention, the specific

forms this took, and especially the limitations on the effectiveness of such intervention, would not be a congenial undertaking.

More promising than pluralism for explaining the transformations of the New Deal era are neo-Marxist theories of "the capitalist state." They at least raise the right order of issues and establish some of the analytical terms necessary for understanding such periods of institutional change. At the very center of neo-Marxist analysis is the relationship of political processes and state actions to the capitalist economy and to basic class relations in capitalist society. According to neo-Marxists, a period of economic crisis such as the Great Depression is certain to spur socioeconomically rooted political conflicts and to create pressures for unusual degrees and kinds of state action. Moreover, any neo-Marxist explanation of the ensuing political conflicts and state actions would refer (in one way or another) to class actions, class conflicts, class interests, and, above all, in advanced capitalist societies, to the actions, conflicts, and interests of capitalists and the industrial working class.

Beyond such fundamentals, however, there is not much agreement among the various neo-Marxist approaches.[5] To discuss the usefulness of these theories in any depth it is necessary to identify sub-types and select examples appropriate to the particular purpose at hand. My interest here is in the tools neo-Marxist theories may have to offer for analyzing political conflicts and processes of state intervention within the bounds of advanced ("monopoly") capitalism. For this purpose, I shall explore particular examples of three broad types of neo-Marxist theories: "instrumentalist," "political-functionalist," and "class struggle." For Marxist "instrumentalist" theory, I shall especially emphasize works by U.S. historians of "corporate liberalism."[6] For Marxist "political functionalism" (my label), I shall use

---

[2] See Lester V. Chandler, *America's Greatest Depression 1929–1941* (New York: Harper and Row, 1970).

[3] David B. Truman, *The Governmental Process,* 2nd ed. (New York: Knopf, 1971; originally 1951).

[4] Even a very sophisticated developmentalist argument, such as Samuel Huntington, "Political Modernization: America vs. Europe," chap. 2 in *Political Order in Changing Societies* (New Haven: Yale University Press, 1968), still tends to explain macrohistorical change (or its absence) in vague evolutionist terms, referring to the "needs" of society. Thus while Huntington brilliantly describes America's enduringly peculiar "Tudor" polity, his explanation for why America has no strong state is that it hasn't "needed" one, either to maintain national unity or to ensure economic growth. Aside from its crudeness, this explanation leaves one wondering about the Civil War, when unity broke down, and the Depression, when economic growth did. Society's "needs" must not be a sufficient explanation for political structures, their continuities and transformations.

[5] Two good surveys of the literature are David A. Gold, Clarence Y. II, Lo, and Erik Olin Wright, "Recent Developments in Marxist Theories of the Capitalist State," *Monthly Review* 27, no. 5 (October 1975): 29–43, and 27, no. 6 (November 1975): 36–51; and Bob Jessop, "Recent Theories of the Capitalist State," *Cambridge Journal of Economics* 1, no. 4 (December 1977): 353–73.

[6] I draw especially upon corporate-liberal arguments about the New Deal by Ronald Radosh, "The Myth of the New Deal," in *A New History of Leviathan: Essays on the Rise of the Corporate State,* ed. Radosh and N. Rothbard (New York: Dutton, 1972), pp. 146–87; and G. William Domhoff, "How the Power Elite Shape Social Legislation," *The Higher Circles: The Governing Class in America* (New York: Vintage Books, Random House, 1971), chap. 6.

theoretical arguments from the early work of Nicos Poulantzas.[7] And for one kind of "class struggle" theory, I shall use Fred Block's easy "The Ruling Class Does Not Rule," the arguments of which were developed with reference to twentieth-century U.S. history, including the New Deal.[8] Each of the three theories to be discussed posits a distinctive combination of class and state actions through which a major capitalist economic crisis, such as the Great Depression, should generate political transformations and government interventions sufficient to ensure sociopolitical stability and renewed capital accumulation. For each perspective, my concern will be to see what the theory and the history of the New Deal have to say to one another. Particular emphasis will be placed upon the National Industrial Recovery Act (NIRA) of 1933–35 and the Wagner National Labor Relations Act, for these acts are especially relevant to any assessment of the interrelations of the capitalist class, the industrial working class, and the national government during the New Deal.

Passed in June 1933 at the end of the first "Hundred Days" of New Deal legislation, the National Industrial Recovery Act was envisaged as a joint business-government effort to promote national economic recovery. To ensure the political support of organized labor, a provision of the NIRA, section 7a, endorsed the right of industrial workers "to organize and bargain collectively through representatives of their own choosing." However, most of the act addressed the declared needs of businessmen. Industries were freed from antitrust restrictions and prompted to draw up "codes of fair competition" to be approved and enforced by a new National Recovery Administration (NRA). The codes

regulated hours of work and wage rates for labor, and they raised prices and controlled levels of production in an effort to guarantee profits for capitalists. The idea was to bring about economic recovery by stabilizing levels of production and employment and restoring "business confidence."

The Wagner Act was the most innovative accomplishment of the second, reformist phase of the New Deal. Enacted in July 1935, it reiterated and put teeth into the promises earlier made in section 7a of the NIRA. Industrial workers could join unions and bargain collectively, free from harassment by their employers. A National Labor Relations Board was established with full legal authority to determine collective bargaining units, to hold elections to certify union representatives on a majority basis, and to investigate allegations of unfair labor practices by employers. Through the Wagner Act, in short, the U.S. national government gave legal and administrative support to the widespread establishment of industrial labor unions.

CORPORATE LIBERALISM AND THE NEW DEAL

In any discussion of neo-Marxist theories of the capitalist state, Marxist instrumentalisms are the place to begin, for they have been the take-off point for most recent debates. The somewhat dubious honor of embodying the generic outlines of this much-maligned approach has invariably been accorded to the pioneering book by Ralph Miliband entitled *The State in Capitalist Society*. In truth this book invokes arguments about politics and the state that have since been crystallized into virtually every major neo-Marxist position on these topics. Nevertheless, Miliband's primary purpose in the book is to debunk pluralism by showing that it systematically underestimates the preponderate, self-interested political influence of members of the capitalist class. As Miliband puts it: "What is wrong with pluralist-democratic theory is not its insistence on the fact of competition [that is, open political competition over state policies in capitalist democracies] but its claim (very often its implicit assumption) that the major organized 'interests' in these societies, and notably capital and labour, compete on more or less equal terms, and that none of them is therefore able to achieve a decisive and permanent advantage in the process of

---

[7] Nicos Poulantzas, *Political Power and Social Classes*, trans. Timothy O'Hagen (London: New Left Books, 1973); and idem "The Problem of the Capitalist State," *Ideology in Social Science*, ed. Robin Blackburn (New York: Vintage Books, Random House, 1973), pp. 238–53. After these works Poulantzas evolved away from political functionalism toward more of a class-struggle approach. But I am only treating the earlier works here.
[8] Fred Block, "The Ruling Class Does Not Rule: Notes on the Marxist Theory of the State," *Socialist Revolution*, no. 33 (May-June 1977) pp. 6–28. Class-struggle versions of neo-Marxism are very diverse, and Block doesn't represent all of them. He just represents an example that I find particularly interesting because the state in Block's theory is not collapsed into class relations, as it appears to be, for example, in the more recent works of Nicos Poulantzas and in some of the German neo-Marxist theories surveyed in John Holloway and Sol Picciotto, eds., *State and Capital: A Marxist Debate* (London: Edward Arnold, 1978).

[9] Ralph Miliband, *The State in Capitalist Society* (New York: Basic Books, 1969), p. 146.

competition."[9] On the contrary, argues Miliband, capitalists, particularly those who control major economic organizations, do enjoy decisive and stable political advantages because of their privileged positions both "inside" and "outside" the state. Inside the state, officials tend either to be from capitalist backgrounds or to enjoy close career or personal ties to capitalists. Such officials, moreover, almost invariably assume the inevitability and the legitimacy of a capitalist economy. Furthermore, says Miliband, "business enjoys a massive superiority *outside* the state system as well, in terms of the immensely stronger pressures which, as compared with labour and any other interest, it is able to exercise in pursuit of its purposes."[10] For capitalists enjoy disproportionate access to organizational resources, and they can credibly clothe their policy demands in "the national interest" and back them up with potent threats of economic or political disruption.

Miliband's purpose is to sketch a broad frame of reference, not to explain any particular kind of political outcome in capitalist societies. However, since the emergence of a New Left historiography in the United States during the 1960s, there has been an especially "strong" variant of instrumentalism specifically designed to explain why and how state intervention has increased during the twentieth century in U.S. capitalism. James Weinstein, William Domhoff, and Ronald Radosh have been among the articulate proponents of this view,[11] and James O'Connor relies in significant part upon it in his recent *Fiscal Crisis of the State*.[12] As Fred Block points out, " . . . the heart of the theory is the idea that enlightened capitalists recognize that crises of capitalism can be resolved through an extension of the state's role."[13] Corporate liberalism, Block notes,

> is a reinterpretation of the meaning of American liberalism. . . . In [the liberal] view, the expansion of the role of the state during the 20th century was a consequence of popular victories that succeeded in making capitalism a more benevolent system. The new theory

reversed the old view, arguing that liberalism was the movement of enlightened capitalists to save the corporate order. In this view, the expansion of the role of the state was designed by corporate leaders and their allies to rationalize the economy and society. Rationalization encompasses all measures that stabilize economic and social conditions so that profits can be made on a predictable basis by the major corporations.[14]

Corporate liberalism seeks to explain particular episodes of capitalist political intervention, those that occur under crisis conditions and involve the deliberate extension of state action by a class-conscious vanguard. Under normal conditions, capitalists may influence the state in disunified fashion in all of the ways Miliband outlines, often working at cross-purposes through leadership posts in the state, personal ties to particular policy makers, or interest-group pressures from without. But, say the theorists of corporate liberalism, when crises of accumulation occur or political challenges from below threaten, capitalists can be expected to act as a class. As James O'Connor puts it, "by the turn of the century, and especially during the New Deal, it was apparent to vanguard corporate leaders that some form of rationalization of the economy was necessary. And as the twentieth century wore on, the owners of corporate capital generated the financial ability, learned the organizational skills, and developed the ideas necessary for their self-regulation as a class."[15] Enlightened leadership for the capitalist class is likely to come from those holding the most strategic and powerful economic positions. These vanguard leaders will realize the necessity of stepped-up state intervention and will use their great resources and prestige to persuade many capitalists to go along and to pressure politicians to implement the needed programs. If necessary, minor co-optive concessions will be offered to small businessmen and workers. The resulting state intervention will, however, primarily work in the interests of large-scale corporate capital.

For theorists of corporate liberalism, therefore, the New Deal is envisaged as a set of clever capitalist strategies to stabilize and revitalize a U.S. economy dominated by large corporations. "The New Deal reforms," writes Ronald Radosh, "were not mere incremental gestures. They were solidly based, carefully

[10] Ibid.
[11] James Weinstein, *The Corporate Ideal in the Liberal State: 1900–1918* (Boston: Beacon Press, 1968). For relevant works by Domhoff and Radosh, see note 6. In a private communication, Bill Domhoff has convinced me that his views about the Wagner Act have developed away from a strictly corporate-liberal position in publications subsequent to *The Higher Circles*. Thus my arguments here apply only to the cited parts of that book.
[12] James O'Connor, *The Fiscal Crisis of the State* (New York: St. Martin's Press, 1973).
[13] Fred Block, "Beyond Corporate Liberalism," *Social Problems* 24 (1976–77): 355.

[14] Ibid., p. 352.
[15] O'Connor, *Fiscal Crisis*, p. 68.
[16] Radosh, "Myth of the New Deal," in *New History of Leviathan*, ed. Radosh and Rothbard, p. 186.

worked out pieces of legislation."[16] Great stress is placed on the ultimate benefits that U.S. corporate capitalism gained not only from government interventions to stabilize particular industries, but also from such widely popular measures as unemployment insurance, social security, and the legalization of unions and collective bargaining. That such measures appeared to be won by democratic pressure only represents an added advantage for capitalists. For in this way, says Radosh, "the reforms were of such a character that they would be able to create a long-lasting mythology about the existence of a pluralistic American democracy. . . ."[17] Business opposition to the New Deal is seen by theorists of corporate liberalism as emanating from "small business types, with their own conservative mentality, [who] responded to the epoch in terms of the consciousness of a previous era."[18] By contrast, far-sighted leaders of big business strongly promoted the necessary reforms. "The moderates in the governing class had to put up a stubborn, prolonged fight until the law would be able to reflect the realities of the new epoch of corporation capitalism."[19]

The corporate-liberal explanation of the New Deal is highly misleading. It can only be substantiated through a purely illustrative and selective citing of facts. When the theory is subjected to a rigorous, skeptical examination, corporate liberalism fails to explain even those aspects of the New Deal that seem most consonant with it.

There *are* facts that fit the corporate-liberal interpretation of the New Deal; indeed, such facts are repeatedly recounted by proponents of the theory. The self-stated aims of the leaders of the New Deal, including Franklin Roosevelt himself, could easily be described as "corporate-liberal," in the sense that the top New Dealers were all out to sustain American capitalism (and democracy) through reform, not to propel the country toward socialism. More to the point, business leaders and spokesmen were visibly involved in the New Deal. Their presence was all-pervasive with respect to the early, comprehensive measure for economic recovery, the National Industrial Recovery Act of 1933–35,[20] and under the National Recovery

Administration, businessmen in each industry drafted and enforced the regulatory codes. Later in the New Deal, the Social Security Act was endorsed by a "Business Advisory Council" of prominent bankers and officers of major corporations.[21] Finally, corporate-liberal theorists correctly point out that throughout the 1930s FDR never ceased wooing business support and that there were always officials with business backgrounds and ties holding high-level positions in the federal administration.

But facts such as these represent only the loosest conceivable evidence for validating the hypothesis that capitalist plans and influence caused the New Deal. (Indeed, by analogous criteria, one could "prove" that Marxist theory was sponsored by capitalists because of Marx's close personal and financial ties to Engels, the son of a capitalist manufacturer!) If we hold corporate liberalism to more rigorous standards of validation, then the key questions become: Was there at work during the 1930s a self-conscious, disciplined capitalist class, or vanguard of major capitalists, that put forward functional strategies for recovery and stabilization and had the political power to implement them successfully? Were most corporate leaders (especially of big, strategic businesses) prepared to make concessions to labor? Did business opposition to the New Deal come primarily from small business? These questions go to the heart of the corporate-liberal claims; if they cannot be answered affirmatively, then the theory does not adequately explain the New Deal.

No part of the New Deal better appears to fit the corporate-liberal model than the National Industrial Recovery Act and the National Recovery Administration (NRA) established under it. Capitalists, above all, those who ran the major corporations in each industry, were by all historical accounts able to get exactly what they wanted out of the NRA, that is, fixed prices and stabilized production. Nevertheless, despite the ubiquitous influence of big businessmen in the formulation and implementation of the NIRA, this part of the New Deal does not measure up as a class-conscious strategy for U.S. corporate capitalism. The policies pursued were inadequate to the needs of the economy and to the interests of big business in general. For the most important fact of all about the NIRA, though, curiously, one that is never discussed by corporate-liberal theorists, is that it *failed* to bring economic recovery through busi-

[16] Ibid.
[18] Ibid., p. 187.
[19] Ibid.
[20] See Ellis W. Hawley, *The New Deal and the Problem of Monopoly* (Princeton, N. J.: Princeton University Press, 1966), chaps. 1–3; and Arthur M. Schlesinger, Jr., *The Coming of the New Deal* (Boston: Houghton Mifflin, 1958), chaps. 6–8.

[21] Radosh, "Myth of New Deal," in *New History of Leviathan*, ed. Radosh and Rothbard, pp. 157–58.

ness-government cooperation. Yet if we probe a bit into the actual state of consciousness and discipline among U.S. capitalists at the time of the NIRA, this failure becomes more understandable. We can see that, ironically, the failure can be partially attributed to the strong and misdirected political influence of (by corporate-liberal criteria) *insufficiently* class conscious capitalists.

U.S. capitalists were ill prepared to act together as a class in the early 1930s.[22] During the height of the Progressive Era (and the heyday of the National Civic Federation), there had been a measure of class unity and discipline, at least among large-scale corporate capitalists. In large part this was because the House of Morgan, autocratically directed by J. P. Morgan himself, enjoyed strong influence on boards of directors of the major corporations in many key industries. By the 1930s, the Morgan hegemony was no longer so absolute. World War I and the patterns of economic growth during the 1920s loosened the dependence of industrial firms upon outside financing. Sheer competitive disunity increased in many industries. Within others there was more unity, as ties among firms were strengthened during the mobilization for World War I and through the trade-association movement sponsored by the Republican administrations during the 1920s. Thus by the end of the decade the highest level of consciousness and discipline that some (by no means all) capitalists enjoyed was focused within single industries, especially those like textiles, where active and reasonably effective trade associations had evolved.[23]

Not surprisingly, therefore, when the Depression struck and business spokesmen began to come forward with plans for government programs to help business, even the most comprehensive visions of "business planning" outlined by Gerard Swope, president of General Electric and Henry Harriman, president of the U.S. Chamber of Commerce, called primarily for coordination within industries.[24] The idea was to give government backing to the efforts of trade associations (or other industry-wide bodies) to regulate competition in the interests of all (and especially the more established) businesses. But these plans had very little to say about how problems of interindustry coordination were to be resolved in the interest of the capitalist class, and the accumulation process, as a whole. At most, Swope and Harriman envisaged mutual consultation by representatives chosen from each industry, but they did not say how particular industries (or dominant enterprises within industries) could be persuaded to accept plans not favorable to their short-term interests.

In truth, the supposedly class-conscious capitalists of the early 1930s were mesmerized by false analogies based upon their experience of business-dominated government intervention during World War I.[25] The War Industries Board (WIB) of 1918 had been run by businessmen-administrators in the interests of the dominant firms in each industry.[26] As William Leuchtenburg puts it, "perhaps the outstanding characteristic of the war [World War I] organization of industry was that it showed how to achieve massive government intervention without making any permanent alteration in the power of corporations."[27] U.S. capitalists applauded this experience of "government intervention." Not only was their autonomy respected, but the happy result was economic prosperity and plentiful profits. In the face of another national crisis after 1929, why not revive the methods that had worked so well in World War I? For the capitalists there was the added advantage that appealing to the "analogue of war" could provide an occasion for nationalistic propaganda: it could pull Americans of all classes together "to do battle against

---

[22] This paragraph draws especially upon David Vogel, "Why Businessmen Distrust Their State: The Political Consciousness of American Corporate Executives," *British Journal of Political Science* 8, no. 1 (January 1978): 70–72; and Gabriel Kolko, *Main Currents in American History* (New York: Harper and Row, 1976), pp. 100–117.

[23] See Louis Galambos, *Competition and Cooperation: The Emergence of a National Trade Association* (Baltimore: Johns Hopkins University Press, 1966); and Robert F. Himmelberg, *The Origins of the National Recovery Administration* (New York: Fordham University Press, 1976).

[24] Gerard Swope, *The Swope Plan* (New York: Business Bourse, 1931); Otis L. Graham, Jr., *Toward a Planned Society* (New York: Oxford University Press, 1976), pp. 24–25; and Kolko, *Main Currents*, pp. 116–20.

[25] William E. Leuchtenburg, "The New Deal and the Analogue of War," in *Change and Continuity in Twentieth-Century America*, ed. John Braeman, Robert Bremner, and E. Walters (Columbus: Ohio State University Press, 1964). This article discusses the appeal of "analogies of war" to virtually all of the sets of actors in the early New Deal.

[26] Robert D. Cuff, *The War Industries Board: Business-Government Relations during World War I* (Baltimore: Johns Hopkins University Press, 1973).

[27] Leuchtenburg, "Analogue of War," in *Change and Continuity*, ed. Braeman, Bremner, and Walters, p. 129.

the economic crisis," a crisis that otherwise might have been blamed on the capitalists themselves.

Still, there was an enormous difficulty in modeling the NRA on the WIB. Government mobilization of industrial resources for war, which inherently involves increasing production through massive federal spending, is not at all equivalent to using government authority to raise prices and stabilize profits, production levels, wages, and employment. In the WIB, businessmen-administrators were asked to allocate plenty and to control rapid expansion in an orderly way, with government purchases offered as inducements. But in the NRA, the job was to discipline businessmen, and labor, in a situation of scarcity and with few positive sanctions. Such policies were certain to exacerbate and politicize economic conflicts. The WIB was therefore a very poor model for capitalists to draw upon in their plans, and demands, for government intervention in the Depression. Moreover, it was unrealistic to expect that the efforts of individual industries to enhance their own profits by increasing their prices would lead to a rise in total real output and employment. Yet business spokesmen convinced themselves and, initially, many politicians that recovery *would* come in this way. Their "trade association consciousness" and their infatuation with the inappropriate WIB model left U.S. capitalists ill prepared to advocate any other more realistic plan for government intervention in the 1930s. The result was prolonged economic crisis and continuing political uncertainties for capitalists.

If the failure of the NRA raises questions about corporate liberalism by demonstrating the inability of U.S. capitalists to pursue a class-conscious strategy for economic recovery, New Deal labor politics even more directly contradict the corporate-liberal model of political change. The history of these policies shows that major industrial capitalists were not prepared to grant concessions to labor; instead undesired policies were forced upon them through the workings of a national political process that they could not fully control.

Even during the honeymoon between business and government at the start of the New Deal, major capitalists and their spokesmen were very reluctant to make concessions to labor, especially not any that would facilitate independent labor unions. As Arthur Schlesinger points out, in the original passage of the NIRA through Congress, the prolabor section 7a was constantly on the verge of being defined out of existence: "The trade association group, evidently feeling that organization was a privilege to be accorded only to employers, accepted the idea of 7a with reluctance;

even the more liberal among them, like Harriman and Swope, had made no provision for organized labor in their own plans. . . . Only the vigilance of Jerome Frank, Leon Keyserling and Senator Wagner and the fear [in Congress] of provoking labor opposition kept it in."[28]

Such good friends as labor had in the early New Deal were not from the ranks of major capitalists, but from within the government.[29] Labor Secretary Frances Perkins was a rallying point for politicians and professionals who wanted to promote welfare measures and national regulation of working conditions, wages, and hours. And Senator Robert F. Wagner of New York spearheaded efforts to guarantee labor's right to collective bargaining with employers through independent union organizations. Wagner was certainly not anticapitalist, but his ideas about reform, recovery, and the rights of labor went well beyond the notions of even the most far-sighted U.S. capitalists. In August 1933, Roosevelt made Wagner the chairman of a National Labor Board (NLB) that was supposed to promote labor's rights under section 7a. The board tried to persuade employers to bargain with unions that were to be certified, after board-supervised elections, as representing a majority of workers. But major employers adamantly refused, and the NLB could not persuade either Roosevelt or the NRA to enforce its decisions. As Senator Wagner saw that friendly persuasion would not work, he and his staff began planning and lobbying within Congress and the Roosevelt administration for strong legislation to enforce union recognition. These efforts eventually culminated in the (Wagner) National Labor Relations Act of July 1935.

By the second half of 1934, business opposition to the New Deal was spreading and becoming more vocal and organized.[30] To be sure, smaller businessmen were

---

[28] Schlesinger, *Coming of New Deal*, p. 99.

[29] Good background on the labor policies of the New Deal is especially to be found in Irving Bernstein, *The New Deal Collective Bargaining Policy* (Berkeley and Los Angeles: University of California Press, 1950); and Murray Edelman, "New Deal Sensitivity to Labor Interests," in *Labor and the New Deal*, ed. Milton Derber and Edwin Young (New York: DaCapo Press, 1972), pp. 157–92.

[30] Ellis Hawley, "The New Deal and Business," in *The New Deal*, ed. Braeman, Bremner, and Brody, vol. 1, *The National Level*, pp. 64–66; and Schlesinger, *Coming of New Deal*, chap. 30; William H. Wilson, "How the Chamber of Commerce Viewed the NRA: A Reexamination," *Mid-America* 44 (1962): 95–108; and Kim McQuaid, "The Frustration of Corporate Revival in the Early New Deal," *The Historian* 41 (August 1979): 682–704.

among the earliest opponents, as they reacted against the competitive advantages secured for large corporations under the NRA.[31] But businessmen across the board were souring on "bureaucracy" and were growing increasingly apprehensive about government regulation as political demands were voiced on behalf of farmers, consumers, and industrial labor. While a few major capitalists continued to speak out for the Roosevelt administration as individuals and through the Business Advisory Council, a much larger number of major capitalists were becoming increasingly hysterical in their opposition to the New Deal. The American Liberty League, launched in 1934, drew its most important support from major financial and industrial interests clustered around DuPont Chemical and General Motors—hardly "small business"![32] What is more, the National Association of Manufacturers (NAM), which prior to the 1930s was predominately a spokesman for small and medium businesses, was transformed during the early 1930s into an anti-New Deal vehicle dominated by big businesses.[33] This is important to note because supporters of corporate liberalism repeatedly dismiss NAM opposition to New Deal policies as representing only the stubbornness of small businessmen.

Many U.S. businessmen ended up opposing the Social Security Act, and virtually all large-scale industrial employers unequivocally opposed the Wagner Act.[34] To say this is not to deny that, eventually, these measures were accepted by most corporate capitalists

in the U.S. Nor is it to deny that these measures ended up, *after* the 1930s, creating conditions favorable to smoother capitalist economic growth and more stable industrial labor relations. But U.S. capitalists did not plan or promote these measures: they could not foresee their ultimately favorable effects, and, in the depressed economic situation and uncertain political climate of the mid-1930s, they feared the immediate ill effects of increased government power within the economy. In the area of labor relations, in particular, U.S. capitalists were comfortably accustomed to running their corporations with a free hand; independent labor unions, they correctly understood, would only circumscribe one of the areas of managerial autonomy that they had enjoyed in the past. That the labor unions would be established through increased federal regulatory powers only made the prospect worse.

To be sure, U.S. capitalists enjoyed great political influence during the 1930s, as they did in previous decades, and have ever since. But corporate liberalism greatly overestimates what U.S. capitalists were able and willing to do during the 1930s to engineer effective, congenial political responses to a capitalist economic crisis. As Ellis Hawley writes:

> Since they [capitalists] seemed to have benefited most from the innovations of the period, the temptation was strong to conclude that they must have planned it that way and used the New Dealers either as their tools or as camouflage for their operations. In reality, so the evidence at hand indicates, they had neither the power, the unity, nor the vision to do this. They could, to be sure, push an initial program upon the new administration, limit the efforts at structural reform, and secure desired stabilization measures for certain types of industries. But they could not make the initial program work or retain the initiative; and instead of seeing that their long-range interests lay with the pattern taking shape after 1934 and moving quickly to adopt it, most of them spent the next six years fighting a bitter and expensive delaying action.[35]

Major New Deal measures were passed and implemented over the opposition of capitalists. Not only did capitalists fail to control the political process during the mid-1930s, they even lost their ability to veto major legislative enactments that touched directly upon their

[31] Small business opposition, pressed especially through Congress, is a major theme in Hawley, *New Deal and Problem of Monopoly*, chap. 4.

[32] George Wolfskill, *The Revolt of the Conservatives: A History of the American Liberty League* (Boston: Houghton Mifflin, 1962); and Frederick Rudolph, "The American Liberty League, 1934–1940," *American Historical Review* 56, no. 1 (October 1950): 19–33. Rudolph writes (p. 22): "The membership of its national advisory council was drawn largely from the successful business interests of the industrial states of the North and East. . . ."

[33] Philip H. Burch, Jr., "The NAM as an Interest Group," *Politics and Society* 4, no. 1 (Fall 1973): 100–105.

[34] On social security see Edwin E. Witte, *The Development of the Social Security Act* (Madison: University of Wisconsin press, 1962), pp. 88–90; and Schlesinger, *Coming of New Deal*, p. 311. On the Wagner Act see Bernstein, *New Deal Collective Bargaining Policy,* passim. The resistance of industrial employers is documented in Daniel A. Swanson, "Flexible Individualism: The American Big Business Response to Labor, 1935–1945," (Undergraduate thesis, Harvard College, Social Studies, 1974). See also Vogel, "Why Businessmen Distrust Their State," pp. 63–65.

[35] Hawley, "New Deal and Business," in *The New Deal*, ed. Braeman, Bremner, and Brody, vol. 1, *The National Level*, pp. 75–76.

accustomed prerogatives. Corporate-liberal theory cannot explain why or how this could happen, just as it cannot account for the failures of the business-sponsored NIRA.

Quite evidently, U.S. politics in the 1930s was more complex than the corporate-liberal perspective maintains. Let us therefore proceed to the "political functionalism" of Nicos Poulantzas.

POLITICAL FUNCTIONALISM AND THE NEW DEAL

Nicos Poulantzas is well known for some basic disagreements with instrumentalist approaches. For Poulantzas, "the direct participation of members of the capitalist class in the State apparatus and in the government, even where it exists, is not the important side of the matter. The relation between the bourgeois class and the State is an *objective relation*. This means that if the *function* of the State in a determinate social formation [that is, in a given society] and the *interests* of the dominant class in this formation *coincide*, it is by reason of the system itself. . . ."[36] In Poulantzas's view capitalists do not need to staff the state apparatus directly; nor must they put deliberate political pressure on government officials. Even without such active interventions, capitalists will still benefit from the state's activities. For the state, by definition, is "the factor of cohesion of a social formation and the factor of reproduction of the conditions of production of a system."[37] State interventions will, in other words, necessarily function to preserve order in capitalist society and to sustain and enhance the conditions for capitalist economic activity.

According to Poulantzas, the state and politics work in opposite ways for the dominant capitalist class and for the working class (and other noncapitalist classes).[38] Because working-class unity is a threat to capitalism, Poulantzas posits that the state functions most fundamentally to "disunite" the workers. It does this, in part, by transforming them into privatized individual citizens, competitive in their economic relations and members of a classless "nation" in political terms. At the same time, the political system (in a democratic capitalist state) allows workers to vote and form interest groups and political parties through which they may be able to achieve limited concessions through nonrevolutionary political struggles. Thus the capitalist state controls workers (indeed all nondominant classes) by promoting their "individualization" and by making necessary co-optive concessions in ways that tend to divide noncapitalists into competing sub-groups.

Poulantzas' state functions the opposite way for the capitalist class. In sharp contrast to Miliband's instrumentalism and to corporate liberalism, Poulantzas holds that neither the political interventions of self-interested capitalists nor the policies formulated by an enlightened corporate vanguard will ensure that the political system functions in the interests of capitalists. Instead this happens only because of the interventions of a "relatively autonomous" state not directly controlled by capitalists. This state organizes the unity of the capitalist class itself, because it is "capable of transcending the parochial, individualized interests of specific capitalists and capitalist class fractions."[39] Simultaneously, the relatively autonomous state also enforces whatever concessions the current state of the political class struggle makes necessary if the dominated classes are to be kept in line.

Poulantzas is not greatly interested in explaining exactly how the capitalist state goes about performing its inherent functions. Historical contingencies such as divisions within the capitalist class and the vagaries of the political class struggle apparently determine, in Poulantzas's view, specifically how the state is structured and how it functions. But, short of revolution, functional outcomes are certain to occur: the bottom line for Poulantzas always seems to be the stability of the capitalist system, the reproduction of capitalist production relations, and the continuation of capitalist class domination. Poulantzas's capitalist state is basically a vehicle of system maintenance.

Corporate-liberal instrumentalists, as we have seen, attempt to explain New Deal measures as the strategies of class-conscious capitalists. More appropriately, Poulantzian theory would stress the political provenance of policies, even of a measure such as the NIRA, which closely conformed to the declared preferences of

---

[36] Nicos Poulantzas, "The Problem of the Capitalist State," *Ideology in Social Science*, ed. Robin Blackburn (New York: Vintage Books, Random House, 1973), p. 245.

[37] Ibid., p. 246.

[38] Nicos Poulantzas, *Political Power and Social Classes*, trans. Timothy O'Hagen (London: New Left Books, 1973). See also Simon Clarke, "Marxism, Sociology and Poulantzas's Theory of the State," *Capital and Class*, no. 2 (Summer 1977), pp. 1–31.

[39] Gold, Lo, and Wright, "Recent Developments," p. 38.

capitalists. From a Poulantzian vantage point, New Deal economic policies were not simply a response to the demands of capitalists; rather they addressed the interests of competing groups both within the ranks of the capitalist class and between capitalists and noncapitalists. This process of placating competing interests through active state intervention was mediated by the Democratic party after its massive electoral victories in 1932. If business strategies and political influence had been all that was necessary to produce an NIRA-type program, then it should have been enacted by the Republicans in late 1931 or during 1932, when Swope and Harriman were first urging their plans. Instead, the NIRA came only after the Democrats and Roosevelt came to power, and even then, the NIRA was not formulated until the end of the "Hundred Days" of early New Deal legislation. The NIRA itself was presented as a consensual, national effort to help businessmen, workers, and consumers, all together. And it represented the culmination of a sweeping legislative program in which the needs of farmers, bankers, home owners, the unemployed, and local governments had been addressed.[40] Just as Poulantzas's theory would suggest, this over-all process of interest aggregation and consensus building, all within the bounds of a taken-for-granted effort to save the existing capitalist economy, no doubt could be undertaken only by the Democratic party led by Franklin Roosevelt. Compared to the Republicans led by Herbert Hoover, the FDR-led Democrats in 1933 were more popularly rooted and sufficiently "relatively autonomous" from pure business domination to enable them to take strong state initiatives in the economic crisis. These initiatives, in turn, promised benefits for practically everyone and rebuilt national morale.

Within the political context thus created, it was possible to formulate and enact the NIRA. In the drafting process, various proposals for the government action to promote recovery were melded together:[41] business schemes for government-backed industrial cartels were the primary basis for Title 1 of the act, yet there was also a Title II establishing the Public Works Administration, which incorporated plans calling for major government spending to stimulate industry. Moreover, section 7a of Title I made promises to labor, and there were also rhetorical concessions to consumers and small businessmen.

The origins, the political context, and the legislative content of the NIRA thus fit Poulantzian political functionalism very well: the state undertook to organize business to promote recovery, and it did so with all of the symbolic trappings and concessions to popular groups that were necessary to present the entire effort as a unified, national battle against the Depression. Indeed, if the early New Deal and the NIRA had only quickly achieved their declared purposes of sociopolitical stability and full economic recovery, the Poulantzian theory would appear to offer a perfect explanation for the New Deal. But in actuality, the NIRA blatantly failed to bring economic recovery, and it deepened conflicts within the capitalist class, between capitalists and the state, and between capitalists and labor. Poulantzian theory predicts functional outcomes of state policies and interventions. It offers little direct theoretical guidance for explaining why and how failures of state policies could occur, especially not failures threatening to capitalists. It offers little guidance for dissecting the concrete course of political and social struggles over time, especially not struggles that lead toward deepening political contradictions as opposed to functional resolutions of crises through stabilizing political actions.[42]

In the context of his polemic against instrumentalism, Nicos Poulantzas has insisted that it does not matter whether capitalists staff or pressure the state. Thus Poulantzas declared in a critique of Ralph Miliband, "If Miliband had first established that the State is precisely *the factor of cohesion of a social for-*

---

[40] Actually, those whose needs were addressed earliest and most thoroughly in the New Deal were commercial farmers. This was not incidental in political terms, for Roosevelt had gained the presidential nomination in 1932 only through support from the South and West. Also, given the disproportionate weight of rural areas in the U.S. national political system of the 1930s, Roosevelt was bound to be especially desirous of attracting voters and placating Congressmen from these areas. It is noteworthy that neo-Marxist theories of politics in advanced capitalism tend to ignore farmers, concentrating instead only on industrial workers and industrial and financial capitalists. But a complete analysis of class and politics in the New Deal would definitely have to look at the relationships of farmers and agricultural laborers to industrial capitalists and workers.

[41] The best discussion is Hawley, *New Deal and Problem of Monopoly*, chaps. 1–2. See also Schlesinger, *Coming of New Deal*, chap. 6.

[42] Analogous criticisms (focused on Poulantzas's own concrete analyses of fascism) are offered by a historian in Jane Caplan, "Theories of Fascism: Nicos Poulantzas as Historian," *History Workshop* 3 (Spring 1977): 83–100. As Caplan says (p. 98), "we must . . . not turn history into a prolonged tautology." Poulantzas's functionalism constantly tends to do this.

mation and the factor of reproduction of the conditions of production of a system that itself determines the domination of one class over the others, he would have seen clearly that the participation, whether direct or indirect, of this class in government *in no way changes things.*"[43] Obviously, this is an extreme formulation. Poulantzas is saying that, no matter what, the state functions automatically to stabilize and reproduce the capitalist system. Yet Poulantzas has also made statements about relations between capitalists and the state apparatus that, if posed as hypotheses about conditions that could vary historically and cross-nationally, would help us explain the failures of the NIRA. The "capitalist State," Poulantzas has suggested, "best serves the interests of the capitalist class only when the members of this class do not participate directly in the State apparatus, that is to say when the *ruling class* is not the *politically governing class.*"[44]

We have already seen that the NIRA as a piece of legislation was drafted and enacted in a way that conforms to the Poulantzian notion of a "relatively autonomous" political process producing state policies that both support capitalism and are democratically legitimate. This was possible in 1933 because the electoral system, the Democratic party, the Roosevelt administration, and the Congress operated to produce the "Hundred Days" and the NIRA legislation. But, interestingly enough, the "relative autonomy" of politics was much less evident in the implementation of the NIRA than it was in its enactment. A silent assumption of Poulantzas's functionalist theory is that there will always be a centralized, bureaucratic administrative apparatus to manage economic interventions on behalf of the capitalist class as a whole.[45] But for understandable historical reasons, the U.S. federal government in the early 1930s lacked any such administrative capacity. The failures of the NIRA to promote economic recovery and to stabilize relationships among businessmen can be attributed in significant part to the absence of effective capacities for autonomous economic intervention on the part of the U.S. federal administration.

The national government with which the U.S. entered the Great Depression was basically formed during the Progressive Era partly in reaction against, and partly upon the foundations of, the uniquely "stateless" governmental system that had held sway in America during the nineteenth century.[46] This nineteenth-century system has aptly been called a "state of courts and parties," because its basic governmental functions were divided between, on one hand, a potent judiciary branch and, on the other, a network of government offices staffed by locally rooted political parties according to their electoral fortunes and patronage requirements. In the expanding, decentralized capitalist economy of nineteenth-century America, this governmental system functioned remarkably well. The courts regulated and defended property rights, and the party-dominated electoral-administrative system freely handed out economic benefits and loosely knit together a diverse society. With the advent of corporate concentration and the emergence of a truly national economy and society, the government of courts and parties began to face national-administrative and policy-making tasks for which it was poorly suited. But the old system managed to remain intact, and block governmental "modernization," as long as its mass-mobilizing political parties were relatively balanced in their political competition (at the national level and in many states outside the South). Only after the massive electoral realignment of 1896 decreased party competition in many formerly competitive states and created a national imbalance strongly in the Republicans' favor, was the way opened for the building of new national administrative systems.

Such administrative expansion came slowly and in fragmented ways during the Progressive Era. Unlike Continental European nations with bureaucratic states inherited from preindustrial, monarchical times, the U.S. national government, starting late in the game and from a low level, developed autonomous administrative capacities only imperfectly and under central executive coordination and control. Presidents (along with groups of professionals) took the lead in promoting federal administrative expansion and bureaucratizing reforms. But Congress resisted efforts at administrative expansion and, at each step, contested the executive branch for control of newly created federal agencies. For, by the early twentieth century, the U.S. had, if anything, even more of a "Tudor polity"[47]—a polity of divided

---

[43] Poulantzas, "Problem of Capitalist State," in *Ideology*, ed. Blackburn, p. 246.
[44] Ibid., p. 246.
[45] This is obviously a very "French" assumption!

[46] This and the following two paragraphs build on Stephen Lee Skowronek's excellent "Building a New American State: The Expansion of National Administrative Capacities, 1877–1920" (Ph.D. diss., Department of Political Science, Cornell University, January 1979), to be published soon by Cambridge University Press.
[47] This phrase comes from Huntington, "Political Modernization: America vs. Europe," in *Political Order in Changing Societies*, chap. 2.

sovereignty among the legislative, executive, and judicial branches and among federal, state, and local governments—than it had during the nineteenth century. In the earlier government of courts and parties, political party discipline had provided a kind of coordination in government. But once parties were weakened and once administrative realms began to be set up beyond the direct patronage controls of the parties, institutional struggles between the president and Congress were unleashed, above all, over how much administrative expansion should occur and under whose control.

In this context, no centrally coordinated, executive-dominated national bureaucratic state could emerge, not even during World War I. Administrative expansion during that crisis was ad hoc and staffed by officials predominately recruited from business.[48] Moreover, it was rolled back by Congress right after the end of the war. What remained were a few (increasingly uncontrollable) independent regulatory agencies and some restricted realms of federal administration with overlapping, cross-cutting lines of control and access to the executive and to Congress. During the 1920s, the Republicans governed within this system, making minimal efforts at institutional innovation and undertaking few federal interventions in the affairs of states, localities, or the private economy. When the Depression hit, therefore, the U.S. had (for a major industrial nation) a bureaucratically weak national government, and one in which existing administrative capacities were poorly coordinated.

This historical background on the U.S. state can help us understand what happened in the implementation of the NIRA during 1933–35 in two main ways. First, it becomes easy to see why the National Recovery Administration, set up under Title I of the NIRA to regulate the industrial economy, had to be created from scratch and through the emergency recruitment of administrators from business backgrounds. There was no pre-existing federal bureaucracy with the manpower and expertise needed to supervise a sudden, massive effort to draw up hundreds of codes to regulate wages, working hours, prices, and production practices in every U.S. industry from steel and automobiles to textiles and consumer services.

The head of the NRA appointed by Roosevelt was General Hugh Johnson, a man with business experience and connections, who had served in the WIB during World War I. Johnson moved quickly to set in motion the process of approving and enforcing codes of fair competition for the various industries. Not taking time to define regulatory standards, Johnson appointed many "deputy administrators." He followed the WIB precedent of recruiting officials from business, very often drawing his deputies from the same industries with which they were then supposed to negotiate over the codes. Moreover, once the codes were approved by the NRA, their enforcement was typically delegated to code authorities dominated by representatives selected by trade associations or other major interests within each industry.[49]

Hastily assembled in these ways from extragovernmental sources of manpower, expertise, and organization, the NRA ended by being, as a contemporary observer noted, little more than "a bargain between business leaders on the one hand and businessmen in the guise of government officials on the other."[50] Obviously there was no "autonomy of the state" in relation to capitalists within the Recovery Administration. In consequence, economically powerful corporations and established trade associations were able briefly to gain legal backing for their own short-term interests, disregarding the legislated provisions for labor to have its own union organizations and representatives on code authorities and overriding the interests of smaller businesses or beleaguered competitors.[51] Yet these short-term advantages came at a price. Government regulation without state autonomy soon left businessmen quarreling among themselves, with the winners unable to enforce their will except through cumbersome legal procedures, and with the losers able to bring counterleverage on the NRA through Congress and courts. (Indeed, the NIRA was eventually declared unconstitutional in response to a suit brought by a small poultry-processing company!) And the NRA codes, once captured by big business, simply functioned to freeze production, guarantee monopoly prices to dominant firms, and undermine general economic expansion. Arguably, a more autonomous form of

---

[48] Cuff, *War Industries Board*.

[49] Good accounts of NRA administration include Hawley, *New Deal and Problem of Monopoly*, chap. 3; Schlesinger, *Coming of New Deal*, chap. 7; and Leverett S. Lyon et al., *The National Recovery Administration: An Analysis and Appraisal*, 2 vols. (Washington D.C.: The Brookings Institution, 1935), chaps. 4–9.

[50] Quoted in Hawley, *New Deal and Problem of Monopoly*, pp. 56–57.

[51] On the economic and political consequences of the NRA, see ibid., pp. 66–71 and chaps. 4–6; Chandler, *America's Greatest Depression*, pp. 229–39; and Schlesinger, *Coming of New Deal*, chaps. 8–10.

state regulation could have kept prices down and facilitated expanded production. In any event, when businessmen themselves became the state, government intervention could do little more than reinforce and freeze the economic status quo, while simultaneously politicizing conflicts among businessmen.

The limited capacities of the U.S. federal government can be used to explain the failure of the NIRA in a second way. Title II of the act called for massive federal expenditures on public-works projects, something that supporters felt would provide employment and help stimulate industry through construction contracts and purchases of materials. General Hugh Johnson fondly hoped to head both the NRA and the Public Works Administration (PWA), and he envisaged quickly spending the $3.3 billion PWA appropriation to help expand the economy even as the industrial regulatory codes were put into effect. Historians often imply that Roosevelt made a mistake in putting the gung-ho General Johnson in charge of the NRA, while handing the PWA to "Honest Harold" Ickes, who proceeded to spend his agency's appropriation very slowly and only on projects of unquestionable soundness.[52] Apparently, historians dream (a bit anachronistically) of a quick, Keynesian fix to the Depression—if only the PWA had had the right man as director. But this fails to take sufficient account of the given administrative and political realities of the time. The administrative means to implement a huge, speedy public-works program were simply not available, as Herbert Stein points out in his remarks on the proposals for $1 billion- to $8.5 billion-dollar programs that were offered from 1929 on:

> As proposals of amounts of money to be spent for federal construction in a short period, perhaps a year or two, these suggestions could not be taken seriously. The federal government could simply not raise its construction expenditures quickly by one or two billion dollars a year, for instance, and have any structures to show for it. Federal construction expenditures were only $210 million in 1930—a small base on which to erect a program of several billion dollars. The larger proposals were intended to finance expansion of state and local public works expenditures, in addition to federal. . . . But even combined federal, state, and local

construction expenditures in 1930 were less than $3 billion.[53]

Arguably, the Roosevelt administration should have thrown administrative regularity to the winds and, in the interests of promoting economic recovery, simply handed public-works funds to businesses or to local governments. This might or might not have rapidly expanded productive economic investments. But politically it would have been disastrous. Virtually everyone inside and outside government at the time believed in "balanced budgets," and especially in a time of national economic crisis, federal expenditures were subject to close critical scrutiny for signs of waste or corruption. In choosing the cautious Harold Ickes to head the PWA, Roosevelt acted in the knowledge that conspicuously wasteful or foolhardy public works expenditures could put the entire program in danger in Congress and perhaps raise doubts about other New Deal legislation as well, including relief expenditures.

The NIRA, in short, failed to regularize relationships among businessmen and failed to promote the economic expansion needed by the capitalist class as a whole in significant part because there was little autonomous administrative capacity in the U.S. national government of the early 1930s. Insofar as Poulantzian theory tends to assume that all capitalist states will automatically have this capacity, or will rapidly generate it if it is needed, the theory becomes misleading. Governmental capacities vary with the political histories of various countries; in turn, these governmental capacities affect what can be done for capitalist economies and for capitalists both in "normal" times and in crisis situations. Functional, adaptive state interventions do not always occur, and a large part of the explanation for whether they do or not, and for the exact forms of state interventions, lies in the prior histories of the state structures themselves.

If Poulantzas's functionalist theory overestimates the automatic ability of capitalist states to unify, organize, and serve the class interests of capitalists, it also underestimates the extent to which political struggles and state actions in capitalist democracies can actually stimulate or accelerate challenges to capitalist prerogatives from below, rather than merely averting challenges from below through minimal, nonthreatening

---

[52] Schlesinger, *Coming of New Deal*, pp. 103–9, is the *locus classicus* of the Johnson-versus-Ickes comparison.

[53] Herbert Stein, *The Fiscal Revolution in America* (Chicago: University of Chicago Press, 1969), pp. 23–24.

concessions. For labor policies under the NIRA ended up promoting the emergence, through bitter conflicts, of independent industrial labor unions. These unions not only encroached upon the formerly near-absolute control of capitalist managers over the workplace, they also organizationally unified industrial workers to a greater degree than ever before in U.S. history.

Of course, the NIRA as originally passed in 1933 was intended to pacify labor, not to encourage industrial conflicts. But the actual effect of the act was to intensify conflicts over its labor provisions among workers, businessmen, and politicians.[54] In part, the declared goals of the NIRA were simply not implemented in the business-dominated NRA. Labor representatives appeared on less than 10 percent of the industrial code authorities, and the probusiness NRA administrators refused to disallow the company unions that managers organized to circumvent section 7a's declaration of labor's right to organize. In many industries, workers went on strike in efforts to secure their rights under the NIRA. Indeed, the impact of the NIRA upon labor was not simply the denial of promises in the actual administrative practices of the NRA. The mere passage of the act raised hopes among labor-union organizers and industrial workers, who redoubled their efforts in the field. Given employer resistance, the predictable result was an accelerating strike wave. Thus the NIRA and the NRA, by their mere existence, tended to encourage and politicize industrial labor disputes—hardly a "functional" outcome for capitalists.

Finally, and perhaps most important of all, the NIRA set in motion an effort to put the full legal backing of the state behind independent labor unions. During the life of the NRA Senator Wagner failed to get cooperation from businessmen, or backing from Hugh Johnson, for his plan to have the National Labor Board supervise elections and certify labor unions on a majority basis as representatives for workers in negotiations with employers. But Wagner's failure simply spurred him to redouble his efforts to legislate this solution over business opposition. And given the independent political leverage available to members of the Congress, Wagner was able to pursue a policy-making strategy at odds with the official attitude of the Roosevelt administration.

For the sake of organized labor, it was a good thing that Wagner was able to push ahead of official New Deal policies. If Roosevelt as president or as head of the Democratic party had been able to control all policy initiatives, the stance of the U.S. state toward labor in the New Deal might have better conformed to Poulantzas's theoretical expectations. For FDR and his labor secretary, Frances Perkins, favored only "paternalistic" concessions to labor, such as legislative measures to regulate wages, hours, and working conditions. They were not particularly friendly to organized labor; nor would they sponsor government measures to increase its power.[55] Roosevelt invariably wanted to "balance" existing pressures from capital and labor, even though capital's economic and organizational power was vastly preponderant. During 1934, Roosevelt intervened in the NRA's consideration of disputes in the auto industry, essentially backing up management's position in favor of "proportional representation" for company versus independent unions, rather than supporting the policy of Wagner's National Labor Board in favor of unified representation through majority election.[56] Not until Wagner had carried his proposals to the verge of sure Congressional victory did FDR endorse strong prolabor measures.

Robert Wagner was a politician bred in the New York Tammany Machine during a period when the machine had begun to sponsor some measure of social reform.[57] During his political career, Wagner developed ties to the American Federation of Labor and to liberal policy associations. And as a senator during the 1920s, he was one of the first congressmen to build an independent staff and to employ and consult professional experts in drafting legislation. Wagner established himself even before the Depression as a major formulator of national economic policies, and he was unusually effective in piloting bills through the Senate.

[54] See Chandler, *America's Greatest Depression*, pp. 231–32; and, in general, the references cited in note 49.

[55] Edelman, "Sensitivity to Labor Interests," in *Labor and the New Deal*, ed. Derber and Young, pp. 161–64, 178–82.

[56] Bernstein, *Turbulent Years*, pp. 172–85.

[57] This paragraph (and other discussion of Wagner) draws on J. Joseph Huthmacher, *Senator Robert F. Wagner and the Rise of Urban Liberalism* (New York: Atheneum, 1971); and Leon H. Keyserling, "The Wagner Act: Its Origin and Current Significance," *The George Washington Law Review* 29, no. 2 (December 1960): 199–233.

Thus Wagner had the policy-formulating capacity, the political connections, and the legislative skills to promote what eventually became the Wagner National Labor Relations Act. His frustrations with the NRA sharpened Wagner's perception of the need for strong, one-sided legislation in favor of unions. And the looseness of presidential control over Congress and of discipline on policy matters within the Democratic party allowed him the political space to move aggressively ahead of Roosevelt. From a capitalist point of view, this meant that the U.S. political system not only inadvertently stimulated industrial conflict, as an unintended effect of the NIRA, but also generated an autonomous political effort, spearheaded by Wagner, to array state power against capitalist prerogatives and preferences. This kind of development does not seem to be envisaged by Poulantzas's theory, which predicts that the capitalist state will invariably act to make the working classes less, not more, threatening to capitalists. Poulantzas's perspective probably underestimates the potential democratic responsiveness of elected politicians in all capitalist democracies. It certainly underestimates for the U.S. political system of the 1930s both the responsiveness of liberals such as Wagner and the autonomous room for maneuvering that members of Congress could enjoy within the U.S. "Tudor polity." In effect, "the state" did not act in a unified way toward labor, and some elements within it were prepared to promote an entirely new system of industrial labor relations for the USA.

This system would ultimately—a decade later—prove acceptable to U.S. capitalists. But in the meantime, as the accompanying figure suggests, New Deal labor legislation (especially section 7a and the Wagner Act) tended to stimulate rather than dampen labor disputes. From 1934 through 1939 labor disputes were primarily about union recognition. Leftist scholars sometimes interpret union recognition as a conservative goal, because they treat struggles for socialism or total workers' control of industry as implicit alternatives, or because they anticipate the stabilizing functions that unions eventually came to play in the U.S. political economy. But in the context of the U.S. in the 1930s, the growth of (noncompany) unions threatened capitalist prerogatives in the workplace, and the disproportionate expansion of industrial as opposed to craft unions united broader sectors of industrial labor than at any previous period in U.S. history. Capitalists (with very few exceptions) regarded all of this as threatening and believed that the federal government was encouraging labor offensives whose results were not fully pre-

dictable or necessarily controllable. For the decade of the Depression, the capitalists were correct in their analysis: "functional" outcomes were by no means certain.

How shall we draw the balance of Poulantzas's political functionalism as an approach to explaining the New Deal? A very welcome aspect of this variant of neo-Marxism is its stress upon what politics and the state do "relatively autonomously" for the economy, for the capitalist class, and for (or to!) the noncapitalists, especially workers. But, unfortunately, what the theory offers with one hand it immediately takes back with the other, for it wants us to believe that the state and politics always do just what needs to be done to stabilize capitalist society and keep the economy going. If this were really true, then state structures, state interventions, and political conflicts would not really be worth studying in any detail, and politics as such would have no explanatory importance. All that we would need to know about the New Deal, or about the NIRA, would be that these were part of a flow of history that eventually worked out splendidly for U.S. capitalists. But, of course, this is not all we need to know, or all we need to explain. To penetrate more thoroughly into the political dynamics of the 1930s, we need a perspective that pays more attention to class and political conflict and assigns greater importance to the autonomous initiatives of politicians. Fred Block's "The Ruling Class Does Not Rule" meets these criteria, and we turn now to an exploration of the strengths and limitations of this third neo-Marxist approach.

CLASS STRUGGLE, STATE MANAGERS, AND THE NEW DEAL

Like Poulantzas, Block launches his attempt to build a theory of the capitalist state with a critique of instrumentalism. Block accepts the reality of capitalist influence in the political process but argues that Marxists must "reject the idea of a class-conscious ruling class" and posit instead "a division of labor between those who accumulate capital and those who manage the state apparatus."[58] Within this division of labor, capitalists are conscious of the specific, short-term economic interests of their firms or sectors, but "in general, they are not conscious of what is necessary to reproduce the social order in changing circumstances."[59] Capitalists

[58] Block, "The Ruling Class Does Not Rule," p. 10.
[59] Ibid.

do not directly control the state, however, for the state is under the direction of the "state managers," defined as "the leading figures of both the legislative and executive branches—[including] the highest-ranking civil servants, as well as appointed and elected politicians."[60] Once we accept the idea of a real division of control between the economy and the state, Block asserts, "the central theoretical task is to explain how it is that despite this division of labor, the state tends to serve the interests of the capitalist class."[61] It is not sufficient simply to posit the "relative autonomy of the state." Instead, an adequate structural theory must spell out causal mechanisms in two distinct areas. "It must elaborate the structural constraints that operate to reduce the likelihood that the state managers will act against the general interests of capitalists."[62] And the theory must also try to explain why, on occasion, state managers actually extend state power, even in the face of capitalist resistance, in order to rationalize or reform capitalism. Rationalization and capitalist reform, Block tells us, refer "primarily to the use of the state in new ways to overcome economic contradictions and to facilitate the [nonrepressive] integration of the working class."[63]

According to Block, it is fairly easy to explain why state managers would normally be very reluctant to act against capitalist interests, even without assuming that class-conscious capitalists run the state. The state in a capitalist society does not directly control economic production, and yet the state managers depend for their power and security in office upon a healthy economy. The state needs to tax and borrow, and politicians have to face re-election by people who are likely to hold them responsible if the economy falters. Thus state managers willingly do what they can to facilitate capital accumulation. Given that most economic investment decisions are controlled directly by private capitalists, state managers are especially sensitive to the overall state of "business confidence," that is, "the capitalist's evaluation of the general political/economic climate." "Is the society stable; is the working class under control; are taxes likely to rise; do government agencies interfere with business freedom; will the economy grow? These kinds of considerations are critical to the investment decisions of each firm. The sum of all of these evaluations across a national economy can be termed the level of business confidence."[64] Normally, state managers will not want to do anything that might hurt business confidence, and so instead of pursuing social reforms or attempting to expand the state's role in the economy, they will confine themselves to formulating policies that are generally supportive of capital accumulation and not seriously objectionable to any major sector of the capitalist class.

But "if the state is unwilling to risk a decline in business confidence, how is it then that the state's role has expanded inexorably throughout the twentieth century?"[65] Block is unwilling to accept the answer offered by corporate-liberal instrumentalists. On the contrary, Block holds that capitalists are almost by definition too short-sighted initially to accept, let alone to promote, major reforms or extensions of state power. Such changes come primarily in opposition to capitalist preferences. And they mostly come when, and because, state managers are strongly prodded to institute reforms by the working class. Class struggle, says Block, pushes forward the development of capitalism. It does this economically by raising wages and thus prompting capitalists to substitute machinery for workers. It does it politically by pressuring state managers to institute economic regulations and social reforms.

According to Block, the biggest spurts forward in state activity come during major crises such as wars or depression. During wars capitalists cannot easily undercut state managers, and during depressions the decline of business confidence is not such a potent threat. Moreover, especially during economic crises, class struggle and pressures from below are likely to intensify. Thus state managers may find it expedient to grant concessions to the working class. Yet they will do so only in forms that simultaneously increase the power of the state itself. What is more, over the longer run, especially as economic recovery resumes or a wartime emergency ends, the state managers will do the best they can to shape (or restructure) the concessions won by the working class in order to make them function smoothly in support of capital accumulation and existing class relations. Thus it can come to pass that reforms and extensions of state power originally won through "pressure from below" can end up being "functional for" capitalism and accepted by many of the very capitalists who at first strongly resisted the changes.

[60] Ibid., p. 8 (fn.).
[61] Ibid., p. 10.
[62] Ibid., p. 14.
[63] Ibid., p. 7 (fn.).

[64] Ibid., p. 16
[65] Ibid., p. 20.

Block's theory of the capitalist state, especially his explanation of major thrusts of capitalist rationalization, is elegant and powerful. In a number of ways, Block's ideas add to our understanding of why the New Deal occurred as it did. Where imprecisions or ambiguities do remain in Block's approach as applied to the New Deal, we can readily pinpoint some promising lines for future theories about political reforms and rationalization within capitalism.

Thinking first about the early New Deal—the "Hundred Days" of legislation culminating in the NIRA—the Block perspective shares some inadequacies with Poulantzian political functionalism, yet also improves upon it in significant ways. To take the inadequacies first: Block does not seem to do any better than Poulantzas in explaining why the NIRA failed to achieve its objectives. Like Poulantzas, Block pitches his theorizing at a high level of abstraction, talking about capitalism in general, and does not investigate existing state structures as constraints upon what state managers can do when they attempt to facilitate capital accumulation (whether through reform or not).

Compared to Poulantzas, the strength of Block's approach as (it might be) applied to the early New Deal lies in Block's greater attention to specific causal mechanisms. Instead of merely positing that the state "must" intervene to save capitalism, Block suggests that U.S. governments during the Depression were spurred to do all they could to facilitate capitalist economic recovery because public revenues and politicians' electoral fortunes depended on such efforts. It also makes sense in terms of Block's theory that both the Hoover administration and, at first, the Roosevelt administration tried to promote recovery in close cooperation with capitalists. For Hoover and Roosevelt wanted to revive business confidence and thus resuscitate private investments.[66]

What is perhaps less clear from Block's perspective is why only FDR and the Democrats (and not Hoover and the Republicans) were willing to promote recovery specifically through increased state intervention in the economy. We can, however, derive a kind of explanation from Block's theory—one that resembles Poulantzas's tendency to root the relative autonomy of the state from capitalists in the pressures generated by "political class struggle" in favor of concessions for noncapitalists. We can argue that the Democratic victory over the Republicans in the elections of 1930 and 1932 was an expression, albeit highly politically mediated, of class-based pressures from below on the U.S. federal government. In response to this pressure, the argument would go, the Democrats were urged, and enabled, to use state power for reformist and regulatory efforts well beyond what the business-dominated Republicans had been willing to undertake, even after the crash of 1929. Since at first hopes were high for quick economic recovery through revived business confidence, Roosevelt made every effort to fashion his first "Hundred Days" of legislation (including the bold National Industrial Recovery Act) not only to meet the reformist demands of farmers, workers, and the unemployed, but also to meet the preferences of many specific groups of capitalists and to enhance the general confidence of businessmen as rapidly as possible. In short, a judicious use of Block's theoretical perspective can go a long way toward explaining the special blend of popular responsiveness and willingness to cooperate with capitalists that characterized the fledgling Roosevelt administration in 1933–34.

Yet, of course, where Block's theory really comes into its own is in the analysis of the major social welfare and labor reforms of the New Deal era. Using Block's theory, there is no need to attribute measures such as the Social Security Act and the Wagner Act either to the far-sighted planning of the capitalist class or to the automatic intervention of a capitalist state smoothly functioning to preserve order and promote economic recovery. Instead, according to Block, these measures were made possible by a conjunction of working-class pressures with the willingness of state managers to increase their own institutional power at a time when capitalist veto power was unusually weak. The reforms provided benefits to many members of the working class, strengthened the state in relation to the working class, and increased the state's capacity to intervene in the capitalist economy. The eventual result was that working-class struggle ended up contributing to the further development of American capitalism.

As a general "explanation sketch" of the causes of the major social reforms of the New Deal and their eventual consequences, this is impeccable. Still it must be emphasized that the very points where Block's class struggle theory of capitalist rationalization becomes most analytically relevant, it also becomes quite vague. What exactly is meant by "class struggle" or "working-class pressure" for reforms? How do varying forms and amounts of working-class pressure affect political and economic outcomes? Equally important, what are the

---

[66] Stein, *Fiscal Revolution*, chaps. 2–5, passim.

likely interrelationships between working-class pressures and the activities of state managers? Do the latter only respond, or are they likely, under certain kinds of circumstances, to *stimulate* pressure from noncapitalists as well?

Merely raising questions such as these suggests that to go from the general "structural" dynamics outlined by Block to actual causal explanations, one would need to specify cross-nationally and historically variable patterns in such things as: the occupational and community situations of the industrial working class; degrees and forms of union organization; the actual and potential connections of working-class voters and organizations to political parties; and the effects of party systems and state structures on the likelihood that politicians' responses to working-class unrest or demands will be reformist rather than repressive.

In the case of the New Deal labor reforms, a number of conditions influenced the nature and pattern of change. The U.S. industrial working class entered the Depression without strong unions and without a labor-based political party. There was, however, a large semi-skilled manufacturing labor force consisting of relatively settled immigrants and their children—a force ripe for mobilization into industrial unions.[67] The Democratic party, meanwhile, was "available" to come to power in the Depression. And insofar as its leadership took a reformist course, it was splendidly positioned to attract industrial working-class votes into a national political party that, nevertheless, could and would remain procapitalist and in many ways quite conservative.

Working-class pressure leading to reforms can entail very different scenarios. It can mean that strong labor unions and a labor or social-democratic or Communist political party impose a more or less anticapitalist reform program on (and through) the government. Or it can mean that spontaneous working-class "disruption," especially strikes, forces specific concessions out of a reluctant government.[68] Neither of these scenarios really fits what happened in the United States during the 1930s. Obviously the industrial working class was organizationally too weak for the first scenario to happen. And we have already seen enough historical evidence on what happened with labor reforms in the New Deal to see that the "disruption" scenario is also inaccurate. Section 7a of the NIRA was originally achieved not by working-class disruptions, but by political lobbying by the American Federation of Labor and by the legislative efforts of Senator Robert Wagner. Once enacted, even though not successfully implemented, section 7a as a specifically political measure had a strong positive impact on labor-union growth in two main ways. First, it encouraged union organizers and emboldened rank-and-file workers with the belief that the national government would now support their efforts to unionize and bargain for economic gains. Second, it started Senator Wagner and others on the road toward the formulation of the Wagner Labor Relations Act, which ended up enforceably legalizing labor unions.

While labor's experiences under the NRA also fueled a growing strike wave in 1933–34, it cannot be plausibly argued that these strikes directly produced the Wagner Act of 1935. By 1934, rising numbers of labor disputes, and the inability of the National Labor Board (set up under the NIRA) to resolve them, did cause Roosevelt and Congress to become increasingly concerned with legislating new means for managing such disputes.[69] But, as the figure on page 66 shows, the immediate fruit of this concern, passed just as strikes came to a peak in mid-1934, was not the Wagner Act. Rather it was Public Resolution number 44, a measure cautiously designed to offend as little as possible major industrialists and conservative politicians.[70] A National Labor Relations Board was set up under the resolution, but it enjoyed no greater power to make employers

---

[67] On the industrial working class see David Brody, "The Emergence of Mass-Production Unionism," pp. 223–62 in *Change and Continuity in Twentieth Century America*, ed. John Braeman, Robert Bremner, and E. Walters (Columbus: Ohio State University Press, 1964); Irving Bernstein, *The Lean Years* (Baltimore: Penguin Books, 1966); Bernstein, *Turbulent Years*; Derber and Young, eds., *Labor and the New Deal*; and Ruth L. Horowitz, *Political Ideologies of Organized Labor: The New Deal Era* (New Brunswick, N.J.: transaction Books, 1978). I draw generally on these works in the discussions of labor that follow.

[68] Such a portrayal of the process of change is offered by Frances Fox Piven and Richard Cloward in *Poor People's Movements: Why They Succeed, How They Fail* (New York: Pantheon Books, 1977), chap. 3. An excellent critique of Piven and Cloward's analyses of events in the 1920s is offered in Timothy George Massad, "Disruption, Organization and Reform: A Critique of Piven and Cloward" (Undergraduate thesis, Harvard College, Social Studies, March, 1978).

[69] Bernstein, *New Deal Collective Bargaining Policy*, pp. 71–72, 77.

[70] On the equanimity of a U.S. Steel vice president about Pulic Resolution no. 44, see the quotation in ibid., p. 81.

accept independent unions than had the National Labor Board. Nevertheless, for whatever reasons, strikes fell off significantly (see the figure below) from the time of the resolution until after the enactment of the Wagner bill a year later, in July 1935.

If working-class pressure helped to produce the Wagner Act, it was pressure registered not only through strikes but also through the major Democratic electoral victories in Congress during the fall elections of 1934. This election strengthened liberals in the Congress and virtually eliminated right-wing Republicans.[71] It came, moreover, just as business opposition to the New Deal was becoming bitter and vociferous. Half a year later, in June 1935, the Supreme Court declared Title I of the NIRA—the early New Deal's major piece of recovery legislation—unconstitutional. It was at this extraordinary political conjuncture, one marked by rhetorical class conflict as well as by FDR's last-minute conver-

sion to the Wagner Act (both because of its Congressional support and because he saw it as a partial substitute for the NIRA), that the various politicians and labor-board administrators who had all along pushed for pro-union legislation were finally able to carry the day and put through Congress the single most important reform of the New Deal era.

Block's theory fits these historical developments, to be sure, but with the important provisos that independent initiatives by liberal politicians within the Democratic party were decisive in the entire sequence from section 7a of the NIRA to the Wagner Act and that the significant working-class pressures were registered electorally as well as expressed in industrial unrest. The U.S. industrial working class of the 1930s was not strong enough either to force concessions through economic disruption alone or to impose a comprehensive recovery program through the national political process. It depended greatly on friendly initiatives and support from within the federal government and the Democratic party. It got these not simply through disruption, but because it represented an attractive potential for electoral mobilization and an interest group that, among others, FDR wanted to conciliate if possible. It also helped labor enormously that business panicked about the New Deal after 1933 and, by going into polit-

---

[71] It is highly unusual for a party in power to gain in "off-year" Congressional elections, yet the Democrats did this in 1934. See John M. Allswang, *The New Deal and American Politics* (New York: Wiley, 1978), p. 30; and James T. Patterson, *Congressional Conservatism and the New Deal* (Lexington: University of Kentucky Press, 1967), pp. 32–33.

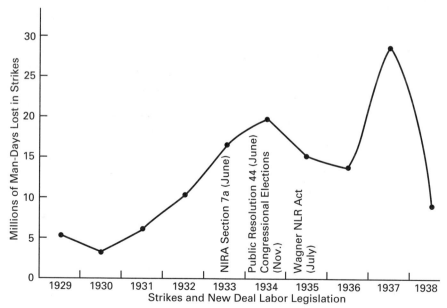

Source: U.S. Bureau of Labor Statistics, *Monthly Labor Review* (Washington: Government Printing Office, 1939), vol. 48, p. 1111.

ical opposition, gave liberals like Wagner even more space for legislative maneuver.

Turning from the causes to the consequences of the labor reforms of the New Deal, we arrive at other important queries that can be raised about Block's general explanation sketch. Do reforms enacted partially in response to demands from below invariably end up "rationalizing" capitalism by allowing state power to be used "in new ways to overcome economic contradictions and to facilitate the integration of the working class"? What determines and, possibly, limits the capacities of state managers to turn reforms and the concomitant enhancement of state power into effective supports for the capitalist economy as a whole?

In his theoretical statements on these issues, Block is not only imprecise; he actually points in contradictory directions. At various places in his article, he asserts that state managers almost by definition have the capacity to work for the general good of the capitalist class and economy:

> Unlike the individual capitalist, the state managers do not have to operate on the basis of a narrow profit-maximizing rationality. They are capable of intervening in the economy on the basis of a more general rationality. In short, their structural position gives the state managers both the interest and the capacity to aid the investment accumulation process.[72]
>
> The more power the state possesses to intervene in the capitalist economy, the greater the likelihood that effective actions can be taken to facilitate investment.[73]

But, at other points, Block admits that the pattern in which working-class pressures that ultimately enhance the state's capacity to manage capital accumulation "is not a smoothly working functional process."[74] He rather weakly alludes to "time lags" and "friction" in the overall process, yet also offers some stronger antifunctionalist formulations:

> There might, in fact, be continuing tensions in a government program between its integrative interest and its role in the accumulation process. [S]ome concessions to working-class pressure might have no potential benefits for accumulation and might simply place strains on the private economy.[75]

The increased capacity of state managers to intervene in the economy during these periods [of crisis and reform] does not automatically rationalize capitalism. State managers can make all kinds of mistakes, including excessive concessions to the working class. State managers have no special knowledge of what is necessary to make capitalism more rational: they grope toward effective action as best they can within existing political constraints and with available economic theories.[76]

With this last statement, Block has come 180 degrees from the notion that the state managers are "capable of intervening in the economy on the basis of a more general rationality" because "their structural position" gives them "both the interest and the capacity to aid the investment accumulation process."[77] Obviously, Block can't have it both ways. Either state managers enjoy the automatically given capacity to rationalize capitalism or their capacities are determined by "existing political constraints." Given that Block footnotes the final quote reproduced above with a reference to the New Deal, it is apparent that he believes "existing political constraints" were important then.[78]

Indeed, during the New Deal, U.S. state managers could not automatically use state power to ensure full economic recovery (and thereby ensure social and political stability). Their efforts were always channeled, shaped, and limited by existing state and party structures not conducive to fully effective state interventions. We have already seen the limitations that an absence of strong, autonomous administrative institutions placed upon the effectiveness of the National Industrial Recovery Act of the early New Deal. Furthermore, even after pressures from below and state initiatives had combined to put through the major social and labor reforms of the post-1934 New Deal, "existing political constraints" still stymied the efforts of the state managers to turn such measures and the political and state power generated by them into effective means for promoting capitalist economic recovery.

Block's theory of capitalist rationalization through class struggle and state-sponsored reforms silently assumes that social democracy is the highest evolution of capitalism and that any major crisis of advanced capitalism resulting in important reforms will ipso facto

[72] Block, "Ruling Class Does Not Rule," p. 20.
[73] Ibid., p. 26.
[74] Ibid., p. 23.
[75] Ibid.

[76] Ibid., pp. 25–26.
[77] Ibid., p. 20.
[78] Ibid., p. 26.

entail a breakthrough toward what C. A. R. Crosland once called a "full employment welfare state."[79] Perhaps the pattern of state intervention implied here could aptly be called "social-democratic Keynesian," because state interventions, regulatory and fiscal together, would promote private accumulation of capital and, at the same time, further the social welfare, the full employment, and the political-economic leverage (that is, through strong unions) of the working class. Now, the interesting thing about the reformist phase of the New Deal (1935–38) is that, although tendencies existed that might conceivably have added up to a social-democratic Keynesian breakthrough, the existing governmental and party structures so patterned political conflicts and so limited the possibilities for political transformations as to prevent any such breakthrough from actually occurring. Instead, the direct consequence of the labor reforms, and of the enhanced labor and liberal power that accompanied them, was not economic recovery through social-democratic Keynesianism but increased social and political tension, leading by 1938–39 to an insecure impasse for the domestic New Deal.

What were the tendencies present in the reformist New Deal that pointed toward a social-democratic Keynesian breakthrough? For one thing, as Block's theory would suggest, the social and labor reforms of the New Deal generated new nexes of political power and interest, binding liberal-Democratic politicians into symbiotic relationships with the welfare and relief agencies of the federal government and binding both urban-liberal politicians and trade-union leaders into a symbiotic relationship with another new organ of state power, the National Labor Relations Board (NLRB). NLRB administrators achieved their entire raison d'être through the spread of labor unions; they had a natural institutional bias (as well as a legal mandate) in favor of protecting all legitimate unions and union drives.[80] Labor unions, in turn, certainly benefited from the protections thus afforded them. Union membership had declined to below 3 million in 1933 but started rising

thereafter and shot up, especially from 1935, to over 8 million in 1939.[81] Both labor unions and the NLRB depended upon liberal-Democratic support in Congress and within presidential administrations. And, of course, liberal-Democratic politicians benefited from monetary contributions and from the electoral mobilization of workers' votes. This mobilization was organized, from 1936 on, through political committees established by union leaders grateful for benefits from the Roosevelt administration and hopeful that further gains could be made for workers (including those unemployed and on relief) through the strengthening of liberal forces in the Democratic party.[82] Indeed, it did seem that liberal Democrats, workers, unemployed people, people on welfare, and federal administrators could all work together fruitfully after 1935–36. Voices like Robert Wagner's called for economic recovery through bolstering the spending power of the working class. Urban liberals in general advocated increased welfare and public works expenditures and proposed substantial new efforts in public housing.[83]

Another major tendency that might have helped produce a breakthrough to social-democratic Keynesianism came from the president himself. After the 1936 election, Roosevelt introduced an executive reorganization plan drafted by a committee of academic experts on public administration. As drafted, this plan was well designed to overcome many built-in obstacles to any strategy (whether social-Democratic or not) of coordinated state intervention in the society and economy.[84] The reorganization plan called for the consolidation of federal administrative organs (including formerly independent regulatory bodies) into functionally rationalized, centrally controlled cabinet departments. It would have enhanced presidential powers of planning and policy coordination by: increasing executive versus Congressional control over the expenditure of budgeted federal funds; establishing a National Resources Planning Board for comprehensive, long-range planning and coordination of federal programs; and greatly

---

[79] From C. A. R. Crosland, *The Future of Socialism* (London: Jonathan Cape, 1956), p. 61. I have taken the expression via Andrew Martin, "The Politics of Economic Policy in the United States: A Tentative View from a Comparative Perspective," Sage Professional Paper: Comparative Politics Series (Beverly Hills: Sage Publications, 1973). My thinking has been greatly influenced by Martin's paper.

[80] Edelman, "New Deal Sensitivity to Labor Interests," in *Labor and the New Deal*, ed. Derber and Young, pp. 170–72.

[81] Derber and Young, eds., *Labor and the New Deal*, pp. 3, 134.

[82] On unions' political activities, see esp. J. David Greenstone, *Labor in American Politics* (New York: Vintage Books, 1970), chap. 2.

[83] Huthmacher, *Wagner and Urban Liberalism*, chaps. 12–13.

[84] Richard Polenberg, *Reorganizing Roosevelt's Government: The Controversy over Executive Reorganization 1936–1939* (Cambridge: Harvard University Press, 1966). Polenberg writes (p. 26): "A powerful president equipped with the personnel, planning, and fiscal control necessary to implement his social program—this was the Committee's aim."

expanding the White House staff directly responsible to the president. All of these measures, taken together, would have gone a long way toward reversing the historically inherited fragmentation of the U.S. federal administration. Since the start of the New Deal, the U.S. federal bureaucracy had, of course, expanded significantly. But the expansion had been piece-meal and, given the competing lines of authority between Congress and the president and the paucity of institutional means of executive coordination available to Roosevelt, the expanded federal government was becoming increasingly unwieldy.

Given that FDR and the Democrats were re-elected by huge popular margins in 1936, the time looked ripe to enhance the Roosevelt administration's ability to institutionalize and expand its reforms. And, to engage in a bit of counterfactual historical speculation, imagine that such a system not only could have been achieved but also that it could, in turn, have been harnessed to a disciplined and thoroughly liberal Democratic party, one devoted to the pursuit of full economic recovery through social spending. Then the institutional and political conditions for a true social-democratic Keynesian breakthrough in the U.S. would have been established. But, of course, things did not turn out this way, largely because of the nature of the Democratic party and the structure of the U.S. national government. The Democratic party absorbed, contained, and rendered partially contradictory the political gains of organized labor and liberals in the 1930s, and the national government blocked FDR's comprehensive scheme for administrative reorganization.

To begin with the failure of comprehensive reorganization, Roosevelt's plan met defeat in Congress above all because it threatened to disrupt well-established patterns of institutional power.[85] Senators and representatives were jealous of Congress's traditional power to "pre-audit" the expenditures of federal agencies, for through such power individuals and committees in Congress could influence programs affecting their state or local constituencies. In addition, both members of Congress and administrators of federal agencies were very nervous about administrative reorganizations that would disrupt existing symbiotic relationships among Congress, bureaucrats, and organized interest groups in the society at large. Predictably, the most intense opposition came from conservatives, for these people worried about the kinds of programs Roosevelt (and the New Dealers in general) might generate through a reorganized federal executive. But not only conservatives opposed the plan; some of Roosevelt's own Cabinet members, acting like any traditional U.S. cabinet heads jealous of their bureaucratic domains, opposed reorganization or failed to support it. Interestingly enough, the "urban liberal" par excellence, Senator Robert Wagner, also opposed the reorganization plan. He was worried about Congressional prerogatives and the administrative independence of the National Labor Relations Board.[86]

The Democratic party also functioned as an obstacle to a social-democratic Keynesian breakthrough in the 1930s. The most basic fact about the New Deal Democratic party was simply that it worked pretty much as all major U.S. political parties have done since about the 1830s.[87] U.S. parties do not formulate explicit, coherent national programs that their members in Congress are then disciplined to support. Rather U.S. parties "aggregate" blocs of voters through very diverse appeals in different parts of the country. Their overriding function is to compete in single-member-constituency, majority-take-all elections in order to place politicians in office from the local to the state to the national level. Once in office, parties exhibit some discipline (especially on procedural matters), but members of Congress are remarkably free as individuals (or ad hoc coalitions) to pursue whatever legislation or whatever administrative measures they believe will appeal to local constituents or to organized groups of financial contributors and voters. Members of Congress may, of course, be unusually attentive during periods of crisis to directives from the president and from House and Senate leaders; this was the case during the "Hundred Days" of 1933. But such extraordinary coordination rarely lasts for long, and there is still unlikely to be a disciplined pursuit of an over-all party program, if only

[85] Ibid., pts. 2, 3. Eventually, parts of the original executive plan were passed by Congress, but these parts simply strengthened the president's staff and modified the cabinet departments somewhat. The changes accomplished were piecemeal—far from the original plan for comprehensive reorganization.

[86] Ibid., pp. 139–40. Polenberg cites Keyserling, "Wagner Act," pp. 203, 207–8, 210–12, on Wagner's views on the NLRB's administrative location. See also Huthmacher, *Wagner and Urban Liberalism*, pp. 243–45.

[87] Theodore J. Lowi, "Party, Policy, and Constitution in America," in *The American Party Systems*, ed. William Nisbet Chambers and Walter Dean Burnham, 2nd ed. (New York: Oxford University Press, 1975), pp. 238–76.

because U.S. presidents, senators, and representatives are elected in diverse ways and by differently structured constituencies.

These institutional givens meant that as liberals, especially from northern urban areas, made gains within the national Democratic party, they could hope to gain *some* legislative and administrative leverage for their various constituents. They could not expect, however, to formulate comprehensive national strategies for a Democratic president and Congress to enact. The existing Congressional-executive system would frustrate any such efforts. Even more important, the Democratic party could maintain a semblance of national unity only by avoiding too many head-on clashes between its entrenched, overwhelmingly conservative southern wing and its expanding liberal urban-northern wing. There were also nonsouthern rural interests in the party, and their representatives were willing to support government programs for farmers but were usually not sympathetic to the needs of urban areas or labor.

Franklin Delano Roosevelt, an immensely popular President, gained the Democratic nomination in 1932 through southern and western support. By 1936 he also enjoyed strong support in urban areas and from organized labor.[88] But it became increasingly difficult for Roosevelt to manage all of these diverse interests under the Democratic umbrella. For a brief time in 1938, he attempted to make the party more consistently liberal by "purging" various very conservative Democrats who had opposed New Deal reforms.[89] But machines or special agglomerations of organized interests at local and state levels control nominations within U.S. parties, which are "national" only in label and for the purpose of electing presidents. So FDR's purge failed, and liberalism—even as an attitude, let alone as a comprehensive program of recovery and reform—could not take over the Democratic party.

Moreover, given the way that the operations of the Democratic party (and the Republican party) intersected with the operation of Congress, liberals (especially urban liberals) were unable to translate electoral

support into truly proportional Congressional leverage. Ironically, efforts by labor and liberals to elect Democrats could even hurt politically, as Edelman explains:

> Both the House and the Senate greatly underrepresent urban areas. The emphasis on local needs therefore means that labor groups are underrepresented, for constituency pressures are more often exerted disproportionately on behalf of farmers and dominant local industries rather than on behalf of worker residential areas in the cities. This bias is greatly emphasized because the constituencies that are "safe" in the sense of predictably returning incumbents to office are also to be found almost entirely in predominantly rural areas: the South, Vermont, Maine, and some parts of the Middle West. Because an individual's influence in Congress depends so enormously on his seniority there, the congressmen from these areas gain disproportionately in influence when their parties win control. Thus a hard-fought Democratic victory in Pennsylvania, New York, Illinois, and California sufficient to enable the Democrats to organize the House and Senate does not benefit these states nearly as much as it benefits Alabama, Mississippi, Florida and other states in which there is little hard campaigning. To this extent AFL and CIO activity in congressional campaigns in the urban areas places some of the anti-labor rural congressmen in a stronger position.[90]

By the very nature of politics, conflicts intensify as a formerly weak interest in a situation of diverging interests grows stronger. As labor and liberal interests gained ground in U.S. politics during the 1930s, conservatives, whether businessmen or rural interests, were bound to oppose them, whatever the institutional arrangements had been. Yet above and beyond this inevitable opposition, the structure and operations of Congress and the Democratic party facilitated the formation of a "conservative coalition" to obstruct or modify many liberal New Deal measures, even as these arrangements made it difficult for liberals to become a national policy-making force.[91] Nor, as we have seen, could liberal programs supported by members of Congress always count on solid support from Roosevelt or his administration. For Roosevelt and his administrators had to worry about maintaining broad support in

[88] Allswang, *New Deal and American Politics*, chaps. 2–4, passim.
[89] On the attempted purge and the reasons for its failure, see ibid., pp. 121–26; and Patterson, *Congressional Conservatism*, chap. 8. On the paradoxical explanation for the one apparent success that FDR had in purging a conservative, see Richard Polenberg, "Franklin Roosevelt and the Purge of John O'Connor: The Impact of Urban Change on Political Parties," *New York History* 49, no. 3. (July 1968): 306–26.

[90] Edelman, "New Deal Sensitivity to Labor Interests," in *Labor and the New Deal*, ed. Derber and Young, pp. 185–86.
[91] Patterson, *Congressional Conservatism*, pp. 334–35.

Congress and about balancing pushes and pulls within the Democratic party as a whole.

Given the structures of politics within which they had to operate, liberals during the New Deal had to settle for doing what pays off in the U.S. political system. They carved out domains of legislation and administration favorable to well-organized constituents and then did their best to defend these against bureaucratic encroachments or opposition within Congress or from the administration.[92]

In sum, "existing political constraints"—specifically, the U.S. government and political parties of the 1930s—limited the possibilities for politicians to use the new political energies and the new domains of state power generated by the reformist New Deal for the successful resuscitation of capitalist accumulation through state spending for (new or much expanded) domestic social programs. By the late 1930s, full economic recovery still eluded the national economy under the New Deal. In the absence of recovery, who could say where U.S. politics might go? Conservatives in Congress were gaining political strength and were increasingly able and willing to block policy initiatives coming from "urban liberals" inside and outside the government and to whittle down welfare and public-works measures sponsored by the president.[93] Labor unions were still not accepted by many industrial employers, and the NLRB and the Wagner Act were coming under increasingly vociferous political attacks.[94]

Yet, of course, the basic social and labor reforms of the liberal New Deal did survive. And full recovery, indeed, spectacularly accelerated growth, was achieved by the U.S. economy. But the intranational structural forces specified in Block's theory, that is, working-class pressures plus the initiatives of state managers, were not alone responsible for this outcome of the 1940s and after. Of the three neo-Marxist theoretical perspectives examined in this paper as a whole, only Block's repeatedly alludes to ways in which transnational structures and conjunctures affect the course of

domestic politics in advanced capitalist nations. Even Block, however, fails to accord such transnational factors the systematic explanatory weight they deserve. It is not only the interplay of capitalists' economic decisions, working-class pressures, and state managers' initiatives that shapes political conflicts and transformations in advanced capitalism. International economic and politico-military relations also matter.

The case of the New Deal certainly dramatizes the importance of both international economics and international politics. Without the virtual collapse of the international monetary system and the sharp contraction of international trade in the early years of the Depression, it is highly doubtful that "political space" could have opened up in the United States for the pursuit of economic recovery and reforms through greater state intervention. Even more important was the impact at the end of the New Deal of the coming of World War II, starting in Europe. Everyone knows that "military Keynesianism"—growing federal expenditures on military preparedness and then war—jolted the national economy out of the lingering Depression at the end of the 1930s.[95] What is perhaps less well known are the crucial ways in which the turn toward military and foreign policy preoccupations and then into war overcame many of the domestic social and political impasses of the later New Deal.[96] There were several key developments. As the Roosevelt administration planned for (and later implemented) wartime industrial mobilization, it sought a rapprochement with big businessmen and tacitly agreed to cease pushing for new labor and social reforms in return for business cooperation. The institutionalization of labor unions was, at the same time, solidified during the war. In return for a no-strike pledge from union leaders, the government required employers to deal with unions and facilitated the enrollment of union members in industries doing war production. Finally, the issues of politics in Congress were partially transmuted from the domestic and economic questions that exacerbated conflicts between rural-conservatives and urban-liberals into more foreign-policy and military related issues that averted (or delayed) some of the old disputes over social reform. Reformers

[92] On the resulting patterns of power see esp. Morton Grodzins, "American Political Parties and the American System," *Western Political Quarterly* 13, no. 4 (December 1960): 974–98; and Grant McConnell, *Private Power and American Democracy* (New York: Vintage Books, 1966).

[93] Patterson, *Congressional Conservatism*, chaps. 6–10; and Richard Polenberg, "The Decline of the New Deal," pp. 246–66, in *The New Deal*, ed. Braeman, Bremner, and Brody, vol. 1, *The National Level*.

[94] Ibid., pp. 315–24; and Huthmacher, *Wagner and Urban Liberalism*, chap. 14.

[95] Robert L. Heilbroner, with Aaron Singer, *The Economic Transformation of America* (New York: Harcourt, Brace Jovanovich, 1977), pp. 205–7.

[96] David Brody, "The New Deal and World War II," pp. 267–309 in *The New Deal*, ed. Braeman, Bremner and Brody, vol. 1, *The National Level*. See also Richard Polenberg, *War and Society: The United States, 1941–1945* (Philadelphia: J. B. Lippincott, 1972).

could no longer use economic crisis as a rationale for social welfare measures. Instead, both liberals and conservatives had to maneuver with the symbols of national unity evoked to sustain the wartime efforts at home and abroad.

What all of this, taken together, amounted to was not at all a defeat or a roll back for the reforms of the New Deal. Rather, most of the reforms were consolidated and retained, but within a new national political context in which business and government were again reconciled. Capitalists learned to live with and use many aspects of the New Deal reforms, even as they retained leverage in the U.S. political system to counter the power of organized labor and to limit future advances by liberals and labor. The full economic recovery, the new governmental tasks, and the new political climate brought by the war, all were important in allowing this denouement. Without the timely arrival of the war, the basic reforms of the New Deal might not have survived—and they might not have proved so "functional" for U.S. capitalism.

CONCLUSION

At the outset I declared three basic aims for this exploratory essay: to show that some current lines of neo-Marxist analysis are more promising than others for explaining the New Deal as an instance of political conflict and transformation within advanced capitalism; to argue that, for such explanatory purposes, no existing neo-Marxist approach affords sufficient weight to state and party organizations as independent determinants of political conflicts and outcomes; and to sketch some of the ways in which U.S. political institutions shaped and limited the accomplishments of the New Deal. In closing, I shall summarize my conclusions on each of these major themes and point out important areas for further investigation and critical discussion.

The evidence of the New Deal reveals the basic inadequacy of those lines of neo-Marxist reasoning that treat political outcomes in advanced capitalism as the enactments of a far-sighted capitalist ruling class or as the automatically functional responses of the political system to the needs of capitalism. Yet there are also more promising lines of analysis within neo-Marxism. Those theorists who assign explanatory importance to class struggle recognize that conflicts between capitalists and noncapitalists affect politics in capitalist societies. They also recognize that politicians (especially in liberal democracies) must respond to the demands of noncapitalists as well as to the demands of capitalists

and the conditions of the economy. Moreover, those theorists who refer to the "relative autonomy of politics" or who assign "state managers" an independent explanatory role are moving toward an approach that can take seriously the state and parties as organizations of specifically political domination, organizations with their own structures, their own histories, and their own patterns of conflict and impact upon class relations and economic development.

Nevertheless, so far, no self-declared neo-Marxist theory of the capitalist state has arrived at the point of taking state structures and party organizations *seriously enough*.[97] Various ways of short-circuiting political analyses have been too tempting. Political outcomes are attributed to the abstract needs of the capitalist system, or to the will of the dominant capitalist class, or to the naked political side-effects of working-class struggles. It is often assumed that politics always works optimally for capitalism and capitalists, leaving only the "how" to be systematically explained. Even those neo-Marxists who have tried to incorporate state structures into their modes of explanation tend to do so only in functionalist or socioeconomically reductionist ways. What is more, almost all neo-Marxists theorize about "the capitalist state" in general, thus attempting to explain patterns of state intervention and political conflict in analytic terms directly derived from a model about the capitalist mode of production as such.

But capitalism in general has no politics, only (extremely flexible) outer limits for the kinds of supports for property ownership and controls of the labor force that it can tolerate. States and political parties within capitalism have cross-nationally and historically varying structures. These structures powerfully shape and limit state interventions in the economy, and they determine the ways in which class interests and conflicts get organized into (or out of) politics in a given time and place. More than this, state structures and

---

[97] There are, however, some very promising pieces of comparative-historical analysis, including Martin, "Politics of Economic Policy in the United States"; Ira Katznelson, "Considerations on Social Democracy in the United States," *Comparative Politics* 11, no. 1 (October 1978): 77–99; Peter J. Katzenstein, ed., *Between Power and Plenty* (Madison: University of Wisconsin Press, 1978), esp. conclusion; and, perhaps the nicest example of all of an approach that combines class and political-structural analysis, Susan S. Fainstein and Norman I. Fainstein, "National Policy and Urban Development," *Social Problems* 26, no. 2 (December 1978): 125–46.

Politics & Society 10, no. 2 (1980): pp. 155–201.

party organizations have (to a very significant degree) independent histories. They are shaped and reshaped not simply in response to socioeconomic changes or dominant-class interests, nor as a direct side-effect of class struggles. Rather they are shaped and reshaped through the struggles of politicians among themselves, struggles that sometimes prompt politicians to mobilize social support or to act upon the society or economy in pursuit of political advantages in relation to other politicians. In short, states and parties have their own structures and histories, which in turn have their own impact upon society.

The New Deal is a difficult case, almost ideal for developing a macro-analytic perspective that points to all of the necessary factors to be considered in explaining transformations of the state and politics within advanced capitalism. Real political changes occurred in the New Deal: the inclusion of some popular interests in a more interventionist "broker state," the incorporation of the industrial working class into the Democratic party, and the expansion of urban-liberal influence within the party. But the political changes that occurred did not please capitalists or ensure capitalist economic recovery or consolidate the basic reforms that were enacted—not until World War II intervened to transform the over-all political and economic context. By using various neo-Marxist explanatory approaches as foils for probing the politics of the New Deal, I have argued that many of the limitations on effective state intervention and on liberal reforms in the New Deal can be traced to the existing U.S. national administrative arrangements, governmental institutions, and political parties. These same structures, moreover, shaped the piecemeal reforms and the partially successful efforts to proffer relief and to promote recovery in response to the Depression. Capitalists, industrial workers, and farmers certainly helped to shape and limit the New Deal, as did the contours of the massive economic crisis itself. But economic and class effects were all mediated through the distinctive structures of U.S. national politics. The immediate changes were not fully intended by anyone, were not consistently in conformance with the interests of any class, and were not smoothly functional for the system as a whole. But the changes did make sense as the product of intensified political struggles and undertakings within given, historically evolved structures of political representation and domination. Such structures are the keys to any satisfactory explanation of the New Deal—and to other episodes, past, present, and future, of political response to economic crisis within capitalism.

READING 5

PROPERTY RIGHTS AND THE ORGANIZATION OF ECONOMIC ACTIVITY BY THE STATE*

John L. Campbell and Leon N. Lindberg

In advanced capitalist society the state helps shape the institutional organization of the economy. We show how the state shapes the economy through the manipulation of property rights. The state's actions create pressures for change that lead actors to look for new forms of economic organization. The state also assists, leads, or constrains the process of selecting new forms of economic organization that emerge in response to these pressures, and it may or may not ratify these new forms. In contrast to the conventional literature on state economy relations that characterizes the U.S. state as having a weak capacity for successful economic intervention, we argue that property rights actions afford the U.S. state a previously unrecognized source of strength. Data come primarily from historical case studies of organizational transformation in the steel, automobile, commercial nuclear energy, telecommunications, dairy, meat-packing, and railroad sectors.

Social scientists have written extensively about the relationship between state and economy in advanced capitalist society. A largely neglected issue is how the state shapes the economy's *organizational structure*—the different institutional arrangements that actors use to coordinate exchange and production, such as markets, vertically integrated corporations, cartels, and so on. This is a surprising omission given recent efforts to "bring the state back in" (Evans, Rueschemeyer, and Skocpol 1985) to political economic analysis. For example, many scholars have

From *American Sociological Review* 55 (October 1990), 634–47. Reprinted with permission of Leon Lindberg and the American Sociological Association.

* Direct all correspondence to John Campbell, William James Hall, Department of Sociology, Harvard University, Cambridge, MA 02138. We would like to thank the following people for comments on earlier drafts: Michael Allen, Patricia Arnold, Kenneth Bickers, Steve Brint, Richard Colignon, Paul DiMaggio, Mauricio Font, Stephan Haggard, Rogers Hollingsworth, Greg Hooks, Rob Kennedy, Helen Mitner, John Portz, David Riesman, Christoph Scherrer, Theda Skocpol, Arthur Stinchcombe, Brigitte Young, and the *ASR* reviewers.

examined the degree to which the centralization of states and economies affects economic policy and growth, but not how policies influence economic centralization *per se* (e.g., Katzenstein 1978).[1]

Furthermore, most of the literature that "brings the state back in" has shown how states intervene in the economy by allocating key resources, such as finance capital, to influence the activities of economic actors (e.g., Cox 1986; Gourevitch 1986; Hall 1986; Katzenstein 1978; Skocpol 1985). It is often argued that states that enjoy relatively few allocative powers, including the United States, are "weak" in that they are often unable to intervene successfully to achieve policy goals (e.g., Shonfield 1965; Thurow 1984; Zysman 1983). However, by emphasizing allocation this literature has neglected another powerful state capacity—the ability to manipulate property rights—that has been important historically in shaping economic organization in the United States (Horwitz 1977; Scheiber 1981).

Only a handful of scholars argues that the state influences economic organization and they refer only sporadically to the fact that the state does this by manipulating property rights (e.g., Hamilton and Biggart 1988; Lazerson 1988; Weiss 1988).[2] Perhaps because their purpose has been to criticize economic, technological, and other nonpolitical theories of economic organization, they have not developed the theoretical implications of this state capacity for theories of the state or state economy relations. The exception is North (1981) and other new institutional historians who argue that, for political reasons, the state tends to create property rights that are inefficient because they constrain economic growth by inadvertently contributing to high transaction costs for economic actors. Following Williamson (1975, 1985), North argues that private actors respond to sluggish growth by building new economic organizations to reduce transaction costs and improve economic performance. For North, the manipulation of property rights by the state creates pressures for organizational change.

There are two problems with this view. On the one hand, organizational change is a process whereby actors select alternative organizational forms in ways that are constrained institutionally (Nelson and Winter 1982). Thus, once property rights are institutionalized they not only trigger, but also constrain this selection process. No one has examined how property rights affect this selection process (see Robbins 1987). On the other hand, political scientists and sociologists have considered how the institutional structure of the state affects the deployment of state policy, and thus, economic activity and performance (e.g., Hall 1986; Skocpol 1985). Yet none of the scholars who argue that the state influences economic organization have discussed how the state's institutional structure influences either the deployment of property rights or the effect of property rights actions on the economy.

We explain how the state shapes the organization of the economy by manipulating and enforcing property rights. We argue that property rights actions by the state not only create pressures for change that cause actors to look for new organizational forms, but they also constrain and influence how actors select different forms. The state creates pressure for change and constrains this selection process not only as an actor but also as an institutional structure—a set of administrative, legislative, and judicial organizations with responsibility for policy-making and implementation. The capacity to establish property rights gives the state a generally unrecognized source of *strength* insofar as it enables state actors to alter the organization of the economy.

---

[1] See Samuels (1987) for further discussion about how state policy *per se*, rather than the transformation of economic institutions, has generally been the dependent variable in political economic research—a serious omission insofar as these transformations have profound and long-lasting consequences for the effectiveness of the state's economic policy and industry's performance.

[2] This is somewhat surprising since property rights are central to classic discussions of state society relations (e.g., Polanyi 1944). Other scholars recognize the importance of the state's manipulation of property rights but fail to appreciate how these actions affect the organization of economic activity. For example, theorists of economic regulation have tried to explain how the state manipulates property rights through regulatory policy (e.g., Bernstein 1977; Downs 1967; Sabatier 1975; Thomson and Krasner 1989), and how these efforts create economic inefficiencies and alter the allocation of wealth (e.g., Peltzman 1976; Posner 1974; Stigler 1975), but not how they influence the organizational structure of the economy. Neo-Marxists focus on how property rights constrain state policy-making, not on how the

---

state's ability to manipulate property rights influences the organization of the economy. They argue that, except during crises, state managers may pursue many policy options as long as they do not undermine the fundamental property rights of the capitalist class—the right and ability of capitalists to continue accumulating capital (e.g., Block 1987; Domhoff 1987; O'Connor 1973; Offe and Ronge 1975).

Property rights actions are state activities that define and enforce property rights, i.e., the rules that determine the conditions of ownership and control of the means of production.[3] Examples of property rights actions include the establishment and enforcement of antitrust, regulatory, labor, and contract law. Most scholars view property rights as defining the relationship between an individual and a commodity, such that someone is said to own or control the means of production to some degree (e.g., Caporaso 1989, p. 143). We contend that property rights also express relationships among people. One person's ownership and control usually corresponds to another's absence of ownership and control. Because property rights specify relations among people, they also define the institutional basis of power relations in the processes of production, exchange, and accumulation. For instance, state antitrust laws prevent producers from colluding against consumers. This conception of property rights is admittedly broad insofar as it includes, in addition to constitutional rights, regulatory and other laws and rules that alter the relationships of exchange, which are rooted in control over property. For example, labor laws affect the power of workers to organize, antitrust laws and price regulations limit the exercise of monopoly ownership rights, and patent laws limit access to new technologies. Hence, the state's ability to define and enforce property rights determines social relations, and therefore, the balance of power among a wide variety of economic actors in civil society.[4] It follows that political struggles among actors outside and within the state influence the state's property rights actions and that the outcomes of these struggles vary over time and across sectors.[5]

We begin with a general discussion of how the state as an actor and an institutional structure influences the organization, or *governance*, of economic activity by establishing and enforcing property rights. Governance refers to the institutionalized economic processes that organize and coordinate activity among a wide variety of economic actors. Second, we show how property rights actions have played important and conceptually distinct roles in the transformation of *governance regimes* in various sectors of the U.S. economy. Governance regimes are combinations of specific organizational forms, including markets, corporate hierarchies, associations, and networks (e.g., interlocking directorates, long-term subcontracting agreements, bilateral and multilateral joint ventures, pools, cartels) that coordinate economic activity among organizations in an industry or economic sector. We refer to these forms individually as *governance mechanisms*.[6] Thus, governance transformations involve the reorganization of a particular governance regime. Corporate hierarchies, for example, may replace a competitive market as the governance mechanism for allocating certain goods or services in a sector. Formal cartels may give way to informal price-leading arrangements for collectively setting prices, and so on. Finally, we examine the implications of the analysis for theories of the state and state economy relations in advanced capitalist societies.

The analysis draws upon case studies and secondary sources that explore governance transformations that occurred in the steel, automobile, commercial nuclear energy, telecommunications, dairy, meat-packing, and railroad sectors in the United States. The case studies represent a cross-section of the U.S. economy. They include manufacturing, agriculture, and infrastructure sectors; capital intensive and labor intensive sectors; sectors that depend in varying degree on sophisticated technology; and sectors founded during the nineteenth century vs. others founded at different times during the

---

[3] State actors do not necessarily manipulate property rights deliberately to influence economic organization, although their actions may have that effect. Judicial decisions, for example, have often unintentionally influenced economic organization in the United States (Scheiber 1981). Hence, we use the term property rights "action" rather than property rights "policy" because "policy" implies that the outcomes of state decision-making are intended.
[4] This argument is based on Hodgson's (1988, Chapter 7) criticism of the orthodox property rights school in economics. For a review of this literature, also see Bowles (1984).
[5] The state does not always establish and enforce property rights in a carefully conceived manner. Often they are devised in an *ad hoc* piecemeal fashion in response to particular problems in the economy. Moreover, the state does not necessarily undertake property rights actions autonomously from the influence of actors

---

in civil society. Recent theory suggests that state autonomy is variable (e.g., Block 1987; Samuels 1987; Skocpol 1985). Although the issue of state autonomy is not a central concern of this paper, we recognize that state actors, not those in civil society, make the final decisions about how to define and enforce property rights—decisions that may be forced upon them by circumstances in the economy beyond their control.
[6] See Lindberg, Campbell, and Hollingsworth (forthcoming) for a discussion and typology of different types of governance mechanisms.

twentieth century. These studies were prepared for a project on the governance of the U.S. economy.[7] Because this paper is primarily theoretical, we use these cases for illustrative purposes only.

Many theorists have criticized the conventional literature on the state's capacity for economic intervention for making sweeping comparative generalizations about national economic policies and policy styles without considering the sectoral variation within national political economies (e.g., Atkinson and Coleman 1989; Cawson 1985; Skocpol 1985; Vogel 1987; Wilks and Wright 1987). The state may manipulate property rights in different ways in different sectors of the economy and this will influence governance regimes in these sectors accordingly.

THE STATE AS AN ACTOR AND AN INSTITUTIONAL STRUCTURE

The notion of state intervention in the economy assumes a clear separation of state and economy in which, for example, markets exist in a truly laissez-faire autonomous condition. Although orthodox economics makes this assumption almost without question, the historical record does not support it (Lazonick 1986; Polanyi 1944). Rather, markets and other forms of economic governance are intimately linked to an ancillary set of institutions, including the state (Granovetter 1985; Hall 1986, Chapter 2). Even Williamson (1985), who argues that alternative forms of economic governance are private responses to market failures, maintains in his general theoretical writings that market transactions are contractually-based. This means the state provides the legal framework within which contracts are written and enforced. As Weiss (1988, p. 162) notes, "Politics does not so much 'triumph' over economic forces. It enters into their overall configuration." The state's influence, quite apart from sporadic interventions, is *always* present in the economy (Block 1986) insofar as it provides an institutional and legal framework that influences the selection of different governance regimes and thereby permanently shapes the economy. The state does this

through the definition and enforcement of property rights as both an actor and a political-institutional structure.

State as Actor

The distinction between the state as an actor and the state as a political-institutional structure is central to our analysis. The state comprises many *actors* (e.g., Evans, Rueschemeyer, and Skocpol 1985; Krasner 1978b; Skowronek 1982; Stepan 1978) who undertake property rights actions that contribute to or block governance transformations. During much of U.S. history the federal government did not interact closely with the economy. Since the Colonial period, however, state and local governments have been intimately involved in shaping economic sectors and industries (Eisinger 1988; Hughes 1977; Walsh 1978). For example, state governments granted special charters and made other property rights decisions after the Civil War that transformed many entrepreneurial firms into large corporate hierarchies (Galambos and Pratt 1988; Horwitz 1977; Hurst 1982; Keller 1981; Sanders 1986). In addition to policy-makers at all levels of government, courts, judges, and the legal profession all played important roles in the development of the U.S. economy (Scheiber 1978, 1980a, 1980b, 1981; Shapiro 1986). For much of the nation's history, the courts were the only state institution that stood above political party domination and performed an integrative state-like function. Courts determined the meaning and effect of laws passed by the legislature, shaped intergovernmental relations, invoked the state's prerogatives over the economy, and became the chief source of economic surveillance. The courts became the American surrogate for the administrative apparatus familiar in European states. Judges in the United States played particularly aggressive roles in policy-making and economic governance (Skowronek 1982).

State as Institutional Structure

The structural features of the state have also been important in shaping the economy through property rights. After all, as Skocpol (1985, p. 21) argues, states affect civil society not only through the goal-oriented behavior of state officials, but also through organizational configurations that encourage or discourage various kinds of political and, we would add, economic group formation. First, the U.S. state is a distinctive

---

[7] The studies, all based on primary and secondary data, were written by Ken Bickers (telecommunications), John Campbell (nuclear energy), Rob Kennedy (railroads), John Portz (meat-packing), Christoph Scherrer (steel and automobiles), and Brigitte Young (dairy). They will appear in Campbell, Hollingsworth, and Lindberg (forthcoming).

configuration of organizations that is predisposed to struggle among state actors. The executive, legislative, and judicial branches tend to clash with each other, as do executive agencies and independent regulatory commissions, and federal, state and local governments (e.g., Markusen 1987; Walker 1981). Insofar as different parts of the state apparatus have overlapping responsibilities for property rights, contradictory property rights actions and political stalemate are possible. Indeed, the institutionally-fragmented nature of the U.S. state has systematically produced these problems in many areas of economic policy-making (Edmonds 1983; O'Connor 1973; Shonfield 1965).

The possibility of contradictory state actions is further enhanced because different parts of the state apparatus provide different *arenas* of political access to societal actors (e.g., Badaracco 1985; Shonfield 1965). To the extent that these actors pursue their interests in different arenas, conflicting property rights actions can be expected. Of course, societal actors who discover new arenas of access or develop new capacities for influencing the policy process may also cause shifts in property rights actions.[8]

A second way in which the institutional structure of the state shapes economic governance is by providing a legal-institutional structure that fosters geographically distinct sets of property rights, and thus, distinctive *locations for economic activity*. National political authority is restricted to the extent that subnational governments exercise authority within their own geographical areas. The existence of fifty separate state governments played an important role in the development of regionally distinct economies (Markusen 1985), politics (Bensel 1984; Markusen 1987; Sanders 1986), and sets of property rights that in turn influenced the location and governance of economic activity. For example, some southern states adopted property rights more favorable to business than those in the North, facilitating the southward migration of industries in pursuit of cheaper labor and less restrictive environmental regulations (Bluestone and Harrison 1982; Goodman 1979; Newman 1984). By changing business charters and laws of incorporation during the nineteenth century, state legislatures in New Jersey and later

Delaware fostered the rise of big enterprises, mergers, and combinations (Hurst 1982, p. 127; Keller 1981, p. 57; Sanders 1986, p. 153). These state-level laws of incorporation "substantially reduced the volume and importance of resource allocation accomplished wholly by market bargaining, and increased allocations made through the discipline of private organizations" (Hurst 1982, p. 50). Because the state's institutional structure facilitates the development of geographically distinct sets of property rights, economic actors enjoy a range of choices concerning where to do business, and as a result, which forms of governance to adopt.

THE STATE AND THE TRANSFORMATION OF GOVERNANCE REGIMES

Governance transformations are typically initiated by private actors responding to changes in markets (e.g., Chandler 1977), technology (e.g., Piore and Sabel 1984), and political or other conditions in their environment. These pressures for change may lead producers or other actors to seek a new governance regime for coordinating economic activity. The development of a new regime involves a complex selection process of trial and error experimentation, formal and informal bargaining and negotiation, and overt struggle and coercion among actors over the shape of a new governance regime. Outcomes of this process depend on the ability of actors to mobilize resources, take advantage of political opportunities, and devise appropriate goals and strategies that break out of existing rules and routines while conforming to the dictates of new environmental factors and existing institutional constraints (e.g., Baumgartner, Burns, and DeVille 1986).[9] The state does not necessarily initiate or lead the transformation process but is often drawn in by other actors or by the imperatives of new political, economic, or technological circumstances.

---

[8] It is not necessary to embrace a pluralist theory of policy-making to recognize there are institutional opportunities (not necessarily equally distributed) for those outside the state to influence the policy process, e.g., by contributing to the creation of contradictory state actions (Friedland, Piven, and Alford 1977).

[9] This characterization of governance transformation parallels that offered by Nelson and Winter (1982) insofar as it recognizes the distinction between pressures for change, on the one hand, and a complex, institutionally constrained selection process, on the other. While they describe an *intra*organizational process of change at the level of the firm, we are concerned with an *inter*organizational process at the level of the economic sector. For a more systematic elaboration of this argument and a discussion of other factors that may generate pressures for change and influence the selection process, see Campbell and Lindberg (forthcoming).

Several clarifications are important. First, in contrast to structural-functional theories of change (e.g., Smelser 1963) we do not suggest that pressures for change always lead to governance transformations. Other factors, including state action, mediate whether change occurs. Second, we do not claim that pressures for change are necessarily exogenous to the governance regime—they may result from intrinsic instabilities within the regime itself. Third, the term "selection process" does not mean that a new governance regime is necessarily well-suited to its environment or that it always relieves the pressures for change. Finally, we do not want to overemphasize the intentions of actors. Although actors may plan the development of some governance mechanisms (e.g., cartels), others may emerge without deliberate foresight (e.g., some markets).

Pressure for Change

The state may deliberately create pressures for governance transformations as an actor by changing, or threatening to change, property rights. For example, to create a market-based governance regime in the commercial nuclear energy sector, Congress passed legislation in 1954 permitting private firms to own nuclear technology and forbidding the federal government from building its own reactors to produce electricity commercially. However, only after Congress threatened two years later to pass new legislation that redefined property rights by mandating the construction of six government-owned commercial plants did utilities seriously consider constructing their own nuclear facilities. This move helped create a market to coordinate further development and dissemination of the technology. In 1957, Congress passed the Price-Anderson Act to further encourage the development of the nuclear energy market by restricting a utility's financial liability in the event of a nuclear accident.

By redefining property rights, the state also fostered a competitive market in the telecommunications sector. AT&T established a monopoly in telephone service during the late nineteenth century, in part because the courts affirmed the company's right to control most of the technology through its hundreds of patents. However, in 1959 the Federal Communications Commission (FCC) ruled that common carriers such as AT&T and other companies should be permitted to use microwave frequencies for communication purposes. The FCC later granted permission to companies such as

Microwave Communications, Inc. (MCI) to connect their microwave systems to AT&T's telephone grid, thus intentionally triggering a dramatic governance transformation whereby a competitive market in long distance service replaced the old AT&T monopoly.

Societal groups may provoke state property rights actions by taking advantage of arenas for public participation in the policy process. Citizen groups and unions worked through Congress and the courts during the 1960s and 1970s to pass and enforce environmental, consumer, and labor legislation regulating the operation of manufacturing facilities and the quality of products (Vogel 1983, 1987). In the automobile sector, manufacturers responded to new strict air quality regulations by establishing in 1967 an Air Pollution Research Advisory Council and an Inter-Industry Emissions Control Program. These were formally organized, collective attempts to develop and cross-license emission control technologies and were a marked departure from the sector's typical form of governance, oligopolistic competition (White 1982). In the nuclear sector, access the policy forums, such as the Atomic Energy Commission, the White House, and the courts, enabled activists outside the state to force the promulgation and enforcement of environmental and other regulations that increased the costs of private radioactive waste management and eventually prevented firms from engaging in this business altogether. As a result, the market for nuclear waste management services collapsed and the federal government assumed responsibility for this activity (Campbell 1988).

The Selection Process

The state may also manipulate property rights as an actor to influence the selection process in several ways. On the one hand, the state often *assists* private actors who are engaged in the selection process. Dairy farmers tried to establish cooperatives and struggled with milk distributors during the 1910s to stabilize milk prices and production levels, but with limited success. One obstacle was that the U.S. Justice Department opposed the formation of dairy cooperatives and collective pricing in the belief that they violated antitrust law. However, under Herbert Hoover's guidance as Commerce Secretary, the Federal Food Administration convinced the Justice Department not to interfere and helped organize price bargaining between the two groups, facilitating the development of a collective governance regime in place of the more market-based system. Similarly, the state offered antitrust exemptions during the 1980s to help major steel producers reorganize governance through mergers and joint ventures to prevent the further erosion of market shares to foreign competitors.

On the other hand, the state may also *lead* the selection process to help a sector cope with pressures for change. The Department of Transportation promoted a Cooperative Automotive Research Program in 1978, a government-industry joint venture designed to improve automobile quality and help the auto industry cope more effectively with foreign competition, which was an important pressure for change during the 1970s (White 1982). Perhaps the most dramatic case of a state-led selection process was in the railroad sector where the federal government created its own rail companies. Amtrak and Conrail, by nationalizing and reorganizing several private railroads in a last-ditch effort to remedy the sector's financial dilemmas and maintain services. In this case, the state's property rights actions shifted control over the means of production from private to public hands and new state-managed corporate hierarchies consolidated previously dispersed firms.

The institutional structure of the state also affects the selection process. Federalism affords subnational governments great leeway in devising property rights and defining distinct locations for economic activity. For example, the Taft-Hartley Act granted state legislatures the right to outlaw union shops, making it extremely difficult for labor to organize in conservative regions not already predominantly unionized, such as southern and western states that often passed right-to-work laws to keep wages low (Newman 1984). In the automobile sector, cheap labor in regions away from Detroit contributed to the development of just-in-time subcontracting in which independent suppliers in the South and West provide parts (just-in-time for assembly) to the large automobile manufacturers. Traditionally, manufacturers had produced these parts within their vertically-integrated firms, but when the sector suffered a profit squeeze during the 1970s and 1980s, subcontracting offered a way to reduce costs.

Similarly, in the steel sector during the 1960s and 1970s lower wages and taxes in the South resulting from differences in state property rights facilitated the establishment of small, independent mini-mills. These new mills created market competition for specialty steel products in a sector that had been dominated by an oligopoly. Movement to the South also helped firms in auto, steel, and meat-packing undermine formally organized, collective governance mechanisms (corporate-union bargaining) and contributed to more market-based mechanisms for establishing wages and benefits. In contrast to cases where state actors help to directly select a specific governance regime, here the state's effect is indirect and *unintentional* because it establishes the range of governance options from which private actors may choose.

One of the most important ways in which the state influences the selection process is through its capacity to ratify or undermine new governance regimes. Ratification occurs when, at the insistence of private or state actors, the government accepts a new regime either by formally approving it or by upholding or supporting resultant transactions. Ratification often involves ruling on property rights. For example, in 1922 Congress passed the Capper-Volstead Act, a property rights action that exempted dairy cooperatives from antitrust prosecution and institutionalized this emergent collective form of governance in the dairy sector.

However, if ratification is not forthcoming, transactions become difficult, the emergent regime is destabilized, and the selection process continues. For instance, scheduling, overcapacity, and other problems plagued the railroad sector during the nineteenth century. Industry leaders created new collective governance mechanisms in the form of associations, pools, and cartels to improve the situation, but these failed as cheating on collective agreements became rampant. Congress tried to support these efforts by passing legislation in 1866 that officially permitted associative behavior among railroads, but these proved to be unenforceable in court because common law held that the agreements were in restraint of trade and therefore illegal (McCraw 1984, p. 49). Although railroads still tried to use these governance mechanisms to solve their problems, they continued to search for more effective ways of rationalizing rail service, specifically through corporate mergers, a governance mechanism that the courts accepted. Hence, railroad pools and associations were *transitional* forms of governance precisely because the state never fully ratified them (e.g., Chandler 1977, Chapter 5).

This example also suggests how the institutional structure of the state influences whether a governance regime is ratified. The U.S. state's organizational configuration as a set of fragmented and decentralized political institutions may undermine the ability of state actors to satisfactorily ratify emergent regimes. In the railroad sector, actors in different parts of the state apparatus, i.e., Congress and the courts, defined and enforced property rights in contradictory ways. As a result, these collective forms of governance were short-lived.

State ratification is conceptually complex because it affects governance transformations in different ways, depending on when it occurs. Although the absence of ratification for an emergent regime prolongs the selection process, if the state withdraws its support from a governance regime it previously supported and that had become firmly institutionalized, this constitutes a new pressure for change. In the telecommunications sector, the Justice Department refused to continue tolerating many of AT&T's monopolistic practices in local service, and, in a deliberate attempt to push the sector in a more market-oriented direction, filed a divestiture suit against the company in 1974. This triggered a search for alternatives—a process that culminated in the break-up of AT&T's local service companies in 1984.

Similarly, at the turn of the century the Attorney General attacked meat-packing pools that were coordinating prices. After the Supreme Court ruled the pools illegal in 1905, a new selection process began in which meat-packers first created a holding company, and then, after two lawsuits challenging the holding company's legitimacy, developed an informal price-leading system. Cattlemen and ranchers used their access to Federal Trade Commission (FTC) officials during the late 1910s to complain about oligopoly pricing and other unfair practices of the big, vertically-integrated meat-packers. In response, the FTC recommended government ownership of the stockyards, distribution outlets, and refrigerator cars. The U.S. Attorney General then sought indictments charging the meat-packers with monopoly and collusion. The meat-packers, believing that changes in their property rights were imminent, quickly agreed to divest their stockyard interests, a compromise that the government accepted. The compromise reduced the amount of vertical integration up-stream, but gave meat-packers control over processing and distribution.

Because ratification often involves the delineation and enforcement of property rights, the courts often play a pivotal role, particularly in the United States where antitrust statutes permit actors to challenge the acceptability of corporate hierarchies and various forms of collective governance. Those who object to a particular form of governance are often the ones who make

these challenges, as in the Justice Department's 1974 attack on AT&T's local service monopoly. However, requests for court ratification also come from dominant actors who benefit from the existing governance regime seeking to use the courts and prevailing property rights as a *defense* against potential governance transformations. In telecommunications, for instance, the Bell system filed hundreds of patent infringement suits during the late nineteenth century against would-be competitors—suits the courts usually upheld, thereby ratifying the corporation's right to monopolize the technology and dominate sectoral governance through a single corporate hierarchy. The construction of this patent wall to preserve its monopoly was a deliberate strategy of the Bell system.[10]

These cases suggest that when the state participates as an actor in the selection of new governance regimes, the resultant regimes may not require formal state ratification. For example, during the search for a commercially viable nuclear energy technology, the state encouraged the formation of several collective research groups that were never challenged and never required formal ratification. Furthermore, few objected formally to the creation of the nationalized railroad companies, Amtrak and Conrail, by the Department of Transportation, although acceptance was probably due as much to the unprofitable nature of these lines as to the state's presence in the selection process. Once Conrail began to generate profits the Reagan administration called for its return to the private sector. In the automobile sector

---

[10] Although North (1981) recognizes the state's pivotal role in the governance process by altering property rights, he fails to acknowledge its role in ratifying new governance regimes. Instead he argues that, in addition to a theory of the state for understanding governance transformations, we need a theory of ideology to account for the willingness of economic actors to abide by the prevailing governance regime—a willingness that he suggests is necessary to stabilize economic activity and avoid chaos in which every transaction is subject to legal challenge and dispute.

However, it is often through the courts that the *state* provides this ideological guidance and stability. The law is often an expression of a society's politically dominant ideology (Hurst 1982; Miliband 1969, pp. 138–45) and it is the courts' job to determine whether a governance regime is ideologically palatable. If the courts find it acceptable, then ratification probably occurs and the regime remains intact, as in the Bell patent cases. If not, regime stability is jeopardized, as when meat-packers were unable to sustain their pooling agreements. Other parts of the state apparatus such as regulatory agencies also provide ideological judgment. In these other institutional locations, however, approval is often much more subtle and politics more important.

the state promoted the Cooperative Automotive Research Program to help coordinate research and development efforts. Once established, no one challenged the sanctity of this government industry venture.

When private actors select new governance regimes without the state's active participation, demands for ratification are more common. In contrast to state-sponsored collective governance in the nuclear and automobile sectors, actors challenged privately organized collective forms of governance, such as railroad pools, cartels, and associations, automobile research organizations (White 1982, p. 437), and meat-packing pools, holding companies, and oligopolies, in court and elsewhere, forcing the state to determine the acceptability of each governance regime. In the steel sector, Chicago-area fabricators convinced the Federal Trade Commission to force steel producers to modify their oligopolistic pricing systems in 1924 and again in 1938 (Markusen 1985, p. 82). When independent telephone companies formed an association to compete with the Bell system in the early 1900s, federal and state authorities ruled the organization violated antitrust laws. The state's presence as an actor in the initial selection of a new governance regime lends a certain legitimacy and, therefore, stability to it.

DISCUSSION

The central concern of this paper has been to show how the state transforms and permanently shapes the organization of the economy through property rights actions. Much of the literature in this area has focused on how the imperatives of economic efficiency (Chandler 1977; Williamson 1985), technological change (Piore and Sabel 1984), profit cycles (Markusen 1985), and other largely *society-centered* conditions create pressures for change. Our analysis suggests that governance transformations may also stem directly from shifts in property rights and from variations in property rights across the institutional terrain of the state. Although we do not reject society-centered arguments, we find clear evidence that governance transformations may also occur for *political* reasons as much as for economic and technological reasons (e.g., Hamilton and Biggart 1988; Lazerson 1988; North 1981; Weiss 1988).

We also suggest several ways in which previous arguments about the state's influence may be improved. Although we agree with North (1981) and others that property rights actions generate pressures for change,

we do not agree that this *necessarily* occurs because the state creates inefficient property rights and high transaction costs or economic stagnation that private actors try to correct by creating new economic institutions. State actors may manipulate property rights in ways that create pressures for change that have nothing to do with transaction-cost or other sorts of economic inefficiencies. For instance, the market for commercial nuclear plants emerged not because utility companies felt it was a more efficient way to organize the production and exchange of nuclear technology, but because impending changes in property rights policies caused utility companies to fear a new source of competition, the federal government. Private actors responded out of a concern with the deliberate exercise of state power, not because of economic inefficiencies or sluggish economic performance. This case also emphasizes that property rights define the institutional basis of power relations in production, exchange, and accumulation, rather than just the relationship of actors to property. The ability to manipulate property rights affords the state important leverage over the balance of power among actors in the economy.

The state also influences the selection process through property rights actions in several ways: as an actor who assists or leads the selection process, as a political-institutional structure that constrains and establishes the range of available governance options, and as an actor who ratifies (or not) emergent governance regimes. Little if any attention has been paid to the many ways in which the state influences the selection process because scholars have not made the conceptual distinction between how the state generates pressures for change and how it influences the selection process. Furthermore, scholars have generally recognized how the state influences governance as an actor (e.g., Hamilton and Biggart 1988; Lazerson 1988; North 1981; Weiss 1988), but not as an institutional structure. This is particularly ironic in North's case, because although he explicitly argues that a complete theory of governance transformation must include a theory of the state, he does not recognize the important role of the state's institutional structure for such a theory—a role others have developed in detail (e.g., Friedland, Piven, and Alford 1977; Katzenstein 1978; Skocpol 1985).

Much of the literature on state economy relations in advanced capitalism argues that the U.S. state is relatively weak because it lacks many capacities for influencing economic activity through the allocation of critical resources. France is often described as a much stronger state because it can allocate finance capital directly to firms and sectors through state-owned credit institutions. States such as the United States that rely heavily on regulatory rather than allocative policy are comparatively weak (e.g., Hamilton and Biggart 1988, pp. 87–8; Samuels 1987, p. 17; Zysman 1983, Chapter 2). However, if state strength is measured by its capacity to trigger and influence institutional transformations in the economy (Krasner 1978b, Chapter 3), the U.S. state derives great strength from its ability to define and enforce property rights through regulatory decisions. For example, FCC decisions to permit independent companies to link their microwave systems to AT&T's telephone grids redefined property rights and fostered a more competitive telecommunications industry. Regulatory and legislative decisions sanctioning dairy cooperatives in the late 1910s and early 1920s aided the development of collective forms of governance in this sector.

In advanced capitalism, all states can define, enforce, and otherwise manipulate property rights. Thus, we do not claim that the U.S. state is stronger *in comparison to other states* than scholars have recognized previously. However, scholars have underestimated the U.S. state's potential strength in *absolute* terms—strength derived from regulatory and other property rights actions. To focus on the degree to which state actors can allocate the flow and direction of important resources is to offer a rather lop-sided analysis of the state's capacity to influence economic activity and affect governance transformations. In short, there is a much wider range of capacities for state strength than the literature commonly acknowledges, particularly with respect to the United States (Ikenberry 1988, p. 203–8).[11]

State strength is also dependent on the organization of actors in society (e.g., Hall 1986; Katzenstein 1978; Krasner 1978b; Samuels 1987; Stepan 1978, p. 84). For example, state actors tend to have greater success in forming and implementing their economic policies if dominant class interests in society are organizationally fragmented (Rueschemeyer and Evans 1985; Samuels 1987). While the state alone does not determine the organizational capacities of private actors, how government officials manipulate property rights, such as through antitrust and labor law, may facilitate or inhibit the collective organization of business and other groups, and, in turn, affect the degree to which state actors influence the subsequent governance transformation process. In the meat-packing industry, for instance, antitrust actions undermined pools and other collective forms of organization that big packers used to coordinate their activity during the early 1900s. Later, when the federal government tried to impose beef-grading schemes and enforce a degree of vertical divestiture, these companies tried to resist and failed because they lacked an effective means of inter-firm coordination. Thus, there are reciprocal influences between the state and the organization of groups in society (Hall 1986, pp. 266–68). This reciprocity influences state strength and is determined in part by the state's ability to establish and enforce property rights.

Through property rights actions, the U.S. state often fostered the development of large corporations and other powerful private organizations that eventually dominated the governance of major economic sectors (Horwitz 1977; Hurst 1960, 1977, 1982; Keller 1981). These organizations occasionally blocked later efforts by the state to transform governance regimes. For instance, selective enforcement of antitrust laws contributed to the formation of large corporate hierarchies in the steel sector early in the twentieth century. Labor legislation in the 1930s contributed to the increased strength of the United Steel Workers' union. When the Carter administration tried to create corporatist bargaining arrangements among these corporations and organized labor in the 1970s to control costs and compete more effectively against foreign companies, the corporations and the union were unified and powerful enough to defeat the Carter proposal for a more collectively organized governance regime. Ironically, the outcome of state strength may in the long run create a potential for state weakness.[12]

---

[11] We are interested here in how different types of policy tools determine state strength. Some scholars argue that the key to state strength is the ability of state actors to make autonomous policy decisions free of the influence of societal groups. In their view, strength increases as state actors develop centralized administrative bureaucracies insulated from the demands of lower levels of government and outside groups and staffed with people sharing a common esprit de corps (e.g., Hall 1986; Katzenstein 1978; Rueschemeyer and Evans 1985). On these dimensions, the U.S. state often appears rather weak (Katzenstein 1978; Krasner 1978a). We maintain that both policy tools and state structure determine state strength.

---

[12] For further criticisms of the literature about strong and weak states, see Atkinson and Coleman (1989), Samuels (1987, Chapter 7), Skocpol (1985), and Wilks and Wright (1987). None addresses property rights as a source of potential state strength.

We have been silent on the causes of state action because we lack the necessary data for a systematic discussion of this issue. However, we offer a few tentative ideas about the causes of state actions that have influenced governance transformations in the United States. The U.S. state promoted the development of collective governance mechanisms, such as associations, in many economic sectors during World War I (Cuff 1973) and the New Deal years (Hawley 1966). Similarly, the federal government became more lenient in its antitrust efforts in the steel sector and permitted cross-licensing and cooperative research programs in the automobile sector when these industries suffered serious declines in the 1970s and 1980s. Thus, it seems that during periods of war or economic crisis the state tends to favor collective governance.

On the other hand, the courts at federal and state levels have usually undermined these efforts (Solo 1974). For instance, courts have typically overturned the attempts of pools, cartels, and trade associations to assume extensive coordinating roles because judges ruled these forms of governance violated antitrust laws or even the constitution (e.g., the Supreme Court's ruling on the National Recovery Administration). These collective forms of governance have also collapsed because courts were unwilling to enforce what they considered illegal contracts (e.g., railroad associations during the late nineteenth century). While economic and geopolitical conditions may influence the *probability* of changes in property rights to facilitate governance transformations, legal and political decisions will determine the *specific outcomes* of struggles over property rights. Whether these decisions are based on the interests of autonomous state actors, classes, or other social groups is an open question.

CONCLUSION

Social scientists have offered a variety of metaphors to capture the relationship between state and economy. Block (1987, pp. 21–2) argues that rather than thinking about the state and the economy as potentially autonomous, it is more fruitful to think of them as permanently connected by a *membrane* that permits their constant interaction. Granovetter (1985) argues that to fully understand economic activity, including its institutional forms, we must examine how that activity is *embedded* in other social relations and institutions. If their empirical content is carefully specified, these metaphors can be very useful in understanding how the state shapes the economy on a continuing basis.

Property rights are an important dimension of both the membrane connecting the state with the economy and the politically defined and enforced social relations within which economic activity is embedded. At a time of great interest in reorganizing U.S. economic institutions to improve economic performance, the importance of understanding how governance regimes change and how the state's property rights actions affect this process could not be greater.

REFERENCES

Atkinson, Michael, and William Coleman. 1989. "Strong States and Weak States: Sectoral Policy Networks in Advanced Capitalist Economies." *British Journal of Political Science* 19:47–67.

Badaracco, Joseph L. 1985. *Loading the Dice: A Five Country Study of Vinyl Chloride Regulation.* Boston: Harvard Business School Press.

Baumgartner, Thomas, Tom Burns, and Philippe DeVille. 1986. *The Shaping of Socio-Economic Systems.* New York: Gordon and Breach.

Bensel, Richard. 1984. *Sectionalism and American Political Development, 1880–1980.* Madison: University of Wisconsin Press.

Bernstein, Marver. 1977. *Regulating Business by Independent Commission.* Westport, CT: Greenwood Press.

Block, Fred. 1986. "Political Choice and the Multiple 'Logics' of Capital." *Theory and Society* 15:175–92.

———. 1987. *Revising State Theory: Essays in Politics and Postindustrialism.* Philadelphia: Temple University Press.

Bluestone, Barry and Bennett Harrison. 1982. *The Deindustrialization of America.* New York: Basic Books.

Bowles, Roger. 1984. "Property and the Legal System." Pp. 187–208 in *What is Political Economy?*, edited by David K. Whynes. New York: Basil Blackwell.

Campbell, John L. 1988. *Collapse of an Industry: Nuclear Power and the Contradictions of U.S. Policy.* Ithaca, NY: Cornell University Press.

Campbell, John L., J. Rogers Hollingsworth, and Leon N. Lindberg. Forthcoming. *Governance of the American Economy.* New York: Cambridge University Press.

Campbell, John L. and Leon N. Lindberg. Forthcoming. "The Evolution of Governance Regimes." In *Governance of the American Economy*, edited by John L. Campbell, J. Rogers Hollingsworth, and Leon N. Lindberg. New York: Cambridge University Press.

Caporaso, James A. 1989. "Property and the Legal System." Pp. 135–60 in *Global Changes and Theoretical Challenges*, edited by Ernst-Otto Czempiel and James A. Roseman. Lexington, MA: Lexington Books.

Cawson, Alan. 1985. "Conclusion: Some Implications for State Theory." Pp. 221–26 in *Organized Interests and the State: Studies in Meso-Corporatism*, edited by Alan Cawson. Beverly Hills, CA: Sage.

Chandler, Alfred D. 1977. *The Visible Hand: The Managerial Revolution in American Business*. Cambridge, MA: Harvard University Press.

Cox, Andrew. 1986. *The State, Finance and Industry*. New York: St. Martin's Press.

Cuff, Robert D. 1973. *The War Industries Board: Business-Government Relations During World War I*. Baltimore: Johns Hopkins Press.

Domhoff, G. William. 1987. "The Wagner Act and Theories of the State: A New Analysis Based on Class-Segment Theory." Pp. 159–85 in *Political Power and Social Theory*, Vol. 6, edited by Maurice Zeitlin. Greenwich, CT: JA1 Press.

Downs, Anthony. 1967. *Inside Bureaucracy*. Boston: Little, Brown, and Company.

Edmonds, Martin. 1983. "Market Ideology and Corporate Power: The United States." Pp. 67–101 in *Industrial Crisis: A Comparative Study of the State and Industry*, edited by Kenneth Dyson and Stephen Wilks. Oxford: Martin Robertson.

Eisinger, Peter. 1988. *The Rise of the Entrepreneurial State*. Madison: University of Wisconsin Press.

Evans, Peter B., Dietrich Rueschemeyer, and Theda Skocpol. 1985. *Bringing The State Back In*. New York: Cambridge University Press.

Friedland, Roger, Frances Fox Piven, and Robert Alford. 1977. "Political Conflict, Urban Structure, and Fiscal Crisis." *International Journal of Urban and Regional Research* 1:447–71.

Galambos, Louis and Joseph Pratt. 1988. *The Rise of the Corporate Commonwealth: U.S. Business and Public Policy in the Twentieth Century*. New York: Basic Books.

Goodman, Robert. 1979. *The Last Entrepreneurs: America's Regional Wars for Jobs and Dollars*. Boston: South End Press.

Gourevitch, Peter. 1986. *Politics in Hard Times: Comparative Responses to International Economic Crises*. Ithaca, NY: Cornell University Press.

Granovetter, Mark. 1985. "Economic Action and Social Structure: The Problem of Embeddedness." *American Journal of Sociology* 91:481–510.

Hall, Peter. 1986. *Governing the Economy: The Politics of State Intervention in Britain and France*. New York: Oxford University Press.

Hamilton, Gary and Nicole Biggart. 1988. "Market, Culture, and Authority: A Comparative Analysis of Management and Organization in the Far East." *American Journal of Sociology* 94:S52–S94.

Hawley, Ellis W. 1966. *The New Deal and the Problem of Monopoly*. Princeton, NJ: Princeton University Press.

Hodgson, Geoffrey M. 1988. *Economics and Institutions: A Manifesto for a Modern Institutional Economics*. Philadelphia: University of Pennsylvania Press.

Horwitz, Morton. 1977. *The Transformation of American Law, 1780–1860*. Cambridge, MA: Harvard University Press.

Hughes, Jonathan R. T. 1977. *The Governmental Habit: Economic Controls from Colonial Times to the Present*. New York: Basic Books.

Hurst, James Willard. 1960. *Law and the Conditions of Freedom in the 19th Century United States*. Madison: University of Wisconsin Press.

———. 1977. *Law and Social Order in the United States*. Ithaca, NY: Cornell University Press.

———. 1982. *Law and Markets in United States History*. Madison: University of Wisconsin Press.

Ikenberry, G. John. 1988. *Reasons of State: Oil Politics and the Capacities of American Government*. Ithaca, NY: Cornell University Press.

Katzenstein, Peter J. 1978. "Conclusion: Domestic Structures and Strategies of Foreign Economic Policy." Pp. 295–336 in *Between Power and Plenty: Foreign Economic Policies of Advanced Industrial States*, edited by Peter J. Katzenstein. Madison: University of Wisconsin Press.

Keller, Morton. 1981. "The Pluralist State: American Economic Regulation in Comparative Perspective." Pp. 56–94 in *Regulation in Perspective: Historical Essays*, edited by Thomas McCraw. Cambridge, MA: Harvard University Press.

Krasner, Stephen D. 1978a. "United States Commercial and Monetary Policy: Unraveling the Paradox of External Strength and Internal Weakness." Pp. 51–88 in *Between Power and Plenty: Foreign Economic Policies of Advanced Industrial States*, edited by Peter J. Katzenstein. Madison: University of Wisconsin Press.

———. 1978b. *Defending the National Interest: Raw Materials Investments and U.S. Foreign Policy*. Princeton, NJ: Princeton University Press.

Lazerson, Mark. 1988. "Small Firm Growth: An Outcome of Markets and Hierarchies." *American Sociological Review* 53:330–42.

Lazonick, William. 1986. "Organizations, Markets, and Productivity." Paper presented at the Economic History Association meetings, Hartford, CT.

Lindberg, Leon N., John L. Campbell, and J. Rogers Hollingsworth. Forthcoming. "Economic Governance and the Analysis of Structural Change in the American Economy." In *Governance of the American Economy*, edited by John L. Campbell, J. Rogers Hollingsworth, and Leon N. Lindberg. New York: Cambridge University Press.

Markusen, Ann. 1985. *Profit Cycles, Oligopoly, and Regional Development.* Cambridge, MA: Massachusetts Institute of Technology Press.

———. 1987. *Regions: The Economics and Politics of Territory.* Totowa, NJ: Rowman and Littlefield.

McCraw, Thomas K. 1984. *Prophets of Regulation.* Cambridge, MA: Harvard University Press.

Miliband, Ralph. 1969. *The State in Capitalist Society.* New York: Basic Books.

Nelson, Richard R. and Sidney G. Winter. 1982. *An Evolutionary Theory of Economic Change.* Cambridge, MA: Harvard University Press.

Newman, Robert J. 1984. *Growth in the American South: Changing Regional Employment and Wage Patterns in the 1960s and 1970s.* New York: New York University Press.

North, Douglass. 1981. *Structure and Change in Economic History.* New York: W. W. Norton.

O'Connor, James. 1973. *The Fiscal Crisis of the State.* New York: St. Martin's Press.

Offe, Claus and Volker Ronge. 1975. "Theses on the Theory of the State." *New German Critique* 6:139–47.

Peltzman, Sam. 1976. "Toward a More General Theory of Regulation." *Journal of Law and Economics* 19:211–40.

Piore, Michael and Charles Sabel. 1984. *The Second Industrial Divide.* New York: Basic Books.

Polanyi, Karl. 1944. *The Great Transformation: The Political and Economic Origins of Our Time.* Boston: Beacon Press.

Posner, Richard A. 1974. "Theories of Economic Regulation." *Bell Journal of Economics and Management Science* 5:337–52.

Robbins, James. 1987. "Organizational Economics: Notes on the Use of Transaction-Cost Theory in the Study of Organizations." *Administrative Science Quarterly* 32:68–86.

Rueschemeyer, Dietrich, and Peter Evans. 1985. "The State and Economic Transformation: Toward an Analysis of the Conditions Underlying Effective Intervention." Pp. 44–77 in *Bringing the State Back In*, edited by Peter Evans, Dietrich Rueschemeyer, and Theda Skocpol. New York: Cambridge University Press.

Sabatier, Paul. 1975. "Social Movements and Regulatory Agencies: Toward a More Adequate—and Less Pessimistic—Theory of 'Clientele Capture'." *Policy Sciences* 6:301–42.

Samuels, Richard J. 1987. *The Business of the Japanese State.* Ithaca, NY: Cornell University Press.

Sanders, Elizabeth. 1986. "Industrial Concentration, Sectional Competition, and Anti-trust Politics in America, 1880–1980." *Studies in American Political Development* 1:142–214.

Scheiber, Harry N. 1978. "American Federalism and the Diffusion of Power: Historical and Contemporary Perspectives." *University of Toledo Law Review* 9:619–80.

———. 1980a. "Federalism and Legal Process: Historical and Contemporary Analysis of the American System." *Law and Society Review* 14:663–722.

———. 1980b. "Public Economic Policy and the American Legal System: Historical Perspectives." *Wisconsin Law Review* 1980:1159–89.

———. 1981. "Regulation, Property Rights, and Definition of 'the Market': Law and the American Economy." *The Journal of Economic History* 41:103–9.

Shapiro, Martin. 1986. "The Supreme Court's 'Return' to Economic Regulation." *Studies in American Political Development* 1:91–141.

Shonfield, Andrew. 1965. *Modern Capitalism: The Changing Balance of Public and Private Power.* New York: Oxford University Press.

Skocpol, Theda. 1985. "Bringing the State Back In: Strategies of Analysis in Current Research." Pp. 3–37 in *Bringing the State Back In*, edited by Peter Evans, Dietrich Rueschemeyer, and Theda Skocpol. New York: Cambridge University Press.

Skowronek, Stephen. 1982. *Building a New American State: The Expansion of National Administrative Capacities. 1877–1920.* New York: Cambridge University Press.

Smelser, Neil J. 1963. *Theory of Collective Behavior.* New York: The Free Press.

Solo, Robert. 1974. *The Political Authority and the Market System.* Cincinnati, Ohio: South-Western Publishing Company.

Stepan, Alfred. 1978. *The State and Society: Peru in Comparative Perspective.* Princeton, NJ: Princeton University Press.

Stigler, George J. 1975. *The Citizen and the State: Essays on Regulation.* Chicago: University of Chicago Press.

Thomson, Janice E. and Stephen D. Krasner, 1989. "Global Transactions and the Consolidation of Sovereignty." Pp. 161–76 in *Global Changes and Theoretical Challenges*, edited by Ernst-Otto Czempiel and James A. Roseman. Lexington, MA: Lexington Books.

Thurow, Lester. 1984. "Building a World Class Economy." *Society* 22(1)16–28.

Vogel, David. 1983. "The Power of Business in America: A Re-appraisal." *British Journal of Political Science* 13:19–43.

———. 1987. "Government-Industry Relations in the United States: An Overview." Pp. 91–116 in *Comparative Government-Industry Relations: Western Europe, the United States, and Japan*, edited by Stephen Wilks and Maurice Wright. New York: Oxford University Press.

Walker, David. 1981. *Toward a Functioning Federalism.* Cambridge, MA: Winthrop.

Walsh, Annmarie Hauk. 1978. *The Public's Business: The Politics and Practices of Government Corporations.* Cambridge, MA: Massachusetts Institute of Technology Press.

Weiss, Linda. 1988. *Creating Capitalism: The State and Small Business Since 1945.* New York: Basil Blackwell.

White, Lawrence. 1982. "The Motor Vehicle Industry." Pp. 411–50 in *Government and Technical Progress: A Cross-Industry Analysis*, edited by Richard Nelson. New York: Pergamon Press.

Wilks, Stephen, and Maurice Wright. 1987. "Conclusion: Comparing Government-Industry Relations: States, Sectors, and Networks." Pp. 274–314 in *Comparative Government-Industry Relations: Western Europe, the United States, and Japan*, edited by Stephen Wilks and Maurice Wright. New York: Oxford University Press.

Williamson, Oliver. 1975. *Markets and Hierarchies: Analysis and Antitrust Implications.* New York: The Free Press.

———. 1985. *The Economic Institutions of Capitalism: Firms, Markets, Relational Contracting.* New York: The Free Press.

Zysman, John. 1983. *Governments, Markets, and Growth.* Ithaca, NY: Cornell University Press.

CHAPTER 3

INSTITUTIONS, ACTORS, AND IDEAS

Social scientists during the nineteenth and early twentieth centuries recognized that politics was shaped in important ways by the structure of political parties, government bureaucracies, and other formal political organizations, as well as by norms and values regarding the purpose of citizenship, government, and civic duty (Weber, 1978). Yet this institutionalist perspective was gradually overshadowed after World War II by theories that focused more on how interest groups, economic elites, and social classes influenced the course of politics. Until the 1970s, society-centered emphases were typical for pluralists and Marxists alike (see the readings in Chapter 2). More recently, however, scholars have reexamined the ways in which politics is influenced by institutions—understood both as organizations and as normative frameworks. State-centered theorists have shifted attention toward analysis of the institutional frameworks within which politics occurs (March & Olsen, 1989).

Society-centered theorists did not always neglect political institutions. During the 1950s, the pioneering pluralist theorist David Truman argued that groups in society constitute the driving force of politics. Depending on their organizational capacities, leadership, and opportunities for gaining access to important political arenas in the government, interest groups secure various concessions and benefits from policymakers. Yet given the proliferation of these competing groups, Truman wondered why their demands did not completely overwhelm policymakers and undermine the effectiveness of government (see also Brittain, 1975; Crozier, Huntington, & Watanuki, 1975; Rose & Peters, 1978). He reasoned that this was due partly to the fact that members of most interest groups value moderation, fairness, and at least a certain amount of equality. They temper their demands accordingly. Furthermore, Truman argued, if citizens discover that government grants consistently greater benefits to one interest group over others, they press their political leaders to correct the situation. In short, Truman argued that American politics proceeds according to certain institutionalized "rules of the game."

More recent efforts to show how politics is institutionally embedded focus less on political values and more on institutional relationships, or "political structures." For example, when Theda Skocpol argues that social scientists should "bring the state back in" to the study of politics and social change, she focuses primarily on institutional patterns. She argues that the ability of state actors to formulate and implement policy depends on the presence of a loyal and skilled administrative staff, the availability of financial and military resources, bureaucratic insulation from the demands of interest groups and social classes, and other institutional conditions—all of which she labels "state capacities." Such capacities, Skocpol argues, vary across nations, across time, and across policy areas within nations. Skocpol further suggests that the institutional structure of the state influences the representation of political interests and patterns of political protest and conflict. Institutions influence the goals and organizational capacities of the social groups that get involved in politics. Indeed, the working class in the United States historically has been unable to organize and sustain a significant political party on the national level, in part because early voting rights for all white males, along with the decentralized structure of U.S. government, encouraged the growth of local political machines that undercut the possibilities for a national working-class party (Katznelson, 1985). Skocpol points to historical-institutionalist arguments of this kind as an example of the new insights we can gain about American politics and beyond by bringing the state back in as a set of institutions interacting with major social groups.

One reason why political institutions receded into the background for a while was that many social scientists, heavily influenced by the underlying behavioral assumptions of neoclassical economics, came to view all political behavior as motivated by rational self-interest. For instance, most Marxists believed that the political actions of capitalists and workers were based on the interests of both groups to maximize their material interests (Cohen & Rogers, 1983; Carnoy, 1984). Similarly, pluralists held that most political groups were organized around the relatively narrow interests of their members. In political science, this "rational choice" perspective has recently blossomed through the development of public choice theory. Some scholars view rational choice approaches as an alternative to all previous theoretical perspectives, while others believe that institutional and rational choice approaches can be fruitfully combined (as, for example, in Stewart & Weingast, 1992).

According to James Buchanan, a Nobel laureate in economics, public choice theory follows traditional economics in assuming that individuals are concerned primarily with fulfilling their personal interests. The society-centered or demand-side version of this theory suggests that individuals in society pursue their interests through voting and other means to secure the material benefits they want from government. As such, the public receives various benefits on demand from government. The state-centered or supply-side version holds that politicians, government bureaucrats, and other state actors who supply benefits to citizens seek to maximize their own interests. They try to secure the most votes, power, and perks, and the largest budgets. In either case, the end result is the same: government grows and becomes bloated by offering more goods, services, and other "rents" to citizens in exchange for their support, and citizens tend to waste more resources trying to get these things from government. In short, self-interested behavior leads to inefficient and wasteful political activity. As a result, Buchanan and other public choice theorists imply that we need to reduce government activity, often by constraining the behavior of state actors by institutional means.

Rational choice theories of politics have come under increasing attack by those who believe that political action is motivated as much by symbolic and altruistic desires as by self-interest (Mansbridge, 1990; March & Olsen, 1989; Thomas Meyer, Ramierz & Boli, 1987). Paul Quirk provides one such challenge, asserting that politicians often set aside personal interests in favor of what they believe to be the public good. He illustrates his argument by focusing on regulatory policy-making in the U.S. Congress. Rather than succumbing to powerful interest group pressure of seeking reelection through the provision of narrow favors to specific industries, as public choice theory might predict, Congress deregulated the airline, trucking, and telecommunication industries in order to pursue the broader goals of fighting inflation, reducing intrusive government regulation, and breaking up powerful industrial monopolies. The reasons for this were complex. Some people in Congress believed that this was what most voters preferred. Others maintained that this was simply the right thing to do and constituted good public policy. Furthermore, Quirk concludes, key congressional leaders believed that it was their responsibility to rise above special interest pressures and serve the general public interest by pressing for this kind of legislation. Quirk's general point is that political actors can be motivated not just by narrow self-interest, but also by broader public concerns. His critique of rational choice assumptions is one that cuts across the debates among pluralists, Marxists, and institutionalists about whether political action is driven by society-centered or state-centered forces.

REFERENCES

Brittain, Samuel. 1975. "The Economic Contradictions of Democracy." *British Journal of Political Science* 5(2): 129–59.

Carnoy, Martin. 1984. *The State and Political Theory*. Princeton, N.J.: Princeton University Press.

Cohen, Joshua, and Joel Rogers. 1983. *On Democracy*. New York: Penguin.

Crozier, Michel, Samuel Huntington, and Joji Watanuki. 1975. *The Crisis of Democracy*. New York: New York University Press.

Katznelson, Ira. 1985. "Working Class Formation and the State: Nineteenth-Century England in American Perspective." In *Bringing the State Back In*, edited by Peter Evans, Dietrich Rueschemeyer, and Theda Skocpol, 257–84. New York: Cambridge University Press.

Mansbridge, Jane J. 1990. *Beyond Self-Interest*. Chicago: University of Chicago Press.

March, James G., and Johan P. Olsen. 1989. *Rediscovering Institutions: The Organizational Basis of Politics*. New York: Free Press.

Rose, Richard, and Guy Peters. 1978. *Can Government Go Bankrupt?* New York: Basic Books.

Stewart, Charles III, and Barry R. Weingast. 1992. "Stacking the Senate, Changing the Nation: Republican Rotten Boroughs, Statehood Politics, and American Political Development." *Studies in American Political Development* 6 (Fall): 223–71.

Thomas, George M., John W. Meyer, Francisco O. Ramierz, and John Boli. 1987. *Institutional Structure: Constituting State, Society and the Individual*. Beverly Hills, Calif.: Sage Publications.

Weber, Max. 1978. *Economy and Society*. Berkeley, Calif.: University of California Press.

BRINGING THE STATE BACK IN: STRATEGIES OF ANALYSIS IN CURRENT RESEARCH

Theda Skocpol

A sudden upsurge of interest in "the state" has occurred in comparative social science in the past decade. Whether as an object of investigation or as something invoked to explain outcomes of interest, the state as an actor or an institution has been highlighted in an extraordinary outpouring of studies by scholars of diverse theoretical proclivities from all of the major disciplines. The range of topics explored has been very wide. Students of Latin America, Africa, and Asia have examined the roles of states in instituting comprehensive political reforms, helping to shape national economic development, and bargaining with multinational corporations.[1] Scholars interested in the advanced industrial democracies of Europe, North America, and Japan have probed the involvements of states in developing social programs and in managing domestic and international economic problems.[2] Comparative-historical investigators have examined the formation of national states, the disintegration and rebuilding of states in social revolutions, and the impact of states on class formation, ethnic relations, women's rights, and modes of social protest.[3] Economic historians and political economists have theorized about states as institutors of property rights and as regulators and distorters of markets.[4] And cultural anthropologists have explored the special meanings and activities of "states" in non-Western settings.[5]

No explicitly shared research agenda or general theory has tied such diverse studies together. Yet I shall argue in this essay that many of them have implicitly converged on complementary arguments and strategies of analysis. The best way to make the point is through an exploration of the issues addressed in a range of comparative and historical studies—studies that have considered states as weighty actors and probed how states affect political and social processes through their

From Peter Evans, Dietrich Rueschemeyer, and Theda Skocpol, editors, *Bringing the State Back In* (New York: Cambridge University Press, 1985), 3–37. Reprinted with the permission of the publishers.

policies and their patterned relationships with social groups. First, however, it makes sense to underline the paradigmatic reorientation implied by the phrase "bringing the state back in."[6]

From Society-Centered Theories to a Renewed Interest in States

There can be no gainsaying that an intellectual sea change is under way, because not long ago the dominant theories and research agendas of the social sciences rarely spoke of states. This was true even—or perhaps one should say especially—when politics and public policy making were at issue. Despite important exceptions, society-centered ways of explaining politics and governmental activities were especially characteristic of the pluralist and structure–functionalist perspectives predominant in political science and sociology in the United States during the 1950s and 1960s.[7] In these perspectives, the state was considered to be an old-fashioned concept, associated with dry and dusty legal-formalist studies of nationally particular constitutional principles. Alternative concepts were thought to be more compatible with scientific, generalizing investigations.[8] "Government" was viewed primarily as an arena within which economic interest groups or normative social movements contended or allied with one another to shape the making of public policy decisions. Those decisions were understood to be *allocations* of benefits among demanding groups. Research centered on the societal "inputs" to government and on the distributive effects of governmental "outputs." Government itself was not taken very seriously as an independent actor, and in comparative research, variations in governmental organizations were deemed less significant than the general "functions" shared by the political systems of all societies.

As often happens in intellectual life, the pluralist and structure–functionalist paradigms fostered inquiries that led toward new concerns with phenomena they had originally de-emphasized conceptually. When pluralists focused on the determinants of particular public policy decisions, they often found that governmental leaders took initiatives well beyond the demands of social groups or electorates; or they found that government agencies were the most prominent participants in the making of particular policy decisions. Within pluralist theoretical premises, there were but limited ways to accommodate such findings.[9] In the classic pluralist studies of New Haven politics, Mayor Richard Lee's strong individual initiatives for urban renewal were extensively documented but not grounded in any overall state-centered analysis of the potential for certain kinds of mayors to make new uses of federal funding.[10] In major works about "bureaucratic politics" such as Graham Allison's *Essence of Decision* and Morton Halperin's *Bureaucratic Politics and Foreign Policy*, government agencies were treated individually, as if they were pure analogues of the competing societal interest groups of classical pluralism.[11] The structure and activities of the U.S. state as a whole receded from view and analysis in this approach.[12]

Like the pluralists, yet on a broader canvas, when structure–functionalist students of comparative political development set out to "apply" their grand theories to Western European history or to particular sets of non-Western polities, they often found poor fits between historical patterns and sequences and those posited by the original concepts and assumptions. "Political development" (itself found to be an overly evolutionist conception) ended up having more to do with concrete international and domestic struggles over state building than with any inherent general logic of socioeconomic "differentiation." Most telling in this regard were the historically oriented studies encouraged or sponsored by the Social Science Research Council's Committee on Comparative Politics toward the end of its life span of 1954–72.[13] In many ways, the ideas and findings about states to be reviewed here grew out of reactions set in motion by such confrontations of the committee's grand theories with case-study and comparative-historical evidence.

Especially among younger scholars, new ideas and findings have also arisen from an alternative theoretical lineage. From the mid-1960s onward, critically minded "neo-Marxists" launched a lively series of debates about "the capitalist state." By now, there are conceptually ramified and empirically wide-ranging literatures dealing especially with the roles of states in the transition from feudalism to capitalism, with the socioeconomic involvements of states in advanced industrial capitalist democracies, and with the nature and roles of states in dependent countries within the world capitalist economy.[14] Neo-Marxists have, above all, debated alternative understandings of the socioeconomic functions performed by the capitalist state. Some see it as an instrument of class rule, others as an objective guarantor of production relations or economic accumulation, and still others as an arena for political class struggles.

Valuable concepts and questions have emerged from these neo-Marxist debates, and many of the compara-tive and historical studies to be discussed here have drawn on them in defining researchable problems and hypotheses. Yet at the theoretical level, virtually all neo-Marxist writers on the state have retained deeply embedded society-centered assumptions, not allowing themselves to doubt that, at base, states are inherently shaped by classes or class struggles and function to preserve and expand modes of production.[15] Many possible forms of autonomous state action are thus ruled out by definitional fiat. Furthermore, neo-Marxist theorists have too often sought to generalize—often in extremely abstract ways—about features of functions shared by *all* states within a mode of production, a phase of capitalist accumulation, or a position in the world capitalist system. This makes it difficult to assign causal weight to variations in state structures and activities across nations and short time periods, thereby undercutting the usefulness of some neo-Marxist schemes for comparative research.[16]

So far the discussion has referred primarily to paradigms in American social science in the period since World War II; yet the reluctance of pluralists and structure–functionalists to speak of states, and the unwillingness even of critically minded neo-Marxists to grant true autonomy to states, resonate with proclivities present from the start in the modern social sciences. These sciences emerged along with the industrial and democratic revolutions of Western Europe in the eighteenth and nineteenth centuries. Their founding theorists quite understandably perceived the locus of societal dynamics—and of the social good—not in outmoded, superseded monarchical and aristocratic states, but in civil society, variously understood as "the market," "the industrial division of labor," or "class relations." Founding theorists as politically opposed as Herbert Spencer and Karl Marx (who now, not entirely inappropriately, lie just across a lane from one another in Highgate Cemetery, London) agreed that industrial capitalism was triumphing over the militarism and territorial rivalries of states. For both of these theorists, nineteenth-century British socioeconomic developments presaged the future for all countries and for the world as a whole.

As world history moved—via bloody world wars, colonial conquests, state-building revolutions, and nationalist anticolonial movements—from the Pax Britannica of the nineteenth century to the Pax Americana of the post–World War II period, the Western social sciences managed to keep their eyes largely averted from the explanatory centrality of states as potent and autonomous organizational actors.[17] It was not that such phenomena as political authoritarianism and totalitarianism were ignored, just that the preferred theoretical explanations were couched in terms of economic backwardness or the unfortunate persistence of non-Western "traditional" values. As long as capitalist and liberal Britain, and then capitalist and liberal America, could plausibly be seen as the unchallengeable "lead societies," the Western social sciences could manage the feat of downplaying the explanatory centrality of states in their major theoretical paradigms—for these paradigms were riveted on understanding modernization, its causes and direction. And in Britain and America, the "most modern" countries, economic change seemed spontaneous and progressive, and the decisions of governmental legislative bodies appeared to be the basic stuff of politics.

As the period after World War II unfolded, various changes rendered society-centered views of social change and politics less credible. In the wake of the "Keynesian revolution" of the 1930s to the 1950s national macroeconomic management became the norm and public social expenditures burgeoned across all of the advanced industrial capitalist democracies, even in the United States. The dismantlement of colonial empires gave birth to dozens of "new nations," which before long revealed that they would not simply recapitulate Western liberal democratic patterns in their political organization or policy choices. Finally, and perhaps most importantly, by the mid-1970s, both Britain and the United States were unmistakably becoming hard-pressed in a world of more intense and uncertain international economic competition. It is probably not surprising that, at this juncture, it became fashionable to speak of states as actors and as society-shaping institutional structures.

Social scientists are now willing to offer state-centered explanations, not just of totalitarian countries and late industrializers, but of Britain and the United States themselves. Fittingly, some recent arguments stress ways in which state structures have distinctively shaped economic development and international economic policies in Britain and America and also ponder how the British and U.S. states might fetter or facilitate current efforts at national industrial regeneration.[18] In short, now that debates about large public sectors have taken political center stage in all of the capitalist democracies and now that Britain and the United States seem much more like particular state–societies in an uncertain, competitive, and interdependent world of many such entities, a paradigmatic shift seems to be under way in the macroscopic social sciences, a shift that involves a fundamental rethinking of the role of states in relation to economies and societies.

The Revival of a Continental European Perspective?

In the nineteenth century, social theorists oriented to the realities of social change and politics on the European continent refused (even after industrialization was fully under way) to accept the de-emphasis of the state characteristic of those who centered their thinking on Britain. Even though they might positively value liberal ideals, Continental students of social life, especially Germans, insisted on the institutional reality of the state and its continuing impact on and within civil society. Now that comparative social scientists are again emphasizing the importance of states, it is perhaps not surprising that many researchers are relying anew—with various modifications and extensions, to be sure—on the basic understanding of "the state" passed down to contemporary scholarship through the widely known writings of such major German scholars as Max Weber and Otto Hintze.

Max Weber argued that states are compulsory associations claiming control over territories and the people within them.[19] Administrative, legal, extractive, and coercive organizations are the core of any state. These organizations are variably structured in different countries, and they may be embedded in some sort of constitutional–representative system of parliamentary decision making and electoral contests for key executive and legislative posts. Nevertheless, as Alfred Stepan nicely puts it in a formulation that captures the biting edge of the Weberian perspective:

> The state must be considered as more than the "government." It is the continuous administrative, legal, bureaucratic and coercive systems that attempt not only to structure relationships *between* civil society and public authority in a polity but also to structure many crucial relationships within civil society as well.[20]

In this perspective, the state certainly does not become everything. Other organizations and agents also pattern social relationships and politics, and the analyst must explore the state's structure and activities in relation to them. But this Weberian view of the state does require us to see it as much more than a mere arena in which social groups make demands and engage in political struggles or compromises.

What is more, as the work of Otto Hintze demonstrated, thinking of states as organizations controlling territories leads us away from basic features common to all polities and toward consideration of the various ways in which state structures and actions are conditioned by historically changing transnational contexts.[21] These contexts impinge on individual states through geopolitical relations of interstate domination and competition, through the international communication of ideals and models of public policy, and through world economic patterns of trade, division of productive activities, investment flows, and international finance. States necessarily stand at the intersections between domestic sociopolitical orders and the transnational relations within which they must maneuver for survival and advantage in relation to other states. The modern state as we know it, and as Weber and Hintze conceptualized it, has always been, since its birth in European history, part of a system of competing and mutually involved states.

Although a refocusing of social scientific interests significantly informed by the Weber–Hintze understanding of states may be upon us, the real work of theoretical reorientation is only beginning to be done. This work is understandably fraught with difficulties, because attempts are being made to think about and investigate state impacts against a background of deeply rooted theoretical proclivities that are stubbornly society-centered. Recent attempts by neo-Marxists and (what might be called) neopluralists to theorize in very general terms about "state autonomy" have not offered concepts or explanatory hypotheses rich enough to encompass the arguments and findings from various comparative-historical studies.[22]

Rather than dwell on the shortcomings of such general theories, however, the remainder of this essay will be devoted to an exploration of what some selected historical and comparative studies have to tell us about states in societal and transnational contexts. Two somewhat different, but equally important tendencies in current scholarship will claim our attention. We shall examine arguments about *state autonomy* and about the *capacities of states* as actors trying to realize policy goals. We shall explore arguments about the *impacts of states on the content and workings of politics.* The overall aim of this exercise is not to offer any new general theory of the state or of states and social structures. For the present, at least, no such thing may be desirable, and it would not in any event be feasible in the space of one essay. Rather, my hope is to present and illustrate a conceptual frame of reference, along with some middle-range issues and hypotheses that might inform future research on states and social structures across diverse topical problems and geocultural areas world.

THE AUTONOMY AND CAPACITY OF STATES

States conceived as organizations claiming control over territories and people may formulate and pursue goals that are not simply reflective of the demands or interests of social groups, classes, or society. This is what is usually meant by "state autonomy." Unless such independent goal formulation occurs, there is little need to talk about states as important actors. Pursuing matters further, one may then explore the "capacities" of states to implement official goals, especially over the actual or potential opposition of powerful social groups or in the face of recalcitrant socioeconomic circumstances. What are the determinants of state autonomy and state capacities? Let us sample the arguments of a range of recent studies that address these questions.

States as Actors

Several lines of reasoning have been used, singly or in combination, to account for why and how states formulate and pursue their own goals. The linkage of states into transnational structures and into international flows of communication may encourage leading state officials to pursue transformative strategies even in the face of indifference or resistance from politically weighty social forces. Similarly, the basic need of states to maintain control and order may spur state-initiated reforms (as well as simple repression). As for who, exactly, is more likely to act in such circumstances, it seems that organizationally coherent collectivities of state officials, especially collectivities of career officials relatively insulated from ties to currently dominant socioeconomic interests, are likely to launch distinctive new state strategies in times of crisis. Likewise, collectivities of officials may elaborate already established public policies in distinctive ways, acting relatively continuously over long stretches of time.

The extranational orientations of states, the c' lenges they may face in maintaining domestic and the organizational resources that collecti state officials may be able to draw on and de of these features of the state as viewe Weberian–Hintzean perspective can help autonomous state action. In an especially combinations of these factors figure in A llen Kay Trimberger's explanations of what be considered extreme instances of autonomous action—historical situations in which strategic es use military force to take control of an entire tional state and then employ bureaucratic means to enforce reformist or revolutionary changes from above.

Stepan's book *The State and Society: Peru in Comparative Perspective* investigates attempts by state elites in Latin America to install "inclusionary" or "exclusionary" corporatist regimes.[23] A key element in Stepan's explanation of such episodes is the formation of a strategically located cadre of officials enjoying great organizational strength inside and through existing state organizations and also enjoying a unified sense of ideological purpose about the possibility and desirability of using state intervention to ensure political order and promote national economic development. For Brazil's "exclusionary" corporatist coup in 1964 and for Peru's "inclusionary" corporatist coup in 1968, Stepan stresses the prior socialization of what he calls "new military professionals." These were career military officers who, together, passed through training schools that taught techniques and ideas of national economic planning and counterinsurgency, along with more traditional military skills. Subsequently, such new military professionals installed corporatist regimes in response to perceived crises of political order and of national economic development. The military professionals used state power to stave off or deflect threats to national order from nondominant classes and groups. They also used state power to implement socioeconomic reforms or plans for further national industrialization, something they saw as a basic requisite for improved international standing in the modern world.

Ellen Kay Trimberger's *Revolution from Above* focuses on a set of historical cases—Japan's Meiji restoration, Turkey's Ataturk revolution, Egypt's Nasser revolution, and Peru's 1968 coup—in which "dynamically autonomous" bureaucrats, including military officials, seized and reorganized state power. Then they used the state to destroy an existing dominant class, a landed upper class or aristocracy, and to reorient national economic development.[24] Like Stepan, Trimberger stresses the formation through prior career terests and socialization of a coherent official elite h a statist and nationalist ideological orientation. also agrees with Stepan's emphasis on the elite's rn to contain any possible upheavals from below. haps because she is in fact explaining a more thoroughly transformative version of autonomous state action to reshape society, Trimberger places more stress than Stepan on the role of foreign threats to national autonomy as a precipitant of "revolution from above." And she highlights a structural variable that Stepan ignored: the relationship of the state elite to dominant economic classes. As Trimberger puts it, "A bureaucratic state apparatus, or a segment of it, can be said to be relatively autonomous when those who hold high civil and/or military posts satisfy two conditions: (1) they are not recruited from the dominant landed, commercial, or industrial classes; and (2) they do not form close personal and economic ties with those classes after their elevation to high office."[25] Trimberger also examines the state elite's relationship to dominant economic classes in order to predict the extensiveness of socioeconomic changes a state may attempt in response to "a crisis situation—when the existing social, political, and economic order is threatened by external forces and by upheaval from below."[26] State-initiated authoritarian *reforms* may occur when bureaucratic elites retain ties to existing dominant classes, as, for example, in Prussia in 1806–1814, Russia in the 1860s, and Brazil after 1964. But the more sweeping structural changes that Trimberger labels "revolution from above," including the actual dispossession of a dominant class, occur in crisis situations only when bureaucratic state elites are free of ties or alliances with dominant classes.[27] As should be apparent, Trimberger has given the neo-Marxist notion of the relative autonomy of the state new analytical power as a tool for predicting the possible sociopolitical consequences of *various* societal and historical configurations of state and class power.[28]

State Autonomy in Constitutional Polities

Stepan and Trimberger deal in somewhat different, though overlapping, terms with extraordinary instances of state autonomy—instances in which nonconstitutionally ruling officials attempt to use the state as a whole to direct and restructure society and politics. Meanwhile, other scholars have teased out more circumscribed instances of state autonomy in the histories of public policy making in liberal democratic, constitutional polities, such as Britain, Sweden, and the United States.[29] In different forms, the same basic analytical factors—the international orientations of states, their domestic order-keeping functions, and the organizational possibilities for official collectivities to formulate and pursue their own policies—also enter into these analyses.

Hugh Heclo's *Modern Social Politics in Britain and Sweden* provides an intricate comparative-historical account of the long-term development of unemployment insurance and policies of old-age assistance in these two nations.[30] Without being explicitly presented as such, Heclo's book is about autonomous state contributions to social policy making. But the autonomous state actions Heclo highlights are not all acts of coercion or domination; they are, instead, the intellectual activities of civil administrators engaged in diagnosing societal problems and framing policy alternatives to deal with them. As Heclo puts it:

> Governments not only "power" (or whatever the verb form of that approach might be); they also puzzle. Policy-making is a form of collective puzzlement on society's behalf; it entails both deciding and knowing. The process of making pension, unemployment, and superannuation policies has extended beyond deciding what "wants" to accommodate, to include problems of knowing who might want something, what is wanted, what should be wanted, and how to turn even the most sweet-tempered general agreement into concrete collective action. This process is political, not because all policy is a by-product of power and conflict but because some men have undertaken to act in the name of others.[31]

According to Heclo's comparative history, civil service administrators in both Britain and Sweden have consistently made more important contributions to social policy development than political parties or interest groups. Socioeconomic conditions, especially crises, have stimulated only sporadic demands from parties and interest groups, argues Heclo. It has been civil servants, drawing on "administrative resources of information, analysis, and expertise" who have framed the terms of new policy elaborations as "corrective[s] less to social conditions as such and more to the perceived failings of previous policy" in terms of "the government bureaucracy's own conception of what it has been doing."[32] Heclo's evidence also reveals that the autonomous bureaucratic shaping of social policy has been greater in Sweden than in Britain, for Sweden's premodern centralized bureaucratic state was, from the start of industrialization and before the full liberalization and democratization of national politics, in a position to take the initiative in diagnosing social problems and proposing universalistic solutions for administering to them.

Heclo says much less than he might about the influences shaping the timing and content of distinctive state initiatives. He does, however, present evidence of the sensitivity of civil administrators to the requisites of maintaining order in the face of dislocations caused by industrial unemployment. He also points to the constant awareness by administrators of foreign precedents and models of social policy. Above all, Heclo demonstrates that collectivities of administrative officials can have pervasive direct and indirect effects on the content and development of major government policies. His work suggests how to locate and analyze autonomous state contributions to policy making, even within constitutional polities nominally directed by legislatures and electoral parties.

Along these lines, it is worth looking briefly at two works that argue for autonomous state contributions to public policy making even in the United States, a polity in which virtually all scholars agree that there is less structural basis for such autonomy than in any other modern liberal capitalist regime. The United States did *not* inherit a centralized bureaucratic state from preindustrial and predemocratic times. Moreover, the dispersion of authority through the federal system, the division of sovereignty among branches of the national government, and the close symbiosis between segments of the federal administration and Congressional committees all help to ensure that state power in the twentieth-century United States is fragmented, dispersed, and everywhere permeated by organized societal interests. The national government, moreover, lacks such possible underpinnings of strong state power as a prestigious and status-conscious career civil service with predictable access to key executive posts; authoritative planning agencies; direct executive control over a national central bank; and public ownership of strategic parts of the economy. Given such characteristics of the U.S. government, the concept of state autonomy has not often been used by scholars to explain American policy developments.

Nevertheless, Stephen Krasner in his *Defending the National Interest* does use the concept to explain twentieth-century continuities in the formulation of U.S. foreign policy about issues of international investments in the production and marketing of raw materials.[33] A clever heuristic tactic lies behind Krasner's selection of this "issue area" for systematic historical investigation: It is an issue area located at the intersection of properly geopolitical state interests and the economic interests of (often) powerful private corporations. Thus, Krasner can ask whether the short-term push and pull of business interests shapes the definition of the U.S. "national interest" with respect to raw materials production abroad or whether an autonomous state interest is consistently at work. He finds the latter pattern and attributes it to actors in a special location within the otherwise weak, fragmented, and societally permeated U.S. government:

> For U.S. foreign policy the central state actors are the President and the Secretary of State and the most important institutions are the White House and the State Department. What distinguishes these roles and agencies is their high degree of insulation from specific societal pressures and a set of formal and informal obligations that charge them with furthering the nation's general interests.[34]

Unfortunately, Krasner does not expand on the concept of "insulated" parts of the state. In particular, he does not tell us whether various organizational features of state agencies make for greater or lesser insulation. Instead, Krasner primarily emphasizes the degree to which different parts of the federal executive are subject to Congressional influences.[35] And he cannot fully dispel the suspicion that the Presidency and the State Department may simply be subject to class-based rather than interest-based business influences.[36] Nevertheless, he does show that public policies on raw materials have been most likely to diverge from powerful corporate demands precisely when distinctively geopolitical issues of foreign military intervention and broad ideological conceptions of U.S. world hegemony have been involved. Thus, Krasner's study suggests that distinctive statelike contributions to U.S. policy making occur exactly in those instances and arenas where a Weberian–Hintzean perspective would insist that they should occur, no matter how unpropitious the overall governmental potential for autonomous state action. As J. P. Nettl once put it, "Whatever the state may or may not be internally, . . . there have . . . been few challenges to its sovereignty *and* its autonomy in 'foreign affairs.'"[37]

My own work with Kenneth Finegold on the origins of New Deal agricultural policies also suggests that autonomous state contributions to domestic policy making can occur within a "weak state." Such autonomous state contributions happen in specific policy areas at given historical moments, even if they are not generally discernible across all policy areas and even if they unintentionally help to create political forces that subsequently severely circumscribe further auton-

omous state action.[38] Finegold and I argue that, by the period after World War I, the U.S. Department of Agriculture was "an island of state strength in an ocean of weakness."[39] We attribute the formulation of New Deal agricultural interventions—policies that responded to a long-standing "agrarian crisis" but *not* simply in ways directly demanded by powerful farm interest groups—to the unique resources of administrative capacity, prior public planning, and practical governmental experience available to federal agricultural experts at the dawn of the New Deal. Our argument resembles Hugh Heclo's findings about innovative civil officials in Britain and Sweden. Essentially, we found a *part* of the early-twentieth-century U.S. national government that allowed official expertise to function in a restricted policy area in ways that were similar to the ways it functioned in Sweden, or in Britain between 1900 and 1920.

In addition, however, we trace the political fate of the New Deal's administrative interventions in agriculture. We show that, in the overall context of the U.S. state structure, this initially autonomous state intervention inadvertently strengthened a particular lobbying group, the American Farm Bureau Federation, and gave it the final increments of electoral and administrative leverage that it needed to "capture" preponderant influence over post-1936 federal agricultural policies. Subsequent state planning efforts, especially those that implied redistribution of economic, racial, or social-class power, were then circumscribed and destroyed by the established commercial farming interests championed by the Farm Bureau.

In short, "state autonomy" is not a fixed structural feature of any governmental system. It can come and go. This is true not only because crises may precipitate the formulation of official strategies and policies by elites or administrators who otherwise might not mobilize their own potentials for autonomous action. It is also true because the very *structural potentials* for autonomous state actions change over time, as the organizations of coercion and administration undergo transformations, both internally and in their relations to societal groups and to representative parts of government. Thus, although cross-national research can indicate in general terms whether a governmental system has "stronger" or "weaker" tendencies toward autonomous state action, the full potential of this concept can be realized only in truly historical studies that are sensitive to structural variations and conjunctural changes within given polities.

Are State Actions "Rational"?

An additional set of comments must be made about the rationality of autonomous state actions. Often such actions are considered more capable of addressing "the capitalist *class* interest" or "society's general interests" or "the national interest" than are governmental decisions strongly influenced by the push and pull of demands from interest groups, voting blocs, or particular business enterprises.[40] In such perspectives, state officials are judged to be especially capable of formulating holistic and long-term strategies transcending partial, short-sighted demands from profit-seeking capitalists or narrowly self-interested social groups. But scholars skeptical about the notion of state autonomy often respond that state officials' own self-legitimating arguments, their claims to know and represent "general" or "national" interests, should not be taken at face value. State officials have no privileged claims to adequate knowledge of societal problems or solutions for them, argue the skeptics. Besides, their legitimating symbols may merely mask policies formulated to help particular interests or class fractions.

Surely such doubts about the superior rationality of state actions deserve respectful attention; yet we need not entirely dismiss the possibility that partially or fully autonomous state actions *may* be able to address problems and even find "solutions" beyond the reach of societal actors and those parts of government closely constrained by them. Partly, the realization of such possibilities will depend on the availability and (even more problematically) the appropriate use of sound ideas about what the state can and should do to address societal problems. Partly, it will depend on the fit (or lack thereof) between the *scope* of an autonomous state organization's authority and the scale and depth of action appropriate for addressing a given kind of problem. Planning for coordinated systems of national transportation, for example, is unlikely to be achieved by state agencies with authority only over particular regions or kinds of transportation, no matter how knowledgeable and capable of autonomous official action those agencies may be. In sum, autonomous official initiatives can be stupid or misdirected, and autonomous initiatives may be fragmented and partial and work at cross-purposes to one another. Notwithstanding all of these possibilities, however, state actions may sometimes be coherent and appropriate.

Still, no matter how appropriate (for dealing with a given kind of crisis or problem) autonomous state activity might be, it can never really be "disinterested" in any meaningful sense. This is true not only because all state actions necessarily benefit some social interests and disadvantage others (even without the social beneficiaries' having worked for or caused the state actions). More to the point, autonomous state actions will regularly take forms that attempt to reinforce the authority, political longevity, and social control of the state organizations whose incumbents generated the relevant policies or policy ideas. We can hypothesize that one (hidden or overt) feature of all autonomous state actions will be the reinforcement of the prerogatives of collectivities of state officials. Whether rational policies result may depend on how "rational" is defined and might even be largely accidental. The point is that policies different from those demanded by societal actors will be produced. The most basic research task for those interested in state autonomy surely is to explore why, when, and how such distinctive policies are fashioned by states. Then it will be possible to wonder about their rationality for dealing with the problems they address—and we will be able to explore this issue without making starry-eyed assumptions about the omniscience or disinterestedness of states.

Can States Achieve Their Goals?

Some comparative-historical scholars not only have investigated the underpinnings of autonomous state actions, but have also tackled the still more challenging task of explaining the various *capacities* of states to implement their policies. Of course, the explanation of state capacities is closely connected to the explanation of autonomous goal formation by states, because state officials are most likely to try to do things that seem feasible with the means at hand. Nevertheless, not infrequently, states do pursue goals (whether their own or those pressed on them by powerful social groups) that are beyond their reach. Moreover, the implementation of state policies often leads to unintended as well as intended consequences, both when states attempt tasks they cannot complete and when the means they use produce unforeseen structural changes and sociopolitical reactions. Thus, the capacities of states to implement strategies and policies deserve close analysis in their own right. Here, I will not attempt any comprehensive survey of substantive findings in this important area of research. Instead, I shall simply indicate some promising ideas and approaches embodied in current investigations of state capacities.

A few basic things can be said about the general underpinnings of state capacities. Obviously, sheer sovereign integrity and the stable administrative–military control of a given territory are preconditions for any state's ability to implement policies.[41] Beyond this, loyal and skilled officials and plentiful financial resources are basic to state effectiveness in attaining all sorts of goals. It is not surprising that histories of state building zero in on exactly these universal sinews of state power.[42] Certain of these resources come to be rooted in institutional relationships that are slow to change and relatively impervious to short-term manipulations. For example, do state offices attract and retain career-oriented incumbents with a wide array of skills and keen motivation? The answer may well depend on historically evolved relationships among elite educational institutions, state organizations, and private enterprises that compete with the state for educated personnel. The best situation for the state may be a regular flow of elite university graduates, including many with sophisticated technical training, into official careers that are of such high status as to keep the most ambitious and successful from moving on to nonstate positions. But if this situation has not been historically established by the start of the industrial era, it is difficult to undo alternative patterns less favorable to the state.[43]

Factors determining a state's financial resources may be somewhat more manipulable over time, though not always. The amounts and forms of revenues and credit available to a state grow out of structurally conditioned, yet historically shifting political balances and bargains among states and between a state and social classes. Basic sets of facts to sort out in any study of state capacities involve the sources and amounts of state revenues and the degree of flexibility possible in their collection and deployment. Domestic institutional arrangements and international situations set difficult to change limits within which state elites must maneuver to extract taxes and obtain credit: Does a state depend on export taxes (for example, from a scarce national resource or from products vulnerable to sudden world market fluctuations)?[44] Does a nonhegemonic state's geopolitical position allow it to reap the state-building benefits of military aid, or must it rely on international bankers or aid agencies that insist on favoring nonpublic investments and restrict the domestic political options of the borrower state?[45] What established authority does a state have to collect taxes, to borrow, or to invest in potentially profitable public enterprises? And how much "room" is there in the existing constitu-

tional–political system to change patterns of revenue collection unfavorable to the state?

Finally, what authority and organizational means does a state have to deploy whatever financial resources it does enjoy? Are particular kinds of revenues rigidly "earmarked" for special uses that cannot easily be altered by official decision makers?[46] Can the state channel (and manipulate) flows of credit to particular enterprises and industrial sectors, or do established constitutional–political practices favor only aggregate categorical expenditures? All of these *sorts* of questions must be asked in any study of state capacities. The answers to them, taken together, provide the best general insight into the direct and indirect leverage a state is likely to have for realizing any goal it may pursue. A state's means of raising and deploying financial resources tell us more than could any other single factor about its existing (and immediately potential) capacities to create or strengthen state organizations, to employ personnel, to coopt political support, to subsidize economic enterprises, and to fund social programs.[47]

State Capacities to Pursue Specific Kinds of Policies

Basic questions about a state's territorial integrity, financial means, and staffing may be the place to start in any investigation of its capacities to realize goals; yet the most fruitful studies of state capacities tend to focus on particular policy areas. As Stephan Krasner puts it:

> There is no reason to assume *a priori* that the pattern of strengths and weaknesses will be the same for all policies. One state may be unable to alter the structure of its medical system but be able to construct an efficient transportation network, while another can deal relatively easily with getting its citizens around but cannot get their illnesses cured.[48]

Those who study a comprehensive state-propelled strategy for change, such as a "revolution from above" or a major episode of bureaucratically sponsored reforms, may need to assess the overall capacity of a state to realize transformative goals across multiple spheres. Moreover, as Krasner points out, it may be useful to establish that "despite variations among issue areas within countries, there are modal differences in the power of the state among [for example] the advanced market-economy countries."[49] Nevertheless, such overall assessments are perhaps best built up from sectorally specific investigations, for one of the most important facts about the power of a state may be its *unevenness* across policy areas. And the most telling result, even of a far-reaching revolution or reform from above, may be the *disparate* transformations produced across sociopolitical sectors.

Thus, in a provocative article, "Constitutionalism, Class and the Limits of Choice in U.S. Foreign Policy," Ira Katznelson and Kenneth Prewitt show how U.S. policies toward Latin America have been partly conditioned by the uneven capacities of the American national government: strongly able to intervene abroad, yet lacking the domestic planning capacities necessary "to direct the internal distribution of costs entailed by a less imperialist foreign policy."[50] To give another example, Alfred Stepan draws many of his most interesting conclusions about the contradictory and unintended results of Peru's episode of "inclusionary corporatism" from a careful analysis of the regime's uneven successes in restructuring the political involvements of various social groups and redirecting the course of economic development in various sectors.[51]

Many studies of the capacities of states to realize particular kinds of goals use the concept of "policy instrument" to refer to the relevant means that a state may have at its disposal.[52] Cross-national comparisons are necessary to determine the nature and range of institutional mechanisms that state officials may conceivably be able to bring to bear on a given set of issues. For example, Susan and Norman Fainstein compare the urban policies of northwest European nations with those of the United States. Accordingly, they are able to conclude that the U.S. national state lacks certain instruments for dealing with urban crises that are available to European states, instruments such as central planning agencies, state-controlled pools of investment capital, and directly administered national welfare programs.[53]

Analogously, Peter Katzenstein brings together a set of related studies of how six advanced industrial-capitalist countries manage the international trade, investment, and monetary involvements of their economies.[54] Katzenstein is able to draw fairly clear distinctions between the strategies open to states such as the Japanese and the French, which have policy instruments that enable them to apply policies at the level of particular industrial sectors, and other states, such as the British and U.S., which must rely on aggregate macroeconomic manipulations of fiscal and monetary parameters. Once again, as in the Fainstein study, it is the juxtaposition of different nations' approaches to a given policy area that allows relevant policy instru-

ments to be highlighted. Neither study, however, treats such "instruments" as deliberate short-term creations of state managers. Both studies move out toward macroscopic explorations of the broad institutional patterns of divergent national histories that explain why countries now have, or do not have, policy instruments for dealing with particular problems or crises.

States in Relation to Socioeconomic Settings

Fully specified studies of state capacities not only entail examinations of the resources and instruments that states may have for dealing with particular problems; they also necessarily look at more than states as such. They examine states *in relation* to particular kinds of socioeconomic and political environments populated by actors with given interests and resources. One obvious use of a relational perspective is to investigate the power of states over domestic or transnational nonstate actors and structures, especially economically dominant ones. What capacities do states have to change the behavior or oppose the demands of such actors or to transform recalcitrant structures? Answers lie not only in features of states themselves, but also in the balances of states' resources and situational advantages compared with those of nonstate actors. This sort of relational approach is used by Stephen Krasner in his exploration of the efforts of U.S. policy makers to implement foreign raw materials policy in interactions with large corporations, whose preferences and established practices have frequently run counter to the state's definition of the national interest.[55]

This is also the sort of approach used by Alfred Stepan to analyze the successes and failures of Peruvian military leaders in using state power to change the patterns of foreign capital investments in their dependent country.[56] Stepan does a brilliant job of developing a consistent set of causal hypotheses to explain the diverse outcomes across industrial sectors: sugar, oil and manufacturing. For each sector, he examines regime characteristics: degree of commitment to clear policy goals, technical capacities, monitoring abilities, state-controlled investment resources, and the state's international position. He also examines the characteristics of existing investments and markets as they impinge on the advantages that either Peru or foreign multinational corporations might hope to attain from any further investments. The entire argument is too complex to reproduce here, but its significance extends well beyond the foreign investment issue area and the Peruvian case. By taking a self-consciously relational approach to the balances of resources that states and multinational corporations may bring to bear in their partially symbiotic and partially conflictual dealings with one another, Stepan has provided an important model for further studies of state capacities in many policy areas.

Another, slightly different relational approach to the study of state capacities appears in Peter Katzenstein's *Between Power and Plenty*, where (as indicated earlier) the object of explanation is ultimately not state *power over* nonstate actors, but nations' strategies for managing "interdependence" within the world capitalist economy. One notion centrally invoked in the Katzenstein collection is that of a "policy network" embodying a patterned relationship between state and society. In Katzenstein's words:

> The actors in society and state influencing the definition of foreign economic policy objectives consist of the major interest groups and political action groups. The former represent the relations of production (including industry, finance, commerce, labor, and agriculture); the latter derive from the structure of political authority (primarily the state bureaucracy and political parties). The governing coalitions . . . in each of the advanced industrial states find their institutional expression in distinct policy networks which link the public and the private sector in the implementation of foreign policy.[57]

Katzenstein argues that the definition and implementation of foreign economic policies grow out of the nexus of state and society. Both state goals and the interests of powerful classes may influence national policy orientations. And the implementation of policies is shaped not only by the policy instruments available to the state, but also by the organized support it receives from key societal groups.

Thus, policy objectives such as industrial reorganization might be effectively implemented because a central state administration controls credit and can intervene in industrial sectors. Yet it may be of equal importance that industries are organized into disciplined associations willing to cooperate with state officials. A complete analysis, in short, requires examination of the organization and interests of the state, specification of the organization and interests of socioeconomic groups, and inquiries into the complementary as well as conflicting relationships of state and societal actors. This is the sort of approach consistently used by the contributors to *Power and Plenty* to explain the foreign economic objectives of the United States, Britain,

Germany, Italy, France, and Japan. The approach is also used to analyze the capacities of these nations' policy networks to implement existing, or conceivable alternative, economic strategies.

The relational approaches of Stepan's *State and Society* and Katzenstein's *Power and Plenty* drive home with special clarity some important points about all current research on states as actors and structures. Bringing the state back in to a central place in analyses of policy making and social change does require a break with some of the most encompassing social-determinist assumptions of pluralism, structure–functionalist developmentalism, and the various neo-Marxisms. But it does not mean that old theoretical emphases should simply be turned on their heads: Studies of states alone are not to be substituted for concerns with classes or groups; nor are purely state-determinist arguments to be fashioned in the place of society-centered explanations. The need to analyze states in relation to socioeconomic and sociocultural contexts is convincingly demonstrated in the best current research on state capacities. And we are about to examine yet another cluster of studies in which a fully relational approach to states and societies is even more essential.

STATES AND PATTERNS OF POLITICS

The previous section focused on the state as a set of organizations through which collectivities of officials may be able to formulate and implement distinctive strategies or policies. When the state comes up in current social scientific discourse, non-Marxists, at least, are usually referring to it in this sense: as an *actor* whose independent efforts may need to be taken more seriously than heretofore in accounting for policy making and social change. But there is another way to think about the sociopolitical impact of the state, an alternative frame of reference not often articulated but perhaps even more important than the view of the state as an actor. This second approach might be called "Tocquevillian," because Alexis de Tocqueville applied it masterfully in his studies *The Old Regime and the French Revolution* and *Democracy in America*.[58] In this perspective, states matter not simply because of the goal-oriented activities of state officials. They matter because their organizational configurations, along with their overall patterns of activity, affect political culture, encourage some kinds of group formation and collective political actions (but not others), and make possible the raising of certain political issues (but not others).

To be sure, the "strengths" or "weaknesses" of states as sites of more or less independent and effective official actions constitute a key aspect of the organizational configurations and overall patterns of activity at issue in this perspective. This second approach is entirely complementary to the ideas we explored in the previous section, but here the investigator's modus operandi is not the same. When the effects of states are explored from the Tocquevillian point of view, those effects are *not* traced by dissecting state strategies or policies and their possibilities for implementation. Instead, the investigator looks more macroscopically at the ways in which the structures and activities of states unintentionally influence the formation of groups and the political capacities, ideas, and demands of various sectors of society. Thus, much of Tocqueville's argument about the origins of the French Revolution dealt with the ways in which the French absolutist monarchy, through its institutional structure and policy practices, unintentionally undermined the prestige and political capacities of the aristocracy, provoked the peasantry and the urban Third Estate, and inspired the intelligentsia to launch abstract, rationalist broadsides against the status quo. Effects of the state permeated Tocqueville's argument, even though he said little about the activities and goals of the state officials themselves.

Comparative Studies of State Structures and Politics in Industrial-Capitalist Democracies

A good way to demonstrate the contemporary fruitfulness of such macroscopic explorations of the sociopolitical effects of states is to sketch some of the findings of comparative-historical scholars who have focused on differences among and within Western advanced industrial-capitalist nations. Analogous effects have been, or could be, found among other sets of countries—for example, among peripheral or "newly industrializing" capitalist nations or among the "state-socialist" countries—but the analytically relevant points would be similar. Thus, I shall confine myself to comparisons among the United States and some European nations, drawing on a number of works to sketch ideas about how the structure and activities of states affect political culture, group formation and collective political action, and the issue agendas of politics.

In a highly unusual and path-breaking essay for its decade, "The State as a Conceptual Variable," J. P. Nettl

delineated a series of institutional and cultural differences in the "stateness" of the United States, Britain, and the continental European nations.[59] Some of his most telling contrasts referred to dimensions of political culture, that is, widely held ideas about the nature and locus of political power and notions about what can be attained in politics and how. In their essay entitled "Constitutionalism, Class, and the Limits of Choice in U.S. Foreign Policy," Ira Katznelson and Kenneth Prewitt apply and extend some of these ideas from Nettl.

Owing to the different historical paths their governmental systems have traversed, argued Nettl, continental Europeans think of "sovereignty" as residing in centralized administrative institutions; Britons focus on political parties in Parliament; and U.S. citizens refuse to designate any concrete body as sovereign, but instead attribute sovereignty to the law and the Constitution. In Europe, according to Nettl, the administrative order is instantly recognizable as an area of autonomous action, and both supporters and opponents of the existing order orient themselves to working through it as the agent of the public good. But in the United States, as Katznelson and Prewitt nicely spell out:

> The Constitution does not establish . . . [an administratively centralized] state that in turn manages the affairs of society toward some clear conception of the public welfare; rather, it established a political economy in which the public welfare is the aggregate of private preferences. . . . The United States is a government of legislation and litigation. . . . Politics becomes the struggle to translate social and economic interests into law. . . . *The political culture defines political power as getting a law passed.*
>
> Dissatisfaction most frequently takes the form of trying to force a new and more favorable interpretation of the Constitution. . . . Never in this endless shuffling does the Constitution itself become the target. Rather, constitutional principles legitimate claims for a fair share of "the American way of life," and constitutional interpretations and reinterpretations are the means for forcing reallocations.[60]

In short, various sorts of states not only conduct decision-making, coercive, and adjudicative activities in different ways, but also give rise to various conceptions of the meaning and methods of "politics" itself, conceptions that influence the behavior of all groups and classes in national societies.

The forms of collective action through which groups make political demands or through which political leaders seek to mobilize support are also partially shaped in relation to the structures and activities of states. This point has been richly established for Western countries by scholars dealing with causes and forms of social protest, with "corporatism" as governmentally institutionalized interest consultation, and with political parties as mediators between electorates and the conduct of state power.

Charles Tilly and his collaborators have investigated changing forms of violent and nonviolent collective protest in France and elsewhere in the West since the seventeenth century. In the process, they have pointed to many ways in which state structures, as well as the actions of state officials, affect the timing, the goals, and the forms of collective protest. Inexorable connections between war making and state making in early modern Europe meant, according to Tilly, that most "collective contention" in those days entailed attempts, especially by regional elites and local communities, to defend established rights against royal tax collectors and military recruiters.[61] Later, nationwide networks of middle- and working-class people in industrializing Britain created the innovative protest forms of the associational "social movement" through interactions with the parliamentary, legal, and selectively repressive practices of the British state.[62] Variations on social-movement "repertoires" of collective action, always adapted to the structures and practices of given states, also spread across many other modern nations. Many additional examples of state effects on collective action could be given from Tilly's work. For many years, he has been a powerful proponent of bringing the state back in to the analysis of social protest, an area of political sociology that was previously dominated by social systems and social psychological approaches.[63]

If studies of collective action are a perennial staple in sociology, studies of interest groups have a comparable standing in political science. Recently, as Suzanne Berger points out, students of Western European countries have ceased to view "interest groups as reflections of society." Instead, they find that "the timing and characteristics of state intervention" affect "not only organizational tactics and strategies," but "the content and definition of interest itself," with the result that each European nation, according to the historical sequence and forms of the state's social and economic interventions, has a distinctive configuration of interests active in politics.[64] In addition, students of interest groups in Western Europe have vigorously debated the causes and dynamics of "corporatist" patterns, in which

interest groups exclusively representing given functional socioeconomic interests attain public status and the right to authoritative participation in national policy making. Some scholars have directly stressed that state initiatives create corporatist forms. Others, more skeptical of such a strong state-centered view, nevertheless analyze the myriad ways in which particular state structures and policies foster or undermine corporatist group representation.[65]

Key points along these lines are driven home when the United States is brought into the picture. In a provocative 1979 essay, Robert Salisbury asked, "Why No Corporatism in America?" and Graham K. Wilson followed up the query in 1982.[66] But scholars agree that such basic (interrelated) features of the U.S. state structure as federalism, the importance of geographic units of representation, nonprogrammatic political parties, fragmented realms of administrative bureaucracy, and the importance of Congress and its specialized committees within the national government's system of divided sovereignty all encourage a proliferation of competing, narrowly specialized, and weakly disciplined interest groups. In short, little about the structure and operations of the American state renders corporatism politically feasible or credible, either for officials or for social groups. Even protest movements in the United States tend to follow issue-specialized and geographically fissiparous patterns. State structures, established interest groups, and oppositional groups all may mirror one another's forms of organization and scopes of purpose.

Along with interest groups, the most important and enduring forms of collective political action in the industrial-capitalist democracies are electorally competing political parties. In a series of brilliant comparative-historical essays, Martin Shefter demonstrates how such parties have come to operate either through patronage or through programmatic appeals to organized voter blocs.[67] Shefter argues that this depended in large part on the forms of state power in existence when the democratic suffrage was established in various nations. In Germany, for example, absolutist monarchs had established centralized administrative bureaucracies long before the advent of democratic elections. Vote-getting political parties, when they came into existence, could not offer the "spoils of office" to followers, because there was an established coalition (of public officials tied to upper and middle classes oriented to using university education as a route to state careers) behind keeping public bureaucracies free of party control. Thus, German political parties were forced to use ideological, programmatic appeals, ranging from communist or socialist to anti-Semitic and fascist.[68] In contrast, Shefter shows how the territorial unevenness of predemocratic central administration in Italy and the absence of an autonomous federal bureaucracy in nineteenth-century U.S. democracy allowed patronage-wielding political parties to colonize administrative arrangements in these countries, thereby determining that voters would be wooed with nonprogrammatic appeals, especially with patronage and other "distributive" allocations of publicly controlled resources.

The full scope of Shefter's work, which cannot be further summarized here, also covers Britain, France, and regional contrasts within the twentieth-century United States. With analytical consistency and vivid historical detail, Shefter shows the influence of evolving state administrative structures on the aims and organizational forms of the political parties that mediate between public offices, on the one hand, and socially rooted electorates, on the other. Unlike many students of voting and political parties, Shefter does not see parties merely as vehicles for expressing societal political preferences. He realizes that they are also organizations for claiming and using state authority, organizations that develop their own interests and persistent styles of work. Lines of determination run as much (or more) from state structures to party organizations to the content of electoral politics as they run from voter preferences to party platforms to state policies.

Structures of public administration and political party organizations, considered together, go a long way toward "selecting" the *kinds* of political issues that will come onto (or be kept off) a society's "political agenda." In his book on policy making in relation to air pollution in U.S. municipal politics, Matthew Crenson develops this argument in a manner that has implications beyond his own study.[69] Boss-run, patronage-oriented urban machines, Crenson argues, prefer to highlight political issues that create *divisible* benefits or costs to be allocated differentially in discrete bargains for support from particular businesses or geographic sets of voters. Air pollution controls, however, generate indivisible *collective* benefits, so machine governments and patronage-oriented parties will try to avoid considering the air pollution issue. Entire political agendas, Crenson maintains, may be dominated by similar types of issues: either mostly "collective" or mostly "specific"/distributional issues. This happens, in part, because the organizational needs of government and parties will call forth similar issues. It also happens

because, once political consciousness and group mobilization are bent in one direction, people will tend to make further demands along the same lines. Once again, we see a dialectic between state and society, here influencing the basic issue content of politics, just previously we have seen state–society interrelations at work in the shaping of political cultures and forms of collective action.

States and the Political Capacities of Social Classes

With so many aspects of politics related to nationally variable state structures, it should come as no surprise that the "classness" of politics also varies in relation to states, for the degree to which (and the forms in which) class interests are organized into national politics depends very much on the prevailing political culture, forms of collective action, and possibilities for raising and resolving broadly collective (societal or class) issues. Marxists may be right to argue that classes and class tensions are always present in industrial societies, but the political expression of class interests and conflicts is never automatic or economically determined. It depends on the capacities classes have for achieving consciousness, organization, and representation. Directly or indirectly, the structures and activities of states profoundly condition such class capacities. Thus, the classical wisdom of Marxian political sociology must be turned, if not on its head, then certainly on its side.

Writing in direct critical dialogue with Marx, Pierre Birnbaum argues that the contrasting ideologies and attitudes toward politics of the French and British working-class movements can be explained in state-centered terms.[70] According to Birnbaum, the centralized, bureaucratic French state, sharply differentiated from society, fostered anarchist or Marxist orientations and political militancy among French workers, whereas the centralized but less differentiated British "establishment" encouraged British workers and their leaders to favor parliamentary gradualism and private contractual wage bargaining.

Analogous arguments by Ira Katznelson in *City Trenches* and by Martin Shefter in an essay entitled "Trades Unions and Political Machines: The Organization and Disorganization of the American Working Class in the Late Nineteenth Century" point to the specifically state-centered factors that account for the cross-nationally very low political capacity of the U.S. industrial working class.[71] Democratization (in the form of universal suffrage for white men) occurred in the United States right at the start of capitalist industrialization. From the 1830s onward, electoral competition incorporated workers into a polity run, not by a national bureaucracy or "establishment," but by patronage-oriented political parties with strong roots in local communities. In contrast to what happened in many European nations, unions and workers in the United States did not have to ally themselves with political associations or parties fighting for the suffrage in opposition to politically privileged dominant classes and an autonomous administrative state. Common meanings and organizations did not bridge work and residence in America, and the early U.S. industrial working class experienced "politics" as the affair of strictly local groups organized on ethnic or racial lines by machine politicians. Work-place struggles were eventually taken over by bread-and-butter trade unions. "In this way," Katznelson concludes, "citizenship and its bases were given communal meaning separate from work relations. The segmented pattern of class understandings in the United States . . . was caused principally by features of the polity created by the operation of a federal constitutional system."[72]

State structures influence the capacities not only of subordinate but also of propertied classes. It is never enough simply to posit that dominant groups have a "class interest" in maintaining sociopolitical order or in continuing a course of economic development in ways congruent with their patterns of property ownership. Exactly how—even whether—order may be maintained and economic accumulation continued depends in significant part on existing state structures and the dominant-class political capacities that those structures help to shape. Thus, in my 1973 discussion of Barrington Moore's *Social Origins of Dictatorship and Democracy*, I argued that the "reformism" of key landed and bourgeois groups in nineteenth-century Britain was not simply a product of class economic interests. It was also a function of the complexly balanced vested political interests those groups had in decentralized forms of administration and repression and in parliamentary forms of political decision making.[73] Likewise, much of the argument in my *States and Social Revolutions* about causes of revolutionary transformations in certain agrarian states rests on a comparative analysis of the political capacities of landed upper classes as these were shaped by the structures and activities of monarchical bureaucratic states.[74]

Again, the point under discussion can be brought home to the United States. Along with the U.S. indus-

trial working class, American capitalists lack the political capacity to pursue classwide interests in national politics. This is one of the reasons invoked by Susan and Norman Fainstein to explain the incoherence and ineffectiveness of contemporary U.S. policy responses to urban crises, which northwest European nations have handled more effectively, to the benefit of dominant and subordinate classes alike.[75] Historically, America's relatively weak, decentralized, and fragmented state structure, combined with early democratization and the absence of a politically unified working class, has encouraged and allowed U.S. capitalists to splinter along narrow interest lines and to adopt an antistate, laissez faire ideology.[76] Arguably, American business groups have often benefited from this situation. Yet American business interests have been recurrently vulnerable to reformist state interventions that they could not strongly influence or limit, given their political disunity or (as at the height of the New Deal) their estrangement from interventionist governmental agencies or administrations.[77] And American business has always found it difficult to provide consistent support for national initiatives that might benefit the economy as a whole.

Obviously, industrial workers and capitalists do not exhaust the social groups that figure in the politics of industrial democracies. Studies of the effects of state structures and policies on group interests and capacities have also done much to explain, in historical and comparative terms, the political involvements of farmers and small businesses. In addition, important new work is now examining relationships between state formation and the growth of modern "professions," as well as related concerns about the deployment of "expert" knowledge in public policy making.[78] Yet without surveying these literatures as well, the basic argument of this section has been sufficiently illustrated.

Politics in all of its dimensions is grounded not only in "society" or in "the economy" or in a "culture"—if any or all of these are considered separately from the organizational arrangements and activities of states. The meanings of public life and the collective forms through which groups become aware of political goals and work to attain them arise, not from societies alone, but at the meeting points of states and societies. Consequently, the formation, let alone the political capacities, of such apparently purely socioeconomic phenomena as interest groups and classes depends in significant measure on the structures and activities of the very states the social actors, in turn, seek to influence.

CONCLUSION

This essay has ranged widely—although, inevitably, selectively—over current research on states as actors and as institutional structures with effects in politics. Two alternative, though complementary, analytical strategies have been discussed for bringing the state back in to a prominent place in comparative and historical studies of social change, politics, and policy making. On the one hand, states may be viewed as organizations through which official collectivities may pursue distinctive goals, realizing them more or less effectively given the available state resources in relation to social settings. On the other hand, states may be viewed more macroscopically as configurations of organization and action that influence the meanings and methods of politics for all groups and classes in society.

Given the intellectual and historical trends surveyed in the introduction to this essay, there can now be little question whether states are to be taken seriously in social scientific explanations of a wide range of phenomena of long-standing interest. There remain, however, many theoretical and practical issues about how states and their effects are to be investigated. My programmatic conclusion is straightforward: Rather than become embroiled in a series of abstruse and abstract conceptual debates, let us proceed along the lines of the analytical strategies sketched here. With their help, we can carry through further comparative and historical investigations to develop middle-range generalizations about the roles of states in revolutions and reforms, about the social and economic policies pursued by states, and about the effects of states on political conflicts and agendas.

A new theoretical understanding of states in relation to social structures will likely emerge as such programs of comparative-historical research are carried forward. But this new understanding will almost certainly not resemble the grand systems theories of the structure–functionalists or neo-Marxists. As we bring the state back in to its proper central place in explanations of social change and politics, we shall be forced to respect the inherent historicity of sociopolitical structures, and we shall necessarily attend to the inescapable intertwinings of national-level developments with changing world historical contexts. We do not need a new or refurbished grand theory of "The State." Rather, we need solidly grounded and analytically sharp understandings of the causal regularities that underlie the histories of states, social structures, and transnational relations in the modern world.

NOTES

This chapter is a revision of "Bringing the State Back In: False Leads and Promising Starts in Current Theories and Research," originally prepared for a Social Science Research Council conference entitled "States and Social Structures: Research Implications of Current Theories," held at Seven Springs Center, Mt. Kisco, New York, February 25–27, 1982. I benefited greatly from conference discussions. Subsequently, reactions from Pierre Birnbaum, David Easton, Harry Eckstein, Kenneth Finegold, and Eric Nordlinger also helped me to plan revisions of the conference paper, as did access to prepublication copies of Stephen Krasner's "Review Article: Approaches to the State: Alternative Conceptions and Historical Dynamics," *Comparative Politics* 16 (2) (January 1984), 223–46 and Roger Benjamin and Raymond Duvall's "The Capitalist State in Context," forthcoming in *The Democratic State*, ed. R. Benjamin and S. Elkin (Lawrence: University of Kansas Press, 1985). Most of all, I am intellectually indebted to discussions and exchanges of memos with all of my fellow members of the 1982–83 Social Science Research Council Committee on States and Social Structures: Peter Evans, Albert Hirschman, Peter Katzenstein, Ira Katznelson, Stephen Krasner, Dietrich Rueschemeyer, and Charles Tilly.

1. Important examples include Alice Amsden, "Taiwan's Economic History: A Case of Etatism and a Challenge to Dependency Theory," *Modern China* 5 (1979): 341–80; Pranab Bardhan, "The State, Classes and Economic Growth in India," 1982–83 Radhakrishnan Memorial Lectures, All Souls College, Oxford; Douglas Bennett and Kenneth Sharpe, "Agenda Setting and Bargaining Power: The Mexican State versus Transnational Automobile Corporations," *World Politics* 32 (1979): 57–89; Peter B. Evans, *Dependent Development: The Alliance of Multinational, State, and Local Capital in Brazil* (Princeton, N.J.: Princeton University Press, 1979); Nora Hamilton, *The Limits of State Autonomy: Post-Revolutionary Mexico* (Princeton, N.J.: Princeton University Press, 1982); Steven Langdon, *Multinational Corporations in the Political Economy of Kenya* (London: Macmillan, 1981); Hyun-chin Lim, "Dependent Development in the World System: The Case of South Korea, 1963–1979" (Ph.D. diss., Harvard University, 1982); Richard Sklar, *Corporate Power in an African State: The Political Impact of Multinational Mining Companies in Zambia*

(Berkeley: University of California Press, 1975); Alfred Stepan, *The State and Society: Peru in Comparative Perspective* (Princeton, N.J.: Princeton University Press, 1978); and Ellen Kay Trimberger, *Revolution from Above: Military Bureaucrats and Development in Japan, Turkey, Egypt, and Peru* (New Brunswick, N.J.: Transaction Books, 1978).

2. Important examples include Douglas Ashford, *British Dogmatism and French Pragmatism: Central-Local Policymaking in the Modern Welfare State* (London: Allen & Unwin, 1983); Pierre Birnbaum, *The Heights of Power: An Essay on the Power Elite in France*, trans. Arthur Goldhammer (Chicago: University of Chicago Press, 1982); David Cameron, "The Expansion of the Public Economy: A Comparative Analysis," *American Political Science Review* 72 (1978): 1243–61; Kenneth Dyson and Stephen Wilks, eds., *Industrial Crisis: A Comparative Study of the State and Industry* (New York: St. Martin's Press, 1983); Peter Hall, "Policy Innovation and the Structure of the State: The Politics–Administration Nexus in France and Britain," *Annals of the American Academy of Political and Social Science* 466 (1983): 43–59; Peter A. Hall, "Patterns of Economic Policy among the European States: An Organizational Approach," in *The State in Capitalist Europe*, ed. Stephen Bornstein, David Held, and Joel Krieger (London: Allen & Unwin, forthcoming); Hugh Heclo, *Modern Social Politics in Britain and Sweden* (New Haven, Conn.: Yale University Press, 1974); Chalmers Johnson, *MITI and the Japanese Miracle: The Growth of Industrial Policy, 1925–1975* (Stanford, Calif.: Stanford University Press, 1982); Peter Katzenstein, ed., *Between Power and Plenty: Foreign Economic Policies of Advanced Industrial States* (Madison: University of Wisconsin Press, 1978); Steven Kelman, *Regulating America, Regulating Sweden: A Comparative Study of Occupational Health and Safety Policy* (Cambridge, Mass.: MIT Press, 1981); Stephen D. Krasner, *Defending the National Interest: Raw Materials Investments and U.S. Foreign Policy* (Princeton, N.J.: Princeton University Press, 1978); Theodore J. Lowi, "Public Policy and Bureaucracy in the United States and France," in *Comparing Public Policies: New Concepts and Methods*, ed. Douglas E. Ashford, vol. 4 of *Sage Yearbooks in Politics and Public Policy* (Beverly Hills, Calif.: Sage, 1978), pp. 177–96; Leo Panitch, ed., *The Canadian State: Political Economy and Political Power* (Toronto: University of Toronto Press, 1977); Theda Skocpol and John Ikenberry, "The Political Formation of the American Welfare State in Historical and Comparative Perspective," *Comparative Social Research* 6 (1983): 87–148; S. Tolliday and J. Zeitlin, eds., *Shop Floor Bargaining and the State: Historical And Comparative Perspectives* (Cambridge and New York: Cambridge University Press, 1984); and John Zysman, *Political Strategies for Industrial Order: State, Market and Industry in France* (Berkeley: University of California Press, 1977).

3. Important examples include Michael Adas, "From Avoidance to Confrontation: Peasant Protest in Pre-Colonial and Colonial Southeast Asia," *Comparative Studies in Society and History* 23 (1981): 217–47; Betrand Badie and Pierre Birnbaum, *The Sociology of the State*, trans. Arthur Goldhammer (Chicago: University of Chicago Press, 1983); Pierre Birnbaum, "States, Ideologies, and Collective Action in Western Europe," *Social Science Journal* 32 (1980): 671–86; Jose Murilo de Carvalho, "Political Elites and State Building: The Case of Nineteenth-Century Brazil," *Comparative Studies in Society and History* 24 (1981): 378–99; Mounira Charrad, "Women and the State: A Comparative Study of Politics, Law, and the Family in Tunisia, Algeria, and Morocco" (Ph.D. diss., Harvard University, 1980); Daniel Chirot, *Social Change in a Peripheral Society: The Creation of a Balkan Colony* (New York: Academic Press, 1976); Stanley B. Greenberg, *Race and State in Capitalist Development* (New Haven, Conn.: Yale University Press, 1980); Michael Hechter, *Internal Colonialism: The Celtic Fringe in British National Development, 1536–1966* (Berkeley: University of California Press, 1975); Ira Katznelson, *City Trenches: Urban Politics and the Patterning of Class in the United States* (New York: Pantheon Books, 1981); Joel S. Migdal, *Peasants, Politics, and Revolution: Pressures toward Political and Social Change in the Third World* (Princeton, N.J.: Princeton University Press, 1974); Gianfranco Poggi, *The Development of the Modern State: A Sociological Introduction* (Stanford, Calif.: Stanford University Press, 1978); Joseph Rothschild, *Ethnopolitics: A Conceptual Framework* (New York: Columbia University Press, 1981); Theda Skocpol, *States and Social Revolutions: A Comparative Analysis of France, Russia, and China* (Cambridge and New York: Cambridge University Press, 1979); Stephen Skowronek, *Building a New American State: The Expansion of National Administrative Capacities, 1877–1920* (Cambridge and New York: Cambridge University Press, 1982); Ezra N. Suleiman, *Politics, Power, and Bureaucracy in France: The Administra-*

tive Elite (Princeton, N.J.: Princeton University Press, 1974); Charles Tilly, ed., *The Formation of National States in Western Europe*, Studies in Political Development no. 8 (Princeton, N.J.: Princeton University Press, 1975); and Charles Tilly, *The Contentious French* (Cambridge: Harvard University Press, forthcoming).

4. See especially Douglass C. North, "A Framework for Analyzing the State in Economic History," *Explorations in Economic History* 16 (1979): 249–59; Douglass C. North, *Structure and Change in Economic History* (New York: Norton, 1981); and Robert H. Bates, *Markets and States in Tropical Africa: The Political Basis of Agricultural Policies* (Berkeley: University of California Press, 1981).

5. See especially Clifford Geertz, *Negara: The Theatre State in Nineteenth-Century Bali* (Princeton, N.J.: Princeton University Press, 1980).

6. Sociologists may recognize that the title of this chapter echoes the title of George C. Homans's 1964 presidential address to the American Sociological Association, "Bringing Men Back In." Of course, the subject matters are completely different, but there is an affinity of aspiration for explanations built on propositions about the activities of concrete groups. This stands in contrast to the application of analytical conceptual abstractions characteristic of certain structure–functionalist or neo-Marxist "theories."

7. Among the most important exceptions were Samuel Huntington's path-breaking state-centered book, *Political Order and Changing Societies* (New Haven, Conn.: Yale University Press, 1968); Morris Janowitz's many explorations of state–society relationships, as in *The Military in the Political Development of New Nations* (Chicago: University of Chicago Press, 1964), and *Social Control of the Welfare State* (Chicago: University of Chicago Press, 1976); and James Q. Wilson's conceptually acute probings in *Political Organizations* (New York: Basic Books, 1973). In his many works in political sociology, Seymour Martin Lipset has always remained sensitive to the effects of various institutional structures of government representation. In addition, Reinhard Bendix consistently developed a state-centered Weberian approach to political regimes as a critical counterpoint to structure–functionalist developmentalism, and S. N. Eisenstadt and Stein Rokkan elaborated creative syntheses of functionalist and Weberian modes of comparative political analysis.

8. For clear paradigmatic statements, see Gabriel Almond, "A Developmental Approach to Political Systems," *World Politics* 16 (1965): 183–214; Gabriel Almond and James S. Coleman, eds., *The Politics of Developing Areas* (Princeton, N.J.: Princeton University Press, 1960); Gabriel Almond and G. Bingham Powell, Jr., *Comparative Politics: A Developmental Approach* (Boston: Little, Brown, 1966); David Easton, "An Approach to the Analysis of Political Systems," *World Politics* 9 (1957): 383–400; and David B. Truman, *The Governmental Process* (New York: Knopf, 1951).

9. Eric A. Nordlinger's *On the Autonomy of the Democratic State* (Cambridge: Harvard University Press, 1981) has stretched pluralist premises to their conceptual limits in order to encompass the possibility of autonomous actions by elected politicians or administrative officials. Tellingly, Nordlinger defines "state autonomy" purely in terms of the conscious preferences of public officials, who are said to be acting autonomously as long as they are not deliberately giving in to demands by societal actors. By insisting that public officials have wants and politically relevant resources, just as voters, economic elites, and organized interest groups do, Nordlinger simply gives officials the same dignity that all actors have in the fluid "political process" posited by pluralism. State autonomy, Nordlinger in effect says, is simply the creative exercise of political leadership. No matter what the organization or capacities of the state, any public official at any time is, by definition, in a position to do this. In my view, the value of Nordlinger's book lies, not in this rather insipid general conclusion, but in the researchable hypotheses about variations in state autonomy that one might derive from some of the typologies it offers.

10. See Robert Dahl, *Who Governs?* (New Haven, Conn.: Yale University Press, 1961); Raymond E. Wolfinger, *The Politics of Progress* (Englewood Cliffs, N.J.: Prentice-Hall, 1974); and Nelson W. Polsby, *Community Power and Political Theory* (New Haven, Conn.: Yale University Press, 1961). In thinking about the missing analytical elements in these studies, I have benefited from Geoffrey Fougere's critical discussion in "The Structure of Government and the Organization of Politics: A Polity Centered Approach" (Department of Sociology, Harvard University, September 1978).

11. Graham Allison, *Essence of Decision: Explaining the Cuban Missile Crisis* (Boston: Little, Brown, 1971); and Morton S. Halperin, *Bureaucratic Politics and Foreign Policy* (Washington, D.C.: The Brookings Institution, 1971).

12. I have benefited from Stephen Krasner's discussion of the bureaucratic politics perspective in *Defending the National Interest*, p. 27. Krasner's own book shows the difference it makes to take a more macroscopic, historical, and state-centered approach.

13. See Leonard Binder, James S. Coleman, Joseph La Palombara, Lucian W. Pye, Sidney Verba, and Myron Weiner, *Crises and Sequences in Political Development*, Studies in Political Development no. 7 (Princeton, N.J.: Princeton University Press, 1971); Gabriel Almond, Scott C. Flanagan, and Robert J. Mundt, *Crisis, Choice, and Change: Historical Studies of Political Development* (Boston: Little, Brown, 1973); Tilly, ed., *Formation of National States*; and Raymond Grew, ed., *Crises of Political Development in Europe and the United States*, Studies in Political Development no. 9 (Princeton, N.J.: Princeton University Press, 1978). The Tilly and Grew volumes openly criticize the theoretical ideas advocated by the Committee on Comparative Politics that sponsored these projects, and Tilly calls for the kind of approach now embodied in the mission of the Committee on States and Social Structures.

14. A sampling of the most important neo-Marxist works includes Perry Anderson, *Passages from Antiquity to Feudalism* (London: New Left Books, 1974) and *Lineages of the Absolutist State* (London: New Left Books, 1974); Gösta Esping-Andersen, Roger Friedland, and Erik Olin Wright, "Modes of Class Struggle and the Capitalist State," *Kapitalistate*, no. 4–5 (1976): 186–220; John Holloway and Simon Picciotto, eds., *State and Capital: A Marxist Debate* (London: Arnold, 1978); Ralph Miliband, *The State in Capitalist Society* (New York: Basic Books, 1969); Nicos Poulantzas, *Political Power and Social Classes*, trans. Timothy O'Hagen (London: New Left Books, 1973); Claus Offe, "Structural Problems of the Capitalist State," *German Political Studies* 1 (1974): 31–57; Göran Therborn, *What Does the Ruling Class Do When it Rules?* (London: New Left Books, 1978); and Immanuel Wallerstein, *The Modern World System*, vols. 1 and 2 (New York: Academic Press, 1974, 1980).

Some excellent overviews of the neo-Marxist debates are those of Martin Carnoy, *The State and Political Theory* (Princeton, N.J.: Princeton University Press, 1984); David A. Gold, Clarence Y. H. Lo, and Erik Olin Wright, "Recent Developments in Marxist Theories of the Capitalist State," *Monthly Review* 27 (1975), no. 5: 29–43; no. 6: 36–51; Bob Jessop, "Recent Theories of the Capitalist State," *Cambridge Journal of Economics* 1 (1977): 353–73; Bob Jessop, *The Capitalist State: Marxist Theories and Methods* (New York: New York University Press, 1982); and Ralph Miliband, *Marxism and Politics* (Oxford: Oxford University Press, 1977).

15. Of all those engaged in the neo-Marxist debates, Fred Block goes the farthest toward treating states as truly autonomous actors. See his "The Ruling Class Does Not Rule: Notes on the Marxist Theory of the State," *Socialist Revolution* 7 (1977): 6–28; and "Beyond Relative Autonomy," in *The Socialist Register 1980*, ed. Ralph Miliband and John Saville (London: Merlin Press, 1980), pp. 227–42. For congruent positions, see also Trimberger, *Revolution from Above*, as well as my own *States and Social Revolutions* (Cambridge and New York: Cambridge University Press, 1979) and "Political Response to Capitalist Crisis: Neo-Marxist Theories of the State and the Case of the New Deal," *Politics and Society* 10 (1980): 155–201. Block and I are jointly criticized for overemphasizing state autonomy in Carnoy, *State and Political Theory*, chap. 8; and Block, Trimberger, and I are all critically discussed in Ralph Miliband, "State Power and Class Interests," *New Left Review*, no. 138 (1983): 57–68.

16. The scope of many neo-Marxist propositions about states makes them more applicable/testable in comparisons *across* modes of production, rather than across nations within capitalism. Therborn, in *Ruling Class*, is one of the few theorists to attempt such cross-mode comparisons, however.

17. I do not mean to imply pure continuity. Around the World Wars and during the 1930s depression, when both British and U.S. hegemony faltered, there were bursts of more state-centered theorizing, including such works as Harold Lasswell's "The Garrison State," *American Journal of Sociology* 46 (1941): 455–68; and Karl Polanyi's *The Great Transformation* (Boston: Beacon Press, 1957; originally 1944).

18. For some suggestive treatments, see Stephen D. Krasner, "United States Commercial and Monetary Policy: Unravelling the Paradox of External Strength and Internal Weakness," in *Between Power and Plenty*, ed. Katzenstein, pp. 51–87; Stephen Blank, "Britain: The Politics of Foreign Economic Policy, the Domestic Economy, and the Problems of Pluralistic Stagnation," in *Between Power and Plenty*, ed. Katzenstein, pp. 89–138; Andrew Martin, "Political Constraints on Economic Strategies in Advanced Industrial Societies," *Comparative Political Studies* 10

(1977): 323–54; Paul M. Sacks, "State Structure and the Asymmetrical Society: An Approach to Public Policy in Britain," *Comparative Politics* 12 (1980): 349–76; and Dyson and Wilks, eds., *Industrial Crisis*.

19. For Max Weber's principal writings on states, see *Economy and Society*, ed. Guenther Roth and Claus Wittich (New York: Bedminster Press, 1968; originally 1922), vol. 2, chap. 9; vol. 3, chaps. 10–13.

20. Stepan, *State and Society*, p. xii.

21. See *The Historical Essays of Otto Hintze*, ed. Felix Gilbert (New York: Oxford University Press, 1975; originally 1897–1932).

22. For discussion of the most important neopluralist theory of state autonomy, see note 9. The works by Poulantzas and Offe cited in note 14 represent important neo-Marxist theories of state autonomy. Poulantzas's approach is ultimately very frustrating because he simply posits the "relative autonomy of the capitalist state" as a necessary feature of the capitalist mode of production as such. Poulantzas insists that the state is "relatively autonomous" regardless of varying empirical ties between state organizations and the capitalist class, and at the same time he posits that the state must invariably function to stabilize the capitalist system as a whole.

23. Stepan, *State and Society*, chaps. 3 and 4. See also Alfred Stepan, "The New Professionalism of Internal Warfare and Military Role Expansion," in *Authoritarian Brazil*, ed. A. Stepan (New Haven, Conn.: Yale University Press, 1973), pp. 47–65.

24. Trimberger, *Revolution from Above*.

25. Ibid., p. 4.

26. Ibid., p. 5.

27. Thus, in commenting on Stepan's work, Trimberger argues that he could have explained the repressive and "exclusionary" nature of the Brazilian coup (in contrast to Peru's "inclusionary" reforms, which included mass political mobilization and expropriation of hacienda landlords) by focusing on the Brazilian military's ties to Brazilian and multinational capitalists. In fact, Stepan does report ("The New Professionalism," p. 54) that Brazilian military professionals received their training alongside elite civilians, including industrialists, bankers, and commercial elites, who also attended the Superior War College of Brazil in the period before 1964.

28. Trimberger's work thus speaks to the problems with Nicos Poulantzas's theory discussed in note 22.

29. For France, there is an especially rich literature on state autonomy, its consequences and its limits. I am deliberately leaving it aside here, because France is such an obvious case for the application of ideas about state autonomy. See the works, however, by Birnbaum, Hall, Suleiman, and Zysman cited in notes 2 and 3, along with Stephen Cohen, *Modern Capitalist Planning: The French Experience* (Berkeley: University of California Press, 1976); and Richard F. Kuisel, *Capitalism and the State in Modern France: Renovation and Economic Management in the Twentieth Century* (Cambridge and New York: Cambridge University Press, 1981).

30. Heclo, *Modern Social Politics*.

31. Ibid., p. 305.

32. Ibid., pp. 305–6, 303.

33. Krasner, *Defending the National Interest*.

34. Ibid., p. 11.

35. See also Krasner, "United States Commercial and Monetary Policy," pp. 51–87.

36. Thus, Krasner has the most difficulty in distinguishing his argument for "state autonomy" from the structural Marxist perspective according to which the state acts for the class interests of capital as a whole. His solution, to stress "nonrational" ideological objectives of state policy as evidence against the class-interest argument, does not strike me as being very convincing. Could an imperialist ideology not be evidence of class consciousness as well as of state purpose: One might stress, instead, the perceived geopolitical "interests" at work in U.S. interventions abroad. "Free-world" justifications for such interventions are not obviously irrational, given certain understandings of U.S. geopolitical interests.

37. J. P. Nettl, "The State as a Conceptual Variable," *World Politics* 20 (1968), 563–64.

38. Kenneth Finegold and Theda Skocpol, "Capitalists, Farmers, and Workers in the New Deal—The Ironies of Government Intervention" (Paper presented at the annual meeting of the American Political Science Association, Washington, D.C., August 31, 1980). Part of this paper was subsequently published as Theda Skocpol and Kenneth Finegold, "State Capacity and Economic Intervention in the Early New Deal," *Political Science Quarterly* 97 (1982): 255–78.

39. Skocpol and Finegold, "State Capacity," p. 271.

40. In contrasting ways, both Krasner's *Defending the National Interest* and Poulantzas's *Political Power and Social Classes* exemplify this point.

41. Or perhaps one should say that any state or state-building movement preoccupied with sheer administrative–military control will, at best, only be able (as well as likely) to implement policies connected to that overriding goal. This principle is a good guide to

understanding many of the social changes that accompany state-building struggles during revolutionary interregnums.

42. See Tilly, ed., *Formation of National States*; Michael Mann, "State and Society 1130–1815: An Analysis of English State Finances," *Political Power and Social Theory* (Greenwich, Conn.: JAI Press, 1980), vol. 1, pp. 165–208; and Stephen Skowronek, *Building a New American State: The Expansion of National Administrative Capacities* (Cambridge and New York: Cambridge University Press, 1982).

43. See Bernard Silberman's important comparative-historical work on alternative modes of state bureaucratization in relation to processes of professionalization: "State Bureaucratization: A Comparative Analysis" (Department of Political Science, the University of Chicago, 1982).

44. Windfall revenues from international oil sales, for example, can render state *both* more autonomous from societal controls and, because social roots and political pacts are weak, more vulnerable in moments of crisis. I argue along these lines in "Rentier State and Shi'a Islam in the Iranian Revolution," *Theory and Society* 11 (1982): 265–83. The Joint Committee on the Near and Middle East of the American Council of Learned Societies and the Social Science Research Council currently has a project entitled "Social Change in Arab Oil-Producing Societies" that is investigating the impact of oil revenues on state-society relationships.

45. See Robert E. Wood, "Foreign Aid and the Capitalist State in Underdeveloped Countries," *Politics and Society* 10(1) (1980): 1–34. Wood's essay primarily documents and discusses the anti-state-building effects of most foreign aid, but it also notes that "the 'overdeveloped' military institutions fostered by aid can provide a springboard for statist experimentation unintended by aid donors" (p. 34). Taiwan and South Korea would both seem to be good examples of this.

46. See John A. Dunn, Jr., "The Importance of Being Earmarked: Transport Policy and Highway Finance in Great Britain and the United States," *Comparative Studies in Society and History* 20(1) (1978): 29–53.

47. For "classic" statements on the social analysis of state finances, see especially Lorenz von Stein, "On Taxation," and Rudolf Goldscheid, "A Sociological Approach to Problems of Public Finance," both in *Classics in the Theory of Public Finance*, ed. Richard A. Musgrave and Alan T. Peacock (New York: Macmillan, 1958), pp. 202–13 and 28–36, respectively.

48. Krasner, *Defending the National Interest*, p. 58.

49. Ibid.

50. Ira Katznelson and Kenneth Prewitt, "Constitutionalism, Class, and the Limit of Choice in U.S. Foreign Policy," in *Capitalism and the State in U.S.–Latin American Relations*, ed. Richard Fagen (Stanford, Calif.: Stanford University Press, 1979), p. 38.

51. Stepan, *State and Society*, chaps. 5–8.

52. This concept is discussed by Peter Katzenstein in *Between Power and Plenty*, pp. 16, 297–98.

53. Susan S. and Norman I. Fainstein, "National Policy and Urban Development," *Social Problems* 26 (1978): 125–46; see especially pp. 140–41.

54. Katzenstein, ed., *Between Power and Plenty*.

55. Krasner, *Defending the National Interest*, especially parts 2 and 3.

56. Stepan, *State and Society*, chap. 7.

57. Katzenstein, ed., *Between Power and Plenty*, p. 19.

58. I am indebted to Jeff Weintraub for pointing out the affinities of this second approach to Tocqueville's political sociology.

59. Nettl, "The State as a Conceptual Variable," pp. 559–92. A recent work pursuing related issues is Kenneth Dyson's *The State Tradition in Western Europe: A Study of an Idea and Institution* (New York: Oxford University Press, 1980).

60. Ira Katznelson and Kenneth Prewitt, "Limits of Choice," in *Capitalism and the State*, ed. Fagen, pp. 31–33.

61. Charles Tilly, *As Sociology Meets History* (New York: Academic Press, 1981), pp. 109–44.

62. Ibid., pp. 145–78.

63. For an overview of Tilly's approach to collective action in critical response to earlier sociological approaches, see *From Mobilization to Revolution* (Reading, Mass.: Addison-Wesley, 1978).

64. Suzanne Berger, "Interest Groups and the Governability of European Society," *Items* (Newsletter of the Social Science Research Council) 35 (1981): 66–67.

65. See Suzanne Berger, ed., *Organizing Interests in Western Europe: Pluralism, Corporatism, and the Transformation of Politics* (Cambridge and New York: Cambridge University Press, 1981); Philippe C. Schmitter and Gerhard Lehmbruch, eds., *Trends toward Corporatist Intermediation*, vol. 1 of *Contemporary Political Sociology* (Beverly Hills, Calif.: Sage, 1979), and Gerhard Lehmbruch and Philippe C. Schmitter, eds., *Patterns of Corporatist Policy-Making*, vol. 7 of *Modern Politics Series* (Beverly Hills, Calif.: Sage, 1982).

66. Robert H. Salisbury, "Why No Corporatism in America?" in *Corporatist Intermediation*, ed. Schmitter and Lehmbruch, pp. 213–30; and Graham K. Wilson, "Why Is There No Corporatism in the United States?," in *Corporatist Policy-Making*, ed. Lehmbruch and Schmitter, pp. 219–36.

67. See Martin Shefter's "Party and Patronage: Germany, England, and Italy," *Politics and Society* 7 (1977): 403–51; "Party, Bureaucracy, and Political Change in the United States," in *The Development of Political Parties: Patterns of Evolution and Decay*, ed. Louis Maisel and Joseph Cooper, vol. 4 of *Sage Electoral Studies Yearbook* (Beverly Hills, Calif.: Sage, 1979), pp. 211–65, and "Regional Receptivity to Reform: The Legacy of the Progressive Era," *Political Science Quarterly* 98 (1983): 459–83.

68. In fact, Shefter shows ("Party and Patronage," p. 428) that parties in the Weimar Republic that might have preferred to use patronage appeals to garner peasant votes were prodded into ideological appeals because bureaucratic autonomy was so great. Thus, they resorted to anti-Semitic and nationalist "ideas" to appeal to the peasantry, a class that is often supposed to be inherently oriented to patronage appeals.

69. Matthew Crenson, *The Un-Politics of Air Pollution: A Study of Non-Decisionmaking in the Cities* (Baltimore, Md.: Johns Hopkins University Press, 1971), especially chaps. 5 and 6.

70. Pierre Birnbaum, "States, Ideologies and Collective Action in Western Europe," *International Social Science Journal* 32 (1980): 671–86.

71. Katznelson, *City Trenches*; and Martin Shefter, "Trades Unions and Political Machines: The Organization and Disorganization of the American Working Class in the Late Nineteenth Century," forthcoming in *Working Class Formation: Nineteenth Century Patterns in Western Europe and the United States*, ed. Ira Katznelson and Aristide Zolberg (Princeton, N.J.: Princeton University Press).

72. Katznelson and Prewitt, "Limits of Choice," p. 30.

73. Theda Skocpol, "A Critical Review of Barrington Moore's *Social Origins of Dictatorship and Democracy*," *Politics and Society* 4 (1973): 1–34.

74. Skocpol, *States and Social Revolutions*.

75. Fainstein and Fainstein, "National Policy and Urban Development."

76. Ibid., pp. 39–40; and David Vogel, "Why Businessmen Distrust Their State: The Political Consciousness of American Corporate Executives," *British Journal of Political Science* 8 (1978): 45–78.

77. See David Vogel, "The 'New' Social Regulation in Historical and Comparative Perspective," in *Regulation in Perspective*, ed. Thomas McGraw (Cambridge: Harvard University Press, 1981), pp. 155–85.

78. See Gerald L. Geison, ed., *Professions and the French State, 1700–1900* (Philadelphia: University of Pennsylvania Press, 1984); Arnold J. Heidenheimer, "Professions, the State, and the Polic(e)y Connection: How Concepts and Terms Evolved over Time and across Language Boundaries" (Paper presented at a panel, Professions, Public Policy and the State, Twelfth World Congress, International Political Science Association, Rio de Janeiro, Brazil, August 12, 1982); Terry Johnson, "The State and the Professions: Peculiarities of the British," in *Social Class and the Division of Labour*, ed. Anthony Giddens and Gavin Mackenzie (Cambridge and New York: Cambridge University Press, 1982), pp. 186–20; Dietrich Rueschemeyer, *Lawyers and Their Society: A Comparative Study of the Legal Profession in Germany and the United States* (Cambridge: Harvard University Press, 1973); Dietrich Rueschemeyer, "Professional Autonomy and the Social Control of Expertise," in *The Sociology of the Professions*, ed. R. Dingwall and P. Lewis (London: Macmillan, 1983); Bernard Silberman, "State Bureaucratization"; and Deborah A. Stone, *The Limits to Professional Power: National Health Care in the Federal Republic of Germany* (Chicago: University of Chicago Press, 1980).

READING 7

THE ECONOMIC THEORY OF POLITICS REBORN

James M. Buchanan

Public choice can help build a political system to channel self-serving behavior of individuals toward the common good. The "new" ideas are as old as Adam Smith, David Hume, and the American Founding Fathers.

From *Challenge* 31(2) 1988: 4–10. Reprinted with the permission of the publisher, M. E. Sharpe, Inc.

The economic theory of politics, or "Public Choice," is a relatively young subdiscipline that has emerged to occupy the attention of scholars in the four decades since the end of World War II. What is there that is peculiarly "economic" about "Public Choice"? Here we can look to British political economist Duncan Black (*Theory of Committees and Elections*, 1958) to put us on the right track. Black stated, very simply, that for his analysis an individual is nothing more than a set of preferences, a utility function, as we call it. Once this apparently innocent definition of an individual is accepted, we are really trapped. If we argue that individuals have *similar* preferences, we are forced into a position where we must explain why. And if we can think of no good reason, we are required to acknowledge that preferences may *differ* among persons.

From these innocent beginnings, the economic theory of politics emerges as a matter of course. The theory is "economic" in the sense that, like traditional economic theory, the building blocks are *individuals*, not corporate entities, not societies, not communities, not states. The building blocks are living, choosing, economizing persons. If these persons are allowed to have *differing* preferences, and if we so much as acknowledge that some aspects of life are inherently collective or social rather than purely private, the central problem for public choice jumps at us full blown. How are differing individual preferences to be reconciled in reaching results that must, by definition, be shared jointly by all members of the community? The positive question is: How *are* the differences reconciled under the political institutions we observe? This question is accompanied by the normative one: How *should* the differences among individuals in desired results be reconciled?

Even at this most elementary level, we must examine the purpose of the collectivity. I have often contrasted the "economic" approach to politics with what I have called the "truth judgment" approach. Individuals may differ in their judgments as to what is "true" and what is not, and it is possible that, occasionally, we may want to introduce institutions that essentially collect or poll the opinions of several persons in arriving at some best estimate of what is "true" or "right." The jury comes to mind as the best example here. The accused is either guilty or not guilty, and we use the jury to determine which of these judgments is "true."

But for matters or ordinary politics, the question is *not* one of truth or falsity of the alternatives. The problem is one of resolving individual differences of preferences into results, and it is misleading to call these results true or false. We can return to the parallel with standard economic theory. A result emerges from a process of exchange, of compromise, of mutual adjustment among several persons, each of whom has private preferences over the alternatives. Further, the satisfaction of these private preferences offers the *raison d'être* for collective action in the first place. The membership of a congregation decides, somehow, that the church-house is to be painted blue rather than green, but it is inappropriate to talk of either color as being the "true" one. The members of a school board decide to hire Mrs. Jones rather than Mr. Brown, but we can scarcely say that the successful candidate embodies "truth."

THE VOTING PARADOX

Let's return to Duncan Black's seminal efforts, as he faced up to the central problem. I am sure that the natural starting place for Black was with ordinary committees that are used to govern many kinds of collective activities. In this, Black was probably influenced by his own participation in the machinery used for making university-college decisions, as Lewis Carroll (of *Alice in Wonderland*) had been influenced by his own share in the committee governance of Christ Church, Oxford. And it is through Duncan Black that we know that the claim to early ideas in voting theory rests largely with Lewis Carroll, who joins the 18th century French nobleman, Condorcet, in making up the two most important figures in the "history of public choice doctrine" prior to the middle years of this century.

How do committees reach decisions when agreement among all members is not possible? Simple observation suggested the relevance of analyzing simple majority voting in formal terms. When he carried out this analysis, Black was, I think, somewhat disappointed even if not surprised when he found that there may exist no motion or proposal (or candidate) from among a fixed set of possibilities that will defeat all others in a series of one-against-one majority tests. There may exist no majority motion. If this is the case, simple majority voting will produce continuous cycling or rotation among a subgroup or subset of the alternatives. The collective outcome will depend on where the voting stops, which will, in turn, depend on the manipulation of the agenda as well as upon the rules of order. The committee member who can ensure that his preferred amendment or motion is voted upon just prior to adjournment often wins the strategic game that majority rules always introduce. (It is interesting, even today, to observe the reactions of fellow committee members when a public choice economist observes that the outcome of deliberation may well be dependent on the voting rules adopted.) The "paradox of voting" became one of the staple ingredients in any subsequent public choice discourse.

Kenneth Arrow confronted a somewhat different and more general problem, although he was to reach the same conclusion (*Social Choice and Individual Values*, 1951). Arrow tried to construct what some economists call a "social welfare function" designed to be useful in guiding the planning authority for a society. He sought to do so by amalgamating information about the separate preferences of individual members, and he was willing to assume that the individuals' preferences exhibit the standard properties required for persons to make ordinary market choices. To his surprise, Arrow found that no such "social welfare function" could be constructed; the task was a logical impossibility, given the satisfaction of certain plausible side conditions. The paradox of majority voting became the more general and more serious impossibility theorem of social or collective choice.

Perhaps it is unfair to both, but I think that Duncan Black would have been happier if he could have discovered that majority voting rules do produce consistent outcomes, and that Kenneth Arrow would have been happier if he could have been able to demonstrate that a social welfare function could be constructed. Black was, and to my knowledge remains, dedicated to government by majority rule; Arrow was, and to my knowledge remains, an advocate of social planning.

Black started immediately to look for the set of conditions that preferences must meet in order for majority voting to exhibit consistency. He came up with his notion of single-peakedness, which means that if all individual preferences among alternatives can be arrayed along a single dimension so that there is a single peak for each voter, there will exist a unique majority motion or proposal (or candidate). This alternative will be that one of the available set of proposals that is most preferred by the median voter. In this setting, majority voting does produce a definitive result, and in so doing it satisfies voters in the middle more than voters at either extreme.

For example, if voters on school budgets can be divided roughly into three groups of comparable size (big spenders, medium spenders, and low spenders), the medium spenders will be controlling under ordinary majority voting, provided that neither the low nor the high spenders rank medium spending lowest among the three budget options. The formal collective or social choice theorists, shocked by the Arrow impossibility theorem, have continued to try to examine the restrictions on individual preferences that might be required to generate consistent social orderings.

THE THEORY OF CONSTITUTIONS

At this point I should introduce my own origins of interest in public choice, and my own contributions, along with those of my colleague, Gordon Tullock. As did Duncan Black, I came to public choice out of intellectual frustration with orthodox pre-World War II public finance theory, at least as I learned it in the English language works of such economists as A. C. Pigou, Hugh Dalton, Harold Graves, and Henry Simons. It made no sense to me to analyze taxes and public outlays independent of some consideration of the political process through which decisions on these two sides of the fiscal account were made. Public finance theory could not be wholly divorced from a theory of politics. In coming to this basic criticism of the orthodoxy, I was greatly influenced by Knut Wicksell on the one hand and by some of the Italian theorists on the other.

One of my first published papers, in 1949, was basically a plea for a better methodology. My initial reaction to Arrow's impossibility theorem was one of nonsurprise. Since political outcomes emerge from a process in which many persons participate rather than from some mysterious group mind, why should anyone have ever expected "social welfare functions" to be internally consistent? Indeed, as I argued in a 1954 paper on Arrow, it seemed to me that if individual preferences are such as to generate a cycle, then such a cycle, or inconsistency, is to be preferred to consistency, since the latter would amount to the imposition of the will of some members of the group on others.

The next stage in my logical sequence came when Gordon Tullock and I started to work on just how majority rules actually work—what economist Dennis Mueller of the University of Maryland has called "positive public choice." Tullock developed his now classic 1959 paper on majority rule and logrolling (see For Further Reading) in which he showed that a sequence of majority votes on spending projects financed out of general tax revenues could overextend the budget and could, indeed, make everyone worse off than they would be with no collective action. Tullock's example was spending on many separate road projects all of which are financed from the proceeds of a general tax, but the same logic can be extended to any situation where there are several spending constituencies that independently influence budgetary patterns.

We came to the view that the apparent ideological dominance of majority rule should be more thoroughly examined. This in turn required us to analyze alternatives to majority rule, to begin to construct an "economic theory of political constitutions," out of which came *The Calculus of Consent* in 1962. This book has achieved a measure of success, of course to our great satisfaction. We used ordinary economic assumptions about the utility-maximizing behavior of individuals, and we sought to explain why specific rules for making collective decisions might emerge from the constitutional level of deliberation.

To pull this explanation off, we needed some means or device that would enable us to pass from individually identifiable self-interest to something that might take the place of "public interest." Unless we could locate such a device or construct, we would have remained in the zero-sum model of politics, where any gains must be matched by losses. We got over this problem by looking at how rules for ordinary parlor games are settled *before* the fall of the cards is known. Uncertainty about just where one's own interest will lie in a sequence of plays or rounds of play will lead a rational person, from his own interest, to prefer rules or arrangements or constitutions that will seem to be "fair," no matter what final positions he might occupy. There is a recognizable affinity between this approach that Tullock and I used in *The Calculus of Consent* and that developed in much more general terms by philosopher John Rawls in his *A Theory of Justice* (1971). Rawls had discussed his central notion of "justice as fairness" in several papers published in the 1950s, and, while our approach came, we think, independently out of our own initial attempt to look for criteria for preferred rules, we do not quibble about the source of ideas. Indeed, the basic ideas in the "justice as fairness" notion can also be found in the work of other scholars that predate Rawls's early papers.

Our book was a mixture of positive analysis of alternative decision rules and a normative defense of certain American political institutions that owe their origins to the Founding Fathers, and to James Madison in particular. We considered that our analysis did "explain" features of the American political heritage that orthodox political science seemed unable to do. Explicitly and deliberately, we defended constitutional limits on majority voting. In a somewhat more funda-mental sense, we defended the existence of constitutional constraints per se; we justified bounds on the exercise of majoritarian democracy.

THE SUPPLY OF PUBLIC GOODS

Black's early work on committees, Arrow's search for a social welfare function, our own work on the economic theory of constitutions, the derivations of these works in such applications as median voter models—all of these efforts were what we should now call demand-driven. By this I mean that the focus of attention was on the ways in which individual preferences might be amalgamated to general collective results on the presumption that the outcomes would be there for the taking. There was almost no attention paid in these works to the utility-maximizing behavior of those who might be called on to *supply* the public goods and services demanded by the taxpayers/voters. There was no theory of public goods supply in the early models of public choice.

To get at the origins of the supply-side models, we must go back to some of the Italian scholars, who quite explicitly developed models of the workings of the state-as-monopoly, analyzed as being separate and apart from the citizenry, and with its own distinct interests. Machiavelli is, of course, the classic source of ideas here, but the discussions of Vilfredo Pareto and Gaetano Mosca about ruling classes, along with the fiscal applications by the public finance theorists such as Antonio De Viti De Marco, Amilcare Puviani, and Mauro Fasiani all deserve mention in any catalogue. From these writers, and independent of them, we may trace the development of rudimentary ideas through Joseph Schumpeter and then to Anthony Downs, who, in his 1957 book, *An Economic Theory of Democracy*, analyzed political parties as analogous to profit-maximizing firms. Parties, said Downs, set out to maximize votes, and he tried to explain aspects of observed political reality in terms of his vote-maximizing models. Perhaps the most important theorem to emerge here was the tendency of parties to establish positions near each other in two-party competition and near the center of the ideological or issue spectrum. Political scientist William Riker in *The Theory of Political Coalitions* (1962) challenged Downs's vote-maximizing assumption. He argued convincingly that parties seek not maximum votes, but only sufficient votes to ensure minimally winning coalitions.

Downs's primary emphasis was on the political party, not on the behavior of the politician or bureaucrat. This gap in early supply-side analysis was filled by Gordon Tullock who, drawing on his own experiences in the bureaucracy of the U.S. Department of State, published *The Politics of Bureaucracy* in 1965, although he had written the bulk of this work a decade earlier. Tullock challenged the dominant orthodoxy of modern political science and public administration, exemplified in the works of Max Weber and Woodrow Wilson, by asking the simple question: What are the rewards and penalties facing a bureaucrat located in a hierarchy and what sorts of behavior would describe his efforts to maximize his own utility? The analysis of bureaucracy fell readily into place once this question was raised. The mythology of the faceless bureaucrat following orders from above, executing but not making policy choices, and motivated only to forward the "public interest" was not able to survive the logical onslaught. Bureaucrats could no longer be labeled "economic eunuchs." It became obligatory for analysts to look at bureaucratic structure and at individual behavior within that structure. Tullock's work was followed by a second Downs book (*Inside Bureaucracy*, 1967), and the modern theory of bureaucracy was born.

As the theory of constitutions has an affinity with the work of Rawls, so the theory of bureaucracy has an affinity with the work of those economists who have been called the "property rights theorists." Among them are Armen Alchian and Harold Demsetz of UCLA, and Roland McKean of Virginia, who initiated analysis of the influence of reward and punishment structures on individual behavior, and especially in comparisons between profit and nonprofit institutions. To predict behavior, either in governmental bureaucracy or in privately organized nonproprietary institutions, it is necessary to examine carefully the constraints and opportunities faced by individual decision makers.

The next step was almost programmed. Once we begin to look at bureaucracy in this way, we can, of course, predict that individual bureaucrats will seek to expand the sizes of their bureaus since, almost universally in modern Western societies, the salaries and perquisites of office are related directly to the sizes of budgets administered and controlled. The built-in motive force for expansion, the dynamics of modern governmental bureaucracy in the small and in the large, was apparent to all who cared to think.

This theory of bureaucratic growth was formalized by economist William Niskanen (*Bureaucracy and Representative Government*, 1971), who developed a model of separate budget-maximizing departments and subdepartments. In the limiting case, Niskanen's model suggested that bureaucracies could succeed in expanding budgets to twice the size necessary to meet taxpayers' genuine demands for public goods and services. In this limit, taxpayers end up by being no better off than they would be without any public goods; all of their net benefits are "squeezed out" by the bureaucrats. The implication is that each and every public good or service, whether it be health services, education, transport, or defense, tends to be expanded well beyond any tolerable level of efficiency, as defined by the demands of the citizenry.

Alongside this theory of bureaucracy, there have been efforts to analyze the behavior of the politicians, the elected legislators who face opportunities to earn "political income." Attempts have also been made to integrate demand-side and supply-side theories into a coherent analysis.

RENT SEEKING

To this point, I have largely discussed what we might call established ideas in public choice, although this epithet should not imply that fascinating research is not continuing in some of the areas mentioned. But let me now briefly introduce an area of inquiry that is a more modern development—"rent seeking." "Profit seeking" might be descriptively more accurate, but "rent seeking" is used here in order to distinguish the activity from profit seeking of the kind we ordinarily examine in the study of markets. Once again we can look to Gordon Tullock for the original work on rent seeking, although he did not originally use the term, and I think that Tullock himself did not fully appreciate the potential promised in his paper, "The Welfare Costs of Tariffs, Monopolies, and Theft," (*Western Economic Journal*, June 1967). Tullock's work was followed by papers from Richard Posner of the University of Chicago Law School, Anne Krueger of the University of Minnesota, who invented the term itself, and others; their efforts have been followed by a genuine flurry of research activity.

The basic notion is a very simple one and once again it represents the transference of standard price theory to politics. From price theory we learn that profits tend to be equalized by the flow of investments among prospects. The existence or emergence of an opportunity for differentially high profits will attract investment until returns are equalized with those generally available in the economy. What should we predict, therefore, when politics creates profit opportunities or rents? Investment will be attracted toward the prospects that seem favorable. If "output" cannot expand, as in the standard market adjustment, we should predict that investment will take the form of attempts to secure access to the scarcity rents. When the state licenses an occupation, when it assigns import or export quotas, when it allocates TV spectra, when it adopts land-use planning, when it employs functionaries at above-market wages and salaries, we can expect resource waste in investments to secure the favored plums. Demands for money rents are elastic. The state cannot readily "give money away," even if it might desire to do so.

The rent-seeking analysis can be applied to many activities of the modern state, including the making of money transfers to specified classes of recipients. If mothers with dependent children are granted payments for being mothers, we can predict that we shall soon have more such mothers. If the unemployed are offered higher payments, we predict that the number of unemployed will increase. Or, if access to membership in recipient classes is arbitrarily restricted, we predict that there will be wasteful investment in rent seeking. As the expansion of modern governments offers more opportunities for rents, we must expect that the utility-maximizing behavior of individuals will lead them to waste more resources in trying to secure the "rents" or "profits" promised by government.

EMPIRICAL PUBLIC CHOICE

I have to this point said little about the empirical testing of these ideas or hypotheses. In the last decade, these empirical tests have occupied much of the attention of public choice economists. Indeed, to the Chicago-based group of scholars who talk about the "economic theory of politics," the ideas traced out above amount to little or nothing until they are tested; their view is that empirical work is the be-all and the end-all of the discipline. Those of us in the Virginia tradition are more catholic in our methodology; we acknowledge the contributions of the empiricists while attributing importance to the continuing search for new theoretical insights. The empiricists, among whom I should list my own colleagues Mark Crain and Bob Tollison in addition to the Chicago group, notably George Stigler and Sam Peltzman, have taken the utility-maximizing postulates and derived implications that are subject to test.

The Chicago-based emphasis has been on economic regulation of such industries as transport, broadcasting, and electricity. What is the economic model for the behavior of the regulator and, through this, for the activities of the regulatory agency? What does the record show? Stigler suggested that the evidence corroborates the hypothesis that regulation is pursued in the interests of the industries that are regulated. Others have challenged Stigler and have tried to test the differing hypothesis that regulation is carried out for the self-interest of the regulatory bureaucracy, which may or may not coincide with the interest of the industry regulated. Little or none of the empirical work on regulation suggests that the pre-public choice hypothesis of regulation in the "public interest" is corroborated. In the long run, this research must have some impact on the willingness of the citizenry, and the politicians, to subject more and more of the economy to state regulation, although the end does not seem yet in sight.

Crain and Tollison have looked carefully at the record for legislatures in the American states. They have used straightforward utility-maximizing models, with objectively measurable arguments in the utility functions, to explain such things as relative salaries of legislators among states, relative occupational categories of legislators, committee structures in legislatures, and varying lengths of legislative sessions. They have developed strong empirical support for the basic hypotheses that politicians respond to economic incentives much like the rest of us.

A different area of empirical work that can be brought within the public choice framework is that on "political business cycles," the alleged attempts by politicians in office to create economic conditions timed so as to further their own electoral prospects. The results seem to be somewhat mixed, and I shall not attempt to offer any judgments on this research here.

NORMATIVE IMPLICATIONS OF PUBLIC CHOICE

My own interests have never been in the empirical tradition, as narrowly defined. I have been more interested in a differing sort of research inquiry that follows more or less naturally from the integration of the demand-side and the supply-side analysis of governmental decision-making institutions. As proofs of the logical inconsistencies in voting rules are acknowledged, as the costs of securing agreement among persons with differing preferences are accounted for, the theory of rules, of constitutions, emerges almost automatically on the agenda for research. But my own efforts have been aimed at going beyond the analysis of *The Calculus of Consent*. I have tried to move cautiously but clearly in the direction of normative understanding and evaluation, to move beyond analysis of the way rules work to a consideration of what rules work *best*. My interest has been in examining the bases for constitutional improvement, for constitutional change, for what I have called "constitutional revolution." My efforts have been motivated by the observation that the American constitutional structure is in disarray; the constraints that "worked" for two centuries seem to have failed. The checks on government expansion no longer seem to exist. The Leviathan-state is the reality of our time.

My book, *The Limits of Liberty* (1975), was devoted to diagnosis of this constitutional failure, a step that I considered to be necessary before reform might be addressed. My subsequent research emerged as a natural follow-up to the diagnosis and appeared, with Richard Wagner as coauthor, as *Democracy in Deficit* in early 1977. The book was an attempt to examine the political consequences of Mr. Keynes, and the central theme was to the effect that an important element of the American fiscal constitution, namely the balanced-budget rule, had been destroyed by the political acceptance of Keynesianism. Economists blindly ignored the asymmetry in application of Keynesian policy precepts, an asymmetry that the most elementary public choice theorist would have spotted. Economists naively presumed that politicians would create budget surpluses as willingly as they create deficits. They forgot the elementary rule that politicians enjoy spending and do not like to tax. In *Democracy in Deficit*, Wagner and I called explicitly for the restoration of budget balance as a constitutional requirement. With Geoffrey Brennan, I published *The Power to Tax* in 1980, which was an attempt to design a "tax constitution." We examined ways and means through which the revenue-grabbing proclivities of governments might be disciplined by constitutional constraints imposed on tax bases and rates.

These efforts, on my part and others', suggest that we proceed from a belief that governments can be constrained. We refuse to accept the Hobbesian scenario in which there are no means to bridle the passions of the sovereign. Historical evidence from America's own two centuries suggests that governments can be controlled by constitutions. In one sense, all of public choice or the economic theory of politics may be summarized as the "discovery" or "rediscovery" that persons should be treated as rational utility-maximizers in all of their behavioral capacities. This central insight, in all of its elaborations, does not lead to the conclusion that all collective action, all government, is necessarily undesirable. It leads, instead, to the conclusion that, because persons will tend to maximize their own utilities, institutions must be designed so that individual behavior will further the interests of the group, small or large, local or national. The challenge to us is one of constructing, or reconstructing, a political order that will channel the self-serving behavior of participants toward common good in a manner that comes as close as possible to that described for us by Adam Smith, with respect to the economic order.

THE WISDOM OF CENTURIES

If we look only at the intellectual developments of the 20th century, public choice is "new," and it has, I think, made a major impact on the way that living persons view government and political process and politicians. The public philosophy of 1987 is very different from the public philosophy of 1948 or 1958. There is now much more skepticism about the capacity or the intention of government to satisfy the needs of citizens.

In one sense, public choice or the economic theory of politics is not new at all. It represents rediscovery and elaboration of a part of the conventional wisdom of the 18th and 19th centuries, and notably the conventional wisdom that informed classical political economy. Adam Smith, David Hume, and the American Founding Fathers would have considered the central principles of public choice theory to be so elementary as scarcely to warrant attention. A mistrust of governmental processes along with the implied necessity to impose severe constraints on the exercise of governmental authority was part and parcel of the philosophical heritage that they shared. This set of attitudes extended at least through the middle years of the 19th century, after which they seem to have been suspended for a hundred years. Perhaps they are on the way to return.

I could scarcely do better in conclusion than to introduce a citation from John Stuart Mill's *Considerations on Representative Government* (1861):

> . . . the very principle of constitutional government requires it to be assumed, that political power will be abused to promote the particular purposes of the holder; not because it always is so, but because such is the natural tendency of things, to guard against which is the especial use of free institutions.

READING 8

DEREGULATION AND THE POLITICS OF IDEAS IN CONGRESS

Paul J. Quirk

In a period of extraordinary policy change from the mid-1970s to the early 1980s, much of the overtly anti-competitive regulatory activity of the United States federal government was reformed or abolished. Stock brokerage commissions, railroad freight rates, interest paid to bank depositors, airline industry routes and fares, trucking industry rates and services, and the services and equipment offered and prices charged by the telecommunications industry, among other things, were largely or entirely freed from government control. The reforms had significant economic consequences. They produced some adverse effects, such as diminished transportation service for certain communities and a trend toward monopolization of some markets. But for the most part, prices fell, services improved, and the pace of innovation increased in the deregulated industries.

Whatever the economic effects, the adoption of pro-competitive deregulation had important lessons for political analysis. In some cases, like banking and stock brokerage, reform was facilitated by economic developments that led segments of the regulated industry or other well-organized interests to demand policy change; to a great extent it represented the ordinary workings of interest-group politics. In several other cases, however, especially airlines, trucking, and (in the crucial initial phases of policy change) telecommunications, deregulation occurred without benefit of significant interest-group support. Indeed, as Martha Derthick and I pointed out in *The Politics of Deregulation*,[1] the political success of deregulation required in each case that a diffuse, unorganized interest in reform (primarily consumers) defeat an intense, well-organized opposition (the regulated industry and its labor unions)— while at the same time overcoming the normal tendency of government organizations to protect their jurisdictions. Instead of interest-group politics, deregulation demonstrated the importance of what Derthick and I called the politics of ideas. It also revealed the inadequacy of self-interest theories of politics.

In this chapter, I describe and explain the response of the United States Congress to the issues posed by deregulation. I argue that despite the expectations of self-interest theorists and some others to the contrary, Congress has a rather robust capacity to serve general interests and respond to ideas. I identify the principal sources of this capacity. Finally, I discuss some broader implications of the analysis for the study of public policy-making.

SELF-INTEREST THEORIES: CAPTURE AND REELECTION

Economic or self-interest theories of politics generally begin by assuming that political actors pursue only self-referential objectives, like reelection or individual economic welfare, and end by concluding that narrow, well-organized interests dominate public policy-making. Two such theories, the capture theory of regulation and the electoral theory of Congress, apply to the congressional response to deregulation.

The capture theory of regulation is stated in an article by economist George Stigler.[2] As the premise of his analysis, notorious for its radical debunking of regulatory politics, Stigler assumed self-interested behavior by both politicians and their constituents. Representatives and political parties, in his view, seek electoral success and the perquisites of office. They do not act on their own views about the merits of policies or therefore respond to preaching; rather they in effect sell political power to any group that purchases policies with votes and resources. A group's ability to offer the requisite payment is the sole basis of an effective political demand.

For their part, constituents are assumed to seek only their individual economic welfare. Their efforts to learn about policy issues or express their preferences, through voting or lobbying organizations, are determined by the individual costs and returns, just as in a

From Jane J. Mansbridge, ed., *Beyond Self-Interest* (Chicago, University of Chicago Press, 1990), 183–99, 330. Reprinted with the permission of the author and the University of Chicago Press. *Editor's note:* This chapter is derived primarily from the author's previous work in Martha Derthick and Paul J. Quirk, *The Politics of Deregulation* (Washington, D.C.: Brookings Institution, 1985), chap. 4; and Paul J. Quirk, "In Defense of the Politics of Ideas," *Journal of Politics* 50 (February 1988): 31–41. It incorporates, with minor revisions, passages from both those works. Documentation of quotations and further evidence about the cases are provided in the original study. The general direction of the argument is a product of the author's collaboration with Martha Derthick, who, along with Jane Mansbridge and Stella Herriges Quirk, also provided helpful comments on an earlier draft.

private market. Unfortunately, any large group of constituents—especially an inclusive group like consumers or taxpayers—faces prohibitive obstacles to generating an effective demand. On most issues members of such a group will have low per capita stakes, high costs of organization and information, and strong incentives for free riding. The principal demands come from narrow interests, such as industries and cohesive occupational groups, that have high stakes, low information costs, and the organization to pursue their collective interests. For an issue of regulatory policy, the dominant group is normally the regulated industry itself, which usually has more at stake than any other affected group.

"As a rule," Stigler concluded, "regulation is acquired by the industry and is designed and operated primarily for its benefit."[3] Rather than benefiting the public, regulation transfers wealth to the industry by protecting it from competition. The principal exception Stigler recognized is that a more powerful industry may obtain regulation of a weaker rival for the purpose of hampering it. Apart from that case, Stigler considered the logic of self-interest to be largely inescapable: to blame a regulatory agency for serving industry, he quipped, is like blaming the Great Atlantic and Pacific Tea Company for selling groceries.

In this unvarnished form, the capture theory was massively inaccurate in its predictions. It failed to account for the existence of many regulatory programs that the regulated industries had strongly resisted (and rival industries had not sponsored); for the tendency even among programs that benefit regulated industries to also benefit certain consumers; and most dramatically, for the wave of consumer, environmental, and civil rights regulation that was well under way when Stigler's article was published in 1971.

Recognizing such discrepancies, economic theorists sympathetic with Stigler's effort have proposed amendments. Peltzman points out that a regulated industry often must share the benefits of regulation with other producers (such as suppliers) or even consumers (say, rural telephone users) with sufficient stakes, organization, and political resources to make effective demands.[4] Giving up even more of Stigler's position, Noll and Owen argue that general interests are occasionally effective in the political process.[5] They attribute this efficacy largely to the activity of entrepreneurial leaders, who, for "political or personal motives," promote policies that elicit widespread support and are designed to serve general interests. Evidently viewing such behavior as marginal and episodic, Noll and Owen appeal to it only as a residual

form of explanation. Other economists have abandoned Stigler's assumptions entirely or have given up explaining the relative power of different interests.[6]

The electoral theory of Congress, developed by David Mayhew and Morris Fiorina,[7] is broadly compatible with the capture theory—although it includes a more refined analysis of the political process and a more qualified view of the dominance of interest groups. Like the capture theory, it starts with the premise that members of Congress seek only reelection. It proceeds by identifying the activities that best serve that objective.

In regard to legislation, the theory suggests, members of Congress earn electoral rewards mainly by servicing organized interest groups and seeking concentrated benefits, like defense contracts or public works projects, for their constituencies. These activities bestow benefits on groups that are capable of recognizing the effort and rewarding it with support. In contrast, members of Congress gain little support by trying to advance broad interests or to implement an ideology. Few voters in congressional elections make their decisions on the basis of broad policy issues or ideologies; apart from issues of exceptional salience, few are even aware of their congressman's positions.

The electoral theorists argue that the main objective guiding the development of Congress's institutional structure has been to help members obtain credit for distributing benefits to interest groups and geographic areas. The standing committees recruit members largely by self-selection and yet have substantial autonomy in policy-making. Such committees give control over programs to the legislators whose constituencies they most affect and thus are ideal vehicles for congressional response to narrow interests.

In short, Congress has an exceedingly limited capacity to serve broad or diffuse interests of the nation as a whole; its central impulse is instead to distribute particularized benefits to specific localities and organized groups. Unlike Stigler's theory, however, the electoral theory of Congress acknowledges certain means by which that impulse is sometimes overcome. Presidents, who are elected nationally, and congressional party leaders, who are concerned with their parties' national reputations, have incentives to pursue general interests. Provided they have sufficient control of Congress, presidents and party leaders can moderate the tendency toward particularism. In certain critical areas of policy, such as the budget and taxes, Congress has given committees unusual authority and special institutional incentives to impose some discipline on the granting of special-interest benefits. And even ordinary members of Congress respond to broadly based interests when the public is aroused. Generally speaking, however, the theory holds that narrow interests are in control.

Taken together, the capture theory of regulation and the electoral theory of Congress have several implications about the prospects for reforming anticompetitive regulatory programs. Deregulation should occur primarily if a regulated industry, perhaps responding to changed economic circumstances, asks for it. It may also occur if some other well-organized group—like potential competitors or business users of a regulated service—stands to gain from deregulation and has sufficient resources and intensity to overcome the regulated industry. Finally, it may occur if the general public demands deregulation and is highly attentive to the issue. In the absence of such favorable circumstances, deregulation should not be possible. Congress in particular should be an institutional bulwark against reform. And within Congress, the committees with jurisdiction should be the main outposts of resistance.

CONGRESS AND DEREGULATION

In the deregulation of airlines, trucking, and telecommunications, none of these expectations was borne out. The regulated industries and their labor unions opposed reform strenuously (even though not always to the bitter end). There was no interest-group support remotely comparable to the opposition. And the general public was largely oblivious to the debates. Yet Congress, led for the most part by the committees, endorsed reform.

Airlines

When Sen. Edward Kennedy first advocated deregulating the airline industry in 1975, the certificated airlines opposed the notion intensely and unanimously. United Airlines predicted that "carrier profits would surely vanish." Some groups peripheral to the industry, like charter operators and commuter airlines, had particular restrictions they wanted relaxed, but they did not form a cohesive coalition and were no match, economically or politically, for the certificated airlines. The public, a Harris poll found, approved of airline regulation by a wide margin.

Importantly, reforms that the Civil Aeronautics Board (CAB) adopted administratively throughout the period of the debate tended to undermine the industry's

position and helped cause its resistance gradually to deteriorate. Yet when the Senate and House committees drafted bills in late 1977 and early 1978, the preponderance of the industry still opposed deregulation. The industry was defeated. Both committees reported bills providing for substantial deregulation, and both bills were strengthened in floor debate. In the end, industry resistance collapsed, enabling the conference committee to abolish economic regulation of the airlines.

Telecommunications

After the Federal Communications Commission (FCC) started to admit new competitors to parts of the telecommunications industry in the early 1970s, the American Telephone and Telegraph Company (AT&T), attacking these "experiments in economics," embarked on a campaign with the independent telephone companies and the industry's unions to block competition by legislation. Deploying the company's massive political resources with such intensity that it was widely criticized as overbearing, AT&T tried to push an anticompetitive bill through Congress—recruiting over two hundred House and Senate cosponsors in 1975 and 1976. The principal interest groups supporting competition, the competitors themselves, were vastly outweighed by AT&T; in fact the new long-distance carriers had no lobbying organization until they formed one to fight the AT&T bill. The public, according to polls, was satisfied with the traditional monopoly.

The communications subcommittees in both Houses dismissed the anticompetitive AT&T bill and instead, with virtually no dissent, set about drafting bills to endorse the FCC's procompetitive policies. As it happened, disagreement on difficult subsidiary issues (in particular, whether to break up AT&T, which of the former monopoly's operations to deregulate, and how to control the restructuring of telephone rates) prevented the passage of legislation. But the subcommittees' response provided a political foundation for court decisions and further FCC rulings that over several years gave competition essentially unlimited scope in the industry.

Trucking

"If we are serious about defeating deregulation, then now is the time to prove our strength," the American Trucking Association (ATA) warned its members just before Senate committee markups on trucking deregulation in 1980. The Teamsters Union also urgently wished to defeat it. Interest-group support for deregulation was again negligible: Although a few segments of the trucking industry (contract carriers, private carriers, and owner-operators) wanted additional leeway for their particular operations, they were indifferent, at best, to wide-ranging deregulation. Nor did the public demand deregulation of the trucking industry; only a small part of the public even knew that it was regulated.

Handling the industry and the Teamsters a sharp defeat, the Senate Commerce Committee reported a bill that, said the ATA, "cuts the heart out of regulation." The Senate passed it without change. However, the House Surface Transportation Subcommittee (part of the client-oriented Public Works Committee) was far more deferential to the industry and was inclined to oppose deregulation. Eventually, the House subcommittee leaders struck a compromise with the reformers. Though moderated in some respects, the resulting bill was still highly deregulatory and led to a substantial restructuring of the industry.

SOURCES OF CONGRESSIONAL SUPPORT

Despite the expectations of the relevant self-interest theories, Congress largely supported procompetitive deregulation. This support reflected both some attractive features of the reform proposals and some dispositions and capacities of the institution and its members. As Derthick and I explain in detail,[8] procompetitive deregulation was in several respects an unusually compelling policy proposal. The reform proposals had strong backing in economic theory and evidence and, accordingly, the virtually unanimous endorsement of economists. The economist's rationale of relying on competition to reduce prices and improve efficiency was comprehensible and convincing to laymen. The proposals fit well into ideological agendas at both ends of the political spectrum: Deregulation appealed to conservatives because it would reduce government control and liberate markets; and it appealed to liberals because it would attack business privilege and benefit consumers. With the exception of telecommunications (the only case where purported cross-subsidies were in fact substantial), reform was relatively free of divisive distributive effects among social groups, geographic regions, or economic sectors; the only clear losers were to be regulated industries and their labor.[9] Finally, even though deregulation was never in itself a salient issue to the general public, it had connections that could be used in political rhetoric with two of the public's major concerns—big government and especially inflation.

All of these attributes of the reform proposals and advocacy helped compensate for the intense interest-group opposition. They were able to do so, however, only because Congress also was able to respond to claims on behalf of general interests. As the evidence in these cases demonstrates, there are at least three important sources of that capacity. In part, though not exclusively, they involve motivation other than self-interest.

The Electoral Efficacy of Broadly Based Interests

To the extent that members of Congress seek reelection, they have a stronger incentive than is often acknowledged to respond to the interests and beliefs of the general public. That incentive is strong enough to affect legislative decisions not only in a handful of exceptionally visible policy conflicts, but even in relatively routine conflicts of which only a small fraction of the electorate is directly aware.

As we have seen, there was hardly any overt public demand for procompetitive reform in the airline, trucking, or telecommunications industries. There was, however, a demand for actions that in some way addressed public concerns about inflation and intrusive government. So reform advocates stressed the links between deregulation measures and those concerns. "It is a rare opportunity for the Senate," Senator Howard Cannon pointed out as he opened floor debate on the trucking bill, "to be able to do something more than merely pay lip service to reducing Government regulation and do something concrete to fight inflation." Largely by drawing such connections, advocates of deregulation helped create electoral incentives to support reform.

Such incentives evidently existed even in the case of trucking—the industry farthest removed from the personal concerns of most voters. A number of congressional aides and other informed observers were asked in interviews, around the time of congressional action, whether members of Congress risked the loss of any electoral support if they opposed deregulation of the trucking industry. The observers generally did perceive such risks and attributed them to the voters' agitation about inflation, big government, or excessive regulation. Significantly, these observers did not claim that the electoral risks of opposing deregulation were equivalent to the risks of offending interest groups by supporting it. The risks of supporting deregulation were considered greater. But, in the estimate of one deregulation advocate, the diffuse support balanced the interest-group opposition sufficiently to make the electoral calculation, overall, "a close call."

That members of Congress actually perceived diffuse electoral pressures to support deregulation is illustrated by an episode in the House Surface Transportation Subcommittee. At one point chairman James Howard, an opponent of deregulation, floated the idea of introducing a bill that provided for total deregulation and then modifying it (drastically, he presumed) by amendments in the subcommittee. (He hoped this procedure would force the Carter administration to support weakening amendments, taking some of the heat off of deregulation opponents in the House.) The subcommittee members, however, especially the Republicans, vetoed the strategy. Even though most of them were also sympathetic to the trucking industry and were willing to approve a weak bill, they refused to be put in the position of having to vote openly for amendments restoring regulation.

More important, despite intense and one-sided interest-group pressure to oppose deregulation, majorities in the Senate Commerce Committee and on the Senate floor supported it. They would probably not have done so if there had been no diffuse pressure in favor of deregulation and supporting deregulation had seemed an unmitigated loss in electoral terms.

Why would a member of Congress worry about how voters in the district will react to a relatively obscure issue like trucking deregulation? After all, survey research shows that few voters in congressional elections make their decisions on the basis of even the most salient policy issues, or even know the candidates' positions. Conceivably, members of Congress simply overestimate the voters' concern with issues. More likely, however, they have learned from experience and observation that the voters' response to a policy issue affects a member's prospects for reelection a good deal more often than the prevalence of explicit issue voting would lead one to suppose.

Without detectable issue voting, the voters' response to an issue may have electoral consequences in two principal ways. First, if a member of Congress or a challenger uses an issue effectively in campaign rhetoric, the effect on the voters' images of the candidates and voting decisions may persist long after most of them have forgotten the specific issue. (Indeed, an issue can provide the basis for an effective campaign claim without even being explicitly mentioned.) According to some of the staff of senators who ran for reelection in 1980, the issue of trucking deregulation

received occasional mention in the senate campaigns. To take only one example, one senator included his support for trucking deregulation in a list he often recited of things he had done to fight inflation. Such use of the issue implies at least the perception of an electoral reward.

Second, a relatively small group of opinion leaders may share most of the public's moods and concerns, pay close attention to debates in Congress, and influence voters' images of congressional candidates accordingly, yet without transmitting much information about issues. Newspapers throughout the country editorialized almost uniformly in favor of deregulation. Members of Congress probably assumed that many opinion leaders, and because of them some voters, would respond favorably to support for deregulation.

To account for electoral incentives that could influence decisions on legislation, these implicit forms of issue voting need not affect a large proportion of the electorate. They must merely have an effect on the vote in the same order of magnitude as the effect of the interest-group response at stake in a given decision. Considering the large number of legislative decisions that affect interest groups and the relatively small number of swing voters, an issue-voting effect sufficient to influence those decisions is likely to involve a tiny fraction of the vote—too small for detection in survey research. One part of the explanation of Congress's response to deregulation, then, is that the electoral incentives of members of Congress are considerably less skewed in favor of narrow interests than the economic theorists have supposed.

The Role of Members' Beliefs

Contrary to the economic theories, however, members of Congress do not act almost solely on the basis of electoral calculations. To a great extent they act on their judgments about the merits of issues and conceptions of the public interest.

That they do so (and are presumed by other participants to do so) was again especially evident in the Senate debate on the trucking bill. To begin with, policy advocates—particularly reformers—invested heavily in efforts to persuade senators on the merits. In a close collaboration among the White House, the Department of Transportation, and the Senate Commerce Committee staff, they assiduously gathered evidence, polished arguments, worked out rebuttals to industry claims, planned and sponsored new research, and presented the resulting flood of information—along with summaries and oral briefings—to the Commerce Committee, other senators, and their staffs. Much of the research was designed specifically to answer questions senators had raised.

Accordingly, participants in the conflict saw the members' judgments of the merits as a major influence in their decisions. Even though, as we have seen, senators had some electoral grounds to support deregulation, at least in the trucking case they were widely presumed to have, on balance, even stronger grounds to oppose it. Participants sympathetic to reform often described the choice facing a senator as one of whether to stand up to the interest-group pressures, decide on the merits, and support deregulation or rather bow to those pressures, minimize electoral risk, and oppose deregulation. They showered praise for courage and

independence on senators who supported reform. Such senators, not surprisingly, felt they deserved the praise: "I know I'm going to take heat for this, but damn it, it's right," one told another senator during the vote. Senators who opposed trucking deregulation also professed to be acting out of conviction, of course, but did not make a comparable pitch for moral credit.

Finally, the pattern of roll-call votes in the Senate suggests that support for trucking deregulation was associated with willingness to discount electoral costs. Senators who were up for reelection in 1980, the year of the debate, were substantially less likely to vote for trucking deregulation than those who were up for reelection in 1982 or 1984 or who had announced their retirement from the Senate (see table 1). For example, in the most closely contested floor vote (in which the

T A B L E 1

Senate Voting on Amendments to and Passage of the Motor Carrier Reform Bill in 1980, by Reelection Status and Party

Reelection Status and Party	Processed Foods Amendment[a]		Entry Standard Amendment[b]		Small-Community Entry Amendment[c]		Final Passage	
	For	Against	For	Against	For	Against	For	Against
Running	8	19	10	16	7	19	18	8
	(30)	(70)	(38)	(62)	(27)	(73)	(69)	(31)
Democrat	4	16	5	14	3	16	11	8
	(20)	(80)	(26)	(74)	(16)	(84)	(58)	(42)
Republican	4	3	5	2	4	3	7	0
	(57)	(43)	(71)	(29)	(57)	(43)	(100)	(0)
Not running	40	21	46	18	30	33	52	12
	(66)	(34)	(72)	(28)	(48)	(52)	(81)	(19)
Democrat	18	14	19	14	13	19	23	10
	(56)	(44)	(58)	(42)	(41)	(59)	(70)	(30)
Republican	22	7	27	4	17	14	29	2
	(76)	(24)	(87)	(13)	(55)	(45)	(94)	(6)
Total	48	40	56	34	37	52	70	20
	(55)	(45)	(62)	(38)	(42)	(58)	(78)	(22)

Source: Derthick and Quirk, *The Politics of Deregulation*, p. 134. Authors' calculations based on voting data from *Congressional Quarterly Weekly Report*, vol. 38 (April 19, 1980), p. 1062. The voting data include those who were paired for and against each measure. Votes on amendments, all three of which were defeated, are coded so that a vote "for" indicates support for deregulation. Numbers in parentheses are percentages of the raw totals in each category.

a. Offered by Ernest F. Hollings, Democrat of South Carolina; would have eliminated an expanded agricultural exemption.

b. Offered by Warren G. Magnuson, Democrat of Washington; would have imposed a more restrictive test on applications for entry.

c. Offered by Harrison H. Schmitt, Republican of New Mexico; would have eliminated the requirement to meet a test of public convenience and necessity as it applied to applications to provide service to small communities.

Senate rejected an industry effort to restore regulation of processed foods), senators up for reelection opposed deregulation by about two to one (19 to 8) while those not up for reelection supported it two to one (40 to 21). The same pattern appeared in varying degrees on the two other substantive amendments and on final passage, and was evident within each party. The lesser support for deregulation from senators more immediately at risk suggests that such support was considered to be, on balance, more harmful than beneficial to a senator's electoral prospects—an inference that should apply even to senators up for reelection in later years. (In a few years, the electoral effects presumably would diminish, perhaps sharply, but not disappear, and they certainly would not change directions. If anything, interest groups will have a longer memory than the general public.) Yet more than a majority of senators, including some up for reelection, supported deregulation in crucial votes.

The notion that members of Congress have opinions about public policy and that those opinions are a principal source of their legislative decisions was taken for granted by nearly all academic and other analysts of Congress until quite recently—when some academic analysts began to posit reelection as the objective of all or most legislative decisions.

The reelection assumption could hold for any of three reasons. First, members of Congress could want only to hold office and obtain any benefits that come automatically with doing so. The principal benefit cannot be money income; many members of Congress could earn much more in private life. Rather, this condition would require a specific and peculiar set of tastes for other benefits. Members of Congress would have to want a career of debating public issues, but not one of defending their own convictions about those issues; a sense of participation in policy-making, but not discretion and genuine power; the approval of voters, but not that of congressional colleagues or other elites; and the achievement of getting and keeping office, but no achievement beyond that. It is far more plausible that for many members the opportunities to defend their convictions, exercise power, win respect among the political elite, and make a contribution to the nation's well-being are among the main reasons for wanting the job.

Second, members of Congress could have concerns beyond reelection but be forced to set them aside to stay in office. This notion lacks support, however, in the politics of congressional elections. Reelection depends mainly on campaigns and party fortunes. In view of the large number of significant issues decided in each Congress, the large differences in issue positions even among members with similar districts, and the exceedingly high rate of reelection of congressional incumbents, few issues can pose a substantial threat to a typical member's reelection. The members usually have considerable leeway. It is sometimes urged that many members appear electorally secure only because they bend every effort (and every principle) to achieve security. But the fact that most members are returned to office in no way suggests that a specific pattern of roll-call votes is the basis of their success.

Finally, single-minded reelection seeking could also result if, although members of Congress had concerns beyond holding office and, objectively speaking, had considerable leeway to pursue those concerns, they nevertheless had too strong an aversion to risk to take any unnecessary chances with reelection. In the heat of a reelection campaign, members of Congress are undoubtedly anxious about their prospects. But to suppose that such anxiety pervades members' legislative decisions throughout their terms and regardless of their electoral strength runs against what we know of human decision-making generally and politicians specifically. Cognitive psychology suggests that individuals tend to discount rather than exaggerate low-probability risks. And politicians, however safe their seats eventually become, all chose to start out in what they knew was a risky career.

In the end, there is no compelling ground for assuming that reelection is even the single most important motive in legislative decisions. The goal of reelection undoubtedly often governs a member of Congress's decisions on those occasions when his policy beliefs and electoral interests are in conflict and the electoral stakes are significant. But for most members such occasions may be relatively infrequent, and the latitude to act on the merits far more typical.

The Incentives of Committee Leadership

The leaders of congressional committees and subcommittees, instead of being reliable protectors of committee clients as the electoral theory's view of committees would imply, actually have special incentives and more inclination than other members to act on behalf of general interests.

Partisan and ideological differences among such leaders often obscure their common tendency to serve general interests. That tendency emerged clearly in these cases, however, because of an unusual configuration of conflicting pressures. On the one hand, the interest groups associated respectively with the Republican and Democratic parties—the regulated industries and their labor unions—strongly opposed deregulation. On the other hand, the ideological principles associated respectively with the Republican and Democratic parties—free market conservatism and liberal consumerism, as well as ideologically neutral policy analysis—favored deregulation. Regardless of party or ideology, therefore, those members who were more inclined to deny narrowly based interests and serve broadly based ones tended to support deregulation.

In each of the three cases of deregulation, in both parties and in both houses the leaders of the committees or subcommittees with jurisdiction almost uniformly supported reform. The airline deregulation bill was cosponsored in the Senate by Aviation Subcommittee chairman Howard Cannon and ranking minority member James B. Pearson. After some initial partisan maneuvering, it was cosponsored in the House subcommittee by chairman Glenn Anderson, ranking member Gene Snyder, and other members of both parties.

In telecommunications, support for procompetitive reform held through a succession of committee leaders over three Congresses. Led by chairman Ernest F. Hollings, the Senate subcommittee in 1977 held hearings designed largely to defend the FCC's procompetitive policies against the criticisms leveled by AT&T. For the next six years, subcommittee and full Commerce Committee leaders of both parties— Democrats Cannon and Hollings, and Republicans Bob Packwood, Barry Goldwater, and Harrison H. Schmitt—proposed a series of bills endorsing competition. House subcommittee chairman Lionel Van Deerlin and ranking member Louis Frey worked to kill AT&T's anticompetitive bill, held hearings to defend competition, and attempted a massive procompetitive "rewrite" of the entire communications act. Subsequently, Van Deerlin sponsored procompetitive bills with James M. Collins, Frey's successor as ranking member. Van Deerlin's successor, Timothy E. Wirth, who had been an early advocate of telecommunications competition, took the same view as chairman.

In trucking deregulation, the Senate bill was again sponsored by Howard Cannon, then chairman of the full Commerce Committee, and ranking minority member Bob Packwood; they worked in concert to push a highly procompetitive measure through the Senate. As mentioned earlier, the leadership of the House Surface Transportation Subcommittee was the only exception to the pattern of support. In the clientelist tradition of the full Public Works Committee, subcommittee chairman James Howard, ranking minority member Bud Schuster, and full committee ranking member William Harsha were closely tied to the trucking industry. Yet although they tried to resist deregulation, even they were unwilling to oppose it in open confrontation with the reformers. Rather, they ended up sponsoring a compromise and even demanding a share of the credit for deregulation.

Despite the political benefits available to committee leaders in their relationships with interest groups, they have strong moral, electoral, and institutional incentives to lead their committees to respond effectively to general interests. The circumstances of committee leadership accentuate the same incentives that induce general-interest responses from other legislators. Committee leaders know that their decisions on legislation have major consequences for public policy and the condition of American society. To some extent this encourages greater concern for the public effects of those decisions and a greater disposition to decide on the merits.

With respect to reelection, committee leaders know that their role in the legislative process (which may include introducing the bills, presiding over the committee proceedings, leading the floor debates, and lending their names to the final products) is exceptionally visible and that they are personally identified with the legislation their committees produce. Senator Cannon, for example, observed in an interview that his role in airline and trucking deregulation had gained him a reputation, useful in his home state of Nevada, as an opponent of excessive regulation. Committee leaders are also relatively immune to electoral retaliation by interest groups, which would take a large risk in opposing a committee leader in an election campaign. Thus committee leaders have electoral incentives stronger than those of other members to appeal to the beliefs and interests of the general public.

Institutional inducements for responding to general interests, supplied by Congress itself and the Washington community, are also enhanced for those in positions of leadership. A leader is likely to be more concerned than other members about his prestige in Washington circles. He will want to have a reputation for effective leadership and his committee to have a reputation for significant contributions to public policy. Such reputations are earned mainly by skillful promotion of innovative and responsible legislation, not by dedicated service to special interests.

To be sure, when a committee has a political alliance with an interest group, committee leaders are usually central figures in the arrangement. But when there are pressures or opportunities to pursue broader objectives, the leaders often respond. In addition, they sometimes create these opportunities. The responsiveness of committee leaders to general interests undermines the electoral theory's view of the committee system as mainly a device to deliver benefits to narrow groups.

CONCLUSION

The response of Congress to deregulation and procompetitive reform in the airline, trucking, and telecommunications industries reflects three influences that the economic theories overlook or explicitly deny. First, members of Congress have electoral incentives shaped not only by interest-group demands but, even on issues of low or moderate salience, by the beliefs and preferences of the general public. The fact that such incentives are important implies of course that members of Congress do pursue reelection and, in that respect, is consistent with the self-interest assumption. But the existence of diffuse electoral incentives also implies that voters are concerned with the general consequences of policy choices and thus that they are not self-interested in any strict sense. As the economic theorists have pointed out, voters who sought to enhance their individual economic welfare (and not the welfare of large groups to which they belong) would attend only to issues in which they had exceedingly high per capita stakes.[10] Members of Congress would not have expected such voters to respond to deregulation on the basis of general concerns about inflation, big government, or excessive regulation.

Second, members of Congress do not pursue reelection exclusively. Contrary to the self-interest assumption, many act on judgments about the merits of policy issues or, more generally, conceptions of the public interest. They do so because to act in that manner is one of the major satisfactions of holding office and because, under many circumstances, it causes very slight additional risk of electoral defeat.

Finally, congressional committee and subcommittee leaders, that is, the principal issue-by-issue leaders of the contemporary Congress, have even stronger incentives and a greater inclination to serve general interests than other members. These incentives involve a combi-

nation of self-interested and non-self-interested motivations. Compared with other members, they are likely to feel a stronger sense of duty to serve general interests. They can also obtain greater electoral rewards by appealing to broad segments of the electorate and will face less threat of retaliation from interest groups. And they can earn respect in the Washington community for their leadership.

As a result of this combination of motivations and influences, Congress has the capacity to defeat narrow, well-organized interests and vindicate diffuse, unorganized interests. Put differently, it can act on beliefs and values presumed to express general interests.

One might object that Congress has such a capacity only occasionally, when it enacts "landmark reforms" (so named for their infrequency), that it creates or maintains special-interest benefits far more frequently, and that serving narrow interests is therefore its characteristic mode of policy-making. Undoubtedly, the defeats suffered by powerful, well-organized interests in the deregulation cases were unusual. They were expected by few, if any, informed observers.

The objection, nevertheless, is unwarranted. In focusing merely on the frequency of actions that provide special-interest benefits, it overlooks the disproportionate magnitude of the occasional general-interest reforms, the frequency with which Congress refuses to grant special-interest benefits or deters potential recipients from even asking for them, and the degree to which policies that may look like deference to interest groups arise from widespread beliefs about the workings of markets or the requirements of equity. In addition, a group's ability to preserve special benefits often results in large part from obstacles in Congress to policy change of any kind—the advantage of the status quo—rather than superior resources or political efficacy. Instead of current group power, existing benefits may reflect mainly the past power of interest groups or even the past beliefs of the general public.

Although Congress defers to narrow interests far more often than one would wish—perhaps even enough to suggest a need for structural reform—such deference is by no means consistent or complete. To the contrary, if one looks at the outcomes of congressional policy-making in relation to the actual and potential demand for special-interest benefits, the deference appears quite limited. Congress has established regulatory programs to limit competition, for example, in only a handful of major industries. Some of those were natural monopolies that only later become potentially competitive; most of the others were infrastructure industries first regulated during the Depression, when even economists had abandoned faith in free markets. Most industries, evidently anticipating failure, have not sought direct regulatory restrictions on pricing or entry. Similarly, Congress has either denied or managed to deter requests for trade protection from most industries exposed to import competition, preserving a generally liberal trade policy since the 1930s. The trade bills, criticized as protectionist, that Congress has debated under the pressure of unprecedented trade deficits in recent years have sought to modify that policy at the margins. Until the Reagan administration, Congress had disciplined federal budget policy well enough to reduce the national debt in relation to national income in most periods other than wartime. The legislature's most promiscuous granting of benefits, historically, has perhaps been the creation of special provisions in the tax code. But even before the Tax Reform Act of 1986, Congress limited such provisions sufficiently to keep general tax rates in a supportable range. Moreover, surveys indicated that most of the special provisions had widespread public support.

In short, the capacity of Congress to respond to general interests and to act on ideas about those interests is not limited to rare episodes like the abolition of an anti-competitive regulatory program or the adoption of a major tax reform bill. Though often overridden by special-interest politics, this tendency is regularly a prominent feature of congressional policy-making.

The strength of this capacity has two broad implications for political analysis. On the one hand, it implies that policy debates are less dominated by distributive conflict, and policy outcomes less distorted by narrow functional and geographic interests, than the capture and electoral theories would predict. As a result, it also implies a greater likelihood of responsible, effective public policy and suggests a more sanguine view of the effects of government intervention. A capacity to act on ideas about general interests also points to possibilities for improving policy-making through collective learning—suggesting, for example, that the Depression-era mistake of sacrificing competition to achieve stability may not be repeated, de novo, on a massive scale.

On the other hand, this congressional capacity is reason to look for important sources of policy failure other than excessive regard for special interests. Instead of resulting from the political advantages of narrow groups with respect to organization, information costs, and the like, important failures are likely to reflect other barriers to effective, responsible policy-making. Such barriers include, among others, cognitive biases and limitations that affect both public and elite understanding of policy issues, institutional weaknesses with respect to information gathering or deliberation, and the difficulties of conducting negotiations and achieving constructive outcomes in the conflictual environment of public policy-making. Policy-making may be shaped by ideas about the public interest, but they may not be *good* ideas. The obstacles to a deliberate, informed politics of ideas are more serious threats to the nation's well-being—and more worthy of researchers' attention—than the potential for exploitation and waste that arises in the politics of self-interest.

NOTES

1. Martha Derthick and Paul J. Quirk, *The Politics of Deregulation* (Washington, D.C.: Brookings Institution, 1985).
2. George J. Stigler, "The Theory of Economic Regulation," *Bell Journal of Economics and Management Science* 2 (1971): 3–21. There is also an earlier and quite different capture theory: see Marver H. Bernstein, *Regulating Business by Independent Commission* (Princeton: Princeton University Press, 1955).
3. Ibid., p. 3.
4. Sam Peltzman, "Toward a More General Theory of Regulation," *Journal of Law and Economics* 19 (1976): 211–40.
5. Roger G. Noll and Bruce M. Owen, *The Political Economy of Deregulation: Interest Groups in the Regulatory Process* (Washington, D.C.: American Enterprise Institute, 1983).
6. See, respectively, Michael Levine, "Revisionism Revisited? Airline Deregulation and the Public Interest," *Journal of Law and Economics* 44 (1981): 179–95; and Gary S. Becker, "A Theory of Competition among Pressure Groups for Political Influence," *Quarterly Journal of Economics* 98 (1983): 371–400.
7. David R. Mayhew, *Congress: The Electoral Connection* (New Haven: Yale University Press, 1974); Morris Fiorina, *Congress: Keystone of the Washington Establishment* (New Haven: Yale University Press, 1977).
8. Fiorina, *Congress*, esp. chaps. 2 and 4.
9. The airline and trucking industries argued that small towns and rural areas would suffer under deregulation, but reform advocates presented a good deal of argu-

ment and evidence to the contrary, and managed to
avoid any strong perception of regional conflict. See
Derthick and Quirk, *Politics of Deregulation*, chap. 4.

10. Voters who were literally out to maximize their individual economic welfare presumably would care only
about how issues and candidates' positions affect their
specific interests, such as the income earned in their
industries or occupations. If they wanted to vote that
way, the necessary information would be easily produced and distributed. In fact, interest groups notoriously are unable to control the votes of their members.

PART TWO

THE DEVELOPMENT OF THE NATIONAL POLITY

SOME IMPORTANT DATES

1775–1783	Revolution of the American colonies against Great Britain
1787–1789	Drafting and ratification of the U.S. Constitution
By 1830s	Extension of voting rights to all white men
1828	Election of President Andrew Jackson
1860	Election of President Abraham Lincoln
1861–1865	The Civil War
January 1, 1863	The Emancipation Proclamation: begins the legal process of freeing the slaves
1865–1877	Reconstruction: Union military occupation of the South
1906–1920	The Progressive Era
1917–1919	World War I
1920	Nineteenth Amendment to the U.S. Constitution: voting rights for women
1929–1939	The great depression
1932–1940	The New Deal; the first two terms of President Franklin Delano Roosevelt
June 16, 1933	National Industrial Recovery Act
July 5, 1935	"Wagner" National Labor Relations Act
August 14, 1935	Social Security Act
1939–1945	World War II
1946–1980s	The cold war: United States versus the Soviet Union
1955–1965	Civil rights movement in the South
1960s	"New politics" reforms
July 2, 1964	Civil Rights Act: abolishes segregation
August 6, 1965	Voting Rights Act: enforces voting rights for blacks

People sometimes say that the United States does not have a "state." They have in mind certain important facts about American political development, stretching from the founding of the nation to the present. The American Revolution of 1775 to 1789 freed the thirteen American colonies from British imperial control and brought the former colonists together to create a new government for the "United States." Calling for government "by the people," the new U.S. Constitution prevented the establishment of a monarchy, or a centralized bureaucracy, or a unified parliament. In other words, the Constitution precluded the establishment of any unified center of sovereignty that could govern the entire country from the national capital. Americans were—and still are—distrustful of concentrated governmental power. Thus the Constitution deliberately established a governmental system that divided decision-making among local governments, state governments, and the federal government. Within the federal government, moreover, the president had to share decision-making powers with the Senate, the House of Representatives, and an independent system of courts. Down to the present day, these basic divisions of power continue to exist within U.S. governmental institutions. No monopoly of sovereignty in a national bureaucracy or single center of authority has ever emerged in the United States.

But a "state" does not have to be a centralized national bureaucracy headed by a monarch or a parliament. A state is any set of governmental organizations that collects and spends taxes, maintains order over a given territory, and makes and carries out authoritative decisions for people living in that territory. Of course, the United States has always had a state in this sense of the word. Our job is to understand *what kind* of state the United States has had at each phase of its history, and why that state has changed in important ways through revolution, civil war, foreign wars, and domestic political reforms.

During the nineteenth century, the United States developed what the political scientist Stephen Skowronek (1982, Chap. 2) has aptly called a "state of courts and parties"—a very different kind of state from the monarchies that existed in much of Europe at that time. By the 1830s and 1840s, virtually all American white men, regardless of whether or not they owned property, had gained the right to vote in local, state, and national elections. The United States became the world's first mass democracy. As voting rights expanded, competing political parties came to the fore. These parties were actually networks of local and state party organizations that managed elections and took control of legislative and executive offices throughout the land. Before the Civil War, the dominant parties were the Democrats and the Whigs; after the Civil War, they were the Republicans and the Democrats. These major political parties were "patronage" parties, because they placed their followers in key government offices. They also engineered legislative decisions to distribute benefits (such as land, or regulatory advantages, or pensions) to local groups of loyal voters.

Meanwhile, judges in state and federal courts were also important decision makers. They ruled on cases that argued about property rights, business contracts, the rights of workers or farmers to organize, and the relationship of government to the economy. After the landmark 1803 case of *Marbury v. Madison*, the federal courts, including the U.S. Supreme Court, gained the right to declare "unconstitutional" any laws that the judges decided were not proper under the terms of the U.S. Constitution. This kind of power claimed by American courts is very unusual; judges and courts in other nations usually cannot overrule the decisions of legislatures or the decisions of political parties that gain a majority of votes in elections. In the United States down to the present day, however, courts and judges can make very important political decisions affecting the economy and the rights and welfare of American citizens.

The U.S. state underwent major transformations during, as well as after, the nineteenth century. The election of 1860 put a new political party, the Republicans, in charge of the national government. This soon led to the outbreak of the Civil War, which lasted from 1861 to 1865, culminating in the victory of the Union over the southern Confederacy and the emancipation of African-Americans from slavery. During what is called the "Reconstruction" period, there was a military occupation of the defeated south by the federal government. After Reconstruction ended and voting rights were restored to the south, intense party competition revived between the Democrats and the Republicans. For the rest of the nineteenth century, the two parties vied for control of the national government, the presidency, and the Congress. The Republicans managed to protect their advantage over the Democrats by using the powers of the Congress to manipulate the timing of admission of new states, such as Colorado and Nevada, carved out of the western territories. By admitting to the Union sparsely populated new states that would vote for their party in national elections, the Republicans managed to hold control of the Senate and the presidency for most years after the Civil War (see Stewart & Weingast, 1992, for an analysis of this from a public choice perspective). The Republicans thus were able to continue to use the federal government, even after the Civil War and Reconstruction, to promote northern industrialization through high protective tariffs.

A "new American state" (Skowronek 1982) was gradually built in the twentieth century, especially during the Progressive Era of roughly 1906 to 1920, the New Deal of the 1930s, and the Second World War of 1939 to 1945. Across these historical watersheds, U.S. political structures made a transition *from* a nineteenth-century U.S. federal state characterized by competitive, patronage-oriented political parties, weak bureaucracies, and strong courts and legislatures *to* a twentieth-century U.S. federal state characterized by weakened political parties, less competitive elections, stronger executives, partial and fragmentary bureaucratization at all levels of government, and the rise of associational styles of lobbying by economic interest groups. This transition did not take place all at once, but in various steps and phases.

Around the turn of the twentieth century, the patronage-oriented political parties receded from the dominant place in politics and policy-making that they had held since the 1830s. Elections no longer were so tightly contested in most parts of the country, and citizens did not vote as frequently as they had in the nineteenth century. Indeed, many scholars believe that popular voting has been a less important part of twentieth-century American government than it was when political parties were organizationally robust (see the readings in Chapter 4). Counterbalancing this trend, however, are the important expansions of the eligible electorate that occurred during the twentieth century. Before 1920, American women could vote only in a few states or territories, or in local elections; but the Nineteenth Amendment to the U.S. Constitution in 1920 guaranteed all women the right to vote. Decades later, the civil rights movement led to the 1965 Voting Rights Act, which put the power of the federal government at work to guarantee voting rights for blacks in the South. The United States may have been the world's first mass democracy for white males, but it did not become a full democracy for all of its citizens until the 1960s (Kleppner, 1982; Valelly, 1993).

Especially during the Progressive Era and the New Deal, reform-oriented groups—often dominated by middle-class professionals—argued that new bureaucratic agencies should be created outside of the control of party politicians. Once established, these agencies had to work out relationships with legislatures, courts, and executives. They also had to deal with pressures from business associations and other interest groups that constantly sought to lobby mayors, governors, presidents, and legislators on behalf of particular concerns, especially economic concerns. In an important sense, U.S. government as a whole became even more complex and internally divided during the twentieth century, more so than it had been when the major patronage-oriented political parties tied together the various levels of government and worked out bargains among different groups and sections of the country.

During the New Deal of the 1930s, however, the Democratic party, which had been dominant in the white-ruled South since the 1890s, also benefited from an upsurge of new electoral support from many nonsouthern groups, including workers, farmers, and northern blacks. Responding to the economic emergency and social suffering of the great depression, President Franklin Roosevelt fashioned unprecedented kinds of governmental interventions in the economy and society, including the regulation of banking and industry, the legalization of labor unions by the Wagner Act of 1935, and the establishment of nationwide unemployment, old-age, and public assistance programs through the Social Security Act of 1935. Through these and other programs, the federal government gained new leverage over states, cities, businesses, and citizens; federal bureaucracies expanded; and the president gained authority in relation to the Congress. World War II further enhanced many capacities of the national government. The income tax was extended to cover most American wage and salary earners, thus becoming a major source of revenue for the federal government. A national military buildup occurred, not only to fight World War II and the Korean war, but also to exert American power against the Soviet Union during the cold war.

Few people would argue that the United States since World War II has been without a truly strong national state. Still, government in the United States has retained its historically distinctive institutional features. Congress and the courts have remained influential in national policy-making, often able to rival presidents (as well as each other) in influencing decisions about issues ranging from foreign aid to economic policy to abortion. Local and state governments have also remained vital arenas of politics and policy implementation, and the federal government tries to accomplish many of its goals, not through national administrative action, but by giving funds to states and localities or by regulating their activities. Despite the heightened authority of the president and the enhanced power of the national government that the crises of the twentieth century have furthered, the United States of America remains a country where citizens distrust concentrated sovereignty, and where there are many checks and balances built into the workings of politics at each level of the three-tiered federal system.

REFERENCES

Kleppner, Paul. 1982. *Who Voted?: The Dynamics of Electoral Turnout, 1870–1980.* New York: Praeger.

Skowronek, Stephen. 1982. *Building a New American State: The Expansion of National Administrative Capacities, 1877–1920.* Cambridge, England, and New York: Cambridge University Press.

Stewart, Charles III, and Barry R. Weingast. 1992. "Stacking the Senate, Changing the Nation: Republican Rotten Boroughs, Statehood Politics, and American Political Development." *Studies in American Political Development* 6 (Fall 1992):223–71.

Valelly, Richard. 1993. "Party, Coercion, and Inclusion: The Two Reconstructions and the South's Electoral Politics." *Politics and Society* 21 (March): 37–67.

CHAPTER 4

THE STATE, PARTIES, AND ELECTIONS

How are we to describe and explain the special features of U.S. political institutions from 1789 to the present? How can we situate U.S. political institutions in comparison with those of other industrializing capitalist nations, especially in Europe, and what forces have changed U.S. institutions over time? These are grand questions—the sort that only "big thinkers" in the scholarly world have been able to tackle. Three such thinkers are Samuel P. Huntington, Walter Dean Burnham, and Martin Shefter, each of whom brings a distinctive and valuable perspective to the study of American political development in comparative-historical perspective.

Samuel Huntington (see Reading 9) calls the kind of polity established by the U.S. Constitution a "Tudor polity." His point is that the rebellious American colonists not only broke their new nation away from Europe, but also rejected the kinds of "rationalization" of state authority and "specialization" of governmental functions that were occurring in European states during the course of political modernization. On the continent of Europe, monarchs were the ones who built centralized bureaucracies with concentrated authority to make and implement political decisions; in Britain, there was a revolution against the Stuart kings, and Parliament became the center of national political authority. But the United States, argues Huntington, created a governmental system that resembled England's polity under the Tudor monarchs, before the English revolution brought Parliament to power. The Tudor and the U.S. governments both spread powers among different institutions and levels of government. Huntington believes that America has always retained a "premodern" government with such divided powers and overlapping areas of authority.

Yet there was one dimension on which the United States was the first to undergo political modernization: the expansion of political participation in politics. While kings and propertied classes remained in control in Europe during the nineteenth century, the United States extended voting rights to white men of all economic classes. Violent revolutions were often required to extend political participation in Europe, Huntington argues, but the United States was fortunate to be born with a modern, pluralistic, and consensual society, based in an economy where property ownership was widely dispersed. Huntington argues that America, unlike Europe (and unlike many developing nations today), never needed a centralized state to promote economic development, and did not have to experience violent political conflict in order to overthrow the rule of a monarch or a feudal upper class and bring about full popular participation in national politics. America did not need a strong state to fight foreign wars either.

In fact, Huntington comes very close to arguing that nations get the kinds of governmental institutions they "need" to deal with whatever military or economic challenges they must face, and whatever social divisions they must manage. His perspective on U.S. political development can be criticized for overlooking the massive Civil War that wracked the United States during the 1860s (for other analyses of U.S. political development that feature the Civil War, see Bensel, 1990; Moore, 1966; Shade, 1974). In addition, Huntington downplays the racial, ethnic, regional, and class conflicts that have arisen in every era of American history from the founding of the nation to the present.

Since the nation was founded, elections have been an integral part of American politics, connecting voters to their political representatives. However, the character of elections has changed dramatically—as new groups have gained suffrage, as the organization and constituent bases of parties have shifted, as the tactics and resources of electoral campaigns have evolved, and as new problems have confronted the nation. One of the foremost U.S. authorities on political parties and elections is Walter Dean Burnham, a political scientist noted especially for his analysis of "critical electoral realignments"—sets of elections during which new coalitions and voting patterns emerge that fundamentally alter the course of national politics and public policy. In Reading 10, Burnham identifies five national systems of political party competition: the experimental system of 1789–1820; the democratizing system of 1828–1854/60; the Civil War system of 1860–1893; the industrialist system of 1894–1932; and the New Deal system of 1932 to recent times. Burnham also discusses the social disruptions and economic upheavals that brought about the critical electoral realignments that he holds marked the transitions from each major party system to the next.

Martin Shefter (Reading 11) approaches the periodization and explanation of U.S. political development from an institutionalist, state–society perspective, similar to the perspectives found in readings elsewhere in this collection by Theda Skocpol and David Vogel (among others). Political parties and administrative bureaucracies change in relation to one another over successive phases of a nation's history, Shefter argues. Along with Walter Dean Burnham, Shefter believes that there have been periodic critical realignments in the American electoral system, each of which brings a new dominant political party and a new set of social and economic groups to prominence in the nation's politics. The newly dominant groups attempt to make changes in the organization of political parties or in the organization of governmental administrative agencies, or in both. Attempts are made to change the rules of party politics and administration in ways that give some kinds of policies and groups—and, of course, some styles of doing politics—an advantage over other policies and groups.

Using this analytical scheme, Shefter is able to identify the roots and results of successive major phases of actual and attempted politicogovernmental transformation in American history. The nation was first ruled, he argues, by a regime of notables that deemphasized partisan competition and popular participation in politics, and used elite patronage to fill governmental offices. Then came the Jacksonians, who sought to displace and replace privileged elites, and found it to their advantage to create professionally run, patronage-oriented political parties to compete for power in a cross-class, male, democratic electorate. Eventually mugwump reformers, and then progressive reformers, sought to counter and reduce the power of party politicians whom they considered "corrupt" and inefficient. The mugwumps met with little success, but the progressives eventually took advantage of party weaknesses to institute many electoral and administrative reforms, launching the new American state of the twentieth century.

Shefter traces further transformations in parties and administrative arrangements through the New Deal and down to the new politics reforms of the 1960s. Through all of these transformations, Shefter argues, political parties and electoral democracy have been weakened in the United States. Bureaucratic agencies, meanwhile, have proliferated and become partially independent and competing centers of governmental authority, thus contradicting some of the premises of the original American constitutional vision. Significantly, Shefter's approach to the study of U.S. political development does much more than that of Samuel Huntington to highlight *institutional changes* from the founding of the nation to the present. While Shefter might not deny that elements of a Tudor polity have persisted, he sees much more dynamism than does Huntington. Shefter highlights structural changes in the ground rules of U.S. politics, transformations brought about not only through industrialization and other aspects of economic modernization, but also through critical elections, changes in the organization of political parties, and shifting patterns of bureaucratization.

The final reading in Chapter 4, by Richard Valelly, examines recent trends in the U.S. electoral system against the backdrop of the previous phases of American political history delineated by Burnham and Shefter. As Valelly reports, voter turnout for U.S. national elections has been dropping steadily since 1960. This is particularly disturbing in view of the fact that voter participation in the United States was already even then alarmingly low by international standards. Whereas roughly half of all Americans eligible to vote actually do so in national elections, voter participation often runs as high as 70 percent or 80 percent, and occasionally more than 90 percent, in many other industrial democracies (Piven & Cloward 1988, pp. 5–19). Much higher rates of eligible voter participation also characterized highly competitive U.S. elections during the nineteenth century. Twentieth-century America may be, formally speaking, highly democratic, but it is a democracy in which many citizens choose not to exercise their most basic right, the right to vote.

Survey research suggests that low and declining voter participation reflects a growing dissatisfaction with government (Teixeira, 1992). However, the problem also stems from deeper historical trends in American politics. For instance, Valelly believes that electoral participation has also declined because voters no longer strongly identify with one or the other of the two major parties. Perhaps this has happened because the Democratic party after the 1960s seemed to gravitate toward the kinds of market-oriented economic policies formerly identified with Republicans, rather than pursuing new variants of the government-led policies for which they became known during the New Deal era. Or perhaps declining voter participation can be attributed to the fact that political parties have become much less important in policy-making processes that are dominated by experts, and that often cut across partisan lines (see Heclo, 1978). Citizens may not think that voting matters much in determining what government does.

Perhaps the modest rise in voter turnout for the 1992 presidential election—56 percent of eligible voters participated—represents the end of an era of declining electoral participation. Given that most of the enhanced turnout was in reaction to the unconventional, nonparty candidacy of billionaire Ross Perot, it is surely too soon to conclude that party politics has been revitalized in America (for a discussion, see Burnham, 1993). We cannot yet tell whether gridlock in Washington, D.C., will be overcome now that the Democrats control both the presidency and the Congress. Much may depend on whether President Clinton can make the federal government work to address pressing national problems, and in the process successfully engage voters and the public in the policy-making process.

REFERENCES

Bensel, Richard Franklin. 1990. *Yankee Leviathan: The Origins of Central State Authority in America, 1859–1877.* Cambridge, England, and New York: Cambridge University Press.

Burnham, Walter Dean. 1993. "The Politics of Repudiation, 1992: Edging Toward Upheaval." *The American Prospect* 12 (Winter): 22–33.

Heclo, Hugh. 1978. "Issue Networks and the Executive Establishment." In *The American Political System*, edited by Anthony King, 87–124, Washington, D.C.: American Enterprise Institute.

Moore, Barrington, Jr. 1966. "The American Civil War: The Last Capitalist Revolution." In *Social Origins of Dictatorship and Democracy*, Chapter 3. Boston: Beacon Press.

Piven, Frances Fox, and Richard A. Cloward. 1988. *Why Americans Don't Vote.* New York: Pantheon Books.

Shade, William G. 1974. "'Revolutions Can Go Backwards': The American Civil War and the Problem of Political Development." *Social Science Quarterly* 55(3): 753–67.

Teixeira, Ruy A. 1992. *The Disappearing American Voter.* Washington, D.C.: Brookings Institution.

READING 9

POLITICAL MODERNIZATION: AMERICA VS. EUROPE

Samuel P. Huntington

THREE PATTERNS OF MODERNIZATION

Political modernization involves the rationalization of authority, the differentiation of structures, and the expansion of political participation. In the West, political modernization was spread over many centuries. The sequence and extent of its three components varied significantly in different areas of Europe and North America. Most obviously, the expansion of political participation occurred earlier and far more extensively in America than in Europe. In the eighteenth century political participation in the English colonies, in terms of the suffrage, was already widespread by English standards, not to mention Continental ones. The American Revolution removed the English Crown from the American scene and with it the only possible alternative source of legitimacy to popular sovereignty. The Revolution, as Robert Palmer stresses, made history by establishing the people as the constituent power.[1] All governments derive their just powers from the consent of the governed. Given this principle, little ground existed on which to limit the suffrage. If the people could directly establish a system of government, they certainly could participate in the system so established.

As a result the franchise and other forms of popular participation in government were rapidly expanded with independence. The property qualifications for voting, which in many states did not disenfranchise large numbers of people in any event, were changed first to taxpaying requirements and then abolished altogether. The new states admitted to the union generally came in with no economic restrictions on suffrage. By the 1830s universal white male suffrage was the norm in America. In Europe in contrast, property qualifications remained high. The Reform Act of 1832 expanded the total eligible English electorate from two to four per cent of the total population; in America 16 per cent of

the total population actually voted in the presidential election in 1840. In France high property qualifications existed until 1848 when universal male suffrage was introduced only to be made somewhat less than meaningful with the coming of the Second Empire. Universal male suffrage was introduced in Germany in 1871 but in Prussia the three class system of voting remained in effect until the end of World War I. In the Low Countries and Scandinavia universal male suffrage came at the end of the nineteenth century and in the first decades of the twentieth.

The United States, moreover, pioneered in popular participation in government not only in terms of the number of people who could vote for public officials but also, and perhaps more importantly, in the number of public officials who could be voted on by the people. In Europe suffrage was normally limited to the lower house of the national parliament and to local councils; in America, in contrast, as de Tocqueville observed, "the principle of election extends to everything," and scores of officials at the national, state, and local level were subject to popular approval. De Tocqueville's dramatic contrast between the equality and democracy he saw here and the conditions he knew in Europe was, of course, only one indication of the American lead in expanding participation.

The early widespread political participation in America as contrasted with Europe often leads people to conclude that political modernization in general occurred earlier and more rapidly in the United States than in Europe. Such, however, is far from the case. In fact, the rationalization of authority and the differentiation of structures occurred much earlier and more completely in Europe than in America. The experience of the West, indeed, suggests that an inverse correlation may exist between the modernization of governmental institutions and the expansion of political participation. The former took place much more rapidly in Europe, the latter much more rapidly in America.

In terms of the modernization of governmental institutions, three distinct patterns can be identified: Continental, British, and American.[2] On the Continent the

---

From *Political Order in Changing Societies* (New Haven, CT: Yale University Press, 1968), 93–133. Reprinted with the permission of the publisher

[1] Robert R. Palmer, *The Age of the Democratic Revolution* (2 vols. Princeton, Princeton University Press, 1959–64), *I*, 213ff.

[2] For the sake of clarity, let me make clear the geographical scope I give these terms. With appropriate apologies in Latin Americans and Canadians, I feel compelled by the demands of brevity to use the term "America" to refer to the thirteen colonies which subsequently became the United States of America. By "Europe" I mean Great Britain and the Continent. By "the Continent" I refer to France, the Low Countries, Spain, Portugal, Sweden, and the Holy Roman Empire.

rationalization of authority and the differentiation of structures were dominant trends of the seventeenth century. "It is misleading to summarize in a single phrase any long historical process," Sir George Clark observes,

> but the work of monarchy in the seventeenth century may be described as the substitution of a simpler and more unified government for the complexities of feudalism. On one side it was centralization, the bringing of local business under the supervision or control of the government of the capital. This necessarily had as its converse a tendency toward uniformity.[3]

It was the age of the great simplifiers, centralizers, and modernizers: Richelieu, Mazarin, Louis XIV, Colbert, and Louvois in France; the Great Elector in Prussia; Gustavus Adolphus and Charles XI in Sweden; Philip IV and Olivares in Spain; and their countless imitators among the lesser realms of the Continent. The modern state replaced the feudal principality; loyalty to the state superseded loyalty to church and to dynasty. "I am more obligated to the state," Louis XIII declared on the famous "Day of Dupes," November 11, 1630, when he rejected the Queen Mother and her claims for family in favor of the Cardinal and his claims for the state. "More than any other single day," Friedrich argues, "it may be called the birthday of the modern state."[4] With the birth of the modern state came the subordination of the church, the suppression of the medieval estates, and the weakening of the aristocracy by the rise of new groups. In addition, the century witnessed the rapid growth and rationalization of state bureaucracies and public services, the origin and expansion of standing armies, and the extension and improvement of taxation. In 1600 the medieval political world was still a reality on the Continent; by 1700 it had been replaced by the modern world of nation-states.

The British pattern of institutional modernization was similar in nature to that on the Continent but rather different in results. In Britain, too, church was subordinated to state, authority was centralized, sovereignty asserted internally as well as externally, legal and political institutions differentiated, bureaucracies expanded, and a standing army created. The efforts of the Stuarts, however, to rationalize authority along the lines of Continental absolutism provoked a constitutional struggle,

from which Parliament eventually emerged the victor. In Britain, as on the Continent, authority was centralized but it was centralized in Parliament rather than in the Crown. This, however, was no less of a revolution than occurred on the Continent and perhaps even more of one.

In America, in contrast, political institutions did not undergo revolutionary changes. Instead, the principal elements of the English sixteenth-century constitution were exported to the new world, took root there, and were given new life precisely at the time that they were being abandoned in the home country. They were essentially Tudor and hence significantly medieval in character. The Tudor century saw some steps toward modernization in English politics, particularly the establishment of the supremacy of the state over the church, the heightened sense of national identity and consciousness, and a significant increase in the power of the Crown and the executive establishment. Nonetheless, even in Elizabethan government, the first point of importance is, "the fundamental factor of continuity with the Middle Ages."[5] The sixteenth century, as Chrimes says, saw "The Zenith of the Medieval Constitution." The changes introduced by the Tudor monarchs did not have "the effect of breaking down the essential principles of the medieval Constitution, nor even its structure."[6] Among these principles and institutions were the idea of the organic union of society and government, the harmony of authorities within government, the subordination of government to fundamental law, the intermingling of the legal and political realms, the balance of powers between Crown and Parliament, the complementary representative roles of these two bodies, the vitality of local governmental authorities, and reliance on the militia for the defense of the realm.

The English colonists took these late medieval and Tudor political ideas, practices, and institutions across the Atlantic with them during the great migrations in the first half of the seventeenth century. The patterns of thought and behavior which were established in the New World developed and grew but were not substantially changed during the century and a half of colonyhood. The English generation of 1603–30, Notestein

---

[3] Sir George Clark, *The Seventeenth Century* (New York, Oxford-Galaxy, 1961), p. 91.

[4] Carl J. Friedrich, *The Age of the Baroque: 1610–1660* (New York, Harper, 1952), pp. 215–16.

[5] A. L. Rowse, *The England of Elizabeth* (New York, Macmillan, 1951), p. 262.

[6] S. B. Chrimes, *English Constitutional History* (2d ed. London, Oxford University Press, 1953), pp. 121–23. See also W. S. Holdsworth, *A History of English Law* (3d ed. London, Methuen, 1945), 4, 209 ff.

remarks, was "one in which medieval ideas and practices were by no means forgotten and in which new conceptions and new ways of doing things were coming in. The American tradition, or that part derived from England, was at least in some degree established by the early colonists. The English who came over later must have found the English Americans somewhat settled in their ways."[7] The conflict with the British government in the middle of the eighteenth century served only to reinforce the colonists' adherence to their traditional institutions. In the words of our greatest constitutional historian:

> The colonists retained to a marked and unusual degree the traditions of Tudor England. In all our study of American institutions, colonial and contemporary, institutions of both public law and private law, this fact must be reckoned with. The breach between colonies and mother country was largely a mutual misunderstanding based, in great part, on the fact of this retention of older ideas in the colonies after parliamentary sovereignty had driven them out in the mother country.[8]

In the constitutional debates before the American Revolution, the colonists in effect argued the case of the old English constitution against the merits of the new British constitution which had come into existence during the century after they had left the mother country. "Their theory," as Pollard says, "was essentially medieval."[9]

These ancient institutions and ideas were embodied in the state constitutions drafted after independence and in the Federal Constitution of 1787. Not only is the American Constitution the oldest written constitution in the world, but it is also a constitution that in large part simply codified and formalized on the national level practices and institutions long in existence on the colonial level. The institutional framework established in

1787 has, in turn, changed remarkably little in 175 years. Hence, the American system "can be properly understood, in its origin, development, workings, and spirit, only in the light of precedents and traditions which run back to the England of the civil wars and the period before the civil wars."[10] The American political system of the twentieth century still bears a closer approximation to the Tudor polity of the sixteenth century than does the British political system of the twentieth century. "Americanisms in politics, like Americanisms in speech," as Henry Jones Ford put it, "are apt to be Anglicisms which died out in England but survived in the new world."[11] The British broke their traditional patterns in the seventeenth century. The Americans did not do so then and have only partially done so since then. Political modernization in America has thus been strangely attenuated and incomplete. In institutional terms, the American polity has never been underdeveloped, but it has also never been wholly modern. In an age of rationalized authority, centralized bureaucracy, and totalitarian dictatorship, the American political system remains a curious anachronism. In today's world, American political institutions are unique, if only because they are so antique.

RATIONALIZATION OF AUTHORITY

In seventeenth-century Europe the state replaced fundamental law as the source of political authority and within each state a single authority replaced the many which had previously existed. America, on the other hand, continued to adhere to fundamental law as both a source of authority for human actions and as an authoritative restraint on human behavior. In addition, in America, human authority or sovereignty was never concentrated in a single institution or individual but instead remained dispersed throughout society as a whole and among many organs of the body politic. Traditional patterns of authority were thus decisively broken and replaced in Europe; in America they were reshaped and supplemented but not fundamentally altered. The continued supremacy of law was mated to the decisive rejection of sovereignty.

Undoubtedly the most significant difference between modern man and traditional man is their outlook

[7] Wallace Notestein, *The English People on the Eve of Colonization, 1603–1630* (New York, Harper, 1954), p. xiv. See also Edward S. Corwin, *The "Higher Law" Background of American Constitutional Law* (Ithaca, Cornell University Press, 1955), p. 74.
[8] Charles Howard McIlwain, *The High Court of Parliament and its Supremacy* (New Haven, Yale University Press, 1910), p. 386.
[9] A. F. Pollard, *Factors in American History* (New York, Macmillan, 1925), p. 39. See also Charles Howard McIlwain, *The American Revolution: A Constitutional Interpretation* (Ithaca, Cornell University Press, 1958), and Randolph G. Adams, *Political Ideas of the American Revolution* (3d ed. New York, Barnes and Noble, 1958).

[10] McIlwain, *High Court*, p. 388.
[11] Henry Jones Ford, *The Rise and Growth of American Politics* (New York, Macmillan, 1900), p. 5. See also James Bryce, *The American Commonwealth* (London, Macmillan, 1891), 2, 658.

on man in relation to his environment. In traditional society man accepts his natural and social environment as given. What is ever will be: it is or must be divinely sanctioned; to attempt to change the permanent and unchanging order of the universe and of society is not only blasphemous but also impossible. Change is absent or imperceptible in traditional society because men cannot conceive of its existence. Modernity begins when men develop a sense of their own competence, when they begin to think first that they can understand nature and society, and then that they can control nature and society for their own purposes. Above all, modernization involves belief in the capacity of man by reasoned action to change his physical and social environments. It means the rejection of external restraints on men, the Promethean liberation of man from control by gods, fate, and destiny.

This fundamental shift from acceptance to activism manifests itself in many fields. Among the more important is law. For traditional man, law is an external prescription or restraint over which he has little control. Man discovers law but he does not make law. At most he may make supplementary emendations of an unchanging basic law to apply it to specific circumstances. Such concepts can exist only in a society where government does not make fundamental changes in society. If political bodies are to produce social change, political authority must reside in those bodies and not in external restraints which, more often than not, are identified in practice with the very social order which modernization will change.

In late medieval Europe, law was variously defined in terms of divine law, natural law, the law of reason, common law, and custom. In all these manifestations it was viewed as a relatively unchanging external authority for and restraint on human action. Particularly in England, the dominant concept was "the characteristic medieval idea of all authority as deriving from the law." As Bracton put it, "Law makes the King."[12] These ideas remained dominant through the Tudor years and were in one form or another at the basis of the writings of Fortescue, St. Germain, Sir Thomas Smith, Hooker, and Coke. Even after the Act of Supremacy, Parliament was still viewed as a law-declaring body, not a law-making body. Even during the first phases of the constitutional struggles of the seventeen century, Prynne argued that "the Principal Liberties, Customs, Laws" of the kingdom, particularly those in the *"great Charters,"* are "FUNDAMENTAL, PERPETUAL, AND UNALTERABLE."[13]

The obverse of fundamental law is, of course, the rejection of determinate human sovereignty. For the men of 1600, as Figgis observes, "law is the true sovereign, and they are not under the necessity of considering whether King or Lords or Commons or all three together are the ultimate authority in the state."[14] The sovereignty of law permitted a multiplicity of human authorities, since no single human authority was the sole source of law. Man owed obedience to authority, but authority existed in many institutions: king, Parliament, courts, common law, custom, church, people. Sovereignty, indeed, was an alien concept to the Tudor constitution. No "lawyer or statesman of the Tudor period," as Holdsworth says, "could have given an answer to the question as to the whereabouts of the sovereign power in the English state."[15] Society and government, Crown and people, existed together in harmony in a "single body politic." The Tudor regime, says Chrimes, "was essentially the culmination of the medieval ideals of monarchical government, in alliance with the assent of parliament for certain purposes, and acknowledging the supremacy of the common law where appropriate. No one was concerned about the location of sovereignty within the State."[16] Unlike Bodin and other Continental theorists, sixteenth-century English writers simply denied the existence of sovereignty. The "whole standpoint" of the most notable expounder of the Elizabethan constitution, Sir Thomas Smith, was "nearer that of Bracton than that of Bodin."[17]

Fundamental law and the diffusion of authority were incompatible with political modernization. Modernization requires authority for change. Fundamental changes in society and politics come from the purposeful actions of men. Hence authority must reside in men, not in unchanging law. In addition, men must have

---

[12] Corwin, p. 27.

[13] McIlwain, *High Court*, pp. 51 ff., 65.

[14] John Neville Figgis, *The Divine Right of Kings* (Cambridge, England, Cambridge University Press, 1922), p. 230. See also Christopher Morris, *Political Thought in England: Tyndale to Hooker* (London, Oxford University Press, 1953), p. 1.

[15] Holdsworth, *4*, 208.

[16] Chrimes, pp. 122–23. See also J. B. Black, *The Reign of Elizabeth, 1558–1603* (2d ed. Oxford, Clarendon Press, 1959), p. 206.

[17] John Neville Figgis, "Political Thought in the Sixteenth Century," *The Cambridge Modern History* (Cambridge, 1904), *3*, 748; J. W. Allen, *A History of Political Thought in the Sixteenth Century* (New York, Barnes and Noble, 1960), p. 262.

the power to effect change and hence authority must be concentrated in some determinate individual or group of men. Fundamental and unchanging law may serve to diffuse authority throughout society and thus to preserve the existing social order. But it cannot serve as authority for change except for lesser changes which can be passed off as restoration. The modernization which began in the sixteenth century on the Continent and in the seventeenth century in England required new concepts of authority, the most significant of which was the simple idea of sovereignty itself, the idea that there is, in the words of Bodin, a "supreme power over citizens and subjects, unrestrained by law." One formulation of this idea was the new theory, which developed in Europe in the late sixteenth century, of the divine right of kings. Here, in effect, religious and in that sense traditional forms were used for modern purposes. "The Divine Right of Kings on its political side was little more than the popular form of expression for the theory of sovereignty."[18] The doctrine developed in France after 1594 and was introduced into England by James I. It admirably served the purposes of the modernizing monarchs of the seventeenth century: giving the sanction of the Almighty to the purposes of the mighty. It was a necessary "transition stage between medieval and modern politics."[19]

In addition, of course, other political theorists responded to the needs of the time by furnishing different and more "rational" justifications of absolute sovereignty based on the nature of man and the nature of society. On the Continent, Bodin and the Politiques looked to the creation of a supreme royal power which would maintain order and constitute a centralized public authority above parties, sects, and groups, all of which were to exist only on its sufferance. Bodin's *Republic* was published in 1576; Hobbes' *Leviathan* with its more extreme doctrine of sovereignty appeared in 1651. Closely linked with the idea of absolute sovereignty was the concept of the state as an entity apart from individual, family, and dynasty. Twentieth-century modernizing Marxists justify their efforts by the needs of the party; seventeenth-century modernizing monarchs justified their actions by "reason of state." The phrase was first popularized by Botero in *Della Ragion di Stato* in 1589. Its essence was briefly defined by

another Italian writer in 1614 when he declared, "The reason of state is a necessary violation [*eccesso*] of the common law for the end of public utility."[20] One by one the European monarchs took to legitimizing themselves and their actions by reference to the state.

In both its religious and its secular versions, in Filmer as well as in Hobbes, the import of the new doctrine of sovereignty was the subject's absolute duty of obedience to his king. Both doctrines helped political modernization by legitimizing the concentration of authority and the breakdown of the medieval pluralistic political order. They were the seventeenth-century counterparts of the theories of party supremacy and national sovereignty which are today employed to break down the authority of traditional local, tribal, and religious bodies. In the seventeenth century mass participation in politics still lay in the future; hence rationalization of authority meant concentration of power in the absolute monarch. In the twentieth century, the broadening of participation and the rationalization of authority occur simultaneously, and hence authority must be concentrated in either a political party or in a popular charismatic leader, both of which are capable of arousing the masses as well as challenging traditional sources of authority. But in the seventeenth century the absolute monarch was the functional equivalent of the twentieth century's monolithic party.

On the Continent in the seventeenth century the medieval diffusion of authority among the estates rapidly gave way to the centralization of authority in the monarch. At the beginning of the seventeenth century, "Every country of western Christendom, from Portugal to Finland, and from Ireland to Hungary, had its assemblies of estates."[21] By the end of the century most of these had been eliminated or greatly reduced in power. In France the last Estates General until the Revolution met in 1615, and the provincial estates, except in Brittany and Languedoc, did not meet after 1650.[22] By the seventeenth century only six of the original 22 Spanish kingdoms retained their *cortes.* The *cortes* in Castile was already suppressed; those in Aragon were put down by Philip II; Olivares subordinated Catalonia after a long bloody war. In Portugal the *cortes* met for

---

[18] Figgis, *Divine Right,* p. 237.
[19] Ibid., p. 258. See Allen, p. 386; Charles Howard McIlwain, ed., *The Political Works of James I* (Cambridge, Harvard University Press, 1918).

---

[20] Quoted in Friedrich, pp. 15–16.
[21] Clark, p. 83.
[22] Palmer, *I,* 461: "In 1787 demands were heard for revival of Provincial Estates in various parts of the country. It was a long-delayed reaction against Richelieu and Louis XIV, a demand to make France a constitutional monarchy, not on the English model, but on the model of a France that had long since passed away."

the last time in 1697. In the kingdom of Naples parliamentary proceedings ended in 1642. The Great Elector put down the estates in Brandenburg and Prussia. The estates of Carniola, Styria, and Carinthia had already lost their powers to the Hapsburgs, and during the early part of the century the latter were able to curtail the powers of those in Bohemia, Moravia, and Silesia. The Danish crown became hereditary in 1665, that of Hungary in 1687. Toward the end of the century Charles XI reestablished absolute rule in Sweden.[23] By 1700 the traditional diffusion of powers had been virtually eliminated from continental Europe. The modernizers and state-builders had triumphed.

The tendencies toward the substitution of sovereignty for law and the centralization of authority also occurred in England. James I sundered the Crown from Parliament, challenged the traditional authority of the law and of the judges, advocated the divine right of kings. Kings, he said, "were the authors and makers of the laws and not the laws of the kings."[24] James was simply attempting to modernize English government and to move it along the paths which were already well-developed on the Continent. His efforts at political modernization were opposed by Coke and other conservatives who argued in terms of fundamental law and the traditional diffusion of authority. Their claims, however, were out of date in the face of the social and political changes taking place. "Coke, like most opponents of the King, had not really grasped the conception of sovereignty; he maintained a position, reasonable enough in the Middle Ages, but impossible in a developed unitary state."[25] Centralization was necessary and at times it seemed that England would follow the continental pattern. But in due course the claims for royal absolutism generated counter claims for parliamentary supremacy. When James I, Filmer, and Hobbes put the king above law, they inevitably provoked Milton's argument that "the parliament is above all positive law, whether civil or common, makes or unmakes them both." The Long Parliament began the age of parliamentary supremacy. It was then that England saw "practically for the first time a legislative assembly of the modern type—no longer a mere law-declaring, but

a law-*making* machine."[26] Fundamental law suffered the same fate in England that it had on the Continent, but it was replaced by an omnipotent legislature rather than by an absolute monarchy.

American development was strikingly different from that in Europe. At the same time that the modernizing monarchs were squelching the traditional estates, that men were asserting their power to make law, that Richelieu was building an absolute state in France and Hobbes was proclaiming one in England, the old patterns of fundamental law and diffused authority were transported to a new life in the New World. The traditional view of law continued in America in two forms. First, the idea that man could only declare law and not make law remained strong in America long after it had been supplanted by positive conceptions of law in Europe. In some respects, it persisted right into the twentieth century. Secondly, the old idea of a fundamental law beyond human control was given new authority by identifying it with a written constitution. A written constitution can, of course, be viewed as a contract and as deriving its authority from conscious, positive human action. But it may also and even concurrently be viewed as a codification of limitations already imposed upon government by custom and reason. It was in this latter sense that men accepted the idea of fundamental law in sixteenth- and seventeenth-century England and embodied it in their colonial charters and declarations of rights. The combination of both theories created a situation in which "higher law as with renewed youth, entered upon one of the great periods of its history."[27]

The persistence of fundamental-law doctrines went hand in hand with the rejection of sovereignty. The older ideas of the interplay of society and government and the harmonious balance of the elements of constitution continued to dominate political thought. In England, the ideas of the great Tudor political writers, Smith, Hooker, Coke, "were on the way to becoming anachronisms even as they were set down."[28] In America, on the other hand, their doctrines prospered, and Hobbes remained irrelevant. Neither the divine right of kings, nor absolute sovereignty, nor parliamentary supremacy, had a place on the western shores of the Atlantic. "Americans may be defined," as Pollard

---

[23] See Clark's summary of constitutional trends, pp. 86–87, and also F. L. Carsten, *Princes and Parliaments in Germany* (Oxford, Clarendon Press, 1959), pp. 436–37 and Holdsworth, *4*, 168–72.
[24] James I, "The Trew Law of Free Monarchies," in McIlwain, ed., *Political Works*, p. 62.
[25] Figgis, *Divine Right*, p. 232.

[26] McIlwain, *High Court*, pp. 93–96; italics in original.
[27] Corwin, p. 89.
[28] George H. Sabine, *A History of Political Theory* (rev. ed. New York, Holt, 1950), p. 455.

has said, "as that part of the English-speaking world which instinctively revolted against the doctrine of the sovereignty of the State and has, not quite successfully, striven to maintain that attitude from the time of the Pilgrim Fathers to the present day." The eighteenth-century argument of the colonists with the home country was essentially an argument against the legislative sovereignty of Parliament.

> It is this denial of all sovereignty which gives its profound and permanent interest to the American Revolution. . . . These are American ideas, but they were English before they were American. They were part of that medieval panoply of thought with which, including the natural equality of man, the view of taxes as grants, the laws of nature and of God, the colonists combatted the sovereignty of Parliament. They had taken these ideas with them when they shook the dust of England off their feet; indeed they left their country in order that they might cleave to these convictions. And now they come back bringing with them these and other sheaves, to reconvert us to the views which we have held long since but lost awhile.[29]

To the extent that sovereignty was accepted in America it was held to be lodged in "the people." But apart from rare moments, such as the election of a constituent assembly or the ratification of a constitution, sovereignty could never be exercised by the people. Authority existed in a multiplicity of organs each of which could justify its authority by reference to its source in the people but no one of which could conclusively demonstrate that it was more popular than the others. Popular sovereignty is as nebulous a concept as divine sovereignty. The voice of the people can be about as readily identified as the voice of God. It is thus a latent, passive, and ultimate authority, not a positive and active one.

The difference between American and European development is also manifest in the theories and practices of representation. In Europe, the elimination of the medieval representative bodies, the estates, was paralleled by a decline in the legitimacy accorded to local interests. On the Continent the absolute monarch represented or embodied the state. Beginning with the French Revolution, he was supplanted by the national assembly which represented or embodied the nation. In both instances, the collective whole has authority and legitimacy; local interests, parochial interests, group interests, as Rousseau argued, lacked legitimacy and hence had no claim for representation in the central organs of the political system.

The rationalization of authority in Britain also produced changes in representation which stand in marked contrast to the continuing American adherence to the older traditional concepts. In sixteenth-century England both King and Parliament had representative functions. The king was "the representative head of the corporate community of the realm."[30] The members of Parliament still had their traditional medieval functions of representing local communities and special interests. In the late medieval parliament, "the burgess is his town's attorney. His presence at parliament enables him to present petitions for confirmation of charters, the increase of local liberties, and redress of grievances, and to undertake private business in or near London for constituents."[31] Thus, the king represented the community as a whole, while the members of Parliament represented its component parts. The M.P. was responsible to his constituency. Indeed, an act passed during the reign of Henry V required members of Parliament to reside in their constituency. In the late sixteenth century this legal requirement began to be avoided in practice, but local residence and local ties still remained qualifications for most M.P.s. "The overwhelming localism of representation in Parliament is its dominant feature," writes Rowse of Elizabethan England, "and gives it vigor and reality. Everywhere the majority of members are local men, either gentry of the country or townsmen. The number of official members, privy councillors and such, is very small, and even they have their roots. . . . An analysis of the representation shows a very small proportion of outsiders, and still smaller of officials."[32] The members not only resided in their constituencies and represented the interests of those constituencies, but they were also paid by their con-

[29] Pollard, pp. 31–33. For a perceptive discussion of the implications of this rejection of sovereignty for the way in which the political system has adapted to the most modern of problems, see Don K. Price, *The Scientific Estate* (Cambridge, Harvard University Press, 1965), passim but esp. pp. 45 ff., 58, 75–78, 165–67.

[30] Samuel H. Beer, "The Representation of Interests in British Government: Historical Background," *American Political Science Review, 51* (Sept. 1957), 614.
[31] Faith Thompson, *A Short History of Parliament: 1295–1642* (Minneapolis, University of Minnesota Press, 1953), p. 59.
[32] Rowse, *England of Elizabeth,* p. 306. Cf. A. F. Pollard, *The Evolution of Parliament* (2d ed. rev. London, Longmans, Green, 1926), p. 159, who argues that the nationalizing changes began in the late Tudor years.

stituencies for their services. Each constituency, more-over, was normally represented by two or three members of Parliament.

The constitutional revolution of the seventeenth century dealt the death blow to this "Old Tory" system of representation. It was replaced by what Beer terms the "Old Whig" system, under which the King lost his active representative functions and the M.P. became "the representative of the whole community, as well as of its component interests."[33] Parliament, as Burke phrased it in the classic statement of the Old Whig theory, is "a *deliberative* assembly of *one* nation, with *one* interest, that of the whole—where not local purposes, not local prejudices, ought to guide, but the general good, resulting from the general reason of the whole." Hence the M.P. should not be bound by authoritative instructions from his constituents and should rather subordinate their interests to the general interest of the entire society. With this new concept came a radical break with the old tradition of local residence and local payment. The last recorded instance of a constituency paying its representatives was in 1678. Increasingly during the seventeen century members no longer resided in their constituencies. The statute was "evaded by the admission of strangers to free burghership," and it was finally repealed in 1774.[34] At the same time, the number of multiple-member districts declined, culminating in their complete elimination in 1885. All these developments made Parliament the collective representative of the nation rather than a collection of representatives of individual constituencies. Thus the theory and practice of British representation adjusted to the new fact of parliamentary supremacy.

In America, of course, the Old Tory system took on new life. The colonial representative systems reproduced Tudor practices, and subsequently these were established on a national scale in the Constitution of 1787. America, like Tudor England, had a dual system of representation: the President, like the Tudor king, represented the interests of the community as a whole; the individual members of the legislature owed their primary loyalties to their constituencies. The multi-member constituencies which the British had in the sixteenth century were exported to the colonial legislatures in America, adapted to the upper house of the national legislature, and extended to the state legislatures where they remained in substantial number to the twentieth century.[35] Local residence, which had been a legal requirement and a political fact in Tudor England, became a political requirement and a political fact in America. It reflected "the intense localism . . . which persisted in America after it had been abandoned in the mother country." Thus in Britain many commanding political figures in the nineteenth and twentieth centuries were able to stay in Parliament because they were able to change their constituencies. "What a difference it would have made to the course of English politics," as one commentator observed, "if Great Britain had not thrown off, centuries ago, the medieval practice which America still retains!" Contrariwise, Americans may view with astonishment and disdain the gap which political modernization has created between the British M.P. and his constituents.[36]

DIFFERENTIATION OF STRUCTURE

In comparing European and American developments, a distinction must be made between "functions" and "power." In this chapter, "power" (in the singular) means influence or control over the actions of others; "function" refers to particular types of activity, which may be defined in various ways. "Powers" (in the plural) will not be used, since most authors use it to mean "functions." It is thus possible to speak with the Founding Fathers of legislative, executive, and judicial functions, with Bagehot of dignified and efficient functions, and also of legal and political functions, military and civil functions, domestic and foreign functions. The exercise of any function involves some power. But functions and power are distinct dimensions. Two courts may have similar or identical judicial functions, but one may have much more power than another. Two

---

[33] Beer, pp. 614–15.

[34] Herbert W. Horwill, *The Usages of the American Constitution* (London, Oxford University Press, 1925), p. 169.

[35] Maurice Klain, "A New Look at the Constituencies: The Need for a Recount and a Reappraisal," *American Political Science Review,* 49 (Dec. 1955), passim, but esp. 1111–13. In 1619 the London Company aped English practice when it summoned to the first Virginia House of Burgesses, "two Burgesses from each Plantation freely . . . elected by the inhabitants thereof."

[36] Horwill, pp. 169–70, and see, *contra*, the comments of an American newspaperman covering the 1964 general election: "British members of Parliament aren't oriented toward their constituencies. They don't even have to live in them. . . . Constituencies tend to be regarded as political factors to provide fodder for the national consensus in London. An American Congressman may get 1,500 to 2,000 letters a week from people who elect him. A British MP usually gets no more than 10." Roderick MacLeish, *New York Herald Tribune,* Oct. 11, 1964.

agencies may have similar power, but their functions may differ both in substance and in number. Governmental institutions thus may be equal or unequal in power and specialized or overlapping in function.

In Europe the rationalization of authority and centralization of power were accompanied by functional differentiation and the emergence of more specialized governmental institutions and bodies. These developments were, of course, a response to the growing complexity of society and the increasing demands upon government. Administrative, legal, judicial, military institutions developed as semi-autonomous but subordinate bodies in one way or another responsible to the political bodies (monarch or parliament) which exercised sovereignty. The dispersion of functions among relatively specialized institutions, in turn, also encouraged inequalities in power among the institutions. The legislative or law-making function carried with it more power than the administrative or law-enforcement function.

In medieval government and in Tudor government the differentiation of functions was not very far advanced. A single institution often exercised many functions, and a single function was often dispersed among several institutions. This tended to equalize power among institutions. The government of Tudor England was a "government of *fused* powers" (i.e. functions), that is, Parliament, Crown, and other institutions each performed many functions.[37] In the seventeenth and eighteenth centuries British government evolved toward a concentration of power and a differentiation of function. In Great Britain, as Pollard argues, "Executive, legislature, and judicature have been evolved from a common origin, and have adapted themselves to specific purposes, because without that specialization of functions English government would have remained rudimentary and inefficient. But there has been no division of sovereignty and no separation of powers."[38]

In America, in contrast, sovereignty was divided, power was separated, and functions were combined in many different institutions. This result was achieved despite rather than because of the theory of the separation of powers (i.e. functions) which was prevalent in the eighteenth century. In its pure form, the assignment of legislative, executive, and judicial functions to separate institutions would give one institution a monopoly of the dominant law-making function and thus would centralize power. This was in part what Locke wanted and even more what Jefferson wanted. It was also, of course, found in Montesquieu, but Montesquieu recognized the inequality of power which would result from the strict separation of functions. The "judiciary," he said, "is in some measure next to nothing." Consequently, to obtain a real division of power, Montesquieu divided the legislative function among three different institutions representing the three traditional estates of the realm. In practice in America, as in Tudor England, not only was power divided by dividing the legislative function but other functions were also shared among several institutions, thus creating a system of "checks and balances" which equalized power. "The constitutional convention of 1787," as Neustadt has said, "is supposed to have created a government of 'separated powers' [i.e. functions]. It did nothing of the sort. Rather, it created a government of separated institutions *sharing* powers [functions]."[39] Thus America perpetuated a fusion of functions and a division of power, while Europe developed a differentiation of functions and a centralization of power.

The passion of the Founding Fathers for the division of power, for setting ambition against ambition, for creating a constitution with a complicated system of balances exceeding that of any other, is, of course, well known. Everything is bought at a price, however, and, as many Englishmen have pointed out, one apparent price of the division of power is governmental inefficiency. "The English constitution, in a word," Bagehot argued, "is framed on the principle of choosing a single sovereign authority, and making it good: the American, upon the principle of having many sovereign authorities, and hoping that their multitude may atone for their inferiority."[40] Fifty years later Pollard could similarly point to the separation of powers as "the reason why American efficiency, so marked in private concerns, has been so fettered in government" and why "American politics are unattractive to so many American minds." In due course, however, he hoped that the "American nation will trust a national government with the full powers of sovereignty" and that "The separation of powers will then be reduced to its true proportions as a specialization of functions."[41] Perversely, however,

[37] McIlwain, *High Court*, p. xi; italics in original.
[38] Pollard, *Parliament*, p. 257.

[39] Richard E. Neustadt, *Presidential Power: The Politics of Leadership* (New York, John Wiley, 1960), p. 33; italics in original.
[40] Walter Bagehot, *The English Constitution* (London, Oxford World's Classics, 1949), p. 202.
[41] Pollard, *Parliament*, pp. 255–57.

American institutions continued to divide power and to combine functions. This pattern can be clearly seen in the mixing in the same institution of legislative and judicial functions and of dignified and efficient functions, in the division of the legislative function among many institutions, and in the incomplete differentiation of distinct military institutions.

In medieval government no distinction existed between legislation and adjudication. On the Continent such institutions as the *Justiza* of Aragon and the French *Parlements* exercised important political functions into the sixteenth century. In England, of course, Parliament itself was viewed primarily as a court and not as a legislature down to the beginning of the seventeen century. The courts of law, as Holdsworth observes,

> were, in the days before the functions of government had become specialized, very much more than merely judicial tribunals. In England and elsewhere they were regarded as possessing functions which we may call political, to distinguish them from those purely judicial functions which nowadays are their exclusive functions on the continent, and their principal functions everywhere. That the courts continued to exercise these larger functions, even after departments of government had begun to be differentiated, was due to the continuance of that belief in the supremacy of the law which was the dominant characteristic of the political theory of the Middle Ages.[42]

In England, the supremacy of the law disappeared in the civil wars of the seventeenth century and with it disappeared the mixture of judicial and political functions. English judges followed the course of Bacon rather than Coke and became "lions under the throne" who could not "check or oppose any points of sovereignty." By the eighteenth century, Blackstone could flatly state that no court could declare invalid an act of Parliament, however unreasonable it might be. To admit such a power, he said, "were to set the judicial power above that of the legislature, which would be subversive of all government."[43] Parliament had evolved from high court to supreme legislature.

In America, on the other hand, the mixture of judicial and political functions remained. The judicial power to declare what the law is became the mixed judicial-legislative power to tell the legislature what the law cannot be. the American doctrine and practice of judicial review were undoubtedly known only in very attenuated form in late sixteenth-century and early seventeenth-century England. Indeed, the whole concept of judicial review implies a distinction between legislative and judicial functions which was not explicitly recognized at that time. It is, nonetheless, clear that Tudor and early Stuart courts did use the common law to "controul" acts of Parliament at least to the point of redefining rather sweepingly the purposes of Parliament. These actions did not represent a conscious doctrine of judicial review so much as they represented the still "undifferentiated fusion of judicial and legislative functions."[44] This fusion of legislative and judicial functions was retained by American courts and was eventually formulated into the doctrine and practice of judicial review. The legislative functions of courts in America, as McIlwain argued, are far greater than those in England, "because the like tendency was there checked by the growth in the seventeenth century of a new doctrine of parliamentary supremacy." Unlike English courts, "American courts still retain much of their Tudor indefiniteness, notwithstanding our separation of departments. They are guided to an extent unknown now in England by questions of policy and expediency. The Supreme Court has acted again and again on the principle that it may reverse its decisions, a principle which the House of Lords has definitely accepted as inadmissible."[45] Foreign observers since de Tocqueville have identified the "immense political influence" of the courts as one of the most astonishing and unique characteristics of American government.

The mixing of legal and political functions in American government can also be seen in the consistently prominent role of lawyers in America politics. In fourteenth- and fifteenth-century England lawyers played an important role in the development of parliamentary proceedings, and the alliance between Parliament and the law, in contrast to the separation between the Estates General and the French *parlement*, helped to sustain parliamentary authority.[46] In Elizabethan England lawyers played an increasingly important role in Parliament. In 1593, for instance, 43 per cent of the members of the House of Commons possessed a legal

---

[42] Holdsworth, *4*, 169.

[43] Sir William Blackstone, *Commentaries on the Laws of England*, Thomas M. Cooley, ed. (Chicago, Callaghan, 1876), *I*, 90.

[44] See J. W. Gough, *Fundamental Law in English Constitutional History* (Oxford, Clarendon Press, 1955), p. 27.

[45] McIlwain, *High Court*, pp. ix, 385–86.

[46] Holdsworth, *4*, 174, 184–85, 188–89.

education. The Speaker and the other leading figures in the House were usually lawyers. Subsequently the role of lawyers in the British Parliament declined in significance, reaching a low in the nineteenth century. In the twentieth century only about 20 per cent of the M.P.s have been lawyers. In America, on the other hand, in the colonial governments, in the state governments, and in the national government, the Tudor heritage of lawyer-legislators has continued, with lawyers often being a majority or more of the members of American legislative bodies.[47]

Every political system, as Bagehot pointed out, must gain authority and then use authority. In the modern British system these functions are performed by the dignified and efficient parts of the constitution. The assignment of each function to separate institutions is one aspect of the functional differentiation which is part of modernization. It can be seen most clearly, of course, in the case of the so-called constitutional monarchies, but in some degree it can be seen in almost all modern governments.[48] The American political system, however, like the older European political systems, does not assign dignified and efficient functions to different institutions. All major institutions of the American government—President, Supreme Court, House, Senate, and their state counterparts—combine in varying degrees both types of functions. This combination is, of course, most notable in the Presidency. Almost every other modern political system from the so-called constitutional monarchies of Great Britain and Scandinavia to the parliamentary republics of Italy, Germany, and France before De Gaulle, to the communist dictatorships in the Soviet Union and eastern Europe separates the chief of state from the head of government. In the Soviet system, the differentiation is carried still further to distinguish chief of state from head of government from party chief. In the United States, however, the President unites all three functions, this combination being a major source of his power but also a major limitation on his power, since the requirements of one role often conflict with the demands of another. This combination of roles perpetuates ancient practice. For the Presidency was created, as Jefferson declared in 1787, as an "elective monarchy"; the office was designed to embody much of the power of the British king; and the politics that surround it are court politics.[49]

The Presidency is, indeed, the only survival in the contemporary world of the constitutional monarchy once prevalent throughout medieval Europe. In the sixteenth century a constitutional monarch was one who reigned and ruled, but who ruled under law *(non sub homine sed sub Deo et lege)* with due regard to the rights and liberties of his subjects, the type of monarch Fortescue had in mind when he distinguished *dominium politicum et regale* from *dominium regale*. In the seventeenth century this old-style constitutional monarch was supplanted by the new-style absolute monarch who placed himself above the law. Subsequently, the eighteenth and nineteenth centuries saw the emergence of a new so-called "constitutional monarchy" in which a "dignified" monarch reigned but did not rule. Like the absolute monarch he is a modern invention created in response to the need to fix supreme power in a single organ. The American Presidency, on the other hand, continues the older, original type of constitutional monarchy. In functions and power American Presidents are Tudor kings. In institutional role, as well as in personality and talents, Lyndon Johnson far more closely resembled Elizabeth I than did Elizabeth II. Britain preserved the form of the old monarchy, but America preserved the substance. Today America still has a king, Britain only a Crown.

---

[47] See J. E. Neale, *The Elizabethan House of Commons* (London, Penguin, 1949). pp. 290–95; Rose, p. 307; Thompson, pp. 169–73; Donald R. Matthews, *The Social Background of Political Decision-Makers* (New York, Random House, 1954), pp. 28–31; J. F. S. Ross, *Elections and Electors* (London, Eyre and Spottiswoode, 1955), p. 444; W. L. Guttsman, *The British Political Elite* (New York, Basic Books, 1963), pp. 82, 90, 105; D. E. Butler and Richard Rose, *The British General Election of 1959* (London, Macmillan, 1960), p. 127.

[48] Bagehot, pp. 304. See also Francis X. Sutton, "Representation and the Nature of Political Systems," *Comparative Studies in Society and History, 2* (Oct. 1959), 7: "the kind of distinction Bagehot made when he talked of the 'dignified' and 'efficient' parts of the English constitution is observed clearly in many states. . . . The discrimination of functions here rests, of course, on an analytical distinction relevant in any political system. It is that between symbolic representation and executive control."

---

[49] Thomas Jefferson, Letter to James Madison, Dec. 20, 1787, *Writings* (Washington, D.C., Thomas Jefferson Memorial Association, 1903–05), *6,* 389–90; Ford, p. 293. For an elegant—and eloquent—essay on the President as King, see D. W. Brogan, "The Presidency," *Encounter, 25* (Jan, 1964), 3–7. I am in debt to Richard E. Neustadt for insights into the nature of the American monarchy and into the similarities between White House politics and palace politics. See also Pollard, *Factors in American History*, pp. 72–73: "down to this day the Executive in the United States is far more monarchical and monarchy far more personal than in the United Kingdom. 'He' is a single person there, but 'It' is a composite entity in Great Britain."

In most modern states the legislative function is in theory in the hands of a large representative assembly, parliament, or supreme soviet. In practice, however, it is performed by a relatively small body of men—a cabinet or presidium—which exercises its power in all fields of government activity. In America, however, the legislative function remains divided among three distinct institutions and their subdivisions, much as it was once divided among the different estates and other constituted bodies in late medieval Europe. On the national level this arrangement derives not from the ideas of any European theorist but rather from the "institutional history of the colonies between 1606 and 1776."[50] The relations among burgesses, councils, and governors in the colonies, in turn, reflected the relations among Crown, Lords, and Commons in the late sixteenth century.

In modern politics, the division of power between two bodies in a legislative assembly generally varies inversely with the effective power of the assembly as a whole. The Supreme Soviet has little power but is truly bicameral; the British Parliament has more power but is effectively unicameral. America, however, is unique in preserving a working bicameralism directly inherited from the sixteenth century. Only in Tudor times did the two houses of Parliament become formally and effectively distinguished, one from the other, on an institutional basis. "The century started with Parliament a unitary institution, truly bi-cameral only in prospect." When it ended, the growth in "the power, position, and prestige of the House of Commons" had made Parliament "a political force with which the Crown and government had to reckon."[51] The sixteenth century represented a peak of bicameralism in English parliamentary history. Each house often quashed bills which had passed the other house, and to resolve their differences the houses resorted to conference committees. Originally used as an "occasional procedure," in 1571 the conference committee was transformed into "a normal habit." In Elizabethan Parliaments, conferences were requested by one or the other house on most bills, the conference delegations were at times instructed not to yield on particular items, and when there were substantial differences between the versions approved by the two houses, the conference committee might substantially rewrite the entire bill, at times at the urging

and with the advice of the Queen and her councillors. Although all this sounds very contemporary, it is, in fact, very Tudor, and the conference committee procedure was carried over into the colonial legislatures and then extended to the national level. In Great Britain, however, the practice died out with the rise of cabinet responsibility to the Commons. The last real use of "Free Conferences," where discussion and hence politics were permitted, occurred about 1740.[52]

The participation of two assemblies and the chief executive in the legislative process caused the continuation in America of many other legislative methods familiar to Tudor government. An assembly which legislates must delegate some of its work to subordinate bodies or committees. Committees made their appearance in the Tudor Parliament in the 1560s and 1570s. The practice of referring bills to committees soon became almost universal, and, as the committees assumed more and more of the functions of the House, they became larger and more permanent. The committees were also frequently dominated by those with special interests in the legislation that they considered. Bills concerned with local and regional problems went to committees composed of members from those regions and localities.[53] By the turn of the century the larger committees had evolved into standing committees which considered all matters coming up within a general sphere of business. The active role of the Commons in the legislative process compelled it to resort to this committee procedure. The procedure, in turn, was exported to the colonies in the early seventeenth century—particularly to the Virginia House of Burgesses—where it also met a real need, and 150 years later was duplicated in the early sessions of the national Congress. At the same time in England, however, the rise of the cabinet undermined the committee system which had earlier existed in Parliament; the old standing committees of the House of Commons became empty formalities, indistinguishable from Committees of the Whole House, long before they were officially discontinued in 1832.

The division of the legislative function imposed similar duties upon the Speaker in the Tudor House of Commons and in subsequent American legislatures.

---

[50] Benjamin F. Wright, "The Origins of the Separation of Powers in America," *Economics, 13* (May 1933), 169 ff.

[51] J. E. Neale, *Elizabeth I and Her Parliaments* (New York, St. Martin's, 1958), *I,* 16–17.

[52] Ibid., pp. 235, 287, 387–88, 412–13; G. F. M. Campion, *An Introduction to the Procedure of the House of Commons* (London, Philip Allan, 1929), p. 199; Ada C. McCown, *The Congressional Conference Committee* (New York, Columbia University Press, 1927), pp. 23–37.

[53] Rowse, p. 307.

The Tudor Speaker was a political leader, with a dual allegiance to the Crown and to the House. His success in large measure depended upon how well he could balance and integrate these often conflicting responsibilities. He was the "manager of the King's business" in the House, but he was also the spokesman for the House to the Crown and the defender of its rights and privileges. He could exercise much influence in the House by his control, subject to veto by the House, over the order in which bills were called up for debate and by his influence on the "timing and framing of questions." The struggle between Crown and Parliament in the seventeenth century, however, made it impossible for the Speaker to continue his loyalties to both. His overriding duty was now to the House, and, in due course, the impartiality of Onslow in the eighteenth century (1727–61) became the norm for Speakers in the nineteenth and twentieth centuries. Thus in Britain an office which had once been weighted with politics, efficient as well as dignified, radically changed its character and became that of a depoliticized, impartial presiding officer. In America, on the other hand, the political character of the Tudor Speakership was perpetuated in the colonial assemblies and eventually in the national House of Representatives.[54]

The sharing of the legislative function among two assemblies and the chief executive gives a strikingly Tudor character to the contemporary American lawmaking process. In Elizabethan England, as Rowse observes, the "relations between Crown and Parliament were more like those between President and Congress than those that subsist in England today."[55] The Tudor monarchs had to badger, wheedle, cajole, and persuade the Commons to give them the legislation they wanted. At times they were confronted by unruly Parliaments which pushed measures the monarch did not want or debated issues the monarch wished to silence. Generally, of course, the monarch's "legislative program," consisting primarily of requests for funds, was approved. At other times, however, the Commons would rear up and the monarch would have to withdraw or reshape his demands. Burghley, who was in charge of Parliamentary relations for Elizabeth, "kept a close eye on proceedings and received from the Clerks during the session lists showing the stages of all bills in both

Houses."[56] Elizabeth regularly attempted to win support in the Commons for her proposals by sending messages and "rumors" to the House, by exhorting and instructing the Speaker on how to handle the business of the House, by "receiving or summoning deputations from the Houses to Whitehall and there rating them in person," and by "descending magnificently upon Parliament in her coach or open chariot and addressing them" personally or through the Lord Keeper.[57]

Although the sovereign did not "lack means of blocking obnoxious bills during their progress through the two Houses," almost every session of Parliament passed some bills which the Crown did not want, and the royal veto was exercised. Although used more frequently against private bills than against public ones, important public measures might also be stopped by the Crown. During her reign Elizabeth I apparently approved 429 bills and vetoed approximately 71. The veto, however, was not a weapon which the Crown could use without weighing costs and gains: "politics— the art of the possible—were not entirely divorced even from Tudor monarchy. Too drastic or ill-considered a use of the royal veto might have stirred up trouble."[58] The tactics of a Henry VIII or Elizabeth I in relation to their Parliaments thus differed little from those of a Kennedy or Johnson in relation to their Congresses. A similar distribution of power imposed similar patterns of executive-legislative behavior.

The Tudor monarchs did perhaps have some advantage over American Presidents in that some, although not all, of their Privy Councillors sat in Parliament. These councillors were the principal managers of the Crown's business in Parliament, performing the functions of the majority leaders in Congress. At times, like the majority leaders, they would feel compelled to put their loyalty to the House above their loyalty to the Crown. The practice of Privy Councillors sitting in Parliament, however, was never wholly accepted as desirable, and in the seventeenth century continuing efforts were made to keep "place men" out of Parliament. These culminated in the Act of Settlement of 1701, the relevant provisions of which were subsequently written into the American Constitution, although they almost immediately became ineffective in England. Thus, American practice developed one aspect of the earlier

[54] Neale, *House of Commons*, p. 381 and passim; Holdsworth, *4*, 177; Campion, *2*, 52–54.
[55] Rowse, p. 294.

[56] Neale, *House of Commons*, p. 411.
[57] Rowse, pp. 294–95.
[58] Neale, *House of Commons*, pp. 410–12, and Neale, *Elizabeth I and Her Parliaments*, passim.

English thought and behavior, while later British practice developed another.[59] The relationships between chief executive and legislature, however, made American cabinet and executive officers resemble the English and British cabinets and councils of the sixteenth, seventeenth, and eighteenth centuries. Reflecting this similarity and the drastic change which took place in the role of the British cabinet is the fact that in the United States the executive leadership is still called "the Administration," as it was in eighteenth-century Britain, while in Britain itself, it is now termed "the Government."

The differentiation of specialized administrative structures also took place much more rapidly in Europe than it did in America. The contrast can be strikingly seen in the case of military institutions. A modern military establishment includes a standing army recruited voluntarily or through conscription and commanded by a professional officer corps. In Europe a professional officer corps emerged during the first half of the nineteenth century. By 1870 the major continental states had developed most of the principal institutions of professional officership. England, however, lagged behind the Continent in developing military professionalism, and the United States lagged behind Great Britain. Not until the turn of the century did the United States have many of the institutions of professional officership which the European states had acquired many decades earlier. The division of power among governmental institutions perpetuated the mixing of politics and military affairs and enormously complicated the emergence of a modern system of objective civilian control. In most areas of civil life Americans have been willing to accept functional differentiation and specialized competence as inherent and even desirable aspects of modernization. Even after World War II, however, many Americans still adhered to a "fusionist" approach to civil-military relations and believed that military leadership and military institutions should mirror the attitudes and characteristics of civil society.[60]

American reluctance to accept a standing army also contrasts with the much more rapid modernization in Europe. In the sixteenth century European military forces consisted of feudal levies, mercenaries, and local militia. In England the militia was an ancient institu-tion, and the Tudors formally organized it on a county basis under the Lord Lieutenants to take the place of the private retinues of the feudal lords. This development was a step toward "domestic tranquility and military incompetence," and in 1600, "Not a single western country had a standing army: the only one in Europe was that of the Turks."[61] By the end of the century, however, all the major European powers had standing armies. Discipline was greatly improved, uniforms introduced, regulations formalized, weapons standardized, and effective state control extended over the military forces. The French standing army dates from Richelieu; the Prussian from the actions of the Great Elector in 1655; the English from the Restoration of 1660. In England the county militia continued in existence after 1660, but steadily declined in importance.

In America, on the other hand, the militia became the crucial military force at the same time that it was decaying in Europe. The militia was the natural military system for societies whose needs were defensive rather than offensive and intermittent rather than constant. The seventeenth-century colonists continued, adapted, and improved upon the militia system which had existed in Tudor England. In the next century, they identified militia with popular government, and standing armies became the symbol of monarchical tyranny. "On the military side," as Vagts says, "the war of the American Revolution was in part a revolt against the British standing army."[62] But in terms of military institutions, it was a reactionary revolt. The standing armies of George III represented modernity, the colonial militias embodied traditionalism. The American commitment to this military traditionalism, however, became all the more complete as a result of the War of Independence. Hostility to standing armies and reliance on the militia as the first line of defense of a free people became popular dogma and constitutional doctrine, however much it might be departed from in practice. Fortunately the threats to security in the nineteenth century were few, and hence the American people were able to go through that century with a happy confidence

---

[59] See Campion, pp. 37–38; Pollard, *Parliament*, pp. 237–38; Richard F. Fenno. *The Presidents' Cabinet* (Cambridge, Harvard University Press, 1959), pp. 10–13.
[60] See Huntington, *The Soldier and the State* (Cambridge, Harvard-Belknap, 1957), passim.

---

[61] J. H. Hexter, *Reappraisals in History* (Evanston, Ill., Northwestern University Press, 1962), p. 147, and Clark, p. 84. On the fundamental changes in European military practice, see Michael Roberts, *The Military Revolution: 1560–1660* (Belfast, Queen's University, n.d.).
[62] Alfred Vagts, *A History of Militarism* (rev. ed. New York, Meridian Books, 1959), p. 92. See generally Louis Morton, "The Origins of American Military Policy." *Military Affairs, 22* (Summer 1958), 75–82.

in an ineffective force which was protecting them from a nonexistent danger. The militia legacy, however, remained a continuing element in American military affairs far into the much more tumultuous twentieth century. It was concretely manifest in the political influence and military strength of the National Guard. Even after World War II, the idea that an expert military force is better than a citizen-soldier force had still to win wholehearted acceptance on the western side of the Atlantic.

TUDOR INSTITUTIONS AND MASS PARTICIPATION

Among the peoples of western civilization, the Americans were the first to achieve widespread political participation but the last to modernize their traditional political structures. In America, Tudor institutions and popular participation united in a political system which remains as baffling to understand as it is impossible to duplicate. In Europe, on the other hand, the rationalization of authority and the differentiation of structure clearly preceded the expansion of political participation. How can these differences in political modernization be explained?

In large part, they are directly related to the prevalence of foreign war and social conflict in Europe as contrasted with America. On the Continent the late sixteenth and the seventeenth centuries were periods of intense struggle and conflict. For only three years during the entire seventeenth century was there a complete absence of fighting on the European continent. Several of the larger states were more often at war during the century than they were at peace. The wars were usually complex affairs involving many states tied together in dynastic and political alliances. War reached an intensity in the seventeenth century which it never had previously and which was exceeded later only in the twentieth century.[63] The prevalence of war directly promoted political modernization. Competition forced the monarchs to build their military strength. The creation of military strength required national unity, the suppression of regional and religious dissidents, the expansion of armies and bureaucracies, and a major increase in state revenues. "The most striking fact"

in the history of seventeenth-century conflict, Clark observes,

> is the great increase in the size of armies, in the scale of warfare. . . . Just as the modern state was needed to create the standing army, so the army created the modern state, for the influence of the two causes was reciprocal. . . . The growth of the administrative machine and of the arts of government was directed and conditioned by the desire to turn the natural and human resources of the country into military power. The general development of European institutions was governed by the fact that the continent was becoming more military, or, we may say, more militaristic.[64]

War was the great stimulus to state building.

In recent years much has been written about "defensive modernization" by the ruling groups in nonwestern societies such as Egypt under Mohammad Ali, the eighteenth- and nineteenth-century Ottoman Empire, and Meiji Japan. In all these cases, intense early efforts at modernization occurred in the military field, and the attempts to adopt European weapons, tactics, and organization led to the modernization of other institutions in society. What was true of these societies was also true of seventeenth-century Europe. The need for security and the desire for expansion prompted the monarchs to develop their military establishments, and the achievement of this goal required them to centralize and to rationalize their political machinery.

Largely because of its insular position, Great Britain was a partial exception to this pattern of war and insecurity. Even so, one major impetus to the centralization of authority in English government came from the efforts of the Stuart kings to get more taxes to build and man more ships to compete with the French and other continental powers. If it were not for the English Channel, the Stuart centralization probably would have succeeded. In America, in the seventeenth century, however, continuing threats came only from the Indians. The nature of this threat plus the dispersed character of the settlements meant that the principal

---

[63] Clark, p. 98; Quincy Wright, *A Study of War* (Chicago, University of Chicago Press, 1942), *I*, 235–40. See also Sir George Clark, *War and Society in the Seventeenth Century* (Cambridge, Cambridge University Press, 1958), *passim*.

[64] Clark, *Seventeenth Century*, pp. 98, 101–02. See also Wright, *Study of War, I*, 256: "it would appear that the political order of Europe changed most radically and rapidly in the seventeenth and twentieth centuries when war reached greatest intensity. The seventeenth century witnessed the supercession of feudalism and the Holy Roman Empire by the secular sovereign states of Europe. The twentieth century appears to be witnessing the supercession of the secular sovereign states by something else. Exactly what cannot yet be said."

defense force had to be the settlers themselves organized into militia units. There was little incentive to develop European-type military forces and a European-type state to support and control them.

Civil harmony also contributed significantly to the preservation of Tudor political institutions in America. Those institutions reflected the relative unity and harmony of English society during the sixteenth century. English society, which had been racked by the Wars of the Roses in the fifteenth century, welcomed the opportunity for civil peace that the Tudors afforded. Social conflict was minimal during the sixteenth century. The aristocracy had been almost eliminated during the civil wars of the previous century. England was not perhaps a middle-class society but the differences between social classes were less then than they had been earlier and much less than they were to become later. Individual mobility rather than class struggle was the keynote of the Tudor years. "The England of the Tudors was an 'organic state' to a degree unknown before Tudor times, and forgotten almost immediately afterward."[65] Harmony and unity made it unnecessary to fix sovereignty in any particular institution; it could remain dispersed so long as social conflict was minimal.

The only major issue which disrupted the Tudor consensus, of course, was religion. Significantly, in sixteenth-century English history the Act of Supremacy means the supremacy of the state over the church, not the supremacy of one governmental institution over another or one class over another. After the brief interlude of the Marian struggles, however, the shrewd politicking and popular appeal of Elizabeth restored a peace among religious groups which was virtually unique in Europe at that time. The balance between Crown and Parliament and the combination of an active monarchy and common law depended upon this social harmony. Meanwhile on the Continent, civil strife had already reached a new intensity before the end of the sixteenth century. France alone had eight civil wars during the 36 years between 1562 and 1598, a period roughly comprising the peaceful reign of Elizabeth in England. The following 50 years saw Richelieu's struggles with the Huguenots and the wars of the Fronde. Spain was racked by civil strife, particularly between 1640 and 1652 when Philip IV and Olivares attempted to subdue Catalonia. In Germany, princes and parlia-

ments fought each other. Where, as frequently happened, estates and princes espoused different religions, the controversy over religion inevitably broke the medieval balance of powers between princes and parliaments.[66]

English harmony ended with the sixteenth century. Whether the gentry were rising, falling or doing both in seventeenth-century England, forces were at work in society disrupting Tudor social peace. The efforts to reestablish something like the Tudor balance broke down before the intensity of social and religious conflict. The brief period of Crown power between 1630 and 1640, for instance, gave way "to a short-lived restoration of something like the Tudor balance of powers during the first year of the Long Parliament (1641). This balance might perhaps have been sustained indefinitely, but for the rise of acute religious differences between the Crown and the militant Puritan party in the Commons."[67] In England, as in France, civil strife led to the demand for strong centralized power to reestablish public order. The breakdown of unity in society gave rise to irresistible forces to reestablish that unity through government.

Both Puritan and Cavalier emigrants to America escaped from English civil strife. The process of fragmentation, in turn, encouraged homogeneity, and homogeneity encouraged "a kind of immobility."[68] In America environment reinforced heredity, as the common challenges of the frontier combined with the abundance of land to help perpetuate the egalitarian characteristics of Tudor society and the complexity of Tudor political institutions. And, paradoxically, as Hartz has pointed out, the Framers of the Constitution of 1787 reproduced these institutions on the federal level in the expectation that the social divisions and conflict within American society made necessary a complex system of checks and balances. In reality, however, their Constitution was successful only because their view of American society was erroneous. So also, only the absence of significant social divisions permitted the continued transformation of political

---

[65] McIlwain, *High Court*, p. 336; Rowse, pp. 223 ff.

[66] Friedrich, pp. 20–21; Sabine, pp. 372–73.
[67] Chrimes, p. 138.
[68] Louis Hartz, *The Founding of New Societies* (New York, Harcourt, Brace and World, 1964), pp. 3, 4, 6, 23. Hartz's theory of fragmentation furnishes an excellent general framework for the analysis of the atrophy of settlement colonies, while his concept of the American liberal consensus in large part explains the preservation of Tudor political institutions.

issues into legal ones through the peculiar institution of judicial review.[69] Divided societies cannot exist without centralized power; consensual societies cannot exist with it.

In continental Europe, as in most contemporary modernizing countries, rationalized authority and centralized power were necessary not only for unity but also for progress. The opposition to modernization came from traditional interests: religious, aristocratic, regional, and local. The centralization of power was necessary to smash the old order, break down the privileges and restraints of feudalism, and free the way for the rise of new social groups and the development of new economic activities. In some degree a coincidence of interest did exist between the absolute monarchs and the rising middle classes. Hence European liberals often viewed favorably the concentration of authority in an absolute monarch, just as modernizers today frequently view favorably the concentration of authority in a single "mass" party.

In America, on the other hand, the absence of feudal social institutions made the centralization of power unnecessary. Since there was no aristocracy to dislodge, there was no need to call into existence a governmental power capable of dislodging it.[70] This great European impetus to political modernization was missing. Society could develop and change without having to overcome the opposition of social classes with a vested interest in the social and economic status quo. The combination of an egalitarian social inheritance plus the plenitude of land and other resources enabled social and economic development to take place more or less spontaneously. Government often helped to promote economic development, but (apart from the abolition of slavery) it played only a minor role in changing social customs and social structure. In modernizing societies, the centralization of power varies directly with the resistance to social change. In the United States, where the resistance was minimal, so also was the centralization.

The differences in social consensus between Europe and America also account for the differences in the manner in which political participation expanded. In Europe this expansion was marked by discontinuities on two levels. On the institutional level, democratization meant the shift of power from monarchical ruler to

popular assembly. This shift began in England in the seventeenth century, in France in the eighteenth century, and in Germany in the nineteenth century. Where medieval assemblies survived the age of absolutism, they usually became the vehicle through which popular sovereignty was asserted against royal supremacy. The royal powers and prerogative were gradually limited or terminated; parliament emerged as the dominant institution; and in due course extensions of the suffrage made it representative of the nation.

In countries where assemblies or estates did not survive absolutism, the transition to participant government was more difficult. In these systems, the rationalization of authority and the differentiation of structure had often been carried so far as to close off opportunities for popular participation through traditional institutions. Consequently, the monarchy was often overthrown by revolutionary action and a popularly elected assembly installed in its place: Rousseau was the natural legatee of Richelieu. Countries such as France and Prussia which took the lead in modernizing their political institutions in the seventeenth century thus had the most difficulty in maintaining stable democracy in the twentieth century. Countries where the seventeenth-century tendencies toward absolute monarchy were either defeated (England), stalemated (Sweden), or absent (America), later tended to develop more viable democratic institutions. The continued vitality of medieval estates and pluralistic assemblies is associated with subsequent democratic tendencies. "It is no accident, surely," Carsten observes, "that the liberal movement of the nineteenth century was strongest in those areas of Germany where the Estates survived the period of absolute government."[71] Similarly, in seventeenth-century Spain, Catalonia was the principal locus of feudal opposition to the centralizing and rationalizing efforts of Olivares, but in the twentieth century it has been the principal locus of Spanish liberalism and constitutionalism. In eighteenth-century Europe also, the conservative and even reactionary efforts of the "constituted bodies" to maintain and to restore their privileges laid the basis for later popular participation and popular resistance against despotism.[72]

On the electoral level, the expansion of participation in Europe meant the gradual extension of the suffrage for the assembly from aristocracy to upper bourgeoisie, lower bourgeoisie, peasants, and urban workers. This

---

[69] Louis Hartz, *The Liberal Tradition in America* (New York, Harcourt, Brace, 1955), pp. 9–10, 45–46, 85–86, 133–34, 281–82.
[70] Ibid. p. 43.

[71] Carsten, p. 434; Friedrich, pp. 20–25.
[72] Palmer, *I*, passim, but esp. pp. 323–407.

process is clearly seen in the English reform acts of 1832, 1867, 1884, and 1918. Where no assembly existed, the creation of a popular assembly was also at times accompanied by the introduction of universal male suffrage which, in turn, directly encouraged political instability. In both cases, control of the assembly determined control of the government, and hence struggles over who should vote for the assembly were often intense and sometimes violent. In America, on the other hand, no class differences existed as in Europe, and hence the social basis for conflict over suffrage extensions was less than in Europe. In addition, the continuation of the pluralistic institutions of medieval constitutionalism reduced the apparent significance of suffrage extensions. In a system of checks and balances with many institutions competing for power, it seemed natural enough that at least one of these institutions (usually the lower house of the assembly) should be elected by popular suffrage. Once this was granted, however, the competition between social forces and between governmental institutions produced the gradual democratization of the other institutions.

In America, thus, the unity of society and the division of government made the latter the principal focus of democratization. The American equivalent of the Reform Act of 1832 was the change in the nature of the Electoral College produced by the rise of political parties, and the resulting transformation of the Presidency from an indirectly elected, semi-oligarchical office to a popular one. The other major steps in the expansion of popular participation in the United States involved the extension of the electoral principle to all the state governors, to both houses of the state legislature, to many state administrative offices and boards, to the judiciary in many states, and to the United States Senate. In Europe the broadening of participation meant the extension of the suffrage for one institution to all classes of society while in America it meant the extension of the suffrage by the one class in society to all (or almost all) institutions of government.

Why did the early and rapid expansion of political participation fail to breed violence and instability in the United States? At least in part, the answer lies in the relative complexity, adaptability, autonomy, and coherence of the traditional political institutions which existed in America in the seventeenth and eighteenth centuries. These institutions were, in particular, sufficiently variegated at the local, state and eventually national levels so as to provide many avenues for political participation. The multiplicity of institutions furnished multiple means of access to political power.

Those groups unable to influence the national government might be able to dominate state or local governments. Those who could not elect chief executives might still control legislatures or at least legislative committees. Those who were forever weak numerically might find support in judicial bodies anxious to assert their power and to locate a constituency. With rare exceptions most of the significant social and economic groups in American society in the eighteenth and nineteenth centuries could find some way of participating in government and of compounding this influence with governmental authority.

In Europe the expansion of participation was linked to the centralization of power: "the democratic movement had to be unitary and centralizing, because it had to destroy before it could construct."[73] In America, on the other hand, the expansion of participation was linked with the dispersion of power and the maintenance of the established units of government. Only a modernizing autocrat like Hamilton could advance in America the type of centralization favored by the democrats of Europe. The democratization of many institutions of government, however, equalized their power and thus moderated its own effects. At the same time it also legitimated and reinforced the pluralistic inheritance from the past. As Madison recognized, the most popular branch of government would also be the most powerful one. Time and again the establishment of links between governmental institutions and rising social forces reinvigorated political institutions which, without that connection, would have lost their powers like the monarchs and second chambers of Europe. Thus, the institutional pluralism preserved from the past first encouraged the expansion of political participation and then was strengthened by it.

In Europe the opposition to modernization within society forced the modernization of the political system. In America, the ease of modernization within society precluded the modernization of political institutions. The United States thus combines the world's most modern society with one of the world's more antique polities. The American political experience is distinguished by frequent acts of creation but few, if any, of innovation. Since the Revolution constitutions have been drafted for 38 new political systems, but the same pattern of government has been duplicated over and over again. The new constitutions of Alaska and

---

[73] Ibid., *2,* 350–51.

Hawaii in the 1950s differed only in detail from the constitution of Massachusetts, originally drafted by John Adams in 1780. When else in history has such a unique series of opportunities for political experiment and innovation been so almost totally wasted?

This static quality of the political system contrasts with the prevalence of change elsewhere in American society. A distinguishing feature of American culture, Robin Williams has argued, is its positive orientation toward change. In a similar vein, two observers have noted, "In the United States change itself is valued. The new is good; the old is unsatisfactory. Americans gain prestige by being among the first to own next year's automobile; in England, much effort is devoted to keeping twenty-five-year-old cars in operating condition."[74] In three centuries, a few pitifully small and poor rural settlements strung along the Atlantic seaboard and populated in large part by religious exiles were transformed into a huge, urbanized, continental republic, the world's leading economic and military power. America has given the world its most modern and efficient economic organizations. It has pioneered social benefits for the masses: mass production, mass education, mass culture. Economically and socially, everything has been movement and change. In governmental structure, however, the only significant institutional innovation has been federalism, and this, in itself, of course, was made possible only because of the traditional hostility to the centralization of authority. Fundamental social and economic change has thus been combined with political stability and continuity. In a society dedicated to what is shiny new, the polity remains quaintly old.

The distinctive American contributions to politics are in the organization of popular participation.[75] The one major political institution invented in America is, of course, the political party. Americans created the caucus before the Revolution and committees of corre-spondence during the revolutionary crisis. Upon these beginnings at the end of the eighteenth century they organized the first political parties. American parties, in turn, directly reflect the nature of political modernization in America. They were created in the United States before they appeared elsewhere as a response to the earlier expansion of political participation there. Ambitious politicians had to mobilize and to organize the electorate if they were to succeed in the competition for power. In New York City, in 1800, for instance, the Jeffersonian Republican leaders determined that to win the election they would have to carry New York State and to carry the state they would have to carry New York City. To achieve this end, Aaron Burr in effect innovated the party machine. Burr, as one scholar has said,

> faced severe odds, for the Federalists were ably led by his old adversary, Alexander Hamilton, who had won the previous election decisively, and the Republicans were divided. Burr quietly persuaded the older party leaders to unite on one ticket of eminent local Republicans; shrewdly waited to announce his ticket until after Hamilton had pieced together an inferior one . . . ; organized his lieutenants solidly on a ward-by-ward basis; card-indexed the voters, their political history, attitudes and how to get them to the polls; set up committees to canvass for funds from house to house; put the heat on wealthy Republicans for bigger donations; organized rallies; enlisted in his cause the members of the Tammany Society, then a struggling fraternal group; debated publicly with Hamilton; and spent ten hours straight at the polls on the last day of the three-day election.[76]

The result was a decisive victory for Burr and for the institutional innovations which he brought to American politics.

The early expansion of political participation in America thus explains why mass political organizations originated there. In similar but reverse fashion, the absence of rationalization and differentiation and the continuation of traditional political institutions also explains by American political parties never became as strongly organized as British or Continental parties. The existence of a complex structure of government left fewer functions for parties to perform, and made their general role in the political system less important than it was in Europe. American parties tended to be looser,

---

[74] Robin Williams, *American Society* (2d ed. rev. New York, Knopf, 1961), p. 571; Eli Ginzberg and Ewing W. Reilley, *Effecting Change in Large Organizations* (New York, Columbia University Press, 1957), pp. 18–19.

[75] So also are the distinctive American contributions to the language of politics. As was pointed out above, pp. 140, 151, many of the terms Americans use to describe their governmental institutions were once used in England but have in the course of political modernization dropped from usage there. The opposite is true with respect to the language of political participation and the institutions to organize that participation. Here many of the terms (like the institutions) were either invented in the United States (caucus, gerrymander) or were given a new and specifically political meaning (citizen, primary, machine, boss, spoils, ticket, lobby).

[76] James MacGregor Burns, *The Deadlock of Democracy* (Englewood Cliffs, N.J., Prentice-Hall, 1963), p. 34.

less cohesive, and less disciplined than European parties and they generally avoided involvement in the diversity of ancillary social and economic activities which characterized European parties, particularly of the left. American parties, in some sense, bear the same relation to European parties that American governmental institutions bear to European governmental institutions. In comparison, "American parties have a very archaic general structure."[77] Paradoxically, the form of political organization which originated in America was developed into a much stronger and complex structure in western Europe and was carried to its fullest and most complete development in the Soviet Union.

Modernity is thus not all of a piece. The American experience demonstrates conclusively that some institutions and some aspects of a society may become highly modern while other institutions and other aspects retain much of their traditional form and substance. Indeed, this may be a natural state of affairs. In any system some sort of equilibrium or balance must be maintained between change and continuity. Change in some spheres renders unnecessary or impossible change in others. In America the continuity and stability of governmental institutions has permitted the rapid change of society, and the rapid change in society has encouraged continuity and stability in government. The relation between polity and society may well be dialectical rather than complementary. In other societies, such as Latin America, a rigid social structure and the absence of social and economic change have been combined with political instability and the weakness of political institutions. A good case can be made, moreover, that the latter is the result of the former.[78]

This combination of modern society and Tudor political institutions explains much that is otherwise perplexing about political ideas in America. In Europe the conservative is the defender of traditional institutions and values, particularly those in society rather than in government. Conservatism is associated with the church, the aristocracy, social customs, the established social order. The attitude of conservatives toward government is ambivalent; it is viewed as guarantor of social order; but it also is viewed as the generator of

social change. Society rather than government has been the principal conservative concern. European liberals, on the other hand, have had a much more positive attitude toward government. Like Turgot, Price, and Godwin, they have viewed the centralization of power as the precondition of social reform. They have supported the gathering of power into a single place—first the absolute monarch, then the sovereign people—where it can then be used to change society.

In America, on the other hand, these liberal and conservative attitudes have been thoroughly confused and partly reversed. Conservatism has seldom flourished because it has lacked social institutions to conserve. Society is changing and modern, while government, which the conservative views with suspicion, has been relatively unchanging and antique. With a few exceptions, such as a handful of colleges and churches, the oldest institutions in American society are governmental institutions. The absence of established social institutions, in turn, has made it unnecessary for American liberals to espouse the centralization of power as did European liberals. John Adams could combine Montesquieu's polity with Turgot's society much to the bafflement of Turgot. Nineteenth-century Europeans had every reason to be fascinated by America; it united a liberal society which they were yet to experience with a conservative politics which they had in large part forgotten.

These conservative institutions could well change more rapidly in the future than they did in the past. External security and internal consensus have been the principal factors militating against the modernization of American political institutions. The former disappeared in the early twentieth century; the latter appears at times to be on the verge of disruption. The political institutions suited to a society which did not have to worry about external dangers may be inappropriate for one continually involved in a balance of terror, cold war, and military interventions in distant portions of the globe. So also, the problems of race relations and poverty strengthen demands for action by the national government. The needs of national defense and social reform could undermine the traditional pluralism inherited from the past and hasten the centralization of authority and structural differentiation in American political institutions.

---

[77] Maurice Duverger, *Political Parties* (New York, John Wiley, 1954), p. 22.
[78] Merle Kling, "Toward a Theory of Power and Political Instability in Latin America," *Western Political Quarterly, 9* (March 1956), 21–35.

READING 10

PARTY SYSTEMS AND THE POLITICAL PROCESS

Walter Dean Burnham

A study of the history of American voting alignments . . . reveals that . . . the voting public has made vitally important contributions to American political development approximately once in a generation. Studies of American elections, especially in the past decade, have uncovered a remarkably stable pattern involving two broad types of elections which differ from one another not in degree but in kind. Most American elections, most of the time, are relatively low-pressure events. In such elections the voting decision seems to be a mix of traditional party identifications and short-term, "surge" factors associated with specific candidate or issue appeals.[20] Taken in the aggregate, such elections—whether "maintaining," "deviating," or "reinstating"—are part of a broad pattern of system maintenance.[21] They constitute reaffirmation of a "standing decision," even though the parties themselves may alternate in power as they did in the 1880's or the 1950's.[22]

Approximately once every thirty years, however, an entirely different cycle of elections emerges—a realignment cycle which precipitates massive grass-roots changes in voting behavior and results in a new coalitional pattern for each of the parties. Each of these critical realignments has been associated with a major turning-point in the development of the American political system as a whole. There appears to be a typical pattern in the alignment cycle, although not all of its stages have clearly been followed in each historical realignment. After a more or less extended period of stability, broadly-based discontent with the existing political order begins to emerge and then to crystallize. At a certain point the intrusion of a proximate tension-producing event, in a context of growing discontent, triggers either the creation of new major-party organizations or the capture of one of the old parties by insurgents against the political status quo. This proximate event may be economic, as were the depressions of 1893 and 1929, or political, as were the events leading from the Kansas-Nebraska Act of 1854 to the election of Lincoln; usually it has been a mixture of both elements. In the campaign or campaigns which follow this breakthrough, the insurgents' political style is exceptionally ideological by American standards; this in turn produces a sense of grave threat among defenders of the established order, who in turn develop opposing ideological positions. The elections which follow produce massive realignments of voters, and usually result in a stable majority for one of the parties which endures until the beginning of the next realignment phase a generation later.[23]

This cyclical pattern—long term continuity abruptly displaced by an explosive but short period of change—seems not only to reflect the constituent function of the party systems and the electoral system in the United States, but to be a prime manifestation of the dominance of that function in our politics. The critical realignment, to be sure, drastically reshuffles the coalitional bases of the two parties, but it does far more than this. It constitutes a political decision of the first magnitude and a turning point in the mainstream of national policy formation. Characteristically, the relationships among policy-making institutions, their relative power and decision-making capacity, and the policy outputs they produce are profoundly affected by critical realignments. It was far from coincidence, for example, that the Supreme Court reached its height as an economic policy-maker in a period—1890–1937—which almost precisely covers the period of the partisan alignment of 1894–1932, or that this role became untenable after the next realignment. With characteristic properties such as these, the critical realignment may well be regarded as America's surrogate for revolution. One of

Editor's note: The abridgement of the original article for our current excerpt included deletion of text and corresponding footnotes 1–19.

From William N. Chambers and Walter Dean Burnham, editors, *The American Party System: Stages of Political Development* (New York: Oxford University Press, 1975), 277–307. Reprinted with the permission of the publisher.

[20] Angus Campbell, "Surge and Decline: A Study of Electoral Change," *Public Opinion Quarterly*, XXIV (1960), 397–418.

[21] Angus Campbell *et al.*, *Elections and the Political Order* (New York, 1966), 63–77.

[22] For a useful discussion of the "standing decision," see V. O. Key, Jr., and Frank Munger, "Social Determinism and Electoral Decision: The Case of Indiana," in Eugene Burdick and Arthur J. Brodbeck (eds.), *American Voting Behavior* (Glencoe, 1959), 281–99.

[23] V. O. Key, Jr., "A Theory of Critical Elections," *Journal of Politics*, XVIII (1955), 3–18.

these experiences led directly to the outbreak of civil war, and every one of the others has been marked by acute political tension.[24]

The existence and significance of the critical realignment in American political history provides an excellent point of departure for analyzing our political development in terms of the constituent decisions and institutional modifications which have been associated with it. Examination of American party politics over time reveals the existence of not less than five national party systems. Each of these, to be sure, has constituted a link in a chain of development within the same polity, and thus has numerous properties which it shares in common with the others. But to a marked degree each is also a discrete entity, with characteristic patterns of voting behavior, of elite and institutional relationships, and of broad system-dominant decisions. While a full exploration of these patterns in all their subtlety is the proper subject of a much larger and more detailed study than this, their broad contours can be briefly outlined here.

1. *The experimental system 1789–1820.* In a real sense, the first American party system was a bridge between a pre-party phase in American political development and the recognizably modern parties found in the second and succeeding party systems. All of American political life was experimental and to a degree tentative during this period of nation-building, and the Federalist and Republican parties, as they developed, shared this experimental quality. In a developing society which was overwhelmingly agrarian and spread out along two thousand miles of coastline, a number of fundamental problems had to be faced almost immediately after the establishment of government under the Constitution. Full national independence from Europe—economic and psychological as well as political—remained to be realized. Both living and institutional symbols of a common American nationality had to be forged. In pursuit of the goals of nationality and full independence, it was essential to provide a political framework for "take-off" into sustained economic growth under internally generated capitalist auspices. Finally, certain political issues required authoritative disposition. To what extent, if at all,

should public deference to elite rule, characteristic of eighteenth-century British and colonial politics, be continued as a mainstay of republican institutions? To what extent, if at all, was partisan conflict, both over office and over policy goals, legitimate in itself?

The party system which developed in the 1790's exhibited peculiarities which were intimately associated with the attempt to find solutions to these problems. Both because of the narrow base of the active public in the initial phases of development and because of the primitive communication and transportation facilities of the time, both of the opposing coalitions were organized from the center outward toward the periphery.[25] While the importance of state politics and the significance of regional bastions of support for the Federalist and Republican parties should not be overlooked, these parties apparently were loose amalgamations of state organizations to a smaller extent than were their successors. Second, because of the heavy involvement of coastal America with Europe during the era of the French Revolution, foreign-policy controversy played an enormously salient role in the structuring of party conflict. Third, the deferential tradition was paralleled by a nearly complete identification by each rival group of the national good with their own partisan views; and this significantly affected the behavior of both parties during this period. While this identification with deference and the universal validity of their own policy views affected the Federalists especially adversely by rendering them inflexible and resistant to change, many Jeffersonians also tended to regard their opponents as a "disloyal opposition," and their leadership was hardly free of elitist bias.[26]

It would be a distortion to argue that domestic partisan conflict in this period was confined to the problem of defining how broad the ruling elite should be or what regional and economic interests should be included in it. But in practice it can hardly be argued that the elec-

---

[24] See a preliminary discussion of these characteristics in Walter Dean Burnham, "The Alabama Senatorial Election of 1962: Return of Interparty Competition," *Journal of Politics*, XXVI (1964), 798–829, esp. 822–9.

[25] William N. Chambers, *Political Parties in a New Nation* (New York, 1963), 103–12. See also Noble E. Cunningham, Jr., *The Jeffersonian Republicans in Power, 1801–1809* (Chapel Hill, 1963), esp. 299–305, and Richard P. McCormick, *The Second American Party System* (Chapel Hill, 1966), 19–31.

[26] Cunningham, *The Jeffersonian Republicans in Power, 1801–1809,* 8–9, 303–4. For an interesting discussion of the ambiguous attitude of many Republican leaders concerning expansion of the suffrage, see Chilton Williamson, *American Suffrage from Property to Democracy, 1760–1860* (Princeton, 1960), 138–64.

tion of 1800 produced any revolutionary change in the foundations of national economic policy-making, however important its political effects were. To some degree after 1800, the Jeffersonians were impelled toward active intervention in the economy by the exigencies of foreign affairs, as in the Embargo of 1808. But the rechartering of the Bank of the United States in 1816, as well as the harmony which developed over time between John Marshall's Supreme Court and the other branches of the federal government, are sufficient indications that neo-mercantilism remained on the policy agenda after as well as before 1800. As the democratization of politics in the Jacksonian era was to reveal, such policy could be sustained in an overwhelmingly rural society only so long as systematic partisan mobilization of the vast majority had not yet occurred, and only so long as deference politics continued to display some vitality. In all probability the contribution of greatest lasting significance which the realignment of 1800 made to American political development was the precedent of a peaceful turnover of political power by a Federalist coalition which professed to regard its rival as subversive of the republic. Similarly, the greatest contribution of the parties themselves was to establish the tradition of partisan competition itself, as well as to supply practical working knowledge of such competition to a whole generation of Americans.

After 1800 as well as before, the first party system displayed certain properties which were unique to it and were not clearly transmitted to its successors. First, while contests for the presidency were of major importance in crystallizing party competition nationally, neither the office nor the modes of election involving it were as yet wholly democratized. Legislative choice of presidential electors, like such choice of governors in some states, survived in many states throughout this period. This, coupled with the "inner circle" characteristics of the Republican congressional caucus, permitted a semi-fusion of powers at the federal level which has known no counterpart since the election of Andrew Jackson.[27] Moreover, this system was very incompletely developed. Partisan competition did not spread throughout the country; particularly in the

Southern and frontier regions, what weak foothold the Federalists had had down to 1800 virtually evaporated thereafter.[28] The forces which have operated over the past century to restore party competition were clearly inoperative after 1800. In the period from 1802 to 1822 (excluding the unopposed presidential election of 1820), Jeffersonian Republicans won three-quarters of all contests for presidential electors and congressmen, and four-fifths of all senatorial contests.[29] Finally, of course, the system evaporated in a decade-long, non-partisan "Era of Good Feelings," for which there is no subsequent parallel in American history.

While all party systems can in a sense be regarded as artificial, the extreme imbalance between the components of this first system after 1800 suggests rather strongly that party competition under the first system had accomplished its dominant and relatively narrow purposes by that date. Were it not for disruptive internal pressures generated by repeated collisions with the major powers involved in a European "world war" which lasted until 1815, it seems probable that a non-partisan interregnum would have emerged at least a decade before it did. Once the struggle between uncompromising and moderate elitism had been clearly settled in favor of the latter, there were evidently not enough points of internal conflict at the national level to sustain truly competitive party politics. In this sense, as in others, the first party system left no successors.

2. *The democratizing system, 1828–1854/60.* Of all of the five American party systems, the second was incomparably the most creative from an organizational point of view. The development of national two-party competition centering on a democratized presidency, and growing out of a host of local political alignments, was so massive an undertaking that it required more than a decade to complete after the critical election of 1828. There appear to have been three major stages through which the second party system passed before its dissolution. The first was the period of intense partisan organization between the election of John Quincy Adams in 1825 and his defeat at the polls in 1828. In this phase an extremely heterogeneous opposition to "insider" politics was mobilized around Andrew

---

[27] Binkley, *President and Congress*, 60–82. See also Leonard D. White, *The Jeffersonians* (New York, 1951), 29–59. White also duly notes that very little break in basic administrative patterns occurred after 1800. For a eulogy of Alexander Hamilton delivered by a Republican Secretary of the Treasury, see pp. 14–15 of White's work.

[28] McCormick, *The Second American Party System*, 27–8.
[29] For a statistical confirmation of the existence of forces tending to restore two-party competition, extending back to 1866, see Donald E. Stokes and G. R. Iversen, "On the Existence of Forces Restoring Party Competition," in Angus Campbell *et al., Elections and the Political Order*, 180–93.

Jackson; this "outsider" was virtually compelled to raise the standard of popular revolt in order to unseat the incumbent political elite.[30] The second phase of development, by which time about half of the potential electorate had been mobilized, was the Jacksonian phase proper. This phase was characterized by the emergence of the convention system as a device for presidential nominations independent of Congress or the state legislatures, by an extreme sectionalism in voting patterns, and by the new separation-of-powers conflicts between President and Congress. This phase was also marked by a heavy majority for Jackson's supporters at the polls and a new issue-oriented politics which resulted in a resounding confirmation in 1832 of the "decision of 1828." The third, or mature, phase was inaugurated in 1834 by the founding of the Whig party, and was completed around 1840. The origins of the Whigs involved not only the definitive collapse of Jackson's "Solid South," but the recognition by Jackson's opponents that effective opposition depended on acceptance of both the policy and organizational implications of democratization. Thereafter, as McCormick observes, the second party system was notable for the extreme closeness of the party balance throughout the country and for exceptionally high rates of voter turnout.[31]

The "decision of 1828" generated a number of fundamental changes in institutional relationships and policy outputs. Broadly, it was a decision to democratize political opportunity and—at least rhetorically—to eliminate the last vestiges of elitism and deference politics from the American scene. Democratization in the context of the middle period came to involve a dismantling of neo-mercantilism on the federal level and a general recession of the federal government to an extremely low level of positive activity. During the first half of the lifetime of the second party system, this was to a substantial degree the expression of the agrarian yeoman's political style and political goals, just as Hamilton had feared half a century earlier. Thereafter, the emergence of sectional conflict reinforced the weakness of the federal government—as has been true in some contemporary societies with problems of regional integration—since systematic federal pursuit of any positive domestic policies gravely threatened the increasingly tenuous union between North and South.[32] In this context the presidential nominating convention produced candidates whose chief virtue was their "availability," and whose tenure was exceptionally short. The Senate's role during this period was that of a congress of ambassadors concerned with working out the terms of intersectional compromise. As for the parties themselves, the democratized political atmosphere, the increase in the number and variety of elective offices, and the perpetual mobilization campaigns necessitated the emergence of the plebeian electoral machine staffed by professionals who had to be paid for their services.[33]

The dramatic collapse of the second party system in the period from the mid-1850's to 1860 disclosed its essential fragility. Each party had been put together piecemeal from a bewildering variety of local cleavages and ethno-cultural hostilities. On the national level, each was an electoral machine which sought to make voting capital out of these local antagonisms and the national symbolic rhetoric of the democratic "revolution." But precisely because the two parties were both so nationwide in their coalitional base, they found it increasingly difficult to accommodate sectionally divergent interests among their elites and mass followings.

The weakest link in the system was clearly the Whig party. In retrospect, it seems quite strange that a general sentiment arose in the aftermath of the 1852 presidential election that the party was already moribund, for even in defeat it had received 46.4 per cent of the two-party vote.[34] Yet two major disruptive forces were at work. In the first place, the Whig party below the presidential level was a good deal weaker than it seemed,

---

[30] For a lucid discussion of the organizational effort involved, and Martin Van Buren's key role in it, see Robert V. Remini, *The Election of Andrew Jackson* (Philadelphia, 1963), 51–120.

[31] McCormick, *The Second American Party System*, 329–56.

[32] Studies of elections in certain developing nations can provide interesting comparative insights into the interrelationships between the integrative and policy-making functions under acute conditions of regional heterogeneity. See K. W. J. Post, *The Nigerian Federal Election of 1959* (Oxford, England, 1963), esp. 437–43; and also Leon D. Epstein, "A Comparative Study of Canadian Parties," *American Political Science Review*, LVIII (1964), 46–59.

[33] Still extremely useful for a study of American party development with these particulars in mind is M. Ostrogorski, *Democracy and the Organization of Political Parties* (New York, 1902), vol. II, 207–440.

[34] Arthur C. Cole, *The Whig Party in the South* (Washington, 1913), 274–6. It is particularly suggestive that Whig leadership opinion that the party was dead after the 1852 election was concentrated in the North, and that this conclusion tended to be resisted by Southern Whig leaders with the exception of the group around Alexander H. Stephens.

and this weakness tended to accelerate in every election after 1848. This weakness, and particularly its tendency to increase, probably helped certain Whig elites—especially in the North—to turn their attention to other political combinations which would be more profitable to themselves and the interests which they supported. Second, the structure of opinion on the slavery question and related issues was clearly sharply different among the mass bases of each party. In at least a number of Northern states, the Whigs were the party of the positive liberal state, and this in substantial measure reflected the presence of a large New England subcultural component in their mass base.[35] In the Deep South, on the other hand, there was a significant correlation in many areas between wealth—including slaveholding wealth—and Whig strength in given county units.[36]

It is unlikely that this tendency toward a bimodal opinion structure among the Whigs was duplicated in anything like the same degree in the Democratic party. A posteriori, indeed, it can be noted that the swift and near-total collapse of the Whig party's mass support in the North after the Kansas-Nebraska Act had no counterpart among the Democratic following. Moreover, as elections after 1860 were to demonstrate, the critical split which did come to the Democrats that year was significant as an organizational rupture, but it did not result in permanent mass defections from the Democratic banner.

---

[35] One notes this, for instance, in Benson's estimates of the demographic composition of the major parties in New York around 1844. Benson, *The Concept of Jacksonian Democracy*, 185. The most predominantly Whig area in New York State was also known as the "Burned-over District," because of the plethora of social-reform and millenarian movements which flourished there during the middle period. See Whitney R. Cross, *The Burned-Over District* (Ithaca, N.Y., 1950).

[36] Seymour Martin Lipset, *Political Man* (Garden City, N.Y., 1960), 344–54.

TABLE 1

Partisan Strength in the Second Party System, 1834–53, by Categories of Offices

Office	%Dem.	%Whig	%Other
Presidential electors	53.9	46.1	—
U.S. representatives	54.9	42.6	2.5
U.S. senators	54.8	42.5	2.7
Governors	58.7	39.7	1.6

3. *The Civil War system, 1860–93.* The major "decision" associated with the realignment which culminated in the 1860 election was, of course, the reorganization of the party system and of institutional relationships and policy outputs along explicitly sectional lines. This was the only possible restructuring which could lead to the definitive containment and eventual extinction of slavery and the economic-cultural regime built upon it. Since this intersectional issue was neither "negotiable" nor one which the losing elite groups could permit to be resolved through the electoral process, the inevitable result of organizing the party system in this way was civil war. Put another way around, the only possible way to avert a breakup of the antebellum Union and the violence which followed was—precisely as the conservative compromisers of 1850 had always argued—to declare the entire question of slavery off-limits and thus to prolong the life of the second party system indefinitely. But such an attempt to halt further political development in a broader system undergoing the most dynamic change seems to have been foredoomed to failure. It reckoned without the implications of accelerating cultural, demographic, and economic divergences along regional lines. In fact a classic pre-revolutionary situation had developed by the 1850's. The system as a whole tended to be dominated by political elites who represented a declining sector of the national socio-economic system. Elites who represented the values and interests of dynamically evolving sectors at first resented, and later rose in rebellion against, that traditional dominance.

It may be argued with great plausibility that the American Civil War and its aftermath constituted the only genuine revolution in the history of the country.[37] Certainly during the first half of the Civil War the party system was replete with characteristic deviations from normal patterns, deviations which could be expected in an era of violent transition. With the exclusion of an entire region from access to—much less control over—national policy-making institutions, a radical shift in policy outputs occurred. Not only was slavery given a violent *coup de grace*, but an integrated program of positive federal involvement in the fields of banking and currency, transportation, the tariff, and land grants to smallholders was inaugurated. While on some issues the majority coalition was fragmented, the central

---

[37] A most provocative recent discussion, which raises the largest issues of development, is found in Barrington Moore, Jr., *Social Origins of Dictatorship and Democracy* (Boston, 1966), 111–55.

policy issues of the 1860's were closely integrated. During this era the dominant Republican party was genuinely, if unusually, a policy-making party. On the mass level, the partisan loyalties which were forged during this revolutionary era survived almost unchanged until the 1890's, and in some areas left traces which are still visible today.

It is usual to define the end of Reconstruction as occurring at the time of the famous bargain of 1877 between Northern Republicans and Southern Democrats. In reality, however, the revolutionary phase of this party system had largely run its course by 1870.[38] The administration of Ulysses S. Grant can probably best be regarded as a bridge between the era of convulsive revolution which preceded it and the era of industrializing-elite dominance which followed. Into the 1870's, Republican leaders were preoccupied with the danger that a Southern re-entry into the political system might produce an overthrow of their coalition at the polls and a restoration of the Jacksonian coalition to its former dominance. Nor was this a chimera: the success of the Republican revolution in national policy-making had been predicated upon enormous artificial majorities that were produced in a Congress in which the Southern states were not represented. Indeed, the Republican fears were partially realized after 1872. Southern "Redemption" and the persistence of traditional Northern support for the Democrats resulted in a unique period of partisan deadlock which lasted from 1874 until Republican capture of all branches of the federal government in 1896.

The accelerating influence of industrial capitalism produced results, however, which differed sharply in many respects from those which had been feared by Republican leaders in the Reconstruction era. Both political parties fell substantially under the control of elites who favored industrial development and private enterprise. The Southern Redeemers were not Jacksonians *redivivi*; most of them were upper-class gentlemen who adapted their goals and styles quite well to the new industrial dispensation.[39] Paradoxically, the freezing of alignments along Civil War lines at the mass level gave maximum political latitude to the industrial elites and their partisan assistants to develop the

TABLE 2*

Partisan Strength in the Third Party System, 1854–92, by Categories of Offices

A. 1854–73			
Office	%Dem.	%Rep.	%Other
Presidential electors	29.4	70.0	0.6
U.S. representatives	34.4	58.4	7.2
U.S. senators	32.7	60.7	6.6
Governors	25.6	69.2	5.2

B. 1874–92			
Office	%Dem.	%Rep.	%Other
Presidential electors	50.6	48.3	1.1
U.S. representatives	55.9	41.7	2.4
U.S. senators	47.5	51.0	1.5
Governors	48.9	49.5	1.6

* From *The Era of Reconstruction 1865–1877*, by Kenneth M. Stampp, Copyright © 1965 by Kenneth M. Stampp. Reprinted by permission of Alfred A. Knopf, Inc.

economy on their own terms. As for the Negro, his interests were abandoned by the Republican leadership, in substance if not in rhetoric, as an essential part of the sectional bargain on which the stable deadlock rested. As the nature of the Southern Democratic leadership changed somewhat around 1890 by becoming rather more plebian, it drew the logical consequences implicit in this bargain and, against ineffective Republican resistance on the national level, formally expelled the Negro from the Southern polity. During the 1880's and the 1890's this solution came tacitly to be accepted by the Republicans, by the Supreme Court, and by white public opinion.[40] The modern Solid South thus came into being, and, as a political necessity in a one-party regime, so did the direct primary.

4. *The industrialist system, 1894–1932.* The deadlock of 1874–92, however, was as unstable as the national bipartisan balance which had existed in the 1840's. In both cases a party system whose components were locked in an obsolescent pattern of alignments and partisan ideologies tended increasingly to underrepresent significant disadvantaged elements in the electorate. The processes of industrialization after the Civil War had produced two major strata of the disadvantaged: the farmers, especially in the cash-crop colo-

[38] Kenneth J. Stampp, *The Era of Reconstruction, 1865–1877* (New York, 1965), 186–215.

[39] See, for instance, C. Vann Woodward, *Reunion and Reaction: The Compromise of 1877 and the End of Reconstruction* (Boston, 1951), 23–53.

[40] C. Vann Woodward, *The Burden of Southern History* (Baton Rouge, La., 1960), 69–87. See also *Civil Rights Cases*, 109 U.S. 3 (1883); and *Plessy v. Ferguson*, 163 U.S. 537 (1896).

nial areas of the country, and the growing, ethnically fragmented urban proletariat. As the history of the period from 1877 to 1896 so strikingly reveals, both groups became progressively more alienated from the established order as the Civil War system drew to its close. Suffering from the effects of a long-term crisis in agriculture, the cash-crop farmers in the plains states and the South were already in active rebellion by 1890. Almost immediately thereafter, the second worst industrial depression in American history struck the urban centers. The almost instantaneous result, with a conservative Democratic administration in power, was the collapse of the Democratic party throughout the urban metropole in 1894. As many members of the Northeastern elite feared, the stage was thus set for a political coalition of both disadvantaged elements with the objective of overthrowing industrial-elite rule. The fact that full democratization of politics had uniquely occurred in the United States before the onset of industrialization—and thus that such a mass assault against industrial elites could be conducted with constitutional legitimacy—undoubtedly increased the latter's anxiety. While the Supreme Court did what it could in its classic decisions of 1894–95 to undermine that legitimacy, only a critical realignment could dispose of the issues raised with any finality.[41]

In the event, the insurrection under William Jennings Bryan's leadership proved abortive. Among the factors leading to his defeat, several appear decisive. First, the urban working class was too immature and fragmented internally to work effectively with the agrarian rebels. But more than this, there appears every evidence that the combination of the "Democratic depression" of 1893 and severe ethno-cultural hostilities between new-immigrant workers and old-stock agrarians created an urban revulsion against the Democrats which lasted into the late 1920's.[42] More-

over, the issues which appealed to the dominantly colonial-agrarian clientele of the Bryanites—especially currency inflation—meant nothing, and perhaps less than nothing, to workers whose wages were all too obviously at the mercy of employers and economic conditions. Finally, the essentially nostalgic and colonial character of the insurgents' appeal produced a violently sectional reaction throughout the metropole; the Democratic party in that region sank into an impotence which, save for a limited upswing between 1910 and 1916, lasted for a generation.

The alignment system which was set up during the 1890's marks the point at which American party development began clearly to diverge from developmental patterns in other industrial societies. This system was unique among the five under discussion: it was structured not around competition between the parties, but around the elimination of such competition both on the national level and in a large majority of the states. The alignment pattern was broadly composed of three subsystems: a solidly Democratic South, an almost equally solid Republican bastion in the greater Northeast, and a quasi-colonial West from which protesting political movements were repeatedly launched against the dominant components of the system.[43] The extreme sectionalism of this system can be measured by virtually any yardstick. For example, excluding the special case of 1912, 84.5 per cent of the total electoral vote for Democratic presidential candidates between 1896 and 1928 was cast in the Southern and Border states. Gubernatorial contests during the 1894–1930 period, while showing somewhat greater dispersion of partisan strength, also demonstrate this sectional pattern.

A number of major consequences followed from this pattern of politics. With general elections reduced to formalities in most jurisdictions, the direct primary was developed as an imperfect and ambiguous alternative to party competition. Election turnout dropped precipitately from levels comparable with those of

---

[41] Among the best studies of this interaction are Arnold M. Paul, *Conservative Crisis and the Rule of Law* (Ithaca, N.Y., 1960), esp. 131–235, and Alan F. Westin, "The Supreme Court, the Populist Movement and the Campaign of 1896," *Journal of Politics*, XV (1953), 3–42.

[42] One of the many myths—or, more appropriately, half-truths—which are propagated among liberal historians is the notion that employer coercion or intimidation of urban workers was a dominant factor in the 1896 outcome. See e.g. Ray Ginger, *Altgeld's America* (New York, 1958), 172–9. Quantitative analysis of urban election data—especially over time—indicates how dubious this explanation is. It fails to take into account, first, that the realignment of 1896 endured in the cities with very little change until 1908, and remained substantially dominant until the "Al Smith

revolution" of 1928; and second, the existence even in 1896 of very considerable ethnic differentials in the impact of the campaigns and realignments of this era on the urban vote. For a study which remains a seminal contribution by an historian, see Lee Benson, "Research Problems in American Political Historiography," in Mirra Komarovsky (ed.), *Common Frontiers of the Social Sciences* (Glencoe, 1957), 113–83.

[43] This discussion partly follows E. E. Schattschneider, *The Semi-Sovereign People* (New York, 1960), 78–96. See also his "United States: The Functional Approach to Party Government," in Sigmund Neumann (ed.), *Modern Political Parties* (Chicago, 1956), 194–215.

TABLE 3
Sectionalism and Gubernatorial Elections, 1894–1931

Region	Percentage of Governorships Won By:		
	Dem.	Rep.	Other
South[a]	96.8	2.6	0.6
Border[b]	61.1	38.9	—
Midwest and West[c]	31.0	67.2	1.8
Northeast[d]	16.9	83.1	—
Total U.S.	43.0	56.0	1.0

[a] Eleven ex-Confederate states.
[b] Kentucky, Maryland, Missouri, Oklahoma, West Virginia.
[c] East North Central, West North Central (except for Missouri), Mountain and Pacific census regions.
[d] New England and Middle Atlantic census regions plus Delaware.

present-day Europe: by the 1920's, national turnout ranged from less than one-third in off years to little more than two-fifths in presidential elections. Viewed in terms of the broader political decision-making system as a whole, the substantial disappearance of party competition, the discrediting of party itself as an instrument of government, the progressive fragmentation of Congress during this period, and the large but negative policy role played by the Supreme Court all fitted admirably into the chief function of the fourth party system. That function was the substantially complete insulation of elites from attacks by the victims of the industrializing process, and a corresponding reinforcement of political conditions favoring an exclusively private exploitation of the industrial economy. One is indeed inclined to suspect that the large hole in voter participation which developed after 1900 roughly corresponds to the area in the electorate where a viable socialist movement "ought" to have developed but, for reasons discussed earlier, did not succeed in doing so.[44]

It can nevertheless be argued that the sectionalism of the 1896–1932 alignment significantly advanced the nationalization of American politics. First, the realignment of the 1890's destroyed or submerged a tangled network of diverse patterns of party allegiance which went back to the Civil War or earlier. It thus created both a severe loosening of the grip of traditional voting

patterns and tended to establish broadly regional alignments in their place. Second, the apparently decisive rout of the Democratic party in the industrial-urban centers bore within it the seeds of the party's eventual regeneration. A power vacuum had been created in its state organizations in the Northeast by the desertion of the old, respectable Gold Democratic leadership. This vacuum was in time to be filled by representatives of the newer immigrants.[45] The stage was thus gradually set, via the Democratic convention of 1924 and the "Al Smith revolution" of 1928, for a transition from the old rural-colonial party of Bryan to the winning coalition of rural and urban underprivileged which the party was to become under Franklin Roosevelt.

5. *The New Deal System, 1932–?*. The election of 1928, bringing as it did a huge bloc of new immigrant votes into the political system for the first time, has rightly been called the beginning of critical realignment in the Northeast. Even so, it is doubtful that the extremely stable sectionalism of the fourth party system could have been destroyed by any force less profound than the Great Depression. The extended realignment of 1928–36, associated with that great shock and with the coming of age of the new immigrants, has rightly been called an event "very like the overthrow of a ruling class."[46] Permanent federal involvement in the mixed economy which arose from the ruins was substituted for a business rule which could no longer stay the course. The inevitable institutional modifications emerged; the presidency and its ancillary executive establishment moved into ascendancy as a center of policy planning and initiation, and the Supreme Court's veto over interventionist economic legislation was eliminated. The federal government also promoted the development of countervailing institutions of power in the larger society, especially in the labor field. As the Democratic party became the normal majority party, a substantial class cleavage was added to the traditional mix of voting alignments for the first time. Sectionalism was replaced piecemeal by the emergence of two-party competition where it had not existed for decades. The party system became nationalized, although the organizational structures and functions of the major parties themselves remained largely unchanged.

[44] For a more detailed discussion, see Walter Dean Burnham, "The Changing Shape of the American Political Universe."

[45] An excellent state case study of this process is J. Joseph Huthmacher, *Massachusetts People and Politics, 1919–1933* (Cambridge, Mass., 1959).
[46] Schattschneider, *The Semi-Sovereign People*, 86.

TABLE 4
Gubernatorial Elections in the Fifth Party System, 1932–66

Region	Percentage of Governorships Won By:		
	Dem.	Rep.	Other
South	98.4	1.6	—
Border	80.0	20.0	—
Midwest and West	44.4	53.7	1.9
Northeast	43.4	56.7	—
Total U.S.	57.4	41.6	1.0

It is important to emphasize, however, that the nationalization of party organization and voting alignments which was inaugurated in the 1930's has been a gradual process which is still far from finished. On the state level, years had to pass before the conservative, old-line Democrats who were suddenly propelled to victory during the 1930's were replaced by leaders more in tune with the programs of the national party. Realignment of party organizations and followings along national lines did not spread into a number of states in the far North until the late 1940's and early 1950's.[47] Similar realignment in the South, at least below the presidential level, has begun to have statewide ramifications only since 1960.

Here, as elsewhere in the past, American party development has largely been derivative from major changes in the structure of the socio-economic system. Urbanization and the development of autonomous sources of capital in the former "colonial" areas, along with the enormous shift of middle-class populations southward and westward since the end of World War I, have resulted in a severe erosion of the formerly central distinction between economically developed and underdeveloped regions in the United States. Such postwar changes have helped to provide the social diversification essential to two-party com-

petition. Moreover, the federal government during the past decade has conspicuously reversed the "decision" of the 1890's regarding the exclusion of the Negro from the Southern political system. This reversal is as characteristic of the fifth party system as the former decision was characteristic of the fourth. The original national acceptance of exclusion gave the cue for the organization and maintenance of the restrictive one-partyism which was essential to the classic Southern subsystem. The contemporary national insistence upon the inclusion of the Negro has destroyed most of the rationale for the preservation of that one-partyism.

There is much reason for subdividing the fifth party system into two parts at about the year 1950. The first period was that of the New Deal era proper. Broadly speaking, this was a period in which the major concerns of American politics centered on the domestic issues of prosperity and the full integration of the newer immigrants into American social and political life. As the sustained growth in the American economy after 1941 was still in its infancy, the dominant political themes at this time still turned on scarcity and the attendant problems of class relationships in American society. Despite the intrusion of World War II, foreign-policy issues remained on the whole distinctly peripheral to these concerns. The "American responsibility," about which so much has been heard of late, was barely in gestation among elite circles down until about 1950, and was virtually invisible to the country at large until the outbreak of the Korean War. The election of 1948 may well be remembered in retrospect as the last of the older-style elections: the last before the full emergence of television, the last to turn on explicit class appeals, the last in which the "farm vote" was considered a major factor in the outcome, the last in which foreign-policy issues were conspicuous by their absence from the major-party campaigns.

The period since 1950 may legitimately be described as one of great confusion in American party politics, a period in which the classic New Deal alignment seems to have evaporated without being replaced by an equally structured ordering of politics. The rapid development of public-relations techniques and the projection of candidate "images" have been accompanied at the mass level by a sharp decline in the salience of older-style class cleavages, and an equally significant erosion of party as a dominant factor in electoral decisions. The underlying partisan preferences of the electorate, as survey research has repeatedly demonstrated, have not significantly changed since at least the

---

[47] In New England and elsewhere, as Richard E. Dawson points out in this volume, 1954 appears to have been a breakthrough year. Duane Lockard, *New England State Politics* (Princeton, 1959), 30, 45. In the upper Midwest, the breakthrough came around 1948. John H. Fenton, *Midwest Politics* (New York, 1966), 18–20, 44–64, 87–100.

1940's.[48] But the electorate since 1950 has displayed a willingness to engage in ticket-splitting on an unprecedentedly massive scale. Probably as a consequence of image voting, the partial replacement of patronage politics by ideologically flavored politics, and the penetration of the mass media, short-term influences on voting have grown tremendously in recent years at the expense of long-term continuities.

READING 11

PARTY, BUREAUCRACY, AND POLITICAL CHANGE IN THE UNITED STATES

Martin Shefter

I. INTRODUCTION

Over the past 180 years, five or six distinct party systems have emerged, developed, and decayed in the United States. These successive systems have been distinguished from one another by the issues dividing the major parties, the proportion of the vote each party normally received, and the social composition of each party's electoral base. Equally important, changes have occurred from one party system to the next in the strength of political parties relative to other public institutions and political actors in the United States (Burnham, 1970).

Among the most important institutional changes that have accompanied the emergence of new party systems in the United States have been shifts in the power of political parties relative to public bureaucracies. The relationship between these two institutions is of great significance for a number of reasons. First, it has major consequences for the structure of political parties and for the electoral strategies they are able to pursue. If political parties are the stronger institution, they will be in a position to extract patronage from the bureaucracy and to distribute it to the cadre who conduct their campaigns and the voters who support their candidates; if parties are weaker than bureaucracies, they must find some alternative means of mobilizing popular support (Shefter, 1978a). Second and more generally, the strength of parties relative to bureaucracies has an important bearing upon the character of the political system as a whole, as Figure 1 indicates.

Figure 1 is a simple typology of the relationships that may exist between the power of parties and bureaucracies. Where parties are strong and the bureaucracy is weak (cell I), parties will be in a position to dominate both the electoral and administrative arenas, and, as just noted, to use their power to generate patronage (Tolchin and Tolchin, 1971). Such political systems can be said to be governed by "political machines." Where parties and bureaucracies are both strong (cell II), each institution will be able to dominate its respective arena, to exert some discipline over its members, and to protect its boundaries from lateral penetration. In this situation, parties will not find it possible to obtain patronage from the bureaucracy for distribution to voters, but will be in a position to deliver on whatever promises they make concerning the general policies they intend to enact. Borrowing a term that was popular a generation ago, one can label these "responsible parties." Where the bureaucracy is strong and parties are weak (cell III), executive agencies may be able to resist not only lateral penetration, but also control from above. In this situation, parties will be able neither to extract patronage from the bureaucracy nor to deliver on any promises they may make concerning the implementation of public policy, all they can do is offer voters empty rhetoric or appeal to their supporters' racial, ethnic, or national sentiments. These can be called "irresponsible

		POLITICAL PARTIES	
		STRONG	WEAK
BUREAUCRACY	STRONG	II "Responsible" Party	III "Irresponsible" Party/Bureaucratic State
	WEAK	I Political Machine	IV Regime of Notables Corporatist State Machine of Incumbents

FIGURE 1

From Louis Moisel and Joseph Cooper, editors, *Political Parties: Development and Decoy* (Beverly Hills, CA: Sage Publications, 1978), 211–265. Reprinted with the permission of the publishers.

[48] Philip E. Converse, "The Concept of a Normal Vote," in Angus Campbell *et al.*, *Elections and the Political Order*, 9–39, and esp. 13.

parties" and a regime governed in this way can be termed "bureaucratic state."

The final category (cell IV) is the most complex. If both parties and bureaucracies are institutionally weak, the locus of power depends upon which particular political actors, organizations, or institutions dominate in their stead. Where local dignitaries dominate the electoral arena and use their influence to extract patronage from the bureaucracy for distribution to their personal clients, one may speak of a "regime of notables." Where interest groups have influence over the bureaucracy and are able to help candidates win elections to public office, one may speak of a "corporatist state." Finally, where professional politicians secure elective office by constructing personal campaign organizations and remain in power by intervening before the bureaucracy on behalf of their constituents, one may speak of a "machine of incumbents."

Since the emergence of the first American party system in the 1790s, the power of party relative to bureaucracy in the United States has changed dramatically a number of times, and the American political system could aptly be characterized, at least in part, in each of these ways. In this essay, I seek to account for these patterns of institutional development, transformation, and decay.

My argument, briefly stated, is that changes in relative power of party and bureaucracy in the United States are intimately related to the process of critical realignment in American politics. Critical elections bring to power new political coalitions, some or all of whose members wish to use public authority for new purposes. By altering the relationship between, and the internal structure of, party and bureaucracy, elements of the new majority coalition seek to undermine the position of politicians who held power during the earlier party system, to seize control over the government, and to turn it to the purposes they want it to serve. Or to phrase this in somewhat greater detail, by restructuring the party and the bureaucracy, various contenders for power seek to create an institutional order which will enable them to (1) defeat their opponents in the other party, or in other factions of their own party; (2) subject voters to their discipline; (3) control the use of public authority; and (4) have the structural and technical capacity to perform those functions which the group in question wants the government to serve. Whether reformers in the wake of any given critical election will seek to strengthen or weaken the party as an institution, and to defend or to undermine the autonomy of the bureaucracy, depends primarily upon the structure of

the antecedent regime and the nature of the resources they command.

In the sections below, I will indicate how the major changes that have occurred from one party system to the next in the structure of, and relationship between, party and bureaucracy in the United States can be understood in these terms.

II. THE REGIME OF NOTABLES: THE FEDERALISTS AND JEFFERSONIANS

The first political parties in the United States—the Federalists and the Jeffersonian Republicans—were coalitions of notables. During the period extending from the emergence of the two parties in the 1790s through their collapse in the 1820s, the level of political participation in most areas of the country was low, party organizations were weak or nonexistent, elective offices were monopolized by local notables, and these officials appointed their associates and clients to positions in the bureaucracy.[1] There were, however, some differences between what the Federalists and the Jeffersonians sought to accomplish, the opposition they had to overcome to do so, and the resources they commanded, and these shaped their orientations toward party and bureaucracy.

The Federalists spoke for a rather narrow segment of the American upper class. The central policies of the Washington and Adams administrations. (Hamilton's financial program, the pro-British tilt in foreign relations, and policies with respect to public lands and Indian removal that retarded settlement of the West) served the interests of the nation's mercantile elite, a sector of the economy which had commercial ties with Britain and little geographic presence apart form the coastal regions of New England and the Middle States. Because this sector encompassed such a small proportion of the nation's population (at most 10%), the ideology the party professed and the political techniques upon which it relied were necessarily antidemocratic (Ellis, 1971:Chap. 17).

Though there were some important exceptions, the Federalists, as Ellis (1971:279) observes, "publicly denied the ability of the people to govern themselves, stressed the need for elitist guidance, and never were able to successfully practice the art of popular politics" (cf., Fischer, 1965). Washington, in his farewell address, formulated the classic conservative critique of party, and one element among the Federalists was prepared to use the army, rather than to engage in countermobilization, in order to cope with the Republican opposition. Similarly, the bureaucratic appointment practices of the Federalists were narrowly elitist in their orientation. In selecting individuals to serve in the departments and agencies of his administration, President Washington chose men who in his words were "esteemed and honored by their neighbors," that is, local notables who "placed at the disposal of the [new government] a system of social relations in which they were already superiors, independently of their official tenure."[2] As opposition to Federalist policies congealed, the Washington and Adams administrations, if anything, narrowed their political base, and their patronage practices became more restrictive: they appointed only those notables who supported the administration in its conflicts with the Republicans (Van Riper, 1958:21). This culminated in Adams's midnight appointments. By packing the federal bureaucracy and judiciary with Federalists, Adams sought to ensure that these institutions would remain bastions of Federalism despite the party's repudiation by the majority in the election of 1800.

The majority which supported the Republicans in the critical election of 1800 was composed of two major groups. The first were subsistence farmers who opposed the administration both because they stood outside the market economy and, therefore, could only be injured by Federalist economic policies, and because they were radically democratic in ideology. This group formed the radical wing of the Republican Party. The second was composed of commercial farmers who would profit from trading in a larger market than Britain alone provided. This group, the Republican moderates, was led by planters such as Jefferson and Madison who, because they opposed Federalist policies on behalf of the nation's agricultural majority, were democratic in ideology and were able to successfully play the game of popular politics.

Although radical and moderate Republicans shared an antipathy to the mercantile, pro-British, and anti-democratic orientations of the Federalists, the economic and political orders they favored were not in the least similar. The moderates, unlike the radicals, wanted to build a commercial society and to have the government foster economic development through internal improvements and the chartering of banks. (The Republican moderates differed from the Hamiltonians to the extent that they wanted to develop the economy on an agricultural base and by strengthening the national market, rather than on a mercantile base and by tying the American economy to the British market.) And in the realm of politics, the moderates,

unlike the radicals, regarded as dangerous all forms of political activity conducted apart from the established institutions and leaders of society; they were aghast at the Whiskey Rebellion, uncomfortable with the Democratic-Republican societies, and opposed to constitutional reforms which would radically democratize and decentralize the government.

To implement their program, the moderate Republicans sought to drive from the political arena extremists of both the right and left—the High Federalists and the Old Republicans—and to construct a coalition of moderates from both parties who favored a republican polity, a market economy, and an ordered society. Jeffersonian practices with respect to party and patronage can be understood in light of this goal as well as the resources the Republican moderates were able to command, and the opposition they had to overcome to achieve it. When the Federalists, during the Adams administration, were preparing to use the army to crush opposition (or so it appeared), Madison and Jefferson were willing to ally with the radicals and to mobilize mass support—a strategy which involved creating the Republican Party (Cunningham, 1957). After gaining power, however, the moderates slowly turned away from their alliance with the radicals and sought to conciliate the moderate Federalists. The Republican Party was permitted to decay once its function of defeating the "monarchists" had been fulfilled. As Richard Hofstadter (1969:Chap. 5) has documented, Jefferson, Madison, and Monroe did not regard the Republican Party as a permanent institution, but rather as a temporary expedient to rout the enemies of republicanism and, thereby, to establish the preconditions for a partyless regime.

In a similar vein, Jefferson refused, in the face of substantial pressure, to purge all Federalists from the bureaucracy and judiciary, for fear of alienating those he wished to conciliate. He sought to give the Republicans proportional representation in, rather than total dominance over, the bureaucracy. During his first two years in office, Jefferson replaced somewhat over half the officials appointed by his predecessors—186 of 316 presidential appointees—and then he stopped. In selecting officials to be removed, Jefferson sought in particular to frustrate Adam's effort to turn the judiciary and bureaucracy into a Federalist power base. He refused to recognize the commissions of the midnight appointees, removed Federalist marshals and district attorneys to ensure that Republican suitors would enjoy access to the federal courts, and fired field administrators who used their positions in ways which helped the

Federalists and injured the Republicans. Jefferson appointed only Republicans to the vacancies thus created, but not just any Republicans. In choosing whom to appoint, Jefferson canvassed the Republican notability in the locality in question, and individuals who wished to secure appointments from him submitted petitions and letters attesting to their good character and their acceptability to the respectable men of the community (Cunningham, 1963:Chaps. 2–3; White, 1951:Chap. 24).

The Jeffersonians, then, were very much a party of notables. Where they differed from the Federalists was that their regime was grounded upon a much larger segment of the nation's upper class and that, in order to defeat their opponents, they were prepared to appeal for mass support—a strategy which led them to build the world's first modern party organization (Chambers, 1963). Once their position was secured, however, the Jeffersonians mobilized their followers and recruited public officials through the informal community networks commanded by members of the patriciate and gentry who were loyal to the administration, rather than through a well organized party structure.[3] This system enabled the classes for which they spoke to gain privileged access to public benefits and to use public authority to discipline the groups that were excluded from the Jeffersonian regime. (During the Jeffersonian era, for example, public lands were sold only in large lots to commercial farmers, and federal marshalls appointed by Republican presidents evicted subsistence farmers who were squatting on the public domain.) And because the Jeffersonian notability was rather well educated (it is not coincidental that Jefferson founded a university), the state they staffed in this way was quite competent to administer the mildly mercantilist policies the regime pursued (Aronson, 1964:Chap. 6).

III. PARTY, PATRONAGE, AND POLITICAL MACHINES: THE JACKSONIANS

The system led by the Jeffersonians was overthrown following the election of 1828 by the Jacksonians. The politicians of the Jacksonian Era initiated a process which Luigi Graziano (1978), in a different context, has termed "the emancipation of the state from civil society." They established a party system and a system of public administration which were independent of the informal social hierarchies upon which the Jeffersonians had relied. They did this by creating mass based party organizations, reorganizing the bureaucracy, and perfecting the spoils system.

The Jeffersonian political economy had excluded, or at least disadvantaged, a rather heterogeneous collection of social groups. Chief among these were businessmen seeking to break into the existing order of limited mercantile privilege (the classic example is Wall Street's opposition to the Philadelphia-based Second Bank of the United States); farmers who faced competition in the local markets they once had monopolized from grain transported on government-subsidized canals; master mechanics being squeezed out by merchant-capitalists who were able to obtain credit from publicly chartered banks; and marginal farmers and laborers hurt by the price inflation caused, at least in their view, by the issue of currency by those banks (Lebowitz, 1969; cf. Gatell, 1966). The members of religious and ethnic minorities who were discriminated against by legislation enacted at the behest of more established groups also had reason to be dissatisfied with the prevailing regime.

This heterogeneous collection of social groups was available for mobilization by anti-administration politicians and by political movements which argued that the common source of all their problems was a regime which granted favors to those who occupied privileged political positions and which, in the process, intervened so actively in society that it upset the natural order of things. The Jacksonians proposed a dual remedy for these problems: open up the political system to the people; and limit the powers of government. They sought to implement this program by appealing for popular support apart from established leadership channels (Marshall, 1967). The reforms they sponsored in the electoral and administrative arenas were part and parcel of this effort to overthrow the notables' regime.

The Jacksonians sponsored a number of reforms in the procedures governing the conduct of elections and the recruitment of public officials which made it difficult for local notables to dominate these processes. Under the old regime, restrictions on the franchise, large election districts, the absence of a "top of the ticket" as a focus for popular enthusiasm (presidential electors and governors often were appointed by state legislatures), and, of course, the absence of an organized opposition, together limited the size of the active electorate. The restricted scope of the political universe in conjunction with viva voce voting enabled the leading men of the country to send one of their number to the state legislature. And because state legislatures or their appointees (governors, councils of appointment) commonly selected the heads of state executive departments, judges, and county officials, it was only necessary for the notability to dominate state legislative elections in order to dominate the entire governmental apparatus. The electoral reforms of the Jacksonian Era—white manhood suffrage; the paper ballot; small polling districts; direct election of governors, presidential electors, heads of state executive departments, and local government officials; and short terms of office—swamped the older, elite-dominated mechanisms of election management and political recruitment (McCormick, 1975).

After coming to power by overwhelming their opponents in the electoral arena, the Jacksonians sought to extend their sway over the bureaucracy. The doctrine of rotation-in-office, as is well known, legitimized this effort to expel their predecessors from positions in the bureaucracy. Somewhat less well known are the other moves the Jacksonians made in their effort to sever the ties between the notability and the bureaucracy and to extend their own control over it. In point of fact, the Jacksonians were responsible for the first major episode of administrative reform in American history. Though they were not at all self-conscious about what they were doing, they sought to transform the federal bureaucracy from a structure which operated according to the principles of personal organization into one which operated according to the principles of formal organization. Jacksonian officials such as Amos Kendall drafted administrative reorganization plans that specified the responsibilities attached to positions within the bureaucracy (rather than to the persons occupying these roles); established bureaus organized along functional lines within the executive departments; assigned officials to perform staff (as distinguished from line) responsibilities; created elaborate systems of inspection, reporting, and accounting to monitor departmental field offices; promulgated codes of official ethics; and insisted that officials distinguish sharply between their private funds and public accounts. Matthew Crenson (1975), who describes these reforms in an important recent book, argues, mistakenly in my view, that the Jacksonians established formal bureaucratic structures because rapid social change in the early 19th century had undermined traditional social institutions—the bar, the business community, the local community—and made it impossible to rely on them any longer to enforce standards of probity and good behavior upon bureaucrats.[4] I would argue, rather, that the Jacksonians established formal bureau-

cratic procedures instead of relying on these informal institutions to control the behavior of subordinate officials because these institutions (which continued to flourish well beyond the 1820s and 1830s) were controlled in the main by their political enemies. By removing the bureaucrats appointed by their predecessors, the Jacksonians sought to sever the ties between the bureaucracy, and these traditional social structures; and by reorganizing the bureaucracy, they sought to subject it to the control of the officeholders whom they had elected, the institutions (especially the party organizations) which they commanded, and the social groups for whom they spoke. In other words, the bureaucratic reforms the Jacksonians sponsored served to "emancipate" the output institutions of the state from the informal social hierarchies that an established class of notables controlled, just as the electoral and party reforms they sponsored served to emancipate the input institutions of the state from this segment of civil society.

The electoral and administrative reforms of the Jacksonian Era, then, were part and parcel of the realignment process: they were efforts by a new majority to drive from power the elites who had dominated the earlier regime. As such, they could be supported by all, or at least most, elements of the new majority coalition. Once enacted, however, these reforms had consequences for the distribution of power *within* the majority party. The expansion of the number of public offices subject to popular election, and the shortening of the terms of public officials, made legislators, executives, and judges dependent upon the politicians who organized the enlarged electorates of the period, and turned party management into, if not a full-time profession, then at least a vocation that demanded far more time and attention for its successful performance than had been devoted to it by the gentlemen dilettantes of the earlier regime. At the same time and expulsion of the notables from institutions of policymaking and administration, and the subjection of these institutions to party influence gave middle-class lawyers, editors, and businessmen an incentive to devote themselves to the tasks of party management, because these developments made it possible for such men-on-the-make to live off politics by serving as agents for private interests in their dealings with government (the Jacksonian period saw the rise of the lobby), by moving into and out of public office, and by making personal contacts and obtaining public contracts (e.g., printing contracts) that were useful in their private careers. The Jacksonian reforms, then, placed at the very center of the political system a group of middle-class professional or semiprofessional politicians (Hofstadter, 1969:240–242; cf. Weber, 1958).

The leadership of this group did not go unchallenged. The Jacksonian coalition, as mentioned above, was extremely heterogeneous. It included elements of the business community and the middle class that wanted, as Carl Degler (1956:216) terms it, to "liberate the expanding American economy from the fetters of a dying mercantilist approach to business enterprise," by permitting anyone to obtain a bank or corporate charter (free banking and general incorporation), and by expanding the supply of money and credit. It also included marginal farmers, mechanics, and laborers who wanted to contract the money supply, who regarded all banks and corporations as chartered monopolies, and who supported other policies equally antipathetic to the interests of the first group, such as the 10-hour-day and the right to strike. Many of the spokesmen for this position, especially in the larger cities, were affiliated with the fledgling trade unions of the Jacksonian Era, organizations that were seeking to establish their political hegemony over the working classes. At different times these leaders worked through third parties—organizing the workingmen's parties of the period—or through the Democratic Party—forming its radical wing. To the extent that these leaders mobilized their supporters through craft organizations, their challenge to the professional party politicians of the period was as backward looking as that of the early Whig Party; it harked back to 18th century patterns of working-class political activity (Bridges, 1977).

The middle-class professional politicians in the Democratic party responded to this challenge in a number of ways. They came out in support of some of the policies advocated by the radicals. Such concessions, however, alienated the party's wealthier supporters (Gatell, 1967). It was possible, however, to appeal to the rank-and-file supporters of the radical factions without splitting the Jacksonian movement along class lines by pursuing two alternative strategies. Democratic politicians appealed to working-class voters by stressing the party's stance on religious and cultural issues—its defense of immigrants and Catholics against the attacks of nativists and evangelical Protestants (Montgomery, 1972). And Democratic politicians attempted to steal away the supporters of the radicals by pursuing a strategy of counterorganization. Whereas the radicals sought to organize their followers along craft lines or, more exactly, to politicize preexisting labor organizations, the professional politicians

organized their followers along residential lines (in ward and town committees) and politicized preexisting recreational organizations, such as volunteer fire brigades and militia companies (Katznelson, 1975; Bridges, 1977).

The control that politicians established over the organs of administration and policymaking in the United States during the Jacksonian Era contributed to the success of this strategy of party building. The access they acquired to the bureaucracy enabled them to distribute patronage to the cadre who staffed the party apparatus, as well as to gang leaders, fire captains, and saloon keepers who enjoyed followings among the working classes.[5] Party politicians thereby provided these leaders with a stake in the success of the party organization and with an incentive to bring their followers into its camp. And the influence they enjoyed within city councils and state legislatures enabled party politicians to obtain public subsidies for militia and fire companies and for sectarian charitable institutions with similar consequences.

The party organizations that Jacksonian politicians built, and the bureaucratic reforms they simultaneously sponsored, then, were the means by which a particular political class squeezed out its competitors and came to power in the United States. The construction of a mass-based, geographically organized, the patronage-fueled party apparatus enabled professional politicians who were drawn from, or had ties to the middle class, to establish their hegemony over the working class and to triumph over leaders who depended on two older structures and traditions of political organization—namely, the elite networks of the notables and the autonomous craft organizations of the mechanics. And the building of this apparatus was linked to the bureaucratic reforms of the Jacksonian Era. The cadre who worked for the party organization were compensated for their labors with appointments to positions in the bureaucracy. And the activities of the organization were financed by political assessments levied on the salaries of civil servants.

In the dozen years between 1828 and 1840, the political forces which opposed President Jackson underwent a similar transformation. As had been true of the Jacksonians before them, they were transformed from a diffuse political movement, important elements of which were committed to earlier modes of political organization, into a political party that (a) was mass-based, autonomously organized, and patronage-fueled; (b) appealed to its supporters by focusing as much on ethnocultural concerns as on economic issues; and (c) was led by a corps of semiprofessional politicians drawn chiefly (though not exclusively) from the middle class. This metamorphosis was especially striking in the case of the Whigs because the very animus which had led to the party's formation had been its founders' opposition to the mode of political organization that the Jacksonians employed and the pattern of political activity in which they engaged, namely appeals to a mass public apart from established social hierarchies (Marshall, 1967). However, the imperatives of electoral law and political competition, and the availability of state patronage, enabled the Thurlow Weeds and William Sewards to seize the leadership of the anti-administration forces and to subject the old notability to their discipline, just as these imperatives and resources had enabled the Van Burens and Marcys to squeeze out competitors for leadership of the Jackson movement.

In meaningful sense, then, a new political class came to power in the United States as the second party system emerged. The leaders of the Democratic and Whig parties resembled each other—in terms of their origins and career patterns, the organizations they constructed and the political techniques they employed, and the relations they established with the bureaucracy—more than either resembled the notability that ruled the nation prior to the Jacksonian realignment.[6] There was, moreover, a community of interest within this political class that united it across party lines. As Martin Van Buren recognized, such a leadership group could best maintain control over its followers if an opposition party existed (Hofstadter, 1969:249). The general acceptance by 1840 of the "idea of a party system," to use Hofstadter's phrase, was the ideological expression of the hegemony of this political class, just as the general triumph of the party organizations these politicians constructed over alternative political formations was the institutional expression of its hegemony.

In sum, the electoral and administrative reforms of the Jacksonians emerged out of the efforts of a middle-class leadership group to overturn a previously dominant class of notables by pursuing a strategy of mass mobilization. The party organizations Jacksonian politicians constructed enabled them both to overwhelm these notables and to exert discipline over their political allies. The bureaucratic reforms they sponsored—the spoils system and administrative reorganization—enabled them to drive their opponents from the bureaucracy and to subject it to their own control. The Jacksonians were free to use bureaucratic appointments as a reward for party service to the extent that they wanted the state to perform only a limited range of functions—chiefly, delivering the mails, distributing public lands, collecting tariff revenues, and driving the Indians further west—and these did not require most civil servants to have skills and training beyond those which ordinary citizens possessed, as President Jackson himself observed in his first inaugural address.[7]

IV. THE ATTACK UPON PATRONAGE AND PARTY ORGANIZATION: THE MUGWUMPS

The dozen years which followed the realignment of 1860 were a turning point in American politics: they belonged both to an earlier era and to a later one. Upon coming to power, the Republicans, as had the Jacksonians before them, sought to extend their control over the entire governmental apparatus, and to use the patronage they extracted from the bureaucracy for the purposes of party building. Within a decade, however, an important group of Republicans launched an attack upon the party organization and spoils system, and formulated what would prove to be one of the modern alternatives to that system.

The Republicans who came to power in 1860 were a heterogeneous collection of radicals who wanted to abolish slavery, farmers who supported homestead legislation, manufacturers and workers who wanted tariff protection, and voters who had toyed with nativism in the mid-1850s. They were bound together by the ideology of free labor and by the conviction that the construction of a society organized around this principle was threatened by the "slavepower," which sought to control the western territories and the national government in order to build a society based upon entirely different principles (Foner, 1970). During the 1860s the Republican Party was beset by factionalism; the issues which divided the party's radical, moderate, and conservative factions, however, did not center around questions of patronage and party organization. Thus, upon entering the White House, President Lincoln conducted the most thorough purge of the bureaucracy in the nation's history, and he used the patronage thereby generated to build a party committed to the unionist cause (Carman and Luthin, 1943). This endeavor was supported by radicals, moderates, and conservatives alike.

The very vigor with which the Republicans generated and used patronage for the purposes of party-building in the 1860s, however, had consequences by the 1870s for the character of the party and for the distribution of power within it. It transformed the Republicans from a political movement into a political party and advantaged the professional politicians within it. As Morton Keller (1977:238, 255) notes:

> Party leaders and political organizations hardly were unknown in . . . the 1860s. Nevertheless during the 1870s the character of American politics sharply changed. The passionate, ideologically charged political ambiance of the Reconstruction years gave way to a politics that rested on the perpetuation of party organization rather than the fostering of public policy. . . . These shifts of tone were accompanied by changes of party leadership. In state after state men who placed greater weight on organization than ideology came into or retained power.

The leaders who were squeezed out by these developments—journalists, ideologues, clergymen, and professional men—came to regard the political practices that were responsible for their undoing (to which they formerly had not objected) as profoundly illegitimate. This group of Republicans (who were known at various times as Liberals, Independents, or Mugwumps) was distressed not simply because they had lost influence within the movement they had helped to found, but also because they disagreed with many of the policies enacted by the politicians who belonged to the party's dominant factions, the Stalwarts and the Half Breeds. The leading Liberals and Mugwumps were ardent advocates of hard money, strong proponents of free trade, and hard liners on labor issues (Sproat, 1968). Also as labor conflicts grew more intense in their own communities during the 1870s, they increasingly came to regard as dangerous to property and good order the effort to build a Republican Party in the South on the basis of black votes and in opposition to local elites (Montgomery, 1967). The Stalwarts and the Half Breeds, on the other hand, as professional politicians, sought to fashion compromises on at least the first three of these issues (they did disagree on the Southern question), compromises with which all elements of the party could live, and which would alienate the fewest voters. The Mugwumps labelled such behavior unprincipled.

The Liberals and Mugwumps were the leading advocates of civil service reform in the United States in the 1870s and 1880s; it was they who placed this reform on the political agenda. And, as they themselves explained, their chief motive for so doing was their desire to purify American politics.[8] They argued that if bureaucratic positions were distributed not as a reward for party service, but rather according to merit

as indicated by performance on an open, competitive examination, political competition no longer would center around a struggle for the spoils of office; rather, it would involve the clash of principles. Politicians no longer would be able to entrench themselves in power through what amounted to a system of organized bribery; they would instead have to pay heed to public opinion. Or, to translate this into slightly different language: the party organizations which sustained the incumbent leadership would crumble if deprived of access to patronage, and the politicians affiliated with them would be replaced by the journalists, patricians, and professional men who were opinion leaders in their communities.

In addition to attacking the patronage system, the Mugwump reformers opposed the highly disciplined, "militaristic" pattern of party organization that developed during the 1870s and 1880s (Jensen, 1971). In contrast to the Progressives of the early 20th century, however, they were not opponents of party per se; they were advocates not of *nonpartisanship*, but rather of *bipartisanship* and political *independence.*[9] Indeed, on the individual level, the defining characteristic of an Independent of Mugwump was his willingness to support whichever party nominated the best man. On the organizational level, as well, the Mugwumps sought to break the monopoly that party organizations had on the political loyalties and activities of citizens. They founded one of the first interest groups in American political history, the National Civil Service Reform League, an organization which worked outside party channels to secure the enactment of the policy it advocated, and which was prepared to endorse candidates regardless of party who pledged to vote correctly on this single issue. Finally, on the institutional level, the Mugwumps advocated bipartisan representation on commissions and boards as a solution to the problems of corruption and misgovernment.

The structure of political competition in the United States during the period of the "third party system" makes intelligible both the orientation of the Mugwumps toward political parties, and their ability to secure enactment of the Pendleton Act. During the third party system, the division between the two major parties was the closest it ever has been in American history. The Democrats and Republicans, moreover, were evenly balanced on the state level, as well as nationally, in at least the larger states of the Union. This enabled the Mugwumps to play balance-of-power politics quite successfully, especially so after the last Southern states were "redeemed" in 1877. The Republicans won the

White House in 1876, after losing the popular vote, only because they secured a majority on the commission which certified disputed electoral votes; the switch of fewer than 2,000 votes in New York would have reversed the Republican victory in the 1880 presidential election; and in the elections of 1882, the Republicans suffered serious losses, especially in the states where the Mugwumps were strongest. By supporting the Pendleton Act in the short congressional session of 1882–1883, the Republicans hoped to keep the Mugwumps from deserting the party in 1884. Moreover, they calculated that if the Democrats did win the presidency, the incumbent Republican president could take advantage of the new procedures by freezing Republican patronage appointees into the classified service before the new president was inaugurated.[10]

Although the Mugwumps managed in this way to secure enactment of the Pendleton Act, civil service reform did not alter the structure of party politics in the United States in the direction the reformers desired, at least not during the 19th century. During the 20 years following the passage of the Pendleton Act, the federal bureaucracy grew more rapidly than did the number of positions in the classified civil service, and most of the positions that were placed in the classified service were technical in character, and hence not especially useful for patronage purposes (Sageser, 1935). Moreover, civil service reform made little headway in the 19th century on the state level, the genuine locus of power in the decentralized party system. Only two states (New York and Massachusetts) adopted civil service statutes in the 19th century, and the merit systems in these states were quickly emasculated (Hoogenboom, 1961:260). Consequently, the parties had no less federal or state patronage available to them in 1900 than they had had in 1883. Indeed, the very reason the parties were prepared to live with civil service reform was that it imposed no present costs on them, while it enabled the government to respond to technological change and it defused the opposition of some disgruntled elites. In other words, it permitted the parties to maintain their positions as the central institutions of the American political system through the end of the 19th century.

In sum, the movement for party and bureaucratic reform in the third party system was spearheaded by a political class *manqué* which attacked the patronage system in an effort to deprive the politicians in the dominant party factions of the resources they used to fuel their organizations. Because the major parties were well organized, broadly based, and evenly matched, the reformers pursued their goals by playing balance-of-power politics. Given these structural characteristics of the third party system, all alternative strategies—outmobilizing the dominant party factions, converting their supporters, or demobilizing them—would have been far more difficult, even impossible, to pursue. But for the very reason that the reformers did not acquire for themselves a broader mass base than the factions they opposed, they were not strong enough to defend the entire governmental apparatus against the patronage-seeking politicians who sought to extract resources from it. Only after the realignment of 1896 transformed the structure of party politics in the United States were the opponents of the patronage system able to enjoy greater success.

V. TOWARD A BUREAUCRATIC STATE? THE PROGRESSIVES

In the history of American politics two periods stand out for their institutional creativity—the Jacksonian and Progressive eras. The Jacksonians sponsored a set of institutional reforms which, as noted above, created a party-centered political system in the United States. Following the realignment of 1896, the Progressives launched an attack upon the institutions of Jacksonian democracy and sought to establish in their stead an executive-centered political system.

There is a direct relationship between the realignment of 1896 and the emergence of the Progressive movement. Prior to 1896 the American political system was characterized by high levels of party competition both nationally and in most of the larger states of the Union. The 1896 realignment created a party system that was both regionally based and highly unbalanced. Consequently, in its wake, the great majority of states, and the national government as well, came to be governed by one-party regimes.[11]

This development provided a windfall for the incumbent leadership of whichever was now the dominant party in these one-party states. Moreover, since party politicians in turn-of-the-century America characteristically furthered their careers and strengthened their factions by drawing upon the resources of a major corporation or servicing a major economic interest within their state or city (e.g., the Southern Pacific Railroad in California, the Louisville & Nashville in Kentucky, traction and elevated railway companies in New York City), these developments provided a windfall for the sector of the business community that happened to be allied with the incumbent leadership of the locally dominant party (Mowry, 1951:Chap. 1; Woodward, 1951:377ff.; Shefter, 1976a:37f.).

What is a windfall for one set of political leaders and economic interests can be a disaster for other leaders and competing interests. The emergence of one-party regimes after the election of 1896 rendered the minority party useless as a vehicle through which individuals and groups that did not enjoy preferential access to the dominant party could challenge those that did; it made it impossible for them to pursue a balance-of-power strategy akin to the one the Mugwumps had employed. The political actors who found it impossible to advance their interests *within* the party system were joined together by the Progressives in an attack *upon* the party system.

The Progressive movement, far more than the supposedly boss-dominated party machines it attacked was closely associated with the careers of individual politicians, such as Robert LaFollette of Wisconsin, Hiram Johnson of California, Albert Cummins of Iowa, William U'Ren of Oregon, and Theodore Roosevelt in national politics. These political entrepreneurs commonly had found their personal careers frustrated by the leadership of the dominant party or had been recruited into politics entirely outside party channels (e.g., Thelen, 1976:Chap. 2; Mowry, 1951:106–113). They drew their political following from among those groups that did not enjoy privileged access to the locally dominant party—among shippers in states where the party was tied to a railroad, among firms that sold in national markets in cities where the machine was tied to businesses which sold in local markets, among the native middle classes where the party drew support from the ethnic working classes.[12] The ideology that bound the movement together was formulated by a class of intellectuals and professionals who argued that a government which was dominated by a party machine, and which consequently enacted only those policies which served the interests that were tied to the machine, was both corrupt and irrational. Not only did such a government benefit some groups at the expense of others, it also failed to intervene in the economy and in society when such intervention would serve the long-run interests of all groups (Wiebe, 1967:Chap. 7). In lieu of such a regime, the Progressives proposed to create a set of institutions that would respond directly to the voice of the people, rather than filtering it through party, and that would pay heed to the dictates of science (Haber, 1964).

Once the ideology and the institutional reforms of the Progressives had been developed in this core set-

ting—in one-party states and cities—they were picked up by politicians and businessmen who found them useful in their struggles against incumbent party leaders in other cities and states, and in national politics. (Significantly, many Progressive reforms were labelled by their state or city of origin: the "Oregon idea," the "DesMoines plan.") The diffusion of the Progressive program was so rapid and widespread because the reformers established a network of organizations, such as the National Municipal League, and publications, such as the *National Municipal Review*, for this very purpose, and they were linked to others (namely, professional associations and national magazines) in whose interest it was to advance the cause. In all settings, however, the central thrust of Progressivism was an attack upon the political party—which since the Jacksonian period had been the central institution of American government—and an effort to create an executive establishment to supplant the party in this pivotal position in the American political system.

For each of the major institutional reforms of the Jacksonian era, the Progressives sponsored an equal and opposite reform. The Jacksonians had increased the number of executive offices subject to popular election; the Progressives sought to reduce that number and to create the position of chief executive through such reforms as the short ballot and the strong mayor plan of municipal government. The most extreme version of this strand of reformism—the city manager plan of government—removed even the position of chief executive from direct popular election. The Jacksonians extended the franchise; the Progressives contracted it through registration, literacy, and citizenship requirements (Burnham, 1970:76–79). The Jacksonians established party conventions to nominate candidates for elective office; the Progressives replaced them with primary elections. The Jacksonians created a hierarchical structure of party committees to manage the electorate; the Progressives sought to destroy these party organizations or at least to render their tasks more difficult through such reforms as nonpartisan municipal government, and the separation of local, state, and national elections. Finally, the Jacksonians established a party press and accorded influence to the political editor; the Progressive movement was linked with the emergence of a self-consciously independent press (magazines as well as newspapers) and with muckraking journalists.

The bureaucratic reforms of the Progressives were part and parcel of this more general program of institutional destruction and creation. Civil service reform was the Progressives' effort to destroy the spoils system of the Jacksonians. The Jacksonians had subordinated the bureaucracy as an institution to the political party. By appointing individuals to public jobs in exchange for party service, they were violating the institutional integrity of the bureaucracy for the purposes of strengthening the party. A major reason why the Progressives advocated the creation of an autonomous mechanism and set of procedures for recruiting personnel into the bureaucracy—namely, a civil service commission which would appoint candidates to positions on the basis of their performance on competitive examinations—was to deprive incumbent party leaders of access to the bureaucracy. Deprived of access to the resources necessary for their maintenance, the locally dominant party organization would crumble, and the field would be clear for the reformers to assume power by relying on the organizations and institutions which *they* controlled—the nonpartisan press, chambers of commerce, civic associations, and so forth. To this extent, the Progressive attack upon patronage resembled the one launched by the Mugwump reformers a generation earlier.

In addition, however, there was an affirmative component to the bureaucratic reforms of the Progressives, a component which had not been present in the earlier Mugwump movement for good government. The Progressives sought not simply to destroy the political party, or even to reduce radically the role it played in American government; they sought to create in its stead an administrative arm of government that would be subject to the authority of a chief executive. Toward this end, administrators and professors who were affiliated with the Progressive movement formulated the principles and practices of what came to be called "personnel administration": position-classification plans, career and salary plans, uniform promotion regulations, retirement and pension plans, efficiency reports, and so forth (Van Riper, 1958:191–198). They also formulated the doctrines and techniques of what came to be known as "administrative management." The Committee on Department Methods (Keep Commission) appointed by President Roosevelt in 1905 was the first task force or agency in American history commissioned by a president to inquire into, and recommend improvements in, federal administrative practices (Kraines, 1970; Pinkett, 1965). In Herbert Emmerich's words (1971:39), it "stimulated management improvements in bureau after bureau in such varied fields as accounting and costing, archives and records administration, simplification of paper work, use of office machinery, personnel administration, procurement and supply, and contracting pro-

cedures." Roosevelt also was the first president to request from Congress authority to reorganize administrative agencies by executive order. And the Commission on Economy and Efficiency (Taft Commission), appointed by his successor, recommended among other things the creation of a central budget bureau to prepare an executive budget and of a central personnel bureau to develop efficiency records, position classifications, and rules governing the discipline of civil servants that would extend over all federal administrative agencies and employees (Van Riper, 1958:219–223). On the city and state levels, the Progressives sponsored a parallel series of reforms in an effort to create a unified executive branch out of the dozens of commissions and departments that floated somewhere between the city council and the mayor or the state legislature and the governor (Schiesl, 1977).

These reforms, when fully implemented, were to have major consequences for the political influence of various groups in American society, for the relative power of the nation's governmental institutions, and for the strength of the government and for the role it was able to play both in the domestic and international arenas. These consequences were closely intertwined, and can scarcely be discussed apart from one another. Consider first their political implications. An executive establishment which stood outside the domain of partisan conflict would be in a position to exercise stewardship over the economy as a whole, and would also be in a position to advance the national interest (as that interest was understood by whomever controlled the executive) in the international economy and state system. An executive with such responsibilities would be compelled to pay heed to various interests as much in proportion to their importance in their economy, as in proportion to their weight in the electorate (cf. Maier, 1975:9–15). Such a view of presidential responsibilities was expressed by Theodore Roosevelt in his well known stewardship theory of the presidency. And significantly, it was during the administrations of Roosevelt and his two successors, and with their full cooperation, that the first institutions of functional (or corporatist) representation developed in the United States (McConnell, 1966; Weinstein, 1968). In a similar vein, it was during their administrations that universities, professional associations, and Wall Street law firms and investment banks took their place beside the party as a channel for recruitment into the executive branch, and that the in-and-outer (e.g., Clifford Pinchot, Henry Stimson, James Garfield, Felix Frankfurter) made his appearance beside the patronage appointee in high level government positions (Van Riper, 1958:206). The construction of an executive branch, then, was the work of men who commanded the great national institutions that were coming to play an increasingly important role in the American economy and society, and it provided a channel through which these men could influence public policy. Or to phrase this in slightly different terms, it was during the Progressive era that the executive acquired a constituency among the nation's "cosmopolitan" elite which, as Samuel P. Huntington notes, was to sustain it for the next 50 years, and, correlatively, that the Congress became the refuge of the nation's "parochial" elites (Huntington, 1973).

The administrative reforms of the Progressives increased the control that the president, and the groups which enjoyed access to the presidency, were able to exercise over the administrative apparatus of government, at the expense of the institutions and groups that competed with them for influence over it—the Congress, the political party, and most importantly, the bureaucrats themselves. Administrative reform involved the imposition of uniform procedures upon the bureaucracy—procedures, as mentioned above, governing accounting, records keeping, employee evaluation, promotions, salary scales, and so on. What these reforms meant concretely was that agency heads, chief clerks, and lower level bureaucrats no longer would have as much control as they formerly had over how their office accounts would be kept, which records would be retained, how the work of their subordinates was to be evaluated, who would be promoted, and over the salaries that individual bureaucrats would receive. At the same time, Presidents Roosevelt and Taft promulgated a series of executive orders—the most famous of which were Teddy Roosevelt's "gag orders"—which sought to restrict the lobbying and campaign activities of civil servants, as well as some more conventional union activities, that is, which sought to limit the ability of bureaucrats to win salary increases by working through the Congress, political parties, or labor unions, rather than by conforming to the uniform rules and standards the administrative reformers were seeking to impose on them.[13]

Finally, the administrative reforms of the Progressives increased the technical competence and the organizational coherence of the bureaucracy, and thereby endowed the government with the capacity to intervene far more actively in the economy and society. The Progressives, to be sure, were not New Dealers, and there were substantial disagreements among them (especially between the Western insurgents who rallied behind La

Follette and the Easterners who looked to Teddy Roosevelt for leadership) concerning the policies the government should pursue. Nonetheless public officials who were commonly identified as Progressive generally sought to extend the sway of governmental regulations over the economy, and to implement "reforms" in the areas of public health, education, welfare, and morals, and in the management of the public domain.

In conclusion, then, Progressivism was a movement of political leaders and groups who did not enjoy privileged access to the one-party regimes that emerged in the wake of the 1896 realignment. As had been true of the Mugwumps before them, the Progressives attacked the patronage system and political machines in an effort to dry up the resources and destroy the organizations that incumbent politicians used to maintain themselves in power. There were important differences between the Progressives and Mugwumps, however, which enabled the latter movement to be more successful than the earlier one. The Mugwumps had been closely associated with one segment of the nation's upper class—the mercantile and financial elite of the Northeast—and their reformism was in part an attack upon the politicians who played a mediating role in conflicts between this elite and other sectoral and sectional interests over monetary and trade policy (Sharkey, 1959:Chap. 7). The Progressives, by contrast, did not play the role of intransigent ideologues in such intraclass conflicts. To the contrary, by attempting to create an executive branch which was insulated from partisan influences and the vagaries of electoral competition, they were seeking to establish a governmental institution which would be in a position to take account of all major interests within the economy, and which could supplant the party as the central mediating institution of American government. In addition, the advisory commissions and legislative reference bureaus and municipal research bureaus the Progressives established provided the professional and managerial classes with channels of access to the government; and the civil service reforms they sponsored advantaged the middle class in the competition for positions on the public payroll. Taken together, the managerial and personnel reforms of the Progressives endowed the government with the capacity to administer the regulatory and social overhead programs whose enactment was supported by many of the nation's major business leaders, as well as by groups further down the social scale (Hays, 1958; Lazerson, 1971; Weinstein, 1968). In other words, it was the political genius of the Progressives to discover the terms upon which some of the economic and regional cleavages that had divided the American upper classes in the 19th century could be overcome, and some popular backing could be acquired for an attack upon entrenched political machines.

The Progressive attack upon existing party and bureaucratic institutions, however, encountered substantial resistance. On the national level, the defenders of existing administrative arrangements, by working through the Congress, were able to defeat, or at least to delay, enactment of the major reform proposals of the Keep and Taft commissions. On the state and local levels, the Progressives enjoyed considerable success in those states and cities, chiefly in the West, where the locally dominant parties did not rest on a broad and well-organized popular base. Where the incumbent leadership had mobilized such support during the previous party system, however, it was able to survive the challenge of the Progressives with only temporary losses (Shefter, 1976b).

VI. TOWARDS A RESPONSIBLE PARTY SYSTEM? THE NEW DEAL

The second major wave of party and bureaucratic reforms in this century occurred in the aftermath of the New Deal realignment. On the national level, Franklin D. Roosevelt, in 1937, asked Congress to enact the most comprehensive package of administrative reforms since the proposals of the Taft Commission in 1912. And on the state level, as James Sundquist (1973:Chap. 11) has noted, struggles between reform Democrats and the regular or machine faction of the party erupted in dozens of states as "aftershocks" of the New Deal realignment. Moreover, the number of states adopting merit civil service systems shot up dramatically following the realignment. In the 16 years following 1933, 11 states enacted civil service statutes, whereas in the 16 years preceding the realignment only one state had done so.[14]

The relationship between the New Deal realignment and the party and bureaucratic reform movements which followed it is broadly similar to that between the realignment of 1896 and the reform struggles of the Progressive Era. In both cases, reform movements were spearheaded by elements of the new majority party who wanted to turn the government to new purposes, and who sought, by attacking the patronage system and reorganizing the bureaucracy, both to undermine the politicians who opposed them and to extend their own

control over institutions of government. There were, however, some important differences between the New Dealers and Progressives. Most importantly, New Deal liberals were prepared to pursue a strategy of mass mobilization and popular organization in order to overwhelm their rivals. In addition, on questions of political and administrative organization, F.D.R., as the conventional wisdom asserts, was a thorough pragmatist. He was, for example, quite willing to collaborate with machine politicians who supported his administration. These considerations—the quest for power and control, the strategy of mass organization, and political opportunism—explain variations through time and across space in the party and administrative reforms the New Dealers pursued.

On the national level, administrative and political reform was of little concern to F.D.R. during the period of the "first" New Deal. To the contrary, positions in 60 of the 65 new administrative agencies created during the president's first two years in office were exempted from the classified civil service, and many of these new agencies were located outside the departmental structure of the executive branch (Van Riper, 1958:320). The president's associates frankly admitted that administrative reorganization was too touchy a problem to tackle prior to F.D.R.'s reelection, for, as they correctly predicted, it would generate furious opposition on the part of the interests threatened by it (Polenberg, 1966:10). F.D.R. only appointed a commission to study executive reorganization in 1936, and he only submitted a reorganization bill to Congress in January 1937, after he had won his second term (Karl, 1963).

Chronologically and politically, F.D.R.'s administrative reforms belonged to the second phase of the New Deal—the phase extending from the Wagner Act and Social Security Act of 1935, through the court packing and reorganization bills of 1937, to the congressional purge of 1938—and were part and parcel of an effort to institutionalize both the programs of the New Deal and the power of the New Dealers. The Reorganization Act would institutionalize the *programs* of F.D.R.'s first term by creating two new cabinet departments to administer the public welfare and the public works programs that had been enacted from 1933 to 1936, and by granting the president the authority to integrate other New Deal programs into the existing departmental structure. As the conservative opponents of the reorganization bill well recognized, these provisions would transform programs that had been enacted as emergency measures into permanent features of the American governmental system (Polenberg, 1966:167).

The reforms of 1935–1938 would institutionalize the *power* of the New Dealers by establishing a set of institutions which would link the administration to a mass constituency, and would enable it to assert its control over the entire governmental structure; that is, would perform for the administration precisely those functions served by the party organization in cities and states governed by centralized political machines (Merton, 1957:70–81). The first of these purposes was served by the National Labor Relations Act, which established procedures for organizing the industrial working class into unions that, as could be anticipated, were to become staunch supporters of the administration responsible for their creation, and by the Social Security Act, which established a bureaucracy to provide benefits to the poor and working class in times of need—assistance that formerly had been provided, if at all, only by political machines (Greenstone, 1969: Chap. 2). Significantly, under amendments to the Social Security Act enacted in 1939, the Social Security Board required states to establish merit systems covering the employees who administered the program on the state and local level, a requirement which was policed by a Division of State Merit Systems and which led to the creation of the first civil service systems in most states of the union (Civil Service Assembly, 1940). In this way, the framers of the act sought to ensure that locally dominant political forces would not gain control of the administration of the program and be strengthened by it. Rather, they wanted the flow of these new benefits to be controlled from the center, and the political advantages of the program to accrue to the administration which enacted it.

The second of the abovementioned purposes—the creation of a set of institutions that would enable the administration to extend its control over the entire administrative apparatus—was served by the Executive Reorganization Act of 1937. The Reorganization Act would expand the White House staff; extend the merit system and replace the Civil Service Commission with a single personnel director appointed by the president; transfer the preauditing function from the Comptroller-General (and the Congress) to the Budget Bureau (and the President); create a central planning agency in the Executive Office; and place all administrative agencies, including the independent regulatory commissions, under one of the cabinet departments (Emmerich, 1971: Chap. 3). Together these reforms would endow the administration with the institutional capacity to control the initiation, coordination, and implementation of public policy—a capacity whose only precedent in the political experience of the United States, again, was the control exercised by the party apparatus in cities ruled by centralized machines.

On the state and local levels, the New Deal realignment generated major struggles for control over the Democratic party between political forces committed to the programs of the national administration and the party's incumbent leadership. These aftershocks of the New Deal realignment occurred in some states while F.D.R. was still in the White House, while in others they did not erupt until 15 or 20 years after his death (Sundquist, 1973:Chap. 11). The timing and the character of these struggles for power depended upon the stance the incumbent Democratic leadership took with respect to the national administration and the techniques it employed to maintain itself in power. Where incumbent machine politicians supported the New Deal (e.g., Chicago, Pittsburgh) F.D.R. was perfectly willing to use the patronage generated by New Deal programs to strengthen local party machines (Stave, 1970). Where the incumbent Democratic leadership was hostile to the national administration and commanded a broadly based, patronage-oriented party machine (e.g., Tammany Hall in New York City), the liberals organized through third party organizations or reform clubs (e.g., the American Labor Party and later the Democratic reform movement in New York). In these cities, the conflict between insurgents and incumbents resembled the battles between reformers and political machines during the Progressive era: the insurgents attacked the patronage system in an effort to dry up the resources upon which their opponents relied; they challenged the legitimacy of the party organizations their opponents led, accusing them of "bossism"; and they sought to demobilize their opponents' followers more than to bring new groups into the electorate (Wilson, 1962). Finally, where the incumbent Democratic leadership was hostile or indifferent to the New Deal and did not command a mass-based party organization (e.g., Michigan, Minnesota), the liberals were able with little difficulty to take over the Democratic caucus structure by allying with labor unions and farm organizations that had benefited from New Deal programs. In these states, factional struggles within the Democratic party took the form of a straight ideological conflict between liberals and conservatives; the issues of "bossism" and corruption did not occupy center stage (Fenton, 1966:Chaps. 2–3). Indeed, for the very reason that in these states liberals in the New Deal era (unlike the Progressives 30 or 40 years earlier) were able to gain power *through* the existing party system and party structures, they were not (again in contrast to the Progressives) opponents of party per se. To the contrary, they became advocates of party government, by "responsible," issue-oriented parties (Sawyer, 1960).

In states and cities, then, attacks upon the patronage system and efforts to construct issue-oriented party organizations in the wake of the 1932 realignment were led by New Deal liberals who sought in these ways to undermine the incumbent party leaders who opposed them and to gain power locally. In addition to these short-run political considerations, there were several long-run considerations which led the middle-class liberals who played such a prominent role in the New Deal coalition to favor bureaucratic and party reform. New Deal liberals wanted the government to play a rather active role in society, and a "modern personnel system" (competitive examinations, educational requirements, in-service training) was more likely than a patronage system to recruit civil servants who had the technical proficiency to perform the tasks they wanted the government to perform. It also should be noted, however, that these recruitment procedures would skew the distribution of public jobs to the advantage of the upwardly mobile semiprofessionals—teachers, social workers, etc.—who were an important element of the liberal constituency. And these personnel practices were a means of ensuring that the civil servants who administered New Deal programs at the grass roots would be socialized into the values and doctrines of the professionals who had initially drafted them, rather than the values of old-line politicians or "parochial" elites in local communities throughout the nation. Moreover, the greater the scale of government, the more compelling are arguments for administrative "coordination" and "rationalization," and the administrative reorganizations proposed by bureaucratic reformers during the New Deal era would, indeed, achieve gains in these respects. It must also be noted, however, that these reforms would transfer the tasks of coordination (and the power that inevitably flows to whomever coordinates the work of others) from politicians and political brokers to professional public administrators.

In addition, the long-run political interests of middle-class liberals would be served if America's decentralized, patronage-oriented party organizations were replaced by more disciplined, issue-oriented parties. Candidates who appeal for votes by promising to enact new programs, and incumbents who campaign for reelection by pointing to the new policies they have enacted, have need for the advice of professionals, tech-

nocrats, and administrators who are the most fertile source of ideas for new public policies. Presidential or mayoral "task forces" (the President's Committee on Income Security, which drafted the Social Security Act, was one of the earliest examples) accord far more influence to these groups than had the traditional mechanisms of policy formation in the United States, which were centered in legislatures and staffed by politicians. And to the extent that liberals were confident that the policies they favored enjoyed the support of a majority of the national electorate, they lamented the absence in the United States of a "responsible party system"—one which would enable a president elected by that majority and by virtue of his supporting those policies to extend his sway over the Congress.

In politics, the pursuit of short-run gains commonly prevails over long-run strategic considerations. Although the long-run interests of middle-class liberals would be served by the implementation of a full-scale program of bureaucratic and party reform, skilled political brokers during the postwar decades were able to integrate them into regimes that gave them something of what they wanted, but not everything. Mayors such as Richard Lee in New Haven, Robert Wagner in New York, and Richard Daley in Chicago were able to construct remarkably stable political coalitions, and to win reelection for term after term in the 1950s and early 1960s, by dividing the municipal government into "islands of functional power," and granting the party organization access to the patronage of only certain municipal departments, while the agencies and programs that were of greatest interest to would-be reformers (urban renewal, education, social welfare) were placed under the control of professionals, civil servants, civic leaders, and the downtown business community (Lowi, 1967). It is little wonder that the three seminal studies of urban politics published in 1960–1961—the books by Robert Dahl (1961), Edward Banfield (1961), and Wallace Sayre and Herbert Kaufman (1960)—found the pluralist framework so useful! In the mid-1960s, however, these coalitions fell apart.

VII. THE NEW POLITICS MOVEMENT

The third major movement for party and bureaucratic reform in this century, the New Politics movement, emerged during the 1960s and has had repercussions down to the present day.[15] Like its predecessors, the New Politics movement has sought in a number of fundamental ways to reform the procedures governing the selection of candidates for elective office and the recruitment of administrative officials; to alter the structure of authority within parties and bureaucracies; and to bring about changes in the way elected officials, bureaucrats, and private interests deal with one another. In contrast to the party and bureaucratic reform movements which preceded it, however, the New Politics movement did not emerge in the wake of a critical election. Nonetheless, I would argue that the reform movement of the 1960s can be understood in terms similar to those I have used to analyze earlier movements for party and bureaucratic reform. The difference between the New Politics movement and its predecessors with respect to the timing of its emergence is a function of the distinctive character of the post-New Deal party system—one in which the role of political parties and elections was rather circumscribed. This will become clear, I trust, as I describe the way the New Politics movement unfolded in the 1960s.

The reform movement of the 1960s was initially triggered by the Democratic victory in the 1960 presidential election. The election of 1960 was *not* a realigning election. The coalition which placed John Kennedy in the White House was very much in the New Deal mold; he was supported disproportionately by union members, city dwellers, Catholics, blacks, and Southerners (Axelrod, 1972:14). In organizational terms the Democratic party of 1960 also conformed to the pattern that had been established under F.D.R.: its cadre were an amalgam of old line politicians, union leaders, and upper-middle class liberal activists.

This influence of this last group was greater at the peak of the political system than at its base. If for no other reason than to retain the loyalty of this element of their constituency, Presidents Kennedy and Johnson were constantly in the market for "program material," proposals for new programs and policies. As a number of scholars have noted, the major urban programs of the New Frontier and Great Society were drafted not in response to demands from their presumed beneficiaries—black slum dwellers—but rather on the initiative of presidentially appointed task forces (Marris and Rein, 1973; Piven and Cloward, 1971). The members of these task forces were in the main "professional reformers"—academics, foundation officials, senior civil servants, representatives of professional associations, and so forth (Moynihan, 1969:Chap. 2; Beer, 1973:75).

On the local level, the picture was quite different. As mentioned above, in most large cities after World War II a rather stable accommodation had been achieved

among the major contenders for local power—party politicians, businessmen, union leaders, newspaper publishers, middle income homeowners, the ethnic working classes. Writing at that time, Robert Salisbury (1964) described this pattern of accommodation as "the new convergence of power," and roughly speaking these forces converged around a program of urban renewal in the Central Business District for the business community and construction unions, low taxes for homeowners, and secure jobs in the municipal civil service for the lower-middle class and upwardly mobile members of the working class. Upper-middle class professionals had some influence over municipal agencies, but this was sharply constrained by the desire of mayors to keep taxes low, and of the municipal civil service to control its own work routines and to determine the standards which would govern the hiring, promotion and firing of public employees (Sayre and Kaufman, Chap. 11).

Upper-middle class liberals sought to use the access they enjoyed to the Kennedy and Johnson administrations to circumvent these local accommodations and to extend their influence over the agencies of municipal government. The presidential task forces that drafted New Frontier and Great Society legislation argued that municipal bureaucracies did not command the resources, the talent, or the initiative that was necessary to solve the "urban crisis." To deal with this problem, they proposed to extend federal grants-in-aid to local governments to support "innovative" programs. To obtain these grants, cities found it necessary either to establish independent agencies under the control of the local counterparts of the officials in Washington who dispensed this money, or to have existing municipal departments contract with consulting firms or hire administrators who shared the outlook and knew the vocabulary of the dispensers of the federal grants. The "grantsmen" who were most successful in obtaining federal funds, naturally were those whose educational backgrounds, social origins, and institutional affiliations were similar to the federal grant givers, and who proposed to spend federal monies for purposes their Washington counterparts favored. In other words, the grant-in-aid programs of the Kennedy and Johnson administrations were the means by which upper-middle-class professionals—and their political allies— used their access to the White House to extend their control over the policies, programs, and hiring practices of municipal agencies.[16]

Blacks were useful allies in the endeavor. The attack upon municipal bureaucracies was justified, in part, by the assertion that they were "insensitive" and "unresponsive" to the needs of the black community. Blacks had strong reasons to join this attack because the mechanisms of community participation that were attached to Great Society programs provided them with channels through which they both could influence the way municipal departments distributed their benefits and could obtain access to the patronage that was directly controlled by federally funded community action agencies, model cities boards, neighborhood service centers, and community development corporations. These mechanisms of community participation furthermore legitimized federal intervention in local affairs apart from elected local governments, and they provided an institutional framework through which blacks could be organized to provide local political support for these programs.

The attack upon municipal bureaucracies conducted through the Great Society programs of the 1960s, then, was an effort by one segment of the old New Deal coalition—upper-middle-class liberals and blacks—to extend its control over the institutions of local government at the expense of other segments of that coalition. It was through this struggle for power at the periphery of the political system that the elements of the upper middle class which were to rally behind the New Politics movement—the "new class" or the "conscience constituency"—first became aware of themselves as a distinctive political force.[17]

The second phase of the New Politics movement was triggered by President Johnson's escalation of the war in Vietnam. Vietnam turned upper-middle-class liberal Democrats against their party's national leadership, and at that point the struggle for influence at the periphery of the political system became an all-out battle for control at the center. The New Politics movement sponsored a series of party and bureaucratic reforms which were part and parcel of this effort to undermine the power of its erstwhile allies, and to construct a regime that the social forces for which it spoke could dominate.

The party reforms sponsored by the New Politics movement following the defeat of the antiwar candidates at the 1968 Democratic National Convention were the most comprehensive since those of the Progressive Era. Chief among them were rules requiring that delegations to future national conventions be composed of blacks, women, and youths in a "reasonable relationship to their presence in the population of the State"; encouraging states to select convention delegations through primary elections or open caucus proce-

dures; and discouraging the slatemaking efforts of party organizations (Ranney,1975). Organizations such as Common Cause also sponsored a number of reforms in the area of campaign finance: public subsidies to candidates, limitations on individual contributions, public disclosure of the names of contributors. Through these reforms the New Politics movement weakened the position of its major competitors for influence within the Democratic Party—big city party organizations, labor unions, business—and enhanced the importance of middle class issue-oriented activists, and the influence of three of the major movements with which it was allied, namely, the civil rights movement, the women's movement, and the youth movement.

In addition to reforming the parties, the New Politics movement also sought to bring about changes in the structure of the federal bureaucracy and the conduct of administrative agencies. Indeed, as James Q. Wilson has noted, the "bureaucracy problem," which since the New Deal had been a concern of the Right, became in the 1960s, a concern of the Left (Wilson, 1967). Practices that formerly had been the subject only of academic analysis became matters for journalistic exposure—the interchange of personnel between administrative agencies and the industries they regulated; the cocoon of minimum rates, entry restrictions, public subsidies, and tax benefits that had been placed around one sector of the economy after another since the New Deal; the mutually beneficial relationships that had developed between executive agencies, congressional committees, and private interests. Common Cause, the Nader organization, and various groups in the consumer and environmental movement have attempted to put an end to these practices by sponsoring sunshine laws, inserting strict standards in regulatory statutes, subjecting administrative agencies to close judicial supervision, and by providing for "consumer" or "public" representation in the administrative process.

Finally, the New Politics movement launched a full-scale attack upon the national security establishment as well as upon agencies in the domestic sector. As in that sector, practices which previously had aroused little journalistic attention or public opposition now were labelled as improper: the Pentagon's tolerance of cost overruns in weapons procurement contracts, the public relations campaigns and lobbying efforts of the Pentagon, the hiring of retired military officers by defense contractors, the failure of Congress to monitor the activities of the CIA and other intelligence agencies. The new Politics movement sought to subject the "military-industrial complex" to stricter external control, and more generally to reduce its size (by "reordering national priorities") and limit the role it had come to play in the nation's life during the Cold War years.

By attacking these practices, the New Politics movement was attempting to disrupt the structure of accommodations through which the New Deal coalition had come to terms with the major established social forces in American society in the 1940s. This grand coalition was initially forged by F.D.R. in order to mobilize the entire nation behind the effort to win World War II; F.D.R.'s part of the bargain was to transform himself from Dr. New Deal into Dr. Win-the-War. After Germany and Japan had been defeated, however, the wartime coalition was subject to enormous strains: conservative, isolationist Midwesterners fought bitterly with moderate, internationalist Easterners for control of the Republican party; and the New Deal coalition split into a left wing, center, and a right wing faction (i.e., Progressives, Fair Dealers, and Dixiecrats). In order to cope with the Soviet threat to American interests in Europe in the late 1940s, Truman, with the support of liberal and moderate internationalists in both parties, sought to reconstitute the bipartisan coalition (Westerfield, 1955). By the early 1950s, the moderates had emerged on top in both parties and a bipartisan consensus on national security issues came to prevail in American politics, but only after major concessions were made to the conservatives (left wingers were purged from the bureaucracy and the labor unions, the Democrats abandoned their efforts to revive the New Deal, the civil rights issue was dropped), and of greatest relevance here, after NSC-68 was implemented and a massive and permanent military establishment was created (Huntington, 1961:47–63). The creation of this military apparatus, and the development of all the practices to which the New Politics movement later objected, made it possible to give all the major actors in American politics a stake in the nation's national security policies, and therefore in its postwar regime. Elected officials were given access to a huge pork barrel, which incumbents could use to enhance their political security (Dexter, 1963). National defense made it politically possible for public expenditures to be maintained at a level which kept unemployment reasonably low, wages reasonably high, and labor reasonably happy. And through the procurement of weapons and supplies, those elements of the American business community which had been most strongly identified with the isolationist wing of the Republican Party— namely, Midwestern industrialists as opposed to Eastern financial and commercial interests—were rec-

onciled to internationalism and big government.[18] In other words, the attack which the New Politics movement launched against the military-industrial complex in the late 1960s was the institutional variant of its challenge in the ideological realm to the Cold War consensus on foreign policy: by attacking the military-industrial complex, the New Politics movement was seeking to undermine the agencies and the organizational patterns through which the grand coalition behind that consensus had become institutionalized.

In the area of domestic policy, a rather similar pattern of accommodations between the New Deal coalition and its erstwhile opponents emerged during the postwar period, and the persistent charge made by the New Politics movement, that agencies in the domestic sector were serving "private interests" rather than the "public interest," can be understood as an effort to disrupt these accommodations. The regulatory and expenditure programs enacted by Democratic congressional majorities during the postwar decades, as studies by economists and political scientists have repeatedly demonstrated, generally redistributed income to the more established or wealthier members of each of the major segments of American society and each of the major sectors of the American economy (Boulding and Pfaff, 1972; Banfield, 1974;Chap. 1; Ross and Passell, 1973:61–89). On the local level, federal redevelopment and highway programs financed the grand political coalitions that enabled Democratic mayors to secure reelection term after term. On the national level, their effect was quite similar. As David Mayhew's (1966) study of roll-call voting in the postwar congresses indicates, what distinguished Democrats from Republicans was their willingness to enter into logrolling arrangements to pass legislation of this character across a broad range of issue areas. This enabled the Democrats to become a permanent majority party (indeed, the regime party) during the postwar era, and it enabled individual Democratic congressmen to acquire an extraordinary measure of political security. Or perhaps it might be more accurate to say that the Democratic party became the institution through which a "machine of the incumbents" emerged in American national politics during the postwar era. In recent decades, congressmen from both parties have secured reelection by entering into logrolling deals, negotiated by the Democratic congressional leadership, to pass legislation which serves the major producer interests in their constituencies, and by interceding before executive agencies to obtain "particularized" benefits for individual firms and voters in their districts (Mayhew, 1974; Evans and Novak, 1971). It is, of course, precisely this pattern of political behavior—logrolling; alliances between congressional committees, executive agencies, and producer interests; the receipt of campaign contributions for favors rendered—that the New Politics movement considers to be antithetical to the "public interest." By attacking these arrangements and the agencies implicated in them, the New Politics movement was seeking to undermine the practices and institutions which sustained its opponents in power.

If the political accommodations and the institutional arrangements underlying America's postwar regime can account for the *targets* the New Politics movement chose to attack, the composition of the coalition the movement assembled can account in large measure for the *content* of the administrative reforms it proposed. A comparison between the New Politics movement and the reform movements that immediately preceded it is instructive in this regard, because the administrative arrangements the movement endorsed are substantially different from those advocated by Progressive and New Deal administrative reformers. First, the New Politics movement has severely criticized the public personnel system established at the behest of earlier administrative reformers, one built around competitive examinations and a career civil service. As an alternative to the former the movement has advocated various mechanisms of affirmative action and community control. And as an alternative to the latter, the movement has advocated that the performance of many public tasks be delegated to nongovernmental institutions whose employees are not career civil servants. Second, the New Politics movement has challenged what has been *the* central tenet of administrative reorganization throughout this century: unity of command. It has opposed presidential efforts to centralize control over the bureaucracy, and has supported efforts to extend the influence of Congress, the judiciary, and the press (Glazer, 1975; Tugwell and Cronin, 1974; Wise, 1973).

These differences between the bureaucratic reforms advocated by the New Politics movement and those endorsed by earlier administrative reformers are to be explained to a considerable degree by differences in the social and institutional bases of these movements. In contrast to the Progressives and New Dealers, who drew mass support from a middle class and upwardly mobile working class whose members could expect to secure civil service jobs through competitive examinations, the New Politics movement sought to win support of blacks, who were excluded from public jobs by

such examinations, and from members of the upper middle class who had little interest in moving slowly up the ladder in career civil service systems. The black members of this coalition would benefit in obvious ways, however, from the explicit racial criteria in affirmative action programs, and from the implicit ones in community control plans. And upper-class members of this coalition would benefit quite directly if public responsibilities were delegated, and public monies allocated, to the institutions with which they were affiliated—alternative schools, consulting firms, legal services clinics, public interest law firms, and so forth.

In a similar vein, bureaucratic reformers who were associated with the Progressive and New Deal movements sought to increase the administrative powers of chief executives because both movements (by pursuing rather different strategies, to be sure) reasonably could hope to elect presidents, governors, and mayors. The New Politics movement, by contrast, rarely could command a majority of votes in general elections, and it was either unwilling or unable to do what was necessary to acquire additional support—as the drubbing the McGovernites received in the 1972 presidential election indicates, and as the extremely low rates of turnout in antipoverty elections also suggest. (Indeed, the very demand for guaranteed representation through racial or sexual quotas is an indication that the movement was not prepared to secure representation by seeking to win more votes than its rivals.) Because the movement rarely was able to elect chief executives, it opposed reforms—such as those proposed by the Ash Council in 1970, or the ones President Nixon sought to implement by fiat in 1973—that would increase their administrative powers. To the contrary, the New Politics movement sought to reduce the powers of the presidency, and to increase the influence within the administrative process of the institutions with which the movement was allied or to which it enjoyed access. Thus, the movement has sought to subject the bureaucracy to increased public scrutiny, and to influence its behavior through "investigative reporting" and Naderite exposés, because it is closely associated with an important element of the national press (Weaver, 1974). Civil rights, environmental, and consumer groups have attempted to subject the bureaucracy to tighter supervision by the courts because they command considerable legal talent, and because the federal judiciary (in *its* search for a constituency) in recent years has loosened requirements for standing, considerably narrowed the scope of the doctrine of political questions, and enriched the range of remedies it is prepared to consider in class action suits (Orren, 1976). And after decades of seeking to limit the powers of Congress, liberals recently have sought to expand Congress's powers over the administration—especially in the areas of budgeting and impoundments, investigations and executive privilege—because over the past 10 years increasing numbers of senators and representatives have associated themselves with the issues and political orientations of the New Politics movement (Fiorina, 1977).

Finally, the New Politics movement has sought to deal with the problem of administrative clientelism—the "capture" of regulatory and administrative agencies by producer interests—not by increasing the president's authority over "the headless fourth branch of government," which was the solution proposed by New Deal administrative reformers, but rather by establishing various mechanisms to represent the "consumer interest" or the "public interest" in the administrative process. In practice this means they have attempted to secure appointments to administrative positions for representatives of public interest groups, and they have sought to create new administrative agencies (e.g., a Consumer Protection Agency) which will serve as official spokesmen for their groups. That is, unable to defeat in the electoral arena the productive coalition which served as the constituency for America's postwar regime, they have sought to deal the social forces for which they speak into the pluralist game.

In conclusion, then, there are certain broad similarities between the contemporary movement for party and bureaucratic reform and the movements which immediately preceded it. Like its predecessors, the New Politics movement was led by a coalition of groups (the upper middle classes and their black allies) within the majority party (the Democrats) that sought to extend its influence over the institutions of local and national government at the expense of the political forces (producer interests, including organized labor) that previously had been dominant. And the reforms the New Politics movement advocated, like those sponsored by its predecessors, would deprive the previously dominant political forces of some of the resources (e.g., the military pork barrel) that had sustained their power; would enhance the influence of the organizations (e.g., public interest groups) the reformers established and the institutions (e.g., the press) with which they were allied; and would provide these organizations and the social groups for whom the reformers spoke with privileged access to public authority (e.g., through consumer representation) and to public resources (e.g., through the "social" pork barrel) (see Stockman, 1975).

The distinctive characteristics of the recent wave of reformism can be understood in light of the distinctive characteristics of America's postwar, pluralist regime. As mentioned at the beginning of this section, the New Politics movement, unlike the other movements discussed in this essay, did not erupt in the wake of a realignment in the party system. It did not conform to this pattern because political parties have played a far less significant role in American government and politics in recent decades than at any time since the Jacksonian Era (Burnham, 1975:305f.). This in part was a tribute to the success of earlier bureaucratic reform movements, which had succeeded in creating an executive establishment largely insulated from the influence of party politics and directly linked to other major national institutions. This transformation in the institutional substructure of American politics explains how upper-middle-class liberals, who were affiliated with some of these institutions, could seek to use the national government to extend their influence over local bureaucracies in the early 1960s, even though they had little in the way of a local electoral base. And it explains how a full-scale struggle for control of the federal government could erupt in the mid-1960s when a number of national institutions, beginning with universities and the press, turned against the war in Vietnam, and sought to drive from power the incumbent leadership of the Democratic party, and to contain the power of the national security establishment. The party and bureaucratic reform movements of the past 15 years, as I have argued, emerged from, and were part and parcel of, these struggles for power (Hodgson, 1973).

VIII. CONCLUSION

As the analysis above indicates, the relationship between political parties and public bureaucracies in the United States, and the structure of these two institutions, has changed substantially a number of times over the past two centuries. The explanation most commonly offered for these institutional developments is that they are responses to changes in American society: shifts in the percentage of the population engaged in agriculture, industry, and the professions; the influx of European immigrants and then their assimilation into the middle class; the increasing scale and complexity of the tasks government must perform, and so forth. It would be foolish to deny that social changes such as these have played a role in the institutional transformations described in this essay. But they constitute at most half the story. For, as I have argued, changes in the structure of party and bureaucracy, and in the relationship between these institutions, have had major implications for the distribution of power in the United States. And the groups sponsoring institutional reforms, as well as those who resist them, have not been unaware of these implications.

There is no need to repeat here what I argued above. Suffice it to say that my central theme has been that efforts to reform the structure of party and bureaucracy have been part and parcel of the struggle for power in American politics. These reform movements cluster in the wake of realigning elections as elements of the new majority party seek, in the first place, to deprive the politicians who had played a major role in the earlier party system of access to the resources upon which they had relied to maintain themselves in power, and in the second place, to build an institutional order which they (the reformers) can dominate.

In other words, the emergence, development, and decay of the successive American party systems has involved not only fluctuations in the relative strength of the two major parties, but also in the relationship between political parties and other institutions: as one party system is succeeded by another, changes occur both in the balance of power *within* the party system, and in the balance of power *between* parties and other public institutions. And this finding leads to the following general conclusion: *In American politics institutional conflicts are the functional equivalent of party conflicts.*

In asserting this proposition, I mean not only that controversies over the structure of institutions and conflicts between institutions are an integral part of the cycle of party realignment in the United States, but also that the outcome of these controversies and the very way they are resolved have their equivalents in the way governmental authority is allocated through a party system. Political institutions, as I have stressed in this essay, inevitably favor some interests over others: they elevate one set of spokesmen for a social group in preference to competing leaders; they skew the distribution of public benefits to the advantage of some segments of the population and the disadvantage of others; they give some interests preferential access to public authority at the expense of competing interests. This means that efforts to alter the relative power of different institutions (such as parties and bureaucracies), or to reform their structure so they will embody a new set of interests, can have consequences for the distribution of political power and public benefits as great as those

occurring when one party trounces its rivals in the electoral arena.

Reform movements, however, rarely enjoy victories of this magnitude: institutional reformers generally are compelled to enter into compromises with their opponents, or at least to resign themselves to less than a total victory. For example, the Mugwumps succeeded in placing certain federal agencies under the jurisdiction of the Civil Service Commission, while others continued to serve as sources of party patronage; the Progressives triumphed in some states, but failed completely in others; during the post-New Deal period middle-class liberals enjoyed a measure of influence over certain municipal agencies in most large cities, while others remained under the control of old-line politicians; and most recently, the New Politics movement has enjoyed remarkable success in opening up some federal agencies (e.g., the FCC) to the influence of public interest groups, while others (e.g., the Agriculture Department) continue to operate pretty much as before. Or to describe these outcomes in more general terms, in the aftermath of critical elections and of the institutional conflicts which follow them, the governmental structure of the United States has been divided along functional (and/or geographic) lines, different government agencies (and/or state and local governments) have been parcelled out various contenders for power, and a coalition regime has been established. The process through which this has occurred in the United States is different in form, but not entirely different in substance or outcome, from the bargaining process which occurs in fragmented multiparty systems, where *after* elections have been conducted, the political parties and political factions jockey for advantage, seek to gain control of important government ministries, and ultimately resolve their differences by forming a coalition government. Thus, not only are institutional conflicts an integral part of the cycle of party realignment in the United States, but the process through which they are resolved and the regime which is established in their wake is equivalent to the way public authority is allocated through party systems that, on their face, do not resemble the American.

This last observation indicates that institutional conflicts can serve not only as a continuation of party warfare by other means, but also as a substitute for it. Groups which are unable to gain political power by seizing control of a political party or constructing a new one, and using it to overwhelm the incumbents at the polls (a strategy of *mobilization*) can adopt two alternative strategies. They can pursue a strategy of *demobi-*

lization: sponsoring electoral reforms which effectively disenfranchise the voters who are likely to support their opponents, or sponsoring bureaucratic reforms which deprive the incumbents of the resources they use to link themselves to a mass base. Alternatively, they can pursue a strategy of *circumvention:* outflanking incumbent politicians by establishing executive agencies which stand outside the domain of electoral and party politics, and which provide the reformers with privileged access. The conflicts generated by mobilizing strategies are conducted within the party and electoral system; those generated by demobilizing or flanking strategies take the form of institutional conflicts—either disputes over the proper structure of institutions or conflicts between political institutions.

With the partial exception of the New Deal, reformers over the past century have pursued the second and third of these strategies to a greater extent than the first, and consequently, the locus of political conflict—and of the bargaining and the accommodations which resolve these conflicts—increasingly has moved outside the party system in the United States. Nothing illustrates the extent to which this trend has progressed quite so clearly as Watergate. President Nixon, claiming a mandate from his landslide victory in the 1972 election, sought at the beginning of his second term to centralize his control of the entire administrative apparatus of the federal government, at the expense of the institutions with which his opponents were affiliated—the Congress, the press, and the bureaucracy itself (Nathan, 1975; Aberbach and Rockman, 1976). These institutions and political forces launched a counterattack; they argued that the president's efforts to centralize power violated the constitution. Assisted, to be sure, by Nixon's having clearly broken a criminal law, they were able to secure his removal from office. A number of aspects of this struggle for power are especially noteworthy: it was conducted almost entirely outside the realm of electoral politics; political parties played at most a secondary role in it; it took the form in large measure of an institutional conflict; and the institutions opposing the president, by driving him from office, proved themselves to be powerful enough to reverse a decision (tainted though it might have been) made earlier in the electoral arena.

NOTES

1. On the "gentleman freeholders" of Virginia, see Sydnor (1952); on the "patriciate" of New Haven, see Dahl (1961:Chap. 2). New York and Pennsylvania were, to some extent, exceptions to this pattern: party organizations were somewhat stronger and a partisan spoils system was more fully developed than elsewhere in the country. See Hofstadter (1969:213) and Fish (1905:Chap. 1).

2. Dibble (1965:884f), cited in Crenson (1975:171). Dibble is speaking here of the Justices of the Peace in Elizabethan England, but, as Crenson observes, the same can be said of the notables appointed to office by Washington.

3. Indeed, Presidents James Monroe and John Quincy Adams even reappointed civil servants who were politically hostile to their administrations, although they could have been replaced under the Tenure of Office Act of 1820. See White (1951:Chap. 26).

4. Crenson's explanation for "the rise of bureaucracy in Jacksonian America" is rather similar to the explanation for the contemporaneous "discovery of the asylum" proposed by David Rothman (1971). Rothman's analysis has been criticized tellingly by Christopher Lasch (1974:316), and I draw upon Lasch's argument in my remarks below.

5. Ward heelers, gang leaders, and saloon keepers were "natural leaders" within the city's immigrant and working-class districts, and their rise to positions of power during the Jacksonian Era thus has been attributed by many scholars to the parochial and ethnic loyalties of the city's lower classes. They were not, however, the only leaders: the city's patriciate long had claimed that title, and in the 1820s and 1830s trades union leaders and even some radical intellectuals (e.g., Robert Dale Owen, George Henry Evans) sought to assert such a claim. Why did the former set of leaders prevail and the latter lose? To say that this occurred because ethnic loyalties were more salient to voters than class identifications, or that the American political culture was becoming less "deferential" and more "participant" during this Age of Egalitarianism (as do Lee Benson [1961], Ronald Formisano [1974], and other scholars of the "ethnocultural" school) is simply to describe the phenomenon that requires explanation, rather than to offer an explanation for it. A genuine explanation would have to consider the way in which changes in formal electoral arrangements, the availability of organizational resources, the behavior of elites, and the social structure worked to the advantage of one set of leaders and to the disadvantage of others. The excellent studies by David Montgomery (1972) of Philadelphia, and Amy Bridges (1977) of New York are exemplary in this

respect. I am suggesting that the availability of patronage and public subsidies helped sustain the organizations led by one type of working-class political leader, while at the same time changes in the economy and social structure were undermining the organizations led by competing leaders, as Montgomery and Bridges indicate.

6. As White (1954:Chap. 16) points out, the spoils system became increasingly extensive during the years of the second party system regardless of the party in power.

7. Even at its height, the spoils system did not extend to the more technical branches of the civil service, and a system of examinations was instituted to fill some of these positions. See White (1954:Chap. 19).

8. My argument in this paragraph and the ones following concerning the politics of civil service reform in the late 19th century draws heavily upon the as yet unpublished work of Stephen Skowronek on this topic. Skowronek's work promises to be extremely important, and I am grateful to him for graciously sharing his ideas with me.

9. See the statement of George William Curtis, the president of the National Civil Service Reform League, quoted in White (1958:300).

10. Two other conditions contributed to the willingness of the major parties to enact the civil service reforms the Mugwumps advocated. First, the parties were coming to rely more heavily upon contributions from businessmen, and less heavily upon political assessments levied on the salaries of civil servants, to finance their campaigns. Second, the Pendleton Act received the support of merchants who wished to increase the efficiency of the largest post offices and customs houses. Significantly, the only positions outside Washington mandated for inclusion in the classified service by the act were those in post offices and customs houses employing more than 50 persons.

11. In cities where centralized one-party regimes were established before 1896, opposition to the locally dominant political machines took the form of an antiparty or nonpartisan reform movement prior to that date. On the emergence of the nonpartisan reform movement in New York City following the critical municipal election of 1888, see Shefter (1976a) and Shefter (1978b).

12. Scholars who have attempted to provide a sociological rather than a political analysis of Progressivism assume a priori (and incorrectly) that the same social groups rallied behind the movement in all areas of the country. Because the Progressives generally drew

their support from among groups that did not enjoy privileged access to the locally dominant regime, it has been possible for historians studying different cities, states, and levels of government to find data supporting such divergent conclusions as that Progressivism was fundamentally a movement of a declining upper class, a rising business and professional elite, or of the working class. See, e.g., Hofstadter (1955), Hays (1965), and Rogin and Shover (1970).

13. In this respect, the administrative reforms of the Progressives were parallel to the managerial reforms that the Taylorites were advocating in private industry. As Christopher Lasch (1974:Chap. 7) has argued, these new managerial techniques enabled the directors and executives of corporations to extend their control over the organization of production and the pacing of work, an effort which entailed the destruction of older craft modes of organization and the defeat of the union efforts to assume these prerogatives. Moreover, the very groups that sponsored this effort in the private sector—an emerging *national* upper class and an increasingly self-confident professional class—advocated, and would benefit from, administrative reforms in the public sector. To this extent, the administrative reforms of the Progressives can be understood as an effort by a would-be governing class to assume control of the means of administration as well as the means of production, divesting in the process the groups that formerly had exercised this control. In the private sector, those who were squeezed out through this process attempted to protect themselves through strikes, an effort which generally failed. In the public sector, they sought to protect themselves by appealing to the Congress or to old-line party organizations, an effort which met with far greater success. (Congress, for example, refused to establish a Bureau of Efficiency under the control of the president, as the Taft Commission had requested, and it did not pass the Classification Acts until the White House was occupied by a conservative Republican.) Through this process, Congress came to represent the interests of "parochial" elites and social groups, and social conflicts came to be expressed as institutional conflicts. It is in *this* context that the "institutionalization" of the House of Representatives occurred. Cf., Huntington (1973) and Polsby (1968).

14. The contrast between the number of states adopting the merit system in 1933–1949 and in 1917–1933 cannot be attributed to the various social changes that supposedly render the patronage system obsolete and reduce its popular appeal (e.g., the increas-

ing complexity of government in the modern era, the assimilation of immigrants) because more states (namely, six) adopted the merit system during the still earlier period, 1900–1916, than during 1917–1933.

15. In speaking of the New Politics movement, I am referring to the congeries of groups that took the liberal position on "the social issue" and on foreign policy questions during the 1960s and 1970s—in particular, the antiwar, civil rights, environmental, consumer, and women's liberation movements—as well as organizations, such as Common Cause, concerned more narrowly speaking with questions of electoral and administrative reform. Its boundaries on both the left and right can roughly be delimited by support for George McGovern's bid for the 1972 Democratic presidential nomination. I fully recognize that defined in this way the New Politics movement was extremely heterogeneous and did not speak with a single voice. (The same can be said, of course, of the Jacksonian movement or the Progressive movement, for this is one of the characteristics that distinguishes a political movement from a political organization.) Nonetheless, most of the groups and individuals falling within my definition supported each of the reforms I discuss in this section. On "movement politics," see Lowi (1971).

16. My argument here is consistent with that offered by Piven and Cloward (1969:Chap. 9). My interpretation of the Great Society differs from theirs, however, in two respects: they speak of the national administration as a unitary force; and they assume that the payoff which the proponents of the Great Society expected to reap from its programs was electoral support in national elections. But as Marris and Rein (1973:246 n.7) correctly observe, they offer no evidence to support their supposition that votes were central in the minds of those who planned these programs. I am suggesting, rather, that at least after 1965 the grant-in-aid programs of the Great Society were pet projects not of *the* administration (the president increasingly found them an embarrassment) but rather of the administration's liberal wing. These programs were a sincere effort on the part of upper-middle class liberals to assist the poorest city dwellers, namely blacks. What this entailed, in their understanding, was getting city bureaucracies to adopt the latest and best ideas, that is, their own ideas. And what this meant in practice was extending their own influence, and the influence of their local political allies, over municipal agencies and governments.

17. Although there are many insightful observations on the "new class" in the social science literature, to my knowledge there has yet to be published a scholarly analysis of the social bases of the New Politics movement. I would hypothesize that at the core of the movement stood upper-middle class professionals and young people who were affiliated with institutions in the "grants economy"—universities, government agencies, foundations, consulting firms, churches, charitable institutions, and so forth. This collection of individuals became self-conscious in the course of fighting against the domestic and foreign policies which tied together the coalition of producer interests (including labor) which, as I will note below, played a central role in American politics in the post-New Deal era. The New Politics movement's efforts to "reorder national priorities" (e.g., by reducing the size of the military establishment, enacting a "Marshall Plan for the cities," protecting the environment even at the cost of industrial growth) would reallocate political power, public benefits, and the use of the public domain to the disadvantage of the industrial sector and to the advantage of the institutions with which the members of the new class were affiliated. These policies could also be supported by members of the upper-middle class who worked for profit-making institutions (e.g., newspapers, law firms, financial institutions, advertising agencies) but whose livelihood was not tied in immediate and obvious ways to the prosperity of the industrial sector and to public policies (e.g., weapons procurement, highway construction, the licensing of power plants) contributing to that prosperity. For a compelling general statement on the role of political conflict in the process of class formation, see Lasch (1972:48 n. 1); on the "grants economy" see Boulding (1973). For analyses of the "new class" and its politics see Bazelon (1967) and Apter (1964).

18. A major scholarly debate has arisen concerning the politics and diplomacy behind American policy in the early years of the Cold War. For a review of the controversy, see Smith (1976).

REFERENCES

Aronson, S. (1964). Status and kinship in the higher civil service. Cambridge: Harvard University Press.

Aberbach, J., and Rockman, B. (1976). "Clashing beliefs within the executive branch: The Nixon administration bureaucracy." American Political Science Review, 70(June): 456–468.

Apter, D. (1964). "Ideology and discontent." Pp. 15–43 in D. Apter (ed.), Ideology and discontent. Glencoe, Ill: Free Press.

Axelrod, R. (1972). "Where the votes come from: An analysis of electoral coalitions 1952–1968." American Political Science Review, 66(March):11–20.

Banfield, E.C. (1961). Political influence. New York: Free Press.

——— (1974). The unheavenly city revisited. Boston: Little, Brown.

Bazelon, D.T. (1967). Power in America: The politics of the new class. New York: New American Library.

Beer, S. (1973). "The modernization of American federalism." Publius, 3(fall):49–95.

Benson, L. (1961). The concept of Jacksonian democracy: New York as a test case. Princeton, N.J.: Princeton University Press.

Boulding, K. (1973). The economy of love and fear. Belmont, Calif.: Wadsworth.

Boulding, K., and Pfaff, M. (eds., 1972). Redistribution to the rich and the poor. Belmont, Calif.: Wadsworth.

Bridges, A. (1977). "The working classes in ante-bellum urban politics, New York City 1828–1863." Unpublished paper. University of Chicago Department of Political Science.

Burnham, W.D. (1970). Critical elections and the mainsprings of American politics. New York: W.W. Norton.

——— (1975) "Party systems and the political process." Pp. 277–307 in W.D. Burnham and W.N.Chambers (eds.), The American party systems: Stages of political development (2nd ed.). New York: Oxford University Press.

Carman, H.J., and Luthin, R. H.(1943). Lincoln and the patronage. New York: Columbia University Press.

Chambers, W.N. (1963). Political parties in a new nation. New York: Oxford University Press.

Civil Service Assembly (1940). Civil service agencies in the United States, A 1940 census. Pamphlet No. 16. Washington, D.C.: U.S. Government Printing Office.

Crenson, M. (1975). The federal machine: Beginnings of bureaucracy in Jacksonian America. Baltimore: Johns Hopkins University Press.

Cunningham, N. (1957). The Jeffersonian Republicans, The formation of party organization, 1789–1801. Chapel Hill: University of North Carolina Press.

——— (1963). The Jeffersonian Republicans in power, 1801–1809. Chapel Hill: University of North Carolina Press.

Dahl, R.A. (1961). Who governs? New Haven, Conn.: Yale University Press.

Degler, C.N. (1956). "The Locofocos: Urban 'agrarians'." Journal of Economic History, 16(September):322–333.

Dexter, L.A. (1963). "Congressmen and the making of military policy." Pp. 305–324 in R.L. Peabody and N.W. Polsby (eds.), New perspectives on the House of Representatives. Chicago: Rand McNally.

Dibble, V. (1965). "The organization of traditional authority: English country government, 1558–1640." Pp. 879–909 in J.G. March (ed.), Handbook of organizations. Chicago: Rand McNally.

Ellis, R.E. (1971). The Jeffersonian crisis: Courts and politics in the young republic. New York: W.W. Norton.

Emmerich, H. (1971). Federal organization and administrative management. University: University of Alabama Press.

Evans, R., and Novak, R. (1971). "The Johnson system." Pp. 225–241 in R.E. Wolfinger (ed.), Readings on Congress. Englewood Cliffs, N.J.: Prentice-Hall.

Fenton, J. (1966). Midwest politics. New York: Holt, Rinehart and Winston.

Fiorina, M. (1977). Congress: Keystone of the Washington establishment. New Haven, Conn.: Yale University Press.

Fischer, D.H. (1965).The revolution of American conservatism: The Federalist Party in the era of Jeffersonian democracy. New York: Harper and Row.

Fish, C.R. (1905). The civil service and the patronage. New York: Longmans, Green.

Foner, E. (1970).Free soil, free labor, free men: The ideology of the Republican Party before the Civil War. New York: Oxford University Press.

Formisano, R. (1974). "Deferential-participant politics: The early republic's political culture, 1789–1840." American Political Science Review, 78(June):473–487.

Gatell, F.O. (1966). "Some sober second thoughts on Van Buren, the Albany Regency, and the Wall Street conspiracy." American Historical Review, 53(June):19–40.

——— (1967). "Money and party in Jacksonian America: A quantitative look at New York City's men of quality." Political Science Quarterly, 82(June):235–252.

Glazer, N. (1975). "Towards an imperial judiciary?" Public Interest, 41(fall):104–123.

Graziano, L. (1978). "Center-periphery relations and the Italian crisis: The problem of clientelism." In S. Tarrow el al. (eds.), Territorial politics in industrial nations. New York: Praeger.

Greenstone, D. (1969) Labor in American politics. New York: Knopf.

Haber, S. (1964). Efficiency and uplift: Scientific management in the Progressive Era, 1890–1920. Chicago: University of Chicago Press.

Hays, S.P. (1958). Conservation and the gospel of efficiency. Cambridge: Harvard University Press.

——— (1964). "The politics of reform in municipal governments in the Progressive era." Pacific Northwest Quarterly, 55(October):157–169.

Hodgson, G. (1973). "The establishment." Foreign Policy, 10(spring):3–40.

Hofstadter, R. (1955). The age of reform: From Bryan to F.D.R. New York: Knopf.

——— (1969). The idea of a party system: The rise of legitimate opposition in the United States. Berkeley: University of California Press.

Hoogenboom, A. (1961). Outlawing the spoils: A history of the civil service reform movement. Urbana: University of Illinois Press.

Huntington, S.P. (1961). The common defense. New York: Columbia University Press.

——— (1973). "Congressional responses to the twentieth century." Pp. 6–38 in D. Truman (ed.), Congress and America's future (2nd ed.). Englewood Cliffs, N.J.: Prentice-Hall.

Jensen, R. (1971). The winning of the midwest. Chicago: University of Chicago Press.

Karl, B. (1963). Executive reorganization and reform in the New Deal. The genesis of administrative management, 1900–1939. Cambridge: Harvard University Press.

Katznelson, I. (1975). "Community conflict and capitalist development." Paper presented at annual meeting, American Political Science Association, San Francisco.

Keller, M. (1977). Affairs of state: Public life in late nineteenth century America. Cambridge: Belknap-Harvard University Press.

Kraines, O. (1970). "The president versus congress: Keep Commission 1905–1909. First comprehensive presidential inquiry into administration." Western Political Quarterly, 23(March):5–54.

Lasch, C. (1972). "Toward a theory of post-industrial society." Pp. 36–50 in M.D. Hancock and G. Sjoberg (eds.), Politics in the post-welfare state. New York: Columbia University Press.

——— (1974). The world of nations. New York: Vintage.

Lazerson, M. (1971). Origins of the urban school. Cambridge: Harvard University Press.

Lebowitz, M.A. (1969). "The Jacksonians: Paradox lost?" Pp. 65–89 in B. Bernstein (ed.), Towards a new past. New York: Vintage.

Lowi, T. (1967). "Machine politics—old and new." Public Interest, 9(fall):83–92.

——— (1971). The politics of disorder. New York: Basic Books.

Maier, C. (1975). Recasting bourgeois Europe. Princeton, N.J.: Princeton University Press.

Marris, P., and Rein, M. (1973). Dilemmas of social reform (2nd ed.). Chicago: Aldine.

Marshall, L. (1967). "The strange stillbirth of the Whig Party." American Historical Review, 72(January): 445–468.

Mayhew, D. (1966). Party loyalty among congressmen. New Haven, Conn.: Yale University Press.

——— (1974). Congress: The electoral connection. New Haven, Conn.: Yale University Press.

McConnell, G. (1966). Private power and American democracy. New York: Knopf.

McCormick, R.P. (1975). "Political development and the second party system." Pp. 90–116 in W.D. Burnham and W.N. Chambers (eds.), The American party systems. New York: Oxford University Press.

Merton, R. (1957). Social theory and social structure. New York: Free Press.

Montgomery, D. (1967). Beyond equality: Labor and the radical Republicans 1862–1872. New York: Knopf.

——— (1972). "The shuttle and the cross: Weavers and artisans in the Kensington riots of 1844." Journal of Social History, 5(summer):411–446.

Moynigan, D.P. (1969). Maximum feasible misunderstanding. New York: Free Press.

Mowry, G.E. (1951) The California progressives. Berkeley: University of California Press.

Nathan, R.P. (1975). The plot that failed: Nixon and the administrative presidency. New York: John Wiley.

Orren, K. (1976). "Standing to sue: Interest group conflict in the federal courts." American Political Science Review, 70(September):723–741.

Pinkett, H.T. (1965). "The Keep Commission, 1905–1909: A Rooseveltian effort for administrative reform." Journal of American History, 52(September):297–312.

Piven, F.F., and Cloward, R.A. (1971). Regulating the poor: The functions of public welfare. New York: Pantheon.

Polenberg, R. (1966). Reorganizing Roosevelt's government: The controversy over executive reorganization, 1936–1939. Cambridge: Harvard University Press.

Polsby, N. (1968). "The institutionalization of the U.S. House of Representatives." American Political Science Review 62(March):144–168.

Ranney, A. (1975). Curing the mischief of faction: Party reform in America. Berkeley: University of California Press.

Rogin, M.P., and Shover, J. (1970). Political change in California. Westport, Conn: Greenwood.

Ross, L., and Passell, P. (1973). The retreat from riches: Affluence and its enemies. New York: Viking.

Rothman, D. (1971). The discovery of the asylum: Social order and disorder in the new republic. Boston: Little, Brown.

Sageser, A.B. (1935). The first two decades of the Pendleton Act. Lincoln: University of Nebraska.

Salisbury, R. (1964). "Urban politics: The new convergence of power." Journal of Politics, 26(November):775–797.

Sawyer, R.L. (1960). The Democratic State Central Committee in Michigan, 1949–1959: The rise of the new politics and the new political leadership. Ann Arbor: University of Michigan Institute of Public Administration.

Sayre, W., and Kaufman, H. (1960). Governing New York City. New York: Russell Sage.

Schiesl, M.J. (1977). The politics of efficiency: Municipal administration and reform in America: 1880–1920. Berkeley: University of California Press.

Sharkey, R. (1959). Money, class and party: An economic study of civil war and reconstruction. Baltimore: Johns Hopkins University.

Shefter, M. (1976a). "The emergence of the political machine: An alternative view." Pp. 14–44. in W. Hawley and M. Lipsky (eds.), Theoretical perspectives in urban politics. Englewood Cliffs, N.J.: Prentice-Hall.

_____ (1976b). "Party organization, electoral mobilization, and the conditions of reform success." Unpublished paper. Cornell University Department of Government.

_____ (1978a). "Party and patronage: Germany, England, Italy." Politics and Society, 7(Winter):403–451.

_____ (1978b). "The electoral foundations of the political machine: New York City, 1884–1897." In J. Silbey et al. (eds), The history of American electoral behavior, Princeton, N.J.: Princeton University Press.

Smith, G.S. (1976). "'Harry, we hardly know you': revisionism, politics and diplomacy, 1945–1954. A review essay." American Political Science Review, 70(June):560–583.

Sproat, J. (1968). The "best men": Liberal reformers in the gilded age. New York: Oxford University Press.

Stave, B. (1970). The New Deal and the last hurrah: Pittsburgh machine politics. Pittsburgh: University of Pittsburgh Press.

Stockman, D. (1975). "The social pork barrel." Public Interest, 39(spring):3–30.

Sundquist, J. (1973). Dynamics of the party system. Washington, D.C.: Brookings.

Sydnor, C.S. (1952). Gentlemen freeholders: Political practices in Washington's Virginia. Chapel Hill: University of North Carolina Press.

Thelen, D.P. (1976). Robert M. LaFollette and the insurgent spirit. Boston: Little, Brown.

Tolchin, M., and Tolchin, S. (1971). To the victor . . . political patronage from the clubhouse to the White House. New York: Random House.

Tugwell, R., and Cronin T. (1974). The presidency reappraised. New York: Praeger.

Van Riper, P. (1958). History of the United States civil service. Evanston, Ill.: Row Peterson.

Weaver, P.A. (1974). "The new journalism and the old: Thoughts after Watergate." Public Interest, 35(spring): 67–88.

Weber, M. (1958). "Politics as a vocation." Pp. 77–128 in H. Gerth and C. W. Mills (eds.), From Max Weber. New York: Oxford University Press.

Weinstein, J. (1968). The corporate ideal in the liberal state: 1900–1918. Boston: Beacon Press.

Westerfield, H.B. (1955). Foreign policy and party politics: From Pearl Harbor to Korea. New Haven, Conn.: Yale University Press.

White, L.D. (1951). The Jeffersonians: A study in administrative history, 1801–1829. New York: Macmillan.

_____ (1954). The Jacksonians: A study in administrative history, 1829–1860. New York: Macmillan.

_____ (1958). The Republicans: A study in administrative history, 1869–1901. New York: Macmillan.

Wiebe, R.H. (1967). The search for order, 1877–1920. New York: Hill and Wang.

Wilson, J.Q. (1962). The amateur Democrat: Club politics in three cities. Chicago: University of Chicago Press.

_____ (1967). "The bureaucracy problem." Public Interest, 6(winter):3–9.

Wise, T. (1973). The politics of lying. New York: Random House.

Woodward, C.V. (1951). Origins of the new South, 1877–1913. Baton Rouge: Louisiana State University Press.

READING 12

VANISHING VOTERS

Richard M. Valelly

Electoral participation is vital to political democracy. Yet in the past quarter century our rate of voting participation has dropped sharply and shows no signs of rebounding. In 1988 just 50.2 percent of voting-age adults voted for President, down from 62.8 percent in 1960. Voting for lesser offices, chronically lower than presidential voting, has fallen dramatically as well. In 1986 only 33.4 percent of the voting-age population participated in House elections. The last time half the eligible population cast ballots in House elections in a presidential year was 1972.

Turnout in 1988 came startlingly close to the depressed levels of 1920 and 1924, the all-time lows for the twentieth century, when a majority of the voting-age population did not vote. If present trends continue, in 1992 a majority of voting-age adults will again sit out the presidential election. Yet unlike the early 1920s, when turnout rates dropped after the Nineteenth Amendment expanded the electorate to include women, no abrupt event in the current electoral era explains the non-participation of half the citizenry.

Scholars do not agree on why voting participation has dropped so sharply since 1960. Several popular theories suggest different remedies—or in some cases no

From *The American Prospect* 1(Spring) 1990: 140–150. Copyright © 1990 by New Prospect Inc. Reprinted with the permission of the publishers.

Sources: U.S. Bureau of Census, *Statistical Abstract of the United States: 1989* (109th edition) (Washington, D.C.: 1989), 258. Norman J. Ornstein, Thomas Mann, Michael J. Malbin, *Vital Statistics on Congress*, (Washington, D.C.: 1989). 46.0

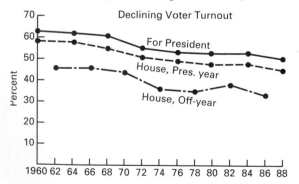

remedy. There is, however, one well-established fact. Though non-voting has spread through all social classes, in our time the poor, the uneducated, and the young are least likely to vote. E.E. Schattschneider, a leading American political scientist in the 1950s and 1960s, presciently suggested in his classic essay *The Semisovereign People* that those who vote in America may constitute "the largest, most broadly-based, ruling oligarchy in the world." That ironic characterization still aptly describes American politics.

EXPLAINING VOTING DECLINE

Ruy Teixeira's *Why Americans Don't Vote*, the work of Paul Abramson and John Aldrich, and Raymond Wolfinger and Steven J. Rosenstone's *Who Votes?* exemplify one leading school of thought. They explain the propensity to vote mainly in terms of voter traits, such as income, occupation, education, and partisanship. A rather different, more conspicuously historical and structural approach, can be found in Walter Dean Burnham's work. Burnham and those influenced by him, such as Paul Kleppner and the historian Michael McGerr, argue that the dynamics of turnout decline since 1960 are linked to the overall path of party and electoral change since the late 1890s. A variation on this view, exemplified by Frances Fox Piven and Richard Cloward's *Why Americans Don't Vote*, embellishes Burnham's approach to argue that low turnout since 1960 results from explicit political efforts to keep poorer, less educated, and minority voters out of politics.

Others writing in this broad tradition hold that turnout has fallen, particularly among lower-class voters, because the Democrats have moved to the right, abandoning their working-class and poor constituencies as they have become more like Republicans. For these constituencies, party politics now only offers "echoes," not "choices," according to Thomas Ferguson and Joel Rogers, among others. However, as I argue, important differences between the parties persisted, but the policies adopted by Democrats in the sixties weakened their ties to their historic constituencies and thus depressed turnout of their potential base.

Many political scientists of diverse schools now see a microeconomic cost-benefit calculus in the decision to vote. Voting, while easy, does cost time and may require some sacrifice of income or leisure. Sorting out the candidates and issues also takes time and energy; these are "information costs." Yet the individual benefits of voting are nearly zero, since the actual contribution of a single vote to a policy outcome is obviously extremely small. A strictly rational view would predict zero turnout, since if each person precisely calculated his or her costs and benefits, no one would vote. Of course, in crude form this insight borders on the tautological: if someone does not bother to vote, the cost must not be worth the benefit. But when married to an analysis of voter traits, the cost-benefit view can be illuminating, since certain traits help voters to pay the "costs of participation." And when incorporated into historical-structural interpretations, the cost-benefit perspective shows that the evolution of electoral politics has periodically changed the individual logic of voting.

THE "VOTER TRAITS" APPROACH

In *Who Votes?* Wolfinger and Rosenstone refined a standard proposition, namely, that "haves" are more likely to vote than "have-nots." They found that the most potent predictor of voting was not income or occupational status but education. The more their years of schooling, the more likely Americans are to vote. By contrast, past a certain threshold level, income has no impact on turnout. (While occupational status has a more powerful effect, it is nowhere near as great as the effect of education.) Education appears to be so powerful a predictor because it promotes civic-mindedness and better enables citizens to follow politics and navigate the complexity of voter registration.

Plausible as these propositions were, they also posed a puzzle. Because the population has become better educated, turnouts should have risen since 1960. Also, outside the South the average presidential turnout from 1840 to 1896 was about fourteen percentage points higher than average presidential turnout from 1900 to 1984, yet twentieth-century Americans are better educated.

A version of the "voter traits" approach, exemplified by the work of Teixeira, resolves the puzzle. This approach links turnout to changes in attitudes, such as depth of partisanship and sense of political efficacy. Teixeira proposes that recent turnout decline reflects a crisis in the "system of the 1950s," when the relatively strong partisan identities created in the 1930s and 1940s still persisted. In those years, voters had a high sense of political efficacy and consequently were willing to pay the costs of participation.

Political parties in the United States, unlike most advanced industrial democracies, do not work hard to mobilize voters. Compared to Europeans, few Americans are formal party members. America is unique in the registration burdens it places on voters. Nonetheless, the relatively strong partisan identities left over from the New Deal and a correspondingly high sense of political efficacy compensated for these obstacles to participation and helped to produce the modern turnout peak that occurred in 1960.

Since 1960, though, voters have lost their previous sense of partisan identity and political efficacy. The American population has become more mobile, more single, and on average younger, all voter traits that tend to lower turnout. But Americans have also become better educated and more prosperous, which should increase turnout. In 1960, for instance, about half the voting age population had less than a high school education; by 1980 only 26 percent fit into that category, and the number with 16 or more years of education had nearly doubled. So changing demographic traits could not fully explain turnout decline; changing attitudes, according to Teixeira, were the key.

Teixeira reports that in 1960 only about 15 percent of the voting age population reported agreeing with two standard statements used in surveys: "People like me don't have any say about what the government goes" and "I don't think public officials care much what people like me think." By 1980 about 32 percent of the population agreed with both statements, while the proportion who disagreed dropped from 61 to 34 percent. The percentage reporting strong partisanship dropped from 36 to 26 percent.

Teixeira proposes that these attitudinal changes resulted in large part from the turmoil of American politics since 1960 and, to a degree, from the rising influence of the broadcast media. John F. Kennedy's assassination, the Warren Commission, the Chicago riot of 1968, George Wallace's third-party run in 1968, the assassinations of Robert Kennedy and Martin Luther King, Jr., Vietnam, Watergate, Vice President Agnew's difficulties with the law, President Nixon's resignation, Ford's pardon, Carter's ineptitude—these events apparently left voters skeptical and uncertain, without strong partisan identities or a sense of political efficacy. Increasingly, media campaign professionals took control of the interpretation of events, and while television became more important, the percentage of Americans who read newspapers declined. Watching TV does not appear to be a perfect substitute for reading. When people read less, they are more likely to find politics confusing. The net result of all these changes was lower turnout.

The strength of Teixeira's analysis is conceptual and methodological. He takes into account the demographic approach of Wolfinger and Rosenstone and the work of others, such as Abramson and Aldrich, who emphasize voter attitudes. In this new synthesis, political disorientation resulting from turmoil and from a decline in campaign newspaper reading overwhelmed the "upgrading" effect of demographic changes, such as greater education. The idea that turnout decline since 1960 reflects the erosion of an earlier "system," the system of the 1950s, is a coherent way to make sense out of the diverse demographic, electoral, and political facts of the last three decades.

THE RISE OF STRONG PARTIES

But where did Teixeira's "system of the 1950s" come from? Why did political parties evolve into organizations that did not work hard to mobilize voters? What were the origins of personal registration and other electoral practices that increase the "costs of participation"?

Burnham and his school trace the collapse in turnout since 1960 to a long historical shift in electoral politics. By the mid-nineteenth century, the professional party politicians who began to revolutionize American politics in the 1820s were producing an average presidential turnout of 74 percent, up from 25 percent at the beginning of the century, when the electorate was much more limited. That achievement was all the more remarkable in light of rapid population growth. Turnout in non-presidential elections was also very high, apparently averaging about 68 percent. Through torchlight parades, festivities, and marching companies, party professionals created a politics that made partisanship *the* crucial determinant of an adult's political identity. During political campaigns they involved entire communities of men, women, and children in a continuous, public display of partisanship.

The Civil War—in part a war between the Democratic and Republican parties—only deepened the hold of partisanship. In post-bellum decades partisan identity was so strong and deep in Northeastern and Midwestern states that political independence in an adult male was widely considered effeminate. A wildly partisan press reinforced such attitudes. As Kleppner argues, ethnicity and small-town and religious values also reinforced partisanship, since parties, at the state level, often consciously sought to appeal to different religious and ethnic groups by staging legislative quarrels over temperance, parochial education, and Sunday

closing laws. Not surprisingly, presidential turnout reached record highs during these decades, between 78 and 82 percent, even as the voting age population expanded.

While there was vote fraud, most analysts do not believe it was so widespread from 1840 to 1896 as to account fully for the difference between nineteenth- and twentieth-century presidential turnout. Indeed, since parties were competitive, they had strong incentives to monitor each other and to keep fraud to a minimum.

REFORM AND RETRENCHMENT

By the 1890s three key groups came to see this highly participatory political system as dangerous. Because American electoral democracy so effectively mobilized ordinary people, it had always potentially threatened concentrations of wealth. That potential threat became more palpable at the end of the nineteenth century as disaffected economic groups, such as the Knights of Labor and farmers' alliances, turned to electoral politics, culminating in the Populism of the 1890s.

To antiparty reformers and to Protestant, middleclass Americans, the ubiquity of patronage and the emphasis on spectacle and display also seemed a threat to rational government. They wanted to reduce the role of parties and rely more on disinterested, nonpartisan administration to cope with the strains of urban life, industrial disorder, and immigration.

Finally, to conservative Southerners, a vigorous, unfettered party politics endangered the stability of the South's social hierarchies. From 1868 to 1892 both white and black presidential turnout in the South was at least as high as it is now and probably higher, despite violence and other efforts to restrict turnout. The Populist strategy of building a class-based, cross-racial coalition of poor farmers threatened conservative Democrats and their economic allies.

Through gradual changes on a number of fronts, the groups that were dissatisfied with high participation prevailed. In the pivotal 1896 election, the Democrats embraced some of the Populist rhetoric but lost the White House for nearly two decades. The ensuing realignment left the Democrats strong inside the South, but Republicans strong in every other region, and as a result created enough regional one-party dominance to reduce popular interest in politics, particularly state and local elections. The reduced stimulus of less party competition weakened the hold of what Kleppner calls "party norms" on the electorate. Turnout dropped.

The elections of 1896 also set the stage for attacks on earlier electoral traditions. The sway of the two parties in their different regions made it easier to change the rules of electoral politics. In the South, after the collapse of Populism, Bourbon Democrats were free to revive white supremacist violence and to push blacks out of politics. But the new rules they imposed, including poll taxes and literacy tests, excluded poor whites as well.

Outside the South, new rules also made participation more costly. Legislatures established personal registration during workdays. At that time workers had neither an eight-hour day nor an hour off for lunch. Between 1900 and 1930 the percentage of counties outside the South with personal registration jumped 72 percent, according to Kleppner. Nor did legislatures require registration opportunities to be fairly distributed by neighborhood. As Piven and Cloward stress, personal registration depressed worker presence in politics, so that rational politicians increasingly directed their appeals to middle-class concerns. In turn, the absence of populist or collectivist appeals continued to discourage worker involvement in politics until the New Deal.

One-party politics in the states also heightened the attractiveness of Progressive reforms aimed at weakening parties further. These new provisions for referenda, recalls, party primaries, and nonpartisan elections changed the previous partisan simplicity of politics. They also, if unintentionally, raised the "information costs" of political involvement.

McGerr convincingly argues that politics became more *culturally distant* from ordinary voters. Party politics once physically involved "the people" in floats, parades, and public gatherings lasting for days of political song and speech. But the new style was more remote. It was an "advertised politics," consciously modeled on mass marketing techniques. In their private worlds, voters would presumably ponder their choices as voter-consumers. The press also changed. Now nonpartisan papers responsibly arrayed facts about politics before a passive electorate.

These changes created a new political context for voting. The handful of Northeastern and Midwestern states and cities where political machines remained had diminishing influence. The machines were isolated remnants of the nineteenth-century system. The addition in 1920 of millions of relatively apolitical female

voters sharply depressed presidential turnout to roughly 49 percent in 1920 and 1924. However, the drama of the 1928 Smith-Hoover contest, followed by the New Deal, rekindled political passions, bringing presidential turnout up over 62 percent in 1940. But the New Deal left intact the Southern regime, the registration rules obstructing participation, and a lower level of partisanship in the population as a whole.

Nonetheless, from the 1940s to the early 1960s, the parties again resembled the "team" parties of the nineteenth century. The alliance between Democrats and organized labor's political action committees introduced a new approach at the national level to the mobilization of voters. But since the early 1960s, the Democratic-labor alliance has been undermined by labor's growing weakness, and "advertised politics" has become increasingly dominant. While serious issue differences between the parties persist, campaigns are obsessively organized around the promotion of a candidate's persona, constant fund-raising, the development of campaign momentum by paid consultants, and the use of broadcast media. Paradoxically, the permanent campaign, in Sidney Blumenthal's phrase, has demobilized the electorate.

The work of Burnham, Kleppner, McGerr, Piven and Cloward, and others thus casts a searching light on the larger historical conditions that explain why postwar American voters would respond to confusing political events and to television by losing their sense of partisanship and political efficacy. The party identification and sense of efficacy that characterized the "system of the 1950s" now look relatively fragile. After all, the Civil War, the turmoil of the post-bellum decades, and the Compromise of 1877, when Democrats and Republicans brokered a presidential election behind closed doors, did not shock Americans into weaker partisanship and political disorientation.

IDEOLOGY AND DEMOCRATIC DECLINE

Do conflicts over issues and ideology have anything to do with the collapse in turnout since 1960? Burnham and many working in his tradition argue that since the New Deal, and especially since the 1970s, the Democrats have moved to the right, abandoning both working-class and middle-class Americans concerned about corporate power and government provision of economic security. In response, these people have stopped voting, or they have never started when they have come of voting age. In "The Turnout Problem" and "The Eclipse of the Democratic Party," Burnham explains the move to the right as the result of the inherent instability of a center-left party in a weakly politicized market society. In *Right Turn*, Ferguson and Rogers emphasize pressure from business on the Democrats to move to the right to lower the cost to business of welfare-state measures in the face of international competition.

Yet, as voters recognize, the philosophies of the two parties are different. The Democratic Party did not turn less liberal; it embraced a different version of liberalism that has demobilized its potential electorate. Ira Katznelson and Margaret Weir argue that the Keynesian approach adopted during the Kennedy-Johnson era, which emphasized market-led growth rather than political alleviation of unemployment through increased public spending, and the Great Society, which conceived poverty as a residual, largely racial problem in an otherwise healthy economy, undercut a potential class-based alliance among black and white voters. Democrats targeted social policies on the supposed few unable to get into the mainstream education, labor, and housing markets because of poverty or racial discrimination.

This renewed emphasis on welfare policy departed from the approach of Roosevelt and Truman. Rather than offering protections to the majority, the Democrats now seemed chiefly concerned about the minority below the poverty line. Much of the increased nonvoting may simply result from the Democrats' letting down their historic working- and middle-class constituencies, not by moving right, but by substituting a new approach to welfare for the old one. The Democrats fumbled their chance to rebuild their majority coalition.[1]

The Democrats might not have suffered politically if the economy had continued to perform well. But when inflation, the deficit, and competitiveness emerged as issues in the 1970s and 1980s, the Democrats could no longer present their social policies as essential for prosperity. Rather, they have presented them as moral imperatives but fiscal luxuries. Such policies were affordable in an expansive era, but not in times of austerity. The Democrats have forgotten how to attract key constituencies by making arguments other than "compassion." Consequently, they have proved unable to resist calls for less government, budget-balancing, and deregulation. Fighting to retain the social policies they created has seemed irresponsible at worst and backward-looking at best, if not impolitic in the face of a tax revolt.

The Democrats' party organization has deepened their difficulty in developing new policies that might rebuild their historic constituencies. The national Democrats are now a fairly cohesive legislative party. They have organized themselves around their congressional power, particularly in the House, establishing caucus government and a firm grip on the committees. But to be a legislative party requires congressional Democrats to get reelected, and to do that they need "permanent," well-funded campaigns and predictable electoral bases. These imperatives make it risky and difficult to adopt new approaches to social and macroeconomic policy. The permanent congressional campaign absorbs time and energy and compromises policy commitments. Building a war chest primarily from well-heeled donors to scare away potential challengers is not an activity that encourages deep reflection on social change.

IMPLICATIONS

Can the turnout decline be reversed? Some observers think it cannot, except under very unlikely conditions. Others are more optimistic and activist. The "voter traits" approach implies that raising turnout may be virtually impossible, especially if the attitudes Teixeira describes have taken on a life of their own. The continuing turnout depression in the last decade, after the political turmoil of the 1960s and 1970s subsided, gives little basis for optimism. The historical-structural approach is also discouraging. The evolution of electoral politics may have permanently reduced the participatory potential of American electoral politics. Party politics, nineteenth-century style, is clearly impossible. In the present context, rational politicians will not agree to give up their candidate-centered approach to elections and submit themselves to the discipline of an inner circle of national party leaders. Social democratic politics, approximated by the Democrats' alliance with the CIO between 1936 and 1948 and the AFL-CIO in

---

[1] Margaret Weir, "The Federal Government and Unemployment: The Frustration of Policy Innovation from the New Deal to the Great Society," in Margaret Weir, Ann Shola Orloff, Theda Skocpol, eds., *The Politics of Social Policy in the United States* (Princeton University Press, 1988); Ira Katznelson, "Was the Great Society A Lost Opportunity?" in Steven Fraser and Gary Gerstle, eds., *The Rise and Fall of the New Deal Order: 1930–1980* (Princeton University Press, 1989).

the 1950s and 1960s, appears unlikely. Many Democrats now see labor as too weak to be much good to them; political professionals now widely regard Mondale's alliance with labor in 1984 as a major cause of his resounding defeat.

The Piven and Cloward approach, with its emphasis on the demobilizing consequences of personal registration, does offer a clear prescription: scrap all personal registration and other unwarranted barriers to voting. Approaches that emphasize the effect of the Democratic Party's modernation also suggest a simple solution: go left. Yet there are good reasons for doubting that these ideas would have much net impact.

Piven and Cloward have tried to carry out a strategy based on their understanding of the causes of low participation. They have founded the Human/SERVE Campaign (Human Service Employees' Registration and Voter Education Campaign) to push for simpler registration procedures and to offer registration assistance to clients at welfare offices, motor vehicle bureaus, and other public agencies. Proposed federal legislation would encourage "mail-in" registration and require the states to provide "motor-voter" registration (enabling citizens to register to vote when obtaining or renewing a driver's license).* The total, five-year cost of this reform, according to an estimate from the Congressional Budget Office would run between $215 million and $250 million.

Currently several states and the District of Columbia have strong forms of motor-voter registration, combining the two kinds of registration on the same form or containing a "prompt question" on a motor vehicle form that triggers voter registration assistance by the registry clerk. About twenty other states are actively considering similar programs.

The Human/SERVE campaign for registration reform presumes that once registered, people are very likely to vote. About 80 to 85 percent of registrants vote, Piven and Cloward believe. Some data, however, suggest that voting by registrants is down 15 percent since 1960. But Piven and Cloward make a convincing case that this apparent drop in registrant voting results from failures by state election officials to purge registrants who have moved or died. Census surveys continue to show a strong link between registration and voting. So getting rid of legal obstacles to voting *should*

significantly increase turnout, just as Piven and Cloward claim. The increase might be as high as 11 percent of the eligible electorate, or about 20 million voters.[2]

Easing registration procedures is surely one step toward fixing the turnout problem. But changes in other national policies are necessary as well to alter the sense of inefficacy and alienation that undergirds non-voting. Voting turnout might increase if we pursued a new generation of policies that fostered a sense of civic membership. Universal worker training and retraining opportunities might restore a link between the citizen as worker and the citizen as voter. Improved primary and secondary schools would help restore voter confidence in public institutions generally. I am not offering a policy platform, only emphasizing that policy ideas should be weighed for their contribution to rebuilding the sense of civic efficacy that invites participation in politics. Registration reform alone, if Teixeira is right, will not motivate people to vote.

Non-voters' policy preferences are, moreover, a slippery question. Piven and Cloward want registration reform not for aesthetic reasons; they have a political agenda. They want to bring poor people back into politics to move the Democratic Party to the left. Yet their critics, including Teixeira, have convincingly pointed out that even extraordinarily high turnout rates among poor, Hispanic, and black adults eligible to vote would not have won the 1988 election for Dukakis and Bentsen.[3]

Teixeira argues that the broad, downward trend of non-voting is not limited to the poor; it is far more widespread. To be sure, this point is irrelevant to the Piven and Cloward strategy. Simply winning elections for the Democrats is not their goal. They want to change the agenda of public debate and get the parties to disagree over social and economic policy in new ways. Such change, in turn, would open up American politics to previously foreclosed possibilities. In such a

---

* As this article went to press, the House of Representatives passed a motor-voter registration bill, but the bill faced uncertain prospects in the Senate.

[2] Frances Fox Piven and Richard A. Cloward, "Government Statistics and Conflicting Explanations of Nonvoting," *PS: Political Science & Politics* 12 (September 1989): 580–588. See Burnham, "The Turnout Problem," for other estimates, which tend to be lower than 11 percent.

[3] See Ruy A. Teixeira, "Registration and Turnout," *Public Opinion* January/February 1989, 12–13, 56–58. The Democratic Leadership Council has also implicitly criticized the Piven-Cloward approach. See William A. Galston, "Rebuilding a Presidential Majority," *The Mainstream Democrat* September/October 1989, 10–13.

context, turnout rates might surpass those of the 1930s and 1950s.

Implicitly, though, Piven and Cloward are assuming that non-voters are likely to be farther to the left than voters and more likely to vote Democratic—if Democrats begin responding to economic needs of current non-participants. Surveys do not show strong policy differences, however, between voters and non-voters. Non-voters, on balance, are only mildly pro-Democratic. There may well be serious measurement error in surveys of non-voters. Non-voters who cooperate with surveys are probably not typical of the larger population of non-voters, who are cynical and politically alienated. But this survey evidence cannot yet be dismissed. It has striking implications, as well, for the position that turnout will increase if the Democratic Party moves left or if it develops a different approach to social policy. Non-voters do not secretly have intense partisanship, held in reserve until some change in the political agenda or some invitation to participate unlocks their passions. They do not vote in part because they lack strong political affiliations. Partisanship among the non-voters would have to be constructed, and that will be difficult.

THE FUTURE OF NON-VOTING

If the past is a guide, transforming our participatory structure will require a debate about turnout. Years of intense debate about the political functions of parties preceded the last, great transformation of party politics. Between the 1870s and the 1900s, such magazines as the *Nation,* the *Atlantic Monthly*, and *Harper's Weekly* discussed the dangers of strong party politics. The editors of large newspapers grew hostile to parties as they responded to the emergence of local reform organizations, such as the City Reform Club established in New York City in 1882 by Theodore Roosevelt. A rising class of social scientists and academic leaders, gathered into professional organizations, also attacked parties. In time, too, military officers (who had organized themselves into their own special associations) turned against strong parties, seeing them as obstacles to the professionalization of the armed services. The hostility to democracy that informed much of this late nineteenth century debate now seems offensive. Yet we live, ironically, in a world created in part by such public argument against the old electoral regime.

There will be no contemporary debate if the collapse in turnout since 1960 is taken lightly. We cannot say, as some have, that non-voting reflects complacency and even contentment among the population. As Piven and Cloward drily remark, "no one has satisfactorily explained why 'the politics of happiness' is so consistently concentrated among the least well off." Others say that non-voting prevents fascism and demagoguery, yet there is no tradition in America of caesarist politicians succeeding on a national scale. Finally, certain writers insist non-voting is healthy because high levels of participation overload democratic government. This argument appeals to those who see the general public as made up of grabby people willing to bankrupt government with insatiable demands. But some of the grabby people are those with the power to abuse deposit insurance or to alter the tax code to their benefit. Broader electoral participation would curb such self-seeking demands on our scarce public resources. In the end, it is awfully hard to contend that non-voting is good for democracy.

The "party of voters" would do well to appreciate its self-interest in bridging the divide that separates it from the "party of non-voters." While turnout has dropped, the demands on government have grown in this century. If democratic government is to take on the tasks demanded of it, it needs to seek out the voices and the votes of people who now feel they simply do not count.

As in the past, the expansion of participation can help to turn the subjects of administration into citizens capable of self-government. It can create a hardy sense of membership in a political community. Our electoral politics now fails to realize the empowering possibilities of democratic life. We need to recreate the popular ownership of electoral politics that we once had— indeed, that America pioneered. Otherwise, the likely low turnout in the 1990 and 1992 elections will be accepted as routine, and America will increasingly look like Schattschneider's "broadly-based oligarchy."

WORKS DISCUSSED IN THIS ESSAY

Paul R. Abramson and John H. Aldrich, "The Decline of Electoral Participation in America," *American Political Science Review* 76(September, 1982):502–521.

Walter Dean Burnham, "The Turnout Problem," in A. James Reichley, ed., *Elections American-Style* (Brookings, 1987).

Walter Dean Burnham, "The Eclipse of the Democratic Party," *Democracy*, July 1982.

Walter Dean Burnham, *The Current Crisis in American Politics* (Oxford University Press, 1982).

Thomas Ferguson and Joel Rogers, *Right Turn: The Decline of the Democrats and the Future of American Politics* (Hill and Wang, 1987).

Paul Kleppner, *Who Voted? The Dynamics of Electoral Turnout, 1870–1980* (Praeger, 1982).

Michael E. McGerr, *The Decline of Popular Politics: The American North, 1865–1928* (Oxford University Press, 1986).

Frances Fox Piven and Richard A. Cloward, *Why Americans Don't Vote* (Pantheon Books, 1989).

E.E. Schattschneider, *The Semisovereign People: A Realist's View of Democracy in America* (The Dryden Press, 1975).

Ruy A. Teixeira, *Why Americans Don't Vote: Turnout Decline in the United States 1960–1984* (Greenwood Press, 1987).

Raymond E. Wolfinger and Steven J. Rosenstone, *Who Votes?* (Yale University Press, 1980).

CHAPTER 5

SOCIAL GROUPS IN AMERICAN POLITICS

Throughout the twentieth century, virtually all western European countries have had political parties dedicated to representing the interests of the working class. In many countries, these parties have played important roles in national politics. For example, the Social Democratic party in Sweden dominated politics from the 1930s to the 1980s, and the Labour party has been very influential in British politics. Why is it, then, that the United States has never had a strong working-class party? For that matter, why is it that, except during the New Deal in the 1930s, there has never been any sustained left-of-center, progressive force in American politics?

"American exceptionalism" is often attributed to social, cultural, and economic factors that have prevented industrial workers and other less privileged groups from becoming politically class conscious and organized (for various arguments, see Davis, 1986; Hartz, 1955; Laslett & Lipset, 1974). Some scholars argue that the failure to create sustained working-class parties was due to the absence of a landed aristocracy in America, whereas in Europe, both workers and the bourgeoisie became "class conscious" through centuries of struggle against feudalism. Other writers hold that the political organization of workers was undermined by the conservativism of early trade union leaders, such as Samuel Gompers of the American Federation of Labor and others who did their best to keep union from allying with socialists, Communists, or progressive intellectuals. Still other scholars argue that working-class political solidarity failed to blossom because workers could flee as individuals to the frontier, rather than collectively struggling to improve their lives in the cities. Scholars also contend that the cultural traditions of American workers, particularly a strong sense of individualism among native-born workers, and ethnic divisions between native and immigrant workers, inhibited collective political organization.

Many of these social, cultural, and economic factors no doubt have been important. Recently, however, various scholars have begun to investigate ways in which the institutional arrangements of the U.S. state and electoral system have militated against the political organization of workers and other groups that might have pursued progressive political agendas. William Forbath (1991) and Victoria Hattam (1993) have explored the ways in which the sovereignty of the U.S. courts discouraged nineteenth-century workers' organizations from seeking to improve their members' lives through legislation and electoral participation. The courts, after all, could overrule prolabor laws that the judges deemed "unconstitutional," so trade unionists decided that it made more sense to rely on strikes and bargains with employers to improve wages and working conditions. What is more, as Ira Katznelson (1985) and others have pointed out, like all adult white males, American workers who fit into this category enjoyed the right to vote from the 1830s onward. Unlike European workers, the Americans did not have to organize class-conscious political movements in order to win the right to participate in electoral politics. Instead, local groups of workers and other popular groups were mobilized by the patronage-oriented parties of the nineteenth century into cross-class electoral alliances defined primarily on ethnic and religious lines. Workers received benefits from government, especially at the local level. But they accrued such benefits as Democrats and Republicans, and as members of local ethnoreligious coalitions, rather than through class-specific political organizations.

The readings in Chapter 4 argued that the political consciousness of various groups in American society and their organization have been influenced not only by their social and economic positions, but also by the historically changing structures and activities of the U.S. state and political parties. In this chapter, we explore the factors that have influenced the political ideas and activities of major socioeconomic classes and of American women during the nineteenth and early twentieth centuries. (Part 4 of this Reader looks in analogous terms at the social and political factors that have influenced African-American and feminist politics in more recent decades.)

One of the paradoxes of American politics is that progressive political movements representing workers and farmers proliferated during the nineteenth and early twentieth centuries, but never gained much influence at the national level. Organizations such as the Knights of Labor, the Farmers' Alliance, the Populists, the International Workers of the World, the Socialist Workers Party, the Nonpartisan League, and the Farmer-Labor party helped to define the political landscape and to raise the political hopes of many less privileged groups. Some of these movements gained more than ephemeral influence in particular cities or states, but they did not displace the major national parties and had largely disappeared by the late 1920s.

Dispositions to class action frequently existed among popular groups in late–nineteenth- and early–twentieth-century America, argues Richard Oestreicher (Reading 13). But the institutional arrangements of politics presented a variety of barriers to the formation of working-class political parties—which would, in turn, have encouraged and sustained political class consciousness. Winner-take-all elections, rather than elections in which parties win seats in the legislature according to their proportion of the vote, made it difficult for third parties to sustain electoral support. The problems of mobilizing people across a large number of states, coupled with the limited resources available to popular organizations, made it hard to mount national political campaigns. The decentralized federal structure of the U.S. state afforded state and local governments considerable scope for distributing benefits and services. Patronage-oriented politics—monopolized by the major parties—encouraged leaders and particular subgroups of workers and farmers to ally with people of other classes at the local and state levels, in order to reap these benefits from government. Mainstream party politicians mobilized supporters along ethnic and religious, rather than class, lines. This encouraged strong group consciousness of a sort, but not national working-class solidarity along the lines that emerged in many European polities in the late nineteenth and early twentieth centuries.

Revolving around parties, official patronage, saloons, and local political clubs, U.S. electoral politics was mostly a set of "fraternal" activities that excluded women. Formally, this situation did not change much until women won the right to vote in 1920, and even then the major parties remained male dominated. Nevertheless, American women had had a long tradition of civic engagement—especially middle-class white women, who enjoyed high levels of education by the international standards of the 1800s and early 1900s. As Paula Baker shows

(Reading 14), even during the era of American history when women were supposed to be "at home," they asserted a moral presence in politics through clubs and other voluntary organizations. Nineteenth-century moral-reform societies provided aid to elderly and poor women, and to children, orphans, and prostitutes. Such societies advocated the abolition of slavery, fought for temperance legislation, and organized to win the vote for women.

Furthermore, when it became apparent that the problems faced by women and families could not be addressed by voluntary means alone, nationwide federations of local women's clubs began to press local, state, and national governments to provide social benefits and services, and to regulate the emerging industrial order. As Theda Skocpol explains in Reading 29 in Chapter 9, women's voluntary politics helped to achieve many "maternalist" social policies for women workers and mothers and children. In Baker's terms, early twentieth-century U.S. government became "domesticated." The barriers between men and women's styles of politics began to erode as women sought the vote and men engaged in educational and lobbying styles of politics. Ironically, once women were brought into the formal electoral system, once they had won the right to vote in 1920, their gender solidarity began to erode. Divisions grew on partisan and class lines, and on ideological lines between women who advocated special legal protections and modern-style feminists who advocated equal rights and opportunities for men and women (see Chapter 8). By 1920, therefore, not only had women succeeded in changing the course of twentieth-century politics, but the new political realities had also changed the possibilities and dilemmas for women.

In addition to influencing the consciousness and organization of workers and women, the changing structures of American politics have also affected the political orientations of the business community. In David Vogel's view (Reading 15), the American bourgeoisie never had to organize itself to overthrow a landed aristocracy or to overcome serious obstacles to private ownership. Capitalists were, from an early time, wary of popular political movements, which, in a democracy, might give rise to political demands for business regulation. What is more, argues Vogel, American businesspeople never learned to cooperate with a strong bureaucratic state—in large part because major corporations developed national bureaucratic organizations earlier than did the U.S. national state itself, which developed few administrative capacities until the 1930s. Overall, argues Vogel, U.S. capitalists have rarely achieved any unified political class consciousness. Instead, they are ideologically distrustful of government power, yet at a practical level are always willing to manipulate agencies or politicians to gain particular, short-term advantages for specific firms or industries. Vogel presents a picture of considerable business influence within American politics, but argues that such influence is not a unified, class-conscious force.

As Vogel claims, national states in other countries have historically played a more active role in orchestrating the development of capitalism (Gerschenkron, 1962). He is also correct in saying that interest groups antagonistic to business have gained access to policymakers more readily in the United States than in some other countries (Atkinson & Coleman, 1989), and that the American business community is comparatively disorganized (Campbell, Hollingsworth, & Lindberg, 1991; Katzenstein, 1978). Still, some scholars would disagree with Vogel's downplaying of the political predominance of business (see especially Reading 3 by Domhoff in Chapter 2). Research suggests that business leaders use informal networks of influence to compensate for their lack of formal political organization (see Useem, 1984). Nevertheless, Vogel has raised an important set of issues for debate and research. He asks us to consider not only how U.S. business interests have influenced the state and politics, but how these political arrangements, in turn, have influenced the goals, consciousness, and group capacities of particular business groups, and of the capitalist class as a whole. Business, like other groups in American society and politics, is affected by the U.S. state with which it interacts.

Indeed, the distinctive character of American politics encompasses the ways public policies are created, as well as patterns of group involvement in politics. In countries where social classes are organized through centralized labor union federations and "peak" business associations, and where these organizations are closely affiliated with political parties, national policy formulation is usually a matter of "corporatist" negotiation, bargaining, and consensus building among dominant economic interests. In national polities organized along corporatist lines, policymakers may be able to pursue long-range goals (cf. Goldthorpe, 1984; Lindberg & Maier, 1985; Schmitter & Lehmbruch, 1979). In the United States, however, interest groups are much more fragmented and disconnected from political parties; and the state itself is split up into many agencies, branches, and levels of government. Diffuse networks of interest groups, bureaucrats, and politicians, each with a personal narrow agenda, have become central actors in the U.S. policy-making process. Decision-making tends to be shortsighted, contentious, and prone to political stalemate, as shifting coalitions of interest groups check and balance one another. This situation has often made it difficult for U.S. leaders to deal effectively with economic, energy, and environmental problems; that is, with any difficulties that may call for long-term planning by government and societal actors (Campbell, 1988; Dyson & Wilks, 1983; Katzenstein, 1978; Lundqvist, 1980; Richardson, 1982).

Many social scientists have suggested that "policy networks" influence official decision-making in Washington, D.C., and across the levels of the U.S. federal government (see Gais, Peterson, & Walker, 1984; Heclo, 1978; Laumann & Knoke, 1987). Initially, such networks were called "iron triangles," and were said to consist of just a few congressional committees, a handful of special-interest groups, and one or two administrative agencies—all allied to dominate decision-making in a given policy area. The most notorious of these troikas included the Pentagon, the defense industry, and the armed services and military appropriations committees in Congress that administered defense-spending policy after World War II (Adams, 1983). However, scholars have found that policy networks have become more complex and open-ended in recent years, especially with respect to domestic politics (see especially Heclo, 1978).

Reading 16 by Robert Salisbury explains why the United States never developed a corporatist system. In a large, diverse country such as this, Salisbury tells us, it is difficult for workers, farmers, business leaders, or anyone else to agree on unified definitions of group interests. Americans are suspicious of big, monopolistic groups, particularly the centralized and internally disciplined associations and unions that provide the institutional basis for corporatist negotiations in other nations. Nor have U.S. government officials been willing to grant monopolistic status to business associations; indeed, under the American legal system, antitrust prosecutions have often been initiated to break up business combinations. Most fundamentally, divisions of sovereignty within U.S. political institutions make it difficult to organize corporatist bargaining. Because a variety of government agencies often share authority in the same policy area, competing special-interest groups—not just within the ranks of business, but within the ranks of other social and economic categories as well—are encouraged to proliferate and gain access to particular policy-making processes. Business interests, for example, can gain more by lobbying parts of government on an industry-by-industry, or even firm-by-firm, basis, than by uniting into classwide business organizations. And the same is true for many other social groups. For all these reasons, Salisbury explains, there has been no corporatism in the United States, and there probably never will be.

REFERENCES

Adams, Gordon. 1983. "The Iron Triangle: Inside the Weapons Elite." Pp. 241–248 in *The Big Business Reader*, edited by Mark Green. New York: Pilgrim.

Atkinson, Michael, and William Coleman. 1989. "Strong States and Weak States: Sectoral Policy Networks in Advanced Capitalist Economies." *British Journal of Political Science* 19(1): 47–67.

Campbell, John L. 1988. *Collapse of an Industry: Nuclear Power and the Contradictions of U.S. Policy.* Ithaca, N.Y.: Cornell University Press.

Campbell, John L., J. Rogers Hollingsworth, and Leon N. Lindberg, editors. 1991. *Governance of the American Economy.* New York: Cambridge University Press.

Davis, Mike. 1986. *Prisoners of the American Dream.* London: Verso.

Dyson, Kenneth, and Stephen Wilks, editors. 1983. *Industrial Crisis: A Comparative Study of the State and Industry.* Oxford: Martin Robertson.

Forbath, William. 1991. *Law and the Shaping of the American Labor Movement.* Cambridge, Mass.: Harvard University Press.

Gais, Thomas L., Mark A. Peterson, and Jack Walker. 1984. "Interest Groups, Iron Triangles, and Representative Institutions in American National Government." *British Journal of Political Science* 14: 161–85.

Gerschenkron, Alexander. 1962. *Economic Backwardness in Historical Perspective.* Cambridge, Mass.: Harvard University Press.

Goldthorpe, John, editor. 1984. *Order and Conflict in Contemporary Capitalism: Studies in the Political Economy of Western European Nations.* New York: Oxford University Press.

Hartz, Louis. 1955. *The Liberal Tradition in America.* New York: Harcourt, Brace.

Hattam, Victoria. 1993. *Labor Visions and State Power.* Princeton, N.J.: Princeton University Press.

Heclo, Hugh. 1978. "Issue Networks and the Executive Establishment." In *The American Political System,* edited by Anthony King, 87–124. Washington, D.C.: American Enterprise Institute.

Katzenstein, Peter J., editor. 1978. *Between Power and Plenty: Foreign Economic Policies of Advanced Industrial States.* Madison: University of Wisconsin Press.

Katznelson, Ira. 1985. "Working Class Formation and the State: Nineteenth-Century England in American Perspective." Pp. 257–84 in *Bringing the State Back In,* edited by Peter Evans, Dietrich Rueschemeyer, and Theda Skocpol. New York: Cambridge University Press.

Laslett, John, and Seymour Martin Lipset. 1974. *Failure of a Dream? Essays in the History of American Socialism.* Garden City, N.Y.: Anchor Press.

Laumann, Edward O., and David Knoke. 1987. *The Organizational State: Social Choice in National Policy Domains.* Madison: University of Wisconsin Press.

Lindberg, Leon N., and Charles S. Maier, editors. 1985. *The Politics of Inflation and Economic Stagnation.* Washington, D.C.: Brookings Institution.

Lundqvist, Lennart J. 1980. *The Hare and the Tortoise: Clean Air Policies in the United States and Sweden.* Ann Arbor: University of Michigan Press.

Richardson, Jeremy, editor. 1982. *Policy Styles in Western Europe.* London: Allen and Unwin.

Schmitter, Philippe C., and Gerhard Lehmbruch. 1979. *Trends Toward Corporatist Intermediation.* Beverly Hills, Calif.: Sage.

Useem, Michael. 1984. *The Inner Circle: Large Corporations and the Rise of Business Political Activity in the U.S. and U.K.* New York: Oxford University Press.

READING 13

URBAN WORKING-CLASS POLITICAL BEHAVIOR AND THEORIES OF AMERICAN ELECTORAL POLITICS, 1870–1940

Richard Oestreicher

Despite repeated pleas for scholarly exorcism, the ghost of American exceptionalism still hovers over discussions in American history, sometimes in the perennial revivals and permutations of Werner Sombart's "Why Is There No Socialism in the United States?" often more broadly in debates about the central dynamics of American politics and culture. Exorcism is misguided. Exceptionalism has been a recurring topic—and not only for historians—because it evokes such a central theme in national symbolism and identity: the contrast between the Old World and the New, America as the city on the hill.[1]

But to the extent that discussion focuses on the absence of a significant labor or socialist party, it usually suffers from the teleological assumption that all capitalist societies should proceed through the same preconceived historical stages and collapses analysis of the salience of class to politics and culture into the single question of socialist voting. Discussions of American exceptionalism have rarely been grounded in empirical international comparisons. Depending on which time period we choose, which countries we pick, and which characteristics we compare, the degree of American exceptionalism varies widely.[2]

Such comparison is beyond the scope of this essay, but perhaps I can highlight the need for comparison by focusing on a theme that arguments about the absence of socialism often bypass: how, when, and to what degree has class been relevant to American politics and culture? That question may also be the kind of integrative theme that will help remedy the widely deplored fragmentation of social history. Let us look at two prominent new social history topics—the new labor history and the new political history—and ask ourselves how synthesizing them might lead to better answers to the questions of the extent to which American capitalism has shaped the political consciousness of American workers and the structure of political power.[3]

From *The Journal of American History* 74(4)1988: 1257–86. Reprinted with the permission of the author and the American Sociological Association.

Earlier versions of this essay were presented to the Labor History Group of the Pittsburgh Center for Social History and at the annual meeting of the Organization of American Historians in April 1986. The ideas in the essay have been stimulated by discussions with many of my faculty colleagues and graduate students at the University of Pittsburgh, especially Loomis Mayfield, Joe White, Joel Sabadasz, Steve Sapolsky, Maurine Weiner Greenwald, Sy Drescher, and Peter Karsten.

[1] Recent efforts to grapple with American exceptionalism in labor and political history include Sean Wilentz, "Against Exceptionalism: Class Consciousness and the American Labor Movement, 1790–1920," *International Labor and Working Class History* (no. 26, 1984), 1–24; Nick Salvatore, "Response," *ibid.*, 25–30; Michael Hanagan, "Response," *ibid.*, 31–36; David Montgomery, "Why Is There No Socialism in the United States? Report on Conference in Paris," *ibid.*, (no. 24, 1983), 67–68; John Patrick Diggins, "Comrades and Citizens: New Mythologies in American Historiography," *American Historical Review*, 90 (June 1985), 614–38; and Leon Fink, "Looking Backward: Reflections on Workers' Culture and the Conceptual Dilemmas of the New Labor History," paper presented at a conference, "The Future of American Labor History: Toward a Synthesis," DeKalb, Illinois, Oct. 1984 (in Richard Oestreicher's possession).

[2] To cite one example, strike frequency in the United States (workers involved per 100,000 nonagricultural wage earners) from 1902 to 1905 was *higher* than in nine out of ten European countries for which data is available. (Among Austria, Belgium, Denmark, France, Germany, Italy, the Netherlands, Norway, Sweden and Great Britain, only Italy had a higher frequency.) The U.S. figure was nearly double the annual mean for the ten European countries (3450 versus 1898). P. K. Edwards, *Strikes in the United States, 1881–1974* (New York, 1981), 254; Peter Flora, Franz Kraus, and Winifred Pfenning, *State, Economy, and Society in Western Europe, 1815–1975: A Data Handbook in Two Volumes* (2 vols., Frankfurt, 1987), II, 693, 697, 701, 711, 717, 727, 733, 739, 743, 753. On the ambiguity of the concept of American exceptionalism, see Ira Katznelson, *City Trenches: Urban Politics and the Patterning of Class in the United States* (New York, 1981), 6–8; and Fink, "Looking Backward," 2–3, 8–13.

[3] Among the many pleas for synthesis in labor history, see David Brody, "The Old Labor History and the New: In Search of an American Working Class," *Labor History*, 20 (Winter 1979), 111–26; David Montgomery, "To Study the People: The American Working class," *ibid.*, 21 (Fall 1980, 485–512; Ronald W. Schatz, "Labor Historians, Labor Economics, and the Question of Synthesis," *Journal of American History*, 71 (June 1984), 93–100. The late Herbert Gutman argued that any synthesis of labor or working-class history should be integrated with a larger synthesis of American history. Herbert G. Gutman, *Work, Culture, and Society in Industrializing America: Essays in American*

Both groups of historians develop key themes most thoroughly in their works on the Northeast and the Midwest from the Civil War to the Great Depression. In those years the United States completed its transition from an agricultural to an industrial economy, became the world's leading industrial producer, and shifted from small-scale artisanal production to large-scale mechanized mass production. American industry concentrated in a belt, starting on the fringes of the Great Plains, running in an arc between the Great Lakes and the Ohio Valley, and then up the Atlantic Coast through New England.[4]

What do labor historians have to say about the consciousness of urban workers in that region between 1870 and 1940? Rejecting the classlessness asserted by consensus historians and the job consciousness emphasized by labor economists of the Wisconsin school, labor historians have, with few recent exceptions, argued for a Thompsonian American working class, different certainly from the working class predicted by classical Marxism but, in its own way, class-conscious nonetheless.[5] The crucial factor in American working-

class development, according to this argument, was the contradiction between republican traditions of individual rights and personal independence and the realities of increasingly regimented lives and authoritarian work disciplines. When labor organizer George E. McNeill declared in 1877 "an inevitable and irresistible conflict between the wage-system of labor and the republican system of government," he was expressing, according to labor historians, one of the most common themes in nineteenth-century working-class rhetoric.[6]

Such a conflict did take place, labor historians argue, with twists and turns, with ebb and flow, but with continuity and historical force as well. In an impressive array of detailed studies of work habits, culture, and community life they have demonstrated how, as David Montgomery put it, working-class republicanism gave a broad range of seemingly disparate and sectorally divided activities a "distinctive quality of moral universality." Advocates of working-class republicanism, like William Sylvis, president of the Iron-Moulders International Union and the National Labor Union viewed labor as "the foundation of the entire political, social, and commercial structure," the source of all wealth and the basis of the republic. But, claimed Homestead's steelworkers in 1892, the centralization of capital gave

Working-Class and Social History (New York, 1976), xi–xiv; MARHO, ed., *Visions of History* (New York, 1983), 203–5. Essays on synthesis of American history include Thomas Bender, "Wholes and Parts: The Need for Synthesis in American History," *Journal of American History*, 73 (June 1986), 120–36; Nell Irvin Painter, "Bias and Synthesis in History," *ibid.*, 74 (June 1987), 109–12; Richard Wightman Fox, "Public Culture and the Problem of Synthesis," *ibid.*, 113–16; Roy Rosenzweig, "What *Is* the Matter with History?" *ibid.*, 117–22; Thomas Bender, "Wholes and Parts: Continuing the Conversation," *ibid.*, 123–30; James Henretta, "Social History as Lived and Written," *American Historical Review*, 84 (Dec. 1979), 1293–1322; Oliver Zunz, "The Synthesis of Social Change: Reflections on American Social History," in *Reliving the Past! The Worlds of Social History*, ed. Oliver Zunz (Chapel Hill, 1985), 53–114; and Samuel P. Hays, "Three Decades of the New Social History in the United States: An Assessment," in *Socialgeschichte*, ed. Jurgen Kocka (Darmstadt, West Germany, 1987). Hays has given thought to the concept of integrative themes. See Samuel P. Hays, "Theoretical Implications of Recent Work in the History of American Society and Politics," *History and Theory*, 26 (no. 1, 1987), 15–31.
[4] On this region as the financial-industrial "metropole" of the United States, see Walter Dean Burnham, "The System of 1896: An Analysis," in *The Evolution of American Electoral Systems*, ed. Paul Kleppner (Westport, 1981), esp. 152–53.
[5] The Wisconsin school's tradition is most clearly and explicitly presented in Selig Perlman, *A Theory of the Labor Movement* (New York, 1928). A perceptive critique is Andy Dawson, "History and Ideology: Fifty Years of 'Job Consciousness,'" *Literature and History*, 8 (Autumn 1978), 223–41.

[6] For views of the American working-class influenced by the work of E. P. Thompson, see Michael H. Frisch and Daniel J. Walkowitz, eds., *Working-Class America: Essays on Labor, Community, and American Society* (Urbana, 1983); and Wilentz, "Against Exceptionalism." Their theoretical position derives from E. P. Thompson, *The Making of the English Working Class* (New York, 1963), esp. 9–11. His conception of class has provoked a vigorous debate among European Marxists between Thompsonian "culturalists" and critics who accuse them of underestimating the material and structural underpinnings of class ("structuralists"). A vitriolic attack on the "culturalist" tendency among American radical historians in Elizabeth Fox-Genovese and Eugene Genovese, "The Political Crisis of Social History: A Marxian Perspective," *Journal of Social History*, 10 (Winter 1976), 205–20. Michael Katz, Michael Doucet, and Mark Stern, *The Social Organization of Early Industrial Capitalism* (Cambridge, Mass., 1982) attempt to combine structuralist and culturalist arguments. For arguments against too literal a transposition of the Thompsonian model to American working class development, see Richard Oestreicher, "Industrialization, Class, and Competing Cultural Systems: Detroit Workers, 1875–1900," in *German Workers in Industrial Chicago, 1850–1910: A Comparative Perspective*, ed. Hartmut Keil and John B. Jentz (DeKalb, 1983), esp. 52–53, 68–69. George E. McNeill, *The Labor Movement: The Problem of To-Day* (New York, 1891), 459.

industrialists "an enormous and despotic power over the lives and fortunes of their employees . . . a power which eviscerates our national Constitution and our common law, and . . . is coming to mean in effect nothing less than the right to manage the country to suit themselves." Workers' defense of their rights and their livelihoods, such activists argued, was a defense of the republic itself. "We are devoted to the maintenance of republican institutions," wrote Edward Bellamy in 1890, "against the revolution now being effected by the money power . . . who are overthrowing the republic."[7]

Workers' desires to recapture control over their labor and their republic, both slipping from their grasp, gave larger meaning to even the most narrowly job-conscious demands and underlay diverse phenomena not previously thought of in class terms: debates over parks and the uses of other public spaces, conflicts about drinking habits and recreational styles, ways of organizing family life and defining gender roles, reactions to slavery and Reconstruction.[8] From the Jacksonian artisans in the workingmen's parties and the National Trades Union who challenged entrepreneurial master craftsmen and merchant capitalists in dozens of northeastern cities, to the railroad workers of 1877 who sparked the largest strike anywhere in the world in the nineteenth century, to the pervasive sweep of fifteen thousand Knights of Labor assemblies into virtually every industrial town in the United States in the 1880s, American workers asserted and reasserted a republican critique of American capitalism.[9]

The rise of large-scale corporate mass production in the second industrial revolution that began shortly before the turn of the century undermined the artisanal basis of this working-class republicanism, attracted a new immigrant working class for whom republican rhetoric had far less emotional resonance, and altered the political terrain of all political and economic struggles. Yet Montgomery argues that earlier traditions of working-class republicanism meshed with responses to mass production in a new class consciousness, evident after World War I in the most widespread expressions of working-class militancy and solidarity in American history. Beginning with a challenge to the exceptionalist framework, writes Sean Wilentz, "we end with the proposition that there is a history of class consciousness in the United States comparable to that of working-class movements in Britain and on the Continent." While many new labor historians still raise doubts about Wilentz's comparison, especially for the years after 1920, few have seriously challenged the first half of his statement "there is a history of class consciousness in the United States" or the orthodoxy of a dis-

---

[7] David Montgomery, "Labor and the Republic in Industrial America, 1860–1920," *Le mouvement social* (no. 111, 1980), 204. Sylvis and Bellamy quoted by Fink, "Looking Backward," 7–8; Homestead workers quoted by Paul Krause, "Labor Republicanism and '*Za Chlebom*': Anglo-American and Slavic Solidarity in Homestead," in *"Struggle a Hard Battle"*: *Essays on Working-Class Immigrants*, ed. Dirk Hoerder (De Kalb, 1986), 143–69, 162.

[8] Roy Rosenzweig, "Middle-Class Parks and Working-Class Play: The Struggle over Recreational Space in Worcester, Massachusetts, 1870–1910," *Radical History Review*, 21 (Fall 1979), 31–46; Betsy Blackmar, "Rewalking the 'Walking City': Housing and Property Relations in New York, 1780–1840," *ibid.*, Frank Couvares, *The Remaking of Pittsburgh: Class and Culture in an Industrializing City, 1877–1919* (Albany, 1984); Paul Faler, *Mechanics and Manufacturers in the Early Industrial Revolution: Lynn, Massachusetts, 1780–1860* (Albany, 1981), 100–138; Bruce Laurie, *Working People of Philadelphia, 1800–1850* (Philadelphia, 1980), 107–33; David Brundage, "The Producing Classes and the Saloon: Denver in the 1880s," *Labor History*, 26 (Winter 1985), 29–52; Susan Levine, "Labor's True Woman: Domesticity and Equal Rights in the Knights of Labor," *Journal of American History*, 70 (Sept. 1983), 323–39; David Montgomery, *Beyond Equality: Labor and the Radical Republicans, 1862–1872* (New York, 1967).

[9] On Philadelphia, see David Montgomery, "The Shuttle and the Cross: Weavers and Artisans in the Kensington Riots of 1844," *Journal of Social History*, 5 (Summer 1972), 411–43; and Laurie, *Working People of Philadelphia*, 85–104; on New York, Sean Wilentz, *Chants Democratic: New York City and the Rise of the American Working Class, 1788–1850* (New York, 1984), esp. 172–254. None of the recent community studies of the Jacksonian era gives an adequate sense of the overall scope and extent of these movements. Still useful are Edward Pessen, *Most Uncommon Jacksonians: The Radical Leaders of the Early Labor Movement* (Albany, 1967), 3–51; John R. Commons et al., *History of Labour in the United States* (4 vols., New York, 1918–1935), I, 260–68; 285–318, 350–437; and Philip S. Foner, *History of the Labor Movement in the United States* (6 vols., New York, 1947–1982), I, 121–42. The estimate of 15,000 local Knights of Labor assemblies is a total of all known assemblies existing between 1869 and 1896. About 8–9,000 were operating in 1886, the Knights' peak year, with assemblies in 97% of all cities and towns with populations over 8,000 in 1890. Jonathan E. Garlock, "A Structural Analysis of the Knights of Labor: A Prolegomenon to the History of the Producing Classes" (Ph.D. diss., University of Rochester, 1974); Jonathan E. Garlock, "Knights of Labor Data Bank," computerized data base (Interuniversity Consortium for Political Research, Ann Arbor).

tinctively working-class brand of republicanism as its basis.[10]

Like the new labor historians, new political historians have developed an orthodoxy—the so-called ethnocultural interpretation of American politics—that challenges basic postulates of the consensus historians against whom both groups have reacted, but their analysis of urban working-class political behavior in the late nineteenth and early twentieth centuries appears to describe a completely different country from the one inhabited by the people Montgomery and Wilentz studied. The political historians began with a concern similar to that of labor historians: How can we understand the values and political motivations of ordinary people? Social analysis of electoral behavior, they argued, could be one of the most fruitful ways of getting at popular values, culture, and consciousness.[11]

Quantification was a critical issue for the new political historians. Most previous political history, they proclaimed, depended on impressionistic argument by example. When subjected to statistical tests, many hallowed notions proved to be false. Echoing the behaviorist social scientists who had inspired them, political historians argued that the way to learn what people (or

at least white males) really believed is to look accurately at what they did.

What did the electorate do, according to such political historians as Lee Benson, Richard Jensen, and Paul Kleppner? Through most of the nineteenth century, most men who were eligible voted. They voted consistently straight party tickets, choosing one or the other on the basis of cultural and emotional loyalties that reflected the fundamental concerns of family, church, tradition, and daily life. In the early twentieth century, while the ideological nature of partisanship shifted slightly, voters, including women after 1920, continued to vote along ethnoculturally based partisan lines. Such consistent electoral behavior demonstrated that Americans, contrary to consensus theorists, were bitterly divided about basic values and loyalties. But until the 1930s cultural issues aroused voters more consistently than economic issues or class interests. Class identities did not determine votes for most voters in most elections. Even when economic issues were quite important, as they were during the depression of the 1890s, economic classes divided their votes between the major parties. The fault lines of partisanship did not coincide with class lines.[12]

Political parties, nonetheless, symbolized "irreconcilable belief systems" and resembled "political churches" mobilized around diametrically opposed reactions to the "strident Yankee moralism" of pietistic Protestants.[13] Pietists wished to purge sin not only from their own hearts but also from their neighbors'. The state, pietists believed, should supervise and regulate personal behavior or at least prevent sinners from engaging in public affronts to decency and virtue. The Republican party, the political vehicle for that crusade

[10] David Montgomery, *Workers' Control in America: Studies in the History of Work, Technology, and Labor Struggles* (Cambridge, Eng., 1979), 91–112; Wilentz, "Against Exceptionalism," 18. Salvatore, "Response"; Hanagan, "Response"; Steven Sapolsky, "Response," *International Labor and Working Class History* (no. 27, 1985), 35–38.

[11] The most influential of the new political historians challenges the appropriateness of the "ethnocultural" label; Paul Kleppner, *The Third Electoral System: 1853–1892* (Chapel Hill, 1979), 358–60. But most historians now use it regardless of their positions on the issues. Among the key works contributing to the reformulation of analysis of electoral behavior between 1870 and 1940 are Paul Kleppner, *The Cross of Culture: A Social Analysis of Midwestern Politics, 1850–1900* (New York, 1970); Richard Jensen, *The Winning of the Midwest: Social and Political Conflict, 1888–1896* (Chicago, 1971); Walter Dean Burnham, *Critical Elections and the Mainsprings of American Politics* (New York, 1970); Kleppner, *Third Electoral System*; Samuel T. McSeveney, *The Politics of Depression: Political Behavior in the Northeast, 1893–1896* (New York, 1972); Paul Kleppner, *Who Voted? The Dynamics of Electoral Turnout, 1870–1980* (New York, 1982); James Sundquist, *Dynamics of the Party System: Alignment and Realignment of Political Parties in the United States* (Washington, 1983); Walter Dean Burnham, "The Changing Shape of the American Political Universe," *American Political Science Review*, 59 (March 1965), 7–28; Paul Kleppner, "From Ethnoreligious Conflict to 'Social Harmony': Coalitional and Party Transformations in the 1890s," in *Emerging Coalitions in American Politics*, ed. Seymour Martin Lipset (San Francisco, 1978), 41–59; Walter Dean Burnham, "The System of 1896: An

Analysis," in *Evolution of American Electoral Systems*, ed. Kleppner, 147–202; and Joel Silbey, Allan Bogue, and William Flanigan, *The History of American Electoral Behavior* (Princeton, 1978). For works by the most prominent early exponents of social analysis of politics, see Lee Benson, "Research Problems in American Political Historiography," in *Common Frontiers of the Social Sciences*, ed. Mirra Komarovsky (Glencoe, 1957), 113–83; and Samuel P. Hays, *American Political History as Social Analysis: Essays* (Knoxville, 1980), 66–132. For the intellectual and historiographical origins of Hays's thinking, see *ibid.*, 3–45.

[12] Kleppner, *Third Electoral System*, 360–64, 367–68; Jensen, *Winning of the Midwest*, xi, xiv. For a general theory to explain this pattern, see Lee Benson, "Group Cohesion and Social and Ideological Conflict," *American Behavioral Scientist*, 16 (May–June 1973), 741–67.

[13] Kleppner, "From Ethnoreligious Conflict to 'Social Harmony,'" 45, 50.

in the late nineteenth century, could depend on the support of the overwhelming majority of northern native Protestants as well as immigrant Protestants with a similar theological orientation. Workers, farmers, and businessmen of such ethnocultural backgrounds supported the Republicans in similar proportions.

Arrayed against these cultural imperialists was a Democratic coalition of the targets of pietistic wrath: slaveholders and later most white southerners, Catholics, nonpietistic Protestant immigrants (especially ritualists, mainly German Lutherans, whose attitudes toward state regulation of personal behavior were similar to those of the Catholics), drinkers, and the wider urban subcultures of plebeian sensual pleasures. Personal liberty, the Democratic watchword, suggests how this diverse coalition was held together by common resistance to the pietistic cultural police. Immigrant and Catholic businessmen were just as ready as their working-class neighbors to man Democratic barricades of cultural defense.[14]

The moral intensity of partisan identifications was reinforced, according to the new political historians, by day-to-day living experiences, familial obligations, and kin networks. Associational life overwhelmingly reproduced ethnocultural boundaries and mirrored ethnically segregated residences. People rarely married across ethnocultural boundaries. In this environment, changing parties constituted treason to family, kin, and neighborhood; group solidarity within a balanced and competitive political system made electoral participation a moral duty. "Catholics," noted a Wisconsin priest in 1889, "think that one is not a Catholic if he is a Republican." A Norwegian pietist criticized the inconsistency of going "to the Lord's table on Sunday and vot[ing] for Cleveland on Tuesday."[15]

Events in the 1890s, Kleppner and Jensen argue, disrupted the previous stability and equal balance of these political churches. The organization of the Populist

party with its regionally concentrated political base, the emergence of a new breed of Republican politicians dedicated to broadening the party's appeal by moderating the intensity of ethnoreligious conflicts, and the sudden shock of the severe mid-decade depression all combined in the critical election of 1896 to produce a major political realignment and a new party system.[16]

Earlier ethnocultural loyalties still influenced most voters after 1896, but the Republicans maintained their decisive 1896 majority by moderating ethnocultural imagery, especially to new immigrants, and projecting themselves as the party of economic growth, full employment, and the "full dinner pail." Democratic efforts to incorporate the American Federation of Labor (AFL) into the party's political coalition, while significant in a few cities, had only a modest impact on the national party balance. The highly competitive pre-1896 party system was replaced by a regionally structured system of one-party supremacy with only scattered areas of serious electoral competition. Declining political competitiveness, along with more restrictive election laws and the changing demography of the electorate, produced a marked long-term drop in turnout.[17]

---

[14] *ibid*, 45, 49–51; Paul Kleppner, "Partisanship and Ethnoreligious Conflict: The Third Electoral System, 1853–1892," in *Evolution of American Electoral Systems*, ed. Kleppner, 134–36.

[15] Kleppner, *Who Voted?* 46; Kleppner, "Partisanship and Ethnoreligious Conflict," 139; Kleppner, *Third Electoral System*, 368. Greater documentation of the linkages between religious and political ideologies and patterns of day-to-day life could strengthen the political historians' case. Ethnic and social historians have traced some linkages. See John Bodnar, *The Transplanted: A History of Immigrants in Urban America* (Bloomington, 1985), 89–91, 94–115, 126–30, 197–204; and Olivier Zunz, *The Changing Face of Inequality: Urbanization, Industrial Development, and Immigrants in Detroit, 1880–1920* (Chicago, 1982).

[16] These themes are summarized in Kleppner, "From Ethnoreligious Conflict to 'Social Harmony,'" McSeveney places more emphasis on the depression but sees economic issues filtered through ethnocultural loyalties. See McSeveney, *Politics of Depression*. For a dissent from the ethnocultural point of view that questions the pietist-ritualist distinction and the extent of realignment and places greater emphasis on economic and class distinctions, see Allan J. Lichtman, "Political Realignment and 'Ethnocultural' Voting in Late Nineteenth Century America," *Journal of Social History*, 16 (Spring 1983), 55–83.

[17] There is debate about the relative importance of four major causes of declining turnout: declining competitiveness, black disenfranchisement, changing demography of the electorate (more immigrants, low turnout among women after their enfranchisement), and rules changes (e.g., registration and residency requirements, redistricting, nonpartisan ballots). See Kleppner, *Who Voted?* 55–82. Some historians see rules changes as ruling-class efforts to limit working-class and immigrant political influence; others see such limitation as an unintended consequence of changes sought for other reasons. Lichtman, "Political Realignment and 'Ethnocultural' Voting," 57–63; Marc Karson, *American Labor Unions and Politics, 1900–1918* (Carbondale, 1958), 64–73; Gwendolyn Mink, *Old Labor and New Immigrants in American Political Development: Union, Party, and State, 1875–1920* (Ithaca, 1986), 204–35; Kleppner, "From Ethnoreligious Conflict to 'Social Harmony'" 44–49, 58–59; Burnham, "System of 1896," 148–49, 162–98; Jerrold G. Rusk, "Comment: The American Electoral Universe: Speculation and Evidence," *American Political Science Review*, 68 (Sept. 1974), 1029–49; Walter Dean Burnham, "Rejoinder to 'Comments' by Philip Converse and Jerrold Rusk," *ibid*., 1050–57.

As a result, by the beginning of the Great Depression, an enormous pool of potential voters—disproportionately young, working-class, and ethnic—rarely voted and had not developed clear partisan identities.[18] When an initial shift toward the Democrats in response to the depression revived the Democratic party, Democratic politicians seized the opportunity to cement the loyalties of this potential political base. Nearly all economic groups veered toward the Democrats in 1932, but after 1933 voters' responses to New Deal programs diverged sharply. The unemployed, relief recipients, low-income households, and blue-collar workers registered overwhelming approval in 1936 and 1940, while business people, professionals, white-collar workers, and upper- and middle-income households all expressed increasing disapproval. In 1936 the difference in the percentage voting Democratic between upper- and lower-income households was 34 percentage points; in 1940 40 percentage points; between business and unskilled workers 34 points in 1936, 33 in 1940.[19]

The new Democratic coalition also had a decidedly ethnic basis as blacks, Jews, Italians, and eastern Europeans all shifted sharply toward the Democrats, but since all those groups (except the Jews) were disproportionately working-class, ethnic and working-class contributions to realignment represented complementary and reinforcing influences rather than countervailing pressures. Religion also still played a fundamental role. Unskilled and semiskilled Catholics were 25 percentage points more Democratic in the 1940 election than non-southern white Protestant unskilled and semiskilled workers (who gave 51 percent of their votes to the Republicans). But among both Catholics and non-southern white Protestants, unskilled and semiskilled workers were decisively more Democratic than upper middle-class professionals and business executives: 29 points more Democratic among non-

southern Protestants, 32 points more Democratic among Catholics. Those cleavages persisted over the next generation, the only era in American political history, according to this group of political historians, when class played an important role in determining the prevailing pattern of partisan political preferences.[20]

How are we to reconcile the apparently fundamental contradictions between these images of the political consciousness of urban workers? Prior to the 1930s, the ethnocultural political historians find little evidence of either the working-class republicanism or the class conflict emphasized by the new labor historians. And in the one era in which the political historians view the New Deal as a co-optive integration of workers into a multi-class coalition destructive of working-class consciousness.[21]

For the most part, the two groups have ignored each other. Kleppner mentions a few of the labor historians disapprovingly in footnotes but does not treat their arguments or evidence extensively. In 1980 Montgomery urged his fellow labor historians to think seriously about the arguments of ethnocultural political historians, but few have taken his advice. One possible explanation for the discrepancies between the new political and the new labor historians is that one group or the other is simply wrong. Yet although methodological criticisms have seriously challenged parts of their arguments, the fundamental discoveries of both groups have been reproduced again and again in one

---

[18] Kleppner, *Who Voted?* 63–70; Samuel Lubell, *The Future of American Politics* (New York, 1965), 43–68; Kristi Andersen, *The Creation of a Democratic Majority, 1928–1936* (Chicago, 1979), 15–17, 48–49, 67–69, 110–16.
[19] Kleppner, *Who Voted?* 83–111; Andersen, *Creation of a Democratic Majority*, 100–110; Bruce Stave, *The New Deal and the Last Hurrah: Pittsburgh Machine Politics* (Pittsburgh, 1970), esp 40–52; Sundquist, *Dynamics of the Party System*, 198–239; Edward G. Benson and Paul Perry, "Analysis of Democratic-Republican Strength by Population Groups," *Public Opinion Quarterly*, 4 (Sept. 1940), 467.

[20] Lubell, *Future of American Politics*, esp. 45–55; Everett Carll Ladd, Jr., and Charles D. Hadley, *Transformations of the American Party System: Political Coalitions from the New Deal to the 1970s* (New York, 1978), 51–53, 57–87; John L. Shover, "The Emergence of a Two-Party System in Republican Philadelphia, 1924–1936," *Journal of American History*, 60 (March 1974), 985–1002; Richard Jensen, "The Cities Reelect Roosevelt: Ethnicity, Religion, and Class in 1940," *Ethnicity*, 8 (June 1981), 189–95.
[21] The co-optive impact of the New Deal on working-class consciousness is forcefully argued in Mike Davis. "The Barren Marriage of American Labour and the Democratic Party," *New Left Review*, 124 (Nov.–Dec. 1980), 43–84; and Mike Davis, *Prisoners of the American Dream: Politics and Economy in the History of the U.S. Working Class* (London, 1986), esp. 93–101. David Montgomery notes gains as well as losses from the "barren marriage," but his argument is consistent with that of Davis. Montgomery, *Workers' Control in America*, 153–80. For a summary and critique of the "corporate-liberal" class co-optation argument, see Stanley Vittoz, *New Deal Labor Policy and the American Industrial Economy* (Chapel Hill, 1987).

case study after another. Their key findings should be accepted.[22]

For at least two and one-half out of the three key questions on which they have most closely focused, the new political historians are undoubtedly right. They are right about who voted, right about how they voted, and right, as far as they go, about why they voted that way. The apparent contradiction between the two images of political consciousness cannot be reconciled by dismissing the political historians. Their explanation of voter motivation is insufficient, but the critical issue that raises, the relationships between voting and the structure of power in American politics, must be addressed directly, not by further debates about the political historians' empirical description of voting behavior. It is here that integration of political and labor history might be most fruitful.

The new labor historians are also, for the most part, right as far as they go. Across the entire industrial heartland, throughout the nineteenth century, in every community they have studied, they have found hundreds of examples of influential individuals whose language echoed George McNeill's declaration of the irreconcilability of republicanism and wage labor. That the symbolism, language, and analysis of so many workers—from Jeffersonian Baltimore or New York to Jacksonian New York, Philadelphia, Lynn, or Newark to Reconstruction Troy or Albany to Gilded Age Detroit, Chicago, Kansas City, Rutland, Boston, Cincinnati, or Homestead—were so consistent demonstrates the widespread existence of a class-conscious artisanal republicanism in nineteenth-century America.[23]

We can still ask *how* widespread? How representative was artisanal republicanism of the entire working class? Few of the new labor historians have addressed the question systematically enough. A long list of examples establishes the existence of class consciousness, but it does not establish its relative place within a larger cultural and intellectual milieu of competing currents and loyalties. New labor historians have not fully situated their examples of class-conscious behavior within a more comprehensive social anthropology of the working class. They have hedged on whether there was a distinction between the labor movement, or even the broader penumbra of movement culture associated with it, and the working class.

To some degree, the reluctance to draw a sharp distinction between movement culture and working-class culture indicates adoption of E. P. Thompson's conception of class, in which overt manifestations of class conflict or class-conscious rhetoric reflect the underlying experiences inherent in the class relationship. The strongest evidence for such linkages lie in the work habits and collective norms they have uncovered that governed the pace and level of output, among both nineteenth-century artisans and early twentieth-century factory workers. Nearly all nineteenth-century crafts developed work cultures that dictated codes of acceptable conduct, standards of workmanship that limited

[22] Kleppner, *Third Electoral System*, 360, 370; Montgomery, "To Study the People," 507. Critiques of ethnocultural political history include James E. Wright, "The Ethnocultural Model of Voting: A Behavioral and Historical Critique," *American Behavioral Scientist*, 16 (May–June 1973), 653–74; Lichtman, "Political Realignment and 'Ethnocultural' Voting," 55–82; Richard L. McCormick, "Ethno-Cultural Interpretations of Nineteenth Century American Voting Behavior," *Political Science Quarterly*, 89 (June 1974), 351–77. Critiques that challenge the core assumptions of the labor historians are Diggins, "Comrades and Citizens," 614–38; Rowland Berthoff, "Writing a History of Things Left Out," *Reviews in American History*, 14 (March 1986), 1–16; and Aileen S. Kraditor, *The Radical Persuasion, 1890–1917: Aspects of the Intellectual History and Historiography of Three American Radical Organizations* (Baton Rouge, 1981), esp. 1–110, 297–321.
[23] Charles G. Steffen, *The Mechanics of Baltimore: Workers and Politics in the Age of Revolution* (Urbana, 1984); Howard B. Rock, *Artisans of the New Republic: The Tradesmen of New York*

City in the Age of Jefferson (New York, 1979); Wilentz, *Chants Democratic*, Laurie, *Working People of Philadelphia*; Alan Dawley, *Class and Community: The Industrial Revolution in Lynn* (Cambridge, Mass., 1976); Faler, *Mechanics and Manufacturers in the Early Industrial Revolution*; Susan E. Hirsch, *The Roots of the American Working Class* (Philadelphia, 1978); Daniel J. Walkowitz, *Worker City, Company Town: Iron and Cotton-Worker Protest in Troy and Cohoes, New York, 1855–1884* (Urbana, 1978); Brian Greenberg, *Worker and Community: Response to Industrialization in a Nineteenth-Century American City, Albany, New York, 1850–1884* (Albany, 1985); Couvares, *Remaking of Pittsburgh*; Richard Oestreicher, *Solidarity and Fragmentation: Working People and Class Consciousness in Detroit 1875–1900* (Urbana, 1986); Richard Schneirov, "The Knights of Labor in the Chicago Labor Movement and in Municipal Politics, 1877–1886" (Ph.D. diss., Northern Illinois University, 1984); Leon Fink, *Workingmen's Democracy: The Knights of Labor and American Politics* (Urbana, 1983); Jama Lazerow, "'The Workingman's Hour': The 1886 Labor Uprising in Boston," *Labor History*, 21 (Spring 1980); Paul Krause, "Steelworkers, Steel Work and the Political Economy of Steel Production in Homestead, Pa., 1880–1892: Social Origins of Labor Insurgency in the Gilded Age," draft, Ph.D. diss., Duke University, 1985 (in Oestreicher's possession); Linda Schneider, "The Citizen Striker: Workers' Ideology in the Homestead Strike of 1892," *Labor History*, 23 (Winter 1982); Stephen J. Ross, *Workers on the Edge: Work, Leisure, and Politics in Industrializing Cincinnati, 1788–1890* (New York, 1985).

pace, and time-honored distractions like the mid-morning mug or the cigar makers' reader.[24] Widespread complaints about informal collective limitations of output in early twentieth-century management literature suggest those habits were as common in the age of mass production as they had been generations earlier. Such practices constituted a workers' moral economy that directly confronted employers' efforts to maximize output and efficiency and directly contradicted the acquisitive ethic of individual gain. The connection between the movement culture of the labor movement and wider arenas of working-class experience is also illustrated by labor organizations' ability to command support for their ideals beyond their own membership: nonunionized workers' respect for picket lines or willingness to honor boycotts.[25]

Yet even if such collective work cultures and expressions of solidarity represented virtually universal working-class norms in the times and places that labor historians have studied most closely, it is still possible that from a *long-term national* perspective those industries and towns constitute minorities divergent from a far less class-conscious working-class majority. Historians of work cultures have tended to focus on small units where the sources and consequences of individual behavior and individual attitudes can be analyzed. The overwhelming majority of their works have been case studies, sometimes concentrating on only one or two factories, more often in small industrial towns than in big cities, rarely over long periods of time. In contrast, because political historians focus on political outcomes (for example, who wins elections) and majority opinion, they have concentrated on long-term shifts in the main tendencies in voting behavior in states, regions, or the whole country. Although work cultures, cooperative practices, and gestures of solidarity may fundamentally shape the day-to-day functioning of a

factory or decisively affect the immediate outcome of a local strike or boycott, they may, nonetheless, recede into relative insignificance when submerged in the long-term electoral behavior of an entire state or region.

A somewhat different response to the contradiction between the political and labor historians' descriptions of working-class consciousness is to accept the validity of the findings of both groups and to argue that the discrepancy represents real differences in the attitudes and behavior of the same people in different contexts. As Ira Katznelson, a leading exponent of that theory explains, among American workers there has historically been a "radical separation in people's consciousness, speech, and activity of the politics of work from the politics of community. . . . Most members of the working class thought of themselves as workers at work, but as ethnics (and residents of this or that residential community) at home." Separate spheres. Unions organized workers at work around a trade-union consciousness growing out of work experiences, but voting took place in geographic units organized around ethnically homogeneous, but economically heterogeneous, neighborhoods whose residents voted as ethnic blocs in response to neighborhood concerns.[26]

Both explanations—that proponents of class-conscious work cultures constituted minorities of a larger national working class and that working-class consciousness differed at home and at work—are at least partially true, but neither strikes me as sufficient. If workers who engaged in cooperative work practices, honored picket lines, or supported boycotts were minorities, the evidence of such activities uncovered by each new case study suggests that, at least in such peak periods of labor insurgency as the mid-1880s or the World War I era, they were very large minorities, forming a countable proportion of the electorate even in very large political units. If political historians find little evidence of class consciousness in aggregate electoral behavior in such periods, it cannot be because the number of strikers, boycotters, or stint setters was statistically inconsequential.

The second explanation, "radical separation" between work and home, appears to fit the conflicting characterizations of labor and political historians: high mobilization around class-based cultural norms on the shop floor but little class polarization at the polling place. But does such a behavioral description reflect a

---

[24] For an influential introduction to discussion of such work cultures, see Gutman, *Work, Culture and Society in Industrializing America*, 3–78. That essay stimulated a search for similar examples. On the moral assumptions of such work cultures, see the works cited in note 23, above.

[25] Montgomery, *Workers' Control in America*, 32–47, 113–38. For a different image of managerial attitudes, see Daniel Nelson, *Managers and Workers: Origins of the New Factory System in the United States, 1880–1920* (Madison, 1975), 55–78. On the relationships between union activities and a "social and industrial morality sanctioned by all workers," see Abraham Bisno, *Union Pioneer: An Autobiographical Account of Bisno's Early Life and the Beginnings of Unionism in the Women's Garment Industry* (Madison, 1967), 227–32.

[26] Katznelson, *City Trenches*, 18.

radical separation of *consciousness* as Katznelson and other exponents of that theory claim? Most recent family and ethnic historians argue that working-class family members collectively pursued a common set of family priorities in the differing arenas in which men and women, old and young, functioned. Behavior varied according to age, gender, stage of life cycle, and context, but attitudes and goals remained the same.

In late nineteenth-century Detroit, immigrant workers and their children did function simultaneously in competing cultural systems appealing to contradictory loyalties. As workers, they participated in a class-based oppositional subculture like those new labor historians have described. As ethnics, they were members of ethnic cultural systems and belonged to ethnically based churches and voluntary associations led by middle-class ethnic elites who were often hostile to unions. And to the extent that they accepted doctrines of individual upward mobility, many immigrant workers absorbed the acquisitive and individualistic ethos of the native middle class.[27]

Multiple cultural systems offered workers different strategies for survival and self-improvement, but the impact of the differing possibilities rarely broke down into such a simple dichotomy as labor at work and ethnic at home. Immigrant workers responded differently to differing possibilities and circumstances in concrete and specific circumstances. In the late 1880s, German workers in Detroit joined in antiprohibition campaigns with the same middle-class ethnic leaders whom they battled bitterly on other occasions. In 1891 many of the workers who fought enthusiastically in behalf of striking streetcar drivers crossed picket lines of German and Polish strikers in a large railroad-car-construction factory strike a few days later. Detroit workers were not exclusively labor at work and ethnics at home. They were also ethnics at work and labor at home.[28]

Similarly Jews and Italians on New York's Lower East Side in the Progressive Era were ethnics, as well as labor, at work. Because they were Jews, Jews over-whelmingly supported radical needle trades unions. Because they were Italians, Italians who labored under the same regime supported the same unions far less. And Jewish housewives who organized rent strikes and meat boycotts and led food riots behaved more than a little like labor at home.[29]

Understanding how workers chose between different strategies both at work and at home suggests a third way to reconcile the differences between the political and labor historians. Consider the following hypothesis: From the 1870s until the 1930s, class sentiments were widespread among American workers, but before the 1930s the structure of political power in American society and the personal familial priorities of workers made it harder to mobilize class sentiments in the political arena than in the workplace. The argument for the hypothesis has four parts:

1. Class sentiments are different from political consciousness.
2. Political consciousness is as much a result of political mobilization as a cause of mobilization.
3. In an entrenched party system, with winner-take-all elections and an electorate highly mobilized on a different basis, political mobilization around class sentiments demanded far greater resources and involved greater risks than the labor movement was able or willing to muster while workplace mobilization around work-related issues needed far fewer resources. Without a tradition of successful political mobilization, class sentiment could not be translated into an articulated political consciousness.
4. The majority of American workers in those years, especially in the cities of the Northeast and Midwest, were immigrants, children of immigrants, or recent rural-to-urban migrants with limited organi-

---

[27] Oestreicher, "Industrialization, Class, and Competing Cultural Systems," esp. 59–65; Oestreicher, *Solidarity and Fragmentation*, 36–39. See also John J. Bukowczyk, "The Transformation of Working-Class Ethnicity: Corporate Control, Americanization, and the Polish Immigrant Middle Class in Bayonne, New Jersey, 1915–1925," *Labor History*, 25 (Winter 1984), 53–82.

[28] Oestreicher, "Industrialization, Class, and Competing Cultural Systems," 53–59; Oestreicher, *Solidarity and Fragmentation*, 43–52, 222–33.

[29] On the importance of cultural differences in the radical needle trades unions, see Steve Fraser, "Dress Rehearsal for the New Deal: Shop-Floor Insurgents, Political Elites, and Industrial Democracy in the Amalgamated Clothing Workers," in *Working-Class America*, ed. Frisch and Walkowitz, esp. 228–32; and Gerald Sorin, *The Prophetic Minority: American Jewish Immigrant Radicals, 1880–1920* (Bloomington, 1985), 23–33, 114–20, 136–38, 163–68. On rent strikes and meat boycotts, see Elizabeth Ewen, *Immigrant Women in the Land of Dollars: Life and Culture on the Lower East Side, 1890–1925* (New York, 1985), 126–27; Dana Frank, "Housewives, Socialists, and the Politics of Food: The 1917 New York Cost-of-Living Protests," *Feminist Studies*, 11 (Summer 1985), 255–85; and William Frieburger, "War, Prosperity, and Hunger: The New York Food Riots of 1917," *Labor History*, 25 (Spring 1984), 217–39.

zational resources and the desire to adapt to existing power in ways that would facilitate, rather than threaten, their priorities of family integrity, economic well-being and cultural defense. That frame of mind further limited the possibilities of mobilizing workers politically outside the existing partisan alignment.

By class sentiment I mean a relatively unfocused sense of grievance, for example, a feeling that workers were treated unfairly and unequally, were underpaid and overworked, and a positive response to notions like "we have to stick together" or to phrases like the "rights of labor." Such sentiment, even if widespread, does not automatically translate into any particular strategy or action. For class sentiment (or sentiments based on ethnicity, religion, race, or gender) to lead to strategy and action, it must be linked to particular symbols and programs and mobilized by specific individuals and organizations.

Political consciousness is the ideological linkage of sentiment and world view with a specific partisan identification or political loyalty. For most people that linkage takes place, not as a result of pure reflection or rational analysis of competing programs, but as a result of repeated political participation. A variety of personal experiences and attributes—race, gender, stage of life cycle, personal community networks, family structure, and religious training, as well as class—may shape individual values and predispose individuals toward a particular political orientation, but most people do not systematically articulate their values and sentiments politically outside the context of formal political activity. Consciousness is as much a product of political mobilization as a cause of mobilization.[30]

Political mobilization is the process through which politicians or activists organize and rally potential voters to support candidates and programs. Political mobilization is a necessary (but not sufficient) condition for any sentiment, value, feeling, symbol, issue, or program to become politically salient. Even in a demo-cratic society mobilization is not a spontaneous process. Political systems are never collections of equal citizens who simply agglomerate themselves around common sentiments. They are systems of power in which politicians and activists with dramatically unequal power struggle to produce some outcomes and to prevent others.

Mobilization takes place within a structure of political power that individuals cannot alter in the short run. In the United States in the late nineteenth and early twentieth centuries, all would-be political mobilizers faced four critical realities: the entrenched two-party system, the winner-take-all method of conducting elections and allocating representation, the multiple tiers of a federal structure, and differential access to political resources. Since the collapse of the second American party system in the 1850s, no new political aspirant in American politics—no party, no politician, no social movement—has gained significant national political power except through the Democratic or the Republican party. Even an ex-president and the most popular political figure of the entire era, Theodore Roosevelt, despite abundant funding, could do no more than split the Republican vote in 1912 and throw the election to the Democrats.

Winner-take-all elections enhanced the stability of the two-party system and made it more difficult for minor parties and insurgent social movements to establish their political credibility. A minority showing in an American election produces no seats, no officeholders. The 6 percent Socialist vote in 1912 gave the American Socialist party no congressional seats. In December 1910 the British Labour party received 6.4 percent of the national vote and elected forty-two members of Parliament.[31] Even when political insurgents could mobilize local majorities and elect local officials, the policy-making power of local officeholders was limited by the tiers of the federal system. In a parliamentary system, especially if the major parties were relatively balanced as in Britain, local majorities could give minor parties policy-making leverage in Parliament. In the American federal system, the power of local officials was sharply circumscribed by higher levels of

---

[30] Voting behavior studies by political scientists demonstrate, for example, that for the majority of voters partisanship shapes opinions on issues more than the other way around. See Norman R. Luttberg, ed., *Policy: Models of Political Linkage* (Itasca, Ill., 1981). For a historical case study arguing this position, see Amy Bridges, *A City in the Republic: Antebellum New York and the Origins of Machine Politics* (Cambridge, Eng., 1984). On the prerequisites for mass politicization, see Lawrence Goodwyn, *The Populist Moment: A Short History of the Agrarian Revolt in America* (Oxford, 1978), xvii–xx.

[31] The Socialists did elect one congressman in 1910 and one in each election from 1914 through 1928. James Weinstein, *The Decline of Socialism in America, 1912–1925* (New York, 1967), 107, 169; Chris Cook and John Paxton, *European Political Facts, 1848–1918* (New York, 1978), 137.

power and by the courts. Given the scope of American politics, and the necessity to contest for power at multiple levels, any electoral initiative was very expensive. No union, no minor party, no social movement could approach the economic resources that businesses and corporations could provide to the established parties.

In the workplace, labor organizations could draw on class sentiment and direct it toward immediate grievances in surroundings familiar to workers and on terrain where they had at least potential organizational advantages. In smaller factories—where most successful labor organizing took place before the 1930s— although fear of firing constituted a powerful source of intimidation, the economic and political resources of employers were usually modest and the knowledge of skilled workers was often indispensable. Organizational efforts could start with a handful of activists and address very limited areas—particular grievances in a single shop or even a section of a shop—and build piecemeal as initial successes attracted more followers and built confidence. Although unions could not prosper unless they expanded widely enough to control employment in segments of an industry, initial success did not generally depend on simultaneous mobilization of many people in many places. And within the shop-floor culture of an unorganized factory, where the employer and his agents were an adversary force, unions filled an organizational vacuum. Only rarely did other organizations compete with them for the right to redress workers' shop-floor grievances.

In contrast, even modest political efforts demanded extensive simultaneous organizational commitments and faced stiff competition from established parties with vastly greater resources. The smallest units of urban political competition, even single aldermanic wards, were dramatically larger than the largest factories. And if political efforts were to be more than symbolic, that is, if they were seriously directed toward using the political system to redress grievances through changes in legislation and public policy, they had to take place simultaneously across many political units. The locus of effective policy-making power was, at a minimum, the city, and more often the state or the nation. Even in a local campaign in a medium-sized factory town, to talk to a majority of voters before an election, to transport supporters to the polls, to place a single poll worker at every precinct, to hand out tickets, and to insure that votes were actually counted demanded hundreds of political workers. A campaign in a big city like New York or Chicago could not be credibly undertaken without thousands of campaigners.

By the Gilded Age, the first time the working class was sufficiently numerous to represent a potential national political force, workers were already deeply involved in an entrenched ongoing political system.[32] The kinds of talented and ambitious working-class personalities who were struggling to establish the Social Democratic parties of the Second International were by then successful machine politicians in the United States. Urban machine politicians responded flexibly to a range of working-class grievances, both day-to-day problems of individuals at a neighborhood level and, when confronted by strong unions, policy demands in the administrative and legislative realms.[33] Such responses, however, functioned more to identify class sentiments with existing partisan loyalties than to focus class sentiments toward a more explicitly class-based political consciousness. By providing potential access to power, political machines undercut some of the reasons for alternative forms of working-class political mobilization at the same time that they dramatically raised the costs of effective alternative mobilization. Any effort to mobilize workers politically independent of, or against, existing party organizations faced not only the bourgeois resistance one would expect to any challenge to capitalist power in a capitalist system, but also the implacable opposition of armies of working-class and lower middle-class political professionals who correctly viewed attempts to restructure the basis of party politics as threats to their livelihood.

The reluctance of Samuel Gompers, other top AFL officials, and many other labor leaders to commit their unions wholeheartedly to more than occasional endorsements of "friends of labor" was based in part on

---

[32] Industrial wage earners formed 27% of the workforce in 1870; blue-collar workers (including those in domestic service but excluding agricultural laborers) between 48% and 51% of the workforce from 1910 through 1940. See Montgomery, *Beyond Equality*, 448–52; Stanley Lebergott, *Manpower in Economic Growth* (New York, 1964), 510–18; and Alba M. Edwards, *Population: Comparative Occupational Statistics for the United States, 1870–1940* (Washington, 1943), 63–72, 187.

[33] On the Magee-Flinn machine in Gilded Age Pittsburgh, see Krause, "Steelworkers," ch. 4, 60–67; Couvares, *Remaking of Pittsburgh*, 64–65. On the Pendergast machine in Kansas City, Mo., in the 1920s and 1930s, see Gary M. Fink, *Labor's Search for Political Order: The Political Behavior of the Missouri Labor Movement, 1890–1940* (Columbia, 1973), 120–27. On Tammany Hall and New York City workers, see Irwin Yellowitz, *Labor and the Progressive Movement in New York State, 1897–1916* (Ithaca, 1965), 158–87.

the fear that the divided partisan allegiances of their members would embroil unions in disruptive internal bickering. But it was also based on a coolly calculated cost-benefit analysis. Political confrontation not only stretched organizational resources, but also risked unions' influence over elected officials who could shield unions from court actions; use state regulation, immigration restrictions, and public contracting to protect and enhance craft labor markets; and limit use of the police to break strikes. Especially after hostile court decisions, such as the Danbury Hatters case (*Loewe v. Lawlor*) and the *Buck's Stove and Range* cases, threatened the legality of unions, Gompers recognized that the AFL had to intervene politically in its own behalf. Convinced that socialist or third party campaigns had no hope of electoral victory and that without timely political relief the survival of unions was questionable, he sought political commitments by major Democratic politicians for a limited agenda of trade-union objectives: freedom from court injunctions, relief from antitrust suits under the Sherman Act, and immigration restriction.[34]

Working-class political insurgents repeatedly mobilized large numbers of voters against established politicians and political machines, sometimes with trade-union support, sometimes over the objections of union leaders, but successful political mobilization involved more than bringing enough voters to the polls to make a credible showing in a single election. Only if political challengers could establish a meaningful niche in the structure of power could they maintain their capacity to mobilize voters in the future. Failing that, they and their initial political base were either absorbed into preexisting coalitions or destroyed. That inescapable reality repeatedly undercut successful political insurgencies, from the workingmen's parties of the 1830s, whose organizational death was insured far more by that necessity than by the clever scheming of political manipulators, to the Populists of the 1890s, driven to a suicidal fusion with the Democrats by their inability to establish stable political power on their own.[35]

The contrast between the repeated failures of such political insurgencies and the ability of the established parties to deliver electoral victories and tangible benefits became an important political tradition and a source of factional advantage for "realists" in debates within the labor movement. Such traditions, developed through repeated experiences, become a part of history, shaping consciousness in the future. Once some political possibilities have been chosen, others become more difficult.

The structural impediments to working-class political mobilization were compounded by the particular cultural backgrounds and priorities of the majority of American urban working-class voters in the late nineteenth and early twentieth centuries. For most of the century after 1850, the majority of the working class were immigrants or the children of immigrants. Such preponderance was even more marked in the major cities of the Northeast and Midwest. Even within the native-stock minority of the working class, rural-to-urban migrants generally outnumbered those who had been born and bred in urban working-class families. Indeed, as late as 1952 only 46 percent of married working-class household heads had working-class fathers (33 percent of fathers had been farmers). Most American workers between 1870 and 1940 were not hereditary proletarians but people in transition.[36]

Despite economic opportunities and the wonders of a consumer culture, capitalist urban America was a hostile place for immigrant workers. To survive, to keep families intact, and to defend cultural traditions, union and political efforts had to be balanced against the necessity of adapting to preexisting structures of superior power. Equally important, among the southern and

---

[34] Christopher L. Tomlins, *The State and the Unions: Labor Relations, Law, and the Organized Labor Movement in America, 1880–1960* (Cambridge, Eng., 1985), 61–67; *Loewe v. Lawlor*, 208 U.S. 274 (1908); *Buck's Stove and Range Company v. American Federation of Labor*, 35 Washington Law Reporter 525 (1907); Karson, *American Labor Unions and Politics*, 30–73, 117–49; Mink, *Old Labor and New Immigrants*, 39–44, 165–67, 204–41.

[35] For emphasis on such manipulation, see Wilentz, *Chants Democratic*, 201–16. Norman Pollack, *The Populist Response to Industrial America: Midwestern Populist Thought* (Cambridge, Mass., 1962), 107–43; Goodwyn, *Populist Moment*, 215–63. Pollack describes fusion as the last gasp of Populist radicalism; Goodwyn sees it as the capture of genuine Populism by an ersatz "shadow movement."

[36] For example, in 1900 immigrants and native whites of foreign parents made up 56% of employees in manufacturing; in 1920 51%. U.S. Department of Commerce and Labor, Census Bureau, *Special Report on Occupations at the Twelfth Census* (Washington, 1904), cxiii; U.S. Department of Commerce, Bureau of the Census, *Fourteenth Census, Population 1920: Occupations* (Washington, 1923), 34. Richard F. Hamilton, *Class and Politics in the United States* (New York, 1972), 309.

eastern Europeans who made up the majority of the enormous immigrant stream just after the turn of the century, personal adaptive strategies often reflected the intention to return home after accumulating a cash take in America. Such sojourners sought, above all else, uninterrupted employment and avoided challenges to authority that might interrupt savings and delay the return home.[37] To stress adaptation is not to argue passivity. One of the achievements of the new labor historians has been their documentation of the extent of informal individual resistance, collective control struggles, and overt class conflict. Workers shaped the institutions of power as they were being shaped by them, but most of the time it was an unequal struggle.

Certainly this profile does not encompass all American workers between 1870 and 1940. Regional working-class subcultures had their own priorities, often quite different from those of the ethnic majorities in northeastern and midwestern cities. Among immigrant workers of many nationalities, significant minorities of politically conscious radicals sometimes exercised considerable political influence.[38] Many skilled workers still nurtured a craft pride that made their work far more a source of emotional identity and far less an instrument of other goals than the model of strategic adaptation would suggest. Such feelings had much to do with the survival of artisanal republicanism long after a workshop economy was only a distant memory. But if the profile approaches, at least to some degree, the frame of mind of the majority of American workers from the Gilded Age through the Great Depression, it suggests how the majority of potential working-class voters approached political choices.

In an ethnically polarized society, ethnically and religiously derived issues like prohibition, enforced sabbath observance, Bible reading in schools, immigration restriction, and bilingualism, as the political histo-rians have argued, mattered deeply to most Americans because they reflected the tensions of daily life and directly affected the quality of life. Who would be their neighbors? Would public behavior disrupt that which they held dear? Would their children be educated to respect or to scorn the traditions of their parents? Would do-gooders restrict limited and much-needed opportunities for recreation? Would families separated by migration be reunited? What political historians like Kleppner and Jensen say about those issues is consistent with what ethnic historians tell us about the motivations of most immigrant workers and their children. Many new labor historians, despite their interest in working-class culture, seem skeptical that such issues had genuine cultural roots within the working class. The political historians' ethnocultural basis of politics was not a conspiracy designed to deflect workers from real economic or class issues. When politicians addressed ethnocultural issues, they gave the people what they wanted.

But the people were not free to choose. Politicians did not give the people all they wanted but only those parts that would continue to get the politicians elected, not antagonize the rest of their electoral coalition, and not arouse decisive opposition from powerful business interests. Ethnocultural issues were not *all* that people wanted. Economic issues like taxation, allocation of public services, public regulation, and, above all, employment were consistent themes in urban and national politics, but working-class voters could not choose which policy alternatives would be presented to them. Politicians who addressed economic issues usually did so as brokers between their constituencies and economic elites, not as spokesmen of workers. That Catholics and Protestants concerned about schooling chose politicians on the basis of which Bible they advocated does not tell us very much about what else they wanted, or how they would have weighed Bible reading against the rights of labor.

Usually, the political system offered clear choices about the former but not the latter. If voters split according to ethnicity and religion rather than class or economics, that may tell us more about the political system than about the relative preferences of voters for ethnocultural or class loyalties.

Between 1870 and the 1920s, millions of working-class voters who chose politicians representing Protestant or Catholic Bibles, prohibition or antiprohibition, also marched on Labor Day, joined systematic work slowdowns, struck for the eight-hour day, fought street battles with strikebreakers and soldiers, boycotted scab

---

[37] Half the southern Italians and over two-thirds of some eastern European nationalities who entered the U.S. between 1900 and 1910 returned home. Bodnar, *Transplanted*, 53–54; John Bodnar, Roger Simon, and Michael P. Weber, *Lives of Their Own: Blacks, Italians, and Poles in Pittsburgh, 1900–1960* (Urbana, 1982), 122–29; Thomas J. Archdeacon, *Becoming American: An Ethnic History* (New York, 1983), 139.

[38] For portraits of the differing political and cultural attitudes of southern workers, see David L. Carlton, *Mill and Town in South Carolina, 1880–1920* (Baton Rouge, 1982); and Jacquelyn Dowd Hall, "Disorderly Women: Gender and Labor Militancy in the Appalachian South," *Journal of American History*, 73 (Sept. 1986), 354–82. On immigrant radicalism, see Hoerder, ed., *"Struggle a Hard Battle."*

breweries, and refused nonunion cigars. If as many of
them chose Republicans as chose Democrats, perhaps
that was because they saw no meaningful difference
between the two on the rights of labor, but real and
important cultural differences. And as immigrants and
migrants trying to adapt to a hostile urban life, perhaps
it made more sense, if they voted at all, to get what they
could from potential winners, rather than to support
sure losers on idealistic or ideological grounds. In partisan, winner-take-all elections in which parties did not
present class-differentiated appeals, neither measurements of the impact of class on votes for major party
candidates nor measurements of the votes for minor
working-class parties across the entire electorate indicate the relative importance of class-based issues and
symbols to working-class voters.

Although such reasoning is plausible, how do we
know there was a reservoir of untapped class feeling
among the urban working-class electorate that could
not be mobilized because labor organizations had insufficient resources (or will) to overcome the twin impediments of the structure of political power and the
cultural horizons of immigrant workers? Beyond labor
historians' demonstration that protest behavior was
enmeshed in broad cultural traditions and deep emotional loyalties, two other lines of analysis might allow
us to judge whether there was indeed an untapped
reservoir of class sentiment between 1870 and 1930.
First we could systematically analyze political situations where credible class appeals were presented to
working-class voters; that is, where they were sponsored or endorsed by powerful organizations or where
candidates had a believable chance of winning. Second,
we could analyze electoral alignments after 1930, an
era where such class sentiment was politicized by the
Democratic party, looking backward for foreshadowings of the New Deal coalition and indicators of
untapped class consciousness in patterns of previous
nonparticipation among working-class voters who supported the Democrats after 1930.

For the first, we could catalogue the various political
forces that periodically mobilized working-class voters
around explicitly prolabor programs or vaguer class-
tinged language. Such a catalogue suggests a significant untapped reservoir of class feelings, but also that
reservoir's limits. At least six varieties of political
activity, and a much wider array of parties and personalities, might be included: populist farmer-laborism,
local independent laborism, socialism, trade unionists
running as major party nominees, major party "friends
of labor" running with union endorsements, and non-

labor political mavericks challenging political establishments with prolabor rhetoric. Populist farmer-
laborism, independent laborism, and socialism have
received the most scholarly attention. Farmer-laborism
is the only one of the three that repeatedly approached
national proportions. From the 1870s through the
1920s, Labor Reformers, Greenbackers, Populists, and
Progressives, using the political categories of Jeffersonian artisanal republicanism, traced working-class
and agrarian distress to political corruption by non-
producers whose control of the state allowed them to
extort the labor of producers. All producers—farmers,
workers, and productive small entrepreneurs—had to
unite politically to drive out the monopolistic cor-
rupters and to replace their regime with a cooperative
commonwealth. From the Massachusetts Labor Reform
party, which elected twenty-two state legislators in
1869, to the national Greenback Labor party, which
polled one million votes in 1878, the Populist revolt of
the 1890s, and the La Follette Progressive party, which
received 16.6 percent of the vote in 1924, that tradition
served as a recurring counterpoint to the dominant ethnocultural themes of American politics. Independent
laborism might be thought of as a localized, urban,
trade-unionist variant of farmer-laborism, merging with
agrarian and middle-class populist currents at the peaks
of farmer-laborism in 1878, 1894, and 1924. Outside
such alliances it had less national visibility, but it was
also a recurring tendency in such contests as the successful mayoral campaign of Hiram Breed in Lynn,
Massachusetts, in 1860, in the more than two hundred
tickets sponsored by the Knights of Labor in the mid-
1880s, the forty local labor parties who formed a
national labor party in 1919 before collapsing into the
movement that backed Robert M. La Follette for president, and the Minnesota Farmer-Labor and New York
American Labor parties of the New Deal era. In their
later stages such parties drew inspiration from the successes of the British Labour party as well as the earlier
populist tradition. Although heavily influenced by
German Marxism, American socialism might also be
thought of as a special case of populist republicanism,
as Nick Salvatore's recent biography of Eugene V. Debs
argues.[39]

---

[39] Nathan Fine, *Labor and Farmer Parties in the United States,
1828–1928* (1928; reprint, New York, 1961), 29–30, 64–66;
David Brody, "On the Failure of U.S. Radical Politics: A Farmer-
Labor Analysis," *Industrial Relations*, 22 (Spring 1983), 141–63,

The other three varieties of political activity are less generally thought of as forms of working-class politics. Their ideological character and relationship to working-class discontent is less obvious, but they are also recurring themes. William McCarthy, a former pressman, elected mayor of Pittsburgh in 1865; Martin Foran, a former International Coopers' Union president, who represented Cleveland in Congress; Eugene V. Debs, elected as an Indiana Democratic legislator in 1884; United Mine Workers Secretary-Treasurer Thomas Kennedy, who was elected lieutenant governor of Pennsylvania in 1936, are examples of the many labor leaders both major parties have periodically elected to local, legislative, and occasionally state offices. Whether such candidacies represented more than personal ambition or mobilized working-class voters who would not have voted the party label anyway is not always clear. Certainly party managers in tightly contested regions with a significant working-class vote sought out talented labor leaders as potential candidates. The sources of electoral support for such candidates need to be more carefully studied. The same is true for the many politicians elected as "friends of labor." Some scholars have suggested that the value of labor endorsements was primarily organizational and financial, not electoral, but studies of particular politicians, like Mayor Hazen S. Pingree of Detroit and California senator and governor Hiram W. Johnson have argued that labor and working-class support was a critical part of larger political coalitions. The roles of such mavericks as Massachusetts congressman and governor Benjamin Butler and newspaper magnate and presidential hopeful William Randolph Hearst are even more problematic, but conservative contemporaries who labeled them scoundrels and demagogues did so primarily because they believed Butler and Hearst were opportunistically and irresponsibly appealing to working-class anger. Their critics were probably right about the opportunism; if they were also right about the sources of support, the successes of Butler and Hearst—both potent political forces—do reveal untapped class sentiments.[40]

These movements, parties, and politicians display a range of programs, appeals, and rhetoric that defies attempts to discover an underlying ideological coherence, but they do have some common characteristics. First, support in their key areas of activity was dramatically higher than national or regional averages of their strength across the entire electorate would lead one to expect. The high totals in localities where class-oriented campaigns were serious political competitors maybe a better measure of class sentiment in the electorate than averages across entire states and regions. Greenback-Labor presidential candidates received 1 percent of the national vote in 1876 and 3 percent in 1880. But that party elected Knights of Labor leader Terence V. Powderly mayor of Scranton, Pennsylvania, with a 55 percent majority in 1878, captured half the votes in 228 eastern Pennsylvania anthracite coal towns in 1877 and 1878, and captured nearly a third in Pittsburgh and Allegheny City in the same years. Labor parties captured only 1.2 percent of the total vote in 1886, according to Kleppner's estimate, but they received a third of the vote in New York and Chicago and won in Milwaukee and many smaller industrial towns.[41] The Socialist Labor party measured its national totals in fractions of a single percentage point but elected aldermen or state legislators in the late 1870s in Chicago, St. Louis, Milwaukee, Detroit, and Louisville. The Populists, who drew negligible percentages in eastern and midwestern industrial areas in 1892 when their southern and western agrarian strength gave them

esp. 144, 151; Dawley, *Class and Community*, 102–4; Fink, *Workingman's Democracy*, 26–29; Stanley Shapiro, "'Hand and Brain': The Farmer-Labor Party of 1920," *Labor History*, 26 (Summer 1985), 405–22; Sapolsky, "Response," 35–38; Nick Salvatore, *Eugene V. Debs: Citizen and Socialist* (Urbana, 1982).
40 Montgomery, *Beyond Equality*, 211, 214–15, 390–91; Salvatore, *Eugene V. Debs*, 41–42; McAlister Coleman, *Men and Coal* (New York, 1943), 18, 170. Oestreicher, *Solidarity and*

Fragmentation, 120–22, 181–82, 186, 195–96, 234–37; Melvin G. Holli, *Reform in Detroit: Hazen S. Pingree and Urban Politics* (New York, 1969), 11–13, 19–20, 133–35, 138–56; John L. Shover, "The Progressives and the Working Class Vote in California," *Labor History*, 10 (Fall 1969), 584–601; Mary Ann Mason Burki, "The California Progressives: Labor's Point of View," *ibid.*, 17 (Winter 1976), 24–37; William D. Mallam, "Butlerism in Massachusetts," *New England Quarterly*, 33 (June 1960), 186–206; Yellowitz, *Labor and the Progressive Movement in New York State*, 188–215.
41 Michael Nash, *Conflict and Accommodation: Coal Miners, Steel Workers, and Socialism, 1890–1920* (Westport, 1982), 66, 173; Richard Oestreicher, "Terence V. Powderly, the Knights of Labor and Artisanal Republicanism," in *Labor Leaders in America*, ed. Melvyn Dubofsky and Warren Van Tine (Urbana, 1987), 39–40; John D. French, "Reaping the Whirlwind: The Origins of the Allegheny County Greenback Labor Party in 1877," *Western Pennsylvania Historical Magazine*, 64 (April 1981), 117–18. Kleppner does not explain how his figure was calculated, and I doubt its accuracy since Henry George received 67,930 votes in his New York City mayoral race and the Chicago Labor Party candidates about 25,000, together nearly 1% of the national vote. Kleppner, *Third Electoral System*, 274.

8.5 percent of the national vote, received 15 percent of the total votes in 513 Ohio, Illinois, and Pennsylvania coal towns in 1894 and 25 percent in 228 Pennsylvania anthracite towns in 1897. Debs, who drew 6 percent in the Socialist party's peak national showing in 1912, averaged more than four times that percentage in 16 western Pennsylvania steel towns in 1912. Although the National Labor party organized in 1919 received less than 1 percent of the 1920 presidential vote, President John Fitzpatrick of the Chicago Federation of Labor, their Chicago mayoral candidate in 1919, received 8 percent, while eight labor mayors were elected in other Illinois towns. And Robert M. La Follette, although his support was most concentrated in rural parts of the Midwest and Great Plains, did surprisingly well in some industrial areas, receiving, for example, 36 percent in Pittsburgh and 44 percent in Cleveland, more than double his national average.[42]

A second common characteristic, which strikingly suggests that such campaigns tapped into class sentiments not reflected by normal partisan alignments, is the surge-like quality of nearly all of the exceptionally high totals. Challengers seemed to come out of nowhere to upset normal political alignments; the result was sometimes sufficiently threatening to stimulate a temporary merger of the two major parties against the outsiders (as in the 1887 Chicago mayoral campaign or several of the campaigns of Milwaukee's Socialists). But support usually disappeared nearly as quickly as it had appeared. The pattern of sharp but transitory outbursts does suggest the existence of pools of untapped class sentiment. But the pattern is also consistent with the frequently advanced explanation of the outbursts as protest votes aroused by mass strikes, depressions, and wars. More detailed community studies of such elections reveal an additional factor that the protest vote hypothesis overlooks: the importance of organizations capable of political mobilization. Surges did not take place evenly across regions most affected by strikes and depressions; they peaked in communities where labor (or other) organizations were strong enough to take advantage of the opportunity. Powderly's 1878 mayoral campaign drew on one of the best-organized Knights of Labor districts in the country. The Pittsburgh Green-

back Labor party of the late 1870s had the organizational resources of two of the most powerful craft unions in the country, the Amalgamated Association of Iron and Steel Workers and the Window Glass Workers. The independent labor parties of the mid-1880s were arms of the Knights of Labor, and their local electoral fortunes paralleled those of that order. Successful local socialist campaigns in the Debs era followed prior organization of strong party locals. Organization, by itself, could not produce electoral surges. In all those cases, the organizations had tried before, less successfully, to mobilize working-class voters. Both organization and additional stimuli were necessary—the combination of the two made surges of class voting possible.[43]

Third, studies of the electoral bases of such campaigns reveal that class sentiments were not distributed equally across the potential working-class electorate but concentrated in particular nationalities of workers and in particular economic sectors. Kleppner's measurement of county-level variations in the extent of Greenback, independent labor, and Populist voting between 1876 and the early 1890s indicate ethnic differences within the working class even during periods of class mobilization. With many local exceptions, such voting was weakest among Yankees, erratic among Germans and Irish Catholics, and strongest among Scandinavians. Detailed studies of the 1886 United Labor campaigns in New York and Chicago depict them as alliances between German working-class radicals and Irish working-class nationalists.[44] My studies of Detroit and Pittsburgh labor voting reveal important variations

---

[42] Fine, *Labor and Farmer Parties*, 43, 55, 397; Fink, *Workingmen's Democracy*, 26–32, 178, 197–98; Nash, *Conflict and Accommodation*, 54, 55, 66, 116–18, 171–74; Shapiro, "'Hand and Brain,'" 405, 412; Stave, *New Deal and the Last Hurrah*, 36.

[43] Oestreicher, "Terence V. Powderly," 39–44; Samuel E. Walker, "Terence V. Powderly, 'Labor Mayor': Workingmen's Politics in Scranton, Pennsylvania, 1870–1884" (Ph.D. diss., Ohio State University, 1973); French "Reaping the Whirlwind," 99–106, 116–18; Krause, "Steelworkers," ch. 4; John William Bennett, "Iron Workers in Woods Run and Johnstown: The Union Era, 1865–1895" (Ph.D. diss. University of Pittsburgh, 1977), 219–39, 275–93; Fink, *Workingmen's Democracy*, 18–20, 25–32; Montgomery, "To Study the People," 506; Oestreicher, *Solidarity and Fragmentation*, xvii, 96, 114–15, 119–21, 209–14; Errol Wayne Stevens, "Labor and Socialism in an Indiana Mill Town, 1905–1921," *Labor History*, 26 (Summer 1985), 353–83.

[44] Kleppner, *Third Electoral System*, 285–88; Martin Shefter, "The Electoral Foundations of the Political Machine: New York City, 1884–1897," in *History of American Electoral Behavior*, ed. Silbey, Bogue, and Flanigan, 282, 286–90; David Scobey, "Boycotting the Politics Factory: Labor Radicalism and the New York City Mayoral Election of 1886," *Radical History Review* (nos. 28–30, 1984), 280–325; Schneirov, "The Knights of Labor in the Chicago Labor Movement," 483–547.

within the working class, but also the importance of organizational factors. In Detroit between 1877 and 1884, a succession of local socialist and labor campaigns, which drew between 7 and 10 percent of the voters, depended on German skilled workers for the majority of their votes. Only in 1886, after Knights of Labor membership had increased more than 1000 percent in the previous year, did the local labor party expand its vote to 14 percent and broaden its base to include Poles and skilled and unskilled workers of all nationalities.[45] In Pittsburgh the 1877–1878 Greenback Labor votes were class votes, with only minor differences in the propensity of different nationalities of workers to support the ticket, but the organizational roots are suggested by the disproportionate concentration of iron and steel workers and glassworkers among Greenback Labor voters. In succeeding Pittsburgh Greenback campaigns, as the overall Greenback vote declined, the proportionately higher support among iron and glassworkers became more pronounced.[46] We

need more detailed quantitative studies of such local campaigns before we can confidently generalize from those examples. But they suggest that while there was untapped class sentiment in the electorate, even in explicitly class-oriented campaigns, ethnocultural factors and organizational resources shaped the potential base of working-class support.

Retrospective analysis of the roots of the New Deal coalition is similarly consistent with the hypothesis that untapped class sentiment existed within the working-class electorate well before the Great Depression. For some time before 1932, the electoral behavior of urban working-class voters, especially those of new immigrant stock, had provided erratic but persistent harbingers of the coming national political realignment. In some cities the immigrant stock working-class wards and precincts that showed very high Democratic votes in 1932 and 1936 also gave high votes to Democrats as far back as 1916, to Debs in 1912, and to La Follette in 1924. In Pittsburgh, the La Follette vote correlated .84 with the 1932 Roosevelt vote and .61 with the 1936 vote (.71 if we omit two black wards that went strongly for Roosevelt in 1936 but not for La Follette in 1924).[47]

But before the 1930s the turnout of immigrant stock urban workers was generally very low, and their occasional surges to particular candidates were too weak and too varied from one community to another to alter national outcomes. When they did vote, they showed marked partisan inconsistency, turning out occasionally for attractive candidates, not voting or switching allegiance in subsequent campaigns. In 1928, for example,

---

[45] Regression equations for the 1884 labor vote yield standardized coefficients of .342 for percent working class in a precinct and .350 for percent German with working class and Germans as the independent variables. In 1886 the coefficients were .425 for percent working class, .302 for percent German, and .136 for a proxy variable designed to measure the impact of the 1886 strikes (the number of factories with 100 or more workers in a precinct or adjoining precincts that were on strike in 1886). While the crudity of the proxy demands caution, the result suggests the 1886 strikes had a modest effect on the labor vote. Oestreicher, *Solidarity and Fragmentation*, 119–23, 140n, 54, 141n, 58–64, 184–85, 216.

[46] The conclusions are based on a statistical analysis of Pittsburgh and Allegheny City Greenback Labor voting between 1877 and 1882. Data for the analysis were collected by students in my graduate seminar on Pittsburgh labor politics, winter 1984. I would like to thank Cindy Davidson, Gary Esneault, Scott Foreman, Phil Garrow, and Loomis Mayfield. The following list gives some indication of the results. It shows the correlation, or strength of association, of the percentage of Greenback Labor vote in a ward with the proportion of types of potential voters in a ward. A correlation of 1.00 indicates perfect correlation; −1.00 a perfect negative correlation; 0.00 no correlation.

Pearson's r of 1877 Greenback Labor vote (state judge) with

working class:	.61
high white collar:	−.49
iron and steel workers:	.68
glassworkers:	.47
native-stock white workers:	−.36
German-stock workers:	.20
Irish-stock workers:	.12
British-stock workers:	.41

The high value for British-stock workers reflects the relatively large number of skilled iron workers and glassworkers in that ethnic group. Results for other 1877 and 1878 labor candidates were similar. In multiple regression equations the highest correlations with labor vote in 1877 and 1878 were for unskilled workers and glassworkers, while weaker (but still statistically significant) predictors were iron and steel workers, and British-born workers. The relationship to skilled workers, other than glassworkers, was weak. By 1882, all of the ethnic variables except the British showed even weaker correlations to the labor vote than in 1877–1878, but the relationship to the British had increased. In both simple correlations and multiple regressions, the importance of overall class variables had declined relative to the importance of the sectoral variables (especially glassworkers and, to a lesser extent, iron and steel workers).

[47] Stave, *New Deal and the Last Hurrah*, 35–40, 196–213, 224; Burnham, *Critical Elections*, 20–25, 55–59; Allan J. Lichtman, *Prejudice and the Old Politics: The Presidential Election of 1928* (Chapel Hill, 1979), 199–230.

61 percent of those who voted for Alfred E. Smith had never voted for a presidential candidate before.[48]

Voting by urban workers of immigrant stock also showed an undertone of class sentiment in the 1920s, weaker than in the 1930s, but foreshadowing the class basis of the New Deal alignment. Allan Lichtman detected statistically significant indications of class cleavage in county-level variations in the voting of the 2058 non-southern counties in both 1924 and 1928, elections which have generally been thought of as archetypal examples of the supremacy of such cultural issues as Prohibition, nativism, religion, rural-urban differences, and reactions to the Ku Klux Klan. Such indications of class sentiment were much clearer in some cities than in others. In Pittsburgh, the 1924 La Follette vote correlated with a proxy for class, median rental value per ward, nearly as strongly as the 1936 Roosevelt vote did ($-.60$ for La Follette, $-.72$ for Roosevelt in 1936). In Philadelphia, where the Republican machine held onto the allegiance of inner-city lower-class voters, economic cleavages in voting were weak even in 1936.[49]

The catalog of sporadic class-oriented political challenges from the 1870s through the 1920s and the foreshadowings of the New Deal coalition support three important conclusions. First, the widespread nature of these efforts, their variety, and their typically explosive surges suggest that at least diffuse forms of class sentiment were endemic among the urban working-class electorate. Such class sentiments were usually only weakly expressed in the political system, at least in part because politicians and business elites consciously sought to prevent their expression. However, combinations of exceptional circumstances, such as severe economic distress, bitter strikes, particularly unpopular actions by incumbents, especially effective working-class sentiments that were otherwise politically latent. Even when such challenges were not immediate, urban politicians usually recognized the need to show enough respect for working-class grievances not to arouse anger.[50]

Second, the erratic, and in the end unsuccessful, nature of nearly all the class-oriented challenges demonstrates that the intensity of such sentiment was almost never sufficient to overcome the institutional and organizational barriers to its mobilization. Third, the variations in the surges of class-oriented political challenges and the foreshadowings of the New Deal coalition should alert us to the importance of organizational factors for political mobilization and arouse doubts that a liberal tradition, or some other underlying ethos in American culture, precluded the development of class consciousness in American society. Class sentiment existed. Indeed, major politicians in both parties throughout the years from 1870 to 1940 were well aware that class feeling occasionally exploded in unpredictable surges of political protest. They cultivated important labor leaders, promised full employment, and symbolically stroked workers with platitudes about the nobility of honest labor. Politicians seem to have taken the existence of class sentiment more seriously than many political historians.[51]

But the structure of political power, the way in which politics was conducted, prevented the ideological articulation of such sentiment. For those who sought to mobilize workers politically on an explicitly class basis political reality created a chicken-and-egg dilemma. The most powerful source of partisan political loyalties and of the articulation of sentiment into ideology is the political system itself, the ability, as a result of electoral victories, to deliver rewards in the form of policy, patronage, and psychically gratifying symbols. Because they could not win elections, would-be mobilizers of class sentiment were denied this

---

[48] Kleppner, *Who Voted?* 63–67; Shover, "Emergence of a Two-Party System," 1000–1002; Norman H. Nie, Sidney Verba, and John R. Petrocik, *The Changing American Voter* (Cambridge, Mass., 1976), 91–92; Andersen, *Creation of a Democratic Majority*, 48–52.

[49] Lichtman's results are based on six indirect proxies for class: per capita retail purchases, 1929; percentage of income tax payers, 1928; percentage of high school graduates, 1940; median housing value, 1930; percentages with telephones and radios, 1930. Given the indirect nature of these proxies his arguments about class voting in the 1920s can be taken as only suggestive. The results are least significant for per capita retail purchases and median housing value, the two proxies which are probably least indirect. Lichtman, *Prejudice and the Old Politics*, 166–98; Stave, *New Deal and the Last Hurrah*, 207, 228; Shover, "Emergence of a Two-Party System," 996–98.

[50] For a study of how late nineteenth-century Chicago politicians responded to working-class political pressure, see Richard Schneirov, "Haymarket and the New Political History Reconsidered: Workers' Class Presence in Chicago's Municipal Politics, 1873–1894," paper presented at the annual meeting of the Organization of American Historians, New York, April 1986.

[51] On politicians' prolabor symbolism, see Roger A. Fischer, *Tippecanoe and Trinkets Too: The Material Culture of American Presidential Campaigns, 1828–1984* (Urbana, 1987).

opportunity. But they could rarely win elections precisely because they lacked the power to reward that comes with prior electoral success. Even when occasional surges of class sentiment carried them into office, they were unable to deliver, their effective power limited by their isolation within a larger political system in which all other levels of power were still controlled by political forces hostile to their objectives and able to exercise de facto veto power over all but the most superficial political changes.

Perhaps the most revealing demonstration of this vicious circle was the experience of the handful of Socialist mayors elected in the Debs era. Despite mayoral victories, they failed to elect city council majorities and hence could not seize the control of administrative agencies necessary to implement local reform programs and appoint their own loyalists. Unable to deliver either patronage to supporters or reforms to voters, they could not translate their electoral victories into a stable political base, and they found themselves voted out in the next election.[52] Recognizing the dilemma, most labor leaders sought the political concessions they deemed essential to their organizations through alliances with major-party politicians and discouraged ideologically inspired attempts to mobilize working-class voters against the major parties. Except under unusual circumstances, until the 1930s class sentiment had no place to go politically.

When the New Deal coalition finally emerged in the 1930s, it drew on the previously unmobilized pockets of class sentiment. Only in the 1930s, when a major portion of the Democratic party, including the president, combined explicitly class-tinged rhetoric and symbolism with an economic program designed to protect some of the rights of labor and address sources of working-class insecurity, did class sentiment have a place in the American political arena. Over the course of the 1930s sentiment did indeed become translated into political consciousness as the class basis of parti-

sanship became successively more marked from election to election, peaking in the late 1940s. Although the New Deal coalition has been slowly demobilizing ever since, the class-based symbolism of the 1930s and 1940s still shapes the images of both parties and still influences some voters even today.

This analysis still leaves many crucial questions unanswered. Three avenues of further analysis and testing are particularly important. First, we need to think more systematically about the relationships between political structure and political consciousness, whether class consciousness or any other kind. Most practitioners of the new labor and the new political history, myself included, share a moral commitment to a liberal-rationalist model of politics that makes them reluctant to confront the extent to which values, opinions, and behavior are shaped by power rather than free and rational choice. We are all prisoners of history, our options limited by the world into which we are born.[53]

Second, any analysis of working-class political behavior in the years from 1870 to 1940 must consider the crucial importance of regionalism, something virtually ignored in this essay.

Finally, the key arguments of this essay depend on further analysis of what happened in the 1930s (and after). While political historians and political scientists have studied the New Deal realignment extensively, they have devoted the greatest attention to questions of timing related to critical election theory. There are fewer case studies of the basis of partisanship and voting than for much of the nineteenth and early twentieth centuries, especially studies that might tell not only how people voted, but how the new political coalition was actually mobilized. That the depression provided Democratic politicians with an opportunity to revive their nearly moribund party does not explain how they went about it. For example, in many previously Republican western Pennsylvania industrial towns, Franklin D. Roosevelt's initial national victories did not translate into stable Democratic realignment until after locals of the Steel Workers Organizing Com-

---

[52] For studies of local socialist administrations that faced these difficulties, see Stevens, "Labor and Socialism in an Indiana Mill Town," esp. 373–80; Ronald Edsforth, *Class Conflict and Cultural Consensus: The Making of a Mass Consumer Society in Flint, Michigan* (New Brunswick, 1987), 54–69; Chad Gaffield, "Big Business, the Working Class, and Socialism in Schenectady, 1911–1916," *Labor History*, 19 (Summer 1978), 350–72; and Douglas E. Booth, "Municipal Socialism and City Government Reform: The Milwaukee Experience, 1910–1940," *Journal of Urban History*, 12 (Nov. 1985), 51–74.

[53] The works of historical sociologists and political scientists emphasizing a "state-centered" or "polity-centered" approach to political history seem promising. See Ann Shola Orloff and Theda Skocpol, "Why Not Equal Protection? Explaining the Politics of Public Social Spending in Britain, 1900–1911, and the United States, 1880–1920," *American Sociological Review*, 49 (Dec. 1984), 726–50; and Peter B. Evans, Dietrich Rueschemeyer, and Theda Skocpol, *Bringing the State Back In* (Cambridge, Eng., 1985).

mittee (SWOC) entered local politics.[54] We need to know much more about the mechanics of working-class political mobilization and the emotional and cultural meanings that newly mobilized working-class voters attached to the Democratic party before we will fully understand the New Deal political realignment.

That the agent of working-class political mobilization after 1930 was the Democratic party, still a cross-class coalition of ideologically contradictory elements, has been enormously significant for the nature of public policy and the tone of politics and culture in the United States. The form class consciousness takes, the language and categories of analysis used to articulate it, may be politically decisive. But the class character of New Deal political alignments does suggest that what has been most exceptional about modern American politics, compared to west European politics in the same era, is not the relevance of class, but the particular form and role class consciousness has taken. The cultural meaning and political significance of a Democratic vote in the United States was quite different from the meaning and significance of a vote for Labour or for the German Social Democratic Party (SPD), but by the late 1940s, the level of class differentiation in voting in America was as high as in Britain or on the Continent.[55]

For the years between 1870 and 1930 a synthesis of the new political and new labor history points in a sim-

ilar direction. American workers in those years brought particular cultural traditions and practical priorities to their industrial experiences, but the ideological implications of those traditions and priorities were ambiguous. Culture is not the same as ideology. Cultures are vast and internally contradictory arrays of memories, symbols, ideas, and practices susceptible to a range of ideological interpretations. Working-class cultures always include tendencies toward class solidarity and tendencies toward class fragmentation. Working-class culture can thus be thought of as a set of contingencies, of possibilities. Which possibilities will develop and thrive depends on historical context and the actions of the specific historical actors within a particular context. Many American workers from 1870 to 1930, like many workers everywhere else, had grievances and felt anger as a result of their position in a class relationship. What was most distinctive about the political behavior of American workers in those years was the way in which the fit between their particular motivations and personal agendas and the structure of power in American society limited the translation of class sentiments into political consciousness.

---

[54] The importance of the Steel Workers Organizing Committee in the local politics of several western Pennsylvania steel towns was brought to my attention by Joel Sabadasz, who is writing a dissertation on steelworkers in three towns in the 1930s and 1940s. See Karen Steed, "Unionization and the Turn to Politics: Aliquippa and the Jones and Laughlin Steel Works, 1937–1941," seminar paper, University of Pittsburgh, 1982 (in Oestreicher's possession); and George Powers, *Cradle of Steel Unionism: Monongahela Valley, Pa.* (East Chicago, 1972), 131–42.

[55] One widely used measure of class differentiation is Robert R. Alford's index of differentiation: the percentage of blue-collar workers who express a preference for the left or workers' party (in the U.S., the Democratic party) minus the percentage of the rest of the electorate expressing preference for that party. Alford's index for the Democratic party varied between 14 and 25 in six surveys from 1936 through 1944 with a mean of 18. In 1948 it peaked at 41 (44 excluding nonvoters). From 1952 through 1960 the mean was 16 and the range was 13 to 23. For Great Britain the range from 1943 through 1951 was 23 to 42 with a mean of 35.5, but for the German SPD in 1953 the index was only 19. Robert R. Alford, *Party and Society: The Anglo-American Democracies* (Chicago, 1963), 348–49, 352–53; Juan J. Linz, "Cleavage and Consensus in West German Politics: The Early Fifties," in *Party Systems and Voter Alignments: Cross-National Perspectives*, ed. Seymour M. Lipset and Stein Rokkan (New York, 1967), 287; Hamilton, *Class and Politics in the United States*, 190–93.

READING 14

THE DOMESTICATION OF POLITICS: WOMEN AND AMERICAN POLITICAL SOCIETY, 1780–1920

Paula Baker

On one subject all of the nineteenth-century anti-suffragists and many suffragists agreed: a woman belonged in the home. From this domain, as wife, as daughter, and especially as mother, she exercised moral influence and insured national virtue and social order. Woman was selfless and sentimental, nurturing and pious. She was the perfect counterpoint to materialistic

---

From *The American Historical Review* 89(5)1984: 620–47. Reprinted with the permission of the author.

A number of individuals commented on earlier versions of this essay, including Dee Garrison, Kathleen W. Jones, Suzanne Lebsock, Richard L. McCormick, Wilson Carey McWilliams, John F. Reynolds, Thomas Slaughter, and Warren I. Susman. I am grateful for their criticism, advice, and encouragement.

and competitive man, whose strength and rationality suited him for the rough and violent public world. Despite concurrence on the ideal of womanhood, anti-suffragists and suffragists disagreed about how women could best use their power of moral superiority. Suffragists believed that the conduct and content of electoral politics—voting and office holding—would benefit from women's special talents. But for others, woman suffrage was not only inappropriate but dangerous. It represented a radical departure from the familiar world of separate spheres, a departure that would bring, they feared, social disorder, political disaster, and, most important, women's loss of position as society's moral arbiter and enforcer.[1]

The debates over female suffrage occurred while the very functions of government were changing. In the late nineteenth and early twentieth centuries, federal, state, and municipal governments increased their roles in social welfare and economic life. With a commitment to activism not seen since the first decades of the nineteenth century, Progressive-era policy makers sought ways to regulate and rationalize business and industry. They labored to improve schools, hospitals, and other public services. These efforts, halting and incomplete as they were, brought a tradition of women's involvement in government to public atten-

tion.[2] Indeed, from the time of the Revolution, women used, and sometimes pioneered, methods for influencing government from outside electoral channels. They participated in crowd actions in colonial America and filed quasi-governmental positions in the nineteenth century; they circulated and presented petitions, founded reform organizations, and lobbied legislatures. Aiming their efforts at matters connected with the well-being of women, children, the home, and the community, women fashioned significant public roles by working from the private sphere.[3]

The themes of the debates—the ideology of domesticity, the suffrage fight, the re-emergence of governmental activism, and the public involvement of nineteenth-century women—are familiar. But what are the connections among them? Historians have told us much about the lives of nineteenth-century women. They have explained how women gained political skills, a sense of consciousness as women, and feelings of competence and self-worth through their involvement in women's organizations. But as important as

---

[1] Accounts of the suffrage campaign include William H. Chafe, *Women and Equality* (New York, 1977); Carl N. Degler, *At Odds: Women and the Family in America from the Revolution to the Present* (New York, 1980), chap. 14; Ellen Carol DuBois, *Feminism and Suffrage: The Emergence of an Independent Women's Movement in America, 1848–1869* (Ithaca, N.Y., 1978); Eleanor Flexner, *Century of Struggle: The Woman's Rights Movement in the United States* (Cambridge, Mass., 1958); Alan P. Grimes, *The Puritan Ethic and Woman Suffrage* (New York, 1967); Aileen S. Kraditor, *The Ideas of the Woman Suffrage Movement, 1890–1920* (New York, 1965); David Morgan, *Suffragists and Democrats in America* (East Lansing, Mich., 1970); William L. O'Neill, *Everyone Was Brave: A History of American Feminism* (Chicago, 1969); Ross Evan Paulson, *Woman's Suffrage and Prohibition* (Glenview, Ill., 1973); and Anne F. Scott and Andrew M. Scott, *One-Half of the People: The Fight for Woman's Suffrage* (Philadelphia, 1975). Important treatments of the ideology of domesticity include Nancy F. Cott, *The Bonds of Womanhood: Woman's Sphere in New England, 1790–1835* (New Haven, 1975); Daniel Scott Smith, "Family Limitation, Sexual Control, and Domestic Feminism in Victorian America," in Mary Hartman and Lois W. Banner, eds., *Clio's Consciousness Raised* (New York, 1974), 119–33; Kathryn Kish Sklar, *Catherine Beecher: A Study in American Domesticity* (New Haven, 1973); and Barbara Welter, "The Cult of True Womanhood, 1820–1860," *American Quarterly*, 18 (1966): 151–74.

[2] Syntheses of the vast number of works on Progressive reform include John W. Chambers II, *The Tyranny of Change: America in the Progressive Era, 1900–1917* (New York, 1980); Otis L. Graham, *The Great Campaign: Reform and War in America, 1900–1928* (Englewood Cliffs, N.J., 1971); Arthur S. Link and Richard L. McCormick, *Progressivism* (Arlington Heights, Ill., 1983); Samuel P. Hays, *The Response to Industrialism, 1885–1914* (Chicago, 1957); William L. O'Neill, *The Progressive Years: America Comes of Age* (New York, 1975); and Robert Wiebe, *The Search for Order, 1877–1920* (New York, 1967). For a good recent review essay, see Daniel T. Rodgers, "In Search of Progressivism," *Reviews in American History*, 10 (1982): 113–32.
[3] Numerous works have appeared over the past decade that deal with the public activities of middle-class women. These works most often examine particular groups and attempt to trace the development of a feminist consciousness in the nineteenth century. See, for example, Barbara Berg, *The Remembered Gate— Origins of American Feminism: Women and the City, 1800–1860* (New York, 1978); Karen Blair, *The Clubwoman as Feminist: True Womanhood Redefined, 1868–1914* (New York, 1980); Ruth Bordin, *Woman and Temperance: The Quest for Power and Liberty, 1873–1900* (Philadelphia, 1981); Mari Jo Buhle, *Women and American Socialism, 1870–1920* (Urbana, Ill., 1981); Cott, *The Bonds of Womanhood*; Barbara Leslie Epstein, *The Politics of Domesticity: Women, Evangelism, and Temperance in Nineteenth-Century America* (Middletown, Conn., 1981); Estelle B. Freedman, "Separatism as Strategy: Female Institution-Building and American Feminism, 1870–1930," *Feminist Studies*, 5 (1979): 512–29; Linda K. Kerber, *Women of the Republic: Intellect and Ideology in Revolutionary America* (Chapel Hill, N.C., 1980); William Leach, *True Love and Perfect Union: The Feminist Reform of Sex and Society* (New York, 1980); Gerda Lerner, "The Lady and the Mill Girl: Changes in the Status of Women in the

these activities were, women were also shaped by—and in turn affected—American government and politics. Attention to the interaction between women's political activities and the political system itself can tell us much about the position of women in the nineteenth century. In addition, it can provide a new understanding of the political society in which women worked—and which they helped change.[4]

In order to bring together the histories of women and of politics, we need a more inclusive definition of politics than is usually offered. "Politics" is used here in relatively broad sense to include any action, formal or informal, taken to affect the course or behavior of government or the community.[5] Throughout the nineteenth century, gender was an important division in American

politics. Men and women operated, for the most part, in distinct political subcultures, each with its own bases of power, modes of participation, and goals. In providing an intellectual and cultural interpretation of women and politics, this essay focuses on the experiences of middle-class women. There is much more we need to learn about the political involvement of women of all classes in the years prior to suffrage; this essay must, therefore, be speculative. Its purpose is to suggest a framework for analyzing women and politics and to outline the shape that a narrative history of the subject could take.

The basis and rationale for women's political involvement already existed by the time of the Revolution.[6] For both men and women in colonial America, geographically bounded communities provided the fundamental structures of social organization. The most important social ties, economic relationships, and political concerns of individuals were contained within spatially limited areas. Distinctions between the family and community were often vague; in many ways, the home and the community were one.[7] There were, to be sure, marked variations from place to place; community ties were weaker, for example, in colonial cities and in communities and regions with extensive commercial

---

Age of Jackson," 15–30, "Community Work of Black Club Women," 83–93, "Political Activities of Anti-Slavery Women," 94–111; and "Black and White Women in Confrontation and Interaction," 112–28, in her *The Majority Finds Its Past: Placing Women in History* (New York, 1979); J. Stanley Lemons, *The Woman Citizen: Social Feminism in the 1920s* (Urbana, Ill., 1973); Keith E. Melder, *Beginnings of Sisterhood: The American Woman's Rights Movement, 1800–1850* (New York, 1977); Mary Beth Norton, *Liberty's Daughters: The Revolutionary Experience of American Women, 1750–1800* (Boston, 1980); Mary P. Ryan, *Cradle of the Middle Class: The Family in Oneida County, New York, 1790–1865* (Cambridge, Mass., 1981); and Anne Firor Scott, *The Southern Lady: From Pedestal to Politics, 1830–1930* (Chicago, 1970). A number of contemporary accounts are especially useful. See Mary R. Beard, *Women's Work in Municipalities* (New York, 1915); Jane Cunningham Croly, *The History of the Women's Club Movement in America* (New York, 1898); Mary A. Livermore, *My Story of the War* (Hartford, Conn., 1896), and "Women and the State," in William Meyers, ed., *Women's Work in America* (Hartford, Conn., 1889); and Frances E. Willard, *Woman and Temperance: Or, the Work and Workers of the Women's Christian Temperance Union* (Hartford, Conn., 1883).

[4] A number of studies examine the treatment of women in American political thought. These include Zillah Eisenstein, *The Radical Future of Liberal Feminism* (New York, 1981); Jean Bethke Elshtain, *Public Man, Private Woman: Women in Social and Political Thought* (Princeton, N.J., 1981); Kerber, *Women of the Republic*; and Susan Moller Okin, *Women in Western Political Thought* (Princeton, N.J., 1979). Historical treatments of women in politics include William H. Chafe, *The American Woman: Her Changing Social, Economic, and Political Roles, 1920–1970* (New York, 1972), 24–47; and Jane Gruenebaum, "Women in Politics" in Richard M. Pious, ed., *The Power to Govern: Assessing Reform in the United States*, Proceedings of the Academy of Political Science, no. 34 (New York, 1981), 104–20; Gerda Lerner, ed., *The Female Experience: An American Documentary* (Indianapolis, 1977), 317–22; and Sheila M. Rothman, *Woman's Proper Place: A History of Changing Ideals and Practices, 1870 to the Present* (New York, 1978), 102–32, 136–53.

[5] "Government" refers to the formal institutions of the state and their functions. "Policy" includes efforts by those within these

institutions as well as by those outside them to shape social or economic conditions with the support of "government."

[6] Cott, *The Bonds of Womanhood*; Kerber, *Women of the Republic*; Norton, *Liberty's Daughters*; and Ryan, *Cradle of the Middle Class*. Also see Linda Grant DePauw, *Founding Mothers: Women in the Revolutionary Era* (New York, 1975); and Joan Hoff-Wilson, "The Illusion of Change: Women and the American Revolution," in Alfred H. Young, ed., *The American Revolution: Explorations in the History of American Radicalism* (DeKalb, Ill., 1976), 383–444. Of these works, only Kerber's and Norton's explicitly set out to answer questions about women and politics, and their analyses differ on important points. On the basis of an examination of women's diaries and other papers, Norton argued that the Revolution and republicanism significantly changed the role of women. Family relationships, for example, grew more egalitarian, and women developed a new appreciation of their competence and skills outside the home. Kerber's analysis of American political thought in relationship to women, however, suggests that neither republicanism nor the Revolution had a positive effect on the role of women. Rather, republican thought assumed women were apolitical. But by the early nineteenth century an ideology of motherhood allowed women to combine domesticity with political action.

[7] Thomas Bender, *Community and Social Change in America* (New Brunswick, N.J., 1978), 68; Paul Boyer and Stephen Nissenbaum, *Salem Possessed: The Social Origins of Witchcraft* (Cambridge, Mass., 1971), 151; Richard L. Bushman, *From Puritan to Yankee: Character and the Social Order in Con-*

and market connections, such as parts of the South.[8] Still, clear separations existed between men and women in their work and standards of behavior, and most women probably saw their part in the life of the community as the less important. A little-changing round of household tasks dominated women's lives and created a routine that they found stifling. Women had limited opportunities for social contact, and those they had were almost exclusively with other women. They turned work into social occasions, and they passed the milestones of their lives in the supportive company of female friends and relatives. But, however confining, separation provided a basis for a female culture— though not yet for female politics.[9]

Differences between men's and women's political behavior were muted in the colonial period, compared with what they later became. In many places, men who did not own land could not vote because governments placed property restrictions on suffrage. Both men and women petitioned legislatures to gain specific privileges or legal changes. Citizens held deferential attitudes toward authority; elections were often community rituals embodying codes of social deference. A community's "best" men stood for election and were returned to office year after year, and voters expected candidates to "treat" potential supporters by providing food and drink before and on election day. Deferential politics, however, weakened by the middle of the eighteenth century. Economic hardship caused some men to question the reality of a harmony of interests among classes, and the Great Awakening taught others to question traditional authorities. Facing a growing scarcity

of land, fathers could no longer promise to provide for their sons, which weakened parental control. This new willingness to question authority of all sorts was a precondition for the Revolution and was, in turn, given expression by republican thought.[10]

Republicanism stressed the dangers posed to liberty by power and extolled the advantages of mixed and balanced constitutions. In a successful republic, an independent, virtuous, watchful, and dispassionate citizenry guarded against the weakness and corruption that threatened liberty. Although interpreted by Americans in different ways, republicanism provided a framework and a rationale for the Revolution. It furnished prescriptions for citizenship and for the relationship between citizens and the state. And it helped unify a collection of local communities racked by internal divisions and pressures.[11]

While the ideology and process of the Revolution forced a rethinking of fundamental political concepts, this re-evaluation did not extend to the role of women. As Linda K. Kerber persuasively argued, writers and thinkers in the republican tradition were concerned more with criticizing a particular political administration than with examining traditional assumptions about the political role of all inhabitants. Given their narrow intentions, they were not obliged to reconsider the position of women in the state. The language of republicanism also tended to make less likely the inclusion of women. Good republicans were, after all, self-reliant, given to simple needs and tastes, decisive, and com-

---

necticut, 1690–1765 (New York, 1970), chaps. 1, 2; John Demos, *A Little Commonwealth: Family Life in Plymouth Colony* (New York, 1970), 182–85, chap. 4; James Henretta, *The Evolution of American society, 1700–1815: An Interdisciplinary Analysis* (Lexington, Mass., 1973), 23–31; Ryan, *Cradle of the Middle Class*, chap. 1; and Michael Zuckerman, *Peaceable Kingdoms: New England Towns in the Eighteenth Century* (New York, 1970).

[8] Bender, *Community and Social Change*, 62–67; Michael Kammen, *Colonial New York* (New York, 1975), 290; Paul G. E. Clemens, *The Atlantic Economy and Colonial Maryland's Eastern Shore: From Tobacco to Grain* (Ithaca, N.Y., 1980); James T. Lemon, *The Best Poor Man's Country: A Geographical Study of Early Southeastern Pennsylvania* (Baltimore, 1972); Edmund S. Morgan, *American Slavery, American Freedom: The Ordeal of Colonial Virginia* (New York, 1975), 149–79; Darrett B. Rutman, *Winthrop's Boston* (Chapel Hill, N.C., 1965); and Sam Bass Warner, Jr., *The Private City: Philadelphia in Three Periods of Its Growth* (Philadelphia, 1968), chap. 1.

[9] Kerber, *Women of the Republic*, chap. 1; and Norton, *Liberty's Daughters*, chaps. 1–3.

[10] Among the many works on colonial political practices, see, for example, Charles S. Sydnor, *Gentlemen Freeholders: Political Practices in Washington's Virginia* (Chapel Hill, N.C., 1952); and Robert Zemsky, *Merchants, Farmers, and River Gods: An Essay on Eighteenth-Century Politics* (Boston, 1971). On changing attitudes toward authority, see Bushman, *Puritan to Yankee*, 138–63, 264–87; Jay Fliegelman, *Prodigals and Pilgrims: The American Revolution against Patriarchal Authority, 1750–1800* (Cambridge, Mass., 1982); Philip J. Greven, Jr., *Four Generations: Population, Land, and Family in Colonial Andover, Massachusetts* (Ithaca, N.Y., 1970), chaps. 7, 8; Robert A. Gross, *The Minutemen and Their World* (New York, 1976); and Gary B. Nash, *The Urban Crucible: Social Change, Political Consciousness, and the Origins of the American Revolution* (Cambridge, Mass., 1979).

[11] Reviews of the literature on republicanism include Robert E. Shalhope, "Toward a Republican Synthesis: The Emergence of an Understanding of Republicanism in American Historiography," *William and Mary Quarterly*, 3d ser., 29 (1972): 49–80, and "Republicanism and Early American Historiography," *ibid.*, 39 (1982): 334–56. The articles in Young's *The American Revolution* illustrate divisions in the republican consensus.

mitted first to the public interest. These were all "masculine" qualities; indeed, "feminine" attributes—attraction to luxury, self-indulgence, timidity, dependence, passion—were linked to corruption and posed a threat to republicanism. Moreover, women did not usually own land—the basis for an independent citizenry and republican government.[12]

Despite their formal prepolitical status, women participated in the Revolution. They were central to the success of boycotts of imported products and, later, to the production of household manufactures. Their work on farms and in businesses in their husbands' absences was a vital and obvious contribution. Women's participation also took less conventional forms. Edward Countryman recounted instances in which groups of women, angered at what they saw as wartime price-gouging, forced storekeepers to charge just prices. During and after the war, women also took part in urban crowd actions, organized petition campaigns, and formed groups to help soldiers and widows. Some even met with legislatures to press for individual demands.[13] Whatever their purposes, all of these activities were congruent with women's identification with the home, family, and community. In boycotts of foreign products and in domestic manufacture during the Revolution, women only expanded traditional activities. In operating farms and businesses, they stepped out of their sphere temporarily for the well-being of their families. Because separations between the home and community were ill defined in early America, women's participation in crowd actions can also be seen as a defense of the home. As Countryman and others pointed out, a communalist philosophy motivated the crowd actions of both men and women. Crowds aimed to redress the grievances of the whole community. Women and men acted not as individuals but as members of a community—and with the community's consent.[14]

Women's political participation took place in the context of the home, but the important point is that the home was a basis for political action. As Kerber and Mary Beth Norton have shown, the political involvement of women through the private sphere took new forms by the beginning of the nineteenth century. Women combined political activity, domesticity, and republican thought through motherhood. Although outside of formal politics, mothering was crucial: by raising civic-minded, virtuous sons, they insured the survival of the republic. On the basis of this important task, women argued for wider access to education and justified interest and involvement in public affairs. As mothers women were republicans; they possessed civic virtue and a concern for the public good. Their exclusion from traditionally defined politics and economics guaranteed their lack of interest in personal gain. Through motherhood, women attempted to compensate for their exclusion from the formal political world by translating moral authority into political influence. Their political demands, couched in these terms, did not violate the canons of domesticity to which many men and women held.[15]

During the nineteenth century, women expanded their ascribed sphere into community service and care of

---

[12] Kerber, *Women of the Republic*, chap. 2.

[13] Edward Countryman, *A People in Revolution: The American Revolution and Political Society in New York, 1760–1790* (Baltimore, 1981), 43–44; Kerber, *Women of the Republic*, chaps. 2–3; Nash, *The Urban Crucible*, chap 7; Norton, *Liberty's Daughters*, chaps. 6–7; and Julia Cherry Spruill, *Women's Life and Work in the Southern Colonies* (Chapel Hill, N.C., 1938; reprint edn., New York, 1972), 232–45.

[14] Countryman, *A People in Revolution*; Eric Foner, *Tom Paine and Revolutionary America* (New York, 1976), chaps. 2, 5; Pauline Maier, "Popular Uprisings and Civil Authority in Eighteenth-Century America," *William and Mary Quarterly*, 3d ser., 27 (1970): 3–35; E. P. Thompson, "The Moral Economy of the English Crowd in the Eighteen Century," *Part & Present*, 50 (1971): 76–136; and Warner, *The Private City*, pt. 1.

[15] Kerber, *Women of the Republic*, chaps, 7, 9; and Norton, *Liberty's Daughters*, chap. 9. Some works suggest that republicanism was not a cause of more egalitarian family relationships, of new education for women to enhance their roles as better wives and mothers, or of women's use of the home to gain political influence. Jay Fliegelman, for example, persuasively argued that by the middle of the eighteenth century the older notion of the patriarchal family was under attack. It was being replaced by a new ideal—one drawn from Locke and the Scottish common-sense philosophers. Examining these writings and popular novels, he showed that the new model, which called for affectionate and egalitarian relationships with children and humane child rearing designed to prepare children for rational independence and self-sufficiency, was in place well before 1776. In fact, the rhetoric of the Revolution was replete with images portraying the importance of personal autonomy and of parental respect for the individuality of children who had come of age. Thus, a cultural revolution against patriarchal authority preceded the Revolution. (Fliegelman's analysis, however, chiefly concerns sons, not daughters, and it deals with questions not directly related to relationships between men and women.) Furthermore, the "republican mother" was not an ideal limited to America. Traian Stoianovitch showed that an ideology of domesticity similar in content to republican motherhood had appeared in a systemized form in France by the late seventeenth century. See Fliegelman, *Prodigals and Pilgrims*; and Stoianovitch, "Gender and Family: Myths, Models, and Ideologies," *History Teacher*, 15 (1981): 70–84.

dependents, areas not fully within men's or women's politics. These tasks combined public roles and administration with nurturance and compassion. They were not fully part of either male electoral politics and formal governmental institutions or the female world of the home and family. Women made their most visible public contributions as founders, workers, and volunteers in social service organizations.[16] Together with the social separation of the sexes and women's informal methods of influencing politics, political domesticity provided the basis for a distinct nineteenth-century women's political culture.

Although the tradition, tactics, and ideology for the political involvement of women existed by the first decades of the nineteenth century, a separate political culture had not yet taken shape. Women's style of participation and their relationship to authority were not yet greatly different from those of many men. Until the 1820s—and in some states even later—property restrictions on suffrage disfranchised many men. Even for those granted the ballot, political interest and electoral turnout usually remained low.[17] During the early years of the republic, deferential political behavior was again commonplace. Retreating from the demands of the Revolutionary period, most citizens once again seemed content to accept the political decisions made by the community's most distinguished men. This pattern persisted until new divisions split communities and competing elites vied for voters' support.[18]

Changes in the form of male political participation were part of a larger transformation of social, economic, and political relationships in the early nineteenth century. The rise of parties and the re-emergence of citizen interest in politics had a variety of specific sources. In some places, ethnic and religious tensions contributed to a new interest in politics and shaped partisan loyalties. Recently formed evangelical Protestant groups hoped to use government to impose their convictions about proper moral behavior on the community, a goal opposed by older Protestant groups and Catholics. Other kinds of issues—especially questions about the direction of the American political economy—led to political divisions. Citizens were deeply divided about the direction the economy ought to take and the roles government ought to play. They thought attempts to tie localities to new networks and markets in commerce and agriculture could lead to greater prosperity, but such endeavors also meant that economic decisions were no longer made locally and that both the social order and the values of republicanism could be in danger. Local party leaders linked these debates to national parties and leaders,[19] and the rise of working men's parties in urban areas seemed to spring from a

---

[16] For the idea that women's political activity through organizations filled an undefined space in American government and politics, see Suzanne Lebsock, *The Free Women of Petersburg: Status and Culture in a Southern Town, 1784–1860* (New York, 1984), chap. 7.

[17] On electoral participation in the early nineteenth century, see Ronald P. Formisano, "Deferential-Participant Politics: The Early Republic's Political Culture," *American Political Science Review* [hereafter, *APSR*], 68 (1974): 473–87; and Paul Kleppner, *Who Voted? The Dynamics of Electoral Turnout, 1870–1980* (New York, 1982), chap. 3: "The Era of Citizen Mobilization, 1840–1900." For a discussion of the increasing rates of participation, their timing, and their causes, see Richard P. McCormick, "New Perspectives on Jacksonian Politics," *AHR*, 65 (1959–60): 288–301.

[18] The rise and decline—indeed, the existence—of deference in male political behavior remains widely debated by political historians. Ronald P. Formisano has provided a good review of this literature in "Deferential-Participant Politics." A number of studies of individual communities illustrate the appearance of competing elites and new community divisions and citizens' demands. See Bender, *Community and Social Change*, 100–08; Michael Frisch, *Town into City: Springfield, Massachusetts, and the Meaning of*

Community, 1840–1880 (Cambridge, Mass., 1972), 32–53, 179–201; and Harry L. Watson, *Jacksonian Politics and Community Conflict: The Emergence of the Second Party System in Cumberland County, North Carolina* (Baton Rouge, La., 1981), 82–108.

[19] I have drawn my discussion of the connections between economic issues and party formation from Watson's *Jacksonian Politics and Community Conflict*, which imaginatively blends many of the themes and approaches historians have most recently advanced to explain nineteenth-century political life. Watson combined a refurbished economic interpretation, the assumption that citizens cared deeply about economic issues, a concern for questions about political culture, attention to republican ideology and quantitative methods, and a social analysis of politics in his account of party formation. Although such assumptions, methods, and concerns will probably continue to influence political historians, a good deal of debate remains about the development of parties and the meaning of partisanship. Richard P. McCormick argued that the legal framework governing elections (as well as the revival of the contest for the presidency) best explains the rising pitch of partisan behavior and that parties were fundamentally electoral machines, unconcerned with issues. See McCormick, *The Second American Party System*. Others, however, have found that ethnic and religious tensions among citizens can account for partisan divisions. See Lee Benson, *The Concept of Jacksonian Democracy: New York as a Test Case* (Princeton, N.J., 1961); Ronald P. Formisano, *The Birth of Mass Political Parties: Michigan, 1827–1861* (Princeton, N.J., 1971); Paul Kleppner, *The Cross of Culture: A Social Analysis of Midwestern Politics, 1850–1900* (New York, 1970); and Michael F. Holt,

similar set of questions and sense of unease about nineteenth-century capitalism.[20]

Whatever their origin, parties also served other less explicitly "political" purposes. The strength of antebellum parties lay in their ability to fuse communal and national loyalties. The major parties were national organizations, but they were locally based: local people organized rallies, printed ballots, worked to gain the votes of their friends and neighbors. Through political activities in towns and cities, parties gained the support of men and translated their feelings into national allegiances.[21] Political organization provided a set pattern of responses to divisive questions, which raised problems to the national level and served to defuse potential community divisions. Indeed, by linking local concerns to national institutions and leaders, parties took national political questions out of the local context.[22] The local base of the Democrats and Whigs allowed them to take contradictory positions on issues in different places. Major party leaders searched for issues that enabled them to distinguish their own party from the opposition, while keeping their fragile constituencies intact. At the same time, local politics returned in most places to a search for consensual, nonpartisan solutions to community questions.[23]

The rise of a national two-party system in the 1820s and 1830s inaugurated a period of party government and strong partisan loyalties among voters that lasted until after the turn of the twentieth century. Parties, through the national and state governments, distributed resources to individuals and corporations, and patronage to loyal partisans. Throughout most of the nineteenth century, roughly three-quarters of the eligible electorate cast their ballots in presidential elections. The organization and identity of the parties changed, but the pre-eminence of partisanship and government-by-party remained. Party identification and the idea of partisanship passed from fathers to sons.[24]

Partisan politics characterized male political involvement, and its social elements help explain voters' enthusiastic participation. Parties and electoral politics united all white men, regardless of class or other differences, and provided entertainment, a definition of manhood, and the basis for a male ritual. Universal white manhood suffrage implied that, since all men shared the chance to participate in electoral politics, they possessed political equality. The right to vote was something important that men held in common. And, as

---

Forging a Majority: The Formation of the Republic Party in Pittsburgh, 1848–1860 (New Haven, Conn., 1969). For recent historiographic analyses of Jacksonian politics, see Ronald P. Formisano, "Toward a Reorientation of Jacksonian Politics: A Review of the Literature, 1959–1975," *Journal of American History* [hereafter, *JAH*], 63 (1976–77); 42–65; and Sean Wilentz, "On Class and Politics in Jacksonian America," *Reviews in American History*, 10 (1982): 45–63. Richard L. McCormick evaluated the work of those offering an ethnic and religious interpretation. See McCormick, "Ethno-Cultural Interpretations of Nineteenth-Century American Voting Behavior," *Political Science Quarterly*, 89 (1974): 351–77.

[20] Discussion of working men's parties include Bruce Laurie, *Working People of Philadelphia, 1800–1850* (Philadelphia, 1980); and Edward Pessen, *Most Uncommon Jacksonians: The Political Leaders of the Early Labor Movement* (Albany, N.Y., 1967), 11–33. The Antimasonic party, strongest in rural areas, offered a moral critique of American politics and society; see Benson, *The Concept of Jacksonian Democracy*, 14–38. Ronald P. Formisano provided an analysis of both parties; see *The Transformation of Political Culture: Massachusetts Parties, 1790s–1840s* (New York, 1983), 197–224.

[21] See Jean H. Baker, *Affairs of Party: The Political Culture of Northern Democrats in the Mid-Nineteenth Century* (Ithaca, N.Y., 1983), chaps. 1, 2; Benson, *The Concept of Jacksonian Democracy*; Formisano, *The Birth of Mass Political Parties*, chaps. 2, 7; and Watson, *Jacksonian Politics and Community Conflict*, 151–86, 269–77, 297–99, 312–13.

[22] For a discussion of the removal of national issues from local politics, see Bender, *Community and Social Change*, 104.

[23] On the positions on issues taken by various parties, see McCormick, *Second American Party System*; and Michael F. Holt, *The Political Crisis of the 1850s* (New York, 1978). Richard P. McCormick's view that parties were primarily electoral machines conflicts with that of Holt, who argued that parties needed clear divisions between them to maintain the voters' interest. For consensual politics at the local level, especially in settled towns, see Hal S. Barron, "After the Great Transformation: The Social Processes of Settled Rural Life in the Nineteenth-Century North," in Steven Hahn and Jonathan Prude, eds., *Rural Societies in Nineteenth-Century America: Essays in Social History* (Chapel Hill, N.C., forthcoming); Bender, *Community and Social Change*, 104–05; and Stuart Blumin, *The Urban Threshold: Growth and Change in a Nineteenth-Century Community* (Chicago, 1976), 144, 148.

[24] For discussions of nineteenth-century voting patterns, see Walter Dean Burnham, "The Changing Shape of the American Political Universe," *APSR*, 59 (1965): 7–28; Paul Kleppner, *Who Voted*, chap. 3; and Richard L. McCormick, "The Party Period and Public Policy: An Exploratory Hypothesis," *JAH*, 66 (1979–80); 279–98. Although they agree on a description of political behavior in the nineteenth century, these accounts differ on periodization, focus, and explanations for the demise of nineteenth-century patterns. I have adopted McCormick's emphases on the continuities of partisan behavior throughout most of the nineteenth century and the links between distribution and partisanship. For the best account of the connections between partisanship and family, see Baker, *Affairs of Party*, chap. 1.

class, geography, kinship, and community supplied less reliable sources of identification than they had at an earlier time, men could at least define themselves in reference to women. Parties were fraternal organizations that tied men together with others like themselves in their communities, and they brought men together as participants in the same partisan culture.[25]

Election campaigns celebrated old symbols of the republic and, indeed, manhood. Beginning as early as William Henry Harrison's log cabin campaign in 1840, parties conducted entertaining extravaganzas. Employing symbols that recalled glorious old causes (first, the Jacksonian period and, later, the Civil War), men advertised their partisanship. They took part in rallies, joined local organizations, placed wagers on election results, read partisan newspapers, and wore campaign paraphernalia. In large and small cities military-style marching companies paraded in support of their party's candidates, while in rural areas picnics and pole raisings served to express and foster partisan enthusiasm.[26]

Party leaders commonly used imagery drawn from the experience of war: parties were competing armies, elections were battles, and party workers were soldiers. They commented approvingly on candidates who waged manly campaigns, and they disparaged nonpartisan reformers as effeminate.[27] This language and the campaigns themselves gathered new intensity in the decades following the Civil War. The men who marched in torchlight parades recalled memories of the war and demonstrated loyalty to the nation and to their party. Women participated, too, by illuminating their windows and cheering on the men; sometimes the women marched alongside the men, dressed as patriotic figures like Miss Liberty.[28] The masculine character of electoral politics was reinforced on election day. Campaigns culminated in elections held in saloons, barber shops, and other places largely associated with men. Parties and electoral politics, in short, served private, sociable purposes.

Just as the practice and meaning of electoral politics changed in the early nineteenth century, so did the function of government. State and local governments gradually relinquished to the marketplace the tasks of regulating economic activity, setting fair prices, and determining product standards. State governments limited the practice of granting corporate charters on an individual basis and, instead, wrote uniform procedures that applied to all applicants. These governments also reduced, and finally halted, public control of businesses and private ventures in which state money had been invested. A spate of state constitutional revisions under-

[25] Daniel Calhoun suggested that fears about gender replaced fears about tyranny in the political thought of the nineteenth century; Calhoun, *The Intelligence of a People* (Princeton, N.J., 1973), 188–205. For a discussion of partisan politics as a way of re-creating fraternal relations, see Wilson Carey McWilliams, *The Idea of Fraternity in America* (Berkeley and Los Angeles, 1973), chap. 3, 243–53. For an account from the Progressive era, see Mary Kingsbury Simkhovitch, "Friendship and Politics," *Political Science Quarterly*, 17 (1902): 189–205.

[26] Descriptions and analyses of campaign rituals include Robert Gray Gunderson, *The Log Cabin Campaign* (Lexington, Ky., 1957), 1–11, 108–47, 210–18; Richard Jensen, *The Winning of the Midwest: Social and Political Conflict, 1888–1896* (Chicago, 1971), 1–33, and "Armies, Admen, and Crusaders: Types of Presidential Election Campaigns," *History Teacher*, 2 (1969): 33–50; Michael E. McGerr, "Political Spectacle and Partisanship in New Haven, 1860–1900," paper presented at the Seventy-Fifth Annual Meeting of the Organization of American Historians, held in Philadelphia, April 1982; and McCormick, *The Second American Party System*, 15–16, 30–31, 75–76, 88, 145, 157–58, 268–76. Lewis O. Saum, drawing on a vast number of diaries, documented citizens' participation in campaigns and their laconic reactions to antebellum politics; Saum, *The Popular Mood of Pre-Civil War America* (Westport, Conn., 1980), 149–57.

[27] Party politicians often spoke of reformers—those men outside of the party—in terms that questioned the reformers' masculinity. Most of all, reformers were seen as politically impotent. Men whose loyalty to a party was questionable were referred to, for example, as the "third sex" of American politics, "man-milliners," and "Miss-Nancys." This suggests that men, like women, were limited in the forms that their political participation could take. Works that note these charges of effeminacy include Lois W. Banner, *Elizabeth Cady Stanton: A Radical for Women's Rights* (Boston, 1980), 43; Geoffrey Blodgett, "Reform Thought and the Genteel Tradition," in H. Wayne Morgan, ed., *The Gilded Age* (2d edn., Syracuse, N.Y., 1970), 56–57; Richard Hofstadter, *Anti-Intellectualism in American Life* (New York, 1963), 179–91; and Alan Trachtenberg, *The Incorporation of America: Culture and Society in the Gilded Age* (New York, 1982), 163–65. In addition to this language, phallic imagery and symbolism had an important place in nineteenth-century electoral politics. Psychohistorians might find a good deal of underlying meaning in the long ballot (reformers favored the short form) and pole raisings, for example, as well as in partisans' charges of sexual impotence. Political historians, however, have as yet failed to examine the rituals and symbols of partisan contests in regard to their sexual connotations.

[28] Formisano, *Transformations of Political Culture*, 266; McGerr, "Political Spectacle and Partisanship,"; and Saum, *The Popular Mood of Pre-Civil War America*, 153.

a feminine identity, both of which were devalued by the individualism that suffrage implied. Separate spheres allowed women to wield power of a sort. They could feel that their efforts showed some positive result and that public motherhood contributed to the common good. Moreover, men were unwilling to vote for suffrage amendments. The late nineteenth century was the golden age of partisan politics: at no time before or since did parties command the allegiance of a higher percentage of voters or have a greater hand in the operation of government. Indeed, in the extremes of political action of both men and women during the late nineteenth century—torchlight parades and the Woman's Parliament—there were hints of earnest efforts to hold together a social and political system that was slipping from control. At any rate, separate political cultures had nearly reached the end of existence.

Throughout the nineteenth century, the charitable work of women aimed to remedy problems like poverty, disease, and helplessness. But after the Civil War the ideas that informed women's efforts, as well as the scope of their work, markedly changed. New perceptions about the function of the state and a transformed vision of society came out of the experience of the war. It had illustrated the importance of loyalty, duty, centralization, and organization and encouraged a new sense of American nationality. Even as the federal government drew back from its wartime initiatives, many Americans were recognizing the shortcomings of limited government. Amid rapid urbanization and industrialization, the economic system nationalized and reached tighter forms of organization. Social thinkers and political activists discovered limits in the ability of traditional Protestantism, liberalism, or republicanism to explain their world. Some even questioned the idea of moral authority it-self and turned to a positivistic interpretation of Spen-cerian sociology, which stressed the inevitability of historical progress and touted science as the height of human achievement. While the system had its critics, it more commonly was justified by a faith in historical progress.[46]

Women's political culture reflected these changes. The work of Northern women in the Sanitary Commission illustrates some of the directions that their politics took. The commission, a voluntary but quasi-governmental organization founded by male philanthropists, set out to supply Northern troops with supplies and medical care. Volunteers, they argued, were too often distracted by the suffering of individuals, and community-based relief got in the way. Unsentimental and scientific, the members of the commission felt they best understood the larger purpose and the proper way to deal with the magnitude of the casualties. Women served as nurses in the commission, as they did in army hospitals and voluntary community relief operations. They moved women's traditional roles of support, healing, and nurturance into the public sphere. At the same time, their experiences taught them the limits of sentiment and the need for discipline. Women such as Clara Barton, Dorothea Dix, Mary Livermore, and Mother Bickerdyke gained public acclaim for their services. Well-to-do Northern women raised a substantial amount of money for the commission by running "Sanitary Fairs." They collected contributions, sold items donated by men and women, and publicly celebrated the Union's cause.[47]

The commission is an important example of women's participation in politics. The acceptance and expansion of the woman's sphere, professionalization, and the advancement of science over sentiment were repeated in other Gilded Age female organizations. Some middle-class groups saw socialism as the solution to heightened class tensions, and, for a time, such groups formed alliances with working-class and socialist organizations. In Chicago, the Illinois Woman's Alliance cooperated with the Trade and Labor Assembly on efforts to secure legislation of interest to both groups. Yet such alliances grew increasingly rare as socialists were discredited.[48]

[46] George M. Frederickson, *The Inner Civil War: Northern Intellectuals and the Crisis of the Union* (New York, 1965); James Gilbert, *Designing the Industrial State: The Intellectual Pursuit of Collectivism in America, 1880–1940* (Chicago, 1972); Peter Dobkin Hall, *The Organization of American Culture, 1700–1900; Private Institutions, Elites, and the Origins of American Nationality* (New York, 1982), 218–70; Thomas L. Haskell, *The Emergence of Professional Social Science: The American Social Science Association and the Nineteenth-Century Crisis of Author-*

ity (Urbana, Ill., 1977); Keller, *Affairs of State*; Leach, *True Love and Perfect Union*; and Trachtenberg, *The Incorporation of America*.
[47] L. P. Brockett and Mary C. Vaughn, *Women's Work in the Civil War* (Philadelphia, 1967); Ann Douglas, "The War Within: Women Nurses in the Union Army," *Civil War History*, 18 (1972): 197–212; Frederickson *The Inner Civil War*, 98–112, 212–16; Livermore, *My Story of the War*; Rothman, *Woman's Proper Place*, 71–74; and Ryan, *Womanhood in America*, 226–28.
[48] Buhle, *Women and American Socialism*; Ann D. Gordon and Mari Jo Buhle, "Gender Politics and Class Conflict: Chicago in the Gilded Age," paper presented at the Upstate Women's History Conference, held in Binghamton, New York, October 1981.

Organized women found a more permanent method in social science. Especially in its early reformist stage, social science tied science to traditional concerns of women.[49] The methods and language of social science—data collection, detached observation, and an emphasis on prevention—influenced the political work of women. In the South, women in church and reform groups adopted these methods to address what they perceived as the important social dislocations created by the Civil War. Gilded Age "friendly visitors" spent time with the poor, gathering information and providing a presumably uplifting example. They did little more, since alms giving was bad for the poor because it discouraged work, and, by standing in the way of progress, it was also a detriment to the race. Even more "scientific," Progressive-era settlement workers later mocked the friendly visitors' pretensions. They saw the Gilded Age ladies as lacking in compassion and blind to the broader sources of poverty and, hence, the keys to its prevention. Later still, professional social workers, further removed from sentimentality, replaced the settlement workers and their approaches.[50] Yet in the Gilded Age, social science provided women with quasi-professional positions and an evolutionary argument for women's rights. It also contributed a logic for joining forces with formal governmental institutions, because social science taught the importance of cooperation, prevention, and expertise. This faith in the scientific method and in professionalism eventually led to a devaluation of voluntary work and to the relinquish-ment of social policy to experts in governmental bureaucracies.[51]

The temperance movement illustrates another way that women fused domesticity and politics. It engaged more women than any other nineteenth-century cause and shows how women could translate a narrow demand into a political movement with wide concerns. Temperance appealed to women because it addressed a real problem—one that victimized women—and because, as a social problem, it fell within the woman's sphere. The temperance movement developed through a number of stages and gained momentum especially during the Second Great Awakening. Its history as a women's movement, however, began with the temperance crusade during the years following the Civil War. In small cities and towns in the East and Midwest, groups of women staged marches and held vigils outside or conducted prayer meetings inside saloons, which sometimes coerced their owners to close. In some places, they successfully enlisted the aid of local governments. In most towns, however, the saloons reopened after a short period of "dry" enthusiasm.[52]

The Women's Christian Temperance Union was a descendant of the temperance crusade. It, too, relied on Protestant teachings, women's sense of moral outrage, and the belief in women's moral superiority. Throughout its history, the WCTU was involved in working for legislation such as high license fees and local option. But under the leadership of Frances Willard, the organization, while still defining temperance as its major goal, moved far beyond its initial concerns and closer to the Knights of Labor, the Populist party, and the Christian Socialists and away from the tactics and ideology of the temperance crusade. Like these Gilded Age protest movements, the WCTU turned a seemingly narrow demand of group interest

---

[49] Social science was for Franklin Sanborn, a leader of the American Social Science Association, "the feminine gender of Political Economy, . . . very receptive of particulars but little capacity of general and aggregate matters." Sanborn, as quoted in Haskell, *Emergence of Professional Social Science*, 137.

[50] On women and social science, see Gordon and Buhle, "Gender Politics and Class Conflict"; Leach, *True Love and Perfect Union*, 316–22, 324–46; and Rothman, *Woman's Proper Place*, 108–12. Transitions in reform thought and tactics are traced in Paul Boyer, *Urban Masses and Moral Order, 1820–1920* (Cambridge, Mass., 1978); Robert H. Bremner, *From the Depths: The Discovery of Poverty in the United States* (New York, 1956); Fredrickson, *The Inner Civil War*, 98–112, 119–216; Roy Lubove, *The Professional Altruist: The Emergence of Social Work as a Career, 1880–1930* (Cambridge, Mass., 1965), 2–20, 81–82, 84; and David P. Thelen, *The New Citizenship: The Origins of Progressivism in Wisconsin, 1885–1900* (Columbia, Mo., 1972). On the South, see James L. Leloudis II, "School Reform in the New South: The Women's Association for the Betterment of Public School Houses in North Carolina, 1902–1919," *JAH*, 69 (1982–83); 886–909; and Scott, *Southern Lady*, chap. 6.

[51] For an examination of changing attitudes about voluntarism, see Kathleen D. McCarthy, *Noblesse Oblige: Charity and Cultural Philanthropy in Chicago, 1849–1929* (Chicago, 1982), esp. 27–50.

[52] On women's activity in early temperance organizations, see Jed Dannenbaum, "The Origins of Temperance Activism and Militancy among American Women," *Journal of Social History*, 15 (1981–82): 235–52; Epstein, *The Politics of Domesticity*, 93–114; and Eliza Daniel ("Mother") Stewart, *Memories of the Crusade: A Thrilling Account of the Great Uprising of the Women of Ohio in 1873 against the Liquor Crime* (Columbus, Ohio, 1889: reprint edn., 1972).

into a critique of American society.[53] Indeed, the ability of the WCTU to cast the traditional concerns of women in terms of a broad vision and of the public good helps explain its success. But that success was in part the result of its flexible organization. Although centrally directed, the WCTU was locally organized, which allowed the branches to determine their own concerns and projects within the general directives of the leadership. Willard's WCTU inaugurated the "Do Everything" policy, which allowed local organizations to choose projects as they saw fit. The WCTU made temperance the basis of demands for a wide range of reforms. Alcohol abuse, they argued, was a symptom, not a cause, of poverty, crime, and injustices done to women. Therefore, the WCTU organized departments in areas such as labor, health, social purity, peace, education, and, eventually, suffrage. The locals were directly involved in electoral politics: small-town women worked for "dry" candidates, while the Chicago Union supported the Socialist party.[54]

The WCTU's call for the vote for women nearly split the organization. It supported suffrage not for the sake of individual rights but because the ballot could allow women to serve better the causes of temperance, the home, and the public good. American politics and economics in the late nineteenth century contained enough examples of the baneful results of unrestrained self-interest, from political corruption to avaricious corporations. The efforts of women to deal locally with social problems were no longer sufficient in a nation where the sources were extralocal, and created by male, self-interested political and economic behavior. Woman's vote, they argued, would express her higher, selfless nature. The WCTU combined the woman's sphere with suffrage under the rubric of "Home Protection," an argument that implied feminine values belonged within traditionally defined politics. While taking traditional domestic concerns seriously, the WCTU taught women how to expand them into wider social concern and political action. With greater success than any other nineteenth-century women's group, it managed to forge the woman's sphere into a broadly based political movement.

Other groups—notably the second generation of woman suffragists and clubwomen—also attempted to combine the woman's sphere and women's rights. In this effort, woman suffrage remained divisive. As DuBois and Carl Degler have shown, the threat woman suffrage posed to the doctrine of separate spheres helps explain why the struggle was so long and bitterly fought. But an examination of the political context can provide further insights. The antisuffragists' most powerful argument was that suffrage was dangerous because it threatened the existence of separate spheres. If women voted, they would abandon the home and womanly virtues. The differences between the sexes would be obscured: men would lose their manhood and women would begin to act like men. Throughout the nineteenth century, those arguments struck a chord. Participation in electoral politics did define manhood. Women also had a stake in maintaining their sphere and the power it conferred. But by the end of the century profound social, economic, and political changes made that antisuffrage argument—and the separate male and female political cultures—less persuasive to many women—and many men.

The nature of electoral politics changed significantly during the early twentieth century. Gone were not only the torchlight parades but also most of the manifestations of the male political culture that those parades symbolized. Voter turnout began to decline, and men's allegiance to political parties waned. In the broadest sense, these changes can be traced to the effects of rapid urbanization and industrialization.[55] In the nineteenth century, partisan politics was a local experience,

[53] Willard attempted to ally the WCTU with the Prohibitionists and later the Populists. For a time, she also considered supporting the Republican party but found it an unreliable partner. On Willard's relationship and that of the WCTU to the parties and reform movements of the Gilded Age, see Jack S. Blocker, Jr., "The Politics of Reform: Populists, Prohibitionists, and Woman Suffrage, 1891–1892," *Historian*, 34 (1975): 614–32; Ruth Bordin, "Frances Willard and the Practice of Political Influence," paper presented at the Seventy-Sixth Annual Meeting of the Organization of American Historians, held in Cincinnati, Ohio, April 1983; Buhle, *Women and American Socialism*, 60–69, 80–89; Epstein, *The Politics of Domesticity*, 137–47; and Joseph R. Gusfield, *Symbolic Crusade: Status Politics and the American Temperance Movement* (Urbana, Ill., 1963), 88–96.

[54] Bordin, *Women and Temperance*; Buhle, *Women and American Socialism*, 54–60, 70–89; Degler, *At Odds*, 338–39; Gordon and Buhle, "Gender Politics and Class Conflict"; and Epstein, *The [Polit]ics of Domesticity*, chap. 5.

[55] Historians and political scientists have devoted a good deal of attention to changing patterns of electoral politics in the early twentieth century. Still, much controversy remains. For different points of view, see Burnham, "The Changing Shape of the American Political Universe"; Philip E. Converse, "Change in the American Electorate," in Angus Campbell and Converse, eds., *The Human Meaning of Social Change* (New York, 1972), 263–337; J. Morgan Kousser, *The Shaping of Southern Politics: Suffrage Restrictions and the Establishment of the One-Party*

resting on certain sorts of community relationships. In the partisan press and campaigns, politics meant economic policy. Locally, such issues were handled in an individualistic, partisan manner; on the national level, abstract discussions of distant economic questions supplied the basis for a partisan faith.

But by the early twentieth century the communities in which voters' loyalties were formed had changed. Men's most important relationships were no longer contained solely within geographically defined localities but were instead scattered over distances. Their political ties were no longer exclusively with neighbors but also with people having similar economic or other interests. Male political participation began to reflect this shift. Men increasingly replaced or supplemented electoral participation with the sorts of single-issue, interest-group tactics that women had long employed. Moreover, political parties that dealt with problems on an individualistic basis now seemed less useful because economic and political problems demanded more than individualistic solutions.[56] The sum of these changes in nineteenth-century patterns of electoral participation was to lessen the importance of partisan politics for men. In hindsight, at least, woman suffrage presented less of a threat to a male political culture and to manhood.

Even more important, the antisuffragists could no longer argue so forcefully that the vote would take women out of the home. Government had assumed some of the substantive functions of the home by the early twentieth century. Politics and government in the nineteenth century had revolved almost entirely around questions of sectional, racial, and economic policies. To be sure, governments, especially at the state level, spent the largest portion of their budgets on supporting institutions like schools, asylums, and prisons.[57] But election campaigns and partisan political discussions largely excluded mention of these institutions. In the Progressive era, social policy—formerly the province of women's voluntary work—became public policy. Women themselves had much to do with this important transition—a transition that in turn changed their political behavior.

Women continued to exercise their older methods of political influence, but now they directed their efforts through new institutions. Women's clubs—united in 1890 as the General Federation of Women's Clubs— were one important means. Beginning as self-improvement organizations, many clubs soon focused on social and cultural change. These women sought to bring the benefits of motherhood to the public sphere. They set up libraries, trade schools for girls, and university extension courses, and they worked to introduce home economics courses, to improve the physical environment of schools, and to elect women to school boards. They also sponsored legislation to eliminate sweatshops and provide tenement-house fire inspection. Clubwomen interested in sanitary reforms helped enact programs for clean water and better sewage disposal. In many cities, they raised money for parks and playgrounds. Clubs were also important in pressing for a juvenile court system and for federal public health legislation, such as the 1906 Pure Food and Drug Act.[58]

But by the Progressive period, these women recog-

South, 1880–1910 (New Haven, Conn., 1974); and Jerrold G. Rusk, "The Effect of the Australian Ballot on Split-Ticket Voting," *APSR*, 64 (1970): 1220–38. Other important works tie changes in electoral politics to the transformation of governance in the twentieth century. See Hays, *Response to Industrialism*; Paul Kleppner, *The Third Electoral System, 1853–1892: Parties, Voters, and Political Cultures* (Chapel Hill, N.C., 1979), and *Who Voted*, chap. 4; Richard L. McCormick, "The Discovery That Business Corrupts Politics: A Reappraisal of the Origins of Progressivism," *AHR*, 86 (1981): 247–74; and Wiebe, *The Search for Order*. The interpretation offered here blends elements of these approaches along with the findings of studies of late nineteenth-century community life. It owes the most to Samuel P. Hays, "Political Parties and the Community-Society Continuum," in William Nisbet Chambers and Walter Dean Burnham, eds., *The American Party Systems: Stages of Political Development* (2d edn., New York, 1975), 152–81.

[56] On the connection between community change and partisan behavior, see Hays, "Political Parties and the Community-Society Continuum"; Kleppner, *Who Voted*; and Paula Baker, "The Culture of Politics in the Late Nineteenth Century: Community and Political Behavior in Rural New York," *Journal of Social History* (forthcoming). The relationship between partisanship and forms of policy making is analyzed in McCormick, "The Party Period and Public Policy."

[57] Gerald N. Grob, "The Political System and Social Policy in the Nineteenth Century: Legacy of the Revolution," *Mid-America*, 58 (1976): 5–19.

[58] Blair, *Clubwoman as Feminist*; Marlene Stein Wortman, "Domesticating the Nineteenth-Century American City," *Prospects: An Annual of American Cultural Studies*, 3 (1977):531–72; Rothman, *Woman's Proper Place*, 102–26, 112–27; and Margaret Gibbons Wilson, *The American Woman in Transition: The Urban Influence, 1870–1920* (Westport, Conn., 1979), 91–99. Women in the South engaged in similar work through women's clubs and church organizations; see Leloudis, "School Reform in the New South"; John Patrick McDowell, *The Social Gospel in the South: The Women's Home Mission Movement in the Methodist Episcopal Church, South, 1886–1939* (Baton Rouge, La., 1982); and Scott, *Southern Lady*, chap. 6.

nized that their efforts—and even public motherhood—were not enough. The scope of these problems meant that reform had to be concerned with more than the care of women and children. Charity had real limits. Problems were not solvable, or even treatable, at the local level. Despite attempts to uplift them, the poor remained poor, and women began to identify the problem as having broader sources. The municipal housekeepers needed the help of the state: alone, they were powerless to remove the source of the problem, only to face the growing number of its victims. As Mary Beard explained in 1915,

> It is the same development which has characterized all other public works—the growth from remedy to prevention, and the growth is stable for the reason that it represents economy in the former waste of money and effort and because popular education is leading to the demand for prevention and justice rather than charity. In this expansion of municipal functions there can be little dispute as to the importance of women. Their hearts touched in the beginning by human misery and their sentiments aroused, they have been led into manifold activities in attempts at amelioration, which have taught them the breeding places of disease, as well as of vice, crime, poverty, and misery. Having learned that effectively to "swat the fly" they must swat its nest, women have also learned that to swat disease they must swat poor housing, evil labor conditions, ignorance, and vicious interests.[59]

What Beard described was the process by which politics became domesticated. Women's charitable work had hardly made a dent in the social dislocations of industrial society. The problems were unsolvable at the local level because they were not local problems. And, since the goal of these women was to prevent abstract, general problems—to prevent poverty rather than to aid poor people—the methods of antebellum organizations would not suffice. Hence the state—the only institution of sufficient scope—had to intervene. Women therefore turned their efforts toward securing legislation that addressed what they perceived to be the sources of social problems—laws to compensate victims of industrial accidents, to require better education, to provide adequate nutrition, and to establish factory and tenement inspection, for example.[60] Clubwomen pointed proudly to playgrounds that they had founded and later donated to local governments.[61] Thus women passed on to the state the work of social policy that they found increasingly unmanageable.

Historians have not yet explicitly addressed the questions of how and why governments took on these specific tasks. In the broadest sense, the willingness of government to accept these new responsibilities has to do with the transformation of liberalism in the early twentieth century. Liberalism came to be understood not as individualism and laissez faire but as a sense of social responsibility coupled with a more activist, bureaucratic, and "efficient" government. This understanding of government and politics meshed nicely with that of women's groups. Both emphasized social science ideas and methods, organization, and collective responsibility for social conditions. Thus there were grounds for cooperation, and the institutions that women created could easily be given over to government. Yet the character of collective action varied. The business corporation created the model for the new liberalism, while politically active women and some social thinkers took the family and small community as an ideal.[62] But whatever the mechanism, as govern-

Middle-class black women worked through separate organizations in the nineteenth century. See Lynda F. Dickson, "The Early Club Movement among Black Women in Denver, 1890–1925" (Ph.D. dissertation, University of Colorado, 1982); Tullia Hamilton, "The National Association of Colored Women's Clubs" (Ph.D. dissertation, Emory University, 1978); and Gerda Lerner, "Community Work of Black Women's Clubs," and "Black and White Women in Interaction and Confrontation." For clubwomen's descriptions of their work, see Croly, *History of the Women's Club Movement*; Gerda Lerner, ed., *Black Women in White America: A Documentary History* (New York, 1972), chap. 8; and Mary I. Wood, *The History of the General Federation of Women's Clubs for the First Twenty-Two Years of Its Organization* (New York, 1912).

⌐ard, *Women's Work*, 221.

[60] *Ibid.*, chap. 6–7; Wilson, *American Woman in Transition*; Rothman, *Woman's Proper Place*, 119–27; and Wortman, "Domesticating the Nineteenth-Century American City."

[61] Wortman, "Domesticating the Nineteenth-Century American City"; and Leloudis, "School Reform in the New South." For contemporary accounts, see Beard, *Women's Work*, chaps. 9–11; Wood, *History of the General Federation*, 120–209; and Dorr, *What Eighty Million Women Want.*

[62] Among the many works that trace the transition in liberal thought, see Theodore J. Lowi, *The End of Liberalism: The Second Republic of the United States* (2d edn., New York, 1979), chaps. 1–3; R. Jeffrey Lustig, *Corporate Liberalism: The Origins of Modern American Political Theory, 1890–1920* (Berkeley and Los Angeles, 1982); William E. Nelson, *The Roots of American Bureaucracy, 1830–1900* (Cambridge, Mass., 1982); and James Weinstein, *The Corporate Ideal in the Liberal State, 1900–1918* (Boston, 1968). Discussions of the family and the

ments took up social policy—in part because of women's lobbying—they became part of the private domain.

The domestication of politics, then, was in large part women's own handiwork. In turn, it contributed to the end of separate political cultures. First, it helped women gain the vote. Suffrage was no longer either a radical demand or a challenge to separate spheres, because the concerns of politics and of the home were inextricable. At the same time, it did not threaten the existence of a male political culture because that culture's hold had already attenuated. The domestication of politics was connected, too, with the changed ideas of citizens about what government and politics were for. Each of these developments, illustrating ties between transformations in politics and the role of women, merits further attention.

Recovering from a period of apathy and discouragement, the women's suffrage campaign enjoyed renewed energy in the early twentieth century. The second generation of suffragists included home protection in their arguments in favor of votes for women. They noted that the vote would not remove women from the home and that electoral politics involved the home and would benefit from women's talents. Suffragists argued that women's work in World War I proved their claims to good citizenship. They also took pains to point out what the vote would not do. Indeed, the suffragists made every conceivable argument, from equal rights to home protection to the need for an intelligent electorate. Such a wide array of practical claims did not necessarily represent a retreat from the radicalism of Elizabeth Cady Stanton's generation. Suffragists often presented arguments in response to accusations by the opposition. If opponents claimed that woman suffrage would destroy the home, suffragists replied that it would actually enhance family life. The suffragists' arguments, moreover, reflected a transition in political thought generally. Just as Stanton's contemporaries spoke in the language of Garrisonian abolitionism, the later suffragists framed their ideas in the language of science, racism, efficiency, and cooperation. This does not make their nativist or racist rhetoric any less objectionable, but it does mean that second-generation suffragists were working within a different cultural and intellectual environment.[63]

But organization, not argumentation, was the key to winning the vote for the second generation. They discarded a state-by-state strategy and concentrated on winning a national amendment. Under the leadership of Carrie Chapman Catt and others, suffragists patterned their organization after a political machine, mimicking male politics. The suffrage campaign features a hierarchical organization, with workers on the district level who received guidance, funds, and speakers from the state organizations, which in turn were supported by the national organization. They conducted petition campaigns to illustrate the support that suffrage had from women and men. They held parades and pageants to demonstrate that support and gather publicity. To be sure, suffragists pointed to the positive results votes for women could bring. But most of all, they aimed to show that woman suffrage—whatever it meant—was inevitable.[64]

Suffragists considered the suffrage referenda in New York to be pivotal tests. Victory there would provide crucial publicity for the cause and lend credence to the

---

small community as a model are provided in Jean B. Quandt, *From the Small Town to the Great Community: The Social Thought of Progressive Intellectuals* (New Brunswick, N.J., 1970); and Wortman, "Domesticating the Nineteenth-Century American City." Although historians have not yet fully described the mechanism by which government took on work that had been the responsibility of voluntary organizations, a few hypotheses seem safe. Municipal governments were undoubtedly responding to demands for better social services—ones in part created by women's attempts to form public opinion. Turning to existing institutions would have been a logical choice for municipal governments. Office holders may also have seen new opportunities for patronage—opportunities that gained importance as older sources (service contracts arranged with private businesses, for example) fell under attack.

[63] The second generation has been presented as conservative even by those historians who have regarded suffrage as a radical demand. See Degler, *At Odds*, 357–61; and Ellen DuBois, ed., *Elizabeth Cady Stanton and Susan B. Anthony: Correspondence, Writings, Speeches* (New York, 1981), 192–93. The most detailed analyses of the suffrage movement's conservative turn are Kraditor, *Ideas of the Woman Suffrage Movement*; and O'Neill, *Everyone Was Brave*.

[64] DuBois pointed out that the second-generation suffragists' insistence on nonpartisanship is an indication that the vote—rather than what women might do with it—was their major goal; *Elizabeth Cady Stanton and Susan B. Anthony*, 182–83. The suffragists' new campaign tactics owed a large debt to the publicity-gathering techniques of the Congressional Union. For a good account of the course of the suffrage campaign, see Carrie Chapman Catt, *Woman Suffrage and Politics: The Inner Story of the Suffrage Movement* (1923; 2d edn., New York, 1926), 189–91, 212, 284–99, 302–15. Also see Flexner, *Century of Struggle*, 262–65, 271, 285; and Sharon Hartman Strom, "Leadership and Tactics in the American Woman Suffrage Movement: A New Perspective from Massachusetts," *JAH*, 62 (1975–76): 296–315.

notion of inevitability. In 1915 the referendum lost by a fairly wide margin in a fiercely fought campaign; only five scattered upstate counties supported the referendum. Two years later, woman suffrage was back on the ballot. This time, the suffragists concentrated their efforts on district work in major cities. Curiously, the election approached with much less fanfare than that of 1915. The suffragists apparently had won their battle of attrition. The amount and tone of the newspaper coverage suggests that woman suffrage was indeed considered inevitable, and the referendum passed, almost entirely because of the support it received in the cities. The election results point to important patterns. The woman suffrage referendum ran poorly in areas where the prohibition vote was high or where high voter turnout and other manifestations of the nineteenth-century culture of politics were still visible. Here, women's suffrage was still a threat. Conversely, it ran well in cities, especially in certain immigrant wards and places where the Socialist vote was high—where nineteenth-century political patterns had never taken hold or had already disappeared. Men who had no stake in maintaining the old culture of politics seemed more likely to support woman suffrage. In the South, where the right to vote was tied to both manhood and white supremacy, woman suffrage also met stiff resistance.[65]

_____

[65] The counties that supported suffrage in 1915 were Chautauqua, Schenectady, Chemung, Broome, and Tompkins. The lowest support for the referenda in both 1915 and 1917—as low as 30 percent—occurred in the counties of Livingston, Yates, Ulster, Lewis, Albany, and Columbia. Preliminary calculations suggest that in places where women's groups had a long history of public action, where men's organizations (such as agricultural societies) had increasing involvement in interest-group politics, and where the Socialist vote was high voters were more likely to support suffrage. The southern-tier counties, for example, illustrate the first two hypotheses. Schenectady County, like certain wards in New York City, supported Socialist candidates. Rough calculations also suggest that comparatively high levels of turnout and low incidence of split-ticket voting occurred in places where suffrage was unpopular. Nearly half of New York's sixty-two counties supported suffrage in 1917, but the greatest gains were made in New York, Bronx, Kings, Richmond, and Westchester counties. For studies of the New York City campaign, see Doris Daniels, "Building a Winning Coalition: The Suffrage Fight in New York State," *New York History*, 60 (1979): 59–88; and Elinor Lerner, "Immigrant and Working-Class Involvement in the New York City Suffrage Movement, 1905–1917: A Study in Progressive Era Politics" (Ph.D. dissertation, University of California, Berkeley, 1981). Both Daniels and Lerner emphasized the support suffrage derived from immigrant groups—especially Jewish voters—and ist voters. Lerner noted that men who voted for suffrage knew many women who were financially independent.

That woman suffrage had little impact on women or politics has been considered almost axiomatic by historians. It failed to help women achieve equality. It did not result in the disaster antisuffragists imagined. Women did not vote as a reform bloc or, indeed, in any pattern different from men. Woman suffrage simply doubled the electorate. Historians have traced the reasons for the negligible impact of woman suffrage to the conservative turn of the second-generation suffragists, including their single-minded pursuit of the vote and home protection arguments. But to dismiss woman suffrage as having no impact is to miss an important point. It represented the endpoint of nineteenth-century womanhood and woman's political culture. In a sense, the antisuffragists were right. Women left the home, in a symbolic sense; they lost their place above politics and their position as the force of moral order. No longer treated as a political class, women ceased to act as one. At the same time, politics was unsexed. Differences between the political involvement of men and women decreased, and government increasingly took on the burden of social and moral responsibility formerly assigned to the woman's sphere.

The victory of woman suffrage reflected women's gradual movement away from a separate political culture. By the early twentieth century, the growing number of women who worked for wages provided palpable examples of the limits of notions about a woman's place. Certainly by the 1920s, the attachment of women to the home could not be taken for granted in the same way it had in the nineteenth century, in part because by the 1920s the home was something of an embarrassment. Many men and women rejected domesticity as an ideal. The "new woman" of the 1920s discarded nineteenth-century womanhood by adopting formerly male values and behavior.[66] To be sure, most women probably did not meet the standard of the "new woman," but that ideal was the cultural norm against

_____

Neither, however, put the race in the context of long-term political patterns.
[66] Paula S. Fass, *The Damned and the Beautiful: American Youth in the 1920s* (New York, 1977). Ironically, motherhood was ritualized and glorified just as the domestic ideal declined. See Kathleen W. Jones, "Mother's Day: The Creation, Promotion, and Meaning of a New Holiday in the Progressive Era," *Texas Studies in Literature and Language*, 22 (1980): 176–96. For a review of the work on women in the 1920s, see Estelle B. Freedman, "The New Woman: Changing Views of Women in the 1920s," *JAH*, 61 (1974–75): 373–93. Also useful is Freda Kirchwey, *Our Changing Morality: A Symposium* (New York, 1924).

which women now measured their behavior. Women thus abandoned the home as a basis for a separate political culture and as a set of values and way of life that all women shared.

Women rejected the form and substance of nineteenth-century womanhood. Municipal housekeepers and charity workers saw that the responsibility for social policy was not properly theirs: only government had the scope and potentially the power to deal with national problems. Society seemed too threatening and dangerous to leave important responsibilities to chance, and women to whom municipal housekeeping was unknown seemed to sense this. They also surrendered to government functions that had belonged to the woman's sphere. Given the seemingly overwhelming complexities and possibilities for grievous errors, women were willing to take the advice of experts and government aid in feeding their families and rearing and educating their children. Tradition offered little guidance; the advice of their mothers, who grew up during the mid- and late nineteenth century, could well have seemed anachronistic in an urban and industrial society. Their own experiences could lead to wrong decisions in a rapidly changing society. Moreover, abandoning the functions of the old-fashioned woman's sphere allowed a new independence. Women made some gains, but they also lost the basis for a separate political culture.[67]

Lacking a sense of common ground, women fragmented politically. Their rejection of the woman's sphere as an organizing principle discouraged women from acting as a separate political bloc. Without political segregation to unite them, differences among groups of women magnified. What benefited professional women might be superfluous, even damaging, to the interests of working-class women. Women did not vote as a bloc on "women's" issues because there were no such issues, just as there were no issues that reflected the common interests of all men. The commonality that women had derived from the home in the nineteenth century disappeared, leaving women to splinter into interest groups and political parties. Organizing a separate women's party held little appeal for women because they could not find issues on which to unite.[68] Women were also no longer "above" politics. Their political behavior benefited from neither the veneration of the home and the moral power it bestowed nor the aura of public concern that their older informal methods of participation communicated.

It almost goes without saying that women gained little real political power upon winning the vote. Men granted women the vote when the importance of the male culture of politics and the meaning of the vote changed. Electoral politics was no longer a male right or a ritual that dealt with questions that only men understood. Instead, it was a privilege exercised by intelligent citizens. Important positions in government and in the parties still went to men. Woman suffrage was adopted just at the time when the influence of parties and electoral politics on public policy was declining. By the early twentieth century, interest groups and the formation of public opinion were more effective ways to influence government, especially the new bureaucracies that were removed from direct voter accountability.[69]

As differences between political participation of men and women lessened in the early twentieth century, the role of government changed. Government now carried moral authority and the obligations it implied. That governments often chose not to use that authority is not the point. What matters is that citizens wanted more from government, in the way of ethical political

---

[67] On the changed relationship between doctors and mothers, see Kathleen W. Jones, "Sentiment and Science: The Late Nineteenth-Century Pediatrician as Mothers' Advisor," *Journal of Social History*, 17 (1983–84): 79–96. Jones stressed the reciprocal relationship between women and professionals, noting that women initially sought experts' advice and helped shape the profession of pediatrics. For accounts of women as more passive recipients of expert intrusion, see Barbara Ehrenreich and Deidre English, *For her Own Good: One Hundred Fifty Years of the Expert's Advice to Women* (Garden City, N.J., 1979); Christopher Lasch, *Haven in a Heartless World: The Family Besieged* (New York, 1977); and Rothman, *Woman's Proper Place*.

[68] Felice Dosik Gordon, "After Winning: The New Jersey Suffragists, 1910–1947" (Ph.D. dissertation, Rutgers University, 1982). In an important recent article, Estelle B. Freedman has argued that women's separate institutions provided a degree of influence lost when women joined organizations that included both sexes; see "Separatism as Strategy."

[69] On the rise of interest groups in politics, see Richard L. McCormick, *From Realignment to Reform: Political Change in New York State, 1893–1910* (Ithaca, N.Y., 1981), 151–55, 173–77, 264–71; Herbert F. Margulies, *The Decline of the Progressive Movement in Wisconsin, 1890–1920* (Madison, Wisc., 1968); and Mansel G. Blackford, *The Politics of Business in California, 1890–1920* (Columbus, Ohio, 1977). The image of the intelligent client—in this case, the voter—was common in the late nineteenth and early twentieth centuries. It applied even to motherhood. See Jones, "Sentiment and Science"; and Rothman, *Woman's Proper Place*, 97–99. A classic study that illustrates men's adoption of women's political tactics is Peter H. Odegard, *Pressure Politics: The Story of the Anti-Saloon League* (New York, 1928).

behavior and of policies that ensured economic and social stability. To exercise moral authority, government needed to behave in moral ways. Citizens expected office holders to separate their public actions from their private interests and wanted a civil service system to limit the distribution of public rewards for party work. Even in the 1920s, citizens held government responsible for encouraging a growing economy and social order. When the methods employed in the 1920s for accomplishing these goals—government orchestration of self-regulating functional groups—proved lacking, government took a larger hand in directing social and economic policy.[70]

Even more fundamentally, Americans' perceptions of the distinctions between the public and private spheres were transformed by the 1920s. Although it has not received sufficient scholarly attention, some of the outlines of this change are discernible. In the nineteenth century, social and cultural separations between what was public and what was private were well-defined, at least in theory. The public world included politics, economics, and work outside of the home, while the private sphere meant the home and family. These sharp delineations provided a sense of stability. The lines were often crossed: women, for example, worked outside of the home. And, while women brought their "private" concerns to the "public" sphere, men's political involvement served private ends. This paradox suggests a rethinking of the meanings of public and private in the nineteenth century, one that has implications for understanding public life in the twentieth. Social definitions of public and private blurred in the twentieth century, re-creating an obfuscation similar to that of colonial America. In a sense, the existence of spheres was denied. The personal was political and the political was evaluated in regard to personal fulfillment. Citizens judged office holders on the basis of personality. Men and women shunned the traditional public world of voting and holding office to concentrate their attention on private life. Although not a descent into confusion (the separations between public and private had also been murky in the nineteenth century), these changes pointed to a complex and vastly different understanding

of the meaning of public and private from the one held by people in the nineteenth century.[71]

Women played important, but different, parts in two major turning points in American political history, transformations that coincided with changes in the roles of women. In the Jacksonian period, the cultural assignment of republican virtues and moral authority to womanhood helped men embrace partisanship and understand electoral politics as social drama. The social service work of female organizations filled some of the gaps created as governments reduced the scope of their efforts. Two political cultures operated throughout the remainder of the nineteenth century. The female culture was based on the ideology of domesticity and involved continual expansion of the environs of the "home." Women carried out social policy through voluntary action. They practiced a kind of interest-group politics, by directing their attention to specific issues and exercising influence through informal channels. Male politics consisted of formal structures: the franchise, parties, and holding office. For many men, this participation was as much social as it was political, and it contributed to a definition of manhood.

Women had a more active part in the political changes of the Progressive period. They passed on their voluntary work—social policy—to governments. Men now sought to influence government through nonelectoral means, as women had long done. Electoral politics lost its masculine connotations, although it did not cease to be male dominated. Voting, ideally, had less to do with personal loyalties than with self-interested choices. Women voted. They did so in somewhat smaller numbers than men, and they held few important party or governmental positions. But sharp separations between men's and women's participation abated. In this process, individual women gained opportunities. "Woman," however, lost her ability to serve as a positive moral influence and to implement social policy.

---

[70] Ellis Hawley, *The Great War and the Search for a Modern Order: A History of the American People and Their Institutions, 7–1933* (New York, 1979), 80–109; and Louis Galambos, *~tition and Cooperation: The Emergence of a National ~sociation* (Baltimore, 1966).

[71] Christopher Lasch, *The Culture of Narcissism: American Life in an Age of Diminishing Expectations* (New York, 1979); and Richard Sennett, *The Fall of Public Man: On the Social Psychology of Capitalism* (1974; 2d edn., New York, 1976). On the transition from "character" to "personality" in twentieth-century culture, a transition that has important implications for the study of politics, see Warren I. Susman, " 'Personality' and the Making of Twentieth-Century Culture," in John Higham and Paul K. Conkin, eds., *New Directions in American Intellectual History* (Baltimore, 1979), 212–26.

Much work on women's political involvement is necessary before we can fully understand the connections between women's activities and American politics. But if either is to be understood, the two must be considered together. Gaining a broader understanding of "politics" is one way to begin doing so. This interpretation should consider the political system as a whole, and include both formal and informal means of influence. It could thus embrace voluntary activities, protest movements, lobbying, and other kinds of ways in which people attempt to direct governmental decisions, together with electoral politics and policy making. In determining what activities might be termed "political" we might adapt John Dewey's definition of the "public." For Dewey, the "public as a state" included "all modes of associated behavior . . . [that] have exclusive and enduring consequences which involve others beyond those directly engaged in them."[72] This understanding suggests that the voluntary work of nineteenth-century women was part of the political system. Although directed at domestic concerns, the activities of women's organizations were meant to affect the behavior of others, as much as—or more than—were ballots cast for Grover Cleveland. Given such a definition of politics, political historians could come to different understandings of the changes in and connections between political participation and policy making. Historians of women could find new contexts in which to place their work. Students of both subjects need to go beyond the definition of "political" offered by nineteenth-century men.

---

[72] John Dewey, *The Public and Its Problems* (New York, 1927), 27. As a refinement, "consequences" might be considered political only if they represent attempts to change prescriptions for behaviors and attitudes that are enshrined in law or custom, whether done through legal or informal means.

READING 15

WHY BUSINESSMEN DISTRUST THEIR STATE: THE POLITICAL CONSCIOUSNESS OF AMERICAN CORPORATE EXECUTIVES

David Vogel

The most characteristic, distinctive and persistent belief of American corporate executives is an underlying suspicion and mistrust of government. It distinguishes the American business community not only from every other bourgeoisie, but also from every other legitimate organization of political interests in American society. The scope of direct and indirect government support for corporate growth and profits does not belie this contention; on the contrary, it makes it all the more paradoxical. Why should the group in American society that has disproportionately benefited from governmental policies continue to remain distrustful of political intervention in the economy?

It is of course possible to attribute at least some of the public distrust of government by members of the business community to political posturing; continually to denounce government is a way of assuring that the policies of government reflect corporate priorities. Wilbert E. Moore suggests:

> When businessmen did, and do, make extreme, ideologically oriented pronouncements on freedom from political interference, it is surely fair to say that they do

From *British Journal of Political Science* 8(1)1978:45–78. Reprinted with the permission of the author and Cambridge University Press.
* A number of people have either heard or read earlier versions of this paper and their comments have greatly assisted me in preparing this one. In addition to my colleagues in the Political, Social and Legal Environment of Business Workshop and the participants in the State and Society Seminar of the Center for European Studies at Harvard University, I would like to acknowledge the contributions of John Zysman, Michael Rogin and Richard Abrams of the University of California at Berkeley, Stuart Bruchey of Columbia University, John Mollenkopf of Stanford University, James O'Conner of the University of California at Santa Cruz, Jeffery Hart and Eric Foner of Princeton University, and Alan Wolfe and Daniel Ellsberg. This paper owes much to their suggestions; its shortcomings reflect my stubbornness. An earlier version of this paper was delivered to the annual meeting of the American Political Science Association in Chicago, 1976.

not mean to be taken with total seriousness . . . Often, in fact, the sayers and the doers are not the same people. . . .[T]he extreme spokesmen of business ideology are more often lawyers and public relations men than they are practicing executives . . . These are generally men, who like professors and Congressmen, "have never met a payroll."[1]

Yet this explanation is unsatisfying. In fact, the gap between what executives or their spokesmen say in public and in private is far less than most students of business appreciate. Neither the public nor the private views of executives are formed in a vacuum; executives tend to believe their own propaganda, if for no other reason than that much of it is actually directed at themselves. A study based on extensive private interviews with chief executives during 1974 and 1975 suggests that, if anything, the private views of corporate executives are more critical of government than their public pronouncements.[2] The lack of acceptance of a large and powerful state is also not confined to small businessmen or reactionary sunbelt capitalists. It also dominates the political and social outlook of the top managers of "Fortune 500" firms.[3] As Clifford Geertz argues, "the function of ideology is to make an autonomous politics possible by providing the authoritative concepts that render it meaningful, the suasive images by means of which it can be sensibly grasped."[4] For virtually all American businessmen, including corporate executives, a critical authoritative concept in terms of which they make sense of the world is the notion of governmental involvement as inimical to a sound economy and incompatible with a free society.

Even if the hostility of businessmen expressed toward their government is considered a rhetorical device designed "to establish and maintain the sub-servience of governmental units to business constituencies to which they are actually held responsible,"[5] as McConnell argues, we still must explain why this particular line has enjoyed such widespread popularity among American corporate executives—in sharp contrast, for example, to the public pronouncements of their counterparts in most other capitalist nations. What is so striking about American business ideology is the remarkable consistency of business attitudes toward government over the last one hundred and twenty-five years. A sense of suspicion toward the state has managed to survive the most impressive and decisive political triumphs. Indeed, the level of public hostility toward government appears to have been particularly high during the 'twenties and the 'fifties—the two decades in this century when corporate political hegemony was most secure.

The dominance of the ideology of Social Darwinism among American businessmen during the latter half of the nineteenth century has been amply documented, and James Prothro's *Dollar Decade* offers a vivid documentation of the anti-governmental nature of corporate thinking during the 'twenties.[6] Studies of executive opinions from the Great Depression through the mid-'sixties present a portrait both of business resentment toward the New Deal and of the unwillingness of executives in the post-war period to abandon the ideal of the self-regulating market. In their extensive and thorough study of corporate attitudes, based on material published between 1935 and 1948, Sutton and his co-authors write in *The American Business Creed*: "Business comments on government are rarely complimentary; that the government should have only limited powers and be restrained in their use is a fundamental and ever-recurring proposition in the business creed. The breech of these principles is viewed as a grave threat to the integrity of the economic system." They conclude:

> But it is the substance of the business creed which provides the most striking evidence of the influence of American traditions. For various reasons, the ideas of

[1] Wilbert Moore, *The Conduct of the Corporation* (New York: Vintage Books, 1962), pp. 278–279.

[2] Leonard Silk and David Vogel, *Ethics and Profits: The Crisis of Confidence in American Business* (New York: Simon and Schuster, 1976). For survey data that confirm the book's portrait of business attitudes toward government, see William Martin and George Cabot Lodge, "Our Society in 1985: Business May Not Like It," *Harvard Business Review*, LIII (1975), 143–52.

[3] A recent poll of "Fortune 500" chief executives conducted by the magazine reported that when asked to identify the biggest "problem faced by business in general" 35.2 per cent named "government" (Charles Burck, "A Group Profile of the Fortune 500 Chief Executives," *Fortune*, 93 (May 1976), 172–7).

[4] Clifford Geertz, "Ideology as a Cultural System," in David E. ...d., *Ideology and Discontent* (New York: Free press, 1964), ... at p. 63.

[5] Grant Mcconnell, *Private Power and American Democracy* (New York: Vintage Books, 1966), p. 294.

[6] The most important studies are: Richard Hofstadter, *Social Darwinism in American Thought* (Boston, Mass.: Beacon Press, 1944); Robert Green McCloskey, *American Conservatism in the Age of Enterprise 1865–1910* (New York: Harper and Row, 1951); James Prothro, *Dollar Decade: Business Ideas in the 1920s* (Baton Rouge: Louisiana State University Press, 1954).

the political economists of the nineteenth century have gained more enduring acceptance in America than in Europe. It is these ideas—of Adam Smith, Ricardo, Malthus, the Mills and their popularizers—which form the preponderant classical strand in the business creed, and give it its most distinctive character in the modern world . . . . It is in its vigorous cries against *government interference* and *socialism* and in its persisting faith in the workability of a vaguely defined *free* economy that the business creed is genuinely distinctive. The Western world has not swung over to totalitarian collectivism but outside America it no longer nourishes a Spencerian distrust of the state and a goal of maximal freedom for private enterprise.[7]

After studying the image of government in a large number of selected business journals published between September 1951 and February 1952, Marver Bernstein states:

The journals selected for analysis generally share a common approach to the role of government and the nature of the economy. Their views may be summarized as follows:

1. The state is intrinsically evil. State intervention in economic affairs is dangerous.
2. Freedom is defined as freedom *from* governmental intervention in economic affairs. Freedom exists naturally as long as government does not destroy it by interfering with economic affairs.
3. There is an exclusive identification of *free enterprise*, i.e., an economy which is unhampered and uncoerced by governmental controls, with freedom, morality, and economic opportunity.
4. All good things flow from the free, unfettered operations of the free enterprise economy. Bad results are attributed to the predicted, inevitable consequences of governmental interference.[8]

In his presidential address delivered to the annual meeting of the American Economic Association in 1962, Edward S. Mason noted:

The relationship between government and business in the United States can only be described as one of latent hostility which occasionally, as in the past year, breaks out into rather more open hostility . . .

It is clear to the most obtuse observer that there is a much more distant relationship between business and government leadership in the United States, than, say, in Britain, France or the Netherlands.

Much more important, in my opinion, is the fact that the really revolutionary changes in the role of government and in the relation of various groups to government produced by the great depression and the war have not yet been fully accepted in this country. Where counter-revolution is still considered to be a possibility no one is quite prepared to lay down his arms.[9]

The most recent book-length study of contemporary corporate ideology arrives at a similar conclusion:

The dominant attitude of corporate executives toward government officials—whether elected or appointed— is one of hostility, distrust, and not infrequently, contempt. (One executive noted: "we do our job and the government messes things up.")

Businessmen share a deep skepticism about the ability of government to do anything efficiently, and they believe that the achievement of society's objectives whenever possible is best left in their hands. The reason for government inefficiency, businessmen invariably insist, is that public decisions are made without the discipline of the marketplace.[10]

The attitude toward international government regulation of American-based multinational corporations provides the most recent illustration of the almost instinctive anti-statist bias integral to American corporate culture. Since multinational corporations are a relatively new phenomenon, the attitude of their executives toward controls by states in the international arena furnishes almost a laboratory setting for recording their true values. Their vision, not surprisingly, involves a world in which business corporations have replaced the nation-state as the effective unit of economic policy and resource allocation. There is nothing particularly international or global about the chairman of Dow Chem-

---

[7] Francis X. Sutton, Seymour Harris, Carl Naysen, and James Tobin, *The American Business Creed* (New York: Schocken Books, 1956), pp. 185, 280–1.

[8] Marver Bernstein, "Political Ideas of Selected American Business Journals," *Public Opinion Quarterly* XVII (1953), 258–67.

[9] Edward Mason, "Interests, Ideologies and the Problem of Stability and Growth," *American Economic Review*, LIII (1963), 1–18. See also Andrew Shonfield, *Modern Capitalism* (New York: Oxford University Press, 1965). For a comprehensive review of recent literature in this area see Thomas DiBacco, "The Political Ideas of American Business: Recent Interpretations," *Review of Politics*, XXX (1968), 51–8.

[10] Silk and Vogel, *Ethics and Profits*, p. 46.

ical's dream of "establishing the world headquarters of the Dow company on the truly neutral ground of . . . an island (owned by no nation), beholden to no nation or society."[11] For all their global-spanning capacities and pretensions to a new world international order free from the strife of nation-states, the ideology of the executives of multinational corporations are as American as free enterprise; they have simply projected American corporate ideology on to the international scene. Visions of a world economy without the intrusion of governments emanate almost exclusively from the executives of American owned and managed multinational corporations. They have become confused with the multinational corporation itself only because multinational corporations are disproportionately American owned and managed.[12]

Throughout the twentieth century, executives have periodically appeared to be on the verge of accepting the legitimacy of governmental participation in economic affairs. The contention that corporate executives have at last come to recognize that government has a critical and legitimate role to play in a modern industrial society is made about both the Progressive period and the mid-'sixties. A number of radical, liberal and populist critics of business wrote in the 'sixties that the emergence of the "managed economy" or the "new industrial state" signified the obsolescence of business's traditional hostility to an activist state.[13]

On the other hand, observers more sympathetic to business took virtually the identical development as a cause for celebration. In a seminal article in the January 1966 issue of *Fortune*, Max Ways, the magazine's senior editor, suggested that there was no longer any tension between rising government expenditures and the preservation of corporate autonomy; under the new arrangement, which he labelled "creative federalism," both would be achieved.[14] A year later, Theodore Levitt,

in an article in *Harvard Business Review*, enthusiastically heralded the results of this new sense of partnership:

> Whether they know it or not, the leaders of the economically most significant sector of the American business community—the top executives of the larger corporations—are just completing what may turn out to be most remarkable ideological transformation of the century, perhaps since the beginning of the corporate economy.
>
> It may seem the height of grandiloquence to say so, but there is abundant evidence that the American business community has finally and with unexpected suddenness actively embraced the idea of the interventionist state.[15]

Not coincidently, the revisionist literature published during this same period makes a similar analysis of business-state relations during the Progressive Era. Both Kolko and Weinstein report the ascendancy of the doctrine of "corporate liberalism" among businessmen during the century's first decade. Sharply departing from the *laissez-faire* ideology of the 1890s, this doctrine accepted a strong national government as critical to political stability and economic growth.[16]

The similarities between the two periods (1965–71, 1902–12) are indeed striking. Both are characterized by the relative absence of industrial strife and general economic prosperity. Both periods also witness the popularity of the doctrine of corporate social responsibility among business leaders, indicating both their optimism about the future of the economy and their willingness to co-operate with government to solve various social problems (largely the assimilation of immigrants in the earlier decade and blacks in the later).[17]

Yet what is noteworthy is how little impact each of these more "enlightened" conceptions of the role of government in the society had upon subsequent business thinking. The First World War, far from marking the beginning of a new stage of political capitalism,

[11] Quoted in Robert Gilpin, *U.S. Power and the Multinational Corporation* (New York: Basic Books, 1975), p. 136.

[12] The notion that multinational corporations are essentially a function of United States' hegemony forms the essential thrust of Gilpin's analysis.

[13] See, for example, Michael Reagan, *The Managed Economy* (New York: Oxford University Press, 1963); John Kenneth Galbraith, *The New Industrial State* (Boston: Houghton-Mifflin, 967); Charles Reich, *The Greening of America* (New York: om House, 1970); Morton Minz and Jerry Cohen, *America ew York: Dial Press, 1971).

vs, "Creative Federalism," *Fortune*, 73 (January 1966), eq.

[15] Theodore Levitt. "The Johnson Treatment," *Harvard Business Review*, XLV (1967), 114–28.

[16] Gabriel Kolko, *The Triumph of Conservativism* (Chicago: Quadrangle Books, 1963); James Weinstein, *The Corporate Ideal in the Liberal State* (Boston, Mass: Beacon Press, 1968).

[17] Morrell Heald, *The Social Responsibilities of Business, Company and Community*, 1900–1960 (Cleveland, Ohio: The Press of Case Western Reserve University, 1970).

instead signified its climax. Cuff's study of the War Industries Board demonstrates what little lasting impact its structure had on the business conception of government's proper role. It would be hard to distinguish Prothro's portrait of the beliefs of businessmen in the 'twenties from descriptions of business views during the 1880s.[18] The early and mid-1970s witness almost an identical backlash to the 'twenties: the revival of fears of too much government regulation, the demand that corporate taxes be reduced and the concern that corporate social responsibility has gotten out of hand. The progressivism of corporate liberalism and the promises of creative federalism, with their more tolerant views of the role of government, were both short-lived. Indeed, it is questionable to what extent they ever actually dominated business thinking.

THE HOSTILITY OF BUSINESS TO GOVERNMENT

While granting both the sincerity and the persistence of executive beliefs, one can still be skeptical about the degree to which they reflect corporate behavior. This argument has been made by many writers on business-government relations. Thus, V. O. Key, Jr., contends: "Despite the extraordinary diversity of their political actions, business spokesmen expound more or less uniformly a philosophy of *laissez-faire*; free competition, free enterprise, and the 'American way.' But this is an orthodoxy of ritual rather than of practice. In their actions businessmen pragmatically advocate state intervention today and nonintervention tomorrow."[19] McConnell writes: "A conclusion that must be drawn from the examination of business politics is that the noisy denunciations of government heard from business spokesmen are not to be taken at face value. It has been seen repeatedly that in day-to-day affairs, business and government are not only hostile but so closely meshed as to be indistinguishable."[20] And from Wilbert Moore: "Business interests have generally sought gov-

ernmental intervention of some kind while generally opposing intervention of other kinds. The examples are so well known as to need no more than bare mention."[21] This contention obviously has a great deal of plausibility. Executives do, in fact, support governmental policies that they perceive to be in their interest and oppose those that they do not; to do otherwise would be rather bizarre. Yet by collapsing the distinction between the interests of business executives and their perception of the impact of governmental policies, this statement begs the real issue, which is: *in terms of what criterion do executives decide whether governmental policies are in their interest?*

The business community has been remarkably consistent in its opposition to the enactment of any government policies that would centralize economic decision making or strengthen the authority of government over the direction of the business system as a whole. It is only with respect to policies that have their impact on a particular firm or industry that its much heralded pragmatism at times comes into play. The criterion by which business evaluates government policy has remained quite firm: does the proposed intervention strengthen or weaken the autonomy of management? There is certainly an element of hypocrisy in businessmen's denunciations of government intervention in the economy; their hostility to government appears to vanish whenever their profits are at stake. Corporate executives tend to resolve their apparent contradiction between their beliefs and their practices by denying that government policies that assist private capital accumulation—either directly or indirectly—actually represent government intervention. This perception should be taken seriously: for the most part, government policies that merit business approval do not interfere with management prerogatives. They do not strengthen the power of government. The patterns of interest-group liberalism or small constituencies, which define much of government subsidy and regulatory activity, represent the usually successful attempts of business to receive the benefits of public support without sacrificing autonomy. For all practical purposes, they *do not involve the extension of public authority or power.*[22]

[18] Robert Cuff, *The War Industries Board* (Baltimore: Johns Hopkins University Press, 1973); Prothro, *Dollar Decade*. For business thinking during the latter part of the nineteenth century, see also Edward Kirkland, *Dream and Thought in the Business Community* (Chicago: Quadrangle Books, 1956).

[19] V. O. Key, Jr., *Politics, Parties and Pressure Groups* (New York: Thomas Crowell, 1964), p. 77.

[20] McConnell, *Private Power and American Democracy*, p. 293.

[21] Moore, *Conduct of the Corporation*, p. 279.

[22] This is the thrust of McConnell's book as well as of Theodore Lowi's *The End of Liberalism* (New York: W. W. Norton, 1969). Lowi writes: "The pluralist's embrace of government turned out to be, in its own way, as antigovernmental as capitalism," p. 47. What weakens both the studies—a weakness made apparent by the contrast between the radicalism of their critique of

McConnell's "large constituencies" or Lowi's "redistributive issues" refer to government policies in which the relevant unit affected by a decision is larger than a particular firm or industry—most likely the entire business system—and it is these politically meaningful extensions of public authority that the overwhelming majority of American corporate executives have, at least initially, opposed. Thus the business community virtually unanimously bitterly opposed government protection of the rights of workers to organize into unions—as well as virtually every extension of the welfare state. Executives did not take the principles of Keynesian economics seriously until the mid-'sixties, nearly thirty years after Keynes first articulated them, and soon before they became obsolete. The principal elements of American post-war foreign policy, namely permanent peacetime military mobilization and foreign aid, were initially greeted with considerable skepticism by executives; they were reluctantly supported only because of the effectiveness of the Truman administration's red scare. The development of the political and military machinery necessary to define and defend the American empire in the post-war period was decisive for U.S. corporate growth. Initially, however, most businessmen opposed the United States government's assumption of an international role because of their hostility to large government expenditures.[23] With the exception of the First World War, American businessmen have not encouraged any of the four major

wars fought by the United States in this century; indeed American involvement in the war that proved the most beneficial to the business system—namely the Second World War—was strongly opposed by substantial segments of the business community. Currently, all but a handful of executives are firmly opposed to any form of governmental planning, an incomes policy or, indeed, any measures that would reduce private control over investment or pricing decisions.

To be sure, an administration very closely linked to business did enact wage-price controls. Yet what is striking is not so much that the controls were enacted—a decision in any event made because of pressure from foreign governments concerned about the dollar—or that they were initially greeted with approval. It is rather how, in spite of the obvious benefits they provided business in its negotiations with labor, corporate executives so quickly turned against them. Three years later, in 1976, the experience with controls was frequently cited by executives as an argument against the bureaucratic inefficiencies and economic distortions similarly deemed to be inherent in planning. The parallel between the reaction of business to wage-price controls and the other even more ambitious peacetime flirtation with public management of wages and prices, namely the National Recovery Act, are rather remarkable considering the forty-year interval between them. In both cases a sense of patriotism led to initial enthusiastic support followed rather quickly by disillusionment and then bitter hostility. Whatever their impact on the viability of American capitalism, they were perceived by businessmen as too great an interference with the autonomy of management.

In examining the position of executives with respect to economic policies, it is important to distinguish between policies that in retrospect appear to have been in the interests of business—and thus have elicited relative support from the business community with the passage of time—and the position of executives at the time when the proposals were first debated and enacted.

---

private–public relations and the innocence of their solutions (McConnell advocates large constituencies, while Lowi calls for the rule of law and judicial democracy) is that the authors confine their analysis of the problem of public control of private power to one case study: the United States. It is this defect, so prevalent among students of American politics, that this essay attempts to overcome.

[23] For a detailed discussion of the deep reluctance with which American businessmen acquiesced in the creation of a strong state in the post-war period in order to conduct foreign policy, see David S. McLellan and Charles E. Woodhouse, "The Business Elite and Foreign Policy," *Western Political Science Quarterly*, XIII (1960), 172–90; Thomas DiBacco, "American Business and Foreign Aid: The Eisenhower Years," *Business History Review*, XLI (1967), 21–35; also see a doctoral dissertation in preparation for the Department of Sociology at the University of California, Berkeley, by Clarence Lo, "The Home Front Quagmire: The Organization of Dissent and Economic Policy During the Korean ——" Franz Schurmann describes a similar gap between political ——siness elites after the Second World War. He writes: "But ——m would cost a lot of money, and business was expected

---

to pay a large share of it. Why should a business sacrifice present earnings earmarked for its own corporate expansion to a federal budget which would give them to foreign governments to generate economic recovery abroad, which would benefit America generally but not necessarily the particular business that had poured its huge corporate taxes into government." *The Logic of World Power* (New York: Pantheon, 1974), p. 27.

One must be careful about reading back the contemporary attitudes of the business community into the past.[24] While some regulatory legislation was clearly initiated by segments of the business community—the laws establishing the Federal Communications Commission and the Civil Aeronautics Board are the most notable examples—their more typical response was one of vehement opposition. While it is always possible to find quotations from various businessmen in support of any proposal, the opinions of all businessmen do not count equally in assessing business opinion. (Indeed, as we will subsequently explore in more detail, many executives whose views appear relatively "enlightened" are generally regarded as deviants by their peers.) Moreover, it is important not to confuse regulations supported by executives because the alternatives appeared more disadvantageous—state workman's compensation and federal environmental protection are examples a half-century apart—with corporate support for government intervention. On balance, the preponderance of corporate opinion has been opposed to the overwhelming majority of governmental regulations that attempt to interfere with business. Pension reform, the FDA, CPSC, OSHA, SEC and the FTC—the list is endless—all were initially regarded with considerable suspicion by the mainstream of corporate opinion.[25]

Studies of American business have suffered from a marked ethnocentric bias. The degree of current business-government integration is remarkable only by contrast with the previous history of government intervention in the economy. The popularity (or to be more precise, notoriety) of Galbraith's notion of a "new industrial state" reveals more about the pattern of American industrialism than it does about the contemporary state of American capitalism. Only in the United States would Galbraith's description of business-government planning and co-ordination seem remarkable or objectionable—to either the left or the right. When all the myriad instances of governmental support of business have been accounted for, the American state remains, by virtually every conceivable qualitative and quantitative criteria, the least interventionist in the advanced industrial world. By focusing on the level of subsidies and regulation—what Lowi terms "distributive" and "regulatory" issues—writers on the American corporation have overlooked the extraordinary passive role of the American state with respect to the direction of economic development.[26] The United States is virtually the only capitalist nation which engages neither in an incomes policy, wage-price controls, nor in national planning; and the degree of state participation in production is smaller in the United States than in virtually any other nation in the world—industrial or nonindustrial. To the extent that the United States has moved toward establishing institutions or mechanisms that make some sort of public economic policy possible—i.e., the enactment of the Federal Reserve System to supervise private banking or the establishment of the Council of Economic Advisors to legitimate fiscal policy—it has done so far later than any other industrial system. The American state still lacks essential information about the basic functioning of the economy and even if that information were available the fragmentation of authority and power within the federal bureaucracy would make any co-ordinated government policy extremely problematic.

---

[24] Thus Robert Lane contends that with the passage of time businessmen become more reconciled to regulation: "the period of impact yields insensibly to a more relaxed period of continuation." See "Law and Opinion in the Business Community," *Public Opinion Quarterly*, XVII (1953), 239–57.

[25] Though his view is somewhat exaggerated, Theodore Levitt's litany contains much truth. He argues:

It is not necessary to recount in detail the dismal record of American business's endless series of lost causes. Whether we talk about the Sherman Antitrust Act or the Federal Reserve Act, of the Federal Trade Commission Act or the National Park Service Acts, of the Child Labor Acts or the Securities Exchange Act, of the Wagner Act or the Fair Labor Standards Act of 1938, of the Old Age and Survivors Insurance Benefits Act or the Federal Housing Acts, of the Marshall Plan or Aid to Dependent Children Act, of the Federal Education Act, the Poverty Program, or Medicare—business as a rule fought these programs and lost. Often it fought them with such gruesome predictions of awful consequences to our private enterprise system that one wonders how the foretellers of such doom can now face themselves in the mirror each morning and still believe themselves competent to make important decisions on major matters in their own companies.

("Why Business Always Loses," *Harvard Business Review*, XLVI (1968), 81–9.)

---

[26] In a seminal article, "American Business Public Policy, Case-Studies and Political Theory." *World Politics*, XVI (1964), 677–715. Theodore Lowi distinguishes among distributive policies—those that affect the revenues of an individual corporation, i.e. contracts, subsidies; regulatory policies—those that affect group interests, i.e. consumer protection laws; and redistributive policies—those that affect the distribution of resources among social classes, i.e. tax policy.

It is revealing that the term American executives use most frequently to describe their system is "free enterprise": one that is hardly in use anywhere outside the borders of the United States. By labeling their system a "free enterprise" system, American businessmen are, however crudely, attempting to distinguish the American corporate system from that of every other capitalist nation. Indeed, with all the interaction between American executives and those of other nations, it is striking what little impact other national patterns of industrial organization have had upon the opinions of American businessmen. Save for a brief flirtation with corporatism in the 1920s and 1930s, the American bourgeoisie has been remarkably immune from the influence of foreign ideologies. On the contrary, it has tended to view the relatively high degree of public and private integration in other capitalist nations—to say nothing of socialist ones—with considerable distaste. The attitude of American businessmen has been far from pragmatic, for by any objective economic criteria the least free economies, those of Japan, France and Sweden, have had a far superior economic performance for most of the post-war period. Their distaste for other systems—all of which are invariably characterized by more extensive government participation in economic decisions—is really one of principle: what is precious about the American system is not so much its superior performance but rather the relative autonomy that its managers enjoy. All of the executives' rhetoric about their links between a free society and a free enterprise system really confuses their position: the true meaning of freedom for the American bourgeoisie is the ability of those who own or control economic resources to allocate or appropriate them as they see fit—without interference from either labor unions or government officials. And, in terms of this criterion, by any comparative standard, they have been remarkably successful in preserving the integrity of the American enterprise. The fundamental direction of the American economy remains more decentralized than in any other industrial nation. The fact that the American state in the 1970s has the weakest control in the capitalist world over corporate investment decisions is in no small measure a reflection of political preferences of its business community: America remains the world's freest economy.

In sum, the anti-statist ideology that characterizes the American bourgeoisie should not be dismissed as ~oric. Not only is it sincerely held, but it does have ~act on the political positions and postures of cor- ~cutives. It is, in short, a political phenomenon ~alysis.

THE NATURE OF AMERICAN ECONOMIC DEVELOPMENT

The relatively extreme value placed by the American bourgeoisie on the principle and practice of autonomy—with its attendant mistrust of government—is a function of the history of American industrialization. The critical period to examine is not the first six or seven decades of the nation's development but rather the period of industrial take-off that began in the 1840s and 1850s and climaxed in the creation of the warfare-welfare state of the 1930s and 1940s. If we define industrial capitalism as a system in which the majority of the work force does not own any means of production but are rather paid industrial employees, then the United States only becomes capitalist sometime around the middle of the nineteenth century.[27]

If we are interested in understanding the consciousness of American capitalists, then it is to the period immediately before the Civil War that we must turn. For this is the period when the role in the economic system that contemporary corporate executives play was created; this is the period of the formation of the American industrial capitalist class and thus the impressionable years of its birth and childhood. The extraordinary lack of impact of the corporate-state cooperation of the pre-Civil War period on the consciousness of American businessmen over the next 125 years surely represents one of the most vivid examples of collective amnesia in American history.[28] It is readily

---

[27] It is difficult to document the birth of American capitalism with precision, but the 1850s appear the most reasonable date. According to George Taylor, the 1850s witnessed "the emergence of the wage earner"—a permanent working class. David Montgomery estimates that 60 per cent of the American labor force was employed by 1860. The above are cited in Eric Foner, *Free Soil, Free Labor, Free Men* (New York: Oxford University Press, 1970), p. 32. Both Stuart Bruchey in the *Roots of American Economic Growth, 1607–1861* (New York: Harper and Row, 1965) and Norman Ware, *The Industrial Worker 1840–1860* (New York: Quadrangle Books, 1964), suggest that by mid-century the fluidity of antebellum American life had become somewhat reduced and that a more rigid industrial class structure was emerging.

[28] See for example, Louis Hartz, *Economic Policy and Democratic Thought* (Chicago: Quadrangle Books, 1968); Oscar Handlin and Mary Handlin, *Commonwealth: A Study of the Role of Government in the American Economy, Massachusetts, 1774–1861* (Cambridge, Mass.: Harvard University Press, 1969); for a more comprehensive summary of this period, see Robert Lively, "The American System: A Review Article," *Business History Review*, March 1955, 81–96. What was distinctive about the pattern of business-government co-operation in pre-Civil War America was that it was largely carried out at the local level. The federal structure thus made the development of national political institutions to

explicable, however, as belonging quite literally to the pre-history of American industrial capitalism. The 1840s and 1850s are the critical period in the history of the American business system; these years witness the formation of the contemporary legal structure of the modern corporation as well as the ideology of its managers and owners.

Students of class consciousness have successfully attempted to explain the varying degrees of class or revolutionary consciousness among the working class in terms of the varying national patterns of industrialization. Presented most vividly by Hartz in *The Liberal Tradition in America* and more systematically documented by Giddens in *The Class Structure of the Advanced Societies*, the argument is a simple one. Giddens writes: "the labor movement tends to be socialist in orientation where it is formed in a society in which there was fairly important post-feudal elements, and will be closely integrated with a political movement to the degree that the active incorporation of the working class within the citizenship state is resisted."[29] Hartz's formulation can be summarized even more tersely: the prior existence of feudalism in capitalist societies is a necessary condition for the emergence of socialism. This framework can be used to understand the variation in political consciousness among the bourgeoisie as well as among the working class. As Giddens suggests, the conditions under which a nation industrializes leave a permanent legacy to its political and economic institutions and to the relationship between them. The pattern of industrialization not only affects a society's subsequent institutional arrangements, as Gerschenkron argues; it also shapes the ideology of those who industrialize it.[30]

The distrust of the state that characterizes the consciousness of the American bourgeoisie is built into the structure of American capitalism; it is as much a characteristic of the American political order as is the absence of an effective and viable socialist tradition. The relationship between institutional structure and ideology is one of interdependency: the institutional structure of a nation's period of industrialization stamps an indelible mark upon the consciousness of its industrializing elites. Their consciousness—in this case, that of the suspicion of government—is created by these structures and in turn influences them.

In the two decades prior to the Civil War, the transformation of the relationship between corporations and the American states set the institutional framework for the subsequent development of the American capitalist system. As the basis of economic growth moved from trade and agricultural exports to industry, the emerging industrial elites began to outgrow the need for governmental participation in economic development. The panic of 1837 contributed significantly to a deterioration of public confidence in public regulation and administration. By the mid-1840s private capital was strong enough to demand successfully that the states significantly reduce their intervention in business matters. Whereas a decade earlier the relative inexperience of native entrepreneurs and their inability to raise capital without public backing fostered a dependence on state and local authorities, by the 'forties their growing self-confidence and ability to attract foreign investment made them look upon government as less unnecessary. Once the construction of the infrastructure was completed and the Indians banished to west of the Mississippi, American capitalists faced none of the obstacles that in most European nations made a strong state critical to industrialization. There was no aristocracy to overthrow, no foreign armies to mobilize against and, most importantly, only one nation that had previously industrialized with which to compete. After the Civil War the federal government did play a vital role in American industrial growth: it subsidized railroad construction, enacted tariffs to protect domestic industry and physically subdued both strikers and Indians. Yet what distinguishes each of these actions, as well as the subsidies that the states continued to offer throughout the nineteenth century, is that they resulted in little interference with managerial autonomy.

As in the case of the First World War, the Civil War had no significant impact on the development of public administration in the United States. Temporarily strengthening its scope and size to defeat the most critical domestic opposition to capitalist growth, the federal bureaucracy rapidly atrophied once its task was completed. The spoils of war and the economic growth it generated were given away to the private sector.

---

construct an infrastructure less necessary; by the 1840s, however, state authorities had become rather weak. It is the nature of the national government's role that is critical to an understanding of the political economy of American industrialism and the attitude of business toward government.

[29] Louis Hartz, *The Liberal Tradition in America* (New York: Harcourt, Brace and World, 1955); Anthony Giddens, *The Class Structure of Advanced Societies* (New York: Harper and Row, 1975), p. 207.

[30] Alexander Gerschenkron, "Economic Backwardness in Historical Perspective," in David Landes, ed., *The Rise of Capitalism* (New York: Macmillan, 1966).

After the 1840s governmental assistance continued but governmental authority declined. Wallace Farnham's essay on the relationship between the federal government and the Union Pacific Railroad demonstrates the pattern quite clearly.[31] "Government giveaway" to "private profit seeking enterprises may be our economic history," as one critic argues, but the critical word is "giveaway."[32] It denotes a fundamentally passive role, in marked contrast to the more pioneering and active efforts of the state in shaping industrial development in most other capitalist—and all socialist—nations. While most other states in capitalist societies increased their role and power as industrialization proceeded, the authority of the American state declined and its size remained relatively small. When seen in comparative terms, it simply had a less necessary role to play. With the defeat of the South, the American bourgeoisie's triumph in civil society was virtually complete. While complaints against the business corporation surface periodically through the latter half of the nineteenth century, they do not present any serious challenge to the growth of national markets or the creation or disciplining of an industrial working class—problems that made a strong state imperative in much of Europe. In sum, to a far greater extent than in any other capitalist nation (with the partial exception of England) the American bourgeoisie succeeded in creating the industrial system by its own initiative. Throughout the period of industrialization the critical decisions about the direction of economic development were in private hands. Compared to that of other capitalist nations, the American state's role was more supportive than directive. The result is that the structure of the American government tends to resemble that of civil society—the precise opposite of the relationship in Japan or France.

The alleged economic incompetence of the American government, so heralded throughout the business community, is also a function of the peculiarities of American industrial development. From the inauguration of the spoils system by Andrew Jackson in the 1830s through the New Deal one hundred years later, the federal government was a stepchild of American society. The kind of talent, ability and energies that went into the creation and initial development of the republic in the late eighteenth and nineteenth centuries—a period of political and governmental competence that is a universally venerated feature of our national heritage—were channeled into the business sector after the nation's first half-century. De Tocqueville wrote: "When public employments are few in number, ill-paid and precarious, whilst the different lines of business are numerous and lucrative, it is to business, and not to official duties, that the new and eager desires engendered by the principle of equality turn from every side."[33]

It was the pursuit of economic gain and material growth that occupied the nation's most talented individuals and consumed most of their political and administrative energies for a little over half the history of the republic. Ironically, it was precisely the widespread acceptance of the principles of democracy in the antebellum period that contributed to the deterioration of the quality of public administration: "democratic ideals of the competence of the common man and rotation of office . . . lessened the chance of the states developing able and prestigious administrative bureaucracies." Hartz concludes:

> Political thought, not inexplicably in light of the general triumph of democratic ideals, was gradually overwhelmed by an exaggerated belief in rotation and the joyous acceptance of inexperience . . . Business thought . . . was never overwhelmed in such a way despite the mass faith in opportunities for sudden wealth . . . In the halcyon world of the fifties, it may have been believed that anyone could win a fortune by investing in railroad securities, but it was not believed that the mandates of natural law required the annual election of locomotive engineers.[34]

The relative retardation of the development of national political institutions in the United States has no parallels in any other capitalist nation. By 1910 the crit-

---

[3] Wallace Farnham, "The Weakened Spring of Government: A [...]v in Nineteenth Century American History," *American Historical Review*, LXVIII (1963), 662–80.

[...]zelon, *The Paper Economy* (New York: Vintage Books,

---

[33] Alexis de Tocqueville, *Democracy in America*, Vol. II (New York: Schocken Books, 1961), p. 298. For over one hundred years—from the inauguration of the spoils system in 1829 to the arrival of FDR's "Brain Trust" in the 1930s—the best and the brightest devoted their energies almost exclusively to the private sector.

[34] Thomas Cochran, *Business in American Life: A History* (New York: McGraw-Hill, 1972), p. 124; Hartz, *Economic Policy*, p. 31.

ical features of a modern corporate structure were firmly established in the United States: these included large-scale bureaucratic industrial organizations, relatively large concentrations of wealth in the hands of corporate shareholders, and oligopolistic market structures. A surprisingly large number of the current "Fortune 500" also dominated the American economy in 1909: American Tobacco, Armour and Co., Standard Oil (now Exxon), United Fruit (now United Brands), U.S. Rubber, Dupont, Singer, U.S. Steel, Westinghouse, General Electric, American Can.[35] By contrast, the modern American bureaucratic state—professionally administered and collecting and distributing a significant share of national wealth—really dates from the presidency of FDR. Not until the late 'thirties did the annual revenues of the federal government rival those of the assets of the largest industrial corporation. In an almost literal sense, public bureaucracy in the United States is only half as old as its counterpart in the private sector; most corporations are far older than the government agencies of comparable importance. If one dates the emergence of the first national bureaucratic institution in American society from the development of the railroads in the 1870s and 1880s, the contrast becomes even more dramatic: the public sector does not become equally organized for another half-century.[36]

In every other capitalist nation, a strong bureaucratic state either precedes or emerges alongside the multidivisional firm; in the United States the pattern is reversed. The impact of this fact on the attitude of the bourgeoisie toward the state is decisive. In the United States the professionally managed, oligopolistic, multidivisional firm literally exists for a generation without the modern equivalent of the state. Whatever may be the interdependence of the corporation and the government that has developed over the last generation, the former existed for a significant amount of time without the latter: executives perceive the modern warfare-welfare state as an upstart. Just as the aristocracy in Europe looked down upon the bourgeoisie as *nouveau*—and indeed, after centuries of intermarriage and extensive political and economic ties, continues to do so—so the American bourgeoisie regards state officials with a sort

of contempt; they are newcomers to American institutional life whose later arrival testifies to their inexperience and irrelevance to economic development. Witness the following statement of Rawleigh Warner, Jr., Chairman of the Board of Mobil, an unusually articulate and well-educated executive:

> We have been through a period of everybody talking about the shortcomings of our system. But if you go back before the last 30 or 40 years—before the day of increasing government controls—our system, in spite of some obvious inequities, had produced more wealth and spread it over more people than any other system ever devised. We need to criticize our system, but we need to keep some basic, positive facts in mind.[37]

BUSINESS AND DEMOCRACY IN AMERICA

The attitude of American businessmen toward government cannot be fully explained with reference to the relatively passive and limited role of the state in American industrial development; it is also critically linked to the legitimacy of democratic traditions in America. In no nation have the principles and practices of democracy and of the free market been as intricately connected as in the United States. The Jacksonian Revolution was a democratic revolution which prefigured a capitalist one. The movement for general incorporation that would transform state mercantilism into competitive capitalism effectively mobilized the nascent capitalist class as well as small farmers and urban workers. They were united around the principle of equality of economic opportunity—a convergence of the concepts of economic and political liberty expressed in Henry Clay's phrase "the self-made man."[38]

---

[35] Alfred D. Chandler, Jr., "The Beginnings of Big Business in American Industry," *Business History Review*, XXXIII (1959), 1–31.

[36] Chandler, *Strategy and Structure* (Cambridge, Mass.: MIT Press, 1962).

[37] Rawleigh Warner, Jr., "On Business and Education," *Princeton Alumni Weekly*, 76: 12 (26 January 1976), 8–12.

[38] Quoted in John William Ward, "The Ideal of Individualism and the Reality of Organization," in Earl Cheit, ed., *The Business Establishment* (New York: Wiley, 1964), p. 51. See also James Willard Hurst, *Law and the Conditions of Freedom* (Madison: The University of Wisconsin Press, 1956). On p. 16 Hurst writes:

> Thus the grant of corporate status became a notable issue in the years of Jacksonian Democracy. This did, indeed, involve serious issues concerning the power structure of the society; the Jacksonian polemics on this score forecast the issues in the background of the Granger movement and the Sherman Act. But, aside from the sensitive matter of banks, currency, and credit, the demand for freer incorporation, deep down, fitted th dominant temper of the times, Jacksonian as well as Whig.

As the pace of American industrialization accelerated in the latter third of the nineteenth century, however, the principles of democracy and capitalism came into conflict. By 1880 the number of Americans who were self-employed was reduced to barely one-third of the work force. Of these a significant proportion were small farmers and merchants, without effective market power against the industrial enterprises that produced a steadily growing share of national wealth. The occupational and economic structure of industrial America has effectively undermined the identity of business and popular interests: the Civil War was the last domestic political struggle in which all the interest groups of the market economy—from small farmer to wage earner to industrialist (outside the South)—were united. From the perspective of those who did not own or manage large-scale economic institutions—most notably the farmer, industrial worker and self-employed professional—the successful industrialists and financiers of the 1880s no longer reflected democratic economic and political aspirations. They were now regarded as an obstacle to their realization.

In the late nineteenth century self-employed farmers became the first of many groups excluded from the corporate umbrella to equate an increase in state control over business with democratic aspirations. This development coincides with and parallels a significant increase in anti-state rhetoric on the part of businessmen—even as the federal government begins to play a supportive role in industrialization. The two are closely linked: the American business community's mistrust of the state is significantly a function of its perception of the state as democratic—and thus, after 1850 in principle and after 1880 in fact, open to popular pressures hostile to industrial elites. McCloskey writes:

> With respect to program, the most obvious example of such alteration is to be found in the shifting conservative attitude toward government intervention in business affairs. Hamilton, of course, had proposed the active cooperation of business and government for the greater glory of both the commonwealth and the propertied interests; and this Hamiltonian ideal, while never unanimously approved, was an element in conservative doctrine throughout the first seventy-five years of the Republic. After the Civil War, however, it became clear that capitalism was now strong enough to get along without more active assistance from government than it ʾʾeady enjoyed. Equally important, it began to appear ʾ a partnership between government and business ʾer of gratuitous political interference was

becoming too serious to justify the risk. The idea of a positive relationship between government and economic life thus fell out of favor among those who underwrote the conservative program.

> ʾ . . . The advantage of the propertied interests was the aim of both the Hamiltonian and the post-bellum programs, and the difference was only in the choice of means. *The change had been impelled partly by a broadening of government's popular base, which aggravated the threat of encroaching legislation,* and partly by an unexampled increase in the independence and vitality of the business community.[39] [Emphasis added.]

Regardless of the actual distribution of political power in the United States, the USA has from the beginning of its history been one of the world's most thoroughly democratic societies. In no other society have democratic aspirations and ideals so thoroughly permeated the political culture. Critical to the hegemony of the liberal tradition in American society is popular acceptance of the state as an effectively neutral mechanism, beholden not to privileged interests but to the will of the people; it is not a coincidence that the doctrine of pluralism has enjoyed its greatest vogue among social scientists in the United States. Similarly, one of the most characteristic and recurrent political doctrines in American history, populism, both requires and celebrates popular participation in the governmental process.

Efforts from both the left and the right to disentangle the government from the democratic process in the United States are unconvincing. It is impossible to understand the meaning of government to American citizens—including to corporate executives—without appreciating its thoroughly democratic associations: in the United States to be antistatist is also to be antidemocratic. The opposite is true: to favor a positive state role in society is to be prodemocratic. Other combinations certainly can and do exist. Fascism, for example, is prostatist and antidemocratic while anarchism reflects precisely the opposite relationship. Neither ideology, however, has had an important impact on the American political consciousness.

It is the relatively democratic nature of the American state—embedded in popular ideals and in legal institutions prior to the development of industrial capi-

---

[39] McCloskey, *American Conservatism in the Age of Enterprise*, pp. 23–4.

talism—that is in large measure responsible for the particular vehemence of the American bourgeoisie's antagonism toward an expansion of governmental authority. During the latter half of the nineteenth century, this relationship was acknowledged frankly by businessmen and their spokesmen: Social Darwinism was both antigovernmental and antidemocratic. This attitude persists, though it is expressed a bit less crudely and openly, in the twentieth century. Describing the business ideology of the 1920s, Prothro writes:

Despite the high enthusiasm with which business viewed the increasing exaltation of economic superiority during the 1920s, the[y were] permeated by a nagging and persistent fear of the capacity of government to subvert this natural development . . . *The conspicuous antigovernmental orientation of business organizations is itself an incident of the more basic fear that popular control will, through the device of universal suffrage, come to dominate the governmental process.* Although economic success is perfectly geared to the nature of man, political power is dependent upon an artificial arrangement which runs directly counter to the laws of nature and which gives full play to the corruptibility of the masses. The unconscionable attempt of the masses, misguided by parasitic politicians, to better their lot through political processes constitutes the most unnerving of all the violations of fair play. Government is capable of meritorious service in the cause of *right*, but politics as it is practiced in the twentieth century offers the constant threat of intruding the mass man's delusions into the social order.[40] [Emphasis added.]

The following quotations, recorded at a series of private meetings of corporate executives half a century later, suggest both the continuity and the consistency of an antidemocratic ethos within the business community:

The normal end of the democratic process gives unequal people equal rights to pursue happiness in their own terms. There is a difference between the free enterprise system and a democracy which we also espouse.

We are dinosaurs, at the end of an era. There is a shift of power base from industry and commerce to masses who cannot cope with the complexities of the modern world. Dolts have taken over the power structure.

One-man-one-vote will result in the eventual failure of democracy as we know it.

In this good, democratic country where every man in allowed to vote, the intelligence and property of the country is at the mercy of the ignorant, idle and vicious. [This last statement was actually made in 1868.][41]

The fears of executives about the dangers that the democratic process poses for capital accumulation seem to bear only the most casual relationship to political reality: the periods when the political hegemony of business was at its height, namely the 1870s, 1920s and 1950s, reveal no reduction in business suspicion of the governmental process. The nagging sense of political insecurity that has been so characteristic of American businessmen since the Civil War reflects the fact that, perhaps more than any other faction in the history of American society, business executives have never doubted the persuasiveness of the high-school civics textbooks' description of the American political process. Accepting their nation's most powerful legitimating ideology, they remain concerned that governmental policy will indeed come to reflect popular preferences. Their hostility to both the ideal and the idea of government involvement in the economy is significantly due to their lack of confidence in their ability to dominate the political process. Unlike France, Germany and Japan, we have no tradition of a strong and autocratic state or of a bureaucracy independent of popular pressures.[42]

In the last decades of the nineteenth century, movements of agrarian discontent were relatively successful in using the political process, particularly at the state level, to curb at least some of the more flagrant abuses of corporate power. The establishment of the Interstate Commerce Commission and the passage of the Sherman Act partially reflected these antibusiness political pressures. Yet for a period of thirty-six years, between 1896 and 1932, corporate interests were relatively immune from effective popular control. Many of the reforms of the Progressive Era significantly reduced anti or noncorporate political participation. Samuel Hays documents this process at the municipal level while Walter Dean Burnham's study, *Critical Elections*

---

[40] Prothro, *Dollar Decade*, pp. 53–4.

[41] These quotations are from Silk and Vogel, *Ethics and Profits*, pp. 188, 194.

[42] Contrast, for example, Lowi's pattern of interest-group liberalism with Ezra Suleiman's study of the French bureaucracy in *Politics, Power and Bureaucracy in France* (Princeton, N.J.: Princeton University Pres, 1974).

and the Mainsprings of American Politics, demonstrates the role of Bryan's nomination and subsequent
defeat in 1896 in effectively depriving the United States
of a two-party system for over a generation.[43] Whatever
the origin or effectiveness of its reforms, the Progressive Era produced no institutional force or political faction capable of challenging effectively corporate
interests and goals. On the contrary, the 'twenties illustrate vividly how quickly executives were able to forget
the lessons of Progressive reform. The left, including
the Socialist party and the Industrial Workers of the
World, was destroyed, the intelligentsia was intimi-
dated, the farmers were rendered impotent, the trade-
union movement was broken. Equally important, the
Supreme Court effectively struck down popular efforts
to control business. The 'twenties remain the golden
age of corporate capitalism.

It is in this context that the full significance of the
New Deal, and the subsequent history of American politics, must be appreciated. For most of the history of
capitalism, the large business corporation in the United
States effectively enjoyed a monopoly of the political
and institutional power without parallel in the capitalist
world in the twentieth century. The history of the last
forty years, however, has witnessed the mobilization,
organization and institutionalization of a wide diversity
of nonbusiness and anticorporate interest. What is critical about the business perception of these institutions—which include the welfare-state and regulatory
state bureaucracies, organized labor, the welfare-rights
movement, the consumer movement and the environmental movement—is that the existence and purpose of
each of them is critically connected with an activist
state. Not only is virtually every institution or organization that contemporary businessmen consider opposed
or indifferent to their needs and values a product of
the last forty years; each of them can date its origin to
periods of an expanding and increasingly powerful state whose expansion and strength can in turn be
traced to the political mobilization of nonbusiness
constituencies. To focus on the economic impact of
the New Deal and the Great Society really misses
the essential drama of these reform periods for business executives: they spawned institutional and organi-

zational sources of power outside direct corporate
purview.

The critical key to understanding why businessmen
are more antistatist than virtually any other major
interest in American society lies in the unique role of
the state at their institution's birth. Business—both
large and small—developed during a period when the
state was relatively weak and small: in the case of virtually all other major national institutions, the state and
the political process played a critical role in their formation.

The relationship between organized labor and the
Wagner Act, between welfare rights and social welfare
organizations and the Great Society, and between the
environmental movement and the government legislation of the early 'seventies is symbiotic. For nonbusiness institutions and organizations, their very political
existence is closely bound up with governmental decisions and with the extension of the power and size of
the federal government. Whatever the disappointments
of these factions in achieving their policy goals—and
obviously they are greater than that of business—they
rarely succumb to the kind of antistatist hysteria that
has been a staple of corporate ideology since the 1840s.
Their occasional flights of radical rhetoric notwithstanding, their leadership as well as their rank and file
essentially identify their political welfare with that of a
large, strong government. Relatively powerless within
civil society, they rely upon the political process to provide them with whatever protection they can secure
against the interests and power of corporate capital.

The relative hostility of executives toward the government and the democratic process thus reflects a
broader intolerance toward all nonbusiness institutions
and nonmarket roles. American corporate executives
have been spoiled. Capitalism in America did not grow
out of a heritage of feudalism. The American business
community has not had the historical experience of
coexisting or competing with a plurality of other institutions, such as an established military, established
clergy, established state, established universities or,
more importantly, an established aristocracy. From the
Civil War through the New Deal, American business
really confronted no effective economic or political
competitors to its expansion and prestige. The victory
of the North in the Civil War eliminated the most
important alternative mode of production to industrial
capitalism, and a generation later financial and industrial concentration reduced the second—independent
commodity production—to a secondary role. From the
1870s through the early 1930s, the only national insti-

---

[43] Samuel Hays, "The Politics of Reform in Municipal Government in the Progressive Era," *Pacific Northwest Quarterly*, LV
157–69; Walter Dean Burnham, *Critical Elections and the
Mainsprings of American Politics* (New York: W. W. Norton,

tution in American society (with the exception of the church) was the large business corporation. (The percentage of the gross national product produced by small businesses in the United States is among the lowest in the capitalist world.[44] And the United States was one of the last industrial nations to unionize.)

The New Deal can thus be seen as the major discontinuity in the development of American capitalism. Whatever the merits of the revisionist arguments with respect to the Progressive Era, they are fundamentally misleading as an analysis of the New Deal. Unlike the Progressive Era, the New Deal did not simply enact reforms which could then be ignored when the political pendulum shifted to the right; it created three central institutions in American life that survived it: trade unions, a federal bureaucracy and, indirectly, a number of relatively independent universities. (In this context it is significant that the New Deal marks the entrance of academics to positions of prominence in American public life; the reform agencies of the Progressive Era were staffed largely by businessmen.) A conservative counter-offensive was waged by business after both world wars. What prevented 1946 from being a repetition of 1919 was largely the institutional innovations of the New Deal, not the relative enlightenment of the post-Second World War business community. In sharp contrast to those of the Progressive Era, the reforms of the New Deal were the result of a relative politicization of American public life; they were largely inspired by popular pressures.

In this sense, the New Deal confirms the corporate perception that in America the intervention of the state is linked to its democratic nature: the major expansion of the authority and the size of government in the history of American capitalism occurred precisely during the period when direct corporate political influence was weakest and popular antibusiness pressures strongest. It

is not surprising that the reforms of the second Roosevelt met with far more extensive hostility from business than those of the first. The former were less under their control and thus resulted in a relative strengthening of the authority of government.

CORPORATE CLASS CONSCIOUSNESS

Ideologies appear wherever systematic factual assertions about society contain (usually by implication) evaluations of the distributions of power in the societies in which these assertions are developed and propagated. We may suppose that a group generally accepts a view of society consonant with its interests; we need not think that ideologies are consciously fashioned to serve these interests or that groups are incapable of acting upon beliefs which appear to contradict these interests. [Norman Birnbaum[45]]

The attitudes of business toward government and the democratic process can also be understood in more theoretical terms. Giddens makes a useful distinction between "class awareness" and "class consciousness." Class awareness exists in any structurally differentiated society. It is characterized by a "common awareness and acceptance of similar attitudes and beliefs, linked by a common style of life, among members of [a] class." It does not require recognition that there may exist other classes; indeed, in the case of the middle class, "it may take the form of a denial of the existence or reality of classes."[46] Class consciousness, on the other hand, involves at a minimum, a conception of class identity and therefore of class differentiation. It may also involve a conception of class conflict when, Giddens continues, "perception of class unity is linked to a recognition of opposition of interest with another class or classes."[47] Another sociologist, Morris Rosenberg defines class consciousness in similar terms:

> Class consciousness . . . refers to the individual's psychological *perception* of his own position in the class structure. It contains a number of minimum elements: the individual must identify himself with the class to which he belongs according to the objective definition; he must feel united with others in the same objective

[44] Note by contrast Suzanne Berger's study of the importance of small-scale enterprise to the Italian economy in "The Uses of the Traditional Sector: Why the Declining Classes Survive," unpublished paper. Although this paper focuses on the attitudes of the executives of relatively large firms, the contrast in the attitude of American small businessmen toward government with that of their economic counterparts in France and Italy is even more striking. American small businessmen are fierce individualists, bitterly resentful of government interference in their affairs. On the other hand, the traditional sectors in France and Italy are utterly dependent on government assistance and protection and much of their energy is directed toward securing public benefits. See John H. Bunzel, *The American Small Businessman* (New York: Knopf, 1962).

[45] Norman Birnbaum, "The Sociological Study of Ideology," *Current Sociology*, IX (1960), 91–117.
[46] Giddens, *Class Structure*, p. 111.
[47] Giddens, *Class Structure*, p. 112.

position; and he must feel separated from, or must disidentify with, people in a different objective class position. These cognitive factors represent sentiments of awareness. They are often viewed as overlaid with affect, leading to characteristics such as intra-class friendship and inter-class antagonism and resentment.[48]

The particular conditions of American industrialization have fostered class awareness, not class consciousness, among businessmen. The American business community, unlike its counterparts in most other capitalist nations, did not have to engage in a political and military struggle to break down barriers to the development of a market economy. Unlike the French or the British bourgeoisie who had to organize themselves as a class to struggle against a restrictive and repressive feudal system, American businessmen confronted no such obstacle: from the very beginning of our nation's history, American businessmen confronted a climate extraordinarily sympathetic to individual enterprise and economic development. Never having confronted a systemic obstacle to their ownership of the forces of economic production, businessmen in America have no revolutionary tradition. Their sense of themselves as a coherent political and social entity was not forged in a baptism of fire. On the contrary, American capitalist ideology traces its intellectual origins to the age of Jackson. The suspicion of governmental authority that characterizes the Jacksonian hostility to corporate charters was profoundly individualistic in orientation: government was seen as inhibiting individual opportunity. While businessmen remained committed to this negative view of government long after it had been stripped of its democratic associations—and implications—the Jacksonian classless imagery of the people versus the money power remains central to business thinking. American corporate executives are Jacksonian populists: they remain committed to the ideal of individual liberty and enterprise.[49]

The extent to which capitalism has been ideologically unchanged in America—either by an aristocracy or by a socialist working-class movement—has also inhibited American businessmen from developing a stronger sense of internal unity. The sense of classlessness that pervades American society, cited so frequently by both defenders and critics of America's unique political tradition, not only made American unions relatively indifferent to socialist ideology; the individualistic ethic that is so critical a component of the liberal tradition also inhibits a sense of solidarity within the bourgeoisie. Nearly one hundred and fifty years ago, de Tocqueville remarked:

> To tell the truth, though there are rich men, the class of rich men does not exist; for these individuals have no feelings or purposes, no traditions or hopes, in common; there are individuals, therefore, but no definitive class . . . The rich are not compactly united among themselves.
>   . . . In their intense and exclusive anxiety to make a fortune, they lose sight of the close connection which exists between the private fortune of each of them and the prosperity of all . . . The discharge of political duties appears to them to be a troublesome annoyance, which diverts them from their occupations and business . . . These people think that they are following the principle of self-interest, but the idea they entertain of that principle is a very rude one; and the better to look after what they call their business, they neglect their chief business, which is to remain their own masters.[50]

The member of the bourgeoisie occupies two roles simultaneously, that of businessman and that of capitalist. In the former role he relates to other firms and industries as competitors, while in the latter he is concerned about the relationship of the business system to the rest of society. One relationship emphasizes his individuality and independence: the other stresses the dependence of his economic position upon the maintenance of the socioeconomic system of capitalism. Tension between these roles is built into the nature of a market society. The interests of business as a whole are quite distinct from the sum of the objectives of each firm or industry and are often incompatible with the goals of any particular enterprise.

Examples of this contradiction are numerous. Polanyi demonstrates that capitalism itself was made possible only when the central authority of the state, placing the long-term interests of the emerging system above that of individual craftsmen, merchants and

---

[48] Morris Rosenberg, "Perceptual Obstacles to Class Consciousness," *Social Forces*, XXXII (1953), 22–7.

[49] The literature on the individualistic strain in American business ideology is extensive. See Ward, "The Ideal of Individualism," p. Also see Irvin Wyllie, *The Self-Made Man in America* (New ~wick, N.J.: Rutgers University Press, 1954); John Cawelti, *of the Self-Made Man* (Chicago: University of Chicago

---

[50] De Tocqueville, *Democracy in America*, pp. 167, 193.

farmers, severely curtailed local monopolistic restrictions on the free flow of land, labor and capital.[51] More recently, a number of executives have been distressed by the habit of firms in financial trouble of going to the government for subsidies and bailouts—at the very time when the overwhelming majority of executives are campaigning for a reduction of government interference in the economy.[52] Corporate corruption can also be understood in similar terms: it is the process by which individual corporations place their immediate economic welfare ahead of the public reputation of the business community and the public's confidence in the integrity of government officials. The process by which executives advance their common or class interests is thus by no means an automatic one: the discipline of the market so heralded by Adam Smith clearly has no counterpart when it comes to a wide variety of critical public policy issues.

The lack of systemic challenges to corporate expansion during the nineteenth century meant that executives were free, to a far greater extent than during the comparable period of industrialization in any other capitalist nation, to pay disproportionate attention to their roles as businessmen. Business did require governmental assistance, but mostly on an *ad hoc* basis. Because its role was largely passive, the lack of uniform and consistent public policies did not retard industrial development; the anarchy of the marketplace could easily be transplanted to the public realm. The contemporary result is predictable: the American bourgeoisie has become the most fragmented in the capitalist world. The business community is largely a community in name only; its internal structures of authority remain remarkably decentralized: investment decisions are made by firms or industries relatively independently of each other. The largest important unit of political activity in the United States is the trade association,

although for those industries dominated by large firms even industry-wide organizations are not particularly important.

It is not only that American executives, by virtue of their fiercely competitive spirit, at times behave irresponsibly toward the society as a whole: they often behave irresponsibly toward each other. American businessmen, for example, are far more likely than their counterparts in most other capitalist nations to drive their competitors into bankruptcy. These tensions within the business community are naturally exacerbated by adversity. The last few years have witnessed a growing readiness to name competitors' products in advertisements and an astonishing increase in private antitrust suits—developments suggesting that the mores of the marketplace are not conducive to a sense of community. As one executive recently put it, "We don't have a business community. Just a bunch of self-interested people."[53]

Their lack of solidarity is relatively less important for American businessmen. As long as a consciousness of class interests—and thus class conflict—is absent from virtually all other political groups in American society, then its lack among businessmen is not a particular handicap; each executive can blindly pursue his narrow self-interest, both inside and outside the marketplace, in the belief that all other Americans, however some social scientists might like to divide them into owners and workers, are doing the same. Moreover, to the extent that businessmen both believe and act as if America were a classless society, they also inhibit the emergence of class consciousness among their employees; both the bourgeoisie and the working class can openly and honestly share the belief that their life-chances are a function of their individual efforts.

Even in a society whose major political participants are oblivious of their class roles, issues periodically emerge that do affect the interests of business as a whole. It is with respect to some of these kinds of issues that American businessmen tend to act irrationally from the point of view of the economic and political viability of the business system. The liberal tradition, with its focus on the self-sufficiency and autonomy of the individual, inhibits American businessmen from appreciating and making political judgements on the basis of their common or class interests; their unit of analy-

---

[51] Karl Polanyi, *The Great Transformation* (Boston, Mass.: Beacon, 1944), p. 19. See especially Chaps. 3–10.

[52] Treasury Secretary Simon notes:

. . . if you believe in a free marketplace and in the right to succeed in business, you also must accept the other side of the coin, the right to go out of business . . . I believe that if companies fail to adapt to changes in competitive conditions . . . they have no claim to public support . . . [T]he public should not be fleeced of taxes to keep any business alive that, like the dinosaur, has outlived its usefulness.

Quoted in John Minahan, "Is Free Market A Dirty Word?" *Saturday Review*, II: 21 (12 July 1975), 18–19.

---

[53] Silk and Vogel, *Ethics and Profits*, p. 179.

sis remains rooted in the enterprise. They remain the victims of ideas over which they have no control and which are often obsolete. A classic example of this systemic irrationality is the thirty-year struggle of American businessmen against Keynesian economics. It was only with extreme reluctance that the majority of top executives in the 1960s and 'seventies began to recognize that what was rational from the perspective of the individual firm was irrational from the perspective of the economic interests of business as a whole.

American businessmen appear to behave quite rationally toward government when the interests of their firm or industry are at stake, yet their understanding of the American business system remains remarkably shortsighted and provincial: they confuse their role as businessmen with their interests as capitalists. It is in terms of this dichotomy that the American businessman's distrust of government and the democratic process can be more fully explained. From the point of view of the individual enterprise, the governmental process is indeed fraught with uncertainty; on balance, governmental intervention in the economy does indeed undermine entrepreneurial autonomy, and noncorporate interests have in fact benefited from the increasing size and scope of governmental authority. Yet, when measured not against the individualistic ideal of 1830 but rather in the light of the realities of political life in advanced capitalist societies, both a relatively strong government and a relatively responsive political system have proven extremely functional for the development of American capitalism. It is not that businessmen fail to recognize specific acts of public assistance; most executives have nothing but kind words to say about those particular agencies or programs that play a constructive role in the life of their companies. Industries may be embarrassed by protective regulations or subsidies, but they are not opposed to them. It is rather that they see these policies as exceptional. They do not understand that the American capitalist system requires a large degree of state intervention for its very survival; they only want to support those policies and agencies that directly benefit their firm or industry. To analyze governmental activities on a case-by-case basis thus loses the forest for the trees: it does not understand that the steady expansion of business-government interaction—whether inspired by businessmen or their critics—represents of a broader dynamic that can be observed in every industrial society. It is a dynamic that, at least present, has not only proven compatible

with private accumulation but may well be essential to it.[54]

A similar confusion informs the attitude of American businessmen toward democracy. The pre-eminent position of the principles and processes of democracy in the American political system has proved particularly compatible with corporate profits and growth. Whatever may be inconveniences of a relatively open and responsive governmental system to the achievement of specific corporate objectives—and they are often considerable—they are clearly the price the American bourgeoisie pays for a luxury enjoyed by no other business community in the advanced capitalist nations—the absence of a socialist opposition. American executives continually complain about the large number of organizations and interest groups that routinely turn to the state to redress their grievances against the corporation, but this state of affairs is certainly preferable to one in which these non or antibusiness factions did not use the political process because they perceived it as fixed against them. The latter would seriously undermine the political stability upon which a sound economic system depends. Judging all governmental decisions in terms of their economic impact on their own firms, American executives remain insensitive to the interdependency of the legitimacy of both institutions.

THE CONTEMPORARY DYNAMIC

What are the political implications of the relative lack of class consciousness of American corporate executives? The first challenges that business confronted, which required a positive rather than a passive state role, took place at the turn of the century. The transition

---

[54] See, for example, James O'Connor, *The Fiscal Crisis of the State* (New York: St Martin's Press, 1973), p. 197. Also see Galbraith, *The New Industrial State*. This point is admittedly a controversial one. An observer more sympathetic to business writes:

The thoughtful and fair-minded reader will grant the difficulty of proving that the legislation business opposed has in any way seriously damaged our economy.

. . . [W]ith all his calculating pragmatism, all his unsentimental zeal to junk what is old and decaying, and all his eagerness to find and adopt new things for his business, the modern executive acts in a contradictory manner when it comes to new ideas about social reform and relations between business and government. He welcomes new things in his business, but not in the relationship of his business to his government and his society.

(Theodore Levitt, "Why Business Always Loses," pp. 83–84.)

from competitive or *laissez-faire* to corporate or monopoly capitalism generated social and economic tensions that required a conception of both corporate and governmental responsibilities that transcended an entrepreneurial or individualist ethos. Co-ordination and co-operation, both among firms and between corporations and the government, was required. If executives were to meet these challenges successfully, the business community had to become somewhat more conscious of its class or common interests.

The Progressive Era represents American businessmen's finest hour. While the revisionists exaggerate the extent to which most executives actually endorsed the reforms enacted during this period, Kolko's *The Triumph of Conservatism* does document that in the case of the most important reforms—the Clayton Antitrust Act, the Federal Trade Commission and the Federal Reserve Act—at least a handful of particularly powerful and prominent executives were capable of looking beyond the interests of their own firms to that of the business system as a whole. The doctrine of corporate liberalism, described in Weinstein's *The Corporate Ideal in the Liberal State*, was a class-conscious ideology: it accepted a more powerful state role and was thus contrary to the judgement of most businessmen who remained classical conservatives.[55] Those socially conscious executives who accepted its tenets were able to play a leadership role in enacting reforms that contributed to the stability of the business system for a generation.

It is a mistake, however, to generalize the conclusions of the revisionists to political reforms after the Progressive period. The enlightened business leadership of the Progressive Era was made possible by an unusual centralization of authority within the business community during this period. Not only were most major industries dominated by a single entrepreneur, but at the apex of the system stood a few individuals whose personal stature and economic power fully enabled them to understand and represent the interests of business as a whole. It is thus not surprising that the first attempt at corporate public relations was initiated by John D. Rockefeller after the Colorado mine massacre. At the height of his power, J. P. Morgan dominated the American business community to a greater extent than any individual previously or subsequently.

The most delicate negotiations, regarding the boundaries of government intervention in the economy could be resolved by private conversations between President Theodore Roosevelt and J. P. Morgan—with each individual confident that he had the power to dominate his respective constituencies. In addition, during this period—and neither before nor after—the markets of the largest firms were coextensive with that of the nation as a whole, and thus the interests of the largest firms tended to merge with those of the national economy. The result was that its relative lack of class consciousness was not a handicap to business during the Progressive Era: the individual interests of many of the most powerful capitalists were themselves coincidental with that of the larger industrial system.

Since the 1920s four developments have markedly reduced the ability of corporate executives to generate their own political leadership: the decline of the dominance of the Morgan financial interests, the reduction in market control of many of the turn-of-the-century monopolies, e.g., Standard Oil, U.S. Steel, International Harvester; the displacement of entrepreneurs by professional managers; and the internationalization of U.S. corporations. The impact of the first two developments is obvious: they significantly decentralized authority within the corporate system, making it less likely that the position of any one firm could provide a point of departure for understanding the needs of business as a whole. Most of the voluminous literature on the separation of ownership and control is concerned with its impact on corporate economic behavior; what has been overlooked is its impact on corporate political consciousness.[56] This is serious: the managerial revolution severely undermined the formation of corporate class consciousness and business solidarity.

Unlike entrepreneurs, the views of managers tend to be relatively unoriginal and predictable. Their selection process encourages a bureaucratic mentality. While a handful do go on to distinguished careers in public or university life, most develop perspectives that are peculiarly and uniquely suited to the preservation and growth of the specific enterprise to which they have devoted most of their adult lives; there is nothing in their training or selection process that encourages a

---

[55] Kolko, *Triumph and Conservatism*, and Weinstein, *The Corporate Ideal.*

[56] For the most recent and thorough review of this debate and its significance, see Maurice Zeitlin, "Corporate Ownership and Control: The Large Corporation and the Capitalist Class," *American Journal of Sociology*, LXXIX (1974), 1073–119.

broader political sophistication or the ability to exercise political leadership.[57] While most of them commonly hold equity interests in the firms they administer, these interests are only rarely sufficient for control: the managers remain fundamentally trustees for the firm's owners and are indeed legally required to act according to their best judgement of the owner's interests. Unlike the owner-manager, the professional manager thus cannot even unequivocally speak for the firm he represents; his shareholders—whether individual or institutional—constantly look over his shoulder and make his role analogous to that of a paid employee. In sum, corporate executives are not a bourgeoisie in the nineteenth century sense of the term. They are united neither by kinship ties nor a unique class-generated ethos. Hacker concludes: "Even though their paths undoubtedly cross in the course of business, our top managers are not linked together in ways that make them a cohesive culture. Nor do they have the kind of self confidence that

characterizes a bourgeoisie. Balzac would find nothing to write about here."[58]

The growing anonymity of corporate executives since the 1930s, has been compounded by recent increases in the rate of turnover of occupants of executive suites. Due to the political and economic pressures that have beset business over the last few years, the average tenure of a chief executive officer has declined from five to seven years to between three and five. Four years is barely time enough to master the operations of an international, multidivisional enterprise, let alone to develop an appreciation of the problems faced by the capitalist system. High rates of management turnover are simply not conducive to the development of class consciousness. On the contrary, they encourage an ever greater focus on short-run profit maximization.

A critical factor that underlies the defensiveness of American corporate executives since the New Deal is that they have been incapable of generating their own political leadership. They have been forced to confront systemic challenges at least as serious as during the Progressive Era with an internal structure of leadership and authority that in many ways is as fragmented as that of the late nineteenth century. The growing role of government in the American economy since the 'thirties can be understood as a structural response to the inability of American businessmen to look after their own interests and those of American capitalism. The New Deal not only saved the business system, it saved it in spite of the virtually unanimous opposition of businessmen themselves. That the business system has functioned comparatively well during the last four decades is in no small measure due to the important political defeats that business has experienced; the success of many of the liberal challenges to business has proven functional to American economic growth and political stability. To some extent business wins when it loses: liberal political constituencies—often critical of specific business policies though sympathetic to the capitalist system—have played an important role in balancing the too-rigid antistatist outlook of the business community. The state, guided to an important extent by the pressures and power of noncorporate constituencies most notably the liberal intelligentsia and the trade union movement, has taken upon itself the responsibility for articulating and implementing the

---

[57] Most studies of top management emphasize the insularity of the typical chief executive. Thus, Levitt writes:

One of the most distressing facts about so many highly intelligent business leaders I know—men whom I respect and admire—is how poorly informed they are about matters on which they have strong views. A weekly inside-dope newsletter from Washington, speeches by like-minded sycophants at association meetings and luncheon clubs, and the business press are generally very inadequate for a man's continued education about the realities of our world . . .

It is no surprise therefore that the usual executive is a poor pragmatist when it comes to the externals. He simply lacks the equipment. Preoccupied with internal change and uncertainty, he generally denounces any external changes being proposed. (Levitt, "Why Business Always Loses," pp. 83–4.)

Similarly, Andrew Hacker notes:

The difficulty, when all is said and done, is that corporation executives are not very interesting people. And not the least reason for their blandness is the sort of individuals they have to become in order to get where they do . . . There is not much point, then, in musing about how nice it would be if our corporate managers underwent more instruction in moral philosophy or modern sociology. The simple fact is that they are busy men, on the way up during most of their formative years, and the exigencies of the climb compel them to think of themselves rather than for themselves.

Andrew Hacker, "The Making of a [Corporation] President," in Harry Trebling, ed., *The Corporation in the American Economy* (Chicago: Quadrangle Books, 1970), pp. 74–5. See also Clarence Randall, "Business Too Has Its Ivory Towers," in Trebing, *The Corporation,* For similar appraisals, see C. Wright Mills, *The Power Elite* (New York: Oxford University Press, 1957), Chap. 6, "Chief Executives"; and David Finn, *The Corporate Oligarch* (New York: Clarion, 1969).

---

[58] Andrew Hacker, "Is There a Ruling Class," *New York Review of Books,* 22: 7 (1 May 1975), 9–13.

needs of the business system as a whole. The governmental process mediates between the subjective preferences of businessmen and the long-term interests of the business system. Elected and appointed government officials are usually more sophisticated and enlightened than mainstream Dallas Country Club opinion and it is they who represent the objective interests of the American bourgeoisie. Moreover, it is service in critical policy-making positions in government that gives many businessmen a more informed sense of the realities of American political life and an understanding of the political and social environment of the business system. This frequently distances them from their fellow executives whose world view remains more narrowly economic.

The importance of government to business is not adequately measured by the number of former or future executives holding public positions. For the most part these officials simply reproduce the competitive divisions of the marketplace in the public sector. Their influence on government policies is by no means inconsequential, but their decisions most directly affect the interests and preoccupations of relatively narrow, and often competing, business constituencies. The class or systemic interests of business actually preoccupy a relatively small group of government officials and institutions, most notably the Office of the President, the Council of Economic Advisors, the Federal Reserve Board, the Office of Management and Budget, the National Security Council and the holders of the top positions in the Departments of State, Treasury and Defense. It is the prominent role of businessmen in these positions—people such as Charlie Wilson, Douglass Dillon, Robert McNamara. David Packard, Roy Ash, John Connally, Dean Acheson, Averell Harriman—that has given rise to an extensive literature on the cohesion and interpenetration of business and government elites.[59] The conclusions of much of this literature oversimplify the dynamics of business-government relations in the post New Deal era. These higher level policy-makers do not serve the critical and long-term interests of American business by using their public

positions to advance their interests as businessmen. On the contrary, they perform a constructive role in their context precisely to the extent to which they are able to transcend their role as businessmen and formulate a broader strategy for defining and coping with the interests of the American capitalist system—interests that include a legitimate role for public authority and thus are often contrary to the preferences of most businessmen. The growing importance of government over the last four decades has thus made the lack of corporate class consciousness a manageable problem for the American business system; the political system has provided business with the leadership that it is incapable of generating on its own.

A similar analysis clarifies the role of private research organizations, such as the Conference Board, the Council on Foreign Relations, the Brookings Institution and the Committee for Economic Development. These organizations have frequently been referred to as conduits between the two sectors; they allegedly provide a vehicle through which corporate interests can be articulated and transformed into public policy. To the extent that they help the American political and economic system function more effectively, however, they do so by not mirroring the views and opinions of their business membership. On the contrary, their role is an educational one. They provide a forum through which political leaders, relatively sophisticated executives and, most importantly, their own highly professional staffs (frequently supplemented by outside consultants) can enlighten businessmen as to the political and economic realities of their domestic and international environment. The public reports of these organizations are invariably more sophisticated than the executives whose corporations provide much of their funding; they do not so much reflect corporate preferences as shape them. By contrast, the Chamber of Commerce of the United States, the National Association of Manufacturers and almost all trade associations have minimal impact on the broader issues of government involvement in society largely because their staffs too closely echo the views of their membership. A similar analysis can be made of the numerous, well-publicized conferences at which executives allegedly use the informal social atmosphere to increase their access to public decision making. In fact, the exchange of influence is probably reversed: they provide the opportunity for government officials and other business leaders to raise the consciousness of the majority of business participants.

---

[59] Literature in this tradition includes G. William Domhoff, *Who Rules America?* (Englewood Cliffs, N.J.: Prentice-Hall, 1967); David Horowitz, ed., *Corporations and the Cold War* (New York and London: Monthly Review Press, 1969); Wright Mills, *The Power Elite*; Ralph Miliband, *The State in Capitalist Society* (New York: Basic Books, 1969).

The businessmen who occupy positions of leadership within the business community and society—either by virtue of their public stature or their position as head of powerful non-profit institutions, including government, universities, foundations, research organizations, etc.—are not typical businessmen; public roles and settings, except perhaps at a local level, make most corporate executives uncomfortable. Rather, business leadership tends to be disproportionately drawn from the legal profession (McCoy, Dulles) and investment banking (Simon, Dillon). To the extent that corporate executives do play a prominent public role, they tend to be either bankers (Champion, Lundborg) or sons of successful entrepreneurs (David Rockefeller, Edgar Kaiser, Irwin Miller, Thomas Watson Jr., Henry Ford, II). Those in the first three categories are by nature positioned to promote an understanding of business problems as a whole while those in the latter are members of an authentic bourgeoisie. It may be more than coincidence that American business was saved during the 1930s under the leadership of a member of one of the nation's most aristocratic families.

CONCLUSION

Our argument is that American businessmen, throughout most of their history and particularly over the last forty years, have proven incapable of understanding adequately the economic and political requirements of the socio-economic system upon whose political stability and economic growth their own social existence rests. Not only is there nothing automatic about the process by which members of the bourgeoisie become aware of their class interests but, on the contrary, the process if highly problematic. Although our discussion of this issue has been confined to the United States, our conclusion raises a much broader issue: to what extent have students of capitalism systematically exaggerated the political capacities of the business community? Should Marx's description of the political immobilization of the French bourgeoisie in *The Eighteenth Brumaire of Louis Bonaparte* be seen as prototypical rather than unusual?[60] Ironically, did Marx

himself, in his attempt to use the French and British bourgeois revolutions of the seventeenth and eighteenth centuries as a model for the impending proletarian revolutions, contribute to an overestimation of the ability of the bourgeoisie to identify their common interests and effectively mobilize around them?

Indeed, a recent study by Saboul of the French Revolution[61]—traditionally viewed by both non-Marxist and Marxists as the classic bourgeois revolution—argues that the political, economic and social reforms that destroyed the aristocratic, quasi-feudal order and established the foundation for capitalism were neither initiated nor supported by the bourgeoisie; they were achieved in spite of them. Similarly, both Joseph Schumpeter's *Capitalism, Socialism, and Democracy* and Barrington Moore's *Social Origins of Dictatorship and Democracy*, in their seminal comparative analysis of the dynamics of modern capitalism, place relatively little emphasis on the historical role of business communities.[62] Moore accounts for the development of both democracy and fascism largely in terms of the relationship between the landed aristocracy and the peasants; the preferences of the bourgeoisie play a passive role. Schumpeter contends that in Europe it is the aristocracy that has provided the political leadership in capitalist societies. Reaching conclusions remarkably similar to those of de Tocqueville, he writes:

> Of the industrialist and merchant the opposite is true. There is surely no trace of any mystic glamour about

---

[60] An important school of contemporary Marxist thought, structuralism, argues roughly this position. See Nicos Poulantzas, *[Po]litical Power and Social Classes* (London: New Left Books, [   ]. Structuralism argues that the "only way [the long-term [interest?] of the capitalist system] can be protected . . . is through [the au]tonomy of the state, through a state structure which [tra]nscending the parochial, individualized interests

of specific capitalists and capitalist class fractions." David Gold, Clarence Lo, Erik Olin Wright, "Recent Developments in Marxist Theories of the Capitalist State," *Monthly Review*, 27:5 (October 1975), 29–41. Not surprisingly, Poulantzas draws heavily on *The Eighteenth Brumaire* for his argument. An interesting sidelight about this issue is presented in Anthony Sampson's study of the multi-national oil corporations, *The Seven Sisters* (New York: Viking, 1975), p. 310: "Dr. Kissinger, after one meeting with the oilmen (during the negotiations with OPEC), was heard to complain that they were a living disproof of the maxim of Marx, that the captains of industry always know in the end where their true political interests lie." The Secretary is evidently unfamiliar with recent developments in the Marxist theory of the state.

[61] Albert Soboul, *The French Revolution*, translated from French by Allen Forrest and Colin Young (London: New Left Books, 1974).

[62] Joseph A. Schumpeter, *Capitalism, Socialism, and Democracy* (New York: Harper Torchbooks, 1942): Barrington Moore, Jr., *Social Origins of Dictatorship and Democracy* (Boston, Mass.: Beacon Press, 1966).

him which is what counts in the ruling of men. The stock exchange is a poor substitute for the Holy Grail. We have seen that the industrialist and merchant, as far as they are entrepreneurs, also fill a function of leadership. But economic leadership of this type does not readily expand, like the medieval lord's military leadership, into the leadership of nations. On the contrary, the ledger and the cost calculation absorb and confine.

I have called the bourgeois rationalist and unheroic. He can only use rationalist and unheroic means to defend his position or to bend a nation to his will. Nor are his experiences and habits of life of the kind that develop personal fascination. A genius in the business office may be, and often is, utterly unable outside of it to say boo to a goose—both in the drawing room and on the platform. Knowing this he wants to be left alone and to leave politics alone.

*   *   *   *   *   *

. . . The inference is obvious: barring such exceptional conditions, the bourgeois class is ill equipped to face the problems, both domestic and international, that have normally to be faced by a country of any importance . . . But without protection by some non-bourgeois group, the bourgeoisie is politically helpless and unable not only to lead its nation but even to take care of its particular class interest.[63]

If the above analysis is correct, we would expect that the economic system will perform better when business plays a less direct role in the formation of public policy. In fact, since the 1930s, corporate profits have been consistently higher under Democratic than under Republican administrations; yet the latter are more likely to reflect the political preferences of the business community.

Our analysis generates the following working hypotheses about the political consciousness of businessmen in advanced industrial societies. Since our data are largely confined to the American experience, they should be regarded as tentative.

1. The mistrust of the state by businessmen is a function of the state's previous role in industrial development: the greater the state's leadership and direction, the greater the cohesiveness between pre-

sent business and governmental elites.[64] Put differently, the weaker the authority of the state with respect to industrial policy, the greater the likelihood that contemporary businessmen will oppose extensions of the state's authority.

2. The ideological hostility of businessmen toward their state is a function of their state's democratic heritage; the greater the responsiveness of the state to popular or interest-group pressures, the more likely it is that businessmen will find increased state authority over economic decisions threatening.

3. The smaller the state's previous role in industrial development, the greater the fragmentation of authority within the business community.

Our essay stresses the uniqueness of the American business system in order to underline the usefulness of understanding the nature of American capitalism in comparative terms. In terms of the above hypotheses, France, Germany and Japan would represent cases at the opposite ends of the continuum. In each nation the state played a leadership role in industrialization, virtually creating the business community. In addition, each state (Prussia in the case of Germany) had strong autocratic traditions that in France and Japan continue into the present. There is, in fact, relatively little principled opposition toward strong government by French, German or Japanese businessmen. In addition, economic decision making is relatively concentrated in the banks in Germany and in the state in Japan and France.

Britain falls somewhere in the middle of the continuum, though its experience more closely resembles the United states than that of the nations on the continent. The British state played a supportive role in the early stages of capitalist development, but its participation was far less than in those nations that industrialized

---

[63] Schumpeter, *Capitalism, Socialism, and Democracy*, pp. 137–8.

[64] John Zysman advances a similar hypothesis:

One could hypothesize, for example, that where institutional structures for state leadership in industry already exist, conservative groups will use these structures to maintain stability and thus preserve their power. Where such structures are absent, not having emerged naturally as a part of the nation's industrial development, conservative groups will resist their creation and often see the state as a potential weapon in the hands of their political enemies not a potential ally. Changing the structure of industrial power and the instruments for exercising it is likely to be viewed as an attack on the position, privileges, and power of existing elites not simply a technical rearrangement for more effective industrial management.

(John Zysman, "Financial Markets and Industrial Policy: The Structural Basis of Domestic and International Economic Strategies," unpublished paper, p. 15.)

after it. Nonbusiness institutions, including the government, were not allowed to atrophy as in the United States; throughout the period of industrial development they continued to attract competent leadership and were accorded relatively high prestige. The British government was certainly more closely identified with democratic traditions and more responsive to mass pressures than the French, German or Japanese, but clearly less closely than the American. In fact, businessmen in Britain have felt relatively less comfortable with their government than in most capitalist nations: at least some of the antistatist ideology of the executives of multinational corporations can be traced to British-based firms. (Britain is the second largest home of multi-national corporations.) On the other hand, economic and political elites are far closer than they are in the United States, and British businessmen express far less mistrust of their government than their American counterparts; indeed, if anything, the contempt flows in the opposite direction. Finally, the fragmentation of economic and political decision making is second only to the United States.[65]

Having begun with ideology, we conclude with social structure. The perception of the American state that is shared by American corporate executives is a function of its particular role in the development of American capitalism. The social and economic conditions of nineteenth century America, as well as the international economic environment, made the emergence of a strong national state less critical to industrial growth. The relative conservatism of the American working class meant that the American bourgeoisie did not need a powerful central authority to preserve industrial order while, on the other hand, the relative openness of the American governmental system meant that business could not trust public authorities to safeguard their immediate interests.

The weakness of the American state is a function of the strength of American capitalism—both politically

and economically. Domestically in the latter half of the nineteenth century and internationally since the Second World War, the American state could largely confine its role to that of an umpire because the private sector was strong enough to compete successfully. American multinational-corporation managers could transfer the suspicion of government of their forefathers to the international arena because their power *vis-à-vis* foreign firms was roughly analogous to their strength with respect to noncapitalist forces in late nineteenth century America: for a generation after the Second World War, all the world had become like pre-New Deal industrial America. While American businessmen occasionally complain that the American government gives its nationals far less direct political and economic assistance than do those of the other capitalist governments, the relative distance between business and the U.S. government abroad is characteristic of the United States' role as a hegemonic power; it projects the historic structure of American business-state relations on an international scale. *In this sense, an anti-statist ideology is a luxury that can only be enjoyed by a relatively powerful and successful bourgeoisie.* Because its structure of authority is particularly fragmented, i.e. investment decisions are relatively decentralized and the American business community lacks the authority to discipline its own members, corporate executives find it difficult to act collectively. Their individualistic ideology both reflects and reinforces this objective reality. To the extent that the challenges that confront American business are best handled by a relatively decentralized, competitive business structure, the American model will remain viable and the lack of solidarity and institutional cohesion within the American business community will prove functional for the business system. This state of affairs has clearly characterized the greater part of American economic development until the present.

On the other hand, American business currently faces a number of difficulties, including a relatively unstable business cycle, "stagflation" and problems of international resource scarcity and foreign competition that may now make a collective or disciplined response more appropriate. If this is true, then American businessmen will face far greater difficulty than their counterparts in other capitalist nations whose pattern of economic development renders the principle and practice of strong state authority, or at least extensive private–public co-ordination, more acceptable. One can predict that, if domestic political or international economic pressures force the American state significantly

---

[65] The above paragraph draws upon Edwin M. Epstein, "The Social Role of Business Enterprise in Britain: American Perspective," *Journal of Management Studies* (forthcoming). Epstein writes; "It will be recalled that the first British Factories Acts were passed nearly a half-century before their American analogues. While a restless or over-energetic state is still instinctively the ʰbject of suspicion post-World War II Britain is unquestionably a ʷd economy and is accepted as properly so by all but the most ʷary elements of the political and business communities." British economic and political elites are far more ʰve than in the United States.

to increase its authority over business decisions, American executives will find the adjustment a painful one. Having enjoyed a relatively high degree of freedom from outside interference, they will find its diminution particularly difficult to accept.

READING 16

WHY NO CORPORATISM IN AMERICA?

Robert H. Salisbury

In the early 1970s, after President Nixon had created tripartite machinery to bring labor, business, and government together to try to halt inflation, several scholars proclaimed that the corporate state had arrived in America [Fusfeld, 1972: 1–20; Peterson, 1974: 483–506]. For the most part it was the strength of corporate business in the circles of decision that most impressed these observers, but the new institutional arrangements were taken to be confirming evidence of corporatist tendencies stretching back through World War II, the National Recovery Administration, all the way to Theodore Roosevelt. But the evidence quickly disintegrated. Official labor-management collaboration in an incomes policy was ended and the machinery abandoned. Part of the reason could be found in the curious weakness of those peak associations that would be expected, in a corporatist system, to play crucial roles. Despite the temptations to seek unity, major sectoral groups remained divided.

In January 1977, a small newspaper item announced that the National Association of Manufacturers and the US Chamber of Commerce had suspended talks about the possible merger of their two organizations. Later in the Spring, accompanying the access in of Douglas Fraser to the presidency of the United Auto Workers were speculations about whether the union would now reenter the AFL-CIO. These two stories were among the recent examples of a phenomenon that has long

been known but not much examined: peak interest group associations in the United States have great difficulty achieving enough comprehensiveness of membership to be able effectively to represent their respective sectors in the political process. The analysis of this condition provides the basis for this paper.

To begin, let us say what we mean by the notion of peak association. Comparativists may not think there is much difficulty here. In Britain such groups as the National Farmers Union, the Confederation of British Industries or the Trades Union Congress include some 80–90 percent of their respective potential members. In West Germany the *Spitzenverbände* must be consulted in drafting legislative proposals. And elsewhere in Western Europe the phenomenon is not only familiar, it is a critical organizational ingredient in the emergence of what Schmitter calls societal corporatism. But in the United States it is not quite so clear which organizations are the "peaks," and so we must seek a definition for our term.

It turns out that the interest group literature does not provide much help. The term "peak association" is used, often in passing, by such scholars as Key [1964] and Eldersveld [1958]. It is employed as an important part of his analysis by Wooten [1970]. But none of these writers defines the words very clearly, and Eldersveld seems to imply that he thinks the notion is unclear. My own previous comments concerning "peak associations" are brief but nearly all of what there is. I suggested that the term referred to "sector-wide organizations which embrace a comprehensive array of constituent sector organizations" [Salisbury, 1975: 187]. This is a reasonable beginning but uncertainties remain. First, it is not clear what is meant by saying that a peak association is composed of other organizations. Indeed, the entire notion of group membership itself is far more ambiguous than is commonly realized. For instance, in the National League of Cities the unit of membership can be either the individual city or the state leagues of municipalities. The American Trucking Associations include both individual firms and specialized associations. And the National Association of Manufacturers has several different kinds of membership. Moreover, there is a considerable difference between a group like the American Farm Bureau Federation, a federation of state farm bureaus, and the Consumer Federation of America, an amalgam of over two hundred very diverse kinds of organizations. Yet both are "organizations of organizations."

A second uncertainty arises over the definition of sector. The term is most commonly employed to refe

From Philippe C. Schmitter and Gerhard Lehmbruch, editors, *Trends Toward Corporatist Intermediation* (Beverly Hills, Calif.: Sage Publications, 1972), 213–30. Reprinted with the permission of the publishers.

to the major sections of economic self-interest in modern industrial society: labor, business and agriculture. What is unclear is how many such sectional or producer groups should be designated as sectors without destroying the meaning of the term. What of the professions? A good case can be made for including medicine, law and education as sectors. Each is reasonably well-bounded. Each has an "interest," a stake in society and in public policy. In recent years the "PIGs," the Public Interest Groups which include public official organizations of mayors, governors, counties, and the like, have certainly emerged as a self-interested set with clear stakes in public policy [Stanfield, 1976]. The Nader groups and Common Cause are probably outside the definition. So perhaps are the environmentalists. Consumers are a borderline case. We need not come to a definitive position on the matter; only indicate the fuzziness of the boundary.

Let us attempt a definition. *A peak association is an organization which purports, and is taken, to speak for a particular sector of society.* The term leaves out those groups who defend the public interest for they deny a "selfish" sectoral concern. The term sector is intended to apply to larger rather than smaller slices of society. Neither the petroleum industry nor Texas constitutes a sector in this sense. The definition involves a reciprocal relationship. A group cannot simply declare itself to be the spokesman of a sector. It must be acknowledged to be so by those to whom it speaks: decision makers, elites more generally, or the broad public. Once the notion of audience response is taken into account, it makes the concept probabilistic rather than definitional. An organization may be acknowledged as the legitimate representative of a sector by some elites but not others. It may be supposed that there are threshold points beyond which a group achieves the status of peak association, and these points are located at the intersection of the organization's actual hegemony in its sector—density of membership, absence of intra-sector rivals, forceful assumption of sector leadership—and the recognition of that hegemony by the relevant "others." Presumably, the greater the hegemony, the fuller the recognition. But the opposite is also true. By conferring recognition on a group as the rightful spokesman of a sector, policy makers may greatly enhance its actual dominance. Indeed, it appears that many of the peak associations in Western Europe reached their hegemonic status with major contributions from the more or less official recognition of key government agencies, especially in the

In the United States, however, it has been unusual for official recognition to be granted any organized interest group, and it has been even more rare for such recognition to be given to groups purporting to speak for an entire sector. There are some examples, however, and let us note them. One of the best known is the support given through the Extension Service to the formation and continuing strength of the American Farm Bureau Federation [Block, 1960]. It took decades for this connection to be severed, and during at least part of the time from the Bureau's establishment in 1919 until the late 1940s there were many, inside of government and out, who asserted or acknowledged the Bureau's suzerainty [McConnell, 1953]. Yet all the while the Grange and the Farmer's Union existed as general farm organizations open to all kinds of farmers, and when there was a major consultation with USDA or Congress about farm policy they too were included [Campbell, 1962]. From the time of the Brannan Plan in 1949 until 1977 the dominant motif of American farm politics was partisan division with each party joined together in close working relationship with a general farm organization, Democrats with the Farmer's Union and Republicans with the AFBF [Key, 1964: 159; Heinz, 1963: 952–78]. Even though the latter was much the larger, it could hardly be regarded as a peak organization when its access depended so heavily on having Republicans in power. And periodic efforts to transcend the partisan division by establishing ad hoc coalitions of farm organizations have all quickly failed as the coalitions find themselves unable to contain the centrifugal forces generated by diverse and conflicting farm interests.

Another substantive area has witnessed several efforts of federal government officials to encourage the formation of interest groups [Ziegler, 1964: 94–109; Fainsod et al., 1959: 467]. First during World War I, again under Secretary of Commerce Hoover in the 20s, during the NRA period of 1933–35, and in World War II trade associations were organized with the active support of government, primarily in order to assist in the administration of federal regulatory programs. At other times federal policy has sought to restrict trade association activities, too, of course, but even during the periods of encouragement there was no sustained move to support or consult with groups that purported to speak for all of industry. Organizational recognition was confined to the level of the specific industry. When Washington officials wanted to acknowledge the importance of business (or labor) as a whole, to confer symbolic recognition, and to consult with private interests about public policy they worked with individuals, like William Knudsen and Sidney Hillman, whom they, the officials, not the sector organizations, chose [Blum, 1976].

A case for full peak status might be made for the AFL-CIO. Certainly since the 1955 merger there has been no rival organization in a position to speak on behalf of all of organized labor. Nevertheless, when compared, say, to the TUC, several points of difference appear. For one, the AFL-CIO includes only about seventy-five percent of unionized workers who consist, in turn, of less than one-fourth of the total work force. Moreover, any labor group that does not include the auto workers, the teamsters, or the mine workers must stand in stark contrast to the TUC in which the three equivalent unions are among the most significant. AFL-CIO hegemony is further reduced by its declining rate of success in winning representation elections. This is not meant to dismiss them as unimportant. Mr. George Meany has certainly had a significant voice in national policy discussions, and Andrew Biemiller leads what is widely regarded as among the most skilled lobbying crews in Washington [Singer, 1976]. But neither lobbying strength nor electioneering clout has been sufficient to assure the AFL-CIO of a decisive, officially acknowledged, voice on labor questions. It is the President who selects the Secretary of Labor and other labor representatives on official bodies, not the AFL-CIO, even when a Democrat is in the White House.

A final example of the difficulties of sustaining peak association status in the United States can be drawn from medicine. When Oliver Garceau's splendid study was published in 1941 there was little doubt of the AMA's dominance over the "medical profession in politics" [Garceau, 1941]. This remained largely true through the 1950s. But it is not true any longer. Rival organizations of doctors have been formed, and other groups with different interests, such as the hospital administrators, have emerged to contest with the AMA for position and power in health policy making.

Thus peak associations in the United States are either weak and incomplete or ineffectual. None can claim quasi-monopolistic hegemony over a significant sector of socio-economic self-interest. Consequently, the United States lacks an essential ingredient of a corporatist polity, "a limited number of singular, compulsory, noncompetitive, hierarchically ordered and functionally differentiated categories . . ." [Schmitter, 1974: 93–4]. Now there is a long tradition among American intellectuals that asks, "Why no Socialism in America?" [Laslett and Lipset (eds.), 1974]. To that query, or perhaps instead of it, we now would ask,

"Why no corporatism in America?" I propose to approach this question from three quite different perspectives: one, macro-social; two, in terms of the patterns of public policy; and three, as a problem in organizational analysis.

SOCIAL DIVERSITY AND INSTITUTIONAL FRAGMENTATION

Perhaps the most immediate and common response to the question of "Why no corporatism?" would be the one that harks back to the *Federalist Papers* and identifies two interrelated factors, social diversity and institutional fragmentation, as primarily responsible. The relative extent of social diversity and its effects in American life can be argued. Beer and Sapolsky, for instance, both point out that British agriculture is also diverse in commodity interest, yet successfully brought under a single organizational tent [Beer, 1958: 130–140; Sapolsky, 1968: 355–76]. How much diversity is too much to contain? To the element of heterogeneity one may add that of sheer size. Compared to the nations of Western Europe the physical scope and diversity of the United States is immense. This is undoubtedly true, yet corporate concentrations of power have emerged, despite the anti-trust laws, in sufficient proportion to suggest that American heterogeneity can be overcome by skillful entrepreneurs.

A variant on the diversity factor, and one of considerable interest, is presented by those who contend that the pace and timing of socio-economic growth significantly affects the prospects for corporatist organization. At one end of the spectrum we find Sweden with its rapid and nationwide advance into mature industrialism. The United States is surely close to the other end [Sharkansky, 1975]. Industrialization struck New England a century and a half before it reached many parts of the South or West; today, while Utah, Wyoming and Montana emerge as fuel-rich industrial sites, the Northeast attempts to shore up its sagging employment prospects. The unevenness of growth is not confined to a single period of history. The late-starting sections do not eventually catch up and smooth out the differences. The Old South may become part of the Sun Belt, but Phoenix remains different from Savannah in the value and interests of those who live there.

Within any given sector, therefore, the tensions among competing groups will be greater and more difficult to reconcile to the extent that historical socio-economic growth and development has been distributed geographically in uneven pattern. If the historical pat

Medical Association. Cambridge: Harvard University Press.

Goodwin, C. D. (1975). Exhortation and Controls. The Search for a Wage-Price Policy, 1945–1971. Washington, DC: Brookings.

Grossman, J. B. (1965) Lawyers and Judges, The ABA and the Politics of Judicial Selection. New York: Wiley.

Hartz, L. (1955) The Liberal Tradition in America. New York: Harcourt, Brace.

Heinz, J. (1962) "The Political Impasse in Farm Support Legislation." Yale Law Journal 71 (April): 952–78.

Key, V. O. Jr. (1964) Politics, Parties and Pressure Groups. 5th ed. New York: Crowell.

Laslett, J. M. and S. M. Lipset (eds.) (1974) Failure of a Dream? Essays in the History of American Socialism. Garden City, New York: Anchor/Doubleday.

Lowi, T. (1969). The End of Liberalism. New York: Norton.

Masters, N. A. et al. (1964) State Politics and the Public Schools. New York: Knopf.

McConnell, G. (1966) Private Power and American Democracy: New York: Alfred A. Knopf.

McConnell, G. (1953) The Decline of Agrarian Democracy. Berkeley: University of California Press.

Olson, M. (1965) The Logic of Collective Action. Cambridge, Mass.: Harvard University Press.

Panitch, L. (1976c) "The Development of Corporatism in Liberal Democracies." Paper presented to the American Political Science Association, September.

Peterson, W. C. (1974) "The Corporate State, Economic Performance and Social Policy." Journal of Economic Issues 8 (June): 483–506.

Presthus, R. (1974) Elites in the Policy Process. London: Cambridge University Press.

Salisbury, R. H. (1975) "Interest Groups" in F. Greenstein and N. Polsby (eds.) Handbook of Political Science. Vol. 4. Reading, Mass.

Salisbury, R. H. (1969) "An Exchange Theory of Interest Groups," in Midwest Journal of Political Science, Vol. 13, February, 1–32.

Sapolsky, H. (1968) "Organizational Competition and Monopoly." Public Policy 17: 55–76.

Schattschneider, E. E. (1960) The Semi-Sovereign People. New York: Holt Rinehart & Winston.

Self, P. and H. J. Storing (1962) The State and the Farmer. London: Allen & Unwin.

Sharkansky, I. (1975) The United States: A Study of a Developing Country. New York: David McKay.

Shonfield, A. (1965) Modern Capitalism, The Changing Balance of Public and Private Power. London: Oxford University Press.

Singer, J. W. (1976) "Buttonholding and Buttering up for Labor—and 'the People'." National Journal (April 24).

Stanfield, R. (1976) "The PIGs: Out of the Sty into Lobbying with Style." National Journal (August 14).

Truman, D. B. (1951) The Governmental Process. New York: Alfred A. Knopf.

Wheeler, C. (1975) White Collar Power. Urbana: University of Illinois Press.

Wilensky, H. (1976) The New Corporatism, Centralization and the Welfare State. Beverly Hills, Calif.: Sage.

Zeigler, H. (1964) Interest Groups in American Society. Englewood Cliffs: Prentice-Hall.

PART THREE

CONTEMPORARY MOVEMENTS FOR SOCIAL AND POLITICAL CHANGE

Social movements—collective efforts to bring about social or political change—proliferated in the United States during the 1960s and 1970s. The civil rights movement challenged the legal and customary practices of racial segregation that prevented black Americans in the South from doing such things as sitting in empty seats at the front of buses or trains, buying lunch at the downtown Woolworth store, or swimming in the local public pool. Civil rights protestors also demanded that the federal government intervene to guarantee voting rights for black citizens—a goal whose achievement promised to change the balance of electoral power in many southern communities and states, and in the nation as a whole (McAdam, 1982).

Often inspired by the example of the civil rights movement, many other movements grew up during the 1960s and 1970s (Matusow, 1984). An exhaustive list would be very lengthy, but a few examples will give an idea of the variety of efforts. Feminist movements sought to combat gender discrimination and to gain equal rights for women (see the readings in Chapter 8). Movements among the very poor included an effort to unionize farm workers in California (Jenkins, 1984) and demands for new rights and benefits for welfare recipients (Bailis, 1974; Piven & Cloward, 1977, Chapter 5). Student movements grew up to oppose U.S. military involvement in Vietnam. Gays and lesbians became self-conscious proponents of homosexual liberation (Adam, 1987). And environmental movements arose to oppose nuclear power (Nelkin & Pollak, 1981), combat pollution, or seek the preservation of natural areas faced with destruction by rapid economic development.

The social sciences have always been affected by cultural shifts and political conflicts in the broader society. Thus it is hardly surprising that new theories about the origins, development, and impact of social movements proliferated from the 1960s onward. Sociologists were among the first to debate the nature of social movements and the reasons for their emergence. A few political scientists also jumped into the discussion—especially to analyze the interaction of protest movements with shifts in electoral behavior, and the impact of movements on government policies. To this day, the study of social movements remains a vital area of investigation and debate in political sociology and political science.

Part 3 of the Reader includes three chapters. Chapter 6 introduces ongoing theoretical debates about the roots and dynamics of social movements. Although particular examples such as the environmental, civil rights, and lesbian feminist movements are used as illustrations, the main point of each is to outline concepts and hypotheses that can be used to explain the emergence and development of a wide range of movements in the United States and other nations.

Chapters 7 and 8 focus, respectively, on the civil rights and black power movements of 1955 to 1970, and the women's liberation movement of the 1960s and 1970s. These movements have had a momentous effect on American society and politics during the past several decades. In each case, we look at the roots of the movement, considering why it emerged at the time and in the form that it did. We also ask how successful each movement was in achieving its initial goals, probing not only the actions of movement adherents themselves, but also the reasons why U.S. political institutions in the 1960s and 1970s made it possible for some movement goals to be realized, while obstructing the achievement of others.

After thus dissecting the civil rights and women's movements in their own terms, we examine additional movements—and political and cultural reverberations—that emerged in response to the initial efforts on behalf of black and women's liberation. Some additional movements continued and redefined the original goals of the earlier movements that helped to inspire them; movements for various sorts of "black power" had this sort of relationship to the original civil rights movement. Other movements or reverberations represented "backlashes" by groups of Americans who felt threatened by some of the achievements or tactics of the original black and women's movements. We consider the reactions of many U.S. white voters to the civil rights and black power movements, as well as the "pro-life" and "STOP ERA" efforts that grew up in reaction to certain feminist achievements.

Indeed, social movements often come in interrelated clusters. By looking at major movements in historical context, as we do in this part of the Reader, we are able to see how later movements build upon, or react against, earlier ones. We also learn new things about the sources of change—and the limits to change—in existing institutions and political processes. Social movements do not either arise or play themselves out in a vacuum. The people who make these movements are inextricably involved with existing social and political structures, even as they seek to change them.

REFERENCES

Adam, Barry. 1987. *The Rise of the Gay and Lesbian Movement*. Boston: Twayne.

Bailis, Lawrence Nail. 1974. *Bread or Justice*. Lexington, Mass.: D.C. Heath and Company.

Jenkins, J. Craig. 1984. *The Politics of Insurgency*. New York: Columbia University Press.

Matusow, Allen J. 1984. *The Unraveling of America*. New York: Harper and Row.

McAdam, Doug. 1982. *Political Process and the Development of Black Insurgency, 1930–1970*. Chicago: University of Chicago Press.

Nelkin, Dorothy, and Michael Pollak. 1981. *The Atom Besieged*. Cambridge, Mass.: MIT Press.

Piven, Frances Fox, and Richard A. Cloward. 1977. *Poor People's Movements: Why They Succeed and How They Fail*. New York: Pantheon Books.

CHAPTER 6

PERSPECTIVES ON SOCIAL MOVEMENTS AND COLLECTIVE ACTION

Theories of social movements offer a variety of perspectives on some basic issues: Why do social movements emerge when and where they do? What sorts of people become involved, and how? Why do movements develop in various ways—grow or recede; achieve their goals or fail to achieve the kinds of changes they aim to accomplish? When movements do achieve initial goals, what happens then? Do they give rise to new efforts to reach similar goals? Do they disappear? Do they provoke reactions from countermovements launched by opponents to the initial goals?

The readings in this chapter present some of the hypotheses about such matters that have been offered by classical theorists of collective behavior, by resource mobilization theorists, by analysts of political opportunity structures, by rational choice theorists, and by so-called "new social movement theorists." The ideas presented by these various groups are not necessarily mutually contradictory. Sometimes they complement one another as explanations of the emergence and course of different types of social movements in the United States and other nations.

Perhaps the best-known theory of social movements today is called "resource mobilization theory." This theory was developed as a critique of, and alternative to, what is sometimes called the "classical approach" to collective behavior and social movements (for examples of the classical approach, see Blumer, 1946; Killian, 1964; Kornhauser, 1959; and Smelser, 1962). For classical theorists, social movements were outbursts of irrational or nonrational behavior outside of the normal channels of institutionalized politics. People were seen as likely to engage in forms of collective behavior, ranging from riots to ideological attacks on established authorities, only if they were experiencing severe forms of psychological strain and social disruption. For example, peasants suddenly forced out of their rural homes by rapid urbanization and industrialization might engage in riots or join revolutions after arriving in cities, as a result of experiencing extreme frustration or disorientation. Exactly how frustrated or disoriented people might become was said to depend on the ideas they developed (or accepted from leaders) to explain their situations; and classical theorists often stressed that these ideas were not fully rational. Once launched, the course of such a social movement would be determined by how effective the "agents of social control" were in defusing frustrations and channeling or repressing the movement.

Resource mobilization theorists disagree with many of the basic propositions of the classical approach—especially with those suggesting how movements emerge and who is likely to engage in protest. Craig Jenkins (see Reading 17) and others who adhere to the resource mobilization approach argue that social movements should be seen as rational, goal-oriented efforts to engage in political conflict for realistic advantages. Protest actions, even those that at first glance seem bizarre, may be the only way in which groups excluded from established institutions and routine decision-making can fight effectively for their interests. For resource mobilization theorists, increased psychological frustration or social strain may not be necessary to explain the emergence of a social movement. In the view of these scholars, there are always social strains and conflicts of interest built into existing social arrangements; there are always frustrated people around. But often less powerful groups are too atomized or demoralized to launch social movements. Resource mobilization theorists would hypothesize, for example, that new immigrants to cities are too disconnected from one another to join in protests about their situation. Movements would be more likely to emerge years later, *after* strong neighborhood ties and local organizations had been established by the migrants. At that point, frustrations might diminish, but the migrants to the cities would have acquired greater solidarity and thus a greater ability to demand changes in their own interest. As this example shows, resource mobilization theorists often make different predictions about the timing and sources of protest than do classical theorists of collective behavior.

From the resource mobilization perspective, potentially aggrieved groups must achieve some degree of solidarity in order to act. Preexisting social networks or organizations are thus likely to be involved in launching social movements (Von Eschen, Kirk, & Pinard, 1971). To survive and develop, moreover, protesting groups must have access to such "resources" as money, skills, or safe places to meet. Sometimes resources are seen as coming from within the aggrieved group itself (see McAdam, 1982, and Reading 22 by Aldon Morris in Chapter 7). At other times, the resources to launch or sustain protests are provided to relatively powerless groups by outside "movement entrepreneurs," or by "conscience constituents" such as middle-class professional people who contribute to movements on behalf of the poor (Jenkins & Perrow, 1977; McCarthy & Zald, 1977). Either way, there must be some resources available to help a group to begin and sustain protest efforts. Furthermore, emerging social movements must perceive "opportunities" to voice protests that will not simply be brutally repressed. There must be an apparent prospect of success, if people are to take the risk of demanding change. To explain social movements, therefore, resource mobilization theorists focus on variations in the human and material advantages accessible to aggrieved groups. These theorists also focus on breakdowns in established orders, or splits among powerful elites, that create new political opportunities for social movements to mobilize.

After a movement has emerged, resource mobilization theorists analyze its course over time by examining interactions with other groups in the environment—not just with the groups "targeted" for protest, but also with possible "third parties" who may become involved and shift the balance of power between the protesting group and the target of its demands. Reading 18 by Michael Lipsky provides an excellent delineation of some of the kinds of third parties that have influenced the success or failure of U.S. protest movements in recent times. One important third party is television, which can shape public sympathies for a movement or its target. Similarly, Reading 23 by Doug McAdam in Chapter 7 analyzes the three-way interactions of the civil rights movement, southern segregationists, and the federal government between the mid-1950s and the mid-1960s. Television broadcasts played an important role in this social movement drama, as well.

The sociopolitical environment within which a movement emerges and develops can be analyzed as a "political opportunity structure." Obviously, that larger environment helps to determine the resources available to those who are being challenged by a social movement; and it influences the third parties who might be available to aid either the movement or its target (see Jenkins & Perrow, 1977). Yet political opportunity structures do not come into play only after a movement has been launched. According to Herbert Kitschelt (Reading 19), a political opportunity structure—such as a government and political party system—can shape the organization, tactics, and goals of the movement itself. This happens when some resources and opportunities for movement action are made available by existing institutional arrangements, but others are closed off.

Kitschelt argues that antinuclear movements, for example, emerged about the same time in European nations and in the United States, yet their strategies varied according to the opportunities they were afforded to voice demands or affect policy implementation. Antinuclear protestors were more likely to use lobbying and lawsuits in America, because the structure of U.S. political institutions made action through legislatures, regulatory bodies, and the courts the promising way to obstruct or delay the construction of nuclear plants. Kitschelt also points out that successful movements often inspire and imitate one another. Thus approaches that have worked for one social movement in a given nation may then be adopted by other movements. Readings in Chapter 8 show that U.S. feminists have used many of the same tactics as U.S. environmentalists, which is not surprising given that both movements have emerged within, and dealt with, the same governmental and political system.

Resource mobilization arguments (and related approaches such as Kitschelt's) have been very influential since the 1970s. But they are not the last word in the study of social movements. In the world of scholarship, no one ever has the last word, because questions and research are always changing. Some of the concerns of the earlier classical approach to social movements recently reemerged in new forms. In particular, some scholars are paying renewed attention to the individual motivations and social beliefs of people who participate in social movements.

We cannot just presume that aggrieved people, even those with some resources and opportunities, will launch or pursue a social movement to change their conditions. This point is brought home by Dennis Chong (Reading 20), who studies the development of the civil rights movement from a rational choice perspective. This approach addresses dilemmas about group action explained in *The Logic of Collective Action* by Mancur Olson, Jr. (1971). A large collection of people—such as farmers, or industrial workers, or blacks in the segregationist South—may have a collective interest in a "public good," such as improved prices, or higher wages and better working conditions, or the abolition of legal segregation. But it is hard to motivate individuals to engage in public-spirited collective action, because every individual has a motivation to be a "free rider," that is, to wait for others to take the risks and bear the costs of the social movement to bring change. The individual who has been a free rider then gets the benefits—the higher prices, or higher wages, or freedom from segregation—without paying any price to help organize a social movement. Olson argues that large groups sometimes organize by providing "selective incentives," such as offering cheap health insurance to all who join a farmers' organization (but not to those who do not join). In this way, they are able to appeal to individuals' self-interest, thus avoiding the free rider problem. But, as Chong points out, the large groups that might launch—and benefit from—social movements often cannot provide selective material inducements to persuade individuals to contribute to the group effort. We need a better answer to the dilemma that Olson poses so well: How do self-interested individuals sometimes come together to launch a large-scale social movement?

According to Chong, social movements often build on existing social relationships—institutions or social networks that may connect people across many settings—to afford individuals psychological benefits for cooperating with others. People will feel good about working with others whom they already know, whose opinions about their conduct they value. Cooperation based on existing ties also helps to assure individuals that others will take risks for change along with them, not abandoning them to face dangers or costs that others shirk. To make this collective dynamic work as an "assurance game," Chong argues, movements must achieve enough initial successes to convince people that participation will be rewarding and effective. Obviously, Chong uses reasoning from the rational choice perspective to reach some of the same conclusions as resource mobilization theorists. His special contribution is to analyze the individual motivations that leaders and followers may have for taking part in costly and risky social movements (see the full analysis in Chong, 1991).

Along with others who call themselves "new social movement theorists" (see Melucci, 1980; Touraine, 1985), Verta Taylor and Nancy Whittier (Reading 21) agree with Chong that we must go beyond the basic resource mobilization emphasis on interests and resources. They look not just at individual motivations, but also at the shared "identities" of the people who become involved in social movements. We cannot take it for granted that we know which groups and individuals may feel aggrieved and will try to work together for change. It may seem obvious that blacks in the South were, over a long period, an oppressed group made up of individuals who usually knew full well that they shared a radically defined disadvantaged situation. Thus they probably constituted a self-conscious group ready to seek change, if and when new resources become available and opportunities arose. But some social movements have arisen out of the efforts of newly defined social identities, such as "lesbian feminist," or out of new ways of looking at the world, such as "environmentalism" or "black is beautiful." According to Taylor and Whittier, social movements have as much to do with the creation and recreation of social identities during the course of the struggle itself as they do with the mobilization of resources to achieve goals for a predefined group.

Based on this insight, Taylor and Whittier outline some questions about cultural meanings that, they argue, we should explore for all social movements. How does the group in question understand the boundaries between itself and the target of its efforts? How does it redefine its group situation as one of social oppression, not individual blame? And how does it make the actions taken by the movement meaningful in a positive way for individual participants? Taylor and Whittier suggest that ways of "being," of understanding "who we are," are just as important to social movements as are ways of "doing," such as mobilizing resources and taking advantages of political opportunities. They apply their perspective to explain the emergence of a new movement, the lesbian feminist movement, which is different from mainstream feminism and the gay liberation movement, although it was influenced by both. The theoretical insights offered by Taylor and Whittier could be used to explore the cultural reworkings influencing the emergence of the movement to achieve "black power" in the aftermath of the southern civil rights movement.

REFERENCES

Blumer, Herbert. 1946. "Collective Behavior." In *New Outline of the Principles of Sociology*, edited by A.M. Lee, 170–222. New York: Barnes and Noble.

Chong, Dennis. 1991. *Collective Action and the Civil Rights Movement*. Chicago: University of Chicago Press.

Jenkins, J. Craig, and Charles Perrow. 1977. "The Insurgency of the Powerless: Farm Workers Movements (1946–1972)." *American Sociological Review* 42: 249–68.

Killian, Lewis M. 1964. "Social Movements." In *Handbook of Modern Sociology*, edited by R.E.L. Faris, 426–55. Chicago: Rand McNally.

Kornhauser, William. 1959. *The Politics of Mass Society*. Glencoe, Ill.: Free Press.

McAdam, Doug. 1982. *Political Process and the Development of Black Insurgency, 1930–1970*. Chicago: University of Chicago Press.

McCarthy, John D., and Mayer N. Zald. 1977. "Resource Mobilization and Social Movements: A Partial Theory." *American Journal of Sociology* 82(6): 1212–41.

Melucci, Alberto. 1980. "The New Social Movements: A Theoretical Approach." *Social Science Information* 19(2): 199–226.

Olson, Mancur, Jr. 1971. *The Logic of Collective Action: Public Goods and the Theory of Groups.* New York: Schocken Books.

Smelser, Neil. 1962. *Theory of Collective Behavior.* New York: Free Press.

Touraine, Alain. 1985. "An Introduction to the Study of Social Movements." *Social Research* 52: 749–87.

Von Eschen, Donald, Jerome Kirk, and Maurice Pinard. 1971. "The Organizational Substructure of Disorderly Politics." *Social Forces* 49(4): 529–44.

READING 17

RESOURCE MOBILIZATION THEORY AND THE STUDY OF SOCIAL MOVEMENTS

J. Craig Jenkins

Abstract

Resource mobilization theory has recently presented an alternative interpretation of social movements. The review traces the emergence and recent controversies generated by this new perspective. A multifactored model of social movement formation is advanced, emphasizing resources, organization, and political opportunities in addition to traditional discontent hypotheses. The McCarthy-Zald (1973) theory of entrepreneurial mobilization is critically assessed as an interpretation of the social movements of the 1960s–1970s, and the relevance of the Olson (1968) theory of collective action is specified. Group organization is argued to be the major determinant of mobilization potential and patterns. The debate between the Gerlach-Hine (1970) and entrepreneurial theories of social movement organization is traced in terms of historical changes in the social movement sector and the persistence of organizational diversity. A model of social movement politics is outlined, building on Gamson's (1975) theory of strategy and Tilly's (1978) polity theory by emphasizing political alliances and processes shaping success and failure. Piven & Cloward (1977) are correct that disruptiveness leads to success and that disruptions can be mobilized without formal organization; they are wrong in asserting that formal organization is necessarily incompatible with mobilization. The future development of resource mobilization theory lies in two directions: extending the polity theory to deal with different states and regimes, including the development of neo-corporatism, and providing a more sophisticated social psychology of mobilization.

THE EMERGENCE OF RESOURCE MOBILIZATION THEORY

Of the wide-ranging effects that the social movements of the 1960s had on sociology, one of the more signifi-

cant was the reorientation of the study of social movements. Traditionally the central problem in the field had been explaining individual participation in social movements. The major formulations—mass society theory, relative deprivation, collective behavior theory—pointed to sudden increases in individual grievances generated by the "structural strains" of rapid social change. While specific hypotheses varied, these traditional theories shared the assumptions that movement participation was relatively rare, discontents were transitory, movement and institutionalized actions were sharply distinct, and movement actors were arational if not outright irrational. The movements of the 1960s dramatically challenged these assumptions. By providing a rich array of experience and enlisting the active sympathies of an enlarged pool of analysts, the movements stimulated a shift in theoretical assumptions and analytic emphases that eventually became formalized in the resource mobilization theory of social movements (Oberschall 1973; Tilly 1978; McCarthy & Zald 1973, 1977; Gamson 1975; Jenkins 1981) and closely allied neo-Marxian formulations (Useem 1975; Paige 1975; Schwartz 1976; Ash-Garner 1977; Piven & Cloward 1977). These new perspectives emphasized the continuities between movement and institutionalized actions, the rationality of movement actors, the strategic problems confronted by movements, and the role of movements as agencies for social change. In specific, these analysts argued that: (*a*) movement actions are rational, adaptive responses to the costs and rewards of different lines of action; (*b*) the basic goals of movements are defined by conflicts of interest built into institutionalized power relations; (*c*) the grievances generated by such conflicts are sufficiently ubiquitous that the formation and mobilization of movements depend on changes in resources, group organization, and opportunities for collective action; (*d*) centralized, formally structured movement organizations are more typical of modern social movements and more effective at mobilizing resources and mounting sustained challenges than decentralized, informal movement structures; and (*e*) the success of movements is largely determined by strategic factors and the political processes in which they become enmeshed.

These new perspectives have, in turn, stimulated a series of critiques, ranging from debates among resource mobilization theorists over the usefulness of particular formulations (Perrow 1979) to arguments by collective behavior theorists that the new perspectives are either not as distinctive as their proponents claim or rest on too narrow a theoretical framework (Turner 1982; Gusfield 1982; Zurcher & Snow 1981). This review draws on these debates and recent empirical studies to outline the basic arguments of resource mobilization theory and to assess critically the contribution of the theory to the major issues in the field: the formation of movements, the process of mobilization, the organization of social movements, and the outcome of challenges.

SOURCES OF CONTENTION: RESOURCE MOBILIZATION VS TRADITIONAL APPROACHES

The clash between resource mobilization theory and traditional approaches, especially collective behavior theories, has stemmed in large part from different conceptions of social movements. Traditional definitions have included any set of noninstitutionalized collective actions consciously oriented towards social change (or resisting such changes) and possessing a minimum of organization (Wilkinson 1971:27; Turner & Killian 1972:246). Social movements are traditionally seen as extensions of more elementary forms of collective behavior and as encompassing both movements of personal change (e.g. religious sects, cults, and communes) and those focused on institutional changes (e.g. legal reforms and changes in political power). Resource mobilization theorists have, in contrast, seen social movements as extensions of institutionalized actions and have restricted their focus to movements of institutional change that attempt to alter "elements of social structure and/or the reward distribution of society" (McCarthy & Zald 1977:1218), organize previously unorganized groups against institutional elites (Gason 1975:16–18), or represent the interests of groups excluded from the polity (Jenkins & Perrow 1977; Tilly 1978, 1979).

Most of the disputes in the field flow from this difference. Institutional change movements tend to conform to the basic resource mobilization model: rational actions oriented towards clearly defined, fixed goals with centralized organizational control over resources and clearly demarcated outcomes that can be evaluated in terms of tangible gains. The premise that social movements are extensions of institutionalized actions is also plausible. The problem arises, however, in applying this model to movements of personal change in which expressive actions are intertwined with rational-instrumental actions. In such movements, goals tend to arise out of interaction; centralized control

is tied to a charismatic leader or is weak; outcomes are diffuse. Continuities between these movements and elementary collective behavior are more apparent.

Given this bifurcation, how can the field develop? One direction is to apply resource mobilization models to the organizational aspects of personal change movements. Recent work by Lofland (1977, 1979), Shupe & Bromley (1979), Liebman (1983), and Hadden & Swan (1981) on religious movement organizations and by Snow, Zurcher & Eckland-Olson (1980) on microstructures of recruitment have already demonstrated the usefulness of resource mobilization models in studying personal change movements. More problematic is the analysis of personal and cultural change in resource mobilization terms. Traditionally resource mobilization theory has been posed in terms of collective actors struggling for power in an institutional context. Microlevel processes have been ignored or treated as simplifying assumptions for a larger-scale analysis (e.g. the rational actor premise; cf. Tilly 1978:119). Gamson, Fireman & Rytina (1982) have provided a start by analyzing micro-mobilization in terms of actions that give rise to rebellion, while Granovetter (1978) has analyzed the logic of collective decision-making. These analyses, however, have not yet been extended to deal with personality transformation or cultural change. In view of the generally limited success of sociologists in dealing with the links between micro- and macro-processes (Collins 1981), this will likely remain a problem in the future.

THE FORMATION OF SOCIAL MOVEMENTS

The sine qua non of the study of social movements has traditionally been the question of why movements form. Traditional explanations have emphasized sudden increases in short-term grievances created by the "structural strains" of rapid social change (Gusfield 1968). In contrast, resource mobilization theorists have argued that grievances are secondary. Tilly (1978), Jenkins & Perrow (1977), and Oberschall (1978a) have argued that grievances are relatively constant, deriving from structural conflicts of interest built into social institutions, and that movements form because of long-term changes in group resources, organization, and opportunities for collective action. While grievances are necessary for movement formation, they are explained either by changes in power relations (Korpi 1974) or by structural conflicts of interest. McCarthy &

Zald (1973, 1977) have taken a slightly different direction, arguing for an entrepreneurial theory of movement formation in which the major factor is the availability of resources, especially cadres and organizing facilities. Grievances are either structurally given or, increasingly in the contemporary setting, manufactured by the mobilizing efforts of movement entrepreneurs. As McCarthy & Zald formulate it, "the definition of grievances will expand to meet the funds and support personnel available" (1973:13).

The debate touched off by these formulations, especially the McCarthy-Zald version, has produced support for both formulations as well as a refined theory of grievances. The strongest support for the McCarthy-Zald theory has come from studies of the "public interest" movement that came to prominence in the 1970s. Berry's (1977:17–27) survey of public interest organizations found that the majority were formed by energetic entrepreneurs acting without significant increases in grievances. Likewise, Schoefield, Meier & Griffin (1979), Simcock (1979), and Wood (1982) have traced the emergence of the environmental movement to a handful of natural scientist and policy researchers who redefined traditional conservationist concerns in ecological terms and mobilized institutional resources. These movements pursued goals linked to the interests of broad, diffuse, disorganized collectivities such as the general public or middle-class consumers who were unlikely to mobilize without the initiative of entrepreneurs.

The entrepreneurial model has also received support from movements of deprived groups such as farm workers (Jenkins & Perrow 1977) and welfare recipients (Bailis 1974; Jackson & Johnson 1974). In these cases, the entrepreneurs had branched out after being cadres in the civil rights and student movements. Both were also centered among deprived groups with few resources, minimal political experience, and little prior organization, making outside organizers critical in the formation of a movement. In fact, such cadre diversification was also critical in launching a wide array of movements among less deprived groups such as women's liberation (Freeman 1973; Evans 1979; Tierney 1982), radical ecology (Wood 1982), and neighborhood and general citizen organizing (Kotz & Kotz 1977; Boyte 1979). In other words, the entrepreneurial model appears most relevant for movements among deprived groups and broad disorganized collectivities. The entrepreneurs are typically generated by the factionalization of previous movements. Significantly, however, major movements do not appear to emerge from the de novo manufacture of grievances by entrepreneurs. As McCarthy & Zald (1973:28) argue, entrepreneurs are more successful by seizing on major interest cleavages and redefining long-standing grievances in new terms.

Recent studies have also demonstrated the significance of increased grievances generated by sudden and major threats to the interests of cohesive and moderately resourceful groups. Useem's (1980) study of the antibusing countermovement in Boston found that relative deprivation created by elite challenges to traditional privileges was significant in explaining participation independent of solidarity levels. While the grievance measures were *post factum*, Walsh's (1981) study of protest groups contesting the reopening of the Three Mile Island nuclear plant has confirmed the importance of crises generated by elite actions. Antinuclear organizations had previously failed to mobilize citizens against the plant until the disaster. Significantly, support came overwhelmingly from middle- and upper-middle class residents who were politically active and highly involved in extralocal community organizations. In other words, "crisis" formation presupposes the existence of resourceful, organized groups. Typically the "crisis" is created by elite actions that threaten a population's way of life and thereby violate institutionalized conceptions of elite responsibilities (Moore 1978).

Studies have also confirmed the argument that long-term changes in the organization, resources, and opportunities of groups give rise to movement formation. Industrial conflicts are more likely among ecologically concentrated workers in large factories and densely populated urban neighborhoods (Lodhi & Tilly 1973; Shorter & Tilly 1974:287–95; Foster 1974; Lincoln 1978). Likewise, the emergence of the civil rights movement in the 1950s stemmed from the urbanization of the southern black population, increased numbers of middle-class and working-class blacks, growing black college enrollments, and the organizational expansion of black churches. These changes simultaneously freed blacks from traditional paternalistic social controls, increased levels of black organization and resources, and placed the black voter in a strategic location in national politics (W. J. Wilson 1973:140–51; Piven & Cloward 1977:189–94; Morris 1980; McAdam 1982). Similarly, Ragin (1979) and Nielsen (1980) have argued that ethnic separatist movements in Western Europe have emerged because of declining status inequalities, especially increases in the resources and ecological concentration of minority groups facilitating their competition for social rewards. In the same vein, sudden increases in the opportunities for cohesive, aggrieved groups can lead to the formation of movements. Large-scale peasant rebellions have typically emerged after the coercive capacity of the state has collapsed, leaving cohesive villages free to act on long-standing grievances (Skocpol 1979). In general, the formation of movements is linked to improvements in the status of aggrieved groups, not because of grievances created by the "revolution of rising expectations" but because these changes reduce the costs of mobilization and improve the likelihood of success.

These studies have also indicated the need for a multifactored approach to the problem of movement formation. Movements are formed through diverse routes depending on the elements absent in the premovement situation. Gamson, Fireman & Rytina (1982:82–93) have provided a suggestive formulation arguing for a "threshold" model of resources. Beyond this threshold additional resources make little difference. Presumably the same applies to grievances, organization and opportunities. Each factor must be present at its threshold level before a movement emerges. At the same time, deficits in some dimensions (e.g. group organization) might be offset by surpluses on other dimensions (e.g. experienced organizers). In general, a multifactored approach is more useful than McCarthy & Zald's exclusive emphasis on organizational resources. At the same time, the classic "structural strain" theories of grievances have been less useful than an approach emphasizing structural conflicts of interest.

THE PROCESS OF MOBILIZATION

Mobilization is the process by which a group secures collective control over the resources needed for collective action. The major issues, therefore, are the resources controlled by the group prior to mobilization efforts, the processes by which the group pools resources and directs these towards social change, and the extent to which outsiders increase the pool of resources.

Little agreement exists on the types of resources that are significant. Several analysts have offered classificatory schemes based upon the usefulness of particular resources in controlling the actions of targets (e.g. Etzioni 1968:388–89; Gamson 1968:100–5). In this vein, Rogers (1974) has distinguished *instrumental* resources used in actual influence attempts from *infra-* resources that condition the use of instrumental resources. Similarly, Jenkins (1982a) has distinguished *power* resources that provide the means for controlling the actions of targets from *mobilizing* resources such as

facilities that provide for mobilizing power resources.

The problem with schemes based on uses, however, is that most resources have multiple uses. Any scheme that ignores the intrinsic features of resources is therefore of limited value. In response, most analysts have simply listed the assets that are frequently mobilized by movements [e.g. McCarthy & Zald's (1977) money, facilities, labor, and legitimacy; or Tilly's (1978:69) land, labor, capital, and technical expertise]. Freeman (1979:172–5) has offered a more useful scheme, distinguishing *tangible* assets such as money, facilities, and means of communication from the *intangible* or "human" assets that form the central basis for movements. Intangible assets include both specialized resources such as organizing and legal skills, and the unspecialized labor of supporters.

The most distinctive contribution of resource mobilization theory has been to emphasize the significance of outside contributions and the cooptation of institutional resources by contemporary social movements. Traditionally, analysts have assumed that resources come from the direct beneficiaries of the social changes pursued and that, since movements lie outside institutionalized politics, they derive their resources from noninstitutional sources. McCarthy & Zald (1973, 1977), however, have argued that the movements of the 1960s and 1970s mobilized a "conscience constituency" of the wealthy and the affluent middle class (including college students) and coopted institutional resources from private foundations, social welfare institutions, the mass media, universities, governmental agencies, and even business corporations. Social movements have therefore shifted from classical social movement organizations (or classical SMOs) with indigenous leadership, volunteer staff, extensive membership, resources from direct beneficiaries, and actions based on mass participation, towards professional social movement organizations (or professional SMOs) with outside leadership, full time paid staff, small or nonexistent membership, resources from conscience constituencies, and actions that "speak for" rather than involve an aggrieved group.

This portrait of recent social movements has been challenged on several points. The general thesis is that these movements did not arise from a genuine "participation revolution" in American politics but merely reflected improved facilitative conditions for professionalized mobilization. Professionals and college students with discretionary time schedules and income, liberal institutions with "slack" resources, and pervasive mass media that could be coopted by enterprising movement entrepreneurs were the major factors behind the stormy 1960s. Evidence on political trends, how-ever, indicates a virtual explosion of unconventional mass political participation between 1960 and 1974. Figure 1 shows that the number of protest demonstra-tions and riots escalated dramatically, peaking in the 1967–1972 period. This "participation revolution" was, in turn, undergirded by a general increase in the mobi-lization for unconventional politics as the number of political ideologues increased from 1% of the citizenry in the 1950s to 19% in 1972, then declining to 7% in 1976 (Nie, Verba & Petrocik 1980:367), membership in political organizations expanded from 2.8% in 1956 to a peak of 4.4% in 1974 (Survey Research Center & Davis et al 1981), and political activists involved in nonelectoral activity rose from 5–12% in the 1950s to 15–20% in the late 1960s and early 1970s (Campbell et al 1960:51–2; Converse 1972:332–6; Rosenau 1974:44–86; Milbrath & Goel 1977:18–19). Simultane-ously, mobilization for routine politics declined as voter turnout slowly declined, partisan independence rose, and general distrust of elected officials and major insti-tutions steadily increased (Ladd & Hadley 1978; Miller, Miller & Schneider 1980:257–9).

While McCarthy & Zald are correct that profes-sional SMOs and the cooptation of institutional resources increased in the 1960s, these features hardly explain the mobilization of generalized political tur-moil in that period. Most of the movements were not

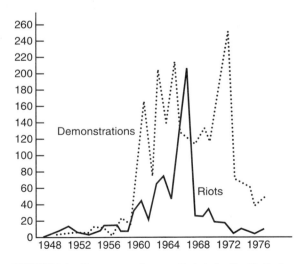

FIGURE 1 Demonstrations and riots in the United States, 1948–1977. From C. L. Taylor and Jodice, D. A., editors, *World Handbook of Political and Social Indicators*, 3rd ed. (New Haven, Conn.: Yale University Press, 1983).

professional SMOs and did not rely on external resources for their crucial victories. Contributors of external resources were largely reactive, not initiatory, and were not consistently beneficial. The civil rights movement was indigenously led by black clergy and students, mobilized resources chiefly through local community networks, and tapped "conscience con-stituents" only after generalized turmoil had already been mobilized (Morris 1980, 1981; McAdam 1982). Moreover, most of the external resources were mobi-lized by the moderate wing of the movement after it had successfully entered the polity and begun institutional-izing the gains of the Civil Rights Acts of 1964 and 1965. Ironically, the militant wing was more dependent on external resources and, partially because of conflicts over the use of these resources, became increasingly radical, eventually turning against their "conscience constituents" and destroying the organizations (Meier & Rudwick 1973; Carson 1981). Nor is the McCarthy-Zald theory fully satisfactory in explaining the middle-class and student involvement in the various movements of the 1960s. By focusing exclusively on economic changes that facilitated involvement (discre-tionary income and time schedules, social reform careers, institutional "slack"), the theory ignores changing cultural values and elite actions that led to an interest in movement politics. The middle-class "partic-ipation revolution" was rooted in the shift towards "postmaterialist" values emphasizing self-fulfillment that supported demands for direct participation in polit-ical decisions and moral concern for the plight of others (Ladd & Hadley 1978; Yankelovich 1974, 1981; Ingel-hart 1977). When elites challenged these values by manipulative acts and outright rejection, the middle class rallied around the movements.

The McCarthy-Zald theory does, however, identify significant aspects of recent social movements. The stu-dent and antiwar movements did rely heavily on the mobilization of transitory teams through coopting the mass media (Oberschall 1978; Gitlin 1980). Addition-ally, the welfare rights movement (Bailis 1974; West 1981), farm worker movement (Jenkins & Perrow 1977; Jenkins 1983), and "older wing" of the women's movement (Freeman 1975) were initiated by movement entrepreneurs who relied heavily on institutional resources. Moreover, the environmental, consumer rights and general "public interest" movements of the 1970s have fit the professional SMO model quite closely (McFarland 1976; Berry 1977; Handler 1978; Weisbrod, Handler & Komesar 1978). Finally, profes-sional SMOs such as Mobilization for Youth (Helfgot 1981) and the Community Action Program (Greenstone

& Peterson 1977; Friedland 1980) did function as social control devices, "diffusing the radical possibilities of dissent . . . by applying large amounts of resources . . . in ameliorative directions" (McCarthy & Zald 1973:26).

If direct beneficiaries have been the major contributors to recent movements, how have they been mobilized? Because of its rationalistic assumptions, the major debate has been over the usefulness of Mancur Olson's (1968) theory of collective action. According to Olson, rational self-interested individuals will not contribute to securing "collective goods" (i.e. nonexcludable benefits) because of the superior rationality of "riding free." Mobilization occurs only if "selective benefits" (i.e. distinct divisible benefits) are offered, the group is sufficiently small that benefits to individuals are greater than the costs of securing the collective good, or the group is "privileged" (i.e. contains individuals sufficiently endowed that the marginal costs of securing the collective good are less than their individual benefit).

All three of Olson's solutions to the problem of collective goods have come under critical attack. The major target has been the "by-product" theory of mobilization based on selective incentives. According to the theory, movement entrepreneurs motivated by the selective incentives of career opportunities offer selective incentives to members for their contributions, creating an expanding cycle of collective actions and further mobilization (Salisbury 1969; Frohlich, Oppenheimer & Young 1971; Oberschall 1973:146–72). The major challenge has centered on the prominence of moral or purposive incentives. Tillock & Morrison (1979) found that members of Zero Population Growth claimed overwhelmingly that a moral commitment to the collective good of population control was their sole motive for support. Moreover, contributions did not vary as a function of the size of chapter membership, casting doubt on the small-group hypothesis. While opinion surveys are a weak method for assessing motives, studies of environmental and public interest organizations by Mitchell (1980) and Berry (1977:36–43) have provided further support against the "by-product" theory. Selective incentives such as membership services and social events are rarely utilized and, in opinion surveys, contributors consistently claim that these are irrelevant to their support. A clue is provided by the framing of membership appeals. Movement entrepreneurs have consistently posed their appeals in terms of "collective evils" such as massive ecological dangers and violations of human rights.

Moralistic concerns are clearly uppermost. Moreover, in such a "no-exit" situation, the distinction between individual and collective benefits is obliterated (Hirschman 1970). However, these studies refute only the stronger version of the free-rider hypothesis— namely, that no one will contribute to the collective goods in the absence of selective benefits (Brubaker 1975). Moreover, these studies have examined only contributors, ignoring the far greater number of non-contributors who will also benefit from the collective good.

What about the weaker version of the free-rider hypothesis—that contributions will be suboptimal in the absence of selective incentives (Samuelson 1954)? In a series of experiments, Marwell & Ames (1979, 1980) have subjected this version to critical scrutiny, finding consistently that over half of all participants have contributed to the collective good without selective incentives. Variations in personal resources, pay off levels, and prior experience did not significantly affect contribution rates. However, group size was significant, smaller groups contributing at higher rates. Whether this was because of greater ease in coordination or due to Olson's small-group effect was unclear. While the isomorphism between experiments and natural settings is never perfect, these were sufficiently realistic that the high levels of contributions cast serious doubt on the free-rider hypothesis. In fact, Marwell (1981) has subsequently posited an intrinsic altruism reinforced by face-to-face interaction.

The Olson theory, however, cannot be dismissed. One case that supports it is the National Welfare Rights Organization experience (Bailis 1974). The NWRO was initiated by professional organizers who used the selective incentive of assistance in securing special cash benefits to mobilize welfare recipients. When organizers shifted to nonmaterial incentives, few prospective members were receptive. In line with Olson's theory, as soon as members learned how to secure the welfare benefits for themselves, contributions to the NWRO trailed off, leaving behind a core of activists motivated largely by the selective benefits of social recognition. When welfare administrators abolished the cash benefit program, the NWRO virtually collapsed.

The Olson theory correctly identifies a major problem but fails to offer an adequate solution. Olson is correct that movements cannot be mobilized around collective material benefits and that free-riding is potentially a major problem. The strongest evidence comes from Walsh & Warland's (1982) study of residents surrounding the Three Mile Island nuclear plant disaster. Free-riding was pervasive; only 13% of those opposed to the restart contributed. Free-riding was largely due to ignorance and calculations of personal interest. Almost half (48%) of the free-riders were unaware of the opposition effort or had not been contacted by movement organizers. The remainder cited personal constraints (24%), distaste for protest tactics and movement leaders (11%), or pessimism about their own political efficacy (5%). In other words, free-riding is probably widespread in natural settings and, while organizing efforts can reduce its frequency, personal calculations of costs and rewards are significant considerations.

How, then, do successful movements overcome the problem? The major method is the development of programs that offer the *collective incentives* of group solidarity and commitment to moral purpose (J. Wilson 1973; Gamson & Fireman 1979; Moe 1980; Jenkins 1982a). Group solidarity and purposive incentives are collective in that they entail the fusion of personal and collective interests. Movement supporters, like all socialized actors, act in terms of internalized values and sentiments as well as calculations of self-interest. The major task in mobilization, then, is to generate solidarity and moral commitments to the broad collectivities in whose name movements act.

The mobilization potential of a group is largely determined by the degree of preexisting group organization. Groups sharing strong distinctive identities and dense interpersonal networks exclusive to group members are highly organized and hence readily mobilized (Tilly 1978:62–3). By providing prior solidarities and moral commitments, these identities and networks provide a basis for the operation of collective incentives. The "bloc recruitment" (Oberschall 1973:125) of preexisting solidary groups is the most efficient form of recruitment and appears to be typical of large-scale institutional change movements (Snow, Zurcher & Eckland-Olson 1980). Conversely, groups with weak identities, few intragroup networks, and strong ties to outsiders are less likely to mobilize. As Foster (1974) found among English industrial workers, communities with strong intraclass networks based on intermarriage and involvement in recreational activities mobilized more readily and more extensively than those with weak networks and/or strong ties outside of their class. Similarly, Jenkins (1982a) found that seasonal farm workers who were immune to the paternalistic ties of their employers and enmeshed in cohesive work and kinship networks were more readily mobilized than

either migrants who lacked intragroup ties or permanent hands who were subject to employer controls.

Recruitment strategies follow the same basic principles. Campaigns centered around purposive and solidary incentives, focused on preexisting or "natural" groups, and linking the vision of change to the preexisting group culture are more effective. Farm worker unions that emphasized "bread and butter" gains were less successful than those that organized solidary events and inaugurated ideological training programs (Jenkins 1982a). Similarly, individual recruitment requires greater resource investments and is much slower than bloc recruitment (Snow, Zurcher & Eckland-Olson 1980; Jenkins 1982a). Likewise, organizers who draw on the cultural symbols of the target population are more successful than those emphasizing abstract ideologies (Brill 1971).

Differential recruitment follows essentially the same outlines. Recruitment tends to select individuals who are more enmeshed in interpersonal networks (Pinard 1971; Leahy & Mazur 1978; Snow, Zurcher & Eckland-Olson 1980), active in political organizations that support social change (von Eschen, Kirk & Pinard 1971; Barnes & Kaase 1979; E. J. Walsh, R. H. Warland, unpublished paper), ideologically committed to social change (Bolton 1972; Fendrich 1974), and structurally available for participation (Orum 1972 Snow, Zurcher & Eckland-Olson 1980). Differential recruitment also changes as movements expand. Early recruits to the student movement came from higher socioeconomic backgrounds, attended elite universities, were more active in political organizations, and were more committed to social change ideologies than later recruits (Lipset 1971:81–8; Wood 1974). Likewise, social classes appear to respond to different incentives. In general, more secure middle- and upper-class groups are more receptive to purposive incentives, while less secure, lower-class groups respond to selective incentives and collective solidarity (J. Wilson 1973:72–73). Similarly, differential participation tends to follow receptiveness to different incentives. Oliver (1982) found that full-time cadres in the neighborhood movement were more ideologically committed, while transitory activists were more concerned about personal benefits. In other words, the monetary rewards that professional staff receive are probably secondary to ideological concern as their low salary levels suggest.

Note that the preceding discussion has ignored the major emphasis in classic studies of differential recruitment—namely, the role of personality characteristics. While personality differences undoubtedly play a role in differential recruitment, existing studies have been inconclusive as to which personality traits are significant and, more importantly, have been methodologically unable to demonstrate that these traits are independent of the social characteristics that lead to differential recruitment and participation.

THE ORGANIZATION OF SOCIAL MOVEMENTS

The major debate over the organization of movements has been between proponents of a centralized bureaucratic model (Gamson 1975; McCarthy & Zold 1973, 1977) and those arguing for a decentralized informal model (Gerlach & Hine 1970). The former argue that a formalized structure with a clear division of the labor maximizes mobilization by transforming diffuse commitments into clearly defined roles and that a centralized decision-making structure increases combat readiness by reducing internal conflicts (Gamson 1975: 89–109). In contrast, Gerlach & Hine (1970:34–56) have argued that decentralized movements with a minimum division of labor and integrated by informal networks and an overarching ideology are more effective. A segmented, decentralized structure maximizes mobilization by providing extensive inter-personal bonds that generate solidarity and reinforce ideological commitments. In addition, such a structure is highly adaptive, encouraging tactical experimentation, competition among subgroups, and lessened vulnerability to suppression or cooptation by authorities.

This debate, however, has been seriously derailed by several misinterpretations. Some analysts (especially Gerlach & Hine) have assumed that the debate centers around identifying the single typical form of movement organization. As Zald & Ash (1966) argued sometime ago, movements adopt different forms depending on their goals. Personal change movements tend to adopt decentralized structures and exclusive membership rules while institutional change movements are typically centralized and inclusive (Curtis & Zurcher 1974). Moreover, analysts have ignored the distinction between social movements (or SMs) defined by broad goals and/or interests, and social movement organizations (or SMOs) defined by particular organizational structures. Since social movements are typically characterized by multiple SMOs, a multi-organizational model allowing the coexistence of diverse types is generally more appropriate in gauging the organization of a single social movement (Zald & McCarthy 1980). Finally, commentators have often taken these formulations as descriptions rather than ideal-typical extremes. Current research indicates that there are also intermediary forms of SMOs: centralized structures with semi-autonomous locals (e.g. the NAACP, the labor movement) and autonomous locals loosely coordinated through federative structures (e.g. SCLC, the tenant movement).

The broadest treatment of movement organization has been the analysis of the modernization of collective action by Charles Tilly (1978) and his associates (Shorter & Tilly 1974; Tilly, Tilly & Tilly 1975; Tilly & Tilly 1981). Building on the classic distinction between communal and associational organization, they have documented the broad shift over the past four centuries from short reactive actions by small-scale informal solidary groups (or communities) to long proactive actions mounted by large-scale special purpose associations. The shift broadly conforms to that from decentralized, informally structured communal movements to centralized, formally structured SMOs. The major sources of this shift have been linked to the broad contours of social development. The growth of industrial capitalism and the building of modern states destroyed the autonomy of small solidary groups and forced claimants to compete in a larger national political arena in which large numbers and bureaucratic structures were keys to success. Furthermore, urbanization and the growth of the mass media reduced the costs of large-scale mobilization, making bureaucratized associations more feasible. Finally, the institutionalization of liberal democracy, especially mass electoral participation, furnished an environment well suited to movement organizations that could mobilize large numbers of supporters. As the traditional communal group gave way to the modern bureaucratized association, the goals and forms of action shifted. Communal actors were "instinctive radicals," treating outside intrusions as fundamental violations, while associations were more moderate, maximizing gains within a given political environment (Calhoun 1982). The former adopted a relatively fixed repertoire borrowed from existing structures of authority while the latter were more flexible, experimenting with different forms of action and, at least in liberal democracies, adopting the mass demonstration because of its advantages in signalling numerical support. McCarthy & Zald's (1973, 1977) professional SMO with its reliance on professional staff, external resources, and transitory teams could be viewed as a direct extension of this general trend.

Yet despite this broad shift, decentralized movements have continued to emerge. Often decentralized structures are a product of deliberate choices by redemptive or personal-change movements attempting to embody ideals in the hope that these will serve as models for emulation. The student movement, and SDS in particular, adopted a decentralized "leaderless" model of democratic structure in order to maximize the values of direct participation and communal involvement and to avoid the dangers of oligarchy and cooptation (Breines 1980, 1982; Case & Taylor 1979). Decentralized structures can also evolve from ecological constraints and inherited models. Judkins (1979), for example, has argued that the geographic dispersion and competitive leadership structure of the contemporary movement on behalf of black lung victims have created a decentralized structure more akin to a federation of chapters than the bureaucratized organization that is claimed to exist. Similarly, Freeman (1979) has argued that the two wings of the women's movement developed different structures because of the political experiences, values, reference standards, and target relations inherited from the initial organizers. While both branches possessed similar resources, the "older" branch (NOW, WEAL, NWPC) was organized by women whose experience lay in conventional reform politics and whose values and reference standards emphasized effectiveness in bringing about institutional changes. Bureaucratic structures were adopted because these were familiar means that had been used by the labor and civil rights movements. The "younger" branch, in contrast, emerged out of the late phases of the student movement and therefore emphasized direct participation and personal transformation in preparation for social revolution. Once set, organizational structures channel actions and are relatively immutable. As the prospects for revolution receded, these decentralized structures channelled action towards personal-change activities such as "consciousness raising" and educational/service projects. Despite rhetorical commitments to institutional change, appropriate actions were organizationally blocked by the decentralized structures.

Within a basic framework, the organizational structures of movements can still evolve. Contrary to the classic Weber-Michels theory, however, change is not inevitably in the direction of greater bureaucratization. As the National Organization for Women expanded in the mid-1970s to become the major organization in the women's movement, it became more internally diverse and developed a more decentralized structure composed of special task forces to accommodate the diverse ideologies and interests of its rapidly growing membership (Carden 1978). Similarly, Hertz (1981) has argued that the growth of the welfare rights movement in the late 1960s produced a multi-organizational field of informally coordinated organizations, providing the movement with the advantages of a decentralized structure. While this created strains because of internal competition for resources, decentralization also reduced factionalist tendencies by allowing activists to pursue diverse concerns. The same could be argued for the multi-organizational civil rights movement during its expansionary phase (McAdam 1982). Likewise, movement organizations can preserve their decentralized communal structures by adopting restrictions on size, using mutual criticism to restrain core activists, remaining economically marginal, relying strictly on internal financing, and attempting to reduce knowledge differentials among participants (Rothschild-Whitt 1979).

These studies have also underlined Zald & Ash's (1966) classic contention that different organizational structures are effective for different tasks. Bureaucratic structures provide technical expertise and coordination essential in institutional change efforts but are less effective at mobilizing "grass roots" participation. Decentralized structures maximize personal transformation, thereby mobilizing "grass roots" participation and insuring group maintenance, but often at the cost of strategic effectiveness. Movement organizations that attempt to combine incongruent elements therefore confront strategic dilemmas. The antinuclear-power movement, for example, has effectively mobilized "grass roots" support because of its decentralized participatory structures but, despite the adoption of innovative methods for making consensual decisions, the process of consulting numerous "affinity groups" has significantly hindered its strategic effectiveness (Barkan 1979). Similarly, major internal strains in SDS eventually led to organizational collapse in the late 1960s, in part because the decentralized structures were ultimately incompatible with the mass mobilization projects undertaken in opposition to the Vietnam War buildup (Gitlin 1980:133–36, 156–62). In fact, Starr (1979) has argued that this organizational dichotomy is so significant that it accounts for the different fates of the various social movements of the 1960s. "Exemplary" organizations such as communes and co-ops collapsed either because they were introverted and socially isolated or because their decentralized structures blocked large-scale mobilization. At the same time, "adversary" organizations that pursued moderate reforms typically survived and became politically incorporated because their centralized structures enabled them to coopt institutional resources (e.g. the alternative media) or required minimal "grass roots" participation (e.g. community organizations and public interest lobbies).

However, most SMOs probably fall somewhere between the bureaucratic and decentralized models. Potentially this affords the mobilization advantages of decentralization as well as the tactical ones of centralization. Moreover, most social movements contain multiple SMOs. The civil rights experience suggests that informal coordination between different SMOs based on shared ideology and goals might afford the advantages of decentralization while simultaneously allowing sufficient centralized thrust to reap the advantages of bureaucratization (McAdam 1982).

THE POLITICS OF SOCIAL MOVEMENTS

Theories of the outcomes of social movements have traditionally been framed in terms of a "closed system" model of development, arguing that movements pass through a standard evolutionary sequence or "life cycle" culminating in either collapse or bureaucratization and institutional accommodation (Hopper 1950; Lang & Lang 1961). In contrast, resource mobilization theorists have adopted an "open system" approach, arguing that the outcomes of movements are critically shaped by the larger political environment. The outcomes of challenges depend not only on strategic choices but also on the stance of political elites and the support/opposition of established interest organizations and other movements. The balance of supports and social controls is, in turn, shaped by changes in governing coalitions, the structure of regimes, and societal changes that give rise to regime crises.

The major debates have centered around Gamson's (1975) relatively elementary analysis of the success and failure of 53 randomly selected movement organizations active in the United States between 1800 and 1945. Gamson measured success by two dimensions: the provision of tangible benefits that meet goals established by the movement organizations, and the formal acceptance of the movement organization by its main antagonist as a valid representative of a legitimate set of interests. Movement outcomes fall into four categories: full success; cooptation (acceptance but no benefits);

preemption (benefits but no acceptance); and failure. In general, successful movement organizations were bureaucratic, pursued narrow goals, employed selective incentives, enjoyed sponsorship, used unruly methods (including violence), and made their demands during periods of sociopolitical crises. Coopted organizations tended to have larger memberships and formalized structures; they mounted their challenges during wartime. Preempted organizations were typically small, centrally controlled, and less active during crisis periods.

While reanalysis has essentially reconfirmed Gamson's major findings (Steedly & Foley 1979), Goldstone (1980) has argued that the organizational and strategic considerations are largely irrelevant once controls have been introduced for the goals (displacement vs nondisplacement of antagonists) and political context (crisis vs noncrisis) of the challenges. Nondisplacement organizations consistently succeed, suggesting that the American polity is highly receptive to reform movements. Success tends to occur during crisis periods, suggesting the movements have little control over their effectiveness. However, Gamson (1980) has effectively challenged these contentions, demonstrating that Goldstone's conclusions are based on an erroneous recoding of several cases, a significant narrowing of the meaning of success, and an ambiguous interpretation of "crisis" periods. Goldstone defines success in terms of any tangible benefits regardless of whether secured from the main or secondary antagonists. Moreover, "crisis" is treated in an ad hoc manner, including not only depressions and wars but virtually any rapid social change affecting the group in question.

In fact, the Gamson model is more vulnerable to the opposite charge, that it employs too narrow a concept of success. Turner & Killian, for example, have offered three criteria of success: benefits for members; changes in power relations; and the realization of a "program for the reform of society" (1972:256). The first two criteria are the most useful for comparative purposes insofar as the latter is relative to the specific movement and constitutes more of an idealized yardstick than a clear criterion. Even using this narrowed range, Gamson's criteria are extremely limited, dealing only with tangible forms of the first and relatively weak measures of the second. While intangible gains such as improved self-images may be less measurable, they are clearly significant movement goals. Even more problematic is Gamson's assessment of changes in power relations. Broadly speaking, changes in social power (cf. Lukes 1974; Domhoff 1979:121–50) can be assessed in three ways: short-term changes in the outcomes of legitimate decisions (e.g. public policy outcomes); alterations in the composition and organization of decision-making elites (e.g. elite circulation and changes in regimes); and long-term changes in the distribution of socially valued goods (e.g. the transformation of class structures and social prestige hierarchies). Formal acceptance is an extremely weak measure of the second dimension. In the post–New Deal period in the United States, for example, political elites have increasingly allowed movement leaders to participate formally in public hearings and legal proceedings. Formal access, however, has not consistently led to tangible policy gains, in part because of the contingencies of policy implementation (Handler 1978). In fact, such formal access has often misled potential supporters into believing that their interests were being taken into account, thereby reducing mobilization and the likelihood of significant gains (Edelman 1971). In other words, cooptation should be deleted from the list of successful outcomes and a broader range of changes in power relations included.

The most direct challenge to the Gamson model has been Piven & Cloward's (1977) argument that poor people's movements derive their gains solely from mass defiance and that building permanent membership organizations is inherently counterproductive, (*a*) because poor people are unable to construct permanent political organizations in the fashion of more well-to-do segments, and (*b*) owing to the demobilizing effects of organization building. Instead of focusing commitments and maximizing strategic flexibility, formalized organizations divert energies from mass defiance and provide political elites with a forum for propagating symbolic reassurances and thereby demobilizing mass defiance. Evidence supporting the theory comes from studies of the policy impacts of the urban riots of the 1960s. With the sole exception of Albritton's (1979), these studies have found that the size and damages of these riots gave rise to the expansion of welfare rolls and expenditures on welfare and related social programs (Button 1978; Jennings 1979; Issac & Kelly 1981; Griffin, Devine & Wallace 1981; Hicks & Swank 1981). Piven & Cloward appear to be correct on two counts: Formalized organization is not a prerequisite for mass defiance, and the institutional disruptions created by mass defiance do give rise to short-term tangible benefits.

The major flaw in the Piven-Cloward theory is the contention that formalized organization is inherently incompatible with mass defiance. Gamson's data, for example, show a positive relation between the degree of organization and unruliness. Of the 53 organizations, those that used violence or other constraints were more likely to be formalized and centrally controlled than the others (62% and 75% vs 45% and 53%). Moreover, several recent poor people's movements have made effective use of formalized organization. The United Farm Workers' Union, for example, has not only constructed a formalized, centrally controlled organization but has used this structure to organize successful mass strikes (Jenkins 1984). Likewise, membership organizing by the welfare rights movement was actually quite effective. At least between 1967 and 1970, organizing chapters and mobilizing mass defiance went hand in hand (West 1981:292–303). The key shift came in 1970 as state legislatures and welfare administrators curtailed the special grant programs that had furnished NWRO organizers with selective incentives, thereby undercutting membership organizing and leaving leaders with few alternatives to legislative lobbying.

While unruliness in general appears to be effective, the picture is more mixed regarding the various forms of disruption. Snyder & Kelly (1976), for example, have argued that while successful strikes in Italy are associated with both collective violence and the size of union membership, it is membership size that explains the link between violence and strike success. The efficacy of violence also depends on the institutional context and goals of the movement. Burstein (1981) has shown that the urban riots may have generated increased welfare spending but they also worked against the passage of civil rights legislation. At the same time, peaceful demonstrations were productive, both directly by pressuring political elites and indirectly by stimulating shifts in public opinion. Similarly, peaceful protests by the anti-war movement between 1964 and 1970 were effective in bringing about a shift in public opinion and legitimizing the option of withdrawal, thereby spurring favorable shifts in Senate voting on Vietnam War motions. After 1970, however, protests were counterproductive as further shifts in public opinion ceased, fiscal considerations became paramount in Congress, and the issue became the nature, pace, and details of withdrawal (Burstein & Freudenberg 1978). The efficacy of violence also depends on the significance of third parties or bystander publics to the outcome. Because violence tends to alienate such third parties, it reduces the likelihood of success in settings in which third party support is critical (Schumaker 1978; Garrow 1978:158–60).

Because mass media coverage is decisive in

informing elites and mass publics about movement actions as well as in forming the morale and self-image of movement activists, the mass media are important actors in political conflicts. Coverage, however, depends upon the structure of the media organizations. Large city newspapers with middle-class and elite readerships and specialized news staffs are more likely than smaller, less professionalized papers to cover protest actions (Goldenberg 1976). Similarly, until the television networks developed professional news staffs in the late 1950s, this medium was unavailable. Subtler are the effects of selective reportage and framing. Under pressure from the Nixon administration in the early 1970s, the national news managers systematically reduced their coverage of mass demonstrations (Hodgson 1976:374–79). In addition, the frames used routinely by the news media in presenting stories impose their own constraints. News must be "novel" and "interesting." Movements must therefore walk the fine line between outlandishness (which alienates third parties but secures coverage) and conventionality (which may be persuasive but is ignored by the media). Moreover, news coverage is often unsuitable for movement proselytizing. News stories emphasize action rather than context, leaving readers ignorant of the causes and goals of the movement. In the long run, media-based mobilization is a weak substitute for more direct methods. Media coverage also tends to make superstars out of movement leaders, aggravating internal rivalries and tendencies towards showmanship, thereby weakening mobilization (Molotch 1979; Gitlin 1980).

Because of the vulnerabilities of media coverage, the most important alliances with third parties are probably formed independently. The successful boycotts of the United Farm Workers, for example, depended on strong support from liberal churches and organized labor, both of which had been sponsors prior to the protest campaigns (Jenkins 1983). Similarly, the increasing political influence of the NAACP during the late 1960s was due in part to the increasing strength and density of interorganizational sponsorship ties that developed independently of media coverage (Aveni 1978).

In general, these studies support Tilly's (1978: 125–33) thesis that entry into the polity by forging alliances with polity members is the central ingredient in success. Polity access creates a qualitative increment in the returns to collective action and shelters the movement against repression. The clearest evidence is provided by Ragin, Coverman & Hayward's (1982) study

of English strikes. After the English working class secured the electoral franchise in 1918, the Labour Party secured parliamentary representation and became strong enough to enter several governing coalitions. Strike success rates increased dramatically and the ratio of resource investments (strike days per man) to strike gains declined sharply.

Which circumstances make for political access? Tilly (1978:213–14) has offered a political interpretation, arguing that the formation of a member/challenger coalition depends largely on the calculus of short–term political advantages for polity members. If the polity is closely divided, members have lost their normal coalition partners, or members find themselves in jeopardy for want of resources, the normally risky strategy of supporting the entry of a movement is more likely to be adopted. If the coalition is successful, the movement secures access and, depending on the base of power, the rules of polity membership are restructured. Others have traced such regime crises to underlying economic transformations. Piven & Cloward (1977), for example, have argued that poor people's movements secure access only during regime crises created by such major economic dislocations as depressions and the wholesale reorganization of regional economies. Major dislocations simultaneously weaken previously dominant groups and exacerbate cleavages among national elites, thereby increasing the likelihood of an elite division that could lead to elite support for movements. Similarly, Skocpol (1979) has argued that social revolutions are created through generalized regime crises, typically induced by fiscal overloads and major losses in warfare that aggravate long-standing conflicts between dominant groups and, by weakening the repressive capacity of the state, open the way for large-scale peasant uprisings.

These formulations can also be extended to deal with the routine shifts in political power that create opportunities for access by reform movements. The processes depend on the rules governing polity access. In liberal democratic regimes, the state is potentially an "alternative power system" regulated by the mobilization of organized numbers (Schattschneider 1960; Wrong 1979:197–217). Polity access is therefore regulated by broad shifts in public opinion and the mobilization of electoral coalitions that bring about changes in governing coalitions. If a favorable governing coalition is in power, reform movements with a large organized membership can offer electoral support in exchange for entry into the polity. For example, the successful entry of the moderate wing of the civil rights movement in the mid-1960s stemmed from routine changes in political power. Following World War II, southern whites gradually became more tolerant of race relations reform, presumably because of the declining significance of the plantation economy to which the Jim Crow system had historically been tied (Burstein 1979). Simultaneously, black migration to northern cities placed black voters in a strategic position in national elections, providing the margin of victory in several major industrial states (Brink & Harris 1964). The increasing "swing" character of the black vote accelerated this tendency, forcing national candidates of both parties to pay increasing attention to it. The final element was the landslide 1964 election, placing a center/left governing coalition firmly in power based on the votes of the white ethnic working class, the solid South, increasing numbers of upper-middle class liberals and, of course, urban blacks. In control of both the Presidency and Congress for the first time since the 1930s, this center/left coalition forced through an extension of the "New Deal revolution" that included the Civil Rights Acts of 1964 and 1965, thereby enfranchising southern blacks and dismantling the Jim Crow system.

Because they shape political opportunities, broad electoral shifts linked to changes in governing coalitions also regulate the expansion and contraction of the social movement sector. The dynamic of expansion is largely created by two factors: the stimulus of increasing opportunities, and the "demonstration effect" of movement success. The dominance of a center/left governing coalition generally increases the opportunities for reform movements by reducing the likelihood of repression and increasing the likelihood of sponsorship by polity members. Likewise, a successful challenge boosts the morale of other challengers, provides models of effective tactics, and frequently frees up institutional resources for other movements. The dynamic also works in reverse. The proliferation of movements can undermine electoral coalitions by interjecting issues that stimulate a backlash by former coalition members who then transfer their electoral support to a center/right governing coalition. Once in power, this new governing coalition moves to demobilize the social-movement sector, stepping up repression against movement activists and attempting to curtail institutional supports for movements. In broad terms, this dynamic appears to fit the expansion and contraction of the social-movement sector during the 1960s and 1970s in the United States (Jenkins 1982b) and appears to be a standard feature of the political process of social reform in liberal democratic regimes (Tarrow 1982).

The rules governing routine political processes also shape the composition of the social-movement sector and its links to electoral processes. In the United States, single-member districts and Presidential government have institutionalized a two-party system with weak party organizations that rely more on patronage than ideology to mobilize support. In several of the Western European liberal democracies, proportional representation and parliamentary government have institutionalized a multi-party system populated by ideological parties with more stable bases of support. As a result of these factors, social movements in the United States are more likely to be independent of partisan alliances, adopting single-issue strategies rather than linking their programs to electoral campaigns and broader ideological definitions of political issues. In this sense, the success of reform movements is probably more dependent on electoral outcomes in Western Europe than in the United States. At the same time, however, the recent development of neocorporatist representation mechanisms in several Western European democracies has worked against this link, reducing the power of party leaders and parliamentary coalitions and strengthening the hand of state managers and the representatives of the dominant private interest associations (Schmitter 1979). The extent to which neocorporatist relations will allow the selective cooptation of new movements or force challengers into broad opposition party efforts in the future remains unclear. If Nelkin & Pollack's (1981) study of the anti-nuclear power movement in West Germany and France is indicative, the central factors will be the centralization of state institutions and the restrictiveness of access to decision-making bodies. The greater prominence of the oppositional Green party movement in West Germany flows from the greater permeability of a federal as opposed to a unitary state and the greater degree of public access to governmental agencies. In this setting, neocorporatism has not successfully deflected the movement.

THE FUTURE OF RESOURCE MOBILIZATION THEORY

The future of resource mobilization theory lies in two directions: extending the basic polity model to deal with a broader variety of regimes, and refining the basic mobilization model by developing a more sophisticated social psychology of collective action. The central concern of the polity model is the link between regime changes and opportunities for political access. Research has been confined largely to liberal democratic regimes, linking movement access to changing electoral alignments, governing coalitions, and the institutional structure of the state. The development of neocorporatism offers the most provocative thesis for future analysis. Will neocorporatism allow governing elites to deflect and selectively coopt movements or force challengers into broader third party coalitions? Where neocorporatism is weakly developed (as in the United States), will partisan coalitions and alliances with polity members continue to regulate the access of single-issue reform movements? The largest vacuum lies in the analysis of authoritarian and one-party regimes. Are liberal democracies actually more permeable? Do elite cleavages within these regimes play the same role as partisan clashes in opening or closing access? Do corporatist devices have the same implications as in liberal democracies?

The central concern of the mobilization model is the link between collective interests and the pooling of resources. Collective interests are assumed to be relatively unproblematic and to exist prior to mobilization, instead of being socially constructed and created by the mobilization process. The critique of the Olson theory, however, suggests that collective interests are often emergent. How are such collective identities formed? Is resocialization central? Is there a logic of emergence that governs the content of such collective identities? Calhoun (1982), for example, has argued that "radical" definitions emerge only among densely connected informal communities that perceive threats as affecting their complete way of life. Paige (1975), in contrast, argues that this is because of the underlying zero-sum conflict of interests prevalent in traditional agrarian production systems. How indeterminant are such collective redefinitions of interests?

Once resource mobilization theory has expanded its scope in these two directions, it will have served its major purpose, linking the study of social movements to a comparative political sociology of states and regimes and to a more sophisticated social psychology of collective action.

Acknowledgment

This article was prepared with support from National Endowment for the Humanities Grant # RS–00119–79. The author benefitted greatly from conversations with Ron Lawson, who, of course, is not responsible for the review's content.

LITERATURE CITED

Albritton, R. B. 1979. Social amelioration through mass insurgency. *Am. Poi. Sci. Rev.* 73:1003–11

Ash-Garner, R. 1977. *Social Movements in America.* Chicago: Rand-McNally. 233 pp.

Aveni, A. 1978. "Organizational linkages and resource mobilization." *Sociol. Q.* 19:185–202

Bailis, L. 1974. *Bread or Justice.* Lexington, MA: Heath. 254 pp.

Barkan, S. E. 1979. Strategic, tactical and organizational dilemmas of the protest movement against nuclear power. *Soc. Probl.* 27:19–37

Barnes, S. H., Kaase, M. 1979. *Political Actions.* Beverly Hills, CA: Sage. 607 pp.

Berry, J. M. 1977. *Lobbying for the People.* Princeton, NJ: Princeton Univ. Press. 331 pp.

Bolton, C. D. 1972. Alienation and action. *Am. J. Sociol.* 78:537–61

Boyte, H. 1979. *The Backyard Revolution.* Philadelphia, PA: Temple Univ. Press. 271 pp.

Breines, W. 1980. Community and Organization. *Soc. Probl.* 27:419–29

Breines, W. 1982. *Community and Organization.* South Hadley, MA: Bergin. 286 pp.

Brill, H. 1971. *Why Organizers Fail.* Berkeley: Univ. Calif. Press. 192 pp.

Brink, W., Harris, L. 1963. *The Negro Revolution in America.* NY: Simon and Schuster. 236 pp.

Brubaker, E. R. 1975. Free ride, free revelation, or golden rule? *J. Law Econ.* 18:147–61

Burstein, P. 1979. Public opinion, demonstrations and the passage of antidiscrimination legislation. *Publ. Opin. Q.* 43:157–72

Burstein, P. 1981. Social protest, public opinion and public policy. Presented at Ann. Meet. Am. Sociol. Assoc., 76th, Toronto, Canada

Burstein, P., Freudenberg, W. 1978. Changing public policy. *Am. J. Sociol.* 84:99–122

Button, J. W. 1978. *Black Violence.* Princeton, NJ: Princeton Univ. Press. 248 pp.

Calhoun, C. 1982. *The Question of Class Struggle,* NY: Oxford Univ. Press. 182 pp.

Campbell, A., Converse, P., Miller, W., Stokes, D. E. 1960. *The American Voter.* NY: Wiley. 264 pp.

Carden, M. L. 1974. *The New Feminist Movement.* NY: Russell Sage

Carden, M. L. 1978. The proliferation of a social movement. *Res. Soc. Movem. Confl. Change* 1:179–96

Carson, C. 1981. *In Struggle*. Cambridge, MA: Harvard Univ. Press. 359 pp.

Case, J., Taylor, R. C. R. 1979. *Coops, Communes and Collectives*. NY: Pantheon. 326 pp.

Collins, R. 1981. The microfoundations of macro-sociology. *Am. J. Sociol.* 86:984–1014

Converse, R. 1972. Change in the American electorate. In *The Human Meaning of Social Change*, ed. A Campbell, P. Converse. NY: Russell Sage. 584 pp.

Curtis, R. L., Zurcher, L. 1974. Social movements. *Soc. Probl.* 21:356–70

Davis, J. A., Smith, T. W., Stephenson, C. B. 1981. *General Social Survey*. Ann Arbor, MI: Inter-Univ. Consort. Pol. Soc. Res. 783 pp.

Domhoff, G. W. 1979. *Who Really Rules?* Santa Monica, CA: Goodyear. 189 pp.

Edelman, M. 1971. *Politics as Symbolic Action*. New Haven: Yale Univ. Press. 178 pp.

Etzioni, A. 1968. *The Active Society*. NY: Free Press, 488 pp.

Evans, S. J. 1979. *Personal Politics*. NY: Knopf. 174 pp.

Fendrich, J. N. 1974. Keeping the faith or living the good life. *Am. Sociol. Rev.* 39:321–47

Foster, J. 1974. *Class Struggle in the Industrial Revolution*. NY: St. Martins Press. 338 pp.

Friedland, R. 1980. Class, power and social control. In *Classes, Class Conflict and the State*, ed. M. Zeitlin, pp. 193–216. Cambridge, MA: Winthrop. 378 pp.

Freeman, J. 1973. The origins of the women's liberation movement. *Am. J. Sociol.* 78:792–811

Freeman, J. 1975. *The Politics of Women's Liberation*. NY: McKay. 196 pp.

Freeman, J. 1979. Resource mobilization and strategy. In *The Dynamics of Social Movements*, ed. M. N. Zald, J. M. McCarthy, pp. 167–89. Cambridge, MA: Winthrop. 274 pp.

Frohlich, N., Oppenheimer, J. A., Young, O. R. 1971. *Political Leadership and Collective Goods*. Princeton, NJ: Princeton Univ. Press. 286 pp.

Gamson, W. 1968. *Power and Discontent*. Homewood, IL: Dorsey. 208 pp.

Gamson, W. 1975. *The Strategy of Social Protest*. Homewood, IL: Dorsey. 217 pp.

Gamson, W. A. 1980. Understanding the careers of challenging groups. *Am. J. Sociol.* 85:1043–60

Gamson, W., Fireman, B. 1979. Utilitarian logic in the resource mobilization perspective. In *The Dynamics of Social Movements*, ed. M. N. Zald, J. M. McCarthy, pp. 8–45. Cambridge, MA: Winthrop. 274 pp.

Gamson, W., Fireman, B., Rytina, S. 1982. *Encounters With Unjust Authority*. Homewood, IL: Dorsey. 171 pp.

Garner, R., Zald, M. N. 1981. Social movement sectors and systemic constraints. CSRO Work. Pap. #238. Ann Arbor, MI: Cent. Res. Soc. Org., Univ. Michigan

Garrow, D. J. 1978. *Protest at Selma*. New Haven, CT: Yale Univ. Press. 383 pp.

Gerlach, L., Hine, V. 1970. *People, Power, Change*. NY: Bobbs-Merrill, 257 pp.

Gitlin, T. 1980. *The Whole World Is Watching*. Berkeley: Univ. Calif. Press. 327 pp.

Goldenberg, E. 1976. *Making the News*. Lexington, MA: D. C. Heath. 187 pp.

Goldstone, J. A. 1980. The weakness of organization. *Am. J. Sociol.* 85:1017–42

Granovetter, M. 1978. Threshold models of collective behavior. *Am. J. Sociol.* 83:1420–43

Griffin, L. J., Devine, J., Wallace, M. 1981. Accumulation, legitimation and politics. Presented at Ann. Meet. Am. Sociol. Assoc., 76th, Toronto, Canada

Gusfield, J. 1968. The study of social movements. In *Encyclopedia of the Social Sciences*. NY: Macmillan. 14:445–52

Gusfield, J. R. 1982. Social movements and social change. *Res. Soc. Movem., Confl. Change* 4:283–316

Hadden, J. K., Swan, C. E. 1981. *Prime Time Preachers*. Reading, MA: Addison-Wesley. 217 pp.

Handler, J. F. 1978. *Social Movements and the Legal System*. NY: Academic. 252 pp.

Helfgot, J. H. 1981. *Professional Reforming*. Lexington, MA: D. C. Heath. 218 pp.

Hertz, S. H. 1981. *The Welfare Mothers Movement*. Washington, DC: University Press of America. 193 pp.

Hicks, A., Swank, D. 1981. Paying off the poor. Presented at Ann. Meet. Am. Sociol. Assoc., 76th, Toronto, Canada

Hirschman, A. Q. 1970. *Exit, Voice and Loyalty*. Cambridge, MA: Harvard Univ. Press. 178 pp.

Hodgson, G. 1976. *America In Our Time*. NY: Doubleday. 564 pp.

Hopper, R. D. 1950. The revolutionary process. *Soc. Forces* 28:270–79.

Ingelhart, R. 1977. *The Silent Revolution*. Princeton, NJ: Princeton Univ. Press. 278 pp.

Issac, L., Kelly, W. R. 1981. Racial insurgency, the state and welfare expansion. *Am. J. Sociol.* 86:1348–86

Jackson, L. R., Johnson, W. A. 1974. *Protest by the Poor*. Lexington, MA: D. C. Heath. 286 pp.

Jenkins, J. C. 1981. Sociopolitical movements. *Handb. Pol. Behav.* IV:81–153

Jenkins, J. C. 1982a. The transformation of a constituency

into a movement. In *The Social Movements of the 1960s and 1970s*, ed. J. Freeman. NY: Longmans. 397 pp.

Jenkins, J. C. 1982b. Resource mobilization theory and the movements of the 1960s. Presented at Ann. Meet. Am. Sociol. Assoc., 77th, San Francisco

Jenkins, J. C. 1984. *The Politics of Insurgency*. NY: Columbia Univ. Press

Jenkins, J. C., Perrow, C. 1977. Insurgency of the powerless. *Am. Sociol. Rev.* 42:249–68

Jennings, E. T. 1979. Urban riots and welfare policy change. In *Why Policies Succeed or Fail*, ed. H. Ingram, D. Mann. Beverly Hills, CA: Sage. 215 pp.

Judkins, 1979. The black lung movement. *Res. Soc. Movem., Confl. Change* 2:78–96

Kotz, N., Kotz, M. 1977. *A Passion for Equality*. NY: Norton. 372 pp.

Korpi, W. 1974. Conflict, power and relative deprivation. *Am. Pol. Sci. Rev.* 68:971–84

Ladd, E. C., Hadley, C. D. 1978. *Transformations of the American Party System*. NY: Norton. 385 pp.

Lang, K., Lang, G. 1961. *Collective Dynamics*. NY: Crowell. 563 pp.

Leahy, P., Mazur, A. 1978. A comparison of movements opposed to nuclear power, floridation and abortion. *Res. Soc. Movem., Confl. Change* 1:121–39

Liebman, R. 1983. Mobilizing the Moral Majority. In *The New Christian Right*, ed. R. C. Liebman, R. Wuthrow. Hawthorne, NY: Aldine

Lincoln, J. R. 1978. Community structure and industrial conflict. *Am. Sociol. Rev.* 43:199–220

Lipset, S. M. 1971. *Rebellion in the University*. Chicago: Univ. Chicago Press. 310 pp.

Lodhi, A. Q., Tilly, C. 1973. Urbanization, crime and collective violence in 19th century France. *Am. J. Sociol.* 79:296–318

Lofland, J. 1977. *Doomsday Cult*. NY: Irvington. 362 pp. 2nd ed.

Lofland, J. 1979. White-hot mobilization. In *The Dynamics of Social Movements*, ed. M. N. Zald, J. M. McCarthy, pp. 157–66. Cambridge, MA: Winthrop. 274 pp.

Lukes, S. 1974. *Power*. NY: Macmillan. 64 pp.

Marwell, G. 1981. Altruism and problem of collective action. In *Cooperation and Helping Behavior*, ed. V. Derlega, J. Grzelak, pp. 13–37. NY: Academic. 186 pp.

Marwell, G., Ames, R. 1979. Experiments in the provision of public goods, I. *Am. J. Sociol.* 84:1335–36

Marwell, G., Ames, R. 1980. Experiments on the provision of public goods, II. *Am. J. Sociol.* 85:926–37

McAdam, D. 1982. *Political Process and the Development of Black Insurgency*. Chicago: Univ. Chicago Press. 304 pp.

McCarthy, J., Zald, M. N. 1973. *The Trend of Social Movements*. Morristown, NJ: General Learning. 30 pp

McCarthy, J., Zald, M. N. 1977. Resource mobilization and social movements. *Am. J. Sociol.* 82:1212–41

McFarland, A. S. 1976. *Public Interest Lobbies*. Washington, DC: Am. Enterpr. Inst. 141 pp

Meier, A., Rudwick, E. 1973. *CORE*. NY: Oxford Univ. Press. 563 pp.

Milbrath, L., Goel, M. L. 1977. *Political Participation*. Chicago: Rand McNally. 178 pp.

Miller, W. E., Miller, A. H., Schneider, E. J. 1980. *American National Election Studies Sourcebook, 1952–1978*. Cambridge, MA: Harvard Univ. Press. 306 pp.

Moe, T. M. 1980. *The Organization of Interests*. Chicago, IL: Univ. Chicago Press. 227 pp.

Molotch, H. 1979. Media and movements. In *Dynamics of Social Movements*, ed. M. N. Zald, J. M. McCarthy, pp. 71–93. Cambridge, MA: Winthrop. 274 pp.

Moore, B. 1978. *Injustice*. White Plains, NY: Sharpe. 540 pp.

Morris, A. 1980. *The Origins of the Civil Rights Movement*. PhD thesis. State Univ. New York, Stony Brook.

Morris, A. 1981. Black southern student sit-in movement. *Am. Sociol. Rev.* 46:744–67

Nelkin, D., Pollack, N. 1981. *The Atom Besieged*. Cambridge, MA: MIT Press. 362 pp.

Nie, N. H., Verba, S., Petrocik, J. R. 1980. *The Changing American Voter*. Cambridge, MA: Harvard Univ. Press. 398 pp.

Nielsen, F. 1980. The Flemish movement in Belgium after World War II. *Am. Sociol Rev.* 45:76–94

Oberschall, A. 1973. *Social Conflict and Social Movements*. Englewood Cliffs, NJ: Prentice-Hall. 371 pp.

Oberschall, A. 1978a. Theories of social conflict. *Ann. Rev. Sociol.* 4:291–315

Oberschall, A. 1978b. The decline of the 1960s social movements. *Res. Soc. Movem., Confl. Change* 1:257–89

Oliver, P. 1982. The mobilization of paid and volunteer activists in the neighborhood movement. Presented at Ann. Meet. Am. Sociol. Assoc., 76th, Toronto, Canada

Olson, M. 1968. *The Logic of Collective Action*. NY: Schocken, 166 pp.

Orum, A. 1972. *Black Students in Protest*. Washington, DC: Am. Sociol. Assoc. 89 pp.

Paige, J. 1975. *Agrarian Revolution*, NY: Free Press, 435 pp.

Peterson, P., Greenstone, J. D. 1977. Racial change and citizen participation. In *A Decade of Federal*

Antipoverty Programs, ed. R. H. Havemen, pp. 241–78. NY: Academic, 378 pp.

Perrow, C. 1979. The sixties observed. In *The Dynamics of Social Movements*, ed. M. N. Zald, J. M. McCarthy, pp. 192–211. Cambridge, MA: Winthrop, 274 pp

Piven, F., Cloward, R. 1977. *Poor People's Movements*. NY: Pantheon. 381 pp.

Pinard, M. 1971. *The Rise of a Third Party*. Englewood Cliffs, NJ: Prentice-Hall. 233 pp.

Ragin, C. C. 1979. Ethnic political mobilization. *Am. Sociol. Rev.* 44:619–34

Ragin, C. C., Coverman, S., Hayward, M. 1982. Major labor disputes in Britain, 1902–1938. *Am. Sociol. Rev.* 47:238–52

Rogers, M. 1974. Instrumental and infra-resources. *Am. J. Sociol.* 79:1418–33

Rosenau, J. 1974. *Citizenship Between Elections*. NY: Free Press, 562 pp.

Rothschild-Whitt, J. 1979. Conditions for democracy. See Case & Taylor 1979. pp. 215–44

Salisbury, R. H. 1969. An exchange theory of interest groups. *Mid. J. Pol. Sci.* 13:1–32

Samuelson, P. A. 1954. The pure theory of public expenditure. *Rev. Econ. Stat.* 36:387–90

Schattschneider, E. E. 1960. *The Semi-Sovereign People*. NY: Holt, Reinhart and Winston. 186 pp.

Schmitter, P. 1979. Models of interest intermediation and models of societal change in western Europe. In *Trends Towards Corporatist Intermediation*, ed. P. Schmitter, G. Lehmbruck, pp. 119–46. Beverly Hills, CA: Sage. 323 pp.

Schoefield, A. C., Meier, R. J., Griffin, R. J. 1979. Constructing a social problem. *Soc. Probl.* 27:38–62.

Schumaker, P. D. 1978. The scope of political conflict and the effectiveness of constraints in contemporary urban protest. *Sociol. Q.* 19:168–84

Schwartz, M. 1976. *Radical Protest and Social Structure*. NY: Academic. 302 pp.

Skocpol, T. 1979. *States and Social Revolutions*. NY: Cambridge Univ. Press. 407 pp.

Shorter, N., Tilly, C. 1974. *Strikes in France*. NY: Cambridge Univ. Press. 254 pp.

Simcock, B. L. 1979. Developmental aspects of antipollution protest in Japan. *Res. Soc. Movem., Confl. Change* 2:83–104

Snow, D. A., Zurcher, L. A., Ekland-Olson, S. 1980. Social networks and social movements. *Am. Sociol. Rev.* 45:787–801

Snyder, D., Kelly, W. R. 1976. Industrial violence in Italy, 1878–1903. *Am. Sociol. Rev.* 82:131–62

Starr, P. 1979. The phantom community. See Case & Taylor 1979, pp. 245–73

Steedly, H. R., Foley, J. W. 1979. The success of protest groups. *Soc. Sci. Res.* 8:1–15

Tarrow, S. 1982. Social movements, resource mobilization and reform during cycles of protest. West. Stud. Prog. Proj. Soc. Protest and Policy Innov. Work. Pap. #1. Ithaca, NY: Cornell Univ.

Taylor, C. L., Jodice, D. A. 1983. *World Handbook of Political and Social Indicators III*. New Haven, CT: Yale Univ. Press. 587 pp.

Tierney, K. J. 1982. The battered women movement and the creation of the wife beating problem. *Soc. Probl.* 29:207–20

Tillock, H., Morrison, D. E. 1979. Group size and contributions to collective action. *Res. Soc. Movem., Confl. Change* 2:131–58

Tilly, C. 1978. *From Mobilization to Revolution*. Reading, MA: Addison-Wesley. 349 pp.

Tilly, C. 1979. Social movements and national politics. CRSO Work. Pap. #197. Ann Arbor, MI: Cent. Res. Soc. Org., Univ. Michigan

Tilly, C., Tilly, L., Tilly, R. 1975. *The Rebellious Century*. Cambridge, MA: Harvard Univ. Press. 357 pp.

Tilly, C., Tilly, L. 1981. *Collective Action and Class Conflict*. Beverly Hills, CA: Sage. 354 pp.

Turner, R. 1982. Collective behavior and resource mobilization as approaches to social movements. *Res. Soc. Movem., Confl. Change*. 4:1–24

Turner, R., Killian, L. 1972. *Collective Behavior*. Englewood Cliffs, NJ: Prentice-Hall. 435 pp.

Useem, B. 1980. Solidarity model, breakdown model, and the Boston anti-bussing movement. *Am. Social Rev.* 45:357–69

Useem, M. 1975. *Protest Movements in America*, Indianapolis, IN: Bobbs-Merrill, 66 pp.

von Eschen, D., Kirk, J., Pinard, M. 1971. The organizational substructure of disorderly politics. *Soc. Forces* 49:529–44

Walsh, E. J. 1981. Resource mobilization and citizen protest in communities around Three Mile Island. *Soc. Probl.* 26:1–21

Weisbrod, V., Handler, J., Komesar, N. K. 1978. *Public Interest Law*. Berkeley: Univ. Calif. Press. 580 pp.

West, G. 1981. *The National Welfare Rights Movement*. NY: Praeger. 451 pp.

Wilkinson, P. 1971. *Social Movements*. London: Pall Mall. 176 pp.

Wilson, J. Q. 1973. *Political Organizations*. NY: Basic. 359 pp.

Wilson, W. J. 1973. *Power, Racism and Privilege*. NY: Free Press. 224 pp.

Wood, J. 1974. *The Sources of American Student Activism*. Lexington, MA: Heath. 172 pp.

Wood, P. 1982. The environmental movement. In *Social Movements*, ed. J. L. Wood, M. Jackson, pp. 201–20. Belmont, CA: Wadsworth

Wrong, D. 1979. *Power*. NY: Harper and Row, 326 pp.

Yankelovich, D. 1974. *The New Morality*. NY: McGraw-Hill. 166 pp.

Yankelovich, D. 1981. *New Rules*. NY: Random House. 378 pp.

Zald, M. N., Ash, R. 1966. Social movement organizations. *Soc. Forces* 44:327–41

Zald, M. N., McCarthy, J. 1980. Social movement industries. *Res. Soc. Movem., Confl. Change* 3:1–20

Zurcher, L. A., Snow, D. A. 1981. Collective behavior: social movements. In *Social Psychology*, ed. M. Rosenberg, R. Turner, pp. 447–82. NY: Basic. 578 pp.

READING 18

PROTEST AS A POLITICAL RESOURCE*

Michael Lipsky

The frequent resort to protest activity by relatively powerless groups in recent American politics suggests that protest represents an important aspect of minority

From *American Political Science Review* 62(1968): 1144–58.

*This article is an attempt to develop and explore the implications of a conceptual scheme for analyzing protest activity. It is based upon my studies of protest organizations in New York City, Washington, D.C., Chicago, San Francisco, and Mississippi, as well as extensive examination of written accounts of protest among low-income and Negro civil rights groups. I am grateful to Kenneth Dolbeare, Murray Edelman, and Rodney Stiefbold for their insightful comments on an earlier draft. This paper was developed while the author was a Staff Associate of the Institute for Research on Poverty at the University of Wisconsin. I appreciate the assistance obtained during various phases of my research from the Rabinowitz Foundation, the New York State Legislative Internship Program, and the Brookings Institution.

group and low income group politics.[1] At the same time that Negro civil rights strategists have recognized the problem of using protest as a meaningful political instrument,[2] groups associated with the "war on poverty" have increasingly received publicity for protest activity. Saul Alinsky's Industrial Areas Foundation, for example, continues to receive invitations to help organize low income communities because of its ability to mobilize poor people around the tactic of protest.[3] The riots which dominated urban affairs in the summer of 1967 appear not to have diminished the dependence of some groups on protest as a mode of political activity.

This article provides a theoretical perspective on protest activity as a political resource. The discussion is concentrated on the limitations inherent in protest which occur because of the need of protest leaders to appeal to four constituencies at the same time. As the concept of protest is developed here, it will be argued that protest leaders must nurture and sustain an organization comprised of people with whom they may or may not share common values. They must articulate

[1] "Relatively powerless groups" may be defined as those groups which, relatively speaking, are lacking in conventional political resources. For the purposes of community studies, Robert Dahl has compiled a useful comprehensive list. See Dahl, "The Analysis of Influence in Local Communities," *Social Science and Community Action*, Charles R. Adrian, ed. (East Lansing, Michigan, 1960), p. 32. The difficulty in studying such groups is that relative powerlessness only becomes apparent under certain conditions. Extremely powerless groups not only lack political resources, but are also characterized by a minimal sense of political efficacy, upon which in part successful political organization depends. For reviews of the literature linking orientations of political efficacy to socioeconomic status, see Robert Lane, *Political Life* (New York, 1959), ch. 16; and Lester Milbrath, *Political Participation* (Chicago, 1965), ch. 5. Further, to the extent that group cohesion is recognized as a necessary requisite for organized political action, then extremely powerless groups, lacking cohesion, will not even appear for observation. Hence the necessity of selecting for intensive study a protest movement where there can be some confidence that observable processes and results can be analyzed. Thus, if one conceives of a continuum on which political groups are placed according to their relative command of resources, the focus of this essay is on those groups which are near, but not at, the pole of powerlessness.

[2] See, e.g., Bayard Rustin, "From Protest to Politics: The Future of the Civil Rights Movement," *Commentary* (February, 1965), 25–31; and Stokely Carmichael, "Toward Black Liberation," *The Massachusetts Review* (Autumn, 1966).

[3] On Alinsky's philosophy of community organization, see his *Reveille for Radicals* (Chicago, 1945); and Charles Silberman, *Crisis in Black and White* (New York, 1964), ch. 10.

goals and choose strategies so as to maximize their public exposure through communications media. They must maximize the impact of third parties in the political conflict. Finally, they must try to maximize chances of success among those capable of granting goals. The tensions inherent in manipulating these four constituencies at the same time form the basis of this discussion of protest as a political process. It is intended to place aspects of the civil rights movement in a framework which suggests links between protest organizations and the general political processes in which such organizations operate.

I. "PROTEST" CONCEPTUALIZED

Protest activity as it has been adopted by elements of the civil rights movement and others has not been studied extensively by social scientists. Some of the most suggestive writings have been done as case studies of protest movements in single southern cities.[4] These works generally lack a framework or theoretical focus which would encourage generalization from the cases. More systematic efforts have been attempted in approaching the dynamics of biracial committees in the South,[5] and comprehensively assessing the efficacy of Negro political involvement in Durham, N.C. and Philadelphia, Pa.[6] In their excellent assessment of Negro politics in the South, Matthews and Prothro have presented a thorough profile of Southern Negro students and their participation in civil rights activities.[7]

Protest is also discussed in passing in recent explorations of the social-psychological dimensions of Negro ghetto politics[8] and the still highly suggestive, although pre-1960's, work on Negro political leadership by James Q. Wilson.[9] These and other less systematic works on contemporary Negro politics,[10] for all of their intuitive insights and valuable documentation, offer no theoretical formulations which encourage conceptualization about the interaction between recent Negro political activity and the political process.

Heretofore the best attempt to place Negro protest activity in a framework which would generate additional insights has been that of James Q. Wilson.[11] Wilson has suggested that protest activity be conceived as a problem of bargaining in which the basic problem is that Negro groups lack political resources to exchange. Wilson called this "the problem of the powerless."[12]

While many of Wilson's insights remain valid, his approach is limited in applicability because it defines protest in terms of mass action or response and as utilizing exclusively negative inducements in the bargaining process. Negative inducements are defined as inducements which are not absolutely preferred but are preferred over alternative possibilities.[13] Yet it might be argued that protest designed to appeal to groups which oppose suffering and exploitation, for example, might be offering positive inducements in bargaining. A few Negro students sitting at a lunch counter might be engaged in what would be called protest, and by their actions might be trying to appeal to other groups in the system with positive inducements. Additionally, Wilson's concentration on Negro civic action, and his exclusive interest in exploring the protest process to explain Negro civic action, tend to obscure comparison with protest activity which does not necessarily arise within the Negro community.

---

[4] See, e.g., Jack L. Walker, "Protest and Negotiation: A Case Study of Negro Leadership in Atlanta, Georgia," *Midwest Journal of Political Science*, 7 (May, 1963), 99–124; Jack L. Walker, *Sit-Ins in Atlanta: A Study in the Negro Protest*, Eagleton Institute Case Studies, No. 34 (New York, 1964); John Ehle, *The Free Men* (New York, 1965) [Chapel Hill]; Daniel C. Thompson, *The Negro Leadership Class* (Englewood Cliffs, N.J., 1963) [New Orleans]; M. Elaine Burgess, *Negro Leadership in a Southern City* (Chapel Hill, N.C., 1962) [Durham].

[5] Lewis Killian and Charles Grigg, *Racial Crisis in America: Leadership in Conflict* (Englewood Cliffs, N.J., 1964).

[6] William Keech, "The Negro Vote as a Political Resource: The Case of Durham" (unpublished Ph.D. Dissertation, University of Wisconsin, 1966); John H. Strange, "The Negro in Philadelphia Politics 1963–65" (unpublished Ph.D. Dissertation, Princeton University, 1966).

[7] Donald Matthews and James Prothro, *Negroes and the New Southern Politics* (New York, 1966). Considerable insight on these data is provided in John Orbell, "Protest Participation among Southern Negro College Students," this REVIEW, 61 (June, 1967), 446–456.

[8] Kenneth Clark, *Dark Ghetto* (New York, 1965).

[9] *Negro Politics* (New York, 1960).

[10] A complete list would be voluminous. See, e.g., Nat Hentoff, *The New Equality* (New York, 1964); Arthur Waskow, *From Race Riot to Sit-in* (New York, 1966).

[11] "The Strategy of Protest: Problems of Negro Civic Action," *Journal of Conflict Resolution*, 3 (September, 1961), 291–303. The reader will recognize the author's debt to this highly suggestive article, not least Wilson's recognition of the utility of the bargaining framework for examining protest activity.

[12] *Ibid.*, p. 291.

[13] *Ibid.*, p. 291–292.

Assuming a somewhat different focus, protest activity is defined as a mode of political action oriented toward objection to one or more policies or conditions, characterized by showmanship or display of an unconventional nature, and undertaken to obtain rewards from political or economic systems while working within the systems. The "problem of the powerless" in protest activity is to activate "third parties" to enter the implicit or explicit bargaining arena in ways favorable to the protestors. This is one of the few ways in which they can "create" bargaining resources. It is intuitively unconvincing to suggest that fifteen people sitting uninvited in the Mayor's office have the power to move City Hall. A better formulation would suggest that the people sitting in may be able to appeal to a wider public to which the city administration is sensitive. Thus in successful protest activity the *reference publics* of protest *targets* may be conceived as explicitly or implicitly reacting to protest in such a way that target groups or individuals respond in ways favorable to the protesters.[14]

It should be emphasized that the focus here is on protest by relatively powerless groups. Illustrations can be summoned, for example, of activity designated as "protest" involving high status pressure groups or hundreds of thousands of people. While such instances may share some of the characteristics of protest activity, they may not represent examples of developing political resources by relatively powerless groups because the protesting groups may already command political resources by virtue of status, numbers or cohesion.

It is appropriate also to distinguish between the relatively restricted use of the concept of protest adopted here and closely related political strategies which are often designated as "protest" in popular usage. Where groups already possess sufficient resources with which to bargain, as in the case of some economic boycotts and labor strikes, they may be said to engage in "direct confrontation."[15] Similarly, protest which represents efforts to "activate reference publics" should be distinguished from "alliance formation," where third parties are induced to join the conflict, but where the value orientations of third parties are sufficiently similar to those of the protesting group that concerted or coordinated action is possible. Alliance formation is particularly desirable for relatively powerless groups if they seek to join the decision-making process as participants.

The distinction between activating reference publics and alliance formation is made on the assumption that where goal orientations among protest groups and the reference publics of target groups are similar, the political dynamics of petitioning target groups are different than when such goal orientations are relatively divergent. Clearly the more similar the goal orientations, the greater the likelihood of protest success, other things being equal. This discussion is intended to highlight, however, those instances where goal orientations of reference publics depart significantly, in direction or intensity, from the goals of protest groups.

Say that to protest some situation, A would like to enter a bargaining situation with B. But A has nothing B wants, and thus cannot bargain. A then attempts to create political resources by activating other groups to enter the conflict. A then organizes to take action against B with respect to certain goals. *Information concerning these goals must be conveyed through communications media* (C, D, and E) to F, G, and H, which are B's *reference publics*. In response to the reactions of F, G, and H, or in anticipation of their reactions, B responds, *in some way*, to the protesters' demands. This formulation requires the conceptualization of protest activity when undertaken to create bargaining resources as a political process which requires communication and is characterized by a multiplicity of constituencies for protest leadership.

A schematic representation of the process of protest as utilized by relatively powerless groups is presented in Figure 1. In contrast to a simplistic pressure group model which would posit a direct relationship between pressure group and pressured, the following discussion is guided by the assumption (derived from observation) that protest is a highly indirect process in which communications media and the reference publics of protest

---

[14] See E. E. Schattschneider's discussion of expanding the scope of the conflict, *The Semisovereign People* (New York, 1960). Another way in which bargaining resources may be "created" is to increase the relative cohesion of groups, or to increase the perception of group solidarity as a precondition to greater cohesion. This appears to be the primary goal of political activity which is generally designated "community organization." Negro activists appear to recognize the utility of this strategy in their advocacy of "black power." In some instances protest activity may be designed in part to accomplish this goal in addition to activating reference publics.

[15] For an example of "direct confrontation," one might study the three-month Negro boycott of white merchants in Natchez, Miss., which resulted in capitulation to boycott demands by city government leaders. See *The New York Times*, December 4, 1965, p. 1.

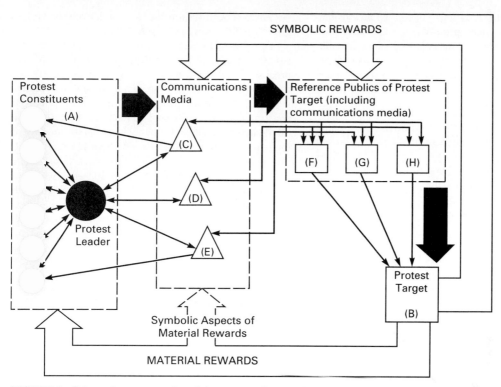

FIGURE 1 Schematic representation of the process of protest by relatively powerless groups.

targets play critical roles. It is also a process characterized by reciprocal relations, in which protest leaders frame strategies according to their perception of the needs of (many) other actors.

In this view protest constituents limit the options of protest leaders at the same time that the protest leader influences their perception of the strategies and rhetoric which they will support. Protest activity is filtered through the communications media in influencing the perceptions of the reference publics of protest targets. To the extent that the influence of reference publics is supportive of protest goals, target groups will dispense symbolic or material rewards. Material rewards are communicated directly to protest constituents. Symbolic rewards are communicated in part to protest constituents, but primarily are communicated to the reference publics of target groups, who provide the major stimuli for public policy pronouncements.

The study of protest as adopted by relatively powerless groups should provide insights into the structure and behavior of groups involved in civil rights politics and associated with the "war on poverty." It should

direct attention toward the ways in which administrative agencies respond to "crises." Additionally, the study of protest as a political resource should influence some general conceptualizations of American political pluralism. Robert Dahl, for example, describes the "normal American political process" as

> one in which there is a high probability that an active
> and legitimate group in the population can make itself
> heard effectively at some crucial stage in the process of
> decision.[16]

Although he agrees that control over decisions is unevenly divided in the population, Dahl writes:

> When I say that a group is heard "effectively" I mean
> more than the simple fact that it makes a noise; I mean
> that one or more officials are not only ready to listen to
> the noise, but expect to suffer in some significant way
> if they do not placate the group, its leaders, or its most

---

[16] *A Preface to Democratic Theory* (Chicago, 1956), pp. 145–146.

vociferous members. To satisfy the group may require one or more of a great variety of actions by the responsive leader: pressure for substantive policies, appointments, graft, respect, expression of the appropriate emotions, or the right combination of reciprocal noises.[17]

These statements, which in some ways resemble David Truman's discussion of the power of "potential groups,"[18] can be illuminated by the study of protest activity in three ways. First, what are the probabilities that relatively powerless groups can make themselves heard effectively? In what ways will such groups be heard or "steadily appeased"?[19] Concentration on the process of protest activity may reveal the extent to which, and the conditions under which, relatively powerless groups are likely to prove effective. Protest undertaken to obstruct policy decisions, for example, may enjoy greater success probabilities than protest undertaken in an effort to evoke constructive policy innovations.[20]

Second, does it make sense to suggest that all groups which make noises will receive responses from public officials? Perhaps the groups which make noises do not have to be satisfied at all, but it is other groups which receive assurances or recognition. Third, what are the probabilities that groups which make noises will receive tangible rewards, rather than symbolic assurances?[21] Dahl lumps these rewards together in the same paragraph, but dispensation of tangible rewards clearly has a different impact upon groups than the dispensation of symbolic rewards. Dahl is undoubtedly correct when he suggests that the relative fluidity of American politics is a critical characteristic of the American political system.[22] But he is less precise and less convincing when it comes to analyzing the extent to which the

system is indeed responsive to the relatively powerless groups of the "average citizen."[23]

The following sections are an attempt to demonstrate the utility of the conceptualization of the protest process presented above. This will be done by exploring the problems encountered and the strains generated by protest leaders in interacting with four constituencies. It will be useful to concentrate attention on the maintenance and enhancement needs not only of the large formal organizations which dominate city politics,[24] but also of the ad hoc protest groups which engage them in civic controversy. It will also prove rewarding to examine the role requirements of individuals in leadership positions as they perceive the problems of constituency manipulation. In concluding remarks some implications of the study of protest for the pluralist description of American politics will be suggested.[25]

II. PROTEST LEADERSHIP AND ORGANIZATIONAL BASE

The organizational maintenance needs of relatively powerless, low income, ad hoc protest groups center around the tension generated by the need for leadership to offer symbolic and intangible inducements to protest participation when immediate, material rewards cannot be anticipated, and the need to provide at least the promise of material rewards. Protest leaders must try to evoke responses from other actors in the political

---

[17] *Ibid.*

[18] *The Governmental Process* (New York, 1951), p. 104.

[19] See Dahl, *A Preface to Democratic Theory*, p. 146.

[20] Observations that all groups can influence public policy at some stage of the political process are frequently made about the role of "veto groups" in American politics. See *Ibid.*, pp. 104 ff. See also David Reisman, *The Lonely Crowd* (New Haven, 1950), pp. 211 ff., for an earlier discussion of veto-group politics. Yet protest should be evaluated when it is adopted to obtain assertive as well as defensive goals.

[21] See Murray Edelman, *The Symbolic Uses of Politics* (Urbana, Ill., 1964), ch. 2.

[22] See Dahl, *Who Governs?* (New Haven, 1961), pp. 305 ff.

[23] In a recent formulation, Dahl reiterates the theme of wide dispersion of influence. "More than other systems, [democracies] . . . try to disperse influence widely to their citizens by means of the suffrage, elections, freedom of speech, press, and assembly, the right of opponents to criticize the conduct of government, the right to organize political parties, and in other ways." *Pluralist Democracy in the United States* (Chicago, 1967), p. 373. Here, however, he concentrates more on the availability of options to all groups in the system, rather than on the relative probabilities that all groups in fact have access to the political process. See pp. 372 ff.

[24] See Edward Banfield, *Political Influence* (New York, 1961), p. 263. The analysis of organizational incentive structure which heavily influences Banfield's formulation is Chester Barnard, *The Functions of the Executive* (Cambridge, Mass., 1938).

[25] In the following attempt to develop the implications of this conceptualization of protest activity, I have drawn upon extensive field observations and bibliographical research. Undoubtedly, however, individual assertions, while representing my best judgment concerning the available evidence, in the future may require modification as the result of further empirical research.

process, at the same time that they pay attention to participant organizational needs. Thus relatively deprived groups in the political system not only receive symbolic reassurance while material rewards from the system are withheld,[26] but protest leaders have a stake in perpetuating the notion that relatively powerless groups retain political efficacy despite what in many cases is obvious evidence to the contrary.

The tension embraced by protest leaders over the nature of inducements toward protest participation accounts in part for the style adopted and goals selected by protest leaders. Groups which seek psychological gratification from politics, but cannot or do not anticipate material political rewards, may be attracted to militant protest leaders. To these groups, angry rhetoric may prove a desirable quality in the short run. Where groups depend upon the political system for tangible benefits, or where participation in the system provides intangible benefits, moderate leadership is likely to prevail. Wilson has observed similar tendencies among Negro leaders of large, formal organizations.[27] It is no less true for leadership of protest groups. Groups whose members derive tangible satisfactions from political participation will not condone leaders who are stubborn in compromise or appear to question the foundations of the system. This coincides with Truman's observation:

> Violation of the "rules of the game" normally will weaken a group's cohesion, reduce its status in the community, and expose it to the claims of other groups.[28]

On the other hand, the cohesion of relatively powerless groups may be strengthened by militant, ideological leadership which questions the rules of the game and challenges their legitimacy.

Cohesion is particularly important when protest leaders bargain directly with target groups. In that situation, leaders' ability to control protest constituents and guarantee their behavior represents a bargaining strength.[29] For this reason Wilson stressed the bargaining difficulties of Negro leaders who cannot guarantee constituent behavior, and pointed out the significance of the strategy of projecting the image of

group solidarity when the reality of cohesion is a fiction.[30] Cohesion is less significant at other times. Divided leadership may prove productive by bargaining in tandem,[31] or by minimizing strain among groups in the protest process. Further, community divisions may prove less detrimental to protest aims when strong third parties have entered the dispute originally generated by protest organizations.

The intangible rewards of assuming certain postures toward the political system may not be sufficient to sustain an organizational base. It may be necessary to renew constantly the intangible rewards of participation. And to the extent that people participate in order to achieve tangible benefits, their interest in a protest organization may depend upon the organization's relative material success. Protest leaders may have to tailor their style to present participants with tangible successes, or with the appearance of success. Leaders may have to define the issues with concern for increasing their ability to sustain organizations. The potential for protest among protest group members may have to be manipulated by leadership if the group is to be sustained.[32]

The participants in protest organizations limit the flexibility of protest leadership. This obtains for two reasons. They restrict public actions by leaders who must continue to solicit active participant support, and they place restraints on the kinds of activities which can be considered appropriate for protest purposes. Poor participants cannot commonly be asked to engage in protest requiring air transportation. Participants may have anxieties related to their environment or historical

---

[26] As Edelman suggests, cited previously.

[27] *Negro Politics*, p. 290.

[28] *The Governmental Process*, p. 513.

[29] But cf. Thomas Schelling's discussion of "binding oneself," *The Strategy of Conflict* (Cambridge, Mass., 1960), pp. 22 ff.

[30] "The Strategy of Protest," p. 297.

[31] This is suggested by Wilson, "The Strategy of Protest," p. 298; St. Clair Drake and Horace Cayton, *Black Metropolis* (New York, 1962, rev. ed.), p. 731; Walker, "Protest and Negotiation," p. 122. Authors who argue that divided leadership is dysfunctional have been Clark, p. 156; and Tilman Cothran, "The Negro Protest Against Segregation in the South," *The Annals*, 357 (January 1965), p. 72.

[32] This observation is confirmed by a student of the Southern civil rights movement:

> Negroes demand of protest leaders constant progress. The combination of long-standing discontent and a new-found belief in the possibility of change produces a constant state of tension and aggressiveness in the Negro community. But this discontent is vague and diffuse, not specific; the masses do not define the issues around which action shall revolve. This the leader must do.

Lewis Killian, "Leadership in the Desegregation Crises: An Institutional Analysis," in Muzafer Sherif (ed.), *Intergroup Relations and Leadership* (New York, 1962), p. 159.

situation which discourages engagement in some activities. They may be afraid of job losses, beatings by the police, or summary evictions. Negro protest in the Deep South has been inhibited by realistic expectations of retribution.[33] Protests over slum housing conditions are undermined by tenants who expect landlord retaliation for engaging in tenant organizing activity.[34] Political or ethical mores may conflict with a proposed course of action, diminishing participation.[35]

On the other hand, to the extent that fears are real, or that the larger community perceives protest participants as subject to these fears, protest may actually be strengthened. Communications media and potential allies will consider more soberly the complaints of people who are understood to be placing themselves in jeopardy. When young children and their parents made the arduous bus trip from Mississippi to Washington, D.C. to protest the jeopardizing of Head Start funds, the courage and expense represented by their effort created a respect and visibility for their position which might not have been achieved by local protest efforts.[36]

Protest activity may be undertaken by organizations with established relationship patterns, behavior norms, and role expectations. These organizations are likely to have greater access to other groups in the political system, and a demonstrated capacity to maintain themselves. Other protest groups, however, may be ad hoc arrangements without demonstrated internal or external relationship patterns. These groups will have different organizational problems, in response to which it is necessary to engage in different kinds of protest activity.

The scarcity of organizational resources also places limits upon the ability of relatively powerless groups to maintain the foundations upon which protest organizations develop. Relatively powerless groups, to engage in political activity of any kind, must command at least some resources. This is not tautological. Referring again to a continuum on which political groups are placed according to their relative command of resources, one may draw a line somewhere along the continuum representing a "threshold of civic group political participation." Clearly some groups along the continuum will possess some political resources (enough, say, to emerge for inspection) but not enough to exercise influence in civic affairs. Relatively powerless groups, to be influential, must cross the "threshold" to engage in politics. Although the availability of group resources is a critical consideration at all stages of the protest process, it is particularly important in explaining why some groups seem to "surface" with sufficient strength to command attention. The following discussion of some critical organizational resources should illuminate this point.

Skilled professionals frequently must be available to protest organizations. Lawyers, for example, play extremely important roles in enabling protest groups to utilize the judicial process and avail themselves of adequate preparation of court cases. Organizational reputation may depend upon a combination of ability to threaten the conventional political system and of exercising statutory rights in court. Availability of lawyers depends upon ability to pay fees and/or the attractiveness to lawyers of participation in protest group activity. Volunteer professional assistance may not prove adequate. One night a week volunteered by an aspiring politician in a housing clinic cannot satisfy the needs of a chaotic political movement.[37] The need for skilled professionals is not restricted to lawyers. For example, a group seeking to protest an urban renewal policy might require the services of architects and city planners in order to present a viable alternative to a city proposal.

---

[33] Significantly, southern Negro students who actively participated in the early phases of the sit-in movement "tended to be unusually optimistic about race relations and tolerant of whites [when compared with inactive Negro students]. They not only *were* better off, objectively speaking, than other Negroes but *felt* better off." Matthews and Prothro, *op. cit.*, p. 424.

[34] This is particularly the case in cities such as Washington, D.C., where landlord-tenant laws offer little protection against retaliatory eviction. See, e.g., Robert Schoshinski, "Remedies of the Indigent Tenant: Proposal for Change," *Georgetown Law Journal*, 54 (Winter, 1966), 541 ff.

[35] Wilson regarded this as a chief reason for lack of protest activity in 1961. He wrote: ". . . some of the goals now being sought by Negroes are least applicable to those groups of Negroes most suited to protest action. Protest action involving such tactics as mass meetings, picketing, boycotts, and strikes rarely find enthusiastic participants among upper-income and higher status individuals": "The Strategy of Protest," p. 296.

[36] See *The New York Times*, February 12, 1966, p. 56.

---

[37] On housing clinic services provided by political clubs, see James Q. Wilson, *The Amateur Democrat: Club Politics in Three Cities* (Chicago, 1962), pp. 63–64, 176. On the need for lawyers among low income people, see e.g., *The Extension of Legal Services to the Poor*, Conference Proceedings (Washington, D.C., n.d.), esp. pp. 51–60; and "Neighborhood Law Offices: The New Wave in Legal Services for the Poor," *Harvard Law Review*, 80 (February, 1967), 805–850.

Financial resources not only purchase legal assistance, but enable relatively powerless groups to conduct minimum programs of political activities. To the extent that constituents are unable or unwilling to pay even small membership dues, then financing the cost of mimeographing flyers, purchasing supplies, maintaining telephone service, paying rent, and meeting a modest payroll become major organizational problems. And to the extent that group finances are supplied by outside individual contributions or government or foundation grants, the long-term options of the group are sharply constrained by the necessity of orienting group goals and tactics to anticipate the potential objections of financial supporters.

Some dependence upon even minimal financial resources can be waived if organizations evoke passionate support from constituents. Secretarial help and block organizers will come forward to work without compensation if they support the cause of neighborhood organizations or gain intangible benefits based upon association with the group. Protest organizations may also depend upon skilled non-professionals, such as college students, whose access to people and political and economic institutions often assists protest groups in cutting across income lines to seek support. Experience with ad hoc political groups, however, suggests that this assistance is sporadic and undependable. Transient assistance is particularly typical of skilled, educated, and employable volunteers whose abilities can be applied widely. The die-hards of ad hoc political groups are often those people who have no place else to go, nothing else to do.

Constituent support will be affected by the nature of the protest target and whether protest activity is directed toward defensive or assertive goals. Obstructing specific public policies may be easier than successfully recommending constructive policy changes. Orientations toward defensive goals may require less constituent energy, and less command over resources of money, expertise and status.[38]

III. PROTEST LEADERSHIP AND COMMUNICATIONS MEDIA

The communications media are extremely powerful in city politics. In granting or withholding publicity, in determining what information most people will have on most issues, and what alternatives they will consider in response to issues, the media truly, as Norton Long has put it, "set . . . the civic agenda."[39] To the extent that successful protest activity depends upon appealing to, and/or threatening, other groups in the community, the communications media set the limits of protest action. If protest tactics are not considered significant by the media, or if newspapers and television reporters or editors decide to overlook protest tactics, protest organizations will not succeed. Like the tree falling unheard in the forest, there is no protest unless protest is perceived and projected.

A number of writers have noticed that the success of protest activity seems directly related to the amount of publicity it receives outside the immediate arena in which protest takes place. This view has not been stated systematically, but hints can be found in many sources. In the literature on civil rights politics, the relevance of publicity represents one of the few hypotheses available concerning the dynamics of successful protest activity.[40]

When protest tactics do receive coverage in the communications media, the way in which they are presented will influence all other actors in the system, including the protesters themselves. Conformity to standards of newsworthiness in political style, and knowledge of the prejudices and desires of the individuals who determine media coverage in political skills, represent crucial determinants of leadership effectiveness.

The organizational behavior of newspapers can partly be understood by examining the maintenance and enhancement needs which direct them toward projects of civic betterment and impressions of accomplishment.[41] But insight may also be gained by analyzing the role requirements of reporters, editors, and others who determine newspaper policy. Reporters, for example, are frequently motivated by the desire to contribute to civic affairs by their "objective" reporting of

---

[38] An illustration of low income group protest organization mobilized for veto purposes is provided by Dahl in "The Case of the Metal Houses." See *Who Governs?*, pp. 192 ff.

[39] Norton Long, "The Local Community as an Ecology of Games," in Long, *The Polity*, Charles Press, ed. (Chicago, 1962), p. 153. See pp. 152–154. See also Roscoe C. Martin, Frank J. Munger, *et al., Decisions in Syracuse: A Metropolitan Action Study* (Garden City, N.Y., 1965) (originally published: 1961), pp. 326–327.

[40] See, e.g., Thompson, *op. cit.*, p. 134, and *passim*; Martin Oppenheimer, "The Southern Student Movement: Year I," *Journal of Negro Education*, 33 (Fall, 1964), p. 397; Cothran, *op. cit.*, p. 72; Pauli Murray, "Protest Against the Legal Status of the Negro," *The Annals*, 357 (January, 1965), p. 63; Allan P. Sindler, "Protest Against the Political Status of the Negroes," *The Annals*, 357 (January, 1965), p. 50.

[41] See Banfield, *op. cit.*, p. 275.

significant events; by the premium they place on accuracy; and by the credit which they receive for sensationalism and "scoops."

These requirements may be difficult to accommodate at the same time. Reporters demand newsworthiness of their subjects in the short run, but also require reliability and verifiability in the longer run. Factual accuracy may dampen newsworthiness. Sensationalism, attractive to some newspaper editors, may be inconsistent with reliable, verifiable narration of events. Newspapers at first may be attracted to sensationalism, and later demand verifiability in the interests of community harmony (and adherence to professional journalistic standards).

Most big city newspapers have reporters whose assignments permit them to cover aspects of city politics with some regularity. These reporters, whose "beats" may consist of "civil rights" or "poverty," sometimes develop close relationships with their news subjects. These relationships may develop symbiotic overtones because of the mutuality of interest between the reporter and the news subject. Reporters require fresh information on protest developments, while protest leaders have a vital interest in obtaining as much press coverage as possible.

Inflated reports of protest success may be understood in part by examining this relationship between reporter and protest leader. Both have role-oriented interests in projecting images of protest strength and threat. In circumstances of great excitement, when competition from other news media representatives is high, a reporter may find that he is less governed by the role requirement of verification and reliability than he is by his editor's demand for "scoops" and news with high audience appeal.[42]

On the other hand, the demands of the media may conflict with the needs of protest group maintenance. Consider the leader whose constituents are attracted solely by pragmatic statements not exceeding what they consider political "good taste." He is constrained from making militant demands which would isolate him from constituents. This constraint may cost him appeal in the press.[43] However, the leader whose organizing appeal requires militant rhetoric may obtain eager press coverage only to find that his inflammatory statements lead to alienation of potential allies and exclusion from the explicit bargaining process.[44]

News media do not report events in the same way. Television may select for broadcast only thirty seconds of a half-hour news conference. This coverage will probably focus on immediate events, without background or explanatory material. Newspapers may give more complete accounts of the same event. The most complete account may appear in the weekly edition of a neighborhood or ethnic newspaper. Differential coverage by news media, and differential news media habits in the general population,[45] are significant factors in permitting protest leaders to juggle conflicting demands of groups in the protest process.

Similar tensions exist in the leader's relationships with protest targets. Ideological postures may gain press coverage and constituency approval, but may alienate target groups with whom it would be desirable to bargain explicitly. Exclusion from the councils of decision-making may have important consequences, since the results of target group deliberations may satisfy activated reference publics without responding to protest goals. If activated reference publics are required to increase the bargaining position of the protest group, protest efforts thereafter will have diminished chances of success.

---

[42] For a case study of the interaction between protest leaders and newspaper reporters, see Michael Lipsky, "Rent Strikes in New York City: Protest Politics and the Power of the Poor," (unpublished Ph.D. dissertation, Princeton University, 1967), pp. 139–49. Bernard Cohen has analyzed the impact of the press on foreign policy from the perspective of reporters' role requirements: see his *The Press and Foreign Policy* (Princeton, N.J., 1963), esp. chs. 2–3.

[43] An example of a protest conducted by middle-class women engaged in pragmatic protest over salvaging park space is provided in John B. Keeley, *Moses on the Green*, Inter-University Case Program, No. 45 (University, Ala., 1959).

[44] This was the complaint of Floyd McKissick, National Director of the Congress of Racial Equality, when he charged that ". . . there are only two kinds of statements a black man can make and expect that the white press will report. . . . First . . . is an attack on another black man. . . . The second is a statement that sounds radical, violent, extreme—the verbal equivalent of a riot. . . . [T]he Negro is being rewarded by the public media only if he turns on another Negro and uses his tongue as a switchblade, or only if he sounds outlandish, extremist or psychotic." Statement at the Convention of the American Society of Newspaper Editors, April 20, 1967, Washington, D.C., as reported in *The New York Times*, April 21, 1967, p. 22. See also the remarks of journalist Ted Poston, *ibid.*, April 26, 1965, p. 26.

[45] Matthews and Prothro found, for example, that in their southwide Negro population sample, 38 percent read Negro-oriented magazines and 17 percent read newspapers written for Negroes. These media treat news of interest to Negroes more completely and sympathetically than do the general media. See pp. 248 ff.

IV. PROTEST LEADERSHIP AND "THIRD PARTIES"

I have argued that the essence of political protest consists of activating third parties to participate in controversy in ways favorable to protest goals. In previous sections I have attempted to analyze some of the tensions which result from protest leaders' attempts to activate reference publics of protest targets at the same time that they must retain the interest and support of protest organization participants. This phenomenon is in evidence when Negro leaders, recognized as such by public officials, find their support eroded in the Negro community because they have engaged in explicit bargaining situations with politicians. Negro leaders are thus faced with the dilemma that when they behave like other ethnic group representatives they are faced with loss of support from those whose intense activism has been aroused in the Negro community, yet whose support is vital if they are to remain credible as leaders to public officials.

The tensions resulting from conflicting maintenance needs of protest organizations and activated third parties present difficulties for protest leaders. One way in which these tensions can be minimized is by dividing leadership responsibilities. If more than one group is engaged in protest activity, protest leaders can, in effect, divide up public roles so as to reduce as much as possible the gap between the implicit demands of different groups for appropriate rhetoric, and what in fact is said. Thus divided leadership may perform the latent function of minimizing tensions among elements in the protest process by permitting different groups to listen selectively to protest spokesmen.[46]

Another way in which strain among different groups can be minimized is through successful public relations. Minimization of strain may depend upon ambiguity of action or statement, deception, or upon effective inter-group communication. Failure to clarify meaning, or falsification, may increase protest effectiveness. Effective intragroup communication may increase the likelihood that protest constituents will "understand" that ambiguous or false public statements have "special meaning" and need not be taken seriously. the Machiavellian circle is complete when we observe that although lying may be prudent, the appearance of integrity and forthrightness is desirable for public relations, since these values are widely shared.

It has been observed that "[t]he militant displays an unwillingness to perform those administrative tasks which are necessary to operate an organization. Probably the skills of the agitator and the skills of the administrator . . . are not incompatible, but few men can do both well."[47] These skills may or may not be incompatible as personality traits, but they indeed represent conflicting role demands on protest leadership. When a protest leader exhausts time and energy conducting frequent press conferences, arranging for politicians and celebrities to appear at rallies, delivering speeches to sympathetic local groups, college symposia and other forums, constantly picketing for publicity and generally making "contacts," he is unable to pursue the direction of office routine, clerical tasks, research and analysis, and other chores.

The difficulties of delegating routine tasks are probably directly related to the skill levels and previous administrative experiences of group members. In addition, to the extent that involvement in protest organizations is a function of rewards received or expected by individuals because of the excitement or entertainment value of participation, then the difficulties of delegating routine, relatively uninteresting chores to group members will be increased. Yet attention to such details affects the perception of protest groups by organizations whose support or assistance may be desired in the future. These considerations add to the protest leader's problem of risking alienation of protest participants because of potentially unpopular cooperation with the "power structure."

In the protest paradigm developed here, "third parties" refers both to the reference publics of target groups and, more narrowly, to the interest groups whose regular interaction with protest targets tends to develop into patterns of influence.[48] We have already discussed some of the problems associated with activating the reference publics of target groups. In discussing the constraints placed upon protest, attention may be focused upon the likelihood that groups seeking to create political resources through protest will be included in the explicit bargaining process with other pressure groups. For protest groups, these constraints are those which occur because of class and political style, status, and organizational resources.

---

[46] See footnote 31 above.

[47] Wilson, *Negro Politics*, p. 225.
[48] See Wallace Sayre and Herbert Kaufman, *Governing New York City* (New York, 1960), pp. 257 ff. Also see Banfield, *op. cit.*, p. 267.

The established civic groups most likely to be concerned with the problems raised by relatively powerless groups are those devoted to service in the public welfare and those "liberally" oriented groups whose potential constituents are either drawn from the same class as the protest groups (such as some trade unions), or whose potential constituents are attracted to policies which appear to serve the interest of the lower class or minority groups (such as some reform political clubs).[49] These civic groups have frequently cultivated clientele relationships with city agencies over long periods. Their efforts have been reciprocated by agency officials anxious to develop constituencies to support and defend agency administrative and budgetary policies. In addition, clientele groups are expected to endorse and legitimize agency aggrandizement. These relationships have been developed by agency officials and civic groups for mutual benefit, and cannot be destroyed, abridged or avoided without cost.

Protest groups may well be able to raise the saliency of issues on the civic agenda through utilization of communications media and successful appeals or threats to wider publics, but admission to policy-making councils is frequently barred because of the angry, militant rhetorical style adopted by protest leaders. People in power do not like to sit down with rogues. Protest leaders are likely to have phrased demands in ways unacceptable to lawyers and other civic activists whose cautious attitude toward public policy may reflect not only their good intentions but their concern for property rights, due process, pragmatic legislating or judicial precedent.

Relatively powerless groups lack participation of individuals with high status whose endorsement of specific proposals lend them increased legitimacy. Good causes may always attract the support of high status individuals. But such individuals' willingness to devote time to the promotion of specific proposals is less likely than the one-shot endorsements which these people distribute more readily.

Similarly, protest organizations often lack the resources on which entry into the policy-making process depends. These resources include maintenance of a staff with expertise and experience in the policy area. This expertise may be in the areas of the law, planning and architecture, proposal writing, accounting, educational policy, federal grantsmanship or publicity. Combining experience with expertise is one way to create status in issue areas. The dispensing of information by interest groups has been widely noted as a major source of influence. Over time the experts develop status in their areas of competence somewhat independent of the influence which adheres to them as information-providers. Groups which cannot or do not engage lawyers to assist in proposing legislation, and do not engage in collecting reliable data, cannot participate in policy deliberations or consult in these matters. Protest oriented groups, whose primary talents are in dramatizing issues, cannot credibly attempt to present data considered "objective" or suggestions considered "responsible" by public officials. Few can be convincing as both advocate and arbiter at the same time.

V. PROTEST LEADERSHIP AND TARGET GROUPS

The probability of protest success may be approached by examining the maintenance needs of organizations likely to be designated as target groups.[50] For the sake of clarity, and because protest activity increasingly is directed toward government, I shall refer in the following paragraphs exclusively to government agencies at the municipal level. The assumption is retained, however, that the following generalizations are applicable to other potential target groups.

Some of the constraints placed on protest leadership in influencing target groups have already been mentioned in preceding sections. The lack of status and resources that inhibits protest groups from participating in policy-making conferences, for example, also helps prevent explicit bargaining between protest leaders and

---

[49] See Wilson, *The Amateur Democrats*, previously cited. These groups are most likely to be characterized by broad scope of political interest and frequent intervention in politics. See Sayre and Kaufman, *op. cit.*, p. 79.

[50] Another approach, persuasively presented by Wilson, concentrates on protest success as a function of the relative unity and vulnerability of targets. See "The Strategy of Protest," pp. 293 ff. This insight helps explain, for example, why protest against housing segregation commonly takes the form of action directed against government (a unified target) rather than against individual homeowners (who present a dispersed target). One problem with this approach is that it tends to obscure the possibility that targets, as collections of individuals, may be divided in evaluation of and sympathy for protest demands. Indeed, city agency administrators under some circumstances act as partisans in protest conflicts. As such, they frequently appear ambivalent toward protest goals: sympathetic to the ends while concerned that the means employed in protest reflect negatively on their agencies.

city officials. The strain between rhetoric which appeals to protest participants and public statements to which communications media and "third parties" respond favorably also exists with reference to target groups.

Yet there is a distinguishing feature of the maintenance needs and strategies of city agencies which specifically constrains protest organizations. This is the agency director's need to protect "the jurisdiction and income of his organization [by] . . . [m]anipulation of the external environment."[51] In so doing he may satisfy his reference groups without responding to protest group demands. At least six tactics are available to protest targets who are motivated to respond in some way to protest activity but seek primarily to satisfy their reference publics. These tactics may be employed whether or not target groups are "sincere" in responding to protest demands.

1. Target groups may dispense symbolic satisfactions. Appearances of activity and commitment to problems substitute for, or supplement, resource allocation and policy innovations which would constitute tangible responses to protest activity. If symbolic responses supplement tangible pay-offs, they are frequently coincidental, rather than intimately linked, to projection of response by protest targets. Typical in city politics of the symbolic response is the ribbon cutting, street corner ceremony or the walking tour press conference. These occasions are utilized not only to build agency constituencies,[52] but to satisfy agency reference publics that attention is being directed to problems of civic concern. In this sense publicist tactics may be seen as defensive maneuvers. Symbolic aspects of the actions of public officials can also be recognized in the commissioning of expensive studies and the rhetorical flourishes with which "massive attacks," "comprehensive programs," and "coordinated planning" are frequently promoted.

City agencies establish distinct apparatus and procedures for dealing with crises which may be provoked by protest groups. Housing-related departments in New York City may be cited for illustration. It is usually the case in these agencies that the Commissioner or a chief deputy, a press secretary and one or two other officials devote whatever time is necessary to collect information, determine policy and respond quickly to reports of "crises." This is functional for tenants, who, if they can generate enough concern, may be able to obtain shortcuts through lengthy agency procedures. It is also functional for officials who want to project images of action rather than merely receiving complaints. Concentrating attention on the maintenance needs of city politicians during protest crises suggests that pronouncements of public officials serve purposes independent of their dedication to alleviation of slum conditions.[53]

Independent of dispensation of tangible benefits to protest groups, public officials continue to respond primarily to their own reference publics. Murray Edelman has suggested that:

> Tangible resources and benefits are frequently not distributed to unorganized political group interests as promised in regulatory statutes and the propaganda attending their enactment.[54]

His analysis may be supplemented by suggesting that symbolic dispensations may not only serve to reassure unorganized political group interests, but may also contribute to reducing the anxiety level of organized interests and wider publics which are only tangentially involved in the issues.

2. Target groups may dispense token material satisfactions. When city agencies respond, with much publicity, to cases brought to their attention representing examples of the needs dramatized by protest organizations, they may appear to respond to protest demands while in fact only responding on a case basis, instead of a general basis. For the protesters served by agencies in this fashion it is of considerable advantage that agencies can be influenced by protest action. Yet it should not be ignored that in handling the "crisis" cases, public officials give the appearance of response to their reference publics, while mitigating demands for an expensive, complex *general* assault on problems represented by the cases to which responses are given. Token responses, whether or not accompanied by more general responses, are particularly attractive to reporters and television news directors, who are able to dramatize individual cases convincingly, but who may be unable to "capture" the essence of general depriva-

---

[51] Sayre and Kaufman, *op cit.*, p. 253.

[52] See *ibid.*, pp. 253 ff.

[53] See Lipsky, *op cit.* chs. 5–6. The appearance of responsiveness may be given by city officials *in anticipation* of protest activity. This seems to have been the strategy of Mayor Richard Daley in his reaction to the announcement of Martin Luther King's plans to focus civil rights efforts on Chicago. See *The New York Times*, February 1, 1966, p. 11.

[54] See Edelman, *op. cit.*, p. 23.

tion or of general efforts to alleviate conditions of deprivation.

3. Target groups may organize and innovate internally in order to blunt the impetus of protest efforts. This tactic is closely related to No. 2 (above). If target groups can act constructively in the worst cases, they will then be able to pre-empt protest efforts by responding to the cases which best dramatize protest demands. Alternatively, they may designate all efforts which jeopardize agency reputations as "worst" cases, and devote extensive resources to these cases. In some ways extraordinary city efforts are precisely consistent with protest goals. At the same time extraordinary efforts in the most heavily dramatized cases or the most extreme cases effectively wear down the "cutting-edges" of protest efforts.

Many New York City agencies develop informal "crisis" arrangements not only to project publicity, as previously indicated, but to mobilize energies toward solving "crisis" cases. They may also develop policy innovations which allow them to respond more quickly to "crisis" situations. These innovations may be important to some city residents, for whom the problems of dealing with city bureaucracies can prove insurmountable. It might be said, indeed, that the goals of protest are to influence city agencies to handle every case with the same resources that characterize their dispatch of "crisis" cases.[55]

But such policies would demand major revenue inputs. This kind of qualitative policy change is difficult to achieve. Meanwhile, internal reallocation of resources only means that routine services must be neglected so that the "crisis" programs can be enhanced. If all cases are expedited, as in a typical "crisis" response, then none can be. Thus for purposes of general solutions, "crisis" resolving can be self-defeating unless accompanied by significantly greater resource allocation. It is not self-defeating, however, to the extent that the organizational goals of city agencies are to serve a clientele while minimizing negative publicity concerning agency vigilance and responsiveness.

4. Target groups may appear to be constrained in their ability to grant protest goals.[56] This may be directed toward making the protesters appear to be unreasonable in their demands, or to be well-meaning

individuals who "just don't understand how complex running a city really is." Target groups may extend sympathy but claim that they lack resources, a mandate from constituents, and/or authority to respond to protest demands. Target groups may also evade protest demands by arguing that "If-I-give-it-to-you-I-have-to-give-it-to-everyone."

The tactic of appearing constrained is particularly effective with established civic groups because there is an undeniable element of truth to it. Everyone knows that cities are financially undernourished. Established civic groups expend great energies lobbying for higher levels of funding for their pet city agencies. Thus they recognize the validity of this constraint when posed by city officials. But it is not inconsistent to point out that funds for specific, relatively inexpensive programs, or for the expansion of existing programs, can often be found if pressure is increased. While constraints on city government flexibility may be extensive, they are not absolute. Protest targets nonetheless attempt to diminish the impact of protest demands by claiming relative impotence.

5. Target groups may use their extensive resources to discredit protest leaders and organizations. Utilizing their excellent access to the press, public officials may state or imply that leaders are unreliable, ineffective as leaders ("they don't really have the people behind them"), guilty of criminal behavior, potentially guilty of such behavior, or are some shade of "left-wing." Any of these allegations may serve to diminish the appeal of protest groups to potentially sympathetic third parties. City officials, in their frequent social and informal business interaction with leaders of established civic groups, may also communicate derogatory information concerning protest groups. Discrediting of protest groups may be undertaken by some city officials while others appear (perhaps authentically) to remain sympathetic to protest demands. These tactics may be engaged in by public officials whether or not there is any validity to the allegations.

6. Target groups may postpone action. The effect of postponement, if accompanied by symbolic assurances, is to remove immediate pressure and delay specific commitments to a future date. This familiar tactic is particularly effective in dealing with protest groups because of their inherent instability. Protest groups are usually comprised of individuals whose intense political activity cannot be sustained except in rare circumstances. Further, to the extent that protest depends upon activating reference publics through strategies which have some "shock" value, it becomes increasingly dif-

---

[55] See Lipsky, *op cit.*, pp. 156, 249 ff.
[56] On the strategy of appearing constrained, see Schelling, *op. cit.*, pp. 22 ff.

ficult to activate these groups. Additionally, protest activity is inherently unstable because of the strains placed upon protest leaders who must attempt to manage four constituencies (as described herein).

The most frequent method of postponing action is to commit a subject to "study." For the many reasons elaborated in these paragraphs, it is not likely that ad hoc protest groups will be around to review the recommendations which emerge from study. The greater the expertise and the greater the status of the group making the study, the less will protest groups be able to influence whatever policy emerges. Protest groups lack the skills and resource personnel to challenge expert recommendations effectively.

Sometimes surveys and special research are undertaken in part to evade immediate pressures. Sometimes not. Research efforts are particularly necessary to secure the support of established civic groups, which place high priority on orderly procedure and policy emerging from independent analysis. Yet it must be recognized that postponing policy commitments has a distinct impact on the nature of the pressures focused on policy-makers.

VI. CONCLUSION

In this analysis I have agreed with James Q. Wilson that protest is correctly conceived as a strategy utilized by relatively powerless groups in order to increase their bargaining ability. As such, I have argued, it is successful to the extent that the reference publics of protest targets can be activated to enter the conflict in ways favorable to protest goals. I have suggested a model of the protest process which may assist in ordering data and indicating the salience for research of a number of aspects of protest. These include the critical role of communications media, the differential impact of material and symbolic rewards on "feedback" in protest activity, and the reciprocal relationships of actors in the protest process.

An estimation of the limits to protest efficacy, I have argued further, can be gained by recognizing the problems encountered by protest leaders who somehow must balance the conflicting maintenance needs of four groups in the protest process. This approach transcends a focus devoted primarily to characterization of group goals and targets, by suggesting that even in an environment which is relatively favorable to specific protest goals, the tensions which must be embraced by protest leadership may ultimately overwhelm protest activity.

At the outset of this essay, it was held that conceptualizing the American political system as "slack" or "fluid," in the manner of Robert Dahl, appears inadequate because of (1) a vagueness centering on the likelihood that any group can make itself heard; (2) a possible confusion as to which groups tend to receive satisfaction from the rewards dispensed by public officials; and (3) a lumping together as equally relevant rewards which are tangible and those which are symbolic. To the extent that protest is engaged in by relatively powerless groups which must create resources with which to bargain, the analysis here suggests a number of reservations concerning the pluralist conceptualization of the "fluidity" of the American political system.

Relatively powerless groups cannot use protest with a high probability of success. They lack organizational resources, by definition. But even to create bargaining resources through activating third parties, some resources are necessary to sustain organization. More importantly, relatively powerless protest groups are constrained by the unresolvable conflicts which are forced upon protest leaders who must appeal simultaneously to four constituencies which place upon them antithetical demands.

When public officials recognize the legitimacy of protest activity, they may not direct public policy toward protest groups at all. Rather, public officials are likely to aim responses at the reference publics from which they originally take their cues. Edelman has suggested that regulatory policy in practice often consists of reassuring mass publics while at the same time dispensing specific, tangible values to narrow interest groups. It is suggested here that symbolic reassurances are dispensed as much to wide, potentially concerned publics which are not directly affected by regulatory policy, as they are to wide publics comprised of the downtrodden and the deprived, in whose name policy is often written.

Complementing Edelman, it is proposed here that in the process of protest symbolic reassurances are dispensed in large measure because these are the public policy outcomes and actions desired by the constituencies to which public officials are most responsive. Satisfying these wider publics, city officials can avoid pressures toward other policies placed upon them by protest organizations.

Not only should there be some doubt as to which groups receive the symbolic recognitions which Dahl describes, but in failing to distinguish between the kinds of rewards dispensed to groups in the political system, Dahl avoids a fundamental question. It is literally fundamental because the kinds of rewards which can be obtained from politics, one might hypothesize, will have an impact upon the realistic appraisal of the efficacy of political activity. If among the groups least capable of organizing for political activity there is a history of organizing for protest, and if that activity, once engaged in, is rewarded primarily by the dispensation of symbolic gestures without perceptible changes in material conditions, then rational behavior might lead to expressions of apathy and lack of interest in politics or a rejection of conventional political channels as a meaningful arena of activity. In this sense this discussion of protest politics is consistent with Kenneth Clark's observations that the image of power, unaccompanied by material and observable rewards, leads to impressions of helplessness and reinforces political apathy in the ghetto.[57]

Recent commentary by political scientists and others regarding riots in American cities seems to focus in part on the extent to which relatively deprived groups may seek redress of legitimate grievances. Future research should continue assessment of the relationship between riots and the conditions under which access to the political system has been limited. In such research assessment of the ways in which access to public officials is obtained by relatively powerless groups through the protest process might be one important research focus.

The instability of protest activity outlined in this article also should inform contemporary political strategies. If the arguments presented here are persuasive, civil rights leaders who insist that protest activity is a shallow foundation on which to seek long-term, concrete gains may be judged essentially correct. But the arguments concerning the fickleness of the white liberal, or the ease of changing discriminatory laws relative to changing discriminatory institutions, only in part explain the instability of protest movements. An explanation which derives its strength from analysis of the political process suggests concentration on the problems of managing protest constituencies. Accordingly, Alinsky is probably on the soundest ground when he prescribes protest for the purpose of building organiza-

tion. Ultimately, relatively powerless groups in most instances cannot depend upon activating other actors in the political process. Long-run success will depend upon the acquisition of stable political resources which do not rely for their use on third parties.

READING 19

POLITICAL OPPORTUNITY STRUCTURES AND POLITICAL PROTEST: ANTI-NUCLEAR MOVEMENTS IN FOUR DEMOCRACIES

Herbert P. Kitschelt*

Since the 1960s, successive protest movements have challenged public policies, established modes of political participation and socio-economic institutions in advanced industrial democracies. Social scientists have responded by conducting case studies of such movements. Comparative analyses, particularly cross-national comparisons of social movements, however, remain rare, although opportunities abound to observe movements with similar objectives or forms of mobilization in diverse settings.

A social movement that lends itself to cross-national study is the anti-nuclear power movement, which swept across the political landscapes of America and Europe in the 1970s. In some countries, the nuclear power conflict reached an intensity unprecedented in the history of technology controversies. So far, the opportunity for a theoretically-oriented and controlled comparison of anti-nuclear movements has not been seized, for while case studies of nuclear power conflicts generate a wealth of descriptive detail, individually they are not

---

[57] Clark, *op. cit.*, pp. 154 ff.

From *British Journal of Political Science* 16(1986):57–85. Reprinted with the permission of the author and Cambridge University Press.

*For helpful comments on an earlier version of this paper, I would like to thank Peter Lange, Anthony King, Sidney Tarrow, and two anonymous reviewers for the *Journal*.

suited to the task of arriving at a generalized under-standing of the factors that determine the dynamics of social movements.[1]

This article is an attempt to use some of the rich detail of the existing case studies to construct a systematic comparison of the anti-nuclear power movements in France, Sweden, the United States and West Germany. All four countries have experienced intense conflicts over nuclear technology, but anti-nuclear movements in each have pursued a different strategy and have had a different impact on overall energy policy. I shall argue that a particular set of variables is most useful for explaining these variations, namely, a nation's *political opportunity structure*. Political opportunity structures are comprised of specific configurations of resources, institutional arrangements and historical precedents for social mobilization, which facilitate the development of protest movements in some instances and constrain them in others. While they do not determine the course of social movements completely, careful comparisons among them can explain a good deal about the variations among social movements with similar demands in different settings, if other determinants are held constant. Comparison can show that political opportunity structures influence the choice of protest strategies and the impact of social movements on their environments. The latter, in partic-

ular, is a topic that has received little attention until recently.[2]

The explanation of the strategies and impacts of social movements suggested in this article differs from—but is not necessarily inconsistent with—those advanced by three other theoretical approaches: Marxian-macrosociological, microsociological and resource mobilization. Essentially, what distinguishes the approach taken here is the importance assigned to explaining movement variations, both in terms of mobilization and impact. Marxian-macrosociological analysis, for example, links the emergence of social movements to various stages in the development of socio-economic modes of production; and those following this approach have viewed the anti-nuclear movement as a member of a larger class of "new social movements" that has been spawned by the systems of bureaucratic and technological control that regulate social life in late capitalism.[3] What proponents of this

[1] The non-theoretical literature includes several useful handbooks, written by anti-nuclear activists, about the development of nuclear power conflicts in a number of countries, as well as several descriptively rich comparative analyses written by academic observers. Representative handbooks include: Projektbereich Ökologie der Vereinigten deutschen Studentenschaft, Bochum, *Atomenergie International: Atomprogramme und Wilderstand in 28 Ländern* (Bochum: Druckladen, 1978); Anna Gyorgy and friends, *No Nukes: Everyone's Guide to Nuclear Power* (Boston: South End Press, 1979); and Lutz Mez, ed., *Der Atomkonflikt* (West Berlin: Olle und Wolters, 1979). Representative academic analyses include: John Surrey and Charlotte Huggett, "Opposition to Nuclear Power: A Review of International Experience," *Energy Policy*, IV (1976), 286–307; Dorothy Nelkin and Michael Pollak, "The Politics of Participation and the Nuclear Debate in Sweden, the Netherlands, and Austria," *Public Policy* XXV (1977), 333–57; also "The Political Parties and the Nuclear Energy Debate in France and Germany," *Comparative Politics*, XII (1980), 127–41; and also *The Atom Besieged: Extraparliamentary Dissent in France and Germany* (Cambridge, MA: MIT Press, 1981); and Jim Falk, *Global Fission: The Battle Over Nuclear Power* (Melbourne: Oxford University Press, 1982).

[2] Societal impacts of social movements are a concern of the following recent literature: William Gamson, *The Strategy of Social Protest* (Homewood, IL: Dorsey, 1975); Gary Marx and James Wood, "Strands of Theory and Research in Collective Behavior," *Annual Review of Sociology*, 1 (1975), 363–428; Frances Fox Piven and Richard Cloward, *Poor People's Movements: Why They Succeed, How They Fail* (New York: Pantheon, 1979); Ted Robert Gurr, "On the Outcomes of Violent Conflict," in Ted Robert Gurr, ed. *Handbook of Political Conflict* (New York: Free Press, 1980), pp. 238–94; Doug McAdam, *Political Process and the Development of Black Insurgency, 1930–1970* (Chicago: University of Chicago Press, 1982); and Sidney Tarrow, *Social Movements: Resource Mobilization and Reform During Cycles of Protest: A Bibliographic and Critical Essay*, Western Societies Program, Occasional Paper No. 15, Center for International Studies (Ithaca, NY: Cornell University, 1982).

[3] Key contributions to this perspective include: Alain Touraine, *The Self-Production of Society* (Chicago: University of Chicago Press, 1977), Chap. 6; Alain Touraine, *The Voice of the Eye* (Cambridge: Cambridge University Press, 1981); Alain Touraine, Zsuza Hegedus, François Dubet and Michel Wieviorka, *La Prophétie Anti-Nucléaire* (Paris: Edition du Seuil, 1980); Alberto Melucci, "The New Social Movements: A Theoretical Approach," *Social Science Information*, XIX (1980), 199–226; Jürgen Habermas, *Theorie des kommunikativen Handelns*, Volumes 1 and 2 (Frankfurt: Suhrkamp, 1981); Klaus Eder, "A New Social-Movement?," *Telos*, 52 (1982), 5–20; and Claus Offe, "New Social Movements as a Meta-Political Challenge" (unpublished paper, Universität Bielefeld, June 1983). A critical review of the literature is found in Jean Cohen, "Between Crisis Management and Social Movements: The Place of Institutional Reform," *Telos*, LII (1982), 21–40.

approach do not explain is why the various national anti-nuclear protests have had such dissimilar careers, in terms of both differential articulation and impact, in otherwise similarly constituted capitalist societies.

Insensitivity to the importance of explaining movement variations also characterizes microsociological approaches, which seek to explain the mobilization of protest and its impact on policy and institutions as direct consequences of the number and intensity of social "strains" and "grievances" or of the relative deprivation experienced by particular social groups.[4] As has often been noted, strains or deprivations in and of themselves seldom explain variations in the dynamics of social movements. This is certainly true for the cases under study; each country's energy program presented its citizens with similar levels of grievances, but the national movements that emerged developed in distinct ways. As will be shown, political opportunity structures functioned as "filters" between the mobilization of the movement and its choice of strategies and its capacity to change the social environment. At most, we can say that the existence of strain and relative deprivation is a necessary but not a sufficient condition of social protest.[5]

The explanatory approach suggested here is loosely linked to the relatively recently elaborated resource-mobilization perspective in social protest research,

which conceives of social movements as collective and rational decision-makers that mobilize their followers and promote their causes with the best available strategies given limited cognitive and material resources.[6] Most of the empirical studies that adopt this perspective, however, concentrate on those internal variables of movement mobilization that are deemed to be within an incipient movement's discretion, e.g., incentive structure in membership recruitment, internal organization, specification of goals and skills in forming coalitions with allies. In contrast, the emphasis of the present comparison of anti-nuclear movements is on relating the strategic choices and societal impacts of movements to specific properties of the external political opportunity structures that movements face. Such institutional constraints have often been simply assumed, rather than systematically and comparatively used to explain social movements' trajectories.[7]

A comparison of anti-nuclear protest movements in France, Sweden, the United States and West Germany is well-suited to discovering the effects of institutional constraints on social movement mobilization for several reasons. First of all, these four anti-nuclear movements share similar operational objectives, namely, to prevent the completion of nuclear power plants under construction, to prevent work from beginning on planned projects and, ultimately, to shut down existing nuclear facilities. Secondly, in all of the cases, nuclear power conflicts grew from localized, segmented conflicts about specific power plants into national movements and controversies in the same time period, soon

---

[4] This perspective is labelled as "Durkheimian" in Charles Tilly, *From Mobilization to Revolution* (Reading, MA: Addison-Wesley, 1978). It has been adopted and refined by authors as diverse as the structural-functionalist Neil Smelser in *Theory of Collective Behavior* (New York: Free Press, 1962) and the behavioralist Ted Robert Gurr in *Why Men Rebel* (Princeton, NJ: Princeton University Press, 1970). Critical assessments of the relative deprivation perspective are found in Michael Useem, *Protest Movements in America* (Indianapolis: Bobbs-Merrill, 1975) and J. Craig Jenkins, "Sociopolitical Movements," in Samuel R. Long, ed., *The Handbook of Political Behavior*, Vol. 4 (New York: Plenum Press, 1981).

[5] Early critics of the social strain and relative deprivation theories rejected their validity out of hand, but some contemporary critics accept the intensification of grievances as one of several determinants of social movement mobilization. For example, see E. J. Walsh, "Resource Mobilization and Citizen Protest in Communities Around Three Mile Island," *Social Problems*, XXIX (1981), 1–21; Harold R. Kerbo, "Movements of 'Crisis' and Movements of 'Affluence': A Critique of Deprivation and Resource Mobilization Theories," *Journal of Conflict Resolution*, XXVI (1982), 645–63; and Keith Webb, *et al.*, "Etiology and Outcomes of Protest: New European Perspectives," *American Behavioral Scientist*, XXVI (1983), 311–31.

[6] Key contributions to the resource mobilization perspective are Anthony Oberschall, *Social Conflict and Social Movements* (Englewood Cliffs, NJ: Prentice-Hall, 1973); William Gamson, *The Strategy of Social Protest* (Homewood, IL: Dorsey, 1975); and John D. McCarthy and Mayer Zald, "Resource Mobilization and Social Movements: A Partial Theory," *American Journal of Sociology*, LXXXII (1977), 1212–41.

[7] McCarthy and Zald, "Resource Mobilization and Social Movements," p. 1236, for instance simply state that they have assumed the "modern American context" for their theory. But the institutional context is, as Piven and Cloward, pp. 15–37; point out, an important determinant of movement mobilization that may vary. A greater emphasis on external political opportunity structures is found in some of the recent social movement research. See McAdam, *Political Process and the Development of Black Insurgency*; Tarrow, *Social Movements*; and Tilly, *From Mobilization to Revolution*, Chap. 4.

after the first energy crisis of 1973–74.[8] (Anti-nuclear movements are treated here as complex aggregations of protest events at the level of entire countries, not as sequences of separable protest episodes at a more disaggregated level.) Thirdly, the objective "threat" of nuclear power was about the same in each country in that all governments were firmly committed to nuclear programs of approximately the same size and growth rates at the time that anti-nuclear protest became a national phenomenon. Each country, for example, expected to install one to two gigawatts of nuclear elec-

tricity generation capacity per million inhabitants by the late 1980s. Finally, as we shall see, the subjective sense of deprivation and grievance also was quite similar. This assessment is supported by data about the social base of the movements indicating that the primary recruits were professionals and (public) service sector employees, farmers and property owners in the vicinity of proposed nuclear sites, students and young radicals, making each national movement an expression of "middle-class radicalism."[9] They shared not only similar social bases but similar opponents: each faced a pro-nuclear coalition comprised of nuclear scientists, engineering firms, utilities and promotional or regulatory state agencies.[10]

EXPLAINING STRATEGIES AND IMPACTS OF SOCIAL MOVEMENTS

Political opportunity structures can further or restrain the capacity of social movements to engage in protest activity in at least three different ways. Firstly, mobilization depends upon the coercive, normative, remunerative and informational resources that an incipient movement can extract from its setting and can employ in its protest. In Western democracies, non-violent resources are crucial for the emergence of protest. Thus, if movements can appeal to widely shared norms, collect adequate information about the nature of the grievance against which they protest and raise the money to disseminate their ideas and information, the chances of a broad mobilization increase. Secondly, the access of social movements to the public sphere and political decision-making is also governed by institutional rules, such as those reinforcing patterns of interaction between government and interest groups, and

---

[8] If the paper focused on the explanation of early nuclear power conflicts, a more disaggregate level of analysis would have been in order: site-specific variables, such as the absence or presence of other industrial polluters, including nuclear ones, at a prospective plant site; patterns of rural settlement; fiscal side-payments to communities willing to host nuclear facilities; and the secretiveness of decision-making among local political and economic elites have been found to be reliable predictors of protest in numerous case studies. For France, see Didier Anger, *Cronique d'une lutte: le combat anti-nucléaire à Flamanville et dans La Hague* (without location: Jean-Claude Simoën, 1977); Phillipe Garraud, "Politique électro-nucléaire et mobilisation: la tentative de constitution d'enjeu," *Revenue française de science politique*, XXIX (1979), 448–74; Thierry Jund, *Le Nucléaire contre l'Alsace* (Paris: Syros, 1977); N. J. D. Lucas, *Energy in France: Planning, Politics and Policy* (London: Europa Publications, 1979), pp. 188–212; and Alexandre Nicolon, Nicolon, *Nucléopolis: materiaux pour l'analyse d'une société nucléaire* (Grenoble: Presses Universitaires de Grenoble, 1979). For Sweden, see Lennart Daleus," A Moratorium in Name Only," *Bulletin of the Atomic Scientist*, XXXI (1975), 27–33. For the United States see Lyton Caldwell, Lynton Hayes, and Isabel MacWhirter, *Citizens and the Environment: Case Studies in Popular Action* (Bloomington, IN: Indiana University Press, 1976), Chaps, 3, 6, 7 and 8; Steven del Sesto, *Science, Politics and Controversy: Civilian Nuclear Power in the United States, 1947–1974* (Boulder, CO: Westview, 1979), Chap. 6; Stephen Ebbin and Raphael Kasper, *Citizen Groups and the Nuclear Power Controversy: Uses of Scientific and Technical Information* (Cambridge, MA: MIT Press, 1974); Gyorgy *et al., No Nukes*; Robert E. Kasperson et al., "Public Opposition to Nuclear Energy: Retrospect and Prospect," *Science, Technology and Human Values*, V (1980), 11–23; and Dorothy Nelkin, *Nuclear Power and Its Critics: The Cayuga Lake Controversy* (Ithaca, NY: Cornell University Press, 1971). For West Germany, see Battelle Institut, *Bürgerinitiativen im Bereich von Kernkraftwerken* (Bonn: Bundesministerium für Forschung und Technologie, 1975); Herbert Kitschelt, *Kernenergiepolitik: Arena eines gesellschaftlichen Konflikts* (Frankfurt: Campus, 1980), Chaps. 5.2 and 5.4; Dieter Rucht, *Von Whyl nach Gorleben: Bürger gegen Atomprogramm und nukleare Entsorgung* (Munich: Beck, 1980); and Joachim Schritt, *Bauern gegen Atomanlagen* (Offenbach: Verlag 2000, 1977).

[9] Reliable quantitative data about the social background of anti-nuclear activists are hard to come by. But the case studies referred to in fn. 4 consistently identify these three groups of activitist.

[10] The alliances of pro-nuclear interests were very similar in all four countries during the early stages of the nuclear power debate. However, the reasons why these clusters of industrial and administrative interests are the logical outcome of nuclear technology development in the countries compared here are discussed in Herbert Kitschelt, "Structures and Sequences of Nuclear Energy Policy-Making: Suggestions for a Comparative Perspective," *Political Power and Social Theory*, III (1982), 271–308.

electoral laws.[11] These rules allow for, register, respond to and even shape the demands of social movements that are not (yet) accepted political actors. They also facilitate or impede the institutionalization of new groups and claims. Thirdly, a social movement faces opportunities to mobilize protest that change over time with the appearance and disappearance of other social movements. The mobilization of one movement, for example, may have a "demonstration effect" on other incipient movements, encouraging them to follow suit. And the simultaneous appearance of several movements contesting the institutions of social control often presents the best opportunity to maintain movement momentum and to change established policies.[12]

In the four countries compared here, the temporal opportunity structures encountered by the anti-nuclear movements were quite similar; the protests reached a peak in the second half of the 1970s and they grew out of the broader environmental movement. Crucial differences, however, characterize the resource and institutional opportunity structures they faced.[13] These configurations, which are relatively inert over time, may also be labelled as the "political regimes" prevailing in each country. While they are not immutable, they respond only slowly to new policy demands. And inasmuch as they pattern policy demands and options independently of the preferences of shifting coalitions of interested political actors and social forces, they inject a decidedly non-pluralistic element into the policy formation process.

Students of social movements at times distinguish relatively "open" political opportunity structures from relatively "closed" ones and note that the dominance of one type or the other sets limits to the responsiveness that movements can expect.[14] A particularly useful outgrowth of this research is the identification of a curvilinear relationship between openness and movement mobilization, which shows that very closed regimes repress social movements, that very open and responsive ones assimilate them, and that moderately repressive ones allow for their broad articulation but do not accede readily to their demands.

This conceptualization of opportunity structures is useful but somewhat one-sided, for it considers only the input processes of political decision cycles. The other side of the coin is that the capacity of political systems to convert demands into public policy also affects social movement mobilization and impact: the output phase of the policy cycle also shapes social movements and offers them points of access and inclusion in policymaking.[15] Indeed, this conclusion is supported by the many case studies which show that policies are often entirely renegotiated as they are implemented.[16] Thus, the capacity of political opportunity structures to implement policies—as well as their openness to societal demands—ought to be seen to determine the overall responsiveness of politics to social movements.

While it is certainly the case that political opportunity structures vary among policy arenas within the same political regime, system-wide political properties and national "policy styles" also play key roles in determining the dynamics of social movements. The nature of these properties and styles are of crucial importance because representatives of entirely new demands often cannot participate effectively in highly differentiated policy arenas and instead must appeal to actors and institutions in politics, such as parties, parliaments and courts, whose authority and decision procedures at least partially transcend those of particular policy arenas.

In this respect, at least four factors determine the openness of political regimes to new demands on the input side. (1) The number of political parties, factions, and groups that effectively articulate different demands

---

[11] The concept of political opportunity structure is used here in a broader sense than that conveyed by "state structure," a concept that has been used, and criticized, in recent discussions in the field of comparative public policy. See John Zysman, *Governments, Markets and Growth* (Ithaca, NY: Cornell University Press, 1983), pp. 291–300 and 347–9. Opportunity structure encompasses the concept of "dominant policy style." The latter is developed for a number of countries in Jeremy Richardson, ed., *Policy Styles in Western Europe* (London: George Allen & Unwin, 1982). A recent analysis in this vein of labour movements is found in Peter Lange, George Ross and Maurizio Vannizelli, *Unions, Change and Crisis: French and Italian Union Strategy and the Political Economy, 1945–1980* (London: Allen & Unwin, 1982).

[12] The concepts of movement cycles and reform cycles are developed in Tarrow, *Social Movements*, pp. 35–46.

[13] Structures are those processes in a system that change at a rate so slow as to be fixed for the study of events that transpire over a short period of time. See Karl Deutsch, "The Crisis of the State," *Government and Opposition*, XVI (1981), 331–41, at p. 332.

[14] The distinction drawn between open and closed opportunity structures is used in Peter K. Eisinger, "The Conditions of Protest Behavior in American Cities," *American Political Science Review*, LXVII (1973), 11–28.

[15] This term is used in Judith May and Aaron Wildavsky, eds. *The Policy Cycle* (Beverly Hills, CA: Sage, 1978) to describe public policy processes in terms of steps and stages.

[16] This point is frequently stressed in implementation research. See Eugene Bardach, *The Implementation Game* (Cambridge, MA: MIT Press, 1977).

in electoral politics influences openness. The larger this number, the more "centrifugal" a political system tends to be and the more difficult it is to confine electoral interest articulation to the "cartel" of entrenched interests that is represented by the established, bureaucratized parties. (2) Openness increases with the capacity of legislatures to develop and control policies independently of the executive. This is the case because a legislature is by definition an electorally accountable agent and is therefore much more sensitive to public demands, whereas only the uppermost positions in the executive are subject to such direct public pressure. (3) Patterns of intermediation between interest groups and the executive branch are another element shaping political openness. Where "pluralist" and fluid links are dominant, access for new interests to the centres of political decision-making is facilitated. (4) Finally, political openness not only requires opportunities for the articulation of new demands, but new demands must actually find their way into the processes of forming policy compromises and consensus. For this to occur, there must be mechanisms that aggregate demands. Openness is constrained when there are no viable procedures to build effective policy coalitions.

In a similar vein, three operational dimensions characterize the capacity of political systems to implement policies. (1) National policies are implemented more effectively when the state apparatus is centralized. A complicated division of jurisdiction between a multitude of semi-independent government agencies and a federal stratification of state authority tends to make policy implementation more cumbersome. (2) Simultaneously, government control over market participants is a key variable for government effectiveness in many policy areas.[17] The degree of state control over the finance sector, the relative size of the public sector's share of GNP and its share of total employment, and the state's co-ordination, control or exclusion of economic interest groups in policy-making, are some of the factors that influence policy effectiveness. The greater is the control of economic resources and decision centres through political institutions, the more limited are the resources available with which to challenge policies. (3) Policy effectiveness is also determined by the relative independence and authority the judiciary enjoys in

the resolution of political conflict. Policy implementation becomes more hazardous and cumbersome if courts are forums of political arbitration removed from executive branch control.

Differences in the openness and capacity of political regimes are continuous rather than discrete variables. Given the number of variables on each dimension, many combinations of openness and implementation capacity may occur. Nevertheless, for comparative purposes, one may roughly dichotomize each of the political input and capacity variables. Doing so shows that each of the four countries included in the present study represents a different configuration of regime properties (see Table 1). Space constraints rule out a detailed defence of this classification of opportunity structures, let alone an analysis of each structure's historical origins or regime changes.[18] Some classifications, however, are likely to be contested and therefore deserve a brief discussion.

With respect to *France*, there is a broad agreement on the effectiveness, though not the efficiency, of national policy-making. More debatable is the characterization here of the French political system as closed. There are, however, several features of policy-making that support this characterization: the executive branch is clearly dominant over a weak legislature and there is policy-making access for only a select number of interest groups. Moreover, the party system of the Fifth

---

[18] The divergent features of political regimes found among advanced industrial democracies can be traced back to the circumstances surrounding their state-building, their location in the world economy, the timing and speed of their industrialization, and the formation of class and group coalitions promoting specific regime forms. For the purposes of this article, however, the varying outcomes of political development in the four countries are taken as givens.

---

[17] This variable permits only a restricted, though important, scope of generalization across policy areas. While it is important as a determinant of most economic and social policies, there are obviously other policy areas where it does not come into play as a determinant of policy formation.

TABLE 1

Political Opportunity Structures in France, Sweden, West Germany and the United States

		Political input structures	
		Open	**Closed**
Political output structures	**Strong**	Sweden	France
	Weak	United States	West Germany

Republic exhibits centripetal tendencies. Increasingly, this has meant that two blocs, organized along the fundamental socio-economic cleavages of French society, vie for political power. Thus, the two main competitors in the party system have had difficulty in accommodating the demands generated by the cross-cutting cleavages as of the "new politics."[19]

Sweden's political capacity may not be as high as that of France, but its unitary public administration, weak political judiciary and fairly high degree of control and concentration of the economy justify its characterization as a "high effectiveness" polity, as compared with either West Germany or the United States. More questions, though, can be raised about the openness of Swedish politics. While societal corporatism may indicate the opposite, Sweden's relatively differentiated, fractionalized party system and its consensus-orientated, responsive bureaucracy are all factors that weigh in favour of characterizing it as open. This is further supported by the fact that hitherto unrepresented new-politics issues, such as demands for participatory democracy, rights for students, the emancipation of women, comprehensive aid to less developed countries and, more recently, civil and socio-economic rights for immigrants have all been attentively registered by the political parties and have triggered policy innovations.[20] In both respects, Sweden's political process displays relatively great openness.[21]

America's political input structures exhibit fairly great openness to interest articulation but far less openness with respect to the aggregation of new demands. The comparatively strong position of the Congress, the lack of tightly integrated political parties, the relative openness of a deeply fragmented administration, all testify to the openness of politics in the United States. But the lack of structured systems of intermediation between interest groups, legislators and the political bureaucracy imposes severe constraints on the capacity for political aggregation and innovation. New demands often "evaporate" in the pluralist process of coalition formation or later on when a weak state agency has to renegotiate a policy with organized interests. The executive branch is territorially and substantively fragmented, has little control over the economy and must face an autonomous judiciary.[22]

The description of *West Germany* as a polity with a "weak" capacity breaks with the efficiency myth with which German politics has often been falsely associated. The jurisdictional and territorial fragmentation of the state is great, the judiciary is quite autonomous, and the state is restricted with respect to both the choice of instruments and the resources at its disposal in the control of private market actors. At the same time, its centripetal party system, organized along class and religious cleavages, weak legislature and inaccessible executive make West German political input structures appear more like those of the closed French system

[19] Useful analyses of the French political system are found in Philip G. Cerny and Martin A. Schain, eds. *French Politics and Public Policy* (New York: St. Martin's Press, 1980); William Andrews and Stanley Hoffman, eds., *The Fifth Republic at Twenty* (Albany, NY: State University of New York Press, 1981); Stephen Cohen and Peter Gourevitch, eds, *France in a Troubled World Economy* (London: Butterworth Scientific, 1982); and Douglas Ashford, *Policy and Politics in France* (Philadelphia, PA: Temple University Press, 1982).

[20] Compare, for the assimilation of Swedish movements in the late 1960s, Olof Ruin, "Participatory Democracy and Corporatism: The Case of Sweden," *Scandanavian Political Studies*, IX (1974), 171–84. Early socio-economic reforms and a better representation of women in politics have even pre-empted a strong women's movement in Sweden. Compare: Maud Edwards, "Sweden," in Joni Lovenduski and Jill Hills, eds. *The Politics of the Second Electorate: Women and Public Participation* (London: Routledge & Kegan Paul), pp. 208–27; Hilda Scott, *Sweden's "Right to be Human": Sex Role Equality: The Goal and the Reality* (Avondale, NY: M. E. Sharpe, 1982).

[21] For Sweden, see Neil Elder, *Government in Sweden: The Executive at Work* (Oxford: Pergamon, 1970); M. Donald Hancock, *Sweden: The Politics of Postindustrial Change* (Hinsdale, IL: The Dryden Press, 1972); and Thomas J. Anton, *Administered Poli-*

tics: Elite Political Culture in Sweden (Boston: Nijhoff, 1980). Several works note a marked decline in Sweden's capacity to build consensus and implement public policy. As similar trends also have been observed in other countries, the distance between the predominant Swedish "policy style" and other regimes, nevertheless, may not have disappeared. See Gunnel Gustafsson and Jeremy Richardson, "Concepts of Rationality and the Policy Process," *European Journal of Political Research*, VII (1979), 415–36; Olof Ruin, "Sweden in the 1970s: Policy-making Becomes More Difficult," in Richardson, ed., *Policy Styles in Western Europe*, pp. 141–67; and Neil Elder, Alastair H. Thomas and David Arter, *The Consensual Democracies?* (Oxford: Martin Robertson, 1982).

[22] For the American political system, see Walter Dean Burnham, *Critical Elections and the Mainsprings of American Politics* (New York: Norton, 1971); Harold Seidman, *Politics, Position and Power: The Dynamics of Federal Organization*, 2nd edn (New York: Oxford University Press, 1975); Anthony King, ed., *The New American Political System* (Washington, DC: American Enterprise Institute for Public Policy Research, 1978); and James Sundquist, *The Decline and Resurgence of Congress* (Washington, DC: Brookings, 1981).

than those of the more open American and Swedish polities.[23]

How do these different national political opportunity structures affect the strategies and impacts of social movements? Two major hypotheses guide the present comparison of anti-nuclear movements. Firstly, with respect to strategies, political opportunity structures set the range of likely protest activities. For instance, when political systems are open and weak, they invite *assimilative* strategies; movements attempt to work through established institutions because political opportunity structures offer multiple points of access. In contrast, when political systems are closed and have considerable capacities to ward off threats to the implementation of policies, movements are likely to adopt *confrontational*, disruptive strategies orchestrated outside established policy channels.

Secondly, political opportunity structures facilitate or impede movement impacts, among which we may distinguish three types: procedural, substantive and structural.[24] Procedural impacts or gains open new channels of participation to protest actors and involve their recognition as legitimate representatives of demands. Substantive gains are changes of policy in response to protest. And structural impacts indicate a transformation of the political opportunity structures themselves as a consequence of social movement activity.

To elaborate further, the second hypothesis leads us to expect procedural gains to covary with the openness of political systems. Thus, open regimes should be more willing to accept new groups, as it is likely that at least some established political actors will seek to strengthen their own positions by allying themselves with the newcomers. This incentive is missing in closed systems, where policy-making is the prerogative of a circumscribed cartel of political actors. For substantive gains to be made, a polity must have not only relatively open institutions and policy-making procedures but a high capacity to implement policies. The more open-

ness and capacity converge, the greater the likelihood of policy innovation. A variation should occur when a regime is closed and strong. In this instance, movement activities may prompt a limited range of elite-initiated reforms. Substantive gains are least likely to be found in weak regimes, be they open or closed. Here the likely outcome of protest activity is political stalemate, a situation in which neither old nor new policies can be implemented successfully. Finally, structural impacts will figure when a political system cannot bring about either procedural or substantive reforms. In this instance, a social movement will try to broaden its demands to include those for altering the existing political system fundamentally.

According to the logic of these hypotheses, social movements in the four cases under consideration ought to pursue distinct and different strategies and to have different policy impacts. These expectations are summarized in Table 2. Bearing them in mind, we turn now to the empirical data about the careers of anti-nuclear movements in France, Sweden, the United States and West Germany.

STRATEGIES OF ANTI-NUCLEAR MOVEMENTS

What strategies have anti-nuclear protesters adopted? Assimilative strategies have included lobbying, petitioning government bodies, influencing public policy through referendum campaigns and partisan involvement in electoral contests. Additionally, movements have tried to affect policy implementation by participating in licensing procedures and litigation. Confrontational strategies have included public demonstrations and acts of civil disobedience, exemplified by occupations of nuclear plant sites and access roads. But the national movements have not chosen equally from among these two types of protest. Moreover, as Table 3 shows, the choice of strategy does not vary at random. Rather, it varies with the specific type of political opportunity structure.

In the political systems where open decision-making processes prevail, anti-nuclear activists attempted to influence, directly and indirectly, legislatures and elections early on in the policy conflict. Thus, in the United States, environmental interest groups adopted an assimilative strategy that included, at the federal level, lobbying in Congressional committees and attempting to influence key sets of actors in the executive branch such as the Council on Environmental Quality, the Environmental Protection Agency and, to a lesser extent, the

---

[23] Useful analyses of policy-making in West Germany are found in Renate Mayntz and Fritz Scharpf, *Policy-Making in the German Federal Bureaucracy* (New York: Elsevier, 1975); David Conradt, *The German Polity*, 2nd edn (New York: Longman, 1982); Kenneth Dyson, "West Germany: The Search for a Rationalist Consensus," in Richardson, ed., *Policy Styles in Western Europe*, pp. 16–46.

[24] Gamson, *The Strategy of Protest*, Chap. 3, introduced the important distinction between procedural and substantive impacts or "gains" of movements, but omitted structural impacts on the political regimes themselves.

TABLE 2

Hypotheses About the Relationship Between Political Opportunity Structures and the Dynamics of Social Movements

		Political input structures	
		Open	**Closed**
Political output structures	**Strong**	(1) Assimilative movement strategies dominant (2) Significant procedural gains (3) High substantive policy innovation (4) Few structural pressures (Sweden)	(1) Confrontational movement strategies dominant (2) Few procedural impacts (3) Limited substantive elite reform; low-medium innovation (4) Strong structural pressures (France)
	Weak	(1) Assimilative movement strategies dominant (2) Significant procedural impacts (3) Substantive impacts: tendency towards policy stalemate; medium-low innovation (4) Few structural pressures (United States)	(1) Confrontational and assimilative movement strategies (2) Few procedural impacts (3) Few substantive impacts, tendency towards policy stalemate; very low innovation (4) Strong structural pressures (West Germany)

TABLE 3

Strategies of Anti-Nuclear Protest Mobilization in France, Sweden, the United States and West Germany

	Assimilative strategies aimed at political inputs		Assimilative strategies aimed at political outputs		Confrontational strategies against political process
	Lobbying/ petitioning	**Elections/ referendums**	**Interventions in licensing procedures**	**Litigation in courts**	**Public demonstration, acts of civil disobedience**
United States	high	high	high	high	low
Sweden	high	high	low	low	medium
West Germany	low	low (later : high)	high	high	high
France	low	low (later : high)	low	low	high

Nuclear Regulatory Commission. At the state level, these groups were successful in placing several anti-nuclear referendums on the ballot. And, at both levels, environmental groups sought to influence elected representatives by publicizing their voting records on nuclear and environmental matters.[25] In Sweden, anti-nuclear protesters organized themselves as public interest groups. Unlike their American counterparts, they preferred to work directly through the established party system rather than through either the legislature or the bureaucracy.[26] Both the Centre party, whose electoral base is essentially middle-class and whose constituency includes many young, educated people who are attracted to the issues of social decentralization and self-management, and the Eurocommunist Swedish Communist party adopted anti-nuclear positions in the mid-1970s. Other significant arenas of political participation included the several investigative government commissions on nuclear policy that sat during the course of the controversy and the national referendum on the nuclear program in 1980.

By contrast, in political systems where the established channels of political articulation offer few opportunities to voice protest, movements opted for more confrontational "outsider" strategies. For instance, no major party in either France or West Germany adopted a clear-cut anti-nuclear position during the controversy.[27] In both countries parliament exercised next to

no control over nuclear policy, and executive agencies were inaccessible to the nuclear opposition, rendering lobbying strategies futile. Finally, neither in West Germany, where the Basic Law rules out plebiscites, nor in France, where political elites stood in the way, could anti-nuclear groups dramatize their demands through national referendums. In France, the Socialists raised the idea of a referendum while in opposition but quickly abandoned it once in office. Given the inaccessibility of the existing political input structures, anti-nuclear movements in both countries began to press for structural change through the new anti-nuclear ecology parties of the late 1970s.

Variations in movement strategies also hold good with respect to the implementation of nuclear policy. In the United States and West Germany, each with weak implementation capacities, an arm's length relationship between government and the nuclear industry prevails. At least on paper and in the formal decision-making procedures, state regulators are neutral referees in conflicts between the industry and its critics. Licensing procedures, therefore, allowed nuclear critics to intervene in public investigative hearings and to sue against regulatory decisions. However, procedures are cumbersome and involve a plethora of competing agencies. In the United States and to a lesser extent in West Germany, intervention in licensing activities emerged as a major strategy of anti-nuclear groups and legal councillors.[28] Moreover, in both countries, the courts became a central battlefield in the controversy.[29] Although court action was frequently responsible for significant delays in nuclear construction projects, the courts were rarely

---

[25] In addition to those listed in fn. 2, detailed analyses of the nuclear power conflict in the United States are found in: Dorothy Nelkin and Susan Fallows, "The Evolution of the Nuclear Debate: The Role of Public Participation," *Annual Review of Energy*, III (1978), 275–312; and Jerome Price, *The Anti-nuclear Movement* (Boston: Twayne Publishers, 1982).

[26] For the Swedish nuclear controversy, see Daleus, "A Moratorium in Name Only," Nelkin and Pollak, "The Politics of Participation," Dean Abrahamson, "Governments Fall as Consensus Gives Way to Debate," *Bulletin of the Atomic Scientist*, XXXV (1979), 30–7; Ann-Marie Westmann, 'Schweden, Wohfahrtsstaat am Scheideweg', in Mez. *Der Atomkonflikt*, pp. 229–40; and Hans Zetterberg, *The Swedish Public and Nuclear Energy: The Referendum of 1980* (Tokyo: United Nations University, 1980).

[27] The role of political parties in West German and French nuclear power controversies is analyzed in Alexandre Nicolon and Marie-Josephe Carrieu. "Les parties face au nucléaire et la contestation," in Fagnani and Nicolson, *Nucléopolis*, pp. 79–159; Nelkin and Pollak, "The Political Parties and the Nuclear Energy Debate in France and Germany," and Kitschelt, *Kernenergiepolitik*, Chap. 5.5.

[28] For the United States, see Ebbin and Kasper, *Citizen Groups and the Nuclear Power Controversy*; and Elizabeth S. Rolph, *Nuclear Power and the Public Safety: A Study in Regulation* (Lexington, MA: Lexington Books, 1979). For West Germany, see Kitschelt, *Kernenergiepolitik*, Chap. 4. Licensing procedures in the United States, West Germany, France and Sweden are compared in Lutz Hoffmann *et al.*, *Faktoren der Standortwahl für Kernkraftwerke in ausgewählten Industriestaaten* (Bonn: Bundesministerium für Raumordnung, 1978).

[29] The role of litigation in West German and American anti-nuclear activities is discussed in Constance Ewing Cook, *Nuclear Power and Legal Advocacy: The Environmentalists and the Courts* (Lexington, MA: Lexington Books, 1980); Kitschelt, *Kernenergiepolitik*, Chap. 5.4; Nelkin and Pollack, *The Atom Besieged*, Chap. 11.

inclined to rule in the plaintiff's favour.[30] Thus, anti-nuclear activists realized that licensing skirmishes and litigation could only temporarily stave off nuclear projects and that other means of achieving their cancellation or shut-down were required.

In France and Sweden, in contrast, relatively effective public implementation capacities prevented intervention in the regulatory machinery. Both countries disallow broad political participation in licensing procedures and conduct no public hearings about licensing applications.[31] The protesters therefore had to look for other promising strategies to alter the course of nuclear policy.

The frequency of confrontational protest behaviour also supports the contention that a link exists between movement strategies and opportunity structures.[32] Confrontational incidents are most common in the regimes I have categorized as closed, as a measure of demonstration activity in the four countries indicates. In France, between 1975 and 1977, approximately 175,000 people rallied against nuclear power in ten demonstrations. Determined police action against the demonstrators subsequently led to a decline in such mass events. In West Germany, the intransigence of political elites provoked demonstrations too, but a weak state did not act decisively to quell the unrest. From February 1975 to April 1979, approximately 280,000 people participated in seven demonstrations at nuclear sites. Several site occupations were also attempted. In the aftermath of the Three Mile Island accident, in the fall of 1979, approximately 120,000 attended a Bonn demonstration against nuclear power. Several large demonstrations have taken place since then.

In the less intransigent Swedish and American systems, demonstrations have played only a minor role. Two, attended by between 10,000 and 15,000 people from Sweden and Denmark, were held in 1976 and 1977 to protest against the construction of the Barseback nuclear complex. In the United States, demonstrations and civil disobedience were strategies "imported" from Western Europe. Despite its head start in the late 1960s, the American anti-nuclear movement staged its first large-scale demonstration only in 1978, at the site of the Seabrook plant in New England.[33] To be sure, the accident at Three Mile Island in March 1979 was followed by a number of demonstrations with large turnouts, such as those in New York City, Washington, DC, and San Francisco, but occurring as they did, in the wake of what was depicted as a near national disaster, they must be viewed as temporary aberrations from the prevailing American pattern of assimilative protest.

Overall, there is convincing evidence that political opportunity structures direct the paths of social mobilization taken by the various national nuclear protest movements. It is a different matter, however, whether even strategies well-adapted to differing political regimes necessarily produce success in terms of procedural, substantive or structural impacts.

POLITICAL OPPORTUNITY STRUCTURES AND SOCIAL MOVEMENT IMPACTS

If political opportunity structures shape the impact of anti-nuclear movements on policy, we should not expect policy impacts to be attributable to the overall scale and intensity of protest but rather to vary, within limits, independently of them. High mobilization does not necessarily lead to profound impacts if the political opportunity structures are not conducive to change. Conversely, lower mobilization may have a disproportionate impact owing to properties of the political opportunity structure.

To test this argument, one would ideally need a good common measure of overall movement strength in each country. However, given the numerous protest strategies adopted, such a measure is difficult to find. Poll information on opinions about nuclear energy provides

[30] The effectiveness of litigation and the importance of the courts in the anti-nuclear movement's strategy has sometimes been overestimated, e.g., by Nelkin and Pollack, *The Atom Besieged*. There is not a single instance in either country where appeals courts have permanently revoked nuclear construction or operation licences. A discussion of the limits of the litigation strategy and the disillusionment it brings appears in Herbert Kitschelt, 'Justizapparate als Konfliktlösungsinstanz?' *Demokratie and Recht*, VII (January 1979), 3–22; and in Lettie McSpadden-Wenner, "Energy Environmental Trade-Offs in the Courts: Nuclear and Fossil Fuels," Regine Axelrod, ed., *Environment, Energy, Public Policy* (Lexington, MA: D. C. Heath, 1981), pp. 81–109.

[31] The French licensing procedure is discussed in Jean-Marie Colson, *Le Nucléaire sans les Français: Qui decide? Qui profite?* (Paris: Maspero, 1977), pp. 101ff.

[32] These correlations between political structures and protest activity also appear in earlier movements from which anti-nuclear groups recruited some of their participants. Student movements in the late 1960s, for instance, were more militant and embittered in West Germany and France than in Sweden or in the United States.

[33] The Seabrook controversy is discussed in Steven Barkan, "Strategic, Tactical and Organizational Dilemmas of the Protest Movement Against Nuclear Energy," *Social Problems*, XXVII (1979), 19–37; and in Harvey Wasserman, *Energy War: Reports from the Front* (New York: Lawrence Hill, 1979).

a very rough indicator; but polls are extremely sensitive to the way questions are phrased and are, at best, indirectly related to anti-nuclear protest activities.[34] Moreover, poll findings are not stable over time and are vulnerable to a public issue-attention cycle.[35] That said, and allowing for the lack of strictly comparable cross-national surveys, several tentative generalizations can be drawn from opinion surveys taken during the late 1970s, at the height of the public controversy.[36] Anti-nuclear sentiments appear to have peaked once around 1976 and again in 1979, after the Three Mile Island accident, France being an exception in the latter instance. At these peaks, a plurality of respondents in all countries favoured nuclear power (35 per cent to 50 per cent of respondents), sizeable minorities opposed it (30 per cent to 45 per cent), and significant, but over time declining, groups expressed no opinion (10 per cent to 30 per cent). Anti-nuclear preferences reached a plurality only for a brief period following the Three Mile Island accident. Since 1979, they have declined in all four countries. Survey findings as similar as these can clearly shed little light on the significantly different policy impacts of anti-nuclear protests in France, West Germany, the United States and Sweden.

More direct measures of protest mobilization also do not yield plausible associations with movement impacts. The number of participants in the various protest activities, for instance, even when standardized for country size, turns out to be a poor predictor of movement impact. The United States has had a comparatively low level of mobilization, but its nuclear program is stalemated. France, in contrast, has had much greater mobilization, but its program has experienced little disruption. Also, the number and total membership of anti-nuclear protest organizations does not yield a reliable independent measure of protest intensity, because cross-national variations reflect varying opportunity structures rather than varying intensities of mobilization. This caveat is borne out in the open Swedish and American regimes, where protests are more formally organized and rely heavily on established nature-protection lobbies. These lobbies are much less important in France and West Germany.

Any assessment of the overall strength of the anti-nuclear movement must further consider the complication that "power" and "strength" are relational concepts, which measure not only the resources and activities of anti-nuclear groups but also those of the pro-nuclear advocates. If, for instance, governments had changed their evaluation of nuclear power autonomously, not merely as a reaction to the more or less effective veto-power of anti-nuclear protesters, then less pro-nuclear policies would indicate an intrinsic weakening of the pro-nuclear advocates, not the strength of anti-nuclear protest or opportunity structures conducive to the exercise of veto-power. Empirically, though, there is little evidence for autonomous change in the positions, preferences and resources of the nuclear advocates in the four countries during the protest period. Everywhere, nuclear manufacturing industries, electric utilities and state agencies promoting nuclear power remained firmly committed to the new technology. For example, industrial policies in both Sweden and France targeted nuclear plant manufacture as a major export industry and, therefore, it enjoyed a secure political position. The wholly or partially nationalized electric utilities were also strong lobbyists. Nevertheless, the outcome of the nuclear controversy in the two countries differs dramatically with respect to the long-term future of their nuclear industries.[37]

---

[34] Survey questions have been manipulated so as to create a virtual "politics of nuclear polling," with advocates and opponents of nuclear power using the surveys most favourable to their own position. This is discussed in Otwin Renn, *Kernenergie aus der Sicht der Bevölkerung* (Jülich: Kernforschungsanlage Jülich, 1977), pp. 47–9.

[35] The concept of the 'issue attention cycle' for social movements is developed in Anthony Downs, "Up and Down with Ecology: The 'Issue Attention Cycle.'", *Public Interest*, XXVIII (1972), 38–50.

[36] For opinion surveys about nuclear energy issues, see Gerald Duménil, "Energie nucléaire et opinion publique," pp. 317–74 in Fagnani and Nicolon, *Nucléopolis* (France); Barbara Farah *et al.*, *Public Opinion About Energy: A Literature Review* (Golden, CO: Solar Energy Research Institute, 1979)(United States); Renn, *Kernenergie aus der Sicht der Bevölkerung* and *Wahrnehmung und Akzeptanz technischer Risiken* (Jülich: Kernforschungslage Jülich, 1981)(Germany); and Hans Zetterberg, *The Swedish Public and Nuclear Energy* (Sweden).

[37] It has also been argued that weakness of a nation's energy sector, above all the absence of strong oil companies, explains why governments protect nuclear and other energy policies more from movement challenges than do countries with strong, indigenous energy industries. For this argument, see Peter Gourevitch, "The Second Image Reversed: The International Sources of Domestic Politics," *International Organization*, XXXII (1978), 881–911, esp. p. 906. At first blush, this model seems to explain the differences between France and the United States. The weak French energy sector requires firm government support, whereas the United States can afford a more pluralist style because its energy sector is strong and can fight for itself. The model fails to explain, however, why West Germany and Sweden, each with comparatively weak energy industries, were unable to imitate the French strategy and, instead, retreated, each in its own particular way, from an all-out, long-term commitment to nuclear power.

Overall, the evidence about mobilization does not support an explanation of differential movement impact based solely on the relative internal strengths and weaknesses of the movements and their pro-nuclear opponents. The alternative to this approach is to try to capture the dynamic interplay between movement mobilization and regime response by examining systematically the types of impacts anti-nuclear movements have had. To this I now turn.

PROCEDURAL IMPACTS

Anti-nuclear movements have made procedural inroads when they have been able to gain greater access to formal political decision-making. At one end of the spectrum, procedural impacts in France have been virtually non-existent. Because the French party system is organized along a bipolar socio-economic cleavage, its parties have been reluctant to represent anti-nuclear demands. This is well illustrated by the inability of either the Socialists or the Communists to respond to the protest. The Socialists, for example, temporarily flirted with the anti-nuclear cause in the 1978 and 1981 campaigns but once in government quickly backed away. Vacillation also characterized the position of the Socialist-leaning labour union, whose leadership was sceptical about the merits of nuclear power but was unable to generate widespread support for an anti-nuclear position. The Communist party and its labour union, which is firmly entrenched in the utility and energy industries, were even less accessible.

The anti-nuclear movement also met with indifference and worse from the various state authorities. During the Giscard administration, for instance, the nuclear issue was never discussed at length in the French legislature. Once elected, the Socialist government rid itself of the internally divisive issue in an early and brief parliamentary debate in October 1981. At that time, the new government simply decided to continue the nuclear policy of its conservative predecessor and gave little consideration to the dissenting minority within its own parliamentary party. Furthermore, no efforts were made to represent anti-nuclear interests in arenas of quasi-corporatist decision-making or to organize a national plebiscite to resolve the conflict.[38] The

French anti-nuclear movement also failed to gain access to executive branch agencies and, although the government streamlined nuclear licensing procedures and made them more comprehensive in the late 1970s, the new rules still prevented the opposition from participating in public licensing hearings and from appealing effectively to the courts.[39] Finally, the French state responded to anti-nuclear demonstrations and civil disobedience with a dose of retaliation so heavy—as in its response to the 1977 demonstration against the new fast breeder reactor in Malville—that anti-nuclear activities have since been effectively discouraged.

The anti-nuclear movement in West Germany did not fare much better with the established political parties than did its French counterpart. The conservative opposition parties were clearly in favour of nuclear power. The German labour unions were also strongly supportive of the expansive nuclear program. And although the parties in the Social Democratic–Free Democratic coalition government were internally divided between pro-union and pro-business nuclear advocates and important oppositional minorities, a situation that led to a temporary policy stalemate, they never unequivocally represented the anti-nuclear position. Moreover, the parties were unable to influence the firmly pro-nuclear policies of the Social Democratic–Free Democratic government. It is therefore not surprising that parliamentary debates on nuclear energy during the period never effectively gave voice to the anti-nuclear position. A parliamentary commission on nuclear energy which included pro- and anti-nuclear "experts" was convened in 1979, late in the controversy. It issued a strategically ambivalent mid-term report in 1980, which pro-government partisans hoped would draw anti-nuclear sympathizers over to the government parties in that year's national election.[40] After the election, in 1982, however, a broad majority of

---

[38] The new Socialist government allowed consultative local referendums on nuclear power projects. But this provision was far less sweeping than it sounds, for referendums may be overruled by decisions of regional political bodies, and the reform was accompanied by government and electric utility threats of economic hardship for uncooperative regions. The licensing reform by the Socialist government is described in M. Rappin. "Dezentralisierung des französischen Genehmigungsverfahrens," *Atomwirtschaft-Atomtechnik*, XXVII (1982), 39–41.

[39] For the litigation initiated by French anti-nuclear activists, see Colson, *Le Nucléaire sans les Français*, pp. 139–50, and Nelkin and Pollak, *The Atom Besieged*, Chap. 11.

[40] The political dynamics of this commission are analysed in Herbert Kitschelt, Der Zwischenbericht der Enquete-Kommission "Zukunftige Kernenergiepolitik": Stagnation oder Innovation in der politischen Ökonomie des westdeutschen Energiesektors?" *Jarhbuch Technik und Gesellschaft*, 1(1982), 165–91.

commissioners endorsed the planned nuclear program, almost in its entirety. Overall, the anti-nuclear movement in West Germany made no gains in procedural representation, for its mobilization failed to open any new party, legislative, corporist or (constitutionally forbidden) plebiscitarian avenues of representation.

The obstacles encountered by the West German nuclear program were in fact generated at the implementation end of the policy process, by procedures that were neither fully open nor closed to public participation. The existing licensing procedures were fragmented and did slow the program down, but opponents were not able to use these weaknesses purposively to pursue their own policy agenda because they were unable to extend their procedural participation, e.g., through more extensive citizens' rights to sue collectively against industrial projects (*Verbandsklage*). Until 1981, however, when the movement began to wane, the government was unable to take the decisive measures necessary to tip the scales firmly in favour of the program's proponents by, for instance, streamlining the licensing procedure and restricting the opportunities for procedural obstruction that the anti-nuclear activists enjoyed. By neither consistently repressing anti-nuclear protesters nor granting them new democratic rights, the state may have unwittingly fueled the movement's mobilization and thwarted the nuclear program.

The United States, while also a case of policy stalemate, exhibits opportunity structure features that distinguish it from West Germany. America's "decomposed" party system began to assimilate anti-nuclear demands with relative ease in the early 1970s. Then, in 1976, the anti-nuclear movement succeeded in placing anti-nuclear referendums on the ballot in a number of states. This action and the electoral response were measures of public opinion that further sensitized legislators to the issue. Partly as a consequence, more members of Congress, regardless of party affiliation, shifted to an anti-nuclear position. Anti-nuclear activists also strengthened their position in the executive branch. During the Carter presidency, the zenith of the conflict, several anti-nuclear activists were appointed to high-ranking positions in energy and environmental agencies. Even so, they could not conquer entrenched pro-nuclear bastions. The intensifying nuclear power debate led instead to a progressive fragmentation of political power and a stalemate in both Congress and the administration, which prevented adoption of any coherent nuclear policy. Numerous changes in the organization and jurisdiction of legisla-

tive and administrative bodies in the nuclear arena illustrate this process.[41] Few new policy initiatives were undertaken, and key political actors were unable to forge lasting and effective coalitions. With respect to the reform of nuclear licensing procedures, for instance, neither advocates nor opponents of nuclear power were able to make decisive gains. Although pro-nuclear forces in the United States have regained strength during the Reagan presidency, the stalemate has not been broken and no stable governance of nuclear energy is in sight. The American political opportunity structure has thus facilitated the partial, though inconsistent, inclusion of the anti-nuclear opposition in decision-making arenas.

At the end of the input spectrum furthest removed from France lies Sweden, which exhibits the greatest degree of procedural responsiveness. The anti-nuclear opposition there was represented by two opposition parties (the Communist and the Centre) as early as 1973, and parliament served as a forum for the nuclear debate. Moreover, the pro-nuclear Social Democratic government financed a broadly participatory national debate on the issue. This debate especially had dramatic consequences for the Swedish nuclear energy program, for it intensified and crystallized the public's anti-nuclear sentiments, which in turn contributed to the defeat of the Social Democrats in the 1976 election.[42] The new government, headed by a prime minister opposed to nuclear energy, was, however, divided on the issue. The government tried at first to end the deadlock by adopting the quasi-corporatist strategy of appointing an energy commission, which was staffed by the chief antagonists in the controversy. But when this effort failed, along with efforts to negotiate a viable policy compromise between the ruling parties, the government collapsed in 1978. The 1979 accident at Three Mile Island injected a new urgency into the debate, which prompted all parties to agree to a national referendum, to be held after the upcoming election, that

---

[41] There are several overviews of American nuclear energy policy that place it in the more comprehensive setting of American energy policy: Irwin C. Bupp and Jean-Claude Derian, *Light Water: How the Nuclear Dream Dissolved* (New York: Basic Books, 1978), Chaps. 8 and 10; Walter Rosenbaum, *Energy, Politics and Public Policy* (Washington, DC: Congressional Quarterly Press, 1981); John Chubb, *Interest Groups and the Bureaucracy: The Politics of Energy* (Stanford, CA: Stanford University Press, 1983), Chaps. 4 and 6.

[42] Compare Nelkin and Pollak, "The Politics of Participation."

would remove the issue from the realm of ordinary political campaigning. In summary, the Swedish anti-nuclear movement found that its political opportunity structure offered an eclectic variety of participatory avenues: electoral, corporatist and plebiscitarian. What it did not find, however, were similar opportunities to influence implementation—for example, to intervene in nuclear plant licensure proceedings. In this respect, Sweden is much like France.

SUBSTANTIVE POLICY IMPACTS

What kind of policy impacts have anti-nuclear movements sought? On the one hand, anti-nuclear activists have sought the suspension of nuclear power plant licensing and construction, and, in certain instances, the shut-down of already-operating plants. On the other hand, they have called for a reorientation of energy policies towards energy conservation and research on renewable energy resources. While these goals have been pursued by activists in all of the four countries under consideration, the degree to which they have been successfully pursued varies widely. It is to this variation that we now turn.

That at least several of the movements have been rewarded by scaled-down nuclear programs is clear from Tables 4 and 5, which provide, respectively, information about the number of commercial nuclear power plants under construction or already in operation in each country during the period from 1974 to 1984, and information about the number of planned nuclear stations not yet under construction. Not surprisingly, the regimes most tolerant of the anti-nuclear opposition,

TABLE 4
Commercial Nuclear Power Plants in Construction, Operation, or Decommissioned

	1974	1977	1980	1984
France	10	30	44	54
Sweden	10	12	12	12
United States	87	136	140 (144)*	125 (144)*
West Germany	15	18	19	21

*The higher figure includes plants under construction, but temporarily mothballed (1984:9) or permanently abandoned (1984:10).
Sources: calculations based on raw data from *Nuclear News*, "The World List of Nuclear Power Plants," Vol. XVII (1974), No. 10; Vol. XX (1977), No. 10; Vol. XXIII (1980), No. 10; Vol. XXVII (1984), No. 2.

TABLE 5
Nuclear Power Plants Planned but not yet Under Construction

	1974	1977	1980	1984
France	15	2	3	0
Sweden	2	0	0	0
United States	125	64	14 (28)*	2
West Germany	4	8	4 (8)*	2

*Figures in brackets include plants without definite construction schedule.
Sources: as for Table 4.

Sweden and the United States, are also the ones with a steady or declining number of plants planned and built in the last decade. West Germany's program is also, if only temporarily, restrained. And, of the four, only France's program continues to grow and to grow rapidly. But what specific attributes of political opportunity structures have made some movements more successful than others in achieving this portion of the anti-nuclear agenda?

One might be tempted to suppose that a simple drop-off in demand for additional electricity explains the differences between the four countries. But growth of electricity demand has also slowed down dramatically in France, where the nuclear program has continued apace. German and American utilities still deplore the expected "shortfall" of, in their view, potentially inexpensive nuclear base load capacity. Moreover, in all four countries, utilities did not expect declining growth rates in the 1970s and planned many new nuclear stations. In France, however, a political–economic regime intransigent to anti-nuclear activists was able to realize such plans and overbuild nuclear capacity to an extent that it precipitated a financial crisis of the nationalized Electricité de France.[43] In West Germany, the United States and Sweden, effective anti-nuclear opposition "saved" utilities from making investments that would have appeared uneconomic in retrospect. Why did this happen?

---

[43] These financial difficulties in Stephen Cohen, "Informed Bewilderment: French Economic Strategy and the Crisis," in Cohen and Gourevitch, *France in a Troubled World Economy*, pp. 21–48; and in Herbert Kitschelt, *Politik und Energie: Energie-Technologiepolitiken in den USA, der Bundesrepublik Deutschland, Frankreich und Schweden* (Frankfurt: Campus Verlag, 1983), pp. 249–51.

Where political opportunity structures were conducive to popular participation, anti-nuclear activists could impose economic penalties on nuclear builders, by slowing the construction of plants being built and increasing the risk of future investments. In the United States, Sweden and West Germany, anti-nuclear activists were continually able to raise the costs of plants, but those in France were unable to do this. Greater responsiveness to the anti-nuclear opposition invariably led to extremely tight and often changing safety regulations.[44] Once formulated, these new safety standards allowed opponents to intervene to insist that they be complied with. The two factors reinforced each other; when nuclear regulatory agencies tightened their safety standards, opponents felt justified in their suspicions and pressed for additional requirements or else requested that existing plants be upgraded to meet the latest standards. Thus, new safety standards and the delays they brought with them—both resulting from relatively open political opportunity structures—increased the capital costs and finance charges on borrowed capital incurred by the builders of nuclear plants.

Table 6 shows that construction schedule delays were most pronounced in the United States and West Germany, both of which have fragmented implementation structures.[45] Here, in addition to licensing procedures, the courts also contributed to the delay problem when they suspended construction work during litigation. Much shorter delays were typical in France and Sweden, where tight implementation procedures offer few opportunities for outside intervention. The contrast is best illustrated with a comparison of average completion times; in the United States, it takes twelve to fourteen years to complete a commercial nuclear plant, while in France it takes only six.

In Sweden, nuclear policy was changed not by disrupting the policy implementation process but by working through the "input side" of politics. As a result of a difficult and long drawn-out process of mutual adjustment among opposing groups, not a single political party continued to advocate further expansion of the nuclear program when the national referendum was held in March 1980. Although anti-nuclear activists did not succeed in persuading a majority of the voters to support an immediate halt to all construction activity and dismantling of existing plants, the Swedish government has taken the magnitude of public opposition into account and has ordered no new plants, a move that is certain to guarantee the demise of the Swedish nuclear industry. The strength of the "input side" of Swedish politics is also demonstrated by that country's ability to respond positively to the other half of the anti-nuclear agenda, which calls for an energy policy orientated towards conservation and the development of renewable fuels, especially biomass.

Why such a basic shift in overall energy strategy has not occurred in either the United States, West Germany or France is again to be traced back to variations in national opportunity structures. Energy conservation programs, for instance, working through incentives, taxes, regulation and state investment in infrastructure have been most aggressively pursued in the "high intervention" political economies of Sweden and France.[46]

---

[44] This process was accompanied by increasing outlays for nuclear safety research that led to further regulatory requirements and delays of nuclear power plants. See Barry Weingast, "Congress, Regulation and the Decline of Nuclear Power," *Public Policy*, XXVIII (1980), 231–55.

TABLE 6

Average Construction Delays of All Nuclear Power Plants Under Construction or in Commercial Service (Months)*

	1974	1977	1980	1984
France	0.7	3.6	7.1	11.3
Sweden	2.7	4.9	15.9	19.8
United States	20.0	35.9	49.4	53.1
West Germany	6.1	13.8	30.6	42.4

*Delays for each plant were measured as number of months behind construction schedule expected at that time when the plant order was given. For each country, delays were calculated only for plants already in operation or under construction and still scheduled to be completed. Plants where construction has not yet begun or plants mothballed while under construction are not included.
Sources: calculations based on sources given in Table 4.

---

[45] These data would be even more striking if only plants originally scheduled for completion between 1976 and 1980 had been included. By the 1980s, after the controversy's peak, plants were delayed an average of 73.7 months in the United States, 42.2 months in the Federal Republic, 15.9 months in France, and 17.2 months in Sweden. By 1984, some time after the peak of the nuclear controversy, delays for this group of power plants had increased still further: 86 months in the United States, 56 in West Germany, 26 in Sweden, and 16 in France. Data are calculated according to sources and procedures described under Table 6.

[46] For a more detailed analysis of energy conservation policies, compare: International Energy Agency, *Energy Conservation: The Role of Demand Management in the 1980s* (Paris: OECD, 1981), and Kitschelt, *Politik und Energie*, Chap. 4.1.

In Sweden, the trade-off between nuclear power and conservation has been direct. In France, however, the commitment to conservation complements the government's existing one to nuclear power and, at least indirectly, is attributable to elite efforts to appease the anti-nuclear opposition without yielding to its key demands.[47] In the United States and West Germany, conservation policies have scarcely been pursued beyond allowing free market mechanisms to increase the prices of scarce resources.

Government research in energy conservation and renewable energy technologies exhibits similar patterns. While governments in all four countries targeted their financial support almost exclusively on nuclear research until the mid-1970s, funding of new energy technologies managed to take off in the two open regimes. In contrast to Sweden, the research program in the United States has been beset with problems, most of which stem from this new research area's unstable supporting coalition and to inefficient program implementation.[48] Using budget outlays for nuclear and renewable energy technologies as an indicator, Table 7 illustrates the differences between the energy technology policies of the four countries.

Is it not possible to explain all the changes in nuclear and energy technology policy through shifting electoral fortunes and changes of governments, rather than through the more stable political opportunity structures? For France and Germany, the answer must be no. Changes from a conservative–liberal to a socialist government and vice versa made little difference to energy policy. Even in the United States, four different presidents (Nixon, Ford, Carter and Reagan) declared themselves more or less enthusiastically in favour of nuclear energy, but none was able to create an effective coalition to support it. Generally, long-term energy strategies appear to be difficult to maintain in the fluid American system of policy formation, as both the rapid rise and demise of renewable energy research and of the nuclear fast breeder reactor technology demonstrate.

The only case broadly consistent with the importance of elections and changes of government is that of Sweden, where a government change in 1976 did precipitate a shift in energy policy. However, this case is not inconsistent with our competing regime hypothesis, for the latter would also predict policy changes to occur as a consequence of electoral and government changes whenever political regimes are open and have the capacity for effective policy implementation. But, even in Sweden, electoral politics is of only limited significance for policy innovation because policy changes are frequently built on much broader than minimum winning coalitions, as evidenced by the unanimous decision of the political parties in 1980 not to pursue nuclear power beyond the twelve-reactor program.

Differences in nuclear policy among the four countries are also not entirely explained by the import dependence argument, which predicts intransigent pursuit of nuclear energy whenever dependence is high.

---

[47] See Lucas, *Energy in France*, pp. 152–6.

[48] An instructive analysis of the budget decisions for solar energy by the US Congress is provided by W. Henry Lambright and Albert Teich, "Policy Innovation in Federal Research and Development: The Case of Energy Research and Development," *Public Administration Review*, IXL (1979), 140–7. A detailed comparative analysis of the formation and implementation of energy technology policies can be found in Kitschelt, *Politik und Energie*, Chap. 6.

TABLE 7

Public Energy Research and Development Expenses in the Four Countries in 1979 (Per Thousandths of GNP)

	Nuclear fission	Renewables/ energy conservation	Overall energy technology expenditures
Sweden	0.14	0.65	1.05
United States	0.49	0.36	1.61
France	0.72	0.28	1.54
West Germany	0.83	0.12	1.39

Sources: International Energy Agency, *Energy Research, Development, and Demonstration in the IEA Countries 1979* (Paris: Organization for Economic Cooperation and Development, 1980): Organization for Economic Cooperation and Development. *OECD Energy Balances 1976–1980* (Paris: OECD, 1982).

Thus, the French, Swedish and West German dependence levels on imported oil are too similar to justify the significant differences that can be found in their respective nuclear policies.[49] Moreover, in Sweden uranium deposits are the only significant indigenous non-renewable fuel reserve. Despite this, Sweden is attempting to withdraw from the nuclear economy. In the American case, energy import sensitivity and vulnerability is much lower than in Europe, but the United States' role as the hegemonic Western power and the absolute magnitude of American energy imports in world trade render the long-term question of energy supply no less significant in the United States than in Europe.[50]

Raw figures about foreign energy dependence and national energy resources are, by themselves, not likely to explain public policy. A shortcoming of both resource dependence and change of government explanations is that they are not sophisticated enough to reconstruct the actual process of nuclear power policy formation. Opportunity structures come much closer to explaining the process through which a new policy is learned or an old policy is reaffirmed in the face of challenging political demands.

STRUCTURAL IMPACTS OF ANTI-NUCLEAR MOVEMENTS

Aside from the procedural and substantive impacts, the impact of anti-nuclear movements on political regimes themselves may vary between countries, depending on the type of opportunity structure that exists. The less innovative and more immobile a political regime, the greater the risk that this inflexibility itself will trigger demands that go beyond the immediate policy issue to ones threatening the legitimacy of the regime.

Changes in political implementation capacities resulting from anti-nuclear protest are difficult to detect in the four countries for the 1973–83 period. Everywhere, the inertia of administrative institutions and the economic power of the established actors in the energy sector are formidable. Structural impacts do, however, stand out with respect to the four countries' input patterns. Where the political input structures are closed, noteworthy efforts have been made to realign the party system. New "green" or ecological parties have appeared and adopted the nuclear issue as a major plank in their political programs.[51] These parties tend not to be organized along traditional cleavages of class, religion and ethnicity.[52] Instead, they are mobilized on the basis of alleged inequalities of "qualitative" and "reproductive" life chances, which are created by the subordination of nature and society to large-scale economic enterprise and bureaucratic state institutions.[53]

We would expect ecological parties to be stronger in regimes that are less responsive to anti-nuclear demands, such as those of France and West Germany, and weaker or non-existent in more innovative ones, such as those of Sweden and the United States. In fact, the West German ecology party, *Die Grünen*, founded in the late 1970s, has managed to win more than 5 per cent of the vote in most West German state elections since 1979. In the March 1983 federal election, for example, it received 5.6 per cent of the popular vote, and in the European election of 1982 8.2 per cent. In France, ecological voting lists experienced remarkable successes in the local elections of 1977. They were less successful in the 1978 National Assembly elections, however, when they could not agree on either participation in the election or a common campaign strategy. Nevertheless, the ecological candidate in the French presidential election of 1981, Brice Lalonde, received almost 4 per cent of the vote on the first ballot. The two ecological parties participating in the 1984 election together won 6.7 per cent of the vote.

---

[49] Large German coal deposits do not improve this picture dramatically. Because mining and burning coal have deleterious environmental and economic consequences, Germany has been hesitant to exploit this resource at an accelerated pace.

[50] An assessment of the world energy situation after the second oil crisis of 1978–80 is found in Daniel Yergin and Martin Hillenbrand, eds., *Global Insecurity: A Strategy for Energy and Economic Renewal* (Boston: Houghton Mifflin, 1982).

[51] For discussions of ecological parties, see Claude-Marie Vadrot, *L'Écologie: histoire d'une subversion* (Paris: Syros, 1978); Garraud, "Politique electro-nucléaire et mobilisation"; Roland Roth, ed., *Parlamentarisches Ritual und politische Alternativen* (Frankfurt: Campus Verlag, 1980); Jörg Mettke, ed., *Die Grünen: Regierungspartner von morgen* (Reinbek: Rowohlt, 1982); Ferdinand Müller-Rommel, "'Parteinen neuen Typs' in Westeuropa: eine vergleichende Analyse," *Zeitschrift für Parlamentsfragen*, XIII (1982), 369–90; and Horst Mewes, "The West German Green Party," *New German Critique*, XXVIII (1983), 51–83.

[52] The new parties thus destabilize the formation of cleavages that have been institutionalized in West European party systems throughout most of this century. Compare Seymour Martin Lipset and Stei Rokkan, eds., *Party Systems and Voter Alignments* (New York: Free Press, 1967).

[53] This argument is elaborated in the theories referred to in fn. 3.

In contrast, green parties in the United States and Sweden have received little support. The Swedish ecological party failed to receive 2 per cent of the vote in the Rijksdag election of 1982 and has remained well below the minimum 4 per cent threshold it needs for representation in parliament. The closest equivalent to an ecology party in the United States, the Citizens' party, is insignificant.

Although there is a striking correlation between the performance of ecological parties and the outcomes of the nuclear conflict in the early 1980s, one is well advised not to interpret the new parties as "single issue" formations. Thus, the nuclear conflict and political opportunity structures may offer a good explanation of the emergence of such parties in a specific historical period, but a multitude of other factors may influence their future course.[54]

CONCLUSION

This comparison of nuclear power conflicts in four countries shows that the mobilization strategies and impacts of social movements can, to a significant degree, be explained by the general characteristics of domestic political opportunity structures. Furthermore, the cases show that governments do not necessarily engage in a reactive process of learning when faced with unexpected opposition to a policy. In the case of nuclear energy, the capacity to learn from the experience of manifest conflict did not simply follow from the magnitude of protest. Rather, it was shaped in certain pre-established ways by the channels and opportunities that political regimes offered to opponents to disseminate their message and disrupt established policies. Variations of such institutional rules led to different dispositions of governments to defend or revise policies. Where political input structures were open and responsive to the mobilization of protest, as in Sweden and to a lesser extent in the United States, a search for new policies was triggered. Where they were closed, as in

France and West Germany, governments insisted more intransigently on a predetermined policy course. Where state capacities to implement policies were weak, as in the United States and West Germany, the nuclear protest movement had at least a chance to disrupt the policy against which it was mobilized. Where political capacities were stronger, as in Sweden and France, nuclear policy was shielded from most of the attacks on its implementation. The combination of political input and output structures in each country sets limits on policy innovation. Where openness was high and capacity strong, innovation tended to be greater. Sweden approximates this configuration best. Where the reverse configuration existed, policy-making immobility prevailed. This is especially patent in the West German case, and to a lesser extent in the United States. Under these conditions, established policies were stalemated, and new policies could not be agreed upon or implemented.

Theories are fruitful only if they can be applied to cases beyond the ones they were first designed to explain. In extending the logic of the present argument to nuclear power conflicts in other countries, one must, however, take into account the possibility that several factors, controlled in this study, might vary in a larger sample of cases, most notably the relative size of nuclear programs and the intensity of anti-nuclear mobilization. This qualification underlines again the caveat that the regime hypothesis does not explain differences of social movement mobilization and energy strategies in their entirety.

Beyond the nuclear case, it is conceivable that the regime hypothesis can explain the strategies and impacts of other movements concerned with qualitative life-chances and the physical structuring of the social environment. Many of these conflicts cut across the social cleavages currently institutionalized in party systems, arenas of functional interest group representation and administrative agencies. Political regimes have a varying propensity to innovate in procedural, substantive and structural ways when confronted by challenging new groups. Energy policy aside, environmental protection, consumer safety regulation, information systems control, genetic engineering regulation, military technology and strategic planning, urban development and transportation planning are but a few examples of issue areas that may precipitate new social movements with dynamics similar to those of anti-nuclear movements.

---

[54] Thus, ecological parties in countries with weak nuclear conflicts or with opportunity structures not conducive to the formation of new parties will benefit in the future from a demonstration effect provided by the successful ecological parties, especially the West German party. A more exhaustive comparative analysis of ecological parties in different countries would require a detailed examination of the socioeconomic development, the political culture and the system of party competition in each instance.

COLLECTIVE ACTION AND THE CIVIL RIGHTS MOVEMENT

Dennis Chong

The story is told. I think I now see the judicious reader putting on his spectacles to look for the moral.
—CHARLOTTE BRONTË, *SHIRLEY*

By the time the civil rights movement had run its course, it had permanently changed the nature of social relations in this country. So great was its impact that some writers marked the movement's demise in the late 1960s as the end of the "Second American Revolution."

For centuries the race problem had been the shame of the nation. Blacks remained a subjugated caste in a country that prided itself on its egalitarian tradition. Despite glimmers of hope during Reconstruction that this contradiction between ideal and reality would be erased, almost a century later, black Americans continued to be segregated from the rest of society and denied their political rights. Clearly white America was not about to extend its hand to bring blacks into the social, political, and economic mainstream without a struggle.

To win their rights, blacks had to organize and press their demands for reform. World War II and all the changes it wrought played a major part in providing the impetus for the black revolt, which sputtered and stalled before finally taking hold—if we can ever pinpoint such things—in that dramatic moment when seamstress and NAACP veteran Rosa Parks refused to give up her seat to a white passenger on a local bus, the incident that sparked the Montgomery bus boycott. She had, in the felicitous phrase of Martin Luther King, Jr., simply been "captured by the zeitgeist—the spirit of the times."

The Montgomery campaign provided an auspicious beginning to the civil rights movement. Because it attracted nationwide attention, the boycott gave blacks throughout the country a model of social change built around the use of nonviolent collective action. James Forman ([1972] 1985) writes that "the boycott woke me to the real—not merely theoretical—possibility of

From *Collective Action and the Civil Rights Movement* (Chicago and London: University of Chicago Press, 1991), 230–40.

building a nonviolent mass movement of Southern black people to fight segregation" (85). John Lewis recalls being enthralled as a youngster by news of the Montgomery boycott: "In the papers that we got in the public schools system in the library, I read *everything* about what was happening there, and it was really one of the most exciting, one of the most moving things to me to see just a few miles away the black folks of Montgomery stickin' together, refusing to ride segregated buses, walking the streets. It was a moving movement" (Raines 1977, 73).

However, the boycott was only the first act of a drama that would take a decade to unfold. Before it was over, this morality play would be replete with heroes and villains, examples of courage, selflessness, and sacrifice, but also of cruelty, brutality, and hatred, crisis points and turning points, moments of despair and defeat, exuberance and victory.

While all good stories deserve retelling, my intent has not been to recount the history of the civil rights movement. There already exist many excellent accounts detailing the personalities, politics, and events of that period. Instead I have used examples drawn from that and other movements throughout the book to illustrate a general model of the dynamics of public-spirited collective action. Therefore while my reference point for much of the discussion has been the civil rights movement, the arguments I made and the models I proposed pertain to the broader issue of mass political activism.

Two questions have guided this inquiry. First, what determines whether rational individuals will participate in public-spirited collective action? Second, how do individual decisions to join (or quit) a movement translate into collective outcomes?

To summarize, I argued that many of the choices facing participants in public-spirited collective action can be represented in game-theoretic terms. In the study of collective action in general, this in itself is not a new point of departure. Other analysts have commonly modeled instances of collective action as a prisoner's dilemma game. In this well-known game, it is in each player's self-interest not to cooperate with the other players irrespective of their cooperative or uncooperative behavior. Unfortunately, if each player acts selfishly, the collective outcome—mutual defection—is less desirable than if all had cooperated. Individual rationality defeats collective rationality.

Collective action in pursuit of public goods often constitutes a multiple-player prisoner's dilemma (or collective action) problem. Since noncontributors cannot be excluded from enjoying public goods to the same extent as contributors, no one has an incentive to contribute to the collective provision of the public good. Each individual instead prefers to let others supply the public good while he enjoys a free ride. Consequently collective action is difficult to initiate because people must be given some added incentive (a "selective incentive") to participate over and above the rewards they will derive from attaining the collective goal itself.

Public-spirited collective action, however, offers little in the way of direct tangible selective incentives. Rather, the most prominent benefits are usually social and psychological. Many people participate in causes out of a sense of obligation to their families, friends, and associates; they go along to get along, to repeat a trite but true aphorism. Because we frequently depend on others for our own well-being and comfort, our self-interest is often served by looking out for and caring for the interests of others. Decency, honesty, and fair play may be instrumental in satisfying many personal needs and interests in communities in which both good and bad faith are reciprocated in kind. For this reason, collective action is best examined within the context of ongoing social relationships and is more accurately modeled as an iterated game. One's best strategy must take into account the repeated exchanges and encounters that one will have with other members of the community. Consequently it can be in one's long-term interest to cooperate in collective endeavors if noncooperation results in damage to one's reputation, ostracism, or repudiation from the community.

We should note that opportunities for publicly validating one's social and political credentials and convictions do not appear very frequently in our lives. In our mundane affairs, we occasionally find ourselves in situations where we can play the Good Samaritan, come forth and perform a selfless deed for our fellow man, or be a minor hero in righting a small injustice. Whether we choose to do so in such circumstances reveals the kind of people we are, our virtues, our characters, and our moralities. But fairly or unfairly, these local dramas are not usually considered the litmus tests of our moral resolve. Those tests are administered in conjunction with the grand issues of our day involving the lives and fates of masses of people. Consequently one's ethical and political preferences can often be expressed only in the context of significant public, political, and social affairs.

The psychological benefits of participating in collective action are more difficult to specify. They pertain to the satisfaction people receive from being a part of a collective experience, especially when that experience has historic connotations. The civil rights movement was a great event, and one that many blacks as well as whites were sure not to miss. Political participation also instills feelings of efficacy, self-esteem, righteousness, and competence that are part and parcel of playing an active role in the affairs of society. Those who engage in political activism primarily to extract the psychological or expressive benefits may be behaving noninstrumentally in relation to the collective goals of the movement but instrumentally in a narrowly rational sense in relation to a variety of personal aspirations.

I argued that the promise of social and psychological benefits for cooperating in collective action alters the choices facing the potential activist. Instead of preferring to free ride regardless of how others behave, he prefers to act in conformity with others: if others cooperate, he wishes to cooperate; if they act selfishly, he wants to do the same. People in the civil rights movement did not choose free ridership; on the contrary, they preferred participation to inactivity under the right condition—the condition being, I argued, that enough others also participate to make collective action successful. For this reason I made the case that public-spirited collective action is better modeled as an assurance game in which people find it in their interest to personally participate when others do likewise. They still face many collective action problems, but these are a kind different from those posed by the prisoner's dilemma.

A group that is trying to organize must be able to develop the prospects of collective action to a point where people feel obligated to cooperate and eager to participate in the cause. Social obligation is greatest in conjunction with movements that promise to reap benefits for the entire group. When collective action by a group can wrest concessions from the government or the opposition, then members of that group face a test of their character and resolve. But when collective action constitutes at best an ineffective symbolic protest, many will in good conscience refrain from participating.

By the same token, the participatory or expressive benefits of political activism will be trimmed when collective action garners few victories. Individuals who become involved for the collective and historic experience will withdraw disappointed unless they are periodically reinforced by gains made through collective action.

The conditional status of the rewards offered for political activism makes the organization of collective action challenging, even though people feel obligated or pressured by others not to free ride and even though they may derive considerable satisfaction from being involved in a cause. If collective action is to materialize under these circumstances, some group of leaders typically will have to step into the breach and build the movement to a point where others find it a worthy investment.

The game-theoretic analysis provided a simple schema for understanding the choices facing potential participants in collective action. The assurance problem highlighted the catch-22 facing groups that are trying to organize. In order to have any chance of winning concessions from the authorities, the group first has to organize and press its demands in the political arena; but the incentive for individuals to cooperate in an organized movement depends first on a demonstration that collective action is a worthwhile investment.

How do groups escape this catch-22? For this part of the analysis, I moved from games to a dynamic model using difference equation in order to model explicitly those factors that affect how the assurance problem (or game) confronting political activists will be played out. The model was used to explain a variety of disparate observations about collective action based on a small, consistent set of assumptions about the factors that motivate individuals to participate.

The model represents the assurance problem in terms of a supply-and-demand relationship between a group that is seeking social change and the authorities that are capable of providing it. According to the model, two principal factors inspire political activism: successful examples of collective action and successful past political mobilization. Both developments increase the prospects and therefore the attractiveness of collective action to those contemplating whether or not to participate.

The model also distinguishes the behavior of leaders from that of the followers in a social movement. Leaders become involved irrespective of the degree of success and the level of mobilization previously established by the movement. Followers, on the other hand, join collective action only in response to success and the existing level of mobilization. In other words, leaders act autonomously, while followers jump on the bandwagon, as well as respond to the contagion of the movement.

I made a number of deductions from this simple supply-and-demand model of collective action. These included a specification of the equilibrium level of political mobilization; the conditions under which the level of mobilization will stabilize at this equilibrium value; and the circumstances in which the level of mobilization will rise or decline monotonically, or oscillate, within or without bounds, over time.

Two conclusions pertaining to the initiation of collective action are of particular importance. First, "unconditional cooperators," whose actions are not contingent upon the actions of others, are usually needed to initiate collective action. Such individuals step into the breach and pay the heavy start-up costs, while everyone else waits for more favorable circumstances before contributing. Second, in the absence of immediate concessions, the movement will have to expand on the basis of factors other than its record of success. When there are few if any victories to publicize, nonparticipants are not able to jump on the bandwagon of success; instead, if the movement is to grow, they must join because of the contagiousness of the movement itself: in short, they must choose to participate because they think that enough other people are participating to make collective action worthwhile.

Moreover, participants cannot be too easily frustrated by their lack of success. A working assumption of the dynamic model is that the resilience of the protesters is directly correlated with the responsiveness of the authorities. What we saw, however, is that the linkage will have to be severed if the nascent movement is to survive beyond the initial period when resistance to political pressure is strongest. Unless the activists are sufficiently determined to weather the early storm, collective action will in all probability collapse.

The dynamics of collective action are such that we can expect a variety of strategies to be employed by political activists in their efforts to build and sustain a movement. Quick victories will be sought in order to buoy the spirits of the rank and file. The leaders of the movement will express optimism about the effectiveness of collective action; they will also exaggerate the degree of popular support behind the movement, the size of their organizations, and the number of participants at rallies and demonstrations in order to bolster perceptions of the movement's potential among both followers and the opposition. The more successful the movement is believed to be, the more attractive it becomes to potential supporters and the more attention it will receive from the authorities.

In addition to trying to intimidate the authorities, the leadership will portray them as being pliable and susceptible to political pressure. The message to the rank and file will be that coordination will be rewarded with significant concessions; collective action will not be a futile gesture.

Tactics that work will diffuse and be imitated by different branches of the movement. Moreover, tactics that are effective in one setting will prove increasingly effective in subsequent confrontations until unfriendly authorities learn new methods to counteract them. Before such countermeasures are developed, the authorities will realize that it is in their interest to avoid a protracted conflict in which they will ultimately be the losers.

For their part, unsympathetic authorities will try to stonewall the activists by avoiding negotiations with them and denying them the concessions that would breathe new life into the movement. They may try to repress key leaders within the movement and interfere with the development of political and social organizations.

The end result of these strategies is a contest of wills in which each side attempts to outlast the other. The activists try to sustain their pressure long enough to force the authorities to the bargaining table, while the authorities implement measures that increase the cost of participation and discourage the protesters from persisting.

In my analysis of the origins of the civil rights movement, I showed that political mobilization was facilitated by the development of strong organizations and effective leadership as well as the ability of forerunners of the movement to win both symbolic and substantive concessions from local authorities and the federal government.

Black organizations and institutions helped to coordinate the preferences and actions of those who supported the civil rights movement. The growth of these organizations, such as the church, black colleges, and civil rights groups, was facilitated by the large-scale migration of blacks, starting in the 1930s, from the rural South to southern cities and urban centers in the North in pursuit of industrial and wartime employment. The black population became geographically concentrated as a result and began to acquire the financial resources necessary to develop and nurture the indigenous institutions and organizations that were essential to the movement. The segregation of blacks in the cities reduced their susceptibility to racial violence and oppression and gave them the autonomy needed to undertake a challenge to the social order.

But spontaneous collaboration did not occur within the civil rights movement, nor is it likely to occur in any instance of collective action that demands a substantial investment from the participants. Before the civil rights movement was possible, black leaders, civil rights organizations, and other liberal elites such as the scien-

tific and intellectual communities had the difficult task of defining, and often reformulating, the nature of the race problem in this country. Large segments of the black population that had been persuaded by the prevailing propaganda to blame themselves habitually for their inferior status had to be taught to locate the source of their problems within the institutions of society.

In general, absolute levels of economic deprivation, inequality of opportunity, government incompetence, or a variety of other indicators of social decline are not as important in generating social unrest as the manner in which people come to interpret these facts. This is because the health of a nation is measured against standards that people set according to their notion of what social conditions are conceivable or possible within the context of the times. Feelings of deprivation and dissatisfaction are thus a consequence of counterfactual images that people hold of the way society ought to be, or could be, with the right leadership or the proper system of organization. Naturally these standards of comparison have been appropriately modified as the conditions of living have been generally improved throughout the world during the modern era. The same material circumstances that have given rise in the twentieth century to feelings of outrage and injustice and ultimately to social movements and revolts would have been construed in earlier centuries as the height of comfort and privilege.

For this reason we ought to be highly skeptical about the possibility of discovering any constant combination of objective factors in a society which will predictably set off a chain of events leading up to a collective movement. Rather, we will have to consider not only the conditions of the society but also the symbolic interpretations and judgments that people at that time make of them (Boulding 1956). All this, of course, is just another way of saying that people tend to experience relative deprivation rather than any absolute level of deprivation measured against a constant reference point. James C. Davies (1962) has captured this idea neatly in discussing the importance people place on the contrast between their expectations for themselves and the actual quality of their lives; when the gap exceeds some tolerable threshold, people are driven to do something in order to redress the imbalance.

Under this assumption, collective action can be stimulated in quite a variety of different objective circumstances—even, paradoxically, when economic growth is on the rise; such "revolutions of rising expectations" occur when the rate of social and economic improvement is not fast enough in the minds of the citizens. Without suggesting that the momentous English, American, French, and Russian revolutions were attributable solely to this factor, Crane Brinton (1938) points out that each of the revolts occurred at a time when the material condition of life in the society was on the whole improving.

World War II not only had a structural impact, causing massive relocation of blacks in response to the demands of the war economy, it also had monumental psychological ramifications. The wartime economy raised the economic status and standard of living of blacks, and in the process elevated the expectations they had concerning the quality of their lives. The new life circumstances of blacks in the rapidly modernizing industrial cities were accompanied by a revised outlook on their place in American society. "Freed from the confines of a rigid caste system and subject to urban formative experiences, blacks developed new norms and beliefs. Aggression could be turned against one's oppressor rather than against one's self, more employment and educational opportunities could be secured, and political power could be mobilized" (Sitkoff 1981, 15). The country as a whole had undergone the collective experience of defending liberty and democracy against the forces of fascism and totalitarianism. The war had been more than a physical contest between opposing military forces, it had also been a propaganda war of competing ideals and ideologies. For the country in general, but especially for black Americans, the war experience heightened the contrast between the ideals of American society and the harsh realities—segregation, discrimination, mob violence, lynchings, and political disenfranchisement—that it offered to its black citizens.

In his fine study of the civil rights movement, McAdam (1982) explicitly partitions these two factors. The institutional changes in the black community, he writes, only created the "structural potential" for collective action. In other words, while preestablished organizations, associations, and social networks ease the task of mobilizing people for collective action, they do not ensure that people will actually take the initiative. For the movement to take off, members of the aggrieved group also have to share a belief that collective action is an effective method of addressing their problems (105–6).

However, optimism among civil rights activists about the effectiveness of collective action could not have been sustained indefinitely without a real increase in the federal government's responsiveness to the plight of blacks. Organization without access is a dead end.

The lifeblood of collective action is its ability to extract concessions—symbolic as well as tangible—from the opposition or the government. The expressive benefits that political activists receive from simply voicing their demands are always short-lived in the absence of identifiable effects. Until the 1930s, Congress, the courts, and the administration were at best indifferent and at worst hostile to the interests and aspirations of black Americans. This situation did not change until civil rights organizations gained strength and the black population acquired electoral power as a consequence of their migration into northern cities. These developments, in conjunction with the liberally disposed FDR administration, gave blacks a degree of access to government that they had never before enjoyed.

The increased responsiveness of all three branches of the federal government in the 1930s and 1940s to black demands fueled the organizational efforts of the inchoate civil rights movement. As blacks saw their efforts paying dividends, they stepped up their pressure and broadened their demands for social change. The spiraling relationship between supply and demand peaked in the first half of the 1960s during the Johnson and Kennedy administrations. This was the heyday of the movement, when the federal government finally realized that it would have to take the initiative and intervene aggressively in the South, and when the civil rights movement attracted the sympathy and support of large segments of the population throughout the country. In this brief but brilliant phase, the civil rights movement captured both the support of large segments of the public and the sponsorship of the government.

But why did the movement collapse? Only because it succeeded too well. Successful collective action pays a stream of material, social, and psychological benefits to participants in the movement. As the goals of the movement are achieved, however, new and equally attractive—and equally feasible—goals have to be devised to ensure the continued contribution of current members. Unless the new generation of goals displays the same luster as the earlier goals, participation in the movement will no longer carry the same participatory benefits that accrue to those who take part in "historic" or memorable causes. Furthermore, if the new set of goals are not as practicable as the earlier ones, then supporters of the cause will feel less obligated to lend their time and energy to fighting for them. Most people are reluctant to participate in lost causes. Unfortunately, to tired radicals who are satisfied with their efforts or disappointed over the impact of their achievements, no new agenda may be sufficiently attractive for them to want to sustain their level of commitment and participation. Consequently in the latter stages of the movement, the benefits of cooperation become almost as obscure as they were in the initial period of collective action when little of consequence could be gained through collaboration.

Many of these problems arose at the close of the civil rights movement. The success of the movement produced contentment in some and frustration in others. There was renewed disagreement over the best strategy to further the cause. The movement ran short of ideas and projects that could involve mass participation; and it encountered a new set of problems that was even more resistant to resolution than legalized segregation and discrimination. Therefore it is no surprise that this new phase of the movement proved less compelling than the last. Problems with long-term solutions do not lend themselves to the short-term reinforcement schedule that is often required to nurture large-scale political activism. In the absence of such periodic rewards, the benefits of participation diminish, and the obligation to contribute weakens.

REFERENCES

Boulding, Kenneth E. 1956. *The Image: Knowledge in Life and Society*. Ann Arbor: University of Michigan Press.

Brinton, Crane. 1938. *The Anatomy of Revolution*. New York: Norton.

Davis, James C. 1962. "Toward a Theory of Revolution." *American Sociological Review* 27(1)5–18.

Foreman, James. [1972] 1985. *The Making of Black Revolutionaries*. Washington, D.C.: Open Hand Publishing.

McAdam, Doug. 1982. *Political Process and the Development of Black Insurgency 1930–1970*. Chicago: University of Chicago Press.

Raines, Howell. 1977. *My Soul is Rested*. New York: G.P. Putnam's Sons.

Sitkoff, Harvard. 1981. *The Struggle for Black Equality: 1954–1980*. New York: Hill and Wang.

READING 21

COLLECTIVE IDENTITY IN SOCIAL MOVEMENT COMMUNITIES: LESBIAN FEMINIST MOBILIZATION

Verta Taylor and Nancy E. Whittier

Understanding the relationship between group consciousness and collective action has been a major focus of social science research (Morris 1990). The resource mobilization and political process perspectives, in contrast to earlier microlevel analyses, have shifted attention to the macrolevel, deemphasizing group grievances and focusing instead on the external political processes and internal organizational dynamics that influence the rise and course of movements (Rule and Tilly 1972; Oberschall 1973; McCarthy and Zald 1973, 1977; Gamson 1975; Jenkins and Perrow 1977; Schwartz 1976; Tilly 1978; McAdam 1982; Jenkins 1983; Morris 1984). But the resource mobilization and political process theories cannot explain how structural inequality gets translated into subjectively experienced discontent (Fireman and Gamson 1979; Ferree and Miller 1985; Snow et al. 1986; Klandermans 1984; Klandermans and Tarrow 1988; Ferree, this volume). In a recent review of the field, McAdam, McCarthy, and Zald (1988) respond by offering the concept of the micro-mobilization context to characterize the link between the macrolevel and microlevel processes that generate collective action. Drawing from a wide range of research documenting the importance of preexisting group ties for movement formation, they view informal networks held together by strong bonds as the "basic building blocks" of social movements. Still missing, however, is an understanding of the way these networks transform their members into political actors.

European analyses of recent social movements, loosely grouped under the rubric "new social movement theory," suggest that a key concept that allows us to understand this process is collective identity (Pizzorno 1978; Boggs 1986; Cohen 1985; Melucci 1985, 1989; Touraine 1985; B. Epstein 1990). Collective

From Aldon Morris and Mueller, Carol, editors, *Frontiers in Social Movement Theory* (New Haven, Conn: Yale University Press, 1992), 104–29. Reprinted with the permission of the publishers.

identity is the shared definition of a group that derives from members' common interests, experiences, and solidarity. For new social movement theorists, political organizing around a common identity is what distinguishes recent social movements in Europe and the United States from the more class-based movements of the past (Kauffman 1990). It is our view, based on existing scholarship (Friedman and McAdam, this volume; Fantasia 1988; Mueller 1990; Rupp and Taylor 1990; Whittier 1991), that identity construction processes are crucial to grievance interpretation in all forms of collective action, not just in the so-called new movements. Despite the centrality of collective identity to new social movement theory, no one has dissected the way that constituencies involved in defending their rights develop politicized group identities.

In this chapter, we present a framework for analyzing the construction of collective identity in social movements. The framework is grounded in exploratory research on the contemporary lesbian feminist movement in the United States. Drawing from Gerson and Peiss's (1985) model for analyzing gender relations, we offer a conceptual bridge linking theoretical approaches in the symbolic interactionist tradition with existing theory in social movements. Our aim is to provide a definition of collective identity that is broad enough to encompass mobilizations ranging from those based on race, gender, ethnicity, and sexuality to constituencies organized around more focused visions.

After discussing the data sources, we trace the evolution of lesbian feminism in the early 1970s out of the radical branch of the modern women's movement and analyze lesbian feminism as a social movement community. Substantively, our aim is to demonstrate that lesbian feminist communities sustain a collective identity that encourages women to engage in a wide range of social and political actions that challenge the dominant system. Theoretically, we use this case to present an analytical definition of the concept of collective identity. Finally, we conclude by arguing that the existence of lesbian feminist communities challenges the popular perception that feminists have withdrawn from the battle and the scholarly view that organizing around identity directs attention away from challenges to institutionalized power structures (B. Epstein 1990). . . .

THE LESBIAN FEMINIST SOCIAL MOVEMENT COMMUNITY

Analyzing the historical evolution of organizational forms in the American women's movement, Buechler

(1990) proposes the concept of a social movement community to expand our understanding of the variety of forms of collective action. Buechler's concept underscores the importance to mobilization of informal networks, decentralized structures, and alternative institutions. But, like most work in the resource mobilization tradition, it overlooks the values and symbolic understandings created by discontented groups in the course of struggling to achieve change (Lofland 1985).

Here it is useful to turn to recent literature on lesbian communities that emphasizes the cultural components of lesbian activism, specifically the development of counterinstitutions, a politicized group identity, shared norms, values, and symbolic forms of resistance (Wolf 1979; Krieger 1983; Lockard 1986; Davis and Kennedy 1986; Phelan 1989; Esterberg 1990). From this perspective, we expand on Buechler's model by defining a social movement community as a network of individuals and groups loosely linked through an institutional base, multiple goals and actions, and a collective identity that affirms members' common interests in opposition to dominant groups.

We describe lesbian feminism as a social movement community that operates at the national level through connections among local communities in the decentralized, segmented, and reticulated structure described by Gerlach and Hine (1970). Like other new social movements, the lesbian feminist movement does not mobilize through formal social movement organizations. Rather, structurally the movement is composed of what Melucci (1989) terms "submerged networks" propelled by constantly shifting forms of resistance that include alternative symbolic systems as well as new forms of political struggle and participation (Emberley and Landry 1989). Although participants use different labels to describe the movement, we are interested here in the segment of the contemporary women's movement characterized as "cultural feminism" (Ferree and Hess 1985; Echols 1989) or "lesbian feminism" (Adam 1987; Phelan 1989). We prefer "lesbian feminism" for three reasons. It is the label most often used in movement writings, although participants also refer to the "women's community," "feminist community," and "lesbian community." Second, it locates the origins of this community in the contemporary women's movement. Finally, the term makes explicit the vital role of lesbians in the women's movement. The term "cultural feminism" erases the participation of lesbians and obscures the fact that a great deal of the current criticism leveled at cultural feminism is, in reality, directed at lesbian feminism.

Scholars have depicted the women's movement that blossomed in the 1960s and 1970s as having two segments, a women's rights or liberal branch and a women's liberation or radical branch (Freeman 1975). The liberal branch consisted primarily of national-level, hierarchically organized, formal organizations like the National Organization for Women (NOW) that used institutionalized legal tactics to pursue equal rights (Gelb and Palley 1982). The radical branch emerged in the late 1960s out of the civil rights and New Left movements and formed a decentralized network of primarily local, autonomous groups lacking formal organization and using flamboyant and disruptive tactics to pursue fundamental transformation of patriarchal structures and values (Hole and Levine 1971; Evans 1979). It is impossible to comprehend contemporary lesbian feminism without locating it in the radical feminist tradition.

Ideologically and strategically, radical feminism opposed liberalism, pursued social transformation through the creation of alternative nonhierarchical institutions and forms of organization intended to prefigure a utopian feminist society, held gender oppression to be primary and the model of all other forms of oppression, and emphasized women's commonality as a sex-class through consciousness raising. Although it coalesced around common issues such as rape, battering, and abortion, radical feminism was never monolithic (Jaggar and Struhl 1978; Ferree and Hess 1985). By the mid-1970s, radical feminism confronted an increasingly conservative and inhospitable social climate and was fraught with conflict over differences of sexuality, race, and class (Taylor 1989a). Recent scholarship argues that the most important disputes focused on the question of lesbianism (Echols 1989; Ryan 1989).

Conflict between lesbian and heterosexual feminists originated in the early 1970s. Although women who love other women have always been among those who participated in the feminist struggle, it was not until the emergence of the gay liberation movement that lesbians demanded recognition and support from the women's movement. Instead they encountered overt hostility in both the liberal and radical branches. The founder of NOW, Betty Friedan, for example, dismissed lesbianism as the "lavender herring" of the movement. Since charges of lesbianism have often been used to discredit women who challenge traditional roles (Rupp 1989; Schneider 1986), feminists sought to avoid public admission that there were, in fact, lesbians in their ranks.

Echols (1989) traces the beginning of lesbian feminism to 1971 with the founding of the Furies in Washington, D.C. This was the first separate lesbian feminist group, and others formed shortly after in New York, Boston, Chicago, San Francisco, and other urban localities around the country. The Furies is significant because it included women such as Charlotte Bunch, Rita Mae Brown, and Colletta Reid who, along with Ti-Grace Atkinson, ex-president of the New York Chapter of NOW and founder of the Feminists, articulated the position that would lay the foundation for lesbian feminism (Hole and Levine 1971; Atkinson 1974; Bunch 1986). They advocated lesbian separatism and recast lesbianism as a political strategy that was the logical outcome of feminism, the quintessential expression of the "personal as political." As a result, heterosexual feminists found themselves increasingly on the defensive.

If early radical feminism was driven by the belief that women are more alike than different, then the fissures that beset radical feminism in the mid-1970s were about clarifying the differences—on the basis of race, class, and ethnicity as well as sexual identity—among the "group called women" (Cassell 1977). Recent scholarship argues that such conflict ultimately led to the demise of radical feminism and the rise of what its critics have called "cultural feminism," leaving liberal feminism in control of the women's movement (Echols 1989; Ryan 1989).

We agree with the dominant view that disputes over sexuality, class, and race contributed to the decline of the radical feminist branch of the movement. We do not, however, agree that radical feminism was replaced by a cultural haven for women who have withdrawn from the battle (Snitow, Stansell, and Thompson 1983; Vance 1984; Echols 1989). Rather, we hold that radical feminism gave way to a new cycle of feminist activism sustained by lesbian feminist communities. These communities socialize members into a collective oppositional consciousness that channels women into a variety of actions geared toward personal, social, and political change.

Although no research has been undertaken to document the extent of lesbian communities across the nation, existing work has focused on a number of different localities (e.g., Barnhart's [1975] ethnography of Portland, Wolf's [1979] study of San Francisco, Krieger's [1983] ethnography of a midwestern community, Lockard's [1986] description of a southwestern community). White (1980) describes the major trendsetting centers of the gay and lesbian movement as

Boston, Washington, San Francisco, and New York. Although our analysis is exploratory and based on only seventeen communities, our data suggest that developments in the major cities are reflected throughout the United States in urban areas as well as in smaller communities with major colleges and universities.

COLLECTIVE IDENTITY: BOUNDARIES, CONSCIOUSNESS, AND NEGOTIATION

The study of identity in sociology has been approached at the individual and systemic levels as well as in both structural and more dynamic social constructionist terms (Weigert et al. 1986). New social movement theorists, in particular Pizzorno (1978), Boggs (1986), Melucci (1985, 1989), Offe (1985), and Touraine (1985), take the politics of personal transformation as one of their central theoretical problematics, which is why these approaches are sometimes referred to as "identity-oriented paradigms" (Cohen 1985). Sometimes labeled postmodernist, new social movement perspectives are social constructionist paradigms (B. Epstein 1990). From this standpoint, collective political actors do not exist de facto by virtue of individuals sharing a common structural location; they are created in the course of social movement activity. To understand any politicized identity community, it is necessary to analyze the social and political struggle that created the identity.

In some ways, the most apparent feature of the new movements has been a vision of power as operating at different levels so that collective self-transformation is itself a major strategy of political change. Reviewing work in the new social movement tradition suggests three elements of collective identity. First, individuals see themselves as part of a group when some shared characteristic becomes salient and is defined as important. For Touraine (1985) and Melucci (1989), this sense of "we" is evidence of an increasingly fragmented and pluralistic social reality that is, in part, a result of the new movements. A crucial characteristic of the movements of the seventies and eighties has been the advocacy of new group understandings, self-conceptions, ways of thinking, and cultural categories. In Touraine's model, it is an awareness of how the group's interests conflict with the interests of its adversaries, the adoption of a critical picture of the culture as a whole, and the recognition of the broad stakes of the conflict that differentiate contemporary movements from classical ones. Thus, the second component of collective identity is what Cohen (1985) terms "con-

sciousness." Consistent with the vision of the movements themselves, Melucci defines a movement's "cognitive frameworks" broadly to include not only political consciousness and relational networks but its "goals, means, and environment of action" (1989, 35). Finally, for new social movement theorists, the concept of collective identity implies direct opposition to the dominant order. Melucci holds that social movements build "submerged networks" of political culture that are interwoven with everyday life and provide new expressions of identity that challenge dominant representations (1989, 35). In essence, as Pizzorno (1978) suggests, the purposeful and expressive disclosure to others of one's subjective feelings, desires, and experiences—or social identity—for the purpose of gaining recognition and influence is collective action.

Our framework draws from feminist theoretical approaches in the symbolic interactionist tradition (Gerson and Peiss 1985; Margolis 1985; West and Zimmerman 1987; Chafetz 1988). These formulations differ from structural and other social psychological approaches that tend to reify gender as a role category or trait of individuals. Instead, they view gender hierarchy as constantly created through displays and interactions governed by gender-normative behavior that comes to be perceived as natural and normal. Gerson and Peiss (1985) offer a model for understanding how gender inequality is reproduced and maintained through social interaction. Although they recognize the social change potential of the model, they do not address this aspect systematically.

Building on their work, we propose three factors as analytical tools for understanding the construction of collective identity in social movements. The concept of *boundaries* refers to the social, psychological, and physical structures that establish differences between a challenging group and dominant groups. *Consciousness* consists of the interpretive frameworks that emerge out of a challenging group's struggle to define and realize its interests. *Negotiation* encompasses the symbols and everyday actions subordinate groups use to resist and restructure existing systems of domination. We offer this scheme as a way of analyzing the creation of collective identity as an ongoing process in all social movements struggling to overturn existing systems of domination.

Boundaries

Boundaries mark the social territories of group relations by highlighting differences between activists and the web of others in the contested social world. Of course, it is usually the dominant group that erects social, political, economic, and cultural boundaries to accentuate the differences between itself and minority populations. Paradoxically, however, for groups organizing to pursue collective ends, the process of asserting "who we are" often involves a kind of reverse affirmation of the characteristics attributed to it by the larger society. Boundary markers are, therefore, central to the formation of collective identity because they promote a heightened awareness of a group's commonalities and frame interaction between members of the in-group and the out-group.

For any subordinate group, the construction of positive identity requires both a withdrawal from the values and structures of the dominant, oppressive society and the creation of new self-affirming values and structures. Newer approaches to the study of ethnic mobilization define ethnicity not in essentialist terms but in relation to socially and politically constructed boundaries that differentiate ethnic populations (Barth 1969; Olzak 1983). This is a useful way of understanding the commonalities that develop among members of any socially recognized group or category organized around a shared characteristic. It underscores the extent to which differentiation and devaluation is a fundamental process in all hierarchical systems and has two advantages over other approaches (Reskin 1988).

First, the concept of boundaries avoids the reification of ascriptive and other differentiating characteristics that are the basis for dominance systems (Reskin 1988); second, it transcends the assumption of group sameness implied by single-factor stratification systems because it allows us to analyze the impact of multiple systems of domination based on race, sex, class, ethnicity, age, sexuality, and other factors (Morris 1990). These distinct hierarchies not only produce differentiation within subordinate groups but affect the permeability of boundaries between the subordinate and dominant groups (Collins 1989; Morris 1990; Zinn 1990).

Boundary markers can vary from geographical, racial, and religious characteristics to more symbolically constructed differences such as social institutions and cultural systems. Our analysis focuses on two types of boundary strategies adopted by lesbian feminists as a means of countering male domination: the creation of separate institutions and the development of a distinct women's culture guided by "female" values.

Alternative institutions were originally conceived by radical feminists both as islands of resistance against patriarchy and as a means to gain power by improving women's lives and enhancing their resources (Taylor 1989a; Echols 1989). Beginning in the early 1970s, radical feminists established separate health centers, rape crisis centers, battered women's shelters, bookstores, publishing and record companies, newspapers, credit unions, and poetry and writing groups. Through the 1980s, feminist institutions proliferated to include recovery groups, business guilds, martial arts groups, restaurants, AIDS projects, spirituality groups, artists' colonies, and groups for women of color, Jewish feminists, disabled women, lesbian mothers, and older women. Some lesbian feminist groups were not entirely autonomous but functioned as separate units or caucuses in existing organizations, such as women's centers and women's studies programs in universities.

As the mass women's movement receded in the 1980s, the liberal branch abandoned protest and unruly tactics in favor of actions geared toward gaining access in the political arena (Rupp and Taylor 1986; Mueller 1987; Echols 1989). An elaborate network of feminist counterinstitutions remained, however, and increasingly were driven by the commitment of lesbian feminists. This is not to say that they were the sole preserve of lesbians. Rather, it is our view that what is described generally as "women's culture" to emphasize its availability to all women has become a predominantly lesbian feminist culture.

A number of national events link local lesbian feminist communities, including the annual five-day Michigan Womyn's Music Festival attended by four thousand to ten thousand women, the National Women's Writers' Conference, and the National Women's Studies Association Conference. In addition, local and regional events and conferences on the arts, literature, and, in the academic professions, feminist issues proliferated through the 1980s. National newspapers such as *Off Our Backs*, national magazines such as *Outlook*, publishing companies such as Naiad, Persephone, and Kitchen Table Women of Color presses, and a variety of journals and newsletters continue to publicize feminist ideas and activities. In short, throughout the 1980s, as neoconservatism was winning political and intellectual victories, lesbian feminists struggled to build a world apart from male domination.

The second boundary that is central to lesbian feminist identity is the creation of a symbolic system that affirms the culture's idealization of the female and, as a challenge to the misogyny of the dominant society, vilifies the male. Perhaps the strongest thread running through the tapestry of lesbian feminist culture is the belief that women's nature and modes of relating differ fundamentally from men's. For those who hold this position, the set of traits generally perceived as female are egalitarianism, collectivism, an ethic of care, a respect for knowledge derived from experience, pacifism, and cooperation. In contrast, male characteristics are thought to include an emphasis on hierarchy, oppressive individualism, an ethic of individual rights, abstraction, violence, and competition. These gender boundaries are confirmed by a formal body of feminist scholarship (see, e.g., Rich 1976, 1980; Chodorow 1978; Gilligan 1982; Rubin 1984; Collins 1989) as well as in popular writings (see, e.g., Walker 1974; Daly 1978, 1984; Cavin 1985; Dworkin 1981; Johnson 1987). Johnson, for example, characterizes the differences between women and men as based on the contrast between "masculine life-hating values" and "women's life-loving culture" (1987, 226).

Our interviews suggest that the belief that there are fundamental differences between women and men is widely held by individual activists. One lesbian feminist explains that "we've been acculturated into two cultures, the male culture and the female culture. And luckily we've been able to preserve the ways of nurturing by being in this alternative culture."

Because women's standards are deemed superior, it is not surprising that men, including older male children, are often excluded from community events and business establishments. At the Michigan Womyn's Music Festival, for example, male children over the age of three are not permitted in the festival area, but must stay at a separate camp. Reversing the common cultural practice of referring to adult women as "girls," it is not unusual for lesbian feminists to refer to men, including gay men, as "boys."

Maintaining an oppositional identity depends upon creating a world apart from the dominant society. The boundaries that are drawn around a group are not entirely a matter of choice. The process of reshaping one's collective world, however, involves the investiture of meaning that goes beyond the objective conditions out of which a group is created. Seen in this way, it is easy to understand how identity politics promotes a kind of cultural endogamy that, paradoxically, erects boundaries within the challenging group, dividing it on the basis of race, class, age, religion, ethnicity, and other factors. When asked to define the lesbian feminist community, one participant highlights this process by stating that "if there is such a thing as a lesboworld, then there are just as many diversities of communities in that world as there are in the heteroworld."

Consciousness

Boundaries locate persons as members of a group, but it is group consciousness that imparts a larger significance to a collectivity. We use the concept of consciousness to refer to the interpretive frameworks that emerge from a group's struggle to define and realize members' common interests in opposition to the dominant order. Although sociologists have focused primarily on class consciousness, Morris (1990) argues that the term *political consciousness* is more useful because it emphasizes that all systems of human domination create opposing interests capable of generating oppositional consciousness. Whatever the term, the important point is that collective actors must attribute their discontent to structural, cultural, or systemic causes rather than to personal failings or individual deviance (Ferree and Miller 1985; Touraine 1985).

Our notion of consciousness builds on the idea of cognitive liberation (McAdam 1982), frames (Snow et al. 1986), cognitive frameworks (Melucci 1989), and collective consciousness (Mueller 1987). We see the development of consciousness as an ongoing process in which groups reevaluate themselves, their subjective experiences, their opportunities, and their shared interests. Consciousness is imparted through a formal body of writings, speeches, and documents. More important, when a movement is successful at creating a collective identity, its interpretive orientations are interwoven with the fabric of everyday life. Consciousness not only provides socially and politically marginalized groups with an understanding of their structural position but establishes new expectations regarding treatment appropriate to their category. Of course, groups can mobilize around a collective consciousness that supports the status quo. Thus, it is only when a group develops an account that challenges dominant understandings that we can use the term *oppositional consciousness* (Morris 1990).

Contemporary lesbian feminist consciousness is not monolithic. But its mainspring is the view that heterosexuality is an institution of patriarchal control and that lesbian relationships are a means of subverting male domination. The relationship between feminism and lesbianism is well summarized by the classic slogan "feminism is the theory and lesbianism is the practice," mentioned by a number of our informants. Arguing that sexism and heterosexism are inextricably intertwined, lesbian feminists in the early 1970s characterized lesbianism as "the rage of all women condensed to the point of explosion" (Radicalesbians 1973, 240) and held that women who choose lesbianism are the vanguard of the women's movement (Birkby et al. 1973; Myron and Bunch 1975; Daly 1978, 1984; Frye 1983; Hoagland 1988). The classic rationale for this position, frequently reprinted in newsletters and other lesbian publications, is Ti-Grace Atkinson's analogy: "Can you imagine a Frenchman, serving in the French army from 9 A.M. to 5 P.M., then trotting 'home' to Germany for supper overnight?" (1974, 11).

Despite the common thread running through lesbian feminist consciousness that sexual relationships between women are to be understood in reference to the political structure of male supremacy and male domination, there are two distinct strands of thought about lesbian identity. One position holds that lesbianism is not an essential or biological characteristic but is socially constructed. In a recent analysis of the history of lesbian political consciousness, Phelan (1989) argues that lesbian feminist consciousness emerged and has been driven by a rejection of the liberal view that sexuality is a private or individual matter. A classic exposition of the social constructionist position can be found in Rich's "Compulsory Heterosexuality and Lesbian Existence" (1980), which defines lesbian identity not as sexual but as political. Rich introduces the concept of the "lesbian continuum" to include all women who are woman-identified and who resist patriarchy. By locating lesbianism squarely within the new scholarship on the female world, Rich, like other social constructionists, suggests that sexuality is a matter of choice.

If it is not sexual experience but an emotional and political orientation toward women that defines one as lesbian, then, as the song by Alix Dobkin puts it, "any woman can be a lesbian." Lesbian feminist communities in fact contain women who are oriented toward women emotionally and politically but not sexually. These women are sometimes referred to as "political dykes" or "heterodykes" (Clausen 1990; Smeller, unpublished), and community members think of them as women who "haven't come out yet." Some women who have had both male and female lovers resist being labeled bisexual and cling to a lesbian identity. For example, well-known singer and songwriter Holly Near explains: "I am too closely linked to the political perspective of lesbian feminism. . . . it is part of my world view, part of my passion for women and central in my objection to male domination" (1990). The significance of lesbian identity for feminist activists is well summarized by the name of a feminist support group at a major university, Lesbians Who Just Happen to Be Dating Politically-Correct Men.

The second strand of lesbian feminist thought aims to bring sex back into the definition of lesbianism (Treblecot 1979; Califia 1982; Ferguson 1982; Zita 1982; Hollibaugh and Moraga 1983; Rubin 1984; Nestle 1987; Penelope 1990). Criticizing the asexuality of lesbian feminism, Echols suggests that, in contemporary women's communities, "women's sexuality is assumed to be more spiritual than sexual, and considerably less central to their lives than is sexuality to men's" (1984, 60). Putting it more bluntly, sadomasochism advocate Pat Califia characterizes contemporary lesbian feminism as "anti-sex," using the term "vanilla feminism" to dismiss what she charges is a traditionally feminine passive attitude toward sex (1980). These "pro-sex" or "sex radical" writers tend to view sexuality less as a matter of choice and more as an essential characteristic. So, too, do some lesbian separatists, who have little else in common with the sex radicals. Arguing against social constructionism, Penelope (1990) places lesbianism squarely in the sexual arena. She points to the historical presence of women who loved other women sexually and emotionally prior to the nineteenth-century invention of the term *lesbian* and emphasizes that currently there are a variety of ways that women come to call themselves lesbian. In our interviews with lesbian activists, it was not uncommon for women who embraced essentialist notions to engage in biographical reconstruction, reinterpreting all of their prelesbian experiences as evidence of lesbian sexuality.

The emphasis on sexuality calls attention to the unknown numbers of women engaged in same-sex behavior who do not designate themselves lesbian and the enclaves of women who identify as lesbian but have not adopted lesbian feminist ideology and practice. These include lesbians who organize their social lives around gay bars (Nestle 1987), women who remain in the closet, pretending to be heterosexual but having sexual relationships with other women, and women who marry men and have relationships with women on the side. Describing the variousness of the contemporary lesbian experience and the multiple ways women come to call themselves lesbian, one of our interviewees discussed "pc [politically correct] dykes," "heterodykes," "maybelline dykes," "earth crunchy lesbians," "bar dykes," "phys ed dykes," "professional dykes," and "fluffy dykes."

For a large number of women, locating lesbianism in the feminist arena precludes forming meaningful political alliances with gay men. In part, this is because issues of sexual freedom that many feminists have viewed as exploiting women, including pornography, sexual contact between the young and old, and consensual sadomasochism, have been central to the predominantly male gay liberation movement (Adam 1987). Adam, however, suggests that, despite some conflicting interests, the latter part of the 1980s saw growing coalitions between lesbian feminists and gay liberationists surrounding the issues of AIDS. Our data confirm this hypothesis. Yet it is perhaps not coincidental that at a time when lesbian feminist communities serve increasingly as mobilization contexts for the larger lesbian and gay movement, lesbian activists describe a resurgence of lesbian separatism. Calls for more "women only space" pervaded gay and lesbian newsletters by the end of the 1980s (Japenga 1990).

Thus, our analysis suggests that an important element of lesbian feminist consciousness is the reevaluation of lesbianism as feminism. A number of recent studies, though admittedly based on small samples, confirm that the majority of women who openly embrace a lesbian identity interpret lesbianism within the framework of radical feminist ideology (Kitzinger 1987; Devor 1989; Phelan 1989). Removing lesbian behavior from the deviant clinical realm and placing it in the somewhat more acceptable feminist arena establishes lesbian identity as distinct from gay identity. Yet an increasingly vocal segment of lesbian feminists endorses a more essentialist, or what Steven Epstein (1987) terms "modified social constructionist," explanation of lesbianism. They have undoubtedly been influenced by the identity politics of the liberal branch of the gay liberation movement that has, in recent years, advocated that sexuality is less a matter of choice and more a matter of biology and early socialization.

Highlighting the significance of a dominated group's own explanation of its position for political action, Kitzinger (1987) uses the term *identity accounts* to distinguish the range of group understandings that emerge among oppressed groups to make sense of themselves and their situation. Our findings confirm that these self-understandings not only influence mobilization possibilities and directions but determine the types of individual and collective actions groups pursue to challenge dominant arrangements. In the next section, we examine lesbian feminist practice, emphasizing that it is comprehensible only because it presupposes the existence of a theory of lesbian identity.

Negotiation

Viewing collective identity as the result of repeatedly activated shared definitions, as new social movement theorists do, makes it difficult to distinguish between "doing" and "being," or between social movement

organizations and their strategies. Although recent social movement analyses tend to emphasize primarily the political and structural aims of challenging groups, personal transformation and expressive action have been central to most movements (Morris 1984; Fantasia 1988; McNall 1988). The insistence that the construction and expression of a collective vision is politics, or the politicization of the self and daily life, is nevertheless the core of what is "new" about the new social movements (Breines 1982; Melucci 1988; Kauffman 1990). Thus, we propose a framework that recognizes that identity can be a fundamental focus of political work.

Margolis (1985) suggests the concept of negotiation, drawn from the symbolic interactionist tradition, as a way of analyzing the process by which social movements work to change symbolic meanings. Most interactions between dominant and opposing groups reinforce established definitions. Individuals differentiated on the basis of devalued characteristics are continuously responded to in ways that perpetuate their disadvantaged status (Reskin 1988). West and Zimmerman (1987) use the term *identificatory displays* to emphasize, for example, that gender inequality is embedded and reproduced in even the most routine interactions. Similar analyses might be undertaken with regard to class, ethnicity, sexuality, and other sources of stratification. From a social movement standpoint, the concept of negotiations points to the myriad of ways that activists work to resist negative social definitions and demand that others value and treat oppositional groups differently (Goffman 1959).

The analysis of social movement negotiations forces us to recognize that, if not sociologically, then in reality, "doing" and "being" overlap (West and Zimmerman 1987). Yet we need a way to distinguish analytically between the politics of the public sphere, or world transformation directed primarily at the traditional political arena of the state, and the politics of identity, or self-transformation aimed primarily at the individual. We think that the concept of negotiations calls attention to forms of political activism embedded in everyday life that are distinct from those generally analyzed as tactics and strategies in the literature on social movements.

Building on Margolis's (1985) work on gender identity, we suggest two types of negotiation central to the construction of politicized collective identities. First, groups negotiate new ways of thinking and acting in *private* settings with other members of the collectivity, as well as in *public* settings before a larger audience. Second, identity negotiations can be *explicit*, involving open and direct attempts to free the group from domi- nant representations, or *implicit*, consisting of what Margolis terms a "condensed symbol or display" that undermines the status quo (1985, 340). In this section, we identify actions that lesbian feminist communities engage in to renegotiate the meaning of "woman." Opposition to male domination and the societal devalu- ation of women is directed both at the rules of daily life and at the institutions that perpetuate them.

In many respects, the phrase "the personal is polit- ical," coined by radical feminist Carol Hanisch and elaborated in Kate Millett's *Sexual Politics* (1969), is the hallmark of radical feminism (Echols 1989). Influ- enced by the civil rights and New Left movements, feminists began in the late 1960s to form conscious- ness-raising groups designed to reinterpret personal experiences in political terms. Analyzing virtually every aspect of individual and social experience as male-dominated, the groups encouraged participants to challenge prevailing representations of women in every sphere of life as a means of transforming the institu- tions that produced and disseminated them (Cassell 1977). The politicization of everyday life extended beyond the black power and feminist movements into other movements of the 1960s. In contemporary lesbian feminist communities the valorization of personal experience continues to have a profound impact.

Community members see lesbianism as a strategy for feminist social change that represents what one respondent describes as "an attempt . . . to stop doing what you were taught—hating women." Other women speak of the importance of learning to "value women," becoming "woman-centered," and "giving women energy." Being woman-centered is viewed as chal- lenging conventional expectations that women orient themselves psychologically and socially toward men, compete with other women for male attention, and devalue other women. To make a more complete break with patriarchal identities and ways of life, some women exchange their male-given surnames for women-centered ones, such as "Sarachild" or "Black- womyn." Loving and valuing women becomes a means to resist a culture that hates and belittles women. Invoking Alice Walker's (1974) concept of "womanist," one black woman that we interviewed explained, "My lesbianism has nothing to do with men. It's not about not choosing men, but about choosing women."

At the group level, lesbian feminists structure orga- nizations collectively (Rothschild-Whitt 1979) and attempt to eliminate hierarchy, make decisions by con- sensus, and form coalitions only with groups that are

not, as one activist said, "giving energy to the patri- archy." Demands for societal change seek to replace existing organizational forms and values with ones sim- ilar to those implemented in the community (Breines 1982). A worker at a women's festival illustrated the importance of community structure as a model for social change by commenting to women as they left the festival, "You've seen the way the real world can be, and now it's up to you to go out there and change it."

Because a traditionally feminine appearance, demeanor, self-concept, and style of personal relations are thought to be among the mainsprings of women's oppression, lesbian feminist communities have adopted different standards of gender behavior. For example, one of the visions of feminism has been to reconstitute the experience of victimization. Thus, women who have been battered or raped or have experienced incest and other forms of abuse are termed "survivors" to redefine their experiences as resistance to male vio- lence. New recruits to the community are resocialized through participating in a variety of organizations— women's twelve-step programs, battered women's shel- ters, martial arts groups, incest survivors' groups—that provide not only self-help but also a means for women to renegotiate a lesbian feminist identity. The very name of one such organization in New York City, Iden- tity House, is illustrative. Lesbian mothers organize support groups called "momazonians" or "dykes with tykes" to emphasize that motherhood is a crucial locus of contestation. "Take Back the Night" marches against violence, prochoice demonstrations, participation in spontaneous protests, and feminist music, theater, and dramatic presentations are other examples of public arenas for negotiating new standards of gender behavior.

Essential to contemporary lesbian feminist identity is a distinction between the lesbian who is a staunch feminist activist and the lesbian who is not of the van- guard. Thus, commitment to the politics of direct action distinguishes members of the lesbian feminist commu- nity from the larger population of lesbians. One partic- ipant illustrates the importance of this distinction, stating that women "who say that they are lesbians and maybe have sexual relationships with women, but don't have the feminist politics" compose a category who "could have been in the community, but they've opted out." Women even choose partners based on political commitment, noting that "sleeping with a woman who is not a feminist just doesn't work for me; there's too much political conflict." The tendency to choose life partners and form other close personal relationships based on shared political assumptions is not, however, unique to lesbian feminism but has been reported in relation to other movements as well (Rupp and Taylor 1987; McAdam 1988). In short, negotiating new gender definitions is central to lesbian feminist collective identity.

Challenging further the notion of femininity as frailty, passivity, and preoccupation with reigning standards of beauty, many women wear clothing that enables freedom of movement, adopt short or simple haircuts, walk with firm self-assured strides, and choose not to shave their legs or wear heavy makeup. Devor (1989) terms this mode of self-presentation "gender blending," arguing that it represents an explicit rejection of the norms of femininity and, by extension, of women's subjugation. By reversing reigning cultural standards of femininity, beauty, and respectability, lesbian feminists strike a blow against female objectification. How central this is to lesbian feminist identity is illustrated by a lesbian support group at a major university with the name Women in Comfortable Shoes.

Because appearance and demeanor are also implicit means of expressing one's opposition, community members' presentation of self is subject to close scrutiny or, to use the vernacular of the activists themselves, is monitored by the "pc police." Women who dress in stereotypically "feminine" ways are often criticized and admit to feeling "politically incorrect." As one respondent commented, "I've always had a lot of guilt feelings about, why don't I just buckle down and put on some blue jeans, and clip my hair short, and not wear makeup, and go aggressively through the world." Some of our interviewees report a return to gendered fashion in contemporary lesbian communities. Women who identify as sex radicals, in particular, have adopted styles of dress traditionally associated with the "sex trade," or prostitution, such as miniskirts, low-cut tops, and fishnet stockings, sometimes combined with more traditionally masculine styles in what is known as a "gender fuck" style of dressing. Suggesting that "the most profound and potentially the most radical politics come directly out of our own identity" (Combahee River Collective 1982), African-American feminists criticize the tendency of many white lesbian feminists to dictate a politics based on hegemonic cultural standards. Some women who are identifiably butch and dress in studded leather clothing and punk and neon haircuts offer class-based motivations for their demeanor, and African-American, Asian-American, and Latina lesbians embrace different cultural styles. In short, the changes in appearance and behavior women undergo as they come out cannot be fully understood as individually chosen but are often the ultimatum of identity communities (Krieger 1982).

We have presented three dimensions for analyzing collective identity in social movements: the concepts of boundaries, consciousness, and negotiation. Although we have treated each as if it were independent, in reality the three interact. Using these factors to analyze lesbian feminist identity suggests three elements that shape the social construction of lesbian feminism. First, lesbian feminist communities draw boundaries that affirm femaleness and separate them from a larger world perceived as hostile. Second, to undermine the dominant view of lesbianism as perversion, lesbian feminists offer identity accounts that politicize sexuality. Finally, by defining lesbians as the vanguard of the women's movement, lesbian feminists valorize personal experience, which, paradoxically, further reifies the boundaries between lesbians and nonlesbians and creates the impression that the differences between women and men and between lesbian and heterosexual feminists are essential.

CONCLUSION

The concept of collective identity is associated primarily with the social movements of the 1970s and 1980s because of their distinctive cultural appearance. It is our hypothesis, however, that collective identity is a significant variable in all social movements, even among the so-called traditional nineteenth-century movements. Thus, we frame our approach broadly to apply to oppositional identities based on class, race, ethnicity, gender, sexuality, and other persistent social cleavages. Certainly any theory derived from a single case is open to criticism. But recent research in the resource mobilization tradition points to the impact that changes in consciousness have on mobilization (Klein 1984; Downey 1986; Mueller 1987; McAdam 1988).

There is a growing realization among scholars of social movements that the theoretical pendulum between classical and contemporary approaches to social movements has swung too far. Social psychological factors that were central to collective behavior theory (Blumer 1946; Smelser 1962; Killian 1964; Turner and Killian 1972) have become the theoretical blind spots of resource mobilization theory. Ignoring the grievances or injustices that mobilize protest movements has, as Klandermans (1986) suggests, stripped social movements of their political significance. In contrast to the structural and organizational emphases of resource mobilization theory, new social movement theory attends to the social psychological and cultural discontent that propels movements. But it provides little understanding of how the injustices that are at the heart of most movements are translated into the everyday lives of collective actors. Our analysis suggests that the study of collective identity, because it highlights the role of meaning and ideology in the mobilization and maintenance of collective action, is an important key to understanding this process.

REFERENCES

Adam, Barry D. 1987. *The Rise of a Gay and Lesbian Movement*. Boston: Twayne.

Atkinson, Ti-Grace. 1974. *Amazon Odyssey*. New York: Link Books.

Barth, F. 1969. "Introduction." In *Ethnic Groups and Boundaries*, ed. F. Barth. Boston: Little, Brown, 1–38.

Birkby, Phyllis, Bertha Harris, Jill Johnston, Esther Newton, and Jane O'Wyatt. 1973. *Amazon Expedition: A Lesbian Feminist Anthology*. New York: Times Change Press.

Blumer, Herbert. 1946. "Collective Behavior." In *New Outline of the Principles of Sociology*, ed. A. M. Lee. New York: Barnes and Noble, 1970–222.

Boggs, Carl. 1986. *Social Movements and Political Power*. Philadelphia: Temple University Press.

Breines, Wini. 1982. *Community and Organization in the New Left, 1962–68*. New York: Praeger.

Buechler, Steven M. 1990. *Women's Movements in the United States*. New Brunswick, N.J.: Rutgers.

Bunch, Charlotte. 1986. "Not for Lesbians Only." In *Feminist Frontiers II*, ed. Laurel Richardson and Verta Taylor. New York: Random House, 452–54.

Califia, Pat. 1980. "Feminism vs. Sex: A New Conservative Wave." *Advocate*, February 21.

_____. 1982. "Public Sex." *Advocate*, September 30.

Cassell, Joan. 1977. *A Group Called Women: Sisterhood and Symbolism in the Feminist Movement*. New York: David McKay.

Cavin, Susan. 1985. *Lesbian Origins*. San Francisco: Ism Press.

Chafetz, Janet Saltzman. 1988. *Feminist Sociology*. Itaska, Ill.: F.E. Peacock.

Chodorow, Nancy. 1978. *The Reproduction of Mothering: Psychoanalysis and the Sociology of Gender*. Berkeley: University of California Press.

Clausen, Jan. 1990. "My Interesting Condition." *Outlook* 2:11–21.

Cohen, Jean L. 1985. "Strategy or Identity: New Theoretical Paradigms and Contemporary Social Movements," *Social Research* 52:663–716.

Collins, Patricia Hill. 1989. "The Social Construction of Black Feminist Thought." *Signs* 14, no. 4:745–73.

Combahee River Collective. 1982. "A Black Feminist Statement." In *But Some of Us Are Brave: Black Women's Studies*, ed. Gloria T. Hull, Patricia Bell Scott, and Barbara Smith. Old Westbury, N.Y.: Feminist Press, 13–22.

Daly, Mary. 1984. *Pure Lust: Elemental Feminist Philosophy*. Boston: Beacon Press.

Devor, Holly. 1989. *Gender Blending*. Bloomington: Indiana University Press.

Downey, Gary L. 1986. "Ideology and the Clamshell Identity: Organizational Dilemmas in the Anti–Nuclear Power Movement." *Social Problems* 33:357–73.

Dworkin, Andrea. 1981. *Pornography and Silence: Culture's Revenge against Nature*. New York: Harper and Row.

Echols, Alice. 1984. "The Taming of the Id: Feminist Sexual Politics, 1968–83." In *Pleasure and Danger: Exploring Female Sexuality*, ed. Carole S. Vance. Boston: Routledge and Kegan Paul, 50–72.

Emberley, Julia, and Donna Landry. 1989. "Coverage of Greenham and Greenham as 'Coverage.'" *Feminist Studies* 15:485–98.

Epstein, Barbara. 1990. "Rethinking Social Movement Theory." *Socialist Review* 20:35–66.

Epstein, Steven. 1987. "Gay Politics, Ethnic Identity: The Limits of Social Constructionism." *Socialist Review* 17:9–54.

Esterberg, Kristin Gay. 1990. "Salience and Solidarity: Identity, Correctness, and Conformity in a Lesbian Community." Paper presented at the annual meeting of the American Sociological Association, August 11–15, Washington, D.C.

Evans, Sarah. 1979. *Personal Politics*. New York: Vintage.

Fantasia, Rick. 1988. *Cultures of Solidarity*. Berkeley: University of California Press.

Ferguson, Ann. 1982. "Patriarchy, Sexual Identity, and the Sexual Revolution." In *Feminist Theory: A Critique of Ideology*, ed. Nannerl O. Keohane, Michelle Z. Rosaldo, and Barbara L. Gelpi. Chicago: University of Chicago Press, 147–61.

Ferree, Myra Marx, and Beth B. Hess. 1985. *Controversy and Coalition: The New Feminist Movement*. Boston: Twayne.

Ferree, Myra Marx, and Frederick D. Miller. 1985. "Mobilization and Meaning: Some Social-Psychological Contributions to the Resource Mobilization Perspective on Social Movements." *Sociological Inquiry* 55:38–61.

Fireman, Bruce, and William Gamson. 1979. "Utilitarian Logic in the Resource Mobilization Perspective." In *The Dynamics of Social Movements*, ed. Mayer N. Zald and John D. McCarthy. Cambridge, Mass.: Winthrop, 8–44.

Freeman, Jo. 1975. *The Politics of Women's Liberation*. New York: David McKay.

Frye, Marilyn. 1900. "Do You Have to Be a Lesbian to Be a Feminist?" *Off Our Backs* 20:21–23.

Gamson, William A. 1975. *The Strategy of Social Protest*. Homewood, Ill.: Dorsey Press.

Gelb, Joyce, and Marian Lief Palley. 1982. *Women and Public Policy*. Princeton: Princeton University Press.

Gerlach, Luther P., and Virginia H. Hine. 1970. *People, Power, Change: Movements of Social Transformation*. Indianapolis: Bobbs-Merrill.

Gilligan, Carol. 1982. *In a Different Voice*. Cambridge, Mass.: Harvard University Press.

Goffman, Erving. 1959. *The Presentation of Self in Everyday Life*. Englewood Cliffs, N.J.: Prentice-Hall.

Hoagland, Sarah Lucia. 1988. *Lesbian Ethics: Toward New Value*. Palo Alto, Calif.: Institute of Lesbian Studies.

Hollibaugh, Amber, and Cherrie Moraga. 1983. "What We're Rollin' Around in Bed With: Sexual Silences in Feminism." In *Powers of Desire*, ed. Ann Snitow, Christine Stansell, and Sharon Thompson. New York: Monthly Review Press, 394–405.

Jaggar, Alison M., and Paula Rothenberg Struhl. 1978. *Feminist Frameworks*. New York: McGraw-Hill.

Japenga, Ann. 1990. "The Separatist Revival." *Outlook* 2:78–83.

Jenkins, J. Craig. 1983. "Resource Mobilization Theory and the Study of Social Movements," *Annual Review of Sociology* 9:527–53.

Jenkins, J. Craig, and Charles Perrow. 1977. "Insurgency of the Powerless: Farm Workers Movement (1946–72)." *American Sociological Review* 42:249–68.

Kauffman, L. A. 1990. "The Anti-Politics of Identity." *Socialist Review* 20:67–80.

Killian, Lewis M. 1964. "Social Movements." In *Handbook of Modern Sociology*, ed. R.E.L. Faris. Chicago: Rand McNally, 426–55.

Kitzinger, Celia. 1987. *The Social Construction of Lesbianism*. London: Sage.

Klandermans, Bert. 1984. "Mobilization and Participation: Social-Psychological Expansions of Resource Mobilization Theory." *American Sociological Review* 49:583–600.

_____. 1986. "New Social Movements and Resource Mobilization: The European and American Approach." *Journal of Mass Emergencies and Disasters* 4:13–37.

Klandermans, Bert, and Sidney Tarrow. 1988. "Mobilization into Social Movements: Synthesizing European and American Approaches." In *From Structure to Action: Comparing Movement Participation across Cultures*. International Social Movement Research, vol. 1, ed. Bert Klandermans, Hanspeter Kriesi, and Sidney Tarrow. Greenwich, Conn.: JAI Press, 1–38.

Klein, Ethel. 1984. *Gender Politics*. Cambridge, Mass.: Harvard University Press.

Krieger, Susan. 1982. "Lesbian Identity and Community: Recent Social Science Literature." *Signs* 8:91–108.

Lofland, John. 1979. "White-Hot Mobilization: Strategies of a Millenarian Movement." In *Dynamics of Social Movements*, ed. Mayer N. Zald and John D. McCarthy. Cambridge, Mass.: Winthrop, 157–66.

_____. 1985. "Social Movement Culture." In *Protest*, ed. John Lofland. New Brunswick, N.J.: Transaction Books, 219–39.

Margolis, Diane Rothbard. 1985. "Redefining the Situation: Negotiations on the Meaning of Woman." *Social Problems* 32:332–47.

McAdam, Doug. 1982. *Political Process and the Development of Black Insurgency, 1930–70*. Chicago: University of Chicago Press.

_____. 1988. *Freedom Summer*. New York: Oxford University Press.

McAdam, Doug, John D. McCarthy, and Mayer N. Zald, 1988. "Social Movements." In *Handbook of Sociology*, ed. Neil Smelser, Newbury Park, Calif.: Sage, 695–737.

McCarthy, John D. and Mayer N. Zald. 1973. *The Trend of Social Movements in America*. Morristown, N.J.: General Learning Press.

_____. 1977. "Resource Mobilization and Social Movements: A Partial Theory." *American Journal of Sociology* 82:1212–41.

McNall, Scott G. 1988. *The Road to Rebellion: Class Formation and Populism, 1865–1900*. Chicago: University of Chicago Press.

Melucci, Alberto. 1985. "The Symbolic Challenge of Contemporary Movements." *Social Research* 52:781–816.

_____. 1988. "Getting Involved: Identity and Mobilization in Social Movements." In *From Structure to Action: Comparing Movement Participation across Cultures*. International Social Movement Research, vol. 1, ed. Bert Klandermans, Hanspeter Kriesi, and Sidney Tarrow, Greenwich, Conn.: JAI Press, 329–48.

_____. 1989. *Nomads of the Present: Social Movements*

and Individual Needs in Contemporary Society. Philadelphia: Temple University Press.

Millett, Kate. 1969. *Sexual Politics*. New York: Ballantine.

Morris, Aldon D. 1984. *The Origins of the Civil Rights Movement*. New York: Free Press.

————. 1990. "Consciousness and Collective Action: Towards a Sociology of Consciousness and Domination." Paper presented at the annual meeting of the American Sociological Association, August 9–13, San Francisco.

Mueller, Carol McClurg. 1987. "Collective Consciousness, Identity Transformation, and the Rise of Women in Public Office in the United States." In *The Women's Movement of the United States and Western Europe*, ed. M. F. Katzenstein and C. M. Mueller. Philadelphia: Temple University Press, 89–108.

————. 1990. "Collective Identities and the Mobilization of Women: The American Case, 1960–1970." Paper presented at the colloquium on New Social Movements and the End of Ideology, July 16–20, Univerisidad Internacional Menendez Pelayo.

Myron, Nancy, and Charlotte Bunch. 1975. *Lesbianism and the Women's Movement*. Baltimore: Diana Press.

Near, Holly. 1990. *Fire in the Rain, Singer in the Storm*. New York: Morrow.

Nestle, Joan. 1987. *A Restricted Country*. Ithaca, N.Y.: Firebrand Books.

Oberschall, Anthony. 1973. *Social Conflict and Social Movements*. Englewood Cliffs, N.J.: Prentice-Hall.

Offe, Claus. 1985. "New Social Movements: Challenging the Boundaries of Institutional Politics." *Social Research* 52:817–68.

Olzak, Susan. 1983. "Contemporary Ethnic Mobilization." *Annual Review of Sociology* 9:355–74.

Penelope, Julia. 1990. "A Case of Mistaken Identity." *Women's Review of Books* 8:11–12.

Phelan, Shane. 1989. *Identity Politics: Lesbian Feminism and the Limits of Community*, Philadelphia: Temple University Press.

Pizzorno, Alessandro. 1978. "Political Science and Collective Identity in Industrial Conflict." In *The Resurgence of Class Conflict in Western Europe since 1968*, ed. C. Crouch and A. Pizzorno. New York: Holmes and Meier, 277–98.

Radicalesbians. 1973. "The Women Identified Woman." In *Radical Feminism*, ed. Anne Koedt, Ellen Levine, and Anita Rapone. New York: Quadrangle, 240–45.

Reskin, Barbara. 1988. "Bringing the Men Back In: Sex Differentiation and the Devaluation of Women's Work." *Gender and Society* 2:58–81.

Rich, Adrienne. 1976. *Of Women Born*. New York: Norton.

————. 1980. "Compulsory Heterosexuality and Lesbian Existence." *Signs* 5:631–60.

Rothschild-Whitt, Joyce. 1979. "The Collectivist Organization: An Alternative to Rational-Bureaucratic Models." *American Sociological Review* 44:509–27.

Rubin, Gayle. 1984. "Thinking Sex: Notes for a Radical Theory of the Politics of Sexuality." In *Pleasure and Danger*, ed. Carol S. Vance. Boston: Routledge and Kegan Paul, 267–319.

Rule, James, and Charles Tilly. 1972. "1830 and the Unnatural History of Revolution." *Journal of Social Issues* 28:49–76.

Rupp, Leila J. 1989. "Feminism and the Sexual Revolution in the Early Twentieth Century: The Case of Doris Stevens." *Feminist Studies* 51:289–309.

Rupp, Leila J., and Verta Taylor, 1986. "The Women's Movement since 1960: Structure, Strategies, and New Directions." In *American Choices: Social Dilemmas and Public Policy since 1960*, ed. Robert H. Bremner, Richard Hopkins, and Gary W. Reichard. Columbus: Ohio State University Press, 75–104.

————. 1990. "Women's Culture and the Persisting Women's Movement." Paper presented at the annual meeting of the American Sociological Association, Washington, D.C., August 12.

Ryan, Barbara. 1989. "Ideological Purity and Feminism: The U.S. Women's Movement from 1966 to 1975." *Gender and Society* 3:329–57.

Schneider, Beth. 1986. "I Am Not a Feminist But . . ." Paper presented at the annual meeting of the American Sociological Association, New York, September 2.

Schwartz, Michael. 1976. *Radical Protest and Social Structure: The Southern Farmers' Alliance and the One-Crop Tenancy System*. New York: Academic Press.

Smeller, Michelle M. Unpublished, "From Dyke to Doll: The Processual Formation of Sexual Identity." Ohio State University.

Smelser, Neil. 1962. *Theory of Collective Behavior*. New York: Free Press.

Snitow, Ann, Christine Stansell, and Sharon Thompson. 1983. *Powers of Desire: The Politics of Sexuality*. New York: Monthly Review Press.

Snow, David A., E. Burke Rochford, Jr., Steven K. Worden, and Robert D. Benford. 1986. "Frame Alignment Processes, Micromobilization, and Movement Participation." *American Sociological Review* 51:464–81.

Taylor, Verta. 1989a. "The Future of Feminism." In *Feminist Frontiers*, ed. Laurel Richardson and Verta Taylor. New York: Random House, 434–51.

————. 1989b. "Social Movement Continuity: The

Women's Movement in Abeyance." *American Sociological Review* 54:761–75.

Taylor, Verta, and Nancy Whittier. 1992. "The New Feminist Movement." In *Feminist Frontiers: Rethinking Sex, Gender, and Society*, ed. Laurel Richardson and Verta Taylor. New York: McGraw-Hill.

Tilly, Charles. 1978. *From Mobilization to Revolution.* Reading, Mass.: Addison-Wesley.

Touraine, Alain. 1985. "An Introduction to the Study of Social Movements." *Social Research* 52:749–87.

Treblecot, Joyce. 1979. "Conceiving Women: Notes on the Logic of Feminism." *Sinister Wisdom* 11:3–50.

Turner, Ralph H., and Lewis M. Killian. 1972. *Collective Behavior.* 2d ed. Englewood Cliffs, N.J.: Prentice-Hall.

Vance, Carole S. 1984. *Pleasure and Danger.* Boston: Routledge and Kegan Paul.

Walker, Alice. 1974. *In Search of Our Mothers' Gardens.* New York: Harcourt Brace Jovanovich.

Weigert, Andrew J., J. Smith Teitge, and Dennis W. Teitge. 1986. *Society and Identity.* New York: Cambridge University Press.

West, Candace, and Don H. Zimmerman. 1987. "Doing Gender." *Gender and Society* 1:125–51.

White, Edmund. 1980. *States of Desire.* New York: E. P. Dutton.

Whittier, Nancy. 1991. "Feminists in the Post-Feminist Age: Collective Identity and the Persistence of the Women's Movement." Ph.D. diss., Ohio State University.

Zinn, Maxine Baca. 1990. "Family, Feminism, and Race in America." *Gender and Society* 4:68–82.

Zita, Jacquelyn. 1982. "Historical Amnesia and the Lesbian Continuum." In *Feminist Theory: A Critique of Ideology*, ed. Nannerl O. Keohane, Michelle Z. Rosaldo, and Barbara L. Gelpi. Chicago: University of Chicago Press, 161–76.

CHAPTER 7

THE CIVIL RIGHTS MOVEMENT, BLACK POWER, AND WHITE BACKLASH

SOME DATES TO REMEMBER

May 17, 1954	*Brown v. Board of Education of Topeka:* Supreme Court decision outlawing racial segregation in the public schools
1955–1956	Montgomery bus boycott
February 1, 1960	Sit-in in Greensboro, North Carolina; triggers sit-ins across the South
May–August 1961	"Freedom rides" conducted by CORE and SNCC
April–May 1963	Birmingham campaign
August 28, 1963	March on Washington; "I Have a Dream" speech by Dr. Martin Luther King, Jr.
July 2, 1964	Civil Rights Act signed into law by President Lyndon Johnson: outlaws public segregation
January–March 1965	Selma campaign
August 6, 1965	Voting Rights Act of 1965; federal enforcement of black voting rights in the South
August 11–16, 1965	Watts riot in Los Angeles, followed by hundreds of other urban riots, 1965–1968
May 1966	"Black power" declared as an ideal by SNCC chairman Stokely Carmichael
July–August 1966	Chicago campaign
April 4, 1968	Assassination of Dr. Martin Luther King, Jr.
1968	Alabama Governor George Wallace runs for president as an independent candidate, attracting many votes from white southerners and northern white workers
November 1968	Election of Republican president Richard M. Nixon

The civil rights movement has been called the "Second American Revolution," and there are several reasons why this is an appropriate label. From the 1950s to the middle of the 1960s, militant yet nonviolent mass protests shattered legal segregation in the South, freeing southern blacks at last from the legalized repression and exclusion from citizenship rights that they had suffered since the end of the nineteenth century (Valelly, 1993).

Once southern blacks persuaded the federal government to enforce their right to vote, the nation's politics was forever changed. Blacks became majorities or large pluralities in many parts of the South, and this occurred at the same time that black migrations from the rural South to cities enabled them to become pivotal to the Democratic party's electoral fortunes in many northern cities and states. Black influence and racial issues were to become central in American national politics from 1964 onward, especially in presidential elections.

As the civil rights revolution achieved its initial victories, the aspirations of African-Americans rose. Martin Luther King, Jr., sought to move the civil rights movement north, turning it into a general crusade for jobs and justice for the poor, both black and white, and into a crusade against de facto segregation in America's great cities. Impatience for change, along with tensions between the police and ghetto residents, fueled a wave of urban riots in the late 1960s. Some African-Americans became militant advocates of "black power" rather than racial integration, while many others continued to hope for the triumph of King's ideal of an integrated and just society. In the late 1960s, however, many northern whites who had supported the civil rights revolution as long as it was focused on the South began to react against urban riots and black power. In the South and North alike, a white backlash set in, opposing the further vigorous use of federal power to promote racial changes in the United States.

The readings in this chapter graphically portray the momentous social and political transformations of the fight for civil rights and its aftermath. They take us from the southern movement of 1955–1965 thorugh struggles over racial issues in northern cities; and they trace the reverberations of changing race relations in national elections from 1964, through "the Reagan era" of the 1980s, to the political choices of the early 1990s.

As we look back, we can only marvel at how remarkable the mass effort to attain black liberation in the South was! For many decades before the 1930s and 1940s, blacks had suffered pervasive oppression under segregation. They had clear grievances, but had little power to redress them. Most were rural sharecroppers, dependent on white landowners for their livelihood. They could not vote, or form unions, or speak out freely. A black who got "out of place" might be tortured or lynched, but the federal government did nothing to stop the harassment, or even to enforce black voting rights. Then, beginning with the New Deal and World War II, things began to change (McAdam, 1982, Chap. 5). Democratic presidents and federal courts took occasional steps that gave blacks new hope, and the participation of African-Americans as soldiers in World War II had a similar effect. Southern agriculture was mechanized, displacing masses of families from the cotton fields. From the 1940s onward, hundreds of thousands of blacks migrated to cities in the South and the North. In the South, black churches in urban areas became wealthier and more independent, black colleges expanded, and the southern branch of the National Association for the Advancement of Colored People became more aggressive in pressing for court rulings against segregation.

Against the backdrop of these long-term changes, Aldon Morris and Doug McAdam (see Readings 22 and 23) trace the origins and development of the black mass insurgency between 1955 and 1965. Segregation ended only when southern blacks gained the courage to protest outside of "normal" channels, finally making the practice too costly for whites to maintain. Both Morris and McAdam work with ideas about indigenous "resource mobilization" and changing "political opportunity structures." Morris shows in detail how urban black churches in the South served as centers of support for the sit-ins against segregation; and he tells us about the networks of communication formed among ministers, students, and other southern blacks who became leaders in spreading resistance throughout the South after 1960. Nonviolent protest tactics, Morris argues, were especially well suited to a mass movement that depended on leadership from Baptist and Methodist ministers, and on mobilizing ordinary church members to sit in, boycott, or demonstrate—or to offer monetary support to others who did these (often dangerous) things. The reading by Morris can be usefully juxtaposed to the theoretical reading by Dennis Chong in Chapter 6.

McAdam builds on Morris's research and carries the story forward. By analyzing the successive tactics used by civil rights protesters from 1955 into the mid-1960s, he traces the three-way maneuvers among black protestors, southern segregationists, and the federal government. He shows how the civil rights movement won its greatest victories when it was able to use innovative protest tactics—bus boycotts, sit-ins, freedom rides, and community-wide mass demonstrations—to provoke die-hard segrationists to violence. Americans across the nation could see the terrible violence and injustices spawned by segregation in vivid detail on their television screens. The federal government no longer could ignore the situation, but had to step in, with force and new laws, to abolish legal segregation. After the huge "march on Washington" staged by the civil rights movement in the summer of 1963, bipartisan coalitions in the Congress passed the Civil Rights Act of 1964 and the Voting Rights Act of 1965, and President Lyndon Johnson signed them into law.

McAdam provides insights into what happened to black protest after the initial southern victories, when the center of attention shifted to the North. The urban riots of the late 1960s may have been a "tactical innovation" suited to the conditions of poor urban populations, McAdam suggests, and they may have spurred certain governmental programs to help the urban poor. But the riots also destroyed black neighborhoods and invited forcible repression by local, state, and federal authorities, thus closing down opportunities for further urban black protest. Some analysts believe that a continued liberal crusade against urban segregation and injustice might have been possible in the wake of the southern civil rights victories (for an articulate defense of this position, see Orfield, 1988). However, white support for federally mandated changes in the North was much weaker than it was for dismantling southern segregation. Issues of neighborhood segregation, use of busing to implement school integration, calls for black power in the cities, and increasing black access to jobs—all would have to be faced by northern whites and the politicians. What little white enthusiasm there was for resolving such problems quickly dissipated after the outbreak and spread of the riots. Blacks were suddenly perceived as dangerous and ungrateful, and many northern whites joined their southern peers in deciding that the civil rights revolution had "gone too far."

Meanwhile, black impatience with the slow pace of change—especially when it came to alleviating persistent black poverty in both the South and the North—led some groups to champion "black power." This slogan has meant many things since the 1960s. When originally articulated by Stokely Carmichael and the Student Non-Violent Coordinating Committee (SNCC), it was an assertion of black pride and leadership (Carmichael & Hamilton, 1967). Many black intellectuals and students placed the emphasis on controlling their own organizations, and white civil rights activists were expelled from groups like SNCC and the Congress of Racial Equality (CORE). Black power could also mean urban armed struggle, as it did to the Black Panthers. Over time, during the 1970s and 1980s, black power often came to denote the creation of community-based movements dedicated to furthering the autonomy, as well as the electoral and nonelectoral power, of black Americans in the cities (Jennings, 1992).

The impact of social movements for black liberation reverberated far beyond the immediate stakes of southern legal segregation, and of northern poverty and de facto segregation. As Thomas and Mary Edsall explain in Reading 24, the U.S. electoral sytem was transformed by new black votes, rising black aspirations, and growing white disillusionment. Racial changes were not the only upheavals Americans faced from the 1960s onward. There was also U.S. involvement in the Vietnam war, accompanied by rising economic and military costs, a passionate antiwar movement, and the ultimate defeat of American and South Vietnamese forces by the North Vietnamese. In addition, there were dozens of movements demanding new governmentally enforced "rights" for such groups as feminists, prisoners, the disabled, and gays and lesbians—all in addition to the continuation of movements demanding social programs and "affirmative action" for blacks. According to the Edsalls, the effect of these simultaneous developments created profoundly contradictory problems for the Democratic party after 1964.

Not only did white southerners continue to defect from the party (as they had in 1964), but many northern working-class and middle-class whites also began to oppose higher taxes and more federal regulations to help blacks and other "special interests." Democratic presidential candidates, in particular, had a hard time satisfying blacks and whites at the same time. First, the independent 1968 presidential campaign of Alabama Governor George Wallace, and then the increasingly conservative Republican party, managed to attract the defecting white Democrats into what the Edsalls call a "top-down coalition," uniting business interests and ordinary whites against apparent liberal–Democratic support for higher taxes, more regulation, and increased federal intervention to promote racial equality. The new conservative coalition steadily gained electoral strength, until it swept Ronald Reagan and many right-wing congressional candidates into office in 1980.

The Edsalls have a different perspective than does Orfield (1988) on the political possibilities and obstacles faced by the Democratic party after 1964. Orfield holds that vigorous measures against northern racial segregation were possible, and he faults Democratic party leaders for not pursuing them. But the Edsalls argue that even the small steps that were taken by the federal government in the 1960s and the early 1970s—steps such as busing for school desegregation, increased social welfare spending, and "affirmative action" regulations—served to trigger a "chain reaction" of white defections from the Democratic party. Ironically, some of these steps were taken during the Republican presidency of Richard M. Nixon, yet they still tended to redound to the disadvantage of the Democrats in presidential politics because that party was more identified with the goals and mobilization of blacks after 1964 (Carmines & Stimson, 1989).

The Edsalls' diagnosis of Democratic party dilemmas about race is similar to the one offered (in Reading 30 in Chapter 10) by William Julius Wilson, a leading sociologist who has studied the problems of the black urban underclass (Wilson, 1987). Whereas the Edsalls analyzed events from the 1960s to the 1980s, Wilson looks forward into the 1990s. Interestingly enough, the electoral strategy pursued by Democratic presidential candidate Bill Clinton in 1992 seems to have been informed by what observers such as the Edsalls and Wilson have to say. Although the Los Angeles riot occurred during the 1992 presidential campaign, candidate Clinton did *not* talk about urban problems, antipoverty programs, or affirmative action for blacks; and he distanced himself from advocates of black power. He also went out of his way to show sympathy for the concerns of white southerners and northern white workers about high taxes and the need to "reform welfare." When discussing how he might handle America's domestic problems, Clinton highlighted the kinds of "race-neutral" social and economic policies Wilson prescribes as ideal for rebuilding a progressive, cross-racial coalition in the Democractic party.

Bill Clinton won enough votes from both black and white working-class voters to be elected president in November 1992. During his time in office, however, President Clinton faces the challenge of finding ways to use the powers of the federal government to promote progress for blacks and the cause of racial equality, while not triggering another round of "white backlash" against the Democratic party. If he fails at this difficult endeavor, Republicans are waiting in the wings, eager to reconstruct the "top-down" white coalition that worked so well for their party between the 1960s and 1992.

REFERENCES

Carmichael, Stokely, and Charles V. Hamilton. 1967. *Black Power: The Politics of Liberation in America.* New York: Vintage Books.

Carmines, Edward G., and James A. Stimson. 1989. *Issue Evolution: Race and the Transformation of American Politics.* Princeton, N.J.: Princeton University Press.

Edsall, Thomas Bryne, and Mary D. Edsall. 1991. *Chain Reaction: The Impact of Race, Rights, and Taxes on American Politics.* New York: W. W. Norton.

Jennings, James. 1992. *The Politics of Black Empowerment.* Detroit, Mich.: Wayne State University Press.

McAdam, Doug. 1982. *Political Process and the Development of Black Insurgency, 1930–1970.* Chicago: University of Chicago Press.

Orfield, Gary. 1988. "Race and the Liberal Agenda: The Loss of the Integrationist Dream, 1965–1974," In *The Politics of Social Policy in the United States,* edited by Margaret Weir, Ann Shola Orloff, and Theda Skocpol, 313–55. Princeton, N.J.: Princeton University Press.

Valelly, Richard M. 1993. "Party, Coercion, and Inclusion: The Two Reconstructions of the South's Electoral Politics." *Politics and Society* 21 (March): 37–67.

Wilson, William Julius. 1987. *The Truly Disadvantaged: The Inner City, the Underclass, and Public Policy.* Chicago, University of Chicago Press.

READING 22

BLACK SOUTHERN STUDENT SIT-IN MOVEMENT: AN ANALYSIS OF INTERNAL ORGANIZATION*

Aldon Morris

This paper argues that the Southern sit-in movement of 1960, though it appears to have developed in the spontaneous manner described by classic collective behavior theory, actually grew out of pre-existing institutions and organizational forms. The spread of the sit-ins followed the networks of these pre-existing institutional relationships. Factors internal to the black community—churches, colleges, protest organizations, and leaders—were responsible for nurturing and developing the movement. The analysis is based on primary data collected from archives and interviews with civil rights leaders.

Scholars of the Civil Rights movement (Zinn, 1964; Oppenheimer, 1964; Matthews and Prothro, 1966; Meier and Rudwick, 1973; Oberschall, 1973; McAdam, 1979) and Civil Rights activists agree that the black Southern student sit-in movement of 1960 was a crucial development. The sit-ins pumped new life into the Civil Rights movement and enabled it to win unprecedented victories. Moreover, the sit-ins exercised a profound tactical and strategic influence over the entire course of social and political upheavals of the 1960s.

Apart from having a jarring impact on race relations, the sit-ins signaled the possibility of militant action at both Northern and Southern white campuses (Haber, 1966; Obear, 1970; Sale, 1973). A critical mass of the

early leaders of the white student movement acquired much of their training, organizing skills, and tactics from the black activists of the student sit-in movement (Sale, 1973; Westby, 1976). Thus, the beginning of the white student movement as well as the quickened pace of Civil Rights activity can be traced to the black student sit-in movement.

The sit-ins were important because their rapid spread across the South crystalized the conflict of the period and pulled many people directly into the movement. How is such a "burst" of collective action to be explained? A standard account of the sit-ins has emerged which maintains that the sit-ins were the product of an independent black student movement which represented a radical break from previous civil rights activities, organizations, and leaderhsip of the Black community (e.g. Lomax, 1962; Zinn, 1964; Oppenheimer, 1964; Matthews and Prothro, 1966; Meier and Rudwick, 1973; Oberschall, 1973; Piven and Cloward, 1977).

In the standard account, various factors are argued to be the driving force behind the sit-ins, including impatience of the young, mass media coverage, outside resources made available by the liberal white community of the North, and support form the Federal Government. Although these writers differ over the proximate causes of the sit-ins, they nevertheless concur that the sit-ins broke from the organizational and institutional framework of the emerging Civil Rights movement. The data for the present study do not fit this standard account and suggest that a different account and interpretation of the sit-ins is warranted. The purpose of this paper is to present new data on the Southern student sit-in movement of 1960, and to provide a framework that will theoretically order the empirical findings.

THEORETICAL CONTEXT AND PROPOSITIONS

Classical collective behavior theory and the recently formulated resource mobilization theory are the major sociological frameworks that attempt to provide explanations of the origins, development, and outcomes of social movements. Classical collective behavior theory (e.g. Blumer, 1946; Turner and Killian, 1957; Lang and Lang, 1961; and Smesler, 1963) maintains that social movements differ substantially from institutionalized behavior. Social movements are theorized to be relatively spontaneous and unstructured. Movement participants are often portrayed as nonrational actors

From *American Sociological Review* 46 (December 1981): 744–767. Reprinted with the permission of the author and the American Sociological Association.

* Direct all communications to Aldon Morris, Center for Research on Social Organization, University of Michigan, 330 Packard, Ann Arbor, Michigan 48109.

I would like to thank Kim Myles, Walter Allen, Michael Schwartz, Charles Perrow, Lewis Coser, Doug McAdam, Mayer Zald, William Gamson, and Charles Tilly for their helpful comments on this paper. The debt that I owe movement participants who consented to be interviewed will be obvious. A special thanks to Sheila Wilder and Debbie Snovak who labored through several drafts of this paper. Finaly I thank two anonymous ASR Reviewers for extremely valuable comments. This research was partially supported by the ASA Minority Fellowship Program and a grant from the National Science Foundation SOC 76-20171.

functioning outside of normative constraints and propelled by high levels of strain.

Classical collective behavior theorists do not deny that organizations and institutional processes play a role in collective behavior. Rather, organizations and institutional processes emerge in the course of movements and become important in their later stages. The standard account of the sit-ins fits the collective behavior imagery. Indeed, it can be argued that the diverse proponents of the "standard account" have been unduly influenced by classical collective behavior theory; their account largely ignores the organizational and institutional framework out of which the sit-ins emerged and spread.

The resource mobilization explanation (e.g. Oberschall, 1973; Gamson, 1975; Tilly, 1978; McCarthy and Zald, 1973) of social movements differs markedly from classical collective behavior theory. In this view, social movements have no distinct inner logic and are not fundamentally different from institutionalized behavior. Organizations, institutions, pre-existing communication networks, and rational actors are all seen as important resources playing crucial roles in the emergence and outcome of collective action. In contrast to classical collective behavior theory, organizational and institutional structures are argued to be central throughout the entire process of collective action.

In its present formulation, resource mobilization theory is unclear about the type of organization and resources that are crucial for the initiation and spread of collective action. Some theorists (Oberschall, 1973; McCarthy and Zald, 1973; Jenkins and Perrow, 1977) argue that resources and organizations outside the protest group are crucial in determining the scope and outcomes of collective action. External groups and resources are argued to be especially critical for movements of the poor. In other formulations of this approach (e.g. Gamson, 1975; Tilly, 1978), emphasis is placed on the important role that internal organization plays in collective action. However, internal organization is but one of several variables (e.g. repression, bureaucracy, opportunity) that are investigated. In my view such an approach fails to capture the degree to which collective action is dependent on internal organization.

This paper focuses on the central function that internal organization played in the emergence and development of the sit-in movement. My analysis suggests that one-sided emphases on spontaneous processes or outside resources can lead to unwarranted neglect of internal structure. A case will be made that the diffusion of the 1960s sit-ins cannot be understood without treating internal organization as a central variable. The analysis will be guided by three propositions.

Proposition 1. Pre-existing social structures provide the resources and organizations that are crucial to the initiation and spread of collective action. Following Tilly (1978), collective action is defined here as joint action by protest groups in pursuit of common ends. This proposition maintains that collective action is rooted in organizational structure and carried out by rational actors attempting to realize their ends. This proposition is central to resource-mobilization theory and has received considerable support from a number of empirical studies (Oberschall, 1973; Gamson, 1975; Tilly, 1975).

Proposition 2. The extent and distribution of internal social organization will determine the extent to which innovations in collective strategy and tactics are adopted, spread, and sustained. This proposition directs attention to a protest group's internal organization—its "local movement centers." A local movement center is that component of social structure within a local community that organizes and coordinates collective action. A local movement center has two major properties. First, it includes all protest organizations and leaders of a specific community that are actively engaged in organizing and producing collective action. During the sit-ins, the Southern Christian Leadership Conference (SCLC), Youth Councils of the National Association for the Advancement of Colored People (NAACP), Congress of Racial Equality (CORE), and "direct action" churches existed in numerous Southern black communities. A local center within the Civil Rights movement included all these organizations and leaders. Second, a local movement center contains a unit that coordinates protest activities within the local movement and between the local center and other institutions of the larger community. During the Civil Rights movement, a particular church usually served as the local coordinating unit. Through this unit the protest activities of the church community, college community, activist organizations, and their leaders were mobilized and coordinated. Thus, movement centers provide the organization and coordination capable of sustaining and spreading collective action.

Proposition 3. There is an interaction between the type of pre-existing internal organization and the type of innovations in strategy and tactics that can be rapidly adopted and spread by a protest group. This proposition addresses the issue of why a protest group adopts a particular tactical innovation rather than another.[1] Whereas Proposition 2 maintains that diffusion of an innovation in strategy is a function of the development and spread of internal social organization, Proposition 3 specifies that certain types of organization are more conducive than others to the diffusion and adoption of certain types of tactical innovation.

In short, the framework for the analysis of the 1960 sit-ins consists of three interrelated propositions. One, collective action is initiated through pre-existing structures. Two, tactical innovation within a movement is a function of well-developed and widespread internal organization. Three, the type of innovation in strategy and tactics which can be rapidly disseminated and sustained is largely determined by the characteristic internal organization of a protest group.

DATA

This study of the sit-ins is part of a larger study on the origins of the Civil Rights movement (Morris, forthcoming). A substantial part of the data were collected from primary sources—archives and interviews with Civil Rights participants. The archival research was conducted at various sites between May and September of 1978.[2] Thousands of original documents (i.e. memoranda, letters, field reports, organizational histories and directives, interorganizational correspondences, etc.) generated by movement participants were examined. These data contained a wealth of information pertaining to key variables—organization, mobilization, finance, rationality, spontaneity—relevant to the study of movements.

Interviews with participants of the movement constituted the second source of data. Detailed interviews

with over 50 Civil Rights leaders were conducted. Interviews made it possible to follow-up on many issues raised by the archival data; and, since these interviews were semi-open-ended, they revealed unexpected insights into the movement. Whenever statements were heard that seemed novel or promising, interviewees were given freedom to speak their piece.

METHODS

The strategy for the archival research was straightforward. The researcher examined every document possible within the time allocated for a particular site.[3] The main objective was to examine the roles played in the sit-ins by variables associated with Weberian theory and theories of collective behavior and resource mobilization. Following collective behavior theory, I was concerned with the extent to which the sit-ins were spontaneous and discontinuous with established social structure. From Weberian theory I was interested in whether a charismatic attraction between a leader and followers was sufficient to produce the heavy volume of collective action in the 1960 sit-ins. Finally, several issues addressed by resource mobilization theory were of interest. I examined archival sources to ascertain the role of social organization and resources in the sit-ins. Also, I was concerned with whether the leadership, money, and skills behind the sit-ins were supplied by outsiders or by the indigenous Southern black community.

Three strategies were employed in the interview process. First, the researcher attempted to learn as much as possible about the movement from extensive library and archival sources before conducting interviews. This prior knowledge enabled the interviewer to ask specific questions and to assist interviewees in rooting their memories in the social, temporal, and geographical context of their actions twenty years earlier. Prior knowledge enabled the interviewer to gain the respect of interviewees and increased the likelihood that they would approach the interview in a serious manner.

Second, the interviews were semistructured, usually lasting two or three hours. An extended list of questions structured around the variables used in the archival

---

[1] Why, for example, did the "teach-ins" spread rapidly between college campuses during the mid-sixties? This proposition suggests that the teach-in tactic was especially suited to the university-based internal organization of the white student movement. In its essentials the teach-in innovation was academically oriented and could be implemented by academic types who were entrenched in the "movement centers" of the various universities involved in the movement. Lecture halls, libraries, film clips, study groups, seminar notes, etc. were the pre-existing indigenous resources used by agents of the movement via the teach-ins.

[2] King papers at Boston University; SCLC papers at the Southern Christian Leadership Conference headquartered in Atlanta; Rev. Kelly Miller Smith's papers housed at First Baptist Church of Nashville.

[3] All of the King papers at Boston University and all of SCLC's files in Atlanta were examined, as well as the portion of Rev. Smith's papers dealing with the sit-ins.

research were formulated beforehand. The interviewees were instructed to feel free to deviate from the questions and to discuss what they thought to be important. Their "diversions" produced new information.

Third, the interview sample was assembled in two ways. While examining the archival material, the names of leaders associated with various activities turned up constantly. These were the initial individuals contacted for interviews. Once the interview process was underway, interviewees would invariably remark, often in response to queries, "you know, you really should speak to [so-and-so] regarding that matter." Subsequent interviews were arranged with many of these individuals. Thus, the snowball effect was central to the sampling process. Although the activists interviewed came from numerous organizations and represented different, if not conflicting, viewpoints, to our surprise they agreed on many basic issues.

Given that the sit-in movement occurred twenty years ago, it is reasonable to wonder whether interview accounts are reliable and valid. Moreover, there is the suspicion that participants might have vested interests in presenting the "facts" in such a way as to enhance their own status. Such problems of recall and vested interest have been minimized in this research because the anlaysis is not based on any one source. Rather, it is built on an array of published material, archival sources, and accounts of individuals who participated in and were eye-witnesses to the same events. Furthermore, cross references were made throughout the data collection process. Follow-up phone calls were made to clarify ambiguity and to obtain a comprehensive view of the sit-in movement. It appears that neither of these potential trouble spots produced fundamental defects in the data.

EARLY SIT-INS: FORERUNNERS

The first myth regarding the sit-in movement is that it started in Greensboro, North Carolina, on February 1, 1960. This research documents that Civil Rights activists conducted sit-ins between 1957 and 1960 in at least fifteen cities: St. Louis, Missouri; Wichita and Kansas City, Kansas; Oklahoma City, Enid, Tulsa, and Stillwater, Oklahoma; Lexington and Louisville, Kentucky; Miami, Florida; Charleston, West Virginia; Sumter, South Carolina; East St. Louis, Illinois; Nashville, Tennessee; and Durham, North Carolina.[4]

The Greensboro sit-ins are important because they represent a unique link in a long chain of sit-ins. Although this paper concentrates on the uniqueness of the Greensboro link, there were important similarities in the entire chain. While other studies (Southern Regional Council, 1960; Oppenheimer, 1964; Matthews and Prothro, 1966; Meier and Rudwick, 1973) have not totally overlooked these earlier sit-ins, they fail to reveal their scope, connections, and extensive organizational base.

The early sit-ins were initiated by direct-action organizations. From interviews with participants in the early sit-ins (Moore, 1978; McCain, 1978; Lawson, 1978; Smith, 1978; McKissick, 1978, 1979; Luper, 1981; Randolph, 1981; Lewis, 1981) and published works (Southern Regional Council, 1960; Meier and Rudwick, 1973), I found that Civil Rights organizations initiated sit-ins in fourteen of the fifteen cities I have identified. The NAACP, primarily its Youth Councils, either initiated or co-initiated sit-ins in nine of the fifteen cities. CORE, usually working with the NAACP, played an important initiating role in seven of the fifteen cities. The SCLC initiated one case and was involved in another. Finally, the Durham Committee on Negro Affairs, working with the NAACP, initiated sit-ins in that city. From this data, we can conclude that these early sit-ins were a result of a multi-faceted organizational effort.

These sit-ins received substantial backing from their respective communities. The black church served as the major institutional force behind the sit-ins. Over two decades ago, E. Franklin Frazier argued that "for the Negro masses, in their social and moral isolation in American society, the Negro church community has been a nation within a nation" (Frazier, 1963:49). He argued that the church functioned as the central political arena in black society. Nearly all of the direct-action organizations that initiated these early sit-ins were closely associated with the church. The church supplied these organizations not only with an established communication network, but also leaders and organized masses, finances, and a safe environment in which to hold political meetings. Direct-action organizations clung to the church because their survival depended on it.

Not all black churches supported the sit-ins. The many that did often supported sit-ins in a critical but "invisible" manner. Thus, Mrs. Clara Luper, the organizer of the 1958 Oklahoma City sit-ins, wrote that the black church did not want to get involved, but church leaders told organizers, "we could meet in their churches. They would take up a collection for us and

---

[4] I suspect that further research will reveal that sit-ins occurred in more than these fifteen cities between 1957 and 1960.

make announcements concerning our worthwhile activities" (Luper, 1979:3). This "covert" role was central. Interviewed activists revealed that clusters of churches were usually directly involved with the sit-ins. In addition to community support generated through the churches, these activists also received support from parents whose children were participating in demonstrations.

These sit-ins were organized by established leaders of the black community. The leaders did not spontaneously emerge in response to a crisis, but were organizational actors in the full sense of the word. Some sit-in leaders were also church leaders, taught school, and headed up the local direct-action organization, their extensive organizational linkages provided blocks of individuals to serve as demonstrators. Clara Luper wrote, "The fact that I was teaching American History at Dungee High School in Spencer, Oklahoma and was a member of the First Street Baptist Church furnished me with an ample number of young people who would become the nucleus of the Youth Council" (Luper, 1979:1). Mrs. Luper's case is not isolated; leaders of the early sit-ins were enmeshed in organizational networks and were integral members of the black community.

Rational planning was evident in this early wave of sit-ins. During the late fifties, the Revs. James Lawson and Kelly Miller Smith, both leaders of a direct-action organization—Nashville Christian Leadership Council—formed what they called a "nonviolent workshop." In these workshops, Lawson meticulously taught local college students the philosophy and tactics of nonviolent protest (D. Bevel, 1978; Lewis, 1978).[5] In 1959, these students held "test" sit-ins in two department stores. Earlier, in 1957, members of the Oklahoma City NAACP Youth Council created what they called their "project," whose aim was to eliminate segregation in public accommodations (Luper, 1979:3). The project consisted of various committees and groups who planned sit-in strategies. After a year of planning, this group walked into the local Katz Drug Store and initiated their sit-in. In St. Louis in 1955, William Clay organized an NAACP Youth Council. Through careful planning and twelve months of demonstrations, members of this orgnaization were able to desegregate dining facilities at department stores (Meier and Rudwick, 1973:93). In Durham, North Carolina in 1958, black activists of the Durham Committee on Negro Affairs conducted a survey of 5-and-10-cent stores in Durham (Southern Regional Council, 1960). The survey revealed that these stores were heavily dependent on black trade. Clearly, the sit-ins initiated by this group were based on rational planning. A similar picture emerges in Sumter, South Carolina and for all the early sit-ins.

Finally, these early sit-ins were sponsored by indigenous resources of the black community; the leadership was black, the bulk of the demonstrators were black, the strategies and tactics were formulated by blacks, and the finances came out of the pockets of blacks, while their serene spirituals echoed through the churches.[6]

Most of the organizers of the early sit-ins knew each other and were well aware of each other's strategies of confrontation. Many of these activists were part of the militant wing of the NAACP. Following the Montgomery bus boycott, this group began to reorganize NAACP Youth Councils with the explicit purpose of initiating direct-action projects. This group of activists (e.g., Floyd McKissick, Daisy Bates, Ronald Walters, Hosea Williams, Barbara Posey, Clara Luper, etc.) viewed themselves as a distinct group, because the national NAACP usually did not approve of their direct-action approach or took a very ambivalent stance.

These militants of the NAACP built networks that detoured the conservative channels and organizational positions of their superiors. At NAACP meetings and conferences, they selected situations where they could present freely their plans and desires to engage in confrontational politics. At these gatherings, information regarding strategies was exchanged. Once acquainted, the activists remained in touch by phone and mail.

Thus, it is no accident that the early sit-ins occurred between 1957 and 1960. Other instances of "direct action" also occurred during this period. For example,

---

[5] Actual names of movement participants are used in this study rather than pseudonyms. I decided to use actual names because my study focuses on real places, movements, and activists. This approach will assist other researchers in evaluating the interview data, since they will know who said what and can conduct further interviews if the need arises. In addition, the respondents had a story to convey and expressed no desires to remain anonymous.

[6] It could legitimately be argued that outside resources were central to these early sit-ins, given that in some cases CORE was involved. However, it seems that the emerging black, direct-action organizations of the late 1950s and the church served as a resource base for CORE. Thus, CORE, which was very small at the time, "piggybacked" on indigenous resources of the black community. Elsewhere (1980) I have presented supporting data for this argument. Meier and Rudwick's account of early CORE suggests a similar conclusion.

Mrs. Daisy Bates led black students affiliated with her NAACP Youth Council into the all-white Little Rock Central High School and forced President Eisenhower to send in National Guards. CORE, beginning to gain a foothold in the South, had the explicit goal of initiating direct-action projects. We have already noted that CORE activists were in close contact with other activists of the period. Though these early sit-ins and related activities were not part of a grandiose scheme, their joint occurrences, timing, and approaches were connected via organizational and personal networks.

SIT-IN CLUSTER

Organizational and personal networks produced the first cluster of sit-ins in Okalahoma in 1958. By tracing these networks, we can arrive at a basic understanding of this cluster and a clue to understanding the entire sit-in movement.

In August of 1958, the NAACP Youth Council of Wichita, Kansas, headed by Ronald Walters, initiated sit-ins at the lunch counters of a local drug store (Lewis, 1981). At the same time, Clara Luper and the young people in her NAACP Youth Council were training to conduct sit-ins in Oklahoma City. The adult leaders of these two groups knew each other: in addition to working for the same organization, several members of the two groups were personal friends. Following the initial sit-ins in Wichita, members of the two groups made numerous phone calls, exchanged information, and discussed mutual support. This direct contact was important because the local press refused to cover the sit-ins. In less than a week, Clara Luper's group in Oklahoma City initiated their planned sit-ins.

Shortly thereafter, sit-ins were conducted in Tulsa, Enid, and Stillwater, Oklahoma. Working through CORE and the local NAACP Youth Council, Clara Luper's personal friend, Mrs. Shirley Scaggins, organized the sit-ins in Tulsa (Luper, 1981). Mrs. Scaggins had recently lived in Oklahoma City and knew the details of Mrs. Luper's sit-in project. The two leaders worked in concert. At the same time, the NAACP Youth Council in Enid began to conduct sit-ins. A Mr. Mitchell who led that group (Luper, 1981) knew Mrs. Luper well. He had visited the Oklahoma Youth Council at the outset of their sit-in and discussed with them sit-in tactics and mutual support. The Stillwater sit-ins appear to have been conducted independently by black college students.

A process similar to that in Oklahoma occurred in East St. Louis, Illinois. Homer Randolph, who in late 1958 organized the East St. Louis sit-ins, had previ-ously lived in Oklahoma City, knew Mrs. Luper well, and had young relatives who participated in the Oklahoma City sit-ins.

In short, the first sit-in cluster occurred in Oklahoma in 1958 and spread to cities within a hundred-mile radius via established organizational and personal networks. The majority of these early sit-ins were (1) connected rather than isolated, (2) initiated through organizations and personal ties, (3) rationally planned and led by established leaders, and (4) supported by indigenous resources. Thus, the Greensboro sit-ins did not mark the movement's beginning, but were links in the chain. But the Greensboro sit-ins were a unique link which triggered sit-ins across the South at an incredible pace. What happened in the black community between the late 1950s and early 1960s to produce such a movement?

EMERGENCE OF INTERNAL ORGANIZATION

During the mid-fifties the extensive internal organization of the Civil Rights movement began to crystalize in communities across the South. During this period "direct action" organizations were being built by local activists. Community institutions—especially the black church—were becoming political. The "mass meeting" with political oratory and protest music became institutionalized. During the same period, CORE entered the South with intentions of initiating protest, and NAACP Youth Councils were reorganized by young militant adults who desired to engage in confrontational politics.

However, neither CORE nor the NAACP Youth Councils were capable of mobilizing wide-scale protest such as the sit-ins of 1960, because neither had a mass base in the black community. CORE was small, Northern-based, and white-led, largely unknown to Southern blacks. Historically, the NAACP had been unable to persuade more than 2% of the black population to become members. Furthermore, the national NAACP was oriented to legal strategies, not sit-ins. Following the 1954 school desegregation decision, the NAACP was further weakened by a severe attack by local white power structures. Members of the Southern white power structures attempted to drive local branches of NAACP out of existence by labeling them subversive and demanding they make their membership public. NAACP officials usually refused to comply with this demand because their members might suffer physical and economic reprisals if identified. NAACP's opponents argued in the local courts that this noncompliance confirmed their suspicion that NAACP was subversive, and the courts responded by issuing injunctions which prevented NAACP from operating in a number of Southern states. For example the NAACP was outlawed in the state of Alabama from 1956 to 1965 (Morris, 1980). This repression forced the NAACP to become defensively-oriented and to commit its resources to court battles designed to save itself. Thus, neither CORE nor NAACP Youth Councils were able to provide the political base required to launch the massive sit-ins of 1960.

Nevertheless, between 1955 and 1960 new organizational and protest efforts were stirring in Southern black communities. The efforts attracted CORE southward and inspired the direct-action groups in the NAACP to reorganize its Youth Councils. The Montgomery bus boycott was the watershed. The importance of that boycott was that it revealed to the black community that mass protests could be successfully organized and initiated through indigenous resources and institutions.

The Montgomery bus boycott gave rise to both the Montgomery Improvement Association (MIA) and the Southern Christian Leadership Conference (SCLC). The MIA was organized in December 1955 to coordinate the activities of the mass bus boycott against segregated buses and to serve as the boycott's official decision-making body. The MIA was a local church-based Southern organization. Its leaderhsip was dominated by local ministers of Montgomery, with the Rev. Martin Luther King serving as its first president. The dramatic Montgomery boycott triggered similar boycotts in a number of Southern cities. As in Montgomery, these boycotts were organized through the churches, with a local minister typically becoming the official leader. SCLC was organized in 1957 by activist clergymen from across the South to coordinate and consolidate the various local movements. SCLC's leadership was dominated by black ministers with King elected as its first president, and the major organizational posts were filled by ministers who led local movements. Thus, SCLC was organized to accomplish across the South what the MIA had in Montgomery. The emergence of MIA and SCLC reflected the dominant role that churches began to play in confrontational politics by the late 1950s.

The Montgomery bus boycott demonstrated the political potential of the black church and church-related direct-action organizations. By 1955 the massive migration of blacks from rural to urban areas was well underway, and many Southern cities had substantial black populations. The black urban churches that emerged in these cities were quite different from their rural counterparts. The urban churches were larger, more numerous, and better financed, and were presided over by ministers who were better educated and whose sole occupation was the ministry (Mays and Nicholson, 1933; McAdam, 1979; Morris, 1980). Moreover, urban churches were owned, operated, and controlled by the black community.

These churches functioned as the institutional base of the Montgomery bus boycott. They supplied the movement with money, organized masses, leaders, highly developed communications, and relatively safe environments where mass meetings could be held to plan confrontations. This institutional base was in place prior to the boycott. Movement leaders transformed the churches into political resources and committed them to the ends of the movement. The new duty of the church finance committee was to collect money for the movement. The minister's new role was to use the pulpit to articulate the political responsibilities of the church community. The new role of the choir was to weave political messages into the serene spirituals. Regular church meetings were transformed into the "mass meeting" where blacks joined committees to guide protests, offered up collections to the movement, and acquired reliable information of the movement, which local radio and television stations refused to broadcast. The resources necessary to initiate a black movement were present in Montgomery and other communities. They were transformed into political resources and used to launch the first highly visible mass protest of the modern Civil Rights movement.

The important role of the MIA in the emergence of the modern Civil Rights movement is seldom grasped. As a nonbureaucratic, church-based organization, MIA's organizational affairs were conducted like church services rather than by rigid bureaucratic rules, as in the case of the NAACP. Ministers presided over the MIA the way they presided over their congregations. Ultimate authority inhered in the president, Dr. King. Decisions pertaining to local matters could be reached immediately. Diverse organizational tasks were delegated to the rank-and-file on the spot. Rules and procedures emerged by trial and error and could be altered when they inhibited direct action. Oratory, music, and charismatic personalities energized MIA's organizational affairs. The structure of the organization was designed to allow masses to participate directly in protest activities. The MIA proved to be appropriate for confrontational politics because it was mass-based, nonbureaucratic, Southern-led, and able to transform pre-existing church resources into political power.

Southern blacks took notice of the Montgomery movement. Activists from across the South visited Montgomery to observe the political roles of the church and the MIA. For example, when Hosea Williams (at that time, an activist associated with the NAACP in Savannah, Georgia) visited the Montgomery movement, he marvelled at its dynamics:

> You had had NAACP lawsuits, you'd had NAACP chapters, who had much less than 5% participation anyplace. But here's a place [Montgomery] where they got masses of blacks—they couldn't get a church big enough where they could hold mass rallies. And then, none of them [masses] were riding the buses. I was interested in these strategies and their implementation and in learning how to mobilize the masses to move in concert. [Williams, 1978]

Williams, like countless others, did more than marvel. In his words, "I went back to Savannah and organized the Youth Council and nonviolent movement." Thus, another direct-action organization emerged.

Black ministers were in the best position to organize church-related direct-action organizations in the South. Even while the Montgomery movement was in progress, ministers in other cities (e.g., Steele in Tallahassee, Shuttlesworth in Birmingham, and Davis in New Orleans) began to build mass-based movements patterned after the Montgomery movement. These ministers were not only in a position to organize and commit church resources to protest efforts, they were also linked to each other and the larger community via ministerial alliances. In short, between 1955 and 1960 a profound change in Southern black communities had begun. Confrontational politics were thrust to the foreground through new direct-action organizations closely allied with the church.

SCLC AND MOVEMENT CENTERS

The creation of the Southern Christian Leadership Conference (SCLC) in 1957 marked a critical organizational shift for the Civil Rights movement. The ministers who organized SCLC clearly understood the historic and central institutional importance of the church in black society. They knew that the church nurtured and produced most of the indigenous leaders, raised finances, and organized masses, as well as being a major force in other aspects of black culture. By 1957 these ministers, many of whom were leading movements in their local communities, consciously and explicitly concluded that the church was capable of functioning as the institutional vanguard of a mass-

based black movement. Hence, they organized SCLC to be a Southern-wide, church-based protest organization.

Prior to SCLC, the major black protest organization—NAACP—had been closely linked with the church. Yet, before SCLC was created, the NAACP, and not the church, functioned as the organization through which protest was initiated. With the emergence of SCLC, the critical shift occurred whereby the church itself, rather than groups closely linked to it, began to function as the institutional center of protest.

In 1957 organizers of SCLC sent out a call to fellow clergymen of the South to organize their congregations and communities for collective protest. The remarks of Rev. Smith of Nashville typified the action of protest-oriented ministers:

> After the meeting [SCLC organizing meeting] and after the discussion that we had and all that, it became clear to me that we needed something in addition to NAACP. So I came back and I called some people together and formed what we named the Nashville Christian Leadership Council in order to address the same kind of issues that SCLC would be addressing. [Smith, 1978]

Hundreds of ministers across the South took similar action.

From this collective effort resulted what can best be conceptualized as local movement centers of the Civil Rights movement, which usually had the following seven characteristics:

1. A cadre of social-change-oriented ministers and their congregations. Often one minister would become the local leader of a given center and his church would serve as the coordinating unit.
2. Direct action organizations of varied complexity. In many cities local churches served as quasi-direct-action organizations, while in others ministers built complex, church-related organizations (e.g., United Defense League of Baton Rouge, Montgomery Improvement Association, Alabama Christian Movement for Human Rights of Birmingham, Petersburg Improvement Association). NAACP Youth Councils and CORE affiliates also were components of the local centers.
3. Indigenous financing coordinated through the church.
4. Weekly mass meetings, which served as forums and where local residents were informed of relevant information and strategies regarding the movement. These meetings also built solidarity among the participants.

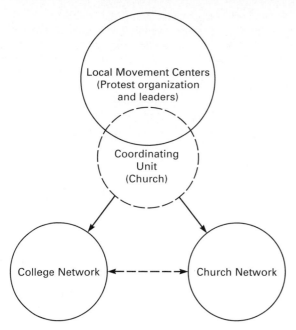

FIGURE 1.   Structure of a Typical Local Movement Center

5. Dissemination of nonviolent tactics and strategies. The leaders articulated to the black community the message that social change would occur only through nonviolent direct action carried out by masses.
6. Adaptation of a rich church culture to political purposes. The black spirituals, sermons, and prayers were used to deepen the participants' commitment to the struggle.
7. A mass-based orientation, rooted in the black community, through the church.

See Figure 1 for a schematic diagram of a typical local movement center.

Most scholars of the movement are silent about the period between the Montgomery bus boycott and the 1960 sit-ins. My analysis emphasizes that the organizational foundation of the Civl Rights movement was built during this period and active local movement centers were created in numerous Southern black communities. For instance, between 1957 and 1960 many local centers emerged in Virginia. Ministers such as Reverends Milton Reid, L. C. Johnson, Virgil Wood, Curtis Harris, and Wyatt Walker operated out of centers in Hopewell, Lynchburg, Portsmouth, and Petersburg. The direct action organizations of these cities were named

Improvement Associations and were patterned after the original MIA. South Carolina also had its movement centers. For example, in 1955–1956, after whites began exerting economic pressure against blacks desiring school integration, the black community of Orangeburg initiated an economic boycott against twenty-three local firms. This extended boycott resulted in a vibrant movement center led by the Reverends Matthew McCollom, William Sample, and Alfred Issac and their congregations. Movement centers emerged in other South Carolina cities, such as Sumter, Columbia, and Florence, organized by James McCain of CORE and activist clergymen.

In Durham, North Carolina, churches that made up the movement center were Union Baptist, pastored by Rev. Grady Davis; Ashbury Temple, pastored by Rev. Douglas Moore; Mount Zion, pastored by Rev. Fuller; St. Marks, pastored by Rev. Speaks; and St. Josephs, pastored by Rev. Swann. Movement centers were also to be found in cities of the deep South such as Montgomery and Birmingham, Alabama; Baton Rouge, Louisiana; and Tallahassee, Florida.

So prevalent were these centers throughout the South that when Gordon Carey, a CORE field investigator, surveyed the situation in 1959, he reported:

> In some Southern cities such as Montgomery, Orangeburg, Tallahassee, and Birmingham nonviolent movements have been and are being carried on. But most of the South, with its near total segregation, has not been touched. Many places have *felt* the *spirit* of Martin Luther King, Jr. but too often this spirit has not been turned into positive action. [Carey, 1959, emphasis added]

The "spirit" to which Carey referred was in fact the church-based movement centers he found throughout the South, most of which were affiliated with or patterned after SCLC.

Elsewhere (Morris, 1980), I have analyzed how, in the late 1950s, these centers were perfecting confrontation strategies, building organizations, leading marches, organizing voter drives, and radicalizing members of the community. Scholars (e.g., Oberschall, 1973:223) persistently dismiss these centers as weak, limited, and unwilling to confront the white power structure. Yet the evidence suggests a different interpretation. For example, Rev. Fred Shuttlesworth and his mass-based movement center continually confronted Bull Connor and the white power structure of Birmingham throughout the late fifties. As a consequence, Shuttlesworth's home and church were repeatedly bombed.

In short, between 1955 and 1960 many local movement centers were formed and hardened. These centers, which included NAACP Youth Councils and CORE chapters, constituted the new political reality of Southern black communities on the eve of the 1960 sit-ins. It was these structures that were able to generate and sustain a heavy volume of collective action.

THE GREENSBORO CONNECTION

On February 1, 1960 Ezell Blair Jr., Franklin McCain, Joe McNeil, and David Richmond, all students at North Carolina Agricultural and Technical College, sat-in at the Woolworth's lunch counter in Greensboro, North Carolina. Though most commentators mark this as the first sit-in, the four protesters knew that they were not the first to sit-in in the state of North Carolina. Sit-in activity in the state had begun in the late fifties, when a young black attorney, Floyd McKissick, and a young Board member of SCLC, Rev. Douglas Moore, and a small group of other young people (including a few whites from Duke University) began conducting sit-ins in Durham.

These early Durham sit-ins were part of the network of sit-ins which occurred between 1957 and 1960. The activists involved in the early sit-ins belonged to the NAACP Youth Division, which McKissick headed, and their own direct-action organization called the Durham Committee on Negro Affairs. During the late fifties, McKissick and Moore's group conducted sit-ins at local bus stations, waiting rooms, parks, hotels, and other places (McKissick, 1978). In 1957, Rev. Moore and others were arrested for sitting-in at a local ice-cream parlor. The subsequent legal case became known as the "Royal Ice Cream Case." McKissick, who also headed the local boy Scout organization, periodically would take the young "all-American scouts into segregated restaurants and order food. In short, this Durham group persistently confronted the white power structure in the late fifties.

The four students who sat-in at Greensboro and sparked the widespread sit-in movement had been members of the NAACP Youth Council, headed by McKissick. According to McKissick, he knew them all well and they knew all about the Durham activities. Martin Oppenheimer (1964:398), an early historian of the sit-ins, confirms this: "All of the boys were, or at some time had been members of an NAACP Youth Council." Indeed, the four students had participated in numerous meetings in social-action oriented churches in Durham. Involvement with the NAACP Youth Council meant that they were not only informed about the Durham sit-ins, but also knew about many of the sit-ins conducted prior to 1960. Thus, the myth that four college students got up one day and sat-in at Woolworth's—and sparked the movement—dries up like a "raisin in the sun" when confronted with the evidence.

The National office of the NAACP and many conservative ministers refused to back the Greensboro sit-ins. The NAACP's renowned team of lawyers did not defend the "Greensboro Four." Nevertheless, on the same day they sat-in, the students contacted a lawyer whom they considered to be their friend, and Floyd McKissick became the lawyer for the "Greensboro Four." The network of college students and adult activists had begun to operate in earnest.

Well-forged networks existed between and among black churches and colleges in North Carolina, facilitated by the large number of colleges concentrated in the state. Indeed, ten black colleges existed within a ten-mile radius of Greensboro (Wolff, 1970:590). Interactions between colleges and churches were both frequent and intense; many colleges were originally founded by the churches. A number of North Carolina churches were referred to as "college churches" because they had large student memberships. These two sets of social organizations were also linked through college seminaries where black ministers received their theological training.

These church-student networks enabled activist-oriented students to become familiar with the emerging Civil Rights movement via local movement centers and made it possible for adult activists to tap the organizational resources of the colleges. Leaders of student governments and other campus groups facilitated student mobilization because they, like the ministers, had organizing skills and access to blocs of people. Moreover, the concentration of colleges in the state provided an extensive network of contacts. Fraternity and sorority chapters linked students within and between campuses, as did dating patterns and joint cultural and athletic events. Finally, intercollegiate kinship and friendship networks were widespread, and student leaders were squarely tied to these networks. Similarly, black communities across North Carolina could be rapidly mobilized through the churches, since churches were linked through ministerial alliances and other networks. By 1960 these diverse and interlocking networks were capable of being politicized and coordinated through existing movement centers, making North Carolina an ideal state for the rapid diffusion of collective action.

TABLE 1.
Number of Cities with Sit-ins and Related Protest Activities, February-March 1960, by State

State	Number
North Carolina	18
Florida	11
Virginia	9
South Carolina	7
Texas	5
Tennessee	4
Alabama	4
Georgia	2
West Virginia	2
Louisiana	2
Arkansas	2
Maryland	1
Ohio	1
Kentucky	1
Total	69

Compiled from: Southern Regional Council. "The student protest movement, winter 1960." SRC-13, April 1 1960 (revised)

Within a week of the Greensboro protest, sit-ins rapidly spread across the South. In an extensive study, the Southern Regional Council (1960) reported that between February 1 and March 31 of 1960, major sit-in demonstrations and related activity had been conducted in at least sixty-nine Southern cities (see Table 1).[7]

BEYOND GREENSBORO

As soon as the sit-ins started in Greensboro, the network of movement centers was activated. In the first week of February, 1960, students continued to sit-in daily at the local Woolworth's, and the protest population began to grow. The original four protesters were joined by hundreds of students from A & T College and several other local black colleges. Black high-school students and a few white college students also joined the protest. Influential local whites decided to close the Woolworth's in Greensboro, hoping to take the steam out of the developing mass-movement. It was too late.

Floyd McKissick, Rev. Douglas Moore, and others who had conducted previous sit-ins formulated plans to spread the movement across the state. They were joined by CORE's white field secretary, Gordon Carey, whose services had been requested by the local NAACP president. Carey arrived in Durham from New York on February the 7th and went directly to McKissick's home, where the sit-ins were being planned. Carey was a good choice because he had knowledge of nonviolent resistance and because of his earlier contact with movement centers in Southern black communities.

On February 8th—exactly one week after the Greensboro sit-ins—the demonstrations spread to nearby Durham and Winston-Salem. McKissick, Moore, Carey, and others helped organize these sit-ins, bringing students from the local colleges to churches where they were trained to conduct sit-ins. For example, the Durham students were trained at the same churches through which McKissick and Moore had planned direct action in the late 1950s. Following training and strategy sessions, the students went to the local lunch counters and sat-in.

The organizing effort was not limited to these two nearby cities. Within the first week of the Greensboro sit-in, McKissick, Carey, and Rev. Moore made contact with activists in movement centers throughout North Carolina, South Carolina, and Virginia, urging them to train students for sit-ins. They not only phoned these activists, but traveled to various cities to provide assistance. Upon arrival they often found sit-in planning sessions already underway. According to Carey (1978), "when we reached these cities we went directly to the movement oriented churches." When asked why, Carey replied, "Well, that's where the protest activities were being planned and organized." Thus, these sit-ins were largely organized at the movement churches rather than on the campuses. To understand the sit-in movement, one must abandon the assumption that it was a collegiate phenomenon. For different reasons, Rev. Moore attempted to convey this same idea in the early days of the sit-ins: "If Woolworth and other stores think this is just another panty raid, they haven't had their sociologists in the field recently" (Moore, 1960). The sit-ins grew out of a context of organized movement centers.

As anticipated above, the Southern Christian Leadership Conference was central to the rise of the 1960 sit-in movement. It is critical to remember that when Rev. Moore and other organizers visited churches in North and South Carolina and Virginia, they discovered that church leaders were already training students for sit-ins. Speaking of the ministers who headed these

---

[7] To appreciate the volume of protest activity engendered by the sit-ins, it is necessary to note that the total number of cities (69) is not a count of actual day-to-day demonstrations, which during these first two months ran into the hundreds if not thousands.

movement churches, Carey (1978) reported, "all of these ministers were active in the Southern Christian Leadership Conference. At least 75% were getting inspiration from King." Additionally, these ministers had contacts with and often were leaders of both CORE and the activist wing of the NAACP.

Since the movement centers were already in place, they served as both receiving and transmitting "antennas" for the sit-ins. As receivers they gathered information of the sit-ins, and as transmitters they rebroadcast information throughout the networks. Because this internal network already existed, information was rapidly channeled to groups prepared to engage in nonviolent collective action.

During the second week of February 1960, plans were formulated to conduct sit-ins in a number of Southern cities. Communication and coordination between the cities was intensified. For example, early in the second week of February, the Rev. B. Elton Cox of High Point, North Carolina, and Rev. C. A. Ivory of Rock Hill, South Carolina, phoned McKissick and other leaders, informing them that their groups were "ready to go" (McKissick, 1978). Cox's group sat-in on February 11th and Ivory's on February 12th. Rev. Ivory organized and directed the Rock Hill sit-ins from his wheelchair. Within the week, sit-ins were being conducted in several cities in Virginia, most of them organized through the dense network of SCLC movement centers in that state (Southern Regional Council, 1960; Walker, 1978).

The movement hot lines reached far beyond the border states of North Carolina, South Carolina, and Virgina. Rev. Fred Shuttlesworth, an active leader of the Birmingham, Alabama, movement center, happened to be in North Carolina when the first wave of sit-ins occurred, fulfilling a speaking engagement for the leader of the High Point sit-ins—Rev. Cox. According to Shuttlesworth, "He [Rev. Cox] carried me by where the people were going to sit-in. . . I called back to Atlanta, and told Ella [Baker] what was going on. I said, 'this is the thing. You must tell Martin [King] that we must get with this, and really this can shake up the world' " (Shuttlesworth, 1978). Baker, the Executive Director of SCLC, immediately began calling her contacts at various colleges, asking them, "What are you all going to do? It is time to move" (Baker, 1978).

Carey and Rev. Moore phoned the movement center in Nashville, Tennessee, and asked Rev. Lawson if they were ready to move. The student and church communities coordinated by the Nashville Christian Leadership Conference answered in the affirmative. According to Lawson,

Of course there was organizing because after the sit-in, the first one in February, people like Doug Moore, Ella Baker, myself, did call around to places that we knew, said, "Can you start? Are you ready? Can you go? And how can we help you?" So there was some of that too that went on. Even there the sit-in movement did not just spread spontaneously. I mean there was a readiness. And then there were, there were phone calls that went out to various communities where we knew people and where we knew student groups and where we knew minister groups, and said, you know, "this is it, let's go." [Lawson, 1978]

When asked, "Why did the student sit-in movement occur?" Lawson replied,

Because King and the Montgomery boycott and the whole development of that leadership that clustered around King had emerged and was ready and was preaching and teaching direct action, nonviolent action, and was clearly ready to act, ready to seed any movement that needed sustenance and growth. So there was . . . in other words, the soil had been prepared. [Lawson, 1978]

These data provide insight into how a political movement can rapidly spread between geographically distant communities. The sit-ins spread across the South in a short period of time because activists, working through local movement centers, planned, coordinated, and sustained them. They spread despite the swinging billy clubs of policemen, despite Ku Klux Klansmen, white mobs, murderers, tear gas, and economic reprisals (Southern Regional Council, 1960; Matthews and Prothro, 1966; Oberschall, 1973). The pre-existing movement centers provided the resources and organization required to sustain the sit-ins in the face of opposition.

SIT-IN CLUSTERS OF 1960

The organizational and personal networks that produced the first cluster of sit-ins in Oklahoma in 1958 have already been described. The cluster concept can be applied to the entire set of sit-ins of February and March 1960. Many of the cities where sit-ins occurred can be grouped by geographic and temporal proximity. A cluster is defined as two or more cities within 75 miles of each other where sit-in activity took place within a span of 14 days. In Table 2, forty-one of the sixty-nine cities having sit-ins during this two-month period have been grouped because they meet these criteria. Within this period 59% of the cities that had sit-

TABLE 2.
Clusters of Cities with Sit-ins and Related Activities, February–March 1960

Cluster	Number of days between first sit-ins within cluster	Maximum number of miles between farthest two cities within cluster
Fayetteville, Raleigh, N.C. (2/9/60–2/10/60)	1	50
Tampa, St. Petersburg, Sarasota, Fla. (2/29/60–3/2/60)	2	50
Montgomery, Tuskegee, Ala. (2/25/60–2/27/60)	2	25
Columbia, Florence, Sumter, S.C. (3/2/60–3/4/60)	2	70
Austin, San Antonio, Tx. (3/11/60–3/13/60)	2	75
Salisbury, Shelby, N.C. (2/16/60–2/18/60)	2	60
Wilmington, New Bern, N.C. (3/17/60–3/19/60)	2	75
Charlotte, N.C., Concord, Rock Hill, S.C. (2/9/60–2/12/60)	3	50
Durham, Winston-Salem, High Point, N.C. (2/8/60–2/11/60)	3	75
Chapel Hill, Henderson, N.C. (2/25/60–2/28/60)	3	50
Jacksonville, St. Augustine, Fla. (3/12/60–3/15/60)	3	40
Charleston, Orangeburg, Denmark, S.C. (2/25/60–2/29/60)	4	70
Daytona Beach, Sanford, Orlando, Fla. (3/2/60–3/7/60)	5	54
Houston, Galveston, Tx. (3/5/60–3/11/60)	6	65
Richmond, Petersburg, Va. (2/20/60–2/27/60)	7	30
Hampton, Norfolk, Portsmouth, Suffolk, Newport News (2/11/60–2/22/60)	11	35

Compiled from: Southern Regional Council. "The student protest movement, winter 1960." SRC-13, April 1 1960

ins and related activity were part of clusters. The percentage of these cities forming sit-in clusters is even more striking in the first month: during February, 76% of cities having sit-ins were part of clusters, while during March the percentage dropped to 44%.

The clustering differentials between the two months can be explained by taking region into account as shown in Table 3. In the first month (February) 85% of the cities having sit-ins were located in Southeastern and border states. This pattern had been established earlier, when most of the pre-1960 sit-ins occurred in border states. Most of the February sit-ins took place in cities of border states because repression against blacks was not as severe there as in the deep South. This made it possible for activists in border states to build dense networks of movement centers. We have already seen that North Carolina, South Carolina, and Virginia had numerous social-action churches and direct-action organizations. By the time the sit-ins occurred in Virginia, SCLC had affiliates throughout the state, and Rev. Wyatt Walker, who was the leader of Virginia's movement centers, was also the state

TABLE 3.

Cities with Sit-ins and Related Activities, February–March 1960, by Geographic Region

	Deep South	Southeastern and Border States	Non-South	All States
February–March 1960				
Number of cities with sit-ins, 2-month total	26	42	1	69
Region's % of 2-month total	38	61	1	100
February 1960				
Number of cities with sit-ins	5	28	0	33
Region's % of Feb. total	15	85	0	100
% of 2-month total occurring in Feb.	19	67	0	48
March 1960				
Number of cities with sit-ins	21	14	1	36
Region's % of March total	58	39	3	100
% of 2-month total occurring in March	81	33	100	52

Compiled from: Southern Regional Council. "The student protest movement, winter 1960." SRC-13, April 1 1960
Note: Deep South states are Alabama, Florida, Georgia, Texas, Arkansas, and Louisiana. Southeastern and Border states are South Carolina, North Carolina, Virginia, Tennessee, Maryland, Kentucky, and West Virginia. The non-South state is Ohio.

Director of CORE and President of the local NAACP. Similar patterns existed in the other border states. Small wonder that in the month of February, 73% of cities having sit-ins were located in Virginia, North Carolina, and South Carolina. Similarly, these cities produced 88% of the February clusters. This clustering reflected both the great density of movement centers and a system of domination less stringent than that of the deep South.

Table 3 reveals that in March a major change took place: the majority of the sit-ins occurred in cities of the deep South. With a few exceptions, the sit-ins in the deep South did not occur in clusters. They occurred almost exclusively in Southern cities where movement centers were already established: Montgomery and Birmingham, Alabama; Baton Rouge and New Orleans, Louisiana; Tallahasee, Florida; Nashville and Memphis, Tennessee; and Atlanta and Savannah, Georgia. Repression would have been too great on student protesters operating outside of the protection of such centers in the deep South. Thus, the decrease in clustering in the deep South reflected both the high level of repression and the absence of dense networks of movement centers. Focusing on the internal movement centers enables us to explain both the clustering phenomenon and its absence.

Given the large proportion of sit-ins occurring in clusters, we can say that they did not spread randomly.

The clusters represented the social and temporal space in which sit-ins were organized, coordinated, spread, and financed by the black community.[8] Within these clusters, cars filled with organizers from SCLC, NAACP, and CORE raced between sit-in points relaying valuable information. Telephone lines and the community "grapevine" sent forth protest instructions and plans. These clusters were the sites of numerous midday and late night meetings where the black community assembled in the churches, filled the collection plates, and vowed to mortgage their homes to raise the necessary bail-bond money in case the protesting students were jailed. Black lawyers pledged their legal services to the movement and black physicians made their services available to injured demonstrators. Amidst these exciting scenes, black spirituals that had grown out of slavery calmed and deepened the participants' commitment. A detailed view of the Nashville sit-ins provides an example of these dynamics, because the Nashville movement epitomized the sit-ins whether they occurred singularly or in clusters.

---

[8] Cities identified as part of a particular cluster may actually be part of another cluster(s). I assume that the probability of shared organization and coordination of sit-ins is high if two or more cities within a 75-mile radius had sit-ins within a two-week period. My data and analysis generally confirm this assumption.

THE NASHVILLE SIT-IN MOVEMENT

A well-developed, church-based movement center headed by Rev. Kelly Miller Smith was organized in Nashville during the late 1950s. The center, an affiliate of SCLC, was called the Nashville Christian Leadership Council (NCLC). Rev. James Lawson, an expert tactician of nonviolent protest, was in charge of NCLC's direct-action committee. Lawson received a call from Rev. Douglas Moore about two days after the Greensboro sit-ins began. The Nashville group was ready to act because a cadre of students had already received training in nonviolent direct action. They had conducted "test sit-ins" in two large department stores in downtown Nashville prior to the 1959 Christmas holidays. Moreover, the group had already made plans in late 1959 to begin continuous sit-ins in 1960 with the explicit intention of desegregating Nashville (Smith, 1978; D. Bevel, 1978). Thus, Greensboro provided the impetus for the Nashville group to carry out its preexisting strategy.

Rev. Smith's First Baptist Church became the coordinating unit of the Nashville sit-in movement. A decision to sit-in at local lunch counters on Saturday, February 13, 1960, was arrived at after much debate. The adults (mostly ministers) of the NCLC met with the students at movement headquarters and tried to convince them to postpone the demonstrations for a couple of days until money could be raised. According to Rev. Smith (1978), "NCLC had $87.50 in the treasury. We had no lawyers, and we felt kind of a parental responsibility for those college kids. And we knew they were gonna be put in jail, and we didn't know what else would happen. And so some of us said, 'we need to wait until we get a lawyer, until we raise some funds.' "

NCLC leaders told the students that they could collect the money through the churches within a week. Then, according to Rev. Smith:

> James Bevel, then a student at American Baptist Theological Seminary, said that, "I'm sick and tired of waiting," which was a strange thing to come from a kid who was only about nineteen years old. You see, the rest of us were older . . . [Bevel said] "If you asked us to wait until next week, then next week something would come up and you'd say wait until the next week and maybe we never will get our freedom." He said this, "I believe that something will happen in the situation that will make for the solution to some of these problems we're talking about." So we decided to go on. [Smith, 1978]

The proximity of four black colleges in Nashville—Fisk University, Tennessee State College, American Baptist Theological Seminary, and Meharry Medical School—facilitated the mobilization of large numbers of students. In its extensive ties between students and churches, Nashville resembled the state of North Carolina. Indeed, John Lewis, James Bevel, and Bernard Lafayette, who became major sit-in leaders, were students at the American Baptist Theological seminary and were taught there by Rev. Smith. Furthermore, they were student leaders:

> John Lewis, Bernard and myself were the major participants in the seminary. All of us were like the top student leaders in our schools. I think John at the time was the president of the Student Council. I was a member of the Student Council. I was one of the editors of the yearbook. Bernard was an editor of the yearbook. So all of us were like the top leaders in our school. [J. Bevel, 1978]

Thus the student leaders could rapidly mobilize other students because they already had access to organized groups. Other writers (Von Eschen et al., 1971; McAdam, 1979) have pointed out that these college networks played a key role in sit-in mobilization. However, the sit-in movement cannot be explained without also noting the crucial interaction between black college students and local movement centers. Speaking of Rev. Smith and his church, Bevel recalled, "the First Baptist basically had the Baptist people who went to Fisk and Meharry and Tennessee State, and the Seminary were basically members of his church" (J. Bevel, 1978). These students had been introduced to the Civil Rights movement while they attended church.

On the first day of the sit-ins in Nashville, students gathered in front of their respective campuses. NCLC sent cars to each college to transport the students to Rev. Smith's church. Again, the major organizational tasks were performed in the church which served as the coordinating unit of the local movement center, rather than on the campuses. Coordination of sit-in activity between the college community and the churches was made less difficult because many of the students (especially student leaders) were immersed in the local movement centers prior to the sit-ins. The pattern of close connection between student demonstrators and adult leaders had already existed in places such as Greensboro and even Oklahoma City in 1958; indeed, this pattern undergirded the entire movement. Rev. Jemison's (1978) remark that the Baton Rouge sit-in demonstrators "were schooled right over there at our church; they were sent out from here to go to the lunch counters" typifies the relationship between the students and the local movement centers.[9] Jemison continued, "The student leaders attended church here. We had close ties because they were worshipping with us while we were working together."

Once the Nashville students arrived at movement headquarters, they particpated in workshops where they learned the strategies of nonviolent confrontation from experts like Rev. Lawson, Rev. Metz Rollins, Rev. C. T. Vivian, and the core group of students that Lawson had already trained. This pool of trained leaders was a pre-existing resource housed by NCLC. After the workshops, the students were organized into groups with specific protest responsibilities, each having a spokesperson who had been trained by Lawson during the late 1950s. They then marched off to confront Nashville's segregated lunch counters and agents of social control.

The adult black community immediately mobilized to support the students. Shortly after the demonstrations began, large numbers of students were arrested. According to Rev. Smith,

> We just launched out on something that looked perfectly crazy and scores of people were being arrested, and paddy wagons were full and the people out in downtown couldn't understand what was going on, people just welcoming being arrested, that ran against everything they had ever seen. . . . I've forgotten how much we needed that day, and we got everything we needed. [That particular day?] Yes, sir. About $40,000. We needed something like $40,000 in fives. And we had all the money. Not in fives, but in bail. Every bit of it came up. You know—property and this kind of thing . . . and there were fourteen black lawyers in this town. Every black lawyer made himself available to us. [Smith, 1978]

Thus, basic, pre-existing resources in the dominated community were used to accomplish political goals. It was suggested to Rev. Smith that a massive movement such as that in Nashville would need outside resources. He replied,

> Now let me quickly say to you that in early 1960, when we were really out there on the line, the community

stood up. We stood together. This community had proven that this stereotyped notion of black folk can't work together is just false. We worked together a lot better than the white organizations. So those people fell in line. [Smith, 1978]

Rev. Smith's comments are applicable beyond Nashville. For example, in Orangeburg, after hundreds of students were arrested and brutalized, the adult black community came solidly to their aid. Bond was set at $200 per student, and 388 students were arrested. Over $75,000 was needed, and adults came forth to put up their homes and property in order to get students out of jail. Rev. McCollom, the leader of the Orangeburg movement center, remarked that, "there was no schism between the student community and the adult community in Orangeburg" (McCollom, 1978). Jim McCain (1978) of CORE, who played a central role in organizing sit-ins across South Carolina and in Florida, reported that community support was widespread. According to Julian Bond (1980), a student leader of Atlanta's sit-ins, "black property owners put up bond which probably amounted to $100,000" to get sit-in demonstrators released from jail.

These patterns were repeated across the South. This community support should not be surprising, considering the number of ministers and congregations involved before and during the movement. Yet, Zinn, an eyewitness to many of these events, wrote, "Spontaneity and self-sufficiency were the hallmarks of the sit-ins; without adult advice or consent, the students planned and carried them through" (1964:29). This myopia illustrates the inadequacies of analyses that neglect or ignore the internal structure of oppressed communities and protest movements.

The continuing development of the Nashville sit-ins sheds further light on the interdependence of the movement and the black community. A formal structure called the Nashville Nonviolent Movement was developed to direct sit-in activities. Its two substructures, the Student Central Committee and the Nashville Christian Leadership Council, worked closely together and had overlapping membership (Reverends Lawson and Vivian were members of both groups). The Central Committee usually consisted of 25 to 30 students drawn from all the local colleges. NCLC represented adult ministers and the black community. The two groups established committees to accomplish specific tasks, including a finance committee, a telephone, publicity, and news committee, and a work committee. The work committee had subgroups responsible for painting

---

[9] For further evidence of the centrality of student-church ties in other cities that had sit-ins see Morris, forthcoming.

protest signs and providing food and transportation. The city's black lawyers became the movement's defense team, students from Meharry Medical School were the medical team.

This intricate structure propelled and guided the sit-in movement of Nashville. A clear-cut division of labor developed between the Central Committee and the NCLC. The Central Committee's major responsibilities were to train, organize, and coordinate the demonstration. The NCLC developed the movement's financial structure and coordinated relations between the community and the student movement. Diane Nash Bevel, a major student leader of the Nashville sit-ins, was asked why the students did not take care of their own finances and build their own relationships with the larger community. She replied,

> We didn't want to be bothered keeping track of money that was collected at the rallies and stuff. We were just pleased that NCLC would do that, and would handle the bookkeeping and all that trouble that went along with having money. . . . Besides, we were much too busy sitting-in and going to jail and that kind of thing. There wasn't really the stability of a bookkeeper, for instance. We didn't want to be bothered with developing that kind of stability. . . . We were very pleased to form this alliance with NCLC who would sponsor the rallies and coordinate the community support among the adults and keep track of the money, while we sat-in and . . . well, it took all our time, and we were really totally immersed in it. My day would sometimes start . . . well we'd have meetings in the morning at six o'clock, before classes, and work steady to extremely late at night, organizing the sit-ins, getting publicity out to the students that we were having a sit-in, and where and what time we would meet. Convincing people, and talking to people, calming people's fears, going to class, at the same time. It was a really busy, busy time for all of the people on the Central committee. We were trying to teach nonviolence, maintain order among a large, large number of people. That was about all we could handle. [D. Bevel, 1978]

Students are ideal participants in protest activities. Usually they do not have families to support, employers' rules and dictates to follow, and crystallized ideas as to what is "impossible" and "unrealistic." Students have free time and boundless energy to pursue causes they consider worthwhile and imperative (Lipset and Wolin, 1965:3; McCarthy and Zald, 1973:10). McPhail's (1971:1069) finding that young, single, unemployed males were ideal participants in civil disorders and

McPhail and Miller's (1973:726) discussion of availability for participation in the assembly process parallels this notion that students are ideal participants in protest activities. Nevertheless, although black students were able to engage in protest activities continuously because of their student status, a one-sided focus on them diverts attention from the larger community, which had undergone considerable radicalization. Speaking of the adults, James Bevel (1978), a student organizer of the Nashville sit-ins, remarked, "But when you talk to each individual, they talked just like we talked—the students. They had jobs and they were adults. But basically, their position would be just like ours. They played different roles because they were in different—they had to relate based on where they were in the community" (J. Bevel, 1978).

The adults of the NCLC organized the black community to support the militant student sit-in movement. Once the movement began, NCLC instituted weekly and sometimes daily mass meetings in the churches. Rev. Smith (1978) recalled,

> Sometimes we had them more than once a week if we needed to. When things were really hot we called a meeting at eight o'clock in the morning. We'd call one for twelve that day, twelve noon, and the place would be full. We had what we called our wire service. People got on telephones, that was our wire service, and they would fill that building. They'd fill that building in just a matter of relatively short time.

At these mass meetings, ministers from across the city turned over the money that their respective churches had donated to the movement. Thousands of dollars were collected at the mass meetings while black adults, ministers, and students sang such lyrics as "Before I'd be a slave, I'd rather be buried in my grave." Then too, bundles of leaflets were given to adults at mass meetings who then distributed them throughout the black community. This shows how the movement built communication channels through which vital information, strategies, and plans were disseminated.

During the Nashville sit-ins, word went out to the black community not to shop downtown.

> We didn't organize the boycott. We did not organize the boycott. The boycott came about. We don't know how it happened. I tell you there are a lot of little mystical elements in there, little spots that defy rational explanation. . . . Now, we promoted it. We adopted it. But we did not sit down one day and organize a boycott. . . . ninety-nine percent of the black people in this commu-

nity stayed away from downtown during the boycott. It was a fantastic thing—successful. It was fantastically successful. [Smith, 1978]

Yet the boycott was largely organized by NCLC. According to Bevel, Dr. Vivian Henderson, who was head of Fisk University's economic department and a member of NCLC, played a key role in the boycott, because

> Vivian Henderson was basically responsible for calling the boycott. He got up at a mass meeting and said, "at least what we could do to support students, if we've got any decency, we can just stop paying bills and just don't shop until this thing is resolved." A very indignant type of speech he made. It just caught on. All the bourgeois women would come to the meeting, and they just got on the phone and called up everybody, all the doctors' wives and things. They just got on the phone and called 300 or 400 people and told them don't shop downtown. Finally there was just a total boycott downtown. There would be no black people downtown at all. [J. Bevel, 1978]

Activists were stationed downtown to insure that blacks knew not to shop. According to Rev. Smith, shortly after the boycott was initiated, merchants began coming to his home wanting to talk. Diane Nash Bevel attributed the boycott's effectiveness to reduced profits during the Easter shopping season. It also changed the merchants' attitude toward the sit-ins.

> It was interesting the difference that [the boycott] made in terms of how the managers were willing to talk with us, because see we had talked with the managers of the stores. We had a meeting at the very beginning and they had kind of listened to us politely, and said, "well, we just can't do it. We can't desegregate the counters because we will lose money and that's the end of it." So, after the economic withdrawal, they were eager to talk with us, and try to work up some solution. [D. Bevel, 1978]

In early 1960 the white power structure of Nashville was forced to desegregate a number of private establishments and public transportation facilities, SNCC's *Student Voice* reported that in Nashville, "A long series of negotiations followed the demonstrations, and on May 10, 6 downtown stores integrated their lunch counters. Since this time others have followed suit, and some stores have hired Negroes in positions other than those of menial workers for the first time" (*Student Voice,* August, 1960). Daily demonstrations by hundreds of students refusing to accept bond so that they could be released from jail, coupled with the boycott, gave blacks the upper hand in the conflict situation. Careful organization and planning was the hallmark of the Nashville sit-in movement.

DISCUSSION AND CONCLUSIONS

Consistent with Proposition 1, I have presented evidence that pre-existing social structures played a central role in the 1960 sit-in movement. Pre-existing activist groups, formal movement organizations, colleges, and overlapping personal networks provided the framework through which the sit-ins emerged and spread. Previous writings on the sit-ins (e.g., Lomax, 1962; Zinn, 1964; Matthews and Prothro, 1966; Killian, 1968; Meier and Rudwick, 1973; Piven and Cloward, 1977) have persistently portrayed pre-existing organization as an after-the-fact accretion on student spontaneity. The dominant view is that SCLC, CORE, NAACP, and community leaders rushed into a dynamic campus movement after it was well underway, while my data provide evidence that those organizational and community forces were at the core of the sit-in movement from its beginning. Thus, pre-existing organizations provided the sit-ins with the resources and communication networks needed for their emergence and development.

Prior to 1960 the sit-in was far from being the dominant tactic of the Civil Rights movement, yet in early 1960, sit-in demonstrations swept through thirteen states and hundreds of communities within two months. Almost instantly sit-ins became the major tactic and focus of the movement. A tactical innovation had occurred.

Consistent with Proposition 2, the data strongly suggest that the 1960 Greensboro sit-in occurred at the time when the necessary and sufficient condition for the rapid diffusion of sit-ins was present. That condition was the existence of well-developed and widespread internal organization. Because this internal organization was already firmly in place prior to 1960, activist groups across the South were in a position to quickly initiate sit-ins. The rapidity with which sit-ins were organized gave the appearance that they were spontaneous. This appearance was accentuated because most demonstrators were students rather than veteran Civil Rights activists.

Yet the data show that the student organizers of the sit-ins were closely tied to the internal organization of the emerging Civil Rights movement. Prior student/ activist ties had been formed through church affiliations and youth wings of Civil Rights organizations. In short, students and seasoned activists were able to rapidly coordinate the sit-ins because both were anchored to the same organization.

Innovations in political movements arise in the context of an active opposition. The organization of the Civil Rights movement provided the resources that sustained diffusion of the sit-ins in the face of attack. This vast internal organization consisted of local movement centers, experienced activists who had amassed organizing skills, direct-action organizations, communication systems between centers, pre-existing strategies for dealing with the opposition, workshops and training procedures, fund-raising techniques, and community mobilization techniques.

The pre-existing internal organization enabled organizers to quickly disseminate the "sit-in" idea to groups already favorably disposed toward direct action. In the innovation/diffusion literature (e.g., Coleman et al., 1957; Lionberger, 1960; Rogers, 1962) a positive decision by numerous actors to adopt a new item is treated as a central problem. In the case of the sit-ins, the adoption problem was largely solved by the pre-existing organization. Since that organization housed groups that had already identified with "confrontational politics," little time was lost on debates as to whether sit-ins should be adopted. Thus, the diffusion process did not become bogged down at the adoption stage.

Repression might have prevented the diffusion process. The authorities and white extremist groups attempted to prevent the spread of the sit-ins by immediately arresting the demonstrators, employing brutal force, and refusing to report the sit-ins in the local press. The organizational efficiency of the movement centers prevailed against the opposition. Existing recruiting and training procedures made it possible for jailed demonstrators to be instantly replaced. When heavy fines were leveled against the movement, activists were able generally to raise large sums of money through their pre-existing community contacts. The pre-existing communication networks easily overcame the problems imposed by news blackouts. Moreover, skilled activists were able to weaken the stance of the opposition by rapidly organizing economic boycotts. Because the internal organization was widespread, these effective counter measures were employed in Black communities across the South. Thus, it was well-developed and widespread internal organization that enabled the 1960 sit-ins to rapidly diffuse into a major tactical innovation of the Civil Rights movement.

Proposition 3 maintains that pre-existing internal organization establishes the types of innovations that can occur within movements. The internal organization that gave rise to the sit-ins specialized in what was called nonviolent direct action. This approach consisted of a battery of tactics that were disruptive but peaceful. The nonviolent approach readily fitted into the ideological and organizational framework of the black church, and provided ministers, students, and ordinary working people with a method for entering directly into the political process.

The movement centers that emerged following the Montgomery bus boycott were developed around nonviolent approaches to social change. Indeed, the primary goal of these centers was to build nonviolent movements. Yet, nonviolent confrontations as a disciplined form of collective action was relatively new to the black masses of the South. The activists within the movement centers systematically introduced blacks to the nonviolent approach. They organized nonviolent workshops and conducted them on a routine basis in the churches and protest organizations. Literature from organizations (e.g., Fellowship of Reconciliation and CORE) that specialized in the nonviolent approach was made available through the centers. Skilled nonviolent strategists (e.g., Bayard Rustin, James Lawson, and Glenn Smiley) travelled between centers training leaders how to conduct nonviolent campaigns. The varied tactics—mass marches, negotiations, boycotts, sit-ins—associated with direct action became common knowledge to activists in the centers. Moreover, in the late fifties activists began experimenting with these tactics and urging the community to become involved with nonviolent confrontations. Meier and Rudwick (1976) have shown that sit-ins at segregated facilities were conducted by black activists in the nineteen forties and late fifties. But this tactic remained relatively isolated and sporadic and did not diffuse throughout the larger community. Meier and Rudwick (1976:384) conclude that diffusion did not occur before 1960 because the white mass-media failed to cover sit-ins. My analysis suggests another explanation: sit-ins prior to 1960 did not spread because the internal organization required for such a spread did not exist. In short, without viable internal social organization, innovations will remain sporadic and isolated. With organization, innovations can spread and be sustained. By 1960 the internal organization of the Civil Rights movement had amassed resources and organization specifically designed to execute nonviolent confrontations.

The sit-in tactic was well suited to the existing internal organization of the Civil Rights movement. It did not conflict with the procedures, ideology, or resources of the movement centers. Indeed, because the sit-in method was a legitimate tactic of the direct-action approach, it was quickly embraced by activists situated in the movement centers. Because these activists were already attempting to build nonviolent movements, they instantly realized that massive sit-ins could have a wide impact. Furthermore, they were well aware that they were in command of precisely the kinds of resources through which the sit-ins could be rapidly diffused. This is why they phoned activist groups and said, "This is it, let's go!" That is, the sit-ins became a tactical innovation within the movement because they fit into the framework of the existing internal organization.

In conclusion, this paper has attempted to demonstrate the important role that internal organization played in the sit-in movement. It is becoming commonplace for writers (e.g., Hubbard, 1968; Lipsky, 1968; Mars and Useem, 1971; McCarthy and Zald, 1973; Oberschall, 1973) to assert that the Civil Rights movement was dependent on outside resources: elites, courts, Northern white liberals, mass media, and the Federal Government. The present analysis suggests that this assertion may be premature, especially when the role of internal organization is ignored. Future research on collective action that treats internal organization as a topic in its own right will further increase our knowledge of the dynamics of social movements.

REFERENCES

Baker, Ella. 1978. Interview. New York, New York.

Bevel, Diane Nash. 1978. Interview. Chicago, Illinois, December 14.

Bevel, James. 1978. Interview. New York, New York. December 27.

Blumer, H. 1946. "Collective Behavior." pp. 165–220 in A. M. Lee (ed.), New Outline of the Principles of Sociology, New York: Barnes & Noble.

Bond, Julian. 1980. Interview. Ann Arbor, Michigan. October 19.

Carey, Gordon. 1959. Report to CORE National Council.

February 21–22. 1978.

———— . Interview. Soul City, North Carolina. November 18 (Follow-up telephone interview November 1, 1979).

Coleman, James S., Eliher Katz, and Herbert Menzel. 1957. "The diffusion of an innovation among physicians." Sociometry 20:253–70.

Frazier, E. Franklin. 1963. The Negro Church in America. New York: Schocken Books.

Gamson, William A. 1975. The Strategy of Social Protest. Homewood, Illinois: Dorsey Press.

Haber, Robert A. 1966. "From protest to radicalism: an appraisal of the student struggle 1960." pp. 41–9 in Mitchell Cohen and Dennis Hale (eds.). The New Student Left. Boston: Dorsey.

Hubbard, Howard. 1968. "Five long hot summers and how they grew." Public Interest 12:3–24.

Jemison, Rev. T. J. 1978. Interview. Baton Rouge, Louisiana. October 16.

Jenkins, J. Craig and Charles Perrow. 1977. "Insurgency of the powerless: farm workers movements (1946–1972)." American Sociological Review 42:249–68.

Killian, Lewis M. 1968. The Impossible Revolution? New York: Random House.

Lang, Kurt and Gladys Lang. 1961. Collective Dynamics, New York: Crowell.

Lawson, James. 1978. Interview. Los Angeles, California. October 2 and 6.

Lewis, John. 1978. Interview. Washington, D.C. November 9.

Lewis, Chester. 1981. Interview. Wichita, Kansas, February 3.

Lionberger, H.F. 1960. Adoption of New Ideas and Practices. Ames: The Iowa State University Press.

Lipset, Seymour Martin and Sheldon S. Wolin. 1965. The Berkeley Student Revolt. Garden City, New York: Doubleday.

Lipsky, Michael. 1968. "Protest as a political resource." American Political Science Review 62:1114–58.

Lomax, Louis E. 1962. The Negro Revolt. New York: New American Library.

Luper, Clara. 1979. Behold the Walls. Jim Wire. 1980. Interview. Oklahoma City, Oklahoma. (Follow-up interview, January 1981).

Marx, Gary T. and Michael Useem. 1971. "Majority involvement in minority movements: civil rights, abolition, untouchability." Journal of Social Issues 27:81–104.

Matthews, Donald and James Prothro. 1966. Negroes and the New Southern Politics. New York: Harcourt, Brace, and World.

Mays, Benjamin and Joseph W. Nicholson. 1933. The Negro's Church. New York: Arno Press and the New York Times.

McAdam, Douglas. 1979. "Political process and the civil rights movement 1948–1962." Ph.D. dissertation. Department of Sociology, State University of New York at Stony Brook.

McCain, James. 1978. Interview. Sumter, South Carolina. November 18.

McCarthy, J. D. and M. N. Zald. 1973. The Social Trends of Social Movements in America: Professionalism and Resource Mobilizaiton. Morristown, N.J.: General Learning Press.

McCollom, Rev. Matthew. 1979. Interview. Orangeburg, South Carolina. October 31.

McKissick, Floyd. 1978. Interview. Soul City, North Carolina. November 18 (Follow-up telephone interview November 2, 1979).

McPhail, Clark. 1971. "Civil disorder participation: a critical examination of recent research." American Sociological Review 36:1058–73.

———.1973. "The assembling process: a theoretical and empircal examination." American Sociological Review 38:721–35.

Meier, August and Elliot Rudwick. 1966. From Plantation to Ghetto. New York: Hill and Wang.

———. 1973. CORE A study in the Civil Rights Movement 1942–1968. Oxford University Press.

———. 1976. Along the Color Line. University of Illinois Press.

Moore, Douglas. 1960. Journal and Guide. Vol. LX, March 5, 1960.

———. 1978. Interview. Washington, D.C. November 1.

Morris, Aldon. 1980. "The origins of the civil rights movement: an indigenous perspective." Ph.D. dissertation. Department of Sociology, State University of New York at Stony Brook.

———. Forthcoming. Origins of the Civil Rights Movement. New York: Free Press.

Obear, Frederick W. 1970. "Student activism in the sixties." Pp. 11–26 in Julian Foster and Durward Long (eds.), Protest: Student Activism in America 1970. New York: William Morrow.

Oberschall, Anthony. 1973. Social Conflict and Social Movements. Englewood Cliffs, N.J.: Prentice-Hall.

Oppenheimer, Martin. 1964. "The southern student movement: year I." Journal of Negro Education 33:396–403.

Piven, Frances Fox, and Richard A. Cloward. 1977. Poor People's Movements. New York: Vintage.

Randolph, Homer. 1981. Interview. East St. Louis, Illinois.

Rogers, Everett M. 1962. Diffusion of Innovations. New York: The Free Press of Glencoe.

Sale, Kirkpatrick. 1973. SDS. New York: Vintage.

Shuttlesworth, Rev. Fred. 1978. Interview. Cincinnati, Ohio. September 12.

Smelser, Neil J. 1963. Theory of Collective Behavior. New York: Free Press.

Smith, Rev. Kelly Miller. 1978. Interview. Nashville, Tennessee. October 13.

Southern Regional Council. 1960. "The student protest movement, winter 1960." SRC-13, April 1.

Student Nonviolent Coordinating Committee. 1960. The Student Voice. August.

Tilly, Charles. 1978. From Mobilization to Revolution. Reading. Massachusetts: Addison-Wesley.

Tilly, Charles, Louise Tilly, and Richard Tilly. 1975. The Rebellious Century 1830–1930. Cambridge, Massachusetts: Harvard University Press.

Turner, Ralph and Lewis Killian. 1957. Collective Behavior. Englewood Cliffs, N.J.: Prentice-Hall.

Von Eschen, Donald, Jerome Kirck, and Maurice Pinard. 1971. "The organizational substructure of disorderly politics." Social Forces 49:529–44.

Walker, Rev. Waytt Tee. 1978. Interview. New York City, New York. September 29.

Westby, David L. 1976. The Clouded Vision: The Student Movement in the United States in the 1960s. London: Associated University Press.

Williams, Hosea. 1978. Interview. Atlanta, Georgia. September 22.

Wolff, Miles. 1970. Lunch at the Five and Ten. New York: Stien and Day.

Zinn, Howard. 1964. SNCC: The New Abolitionists. Boston: Beacon.

READING 23

TACTICAL INNOVATION AND THE PACE OF BLACK INSURGENCY BETWEEN 1955 AND 1970*

Doug McAdam

The pace of black insurgency between 1955 and 1970 is analyzed as a function of an ongoing process of tactical interaction between movement forces and southern segregationists. Given a political system vulnerable to challenge and strong internal organization the main challenge confronting insurgents is a preeminently tactical one. Lacking institutionalized power, challengers must devise protest techniques that offset their powerlessness. This is referred to as a process of tactical innovation. Such innovations, however, only temporarily afford challengers increased bargaining leverage. In chess-like fashion, movement opponents can be expected, through effective tactical adaptation, to neutralize the new tactic, thereby reinstituting the power disparity between themselves and the challenger.

This perspective is applied to the development of the black movement over the period, 1955–1970. Evidence derived from content-coding all relevant story synopses contained in The New York Times Index *for these years is presented showing a strong correspondence between the introduction of new protest techniques and peaks in movement activity. Conversely, lulls in black insurgency reflect the successful efforts of movement opponents to devise effective tactical counters to these innovations.*

Sociological analysis and theory regarding social movements has tended to focus on the causes of insurgency. By comparison, relatively little attention has been devoted to the dynamics of movement develop-

ment and decline.[1] This article represents a modest attempt to address this "hole" in the movement literature by analyzing the effect of one factor on the ongoing development of a single movement. It studies the relationship between *tactical interaction* and the pace of black insurgency between 1955 and 1970.

THE SIGNIFICANCE OF TACTICS AND THE PROCESS OF TACTICAL INTERACTION

The significance of tactics to social movements derives from the unenviable position in which excluded or challenging groups find themselves. According to Gamson (1975:140): "the central difference among political actors is captured by the idea of being inside or outside of the polity . . . Those who are outside are challengers. They lack the basic prerogative of members—routine access to decisions that affect them. The key challenge confronting insurgents, then, is to devise some way to overcome the basic powerlessness that has confined them to a position of institutionalized political impotence. The solution to this problem is preeminently tactical. Ordinarily insurgents must bypass routine decision-making channels and seek, through use of noninstitutionalized tactics, to force their opponents to deal with them outside the established arenas within which the latter derive so much of their power. In a phrase, they must create "negative inducements" to bargaining (Wilson, 1961).

Negative inducements involve the creation of a situation that disrupts the normal functioning of society and is antithetical to the interests of the group's opponents. In essence, insurgents seek to disrupt their opponent's realization of interests to such an extent that the cessation of the offending tactic becomes a sufficient inducement to grant concessions.

Findings reported by Gamson (1975:72–88) support the efficacy of negative inducements or disruptive tac-

From *American Sociological Review* 48 (December 1983): 735–54. Reprinted with the permission of the author and the American Sociological Association.

* Direct all correspondence to: Doug McAdam, Department of Sociology, University of Arizona, Tucson, AZ 85721.

This research was supported in part by NIMH grant No. 5 ROI MH20006 04 SSR. The grant supported a larger study of insurgency in the 1960s directed by Charles Perrow, to whom goes my deep appreciation as well as much of the credit for this work. I would also like to thank Al Bergesen, Neil Fligstein, Lois Horton, Michael Hout, John McCarthy, Victoria Nelson-Rader, Michael Sobel and two anonymous reviewers for their extremely helpful comments on various drafts of this paper.

[1] I am not alone in noting the relative lack of attention paid to the dynamics of movement development and decline in the sociological literature. Gamson (1975), Piven and Cloward (1977), and Snyder and Kelly (1979) have made similar comments in other contexts. The introduction of resource mobilization and other "rationalistic" theories of social movements, however, has helped focus more attention on the ongoing dynamics of movement development. In the work of such theorists as Tilly (1978), McCarthy and Zald (1973, 1977), and others, one begins to discern the outlines of a systematic framework for analyzing not just the emergence but subsequent development/decline of social movements.

tics for many challenging groups. In summarizing his findings, he concludes that "unruly groups, those that use violence, strikes, and other constraints, have better than average success" (Gamson, 1975:87). Piven and Cloward's (1979) analysis of several "poor people's movements" supports Gamson's conclusion. As they note, ". . . it is usually when unrest among the lower classes breaks out of the confines of electoral procedures that the poor may have some influence, for the instability and polarization they then threaten to create by their actions in the factories or in the streets may force some response from electoral leaders" (Piven and Cloward, 1979:15).

In most cases, then, the emergence of a social movement attests to at least limited success in the use of disruptive tactics. To survive, however, a movement must be able to sustain the leverage it has achieved through the use of such tactics. To do it must either parlay its initial successes into positions of institutionalized power (as, for instance, the labor movement did) or continue to experiment with noninstitutional forms of protest. Regarding the latter course of action, even the most successful tactic is likely to be effectively countered by movement opponents if relied upon too long. Barring the attainment of significant institutionalized power, then, the pace of insurgency comes to be crucially influenced by (a) the creativity of insurgents in devising new tactical forms, and (b) the ability of opponents to neutralize these moves through effective tactical counters. These processes may be referred to as *tactical innovation* and *tactical adaptation,* respectively. Together they define an ongoing process of *tactical interaction* in which insurgents and opponents seek, in chess-like fashion, to offset the moves of the other. How well each succeeds at this task crucially affects the pace and outcome of insurgency.

As crucial as this interactive dynamic is, it has received scant empirical attention in the social movement literature.[2] Instead research has tended to focus on the characteristics or resources of either opponents or insurgents rather than the dynamic relationship between the two.

POLITICAL PROCESS AS A CONTEXT FOR TACTICAL INNOVATION

As important as the process of tactical innovation is, it derives much of its significance from the larger political/organizational context in which it occurs. That is, the process only takes on significance in the context of the more general factors that make for a viable social movement in the first place.

Elsewhere (McAdam, 1982) is outlined a *political process* model of social movements that stresses the importance of two structural factors in the emergence of widespread insurgency. The first is the level of indigenous organization within the aggrieved population; the second the alignment of groups within the larger political environment. The first can be conceived of as the degree of organizational "readiness" within the minority community and the second, following Eisinger (1973:11), as the "structure of political opportunities" available to insurgent groups. As necessary, but not sufficient, conditions for social insurgency, both factors are crucial prerequisites for the process of tactical innovation. Indigenous organizations furnish the context in which tactical innovations are devised and subsequently carried out. Such organizations serve to mobilize community resources in support of new tactical forms and to supply leaders to direct their use, participants to carry them out, and communication networks to facilitate their use and dissemination to other insurgent groups.[3] This latter point is especially significant. The simple introduction of a new protest technique in a single locale is not likely to have a measurable effect on the pace of movement activity unless its use can be diffused to other insurgent groups operating in other areas. It is the established communication networks characteristic of existing organizations that ordinarily make this crucial process of diffusion possible.[4]

---

[2] Though hardly a major focus of theoretical attention, the dynamic has at least been acknowledged and discussed by a number of movement theorists. Zald and Useem (1982), for example, apply a similar interactive perspective to the study of the ongoing relationship between movements and the countermovements they give rise to. Such a perspective also informs Tilly's (1978) model of social movements. Finally, elements of an interactive conception of movement development are implied in McPhail and Miller's work (1973) on the "assembling process."

---

[3] In his analysis of the emergence and spread of the sit-in tactic, Morris (1981) offers a richly drawn example of the organizational roots of tactical innovation. In this case it was the indigenous network of southern black churches, colleges and local movement affiliates that supplied the organizational context essential to the successful application and diffusion of the sit-in tactic.

[4] A possible exception to the rule involves the urban riots of the mid to late 1960s. In the case of these loosely organized, more diffuse forms of protest, it is likely that the media—particularly television—served as the principal vehicle of diffusion linking rioters in different cities. Within the same city, however, several authors have noted the importance of indigenous associational networks in the spread of the riot (cf. Feagin and Hann, 1973:48–49; Wilson and Orum, 1976:198).

But the effectiveness of such organizations and the tactical innovations they employ also depend, to a considerable degree, on characteristics of the larger political environment which insurgents confront. Under ordinary circumstances excluded groups or challengers face enormous obstacles in their efforts to advance group interests. They oftentimes face a political establishment united in its opposition to insurgent goals and therefore largely immune to pressure from movement groups. Under such circumstances tactical innovations are apt to be repressed or ignored rather than triggering expanded insurgency. More to the point it is unlikely even that such innovations will be attempted in the face of the widely shared feelings of pessimism and impotence that are likely to prevail under such conditions. Tactical innovations *only* become potent in the context of a political system vulnerable to insurgency. Expanding political opportunities then create a potential for the exercise of political leverage which indigenous organizations seek to exploit. It is the confluence of these two factors that often seems to presage widespread insurgency.

Certainly this was true in the case of the black movement (McAdam, 1982: see especially Chapters 5–7). By mid-century the growing electoral importance of blacks nationwide, the collapse of the southern cotton economy, and the increased salience of third world countries in United States foreign policy had combined to grant blacks a measure of political leverage they had not enjoyed since Reconstruction. Equally significant was the extraordinary pace of institutional expansion within the southern black community in the period of 1930–1960. Triggered in large measure by the decline in cotton farming and the massive rural to urban migration it set in motion, this process left blacks in a stronger position organizationally than they had ever been in before. In particular, three institutions—the black church, black colleges, and the southern wing of the NAACP—grew apace of this general developmental process. Not surprisingly, these three institutions were to dominate the protest infrastructure out of which the movement was to emerge in the period 1955–1960. It is against this backdrop of expanding political opportunities and growing organizational strength, then, that the emergence of the civil rights movement must be seen.

The confluence of indigenous organization and expanding political opportunities, however, only renders widespread insurgency likely, not inevitable. Insurgents must still define the "time as ripe" for such activity and commit indigenous organizational re-

sources to the struggle. Then, too, they must devise methodologies for pressing their demands. It is only at this point that the process of tactical innovation becomes crucial. For if expanding opportunities and established organizations presage movement emergence, it is the skill of insurgents in devising effective protest tactics *and* their opponents, ability to counter such tactics that largely determine the pace and outcome of insurgency. In the remainder of this article attention will center on this dynamic and its effects on the unfolding of black protest activity in this country between 1955 and 1970.

INSTITUTIONALIZED POWERLESSNESS AND THE POLITICS OF PROTEST

By any measure of institutionalized political power blacks were almost totally powerless in the middle decades of this century. Of the nearly eight and three-quarter million voting age blacks in the country in 1950 only an estimated three million were registered to vote (Berger, 1950:26), in contrast to the estimated 81 percent registration rate for whites in 1952 (Danigelis, 1978:762). While no contemporaneous count of black elected officials nationwide is available, the number was certainly very small. At the national level, only two Congressmen—Dawson (R–IL) and Powell (D–NY)—held elective office. Institutionalized political impotence was most extreme for southern blacks. Some ten and a quarter million blacks still resided in the South in 1950, with barely 900,000 of them registered to vote (Bullock, 1971:227; Hamilton, 1964:275). No blacks held major elective office in the region and none had served in Congress since 1901 (Ploski and Marr, 1976). Moreover, with blatantly discriminatory electoral practices still commonplace throughout the region—especially in the Deep South—the prospects for changing this state of affairs were bleak. Yet a scant twenty years later significant change had come to the South. An entire system of Jim Crow caste restrictions had been dismantled. Black voter registration rates had risen from less than 20 percent in 1950 to 65 percent in 1970 (Lawson, 1976:331). The number of black elected officials in the region climbed to nearly 1,900 after the 1970 elections (Brooks, 1974:293). And with the election of Andrew Young and Barbara Jordan, black southerners were represented in Congress for the first time since 1901.

The pressure for these changes came from an indigenous movement organized and led primarily by southern blacks. In the face of the institutional political powerlessness of this population it is important to ask how this pressure was generated and sustained. The answer to this question is, of course, complex. However, any complete account of how blacks were able to mount such a successful insurgent campaign must focus squarely on their willingness to bypass "proper channels" in favor of noninstitutionalized forms of protest. Having "humbly petitioned" the South's white power structure for decades with little results, insurgents logically turned to the only option left open to them: the "politics of protest." It was the potential for disruption inherent in their use of noninstitutionalized forms of political action that was to prove decisive.

METHODS

To measure the pace of black insurgency over this period all relevant story synopses contained in the annual *New York Times Index* (for the years 1955–70) under the two headings, "Negroes–U.S.–General," and "Education–U.S.–Social Integration," were read and content-coded along a variety of dimensions. The decision to restrict coding to these headings was based on a careful examination of the classification system employed in the *Index,* which indicated that the overwhelming majority of events relevant to the topic were listed under these two headings.

To be coded, a story had to satisfy four criteria. It first had to be relevant to the general topic of black civil rights. As a result, a good many other topics were excluded from the analysis, for example, stories reporting the achievements of black athletes or entertainers. Besides this general criterion of relevance, to be coded, synopses also had to be judged unambiguous as to (1) the nature of the event being reported (e.g., riot, sit-in, court decision); (2) the individual(s) or group(s) responsible for its initiation; and (3) geographic location of the event. The former two variables, "type of action" and "initiating unit," figure prominently in the anlaysis to be reported later.

In all better than 12,000 synopses were coded from a total of about 29,000 read. Coding was carried out by the author and a single research assistant. By way of conventional assurances, intercoder reliability coefficients exceeded .90 for all but one variable. For all variables employed in this article, however, reliability ratings exceeded .95.[5]

---

[5] For a more complete discussion of the coding procedures employed in this analysis the reader is referred to McAdam, 1982:235–50.

BLACK INSURGENCY AND THE PROCESS OF TACTICAL INNOVATION

To assess the effect of tactical innovation on the pace of black insurgency between 1955 and 1970 requires that we be able to measure both insurgent pace and innovation. Two code categories noted in the previous section enable us to do so. The variable, "initiating unit," provides us with frequency counts of all civil rights-related actions for all parties to the conflict (e.g., federal government, Martin Luther King, Jr., etc.). One major category of initiating unit employed in the study was that of "movement group or actor." The combined total of all actions attributed to movement groups or actors provides a rough measure of the pace of movement-initiated activity over time. Figure 1 shows the frequency of such activity between October 1955 and January 1971.

What relationship, if any, is there between tactical innovation and the ebb and flow of movement activity? By coding the "type of action" involved in each reported event, we can compare the frequency with which various tactics were used to the overall pace of insurgency shown in Figure 1. Figures 2 and 3 show this specific activity frequencies for five novel tactical forms utilized by insurgents during the course of the movement.

As these figures show, peaks in movement activity tend to correspond to the introduction and spread of new protest techniques.[6] The pattern is a consistent one. The pace of insurgency jumps sharply following the introduction of a new tactical form, remains high for a period of time, and then begins to decline until another tactical innovation sets the pattern in motion again. A more systematic view of this dynamic is provided in Table 1.

Table 1 reports the use of five specific tactics as a proportion of all movement-initiated actions during

---

[6] In most cases the protest techniques were not really new. Indeed, most had been employed by insurgents previously. What distinguished their use from previous applications was the adoption of the tactic by other insurgent groups. The extensiveness of the adoption is largely attributable to the dense network of communication ties that had developed between insurgents by 1960. Morris (1981) provides a detailed illustration of the crucial importance of formal and informal ties in the process of tactical diffusion in his analysis of the spread of the sit-in tactic. His analysis merely underscores a fundamental point made earlier: the significance of the process of tactical innovation depends heavily on the organizational resources available to insurgent groups. A well-developed communication network linking insurgents together is perhaps the most critical of these resources.

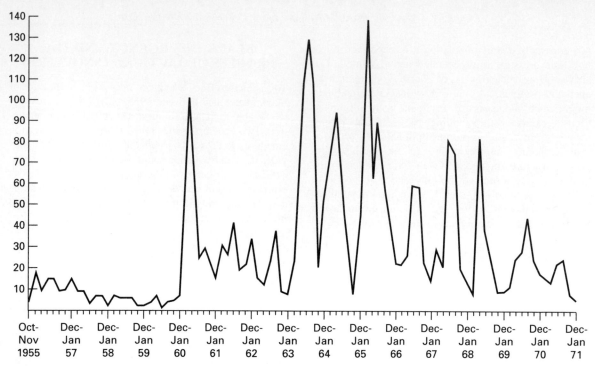

FIGURE 1. Movement-Initiated Actions, Oct–Nov 1955 through Dec–Jan 1971. (*Source: Annual Index* of the *New York Times,* 1955–1971.)

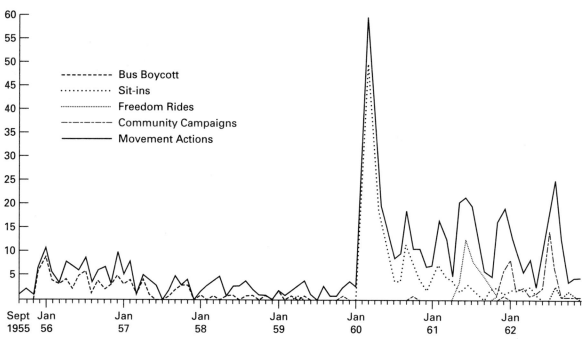

FIGURE 2. Movement-Initiated Actions, September 1955 through December 1962. (*Source: Annual Index* of the *New York Times,* 1955–1962.)

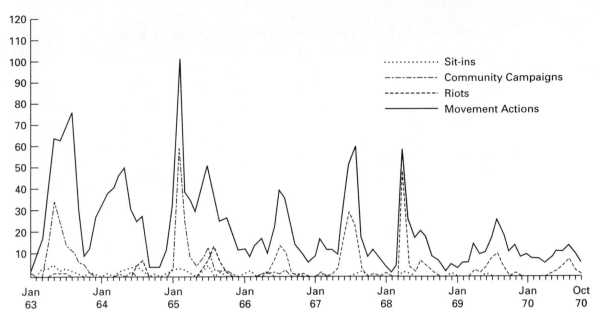

FIGURE 3. Movement-Initiated Actions, January 1963 through October 1970. (*Source: Annual Index* of the *New York Times, 1963–1970.*)

each of the first twelve months following the introduction of each technique. As the "Total" column makes clear, the sheer number of actions is highest immediately following the introduction of a new protest form, as is the proportion of all actions attributed to the new technique. Thus, tactical innovation appears to trigger a period of heightened protest activity dominated by the recently introduced protest technqiue. This is not to suggest that the older tactical forms are rendered obsolete by the introduction of the new technique. Table 1 shows clearly that this is not the case. In only 22 of the 60 months represented in the table did the new tactical form account for better than 50 percent of all movement-initiated actions. On the contrary, tactical innovation seems to stimulate the renewed usage of *all* tactical forms. Thus, for example, the economic boycott, largely abandoned after the bus boycotts, was often revived in the wake of sit-in demonstrations as a means of intensifying the pressure generated by the latter technique (Southern Regional Council, 1961). Then, too, during the community-wide campaign all manner of protest techniques—sit-ins, boycotts, etc.—were employed as part of a varied tactical assault on Jim Crow. This resurgence of the older tactical forms seems to underscore the importance of the process of tactical

innovation. The presumption is that in the absence of the heightened movement activity triggered by tactical innovation the older protest forms would not have reappeared. Their use, then, is dependent on the altered protest context created by the introduction of the new technique.

What of the "valleys" in movement activity shown in Figures 2 and 3? A closer analysis suggests that the lulls in insurgency reflect the successful efforts of movement opponents to devise effective tactical counters to the new protest forms. For a fuller understanding of this interactive dynamic, we now turn to a more detailed qualitative examination of the processes of tactical innovation and adaptation surrounding the protest techniques listed in Table 1.

Bus Boycott

The first such technique was the bus boycott. Certainly the most famous and successful of these boycotts was the one organized in Montgomery, Alabama, (1955–56) by the church-based Montgomery Improvement Association (MIA) led by Martin Luther King, Jr. The technique, however, was not original to Montgomery. In

TABLE 1.

**Tactical Innovations as a Proportion of a Month's Activity by Months
Since First Use of Tactical Form**

Month Since First Use[a]	Bus Boycott	Sit-in	Freedom Ride	Community Campaign	Riot	Total
0	.86 (6/7)	.57 (24/42)	.19 (4/21)	.06 (1/17)	.14 (7/51)	.30 (42/138)
1	.82 (9/11)	.83 (50/60)	.59 (13/22)	.35 (7/20)	.38 (14/37)	.62 (93/150)
2	.67 (4/6)	.91 (30/33)	.45 (9/20)	.64 (9/14)	.21 (5/24)	.59 (57/97)
3	1.00 (5/5)	.74 (14/19)	.54 (7/13)	.20 (2/10)	.04 (1/26)	.40 (29/73)
4	.50 (4/8)	.53 (8/15)	.83 (5/6)	.50 (3/6)	.00 (0/18)	.38 (20/53)
5	.29 (2/7)	.44 (4/9)	.60 (3/5)	.11 (1/9)	.00 (0/11)	.24 (10/41)
6	.83 (5/6)	.40 (4/10)	.00 (0/17)	***	.00 (0/12)	.23 (11/48)
7	.67 (6/9)	.63 (12/19)	.05 (1/20)	***	.00 (0/8)	.37 (22/60)
8	***	.73 (8/11)	.00 (0/14)	.79 (15/19)	.00 (0/14)	.39 (24/61)
9	.67 (4/6)	.36 (4/11)	.00 (0/10)	.23 (6/26)	.00 (0/17)	.20 (14/70)
10	.29 (2/7)	.29 (2/7)	.00 (0/6)	.08 (1/12)	.11 (1/9)	.15 (6/41)
11	***	.62 (5/8)	.00 (0/9)	***	.29 (6/21)	.33 (15/45)

[a]Listed below are the months of first use for the five tactical forms shown in the table:

Bus Boycott:	December, 1955
Sit-in:	February, 1960
Freedom Ride:	May, 1961
Community Campaign:	December, 1961
Riot:	August, 1965

***Fewer than 5 movement-initiated actions.

1953 a similar boycott had been organized by the Rev. Theodore Jemison in Baton Rouge, Louisana.

If not the first, the Montgomery campaign was unique in the measure of success it achieved and the encouragement it afforded others to organize similar efforts elsewhere. In a very real sense the introduction of this technique marks the beginning of what is popularly called the "civil rights movement." From extremely low levels of activism in the early 1950s, the pace of black protest rose sharply in 1956 and 1957.

Consistent with the theme of this article, it is appropriate that we date the beginnings of the movement with a particular tactical, rather than substantive, innovation. After all, the specific issue of discriminatory bus seating had been a source of discontent in the black community for years. Repeated efforts to change such practices had always met with failure until the Montgomery boycott was launched. Why did this tactic succeed where all others had failed? The answer to this question lies in the contrast between the institutional powerlessness of southern blacks at this time and the leverage they were able to mobilize outside "proper channels" by means of the boycott. Outside those channels blacks were able to take advantage of their sizeable numbers to create a significant "negative inducement"

to bargaining. That inducement was nothing less than the economic solvency of the bus lines, which depended heavily—70–75 percent in Montgomery—on their black ridership (Brooks, 1974:110). Such leverage was telling in Montgomery and elsewhere.

The U.S. Supreme Court, on November 13, 1956, declared Montgomery's bus segregation laws unconstitutional. Five weeks later, on December 21, the city's buses were formally desegregated, thereby ending the black community's year-long boycott of the buses. During the boycott an estimated 90–95 percent of the city's black passengers refrained from riding the buses (Walton, 1956).

A similar boycott begun on May 28, 1956, in Tallahassee, Florida, did not result in as clear-cut a victory for insurgents as did the Montgomery campaign. Nonetheless, the boycott once again demonstrated the power of widespread insurgent action by blacks. With blacks comprising 60–70 percent of its total ridership, the city bus company quickly felt the effect of the boycott. Barely five weeks after the start of the campaign, the bus company was forced to suspend service. With revenues cut by an estimated 60 percent, it simply was no longer feasible to maintain bus service (Smith and Killian, 1958). Several months later bus service was resumed, thanks to several forms of public subsidy devised by city officials. Still the boycott held. Finally, following the Supreme Court's ruling in the Montgomery case, organized efforts to desegregate Tallahassee's buses were instituted. Despite continued harassment, legal desegregation had come to Tallahassee. Finally, the impact of the Tallahassee and Montgomery boycotts (as well as those organized elsewhere) was felt in other locales. Apparently fearing similar disruptive boycotts in their communities, at least a dozen other southern cities quietly desegregated their bus lines during the course of the Tallahassee and Montgomery campaigns.

As effective as the boycott proved to be, it was in time effectively countered by southern segregationists. The adaptation to this tactic took two forms: legal obstruction and extra-legal harassment. The latter consisted of violence or various forms of physical and economic intimidation aimed at members of the black community, especially those prominent in the boycott campaigns. In Montgomery,

> buses were fired upon by white snipers; a teenage girl was beaten by four or five white rowdies as she got off the bus. Four Negro churches were bombed at an estimated damage of $70,000, the homes of Ralph Abernathy and Robert Graetz were dynamited . . . and someone fired a shotgun blast into the front door of . . . Martin Luther King's home (Brooks, 1974:119)

Similar responses were forthcoming in Tallahassee and in other boycott cities (Smith and Killian, 1958:13). These incidents had the effect of increasing the risks of participation in insurgent activity to a level that may well have reduced the likelihood of generating such campaigns elsewhere.

These extra-legal responses were supplemented by various "legal" maneuvers on the part of local officials which were designed to neutralize the effectiveness of the bus boycott as an insurgent tactic. Several examples drawn from the Tallahassee conflict illustrate the type of counter moves that were instituted in many southern communities at this time.[7]

—City police initiated a concerted campaign of harassment and intimidation against car pool partici-

pants that included arrests for minor violations and the detention of drivers for questioning in lieu of formal charges.

—The executive committee of the I.C.C., the organization coordinating the boycott, was arrested, tried, and found guilty of operating a transportation system without a license. Each member of the committee received a 60-day jail term and a $500 fine, a sentence that was suspended on condition the defendants engaged in no further illegal activity.

—Following the Supreme Court's desegregation ruling in the Montgomery case, the Tallahassee City Commission met and rescinded the city's bus segregation ordinance replacing it with one directing bus drivers to assign seats on the basis of the "maximum safety" of their passengers. Segregation, of course, was deemed necessary to insure the "maximum safety" of passengers.

Though unable to stem desegregation in the long run, these countermeasures (in combination with the extra-legal techniques reviewed earlier) were initially effective as tactical responses to the bus boycotts.

It wasn't just the short-run effectiveness of these tactical responses, however, that led to the declining pace of black insurgency in the late 1950s (see Figure 2). In point of fact, the bus boycott was a tactic of limited applicability. Its effectiveness was restricted to urban areas with a black population large enough to jeopardize the financial well-being of a municipal bus system. It was also a tactic dependent upon a *well-organized* black community *willing* to break with the unspoken rule against noninstitutionalized forms of political action. This point serves once again to underscore the importance of organization and opportunity in the generation and sustenance of protest activity. Given the necessity for coordinating the actions of large numbers of people over a relatively long period of time, the bus boycott tactic made extensive organization and strong community consensus a prerequisite for successful implementation. Tactical innovation may have triggered the boycott, but once again it was the confluence of existing organization and system vulnerability—in the form of municipal bus lines dependent on black patrons—that provided the context for successful insurgency. Not surprisingly, these conditions were fairly rare in the South of the mid '50s. Therefore, truly mass protest activity had to await the introduction of a protest tactic available to smaller groups of people. That tactic was the sit-in.

---

[7] All of the examples are taken from Smith and Killian's (1958) account of the bus boycott in Tallahassee, Florida, and the conflict that stemmed from it.

The Sit-in

According to Morris (1981), blacks had initiated sit-ins in at least fifteen cities between 1957 and February 1, 1960. The logical question is why did these sit-ins not set in motion the dramatic expansion in protest activity triggered by the February 1 episode in Greensboro, North Carolina? The answer helps once again to illustrate the importance of organization and opportunity as necessary prerequisites for the dynamic under study here. First, as Morris's analysis reveals, the earlier sit-ins occurred at a time when the diffusion network linking various insurgent groups had not yet developed sufficiently for the tactic to spread beyond its localized origins. Indeed, within a narrow geographical area the expected escalation in protest activity *did* occur. For example, in August, 1958, the local NAACP Youth Council used sit-ins to desegregate a lunch counter in Oklahoma City, Oklahoma. Following this success, the tactic quickly spread, by means of organizational and personal contacts, to groups in the neighboring towns of Enid, Tulsa and Stillwater, Oklahoma, and Kansas City, Kansas, where it was used with varying degrees of success (McAdam, 1982:269; Morris, 1981:750; Oppenheimer, 1963:52).

Secondly, the "structure of political opportunities" confronting southern blacks was hardly as favorable in 1957–58 as it was in 1960. Every one of the pre-Greensboro sit-ins occurred in "progressive" border states (e.g., Missouri, Oklahoma, Kansas). This is hardly surprising in light of the strong supremacist counter-movement that was then sweeping the South (Bartley, 1969; McAdam, 1982). Between 1954 and 1958 southern segregationists mobilized and grew increasingly more active in resisting school desegregation and the organized beginning of the civil rights movement. White Citizen Councils sprang up throughout the region and came to exercise a powerful influence in both state and local politics (McMillen, 1971). As part of a general regional "flood" of segregationist legislation, several states outlawed the NAACP, forcing the state organization underground and seriously hampering its operation. But the resistance movement was to peak in 1957–58. Total Citizen Council membership rose steadily until 1958, then fell off sharply thereafter. The volume of state segregation legislation followed a similar pattern, peaking in 1956–57 and declining rapidly during the remainder of the decade. By 1960 a noticable "thaw" was evident in all regions except the "deep South."

Faced, then, with a more conducive political environment and the dense network of organizational ties that make for rapid and extensive diffusion, it is not surprising that the tactic spread as rapidly as it did in the spring of 1960. The events surrounding the Greensboro sit-in are, by now, well known. There on February 1, 1960, four students from North Carolina A and T occupied seats at the local Woolworth's lunch counter. In response, the store's management closed the counter and the students returned to campus without incident. After that, events progressed rapidly. Within a week similar demonstrations had taken place in two other towns in the state. By February 15, the movement had spread to a total of nine cities in North Carolina as well as the neighboring states of Tennessee, Virginia, and South Carolina (McAdam, 1982). By the end of May, 78 southern communities had experienced sit-in demonstrations in which at least 2,000 had been arrested (Meier and Rudwick, 1973:102).

The effect of this tactical innovation on the overall pace of black insurgency is apparent in Figure 2. From low levels of movement activity in the late 1950s, the pace of insurgency increased sharply following the first sit-in in February and remained at fairly high levels throughout the spring of that year. This dramatic rise in movement activity was almost exclusively a function of the introduction and spread of the sit-in as a new tactical form. Not only did local movement groups rush to apply the tactic throughout the South, but these various campaigns soon stimulated supportive forms of movement activity elsewhere. Sympathy demonstrations and the picketing of national chain stores began in the North. At the same time, the existing civil rights organizations rushed to capitalize on the momentum generated by the students by initiating actions of their own (Meier and Rudwick, 1973:101–104; Zinn, 1965:29).

Why did the introduction of this tactic have the effect it did? Two factors seem to be crucial here. The first is the "accessibility" of the tactic. Even a small group of persons could employ it, as indeed was the case in the initial Greensboro sit-in. Nor was the tactic reserved only for use in large urban areas, as was the case with the bus boycott. In the South nearly all towns of any size had segregated lunch counters, thereby broadening the geographic base of insurgency.

The second factor accounting for the popularity of the tactic was simply that it worked. By late 1961, facilities in 93 cities in ten southern states had been desegregated as a *direct* result of sit-in demonstrations (Bullock, 1970:274). In at least 45 other locales the desire to avoid disruptive sit-ins was enough to occasion the integration of some facilities (Oppenheimer, 1963:273). These figures raise another important question: *why* was the tactic so successful? At first blush the underlying logic of the sit-ins is not immediately apparent. Certainly the logic of the boycott does not apply in the case of segregated facilities. Given that blacks were barred from patronizing such facilities in the first place, they could not very well withdraw their patronage as a means of pressing for change. Instead they sought to create a very different inducement to bargaining. By occupying seats at segregated lunch counters, insurgents sought to disrupt the ordinary operation of business to such an extent that the affected stores would feel compelled to change their racial policies.

The hoped-for disruption of business was only partly a function of the routine closing of the lunch counter that normally accompanied sit-in demonstrations. Obviously, the revenues generated by the lunch counter were only a small fraction of the store's total income and insufficient in themselves to induce the store to negotiate with insurgents. For the tactic to work there had to occur a more generalized store-wide disruption of business. This, in turn, depended upon the emergence, within the community, of a general "crisis definition of the situation." When this occurred, the store became the focal point for racial tensions and violence of sufficient intensity to deter would-be shoppers from patronizing the store. An example will help to illustrate this point. It is drawn from an eye-witness account of the violence that accompanied a 1960 sit-in in Jacksonville, Florida. The account reads:

> Near noon on that day the demonstrators arrived at Grant's store . . . Grant's then closed its counters after demonstrators sat-in for about five minutes. The sitters then left. As they proceeded toward other stores, a group of about 350 armed white men and boys began running down the street toward the store. Some Negroes broke and ran. The majority, however, proceeded in good order, until four or five members of the Youth Council also panicked and ran. At this point the mob caught up to the demonstrators. A girl was hit with an axe handle. Fighting then began as the demonstrators retreated toward the Negro section of town . . . A boy was pushed and hit by an automobile . . . By 12:50 only an hour after the first sit-in that day, Police Inspector Bates reported the downtown situation completely out of hand. A series of individual incidents of

mobs catching Negroes and beating them took place at this time. (Oppenheimer, 1963:216)

Clearly, under conditions such as these, shoppers are not likely to patronize the target store let alone venture downtown. The result is a marked slowdown in retail activity amidst a generalized crisis atmosphere. This state of affairs represents a two-fold tactical advance over that evident during a bus boycott. First, the crisis engendered by a boycott affected fewer people directly and took longer to develop than did a sit-in crisis. Second, as Oberschall (1973:268) notes, "the cost of the boycott fell heavily upon the boycott participants, many of whom walked to work over long distances. Only after months had passed did the loss of income from bus fares create a financial situation worrisome to the municipal administration." By contrast, the financial cost of the sit-in campaign was felt immediately by the segregationists themselves, making it a much more direct and successful tactic than the boycott.[8]

As is the case with all tactics, however, the impact of the sit-in was relatively short lived. As Figure 2 shows, following the peak in movement activity during the spring of 1960, the pace of insurgency declined sharply in the summer and fall of the year. Part of this decline

---

[8] Nor was the cost of the sit-ins for the segregationists merely financial. The symbolic consequences were enormous as well. For southern blacks and whites alike the sit-ins served to shatter certain myths that had served for decades to sustain the racial status quo. Southern blacks who had long felt powerless to effect basic changes in "their" way of life were galvanized by the realization that they were in fact doing just that. For their part many segregationists found it increasingly difficult to maintain their long-held invidious moral distinction between blacks and whites as a result of the glaring symbolic contrast evident in the sit-ins. The dilemma is nicely captured by an editorial that appeared in the prosegregationist *Richmond News Leader* on February 22, 1960, in the wake of sit-ins in that city. In part the editorial read:

> Many a Virginian must have felt a tinge of wry regret at the state of things as they are, in reading of Saturday's "sit-downs" by Negro students in Richmond stores. Here were the colored students, in coats, white shirts, ties, and one of them was reading Goethe and one was taking notes from a biology text. And here on the sidewalk outside, was a gang of white boys come to heckle, a ragtail rabble, slack-jawed, black-jacketed, grinning fit to kill, and some of them, God save the mark, were waving the proud and honored flag of the Southern States in the last war fought by gentlemen. Ehew! It gives one pause. (quoted in Zinn, 1965:27)

In accounting for the sit-ins, then, one must consider the symbolic consequences of the demonstrations, no less than the financial cost to the segregationists.

can, of course, be attributed to the effectiveness of the tactic. Having desegregated facilities in so many cities, there were simply fewer targets left to attack. However, far more important than this in accounting for the diminished use of the tactic was the process of tactical adaptation discussed earlier. Having never encountered the tactic before, segregationists were initially caught off guard and reacted tentatively toward it. Over time, however, they devised tactical counters that proved reasonably effective.

In his thorough analysis of the sit-in movement, Oppenheimer (1963) makes reference to this two-stage phenomenon. He distinguishes between several phases in the development of the typical sit-in. The initial or "incipient state" of the conflict is characterized by "the relatively unplanned reaction to the movement of the police in terms of arrests, by the managers of the stores in terms of unstructured and varying counter-tactics which may vary from day to day . . ." (Oppenheimer, 1963:168). However, through this process of trial and error, movement opponents were able to devise consistently effective responses to the sit-in tactic (and share them with one another) during what Oppenheimer calls the "reactive phase" of the conflict. These responses included mass arrests by the police, the passage of state or local anti-trespassing ordinances, the permanent closure of the lunch counters, and the establishment of various biracial negotiating bodies to contain or routinize the conflict. The latter adaptation proved especially effective. By defusing the crisis definition of the situation, the disruptive potential of the sit-in was greatly reduced, resulting in a significant decline in the leverage exercised by the insurgents. Indeed, this must be seen as a general aspect of the process of tactical adaptation regardless of the protest technique involved. All protest tactics depend for their effectiveness on the generation of a crisis situation. Yet prolonged use of the tactic necessarily undercuts any definition of crisis that may have obtained initially. James Laue (1971) has termed this process the "neutralization of crisis." He explains: "crisis tolerances change as communities learn to combat direct action and other forms of challenges. In most cities in the early 1960's, sit-ins were enough to stimulate a crisis-definition, but today they are dealt with as a matter of course and are generally ineffective as a change technique" (Laue, 1971:259). And so it was in the South after the initial wave of sit-ins. As a result, the pace of insurgency dropped sharply and civil rights activists resumed their search for potent new tactical forms.

The Freedom Rides

The tactic that revived the movement was the freedom ride. First used by the Fellowship of Reconciliation in 1947 to test compliance with a supreme Court decision (Morgan *v.* Virginia, 1946) outlawing segregated seating on vehicles engaged in interstate transportation, the tactic was reintroduced by CORE in May 1961. Prompting its reintroduction was another Supreme Court decision—Boynton *v.* Virginia—extending the ban against segregation in interstate travel to terminal facilities as well as the means of transportation themselves. To test compliance with the ruling two CORE-organized interracial groups left Washington, D.C., on May 4, bound, by bus, for New Orleans. The buses never reached their destination. Following the burning of one bus near Anniston, Alabama, and a savage mob attack in Birmingham, the riders had to fly to New Orleans to complete their journey. Nevertheless, the ride had more than accomplished its original purpose. Not only had it dramatized continued southern defiance of the Supreme Court's ruling, but it also served, in the words of a contemporary analyst, "as a shot in the arm to civil rights groups just when interest on the part of Southern Negro students seemed to be flagging . . ." (Oppenheimer, 1963:277).

Figure 2 supports Oppenheimer's assessment. Following the initial wave of sit-ins during the spring of 1960, the pace of movement activity foundered badly. Except for a brief flurry of activity in February–March, 1961, (stimulated, once again, by the introduction of a minor protest technique, the jail-in) the pace of insurgency had dropped to pre–sit-in levels. The initial CORE-sponsored ride changed all this. Inspired by that effort, *and* anxious to capitalize on the momentum it had generated, SNCC activists initiated a second Freedom Ride, which departed from Nashville on May 17. After surviving a mob attack three days later in Montgomery, the second group of riders pressed on to Jackson, Mississippi, where they were arrested and jailed on May 24, on charges of trespassing. Thereafter, the tactic was picked up by groups all over the country. From May to August, separate groups of riders poured into Jackson at the rate of nearly one group a day. By summer's end better than 360 persons had been arrested in connection with the rides (Meier and Rudwick, 1973:140).

In accounting for the impact of the freedom rides one must again point to the ability of insurgents to create a crisis situation of formidable proportions. In this they were helped immeasurably by local segregationists, who responded to the "threat" posed by the rides with a series of highly publicized, violent disruptions of public order. These responses, in turn, prompted a reluctant federal government to intervene in support of the riders. The Justice Department asked a federal district court in Montgomery to enjoin various segregationist groups from interfering with interstate travel; Robert Kennedy ordered 600 marshals to Montgomery to protect the riders; and under administration pressure on September 22, 1961, the Interstate Commerce Commission issued an order barring segregation in interstate travel. Indeed, it seems as if federal intervention had been the goal of insurgents all along. James Farmer, CORE director and chief architect of the rides, described the strategy underlying the campaign: "our intention was to provoke the Southern authorities into arresting us and thereby prod the Justice Department into enforcing the law of the land" (Farmer, 1965:69).

Thus, like the earlier tactics, the rides were used to create a crisis situation. The nature of this crisis, however, was very different from those generated by either the bus boycotts or the sit-ins. It marked the movement's initial use of a protest dynamic whose recognition and conscious exploitation would fuel the heightened pace of insurgency during the period widely regarded as the heyday of the movement. That period begins with the inauguration of John Kennedy as president in January of 1961 and ends with the close of the Selma campaign in May 1965 and the movement's consequent shift to the urban north as a locus of protest activity.

The dynamic in question can be described simply. Impatient with the slow pace of social change achieved through confrontation at the local level, insurgents sought to broaden the conflict by inducing segregationists to disrupt public order to the point where supportive federal intervention was required. This dynamic again emphasizes the crucial importance of political opportunities in setting the context within which the process of tactical innovation operates. With Kennedy's election, the vulnerability of the federal government to this type of pressure increased enormously. Whereas Eisenhower had owed little political debt to black voters or the Democratic South, Kennedy owed much to both groups. The "black vote," in particular, had been widely credited with playing the decisive role in Kennedy's narrow electoral victory over Richard Nixon, the previous fall (c.f. Lawson, 1976:256). Kennedy thus came to office with a need to hold his fractious political coalition together and to retain the support of an increasingly important black constituency. This rendered his administration vulnerable to the "politics of protest" in a way Eisenhower's had never been. Recognition of this vulnerability is reflected in the evolution of the movement's tactics. Whereas the earlier tactics had sought to mobilize leverage at the local level through the disruption of commercial activities, the tactics of the next four years aimed instead to provoke segregationist violence as a stimulus to favorable government action. During this period it was the insurgents' skillful manipulation of this dynamic that shaped the unfolding conflict process and keyed the extent and timing of federal involvement and white opposition. Data presented in Figure 4 supports this contention.

The figure clearly reflects the determinant role of movement forces in shaping the unfolding conflict during the early '60s. In their respective patterns of activity, both segregationist forces and the federal government betray a consistent reactive relationship vis-à-vis the movement. With regard to the first of these groups, the pattern of movement stimulus/segregationist response noted earlier is quite evident. In Figure 4 peaks in segregationist activity are clearly shown to follow similar peaks in black insurgency.

The relationship between the federal government and the movement is a bit more complex. Government activity is still responsive to the pace of black insurgency, but as expected, much of this responsiveness derives from the ability of the movement to provoke disruptive segregationist activity. This can be seen more clearly through a logit regression analysis intended to assess the effect of a variety of independent variables on the odds of a federal civil rights-related action.[9] The odds were computed separately for each of six tactical forms—bus boycotts, sit-ins, freedom rides, and three community-wide protest campaigns in Albany, Birmingham and Selma. For each of the first seven weeks following the initial use of the tactic (or beginning of the campaign), the number of movement *actions* that were followed the very next week by federal *events* in

---

[9] My use of logit regression was motivated primarily by a concern for the likely heteroskedasticity of my data. For an excellent introduction to the technique and its possible uses see Swafford (1980). The unit of analysis in the logit regression was the first seven weeks following the introduction of each protest tactic. The analysis was based on a total of 84 observations.

the same state was recorded."[10] Likewise the number of movement actions that were *not* followed the next week by government events was also noted. The log odds of a movement action being followed by a federal event constitutes the dependent variable in the analysis.

Nine independent variables were utilized in the analysis. Each of the six "tactics" listed above were treated as independent variables. Five dummy variables were created, with "sit-in" employed as the left-out category. Use of sit-in as the omitted category reflects the fact that it had the least effect of any of the tactics on the dependent variable. In addition to these six tactics, three other independent variables were also entered into the analysis. The first was the number of weeks, ranging from 0–6, since the initial use of the tactic. The second was the total number of movement actions during any given week. The final independent variable was the presence of absence of a segregationist *action* during the week following and in the same state as the initial movement action.

As reported in Table 2, the results of the logit regression analysis show clearly that not all of the six tactical forms were equally productive of federal action.

---

[10] In coding story synopses a distinction was made between two general types of movement-related activity. *Statements* referred to any written or oral pronouncements related to the topic of civil rights that were issued by a party to the conflict. *Actions* represented a broad category consisting of all other types of activity *except* for statements. The term *event* was used to designate the total of all statements and actions attributed to a particular initiating unit.

This analysis is based on all *events* initiated by the federal government but only the *actions* attributed to movement and segregationist forces. This convention reflects my conception of the dominant conflict dynamic operative during the early 1960s. Movement and segregationist forces tended to engage in a chesslike exchange of strategic *actions* (e.g., marches, court orders, arrests, sit-ins, beatings) within a localized conflict arena. Much of this local maneuvering, however, was played out for the benefit of federal officials, whose *actions* and *statements* came, in turn, to exert a crucial influence over the course of local events.

A second methodological convention should also be clarified at this point. The decision to lag movement actions one month behind both segregationist actions and government events was made *before* the completion of data collection and was based on my reading of many impressionistic accounts of specific movement campaigns. Those accounts invariably stressed the *delayed reaction* of segregationists to movement activity in their community. Thus, for example, we are told that "Birmingham residents of both races were surprised at the restraint of [Bull] Connor's [Birmingham's notorious chief of police] men at the beginning of the campaign" (King, 1963:69). Once mobilized, however, local segregationists could generally be counted on to respond with the flagrant examples of public violence that made a virtually *instantaneous* federal response necessary.

TABLE 2.

Summary of Logit Regression Analysis of Odds of Federal Action in Relation to Various Independent Variables

Tactic	b	β	F
Bus Boycott	-.344	.132	.681
Freedom Rides	.838**	.155	29.084
Community Campaigns			
Albany	.225	.151	2.206
Birmingham	.806**	.113	50.604
Selma	.854**	.102	69.994
Number of Weeks			
Since First Use	-.744**	.187	15.789
Number of Movement			
Actions	.416*	.150	7.654
Segregationist Response	.593**	.752	62.226
Constant	-1.308	.111	138.401
R^2	.67		

*Significant at the .10 level
**Significant at the .01 level

Indeed, only three of the tactics showed a significant positive relationship with the dependent variable. Not surprisingly, all of these tactics were employed during the Kennedy presidency rather than the "Eisenhower years." As noted earlier, the tactical forms of the "Kennedy years" were designed to prompt favorable federal action by inducing disruptive segregationist violence. Table 2 reflects the operation of this characteristic dynamic.

Both the pace of movement action and the presence or absence of a segregationist response to movement action are significantly related to the odds of federal action. It is the relationship between segregationist action and the odds of a federal response, however, that is the stronger of the two. Federal activity, then, is still responsive to the overall pace of black insurgency, but as expected, much of this responsiveness appears to derive from the ability of the movement to provoke disruptive segregationist activity. More accurately, then, much of the strength of the relationship between federal and movement activity is indirect, with the stimulus to government involvement supplied by the intervening pattern of segregationist activity.

Returning to Figure 4, we can identify four periods that, in varying degrees, reflect this characteristic three-way dynamic linking black protest activity to federal intervention by way of an intermediate pattern of white resistance. The first of these periods, as noted earlier, occurred between May–August, 1961, during the peak of activity associated with the freedom rides.

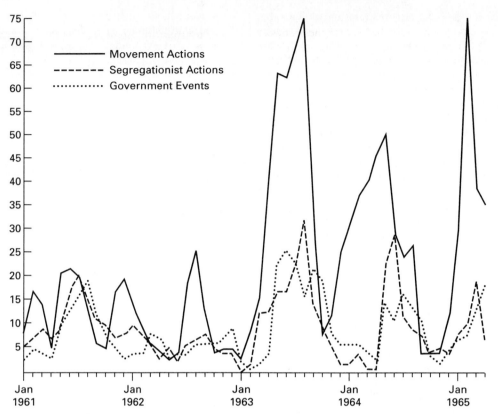

FIGURE 4.   Movement Actions, Segregationist Actions and Federal Government Events, January 1961 through April 1965.*
(*Source: Annual Index* of the *New York Times,* 1961–1965.)

* The final eight months of 1965 have been excluded from this figure because they mark the termination of the dynamic under analysis here. In large measure this is due to the shifting northern locus of movement activity.

However, even this tactic was not able to sustain high levels of insurgency indefinitely. By August the pace of the rides, and movement activity in general, had declined dramatically. In this decline we can once again see the process of tactical adaptation at work. Following the two violence-marred rides through Alabama, and the federal intervention they precipitated, law enforcement officials in Mississippi worked hard to prevent any reoccurrence of violence in their state. In effect, they had learned to short-circuit the dynamic discussed above by failing to respond violently to the demonstrators' tactics. Over time the arrival and arrest of a new group of riders in Jackson took on a fairly routine character. The "crisis atmosphere" that had pervaded the initial rides had again been "neutralized." Fortunately, for insurgents the effectiveness of these counter-maneuvers was negated by the ICC's desegregation order on September 22. The issue of segregation

in interstate transportation was dead. Then too, so was the freedom ride tactic and the momentum it had afforded the movement.

Community-wide Protest Campaigns

With the cessation of the freedom rides there again followed a period of diminished movement activity as insurgents groped to develop new protest tactics. The next breakthrough occurred in December 1961 in Albany, Georgia, with the initiation of the first of what might be called the "community-wide protest campaigns." Such campaigns represented a significant tactical escalation over all previous forms of protest. Instead of focusing on a particular lunch counter, bus terminal, etc., insurgents sought to mobilize the local community for a concerted attack on all manifestations of segregation in the target locale. This escalation was a logical response to the routinization of the other protest methodologies discussed previously. Quite simply, the "crisis tolerance" of local segregationists had increased to the point where bus boycotts, sit-ins or freedom rides were no longer sufficient in themselves to generate the leverage required by insurgents. Nothing short of a community-wide crisis would suffice to precipitate the sort of disruption that would grant insurgents increased leverage to press their demands. Indeed, in Albany not even this escalation in tactics was able to achieve significant progress. Yet, over the next three years this tactic was to be refined through a process of trial and error to the point where it was responsible for the most dramatic campaigns of the entire movement.

The Albany campaign took place during the final two months of 1961 and the summer of the following year. Figure 2 again mirrors a rise in movement activity during these two periods. What was absent during the campaign was the pattern of reactive segregationist violence and subsequent federal intervention evident in the freedom rides. Consistent with this view, Table 2 shows only a weak positive relationship between that campaign and subsequent government action. Accounts of the Albany campaign stress the firm control exercised by Police Chief Laurie Pritchett over events there (Watters, 1971:141–229; Zinn, 1962). While systematically denying demonstrators their rights, Pritchett nonetheless did so in such a way as to prevent the type of major disruption that would have prompted federal intervention. To quote Howard Hubbard (1968:5), "the reason . . . [the movement] failed in Albany was that Chief Pritchett used force rather than violence in controlling the situation, that is, he effectively reciprocated the demonstrators' tactics." Even in "defeat," then, the dynamic is evident. Failing to provoke the public violence necessary to prompt federal intervention, insurgents lacked sufficient leverage themselves to achieve anything more than an inconclusive stand-off with the local segregationist forces in Albany.

The experience of Albany was not without value, however, as the following remarkable passage by Martin Luther King, Jr., attests:

> There were weaknesses in Albany, and a share of the responsibility belongs to each of us who participated. However, none of us was so immodest as to feel himself master of the new theory. Each of us expected that setbacks would be a part of the ongoing effort. There is no tactical theory so neat that a revolutionary struggle for a share of power can be won merely by pressing a

row of buttons. Human beings with all their faults and strengths constitute the mechanism of a social movement. They must make mistakes and learn from them, make more mistakes and learn anew. They must taste defeat as well as success, and discover how to live with each. Time and action are the teachers.

> When we planned our strategy for Birmingham months later, we spent many hours assessing Albany and trying to learn from its errors. (King, 1963:34–35)

The implication of King's statement is that a fuller understanding of the dynamic under discussion here was born of events in Albany. No doubt a part of this fuller understanding was a growing awareness of the importance of white violence as a stimulus to federal action. As Hubbard (1968) argues, this awareness appears to have influenced the choice of Birmingham as the next major protest site. "King's Birmingham innovation was preeminently strategic. Its essense was not merely more refined tactics, but the selection of a target city which had as its Commissioner of Public Safety, "Bull" Connor, a notorious racist and hothead who could be depended on not to respond nonviolently" (Hubbard, 1968:5).

The view that King's choice of Birmingham was a conscious strategic one is supported by the fact that Connor was a lame-duck official, having been defeated by a moderate in a run-off election in early April, 1963. Had SCLC waited to launch the protest campaign until after the moderate took office, there likely would have been considerably less violence *and* less leverage with which to press for federal involvement. "The supposition has to be that . . . SCLC, in a shrewd . . . strategem, knew a good enemy when they saw him . . . one that could be counted on in stupidity and natural viciousness to play into their hands, for full exploitation in the press as archfiend and villain" (Watters, 1971:266).

The results of this choice of protest site are well known and clearly visible in Figure 4 and Table 2. The Birmingham campaign of April–May 1963 triggered considerable white resistance in the form of extreme police brutality and numerous instances of segregationist violence. In turn, the federal government was again forced to assume a more supportive stance vis-à-vis the movement. The ultimate result of this shifting posture was administration sponsorship of a civil rights bill that, even in much weaker form, it had earlier described as politically inopportune (Brooks, 1974). Under pressure by insurgents, the bill was ultimately signed into law a year later as the Civil Rights Act of 1964.

Finally there was Selma, the last of the massive community-wide campaigns. It was in this campaign that the characteristic protest dynamic under discussion was most fully realized. To quote Garrow (1978:227):

> . . . it is clear that by January 1965 King and the SCLC consciously had decided to attempt to elicit violent behavior from their immediate opponents. Such an intent governed the choice of Selma and Jim Clark (Selma's notoriously racist sheriff), and such an intent governed all of the tactical choices that the SCLC leadership made throughout the campaign. . . .

These choices achieved the desired result. Initiated in January 1965, the campaign reached its peak in February and March, triggering the typical reactive patterns of white resistance and federal involvement (see Figure 4 and Table 2). As regards segregationist violence, the campaign provoked no shortage of celebrated atrocities. On March 9, state troopers attacked and brutally beat some 525 marchers attempting to begin a protest march to Montgomery. Later that same day, the Reverend James Reeb, a march participant, was beaten to death by a group of whites. Finally, on March 25, following the triumphal completion of the twice interrupted Selma-to-Montgomery march, a white volunteer, Mrs. Viola Liuzzo, was shot and killed while transporting marchers back to Selma from the state capital. In response to this consistent breakdown of public order, the federal government was once again pressured to intervene in support of black interests. On March 15, President Johnson addressed a joint session of Congress to deliver his famous "We Shall Overcome" speech. Two days later he submitted to Congress a tough Voting Rights Bill containing several provisions that movement leaders had earlier been told were politically too unpopular to be incorporated into legislative proposals. The Bill passed by overwhelming margins in both the Senate and House and was signed into law August 6 of the same year.

However, for all the drama associated with Selma it was to represent the last time insurgents were able successfully to orchestrate a coordinated community-wide protest campaign. Part of the reason for this failure was the growing dissension within the movement. As the earlier consensus regarding goals and tactics gradually collapsed around mid-decade, so too did the ability of insurgents to mount broad-based community campaigns. "The movement—in the special sense of organizations and leaders working together toward agreed goals . . . fell apart after Selma" (Watters, 1971:330).

But growing internal problems were only part of the reason for the movement's diminished use of this tactic. As was the case with earlier innovations, movement opponents learned to counter the specific tactic and in so doing short-circuit the more general protest dynamic under discussion here. The key to both outcomes lay in the opponents' ability to control the violent excesses of the most rabid segregationists. Through the process of tactical interaction they learned to do exactly that. Von Eschen et al. (1969:229–30) explain:

> The response of the movement's opponents was bound to become less extreme. For one thing, a movement is a school in which both the movement and its opponents learn by trial and error the most appropriate moves. Thus, much of the success of the movement had depended on the untutored, emotional responses of the southern police. In time, however, authorities learned that such responses were counter-productive. In some areas, authorities learned responses sufficiently appropriate to deny the movement its instrument of disorder and to totally disorganize its leadership. In Maryland, for instance, Mayor McKeldin responded to CORE's announcement that Baltimore was to become CORE's target city with a warm welcome and an offer of aid, and the temporary chief of police, Gelston, used highly sophisticated tactics to defuse CORE's strategies.

Finally, the increasing northern locus of movement activity made use of the tactic and the characteristic three-way dynamic on which it depended virtually impossible to sustain. The reason centers on the very different form that white resistance took in the North as opposed to the South.

> One of the functional characteristics of the southern segregationists was that they could be counted on, when sufficiently provoked, to create the violent disruptions of public order needed to produce federal intervention. No such convenient foil was available to the movement outside the south . . . Without the dramatic instances of overt white oppression, the movement was deprived of both the visible manifestations of racism so valuable as organizing devices and the leverage needed to force supportive government involvement. Having developed an effective mode of tactical interaction vis-à-vis one opponent, insurgents were unable to devise a similarly suitable response to the changed pattern of northern resistance. (McAdam, 1982:214–15)

Urban Rioting

The last of the major tactical innovations of the period was the urban riot of the mid to late 1960s. Though by no means the first use of the tactic, the Watts riot of 1965 seemed to inaugurate an era of unprecedented urban unrest (see Downes, 1970:352). In the three years following the Watts riot "urban disorders" increased steadily. The peaks in riot activity shown in Figure 3 for the summers of 1966–68 reflect the spread of rioting during this period.

That there were differences between the riots and the tactical forms discussed earlier should be obvious. Most importantly, no evidence has ever been produced to indicate that the riots were deliberately planned or carried out by specific insurgent groups, as were the other tactics. There is little question, however, that the riots came to be *used* rhetorically by black leaders as a tactic and widely interpreted as a form of political protest within the black community (Fogelson, 1971:17). Then, too, the often noted selectivity of riot targets suggests that at the very least the rioters were animated, in part, by a limited political definition of their own actions.

In addition to their political use and interpretation, the riots share two other similarities with the other protest techniques discussed above. First, all occasioned a significant breakdown in public order. And, except for the bus boycotts and sit-ins, all served to stimulate directly supportive federal action.[11] Evidence to support this latter contention is drawn from a number of sources. For example, Button (1978) documents a strong (though by no means consistent) pattern of increased federal expenditure for programs benefiting blacks (and poor whites) in 40 American cities following urban riots in those locales. Consistent with the general thrust of Button's work are the data on school desegregation (U.S. Commission of Civil Rights, 1977:18). They suggest a close connection between disruptive insurgency and the pace of federally sponsored school desegregation efforts. Finally, the work of Isaac and Kelly (1981), and Schram and Turbett (1983), among others, argues for a close connection between

the riots and the expansion in welfare benefits in the late 1960s.

With use, however, all new tactical forms become less efffective, and so it was with the urban riot. After 1965—and especially after 1967—the ameliorative federal response to the riots was increasingly supplanted by a massive control response at all levels of government which was designed to counter the continued threat posed by the disorders. That these efforts had a measurable effect on the actual handling of the riots is suggested by a comparison of data on the 1967 and April 1968 disorders, the latter occurring in the wake of Martin Luther King's assassination.

The first finding of note involves a comparison of the number of law enforcement personnel used in quelling these two sets of disturbances. As shown in Table 3, the force levels used in the 1968 disorders were on the average 50 percent greater than those used the previous year. As Skolnick (1969:173) notes:

> . . . 1968 represented a new level in the massiveness of the official response to racial disorder. In April alone . . . more National Guard troops were called than in all of 1967 . . . and more federal troops as well . . . *Never* before in this country has such a massive military response been mounted against racial disorder.

The presence of increased numbers of enforcement personnel facilitated the more thoroughgoing containment efforts desired by those charged with controlling the disorders. As the data in Table 3 indicate, all major indices of official repression, save one, showed increases between 1967 and April 1968. The average number of injuries per disorder in 1968 was nearly 40 percent higher than in 1967. Even more dramatic was the nearly two-fold increase in the average number of arrests between the two years.

In the face of this massive control response, it is hardly surprising that the intensity and pace of movement activity dropped sharply in the final two years of the period under study (Feagin and Hahn, 1973:193–94; Skolnick, 1969:173). Confronted by government forces increasingly willing and able to suppress ghetto disorders with force, and painfully aware of the costs incurred in the earlier rioting, insurgents gradually abandoned the tactic. In effect, the government's massive control efforts had proven an effective tactical adaptation to the riots. Though no doubt sensible, the abandonment of rioting as a form of protest deprived insurgents of the last major tactical innovation of the era. And with the abandonment of the tactic, insurgency once again declined sharply (see Figure 1).

---

[11] This is not to suggest that the bus boycott and sit-ins were unsuccessful. It must be remembered that, unlike the later tactics, the goal of the boycott and sit-in was not so much to stimulate federal intervention as to mobilize leverage *at the local level* through the creation of negative financial inducements. In this they were largely successful..

TABLE 3.

Comparative Statistics on Racial Disorders During 1967 and April, 1968[a]

	Year 1967	April 1968	Totals
Number of Disorders	217	167	384
Cities	160	138	298
States	34 (+Wash., D.C.)	36 (+Wash., D.C.)	70 (+Wash., D.C.)
Arrests	18,800	27,000	45,800
Avg. No. of Arrests Per Disorder	87	162	119
Injured	3,400	3,500	6,900
Avg. No. Injured Per Disorder	16	22	18
Killed	82	43	125
Property Damage[b]	$69,000,000	$58,000,000	$127,000,000
National Guard			
Times Used	18	22	40
Number Used	27,700	34,900	62,600
Federal Troops			
Times Used	1	3	4
Number Used	4,800	23,700	28,500

Source: Adapted from Lemberg Center for the Study of Violence, "April Aftermath of the King Assassination," Riot Data Review, Number 2 (August 1968), Brandeis University, P. 60, (Mimeographed).
[a]Excluded from the totals reported in this chart are "equivocal" disorders, so termed by the authors of the study because of sketchy information on the racial aspects of the event.
[b]Property damage refers to physical damage to property or loss of stock (usually through looting), estimated in dollars.

The failure of the insurgents to devise new tactical forms must ultimately be seen as a response to the shifting political and organizational realities of the late 1960s and early 1970s. Just as the earlier innovations had depended upon the confluence of internal organization and external opportunity, the cessation of innovation can be seen, in part, as a function of a certain deterioration in these two factors. Organizationally the movement grew progressively weaker as the '60s wore on. In the face of the collapse of the strong consensus on issues and tactics that had prevailed within the movement during its heyday, insurgents found it increasingly difficult to organize the strong, focused campaigns characteristic of the early 1960s. Instead, by 1970, insurgent activity had taken on a more diffuse quality with a veritable profusion of small groups addressing a wide range of issues by means of an equally wide range of tactics. Unfortunately, the diversity inherent in this approach was all too often offset by a political impotence born of the absence of the strong protest vehicles that had earlier dominated the movement.

Second, reversing a trend begun during the 1930s, the "structure of political opportunities" available to blacks contracted in the late 1960s in response to a variety of emergent pressures. Chief among these was the mobilization of a strong conservative "backlash" in this country fueled both by the turbulence of the era and the conscious exploitation of "law and order" rhetoric by public officials. When combined with the emergence of other competing issues and the declining salience of the black vote, this "backlash" served to diminish the overall political leverage exercised by insurgents and therefore the prospects for successful insurgency.

SUMMARY

The pace of black insurgency between 1955 and 1970 has been analyzed as a function of an ongoing process of *tactical interaction* between insurgents and their opponents. Even in the face of a conducive political environment and the presence of strong movement organizations, insurgents face a stern tactical challenge. Lacking institutional power, challengers must devise protest techniques that offset their powerlessness. This has been referred to as a process of *tactical innovation.* Such innovations, however, only temporarily afford challengers increased bargaining leverage. In chesslike fashion, movement opponents can be expected, through effective *tactical adaptation,* to neutralize the new tactic, thereby reinstituting the original power disparity between themselves and the challenger. To succeed over time, then, a challenger must continue its search for new and effective tactical forms.

In the specific case of the black movement, insurgents succeeded in doing just that. Between 1955 and 1965 they developed and applied a series of highly effective new tactical forms that, in succession, breathed new life into the movement. For each new innovation, however, movement opponents were eventually able to devise the effective tactical counters that temporarily slowed the momentum generated by the introduction of the technique. With the abandonment of the riots in the late 1960s, insurgents were left without the tactical vehicles needed to sustain the movement. Reflecting the collapse of the movement's centralized organizational core and the general decline in the political system's vulnerability to black insurgency, by decade's end the movement had not so much died as been rendered tactically impotent.

REFERENCES

Bartley, Numan. 1969. The Rise of Massive Resistance: Race and Politics in the South During the 1950s. Baton Rouge: Louisiana State University Press.

Berger, Morroe. 1950. Equality by Statute, New York: Columbia University Press.

Brooks, Thomas R. 1974. Walls Come Tumbling Down: A History of the Civil Rights Movement, 1940–1970. Englewood Cliffs, NJ: Prentice-Hall.

Bullock, Henry Allen. 1970. "Education: parallel inequality." Pp. 269–79 in Allen Weinstein and Frank Otto Gatell (eds.), The Segregation Era 1863–1954. New York: Oxford University Press.

——. 1971. "Urbanism and Race Relations." Pp. 207–229 in Rupert B. Vance and Nicholas J. Demerath (eds.). The Urban South. Freeport, NY: Books for Libraries Press.

Button, James W. 1978. Black Violence. Princeton, NJ: Princeton University Press.

Danigelis, Nicholas L. 1978. "Black political participation in the United States: some recent evidence." American Sociological Review 43:756–71.

Downes, Bryan T. 1970. "A critical reexamination of social and political characteristics of riot cities." Social Science Quarterly 51:349–60.

Eisinger, Peter K. 1973. "The conditions of protest behavior in American cities." American Political Science Review 76:11–28.

Farmer, James. 1965. Freedom—When? New York: Random House.

Feagin, Joe R. and Harlan Hahn. 1973. Ghetto Revolts. The Politics of Violence in American Cities. New York: Macmillan.

Fogelson, Robert M. 1971. Violence as Protest. Garden City, NY: Doubleday.

Gamson, William A. 1975. The Strategy of Social Protest. Homewood, IL: The Dorsey Press.

Garrow, David J. 1978. Protest at Selma. New Haven, CT: Yale University Press.

Hamilton, C. Horace. 1964. "The Negro leaves the South," Demography. 1:273–95.

Hubbard, Howard. 1968. "Five long hot summers and how they grew." Public Interest 12 (Summer):3–24.

Isaac, Larry and William R. Kelly. 1981. "Racial insurgency, the state, and welfare expansion: local and national level evidence from the postwar United States." American Journal of Sociology. 86:1348–86.

King, Martin Luther, Jr. 1963. Why We Can't Wait. New York: Harper & Row.

Laue, James H. 1971. "A model for civil rights change through conflict." pp. 256–62 in Gary T. Marx (ed.). Racial Conflict. Boston: Little, Brown.

Lawson, Steven F. 1976. Black Ballots: Voting Rights in the South. 1944–1969. New York: Columbia University Press.

Lemberg Center for the Study of Violence. 1968. "April aftermath of the King Assassination." Riot Data Review 2 (August). Waltham, MA: Lemberg Center for the Study of Violence, Brandeis University.

McAdam, Doug. 1982. Politial Process and the Development of Black Insurgency. Chicago: University of Chicago Press.

McCarthy, John D. and Mayer N. Zald. 1973. The Trend of Social Movements in America: Professionalization and Resource Mobilization. Morristown, NJ: General Learning Press.

——. 1977. "Resource mobilization and social movements: a partial theory." American Journal of Sociology 82:1212–41.

McMillen, Neil R. 1971. The Citizens' Council, Organized Resistance to the Second Reconstruction, 1954–1964. Urbana: University of Illinois Press.

McPhail, Clark and David Miller. 1973. "The assembling process: a theoretical and empirical examination." American sociological Review 38:721–35.

Meier, August and Elliott Rudwick. 1973. CORE. A Study in the Civil Rights Movement. 1942–1968. New York: Oxford University Press.

Morris, Aldon. 1981. "Black southern student sit-in movement: an analysis of internal organization." American Sociological Review 46:744–67.

New York Times. 1955–1971. The New York Times Index. New York: New York Times.

Oberschall, Anthony. 1973. Social Conflict and Social

Movements. Englewood Cliffs, NJ: Prentice-Hall.

Oppenheimer, Martin. 1963. The Genesis of the Southern Negro Student Movement (Sit-In Movement): A Study in Contemporary Negro Protest. Unpublished Ph.D. dissertation. University of Pennsylvania.

Piven, Frances Fox and Richard A. Cloward. 1979. Poor People's Movements. New York: Vintage Books.

Ploski, Harry A. and Warren Marr II (eds.). 1976. The Afro American. New York: Bellwether.

Schram, Sanford F. and J. Patrick Turbett. 1983. "Civil disorder and the welfare explosion." American Sociological Review 48:408–414.

Skolnick, Jerome H. 1969. The Politics of Protest. New York: Simon & Schuster.

Smith, Charles V, and Lewis M. Killian. 1958. The Tallahassee Bus Protest. New York: Anti-Defamation League of B'nai B'rith.'

Snyder, David and William R. Kelly. 1979. "Strategies for investigating violence and social change: illustrations from analyses of racial disorders and implications for mobilization research." pp. 212–37 in Mayer N. Zald and John D. McCarthy (eds.). The Dynamics of Social Movements. Cambridge, MA: Winthrop.

Southern Regional Council. 1961. The Student Protest Movement: A recapitulation. Atlanta: Southern Regional Council.

Swafford, Michael. 1980. "Three parametric techniques for contingency table analysis: a nontechnical commentary." American Sociological Review 45:664–90.

Tilly, Charles. 1978. From Mobilization to Revolution. Reading, MA: Addison-Wesley.

U.S. Commission on Civil Rights. 1977. Reviewing a Decade of School Desegregation 1966–1975. Washington, D.C.: U.S. Government Printing Office.

Von Eschen, Donald, Jerome Kirk and Maurice Pinard. 1969. "The disintegration of the Negro nonviolent movement." Journal of Peace Research 3:216–34.

Walton, Norman W. 1956. "The walking city, a history of the Montgomery boycott." The Negro History Bulletin 20 (October, November):17–20.

Watters, Pat. 1971. Down to Now: Reflections on the Southern Civil Rights Movement. New York: Pantheon.

Wilson, James Q. 1961. "The strategy of protest: problems of Negro civil action." Journal of Conflict Resolution 5:291–303.

Wilson, Kenneth L. and Anthony M. Orum. 1976. "Mobilizing people for collective political action." Journal of Political and Military Sociology 4:187–202.

Zald, Mayer N. and Bert Useem. 1982. "Movement and countermovement: loosely coupled interaction." Paper presented at Annual Meetings of the American Socio-

logical Association, San Francisco, CA, September 8, 1982.

Zinn, Howard. 1962. "Albany, a study in national responsibility." Atlanta: Southern Regional Council. 1965. SNCC, The New Abolitionists. Boston: Beacon Press.

READING 24

CHAIN REACTION: THE IMPACT OF RACE, RIGHTS, AND TAXES ON AMERICAN POLITICS

Thomas Byrne Edsall and Mary D. Edsall

The rise of the presidential wing of the Republican party over the past generation has been driven by the overlapping issues of race and taxes. The Republican party has been able to capitalize on these two issues, capturing the White House in five of the last six elections, and shaping a new polarization of the electorate—a polarization which has replaced the traditional New Deal cleavages that sustained the Democratic party from 1932 to 1964.

The overlapping issues of race and taxes have permitted the Republican party to adapt the principles of conservatism to break the underlying class basis of the Roosevelt-Democratic coalition and to build a reconfigured voting majority in presidential elections. Together, the twin issues of race and taxes have created a new, ideologically coherent coalition by pitting taxpayers against tax recipients, by pitting the advocates of meritocracy against proponents of special preference, by pitting the private sector against the public sector, by pitting those in the labor force against the jobless, and by pitting those who bear many of the costs of federal intervention against those whose struggle for equality has been advanced by interventionist government policies.

In a steady evolutionary process, race and taxes have come to intersect with an entire range of domestic issues, from welfare policy to civil-service testing, from drug enforcement to housing regulation, from minority set-aside programs to the decline in urban manufacturing jobs, from prison construction to the globalization of economic competition, from college admissions standards to suburban zoning practices, from highway construction to Federal Communications Commission licensing procedures. In the struggle for government and private-sector resources, race has become a powerful wedge, breaking up what had been the majoritarian economic interests of the poor, working, and lower-middle classes in the traditional liberal coalition. Taxes, in turn, have been used to drive home the cost to whites of federal programs that redistribute social and economic benefits to blacks and to other minorities.

Race and taxes, on their own, have changed the votes of millions of once-Democratic men and women. But it was the collision of race and taxes with two additional forces over the past twenty-five years that created a *chain reaction,* a reaction forcing a realignment of the presidential electorate. These two additional forces were, first, the rights revolution, a revolution demanding statutory and constitutional protections for, among others, criminal defendants, women, the poor, non-European ethnic minorities, students, homosexuals, prisoners, the handicapped, and the mentally ill; and, second, the rights-related reform movement focusing on the right to guaranteed political representation that took root within the Democratic party in the late 1960s and throughout the 1970s.

This chain reaction—a point of political combustion reached as a linked series of highly charged issues collide—acted most powerfully on two key swing voter groups, the white, European ethnic, often Catholic, voters in the North, and lower-income southern white populists. For as long as these voters cast Democratic ballots, the liberal coalition thrived; when they did not, the liberal coalition collapsed. Throughout the 1970s and 1980s, these two key groups of voters, once the mainstay of the New Deal alliance, determined the viability of the conservative presidential majority. The collapse of the political left and the ascendance of a hybrid conservative populism dominated by the affluent have had enormous policy consequences. The holders of power under the new conservative regime encouraged and endorsed, through tax, debt, and budgetary policy, a substantial redistribution of income from the bottom to the top.

The shift in political power has, in turn, helped to erode the belief among working-class whites that the condition of the poor and, more generally, of those in the bottom third of the income distribution is the result of an economic system that needed to be challenged through the Democratic party and through the union movement. Instead, the pitting of whites and blacks at the low end of the income distribution against each other has intensified the view among many whites that the condition of life for the disadvantaged—particularly for disadvantaged blacks—is the responsibility of those afflicted, and not the responsibility of the larger society.

As the civil rights movement became national, as it became clearly associated with the Democratic party, and as it began to impinge on local neighborhoods and schools, it served to crack the Democratic loyalties of key white voters. Crucial numbers of voters—in the white, urban and suburban neighborhoods of the North, and across the South—were, in addition, deeply angered and distressed by aspects of the expanding rights revolution. It has been among the white working and lower-middle classes that many of the social changes stemming from the introduction of new rights—civil rights for minorities, reproductive and workplace rights for women, constitutional protections for the criminally accused, immigration opportunities for those from developing countries, free-speech rights to pornographers, and the surfacing of highly visible homosexual communities—have been most deeply resisted. Resentment of the civil rights movement among key white voters was reinforced and enlarged by cultural and economic conflicts resulting from the rights revolution.

These two forces—race and rights—were, in turn, further charged—that is, were injected with catalytic potential—by the procedural reform movement within the Democratic party. This intraparty reform drive, erupting in the wake of the 1968 convention in Chicago, tapped for Democratic party leadership the ranks of the civil rights, anti-war, women's, and student movements, and became a vehicle for the ascendency of an upper-middle-class, college-educated culturally liberal elite within the Democratic party. This Democratic reform elite, in turn, served as the perfect foil for conservatives seeking to portray the Democratic party as a new establishment intent on imposing an alien—elitist and liberal—racial and cultural agenda on the mass of American voters.

Of the four issues—race, rights, reform, and taxes—race has been the most critical, and the most powerful, in effecting political change. Race has crystalized and provided a focus for values conflicts, for cultural conflicts, and for interest conflicts—conflicts over subjects as diverse as social welfare spending, neighborhood schooling, the distribution of the tax burden, criminal violence, sexual conduct, family structure, political competition, and union membership. Race has provided a mechanism to simultaneously divide voters over values, and to isolate one disproportionately poor segment of the population from the rest of the electorate.

Just as race was used, between 1880 and 1964, by the planter-textile-banking elite of the South to rupture class solidarity at the bottom of the income ladder, and to maintain control of the region's economic and political systems, race as a national issue over the past twenty-five years has broken the Democratic New Deal "bottom-up" coalition—a coalition dependent on substantial support from all voters, white and black, at or below the median income. The fracturing of the Democrats' "bottom-up" coalition permitted, in turn, those at the top of the "top-down" conservative coalition to encourage and to nurture, in the 1980s, what may well have been the most accelerated upwards redistribution of income in the nation's history—a redistribution fed by the tax, spending, and regulatory policies of the Reagan and Bush administrations.

The traditional ideological partisan divide—between Democratic liberalism supportive both of domestic-spending initiatives and of an activist federal regulatory apparatus, on the one hand, and Republican conservatism generally opposed to government regulation and in favor of reduced domestic spending, on the other hand—has been infused, over the past two-and-a-half decades, with racial and race-coded meanings.

For traditional Democratic liberalism, the convictions and resentments of many of its own core voters have become deeply problematic, defying incorporation into party ideology, and precluding, a priori, a functioning biracial political coalition.

In an interview at the campaign headquarters of a GOP state senator in 1988, Dan Donahue, a Chicago carpenter, explained:

> You could classify me as a working-class Democrat, a card-carrying union member. I'm not a card-carrying Republican, yet. . . . We have four or five generations of welfare mothers. And they [Democrats] say the answer to that is we need more programs. Come on . . . . It's well and good we should have compassion for these people, but your compassion goes only so far. I don't mind helping, but somebody has got to help themselves, you've got to pull. When you try to pick somebody up, they have to help. . . . Unfortunately, most of the people who need help in this situation are black and most of the people who are doing the helping are white. . . . We [white, Cook County voters] are tired

of paying for the Chicago Housing Authority, and for public housing and public transportation that we don't use. . . . They hate it [the school board levy] because they are paying for black schools that aren't even educating kids, and the money is just going into the Board of Education and the teachers union.[1]

Dan Donahue's remarks are echoed by significant numbers of working and lower-middle-class white voters across the country—in focus groups, in door to door interviews, in streetcorner and living room conversations.[2]

For the Democratic party, the party that has taken the lead over the past twenty-five years in the struggle for racial equality, the consequences of such division in the electorate have been devastating. Democratic leaders take comfort in poll findings that the electorate remains liberal in its policy commitments, supportive of government spending to rebuild the infrastructure of roads and bridges and to provide improved education, daycare, recreation facilities, public transit, and housing for the homeless. But these leaders neglect underlying information suggesting that a majority of the electorate is unwilling to grant the Democratic party executive-branch authority to set and fund a traditionally liberal agenda—in part out of fear that a Democratic president will raise taxes from the largely white lower-middle and middle classes in order to direct benefits towards the disproportionately black and Hispanic poor—benefits often seen as wastefully spent.

The polarization of the two parties on issues of race had its inception over twenty-five years ago in the most ideological confrontation in twentieth-century American politics, the 1964 presidential election between Lyndon Johnson and Barry Goldwater. Goldwater, the leader of the conservative insurgency that broke the hammerlock of the Eastern Establishment on the presidential wing of the Republican party, publicly defined the Republican party as anti–civil rights with his opposition to the Civil Rights Act of 1964—by far the most salient issue before the nation that year. Johnson, conversely, firmly established the commitment of the Democratic party to civil rights, repeatedly crushing the Southern segregationist wing of the party that had once dominated the Senate.

These partisan divisions were reinforced by a change in the civil rights agenda itself. That agenda shifted away from an initial, pre-1964 focus on government guarantees of fundamental citizenship rights for blacks (such as the right to vote and the right to equal opportunity), and shifted toward a post-1964 focus on broader goals emphasizing equal outcomes or results for blacks, often achieved through racial preferences. These broader objectives were strenuously opposed by conservatives and by the Republican party. Opposition from the right intensified insofar as such objectives required government action to forcibly redistribute private and public goods—goods ranging, on the one hand, from jobs to education to housing, and extending, on the other, so valued intangibles such as cultural authority, prestige, and social space.

The growing saliency of busing throughout the 1970s—when the presidential platforms of each party took sharply opposing stands on perhaps the nation's most divisive question—established one of the most distinct cleavages between the two parties. Affirmative action—and a generally widening system of compensatory preferences favoring blacks over whites—followed on the heels of busing, again splitting the two parties and their presidential platforms, a split that endures to this day.

The contrasting stands of the two national parties on such broad issues as affirmative action and busing have had powerful reverberations into presidential voting patterns, as race has become a pervasive factor in the allocation of limited resources by city, state, and federal governments. Zoning regulations on Long Island, municipal employment residency requirements in black Detroit and in its white suburbs, the location and course offerings of "magnet" schools in Birmingham, the content of promotion exams for New York City police and firemen, the choice of basketball or tennis courts in Los Angeles parks—all of these are racially loaded issues placing black, white, and Hispanic citizens in a distributional competition on an almost daily basis in communities across the country.

These controversies, in turn, affect an extraordinarily broad range of outcomes, from the nature and quality of recreational facilities, to housing, to the caliber of schools, to property values, to the kinds of jobs available, to the sense of security, safety, and even ease enjoyed by ordinary citizens. Central to almost all of these issues are such basic questions as how much taxes are to be raised, for whose benefit; and whose interest will be served in the governmental spending, rule-making, and regulatory processers. At the state and local level, race-freighted issues have not yet been translated into hard and fast, racially-spurred partisan divisions, although that kind of split began to emerge in the 1980s in cities as diverse as Chicago, Birmingham, Philadelphia, and Columbia, South Carolina. But just

as the federal government has been the main advocate of racial equality, so it has been primarily at the federal level that racial cleavages between the two parties have become most apparent: in congressional voting patterns, in the ideological differences between the convention delegates of the two parties, in the two national party platforms, in the thrust and focus of presidential campaigns, and in presidential election-day results.

The commitment of the Democratic party in 1964 to the cause of civil rights, and the opposition of Republican presidential nominee Barry Goldwater to the 1964 Civil Rights Act, set in motion a larger political process. That process altered the core meanings of both liberalism and conservatism, and changed as well the public perceptions of the Democratic and Republican parties. Instead of being seen as advancing the economic well-being of all voters, including white mainstream working and middle-class voters, liberalism and the Democratic party came to be perceived, in key sectors of the electorate, as promoting the establishment of new rights and government guarantees for previously marginalized, stigmatized, or historically disenfranchised groups, often at the expense of traditional constituencies.

In the view of crucial numbers of voters, the Democratic party became the political home of the beneficiaries and advocates of new legal and social rights, from the right to privacy (including the right to sexual privacy) to the rights of blacks, Hispanics, and Asians, to the rights of non-Christian religious minorities. In some respects, the Democratic party became the advocate and champion of a liberal agenda institutionalized by the Warren Court—and for a time by the Burger Court. During the Warren and early Burger years, the Supreme Court expanded far beyond congressional expectation the remedies for discrimination and for racial segregation, and granted legal rights and procedural guarantees to previously unprotected, sometimes unpopular and often controversial groups of once outcast or invisible Americans.

Insofar as the granting of rights to some groups required others to sacrifice tax dollars and authority, to compromise longstanding values, to jeopardize status, power, or the habitual patterns of daily life, this new liberalism became, to a degree, a disruptive force in American life, and particularly so within the Democratic party. At the extreme, liberalism inflamed resentment when it required some citizens—particularly lower-income whites—to put homes, jobs, neighborhoods, and children at perceived risk in the service of bitterly contested remedies for racial discrimination and segregation.

The remedies were established, in the eyes of key voters, not by elected representatives, but by a coercive federal judiciary and by an intrusive federal bureaucracy. The fundamental coalitional structure of the Democratic party, which in the New Deal era had produced an alliance of interests seeking to develop policies and programs benefiting the voting majority, became, in part, a forum for a zero-sum competition. The Democratic party learned only in retrospect to assess the political impact of a mandated redistribution of rights. Only in defeat have Democrats attempted to "read" the political ramifications of an ideology that—no matter how morally coherent or morally justifiable—nonetheless entailed the imposition of substantial costs on voters who had access to election-day retaliation.

The association of the national Democratic party with the newly empowered, frequently controversial groups it sought in the 1960s and 1970s to enfranchise and protect created a backlash among some of the Democrats' traditional constituencies. This backlash was, in turn, fostered and driven for partisan advantage by the Republican opposition. The linkage of the presidential wing of the Democratic party to newly protected groups—often labled by the GOP as "special interests"—became a gold mine for the Republican party. The GOP set out to reinforce that linkage as part of a strategy first developed in the 1960s and early 1970s—a strategy designed to exploit the unpopularity of Democratic elites and of their protégés, and to publicly isolate the national Democratic party from the country's voting mainstream.

To an extraordinary degree, the presidential campaigns of Barry Goldwater, George Wallace, and Richard Nixon in the 1960s and 1970s shaped the rhetoric, themes, and tactics of the Reagan and Bush campaigns of the 1980s. Wallace and Nixon added a new, pejorative meaning to the word "liberal." Under the influence of their rhetoric, liberalism came to connote, for key voters, the favoring of blacks over whites and permissiveness towards drug abuse, illegitimacy, welfare fraud, street crime, homosexuality, anti-Americanism, as well as moral anarchy among the young.

Wallace and Nixon, together with Goldwater—profiting initially from the massive resistance to court-ordered desegregation—established a beachhead in the South for a rapidly evolving presidential Republicanism. Each candidate, including the nominally Democratic Wallace, went on to contribute to a spreading Republican populism, a right-populism attractive to working and lower-middle-class voters seeking to defend themselves from the strictures of a liberal Democratic establishment.

Wallace, of all the candidates seeking to build a right coalition in American politics, provided a sense of moral legitimacy to those whites who felt themselves under siege in the civil rights revolution. Wallace began the process of deflecting attention from blacks, whose own moral claim to equality was indisputable, and instead focused the anger of displaced whites onto a newly conceptualized, liberal establishment—the judges, lawyers, senators, newspaper editors, churchmen, and well-to-do do-gooders who were the champions of the government-led drive to end segregation. Wallace performed for the Republican party a critically important function, pioneering the specter of a new, hated liberal establishment to compete with the reviled corporate upper-class conservative establishment traditionally targeted by American populist politics.

Wallace, in effect, painted the national Democratic party, its elitist cadres, and its government bureaucracies as bastions of entrenched, arrogant privilege; a counterweight to the New Deal left-populist picture of the rich battening on the underpaid labor of the exploited working poor.

In many respects, Ronald Reagan in his quest for the presidency consolidated, updated, and refined the right-populist, race-coded strategies of Wallace and Nixon. The 1980s were marked less by Republican political innovation than by the drive to adjust, renovate, and strengthen messages established in the previous two decades. This drive, in turn, was made possible by the party's well-funded development of powerful new tools of political technology; computerized direct mail, tracking polls, focus groups, marketing techniques, and the manipulation of voter lists, of paid and unpaid television, as well as of demographic, psychological, and geographic data.

In the 1980s, Republicans became master craftsmen, expert at the modernization of political skills introduced into campaigns a generation earlier. What stands out today even more strikingly, however, is the unintenionally cooperative role of the national Democratic party in shaping presidential politics to the advantage of the GOP, as Democrats, over the course of two-and-a-half decades, increased inexorably, their own vulnerability in a political debate structured around the issues of race and taxes.

The race and tax agenda was crucial to the realization of a fundamental goal of the civil rights era Republican party: the "embourgeoisement" of a decisive sector of previously Democratic voters. The issues of race and taxes fostered the creation of a middle-class, anti-government, property-holding, conservative identification among key white voters who had previously seen their interests as aligned with a downwardly-redistributive federal government. This re-identification in the years following 1964—an identification with the importuned rather than with the importuning—was all the more remarkable because it was not accompanied, in many cases, by any genuine movement on the part of such voters into, or even toward, the top half of the income distribution. The "embourgeoisement" of working and lower-middle-class white voters was critical, nonetheless, to the enactment during the Reagan administration of redistributive tax and spending legislation that shifted the rewards of government upwards, from the bottom to the top of the income distribution.

Race and taxes—with their "values," "rights," and redistributive dimensions—functioned to force the attention of the public on the costs of federal policies and programs. Those costs were often first experienced in terms of loss—the loss of control over school selection, union apprenticeship programs, hiring, promotions, neighborhoods, public safety, and even over sexual morals and a stable social order. Those losses or "costs" were then driven home by rising tax burdens to pay for such services as busing, Medicaid, subsidized public housing, law enforcement, prisons, welfare, and new layers of civil rights enforcement at every level of government.

The race and tax agenda effectively focused majority public attention onto what government takes, rather than onto what it gives. For millions of white voters, whose loyalty to the Democratic party had been locked into place by such programs as Social Security, unemployment compensation, the G.I. Bill, and federal mortgage assistance, the post–1964 policy agenda abruptly and negatively transformed their relationship to government.

The costs and burdens of Democratic-endorsed policies seeking to distribute economic and citizenship rights more equitably to blacks and to other minorities fell primarily on working and lower-middle-class whites who frequently competed with blacks for jobs and status, who lived in neighborhoods adjoining black ghettos, and whose children attended schools most likely to fall under busing orders.

The class-tilt of the costs of integration and of racial equality—a disproportionate share of which was borne by low and lower-middle-income whites—turned the resentment of those white working-class voters into a powerful mobilizing force. That resentment was increasingly amplified and channeled by the Republican party, in the wake of the civil rights movement, not just toward blacks, but toward Wallace's original target: the affluent, largely white, universe of liberal "experts" who were pressing the legal claims of blacks and other minorities—experts often sheltered, in their private lives, and largely immune to the costs of implementing minority claims.

The vulnerability of the least-privileged whites to the full impact of the rights-enforcement process provided an ongoing opportunity for the Republican party to reshape public opinion, as Wallace and Nixon had demonstrated, in subtle but critically important ways. In the Wallace tradition, the Republican party was increasingly able to define the Democratic party, its intellectual allies, and the bureaucracy that enforced redistributive laws, as a new left elite—an effective alternative target, as Wallace had shown, to the "fat cat" business class which, between 1929 and 1964, had reliably attracted the lion's share of popular resentment.

The adoption by the post–civil rights GOP of Wallace's demonized "liberal Democratic establishment" facilitated the development of a full-blown Republican-conservative populism. A central pillar of Reagan's success was the skill of his political entourage in manipulating the new Republican agenda of race and taxes in order to portray the Reagan administration as protecting the working man against "big government." Big government was painted, in turn, as fueled by Democrats seeking ever larger infusions of revenue, not only to raise welfare payments and government salaries, but to impose racial preferences on government contracts, on college admissions, and on employment and promotion in the public and private sectors. At the core of Republican-populist strategy was a commitment to resist the forcing of racial, cultural and social liberalism on recalcitrant white, working and middle-class constituencies. Republican-populist strategies and themes were expertly wielded as recently as the 1988 campaign to repackage—and even to reconstitute—George Bush, making possible the "popularization" of his patrician class background, and wiping out the 17-point lead held by the Democratic nominee as late as July of that year.

The development of a Republican populism has been reinforced both by the strategy the party has adopted to stake out the conservative side of racial issues, and by the changing nature of the racial issues themselves. The GOP has positioned itself just where the overwhelming majority of white Americans stand on racial policy: in favor of the principle of equality, but opposed to the enforcement mechanisms developed by the courts and the federal regulatory system. Over the past twenty-five years, poll data reveal that American voters, at least on the record, have moved beyond passive acquiescence in the principles of racial equality, to actual endorsement of those principles.[3] For politicians in virtually every region of the country, a direct appeal to racism would be fatal.

The parties have sharply diverged, however, on such issues as busing and "quotas"—race-based preferential hiring or promotion and affirmative action programs in government spending and in college admissions. The Republican party has firmly established itself as the adversary of these enforcement remedies. This stand places the GOP in support of the position of the majority of the white electorate, and in populist opposition to a powerful federal judiciary and to the civil rights enforcement bureaucracy: the new "establishment."

At the same time, Republican opposition to racial preferences in hiring or promotion or in school admissions is based on the ostensibly egalitarian principle that merit, not special favor, should determine job advancement and access to college—an inherently populist argument.

The Republican party, in developing a populist stance around the issues of race and taxes, has partially resolved one of the central problems facing a political party seeking to build a conservative majority: how to persuade working and lower-middle-class voters to join in an alliance with business interests and the affluent. Opposition to busing, to affirmative action, to quotas, and to housing integration has given a segment of the traditionally Democratic white electorate ideological common ground with business and the affluent in shared opposition to the federal regulatory apparatus. Shared opposition to taxes provides affluent and working-class voters—adversaries in the pre–civil rights era—with a common ground in the fight to restrict the growth of the coercive, redistributive state.

Under the banner of a conservative "egalitarianism," the political right can maintain the loyalty of its low-income supporters by calling for an end to "reverse discrimination," while simultaneously maintaining the loyalty of the richest citizens by shaping to their advantage government policies that provide them with the greatest economic benefits.

As the costs of political initiatives designed to promote racial equality have grown, the national Democratic party has in a number of ways insulated itself from learning about these costs. The party has consequently lost an opportunity to gain better control of the debate and an opportunity to clearly understand the logistics of a modern national majority coalition. The presidential wing of the Democratic party in the late 1960s and early 1970s—the party's reform wing—enacted new rules governing the nomination process. These rules, which seemingly attempted to increase access to the nomination process, in fact functioned to reduce the role of white working and lower-middle-class voters— just the voters who would become pivotal to the outcome of general elections. The presidential selection process was changed, in other words, in a way that cut off feedback and information vital, in terms of successful general election competition, to the party's candidates and to their managers.

The post–1968 Democratic party rules shifted power to constituencies that with rare exception endorsed an agenda of racial, cultural, and social liberalism, while the influence of more conservative interests, particularly of ethnic, working-class leaders, over the selection of the Democratic nominee was substantially reduced.

These leaders represented white voters who were on the frontlines of urban housing integration, who were the subjects of busing orders, who were competitors for jobs as policemen, firemen, and union craftsmen governed by affirmative action consent decrees, and who found the liberal Supreme Court rules on criminal rights, abortion, school prayer, busing, and obscenity incomprehensible. These voters and their political representatives were, and still are, relegated to a largely peripheral status in the Democratic presidential primary competition. And in the absence of these voters from the early stages of the nomination process, Democratic presidential candidates have negotiated that process in the context of an artificially liberal and unrepresentative primary electorate which provides virtually no training for the candidates in the kinds of accommodation and bargaining essential to general election victory.

The political isolation created by the changes in the Democratic nominating rules has coincided over the past two decades with a degree of self-imposed intellectual isolation and intolerance on the part of much of the Democratic party elite—particularly the highly educated, "new class" elite. This isolation and intolerance began to surface in the second half of the 1960s, as many Democratic activists found themselves unable to acknowledge the political and social costs of the liberal agenda. To some degree, events overtook the ability of the new-class, activist, reform wing of the party to respond to the forces accompanying and unleashed by the tide of rising expectations. The outbreak of urban rioting in the 1960s challenged the nonviolent civil rights movements and accelerated the conservative reaction that became known as "white backlash." The enactment of civl rights legislation and of a barrage of measures directed primarily toward helping the black poor coincided with a sharp increase in crime rates, particularly violent crime, in the 1960s.[4] In the same decade, evidence of the deterioration of black family life began to accumulate, as illegitimate birth rates climbed dramatically, as single parenthood became the norm in black communities, and as the number of households on welfare nearly tripled.[5] Social dysfunction among those at the bottom of the income ladder served to blot out—or at the very least, to diminish—public recognition of the extraordinary advances of many working and middle-class blacks in the wake of the civil rights revolution.

Black and white liberals were unable to account for the mounting evidence of violence and social decay, evidence used by conservatives to challenge the legitimacy both of the civil rights movement and of such federal initiatives as the war on poverty, subsidized housing, food stamps, Medicaid, and more generous welfare regulations. Under siege, Democratic liberalism became unreceptive, if not hostile, to new, contradictory, and sometimes frightening information. The public repudiation of racism and the stigmatization of overtly racist expression was a groundbreaking achievement of the 1960s and 1970s. The repudiation of racist expression had an unintended consequence, however, for liberalism and for much of the Democratic party: an almost censorious set of prohibitions against discussion of family structure among the black poor, absent fathers, crime, lack of labor-force participation, welfare dependency, illegitimacy, and other contentious race-freighted issues.

This refusal to address conflicting evidence—of policy failure as well as of policy success—permitted the political right to capture the debate. By the early 1980s, domestic policy making had become dominated by the conservative argument that rising illegitimate birth rates, joblessness, and welfare dependency grew out of—or were reinforced by—economic incentives to bear out-of-wedlock children and the disincentives to work created by the Great Society.

Declining liberal influence over the domestic policy debate meant, in turn, that inadequate recognition was given not only to issues of structural unemployment, low wage scales, and the global transformations that were reshaping American industry, but that inadequate recognition was also given to the successful role of the federal government in expanding the black middle and upper-middle classes. These classes together grew from just 20 percent of black households in 1940, to better than 55 percent in 1980.[6]

While the black middle class grew substantially, conditions in the predominately black and Hispanic underclass grew worse. From prisons to welfare, the government agencies most closely tied to the problems of poverty and of the underclass are now serving constituencies that have a plurality of blacks. In a nation that is 12 percent black and 84 percent white, there were more black prison inmates than white in 1986[7] and, in 1988, more black welfare recipients than white[8]; in 1986, 55.6 percent of all black families with children were one-parent families headed by women[9]; and in 1988, 63.5 percent of all black children were born out of wedlock.[10] According to figures compiled by the Department of Justice in its 1987 criminal victimization survey of 46,000 households—the survey considered by law enforcement professionals to contain the most reliable data on race—30.7 percent of violent crimes in which the race of the offender was identified by the victim were committed by blacks, and a decisive majority of robberies, 59.9 percent, were committed by blacks.[11]

For those committed to racial equality, the trends in crime, welfare dependency, illegitimacy, drug abuse, and joblessness among the worst-off within the black community—in the aftermath of strong anti-discrimination legislation and of expanded social-service entitlements—represent a complex and seemingly intractable set of problems. If the Democratic party does not become a forum for a tough-minded exploration of issues of individual conduct, family structure, patterns of socialization, and other so-called moral/cultural matters—as well as a forum for exploring how such issues interact with larger structural questions of labor markets, wage ladders, deindustrialization, discrimination, etc.—the Democrats will remain vulnerable to challenge—both moral and economic—from the right.

The symptoms of social disorder, which the Democratic left to a large extent has excluded from public debate for most of the past twenty-five years,[12] and which black leaders have resisted talking about in morally unambiguous terms, have become so severe in the nation's cities—and, most difficult of all, so closely associated with race and with liberalism—that continued Democratic avoidance of these issues risks the national party's already-eroded credibility with the voting majority.

The pattern of liberal Democratic neglect of powerful and volatile issues involving race was repeated around a second set of explosive issues, as the party failed during the 1970s to recognize the pressure building towards a full-scale tax revolt. Throughout that decade, inflation and real rising incomes were combining to rapidly push Democratic voters, including many who considered themselves members of the working class, up the bracket system of the federal tax code, forcing them to pay higher and higher marginal rates. Many of these voters, furthermore, saw their rising tax burdens going to finance programs disproportionately serving black and Hispanic constituencies, programs such as low-income health care, public and subsidized housing, the Job Corps, women and infant nutrition programs, Head Start, food stamps, teenage pregnancy counseling, drug rehabilitation, prison construction, and Aid to Families with Dependent Children (AFDC).

In the years just preceding the full-scale outbreak of the tax revolt, when Democrats had the opportunity to adjust the tax structure to take into account the effects of inflation, Democratic attention was diverted by another issue altogther: Watergate. The scandals of the Nixon administration were a short-lived political bonanza for the Democratic party, handing party activists a temporary reprieve—and a set of blinders. Those blinders blocked from view what should have been alarming signs of tax discontent. From 1974 to 1977, major gains in the Senate (five seats) and in the House (a total of fifty seats in the 1974 and 1976 elections)—along with a razor-thin presidential victory in 1976—gave the Democrats false comfort, allowing the party to continue to turn its attention away from the issues of race, values, and taxes.

The party operated on the premise that the public response to Watergate constituted de facto assent to a liberal Democratic agenda, and that the pursuit of such an agenda would lead the Democratic party once again to majority status.

The pitfalls of this strategy became apparent in 1978, and even more so in 1980, when support for the Democrats nose-dived under pressure from a precipitously unraveling economy: unemployment by 1980 had risen to 7.1 percent; inflation had climbed as high as 13.5 percent; regular gasoline, in the midst of spiraling energy costs and a second OPEC oil shock, had reached $1.19 a gallon up from .35 a gallon in 1970 and interest rates had reached an extraordinary 21.5 percent. In the elections of 1978 and 1980, Democrats lost a combined total of fifteen Senate seats, fifty House seats, and the presidency.

The tax revolt, foreshadowing at the state level what would soon become a national issue, forced its way onto the public agenda with the passage in June 1978 of Proposition 13 in California, a referendum measure fixing property taxes at one percent of actual value, barring any new tax hikes, and rolling back real estate assessments to 1976 levels.

Proposition 13 provided, in miniature, an ideal polarizing mechanism for the conservative movement: the only opponents of the tax roll-back measure among all major demographic groups in California were blacks and public employees. At the same time citizen hostility toward government was focused on welfare and public housing, two programs closely associated in the public mind with blacks.

The Republican party moved swiftly to capitalize on Proposition 13, taking the unusual step of making an official party endorsement in the off-year elections of the Kemp-Roth 30 percent across-the-board federal income-tax cut proposed by Republican Representative Jack Kemp of New York and Republican Senator William Roth of Delaware. With the endorsement of Kemp-Roth as a major new Repulican policy initiative calling for significant reductions in the levels of individual taxation, the high-profile, anti-tax and anti-government stand of the GOP was firmly established.

Republican ideological positions in favor of reduced taxes and curtailed government spending place the GOP in a directly adversarial position to the black community. Just as blacks have traditionally been far more supportive of an expansive, interventionist government than whites, they have had strong economic grounds for this position. Not only have a much higher percentage of blacks than of whites received direct government support through welfare, food stamps, Medicaid, and other programs targeted to the poor, over the past three decades, but fully half of all blacks holding professional and managerial-level jobs are employed by local, state, or federal government agencies, compared to just over a quarter of whites.[13] Most of the expansion of black employment in the private sector over the past twenty-five years has, furthermore, been in firms and companies falling under the jurisdiction of the Equal Employment Opportunity Commission (EEOC).[14] For blacks, then, the attack by the GOP on government, on the taxes that support government, and on the governmental regulatory apparatus amounted to a direct assault on the economic underpinnings of the black community.

The relationship of blacks to the federal government, and the dependence of blacks on all levels of government for direct employment, for benefits, and for protection in the courts and in the workplace, reflect the pervasive and mutually reinforcing power of a political agenda based on race and taxes. Race and taxes have been essential, at another level as well, to a key expansion of the Republican coalition: to the initial Republican mobilization in the 1970s of the white fundamentalist Christian community. This mobilization was based, in part, on the willingness of the GOP to vigorously oppose Internal Revenue Service policies prohibiting tax-exempt status for the network of segregated Christian academies that have flourished in the South in the aftermath of stringent federal integration standards for public schools.

Race and taxes, linked together at crucial junctures throughout the political system, have drawn into a coherent framework seemingly disparate issues and values. The forced focus by the Bush 1988 campaign of public attention on Michael Dukakis as a "liberal" and as a "card carrying member of the ACLU" (echoing in "card carrying" the preoccupation of the GOP in the 1950s with Communist party membership), aimed to create a public perception of Dukakis as the exemplar of an elite, rights-oriented, "Harvard Yard boutique" establishment—soft on taxes, soft on "alternate life styles," soft on criminals, soft on defense, and, by implication, soft on social doctrines of forced equality.

The focusing of public attention by the Bush campaign on the prison furlough of Willie Horton tapped not only voter resentment over the prisoners' rights, prison reform, and criminal defendants' rights movements, but tapped these concerns through a particularly threatening and dangerous archetype: of the black man as the rapist of a white woman.

The presence of race and taxes as factors touching upon almost every domestic issue has permitted the Republican party to capitalize on legitimate public concerns in order to conceptualize and construct a majority conservative coalition. For an electorate worried about crime, drugs, rising taxes, and the escalating costs of social-service spending, the Republican issues of strict law enforcement, tightened welfare eligibility, and a reduced poverty-oriented entitlement sector provided ostensibly race-neutral mechanisms to appeal to racially polarized sectors of the electorate.

The power of the joined themes of race and taxes, in concert with the suburban populism of the Republican party, and with the links of the Democratic party to tax-consuming special-interest groups, has resulted in a Republican credibility advantage over the national Democratic party in a number of critical areas. The party standing firm against an array of liberal interests seeking new sources of revenue, and standing firm against a redistributive federal government, is more likely to put its weight behind tough national anti-drug, anti-crime policies than behind civil liberties or criminal rights. The party advocating free-market rather than centralized-government solutions to the problems of racial inequality is more likely, in this view, to be vigilant in conserving American wealth and automony in the face of redistributive claims from a developing world—as vigilant as it is in curtailing domestic social spending.

The public image of the national Democratic party as more permissive on a wide range of domestic issues, including crime, sex, pornography, and drugs, has coincided with a parallel image of the Democratic party as more acquiescent to Third World and other threatening foreign interests. The mutually reinforcing images of domestic and international permissiveness have limited the ability of the Democratic party to capitalize on the dissolution of the Soviet Bloc and on the potential support for redirected—and in the long run possibly reduced—military spending.

Just as a significant segment of the white electorate mistrusts the ability of the national Democratic party to administer improvements in medical care, education, and other domestic programs—goals supported by the public—without distributing benefits most heavily to blacks and to the very poor, the electorate has not been prepared to trust a democratic president to cut back military spending while simultaneously making sure U.S. global concerns are fully protected.

The vulnerability of the Democratic party on this score was powerfully reinforced by the January 1991

House and Senate votes granting President Bush authority to wage war against Iraq in the Persian Gulf. With the near-unanimous backing of the GOP, Bush won the congressional vote, but 45 out of 55 Democratic senators, and 179 out of 265 House Democrats, voted against the war resolution. In the aftermath of Iraq's defeat by the United States, the congressional vote emerged as documentary evidence of Democratic unwillingness to forcibly confront a Third World dictator, and was seen by large numbers of voters as emblematic of Democratic weakness in foreign and military affairs. By March 1991, these developments had functioned to strengthen popular support for the Republican party, and to weaken backing for the Democratic party. When voters were asked in a Washington Post-ABC poll on March 3 and 4, 1991, which party they better trusted to handle the most pressing issues facing the nation, the GOP held a decisive 13 percentage point advantage.

As race and taxes have become organizing issues, the Republican party has achieved a substantial restructuring of the electorate in presidential elections. The Republican presidential coalition, which first emerged in full force in 1972, represents an economic inversion of the New Deal coalition: as Republican presidential candidates have won the support of traditional white Democratic voters at or below the center of the income distribution, the GOP has been able to fashion a presidential voting majority with the strongest levels of backing found among the affluent, smaller majorities in the center, and the weakest margins of support among those at the bottom of the ladder. This is the mirror image of the New Deal coalition, in which a majority was built from the bottom of the income distribution upward.

By constructing a "top-down" coalition around the issues of race and taxes, the Republican party has altered the balance of power in the traditional "have" versus "have-not" political confrontation, so that the segment of the electorate aligning and identifying with the "haves" outnumbers those aligned with the "have-nots." Insofar as the battle for power in American elections is fought out at the margins—in the eight elections since 1960, the winner's margin of victory has averaged 5.1 percent—the race-and-tax agenda, reinforced by culturally potent "rights" and "values" issues, has empowered the Republican party to convert what had been a minority coalition in presidential elections into a majority coalition.

The new Republican presidential majority does not

result from the wholesale conversion of a major segment of the American electorate, but results instead from the piece-by-piece addition of smaller voting blocks, from the shifting of small fractions of the total vote. There has been, for example, what amounts to a realignment of presidential voting in Michigan, a state that voted Democratic in 1960, 1964, and 1968, but voted Republican in 1972, and in every election since then. The presidential realignment of Michigan was driven by the switched allegiance of a relatively small slice of suburban Detroit voters, a switch resulting in large part from an intensely bitter fight over a 1972 court-ordered plan (ultimately rejected by the Supreme Court) to require school busing between Detroit and its surrounding suburbs. While Detroit remained firmly Democratic, the busing fight provoked a realignment in the working-class Detroit suburbs that has transformed the presidential politics of the entire state for at least the past five elections.

Similarly, in the South, the realignment of white fundamentalist Christians between the elections of 1976 and 1980 transformed the presidential election outcome in 1980 in at least seven states. Carter carried Alabama, Arkansas, Kentucky, Mississippi, North Carolina, South Carolina, and Tennessee in 1976, but then lost each of these states to Reagan by a margin of one percent or less—and therefore all of their electoral votes—four years later.

In the winner-take-all system of American politics, changing the outcome of national elections does not require huge percentage shifts within any single voting group. Republican presidential victories have not been dependent on the wholesale conversion, for example, of white working-class voters to the GOP. Republican victories have instead relied on reducing or eliminating Democratic margins among white voters to the degree necessary to convert what was a minority Republican coalition into an election-day majority. The political manipulation of the themes of race and taxes—and of rights and values—is designed to produce relatively modest shifts in a political system where small movements in the electorate determine victory or defeat. Conservative political strategy has been aimed at, in effect, the marginal voter. The target voter is the white, working and lower-middle-class northern or southern populist, and the fundamental strategy is to break him or her loose from traditional Democratic moorings.

Relatively small shifts in voter allegiance can have major consequences. As recently as the Eisenhower and Nixon administrations, the continued presence of a majority in the electorate still committed to the Democratic party, if not to all of its candidates, acted as a brake on conservatism, severely restricting the range of conservative policy initiatives that could be successfully undertaken by the Republican party. Republican gains among voters over the past decade-and-a-half have severely weakened this liberal brake, and the piece-by-piece formation of a presidential majority of "haves" has produced major policy consequences.

The resulting shift to the right has been strengthened, in turn, by the determination of the conservative wing of the Republican party to build the right-leaning coalition in traditional political fashion: by rewarding the loyal and by penalizing the opposition. For the affluent, who form the most loyal members of the new coalition, the Republican party has pressed for enactment of tax cuts skewed in favor of those at the top of the income distribution—from Reagan's $749 billion 1981 tax cut, to Bush's efforts to win approval of a capital-gains tax reduction. For business, particularly business heavily regulated by such adversarial federal agencies as the Environmental Protection Agency (EPA), the Occupational Health and Safety Administration (OSHA), the Federal Trade Commission (FTC), and the anti-trust division of the Justice Department, the Republican party has sought to lessen not only the tax burden, but also to substantially lessen the regulatory burden.

The overlapping areas of domestic spending and civil rights policy have, at the same time, provided Republican strategists with the opportunity to reinforce the loyalty of those voters angered by social-service spending and by what they see as unfair competitive advantages for blacks, and to simultaneously impose penalites on the nation's most Democratic constituencies, the poor and the black.

On this front, the success of the GOP in transforming spending and other race-relevant policies of the federal government has been politically impressive. From 1980 to 1988, for example, discretionary domestic spending as a share of the gross national product was cut by 33.9 percent.[15] The Reagan Justice Department during this period committed itself to dismantling much of the federal civil rights regulatory structure and became the systematic adversary of busing and of affirmative action. The steady stream of conservative Republican appointments to the Supreme Court—Rehnquist, O'Connor, Scalia, and Kennedy—bore fruit in 1989 with a series of five rulings that weakened the legal position of minority and women plaintiffs bringing job discrimination suits, strengthened the leverage of white employees in negotiations

over affirmative action consent decrees, and threatened the future of minority contracting "set-aside" programs developed by state and local governments.[16]

In terms of straightforward economic rewards, the Republican-dominated decade of the 1980s produced one of the most dramatic redistributions of income in the nation's history. While overall family *after-tax* income rose by 15.7 percent, the income of families in the bottom decile fell by 10.4 percent, from $4,791 to $4,295 (in constant 1990 dollars) while the income of those in the top one percent rose by 87.1 percent, from $213,675 to $399,697.[17]

The configuration of elections into majority "top-down" versus minority "bottom-up" confrontations, in effect, permits the GOP to perform the basic function of a political party far more effectively than its Democratic opponents. From 1968 to 1988—the twenty years since the race, tax, and rights agenda superseded an agenda of traditional economic liberalism—the Democratic party has been unable, with the exception of the Carter victory of 1976, to develop a strategy that mobilizes a majority of the electorate in behalf of its presidential candidate.

The building of a majority top-down coalition (incorporating whites from the lower-middle through the upper classes), versus a minority alliance of blacks, Hispanics, the poor, the discriminated-against, and diminishing numbers of whites (excepting a block of well-educated liberals) has proven to be a gold mine for GOP media specialists. Television commercials developed by the Reagan and Bush campaigns, and the institutional television advertising produced by the Republican National Committee throughout the 1980s, crafted powerful campaign messages out of seemingly innocent images of pastoral middle-class life—as in the "It's Morning Again in America" advertisements of the 1984 Reagan campaign. Such a marketing strategy works on the assumption that, buried in the heart of the majority electorate, lies a conviction, sometimes explicit, sometimes implicit, about the values of the Republican party: that the GOP and its presidential candidates are aligned with the fundamental values of the American middle class, and that the Democratic party and its presidential candidates are not.

The 1980 election, unlike previous Republican victories—Eisenhower in 1952 or Nixon in 1968—presented the first successful substantive ideological challenge to New Deal liberalism since its beginning in 1932. In the struggle of the Republican party to achieve majority status, all of the factors favoring partisan realignment coalesced. The tax revolt had by 1980 spread far beyond California's borders; inflation, high interest rates, and unemployment had seriously eroded public trust in the Democratic party to produce prosperity; and the capture of fifty-three American hostages in Iran, the second OPEC oil shock, and the Soviet invasion of Afghanistan, suggested that American international interests were not secure in the hands of a Democratic administration. The 1980 election—in which the GOP took control of the Senate, picked up 35 House seats to gain de facto control of the House, and won 302 state senate and state house seats—represented a repudiation of the national Democratic party that offered the GOP the opportunity to secure a solid majority base in the electorate.

The Republican party won a mandate in 1980 to redirect the course of public policy, and the Reagan administration immediately capitalized on that mandate to win enactment both of the 1981 Conable-Hance tax cut and of the Gramm-Latta budget cuts—major legislation that undermined the liberal principles of progressive taxation and substantially eroded the Great Society programs of the 1960s.

It is one of the ironies of modern politics that it took monetary policies set in motion in 1979 by Paul Volcker, Carter's chairman of the Federal Reserve Board, to stall the newly ascendant GOP and to decisively set back the conservative Republican realignment—monetary policies designed by a Democratic administration to wring rampant inflation out of the economy; policies that led to the brutal recession of 1981–82, with its factory closings, farm bankruptcies, and unemployment rates of 10.5 percent in the month before the 1982 midterm elections.

The loss of conservative momentum during the 1981–82 recession gave the Democratic party the opportunity to regroup. Throughout the 1980s, Democrats learned to use the power of incumbency aggressively, in order to insulate the party from unfavorable trends in public opinion. Incumbency not only gave Democrats access to campaign contributions to tighten control on elective office—access which they learned surprisingly late to take full advantage of—but incumbency also gave them the power to draw U.S. House and state legislative districts favorable to the election of Democrats.

Democratic strategists now privately acknowledge that their control of a majority of legislatures and governorships in 1981 produced post-census congressional redistricting that gave the party control of twenty to twenty-five House seats, most of which would have gone to Republicans had lines been neutrally drawn.

Democratic regrouping in the early 1980s did not, however, involve a serious reassessment of the role of race, rights, or taxes in the collapse of the liberal presidential coalition. Nor did the Democrats make a serious attempt to develop the kinds of policies and political strategies that maintain the allegiance of the poor and of the working class, while muting cultural and values conflicts, racial conflict, and distributional competition. Instead, Democratic party reorganization during the 1980s in many respects involved an intensification of dependence on special interests.

House Democrats, recognizing the threat to their power represented by the 1980 election, sought in the wake of that defeat to enlarge and expand the protective fortress around each Democratic incumbent. Wielding the power of incumbency, House Democrats used implied threats of reprisal, along with numerous concessions to big business, to break the allegiance of the corporate political action committee (PAC) community to the GOP. By 1988, House Democratic incumbents had become, for the first time, more dependent on PACs for financial support than on individual donors.

In securing their hold on Congress, House Democrats, in the course of the 1980s, increasingly became prisoners of the Washington power structure, a dangerous dependence as the public became more and more distrustful of a national policy driven by negotiations between Washington-based interests. The combination of gerrymandered districts with the reliance of House Democrats on PACs and on the perquisites of office meant that the bastion of Democratic strength in Washington was in danger of losing its credibility as a legitimate representative of majority will. Once the party of reform, the national Democrats became by the late 1980s vulnerable to a Republican reform assault, reflected in part by GOP ethics challenges to a number of elected Democrats, including former House Speaker Jim Wright of Texas, Representative Barney Frank of Massachusetts, and former House majority whip Tony Coelho of California.

As Democratic hegemony eroded, and as conflicts over race, rights, and values fractured the once deeply felt loyalty of a plurality of voters to the national Democratic party, Democratic members of the House were forced to rely excessively on an essentially corrupt system of campaign finance, on gerrymandering, on pork-barrel spending, on weak Republican challengers, and on assorted manipulations of the elective process in order to thwart continuing ideological and demographic shifts favoring their opponents.

Democratic dependence on special interests has seriously inhibited the ability of the party to implement innovatively its commitment to America's wage earners, both white and black. The disproportionate influence of special interests has affected not only the economic policy positions but the overall image presented to the public by the national Democratic establishment.

Finally, the dependence on special interests has significantly restricted the range of Democratic responses to a political force of vastly increasing importance over the past fifteen years: the globalization of the economy.

The growth of international competition has directly assaulted a traditional province of the Democratic Party: protective measures designed to insulate vulnerable constituencies from the most destructive elements of unrestrained competition. These measures had amounted over time to a strategy for directing rising wages and steadily improving living conditions toward working-class voters. Democrats had been relatively successful since the New Deal in protecting unions from unbridled competition through a network of regulations and laws, including the National Labor Relations Act and the Davis-Bacon Act.[18] The Democratic party had, furthermore, supported affirmative action, itself a form of protectionist intervention into employment and job promotion markets. In an expanding economy, as long as competition had been largely confined to the territorial United States, these strategies were politically defensible.

As competition became international, however—as factories and production facilities moved to Mexico or overseas, and as corporations and capital traveled at a keystroke from one hemisphere to another—many of the protectionist policies of the Democratic party became futile, and in some cases dangerous to core constituencies.

The failure of Democratic economic policies, and the accompanying political liabilities, became most acute during the Carter years, when the overseas challenge to the domestic auto and steel industries erupted. The economic devastation to Detroit, Cleveland, Buffalo, Pittsburgh, Wheeling (West Virginia), and Birmingham—devastation stretching across the rust and steel belts—was catastrophic to the legitimacy of the national Democratic party. The collapse of heavily unionized industries and the recession of 1980 marked the first substantial Democratic party failure to protect its own voters at the most important level—that of jobs and wages—since the origin of the New Deal coalition.

As House Democrats became dependent on the universe of Washington-based special interests—a universe of interests, epitomized by PACs, generally seeking to preserve existing power arrangements and to prevent innovation—the ability of the Democratic party to respond imaginatively and effectively to the challenge of globalization was limited. In a period of retrenchment, the best organized interests are just those seeking to preserve the status quo; the best organized interests in this case were those dominating the Washington PAC community, a community that had begun, in the early 1980s, to channel more cash to the Democrats. In the process, the Democratic party compounded the loss it had incurred during the Carter years, the loss of perhaps its most precious commodity: the trust of the public in the ability of Democrats to handle the nation's economy. Throughout the latter half of the 1980s, the public in poll after poll was more willing to entrust Republicans with responsibility to provide economic security than the Democrats, and the public saw the GOP as better equipped to represent the interests of the middle classes.[19] The Republican party only began to lose this advantage in 1990 when Bush abandoned his "read my lips—no new taxes" pledge and signed legislation aimed at reducing the federal deficit—legislation to cut spending and raise a broad range of federal taxes.

In many respects, the political consequences of a globalized economy provide a case study of how race interacts catalytically with seemingly race-neutral developments to produce a powerful reaction. Consider, for example, the Detroit metropolitan area, a heavily black city surrounded by largely white, working-class, once-firmly-Democratic suburbs. From the time of the Detroit riots of 1967, through years when a deeply controversial busing proposal appeared likely to force cross-county student transfers, Democratic voting among the white working class steadily eroded. It was when the domestic automobile industry began to collapse in the late 1970s, however, in large part as a result of international competition, that an economic element was added to the persistent racial tension. Studies of the white voters of Macomb County and other suburbs, neighborhoods often dominated by United Auto Workers and auto-industry retirees, found an explosive anger at blacks and at Democratic regimes perceived by such white voters as favoring blacks and as redistributing declining resources to blacks.[20]

Not only in Detroit, but in every beleaguered industrial center, political messages began to be read through a "racial filter." Democratic rhetoric focusing on "fairness" was interpreted by key white voters as meaning "fairness to blacks"—fairness financed with tax dollars extracted from the stagnating and inflation-pinched paychecks of working whites. Already torn loose from their democratic moorings by the racial, cultural, and values conflicts of the 1960s and 1970s, these key voters—soon to be known as "Reagan Democrats"—were further propelled into the arms of the GOP by international economic change; such voters, perceiving themselves as buffeted by economic threat, would come to embrace the GOP at the presidential level, and would periodically abandon their Democratic roots in contests for lower office.

The conflation of rising tax burdens, racial conflict, cultural change, and resource competition has been intensified by the growing public attention paid to the emergence of a heavily black underclass. At a time when the expansion of both the stable black working class and of the black middle class is functioning to cement black-white cooperation and to break up racial stereotypes, the underclass is serving at the other extreme, in the eyes of key voters, to counteract black success and to reinforce the most negative racial stereotypes.

As politics increasingly reflect a struggle over hotly contested cultural and moral values, and at a time when just under 50 percent of the nation's population live in the twenty largest metropolitan areas,[21] the urban underclass has become a driving force, giving much of the "values" debate a racial cast. The underclass, and the desperate tide of black illegitimacy, joblessness, poverty, crime, and welfare dependency in most of the nation's major cities, represent, for many Americans, the most significant and seemingly intractable challenge to traditional majoritarian values. These values, in turn, touch directly on voters' emotionally charged convictions about community, duty, the law, work, the family, sexual conduct, and social responsibility.

Insofar as the national Democratic party, in order to avoid divisive conflict, ignores or neglects majoritarian values issues, Democrats become increasingly vulnerable to accusations of elitism on the one hand, and to charges of moral indifference, on the other—and, finally, to allegations that Democrats are potentially dangerous to America's hard-won competitive leadership position in the world.

As politics are now structured, the pressures for the aggravation of racial conflict are in many respects intensifying. The main force behind the perpetuation of such conflict is the continuing growth of the predominately white suburbs, and the declining political importance of increasingly black and Hispanic central cities. The election of 1992 will be the first in the nation's history in which the suburban vote will constitute an absolute majority. The consequences of this development cannot be overestimated.

At the most critical level, the emergence of a suburban voting majority, often encircling center cities, means that the jurisdictional border between city and county—a boundary with an increasingly minority-dominated, Democratic urban electorate on one side, and a largely white, Republican-leaning suburban electorate on the other—will play a larger and larger role in determining the outcome of national elections.

Just as America's suburbs are becoming functionally independent of center cities, and newly rich in commercial services—with suburban lawyers, doctors, accountants, industrial parks, suppliers, shopping malls, office complexes, hospitals, tennis courts, swimming pools, movie theaters, book stores, and restaurants supplying local consumer needs—suburban voters are also increasingly able to provide for their civic needs through locally based taxes. These locally raised and locally spent taxes will not flow through what are seen by many suburbanites as wasteful Washington bureaucracies and their voracious clienteles.

In the past, public concern over issues such as education, recreation, and the quality of municipal services could be taken advantage of, in political terms, to build a national consensus in support of an activist federal government. Now, the growth of suburbia and of suburban government provides a means to address public concerns, while confining services and benefits to local residents. Affluent counties such as Fairfax (Virginia), Dupage (Illinois), Cobb (Georgia), Montgomery (Maryland), and Orange (California), are the new power centers of American politics. These counties provide avenues for their affluent and middle-class citizens to fulfill civic, social, and communitarian goals through what are often, in effect, racially exclusionary local policies and initiatives.

Partisan competition for the votes of black America has been absent for over a generation, and its absence has corrupted both parties. For the Democratic party, a secure base of support among black voters has stifled innovation, and has eliminated pressure to develop policies that productively reinforce the loyalty of the party's most reliable electorate. The GOP, in turn, has built its success for the past twenty-five years on the basis of racial and cultural flight from the Democratic party, becoming in the process a *de facto* white party.

Partisan competition is perhaps the most effective mechanism with which to force an assault on the problems of poverty, of the underclass, of the working poor, and on such long-range issues as the globalization of the economy. The political marketplace can be a profoundly generative arena and the importance of a healthy partisan competition cannot be overestimated. The failure of the political system to function as a generative force is reflected in part in the deterioration of conditions—of economic security, family, and employment—for those in the bottom third of the income distribution for nearly two decades.

The source of this failure is complex. From the 1930s to the mid-1960s, a period during which the beneficiaries of liberalism were in fact primarily white and constituted a majority of working men and women, the drive to empower those on the margins invigorated liberal Democratic politics. By the 1960s, however, liberalism had begun to press an agenda that increasingly targeted benefits to minorities and provoked often divisive reactions—including cultural and racial antagonisms, anger over reverse discrimination as well as over threatened white hegemony, fear of crime, and distress at continued family dissolution. The struggle to expand and enforce citizenship and constitutional rights became, by the late 1960s, a source of bitter, often subterranean, conflict, dividing rather than strengthening the once-powerful political coalition dominated by those at the bottom.

With liberal constituencies divided, conservatism—committed to protecting the affluent and to dismantling the political alliances of the "have-nots"—is under pressure to mine for profit both racial conflict and the social dysfunction of the very poor, as well as to aggressively adopt positions that capitalize on liberal conflict.

The cold reality is that the presidential realignment of the electorate that began after the election of 1964 has created a politics in which neither national party effectively represents the shared economic interests of the poor and of the working and lower-middle classes. The Democratic party, and many of the voters who traditionally support liberal ideologies and institutions, have been badly wounded by the politics of race, rights, and taxes—and by the dynamic way that these issues have interacted to create a powerful nexus of liabilities for a center-left coalition.

Over the past twenty-five years, liberalism has evaded taking on, and learning from, the experience of voter rejection, as institutional power and a sequence of extraneous events—ranging from Watergate to the 1981–82 recession—have worked to prop up the national Democratic party. For the current cycle to reach completion, and for there to be a breakthrough in stagnant partisan competition, it may be that the Democratic party must go through the kind of nadir—intraparty conflict, challenge to ideological orthodoxy, in short, a form of civil war—experienced by the GOP and the right in the 1960s; that recapturing the ability to build a winning alliance requires learning the full meaning of defeat, developing a conscious awareness of precisely what the electorate will politically support, what it will not, and when—if ever—something more important is at stake.

NOTES

1. Dan Donahue, interview with author, September 1988, at campaign headquarters of state Senator Robert Raica (R) in Chicago.

2. "Research Report: Democrats for the 90's," a report on the views of various voter groups by KRC Research and Consulting, of New York, November 1989; "Report on Democratic Defection," a study of working-class white voters in Detroit suburbs, by The Analysis Group, New Haven and Washington, April 15, 1985; and "Strengthening the Democratic Party through Strategic Marketing: Voters and Donors," a 1985 report for the Democratic National Committee by CRG Research Institute, Washington.

3. Howard Schuman, Charlotte Steeh, and Lawrence Bobo, *Racial Attitudes In America* (Cambridge, MA: Harvard University Press, 1985) 71–138.

4. "Crime and the Administration of Criminal Justice," in *A Common Destiny: Blacks and American Society,* ed. Gerald David Jaynes and Robin M. Williams, Jr. (Washington, D.C.: National Academy Press, 1989), 451–507; and the victimization reports issued by the Department of Justice, Washington, D.C.

5. Bureau of the Census, *Studies in Marriage and the Family,* ser. P-23, no. 162 (Washington, D.C., June 1989); and Department of Labor, Bureau of Labor Statistics, *American Families, 75 Years of Change* (Washington, D.C., March 1990). Cf. additional material cited in Chapters Five and Eight.

6. James P. Smith and Finis R. Welch, *Closing the Gap: Forty Years of Economic Progress for Blacks* (Washington, D.C.: The Rand Corporation, 1986), 12, 13.

7. There were in 1986 (the most recent year for which racial breakdowns of prison populations are available) eleven times as many state prisoners as there were fed-

eral prisoners, according to the Bureau of Justice Statistics, U.S. Department of Justice. State prisoners in 1986 were 45.3 percent black; 39.5 percent white; 12.6 percent Hispanic; and 2.5 percent other races. Federal prisoners in 1986 were 65.7 percent white; 31.8 percent black; and 3.5 percent other. (Federal prison statistics include Hispanics as either white or black.) There were, in 1986, 485,951 state prison inmates, and 36,531 federal prison inmates. Therefore, combining the numbers of state and federal prison inmates, there were more black than white prison inmates. The proportion of minority inmates, according to the Bureau of Justice Statistics, is growing.

Figures are from unpublished data from the Survey of Inmates of State Correctional Facilities, 1986, supplied by the Bureau of Justice Statistics, Department of Justice, by telephone October 1, 1990; and from the Federal Bureau of Prisons, U.S. Department of Justice, supplied by telephone October 1, 1990.

8. In 1988, 39.8 percent of all Aid to Families with Dependent Children (AFDC) recipients were black, 38.8 percent were white, 15.7 percent were Hispanic, and the remaining 5.7 percent were of other races, according to "Characteristics and Financial Circumstances of AFDC Recipients," an annual publication issued by the U.S. Department of Health and Human Services.

9. Bureau of the Census, *Studies in Marriage and the Family, set.* P-23, no. 162 (Washington, D.C., June 1989), 15.

10. National Center for Health Statistics, *Monthly Vital Statistics Report* (Washington, D.C., September 1990), 32. (The percentage of white children born out of wedlock in 1988 was 17.7 percent. The percentage of Hispanic children born out of wedlock was 34 percent in 1988.)

11. Department of Justice, Bureau of Justice Statistics, *Criminal Victimizations in the United States, 1987* (Washington, D.C., June 1989), Table 43, p. 49, and Table 48, p. 52.

12. Among Democratic groups recently attempting to counter the competition from the right is the Democratic Leadership Council and its think-tank offshoot, the Progressive Policy Institute. See for example, the PPI paper released on September 27, 1990: *Putting Children First: A Progressive Family Policy for the 1990s,* by Elaine C. Kamarck and William A. Galston.

The Kamarck-Galston report reads in part:

The path to [a family] policy has been obstructed by the polarized political reaction to the revolution in the American family. Most liberals talk about the economic pressures on families and neglect family values; most conservatives talk about the values and neglect the economics. Liberals tend to reach for bureaucratic solutions even when they are counterproductive; conservatives tend to reject government response even when they would work. Both are wrong. Traditional conservatives' support for families is largely rhetorical; their disregard for new economic realities engenders a policy of unresponsive neglect—expressed for example, in President Bush's misguided veto of the Family Leave Act. Conversely, traditional liberals' unwillingness to acknowledge that intact two-parent families are the most effective units for raising children has led them into a series of policy cul-de-sacs. (p. 1)

13. Selim Jones, employment analyst for the Bureau of the Census, telephone interview with author, September 1989. Among whites holding jobs classified as professional or managerial, 71.5 percent are in the private sector and 28.5 percent are in the public sector. For blacks with similar level jobs, 46.5 percent are in the private sector and 53.5 percent are in the public sector.

In addition, the armed services employ disproportionate numbers of non-civilian blacks: by 1980, more than 22 percent of all active-duty recruits were black, according to "Social Representation in the U.S. Military," Congressional Budget Office, October, 1989.

14. Smith and Welch, *Closing the Gap,* 85–100. The EEOC requires that all companies with over one hundred employees and all contractors doing $50,000 or more a year worth of business with the federal government file annual reports on the racial makeup of their work force.

15. Congressional Budget Office, *The Economic and Budget Outlook: Fiscal Years 1990–1994,* part I, (Washington, D.C., 1989), 135.

16. These five cases—*Wards Cove Packing Co., Inc. v. Atonio; City of Richmond v. J. A. Croson Co.; Martin v. Wilks; Patterson v. McLean Credit Union;* and *Lorance v. AT & T Technologies*—are discussed in Chapter Nine and Chapter Eleven.

17. House Ways and Means Committee, *Overview of Entitlement Programs: The 1990 Green Book,* 101st Cong., 1st sess., June 5, 1990, 1,183.

18. The major exception to Democratic success in protesting the trade union movement was the passage

in 1947 of the Taft-Hartley Labor Act by a Republican-controlled Congress over the veto of Harry S Truman. The legislation prohibited secondary boycotts by unions and allowed states to enact laws barring union shops.

19. Among the most recent polls, at this writing, is "The People, the Press, & Politics 1990," released September 19, 1990, by the Times Mirror Company: "Republicans have a 41%–25% margin as better able to make 'America competitive in the world economy.'

And 40% see Republicans as better able to generate economic growth, compared with only 29% who see that description as better characterizing the Democrats," the poll found (p. 54).

20. For a fuller discussion of focus-group findings of anti-black affect among Michigan voters, see Chapter Seven.

21. Bureau of the Census, *Statistical Abstract of the United States, 1987* (Washington, D.C. 1988), chart 34, "Metropolitan Statistical Areas," p. 28.

CHAPTER 8

FEMINISM AND ANTIFEMINISM

SOME DATES TO REMEMBER

1961	Commission on the Status of Women set up by President John F. Kennedy; 50 state commissions set up, 1962–1967
1963	Final Report of the Commission on the Status of Women
1963	Publication of *The Feminine Mystique* by Betty Friedan
1963	Equal Pay Act
1964	Title VII of the Civil Rights Act outlaws sex discrimination and creates the Equal Employment Opportunity Commission (EEOC)
1966	National Organization of Women (NOW) established
1967–1968	Radical feminist groups founded, often by former activists from the civil rights, anti–Vietnam war, student movements
1968	Women's Equity Action League (WEAL) founded
August 26, 1970	Women's Strike for Equality
1972	Title IX of the Higher Education Act prohibits sex discrimination
March 1972	Equal rights amendment (ERA) approved by Congress; sent to the states for ratification
1972	STOP-ERA founded by Phyllis Schlafly
1973	*Roe v. Wade*: U.S. Supreme Court decision striking down state antiabortion laws as a violation of a constitutional right to privacy
1973–	Expansion of the National Right to Life Committee and other antiabortion groups
1978	Congress extends time for ratification of the ERA until 1982
1977–1982	After 35 of 38 required states had ratified the ERA, no more ratified it prior to 1982

From the nineteenth century to the present, the United States has been the home of the world's largest independent women's movements. Educated, middle-class women have always been at the organizational forefront of these efforts (Chafetz & Dworkin, 1986). Yet there have been crucial changes over time in the social consciousness and political goals of movements dedicated to expanding the influence and opportunities of American women.

Fresh from activism in the antislavery crusades of the day, a handful of precocious U.S. "feminists" declared that "all men and women are created equal" at the Seneca Falls Convention of 1848. Nevertheless, most participants in early U.S. women's movements were *not* feminists who wanted to challenge the division of roles between men and women. During the late nineteenth and early twentieth centuries, middle-class married women formed huge voluntary associations devoted to extending the moral ideals of domesticity and motherhood into public life. These "maternalists" wanted to build upon women's domestic values and duties, not escape them. The roots and legislative achievements of these early women's movements are detailed elsewhere in this Reader, in Reading 14 by Paula Baker in Chapter 5 and Reading 29 by Theda Skocpol in Chapter 9. Many turn-of-the-century maternalists fought for women's suffrage—which was finally guaranteed by the twentieth Amendment to the U.S. Constitution in 1920. Believing that women should remain principally wives and mothers and yet extend their special moral concerns into civic life, the maternalists saw voting as only one of several ways in which to increase female political influence.

From the 1910s onward, modern feminist thought developed in the United States (Cott, 1987). A few groups of women (and some men) argued in favor of equal individual rights for women, and asserted that women should enjoy the same opportunities in the paid economy, and in all spheres of social and political life, as those available to men. Between 1910 and 1960, however, feminists remained few in numbers, confined to elite organizations that lobbied government on behalf of equal rights, often without much success. During this period, there were often conflicts between feminist advocates of equal rights and those who argued that women workers needed special protection under the law. Supporters of protective labor legislation, including Eleanor Roosevelt and most of the other women who were prominent during the New Deal (Ware, 1981), believed that a principled feminist commitment to equal individual rights did not make sense as long as women were burdened with domestic duties and also faced oppressive work conditions in the economy. Not until the 1960s did an equal-rights approach to economic issues become predominant among politically active American women.

Feminism as a truly mass movement began to develop in the United States in the 1960s—in significant part because, by then, changed conditions were making it possible for many middle-class American women to think of themselves as the equals of men and as members of a gender group that was unfairly denied equal opportunities in the society and economy (for explanations along these lines, see Chafetz & Dworkin, 1986; Klein 1984). Not only did American women continue to be very highly educated by world standards, but those who married (the vast majority) were having fewer children and spending much smaller proportions of longer lives engaged in child-rearing activities. Marriage did not provide the economic security it once had, even as late as the 1950s, because the rate of divorce began to rise sharply in the 1960s. Married or divorced, increasing numbers of mothers of small children entered the paid labor force: 12 percent of mothers of preschoolers were employed in 1950, rising to 19 percent by 1960, 30 percent by 1970, and 45 percent by 1980 (Klein, 1984, p. 39). Yet women faced unequal opportunities and very unequal wages in the paid economy. The "equal rights" goals of modern feminism thus became potentially appealing to many people.

Still, changed political opportunities, as well as shifting socioeconomic conditions, were necessary for the emergence of the women's liberation movement. Resources, as well as social strains, had to be present. During the 1960s, both governmental actions and other social movements hastened the evolution of organized collective efforts to achieve women's liberation.

Reading 25 by Jo Freeman analyzes the birth of two, initially separate branches of the U.S. feminist movement. Both branches were prepared to use unconventional protest tactics on behalf of equality for women, going well beyond the polite lobbying of the period from 1925 to 1960 (see Klein, 1984, Chap. 1). One branch of feminism, the "older" and more "formal" branch, was the creation of highly educated, often professional women who were heavily involved in formal politics and wanted stronger government enforcement of women's rights by such agencies as the Equal Employment Opportunity Commission (EEOC). Meanwhile, the other, "younger" branch of "radical" feminism was the creation of women in their twenties. This wing was led by college or university students, or by women who had previously participated in social movements of the 1960s, such as the civil rights and anti–Vietnam war movements.

The younger branch of feminism never coalesced into one focal organization. Not "so much interested in changing the EEOC's enforcement policies as in transforming their own sense of self" (Evans, 1989, p. 279), the younger radical feminists were fervently antibureaucratic, devoted to small "consciousness-raising" groups, and often divided by ideological beliefs. They disagreed about such matters as how to combine women's liberation with leftist politics, and how to manage the differences between lesbian and heterosexual women.

The "older" branch of 1960s feminism, however, did create visible and persistent national organizations—including the Women's Equity Action League, the National Women's Political Caucus, and, above all, the National Organization of Women (NOW). Ironically, NOW was launched in 1966 by people who originally had been brought together on governmentally created public commissions (for further details, see Freeman, 1975). In 1961, newly elected Democratic President John F. Kennedy sought to placate advocates of women's rights by forming a national Commission on the Status of Women; and many states also established such official commissions during the 1960s. As professionals concerned with women's status participated in meetings of—and among—these commissions, they documented legal changes needed to promote women's equality. They also "networked" and shared ideas with one another, and together became frustrated with the slow responses to demands for equality from the U.S. Congress and the federal EEOC (which had been authorized to enforce nondiscrimination laws by the Civil Rights Act of 1964). When official women's commissions proved to be inadequate vehicles for promoting change, Betty Friedan and other women created NOW to pressure government through litigation as well as legislative lobbying. Before long, NOW was also organizing mass demonstrations. Many scholars date the birth of feminism as a mass movement from the August 26, 1970, "Women's Strike for Equality," which NOW orchestrated. Considerable public and media attention was drawn to feminism as thousands of women demonstrated "in support of equal employment and educational opportunities, abortion, and child care" (Klein, 1984, p. 1).

Feminism has made considerable headway in American politics. In other western nations, social conditions often have not been as encouraging, and feminists usually have had to pursue their political goals either through, or in competition with, strong, male-dominated parliamentary political parties and trade union movements (Katzenstein & Mueller, 1987). In contrast, the American polity has weak political parties and unions. With its multiple points of access for organized interest groups, the U.S. political opportunity structure has been relatively open to independently organized feminists prepared to use combinations of protest, lobbying, and legal litigation (for a full elaboration of this point, see Gelb, 1989). American middle-class employed women have thus been able to combine grievances and resources—including social networks, professional training, and a certain amount of disposable income—to create organizations that can effectively agitate public opinion and pressure government on behalf of women's equality. American feminists have been particularly successful in widening opportunities for middle-class women, including those who want to pursue elite careers. But arguably, they have not achieved as much for poor or working-class women as have European feminists, who have worked through strong social democratic political parties (see Gelb, 1989, for a discussion of the achievements of less independently organized feminists in Sweden).

Readings in this chapter discuss shifts in American public opinion in favor of such basic goals as equal pay and equal employment opportunities for women. While many Americans may dislike the label "feminist," many more than in the past now support such ideals. The readings also describe important legislative gains for feminism, ranging from the Equal Pay Act of 1963, through Title IX of the 1972 Higher Education Act, which outlawed sex discrimination in colleges and universities. In its famous *Roe v. Wade* decision in 1973, the U.S. Supreme Court legalized abortion (during early stages of pregnancy), thus partially responding to a key demand of feminists for American women to be able to "control their own bodies." What is more, the U.S. Congress was twice willing (in 1972 and 1978) to endorse the equal rights amendment to the U.S. Constitution, whose ratification by the necessary 38 states became the highest priority of NOW and many other feminist organizations during the late 1970s.

But just as the initial successes of the black civil rights movement of the 1960s aroused opposition among many whites, who dug in their heels against further governmentally sponsored gains for African-Americans, so the initial feminist gains of the 1960s and 1970s spurred the formation of strong antifeminist movements in the United States. Highly visible actions by the federal government triggered key waves of antifeminist mobilization. After the 1973 Supreme Court decision legalizing abortion, opposition swelled under the leadership of the National Right to Life Committee and other groups within the "pro-life" movement. During the 1980s, the antiabortion forces gained considerable legislative and judicial ground. Similarly, after Congress approved the equal rights amendment in 1972, opposition to state-level ratification grew—especially in the South and in swing states such as Illinois. Under the leadership of the conservative activist Phyllis Schlafly, the STOP-ERA movement blocked the final few necessary state ratifications of the amendment—despite all-out mobilization in favor of ratification by the leading feminist organizations. Jane Mansbridge (Reading 27) probes the nature of the ratification struggles and the characteristics of the pro-ERA and anti-ERA forces, in order to explain how the defeat of the ERA came about.

While prominent male-dominated organizations, such as the Catholic Church or conservative political action committees, may well have provided key resources to recent antifeminist movements (Faludi, 1991, Chap. 9), it would be wrong to overlook the support of many American women for these efforts. As Kristin Luker (Reading 26) and Jane Mansbridge explain, many working-class and lower-middle-class women still believe in the ideals of traditional marriage, where husbands are the wage-earning breadwinners and wives are the mothers and homemakers. Traditionalist women, who are often actively religious, not only feel, and regret, the social and economic trends that are making such families difficult to keep together, but they also feel culturally threatened by the rise of feminist movements, which are often led by upper-middle-class women who seem more devoted to careers than to marriage and motherhood. Those who are solely or primarily homemakers feel that their entire way of life is threatened, and they have mobilized politically in response.

Ironically, traditionalist women can sometimes sustain more effective grassroots political efforts than can feminists. The traditionalists are more likely to be homemakers with some time on their hands, whereas the feminists are usually juggling jobs and family responsibilities. And the traditionalists are often tied together across many local communities through Catholic parishes or fundamentalist Protestant churches, while the feminists are more likely to be concentrated in major cities and in national professional associations. Just as the U.S. political opportunity structure is open to pressure from organized feminists, so is it open to counterpressure from organized groups opposed to the goals of feminism. And sometimes the antifeminists can do more in local districts to influence congressional representatives or state legislators.

As both Luker and Mansbridge vividly show, issues about "motherhood" and "equality for women" are highly charged symbolically in U.S. politics today. These not only are issues that divide women from men, but also are issues fueled by moral as well as socioeconomic divisions between sets of women (and their husbands and male friends) who are leading very different kinds of lives within families, churches and associations, and the economy. Contrasting ideals about "women's place" are at stake—and these conflicts over fundamental values are not likely to be fully resolved very soon. In various manifestations, they will be part of American politics for many years to come.

REFERENCES

Chafetz, Janet Saltzman, and Anthony Gary Dworkin. 1986. *Female Revolt: Women's Movements in World and Historical Perspective.* Totowa, N.J.: Rowman and Allanheld.

Cott, Nancy F. 1987. *The Grounding of Modern Feminism.* New Haven, Conn.: Yale University Press.

Evans, Sara M. 1989. *Born for Liberty: A History of Women in America.* New York: Free Press.

Faludi, Susan. 1991. *Backlash: The Undeclared War Against American Women.* New York: Crown Publishers.

Freeman, Jo. 1975. *The Politics of Women's Liberation.* New York and London: Longman.

Gelb, Joyce. 1989. *Feminism and Politics: A Comparative Perspective.* Berkeley: University of California Press.

Katzenstein, Mary Fainsod, and Carol McClurg Mueller. 1987. *The Women's Movements of the United States and Western Europe: Consciousness, Political Opportunity, and Public Policy.* Philadelphia: University of Pennsylvania Press.

Klein, Ethel. 1984. *Gender Politics.* Cambridge, Mass.: Harvard University Press.

Ware, Susan. 1981. *Beyond Suffrage: Women in the New Deal.* Cambridge, Mass.: Harvard University Press.

READING 25

THE WOMEN'S LIBERATION MOVEMENT: ITS ORIGINS, ORGANIZATIONS, ACTIVITIES, AND IDEAS

Jo Freeman

Sometime during the 1920's, feminism died in the United States. It was a premature death—feminists had just obtained that long-sought tool, the vote, with which they had hoped to make an equal place for women in this society—but it seemed an irreversible one. By the time the suffragists' granddaughters were old enough to vote, social mythology had firmly ensconced women in the home, and the very term "feminist" had become an insult.

Social mythology, however, did not always coincide with social fact. Even during the era of the "feminine mystique," the 1940's and 1950's, when the relative numbers of academic degrees given to women were dropping, the absolute numbers of such degrees were rising astronomically. Women's participation in the labor force was also rising, even while women's position within it was declining. Opportunities to work, the trend toward smaller families, plus a change in preferred status symbols from a leisured wife at home to a second car and a color television set, helped transform the female labor force from one of primarily single women under 25, as it was in 1940, to one of married women and mothers over 40, as it was by 1950. Simultaneously, the job market became even more rigidly segregated, with the exception of female professional jobs, such as teaching and social work, which were flooded by men. Thus women's share of professional and technical jobs declined by a third, with a commensurate decline in women's relative income. The result of all this was the creation of a class of highly educated, underemployed, and underpaid women.

ORIGINS IN THE 60'S

In the early 1960's, feminism was still an unmentionable, but it was slowly awakening from the dead. The

first sign of new life was President Kennedy's establishment of a national Commission on the Status of Women in 1961. Created at the urging of Esther Petersen of the Women's Bureau, the short-lived Commission thoroughly documented women's second-class status. It was followed by the formation of a citizen's advisory council and fifty state commissions. Many of the people involved in these commissions, dissatisfied with the lack of progress made on their recommendations, joined with Betty Friedan in 1966 to found the National Organization for Women (NOW).

NOW was the first new feminist organization in almost fifty years, but it was not the sole beginning of the organized expression of the movement. The movement actually has two origins, from two different strata of society, with two different styles, orientations, values, and forms of organization. In many ways there have been two separate movements that have not entirely merged. Although the composition of both branches tends to be predominantly white, middle-class, and college-educated, initially the median age of the activists in what I call the older branch of the movement was higher. Too, it began first. In addition to NOW, this branch contains such organizations as the National Women's Political Caucus, Women's Equity Action League, Federally Employed Women (FEW), and almost 100 different organizations and caucuses of professional women. Their style of organization has tended to be traditionally formal, with elected officers, boards of directors, bylaws, and the other trappings of democratic procedure. All started as top-down organizations lacking a mass base. Some have subsequently developed a mass base, some have not yet done so, and others don't want to.

In 1967 and 1968, unaware of and unknown to NOW or to the state commissions, the other branch of the movement was taking shape. While it did not begin on the campuses, its activators were on the younger side of the generation gap. Although few were students, all were under 30 and had received their political education as participants in or concerned observers of the social-action projects of the preceding decade. Many came direct from New Left and civil rights organizations where they had been shunted into traditional roles and faced with the contradiction of working in a freedom movement but not being very free. Others had attended various courses on women in the multitude of free universities springing up around the country during those years.

During 1967 and 1968 at least five groups formed spontaneously and independently of each other in five different cities—Chicago, Toronto, Detroit, Seattle, and Gainesville, Florida. They arose at a very auspicious moment. The blacks had just kicked the whites out of the civil rights movement, student power had been discredited by SDS, and the organized New Left was on the wane. Only draft-resistance activities were on the rise, and for women whose consciousness was sufficiently advanced, this movement more than any other movement of its time exemplified the social inequities of the sexes. Men could resist the draft. Women could only counsel resistance.

There had been individual temporary caucuses and conferences of women as early as 1964 when Stokeley Carmichael of the Student Nonviolent Coordinating Committee made his infamous remark that "the only position for women in SNCC is prone." But it was not until 1967 that the groups developed a determined, if cautious, continuity and began to expand. In 1968 they held a national conference, attended by over 200 women from around this country and Canada on less than a month's notice. For the next few years they expanded exponentially.

This expansion was more amoebic than organized, because the younger branch of the movement prides itself on its lack of organization. Eschewing structure and damning leadership, it has carried the concept of "everyone doing her own thing" almost to its logical extreme. The thousands of sister chapters around the country are virtually independent of each other, linked only by journals, newsletters, and cross-country travelers. Some cities have a coordinating committee that tries to maintain communication among local groups and to channel newcomers into appropriate ones, but none of these committees has any power over the activities, let alone the ideas, of any of the groups it serves. One result of this style is a very broadly based, creative movement, to which individuals can relate as they desire, with no concern for orthodoxy or doctrine.

Another result is political impotence. It would be virtually impossible for this branch of the movement to join together in a nation-wide action, even assuming there could be an agreement on issues. Fortunately, the older branch of the movement does have the structure necessary to coordinate such actions, and is usually the one to initiate them.

ACTIVITIES

It is a common mistake to try to place the various feminist organizations on the traditional left/right spectrum. The terms "reformist" and "radical" are convenient and fit into our preconceived notions about the nature of political organization, but they tell us nothing relevant. As with most other kinds of categories, feminism cuts across the normal political categories and demands new perspectives in order to be understood. Some groups often called reformist have a platform that would so completely change our society it would be unrecognizable. Other groups called radical concentrate on the traditional female concerns of love, sex, children, and interpersonal relationships (although with nontraditional views). The activities of the organizations are similarly incongruous. The most typical division of labor, ironically, is that those groups labeled radical engage primarily in educational work whereas the so-called reformist ones are the activists. It is structure and style of action rather than ideology that more accurately differentiates the various groups, and even here there has been much borrowing on both sides.

The activities of the two branches have been significantly different. In general, the older branch has stayed with the traditional forms, creating a national structure prepared to use the legal, political, and media institutions of our country. NOW and its subsequent sister organizations have done this with great skill. The Equal Employment Opportunity Commission has changed many of its prejudicial attitudes toward women in its rulings of the last few years. Numerous lawsuits have been filed under the sex provision of Title VII of the 1964 Civil Rights Act. The Equal Rights Amendment has passed Congress. The Supreme Court has legalized some abortions. Complaints have been filed against more than 400 colleges and universities, as well as many businesses, charging sex discrimination. Articles on feminism have appeared in virtually every news medium, and a whole host of new laws have been passed prohibiting sex discrimination in a variety of areas.

The younger branch has been more experimental. Its most prevalent innovation was the development of the "rap group." Essentially an educational technique, it spread far beyond its origins and became a major organizational unit of the whole movement. From a sociological perspective the rap group is probably the most valuable contribution by the women's liberation movement to the tools for social change. As such it deserves some extended attention here.

The rap group serves two main functions. One is simply bringing women together in a situation of structured interaction. It has long been known that people can be kept down as long as they are kept divided from each other, relating more to their social superiors than to their social equals. It is when social development creates natural structures in which people can interact with one another and compare their common concerns that social movements take place. This is the function that the factory served for the workers, the church for the Southern civil rights movement, the campus for students and the ghetto for urban blacks. Women have generally been deprived of structured interaction and been kept isolated in their individual homes, relating more to men than to each other. Natural structures for interaction are still largely lacking, although they have begun to develop. But the rap group has provided an artificial structure that does much the same thing.

The second function of the rap groups is to serve as a mechanism for social change in and of themselves. They are structures created specifically for the purpose of altering the participants' perceptions and conceptions of themselves and of society at large. The process is known as "consciousness-raising" and is very simple. Women come together in groups of five to fifteen and talk to one another about their personal problems, personal experiences, personal feelings, and personal concerns. From this public sharing of experiences comes the realization that what was thought to be individual is in fact common; that what was considered a personal problem has a social cause and probably a political solution. Women see how social structures and attitudes have limited their opportunities and molded them from birth. They ascertain the extent to which women have been denigrated in this society and how they have developed prejudices against themselves and other women.

It is this process of deeply personal attitude change that makes the rap group such a powerful tool. The need for any movement to develop "correct consciousness" has long been known. But usually this consciousness is not developed by means intrinsic to the structure of the movement and does not require such a profound resocialization of one's self-concept. This experience is both irreversible and contagious. Once women have gone through such a resocialization, their views of themselves and the world are never the same again even if they stop participating actively in the movement. Those who do drop out rarely do so without spreading feminist ideas among their own friends and colleagues. All who undergo consciousness-raising feel compelled themselves to seek out other women with whom to share the experience.

There are several personal results from this process. The initial one is a decrease in self- and group-depreci-

ation. Women come to see themselves and other women as essentially worthwhile and interesting. With this realization, the myth of the individual solution explodes. Women come to believe that if they are the way they are because of society, they can change their lives significantly only by changing society. These feelings in turn create a consciousness of oneself as a member of a group and the feeling of solidarity so necessary to any social movement. From this awareness comes the concept of "sisterhood."

The need for group solidarity explains why men have been largely excluded from women's rap groups. Sisterhood was not the initial goal of these groups, but it has been one of the more beneficial by-products. Originally, the idea of exclusion was borrowed from the Black Power movement, which was much in the public consciousness when the women's liberation movement began. It was reinforced by the unremitting hostility of most of the New Left men at the prospect of an independent women's movement not tied to radical ideology. Even when this hostility was not evident, women in virtually every group in the United States, Canada, and Europe soon discovered that when men were present, the traditional sex roles reasserted themselves regardless of the good intentions of the participants. Men inevitably dominated the discussion, and usually would talk only about how women's liberation related to men, or how men were oppressed by the sex roles. In all-female groups women found the discussions to be more open, honest, and extensive. They could learn how to relate to other *women*, not just to men.

Unlike the male exclusion policy, the rap groups did not develop spontaneously or without a struggle. The political background of many of the early feminists of the younger branch predisposed them against the rap group as "unpolitical" and they would condemn discussion meetings which "degenerated" into "bitch sessions." This trend was particularly strong in centers of New Left activity. Meanwhile, other feminists, usually with a civil rights or apolitical background, saw that the "bitch session" obviously met a basic need. They seized upon it and created the consciousness-raising rap group. Developed initially in New York and Gainesville, Fla., the idea soon spread throughout the country, becoming the paradigm for most movement organization.

NOW AND NWPC

These national organizations have and continue to function primarily as pressure groups within the limits of traditional political activity. Diversification in the older branch of the movement has been largely along occupational lines and primarily within the professions. This branch has stressed using the tools for change provided by the system, however limited these may be. It emphasizes short-range goals and does not attempt to place them within a broader ideological framework.

Initially, this structure hampered the development of older branch organizations. NOW suffered three splits between 1967 and 1968. As the only action organization concerned with women's rights, it had attracted many different kinds of people with many different views on what to do and how to do it. With only a national structure and, at that point, no local base, individuals found it difficult to pursue their particular concerns on a local level; they had to persuade the whole organization to support them. This top-down structure, combined with limited resources, placed severe restrictions on diversity and, in turn, severe strains on the organization. Local chapters were also hampered by a lack of organizers to develop new chapters and the lack of a program into which they could fit.

These initial difficulties were overcome as NOW grew to become the largest single feminist organization. While it never hired organizers to develop chapters, the enormous geographical mobility of its members and their desire to create chapters wherever they moved had the same results. Too, NOW benefited greatly from the publicity the movement received in the early seventies. While much of that publicity was a response to the eye-catching tactics of the younger branch, or was aimed at creating "media stars" (none of whom were NOW leaders), NOW was often the only organization with a telephone and a stable address that incipient movement participants could find. Consequently, its membership grew at the same exponential rate the younger branch had experienced in the late sixties.

As the membership grew, the organization became highly decentralized. In 1973, NOW had three national offices with different functions: Administrative in Chicago, Legislative in Washington, D.C., and Public Relations in New York. Its 40,000 members were organized into 700 relatively autonomous chapters and numerous topical task forces. Although it consistently moved in a more radical direction, it had yet to experience another major split.

Within two years, all this changed. With its first contested presidential election in 1974, NOW developed two major factions that fought for control of the organization and very nearly split it into two. Although these factions articulated their concerns ideologically, the fight in fact was not over issues but was a very ordinary attempt by "outs" to become "ins." By 1975 the "insurgent" faction had established solid control, and over the next few years this faction began to centralize NOW. A single office was located in Washington, the national by-laws were re-written to provide for five paid officers, and state organizations were created which deprived local chapters of much of their autonomy.

While this centralization did drain resources and energy from the chapters, it allowed the national office to focus the organization's efforts and thus, on the national level, to increase its power. In the meantime, the issues surrounding the Equal Rights Amendment acquired a national prominence that had not developed when the amendment emerged from Congress in 1972. Under assault from the right wing, who saw the ERA, along with abortion, busing, and gay rights, as leading to the destruction of the family and the American way of life, the Amendment became symbolic of a national struggle unwarranted by its real potential impact. Therefore, when the ERA still lacked three states necessary for ratification one year from the March 22, 1979, deadline, NOW declared it would focus its efforts on the ERA to the virtual exclusion of anything else. In doing so, it repeated the history of the nineteenth-century Woman Movement, which after years of fighting for women's rights on many fronts focused all its efforts on gaining suffrage. With this change, NOW virtually completed its transformation from a social movement organization into an interest group.

The other major national feminist organization, the National Women's Political Caucus, has always been primarily an interest group, even though it emerged out of the women's liberation movement. Formed in 1971 by prominent female politicians, its major aim has been to get more women elected and appointed to public office. Its organization mirrors that of the typical political party, with the effective unit being the state organization and the national office primarily servicing rather than directing the local chapters. Although it has a decidedly feminist bias, its membership is exceedingly diverse with large numbers concerned chiefly with gaining office rather than pushing issues. Without the context of a movement to maintain feminist standards, it would be very easy for the NWPC to become an interest group dedicated solely to the upward mobility of female politicians.

THE SMALL GROUPS

The younger branch has had an entirely different history and faces different prospects. It was able to expand rapidly in the beginning because it could capitalize on the New Left's infrastructure of organizations and media and because its initiators were skilled in local community organizing. Since the primary unit was the small group and no need for national cooperation was perceived, multitudinous splits increased its strength rather than drained its resources. Such fission was often "friendly" in nature, and even when not, served to bring ever-increasing numbers of women under the movement's umbrella.

Unfortunately, these newly recruited masses lacked the organizing skills of the initiators, and, because the very ideas of "leadership" and "organization" were in disrepute, they made no attempt to acquire them. They did not want to deal with traditional political institutions and abjured all traditional political skills. Consequently, the growth of the movement institutions did not go beyond the local level, and they were often inadequate to handle the accelerating influx of new people into the movement. Although these small groups were diverse in kind and responsible to no one for their focus, their nature determined both the structure and the strategy of the movement. To date, the major, though hardly exclusive, activities of the younger branch have been organizing rap groups, putting on conferences, putting out educational literature, and running service projects such as bookstores and health centers. This branch's contribution has lain more in the impact of its new ideas than in its activities. It has developed several ideological perspectives, much of the terminology of the movement, an amazing number of publications and "counter-institutions," numerous new issues, and even new techniques for social change.

Nonetheless, this loose structure is flexible only within certain limits, and the movement has not yet shown a propensity to transcend them. The rap groups have afforded excellent techniques for changing individual attitudes, but they have not been very successful in dealing with social institutions. Their loose, informal structure encourages participation in discussion, and their supportive atmosphere elicits personal insight; but neither is very efficient in handling specific tasks. Thus, although they have been of fundamental value to the development of the movement it is the more structured groups that are the more politically effective.

Individual rap groups tend to flounder when their members have exhausted the virtues of consciousness-raising and decide they want to do something more concrete. The problem is that most groups are unwilling to change their structure when they change their tasks. They have accepted the ideology of "structurelessness" without recognizing the limitations of its uses.

Because "structurelessness" provided no means of resolving political disputes or carrying on ideological debates, the younger branch was racked by several major crises during the early seventies. The two most significant ones were an attempt by the Young Socialist Alliance, youth group of the Socialist Workers' party, to take over the movement, and the so-called gay/straight split. The Trotskyist YSA saw the younger branch of the movement as a potential recruiting ground for socialist converts, and directed its members to join with that purpose in mind. Although YSA members were never numerous, their enormous dedication and their contributions of time and energy enabled them to quickly achieve positions of power in many small groups whose lack of structure provided no means of resisting. However, many New Left women had remained within the younger branch, and their past experience with YSA predisposed them to mistrust it. Not only did they disagree with YSA politics, but they recognized that because YSA members owed their primary allegiance to a centralized national party they had the potential to control the entire movement. The battle that ensued can euphemistically be described as vicious, and it resulted in YSA being largely driven from the younger branch of the movement. (Several years later, in their SWP guise, YSA members began to join NOW, but NOW's structure makes it more difficult to control.) However, the alienation and fragmentation this struggle left in its wake made the movement ill prepared to meet its next major crisis.

The gay/straight split occurred not because of the mere presence of lesbians in feminist groups, but because a vocal group of those present articulated lesbianism as the essential feminist idea. It was argued first that women should identify with, live with, and associate with women only, and eventually that a woman who actually slept with a man was clearly consorting with the enemy and could not be trusted. When this view met the fear and hostility many straight women felt toward homosexuality, the results were explosive.

The gay/straight struggle raged for several years and consumed most of the time and energy of the younger branch. By the time the tensions eased, most straight women had either become gay or left the younger branch. Some joined NOW, some rejoined the New Left, and many simply dropped out of women's groups altogether. Once gay women predominated (by about four to one) in the small groups, their anger toward straight women began to moderate. However, the focus of both the gay and straight women remaining was no longer directed at educating or recruiting non-feminists into the movement, but at building a "women's culture" for those that remained. While a few groups engaged in outreach through public action on issues of concern to all women (e.g., rape) or even on issues concerning straight women exclusively (e.g., wife-beating), most of the small groups concerned themselves with maintaining a comfortable niche for "women-identified women" and with insulating themselves from the damnation of the outside world. Consequently, while the small groups still exist throughout the country, most are hard for the uninitiated to locate and thus their impact on the outside world is now limited.

Their impact on the organizations of the older branch is also limited, as the networks which formerly existed were largely demolished by these crises. A major impetus for NOW's movement in a more radical direction during the early seventies was the pressure it received from the small groups, which frequently accused it of being part of the establishment. The insurgent faction that took control of NOW in the mid-seventies did so on the platform of "out of the mainstream and into the revolution." Once this faction attained power, however, it proceeded to go in the opposite direction, becoming more concerned with respectability in order to appeal to a wide spectrum of women than with developing a consistent feminist interpretation on issues. Without pressure from the younger branch, it found the mainstream more appealing than revolution.

IDEAS

Initially, there was little ideology in the movement beyond a gut feeling that something was wrong. NOW was formed under the slogan "full equality for women in a truly equal partnership with men," and in 1967 the organization specified eight demands in a "Bill of Rights." It and the other organizations of the older branch have largely concluded that attempts at a comprehensive ideology have little to offer beyond internal conflict.

In the younger branch a basic difference of opinion developed quite early. It was disguised as a philosophical difference, was articulated and acted on as a strategic one, but actually was more of a political disagreement than anything else. The two sides involved were essentially the same people who differed over the rap groups, but the split endured long after the groups became ubiquitous. The original issue was whether the fledgling women's liberation movement should remain a branch of the radical left movement or become an independent women's movement. Proponents of the two positions became known as "politicos" and "feminists," respectively, and traded arguments about whether the enemy was "capitalism" or male-dominated social institutions and values. They also traded a few epithets, with politicos calling feminists politically unsophisticated and elitist, and in turn being accused of subservience to the interests of left-wing men. With the influx of large numbers of previously apolitical women, an independent, autonomous women's liberation movement became a reality instead of an argument. The spectrum shifted toward the feminist direction, but the basic difference in orientation remained until wiped out by the debate over lesbian feminism. Those women who maintained their allegiance to the Left then created their own socialist feminist groups or united in feminist caucuses within Left organizations.

Socialist feminism and lesbian feminism are just two of the many different interpretations of women's status that have been developed. Some are more sophisticated than others, and some are better publicized, yet there is no single comprehensive interpretation that can accurately be labeled *the* women's-liberationist, feminist, neofeminist, or radical feminist analysis. At best one can say there is general agreement on two theoretical concerns. The first is the feminist critique of society, and the second is the idea of oppression.

The traditional view of society assumes that men and women are essentially different and should serve different social functions; their diverse roles and statuses simply reflect these essential differences. The feminist perspective starts from the premise that women and men are constitutionally equal and share the same human capabilities; observed differences therefore demand a critical analysis of the social institutions that cause them. Since these two views start from different premises, neither can refute the other in logical terms.

The term "oppression" was long avoided by feminists out of a feeling that it was too rhetorical. But there was no convenient euphemism, and "discrimination" was inadequate to describe what happens to women and what they have in common with other disadvantaged groups. As long as the word remained illegitimate, so did the idea, and that was too valuable not to use. Oppression is still largely an undeveloped concept in which the details have not been sketched, but it appears to have two aspects related much as the two sides of a coin—distinct, yet inseparable. The sociostructural manifestations are easily visible as they are reflected in the legal, economic, social, and political institutions. The sociopsychological ones are often intangible; hard to grasp and hard to alter. Group self-hate and distortion of perceptions to justify a preconceived interpretation of reality are just some of the factors being teased out.

Sexism is the word used to describe the particular kind of oppression that women experience. Starting from the traditional belief of the difference between the sexes, sexism embodies two core concepts. The first is that men are more important than women. Not necessarily superior—we are far too sophisticated these days to use that tainted term—but more important, more significant, more valuable, more worthwhile. This presumption justifies the idea that it is more important for a man, the "breadwinner," to have a job or a promotion, to be paid well, to have an education,and in general to have preference over a woman. It is the basis of men's feeling that if women enter a particular occupation they will degrade it and that men must then leave it or be themselves degraded; it is also at the root of women's feeling that they can raise the prestige of their professions by recruiting men, which they can do only by giving men the better jobs. From this value comes the attitude that a husband must earn more than his wife or suffer a loss of personal status and a wife must subsume her interests to his or be socially castigated. The first core concept of sexist thought, then, is that men do the important work in the world, and the work done by men is what is important.

The second core concept is that women are here for the pleasure and assistance of men. This is what is implied when women are told that their role is complementary to that of men; that they should fulfill their natural "feminine" functions; that they are "different" from men and should not compete with them. From this concept comes the attitude that women are and should be dependent on men for everything, especially their identities, the social definition of who they are. It defines the few roles for which women are socially rewarded—wife, mother, mistress; all pleasing or beneficial to men—and leads directly to the Pedestal theory that extols women who stay in their place as good helpmates to men.

It is this attitude that stigmatizes those women who do not marry or who do not devote their primary energies to the care of men and their children. Association with a man is the basic criterion for a woman's paticipation in this society, and one who does not seek her identity through a man is a threat to the social values. It is similarly this attitude that causes women's-liberation activists to be labeled as manhaters for exposing the nature of sexism. People feel that a woman not devoted to looking after a man must hate men or be unable to "catch" one. The effect of this second core concept of sexist thought, then, is that women's identities are defined by their relationships to men, and their social value is determined by that of the men they are related to.

The sexism of our society is so pervasive that we are not even aware of all its manifestations. Unless one has developed a sensitivity to its workings, by adopting a self-consciously contrary view, its activities are accepted with little question as "normal" and justified. People are said to "choose" what in fact they never thought about. A good example of sexism is what happened during and after World War II. The sudden onslaught of the war radically changed the whole structure of American social relationships as well as the American economy. Men were drafted into the army and women into the labor force. Now desperately needed, women had their wants provided for as were those of the boys at the front. Federal financing of day-care centers in the form of the Lanham Act passed Congress in a record two weeks. Special crash training programs were provided for the new women workers to give them skills they were not previously thought capable of exercising. Women instantly assumed positions of authority and responsibility unavailable to them only the year before.

But what happened when the war ended? Both men and women had heeded their country's call to duty to bring the struggle to a successful conclusion. Yet men were rewarded for their efforts and women punished for theirs. The returning soldiers were given the G.I. Bill and other veterans' benefits. They got their old jobs back and a disproportionate share of the new ones created by the war economy. Women, on the other hand, saw their child-care centers dismantled and their training programs cease. They were fired or demoted in droves and often found it difficult to enter colleges flooded with ex-GIs matriculating on government money. Is it any wonder that they heard the message that their place was in the home? Where else could they go?

The eradication of sexism, and of sexist practices

like those described above, is obviously one of the major goals of the women's liberation movement. But it is not enough to destroy a set of values and leave a normative vacuum. The old values have to be replaced with something. A movement can begin by declaring its opposition to the status quo, but eventually, if it is to succeed, it has to propose an alternative.

I cannot pretend to be definitive about the possible alternatives contemplated by the numerous participants in the women's liberation movement. Yet from the plethora of ideas and visions feminists have thought, discussed, and written about, I think that two predominant ideas have emerged. I call these the Egalitarian Ethic and the Liberation Ethic. They are closely related and merge into what can only be described as a feminist humanism.

The Egalitarian Ethic means exactly what it says. The sexes are equal; therefore sex roles must go. Our history has proven that institutionalized difference inevitability means inequity, and sex-role stereotypes have long since become anachronistic. Strongly differentiated sex roles were rooted in the ancient division of labor; their basis has been torn apart by modern technology. Their justification was rooted in the subjection of women to the reproductive cycle. That has already been destroyed by modern pharmacology. The cramped little boxes of personality and social function to which we assign people from birth must be broken open so that all people can develop independently, as individuals. This means that there will be an integration of social functions and life-styles of men and women as groups until, ideally, one cannot tell anything relevant about a person's social role by knowing that person's sex. But this greater similarity of the two groups also means more options for individuals and more diversity in the human race. No longer will there be men's work and women's work. No longer will humanity suffer a schizophrenic personality desperately trying to reconcile its "masculine" and "feminine" parts. No longer will marriage be an institution in which two half-people come together in hopes of making a whole.

The Liberation Ethic says this is not enough. Not only the limits of the roles must be changed, but their content as well. The Liberation Ethic looks at the kinds of lives currently being led by men as well as women and concludes that both are deplorable and neither is necessary. The social institutions that oppress women as women also oppress people as people and can be altered to make a more human existence for all. So much of our society is hung upon the framework of sex-role stereotypes and their reciprocal functions that the

dismantling of this structure will provide the opportunity for making a more viable life for everyone.

It is important to stress that these two ethics must work in tandem. If the first is emphasized over the second, then we have a women's rights movement, not one of women's liberation. To seek for equality alone, given the current male bias of the social values, is to assume that women want to be like men or that men are worth emulating. It is to demand that women be allowed to participate in society as we know it, to get their piece of the pie, without questioning whether that society is worth participating in. Most feminists today find this view inadequate. Those women who are personally more comfortable in what is considered the male role must realize that that role is made possible only by the existence of the female sex role; in other words, only by the subjection of women. Therefore women cannot become equal to men without the destruction of those two interdependent, mutually parasitic roles. To fail to recognize that the integration of the sex roles and the equality of the sexes will inevitably lead to basic structural change is to fail to seize the opportunity to decide the direction of those changes.

It is just as dangerous to fall into the trap of seeking liberation without due concern for equality. This is the mistake made by many left radicals. They find the general human condition to be so wretched that they feel everyone should devote her/his energies to the millennial Revolution in the belief that the liberation of women will follow naturally the liberation of people.

However, women have yet to be defined as people, even among the radicals, and it is erroneous to assume their interests are identical to those of men. For women to subsume their concerns once again is to ensure that the promise of liberation will be a spurious one. There has yet to be created or conceived by any political or social theorist a revolutionary society in which women were equal to men and their needs duly considered. The sex-role structure has never been comprehensively challenged by male philosophers, and the systems they have proposed have all presumed the existence of a sex-role structure.

Such undue emphasis on the Liberation Ethic can also lead to a sort of Radical Paradox. This is a situation in which the New Left women frequently found themselves during the early days of the movement. They found repugnant the possibility of pursuing "reformist" issues that might be achieved without altering the basic nature of the system, and thus would, they felt, only strengthen the system. However, their search for a sufficiently radical action or issue came to naught and they found themselves unable to do anything out of fear that it might be counter-revolutionary. Inactive revolutionaries are much more innocuous than active reformists.

But even among those who are not rendered impotent, the unilateral pursuit of Liberation can take its toll. Some radical women have been so appalled at the condition of most men, and the possibility of becoming even partially what they are, that they have clung to the security of the role they know while waiting for the Revolution to liberate everyone. Some men, fearing that role-reversal is a goal of the women's liberation movement, have taken a similar position. Both have failed to realize that the abolition of sex roles must be a part of any radical restructuring of society and thus have failed to explore the possible consequences of such role integration. The goal they advocate may be one of liberation, but it does not involve women's liberation.

Separated from each other, the Egalitarian Ethic and the Liberation Ethic can be crippling, but together they can be a very powerful force. Separately they speak to limited interests; together they speak to all humanity. Separately, they afford but superficial solutions; together they recognize that sexism not only oppresses women but limits the potentiality of men. Separately, neither will be achieved because both are too narrow in scope; together, they provide a vision worthy of our devotion. Separately, these two ethics liberate neither women nor men; together, they can liberate both.

READING 26

MOTHERHOOD AND MORALITY IN AMERICA

Kristin Luker

According to interested observers at the time, abortion in America was as frequent in the last century as it is in our own. And the last century, as we have seen, had its own "right-to-life" movement, composed primarily

of physicians who pursued the issue in the service of their own professional goals. When abortion re-emerged as an issue in the late 1950s, it still remained in large part a restricted debate among interested professionals. But abortion as we now know it has little in common with these earlier rounds of the debate. Instead of the civility and colleagueship that characterized the earlier phases of the debate, the present round of the abortion debate is marked by rancor and intransigence. Instead of the elite male professionals who commanded the issue until recently, ordinary people—and more to the point, ordinary women—have come to predominate in the ranks of those concerned. From a quiet, restricted technical debate among concerned professionals, abortion has become a debate that seems at times capable of tearing the fabric of American life apart. How did this happen? What accounts for the remarkable transformation of the abortion debate?

The history of the debate, as examined in previous chapters in this book, provides some preliminary answers. Technological advances in obstetrics led to a decline in those abortions undertaken strictly to preserve the life of the woman, using the narrowly biological sense of the word *life.* These technological advances, in turn, permitted (and indeed forced) physicians over time to make more and more nuanced decisions about abortion and eventually brought to the fore the underlying philosophical issue that had been obscured by a century of medical control over abortion: is the embryo a person or only a potential person? As Chapter Seven has illustrated, once this question is confronted directly, a unified world view—a set of assumptions about how the world is and ought to be organized—is called into play. As that chapter made clear, world views are usually the product of values so deeply held and dearly cherished that an assault upon them is a deeply disturbing assault indeed. Thus to summarize the argument of this book up this point, the abortion debate has been transformed because it has "gone public" and in so doing has called into question individuals' most sacrosanct beliefs.

But this is only part of the story. This chapter will argue that all the previous rounds of the abortion debate in America were merely echoes of the issue as the nineteenth century defined it: a debate about the medical profession's right to make life-and-death decisions. In contrast, the most recent round of the debate is about something new. By bringing the issue of the moral status of the embryo to the fore, the new round focuses on the relative rights of women and embryos. Consequently, the abortion debate has become a debate about women's contrasting obligations to themselves and others. New technologies and the changing nature of work have opened up possibilities for women outside of the home undreamed of in the nineteenth century; together, these changes give women—for the first time in history—the option of deciding exactly how and when their family roles will fit into the larger context of their lives. In essence, therefore, this round of the abortion debate is so passionate and hard-fought *because it is a referendum on the place and meaning of motherhood.*

Motherhood is at issue because two opposing visions of motherhood are at war. Championed by "feminists" and "housewives," these two different views of motherhood represent in turn two very different kinds of social worlds. The abortion debate has become a debate among women, women with different values in the social world, different experiences of it, and different resources with which to cope with it. How the issue is framed, how people think about it, and, most importantly, where the passions come from are all related to the fact that the battlelines are increasingly drawn (and defended) by women. While on the surface it is the embryo's fate that seems to be at stake, the abortion debate is actually about the meanings of *women's* lives.

To be sure, both the pro-life and the pro-choice movements had earlier phases in which they were dominated by male professionals. Some of these men are still active in the debate, and it is certainly the case that some men continue to join the debate on both sides of the issue. But the data in this study suggest that by 1974 over 80 percent of the activists in both the pro-choice and the pro-life movements in California were women, and a national survey of abortion activists found similar results.[1]

Moreover, in our interviews we routinely asked both male and female activists on both sides of the issue to supply information on several "social background variables," such as where they were born, the extent of their education, their income level, the number of children they had, and their occupations. When male activists on the two sides are compared on these variables, they are virtually indistinguishable from one another. But when female activists are compared, it is dramatically clear that for the women who have come to dominate the ranks of the movement, the abortion debate is a conflict between two different social worlds and the hopes and beliefs those worlds support.

WHO ARE THE ACTIVISTS?

On almost every social background variable we examined, pro-life and pro-choice women differed dramatically. For example, in terms of income, almost half of all pro-life women (44 percent) in this study reported an income of less than $20,000 a year, but only one-fourth of the pro-choice women reported an income that low, and a considerable portion of those were young women just starting their careers. On the upper end of the income scale, one-third of the pro-choice women reported an income of $50,000 a year or more compared with only one pro-life woman in every seven.

These simple figures on income, however, conceal a very complex social reality, and that social reality is in turn tied to feelings about abortion. The higher incomes of pro-choice women, for example, result from a number of intersecting factors. Almost without exception pro-choice women work in the paid labor force, they earn good salaries when they work, and if they are married, they are likely to be married to men who also have good incomes. An astounding 94 percent of all pro-choice women work, and over half of them have incomes in the top 10 percent of all working women in this country. Moreover, one pro-choice woman in ten has an annual *personal* income (as opposed to a family income) of $30,000 or more, thus putting her in the rarified ranks of the top 2 percent of all employed women in America. Pro-life women, by contrast, are far less likely to work: 63 percent of them do not work in the paid labor force, and almost all of those who do are unmarried. Among pro-life married women, for example, only 14 percent report any personal income at all, and for most of them, this is earned not in a formal job but through activities such as selling cosmetics to groups of friends. Not surprisingly, the personal income of pro-life women who work outside the home, whether in a formal job or in one of these less-structured activities, is low. Half of all pro-life women who do work earn less than $5,000 a year, and half earn between $5,000 and $10,000. Only two pro-life women we contacted reported a personal income of more than $20,000. Thus pro-life women are less likely to work in the first place, they earn less money when they do work, and they are more likely to be married to a skilled worker or small businessman who earns only a moderate income.

These differences in income are in turn related to the different educational and occupational choices these women have made along the way. Among pro-choice women, almost four out of ten (37 percent) had undertaken some graduate work beyond the B.A. degree, and 18 percent had an M.D., a law degree, a Ph.D., or a similar postgraduate degree. Pro-life women, by comparison, had far less education: 10 percent of them had only a high school education or less; and another 30 percent never finished college (in contrast with only 8 percent of the pro-choice women). Only 6 percent of all pro-life women had a law degree, a Ph.D., or a medical degree.

These educational differences were in turn related to occupational differences among the women in this study. Because of their higher levels of education, pro-choice women tended to be employed in the major professions, as administrators, owners of small businesses, or executives in large businesses. The pro-life women tended to be housewives or, of the few who worked, to be in the traditional female jobs of teaching, social work, and nursing. (The choice of home life over public life held true for even the 6 percent of pro-life women with an advanced degree: of the married women who had such degrees, at the time of our interviews only one of them had not retired from her profession after marriage.)

These economic and social differences were also tied to choices that women on each side had made about marriage and family life. For example, 23 percent of pro-choice women had never married, compared with only 16 percent of pro-life women; 14 percent of pro-choice women had been divorced, compared with 5 percent of pro-life women. The size of the families these women had was also different. The average pro-choice family had between one and two children and was more likely to have one; pro-life families averaged between two and three children and were more likely to have three. (Among the pro-life women, 23 percent had five or more children; 16 percent had seven or more children.) Pro-life women also tended to marry at a slightly younger age and to have had their first child earlier.

Finally, the women on each side differed dramatically in their religious affiliation and in the role that religion played in their lives. Almost 80 percent of the women active in the pro-life movement at the present time are Catholics. The remainder are Protestants (9 percent), persons who claim no religion (5 percent), and Jews (1 percent). In sharp contrast, 63 percent of pro-choice women say that they have no religion,

22 percent think of themselves as vaguely Protestant, 3 percent are Jewish, and 9 percent have what they call a "personal" religion. We found no one in our sample of pro-choice activists who claimed to be a Catholic at the time of the interviews.

When we asked activists what religion they were raised in as a child, however, a different picture emerged. For example, 20 percent of the pro-choice activists were raised as Catholics, 42 percent were raised as Protestants, and 15 percent were raised in the Jewish faith. In this group that describes itself as predominantly without religious affiliation, therefore, only 14 percent say they were not brought up in any formal religious faith. By the same token, although almost 80 percent of present pro-life activists are Catholic, only 58 percent were raised in that religion (15 percent were raised as Protestants and 3 percent as Jews). Thus, almost 20 percent of the pro-life activists in this study are converts to Catholicism, people who have actively chosen to follow a given religious faith, in striking contrast to pro-choice people, who have actively chosen not to follow any.

Perhaps the single most dramatic difference between the two groups, however, is in the role that religion plays in their lives. Almost three-quarters of the pro-choice people interviewed said that formal religion was either unimportant or completely irrelevant to them, and their attitudes are correlated with behavior: only 25 percent of the pro-choice women said they *ever* attend church, and most of these said they do so only occasionally. Among pro-life people, by contrast, 69 percent said religion was important in their lives, and an additional 22 percent said that it was very important. For pro-life women, too, these attitudes are correlated with behavior: half of those pro-life women interviewed said they attend church regularly once a week, and another 13 percent said they do so even more often. Whereas 80 percent of pro-choice people never attend church, only 2 percent of pro-life advocates never do so.

Keeping in mind that the statistical use of averages has inherent difficulties, we ask, who are the "average" pro-choice and pro-life advocates? When the social background data are looked at carefully, two profiles emerge. The average pro-choice activist is a forty-four-year-old married woman who grew up in a large metropolitan area and whose father was a college graduate. She was married at age twenty-two, has one or two children, and has had some graduate or professional training beyond the B.A. degree. She is married to a professional man, is herself employed in a regular job, and her family income is more than $50,000 a year. She is not religiously active, feels that religion is not important to her, and attends church very rarely if at all.

The average pro-life woman is also a forty-four-year-old married woman who grew up in a large metropolitan area. She married at age seventeen and has three children or more. Her father was a high school graduate, and she has some college education or may have a B.A. degree. She is not employed in the paid labor force and is married to a small businessman or a lower-level white-collar worker; her family income is $30,000 a year. She is Catholic (and may have converted), and her religion is one of the most important aspects of her life: she attends church at least once a week and occasionally more often.

INTERESTS AND PASSIONS

To the social scientist (and perhaps to most of us) these social background characteristics connote lifestyles as well. We intuitively clothe these bare statistics with assumptions about beliefs and values. When we do so, the pro-choice women emerge as educated, affluent, liberal professionals, whose lack of religious affiliation suggests a secular, "modern," or (as pro-life people would have it) "utilitarian" outlook on life. Similarly, the income, education, marital patterns, and religious devotion of pro-life women suggest that they are traditional, hard-working people ("polyester types" to their opponents), who hold conservative views on life. We may be entitled to assume that individuals' social backgrounds act to shape and mold their social attitudes, but it is important to realize that the relationship between social worlds and social values is a very complex one.

Perhaps one example will serve to illustrate the point. A number of pro-life women in this study emphatically rejected an expression that pro-choice women tend to use almost unthinkingly—the expression *unwanted pregnancy*. Pro-life women argued forcefully that a better term would be a *surprise* pregnancy, asserting that although a pregnancy may be momentarily unwanted, the child that results from the pregnancy almost never is. Even such a simple thing—what to call an unanticipated pregnancy—calls into play an individual's values and resources. Keeping in mind our profile of the average pro-life person, it is obvious that a woman who does not work in the paid labor force, who does not have a college degree, whose religion is important to her, and who has already committed herself wholeheartedly to marriage and a large

family is well equipped to believe that an unanticipated pregnancy usually becomes a beloved child. Her life is arranged so that for her, this belief is true. This view is consistent not only with her values, which she has held from earliest childhood, but with her social resources as well. It should not be surprising, therefore, that her world view leads her to believe that everyone else can "make room for one more" as easily as she can and that therefore it supports her in her conviction that abortion is cruel, wicked, and self-indulgent.*

It is almost certainly the case that an unplanned pregnancy is never an easy thing for anyone. Keeping in mind the profile of the average pro-choice woman, however, it is evident that a woman who is employed full time, who has an affluent lifestyle that depends in part on her contribution to the family income, and who expects to give a child as good a life as she herself has had with respect to educational, social, and economic advantages will draw on a different reality when she finds herself being skeptical about the ability of the average person to transform unwanted pregnancies into well-loved (and well-cared-for) children.

The relationship between passions and interests is thus more dynamic than it might appear at first. It is true that at one level, pro-choice and pro-life attitudes on abortion are self-serving: activists on each side have different views of the morality of abortion because their chosen lifestyles leave them with different needs for abortion; and both sides have values that provide a moral basis for their abortion needs in particular and their lifestyles in general. But this is only half the story. The values that lead pro-life and pro-choice women into different attitudes toward abortion are the same

---

* As might be imagined, it is not an easy task to ask people who are anti-abortion activists about their own experiences with a certain kind of unanticipated pregnancy, namely, a premarital pregnancy. Most pro-choice people were quite open about having had such pregnancies; as we noted in Chapter Four, their pregnancies—and subsequent abortions—were central to their feelings about abortion. Pro-life women, by contrast, were deeply reluctant to discuss the topic. Several of them, after acknowledging premarital pregnancies, said that they did not want people to think that their attitudes on abortion were merely a product of their personal experiences. Thus we have no comparative figures about the extent to which the values represented here are the product of different experiences or just different opinions. We know only that unanticipated pregnancy was common among pro-choice women, and the interviews suggest that it was not uncommon among pro-life women. The difference in experience is, of course, that those in the first group sought abortions and those in the second group, with only a few exceptions, legitimized their pregnancies with a marriage.

values that led them at an earlier time to adopt different lifestyles that supported a given view of abortion.

For example, pro-life women have *always* valued family roles very highly and have arranged their lives accordingly. They did not acquire high-level educational and occupational skills, for example, because they married, and they married because their values suggested that this would be the most satisfying life open to them. Similarly, pro-choice women postponed (or avoided) marriage and family roles because they chose to acquire the skills they needed to be successful in the larger world, having concluded that the role of wife and mother was too limited for them. Thus, activists on both sides of the issue are women who have a given set of values about what are the most satisfying and appropriate roles for women, and they have made *life commitments that now limit their ability to change their minds.* Women who have many children and little education, for example, are seriously handicapped in attempting to become doctors or lawyers; women who have reached their late forties with few children or none are limited in their ability to build (or rebuild) a family. For most of these activists, therefore, their position on abortion is the "tip of the iceberg," a shorthand way of supporting and proclaiming not only a complex set of values but a given set of social resources as well.

To put the matter differently, we might say that for pro-life women the traditional division of life into separate male roles and female roles still works, but for pro-choice women it does not. Having made a commitment to the traditional female roles of wife, mother, and homemaker, pro-life women are limited in those kinds of resources—education, class status, recent occupational experiences—they would need to compete in what has traditionally been the male sphere, namely, the paid labor force. The average pro-choice woman, in contrast, is comparatively well endowed with exactly those resources: she is highly educated, she already has a job, and she has recent (and continuous) experience in the job market.

In consequence, anything that supports a traditional division of labor into male and female worlds is, broadly speaking, in the interests of pro-life women because that is where their resources lie. Conversely, such a traditional division of labor, when strictly enforced, is against the interests of pro-choice women because it limits their abilities to use the valuable "male" resources that they have in relative abundance. It is therefore apparent that attitudes toward abortion, even though rooted in childhood experiences, are also intimately related to present-day interests. Women who oppose abortion and seek to make it officially unavail-able are declaring, both practically and symbolically, that women's reproductive roles should be given social primacy. Once an embryo is defined as a child and an abortion as the death of a person, almost everything else in a woman's life must "go on hold" during the course of her pregnancy: any attempt to gain "male" resources such as a job, an education, or other skills must be subordinated to her uniquely female responsibility of serving the needs of this newly conceived person. Thus, when personhood is bestowed on the embryo, women's nonreproductive roles are made secondary to their reproductive roles. The act of conception therefore creates a pregnant woman rather than woman who is pregnant; it creates a woman whose life, in cases where roles or values clash, is defined by the fact that she is—or may become—pregnant.

It is obvious that this view is supportive of women who have already decided that their familial and reproductive roles are the major ones in their lives. By the same token, the costs of defining women's reproductive roles as primary do not seem high to them because they have already chosen to make those roles primary anyway. For example, employers might choose to discriminate against women because they might require maternity leave and thus be unavailable at critical times, but women who have chosen not to work in the paid labor force in the first place can see such discrimination as irrelevant to them.

It is equally obvious that supporting abortion (and believing that the embryo is not a person) is in the vested interests of pro-choice women. Being so well equipped to compete in the male sphere, they perceive any situation that both practically and symbolically affirms the primacy of women's reproductive roles as a real loss to them. Practically, it devalues their social resources. If women are only secondarily in the labor market and must subordinate working to pregnancy, should it occur, then their education, occupation, income, and work become potentially temporary and hence discounted. Working becomes, as it traditionally was perceived to be, a pastime or hobby pursued for "pin money" rather than a central part of their lives. Similarly, if the embryo is defined as a person and the ability to become pregnant is the central one for women, a woman must be prepared to sacrifice some of her own interests to the interests of this newly conceived person.

In short, in a world where men and women have traditionally had different roles to play and where male roles have traditionally been the more socially prestigious and financially rewarded, abortion has become a symbolic marker between those who wish to maintain this division of labor and those who wish to challenge it. Thus, on an intimate level, the pro-life movement is women's version of what was true of peasants in the Vendée, the part of France that remained Royalist during the French Revolution. Charles Tilly has argued that in the Vendée, traditional relationships between nobles and peasants were still mutually satisfying so that the "brave new world" of the French Revolution represented more loss than gain, and the peasants therefore resisted the changes the Revolution heralded.[2] By the same logic, traditional relationships between men and women are still satisfying, rewarding, and meaningful for pro-life women, and they therefore resist the lure of "liberation." For pro-choice women, however, with their access to male resources, a division of labor into the public world of work and the private world of home and hearth seems to promise only restriction to "second-class" citizenship.

Thus, the sides are fundamentally opposed to each other not only on the issue of abortion but also on what abortion *means*. Women who have many "human capital" resources of the traditionally male variety want to see motherhood recognized as a private, discretionary choice. Women who have few of these resources and limited opportunities in the job market want to see motherhood recognized as the most important thing a woman can do. In order for pro-choice women to achieve their goals, therefore, they *must* argue that motherhood is not a primary, inevitable, or "natural" role for all women; for pro-life women to achieve their goals, they *must* argue that it is. In short, the debate rests on the question of whether women's fertility is to be socially recognized as a resource or as a handicap.

To the extent that women who have chosen the larger public world of work have been successful, both legally and in terms of public opinion and, furthermore, are rapidly becoming the numerical majority, pro-life women are put on the defensive. Several pro-life women offered poignant examples of how the world deals with housewives who did not have an official payroll title. Here is what one of them said:

> I was at a party, about two years ago—it still sticks in my mind, you see, because I'm a housewife and I don't work—and I met this girl from England and we got involved in a deep discussion about the English and the Americans and their philosophies and how one has influenced the other, and at the end of the conversation—she was a working gal herself, I forget what she did—and she says, "Where do you work?" and I said, "I don't." And she looked at me and said, "You don't work?" and I said, "I don't." And she looked at me and

said, "You don't work?" I said "No." She said, "You're just a housewife . . . and you can still think like that?" She couldn't believe it, and she sort of gave me a funny look and that was the end of the conversation for the evening. And I've met other people who've had similar experiences. [People seem to think that if] you're at home and you're involved with children all day, your intelligence quotient must be down with them on the floor someplace, and [that] you really don't do much thinking or get yourself involved.

Moreover, there are subtle indications that even the pro-life activists we interviewed had internalized their loss of status as housewives. Only a handful of married pro-life activists also worked at regular jobs outside the home; but fully half of those who were now full-time homemakers, some for as long as thirty years, referred to themselves in terms of the work they had given up when they married or had their first child: "I'm a political scientist," "I'm a social worker," "I'm an accountant." It is noteworthy that no one used the past tense as in "I used to be a social worker": every nonemployed married woman who used her former professional identification used it in the present tense. Since this pattern was not noticed during the interviewing, what the women themselves had in mind must remain speculative. But it does not seem unreasonable to imagine that this identification is an unconscious bow to the fact that "just plain" individuals, and in particular "just plain housewives," lack the status and credibility of professionals. Ironically, by calling on earlier identifications these women may have been expressing a pervasive cultural value that they oppose as a matter of ideology. They seemed to believe that when it comes to making public statements—or at least public statements to an interviewer who has come to ask you about your activities in the abortion debate—*what* you are counts more than *who* you are.

Because of their commitment to their own view of motherhood as a primary social role, pro-life women believe that other women are "casual" about abortions and have them "for convenience." There are no reliable data to confirm whether or not women are "casual" about abortions, but many pro-life people believe this to be the case and relate their activism to their perception of other people's casualness.[3] For example:

> Every time I saw some article [on abortion] I read about it, and I had another friend who had her second abortion in 1977 . . . and both of her abortions were a matter of convenience, it was inconvenient for her to be pregnant at that time. When I talked to her I said,

"O.K., you're married now, your husband has a good job, you want to have children eventually, but if you became pregnant now, you'd have an abortion. Why?" "Because it's inconvenient, this is not when I want to have my child." And that bothered me a lot because she is also very intelligent, graduated magna cum laude, and knew nothing about fetal development.

The assertion that women are "casual" about abortion, one could argue, expresses in a short-hand way a set of beliefs about women and their roles. First, the more people value the personhood of the embryo, the more important must be the reasons for taking its life. Some pro-life people, for example, would accept an abortion when continuation of the pregnancy would cause the death of the mother; they believe that when two lives are in direct conflict, the embryo's life can be considered the more expendable. But not all pro-life people agree, and many say they would not accept abortion even to save the mother's life. (Still others say they accept the idea in principle but would not make that choice in their own lives if faced with it.) For people who accept the personhood of the embryo, any reason besides trading a "life for a life" (and sometimes even that) seems trivial, merely a matter of "convenience."

Second, people who accept the personhood of the embryo see the reasons that pro-abortion people give for ending a pregnancy as simultaneously downgrading the value of the embryo and upgrading everything else but pregnancy. The argument that women need abortion to "control" their fertility means that they intend to subordinate pregnancy, with its inherent unpredictability, to something else. As the pro-choice activists in Chapters Four and Five have told us, that something else is participation in the paid labor force. Abortion permits women to engage in paid work on an equal basis with men. With abortion, they may schedule pregnancy in order to take advantage of the kinds of benefits that come with a paid position in the labor force: a paycheck, a title, and a social identity. The pro-life women in this study were often careful to point out that they did not object to "career women." But what they meant by "career women" were women whose *only* responsibilities were in the labor force. Once a woman became a wife and a mother, in their view her primary responsibility was to her home and family.

Third, the pro-life activists we interviewed, the overwhelming majority of whom are full-time homemakers, also felt that women who worked *and* had families could often do so only because women like themselves picked up the slack. Given their place in the social structure, it is not surprising that many of the pro-life women thought that married women who worked outside the home were "selfish"—that they got all the benefits while the homemakers carried the load for them in Boy and Girl Scouts, PTA, and after school, for which their reward was to be treated by the workers as less competent and less interesting persons.*

Abortion therefore strips the veil of sanctity from motherhood. When pregnancy is discretionary—when people are allowed to put anything else they value in front of it—then motherhood has been demoted from a sacred calling to a job.† In effect, the legalization of abortion serves to make men and women more "unisex" by deemphasizing what makes them different—the ability of women to visibly and directly carry the next generation. Thus, pro-choice women are emphatic about their right to compete equally with men without the burden of an unplanned pregnancy, and pro-life women are equally emphatic about their belief that men and women have different roles in life and that pregnancy is a gift instead of a burden.

The pro-life activists we interviewed do not want equality with men in the sense of having exactly the same rights and responsibilities as men do, although they do want equality of status. In fact, to the extent that *all* women have been touched by the women's movement and have become aware of the fact that society often treats women as a class as less capable than men, quite a few said they appreciated the Equal Rights Amendment (ERA), except for its implied stand on abortion. The ERA, in their view, reminded them that women are as valuable *in their own sphere* as men are in theirs. However, to the extent that the ERA was seen as downplaying the differences between men and women, to devalue the female sphere of the home in the face of the male sphere of paid work, others saw it as both demeaning and oppressive to women like themselves. As one of the few married employed pro-life women argued:

> I oppose it [the ERA]. Because I've gotten where I am without it. I don't think I need it. I think a woman should be hired on her merits, not on her sex or race. I

---

* In fact, pro-life women, especially those recruited after 1972, were *less* likely to be engaged in formal activities such as Scouts, church activities, and PTA than their pro-choice peers. Quite possibly they have in mind more informal kinds of activities, premised on the fact that since they do not work, they are home most of the time.

† The same might be said of all sacred callings—stripped of its layer of the sacred, for example, the job of the clergy is demanding, low status, and underpaid.

don't think we should be hiring on sex or on race. I think we should be taking the competent people that are capable of doing the job. . . . I don't think women should be taking jobs from the breadwinner, you know. I still think that our society should be male . . . the male should be the primary breadwinner. For example, my own husband cannot hope for promotion because he is white and Anglo, you know, I mean white male. He's not going to get a promotion. If he could get the promotion that others of different minorities have gotten over him, I probably wouldn't have to work at all. So from my own point of view, purely selfishly, I think we've got to consider it. On the other hand, if I'm doing the same job [as a man], I expect to get the same pay. But I've always gotten it. So I really don't think that's an issue. I see the ERA as causing us more problems than it's going to [solve]. . . . As I see it, we were on a pedestal, why should we go down to being equal? That's my feeling on the subject.

It is stating the obvious to point out that the more limited the educational credentials a woman has, the more limited the job opportunities are for her, and the more limited the job opportunities, the more attractive motherhood is as a full-time occupation. In motherhood, one can control the content and pace of one's own work, and the job is *intrinsically meaningful.* Compared with a job clerking in a supermarket (a realistic alternative for women with limited educational credentials) where the work is poorly compensated and often demeaning, motherhood can have compensations that far transcend the monetary ones. As one woman described mothering: "You have this little, rough uncut diamond, and you're the artist shaping and cutting that diamond, and bringing out the lights . . . that's a great challenge."

All the circumstances of her existence will therefore encourage a pro-life woman to highlight the kinds of values and experiences that support childbearing and childrearing and to discount the attraction (such as it is) of paid employment. Her circumstances encourage her to resent the pro-choice view that women's most meaningful and prestigious activities are in the "man's world."

Abortion also has a symbolic dimension that separates the needs and interests of homemakers and workers in the paid labor force. Insofar as abortion allows a woman to get a job, to get training for a job, or to advance in a job, it does more than provide social support for working women over homemakers; it also seems to support the value of economic considerations over moral ones. Many pro-life people interviewed said that although their commitment to traditional family roles meant very real material deprivations to themselves and their families, the moral benefits of such a choice more than made up for it.

My girls babysit and the boys garden and have paper routes and things like that. I say that if we had a lot of money that would still be my philosophy, though I don't know because we haven't been in that position. But it's a sacrifice to have a larger family. So when I hear these figures that it takes $65,000 from birth to [raise a child], I think that's ridiculous. That's a new bike every year. That's private colleges. That's a complete new outfit when school opens. Well, we've got seven daughters who wear hand-me-downs, and we hope that sometime in their eighteen years at home each one has a new bike somewhere along the line, but otherwise it's hand-me-downs. Those figures are inflated to give those children everything, and I think that's not good for them.

For pro-life people, a world view that puts the economic before the noneconomic hopelessly confuses two different kinds of worlds. For them, the private world of family as traditionally experienced is the one place in human society where none of us has a price tag. Home, as Robert Frost pointed out, is where they have to take you in, whatever your social worth. Whether one is a surgeon or a rag picker, the family is, at least ideally, the place where love is unconditional.

Pro-life people and pro-life women in particular have very real reasons to fear such a state of affairs. Not only do they see an achievement-based world as harsh, superficial, and ultimately ruthless; they are relatively less well-equipped to operate in that world. A considerable amount of social science research has suggested, at least in the realm of medical treatment, that there is an increasing tendency to judge people by their official (achieved) worth.[4] Pro-life people have relatively fewer official achievements in part because they have been doing what they see as a moral task, namely, raising children and making a home; and they see themselves as becoming handicapped in a world that discounts not only their social contributions but their personal lives as well.

It is relevant in this context to recall the grounds on which pro-life people argue that the embryo is a baby: that it is genetically human. To insist that the embryo is a baby because it is genetically human is to make a claim that it is both wrong and impossible to make distinctions between humans at all. Protecting the life of the embryo, which is by definition an entity whose social worth is all yet to come, means protecting others who feel that they may be defined as having low social worth; more broadly, it means protecting a legal view of personhood that emphatically rejects social worth criteria.

For the majority of pro-life people we interviewed, the abortions they found most offensive were those of "damaged" embryos. This is because this category so clearly highlights the aforementioned concerns about social worth. To defend a genetically or congenitally damaged embryo from abortion is, in their minds, defending the weakest of the weak, and most pro-life people we interviewed were least prepared to compromise on this category of abortion.

The genetic basis of the embryo's claim to personhood has another, more subtle implication for those on the pro-life side. If genetic humanness equals personhood, then biological facts of life must take precedence over social facts of life. One's destiny is therefore inborn and hence immutable. To give any ground on the embryo's biologically determined babyness, therefore, would by extension call into question the "innate," "natural," and biological basis of women's traditional roles as well.

Pro-choice people, of course, hold a very different view of the matter. For them, social considerations outweigh biological ones: the embryo becomes a baby when it is "viable," that is, capable of achieving a certain degree of social integration with others. This is a world view premised on achievement, but not in the way pro-life people experience the word. Pro-choice people, believing as they do in choice, planning, and human efficacy, believe that biology is simply a minor given to be transcended by human experience. Sex, like race and age, is not an appropriate criterion for sorting people into different rights and responsibilities. Pro-choice people downplay these "natural" ascriptive characteristics, believing that true equality means achievement based on talent, not being restricted to a "women's world," a "black world," or an "old people's world." Such a view, as the profile of pro-choice people has made clear, is entirely consistent with their own lives and achievements.

These differences in social circumstances that separate pro-life from pro-choice women on the core issue of abortion also lead them to have different values on topics that surround abortion, such as sexuality and the use of contraception. With respect to sexuality, for example, the two sides have diametrically opposed values; these values arise from a fundamentally different premise, which is, in turn, tied to the different realities of their social worlds. If pro-choice women

have a vested interest in subordinating their reproductive capacities, and pro-life women have a vested interest in highlighting them, we should not be surprised to find that pro-life women believe that the purpose of sex is reproduction whereas pro-choice women believe that its purpose is to promote intimacy and mutual pleasure.

These two views about sex express the same value differences that lead the two sides to have such different views on abortion. If women plan to find their primary role in marriage and the family, then they face a need to create a "moral cartel" when it comes to sex. If sex is freely available outside of marriage, then why should men, as the old saw puts it, buy the cow when the milk is free? If many women are willing to sleep with men outside of marriage, then the regular sexual activity that comes with marriage is much less valuable an incentive to marry. And because pro-life women are traditional women, their primary resource for marriage is the promise of a stable home, with everything it implies: children, regular sex, a "haven in a heartless world."

But pro-life women, like all women, are facing a devaluation of these resources. As American society increasingly becomes a service economy, men can buy the services that a wife traditionally offers. Cooking, cleaning, decorating, and the like can easily be purchased on the open market in a cash transaction. And as sex becomes more open, more casual, and more "amative," it removes one more resource that could previously be obtained only through marriage.

Pro-life women, as we have seen, have both value orientations and social characteristics that make marriage very important. Their alternatives in the public world of work are, on the whole, less attractive. Furthermore, women who stay home full-time and keep house are becoming a financial luxury. Only very wealthy families *or families whose values allow them to place the nontangible benefits of a full-time wife over the tangible benefits of a working wife* can afford to keep one of its earners off the labor market. To pro-life people, the nontangible benefit of having children—and therefore the value of procreative sex—is very important. Thus, a social ethic that promotes more freely available sex undercuts pro-life women two ways: it limits their abilities to get into a marriage in the first place, and it undermines the social value placed on their presence once within a marriage.

For pro-choice women, the situation is reversed. Because they have access to "male" resources such as education and income, they have far less reason to believe that the basic reason for sexuality is to produce children. They plan to have small families anyway, and they and their husbands come from and have married into a social class in which small families are the norm. For a number of overlapping reasons, therefore, pro-choice women believe that the value of sex is not primarily procreative: pro-choice women value the ability of sex to promote human intimacy more (or at least more frequently) than they value the ability of sex to produce babies. But they hold this view because they can afford to. When they bargain for marriage, they use the same resources that they use in the labor market: upper-class status, an education very similar to a man's, side-by-side participation in the man's world, and, not least, a salary that substantially increases a family's standard of living.

It is true, therefore, that pro-life people are "anti-sex." They value sex, of course, but they value it for its traditional benefits (babies) rather than for the benefits that pro-choice people associate with it (intimacy). Pro-life people really do want to see "less" sexuality—or at least less open and socially unregulated sexuality—because they think it is morally wrong, they think it distorts the meaning of sex, and they feel that it *threatens the basis on which their own marital bargains are built.*

These differences in social background also explain why the majority of pro-life people we interviewed were opposed to "artificial" contraception, and had chosen to use natural family planning (NFP), the modern-day version of the "rhythm method." To be sure, since NFP is a "morally licit" form of fertility control for Catholics, and many pro-life activists are very orthodox Catholics, NFP is attractive on those grounds alone. But as a group, Catholics are increasingly using contraception in patterns very similar to those of their non-Catholic peers.[5] Furthermore, many non-Catholic pro-life activists told us they used NFP. Opposition to contraception, therefore, and its corollary, the use of NFP, needs to be explained as something other than simple obedience to church dogma.

Given their status as traditional women who do not work outside of the home, the choice of NFP as the preferred method of fertility control is a rational one because NFP enhances their power and status as women. The NFP users we talked with almost uniformly stated that men respect women more when they are using NFP and that the marriage relationship becomes more like a honeymoon. Certain social factors in the lives of pro-life women suggest why this may be so. Because NFP requires abstinence during the fertile period, one effect of using it is that *sex becomes a relatively scarce resource.* Rather than something that is simply there—and taken for granted—sex becomes something that disappears from the relationship for reg-

ular periods of time. Therefore, NFP creates incentives for husbands to be close and intimate with their wives. The more insecure a woman and the less support she feels from her husband, the more reasonable it is for her to want to lengthen the period of abstinence to be on the safe side.* The increase in power and status that NFP affords a woman in a traditional marriage was clearly recognized by the activists who use NFP, as these two quotations suggest:

> The rhythm [method] is the most freeing thing a woman can have, if you want me to tell you the honest-to-God truth. Because if she's married to someone that she loves, and she ought to be, then you know [when she abstains] she's got a romance time, she's got a time when she doesn't have to say she has a headache. He's just go to know, hey, either we're going to have another baby and you're going to pay for it or we're going to read our books tonight. And once in a while we're going to get to read our books, that's the way I look at it. I think it's wonderful, I really do, it might not sound too romantic to people, but it is, this is super romantic.

> You know, if you have filet mignon every day, it becomes kind of disinteresting. But if you have to plan around this, you do some things. You study, and you do other things during the fertile part of the cycle. And the husband and wife find out how much they can do in the line of expressing love for one another in other ways, other than genital. And some people can really express a lot of love and do a lot of touching and be very relaxed. Maybe others would find that they can only do a very little touching because they might be stimulated. And so they would have to find out where their level was. But they can have a beautiful relationship.

NFP also creates an opportunity for both husbands and wives to talk about the wife's fertility so that once again, something that is normally taken for granted can

---

* One NFP counselor described a case to me in which a woman found herself unavailable for sex an average of twenty-five days a month in what seemed a deliberate attempt to use sex to control a spouse's behavior. But the interpretation of oneself as fertile (and hence sexually unavailable unless the spouse wishes to risk the arrival of another child) need not be either calculating or conscious. The more insecure a woman is in her marriage the more insecure she may be about interpreting her fertility signs, both because the insecurity in her marriage translates into a more general insecurity and because she may wish to err "on the safe side" if she is worried about the effects of a pregnancy on a shaky relationship.

be focused on and valued. Folk wisdom has it that men and women use sexuality in different ways to express their feelings of caring and intimacy: men give love in order to get sex and women give sex in order to get love. If there is some truth to this stereotype (and both popular magazines and that rich source of sociological data, the Dear Abby column, suggest that there is), then it means that men and women often face confusion in their intimate dialogues with one another. Men wonder if their wives really want to have sex with them or are only giving it begrudgingly, out of a sense of "duty." Wives wonder if husbands really love them or merely want them for sexual relief. Natural Family Planning, by making sex periodically unavailable, puts some of these fears to rest. Some women said their husbands actually bring them flowers during the period of abstinence. Though husbands were much less forthcoming on this topic, it would seem reasonable that a woman who has been visibly reassured of her husband's caring for her might approach the renewal of sexual activity with the enthusiasm of someone who knows she is cared for as a whole person, to the husband's benefit and pleasure.

Furthermore, a few mutually discreet conversations during our interviews suggest that during abstinence at least some couples find ways of giving each other sexual pleasure that do not involve actual intercourse and hence the risk of pregnancy. Given traditional patterns of female socialization into sexuality and the fact that pro-life women are both traditional and devout women, these periods of mutual caressing may be as satisfying as intercourse for some women and even more satisfying than intercourse for others.*

The different life circumstances and experiences of pro-life and pro-choice people therefore intimately affect the ways they look at the moral and social dilemmas of contraception. The settings of their lives, for example, suggest that the psychological side benefits of NFP, which do so much to support pro-life values during the practice of contraception, are sought in other ways by pro-choice people. Pro-choice people are slightly older when they marry, and the interviews strongly suggest that they have a considerably more varied sexual experience than pro-life people on average; the use of NFP to discover other facets of sexual expression is therefore largely unnecessary for them. Moreover, what little we know about sexual practices in the United States (from the Kinsey Report) suggests that given the different average levels of education and religious devoutness in the two groups, such sexual activities as "petting" and oral-genital stimulation may be more frequently encountered among pro-choice people to begin with.*

The life circumstances of the two sides suggest another reason why NFP is popular among pro-life people but not seriously considered by pro-choice people. Pro-choice men and women act on their belief that men and women are equal not only because they have (or should have) equal rights but also because they have substantially similar life experiences. The pro-choice women we met have approximately the same kinds of education as their husbands do, and many of them have the same kinds of jobs—they are lawyers, physicians, college professors, and the like. Even those who do not work in traditionally male occupations have jobs in the paid labor market and thus share common experiences. They and their husbands share many social resources in common: they both have some status outside the home, they both have a paycheck, and they both have a set of peers and friends located in the work world rather than in the family world. In terms of the traditional studies of family power, pro-choice husbands and wives use the same bargaining chips and have roughly equal amounts of them.[6]

---

*In short, these interviews were describing both "petting" and oral sex. Feminist literature has called to our attention the fact that traditional notions about sexuality are "male-centered": it is assumed that there will be insertion and that there will be a male ejaculation. Ironically, NFP—the birth control method preferred by the devout, traditional women we interviewed—may come very close to achieving the feminist ideal. Under NFP, the "rules" of "regular" sex are suspended, and each couple must discover for themselves what feels good. For a generation of women who were raised when long periods of "necking" and "petting" occurred before—and often instead of—intercourse, NFP may provide a welcome change from genitally centered, male-oriented sexual behavior to more diffuse, body-focused "female" forms of sexual expression.

---

* Kinsey's data suggest that for males the willingness to engage in oral-genital or manual-genital forms of sexual expression is related to education: the more educated an individual, the more likely he is to have "petted" or engaged in oral sex (Alfred Kinsey, *Sexual Behavior in the Human Male*, pp. 337–81, 535–37). For females, the patterns are more complicated. Educational differences among women disappear when age at marriage is taken into account. But as Kinsey notes: "Among the females in the sample, the chief restraint on petting . . . seems to have been the religious tradition against it." The more devout a woman, the less likely she is to have ever petted (Kinsey, *Sexual Behavior in the Human Female*, pp. 247–48).

Pro-choice women, therefore, value (and can afford) an approach to sexuality that, by sidelining reproduction, diminishes the differences between men and women; they can do this *because they have other resources on which to build a marriage.* Since their value is intimacy and since the daily lives of men and women on the pro-choice side are substantially similar, intimacy in the bedroom is merely an extension of the intimacy of their larger world.

Pro-life women and men, by contrast, tend to live in "separate spheres." Because their lives are based on a social and emotional division of labor where each sex has its appropriate work, to accept contraception or abortion would devalue the one secure resource left to these women: the private world of home and hearth. This would be disastrous not only in terms of status but also in terms of meaning: if values about fertility and family are not essential to a marriage, what supports does a traditional marriage have in times of stress? To accept highly effective contraception, which actually and symbolically subordinates the role of children in the family to other needs and goals, would be to cut the ground of meaning out from under at least one (and perhaps both) partners' lives. Therefore, contraception, which sidelines the reproductive capacities of men and women, is both useless and threatening to pro-life people.

THE CORE OF THE DEBATE

In summary, women come to be pro-life and pro-choice activists as the end result of lives that center around different definitions of motherhood. They grow up with a belief about the nature of the embryo, so events in their lives lead them to believe that the embryo is a unique person, or a fetus; that people are intimately tied to their biological roles, or that these roles are but a minor part of life; that motherhood is the most important and satisfying role open to a woman, or that motherhood is only one of several roles, a burden when defined as the only role. These beliefs and values are rooted in the concrete circumstances of women's lives—their educations, incomes, occupations, and the different marital and family choices they have made along the way—and they work simultaneously to shape those circumstances in turn. Values about the relative place of reason and faith, about the role of actively planning for life versus learning to accept gracefully life's unknowns, of the relative satisfactions inherent in work and family—all of these factors place activists in a specific relationship

to the larger world and give them a specific set of resources with which to confront that world.

The simultaneous and on-going modification of both their lives and their values by each other finds these activists located in a specific place in the social world. They are financially successful, or they are not. They become highly educated, or they do not. They become married and have a large family, or they have a small one. And at each step of the way, both their values and their lives have undergone either ratification or revision.

Pro-choice and pro-life activists live in different worlds, and the scope of their lives, as both adults and children, fortifies them in their belief that their own views on abortion are the more correct, more moral, and more reasonable. When added to this is the fact that should "the other side" win, one group of women will see the very real devaluation of their lives and life resources, it is not surprising that the abortion debate has generated so much heat and so little light.

NOTES

1. Granberg, "The Abortion Activists," p. 158.
2. Charles Tilly, *The Vendée.*
3. Many of the pro-life people in this study asserted that women have abortions because they do not wish to have stretch marks or because they want to take a European vacation. While I know of no direct data of how women feel who choose abortions, in the course of research for my previous book (*Taking Chances: Abortion and the Decision Not to Contracept*[1975]), I interviewed over 100 women in deep, unstructured verbatim interviews. In subsequent research, I have talked with or interviewed over 500 women who have had abortions. In my own—and possibly biased—experience, few of these women were "casual" about having an abortion. Some were more conflicted about the abortion decision than others, but for all the women I interviewed, the decision to seek an abortion has been serious, thoughtful, and carefully considered.
4. See, e.g., Fuchs, *Who Shall Live?*; Tristam Engelhardt, *Science, Ethics and Medicine*; Crane, *Sanctity of Social Life*; and Paul Ramsey, *Ethics at the Edges of Life.*
5. Westoff and Bumpass, "Revolution in Birth Control Practices," pp. 41–44.
6. There is a long sociological research tradition on the relative power status of husbands and wives and what contributes to their relative power; see Robert Blood and Donald Wolfe, *Husbands and Wives*; Robert Blood

and Robert Hamlin, "The Effects of the Wife's Employment on the Family Power Structure," pp. 347–52; Phyllis Hallenbeck, "An Analysis of Power Dynamics in Marriage," *Journal of Marriage and the Family* 27 (1966):200–03; and David Heer, "Measurement and Bases of Family Power: An Overview," *Marriage and Family Living* 25 (1963):133–39. For fundamental critiques of this literature, see Constantina Safilios-Rothchild, "Family Sociology or Wives' Family Sociology? A Cross-Cultural Examination of Decision-Making," pp. 290–301; and Dair Gillespie, "Who Has the Power? The Marital Struggle," pp. 445–58.

READING 27

WHY WE LOST THE ERA

Jane J. Mansbridge

The crucial step in building progressive and liberal support for the ERA was the passage of Title VII of the Civil Rights Act of 1964, which prohibited job discrimination on the basis of sex. Title VII had originally been designed to prevent discrimination against blacks, but a group of southern congressmen added a ban on discrimination against women in a vain effort to make the bill unacceptable to northern conservatives. Initially, Title VII had no effect on "protective" legislation. Unions, accordingly, continued to oppose the ERA because they thought it would nullify such legislation. In 1967, when the newly formed National Organization for Women (NOW) gave the ERA first place on its Bill of Rights for Women, several union members immediately resigned.[1] But by 1970 both the federal courts and the Equal Employment Opportunity Commission

From *Why We Lost the ERA* (Chicago: University of Chicago Press, 1986), 18–19, 118–48. Reprinted with the permission of the author and the University of Chicago Press.
Editor's note: In view of the fact that some source material has been deleted and other material consolidated, the original reference numbers have been changed, for the reader's convenience to run consecutively.

(EEOC) had interpreted Title VII as invalidating protective legislation, and had extended most traditional protections to men rather than removing them for women. With their long-standing concern now for the most part made moot, union opposition to the ERA began to wane.[2]

In 1970, the Pittsburgh chapter of NOW took direct action. The group disrupted Senator Birch Bayh's hearings on the nineteen-year-old vote, getting Bayh to promise hearings on the ERA the following spring.[3] This was the moment. Labor opposition was fading, and, because few radical claims had been made for the ERA, conservatives had little ammunition with which to oppose it. In April, the United Auto Workers' convention voted to endorse the ERA.[4] In May, Bayh began Senate hearings on the ERA, and for the first time in its history the U.S. Department of Labor supported the ERA.[5] In June, Representative Martha Griffiths succeeded in collecting enough signatures on a discharge petition to pry the ERA out of the House Judiciary Committee, where for many years the liberal chair of the committee, Emanuel Celler, had refused to schedule hearings because of the persistent opposition by labor movement traditionalists. After only an hour's debate, the House of Representatives passed the ERA by a vote of 350 to 15.

The next fall, the ERA came to the Senate, which, after several days of debate, added by a narrow majority a provision exempting women from the draft.[6] This provision eliminated the only consequence proponents claimed for the ERA that might not have received support from a majority of Americans. However, having consistently insisted on bearing the responsibilities of citizenship as well as the rights, the women's organizations promoting the ERA had decided that women must be drafted. Because an ERA amended to exempt women from the draft was not acceptable to any of the organizations promoting the ERA, Senator Bayh did not bring it to a vote. Instead, without consulting those organizations, he proposed a new wording for the ERA that mirrored the words of the Fourteenth Amendment: "Neither the United States nor any State shall, on account of sex, deny to any person within its jurisdiction the equal protection of the laws." Bayh described his new wording as "recognizing the need for a flexible standard" and "meeting the objections of [the ERA's] most articulate critics,"[7] and he said in a subsequent press interview that the new wording would permit excluding women from the draft.[8] Fearing, on the basis of these remarks, that Bayh would be too flexible in his interpretation of this new wording, the major women's organizations told him that this substitute was not acceptable to them.[9]

In the spring of 1971, the House Judiciary Committee returned to the original 1970 wording of the ERA but adopted the "Wiggins amendment," which said that the ERA would "not impair the validity of any law of the United States which exempts a person from compulsory military service or any other law of the United States or any state which reasonably promotes the health and safety of the people."[10] The women's organizations supporting an ERA concluded, correctly, that the standard of "reasonably" promoting health and safety was no more stringent than the standard the Supreme Court was already using to judge constitutional many laws discriminating against women. Accordingly, they opposed the Wiggins amendment, and under their urging the House rejected it,[11] voting 354 to 23 to adopt the original ERA.

Having passed the House, the ERA went to the Senate, where the Subcommittee on Constitutional Amendments, chaired by ERA opponent Senator Sam Ervin, adopted another substitute: "Neither the United States or any State shall make any legal distinction between the rights and responsibilities of male and female persons unless such distinction is based on physiological or functional differences between them."[12] A majority of the full Committee on the Judiciary, chaired by Senator Bayh, rejected this attempt, so similar to the previous two, and adopted the original wording of the ERA in its definitive March 1972 report.

In the immediately ensuing Senate debate, Senator Ervin introduced eight amendments to the ERA relating to draft and combat, marital and family support, privacy, protections and exemptions, and homosexuality. His goal was twofold. First, he hoped to tempt a majority in the Senate into adopting one or more of the amendments, which would have divided the ERA proponents and at the very least would have delayed the ERA's passage. Second, if the ERA did pass in the Senate, he hoped to focus the upcoming debates in the states on the potentially unpalatable substantive consequences of the ERA. According to Catherine East, an active participant in these events, "proponents could not accept any amendment, even innocuous ones, since an amended ERA would have had to have gone to conference, where hostile House Committee members would most likely have killed it. (Senator Ervin knew this.)"[13] Bayh succeeded in persuading a majority to vote down all the Ervin amendments. On March 22, 1972, the ERA passed the Senate of the United States with a vote of 84 to 8.

As soon as the Senate voted, a secretary in the office of the senator from Hawaii contacted the Hawaii legislative reference bureau, and within twenty minutes the president of the Hawaii state senate presented a resolution to ratify. Five minutes later the resolution, unanimously passed, came before the Hawaii house, receiving equally quick and unanimous treatment.[14] Thus on the very day that the U.S. Senate passed the ERA, Hawaii became the first state to ratify. Delaware, Nebraska, and New Hampshire ratified the next day, and on the third day Idaho and Iowa ratified. Twenty-four more states ratified in 1972 and early 1973. The very earliest states to ratify were all unanimous, and in the other early states the votes were rarely close. Moreover,

> rules were suspended in order to avoid referral to committee. Frequently no or only perfunctory hearings were held on the subject. Floor debate too was brief. . . . Even in those states where open hearings were held, it was not uncommon for only proponents of the amendment to appear as witnesses.[15]

By late 1973, however, the ERA's proponents had lost control of the ratification process. While the national offices of the various pro-ERA organizations could relatively easily coordinate their Washington activities to get the ERA through Congress, they were slow in organizing coalitions in the states. At the end of the 1973 state legislative sessions, only a few states even had active ERA coalitions.[16]

Moreover, in 1973 the Supreme Court decided, in *Roe v. Wade*, that state laws forbidding abortion violated the "right to privacy" implicit in the Constitution. Although the ERA had no obvious direct bearing on whether "abortion is murder," the two issues nonetheless became politically linked. The *Roe* decision took power out of the hands of relatively parochial, conservative state legislators and put it in the hands of a relatively cosmopolitan, liberal U.S. Supreme Court. The ERA would have done the same thing. Furthermore, both were sponsored by what was at that time still called the "women's liberation" movement. Traditionalists saw the "women's libbers" both as rejecting the notion that motherhood was a truly important task and as endorsing sexual hedonism instead of moral restraint. The *Roe* decision seemed to constitute judicial endorsement for these values. Since NOW was not only the leading sponsor of the ERA but the leading defender of abortion on demand, conservative activists saw abortion and the ERA as two prongs of the "libbers'" general strategy for undermining traditional

American values.[17] Unable to overturn the *Roe* decision directly, many conservatives sought to turn the ERA into a referendum on that decision.[18] To a significant degree, they succeeded.[19] The opponents began to organize and convinced the first of several states to rescind ratification—a move that had no legal force but certainly made a political difference in unratified states.

Three more states ratified in 1974, one in 1975, and one—Indiana—in 1977, bringing the total to thirty-five of the required thirty-eight. No state ratified after 1977 despite the triumph of ERA proponents in 1978 in getting Congress to extend the original 1979 deadline until 1982.[20] In 1982 this extension ran out, and the Amendment died. Alabama, Arizona, Arkansas, Florida, Georgia, Illinois, Louisiana, Mississippi, Missouri, Nevada, North Carolina, Oklahoma, Utah, and Virginia had not ratified. All were Mormon or southern states, except Illinois, which required a three-fifths majority for ratifying constitutional amendments and which had a strongly southern culture in the third of the state surrounded by Missouri and Kentucky.[21]

Public Opinion

The first time a polling organization asked the American public about the ERA, in 1970, 56 percent of the people interviewed said they favored ERA. From 1970 to 1982, when the struggle for ratification ended, a majority of adult Americans consistently supported the ERA. In all the important national surveys that asked about the ERA more than once, more respondents favored passage than opposed it. Fifty percent or more favored passage in every survey but one. While responses differed according to the wording of the question, the "average" survey found 57 percent for the ERA, 32 percent opposed, and 11 percent with no opinion.

These surveys, however, were a poor guide to how people would actually act. Time after time in the referenda on state ERAs, feminists experienced the agony of seeing survey support as high as 60 to 65 percent turn, after a brief but bitterly fought campaign, into defeat. In the fall of 1975, two independent polling organizations reported that a majority of people who planned to vote on the state ERAs in the upcoming referenda in New York and New Jersey said they would approve an ERA in their respective states.[22] But in the actual vote on November 4, both state ERAs failed, with 57 percent voting against in New York and 51 percent in New Jersey.[23] In Florida in 1978, preelection surveys showed

the state ERA winning by "two to one," but in the referendum it lost by the same margin—two to one.[24] In a 1980 Iowa survey one month before the referendum, 48 percent of likely voters favored a state ERA and only 23 percent opposed it, but in the referendum itself the state ERA lost by 55 to 45 percent.[25] Finally, in Maine in 1984, a survey taken a month before the referendum indicated that 62 percent of the registered voters would vote for a state ERA; in the election 63 percent voted against it.[26]

Although the ERA was bitterly contested, the conflict did not follow the expected demographic lines. Observers often assumed, for example, that because most ERA activists were women, and because the Amendment was supposed to help women, women would support it more often than men did. In fact, men and women differed hardly at all on the ERA. Activists also believed that differences between men and women on the ERA had an important effect on the "gender gap" in the 1980 Presidential election. But these views came from looking at their own friends, since among the highly educated and politically active, women did support the ERA more than men. In the population as a whole, however, men supported the ERA almost as much as women and voted against Reagan on the basis of their ERA support just as much as women did. Contrary to the activists' beliefs, therefore, the ERA had only a very small effect on the gender gap in the 1980 presidential election.[27]

There were also several reasons to expect the middle class, particularly among women, to have supported the ERA more than the working class. First, people with more education tend to take "progressive" stances regarding "cultural" innovations in gender roles, sexual practices, drug use, and so forth. To the degree that the ERA was a similar "cultural" issue, one would have expected differences by education on the ERA as well. Second, while the ERA affected only governmental laws and practices and not the private sector, 56 percent of the women in the experienced labor force who had college degrees worked for the government in 1970, as did 64 percent of the women with graduate training.[28] (These figures become less startling when one realizes that the governmental sector includes all public school and public university teachers, nurses in public hospitals, and social workers and secretaries at any level of government administration.) One might conclude, on this basis, that middle-class women had a greater stake in the ERA's passage than working-class women. Third, and most important, the activists for the ERA were predominantly middle class, both in comparison with the general population and, to a much lesser degree, in comparison with the anti-ERA activists.[29] (The activists on both sides were predominantly white.)[30] But in spite of all these reasons for expecting predominantly white middle-class support for the ERA, both the working class and blacks were at least as likely to support the ERA as the middle class and whites. In another upset of the ERA-WASP stereotype, Catholics were more likely than Protestants to support the ERA.[31]

Support for the ERA, however, did split along lines that would become familiar in the new politics of the 1980s: religious fundamentalists and heavy church-goers against agnostics and Jews, people with many children against those with none, old people against young, country against city dwellers, and nationwide, southerners against people on the East and West Coasts. The battle against the ERA was one of the first in which the New Right used "women's issues" to forge a coalition of the traditional Radical Right, religious activists, and that previously relatively apolitical segment of the noncosmopolitan working and middle classes that was deeply disturbed by the cultural changes—especially the changes in sexual mores—in the second half of the twentieth century.

The bitterly fought ratification campaign did not, on the best available evidence, have any effect, either positive or negative, on public support for the ERA in the nation as a whole. The 1970 survey question was never repeated, but we have more or less comparable data from 1975 to 1982. With one exception, no survey organization ever found any clear trend in public support for the ERA over this period. The exception was Louis Harris's survey organization. After showing no trend for seven years, Harris suddenly reported a huge leap in support, from 50 to 63 percent, in April 1982. Harris portrayed this thirteen-point change as evidence of a last-minute surge in popular approval for the ERA. In syndicated newspapers across the country, under the headline, "ERA Support Soars as Deadline Nears," Harris declared:

> With less than two months to go before the time allowed for ratification will run out, support for the Equal Rights Amendment has soared to 63–34 percent nationwide, an increase of 13 points just since last January when a much closer 50–46 plurality favored passage of the ERA.[32]

At first glance this increase is puzzling, since none of the other organizations asking comparable questions (Gallup, NBC/Associated Press, and CBS News) found much change in this period. But on closer inspection the explanation becomes clear. Right before its traditional question on the ERA, the Harris organization's April survey asked a new question:

> As you know, the Equal Rights Amendment to the Constitution is being debated across the country. Let me read you the actual wording of that Equal Rights Amendment: "Equality of rights under the law shall not be denied or abridged by the United States or any state on account of sex." Do you favor or oppose that Equal Rights Amendment to the Constitution?

Like other questions that include the actual wording of the Amendment, this one produced a resounding 73 percent approval rate. Harris then asked its traditional "balanced" question about the ERA:

> Many of those who favor women's rights favor the Equal Rights Amendment to the Constitution. This Amendment would establish that women would have rights equal to men in all areas. Opponents argue that women are different from men and need to be protected by special laws which deal with women's status.

The question ended with almost the same words as the preceding question: "Do you favor or oppose the Equal Rights Amendment?" By asking its traditional question right after a question worded so that most respondents committed themselves to the ERA, Harris altered people's answers to the traditional question. When one does not have a strong opinion—and about two-thirds of the people who had an opinion on the ERA said they did not favor or oppose it strongly—a desire to be consistent in one's responses can overwhelm a tentative impulse pro or con.

Since polling is a difficult art, and the Harris organization is not one of its more meticulous practitioners, I would ordinarily attribute this particular gaff to incompetence rather than a deliberate desire to deceive. But the story does not end here. In August 1983, *Business Week* reported,

> Ironically, support for the ERA began to gather new momentum in 1982, just as the campaign for the failed version of the amendment was foundering in state legislatures. The Harris organization, which has polled on the issue several times, reported 50% support for the ERA in January, 1982. By April, when legislatures in key states were in session, pro-ERA sentiment rose to 63%, and support has remained rock-solid.[33]

In 1984, *Ms.* magazine reported, also on the basis of a Harris poll, that "sixty-four percent of American women favor passage of the ERA; a major change from the 48 percent of women who favored it in 1975."[34] What neither *BusinessWeek* nor *Ms.* reported, presumably because Harris had neglected to tell them, was that in the post-1982 polls—from which they derived the belief that support was now "rock-solid" at about 63 percent—Harris had substituted a new question that included three arguments for the ERA instead of one, and stressed economic discrimination, which many strategists agreed was the best way to sell the ERA.[35] Harris often fails to note changes in wording. But Louis Harris is a good liberal and is married to a feminist activist. If a change in wording had produced an apparent *decline* in public support for the ERA, Harris would almost certainly have tried to figure out why and noted the problem. The same is true of ERA activists generally. If Harris had produced a decline of this magnitude, women with experience in survey research would undoubtedly have noticed that no other survey organizations had found such a decline and they would have discounted the Harris results. But because the results matched both their desires and expectations, ERA activists believed them.

In fact, however, even the stable picture painted by most national survey organizations masked a growing gap between the ratified and the unratified states. By 1977 the opponents of the ERA had effectively blocked ratification in the states. Between 1976–1977 and 1980–1981 there was a significant increase in public opposition to the ERA in the unratified states. Those who had previously no opinion were turning from apathy to opposition. In some unratified states support for the ERA also dropped. In two key unratified states, Illinois and Oklahoma, public opposition actually exceeded support by June 1982. Thus, when conservative representatives in the unratified states reported increased opposition to the ERA in their districts in 1977, 1978, and 1982, they were probably right.[36] The national ERA leaders, most of whom lived either in Washington, D.C., or in states that had ratified the ERA, seldom were aware of these developments. Because their friends and acquaintances all supported the ERA, and opinion polls told them that the general public supported it, they tended to dismiss legislators' reports of local opposition as self-serving distortions.

In the late 1970s, attitudes toward the ERA also polarized along party lines. The percentage of Republicans supporting the ERA in the Illinois House of Representatives, for example, fell from 54 percent in 1975 to 41 percent in 1978 to 34 percent in 1982, while the percentage of Democrats supporting the ERA rose from 71 to 73 and finally to 78 percent.[37] In 1980, in a reversal of the party stances that had prevailed in the 1950s and early 1960s, the Republican Presidential candidate and party platform opposed the ERA while the Democrats supported it. By 1981, support or opposition to the ERA had become strongly related to party activism. Democratic activists were much more likely to support the ERA than were Democrats among the public, and Republican activists were much more likely to oppose the ERA than Republicans among the public. Moreover, the closer activists came to a position of party leadership, the more likely they were to take the party position on the ERA. This pattern of polarization among party leaders and activists holds for a wide range of partisan issues.[38] But a constitutional amendment needs an overwhelming majority, so once it becomes a partisan issue its chances of passing are minimal.

IDEOLOGY AND ACTIVISM

Anyone who followed the debate over the ERA is likely to have been impressed by the fact that it was both grossly oversimplified and extremely antagonistic. This chapter will suggest three explanations for this state of affairs. First, the ERA was a public good (or a "public bad") that had to be promoted or defeated by volunteer activity. Because neither passing nor defeating the ERA promised any immediate tangible benefits to activists, both sides recruited activists by appealing to principle.[39] They also exaggerated the ERA's probable long-run effects. Second, because activists were volunteers, they were not subject to much organizational control. Even when an organization wanted to "rein in" activists for pragmatic reasons, it had few good ways of doing so. Abortion funding became linked to the ERA, for example, in part because the ERA organizations could not fully control all the feminist lawyers. Finally, the adversary nature of the political process never encouraged the gladiators on either side to amass information that might weaken their rhetorical stance. The pro-ERA organizations were a great deal more likely to have done extensive legal research, but even they, as we will see, developed blind spots whenever seeing too much might have undermined their position. On the opponents' side, individual and organizational autonomy provided an opportunity to circulate blatant lies without anyone having to take responsibility for them.

The ERA as a Public Good

The American brand of interest group politics has trouble creating what economists call "public goods."[40] A public good is the kind of good—like national defense, clean air, or an open park—that, once available to anyone, will be available to everyone. An individual good, in contrast, can be divided up and distributed to those who are willing to pay for it. Because public goods cannot be sold to individuals on a fee-for-service basis, organizations that provide them have three choices. The most effective is to force individuals to contribute. When unions help all employees in a firm to win better wages or working conditions, for example, they try to force all these beneficiaries of union largess to pay union dues by creating a "union shop." When governments provide everyone with national defense, they force everyone to pay for it through taxation. In a sense, democratic government is an agreement to be coerced for the purpose of producing a large number of desirable results that would never come about without such coercion.

If an organization has no effective means of coercion at its disposal, it can try to link the public good to an individual good. Workers may join a union to get the funeral benefits provided for members only; their dues then support the union's efforts to get "public goods" like pay raises for all. Senior citizens join the American Association of Retired Persons to get access to its insurance and other benefits; the association then spends some of its members' money promoting legislation that benefits not only the members but other old people as well. Gun owners join gun clubs primarily to use the private rifle ranges and skeet shoots; because these clubs are usually affiliated with the National Rifle Association, part of their dues then goes to promote what for them is a public good—legal gun sales. But even this strategy for financing public goods has severe limitations, because it is hard to find individual goods so closely linked to the organization that an individual entrepreneur cannot produce them more cheaply by eliminating the extra cost tacked on to finance the public good.

Finally, an organization seeking to produce public goods can rely on moral exhortation. It can claim that people ought to spend their time and energy promoting a public good because it is right and will benefit many others. Organizations that have to rely on such moral appeals are, at least in an individualistic culture, inherently weak. From a strictly selfish viewpoint it is almost always more rational to let others do the work in such organizations and become a "free rider" who enjoys the benefits of others' labor without contributing oneself. While few people are completely selfish all the time, even fewer are completely devoted to the common good. Organizations that depend on such devotion usually have a capricious, undependable membership. When an organization cannot count on a stable membership, it must devote a tremendous amount of time and effort to soliciting and maintaining the commitment of its members, to the detriment of the time and effort it can spend promoting the public good itself. In contrast, organizations based on the sale of individual goods, whose members continue to pay as long as they want the benefits provided, are usually more stable and have a more predictable flow of funds.

The strength or weakness of a group's organizational base usually translates into political strength or weakness. Trade associations like the National Automobile Dealers Association, whose members gain technical information, access to conventions, and business contacts from their membership, are organizationally strong and politically powerful. Comparable consumer organizations, which can offer few individual benefits, are either nonexistent or organizationally and politically weak.

Although in theory each citizen's interests should count for one and none for more than one in a democracy, in practice well-organized interests count for a great deal more than poorly organized ones. The more an organization can count on a stable membership held together by either coercion or individual benefits, the more it can make its members' interests count in the political process.

For this reason, the major organizations promoting the ERA were shaky at their core. The National Organization for Women (NOW) could offer its members little in the way of individual benefits. To some members—for example, young women, the newly divorced, the newly conscious feminist, or the recent migrant to a new city—the organization could offer new friendships, mutual support, companionship, and solidarity with others like oneself. It could also provide one-time participation in a consciousness-raising group. But members did not need to maintain their formal organizational affiliation to keep getting these benefits. Because NOW had few ongoing individual benefits to offer, its membership drives had to rely on emotional identification and moral exhortation. Whenever women, rightly or wrongly, felt somewhat more threatened, or whenever the president of NOW happened to write a particularly moving letter of appeal, membership in the organization would rise. But as the critical moment faded into history, membership would drop. The organization could offer no individual benefits to make its members feel the rationality of paying their dues consistently year after year.

ERAmerica, and its affiliates like ERA Illinois, had a seemingly more stable base as a coalition of religious, professional, civic, and labor groups. But ERAmerica and its affiliates had the usual problems of broadly based coalitions. Each member organization had priorities different from those of the coalition, few provided consistent financial support, and only one or two tried to enlist their individual members in the work of the coalition—passing the ERA.

The Federation of Business and Professional Women (BPW) had at its disposal the important individual benefit of professional contacts with other women in business, government, and the professions. The League of Women Voters provided relatively isolated homemakers with a chance to maintain adult social contacts, continue their education, and do some good. However, the very emphasis on professional networking and self-help that drew women to BPW also worked against that organization's involvement in state politics—where ERA had to pass—because politics of this sort means conflict, and conflict does not facilitate business contacts. In the same way, the League's specializing in projects that everyone could agree were good (League policy decisions are made by consensus) attracted members who preferred studying "good government" issues to clashing with opposing interests in partisan state politics. Neither BPW nor the League entered easily into the political struggles in state legislatures that the ERA demanded after 1975.

Because the ERA movement had little coercive power and few immediate individual benefits at its disposal, it had to rely on ideological incentives to recruit and maintain activists. People worked for the ERA because they believed in the cause. This meant that the people staffing the organizations that promoted the ERA were not a cross-section of those who favored it. They differed from the rest of the American population in one major respect—they believed in, and wanted to bring about, major changes in the roles of men and women in America.

Because the ERA organizations had to attract their membership primarily with moral and ideological incentives, and because activists were brought into the fray by their sense of injustice rather than by any individual rewards, there were times in which they preferred being right to winning. Moreover, their instincts

about which arguments would appeal to legislators and the public were not very reliable.

The STOP ERA movement had a similar problem, for its job was also to promote a "public good." As a result, the STOP ERA organizations were both weak and ideological in their approach. Although this would have made it difficult for them to pass an amendment, it was not fatal when they had only to stop one.

Participatory Decentralization in the Abortion Decision

In a voluntary association, the initiative for action, the sanction for nonperformance, and the manner in which the work is done all depend heavily on the individual actor. Each actor is relatively autonomous, bound only by the constraints of ideology and solidarity—the incentives for working in the first place. To illustrate this phenomenon of "participatory decentralization," it is instructive to look at the role of feminist lawyers again, this time in the context of the debate about whether the ERA would require the government to pay for abortions on the same basis as other medical procedures.

In theory, feminist lawyers could relate to the ERA in quite diverse ways. When organizations like NOW, League of Women Voters, BPW, or ERAmerica paid a lawyer to act as general counsel or as a consultant, she was supposed to see herself as accountable to the organization's leadership in the same way that any lawyer would be accountable to a client. When a lawyer did unpaid volunteer work, she nominally had the same formal responsibility to her clients, but expected greater autonomy. When there is no quid pro quo, the donor inevitably feels free to consider aspects of a situation other than the client's needs. When a lawyer contributed to the ERA movement through articles in law journals, she was even more autonomous. She was still likely to be deeply committed to the feminist cause, since otherwise she would not commit her academic energies to relatively low-status "women's" subjects which did not give her much academic credit. But she was accountable only to the scholarly community for the accuracy and clarity of her analysis, and was unlikely to feel that her broad commitment to feminism required her to weigh all her words for their possible effects on the ERA's chances of passing.

In practice, these distinct roles often blurred. The small community of Washington and Washington-related feminist lawyers discussed issues among themselves both formally and informally, and many played all the roles I have described at one time or another. As a consequence, even the paid staff lawyers thought of themselves as serving a broader "public" interest, or at least a "feminist" interest, rather than thinking of themselves simply as advocates for their client's own interest, narrowly construed. This helps explain why no staff lawyer, even for the more conservative ERA organizations, raised the possibility of a deferential interpretation of the ERA on the military. In the community of feminist lawyers within which she was operating, that approach was ruled out for reasons that had relatively little to do with the ERA per se.

Toward the end of the ERA campaign, some feminist lawyers also acted relatively autonomously in linking abortion to the ERA. These lawyers were certainly not primarily responsible for the link. Given the strength of support for both the ERA and abortion within NOW, it was impossible after 1973 to keep the two issues entirely separate either in the mind of the public or within NOW. Toward the end of the ERA struggle, for example, Illinois NOW sent a questionnaire to the candidates for reelection to the state legislature, asking for their positions both on the ERA and on abortion. One black woman legislator who supported the ERA criticized this questionnaire sharply:

> [The pro-ERA forces] confused the issues with abortion and ERA. That [abortion] would have been an issue that I would have stayed completely away from. Even though I may be pro-abortion or anti-abortion, it has nothing to do with it [the ERA]. . . . They use their own tactics—[really] the *anti*-ERA people's tactics—to defeat themselves! . . . And you couldn't get them to understand that. . . . Why be concerned on the *same* questionnaire with the ERA and the abortion issue so heavily into it?

Despite mistakes like this, however, most NOW activists, and certainly the more conservative pro-ERA activists, consciously tried to keep the issues of abortion and ERA separate.

Like the combat decision, the series of decisions linking the ERA and abortion involved both feminist lawyers and external events not within the control of the ERA organizations. In this instance, the key event came in 1973, when Justice Blackmun, speaking for seven of the nine justices of the Supreme Court in *Roe v. Wade*, distinguished among the three trimesters of pregnancy, and made the right to an abortion in the first three months a matter of personal autonomy, protected by a right to private decision making that the Court

derived from the Constitution's due process guarantee.[41] Foes of abortion immediately launched a counterattack and succeeded in getting the U.S. Congress and several state legislatures to pass legislation denying public funding to any abortion that did not involve rape, incest, or the potential death of the mother.

Feminist organizations and feminist lawyers did what they could to repel this counterattack. What feminist lawyers could do most easily was to bring suits arguing that federal and state laws that restricted abortion funding were unconstitutional under the Fifth and Fourteenth Amendments of the Constitution, under comparable guarantees in the state constitutions, and under various state ERAs.

For some feminist lawyers, the ERA-abortion connection posed a major political and ethical problem. On the one hand, their commitment to equality for women, to publicly funded abortions, to their clients, and—much less important—to winning important cases and setting judicial precedent all encouraged them to use every argument in their constitutional arsenal against restricting access to abortions. Some believed strongly that the best argument against cutting off abortion funding was that this denied women the equal protection of the laws under the Fourteenth Amendment so long as the government funded other medical procedures for both sexes or for men. Not making that argument when the issues were being litigated for the first time, in the late 1970s and early 1980s, ran the risk of setting a series of possibly irreversible precedents. If the ERA had not been before the states, these lawyers could have proceeded without external hindrance in trying to persuade the Court of their interpretation of the Fourteenth Amendment's equal protection clause. But with the ERA before the states, and with state legislators asking more and more often about the substantive effects of the ERA, the lawyers had to be careful not to frighten potential legislative proponents by suggesting that the equal protection clause—in theory a weaker protection than the ERA—could be linked substantively to abortion. Those feminist lawyers who believed that the ERA added little to the equal protection clause in any case wanted to press ahead with the equal protection analysis, ignoring the political consequences for the ERA. However, in Washington, against some resistance, Eleanor Smeal persuaded the feminist lawyers in the federal abortion funding case not to make this argument.[42] In this way Smeal hoped to keep the ERA and abortion funding separate.

Smeal was less successful in the states. Here, local legal organizations made their own autonomous decisions and based their arguments for abortion funding not only on the potentially dangerous equal protection clause but also, in some states, on the state equal rights amendments. This strategy obviously jeopardized the political future of the federal ERA in the unratified states. In 1978, feminist lawyers in the Hawaiian chapter of the American Civil Liberties Union (ACLU) argued unsuccessfully in the case of *Hawaii Right to Life, Inc. v. Chang* that "[a]bortion is a medical procedure performed only for women; withdrawing funding for abortions while continuing to reimburse other medical procedures sought by both sexes or only by men would be tantamount to a denial of equal rights on account of sex." Withdrawing abortion funding, they argued, would violate not only Hawaii's due process and equal protection clauses, but also its equal rights amendment, which, like the proposed federal ERA, provided that "equality of rights under the law shall not be denied or abridged on account of sex."[43]

In 1980, the lawyers defending federal abortion funding in *Harris v. McRae* lost their case. A majority of the Supreme Court concluded, among other things, that the Constitution's Fifth Amendment (and, in a parallel state case, the Fourteenth Amendment) did not invalidate legislative restrictions on abortion funding. The majority's grounds were that (*a*) Congress had a "legitimate" interest in "protecting potential life," (*b*) restricting funding for abortion bore "a direct relationship" to this legitimate purpose, and (*c*) the classification of poverty (the distinction between "indigent" women and other women) was not a suspect classification requiring a test stronger than that congressional action be rationally related to a legitimate governmental interest.[44]

Once the Court's majority had shown that for them the Fourteenth Amendment's equal protection clause did not bar legislative restrictions on abortion funding, the ACLU would no longer hold back. As the executive director of the Civil Liberties Union of Massachusetts wrote in its newsletter:

> Because a strong coalition is being forged between the anti-ERA coalition and the anti-abortion people, it was our hope to save Medicaid payments for medically necessary abortions through the federal court route without having to use the state Equal Rights Amendment and possibly fuel the national anti-ERA movement. But the loss in *McRae* [the federal abortion funding case] was the last straw. We now have no recourse but to turn to the State Constitution for the legal hook to save Medicaid funding for abortions.[45]

Accordingly, the ACLU argued in the Massachusetts case of *Moe v. Secretary of Administration* that both the Massachusetts state ERA and its due process clause made restricting funding for abortions unconstitutional. Anxious ERA proponents in the key unratified states rejoiced in 1981 when the Massachusetts Supreme Court declared the funding restrictions unconstitutional under the due process clause of the Massachusetts Constitution rather than invoking the state ERA.[46]

ERA supporters in the key nonratified states sometimes felt that they were engaged in a race with the local feminist lawyers who were bringing abortion funding cases in the more liberal ratified states. But no state court actually decided a case regarding abortion funding on the basis of a state ERA prior to the ratification deadline in June 1982. In Connecticut, a lower court found the feminist lawyers' argument that restrictions on abortion funding violated the state ERA "very persuasive," but invalidated those restrictions on other grounds.[47] In Pennsylvania, the courts did not decide on the feminist challenge to state restrictions on abortion funding until after the deadline for ratifying the federal ERA had passed. When the Pennsylvania lower court did finally rule on abortion funding, it struck down the restrictions under the equal protection clause of its state constitution. But it also commented that the argument under the state ERA was "meritorious and sufficient in and of itself to invalidate the statutes before us in that those statutes do unlawfully discriminate against women."[48] This wording, stronger than any prior to June 1982, gave the opposition valuable ammunition in the 1983 Congressional hearings on a new ERA.

In the 1983 House and Senate hearings on the ERA, Ann Freedman, an author of the original *Yale Law Journal* article interpreting the ERA, stated—I believe correctly—that "as a practical matter" the U.S. Supreme Court was unlikely to base its future decisions about abortion funding on the ERA. Rather, the Court would be likely in such cases to continue its elaboration of the right to privacy that provided the basis for *Roe v. Wade.*[49]

Moreover, as Freedman pointed out several times in the Senate hearings, on ambiguous matters the legislative history could be crucial. In 1983, the Congress probably had the power to influence heavily the way any future Supreme Court would decide on this issue. Freedman argued that

> the Senate and the House of Representatives control the meaning. . . . You are the legislators. . . . If the amendment is adopted, it is what the proponents say it means

and what the majority reports or any reports supporting the adoption of the amendment in either House say. And if they are clear about what the amendment means, that will be controlling.[50]

Yet, while it was true as a practical matter that the Supreme Court was unlikely to use the federal ERA to strike down legislative restrictions on abortion, the arguments that feminist lawyers had made in the state courts for an ERA–abortion link were immediately picked up by ERA opponents.[51] These feminist arguments claimed that the ERA would require government funding for abortion at a moment when more than half the public support for the ERA came from people who opposed abortion on demand.[52] In such circumstances, a credible claim that the ERA would mandate abortion funding almost guaranteed that the ERA would neither pass Congress nor be ratified in the states. But when Ann Freedman testified in the House and Senate Hearings that the Supreme Court of the United States would not be likely to use the ERA to mandate funding for abortions, several feminist lawyers treated her testimony as a betrayal.

Here, as on combat, some feminist lawyers had taken a position that would have detrimental consequences for ratification. Both the parallels to the combat decision and the differences from it are striking. In both cases some feminist constitutional lawyers were arguing a position that the Supreme Court of the United States was, as a practical matter, unlikely to take. And in both cases the position they were arguing severely hurt the cause of the ERA in the unratified states. But in the abortion decision, unlike the combat decision, the participants were well aware of the issues. Lawyers who linked the ERA to abortion funding made their decision quite consciously, often after discussion with legal and political leaders in Washington. As might have been predicted, the lawyers most closely connected to the ERA movement argued that there was no practical link. Lawyers in the already ratified states were the ones who made the connection. They knew they were reducing the ERA's chances of passing, but since they thought it unlikely to pass no matter what they did, they decided to proceed.

Participatory Decentralization in the States

The ERA movement depended not just on national experts like lawyers but on every spark of local energy it could inspire. And autonomous action on the local level often affected the course of local debate. Civil dis-

obedience provides the most obvious example. The decision of seventeen women to chain themselves to the rotunda in the Illinois state capital for four days sprang from individual initiative. So did the much publicized thirty-seven-day fast in the same state. These actions affected the ratification debate in a way that no ERA organization could easily alter. Throughout the ERA struggle individuals took actions like these on their own initiative, almost on the spur of the moment, and with as much concern for the personal testimony embodied in the act as for its practical effect on the ERA's chances for ratification.[53]

The costs and benefits of civil disobedience for ratification are hard to calculate. While some of these acts may have reduced the public popularity of the ERA in the short run,[54] the testimony they embodied rekindled the fire in every activist's heart. And because acts like this inspire others in the future, the gain for the movement as a whole may have outweighed small momentary losses in public approval. Certainly the harm to the movement if it had tried to quench such heartfelt gestures would have been incalculable.

The ERA movement had virtually no collective control over any of these acts of civil disobedience. But unlike the lawyers' decisions on what the ERA should be alleged to mean, the pros and cons of visible civil disobedience were discussed at length among the rank and file. If most activists had felt that such actions were hurting the movement, they could have made that conclusion known, either informally or by bringing it up explicitly in their organizations and publications. Because it was a visible, widely understood issue, we can assume that the absence of formal debate on civil disobedience within the organizations reflected widespread acceptance of the tactic.

Pro-ERA marches and demonstrations also provided important opportunities for autonomous action. In the early days of the ERA struggle, pro-ERA demonstrations were open to all. As a consequence, almost every demonstration had a socialist and a lesbian contingent, with banners proclaiming their identities as well as their support for the ERA. After considerable debate, NOW decided not to allow socialist and lesbian banners in its ERA demonstrations. While many disagreed with this decision, it was explicit and relatively participatory.

Here, as in so many other decisions, the initiative first came from peripheral extraorganizational actors, who often simply joined public ERA demonstrations carrying their banners. But in this case the eventual decision was made after lengthy discussion by workers on the front lines. Most pro-ERA organizations first took an activist-pleasing stance and allowed the banners. When the opposition began to publish photographs of these banners and the women carrying them,[55] the pro-ERA groups reversed their policy, often instituting not only a ban on visible lesbian and socialist participation but also a dress code for demonstrations. Although each state followed a slightly different course,[56] the pattern was usually to allow visible socialist and lesbian participation until local evidence convinced most activists that such a course would hurt the ERA. In these decisions, the pressures for ideological purity were the same as in the decisions on combat, the prohibited classification, and abortion funding, but participants eventually had accurate information regarding the alternatives, and personal knowledge of the practical effects of allowing the purists to have their way. Right or wrong, the result was not a decision by accretion.

From the point of view of the movement as a whole, each organization, as well as each individual, was also an autonomous actor. NOW could not keep the president and vice-president of ERA Illinois from attending a Republican fund-raising dinner. ERA Illinois could not keep NOW from calling a demonstration in the last days of the legislative session. By virtue of its size and resources, NOW became the center of the ERA struggle toward the end of this ten-year period. Realizing that it could not maintain its own active membership and at the same time engage in continual compromises with more conservative groups, NOW formally decided in 1978 to discourage coalition activity and to work with other pro-ERA organizations only when those organizations chose to co-sponsor specific actions that NOW had initiated, or when NOW wanted to co-sponsor specific actions initiated by other organizations. This stance freed NOW from whatever control the other pro-ERA organizations had previously exercised over it.

In a system of participatory decentralization, many individuals act relatively spontaneously, subject only to the sanctions of their peers and their consciences. Such a system has the great advantages of flexibility, adaptability, promoting innovation, and generating commitment.[57] But the advantage of not requiring a common line, which encourages innovation, brings with it a corresponding disadvantage: being able to avoid the internal dialogue necessary to hammer out that common line. When individuals and organizations can take action that affects the movement after consulting only their friends, they can avoid many hard questions and have less opportunity to acquire information from outside their group.

In these circumstances, each subgroup reinforces its members' perceptions of reality. Activists fighting for the ERA in the states, for instance, began to see the ERA as an end in itself. Each argument with an angry opponent, each attempt to convince an uncertain neighbor, each phone call to a talk show or letter to the editor, each visit to an irritated legislator made a little scar on the soul, healed only, if at all, by the recounting of similar experiences, the sympathy, and the reaffirmation of the goal that one's friends could provide. As the small but emotionally poignant costs cumulated,[58] and each friend reinforced the other's experience, it is no wonder that for the grass-roots activists the ERA became much more than a practical instrument for improving the lives of American women, much more than a symbol that would inspire women throughout the ages—it became a public symbol of the meaning of one's own life.

These emotional forces sometimes made local activists (including myself, who was only minimally active) care even more about winning than about being right. Getting something *called* the ERA through the legislature, somehow capturing those last two or three votes, became a goal in its own right, worth almost any sacrifice, including perhaps some of the instrumental character of the ERA itself.

Meanwhile, other actors in other parts of the drama were reinforcing in the same way the collective perceptions of their fellows. A number of feminist lawyers believed after 1978 that the ERA was both a lost cause in the states and a minimal addition to constitutional protections. They therefore placed little weight on the way their actions might affect the political fortunes of the ERA. Objectively, they may well have been right. Other lawyers, who thought the ERA meaningless unless it was uncompromising, may also have been right. But they all were living in a different world from the activists on the front lines, just as some activists were living in different worlds from one another. The problems of communicating across the boundaries of these worlds were not just the classic problems of individual autonomy versus the collective good; they were problems of the autonomy of small groups, whose members felt responsible to one another, in a movement that spanned the continent.

The Leadership Question

STOP ERA was able to overcome some of the problems of participatory decentralization by accepting, at least in theory, a relatively hierarchical chain of command centering on one person—Phyllis Schlafly—without whom the opposition would probably not have been able to prevent ratification.

Concentrating much of the responsibility for public debate in one person also meant that Schlafly could perfect her technique, while her opponents, who debated her only once or at the most two or three times, remained comparative amateurs on the ERA issue. Noting Schlafly's increasing skill in debate on the ERA over the years, one state legislator concluded that the pro-ERA forces should also have created a single "spokesman," like Schlafly, who could have honed to perfection the pro-ERA debating position.

Among the ERA forces, the decision not to organize hierarchically was explicit, conscious, and almost unanimous. While one woman sponsor grumbled that "the antis were able to take orders better," most proponents firmly believed in a participatory democracy that spread power among as many different individuals as possible. "Empowering women" was a goal as important as winning the ERA, and empowering women meant, among other things, giving instant responsibility even to the very inexperienced.

As one local NOW leader voiced the dilemma,

NOW Leader: To some extent, some of our principles prevent us from doing some things that Phyllis [Schlafly] has been able to do.

JM: What are some of those principles?

NOW Leader: Well, for example, her never-changing leadership. We think it is very important for lots of people to learn how to do these things. An interesting fact about NOW is that many NOW members are not joiners; they've joined virtually nothing in their lives and probably won't join anything else once they're in NOW. And they don't know basic things about organizations.

. . . What we're about is helping people, empowering them, helping them take control of their own lives, and to the extent that we impose a kind of "follow us to the ends of the earth" kind of mentality or emotional framework on what we're doing, we weaken what we're trying to do. And it's a short-term gain for a long-term

loss. I mean, it's something we're not willing to do. Phyllis doesn't care if the people who follow her ever learn anything. She's content to have them ignorant; we're not. And there's a price you pay for that in media recognition.[59]

When I asked Susan Catania, a key sponsor of the ERA in the Illinois House of Representatives, whether there was anything she thought the pro-ERA forces could have done differently, she expressed almost the same sentiments:

I doubt it. The temptation is to say that either I should have insisted that I be the one to call the shots, or insisted that Eugenia Chapman be the one to call the shots, or insisted that Giddy Dyer do it, because it is so much easier to get it done when one person is making the final decision about everything that is going to happen. But so many women and some men have become politically aware, trained, astute, capable, because of their work for ERA ratification that I don't think I would change it.

As frustrating as it is to have new people coming in constantly, all those people are learning a great deal about how it happens. . . . [But in some ways it is an] uncontrollable mess. It would be much more efficient to have one person running the whole show.[60]

However, while the kinds of people who came to work for the ERA may well have had to learn by doing, Schlafly's hierarchical techniques also seemed to create commitment, release energy, and promote learning, at least for her constituency. Far from indifferent to whether "the people who follow her ever learn anything," Phyllis Schlafly held each year a training conference for members of her Eagle Forum, climaxing in a banquet Saturday evening at which the STOP ERA "commander" formally addressed "her lieutenants." Begun the year after Schlafly lost her bid for president of the National Federation of Republican Women, these conferences had as their goal teaching her stalwarts how to prevent liberal control of Republican party conventions. At first, the conferences attracted only Schlafly's own loyalists in the Republican party, but after the Senate ratified the ERA and it went to the states, they began to attract more and more women.

The training ran the gamut from how to get your anti-ERA message on the "boob-tube," mount an effective letter-writing campaign, testify at public hearings, hold a press conference, set up a phone bank, hold a fund raiser (Schlafly recommended brunches to avoid selling alcohol), to infiltrate the feminist camp to learn ERA strategy.

A video room was open at all hours so participants could watch tapes of Phyllis debating Barbara Walters and Phil Donahue and Birch Bayh and Betty Friedan and a multitude of others. The purpose was not to provide entertainment or a much-needed break. The next day Phyllis would evaluate the women's performance in mock ERA debates. . . . [In workshops] Each woman would be videotaped making a two-minute speech and then watch "instant replays."

At another session a Schlafly aide handed women evaluation forms as they entered the room. Schlafly commanded a leader from every state to stand before the group and, in precisely two minutes, summarize a year's worth of STOP ERA and other "pro-family" activity. Speakers ultimately got their evaluation forms back, on which their peers anonymously evaluated their appearance, the content of their knowledge, poise, hand movements, etc., and then summed it all up with a grade. The person with the highest grade got a prize.[61]

For those who had no principled or emotional objections to the style, hierarchy led to far more learning than ERA proponents imagined.

The worst effect of hierarchy seems to have been the usual one of ignorance of local conditions. Both Ellie Smeal, at the top of a democratic and relatively participatory system, and Phyllis Schlafly, at the top of an autocratic one, experienced this problem. Smeal, for example, told me about the combat issue:

The whole military issue was not raised in the legislatures. It was used by the opposition in campaigns, but it did not cost us votes. The only time we had trouble was in Illinois in 1980. So we had Kathleen Carpenter testify on our side, and it absolutely blew them away. It absolutely wasn't an issue after that.

But Smeal was wrong about combat. Florida, Oklahoma, and Illinois were the only three wavering states that transcribed their debates; in all three, legislators often raised the military issue. And in Illinois, Kathleen Carpenter's 1980 Judiciary Committee testimony was a masterpiece of obfuscation, which left one ERA opponent—a lawyer and a conservative Democrat—saying, "I guess I still do not have an opinion of the bottom line from your testimony about the effect that ERA passage would have with regard to the question of women serving in combat." (This was also my own reaction after reading the testimony several times and even

interviewing Carpenter in person to determine her meaning.) Later, the same legislator declared in debate that he was voting against the ERA because on many questions, including that of women in combat, "the bottom line is 'what does ERA do?' The answer in my opinion is no one knows."[62] Nor, as the debates indicate, did combat stop being an issue in the Illinois legislature after Carpenter's testimony. This kind of misperception of local conditions by top leaders sometimes undermined the morale of state activists, who found it hard to get their insights taken seriously at the Washington office.

Similarly, Schlafly had difficulty understanding how to work effectively in states that had no Southern base. In 1984, Maine Right to Life had put together what its president, Sandra Faucher, called a "tasteful" campaign against the state ERA. In the campaign's television commercial a professor or lawyer read the text of the ERA, listed some possible consequences of the Amendment—like eliminating separate sports teams for boys and girls, ending the primary responsibility of the father for the support of children, homosexual marriages, and abortions paid for by tax dollars—and concluded, "We'd like you to read about this." Faucher says that support for the state ERA, which had begun at 61 percent in mid-June, fell dramatically as soon as the ads began, at times by as much as ten percentage points a week. But then Phyllis Schlafly, with her own small organization, Maine STOP ERA, entered the act and, in Faucher's words, "stopped our momentum dead." Schlafly's group ran a newspaper ad showing two men from New York's Gay Pride parade embracing under the headline: "Who Hid the Sex in Six?" (Six was the referendum number of the ERA). The text ran, in part,

What does the word "sex" [in the language of the ERA] mean? The sex you are, male or female, or the sex you engage in, homosexual, bisexual, heterosexual, sex with children . . . or whatever? . . . One thing is for sure: Militant homosexuals from all over America have made the ERA issue a hot priority. Why? To be able finally to get homosexual marriage licenses, to adopt children and raise them to emulate their homosexual "parents," and to obtain pension and medical benefits for odd-couple "spouses." . . . Vote *NO on 6!* The Pro-Gay E.R.A.

"That almost killed us," said Faucher, "There's a big difference between Iowa's conservative farmland and liberal Maine. . . . [After Schlafly's ad,] our polls showed that we were losing all our upscale better educated Republican types." Faucher was particularly upset because two teenagers had only shortly before this thrown a homosexual man off a bridge, killing him, and sentiment against homophobia was running high in Maine. "She [Schlafly] felt that she knew more than we did," complained Faucher. "But we had *lived* in this state!"[63]

While Schlafly, at the head of an autocratic organization, could simply dismiss information that did not conform to her views, Smeal was constrained by her democratically elected position, her democratically elected board, and her democratic ideals. Smeal's occasional lack of responsiveness to local insight derived in part from the conviction of a charismatic leader that on certain issues she simply knew she was right. It derived in part from the fact that the members of NOW's board and other officials, depending on the president for internal promotion and support in future NOW elections, were sometimes reluctant to contradict her. And it derived in part from the size and diversity of NOW's concerns, which—perhaps in combination with NOW's commitment to involving many people in the day-to-day operations of the organization—made Smeal much more inaccessible to the average member than Phyllis Schlafly was. When I tried to reach Schlafly, for example, it took one phone call. When I tried to reach Smeal, it took months. This meant that the lines of communication from the front lines to the center and back were often poor in NOW and hardly existed in some of the other pro-ERA organizations.

It was true, of course, that once the ERA battle reached what Janet Boles has called the "community conflict" stage[64]—involving amateurs in politics, unconventional tactics, personal slander, and overt hostility—the leadership in both camps could no longer control the actions or the tone of the people who contacted the legislators. The legislators soon came to dislike the personalities and distrust the claims of both sides, encouraged, no doubt, by the fact that these amateur lobbyists were women. When Debrah Bokowski asked legislators in several states to "describe and evaluate" the lobbying efforts of both sides of the ERA issue, a little over half the legislators who answered her request portrayed opponents as uninformed, unreasonable, ineffective, extreme, and emotional. Exactly half the legislators portrayed proponents in equally unflattering terms.[65] Some legislators simply dismissed the activists of both sides:

I think they've both been obnoxious, really. The ladies with the bread and everything else they bring in [the

antis] can be just as irritating as the ones who carry the placards [the pros].

—Female pro-ERA legislator

The activists, the people they [the leaders] bring with them—and this goes for both sides, the pro and the con—are pretty much wild-eyed crazies. You know, they are not professional, in the sense of the professional lobbyists that you, you know, work with normally down there. These people pull at you, yank you, yell, scream, threaten; they all look wild-eyed to me.

. . . these people simply aren't coherent half the time. You can't discuss anything with them. They're just, you know, they just keep at you, and keep at you, and keep at you, just—till you can't get any other work done.

—Female anti-ERA legislator

Even legislators who thought hard about the Amendment discounted the analyses of the citizens on their "side."

Most of the pro-ERA activists are so radical that they contend a great deal more will be accomplished by passage than I think is realistic to assume.

—Female pro-ERA legislator

I've generally been embarrassed by the [arguments] that I've seen publicized on the negative side. They're more . . . comments about brain-less, bra-less broads than ones based on any legal analysis of what the Fourteenth Amendment has and hasn't done and might potentially do in the future, as compared with what the ERA would accomplish.

—Male anti-ERA legislator

Why should activists whose avowed purpose was to pass or defeat a piece of legislation have behaved in ways that so many legislators regarded as foolish? One answer is that the alternative was very difficult and potentially costly. Predicting the substantive effects of the ERA was a difficult, time-consuming task, requiring a relatively dispassionate analysis of the issue. Those in a position to perform the task seldom knew exactly what the result would be, but they knew enough to see that disseminating such information to activists would be risky, since the relative lack of substantive effects would probably convince a lot of activists that they were wasting their time. The benefits of taking this risk were far from obvious, since only a small minority of legislators seemed to care about the Amendment's likely effects. Both sides therefore found it convenient to assume that no one in the legislature cared about the substantive effects and that the ERA's passage or defeat depended entirely on displays of passion and political muscle. Based on my observations in Illinois, I believe this view was probably an overgeneralization. A few waverers really did seem to me to care about what the Amendment would do. But such legislators were certainly a small minority compared to those who had either made up their minds in advance or who responded only to political pressure rather than argument.

However, at a more fundamental level, activists' ignorance about the substantive effects of the ERA was probably an almost inevitable by-product of the way in which they were recruited to the struggle. Because the ERA was a public good, the struggle attracted volunteers with strong ideological preconceptions about its merits and demerits. It promised few immediate changes in anyone's life, so it did not attract pragmatists for whom the tangible short-run costs and benefits were paramount. The volunteers who conducted the battle on both sides could not be subjected to "party discipline" in order to ensure that their actions always promoted the goal of either passing or defeating the ERA. Both sides had to give their volunteers a lot of leeway to do things that made legislative experts on both sides unhappy. In most cases the acts that irritated legislators reflected the fact that working for or against the ERA was not the volunteers' primary goal in life but was, instead, subordinated to a larger agenda. Since legislators seldom shared the agenda of either proponents or opponents, the fact that neither side could conceal these agendas or "stick to the issue" was bound to antagonize legislators who only wanted to get on with their business.

NOTES

1. Marguerite Rawalt indicates that NOW was founded by a group of women dissatisfied with the Interstate Association of State Commissions on the Status of Women for rejecting a resolution endorsing the ERA (Rawalt, "The Equal Rights Amendment, in Irene Tinker, ed., *Women in Washington* [Beverly Hills, Calif.: Sage, 1983], p. 59). For the NOW Bill of Rights, see Robin Morgan, ed., *Sisterhood Is Powerful* (New York: Random House, 1970), pp. 512–514. For the union members' walkout, see the Minutes of the NOW annual meeting, November 19–20, 1967, Schlesinger Library, reported in France Kolb, "How the ERA Passed the Congress," *Radcliffe Quarterly* 68

(March 1982): 11. See also Judith Hole and Ellen Levine, *Rebirth of Feminism* (New York: Quadrangle Books, 1971), p. 68.
2. Peterson, "The Kennedy Commission," in Tinker, ed., p. 31. For the union position as of the 1967, see Mary O. Eastwood, "Constitutional Protection against Sex Discrimination: An Informal Memorandum Prepared for the National Organization for Women Regarding the Equal Rights Amendment and Similar Proposals" (unpublished MS. in the files of Mary Eastwood).
3. Kolb, p. 11.
4. Marguerite Rawalt, Testimony, Equal Rights Amendment Hearings before the Committee on the Judiciary, Subcommittee no. 4, U.S. House of Representatives, March 25, 1971, p. 205.
5. Hole and Levine, p. 56. See also Rawalt, Testimony, p. 204.
6. The vote on this provision, proposed by Senator Ervin, was 36–33. A 50–20 majority also added a school prayer amendment, presumably intended to kill the ERA. The Amendment's supporters did not fight the school prayer amendment because they "felt that with the passage of the Ervin amendment we'd had it" ("Snarl in Senate All But Kills Women's Rights Amendment," *Washington Post*, October 14, 1970, p. 1).
7. *Congressional Record* (hereafter *Cong. Rec.*), October 14, 1970, p. 36863.
8. Senator Birch Bayh, press interview, "Men's Lib Pending," *Washington Daily News*, October 15, 1970, p. 25.
9. Catherine East, "The First Stage," *Women's Political Times* (September 1982): 9. The fact that Senator Ervin was reported as having "applauded the new language" (*Washington Post*, October 15, 1970, p. 1), and as having said that the substitute "would go a long way toward retaining the protective legislation which the states and the federal government have enacted" (*Evening Star*, Washington D.C., October 15, 1970, p. 5), confirmed the women's organizations in their suspicions of a sellout. I would like to thank Catherine East for providing the newspaper clippings referred to in nn. 6–9.
10. Janet K. Boles, *The Politics of the Equal Rights Amendment: Conflict and the Decision Process* (New York: Longman, 1979), p. 39.
11. Catherine East notes that "the Judiciary Committee vote on the Wiggins version was, for the first time, along partisan lines. All the Republicans, except Congressman McClory of Illinois, had voted for the Wiggins version, whereas 13 of the 20 Democrats had

supported the [original] ERA." Catherine East, "The ERA in Congress 1923–1972," unpublished MS., p. 15.

12. East, "The First Stage," p. 10.
13. Ibid.
14. Boles, *Politics*, p. 142.
15. Ibid., pp. 143–144.
16. Ibid., p. 72. See also pp. 62–66, and passim.
17. Gilbert Steiner (*Constitutional Inequality: The Political Future of the Equal Rights Amendment* [Washington, D.C.: Brookings Institution, 1985], pp. 58–66) discusses in more detail the way abortion and the ERA became concatenated.
18. In December 1974, Schlafly's banner headline proclaimed, "ERA Means Abortion and Population Shrinkage," *Phyllis Schlafly Report* 8, no. 5 (December 1974). Her accompanying story cited in support of this claim the arguments of Professor Charles Rice and Dean Clarence Manion of the University of Notre Dame Law School. A month later, Professor Joseph Witherspoon of the University of Texas telegrammed the Texas legislators: "Ratification of the ERA will inevitably be interpreted by the Supreme Court of the United States as an explicit ratification and an approval by the people of the United States of its 1973 decision invalidating state antiabortion statutes . . ." (Professor Joseph Witherspoon, telegram to the Texas state legislators, January 9, 1975, cited in Phyllis Schlafly, *The Power of the Positive Woman* [New Rochelle, N.Y.: Arlington House, 1977], p. 88). And within two weeks Rice wrote the legislators in Indiana: "If the ERA were adopted, it would make clear beyond any doubt that the states would be disabled from prohibiting or even restricting abortion in any significant way" (Professor Charles Rice, letter to Indiana state legislators, January 21, 1975, cited in Schlafly, *Power*, p. 88; see also Steiner, pp. 63–64). According to investigative work by the Lincoln, Nebraska, chapter of NOW, Dean Clarence Manion was a member of the John Birch Society National Council, and Professor Rice appeared with Phyllis Schlafly at a John Birch Society rally in July 1973 (Ann K. Justice, ed., "The Insurance Connection with STOP ERA Forces" [Lincoln, Nebr.: National Organization for Women, 1974], pp. 13, 33).
19. Although the ERA had no bearing on the legality of abortion per se, it did have potential relevance to the question of public funding for abortion. Once conservative legislators began cutting off public funds for abortions, liberal lawyers began looking for constitutional arguments that would make public funding

mandatory. These arguments usually invoked the Fourteenth Amendment to the federal Constitution, but in addition they occasionally invoked state ERAs, and in Pennsylvania a lower court suggested that the state ERA would, in fact, require the state to pay for abortions on the same basis as other medical procedures. But all this came later.

20. I have taken this account largely from Boles, *Politics*, passim, and her Table 1.1, pp. 2–3.
21. The states that refused to ratify were also relatively poor.
22. *New York Times*, November 1, 1975, p. 61. The story does not give any further information on the percentages in the surveys or the names of the polling organizations.
23. For the New York vote, see "Voters Approved Charity Gambling," *New York Times*, December 16, 1975: 1,950,993 against the ERA; 1,470,213 for it. For the New Jersey vote, see "Election Results Certified by State," *New York Times*, December 9, 1975: 860,061 against the ERA; 828,290 for it. For the early returns, see Linda Greenhouse, "Equal Rights Amendments Lose in New York and New Jersey Voting," *New York Times*, November 5, 1975, p. 1.
24. John van Gieson, "'Little ERA,' 7 More Revisions Rejected," *Miami Herald*, November 8, 1978, p. 21A. The story gives no further information on the percentages either in the survey or in the referendum. Gieson attributes the shift to a "last-minute campaign" in which opponents charged that the state ERA "would give homosexuals the right to marry and adopt children."
25. Survey reported in Laurence M. Paul, "Undecided May Hold ERA Fate," *Des Moines Sunday Register*, October 26, 1980, p. 6B, and conducted by the Iowa Poll, October 1–4, 1980; $N = 1,204$; likely voters = 799; wording: "Do you favor or oppose the Equal Rights Amendment to the Iowa Constitution?" Among "all Iowans" the figures were 52 percent favor, 22 percent oppose, and 20 percent undecided. Paul also reported that "in the five years the poll has been asking Iowa's adults about the [Iowa] ERA, support consistently has been in the 60 percent range. In August 1979 the poll found that 60 percent favored the Iowa ERA, 30 percent opposed it and 10 percent had no opinion." The Iowa Poll also asked, "Do you favor or oppose the Equal Rights Amendment to the U.S. Constitution?" (Iowa had ratified the ERA two days after the U.S. Senate in 1972.) Among all adult Iowans, 50 percent favored, 29 percent opposed, and 21 percent were undecided; among likely voters, the

percentages were 46, 34, and 20. Data on the referendum are not final but reported as "with nearly all of the states' precincts reporting," in Jim Healey and Tom Knudson, "Convention and the ERA Are Turned Down" (*Des Moines Register*, November 5, 1980, p. 1A). Healey and Knudson reported that the month between the poll and the vote had been marked by a bitter campaign in which opponents particularly linked the ERA with homosexuality and argued that the ERA would have allowed homosexual marriages, would have forced the state to pay for abortions on demand, and would have led to sexually integrated toilets, hospital rooms, and other facilities.

26. Market Opinion Research Job Number P34243, question 18: "If the election were being held today, would you be voting YES in favor of a state equal rights amendment or voting NO against the amendment?" Yes, in favor, 62 percent; No, against, 23 percent; Don't know/No answer, 15 percent ($N = 600$). Significantly lower approval rates are given by Pat Truman of Maine Stop ERA for the same week (October 3): 33 percent in favor, 34 percent against, and 33 percent undecided. Similarly, Sandra Faucher of Main Right to Life gives figures from the next week (October 9) as 36 percent in favor, 40 percent against, 24 percent undecided. Because Maine Right to Life, which commissioned both the surveys, prefers that the wording and the survey organization involved remain confidential, and because the results differ so dramatically from those obtained by Market Opinion Research, it may be best to treat these results as the artifact of a particular wording. It is worth noting that according to Faucher even their wording produced, four days before the election (October 30), a response of 43 percent in favor, 43 percent against, and 14 percent undecided, which is still noticeably more supportive than the final 63–37 vote against the state ERA in the referendum itself. (The exact percentages in the referendum vary slightly in different reports, presumably due to time differences in the returns reported. I have taken the referendum figures from *Public Opinion* [December/January 1985]: 77: "No" 63.1 percent [333,998], "Yes" 36.9 percent [195,653], with a turnout of 62.5 percent; *Ms.* [December 1984]: 76, reports "No" 64 percent, "Yes" 36 percent.) Referenda votes do not, of course, measure the "true" desires of the public better than survey research. Referenda reflect the desires of those who turn out to vote in what are often off-year elections. They are also extremely susceptible to the effects of short-run, dramatic, and extensive publicity. Moreover, they are notoriously conservative, at least on "social issues." The public's rule of thumb in a referendum seems to be, "When in doubt, vote no." David Butler and Austin Ranney, eds., *Referendums: A Comparative Study of Practice and Theory* (Washington, D.C.: American Enterprise Institute for Public Policy Research, 1978), pp. 16, 83–84.

27. In the *New York Times*/CBS survey of voters leaving the polls in the 1980 Presidential election ($N = 15,201$), 48 percent of the women supported the ERA (18 percent no opinion), compared to 44 percent of the men (16 percent no opinion). (In the twelve years from 1970 to 1982, men had moved slightly toward opposition, and women toward support. Compare this 48/44 ratio in the *New York Times*/CBS 1980 survey and the 70/74 ratio in the 1982 GSS with the first poll on the ERA in 1970 in which only 47 percent of the women favored the ERA, compared to 66 percent of the men. Robert Chandler, *Public Opinion: Changing Attitudes on Contemporary Political and Social Issues* [New York: R. R. Bowker/CBS News *Reference Book*, 1972], p. 47.) In the 1980 *New York Times*/CBS survey, support for the ERA correlated with voting against Reagan .304 ($N = 5,743$) among women and .315 among men ($N = 5,989$). Attitudes toward the ERA account for less than half a point of the nine-point gender gap; interaction with variables including or mentioning the ERA account for another half a point. For a further discussion of these data, see my "Myth and Reality: The ERA and the Gender Gap in the 1980 Election," *Public Opinion* 73 (1985): 64–78. Val Burris, "Who Opposed the ERA? An Analysis of the Social Bases of Antifeminism," *Social Science Quarterly* 64 (1983): 305–317, table 1, also provides data that show a gender gap on the ERA only among people with high incomes and educations. In the middle- and lower-income groups, the relationship is reversed, with men supporting the ERA more than women.

28. U.S. Census of Population: 1970, Subject Reports, Industrial Characteristics, PC(2)–78, 362, table 45. Due to cutbacks in the census, comparable 1980 information is not available at this time.

29. In Texas, Tedin et al. found that in their sample of pro-ERA activists 56 percent had at least a college degree. In their anti-ERA sample, drawn from a group demonstrating at the state capitol and disclosed by their interviews to have been primarily fundamentalist women, only 16 percent had college degrees (Kent L. Tedin et

al., "Social Background and Political Differences between Pro- and Anti-ERA Activists," *American Politics Quarterly* 5 [1977]:395–408). In North Carolina, Theodore S. Arrington and Patricia A. Kyle ("Equal Rights Amendment Activists in North Carolina," *Signs* 3 (1978) 666–680) found that the ERA activist typically had at least a college degree and a professional occupation, and almost three quarters of the married ERA activists had spouses in the professions. Iva E. Deutchman and Sandra Prince-Embury, interviewing six pro-ERA and six anti-ERA leaders, found that all but one of the pro-ERA leaders had graduate degrees, whereas only one of the antis (probably Phyllis Schlafly herself, from other evidence in the article) had a college education ("Political Ideology of Pro- and Anti-ERA Women," *Women and Politics* 2[1982]: 39–55). Pamela Johnston Conover and Virginia Gray, *Feminism and the New Right: Conflict over the American Family* (New York: Praeger, 1983), table 5.4, produce similar educational comparisons for activists who combined both pro- or anti-ERA and abortion activities. See also Carol Mueller and Thomas Dimieri, "The Structure of Belief Systems among Contending ERA Activists," *Social Forces* 60 (1981): 657–675, table 1.

Among women state legislators (in one sense, the most active "activists"), the effect of education in 1977 was fairly dramatic: only 59 percent of the high school graduates (*N* = 27) supported the ERA, compared to 79 percent of those with some college (*N* = 79) and 92 and 90 percent, respectively, of those with a college degree and some graduate education (*N* = 79; 160). Joyce R. Lilie, Roger Handberg, Jr., and Wanda Lowrey, "Women State Legislators and the ERA: Dimensions of Support and Opposition," *Women and Politics* 2 (1982): 23–38, table 2 (61 percent return to a mail survey of the 688 women who in 1977 served in state legislatures). See also Joan S. Carver, "The E.R.A. in Florida" (paper presented at the annual meeting of the Southern Political Science Association, Gatlinburg, Tennessee, 1979, table 2), for the strong effect of education on legislators' votes for the ERA in the Florida House of Representatives from 1973 to 1979.

30. Although neither the Texas nor the North Carolina study looked at race and ethnicity, my own observation of more than a hundred ERA activists in Chicago, where blacks and Hispanics together constitute about half the adult population, turned up only one Hispanic and three black activists. The ERA activists I saw in Chicago were also almost all well educated and female.

31. For parallel findings on the lack of association of ERA attitudes with class, see Conover and Gray, table 6.6, using 1976 and 1980 NES data; and Glenna Spitze and Joan Huber, "Effects of Anticipated Consequences on ERA Opinion," *Social Science Quarterly* 63 (1982): 323–332, table 2, using a 1978 national probability sample. Spitze and Huber also document the small positive association between Catholicism and ERA support.

32. Louis Harris, "ERA Support Soars as Deadline Nears," a Chicago Tribune Syndicate, Inc., release, reprinted in *National NOW Times* (Junes 1982). See also "ERA Support to a Six-Year High," *Chicago Sun-Times*, May 7, 1982, sec. 1, p. 36.

33. *BusinessWeek*, August 1, 1983: 92.

34. Gloria Steinem, "How Women Live, Vote, Think," *Ms.* (July 1984): 54.

35. The new question was the third question asked in April 1982, and was worded:

> Many of those who favor women's rights favor the Equal Rights Amendment to the Constitution. Those who favor ERA argue that unless it is passed, women will continue to receive lower pay for the same work, receive fewer promotions to better jobs, and be discriminated against financially. Opponents argue that the special laws that now exist to protect women are sufficient and no new law is needed. Do you strongly favor, somewhat favor, somewhat oppose, or strongly oppose the Equal Rights Amendment?
>
> —*Harris Survey release, July 16, 1984, telephone survey of "likely voters 18 and over" at 1,259 different sampling points.*

On the basis of the April 1982 sample, in which 63 percent of the public favored ERA on both the "traditional" question and this one, Harris might argue that the new question was a valid continuation of the traditional series. But in April 1982 respondents were answering for the third time in a few minutes the question of whether or not they favored the ERA. It is not surprising, once Harris moved away from the question that used the actual wording of the ERA, that the same people favored the ERA the third time they were asked as favored it the second time.

36. In Oklahoma in 1978, William J. Wiseman, a representative to the Oklahoma legislature from Tulsa County, reported that "my regular polling of the dis-

trict I represent has indicated a remarkable shift over the past four years—from moderate support to strong opposition to the ERA." He testified in the federal hearings on ERA extension that this change in his constituency's opinion, coupled with his own change from believing that the ERA would make sex a suspect classification to believing that "it might also be interpreted to prohibit legal classifications based upon sex, a result which I would strongly oppose," had changed him from voting for ratification in 1974 and subsequent years to opposing it in 1977 and 1978 (statement of William J. Wiseman, Jr., on Equal Rights Amendment Extension, U.S. House of Representatives, Subcommittee on Civil and Constitutional Rights of the Committee on the Judiciary, May 17, 1978, pp. 212–213).

In Illinois in 1977, Representative Griesheimer, a strong ERA opponent, claimed that "I've gone to [the people of my legislative district] three separate times in polls. . . . It's interesting to note that the first time they were polled in March they were in favor of the ratification of the Equal Rights Amendment, that's March of 1973. In July of 1975 they were still in favor of it; and in March of 1976 they turned around and said, 'No, do not ratify' " (Illinois House of Representatives, June 2, 1977, p. 55; see also June 7, 1978, p. 28).

In Illinois in 1978, Representative Mautino, an ERA supporter, reported that in his district "three years ago it was about 65 percent in favor of [the ERA], 35 percent opposed." By May 1978, he said, it was 50.1 percent in favor and 49.9 percent opposed. Mautino then concluded that "in all conscience from all of the information I have evaluated, I will be voting 'yes' on the Equal Rights Amendment" (Representative Mautino, Illinois House of Representatives, June 7, 1978, p. 41).

In Illinois in June 1982, only a few days before the final deadline, Representative Friedrich, an ERA opponent, stated that "the polls in my district have become more and more and more opposed to the ratification of this [the ERA]. The last one was 32 to 1. Before that it had consistently run 2 to 1" (Representative Friedrich, Illinois House of Representatives, June 22, 1982, p. 12).

Most of these representatives were probably referring not to professional surveys in their districts but to questionnaires mailed to their constituencies from their own offices. Such questionnaires are morel likely to be returned by political activists than by representative members of the population, and, as we have

seen, political activists usually take more extreme positions than the average citizen. Thus in a generally conservative district, one would expect an incumbent's mail-back questionnaire survey to overrepresent the anti-ERA positions of conservative activists. This kind of overrepresentation is also inevitable when a legislator sends a questionnaire, as some do, only to his or her own list. However, none of these considerations would explain either the reported shifts over time or the results in what ERA supporter Representative Mautino called his "middle-America" district.

37. Representative Barbara Currie, Illinois House of Representatives, June 8, 1982, pp. 79, 81. These figures differ only slightly from those in Debra L. Dodson, "The Impact of Institutional Factors Upon the Ratification of the Equal Rights Amendment" (paper delivered at the 1982 Midwest Political Science Association meetings). Dodson's careful analysis indicates that the growth in Democratic support derived completely from changes in the "downstate" Democratic vote in the legislature—changes that I would explain by the "Dixiecrat" legislators in that area coming into line with their party's wishes. See also Carver, tables 3 and 4, for polarization in the Florida House, though not in its (much smaller) Senate, from 1973 to 1979.

At the same time, public attitudes toward the ERA were polarizing along party and ideological lines. In national NES samples, the correlations in the predicted direction between attitudes toward the ERA and feelings on a "feeling thermometer" toward "Republicans," "Liberals," "the Women's Liberation Movement," and "Civil Rights Leaders" increased noticeably between 1976 and 1980 (Conover and Gray, table 6.4).

38. The seminal article is Herbert McClosky et al., "Issue Conflict and Consensus among Party Leaders and Followers, *American Political Science Review* 5 (1960): 406–427. For more recent work, see Norman H. Nie, Sidney Verba, and John R. Petrocik, *The Changing American Voter* (Cambridge, Mass.: Harvard University Press, 1976), pp. 200–205, and Sidney Verba and Gary Orren, *Equality in America: The View from the Top* (Cambridge, Mass.: Harvard University Press, 1985), chapter on representation, and citations therein.

39. James Q. Wilson, "Incentive Systems: A Theory of Organization," *Administrative Science Quarterly* 6 (1961): 129–166 (with Peter B. Clark); *The Amateur Democrat* (Chicago: University of Chicago Press, 1962), esp. pp. 156–163; and *Political Organizations*

(New York: Basic Books, 1973), introduced to political science the kind of analysis I employ here. In his terms, the ERA movement relied primarily on "purposive" and secondarily on collective "solidary" incentives. Because the movement combined what Wilson terms "goal-oriented," "ideological," and "redemptive" purposes, it suffered from the inherent contradictions of such a combination. In sociology, Amitai Etzioni's *Comparative Analysis of Complex Organizations* (New York: Free Press [1961], 1975) earlier introduced a similar classification of organizations into those which rely on "coercive," "utilitarian," and "normative" compliance, with the "core" organizations of social movements usually depending heavily on normative compliance (p. 41).

40. Mancur Olson, *The Logic of Collective Action* (Cambridge, Mass.: Harvard University Press, 1965). Many analyses of social movements have used Olson's analysis, almost always pointing out that social movements, precisely because they rely on ideological (or "purposive") and solidarity incentives, fall into a category of organizations that Olson himself decided not to analyze. See, for example, Bruce Fireman and William Gamson, "Utilitarian Logic in the Resource Mobilization Perspective," in Mayer M. Zald and John D. McCarthy, eds., *The Dynamics of Social Movements* (Cambridge, Mass.: Winthrop, 1979); Maren L. Carden *Feminism in the Mid-1970's* (New York: Ford Foundation, 1977); Ralph Turner and Lewis M. Killian, *Collective Behavior* (Englewood Cliffs, N.J.: Prentice-Hall, 1972); Anthony Oberschall, *Social Conflict and Social Movements* (Englewood Cliffs, N.J.: Prentice-Hall, 1973); J. Craig Jenckins, "Sociopolitical Movements," in Samuel Long, ed., *The Handbook of Political Behavior*, vol. 4 (New York: Plenum Press, 1981); Norman Frohlich, Joe A. Oppenheim, and Oran R. Young, *Political Leadership and Collective Goods* (Princeton: Princeton University Press, 1971); and Mary Douglas and Aaron Wildavsky, *Risk and Culture* (Berkeley: University of California Press, 1982). For an excellent review of the literature, see David Knoke and Christine Wright-Isak, "Individual Motives and Organizational Incentive Systems," *Research in the Sociology of Organizations* 1 (1982): 209–254. For an analysis of the anti- and pro-ERA movements and the anti- and pro-abortion movements in Olson's terms, see Conover and Gray, who point out (table 5.7) that in their small sample of activists all twenty-eight members of New Right organizations and all 8 members of liberal organizations gave personal principles or ideology as their primary motive in joining the organization. For the tactics of women's groups trying to represent a diffuse interest with few selective benefits, see Anne E. Costain, "The Struggle for a National Women's Lobby: Organizing a Diffuse Interest," *Western Political Quarterly* 33 (1980): 476–491.

41. *Roe v. Wade*, 410 U.S. 113 (1973).

42. The eventual ACLU decision to stress autonomous decision making free from state intervention rather than sex discrimination in the federal abortion funding case was, however, made on the basis of "what argument was most likely to win. . . . The ERA was not a consideration in how that case was argued—not at all" (telephone interview, with Ruth Bader Ginsburg, November 7, 1985). See also Sylvia Law. 1984. "Rethinking Sex and the Constitution." *University of Pennsylvania Law Review* 132: pp. 981–982.

43. *Hawaii Right to Life, Inc. v. Chang, Director of Social Services and Housing*, Civ. No. 53567, Memorandum in Support of Motion to Intervene, p. 1, cited in *Impact Hearings*, vol. 1, pp. 562, 659–660.

44. *Harris v. McRae*, 448 U.S. 297 (1980), at 325, 326. The state case was *U.S. v. Zbaraz*, 448 U.S. 324 (1980).

45. "From the Executive Director's Desk," *Docket* (newsletter of the Civil Liberties Union of Massachusetts), paper 1980, in *Impact Hearings*, vol. 1, p. 657.

46. *Moe v. Secretary of Administration and Finance*, 417 N.E. 2d 387 (Mass. 1980), quoted in part in *Impact Hearings*, vol 1, p. 657.

47. *Rosie J. Doe et al v. Edward Mahler et al.*, Superior Court, Judicial District of New Haven, Memorandum of Decision on Motions for Class Certification, Motion for Temporary Injunction and Certain Other Motions. October 9, 1981, in *Impact Hearings*, vol. 1, pp. 655–656.

48. John A. MacPhael, Judge of the Commonwealth Court of Pennsylvania, Opinion in *Fischer v. Department of Public Welfare*, 283 C.D. 1981, heard February 7, 1984, in *Impact Hearings*, vol. 1, p. 641.

49. Ann Freedman argued in the 1983 hearings that the Supreme Court would interpret the ERA, as the *Yale Law Journal* article and subsequent expansions of that theory in *Gilbert* argued it should, to prohibit absolutely legislative classification by gender except in cases of privacy, unique physical characteristics, and temporary compensatory treatment to make up for past discrimination. These three exceptions would be subject to strict judicial scrutiny.

She then argued that the ERA would not raise the standard of scrutiny in abortion funding cases beyond the standard the Court had already used in *Harris v. McRae*. This argument assumed that the Court in *Harris* had used a strict scrutiny standard, on the grounds that abortion legislation involves the fundamental right of privacy and the Court uses strict scrutiny in cases that involve a fundamental right *(City of Akron v. Akron Center for Reproductive Health)*. Ann Freedman, Testimony in *Impact Hearings*, vol. 1, pp. 451–454; summarized p. 502; and Letter to Representative John Edwards, Nov. 7, 1983, in *Impact Hearings*, vol. 1, pp. 624–625. Freedman particularly pointed out in her letter to Representative Edwards that if the Supreme Court in *Harris* had wanted to see abortion funding as raising an important issue of sex discrimination, the Court would have used the middle-tier standard it had already created in *Craig v. Boren*, and would have asked whether the Hyde amendment was "substantially related to an important government interest." "Instead," Freedman noted, "the Supreme Court decided the case entirely on privacy grounds and dismissed the sex discrimination argument." *Impact Hearings*, vol. 1, p. 625.

Other lawyers believed that the Court would not feel required by an ERA to change its abortion funding decisions because funding issues preeminently involve the equal protection of the laws: if the state funds one class, it must also fund the others. Under this reasoning, abortion funding issues are essentially Fourteenth Amendment issues.

50. Ann Freedman, Testimony in *Impact Hearings*, vol. 1, pp. 490–491. See also p. 506, where Freedman pointed out that the legislative history had to be made by "a senatorial or congressional proponent." Opponents of the ERA, like Senator Hatch, often suggested incorrectly that arguments by feminist lawyers in the state courts, by feminist organizations, and by opponents in the Congress constituted legislative history.

Senator Hatch, in a particularly distasteful piece of manipulation, claimed that the 1983 legislative history indicated an ERA-abortion link because "Senator Tsongas had the opportunity to disclaim [the ERA-abortion funding link] and failed to" (p. 507). But anyone reading Tsongas's remarks would understand that he intended no such thing. Completely unprepared and on his way to a plane, Tsongas at first answered vaguely to almost every question on the effect of the ERA, suggesting (in words that would later be used against the ERA) that all of these matters would "be settled in the courts." Later when he began to see the trap that Hatch had led him into, he began to backtrack, saying, "I will answer all of your ques-

tions in writing" (p. 31), "Why were not these questions submitted when we would have a chance to review them and give you detailed answers?" (p. 32), and "I simply am asking that the committee give me the right to look at [these questions on the effect of the ERA] and respond to you. I did not anticipate the questions; I did not anticipate the tactics" (p. 39). Out of this material, Senator Hatch's Subcommittee on the Constitution created the following misleading summary:

> *Legislative History*
> The most compelling legislative history on the meaning of an amendment comes from its Congressional proponents. In responding to the alleged ERA/abortion connection, the Senate co-sponsors of the ERA stated as follows: (Sen. Robert Packwood) "I'm not sure how a court would come out on it." (Sen. Paul Tsongas) "This issue would be resolved by the courts."
> —*Impact Hearings,* vol. 1, p. 548.

51. Opponents also picked up a feminist law professor's use of the ERA to support abortion rights in an article in *Ms.* magazine after the 1982 deadline. That article argued that "the separation of abortion from the campaign for the ERA has jeopardized abortion and produced a truncated version of liberation." Rhonda Copelon, "Abortion Rights: Where Do We Go From Here?" *Ms.* (October 1983): p. 146, reprinted in *Impact Hearings*, vol. 1, p. 639. The ERA-abortion link had a continuing impact, for example, on U.S. Representative James Oberstar who voted for the ERA when it came before the U.S. House in November 1983 but changed his mind later, saying he would now support the ERA only with an amendment stating that it did not pertain to abortions (*Eleanor Smeal Report*, April 19, 1984, p. 4).

52. In the 1982 GSS, 52 percent of the people who favored the ERA answered "no" to the question, "Please tell me whether or not you think it should be possible for a pregnant woman to obtain a legal abortion if the woman wants it for any reason."

53. Bernice A. Carroll, "Direct Action and Constitutional Rights: The Case of the ERA," *Organization of American Historians' Newsletter* 11 (1983): 18–21, lists several other instances of direct action in support of the ERA. Carroll, a member of the "Grassroots Group of Second-Class Citizens," which chained itself to the railings before the Illinois State Senate Chamber, concludes that NOW "informally discouraged" civil disobedience and that "in the major ERA campaign

organizations" direct action "was viewed with much doubt, if not hostility." In the discussions in which I participated, I sensed caution but support rather than hostility and, among many, active enthusiasm. In any case, as Carroll reports, direct action provoked "much debate on its wisdom and effectiveness." For the difficulties of controlling autonomous direct action that had potentially negative effects on public opinion, see Deborah L. Rhode. 1983. "Equal Rights in Retrospect." *Law and Inequality* 1: pp. 59–61.

54. In June 1982, when seven women were protesting nonratification through a public fast in the rotunda of the state capitol which seriously weakened their health, Market Opinion Research asked a sample of Illinois voters, "Do you approve or disapprove of the efforts of women's groups over the past two weeks to get the ERA ratified? Sixty-seven percent of the voters opposed those efforts, with only 23 percent favoring them and 11 percent having no opinion ($N = 79$). Women were slightly more likely to oppose (69 percent) than men. Even among ERA supporters, 54 percent opposed.

55. *Phyllis Schlafly Report* 9, no. 11, sec. 2 (June 1976).

56. See comments on Georgia in Boles, *Politics*, pp. 76–77.

57. See Luther P. Gerlach and Virginia H. Hine, *People, Power, Change: Movements of Social Transformation* (Indianapolis: Bobbs-Merrill, 1970), pp. 34–78, esp. pp. 63 ff: "The Adaptive Functions of Decentralized, Segmented, Reticulate Structure." Manfred Kocken and Karl W. Deutsch, "Toward a Rational Theory of Decentralization," *American Political Science Review* 63 (1969): 734–749, point out that decentralized structures are more likely to act with speed, accuracy, innovation, and adaptability. Herbert A. Simon, *Administrative Behavior* (New York: Macmillan, 1960), p. 238, recommends decentralization for speed. Warren G. Bennis and Philip E. Slater, *The Temporary Society* (New York: Harper and Row, 1969), indicate that structures in which participants autonomously determine much of what they do is likely to be innovative and adaptable. Amitai Etzioni, p. 71, citing a study of the League of Women Voters, points out that in organizations where the incentives for participation are nonmaterial (or moral, solidary, purposive, or ideological, depending on one's terminology), high control leads to less loyalty, while decentralization leads to more loyalty.

58. Having paid a price, emotionally or otherwise, people often upgrade in their minds the worth of the good they have paid for. See Leon Festinger, *A Theory of Cognitive Dissonance* (Evanston, Ill.: Row, Peterson, 1957); E. Aronson and J. Mills, "The Effect of Severity of Initiation on Liking for a Group," *Journal of Abnormal and Social Psychology* 59 (1959): 177–181; and, for a recent summary and critique of the literature, Hal R. Arkes and John P. Garske, *Psychological Theories of Motivation*, 2d ed. (Monterey, Calif.: Brooks/Cole Publishing, 1982).

59. The same person told me that "there is always a temptation in a movement, where there's a lot of emotionalism and so on, to take the reins as a charismatic leader and get everybody marching with you, and to order them here and there. And that ability to influence people is heavy stuff, and I think all of us appreciate the dangers in that, and we find ourselves liking it too much. We begin to back off." This recognition and conscious avoidance of the seductions of power was common among the participatory democrats of the American 1960s and 1970s. See my chapter, "The Lust for Power," in *Beyond Adversary Democracy*.

60. Felsenthal, *Sweetheart*, p. 261.

61. Ibid., pp. 267–268.

62. Representative Brummer, Illinois House of Representatives, Judiciary I Committee, Hearings on House Resolution CAI [ERA], April 30, 1980, and Illinois House of Representatives, June 18, 1980, p. 151.

63. See also Carol Mueller & Thomas Dimieri. 1981. "The Structure of Belief Systems among contending ERA Activists." *Social Forces* 60: p. 662, for the tension and lack of communication between anti-ERA groups in Massachusetts in 1976. STOP ERA was hierarchical internally but had the problems of coalitions that all groups experience.

64. Boles, *Politics*, pp. 17–18, applying to the ERA the characterizations of "community conflict" of James S. Coleman, *Community Conflict* (New York: Free Press, 1957), and Robert L. Crain et al., *The Politics of Community Conflict* (Indianapolis: Bobbs-Merrill, 1969). From *Why We Lost the ERA* (Chicago and London: University of Chicago Press, 1986), 18–19, 118–48.

65. Debrah Bokowski, 1982. "State Legislator Perceptions of Public Debate on the Equal Rights Amendment." Paper presented at the annual meeting of the American Political Science Association, Denver.

PART FOUR

THE POLITICS OF
PUBLIC POLICY-MAKING

Government leaders and officials devise public policies for a number of purposes: to acquire the resources needed to keep the government running, to deal with other nations in the world system, and to promote social well-being and economic growth at home. Of course, changing conditions outside of government influence the timing and content of public policies: international crises may occur; the needs of the citizenry may change; the dynamics of the economy may be transformed. But policy responses to such shifting conditions hardly are automatic. Policies are always created, or changed, through *political* discussion and contention.

The various matters we have considered in this Reader—the dynamics of power, group ideas and interests, patterns of political participation, and the rise and impact of social movements—all come into play in the politics of public policy making. What is more, political debates and conflicts about possible public policies occur in and through the distinctive institutions of the U.S. government and political parties. Those historically formed—and changing—institutions place limits on what is likely or possible at any given time. So do previous policies, because governments never devise brand-new policies simply as responses to current problems or balances of power. Future policies always build upon the perceived successes, or try to correct for the perceived failings, of prior policies (Pierson, 1993).

Politicians, bureaucratic officials, professional experts, and politically active groups and social movements—all are possible participants in the policy-making process. Such actors not only contend about *what kind of policy* to choose, but also may influence the *kinds of issues that arise*. Problems can persist for a very long time without ever becoming the focus of public policy. Sometimes powerful actors have a strong stake in keeping an issue "off the agenda" of public debate. At other times, there may be a consensus among experts that, although a problematic condition exists, nothing useful can be done about it through governmental action. So whether an issue comes up at all—and how it is formulated—may be just as important as debates over what to do once a problem is recognized as suitable for government action (Kingdom, 1984). After an issue is on the agenda, discussions, conflicts, and coalitions among interested actors will determine the kinds of alternative responses that are considered, as well as the particular policy that eventually prevails.

This part of the Reader does not attempt to deal with all of the policy issues that have, or might, come up in American politics. That hardly would be possible. Nevertheless, several "policy areas" of considerable importance are discussed, including taxes, social policies, and efforts to manage the development of the national economy. Tax policy takes us to the heart of how government operates: without collecting revenues from economic enterprises and citizens, no government can pay its officials, run its offices, or carry through any other kind of effort. Decisions about amounts and kinds of taxes are politically revealing. They are inherently contentious, not only among social groups, but also between government and citizens. In the case of the United States, the nation itself was born in the course of disputes over "unjust taxation" with Great Britain. Ever since, American businesses and citizens have been resistant to paying taxes. Yet government operates, so political solutions have obviously been found to underpin the raising of revenues.

As for the things governments try to do once they have resources, promoting the social welfare of the citizenry and managing the national economy within a changing world economy today are two of the most important. In western democracies since the middle of the twentieth century, citizens have taken it for granted that their national governments will deal with their needs and challenges in these areas. And Americans are no exception, especially since the advent of the New Deal. Yet there are often institutional and practical limits to what governments can do, and the political conflicts about what is desirable or possible are just as heated with regard to social and economic policies as they are concerning taxes.

The discussions in Chapters 9 and 10 range across U.S. political history and come down to the issues and policy choices that are the focus of public debate in the 1990s. We learn how U.S. governmental institutions, political parties, group involvement in politics, and prior policy choices all have interacted historically to shape patterns of public policy. We also glimpse the debates now going on inside and around the Clinton administration about what to do next to reform health care and other social programs, and to promote employment and international economic competitiveness. The politics of public policy making continues, as leaders and citizens, experts and social groups, all contend over how the government of the United States should define and address the pressing problems of our time.

REFERENCES

Kingdon, John. 1984. *Agendas, Alternatives, and Public Policies*. Boston: Little Brown.
Pierson, Paul. 1993. "When Effect Becomes Cause, 'Policy Feedback' and Political Change." *World Politics* 45 (4): 595–628.

CHAPTER 9

INSTITUTIONS, POLITICS, AND PATTERNS OF POLICY

In the United States, as in other nations, political institutions make a difference in the politics of public policy-making. Government bureaucracies, representative bodies, electoral rules, and political party organizations shape the careers of politicians and officials, making it advantageous and possible for them to pursue certain lines of activity rather than others. Political institutions also influence the ways in which important groups in society—social classes, racial and ethnic groups, gender-based groups—define their political interests and organize collectively to influence political debates and conflicts. By tracing the historical changes in a nation's political institutions, and noticing how they influence the political activities of officials and social groups, we can gain an understanding of how and why the United States has evolved patterns of public policy that are distinctive in comparison with those of other nations, including other industrial democracies.

This "historical and institutional" approach to the explanation of public policy making is used by Sven Steinmo and Theda Skocpol in Readings 28 and 29 respectively. Steinmo examines patterns of taxation and tax politics in the United States as compared with Britain and Sweden, while Skocpol compares American social policies and politics from the nineteenth century to the present with the patterns of policy and politics that have characterized certain western "welfare states" during the same epoch.

Taxes are the "lifeblood" of the state (Braun, 1975, p. 243). Without them, the state cannot provide social programs, maintain roads and bridges, defend the country from military threats, pursue economic policy, or carry out normal governmental operations. During the eighteenth and nineteenth centuries, the federal government in America relied on excise taxes and tariffs for most of its revenue. The amount of revenue it collected from these sources was meager by present-day standards. By the early 1900s, federal, state, and local taxes combined still amounted to only about six percent of the Gross National Product (GNP). However, taxation expanded dramatically after that. The federal government began to collect corporate income taxes in 1909, and four years later started collecting individual income taxes on a permanent basis. During World War II, the individual income tax was expanded to cover most working Americans (Witte, 1985). Other taxes were added along the way, including a variety of payroll taxes such as Social Security, so that by 1986 federal taxes amounted to nearly 20 percent of

GNP, and the combined revenues of all levels of government were more than 30 percent of GNP (Musgrave & Musgrave, 1989, p. 318).

Cross-national comparisons can help us to note what is interesting about any one country. Not surprisingly, Steinmo's juxtaposition of U.S. patterns of taxation and those of Britain and Sweden reveals that U.S. taxes are relatively light. Americans may complain a lot about taxes, but they pay less! (Tax collectors in several western European countries collect between 35 percent and 50 percent of GNP [Heidenheimer, Heclo & Adams, 1983, p. 173].) At the same time, however, corporate taxes on business are heavier overall in the United States than in the other two nations Steinmo studied. At least until recently, U.S. taxes were more "progressive," meaning that the rich paid relatively more than those with lower incomes (although the absolute tax burden was relatively low).

Having established some distinctive patterns for the U.S. case, Steinmo asks *why* national patterns of taxation have developed as they have. Here is where institutions and group politics come in. Because political authority is fragmented by U.S. federalism and divisions of institutional powers, Steinmo argues, there are many opportunities for interest groups to penetrate the policy process and convince policymakers to provide them with various tax loopholes. As a result, much potential revenue fails to be collected. Yet despite the fact that concessions are made to specific firms, for example, there are fewer broad tax write-offs to promote corporate saving and investment than there are in Europe. Democratic pressures do filter through representative institutions in the United States, accounting for the levying of taxes on corporations, and not only on individual citizens.

Given their different institutions and political histories, Britain and Sweden offer clear contrasts to the United States. The tax burden in Britain is moderate and consists of a greater mixture of progressive and regressive taxes. What is more, the British tax system often undergoes dramatic changes. This happens because, in Britain, the ideological differences between the major parties are clear-cut, and the parliamentary electoral system ensures that one party controls both branches of the government. As a result, each time power changes hands, the tax system is revised, and over time a system has evolved that consists of numerous and occasionally contradictory taxes.

Sweden imposes a heavy tax burden, relies primarily on a regressive tax structure, and taxes corporations and wealth lightly. This policy has ensued because the Swedish system of proportional electoral representation, along with a well-organized labor movement, made it possible for the Social Democratic party and its allies to control the national government from the 1930s to the 1980s. Furthermore, Sweden's corporatist system of bargaining ensures that labor unions, business peak associations, and other nationally organized groups are involved when tax policy negotiations take place. Hence, in order to promote jobs and economic growth, labor and the Social Democrats have agreed to tax capital lightly as long as capital and wealth are invested rather than consumed. Sven Steinmo's research thus illustrates the policy differences between a corporatist and an interest-group–dominated political system, as conceptualized by Robert Salisbury in Reading 16 in Chapter 5.

Skocpol's reading continues the comparison of the United States with other western nations. Many western democratic nations proudly proclaim themselves to be "welfare states" that use tax revenues to provide health insurance, old-age pensions, employment training, and other social benefits to all of their citizens (Flora & Heidenheimer, 1981; Furniss & Tilton, 1977). But in the United States, the term "welfare" does not bring positive images to mind. U.S. "welfare recipients," mostly single mothers and their children, are often thought of as "dependents" who are "unwilling to work," and prefer to live on "handouts" from the taxpayers. In contrast to how they feel about welfare, Americans are proud and supportive of their Social Security system for the retired elderly, which is routinely contrasted with Aid to Families with Dependent Children (AFDC) and other "welfare" programs. It is pointed out that Social Security goes only to those who have worked all of their lives (or have been married to such workers), and thus have "earned" the benefits they receive in old age, disability, or widowhood. Social Security, however, is the only really generous and honorable part of the United States' national social-provision agenda. Other programs of the type included in modern European welfare states either are nonexistent in the United States (national health insurance, for example), or are much more fragmentary and less generous, such as unemployment insurance or programs for female-headed families (Kamerman, 1986).

Contemporary American attitudes toward different kinds of public social programs (see Cook & Barrett, 1992) make sense in terms of the history of U.S. social policy. As Skocpol explains, because of its distinctive governmental institutions and political history, the United States did not follow the path of European and other western nations toward the development of a modern welfare state. Working through bureaucratically centralized, parliamentary political systems, politicians, administrative officials, and organized industrial workers in various western nations created pensions and social insurance for industrial workers and their dependents between the 1880s and the 1920s, and then began to expand those social programs in the 1930s and 1940s to fashion comprehensive health, unemployment, and old-age insurance for all citizens. Some nations also established allowances for all families with children, and others committed themselves to sustaining "full employment" economies, in which all who wanted jobs could get them. But the United States did not have a bureaucratic state, or parliamentary politics, or an alliance between trade unions and a working-class–oriented political party. Thus it never developed a full-fledged welfare state along the lines of those that evolved from the late nineteenth century onward in Germany, in Britain, and in Sweden and other parts of Scandinavia.

Some scholars believed that the United States, starting with the New Deal, did establish a European-style welfare state, but in a halfway, "belated" or "incomplete" version (Kudrle & Marmor, 1981). But this view does an injustice to the distinctive kinds of social policies that the United States introduced from the nineteenth century on (for a full elaboration of this argument, see Skocpol, 1992). First and foremost, public schooling was expanded beginning in the 1820s (Heidenheimer, 1981). In the late nineteenth and early twentieth centuries, the United States—while refusing to enact social benefits and labor regulations for male workers as many contemporary European nations were doing—also expanded disability and old-age pensions for military veterans of the Union armies that fought in the Civil War. That is, American men were helped as former soldiers, rather than as workers. Then, during the 1910s and early 1920s, the U.S. federal government and more than 40 states established various protective labor regulations and social benefits for women as mothers or potential mothers. These early "maternalist" social policies (see Skocpol, 1992, Part III) were not sustained or generously funded, but for a while, the United States had a system of public social policies that tried to help mothers and children rather than wage-earning men and their dependents. This was related to the fact that (as we saw in Chapter 5 of this Reader) middle-class married women enjoyed stronger political organization and group consciousness in the early twentieth century than did U.S. industrial workers.

The crisis of the great depression and the New Deal helped to launch the United States onto yet another path of public social provision, which was still quite different from the one being traveled by European welfare states (Weir, Orloff, & Skocpol, 1988). Unemployment insurance for regular workers who lost their jobs, and especially Social Security for retired wage earners, became the most important parts of U.S. social policy from 1935 on. Such workers and their employers were to pay taxes to build up these insurance systems, so that the workers could be helped by government benefits when they lost their jobs temporarily, or when they grew old and retired. "Welfare" grants to the very poor, including mothers and children, also became partly a state and partly a federal responsibility under the terms of the Social Security Act of 1935. These welfare grants were never very generous, however, and they were deliberately treated as less honorable than the "earned" social insurance benefits established in 1935 (Cates, 1983; Heclo, 1986).

It is important to realize that the politicians and experts who designed America's modern system of public social policies in 1935 expected that there would be little need for "welfare" once social insurance programs were fully established. They imagined that all Americans who wanted to work, especially married men, would be able to get jobs in the private economy after the end of the depression. Their families, it was supposed, could depend on a combination of high wages, fringe benefits from private employers, and unemployment and retirement insurance under Social Security. When World War II brought full employment and economic prosperity to America, this assumption seemed entirely realistic. And when a few reformers during the 1940s called for the United States to create a European-style comprehensive welfare state, with public employment programs and more generous social-welfare benefits, their voices were simply ignored (Amenta & Skocpol, 1988). Advocates of adding a new national health insurance system to Social Security were also defeated in the late 1940s (see Starr, 1982, pp. 280–86). At that point, it looked as though most Americans could get their health care paid for through private insurance or employer-paid health coverage.

The framers of Social Security, and those active in the social policy debates of the 1940s, did not expect unemployment and low-wage jobs to become serious problems for many Americans during the decades after World War II. They did not anticipate that massive numbers of poorly educated African-Americans would soon begin to leave southern agriculture to migrate to the cities. They did not predict the changes in the world and U.S. economy that would make high-paying jobs with generous health benefits harder and harder to find from the 1970s on. And they did not foresee the rising rates of divorce and of childbearing out of wedlock, or the increasing numbers of single mothers who would be unable to find jobs that paid enough wages and benefits to sustain themselves and their children. Yet, since the 1960s, all of these developments have been placing enormous strains on the U.S. system of social policies inherited from the New Deal and the 1940s—leading to some of the current political debates and policy proposals that we will sample in Chapter 10.

REFERENCES

Amenta, Edwin, and Theda Skocpol. 1988. "Redefining the New Deal: World War II and the Development of Social Provision in the United States." In *The Politics of Social Policy in the United States*, edited by Margaret Weir, Ann Shola Orloff, and Theda Skocpol, 81–122. Princeton, N.J.: Princeton University Press.

Braun, Rudolf. 1975. "Taxation, Sociopolitical Structure, and State Building: Great Britain and Brandenburg-Prussia." In *The Formation of National States in Western Europe*, edited by Charles Tilly, 243–327. Princeton, N.J.: Princeton University Press.

Cates, Jerry. 1983. *Insuring Inequality: Administrative Leadership in Social Security, 1935–54*. Ann Arbor: University of Michigan Press.

Cook, Fay Lomax, and Edith J. Barrett. 1992. *Support for the American Welfare State: The Views of Congress and the Public*. New York: Columbia University Press.

Flora, Peter, and Arnold J. Heidenheimer. 1981. "The Historical Core and Changing Boundaries of the Welfare State." In *The Development of Welfare States in Europe and America*, edited by P. Flora and A. Heidenheimer, 17–34, New Brunswick, N.J.: Transaction Books.

Furniss, Norman, and Timothy Tilton. 1977. *The Case for the Welfare State*. Bloomington: Indiana University Press.

Heclo, Hugh. 1986. "The Political Foundations of Antipoverty Policy." In *Fighting Poverty: What Works and What Doesn't*, edited by Sheldon H. Danziger and Daniel H. Weinberg, 312–40. Cambridge, Mass.: Harvard University Press.

Heidenheimer, Arnold J. 1981. "Education and Social Security Entitlements in Europe and America." In *The Development of Welfare States in Europe and America*, 269–304. New Brunswick, N.J.: Transaction Books.

Heidenheimer, Arnold, Hugh Heclo, and Carolyn Adams. 1983. *Comparative Public Policy: The Politics of Social Choice in Europe and America*. New York: St. Martin's Press.

Kamerman, Sheila B. 1986. "Women, Children, and Poverty: Public Policies and Female-headed Families in Industrialized Countries." In *Women and Poverty*, edited by Barbara C. Gelpi et al., 41–63. Chicago: University of Chicago Press.

Kudrle, Robert T., and Theodore R. Marmor. 1981. "The Development of Welfare States in North America." In *The Development of Welfare States in Europe and America*, edited by P. Flora and A. Heidenheimer, 81–121. New Brunswick, N.J.: Transaction Books.

Musgrave, Richard A., and Peggy B. Musgrave. 1989. *Public Finance in Theory and Practice*, 5th edition. New York: McGraw-Hill.

Skocpol, Theda. 1992. *Protecting Soldiers and Mothers: The Political Origins of Social Policy in the United States*. Cambridge, Mass.: The Belknap Press of Harvard University Press.

Starr, Paul. 1982. *The Social Transformation of American Medicine*. New York: Basic Books.

Weir, Margaret, Ann Shola Orloff, and Theda Skocpol, editors. 1988. *The Politics of Social Policy in the United States*. Princeton, N.J.: Princeton University Press.

Witte, John. 1985. *The Politics and Development of the Federal Income Tax*. Madison: University of Wisconsin Press.

READING 28

POLITICAL INSTITUTIONS AND TAX POLICY IN THE UNITED STATES, SWEDEN, AND BRITAIN

Sven Steinmo*

This essay addresses one of the broadest and most complex issues faced by students of comparative politics: Why do different democracies pursue different public policies? I address this issue through a comparative examination of the politics and structure of taxation systems in three prominent Western democracies. Despite the paucity of literature that examines taxation from a comparative perspective, taxes provide a peculiarly appropriate arena in which to examine broad comparative questions. Taxation is at the center of ideological debate between left and right in every modern welfare state. Taxation is a critical arena in the politics of who gets what in society and who pays for it in all politics. And, finally, taxes are fundamental to the very size and functioning of government.

Those few analysts who have attempted to explain why public policies vary between advanced democracies have posited three distinct explanations—"interests," "values," and "the state." The first explanation argues that policy outcomes vary because the distribution of power among political interests differs in democratic politics. Groups use their power to further their short-term interests. Thus, since the relative distribution of power between groups differs in these societies, policy outcomes will also differ.[1]

Proponents of the value, or cultural, explanation suggest that policies vary because people in different democracies want different things. The most famous of these arguments is, of course, Louis Hartz's explanation of American exceptionalism. Here, citizens have different expectations about the proper role of government in society, and this general value frames political debate within a polity. Ultimately, different value premises set nations on different policy paths.[2]

The third line of argument emphasizes the role of state institutions and actors in explaining why policies vary in modern democracies.[3] The analysis presented in this paper falls broadly into this category in its attempt to explain variations in tax policies between the United States, Sweden, and Britain.

Institutionalist analysis is not new.[4] Indeed it pulls our attention back to analytic categories that have long been of central interest to political scientists.[5] But it also builds on a critique of the more recently dominant "society-centered" explanations. Institutionalists argue that both the value and interest explanations suffer from at least two basic flaws. First, neither leaves adequate room for the role of the state, either as an independent policy force or as an organizational channel through which political actions must pass. Second, both lack an understanding of how policy preferences and interests are, on the one hand, shaped and, on the other hand, translated into specific policy choices.

From *World Politics* 41 4 (1989):500–35. Reprinted with the permission of The Johns Hopkins University Press.
* The author would like to express his thanks to the several colleagues, as well as the reviewers at *World Politics*, who have read and commented on earlier drafts of this paper. The comments made by John Freeman, Peter Hall, Arnold Heidenheimer, Anthony King, Jonas Pontusson, Kent Weaver, and John Witte have been especially useful.

[1] Pluralists, of course, suggested this explanation several decades ago, but it is continually being reviewed in new versions. Corporatists, for example, generally accept the principle that groups will fight for their short term self interest, but argue that the pluralist characterization of the bargaining process is inaccurate. See Frank Wilson, "Interest Groups and Politics in Western Europe: The Neo-Corporatist Approach," *Comparative Politics* 16, No. 1 (1983). Power Resource theorists use the same basic characterization of politics as the pursuit of economic self-interest and argue that various democracies pursue different public policies because

different groups (now parties) possess different "power resources" with which to fight for their constituency's self-interest. See Francis Castles, "The Impact of Parties on Public Expenditure," in Castles, ed., *The Impact of Parties: Politics and Policies in Democratic Capitalist States* (Beverly Hills: Sage, 1982). See also Walter Korpi, *The Democratic Class Struggle* (London: Routledge, Kegan Paul, 1980).

[2] For perhaps the best recent articulation of the value (or in his words "idea") thesis, see Anthony King's three-part article, "Ideas, Institutions and Policies of Governments: A Comparative Analysis," Parts I, II, and III, *British Journal of Political Science* 3, Nos. 3 and 4 (1973).

[3] See, for example, Eric Nordlinger, *On the Autonomy of the Democratic State* (Cambridge: Harvard University Press, 1981); Peter Katzenstein, *Between Power and Plenty* (Madison: University of Wisconsin Press, 1978); Peter Evans, Dietrich Rueschemeyer, and Theda Skocpol, *Bringing the State Back In* (Cambridge: Cambridge University Press, 1985); Peter Hall, *Governing the Economy: The Politics of State Intervention in Britain and France* (Cambridge: Polity Press, 1986).

[4] James March and Johan P. Olsen, "The New Institutionalism: Organizational Factors in Political Life," *American Political Science Review* 78 (September 1984), 734–49.

[5] See especially E. E. Schattschneider, *The Semi-Sovereign People* (New York: Holt, Reinhart, 1960).

Certainly some "state-centered" explanations can also be criticized for being too narrow. In the early attempts to draw attention to the role of the state and state actors, the significance of social forces and non-state actors in the formulation of public policy was often left undervalued. Few today, however, would argue with the proposition that a more subtle analysis must integrate state/society perspectives in order better to understand how and why democratic governments act the way they act. Such an approach is offered here. My analysis pays attention to the role state actors and their preferences play in public policy making, but at the same time it notes that state actors are rarely particularly autonomous. Instead, they, like the societal actors with which they interact, operate within a particular institutional framework. This institutional framework provides the context in which groups and individuals interpret their self-interest and thereby define their policy preferences. Ideas and/or interests are important for understanding variation in public policy among modern democracies. But the central argument of this paper is that one must ground these variables in the context in which they are defined and interpreted. Neither interests nor values have substantive meaning if abstracted from the institutional context in which humans define them.

Specifically, this paper will demonstrate that the different tax systems found in Sweden, Britain, and the United States can best be explained through an examination of the institutional structures through which these tax systems have been created. We will see, for example, that the Swedish tax system is not particularly progressive, and that Swedish capital is relatively lightly taxed, whereas the United States has a somewhat progressive tax system that taxes capital income more heavily than earned income. Neither interest-group nor value-based explanations can account for these outcomes. But through an examination of how the Swedish corporatist and American pluralist institutions shape the policy preferences of the actors involved in tax policy making we can make sense of these apparently counterintuitive results.

This analysis explicitly rejects an economistic or substantive notion of self-interest. Instead, it takes the individual or group's definition of self-interest as problematical. At the same time, this analysis proposes that neither specific policy preferences nor general political values appear out of thin air. Values and preferences are derived within particular contexts. For those who begin with the understanding of human rationality as fundamentally bounded, this argument will be uncontrover-

sial. It marks a beginning toward a better understanding of the linkage between individual preference formation and broader issues of political behavior and policy outcomes.

Much of the "new institutionalist" literature has either emphasized the autonomy of state actors without clearly specifying what accounts for their varying degrees of autonomy, and/or left open the meaning of institutions. Peter Hall, for example, identifies institutions in the following way:

> The concept of institutions . . . refer[s] to the formal rules, compliance procedures, and standard operating practices that structure the relationship between individuals in various units of the polity and economy. As such, they have a more formal status than cultural norms, but one that does not necessarily derive from legal, as opposed to conventional, standing.[6]

The following analysis, in contrast, emphasizes more conventional variables. Understanding that institutions are part of an interactive relationship with the public policies that emanate from them, and appreciating that the specific loci of decision-making authority for any particular policy arena can vary across polities, this analysis intends to refocus our attention on variables as obvious as constitutional and electoral structures.

I argue that the decision-making models found in the three countries I examine (pluralism, corporatism, and party government) are rooted in different constitutional and electoral structures. American pluralist policy making can only be understood if we first appreciate the constitutional federal structure, the separation of powers, and the consequent diffusion of political authority in the absence of programmatic political parties. Similarly, Swedish corporatism occurs within a constitutional electoral structure in which national political authority is unified in a parliamentary structure, but the power to dominate that system is muted due to proportional representation, which dooms the dominant political party to virtually perpetual minority or coalition governments. Britain's parliamentary system does not force governments into coalition, or indeed into parliamentary compromise. Under the British electoral system, a political party can win substantially less than 50 percent of national popular votes but can still win substantially more than 50 percent of

---

[6] Hall (fn. 3), 23.

parliamentary seats. Party government emanates from this constitutional system.

Having emphasized the importance of constitutional structures, I do not intend here to present an ahistorical or unidimensional analysis. These foundations are necessary but in themselves they are insufficient. We must, in addition, consider the structure of the domestic economy. Most specifically, we are interested in the concentration of power within both labor and the business community. These variables are also somewhat historically determined (e.g., early developers have less centralized economies)[7] but there may also be an interdependence between regime type and public policies that promote and/or inhibit economic concentration. I do not dwell on this variable, however, in large part because it has been the subject of much theoretical and empirical investigation. The correlation between economic structure and regime type is largely uncontroversial.

My argument does not attempt to draw a direct unidimensional link between the electoral structures found in a country and specific tax policy outcomes. It does argue, however, that these structures set the stage for the development of particular decision-making institutions, which must themselves be the subject of empirical investigation. These institutions provide the context in which interest groups, politicians, and bureaucrats define their policy preferences. As Peter Hall writes, "Organization does more than transmit preferences of particular groups, it combines and ultimately alters them."[8] Political institutions, then, are the critical variables for understanding how and why different democratic governments tend to choose different public policies.

COMPARATIVE TAXATION POLICY

As mentioned above, the actual tax systems found in the three countries examined here do not correspond neatly to most people's expectations. Sweden, for example, although famous as the most progressive social welfare state, relies comparatively little on redistributive wealth and property taxes which amount to less than 2 percent of total tax receipts (TTR), little on national progressive income taxes (approximately 14 percent of TTR), and very little on corporate profits taxes (2.4 percent of TTR). Instead, Sweden relies very heavily on regressive value-added taxes (VAT), flat rate local income taxes, and flat rate social security taxes (approximately 20 percent, 28 percent, and 30 percent of TTR respectively). On the other hand, the United States, which is often regarded as a "laggard" welfare state, relies principally on more redistributive taxes, such as progressive income taxes (approximately 35 percent of TTR), corporate profits taxes (10 percent of TTR), and property taxes (10 percent of TTR). Nevertheless, regressive social security and consumption taxes contribute 26 percent and 15 percent of U.S. receipts respectively. Moreover, state and local sales taxes in the United States, like the national VAT in Britain, generally exempt "basic necessities," such as food, in the interests of minimizing their regressive impact. The Swedish VAT, in contrast, is applied at a flat rate on all goods except those designed for investment or export. When all taxes are considered (including state and local taxes), the United States relies substantially more heavily on "redistributive" individual and corporate income taxes and property inheritance and wealth taxes than either Britain or Sweden (see Table 1).[9]

Three Tax Systems?

Precisely because tax policies are so central to the operation of a modern mixed economy, they are profoundly complex. At first this complexity appears to be a dense thicket into which no researcher could hope to penetrate. But after we examine tax structures for some time, we come to appreciate that not all thickets are alike. Indeed clear patterns emerge that allow us to distinguish one tax system from another. Tax structures are not random collections of various revenue sources in which each tax differs fundamentally from the others. Instead each nation's tax system can be distinguished

[7] See Alexander Gershenkron, *Economic Backwardness in Historical Perspective* (Cambridge: Harvard University Press, 1962), for the basic line of argument here.

[8] Hall, "Patterns of Economic Policy: An Organizational Approach," in David Held, ed., *States and Societies* (Oxford: Martin Robertson, 1983), 370.

[9] All data represent 1980 figures. See Organization for Economic Cooperation and Development (OECD) *Long Term Trends in Tax Revenues of OECD Member Countries: 1955–1980* (Paris: OECD, 1981). Sweden has no general property tax. The national wealth tax has been included in the above figures. The U.S. and U.K. had no general wealth taxes in 1980.

TABLE 1

Redistributive Taxes (Income, Corporate Profit, Property, Inheritance, and Wealth) as a Percentage of Total Tax Revenue, 1980

Sweden	44.3%
Britain	49.1
U.S.A.	57.1

Source: OECD (fn. 9).

by its broad patterns. Focusing on these broader patterns enables us to examine and compare the tax systems.

The U.S. tax system is often criticized for being "a perverse welfare system that hands out . . . billion[s] a year, primarily to the rich."[10] And it is commonly assumed that effective U.S. tax rates are regressive. But as Figure 1 indicates, neither assumption is particularly accurate. In our common understanding of "progressive," the effective distribution of taxes appears to be at least as progressive in the United States as in either Sweden or Britain. The U.S. tax system does indeed "hand out billions," and many of these billions go to upper-income groups. But, as John Witte has demonstrated, the poor and middle classes are also massive recipients of tax welfare.[11] Indeed, one of the major distinguishing characteristics of the American tax system is the huge number and amount of tax expenditures that complicate the tax code.[12] No other tax system is as particularistic, nor as complex, as the American. In addition to its complexity and particularism, the American tax system is distinguished by its low revenue yield, its comparatively heavy reliance on progressive sources of

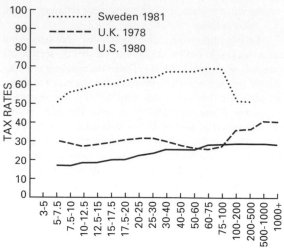

AVERAGE INCOME (U.S. DOLLARS) IN THOUSANDS

FIGURE 1   Total Effective Tax Burden as Percentage of Income (*Sources:* Joseph Pechman, "Taxation," in R. Caves and L. Krause, eds., *Britain's Economic Performance* [Washington, DC: The Brookings Institution, 1980], Table 12. Reprinted with permission of the publishers. For the U.S., data courtesy of Joseph Pechman, The Brookings Institution; for Sweden, Riksrevisionverket, *Statistika Meddelanden,* SOU:1983:7.1, Tables 4.8, 5.1, 10.7, and OECI), *The Impact of Consumption Taxes at Different Income Levels* (Paris: OECD, 1981). (It is assumed here that the distribution of consumption taxes is the same in Sweden as in Norway.) For a more detailed discussion of the effective distributions of taxes in these countries and the assumptions underlying the incidence distributions, see Sven Steinmo, "Taxes, Institutions and the Mobilization of Bias" (Ph.D. diss., University of California, Berkeley, 1987).

revenue, and the significant tax burden borne by the corporate sector.[13]

The Swedish tax system, in contrast, is distinguished by its heavy reliance on relatively regressive forms of taxation and relatively light taxation of capital

---

[10] Michael Harrington, "Do Our Tax Laws Need a Shake-up?" *Saturday Review*, October 21, 1972. Close to two-thirds of taxpayers in the U.S. feel that the current tax system is "unfair"; H and R Block, *The American Public and the Federal Income Tax System* (Kansas City: H and R Block, 1986), 9.

[11] Witte, "The Distribution of Federal Tax Expenditures," *Policy Studies Journal* 12 (September 1983).

[12] The term "tax expenditures" refers to exemptions, deductions, tax limitation, reduced rates, credits, or other special measures in the tax code that effectively reduce the tax burden from some individuals, groups, or companies. Tax expenditures are often called "loopholes" in common parlance. The term "expenditure" has been used to remind us that each of these measures produces a loss of revenue to the treasury and as such constitutes expenditures by the government.

---

[13] King and Fullerton designed a general equilibrium model with which to estimate the effective marginal tax rate on capital income. According to their estimates, the U.S. had the highest tax rate of the three countries I examine here. Though rates varied according to assumptions used, the overall marginal tax rates in 1980 were estimated to be: U.S., 37.2%; Sweden, 35.6%; and Britain, 3.7%. Don Fullerton and Mervyn A. King, *The Taxation of Income From Capital* (Washington, DC: National Bureau for Economic Research, 1983).

Since these estimates were made, significant changes to these tax systems have taken place (see below). Moreover, though the Fullerton and King findings largely support the arguments made

and corporate income. Instead of using taxation as a direct instrument of redistributive policy, Swedish authorities have constructed a tax system that generates huge revenues while at the same time attempting to encourage the concentration of domestic productive investment. In practical terms this has meant that the Swedish tax system taxes average workers exceedingly heavily, yet taxes capital and corporate income remarkably lightly. Of all OECD countries, Sweden's corporate income tax contributes the lowest tax yield, both as a percentage of GDP and as a percentage of total taxation (see Figure 2). Moreover, as several recent studies in Sweden have shown, there are currently so many generous tax expenditures for capital income in Sweden today that, taken together, there is a net revenue loss from capital income taxation.[14]

---

here, we need to be somewhat careful with this type of econometric analysis. For a good overview of general equilibrium analysis and some of its limitations see John Walley, "Lessons from General Equilibrium Models," in Henry Aaron, Harvey Galper, and Joseph Pechman, eds., *Uneasy Compromise* (Washington, DC: The Brookings Institution, 1988), 15–58.

[14] See Gustav Lindencrona, Nils Mattsson, Ingemar Stahl, and Jan Broms, *Enhetlig Inkomst Skatt* [Integrated income tax] (Stockholm: SACO/SR, 1986); or SOU:1986:40, *Utgiftsskatt* [Expenditure tax] (Stockholm: SOU, 1986).

FIGURE 2   Taxes on Corporate Income as Percentage of Total Taxation *(Sources:* OECD [fn. 9], and OECD, *Long-Term Trends in Tax Revenue Statistics of OECD Member Countries:* 1955–1980 (Paris: OECD, 1981), and OECD, *Revenue Statistics of OECD Member Countries 1965–1986* [Paris: OECD, 1987].*

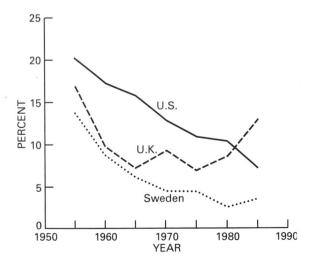

The British tax system is more difficult to characterize than either the Swedish or the American. In many respects, it appears to stand in the middle between them. In revenue terms British taxes are neither as onerous as the Swedish, nor as light as the American (see Table 2). The same can be said with respect to Britain's reliance on progressive rather than regressive taxes (see Table 1). But this does not imply that British taxation is unremarkable. Instead, the British tax system is distinguished by instability and lack of fiscal coherence in its structure. Since World War II at least, British taxes have seesawed: particular taxes have gone up, down, and up again (both in terms of marginal and effective tax rates); new taxes have been introduced, reformed, and repealed; and old taxes have been manipulated in major ways. Seldom, however, do British policy makers pay significant attention to how changes in one tax affect other taxes. Indeed, the ad hoc character of the British tax structure makes it difficult to describe it as a system at all.

TAXING VS. SPENDING?

Before we continue this analysis we must explicitly address an obvious question. Does it make sense to look at taxation policy separately from spending policy? Though it is clear that most students of comparative policy rarely address the flip side of this question—does it make sense to talk about public expenditure policy without explicitly incorporating discussion of the distribution and incidence of tax policies?—this, in itself, does not constitute a sufficient justification for treating taxing and spending in isolation from each other here.

It makes sense to study taxing and spending as discrete realms of activity because in most cases they *are* discrete realms of *political* activity. The fiscal policy literature is dense with exhortations that public policy goals currently pursued in the tax system could more efficiently be pursued via direct spending. But in most cases the political process simply does not work this

TABLE 2

Total Tax Burden as a Percentage of GDP, 1985

Sweden	50.5%
Britain	38.1
U.S.A.	28.7

Source: OECD, *Personal Income Tax Systems: Under Changing Economic Conditions* (Paris: OECD, 1986).

way. The incidence, effect, and distribution of taxes in a society rarely affect, or are affected by, discussions of the distributional effects of public spending programs.

I say rarely and in most cases deliberately. As we shall see, in one case examined here (Sweden), tax and spending choices are explicitly considered together. It is integral to the very argument presented here that the specific decision-making institutions extant in corporatist Sweden encourage the joint consideration of tax and spending decisions. Because these policy arenas are considered together in Sweden, the policy preferences of participants almost inevitably differ from the preferences of policy activists in the United States, the country in which tax and spending decisions are virtually always totally divorced.

TAXATION IN THE UNITED STATES

It will perhaps be surprising to many to discover that the United States has had a relatively progressive tax structure for most of the past seventy years. Few realize that the U.S. federal income tax has had higher maximum tax rates and lower minimum rates for most of the twentieth century than, for example, Social Democratic Sweden. Moreover, due to the absence of a national consumption tax and the low rates of most state and local sales taxes, the U.S. tax system bears very lightly on those with the smallest ability to pay taxes. On the other hand, inheritance and property taxes have been exceptionally steep in the United States for most of this century.[15] Moreover, the nation has consistently forced corporations to bear one of the heaviest shares of the total tax of any industrial democracy.[16] Finally, the United States, currently at least, taxes cap-

ital gains more heavily than any of its democratic counterparts.[17]

But what may be more important than formal tax rates, or even percentage of total tax revenues, for understanding the U.S. tax system (and its problems) are the thousands of exemptions, deductions, credits, minimum taxes, and special rules that litter the tax code. Indeed, these tax expenditures are so significant to the system that they profoundly shape its very structure. First, the United States loses more revenue via tax expenditures than either of the other two systems I examine. In 1986 the revenue lost via tax expenditures equaled 55.3 percent of total federal outlays (excluding tax expenditures) and 100.3 percent of income tax receipts. Second, due to the huge number and highly specific nature of U.S. tax expenditures, no other tax system comes close to being as particularistic and as complex. There are literally thousands of tax expenditures (perhaps more appropriately called loopholes in this context) that are designed to give tax relief to a specific group, interest, or individual. The resulting complexity helps explain why the U.S. income tax has been called the "Lawyers' and Accountants' Relief Act" (Cedric Sandford); "a house of horrors" (Wilbur Mills); and "a disgrace" (Jimmy Carter).

Tax expenditures exist in all Western democracies, but not all countries have loopholes like the United States. Indeed, tax expenditures are substantially different in each country studied here. In both Britain and Sweden it is quite rare for the tax code to specify particular groups, interests, companies, or individuals; this is quite a common U.S. practice. Moreover, while tax expenditures are found in Britain and Sweden, they tend to be focused on those at the upper end of the income scale, whereas U.S. lower- and middle-income taxpayers also benefit mightily from the revenue committees' willingness to provide exceptions to the tax code. Indeed, in both Sweden and Britain today the vast majority of average income tax payers have so few tax loopholes of which to avail themselves that they do not even fill out tax returns at the end of the year.[18]

---

[15] The U.S. topped the OECD list in revenue collections (as a percentage of GNP in 1980) in property taxes (except for Britain); inheritance and gift taxes (except for Belgium); and finally, in corporate profits taxes (except for Norway, Canada, Australia, and Japan).

[16] There is much controversy in the fiscal economics literature over where the actual burden of corporate taxation lies. It is a matter of considerable importance for designing reforms of the tax code whether one believes that consumers, workers, or capitalists bear the burden of this tax. But for a political scientist, who is principally interested in understanding why certain taxes have been chosen, the real incidence is of less significance than the perceived incidence on the part of legislators and voters. On this score there can be little doubt that both politicians and mass voters generally believe that corporate taxes are in the end paid by "the rich" who largely own the corporations.

[17] See Arthur Anderson and Co., "Comparison of Individual Taxation of Long-Term and Short-Term Capital Gains on Portfolio Stock Investments in Seventeen Countries" (Paper prepared for the Securities Industry Association, Washington, DC, April 1987).
[18] Britain has long had a Pay as You Earn (PAYE) system, in which the employer computes the taxes due for the employer with each pay check. Only in very unusual circumstances will an individual even fill out a tax return at year's end. Sweden has recently con-

The specific distribution of effective tax burdens observed in the United States, then, results in large part from the porosity of the major revenue source—the income tax—and the unwillingness of Congress to impose other taxes that, though regressive, would generate more revenue. This in no way implies that the U.S. system of taxing and spending—when taken as a whole—is particularly progressive. But, in this country at least, taxing and spending are definitely not considered together.

PLURALIST TAX POLICY MAKING

When the founding fathers constructed the basic form for the U.S. constitution, they clearly intended to fragment political authority in order to make it difficult for one faction to impose its will on others. Taxation was a particular worry for them. In perhaps the most critical document in American political history, *Federalist* 10, James Madison wrote:

> The apportionment of taxes on the various descriptions of property is an act which seems to require the most exact impartiality; yet there is, perhaps, no legislative act, in which greater opportunity and temptation are given to a predominant party to trample on the rules of justice. Every shilling, with which they overburden the inferior number, is a shilling saved in their pocket.[19]

It would be too simplistic to argue that U.S. tax policy today is a direct reflection of the institutional structures created over two hundred years ago. Such an ahistorical analysis would do great injustice to the dynamics of the political process and to the potential for political change. A more complete explanation would require a more fully elaborated analysis of the development of American political institutions over time[20] and the dynamic interaction of these institutions and the large, fragmented, and expanding

economy.[21] Unfortunately, space does not allow us to delve into this discussion here. Few readers will object, however, to the characterization of the U.S. political process as one in which power is fragmented and authority dispersed. There can be little argument that the United States possesses a "distinctive complex of weak national administration, divided and fragmentary public authority and non-programmatic political parties."[22]

It is these institutional facts that best help us understand the particular tax policy outcomes described above. First let us take the case of the heavy use of particularistic tax expenditures in the United States. The U.S. tax system is not littered with these special amendments because tax policy makers feel that this is a good way to write tax law. Instead, these outcomes are a direct consequence of the fragmentation of U.S. political authority. Whereas tax policy-making powers rest with central government authorities in parliamentary regimes, in the United States it is Congress that writes tax law. Congress, moreover, is itself a highly fragmented decision-making institution. Absent programmatic political parties that can decisively influence representatives' electoral fortunes, members of Congress are tied to their local constituencies in a way that makes them uniquely vulnerable to locally defined demands and special interest group pressures. Lacking strong institutional support and linkages to a national party, individual members of Congress become independent political entrepreneurs. This implies that they must seek support for election from groups that are often particularly interested in specific legislative outcomes. Tax amendments are often high on the agenda of these interest groups.

Each year members of the revenue committees are besieged by requests from particular interest groups, or from other members of Congress on behalf of specific

---

verted to a "no return" system, in which the average taxpayer simply signs a statement testifying that he or she has earned no income other than that reported by his or her employer(s). The individual's tax payment is then computed by the tax authorities at the end of the tax year.

[19] See also *Federalist* Nos. 31, 32, and 33.

[20] See for example, Steven Skowronek, *Building the New American State* (Cambridge: Cambridge University Press, 1982).

---

[21] See Walter Korpi and Michael Shalev, "Strikes, Industrial Relations and Class Conflict in Capitalist Societies," *British Journal of Sociology* 30 (June 1979), 164–87. Theodore J. Lowi also presents a particularly relevant discussion of these variables in "Why Is There No Socialism in the United States? A Federal Analysis" in Robert Golembrewski and Aaron Wildavsky, eds., *The C... Federalism* (New Brunswick, NJ: Transaction Books, 37–54, where he offers a compelling argument link... absence of programmatic parties in the U.S. to federali... in

[22] Margaret Weir and Theda Skocpol, "State Structure ... 3), sibilities for Keynesian Response to the Great D... Sweden, Britain and the United States," in Evans... 136.

interests, for special amendments to the tax code. Because members are dependent upon the support of these same interests for financial and logistic support in their reelection bids, they have a strong incentive to accede to such pressures.[23] For example, Witte reports that of 402 tax expenditures introduced or modified between 1970 and 1981, barely more than 26 percent originated in the administration or with the Internal Revenue Service. The rest were put in the tax code by members of Congress, usually on behalf of some particularly important constituency. Indeed, fully 37 percent of these changes originated on the floor of the House and Senate. "Just as tax politics in general centers on Congress," Witte tells us, "so does the tax expenditure 'problem.'"[24]

Congressional control over tax policy making affects not only the quantity of tax expenditures found in the U.S. tax code, but also their character. This system provides strong incentives for policy makers and interest groups to write very narrow tax legislation. Because political authority is fragmented, it becomes exceptionally difficult to change the basic rules of the tax system, but introducing or amending specific measures to adjust the system on behalf of specific groups can be done relatively easy. Politicians wish to distribute tax benefits for which they can take credit, yet are aware that they cannot give away the bank. Similarly, the incentive structure of this system forces interest groups to fight for particularistic tax measures even when their general ideological positions would tend to favor a more neutral tax system.

Where political authority is more centralized, as in Britain and Sweden, highly specialized interest groups generally have less leverage than they do in the United States. Thus to achieve their tax policy ends they are forced to organize into broader coalitions. The tax policy changes they will demand, then, will necessarily be broader and less particularistic. This is not because football teams, chicken farmers, tuxedo rental companies, or individual taxpayers would not like to have special tax measures benefiting their specific interests (as in the United States), but because interests this narrowly drawn are unlikely to have any significant impact on policy makers in a more centralized political setting.

The fragmentation of tax decision-making authority can thus help to explain another of the distinguishing features of the U.S. tax system: the comparatively heavy taxation of the corporate sector. We tend to find this outcome surprising precisely because we know that the pluralist decision-making process yields power to the well organized and well financed. Why have corporations not benefited mightily from this institutional structure? The answer, of course, is that some companies have. The critical difference is that though the U.S. tax system contains literally hundreds of tax instruments designed to benefit quite specific corporate interests and even specific companies, very broad tax write-offs designed to promote corporate savings and investment have generally been much less common than in Europe. Taken together, these specific tax loopholes cost the Treasury less revenue than broadly based tax expenditures designed to benefit corporations or investment more generally. In Sweden and Britain, in contrast, broad-based tax expenditures that benefit the corporate sector are generally quite common. America's relatively limited experience with accelerated depreciation schedules and investment tax credits pales in comparison to Sweden's historic 100 percent first-year write-offs and the Investment Reserve System,[25] or Britain's Investment and Initial Allowance systems.[26] Thus, in the United States there can be remarkable disparities in effective tax rates borne by particular companies even while the corporate sector as a whole bears a relatively heavy burden.[27]

Another major feature of the U.S. tax system is the absence of a national consumption tax.[28] The lack of such a tax contributes mightily to both the apparent progressivity of effective U.S. tax burdens and to a

---

literature documenting this process is voluminous. See, e.g., e?anley, *The Politics of Finance* (Boston: Little, Brown,
[24] W?, John Witte, *The Politics and Development of the Federal Tax* (Madison: University of Wisconsin Press, 1985). ?3), 322–24.

---

[25] See Sven Steinmo, "So What's Wrong With Tax Expenditures? A Re-evaluation Based on Swedish Experience," *Journal of Public Budgeting and Finance* 6 (Summer 1986).
[26] See Mervyn A. King, *Public Policy and the Corporation* (London: Chapman Hall, 1977).
[27] For a discussion of efficiency losses in the U.S. tax structure and a specific examination of effective rates by asset type, see Jane Gravelle, *Tax Reform Act of 1986: Effective Corporate Rates* (Washington, DC: Congressional Research Service, 1987). Gravelle finds that before the 1986 act effective tax rates by asset type ranged from 1% to 45%. After the reform they ranged from 12% to 40%.
[28] State, local, and federal governments combined in the U.S. collect less revenue in consumption taxes than in any OECD nation (5.2% of GNP in 1985). The OECD average is 11.2%. General sales taxes contribute only 2% of GNP in the U.S., whereas the European Economic Community average is more than 6%.

comparatively low overall tax burden. But what accounts for the absence of this tax? Again, the answer is rooted in the nation's peculiar political institutions. Several presidents have attempted to persuade Congress of the need for such a tax,[29] as has at least one chairman of the Ways and Means Committee. But each time a tax is proposed it is defeated—even when the president's party has had a strong majority in both houses. This could not happen in a parliamentary system.

And why are calls for a revenue-rich consumption tax routinely defeated in the United States? The answer cannot simply be that Americans traditionally oppose this tax, because Swedes and Britons traditionally oppose this type of taxation as well.[30] In both Britain and Sweden central government authorities have enacted consumption tax legislation *over clear public opposition* because the government felt that this tax was necessary for future revenue commitments. This was clearly the logic that motivated several U.S. presidents and high-level revenue officials to propose similar taxes. In the United States, however, opposition interests have unique opportunities to use the cumbersome institutional process created by Madison and his colleagues to veto revenue proposals even when they come from very popular presidents and their parties. Though these vetoes are usually blamed on the wealthy, the corporations, or other special interests (i.e., their vetoes prevent the closing of their loopholes), it is also true that liberal interests and Democratic Party politicians have veto powers. This power has repeatedly been used to prevent the introduction of a national sales tax and the broadening of the tax base.

While one could argue that in the long run revenues raised from a consumption tax or broader tax base would be good for the constituents of the Democratic Left, the fragmentation of authority in the United States leads politicians and interest groups to look at the short rather than the long run. An example will help illustrate this point. In 1985 and 1986, nearly thirty liberal tax policy activists were interviewed on their opinions as to whether the United States should follow Sweden's lead and introduce a value added tax. The answer was nearly always the same. To quote one aide to a prominent liberal senator: "It doesn't matter what they do in Sweden.

That's a different political world. This is America, and no one can guarantee me that the money taxed out of the grocery bills of American workers will ever be used to benefit those same workers. How am I to know whether that tax money will be used for social spending or for more waste at the Pentagon?" A congressional aide reported: "We don't have a deficit problem because our tax system is too easy on workers. Our problem is that we spend too much on the military and that the rich don't pay their fair share."[31]

No matter how persuasive the arguments of academics, economists, Treasury officials, and even presidents that the revenue generated via broader-based taxes could or would be used for such redistributive programs as welfare or health, congressmen respond "not on my constituents you won't." This response is conditioned by the basic fact that they can be held personally responsible for voting for tax increases while they may find it difficult to take credit for popular spending programs.[32] Moreover, the fragmentation of political responsibility in Congress allows politicians simultaneously to support popular spending and oppose unpopular tax increases even while in office.

In sum, Madison's fragmented political institutions provide a profoundly important variable for explaining the complexity, low revenue yield, and ultimately the distribution of effective tax in the United States. The diffusion of political authority and responsibility, and consequent openness to particularistic demands, has encouraged policy activists to pursue their objectives via narrow interest group organizations and to define their objectives as narrowly as possible. Lacking central authority to which to defer, politicians are uniquely vulnerable to these particularistic demands. Since no one is in control, accountability is missing, and it becomes nearly impossible for politicians, interest groups, and bureaucrats to pursue long-range objectives. I have found no evidence to suggest that politicians and/or interest group activists prefer a complex, loophole-ridden tax system. But in the context of the American political structure they continue to circumscribe their policy objectives in ways that have some hope of legislative success.

Barber Conable, when a congressman, explained how the American tax code had developed:

[29] Witte (fn. 23).
[30] See, e.g., Axel Hadenius, *A Crisis of the Welfare State? Opinions about Taxes and Public Expenditure in Sweden* (Stockholm: Almqvist and Wicksell, 1986).

[31] Interviews with author, May 1987.
[32] See Anthony Downs, "Why the Government Budget Is Too Small in a Democracy," *World Politics* 12 (July 1960), 541–63.

Nobody started out with the idea to make a complex tax system. In the early 1920s, the system was simple and comprehensive. Maybe a lot of things were not taxed, but at least everybody was taxed about the same way. Then we found that we had a complicated economy, and that the tax code was unfair to some people, so we made exceptions, and then we made exceptions and exceptions.[33]

The 1986 tax reform, despite its image as a major simplification of the tax code, well illustrates the arguments made above. Indeed, the extent to which the new tax system is distinguished by the same characteristics as the old, despite the radical and comprehensive character of the reform, is nothing short of remarkable.

We have no space here for an elaborate discussion of the 1986 reform, but it yields several useful observations. First, the major policy consequences of the act were to make the tax system *more* progressive than the one it replaced, though clearly not as progressive as many would have liked (see Table 3).

Second, we saw that the United States was distinctive for the heavy tax burden borne by the corporate sector. The reform increased this burden by $120 billion.[34] It is significant that the single largest revenue enhancement on the corporate side was the elimination of the investment tax credit—a general tax expenditure available to a wide variety of corporate interests. Third, the new tax system is even more complex than the one it replaced. Fourth, though a large number of tax loopholes were removed, the U.S. tax system remained radically more particularistic and complex than the others I examine.[35] Lastly, even though the U.S. national government faced a $2 trillion debt and an annual public deficit of nearly $200 billion, the new tax law raised no new revenue.

TAXATION IN SWEDEN

Contrary to expectation, the Swedish tax system is not distinguished by steep progressivity up the entire income scale, nor by heavy-handed treatment of capitalist or capital income. Instead, the hallmarks of the Swedish tax system are its broad base, its high revenue yield, its comparatively generous treatment of corporate and capital income, and its heavy taxation of ordinary workers.

The Swedish tax system reaches very deeply into everyone's pockets, but tries to avoid taxing the investment potential out of the society's capitalists. As a consequence, Swedish authorities have built a broad-based tax system that finances economic redistribution while eschewing the use of symbolic punitive tax rates. "Iron-

[33] Quoted in Charles Daley, *Tax Cuts and Tax Reform: The Quest for Equity* (Washington, DC: American Enterprise Institute, 1978), 20.

TABLE 3

Estimated Change in U.S. Tax Burdens in 1988 by Income Brackets

Income Class	Change in Personal Income and Corporate Income Tax Burdens	Change in Total Federal Tax Burdens
Under $10,000	−32.0%	−12.5%
$10,000–20,000	−8.1	−3.1
$20,000–30,000	−4.1	−1.8
$30,000–40,000	−4.1	−2.0
$40,000–50,000	−6.1	−3.1
$50,000–70,000	+0.7	+0.4
$70,000–100,000	+5.3	+3.9
$100,000–200,000	+6.0	+5.0
$200,000 and above	+9.2	+8.2

Source: Henry Aaron, "The Impossible Dream Comes True: The New Tax Reform Act," *Brookings Review* 5 (Winter 1987), Table 4. Reprinted with the permission of the publishers.

[34] Corporate taxes are expected to rise from 8.2% of total federal revenue in 1986 to 11% by 1988. Thus the corporate tax share of total taxation will be close to the pre-Reagan levels (in 1980 the share was 12.5%). See Congressional Budget Office, *Economic and Budget Outlook: Fiscal Years 1989–93* (Washington, DC: CBO, February 1988). According to Fullerton and Karayannis' model, the marginal effective tax rate on capital income increased from 23.5% in 1981 (which was down from the rate before the Economic Recovery Tax Act of 37.3%) to 42.1% in 1986. See Don Fullerton and Marios Karayannis, "The Taxation of Income from Capital in the United States, 1980–1986" (Paper presented to the International Conference on the Cost of Capital, Cambridge, MA, 19–21 November 1987), Tables IV.1, IV.2, and IV.6.
[35] An incredible array of particular interests (from sports teams to certain Indian tribes to the Gallo wine making family) received special tax favors in 1985 and 1986. For a general analysis of the effects of the 1986 tax reform on tax expenditures see Congressional Budget Office, *Effects of Tax Reform on Tax Expenditures* (Washington, DC: CBO, March 1988).

ically," Rose and Peters note, "taxes are least progressive in Sweden [of all OECD democracies examined] because of the high level of tax paid by ordinary workers."[36] A few examples are illustrative. Sweden bears the dubious distinction of having the heaviest and most regressive consumption tax in the world. The Swedish VAT taxes virtually all goods and services at a flat rate of 23.46 percent, exempts virtually nothing (not even food or clothing), has no reduced rates, and has no specially high rates for luxury goods.[37] The Swedish income tax, similarly, has a much broader base and fewer exemptions or deductions for the average worker than do either the British or U.S. income tax systems.[38] Additionally, the social security tax (which is paid for workers by employers) is almost three times heavier for Swedish workers than it is for either British or U.S. workers.[39]

The paucity of tax expenditures available to workers with average and lower wages has broadened the base of the Swedish tax system and thus has substantially increased tax revenues. However, these same measures have pulled the tax system away from the traditionally important goal of ability to pay, or what Americans would simply call fairness.[40]

At the other end of the scale, however, the Swedish tax system appears less onerous. A 1974 study of the income tax system in Sweden found that "the concept of global progressivity has to be qualified by the fact that the distribution takes place mainly between taxpayers in the middle and low income brackets. That is, tax redistribution has affected basically income concentration beneath a certain level. The redistribution process has 'spared' the highest incomes."[41]

The taxation of the very wealthy in Sweden differs from the taxation of average income earners because capital income receives much more favorable tax treatment than does earned income. This does not necessarily imply that the rich as a group do not pay taxes in Sweden. On the contrary, as a group the rich bear a heavier tax burden than do either their British or U.S. counterparts. Swedish taxes are often blamed when entertainers, movie directors, and tennis players emigrate. Owners of large manufacturing interests, in contrast, are much less inclined to leave Sweden because of heavy taxes.

The key here is that the Swedish tax system has been used to encourage the use of capital (because this contributes to growth and jobs) while taxing stagnant wealth very heavily.[42] The wealthy are able to shield their wealth and income from tax authorities in Sweden by refraining from consuming that wealth and instead placing it in the economy's active working capital stock. In Britain in particular, and the United States to a somewhat lesser extent, the tax system encourages conspicuous consumption on the part of the rich.[43]

Swedish corporations are well treated by any standard, though Swedish formal tax rates on corporate profits do not traditionally differ much from those found in the United States and Britain. Effective tax rates for large, successful Swedish corporations, on the other hand, are very low by international standards. According to the Swedish Department of Industry, the average tax burden borne by Swedish industrial firms in 1981 was between 3 and 13 percent of profits. Jan Södersten has recently recalculated the effective marginal tax rate on capital using King and Fullerton's model and concluded that considering corporate taxes alone, the overall marginal tax rate in 1985 was

---

[36] Richard Rose and Guy Peters, *Can Governments Go Bankrupt?* (New York: Basic Books, 1978), 99.

[37] See Enrique Rodriguez and Sven Steinmo, "The Development of the American and the Swedish Tax Systems: A Comparison," *Intertax*, 1986/3. Of all OECD countries, only Denmark, Norway, and Sweden have no reduced rates for basic necessities. Denmark, Germany, Ireland, Luxembourg, Norway, Sweden, and (currently) Britain have no special high VAT rates on luxury goods.

[38] Aguilar and Gustafsson also find that, as measured by the Kakwanis index, Sweden has the least progressive income tax system of the eight they study. On the other hand, Sweden has the most progressive income distribution. See Renato Aguilar and Björn Gustafsson, "The Role of Public Sector Transfers and Income Taxes: An International Comparison" (Working Paper, Luxembourg Income Study, April 1987).

[39] The Swedish social security tax is less regressive than the British and U.S. equivalents, however. While both the British and U.S. versions have a ceiling, the Swedes tax all earned income at the same rate, but capital income is exempt.

[40] Gustav Lindencrona. "Skatteformagaprincip och individuel beskattning" [The principle of ability to pay and individual taxation], in Lindencrona, ed., *Festskrift til Jan Heller* [Festschrift for Jan Heller] (Stockholm: Norstedt, 1984).

[41] Eduardo Iayos Sola, "The Individual Income Tax and the Distribution of Its Burden: The Swedish Case" (Thesis, University of Stockholm International Graduate School, 1975), 152.

[42] Stagnant wealth refers to wealth that is consumed or saved in nonproductive holdings such as jewelry, large estates, etc. See Steinmo (fn. 25).

[43] See John Kay and Mervyn A. King, *The British Tax System*, 3d ed. (Oxford: Oxford University Press, 1983).

between 0.2 percent and minus 2.6 percent depending on the rate of inflation.[44] "One of the secrets of the Swedish economy is that governments have looked to major corporations to create wealth," Pehr Gyllenhammer, chairman of Volvo and one of Sweden's most powerful industrialists, reported in a recent interview. "There is greater freedom for large corporations in Sweden," he added, "than in the U.S."[45]

Taken together, the numerous mechanisms available to corporate investors in Sweden create a bias in favor of expanding profitable firms with large inventories and/or depreciable assets. It has long been the aim of the government to promote successful corporations and to encourage them to stabilize their investment patterns. Normann and Södersten have shown, for example, that for fifty-one industrial companies examined between 1963 and 1968 effective tax rates and inventory size were negatively correlated. Moreover, expansion rates were positively correlated to both profitability and inventory size, and inversely correlated to the effective tax rate. Finally, and perhaps most surprisingly, profit rates and effective tax rates were inversely related.[46]

In sum, the Swedish tax system encourages the concentration of economic power while it discourages the conspicuous display of wealth. Sweden, in effect, redistributes consumption, not production.

The particular distribution of effective tax burdens for Sweden, then (see Figure 1) is the consequence of a political-economic logic designed to promote stability, economic efficiency, high investment, and growth while concomitantly financing the world's most generous welfare state.

CORPORATISM AND TAX POLICY MAKING

The somewhat counterintuitive structure of the Swedish tax system cannot be explained by a strangely inegalitarian political culture, nor by the presence of popular attitudes favoring capitalists and corporations. Nor does it make sense to describe the Swedish political system as one in which capitalist interests have been politically strong while working-class interests have been weak. Instead, Sweden has developed a remarkably coherent policy-making system in which representatives of labor, business, and the state come together and bargain on a broad array of political-economic policies. The "corporatist" structure provides the context in which these groups define their tax policy goals and has encouraged them to select tax policy objectives that would be quite impossible in a less stable, or less centralized, institutional setting.

The decision-making models observed in Britain and the United States are linked to the structure of electoral representation in these countries. Similarly, in Sweden the development of corporatist institutions depended upon a particular constitutional format, namely, proportional representation.[47] By the time universal suffrage was finally introduced in Sweden (1918), it was clear to the ruling conservative bureaucratic elite that a single-member district, first-past-the-post, winner-take-all electoral system would doom them to electoral insignificance. Proportional representation, then, was seen as a way for this numerically small group to retain some degree of power in the face of obviously hostile and increasingly organized middle- and working-class interests.

Proportional representation frames the structure of political conflict in Sweden in two ways. First, it is largely responsible for the remarkable stability of Swedish national governments. Second, it has forced the dominant political party, the Social Democrats, to rule either as a minority or in a coalition government, even though in the thirteen national elections between

[44] Södersten, "The Taxation of Income from Capital in Sweden" (Paper prepared for the International Conference on the Cost of Capital, Cambridge, MA, 19–21 November 1987). One must remember, however, that the general equilibrium model calculates rates *at equilibrium* and therefore does not necessarily represent an accurate picture of rates paid currently by real corporations. See also Michael McKee, and Jacob Visser, "Marginal Tax Rates on Capital Formation in the OECD" (Paper presented at the same conference). McKee and Visser also conclude that marginal tax rates on capital income are substantially higher in the U.S. than in Sweden, but rates range very widely according to asset type and distributions. According to these authors, effective tax rates can range from 87.5% to minus 169.2% at average inflation in Sweden depending on the source of capital, distribution, and type of investment. In the U.S. the rates could range from 94.8% to minus 131.2% at average inflation.

[45] Quoted in Steve Lohr, "Sweden: Home of Tax Reform, Arms Scandals and a Strong Defense," *New York Times*, September 6, 1987.

[46] See Göran Normann and Jan Södersten, *Skattepolitik resursstyrning och inkomstutjämning* (Tax policy, resource allocation and income leveling) (Stockholm: I.U.I., 1978), 184.

[47] Proportional representation is a necessary but not sufficient prerequisite for the development of societal corporatism. A high degree of economic concentration seems also to be a prerequisite.

1932 and 1973 they received between 41.7 percent to 50.3 percent of the popular vote. They achieved majority status in the Riksdag (Parliament) on only two occasions in this period. These popular vote figures do not substantially differ from those of the British Labour Party during the same period. The Labour Party, however, has been completely shut out of government for more than half the years since World War II.

These basic structural facts fundamentally shape Swedish tax policy decision making because they are the institutional context in which labor, business, and state officials have defined their policy preferences and strategic objectives. As far back as the 1930s, the Social Democrats realized that the electoral structure would prevent them from gaining the sustained majority in the Riksdag necessary to implement most of the redistributive tax policies suggested in their campaign rhetoric and party platforms. It would therefore be necessary for them to find new mechanisms for achieving their general objectives of getting reelected and improving the standard of living of their constituents.

Ernst Wigforss, party theoretician and finance minister from 1932 to 1949, put the party's position in the following way:

> Expressed without euphemisms this means, on the one hand, that those who have power over larger or smaller sectors of the private economy do not base their actions on the assumption that the current tendencies in government are a transitory phenomenon, that a political change will take place within a future near enough that a discussion based on the possibility of concessions, accommodations and compromises becomes unnecessary. On the other hand, it also means that the representatives of political power admit the necessity of maintaining favorable conditions for private enterprise in all those areas where they are not prepared without further ado to replace private enterprise with some form of public operations.[48]

Because authority in Sweden is not fragmented, as in the United States, decision-making power is not diffused, and the government has the power to include or exclude groups and interests from the policy process. But because the government has no majority in the Riksdag, it is forced to seek out compromises and design policies that interests outside the elite of the Social Democratic Party can live with. Thus, the gov-

ernment can dominate, but not predominate in, the policy-making process.

Due to the highly concentrated and centralized structure of Swedish business and labor, which are consequences of Sweden's late development and of specific party policies, Social Democratic governments have had the luxury of being able to consult with a very small group of interest group officials in their attempts to attain their general policy objectives. Elites of these large, hierarchically structured, noncompetitive interest groups could then be incorporated into and given exclusive access to state policy making. As a result, Swedish tax policy makers are neither as distanced from technical expertise outside the government as are the British, nor as swamped by the multitude of different interests that plague the U.S. legislator.

This process provides a forum in which all sides are able to compromise on specific issues because a wide set of issues of concern to them are integrated. The technical experts attempt to find technical solutions to particular problems—solutions that will not impinge negatively on the interests of the other members of the tripartite coalition. This deliberative decision-making structure facilitates long-range planning and encourages technical experts to become policy initiators. I will cite but two examples. In the late 1930s big industry, represented by the Swedish Employers Federation (SAF), asked the government to implement a series of tax breaks that would discriminate in favor of large and successful companies (and thereby discriminate against small, new, or less profitable companies).[49] The Social Democratic government granted the request (in the form of Investment Reserves, Inventory Reserves, and 100 percent first-year depreciation write-offs) in exchange for a survey of private business investment plans and tacit approval of a major expansion of the unemployment insurance program, which was to be administered by the central labor union confederation (LO). Additionally, both sides agreed to a new format for the resolution of labor disputes, thus reducing the occurrence of strikes and lockouts.

In the late 1950s, similarly, the Minister of Finance Gunnar Strång was convinced by two economists from the LO research department that if Sweden was to con-

---

[48] Quoted in Korpi (fn. 1), 48.

[49] These policy ideas were originally suggested by economist Erik Lindhal, who advocated them in a Swedish government research report in the late 1920s. SOU: 1927:33, *Promemorior rorande vissa beskattnings fragor av 1927 are skatte beredning* [Memorandum concerning certain tax questions of the 1927 tax commission] (Stockholm: SOU, 1927).

tinue the expansion of the welfare state, new sources of revenue would be needed given increased opposition to heavier income taxes from both industry and the voters.[50] They advocated the implementation of a national sales tax. Such a tax, however, was vehemently opposed by the labor unions and a majority of Social Democratic voters. But after a year of negotiations with labor union leaders, however, Sträng gained their approval for the new tax by promising that he would quickly expand social spending and in particular initiate a massive program of public housing construction. Labor union members and Social Democratic voters still largely oppose the sales tax, but they do not have the multiplicity of access points necessary to translate this opposition into a veto.

Each of the examples above aptly illustrates some of the main dynamics of Swedish tax policy development. In the context of the highly stable electoral outcomes in Sweden, all groups must calculate their objectives as if the Social Democrats will be in power for a considerable time. Thus both business and labor interests are willing to cooperate in ways that would be anathema in either the United States or Britain. At the same time, the Social Democrats know that they too must compromise given their near-perpetual minority government status. The result is a broadly based, financially lucrative tax system that carefully generates maximum revenues while impinging on Sweden's capacity for economic growth and profit generation as little as possible. Efficiency and revenue-yield considerations permeate the system as a whole.

In sum, the distribution of tax burdens described above is not a contradiction in the Swedish context. The specific tax policy preferences of business, labor, and Social Democratic elites appear perfectly rational when we consider the institutional context in which these preferences are derived. Again, the Swedish case yields yet another example in which policy choices are not simply constrained in different ways by different institutional contexts; instead, *policy preferences differ in different institutional settings*. Political institutions provide the boundaries within which rational actors form their preferences, thus they are integral to the very preferences themselves.

TAXATION IN BRITAIN

The instability of British taxes and the lack of coherence between various parts of the revenue structure are the major hallmarks of the British tax system. Not only are various revenue sources changed with dizzying frequency, but changes in one tax are generally wholly unrelated to the structure of problems of other parts of the tax system. Indeed, the fiscal incoherence of the British tax system and the speed with which it changes make it very difficult to describe. As James and Nobes have observed, "one of the most noticeable characteristics of the British tax system is that it is under continual change. Writing about it is very much like trying to hit a moving target."[51]

But instability and incoherence are very difficult characteristics to verify empirically without a detailed examination of the entire tax structure. Clearly there is no space for such an examination here. While there are certainly dozens of British tax experts and fiscal economists who have decried the instability of the British tax system, this does not definitively prove that their tax system is worse off in this respect than the American, for example. After all, Congress is forever manipulating existing taxes and adjusting the tax code for the benefit of particular constituencies. The difference is that in Britain major changes in specific taxes are quite common and can have fairly profound effects on both the distribution of the tax burden by income class[52] and upon gross revenue totals. In their detailed statistical analysis of the dynamics of the British revenue system, Rose and Karran find that "there is no similarity between aggregate patterns and specific taxes, no collective homogeneity, nor is there absolute or relative stability. . . . When taxes are compared with each other, virtually every test shows that the collective pattern is heterogeneous, not homogeneous. The most striking feature of taxes in Britain is the extent to which they differ."[53]

Without going into great detail, some specific examples of the nature and frequency of the many tax

---

[50] The information in this section was provided by Gunnar Sträng (minister of finance from 1956 to 1976) in an interview with the author, May 1983.

[51] S. James and C. Nobes, *The Economics of Taxation* (London: Philip Allen, 1981), 135.

[52] See Oliver Morrissey and Sven Steinmo, "The Influence of Party Competition on Post War UK Tax Rates," *Politics and Policy* 15, No. 4 (1987).

[53] Richard Rose and Terrence Karran, *Increasing Taxes? Stable Taxes or Both? The Dynamics of United Kingdom Tax Revenues Since 1948*, Center For the Study of Public Policy Monograph No. 116 (Glasgow: CSPP, 1983), 37.

changes made in particular revenue sources in Britain can be instructive. Capital gains taxation, for example, was not introduced until 1965 but was then "reformed" in 1972 and again in 1977 and 1982. The corporate profits tax was first introduced in 1965, and major revisions were introduced in 1972, 1976, and 1983. The VAT was introduced in 1973 (replacing the purchase tax in the same year) and has been "reformed" four times since then. The Selective Employment Tax was created in 1966 and removed in 1973. And the Capital Transfer Tax was introduced in 1976 and reformed to the point of irrelevance in 1980.

The treatment of the corporate sector since World War II provides a particularly good example of the turbulence of British taxation policy. Until 1965 corporate income was taxed under the individual income tax code at the standard, or basic, rate. (This rate was changed five times between 1945 and 1964.) But in addition to this tax, companies were required to pay additional profits taxes on distributed and retained profits. Retained profit tax rates were changed eight times between 1947 and 1964. Distributed profits tax rates were also changed eight times in these seventeen years (but not necessarily in the same eight years). Finally, until 1951, profits taxes were allowable as a deduction against income taxes.[54]

But in addition to the changes in nominal tax rates, British companies were also subjected to numerous tax policy alterations that directly affected the tax treatment of capital investment between 1945 and 1964. Various governments introduced, repealed, increased, and decreased a wide variety of investment allowances, initial allowances, and direct grants for investment. According to the Hansard Society, thirty-eight different changes were made in these various forms of investment subsidies between 1945 and 1972.[55]

In 1965 a separate corporate income tax (somewhat similar to the systems in effect in Sweden and the United States) was introduced by the Labour government. Mervyn King described the history of corporate taxation in the following way:

> The UK experience in the use of taxation to influence corporation behavior is unique. Four major reforms [now six] of the corporate tax system have taken place since the war, the most recent being 1973 [subsequently 1976 and 1984] and tax rates have been altered at frequent intervals. A good illustration of this is afforded by the excitement generated amongst American economists in the 1960's by the investment tax credit and the attempts to assess its effects. A British economist would have shrugged this off as a mere trifle, compared to the changes he had witnessed over the years.[56]

Finally, in 1984, the Conservative government introduced another major overhaul of the taxes on corporations that substantially reduced many of the investment write-offs available to British companies. Thus, surprisingly, the Conservatives substantially increased effective tax rates for British companies and, moreover, substantially increased the tax yield of this revenue source (see Figure 2).

The taxes mentioned above are not unique in Britain. The characterization of the British tax system as unstable, inefficient, and lacking fiscal coherence could go on. Dilnot and his coauthors, for example, bluntly introduced their examination of the British social security system as "another British failure" due to the complex interaction of payments and benefits, their incoherence, and their inefficiency.[57] They show, for example, that due to the complex and ill-planned interaction of social security and income tax in Britain many low-paid workers pay marginal tax rates *in excess* of 100 percent. This means that as their nominal wage increases their standard of living must decrease. Similarly, the histories of consumption taxation, death taxes, and capital gains taxation have also shown these revenue sources to be tumultuous and instable.[58]

Virtually every government since World War II has changed tax rates affecting income from savings, investment, social security, and death. Additionally, special provisions have been introduced, expanded,

---

[54] See King (fn. 26), 258–59.
[55] The student of U.S. tax policy history may be unimpressed. In the U.S. there may be even more specific changes in tax provisions affecting various types of investments in particular industries, particular products, or particular companies in a single year. The difference, however, is that these changes in the British system were quite general and affected all industry—not just particular firms or types of industries as is common in the U.S. Specific changes were also made during these years in favor of particular industries in the U.K. But these were in fact fewer in number than the general changes listed above.

---

[56] King (fn. 26), 5–6.
[57] Andrew Dilnot, John Kay, and Nick Morris, *The Reform of Social Security* (Oxford: Clarendon Press, 1984), 1.
[58] See Morrissey and Steinmo (fn. 52). See also Anne Robinson and Cedric Sandford, *Tax Policy Making in the United Kingdom* (London: Heineman, 1983).

contracted, or repealed for broad constituencies by means of surtaxes, investment surcharges, reduced rates, housekeepers' deductions, Child Relief, Earned Income Credit, Personal Relief, and Old Age Relief, to name but a few.

Table 4 shows how income tax policies made between 1946 and 1975 have affected the personal disposable income (PDI) of several income groups during this period.[59] We see, for example, that tax changes made by both parties reduced the PDI of those in the £100,000 income class by 28.9 percent. Each time the Labour Party entered office, however, it substantially raised income taxes for this group (thus decreasing PDI). But Labour's actions were largely counteracted by Tory tax policies that substantially reduced income taxes for this and all income groups.

Looking back to Figure 1 we see a picture in which no clear pattern emerges.[60] By some measures the system could be considered regressive, by others it could be seen as somewhat proportional. What is most noticeable is that tax rates can go up *or down* as income rises, depending upon the income level. This pattern is not the choice of any particular government. Rather it reflects the layering of different policy preferences by different governments as they each take office in turn. The result is summarized by Kay and King: "The present state of the British tax system is the product of a series of unsystematic and ad hoc measures, many undertaken for excellent reasons—for administrative convenience or to encourage deserving groups and worthy activities—but whose overall effect has been to deprive the system of any consistent rationale or coherent structure."[61]

PARTY GOVERNMENT AND TAX POLICY

It is the British constitutional structure that provides the framework for understanding the country's particular tax policy outcomes. With her winner-take-all, single-member district elections, in the context of a highly centralized political structure, Britain has developed a political process often characterized by the term "party government." Finer has aptly described party government in the following way: "Our system is one of alternating single party governments."[62]

Power is more centralized in party government than it is in either pluralism or corporatism because the electoral structure on which party government is based generally insures that one party will have exclusive control over the government. The electoral system produces a majority for one party in Parliament even when that

---

[59] I use PDI statistics because they encompass a whole range of changes in the income tax, including tax rates, exemption levels, and personal deductions.

[60] It should be noted here that the British figures must be viewed with some caution. Due to the profound secrecy with which British governments view tax information, no direct examinations of tax returns are possible as in the U.S. and Swedish cases. Joseph Pechman's data were derived by applying British taxes to the distribution of incomes found in the Brookings merge file (see Joseph Pechman and Benjamin Okner, *Who Bears the Tax Burden?* [Washington, DC: The Brookings Institution, 1974]). This is not an ideal approach, but it is the only study of total effective tax burdens in the U.K. available.

[61] Kay and King (fn. 43), 18.

[62] Sam Finer, "Adversary Politics and Electoral Reform," in Finer, ed., *Adversary Politics and Electoral Reform* (London: Anthony Wigram, 1975), 6.

TABLE 4

Change in PDI by Party in Power, Single Person, U.K., 1946–1975

	Income				
	Earned			Investment	
	£2,000	£5,000	£10,000	£20,000	£100,000
Labour	3.0%	−12.0%	−25.9%	−55.0%	−139.5%
Conservative	20.7	56.2	88.5	83.0	110.6
Total	23.7	44.2	62.6	28.0	−28.9

Source: Morrisey and Steinmo (fn. 52).
Note: Table gives cumulative change in disposable income from 1946 base level, i.e., total change in disposable income relative to the base year taking all the years in office of each party into consideration.

party has received substantially less than a majority of votes from the electorate. It also makes it exceptionally difficult for third parties to compete successfully. Finally, the institution of strong party discipline under party government further centralizes power in the hands of central government elites in general and the prime minister specifically. All parliamentary systems rely on party discipline, and in all cases this yields great power to those at the top of the hierarchy. It is perhaps an exaggeration to call the British Parliament a rubber stamp, but in comparison to the United States, at least, this characterization does not seem too widely off the mark.

These basic structural features of British party government fundamentally frame the policy preferences and strategic choices of all participants in the policy-making process. Whereas the fragmentation of political authority in the United States facilitates particularistic interest group politics, and the potential stalemate of Sweden's electoral structure encourages compromise, the centralization of national political authority in Britain allows governments to act on their electoral platforms no matter how ill-conceived or antagonistic to the opposition's interests.

First, governments, once elected, have *exclusive* decision-making authority. Though governments can, and sometimes do, consult with interests outside the party when formulating policies they are in no way required to do this, for they are virtually guaranteed passage of the final legislation no matter which groups approve or disapprove.[63] Because the government does not have to consult extensively, it seldom does. Indeed, it is often argued that the government rarely consults with its own party members before initiating major policy initiatives.[64]

Second, because the opposition is fundamentally excluded from the policy-making process it is rarely in touch with the details of current tax policy and is rarely aware of the complications and problems that will result from further changes. Instead, having spent the last several years arguing that everything the current government has done is either incompetent or pernicious, the opposition promises its constituents that it will reverse these evils as soon as it wins the next election. "The hot competition of party politics has fostered the desire to introduce party differences and has afforded little incentive to analyze basic objectives, to assess possibilities and costs in the form of sacrificed alternatives."[65]

When a new government takes office, then, it is under pressure to demonstrate that it is different from, and better than, the government that it replaced. Labour must demonstrate its redistributive commitment (that they will indeed "squeeze the rich until their pips squeak") and the Tories must show how they will unleash market forces and undo the harm to capital inflicted by the last Labour government. But tax systems are complicated affairs, and serious reform takes substantial analysis. Such analysis takes time. Time, unfortunately, is in short supply for governments that have made strong policy promises while campaigning for election.

When the opposition becomes the government it has the legislative power to act out its mandate. The government is pressed to fulfill the promises they made in the heat of the campaign even when better judgment would have them move in other directions. In both U.S. pluralism and Swedish corporatism governments *must* compromise their ideology and policy platforms simply because they need the votes to achieve legislative success. In the British party model, the government always controls a majority of the votes in Parliament. If the government does compromise, it is quickly attacked both by those within the party and also by the opposition for having taken a "U-turn." In short, the British electoral system presents British governments with strong incentives to act on their campaign promises even when these commitments were made with little analysis and though scarcely any attention was paid to their effects on the tax system as a whole.

The very logic of my argument here evokes an interesting puzzle. If British governments are less con-

---

[63] In fact only the topmost elite within the party and the Treasury have any say in tax policy formation. "Revenue changes are solely a tool of macro-economic management considered separately by the Treasury, and announced to the cabinet by the Chancellor in practice for information, not approval—just before the Budget is publicly presented in March or April"; Hugh Heclo and Aaron Wildavsky, *The Private Government of Public Money*, 2d ed. (London: Macmillan, 1981), 179–80.

[64] An example of this can be found as recently as 1984 when the Thatcher government announced on budget day that they would substantially restructure the corporate income tax system. Until that day in March no one outside a very small group of Treasury officials and the prime minister even knew that a reform of the corporate tax system was under consideration. Even the head of the Conservative Party's research department, Peter Cropper, did not know that a corporate tax reform was in the offing until he heard the budget speech on the radio that day.

[65] T. Wilson, "The Economic Costs of the Adversary System," in Finer, ed. (fn. 62), 112.

strained by opposition political forces than Swedish or U.S. governments, what explains the lack of coherence in the British tax system as a whole? Presumably, British governments could simply rewrite the entire tax code and thereby make it even more coherent than the Swedish or U.S. systems. The answer to this puzzle is in part answered in Rose and Karran's recent book, *Taxation by Political Inertia.*[66] In this interesting analysis of the political and economic dynamics of British fiscal policy these authors remind us that while British governments may be less constrained by Parliament than their Swedish and U.S. counterparts, this does not suggest that British governments are wholly unconstrained in their policy choices. There are very strong incentives in any polity to continue to use the revenue system inherited from past governments. Moreover, large-scale restructuring of the tax system involves huge investments of resources (political, intellectual, and financial), whereas the political benefits of such restructuring may be quite marginal if not negative. Most governments, most of the time, are faced with far more immediate problems than that of an incoherent tax structure. Their reluctance to tackle the monumental task of rationalizing the tax system is perhaps further exacerbated by the fact that some of the government's own tax policies may prove to be somewhat less than rational. In sum, from the politicians' point of view the costs outweigh the benefits of truly restructuring the entire tax system. Better, it could be argued, to "fringe tune,"[67] to use taxation as a symbolic issue in which major changes are made in specific taxes, and, finally, leave the technical issues to the bureaucrats.

But, of course, the policy perspectives of bureaucrats are also shaped by the institutional environment in which they live. Whereas in both the United States and Sweden, Treasury or Ministry of Finance officials have taken quite activist positions with respect to reforming and rationalizing their respective tax structures, British officials have developed a culture of agnosticism. This reticence actively to pursue a reform program is not a product of ignorance or even apathy on the part of British officials.[68] Instead, they live in a quite unique institutional environment that discourages policy

activism and encourages policy neutrality. In Sweden, in particular, decades of political stability and single-party dominance have engendered the development of a very active administrative class.[69] This activist position has been fostered, in part, by the perpetual minority status of Social Democratic governments. In this context, ambitious bureaucrats with workable ideas have been strongly encouraged by their political masters.[70] Similarly, in the deadlock of U.S. government by committee, talented fiscal policy experts have often been brought into the Treasury or the Joint Tax Committee to help politicians find technical solutions for profoundly complex tax policy issues. Again, in this context the system rewards innovative and talented officials and their ideas.

In Britain the situation is quite different. Under party government a new election can bring in new political masters who have radically different policy views from those currently in government. The ambitious British official who pursues reform initiatives could well find his ideas are perceived to be on the wrong side of the political fence come the next election. In this context, the rational behavior for officials as a group has been to keep a low profile. This system tends to reward those officials who follow the dictates of their political masters, not those who have ambitious reform ideas of their own.[71]

Finally, because the hands that hold the reins of government can change so dramatically from one year to the next, it is rare for ministers to get to know and trust their official advisers in such a way as to develop the close relationships common in Sweden and (but to a somewhat lesser extent) the United States as well.[72] Dick Taverne describes this as one of the major problems he faced when in the Treasury for the Labour government that took office in 1964. "Indeed, the [Inland] Revenue proved itself expert at showing that all solutions other than their own were utterly unworkable and

---

[66] Richard Rose and Terrence Karran, *Taxation By Political Inertia: Financing the Growth of Government in Britain* (London: Allen and Unwin, 1987).
[67] Ibid., 148.
[68] See, for example, *The Eleventh Report of the Expenditure Committee Session 1976–77.* House of Commons Papers 535 I (London: HMSO, 1977).

[69] Cf. Thomas Anton, Claes Linde, and Anders Mellbourn, "Bureaucrats in Politics: A Profile of the Swedish Administrative Elite," *Canadian Public Administration* 16, No. 4 (1973), 638–39.
[70] In fact it is quite common for talented young officials to be promoted from the supposedly apolitical civil service directly into political positions within the Ministry of Finance.
[71] See Heclo and Wildavsky (fn. 63) for a more detailed view of the administrative practices and culture of the British administrative class.
[72] Since World War II, for example, there have been 17 chancellors of the exchequer. In Sweden there were only 3 ministers of finance in this same period.

total misconceived."[73] This does not mean that the new government's proposals will not be passed, just that they do not necessarily get the whole-hearted support of the technical experts who must translate the general policy aims into specific language.[74] On the other hand, this mutual skepticism means that otherwise politically neutral administrative or technical reforms often may not achieve the political support necessary to translate them into legislation.

Tax Policy Making Under Thatcher

Few will be surprised by the fact that the British tax system has become substantially more regressive in the nearly ten years since Margaret Thatcher's government came into office.[75] Since 1979 the Conservatives have substantially increased consumption taxes, radically decreased marginal and effective income tax rates (especially for those with very large incomes), substantially neutered death and gift taxes[76] and, surprisingly to many, reformed the corporate tax system so that it actually places a heavier tax burden on some types of corporations and generally produces more revenue than the system it replaced.[77] In the tax reform proposed in the 1988 budget, Chancellor Nigel Lawson further radically reduced personal income tax rates for the very wealthy, arguing that this move was made necessary by the reduction of the U.S. tax rate. But, interestingly, whereas the marginal rate cuts for the rich were compensated for in the U.S. case by the elimination of many important tax expenditures favoring the wealthy, in Britain the reduction of tax rates for high-income earners was not complemented by any such reduction. The *Financial Times*, one of Britain's leading conservative newspapers, headlined this version of tax reform in two articles, "Dramatic Gains For the Rich," and "An End To Old Fashioned Egalitarianism."[78]

Thus, the decade of Thatcherism has had important effects on the British tax system. Most would agree that tax policy is more coherent today than it was ten years ago—even if they dislike the direction of change. But it would be incorrect to suggest that the British tax system has become a model of rationality, even if regressive. It is indeed interesting to note that the Conservative government has not been able to reform the system thoroughly even in its own image. The reasons for this are complex, but are consistent with the analysis of how party government affects the actions and perspectives of bureaucratic actors. To undergo major restructuring of a national tax system requires competent technical analysis and long-range planning. The incentive structure facing the British Inland Revenue does not encourage the development of either. One must remember that though we now know that Thatcher won two elections after her initial 1979 victory, no one could reasonably predict this outcome ten or even five years ago. Thus, as discussed above, Inland Revenue civil servants have had every reason to keep their heads low. The many significant tax reforms that have occurred in the past ten years have mostly not been the product of an activist administrative class eager to rationalize its tax system. Instead, these reforms have been pushed by an aggressive political party eager to impose its ideological stamp on the system.

One cannot close this section without mention of the most recent tax reform to be pushed by the Thatcher government—the Poll Tax.[79] This move was so radical, blatantly class-based, and obviously regressive that it nearly evoked a constitutional crisis, with the House of Lords at first refusing to yield its rubber stamp. The government prevailed, however, and is now working out the details of a modern version of a tax that was

---

[73] Taverne, "Looking Back," *Fiscal Studies* 4, No. 3 (1983), 5.

[74] Chancellor Hugh Dalton encountered such opposition to his plan to increase marginal tax rates on the wealthy in 1947 that he was forced to write the proposal himself.

[75] A plethora of evidence has been presented by fiscal economists to demonstrate that effective tax burdens in the U.K. have been dramatically altered in the past decade. See the annual post-budget analysis of the government's tax reforms, published by the Institute for Fiscal Studies in their *Fiscal Studies*. The budget analysis articles are generally included in the second issue of each annual volume and are usually written by Andrew Dilnot et al. Unfortunately, however, no studies have summarized the effects of all revenue changes since 1978.

[76] See Cedric Sandford, "Capital Taxes—Past, Present and Future," *Lloyds Bank Review*, October 1983.

[77] A complete discussion of this apparently unorthodox Conservative tax reform lies outside the scope of this essay. Two important features are worth noting, however. First, the types of companies whose effective tax rates increased the most were large, capital intensive, manufacturing concerns—these corporations are also heavily unionized. Second, though retained profits taxes were increased, the taxation of distributed profits has been made less severe.

[78] *Financial Times*, March 16, 1988.

[79] Specifically, the government has proposed to abolish the existing property tax system (known as rates) and replace it by a head tax. No longer will local taxation be based on propertied wealth, but instead will be based on size of the household.

abolished even before the working class achieved the right to vote.

It perhaps goes without saying that the Labour Party has promised to repeal this tax (as well as reverse the vast majority of Thatcher government tax policies) if and when it regains power. This analysis suggests not only that they will indeed act on these promises, but also that these changes will pull the British tax system further into a maze of incoherence.

TAX POLICY MAKING AND ITS INSTITUTIONAL CONTEXT

I have tried to show how and why the structure of decision making in these three democratic governments has shaped the specific outcomes in one of the most important and controversial arenas of public policy— taxation. My argument has emphasized the constitutional/electoral foundations of these modern decision-making institutions and demonstrated that these institutions shape how groups come to define their policy preferences and strategic objectives. Political institutions are the context in which groups, politicians, and bureaucrats come to define their policy preferences.

In the United States, since no one can control the process because of the constitutional fragmentation of public authority, groups whose influence would be nonexistent in a party government or corporatist regime can exact highly particularistic benefits from tax legislators. Diffusing political power is not the same thing as eliminating it. Congressman Dave Durenberger, a Republican from Minnesota, put the problem for writers on U.S. tax policy succinctly. Arguing that he very much liked the Reagan tax reform plan, he said, "If I thought we had a real chance at tax reform that would reduce the deficit, reduce payroll taxes and reform the income tax, then I would vote against my regional and special interest groups." But because he felt that the plan would not overcome the obstacles put in its way by vested interest groups he added, "I'll vote my constituency. I see most of my colleagues voting the same way."[80]

The structure of the political process in British party government establishes a quite different environment for policy makers. While they are less vulnerable to the particularistic demands of specific interest groups, they are more responsible for acting out their campaign promises. Moreover, because they have exclusive decision-making authority, they are not forced into compromising their policy ambitions as U.S. and Swedish policy makers routinely are. American and Swedish policy makers do not compromise because they like to, or because they are culturally predisposed to consensus building; they compromise over public policy because political realities give them no choice. In party government, policy makers have a choice of whether or not to compromise, and they exercise it only when it suits them. Because the opposition is so totally excluded from the information and expertise of the policy-making process, they can often declare themselves in favor of policies that have substantial practical problems. But once elected they are committed. Thus:

> Both Labour and Conservative parties, while in opposition, have succumbed to the temptation to condemn a large proportion of the government's policies and have promised to reverse many of these policies when they themselves took office. *The result has been a fatal lack of continuity.* (Emphasis added.)[81]

Continuity is a key word for understanding tax policy making in corporatist Sweden. The system of proportional representation has virtually assured stable minority or coalition governments. Lacking governing majorities, successive Social Democratic governments have been forced to reach out to non-socialists and forge compromises and build coalitions. Likewise non-socialists have been forced to accept the inevitability of Social Democratic political dominance and have thus adopted comparatively conciliatory positions. Over time, business, labor, and government elites have come to understand each other's needs—the government and the unions want revenue for social spending, business wants a decent rate of return on capital—and have been able to construct tax policies that broadly accommodate all three major interests.

Few policy-making elites in either the United States or Britain would deny that capitalists require a profit incentive to make them invest, or that investment is necessary for jobs and growth. But in the heat of polit-

---

[80] Quoted in the *San Francisco Examiner*, September 1, 1985, p. A–12.

[81] Michael Stewart, *The Jekyll and Hyde Years: Politics and Economic Policy since 1964* (London: J. M. Dent and Sons, 1977), 241.

ical battle, ideologically charged rhetoric can often steer policy makers in less considerate directions.

CONCLUSION

The argument that political institutions are important in shaping politics (and by implication policy outcomes) is, of course, not new. Aristotle, James Madison, de Tocqueville and E. E. Schattschneider are but a few of those who have long since argued the importance of institutional structure. This essay has attempted to contribute to this body of literature by demonstrating exactly how institutions help shape policy outcomes in a particularly important arena of political life. I have tried to do more than show that different institutional structures bias polities toward some types of interests and away from others. By arguing that institutions provide the context in which political actors make their political choices and define their policy preferences, this analysis takes a step toward a better understanding of the linkage between macrocomparative politics and public policy on the one hand and our increasing understanding of individual human behavior on the other.

I have not argued here that group interests and political values (or ideas) are irrelevant to public policy making. On the contrary, my analysis is centrally concerned with both. But as I argued in the opening sections of this paper, we cannot simply assume certain interests or policy preferences without examining the context in which people make these choices. Similarly, without understanding the institutional context in which general political values are translated into specific policies no one can hope to predict what these policies may be.

This essay, then has very broad implications for the analysis of individual decision making as well as for the study of the modern welfare state. First, although my argument might suggest that institutional structures are intervening variables that filter political demands and thereby help shape policy outcomes, I maintain that the analysis can be pushed further. To do this we must link what we have observed in this study to what we know about human rationality. Simon has shown in his discussions of bounded rationality that the boundaries on rational decision making (intellectual ability, time, information, environment, etc.) are not just constraints on optimal decision making. Instead, these boundaries are integral to the very decision-making process itself. We do not have fixed, economically derived preferences that are somehow constrained; instead, what we want is a part of the environment in which we make

these decisions.[82] Political institutions, then, are part of our preference structure because they are a critical referent in making political choices. To abstract political choices (in the short run) and general political values (in the longer run) from their institutional context is to ignore an absolutely essential variable in our understanding of the source of these preferences.

READING 29

STATE FORMATION AND SOCIAL POLICY IN THE UNITED STATES

Theda Skocpol

Modern "welfare states," as they eventually came to be called, had their start between the 1880s and the 1920s in pension and social insurance programs established for industrial workers and needy citizens in Europe and Australasia. Later, from the 1930s through the 1950s, such programmatic beginnings were elaborated into comprehensive systems of income support and social insurance encompassing entire national populations. In the aftermath of World War II, Great Britain rationalized a whole array of social services and social insurances around an explicit vision of "the welfare state," which would universally ensure a "national minimum" of protection for all citizens against old age, disability and ill health, unemployment, and other causes of insufficient income. During the same period, other nations—especially the Scandinavian democracies—established "full employment welfare states" by deliberately coordinating social policies, first with Keynesian strategies of macroeconomic management and then with targeted interventions in labor markets.

Comparative research on the origins of modern welfare states typically measures the United States against

---

[82] See, for example, Herbert A. Simon, "Human Nature and Politics: The Dialogue of Psychology with Political Science," *American Political Science Review* 79 (June 1985), 293–304.

From *American Behavioral Scientist* 35(4/5) (March/June 1991) Copyright © 1992 by Sage Publications, Inc. Reprinted with the permission of the publishers: 559–84.

foreign patterns of "welfare state development." America is considered a "welfare state laggard" and an "incomplete welfare state" because it did not establish nationwide social insurance until 1935 and because it never has established fully national or comprehensive social programs along European lines. But this approach overlooks important social policies that were distinctive to the United States in the nineteenth and early twentieth centuries. It also distracts us from analyzing why U.S. social policies since 1935 have been characterized by sharp bifurcations between "social security" and "welfare," as well as by persisting federal diversity in certain policy areas.

Early American "social policy" included state and local support for the most inclusive system of primary and secondary public education in the industrializing world (Heidenheimer 1981; Rubinson 1986). It also included generous local, state, and federal benefits for elderly Civil War veterans and their dependents. By 1910, the U.S. federal government was giving old-age and disability pensions to over a third of all elderly men living in the North and to many widows and orphans (and some elderly men in the South) as well (Skocpol forthcoming, chap. 2). In terms of the large share of the federal budget spent, the hefty proportion of citizens affected, and the relative generosity of the benefits by contemporary international standards, the United States had become a precocious social spending state!

In the early 1900s, a number of U.S. trade union officials and reformers hoped to transform Civil War pensions into more universal publicly funded benefits for all working men and their families. But this was not to be. Many social reforms were enacted into law during the progressive era, but not measures calling for new public social spending on old-age pensions or other kinds of working men's social insurance. The United States thus refused to follow other Western nations on the road toward a paternalist welfare state, in which male bureaucrats would administer regulations and social insurance "for the good" of breadwinning industrial workers and their dependents.

Instead, America came close to creating a pioneering maternalist welfare state, with female-dominated public agencies implementing regulations and benefits for the good of women and their children. From 1900 through the 1920s, a broad array of protective labor regulations and social benefits were enacted by state legislatures and the national Congress to help adult American women as mothers or as potential mothers (for full details, see Skocpol forthcoming, Part 3). The most important of these "maternalist" social

policies were mothers' pensions enacted by forty-four states to authorize regular benefits for impoverished widowed mothers, laws enacted by all but two states to limit the hours that women wage earners could work, laws enacted by fifteen states authorizing minimum wages for women workers, and the federal Sheppard-Towner Infancy and Maternity Protection Act of 1921, which authorized the U.S. Children's Bureau to supervise federal matching payments subsidizing local and state programs for maternal health education. Overall, a remarkable number of policies for women and children were enacted in the United States during a period when proposed regulations and benefits for male industrial workers were defeated.

The Great Depression and the New Deal of the 1930s subsequently opened possibilities for old-age pensions and social insurance. In what has been called a "big bang" of national legislation (Leman 1977), the Social Security Act of 1935 created a basic framework for U.S. public social provision that is still in place. Public health insurance was omitted from the Social Security Act, and later schemes for universal national health benefits also failed. Yet three major kinds of nation-spanning social provision were included in the 1935 legislation: federally required, state-run unemployment insurance, federally subsidized public assistance, and national contributory old-age insurance.

Unemployment insurance was instituted in 1935 as a federal-state system. All states were induced to establish programs, but each individual state was left free to decide terms of eligibility and benefits for unemployed workers, as well as the taxes to be collected from employers or workers or both. Unemployment benefits and taxation became quite uneven across the states, and it remained difficult to pool risks of economic downturns on a national basis or to coordinate unemployment benefits with Keynesian demand management. Despite efforts in the 1930s and 1940s to nationalize unemployment insurance and join its operations to various measures of public economic planning, no such explicit joining of "social" and "economic" policy developed in the postwar United States.

Public assistance under the Social Security Act was administered through a set of programs already existing in certain states by the early 1930s, for which the federal government would henceforth share costs. Assistance for the elderly poor and for dependent children (previously "mothers' pensions") were the most important programs to receive new federal subsidies. Free to decide whether they would even have particular programs, the states were also accorded great discretion to decide matters of eligibility and benefits and, in practice, methods of administration. Over time, as old-age insurance expanded to cover virtually all retired employees in the United States, federal old-age assistance became proportionately less important than it was originally. Meanwhile, by the 1960s, the Aid to Dependent Children program (now Aid to Families with Dependent Children [AFDC] providing benefits to caretakers as well as the children themselves) expanded enormously with a predominantly female adult clientele. Labeled "welfare," AFDC has very uneven standards of eligibility, coverage, and benefits across the states, generally providing the least to the poorest people in the poorest states and leaving many impoverished men and husband-wife families without any coverage at all.

Since 1935, the one program originally established on a purely national basis, contributory old-age insurance, has usurped the favorable label "social security" that once connoted the whole and has become the centerpiece of U.S. public social provision. Payroll taxes are collected from workers and their employers across the country. Ultimately, retired workers collect benefits roughly gauged to their employment incomes, with some redistribution toward the low-wage contributors to the system. After 1935, additional programs were added under this contributory insurance rubric: for surviving dependents in 1939; for disabled workers in 1956; and for retirees in need of medical care in 1965. Equally important, "social security" grew in coverage and benefits, as more and more employees and categories of employees were incorporated during the 1950s and benefit levels were repeatedly raised by Congress. By the 1970s, the United States, uneven and often inadequate in the help provided to unemployed and dependent people, had nevertheless become reasonably generous in the benefits offered to retired people of the working and middle classes.

"Welfare" became an explicit area of U.S. political controversy and policy innovation only during the 1960s, when the War on Poverty and the effort to create a "Great Society" were declared. For the first time since 1935, major new programs of needs-tested public assistance were established in the form of in-kind aid through Food Stamps and Medicaid. In 1972, moreover, old-age and other assistance programs (originally established as federal programs under Social Security) were nationalized, ensuring more standardized benefits. Still, the much larger AFDC program remained federally decentralized—and standards for other benefits, such as medical care, are often tied to this uneven stan-

dardbearer of the American welfare system. In turn, U.S. welfare remains, as always, both institutionally and symbolically separate from national economic management, on one hand, and from non-means-tested programs benefiting regularly employed citizens, on the other.

EXISTING THEORIES AND THEIR SHORTCOMINGS

Among many of those seeking to understand the development of social policies in the United States, several approaches currently hold sway. Each offers insights but falls short of offering fully satisfactory explanations of the historical phases and policy patterns just reviewed.

One school of thought can be dubbed the *logic of industrialism* approach (e.g., Cutright 1965; Wilensky and Lebeaux 1965; Wilensky 1975, chap. 2) because it posits that all nation-states respond to the growth of cities and industries by creating public measures to help citizens cope with attendant social and economic dislocations. Once families are off the land and dependent on wages and salaries, the argument goes, they cannot easily cope with disabling accidents at work or with major episodes of illness, unemployment, or dependent elderly relative unable to earn their keep. Social demand for public help grows, and all modern nations must create policies to address these basic issues of social security without forcing respectable citizens to accept aid under the demeaning and disenfranchising rules of traditional poor laws.

Plausible as this sounds, recent cross-national studies on the origins of modern social insurance policies have demonstrated that urbanization and industrialization (whether considered separately or in combination) cannot explain the relative timing of national social insurance legislation from the late nineteenth century to the present (see Flora and Alber 1981; Collier and Messick 1975). The United States in particular does not fit well into the logic of industrialism schema. Not incidentally, proponents of this perspective have tended to include data for "the U.S. case" only when doing cross-national analyses of social insurance for the period after 1935. Before the 1930s, the United States is an awkward outlier. This country was one of the world's industrial leaders, yet "lagged" far behind other nations (even much less urban and industrial ones) when it came to instituting public pensions and social insurance. Nor does this perspective help us to understand why the United States prior to 1935 emphasized public social provision first for veteran soldiers and then for mothers but not for working men.

Another school of thought—let us call it the *national values* approach— accepts many underlying dynamics posited by the logic of industrialism argument but introduces a major modification to explain why some nations, such as Bismarck's Imperial Germany in the 1880s, initiated modern social policies at relatively early stages of urbanization and industrialization, whereas others, most notably the United States, delayed behind the pace of policy innovation that would be expected from the tempos of urbanization and industrialization alone. The answer, say proponents of this approach (e.g., Gronbjerg, Street, and Suttles 1978; Kaim-Caudle 1973; King 1973; Rimlinger 1971), lies in the values and ideologies to which each nation's people adhered as urbanization and industrialization gathered force. Cultural conditions could either facilitate or delay action by a nation-state to promote social security, and cultural factors also influenced the shape and goals of new policies when they emerged. Thus Gaston Rimlinger (1971), one of the ablest proponents of the national values approach, argues that early German social insurance policies were facilitated by the weakness of liberalism and the strength of "the patriarchal social ideal" and "the Christian social ethic" in nineteenth-century Germany (p. 91). In the United States, however, laissez-faire liberal values were extremely strong and a "commitment to individual achievement and self-help" led to a "tenacious" "resistance to social protection" (Rimlinger 1971, 62).

Like the logic of industrialism approach, the national values school fails to notice, let alone explain, U.S. Civil War benefits or social policies for mothers and children. These approaches focus solely on modern social insurance and old-age pensions. Yet even here, general deductions from national values simply cannot give us adequate answers to many crucial questions about timing and programmatic structure.

Laissez-faire liberal values were in many respects more hegemonic and popular in nineteenth-century Britain than they were in the nineteenth-century United States, yet in the years before World War I, Britain enacted a full range of social protective measures, including workers' compensation (1906), old-age pensions (1908), and unemployment and health insurance (1911). These innovations came under the auspices of the British Liberal Party, and they were intellectually and politically justified by appeals to "new liberal" values of the sort that were also making progress among educated Americans around the turn of the cen-

tury. Under modern urban-industrial conditions, the "new liberals" argued, positive governmental means must be used to support individual security, and this could be accomplished without undermining individuals' dignity or making them dependent on the state. If British liberals could use such ideas to justify both state-funded pensions and contributory social insurance this way in the second decade of the twentieth century, why couldn't American progressives do the same? In both Britain and the United States, sufficient cultural transformation within liberalism had occurred to legitimate fledgling welfare states without resort to either conservative-paternalist or socialist justifications (see Orloff and Skocpol 1984 for further elaboration of this argument).

Then, too, when American "New Dealers" of the 1930s at last successfully instituted nationwide social protections justified in "new liberal" terms, why did they end up with the specific array of policies embodied in the Social Security Act? Why was health insurance left aside, despite the availability of liberal rationales for it just as good as those put forward for unemployment and old-age insurance? And why did the public assistance programs subsidized under Social Security actually cement the dependence of many individuals on the arbitrary discretion of state and local authorities, rather than furthering individual dignity and the predictable delivery of citizen benefits as a matter of "rights"? A final query is perhaps the most telling: Given the clear value priority that Americans have always placed on individuals getting ahead through work, why did the New Deal as a whole fail to achieve proposed measures to guarantee jobs for everyone willing to work? Arguably, the social security measures that were achieved were less in accord with long-standing American values than governmental commitments to full employment would have been.

Arguments stressing the impact of either industrialism or national values on social policy development tend to downplay political struggles and debates. During the past fifteen years, however, many historians and social scientists have analyzed the political contributions of capitalists and industrial workers in shaping patterns of social policy since the 1930s in the capitalist democracies. As part of this trend, two sorts of class politics perspectives have been applied to American social politics: One highlights what is called "welfare capitalism," and the other stresses "political class struggle" between workers and capitalists.

Proponents of the *welfare capitalism* approach (e.g., Berkowitz and McQuaid 1980; Domhoff 1970; Ferguson 1984; Quadagno 1984) take for granted that corporate capitalists have dominated the U.S. political process in the twentieth century, and they look (in various ways) for economically grounded splits between conservative and progressive capitalists as the way to explain social policy innovations. Early in this century, the argument goes, certain American businesses preceded the public sector in evolving principles of modern organizational management, including policies for stabilizing and planning employment and protecting the social welfare of loyal employees. Prominent "welfare capitalists" then pressed their ideas upon policy intellectuals and public officials, so that public social insurance measures in key states and at the federal level were supposedly designed to meet the needs of progressively managed business corporations.

This perspective has served as a good lens through which to view the complementarities that have sometimes developed between public social policies—once enacted—and the labor-management practices of American corporations. For example, many American corporations accommodated nicely to Social Security's contributory old-age insurance program, meshing it with their own retirement benefits systems, especially after World War II. But business groups originally opposed the passage of the Social Security Act as well as the passage of most earlier and later federal or state-level social and regulatory measures applicable to men or women workers. However adaptable American capitalists have proven to be after the fact, the historical evidence is overwhelming that they have regularly fiercely opposed the establishment of public social policies. Political processes other than the initiatives of capitalists have nearly always been the causes of U.S. social policy innovations.

The other class politics perspective takes for granted that capitalists everywhere tend to oppose the emergence and expansion of the welfare state. This "social democratic" or *political class struggle* approach has predominated in recent cross-national research on the development of social policies in Europe and the United States (see Bjorn 1979; Castles 1978, 1982; Esping-Andersen 1985; Korpi 1983; Myles 1984; Shalev 1983; Stephens 1979). No attention is paid by these theorists to early U.S. social provision for Civil War veterans, and their worker-centered definitions of modern social provision prevent them from analyzing pioneering U.S. social spending and regulations for mothers and women workers. To explain why American public social provision for working men commenced later and has not become as generous as European

public social provision, this approach underlines the relative weakness of U.S. industrial unions and points to the complete absence of any labor-based political party in U.S. democracy. Given these weaknesses of working-class organization, proponents of this approach argue that U.S. capitalists have been unusually able to use direct and indirect pressures to prevent governments at all levels from undertaking social welfare efforts that would reshape labor markets or interfere with the prerogatives or profits of private business. Only occasionally—most notably during the New Deal and afterwards through the liberal wing of the Democratic Party—have American workers or unions been able to muster sufficient strength to facilitate some innovations or expansions of public social provision.

Certainly, this emphasis on political class struggle between workers and capitalists helps to explain why the United States has not developed a comprehensive full-employment welfare state along postwar Scandinavian lines. Nevertheless, if our intention is not merely to contrast the United States to Europe since World War II but to explain the phases and specific patterns of U.S. social policies since the nineteenth century, then the political class struggle approach is insufficient in several ways. Strict attention to political conflicts of interest between capitalists and industrial workers deflects our attention from other socioeconomic forces that have intersected with the U.S. federal state and with decentralized American political parties to shape social policy making. Until very recently, agricultural interests in the South and the West were crucial arbiters of congressional policy making. Associations of middle-class women were crucial—and often successful—proponents of social provision for women and children during the early twentieth century. And struggles over social welfare or labor market interventions have often involved regional, ethnic, and racial divisions. We need a mode of analysis that will help us understand why social identities and conflicts grounded in gender, ethnicity, and race have been equally or more telling than industrial class conflicts in the shaping of social provision in the United States.

Political class struggle theories have been argued with certain state and party structures in mind, namely, centralized and bureaucratized states with parliamentary parties dedicated to pursuing policy programs in the name of entire classes or other broad, nation-spanning collectivities. For much of Europe, the existence of such features of political organization has given substance to the presumption that the industrial working class may translate its interests into social policies, whenever "its" party holds the reins of national power over a sustained period. But of course the United States has never had a centralized bureaucratic state or programmatic parliamentary parties. Thus the American case highlights the importance of bringing much more explicitly into our explanations of social policy making the historical formation of each national state—as well as the effects of that state's institutional structure on the goals, capacities, and alliances of politically active social groups.

U.S. STATE FORMATION AND PATTERNS OF SOCIAL PROVISION

"State formation" includes constitution making, involvements in wars, electoral democratization, and bureaucratization—large-scale historical processes, in short, whose forms and timing have varied significantly across capitalist industrializing countries. In sharp contrast to many European nations, the United States did not have a premodern polity characterized by monarchical absolutism, a locally entrenched standing army and bureaucracy, or recurrent mobilization for land warfare against equal competitors. Instead, the American colonies forged a federalist constitutional republic and (after some years of continued sparring with Britain) the fledgling nation found itself relatively geopolitically sheltered and facing toward a huge continent available for conquest from militarily unformidable opponents. Wars have never had the same centralizing effects for the U.S. state as they have had for many European states, in part because America's greatest war was about itself and also because mobilization for the two world wars of the twentieth century relied heavily on the organizational capacities of large business corporations and trade associations (Cuff 1973; Vatter 1985). Only after World War II, when the United States took on global imperial functions, did a federal "military-industrial complex" emerge, nourished by the first persistence into peacetime of substantial direct federal taxation.

The American Revolution was a revolt not only against the British Empire but against any European-style notion of concentrated political sovereignty— whether focused in a supreme parliament, as in Britain after the English Revolution, or in an official bureaucracy built up under absolute monarchy, as in much of Continental Europe. After years of political skirmishes between colonists and royal governors, a confederation of thirteen colonies separated Americans from Britain; then the founding fathers sought to cement a precarious

national unity be designing a new federal government. Under the Constitution adopted in 1788, the powers of the states and the central government were carefully divided and balanced against one another in a "compound" arrangement (Scheiber 1978) that left many ambiguities for the future, while the new rules for the federal government spread cross-cutting responsibilities among Congress, the president, and a system of courts. In the words of Samuel P. Huntington (1968), "America perpetuated a fusion of functions and a division of power, while Europe developed a differentiation of functions and centralization of power" (p. 110).

Americans looked to "the Constitution" and "the rule of law," as the loci of fundamental sovereignty. Especially in pre-Civil War America, these functioned as a "roof without walls" in the apt words of John Murrin (1987), as "a substitute for any deeper kind of national identity" because "people knew that without the Constitution there would be no America" (pp. 346–47). Although never-ending rounds of legislation in Congress and the states expressed shifting sets of special interests, the sovereign ideals of constitutionalism and the rule of law could reign impersonally above an economically expansionist and socially diverse country. Only during the Civil War did a Republican-run crusade to save a Northern-dominated nation temporarily transfer the locus of sovereignty to an activist federal government. But even the Civil War did not generate an autonomous federal bureaucracy: The forces of localism, divisions of powers, and distrust of government activism never disappeared, even in the North. The U.S. "Tudor polity" (Huntington 1968) reemerged in full force after the Southern states rejoined the union in the 1870s.

It will not do, however, to leave the matter here, stipulating that Europeans had concentrated sovereignties and a sense of "stateness" while Americans had neither. Stephen Skowronek (1982) places the totality of early American political arrangements in a framework that helps to highlight their distinctive features. Skowronek points out (1982, pp. 19, 24) that America certainly did have a state, both in the sense of "an organization of coercive power" (p. 19) and in the sense of "stable, valued, and recurring modes of behavior within and among institutions" (p. 24):

The early American state maintained an integrated legal order on a continental scale; it fought wars, expropriated Indians, secured new territories, carried on relations with other states, and aided economic development. Despite the absence of a sense of the state, the state was essential to social order and social development in nineteenth-century America. (p. 19)

To be sure, this early American state was not a set of locality-penetrating bureaucracies headed by a monarch or a parliament. Rather, in Skowronek's telling phrase it was a "state of courts and parties" (p. 24). Operating across state and federal levels, courts and parties were the key organizations—and judges and party politicians the crucial "officials in action"—that made up the American state in the nineteenth century: "Party procedures lent operational coherence to the disjointed institutions of the governmental apparatus, [and] court proceedings determined the meaning and the effect of the law itself" (p. 27).

Courts were not very prominent in the original debates over constitutional design, yet as the nineteenth century progressed they carved out a more authoritative role than the Founders had envisaged or than British courts enjoyed. "There is hardly a political question in the United States," observed Alexis de Tocqueville ([1850] 1969, p. 270) "which does not sooner or later turn into a judicial one." To be sure, early American judges and lawyers needed to adjust English common law precedents to U.S. circumstances, and they had to fend off various movements to codify the laws and reduce judicial discretion. Yet these elites and the courts through which they operated also enjoyed important advantages. They could take advantage of their countrymen's regard for the Constitution and legal procedures as common points of reference in a polity wracked with jurisdictional disputes, where fundamental issues regularly required adjudication. And there was no national civil bureaucracy that could compete with the courts by promoting "the national interest" in a more substantive fashion.

Along with courts, political parties and vocationally specialized partisan politicians became the pivots of the nineteenth-century American polity. Ironically, this happened even though the Constitution made no mention of them, given that the Founders disapproved of "the baneful effects of the spirit of party" (George Washington, as quoted in Wallace 1968, 473). Foreign observers of the actual workings of American government noticed the increasing centrality and distinctiveness of U.S. parties. James Bryce (1895) observed in the 1880s that in "America the great moving forces are the parties. The government counts for less than in Europe, the parties count for more" (p. 5). A description of them is therefore a necessary complement to an account of the Constitution and government since

"their ingenuity, stimulated by incessant rivalry, has turned many provisions of the Constitution to unforeseen uses" (p. 3). "The party organizations in fact form a second body of political machinery existing side by side with that of the legally constituted government" such that "the whole machinery, both of national and of state governments, is worked by the political parties" (Bryce 1893, 6). American parties, Bryce (1893) noted, "have been organized far more elaborately than anywhere else in the world, and have passed more completely under the control of a professional class" (p. 6).

The regular American parties of the nineteenth century managed the complex, never-ending processes of nominations and elections for local, state, and national offices. Party conventions became the typical means for nominating candidates, and the nineteenth century's frequent elections required that party supporters be kept in a high state of enthusiasm and readiness through canvasses and rallies. Crucially, from the Jackson era through the end of the century, parties also controlled the staffing and functioning of public administration in the United States (Shefter 1978). Administrative staffing through patronage was complementary to the intensified electoral activities of the new political parties. The opportunity to control the allocation of public offices inspired party cadres and allowed national and state party brokers to offer local loyalists influence over appointments allocated from their levels of government. In turn, public officeholders were highly motivated to contribute portions of their salaries and their time to foster the popularity of their party, for only if their party won the next election would their jobs be safe. Otherwise, the opposite party and all of its appointees would claim the "spoils of office."

Once in place by the 1840s, the parties and their managers proved remarkably resilient, dominating U.S. politics and knitting together the branches and levels of the "Tudor polity" throughout the nineteenth century (Keller 1977; McCormick 1986). The local roots of the parties sunk deep into particular neighborhoods; yet party efforts simultaneously spanned localities within states and, to a remarkable degree, reached across the nation as a whole. Certainly, the party organizations were not top-down hierarchies; rather, they were ramified networks fueled by complex and shifting exchanges of favors for organizational loyalty. As such, however, they successfully linked local to state politicians and kept state politicians in touch with one another and with whatever national officeholders their party might have.

Not until the twentieth century—decades after electoral democratization and well after capitalist industrialization had created private corporate giants operating on a national scale—did the U.S. federal, state, and local governments make much headway in the bureaucratization and professionalization of their administrative functions (Shefter 1978; Skowronek 1982). With the greatest changes coming first at municipal and state levels, bureaucratic-professional transformations happened piecemeal through reform movements spearheaded by the new middle classes. As the various levels of government were thus partially reorganized, the fragmentation of political sovereignty built into U.S. federalism and into the divisions of decision-making authority among executives, legislatures, and courts was reproduced in new ways throughout the twentieth century. American political parties have remained uncoordinated in their basic operations, and in many localities and states, the major parties uneasily combine patronage-oriented and interest-group-oriented modes of operation (Mayhew 1986). Within the federal government, Congress, with its strong roots in state and local political establishments, has remained pivotal in national domestic policy making—even during periods of strong executive initiative such as the New Deal, the two world wars, and the Cold War (Amenta and Skocpol 1988; Fiorina 1977; Grodzins 1960; Huntington 1973; Patterson 1967).

The patterns of U.S. state formation just summarized have conditioned social policy making from the nineteenth century to the present. We can briefly survey some of the most important ways in which this has happened.

Early democratization of the U.S. white male electorate ensured that masses of ordinary Americans could support public schooling as a right of democratic citizenship rather than warily opposing educational institutions imposed from above by officials and upper classes, as happened in Europe (Katznelson and Weir 1985, chap. 2). In the United States, moreover, no national bureaucracy existed to regulate, finance, or serve as a central magnet for educational development, and no single dominant church served as a prop of a counterweight to the state. Thus local and voluntary forces, including Catholic parishes and a multiplicity of Protestant and Jewish sects, took more initiatives than they did in other nations. In a democratic political context, "participatory localism" encouraged many such groups to support free public schools, while others built and defended private schools. Decentralized federalism allowed local, state-level, and private initiatives to compete with one another—and often to imitate one another

as well, in waves of analogous institution building. The result was the world's first system of mass primary and secondary schooling.

In addition, nineteenth-century America's nonbureaucratic and party-centered patronage democracy had a strong proclivity for legislative enactments that would distribute material benefits to many individuals and local communities within the major party coalitions (McCormick 1979). In the context of close electoral competition between the Republicans and the Democrats between 1877 and 1896, patronage democracy fueled the expansion of de facto disability and old-age benefits for those who could credibly claim to have served the Union forces during the Civil War. The Republican Party, especially, enjoyed advantages from expanding access to Civil War pensions (McMurry 1922; Sanders 1980; Bensel 1984, chap. 3). That party could simultaneously promote high tariffs, with benefits finely tuned to reach groups of businesses and workers in various Republican areas of the country, and generous pensions, which spent the "surplus" revenues raised by the tariffs disproportionately on townsmen, farmers, and skilled workers who were also concentrated in Republican-leaning areas of the North. Moreover, during crucial, close-fought elections, the Republicans manipulated the processing of pension applications through the federal Bureau of Pensions in attempts to influence the Republican vote in such tightly competitive states as New York, Ohio, and Indiana.

Once American government began to bureaucratize and professionalize, the surviving structures of patronage democracy and elite perceptions of "corruption" in the Civil War pension system discouraged U.S. progressive liberals from supporting the generalization of veterans' benefits into more universal old-age pensions or working men's social insurance. The absence of strong civil service bureaucracies made it impossible for U.S. advocates of contributory social insurance to imitate the strategies of contemporary British social insurance advocates, who devised plans within national ministries and then persuaded parliamentary politicians to enact them. What is more, progressive reformers were preoccupied with building bureaucratic regulatory agencies that could circumvent the control of patronage-oriented political parties, and they feared that any new forms of public social spending directed at masses of voters would only reinforce party patronage (Orloff and Skocpol 1984; Skocpol 1992, chap 5). The only way that social welfare reforms could be enacted in the United States during the early twentieth century was through waves of similar legislation across many of the state legislatures. But policies that would have entailed new public spending for male voters could not get enthusiastic support from nation-spanning groups active in reformist politics during this period.

Finally, the U.S. state and federal courts also discouraged regulations for working men. Prior to the 1930s, most U.S. courts invoked constitutional principles of "free contract" and "due process" for private property holders to overrule protective labor laws covering adult male workers. Frustrated reformers responded by channeling most of their efforts for regulatory reforms toward protective labor laws covering women workers alone (Skocpol and Ritter, 1991, 56–62). From the time of the 1908 "Lochner" decision, American courts allowed many such laws regulating female labor to stand. Judges accepted the arguments put forward by reformers and women's groups that governments possessed legitimate "police power" to protect future "mothers of the race" from overwork.

During the New Deal and in its aftermath, the United States finally launched nationwide public assistance and social insurance measures, including policies for working men and the elderly. Nevertheless, the Social Security Act was rooted in prior state-level laws or legislative proposals under active debate in the 1930s; and congressional mediation of contradictory regional interests ensured that national standards could not be established in most programs (Skocpol and Amenta 1985). Subsequently, American national mobilization for World War II—a mobilization less total and centrally coordinated by the state than the British mobilization for the same war—did not overcome congressional and local resistance against initiatives that might have pushed the United States toward a nationalized full-employment welfare state. Instead, this pivotal war enhanced federal fiscal capacities and created new possibilities for congressionally mediated subsidies and tax expenditures but did not permanently enhance public instrumentalities for labor market intervention or executive capacities for coordinating social spending with macroeconomic management (Amenta and Skocpol 1988).

Basic structural features of the U.S. state have thus powerfully set overall institutional limits for social provision in the United States. Yet fundamental patterns of state formation are only the starting point for analysis. In addition, political struggles and their policy outcomes have been conditioned by the institutional leverage that various social groups have gained, or failed to gain, within the U.S. polity. By analyzing ways in which America's distinctive state structure has influenced possibilities for collective action and for

political alliances among social groups, we can go even further toward explaining the phases and patterns of U.S. public social provision from the nineteenth century to the present.

U.S. INSTITUTIONS AND SOCIAL GROUPS IN POLITICS

America's precociously democratized federal polity has always made it difficult for either capitalists or industrial workers to operate as a unified political force in pursuit of class projects on a national scale. Ira Katznelson (1981, 1985) and Martin Shefter (1986) have spelled out the situation for workers in a series of important publications. Because in the United States white manhood suffrage and competing patronage parties were in place at the very start of capitalist industrialization, American workers learned to separate their political participation as citizens living in ethnically defined localities from their workplace struggles for better wages and employment conditions. No encompassing "working class politics" emerged; and American trade unions developed no stable ties to a labor-based political party during the period around the turn of the century when European social democratic movements were forged. Nationally, American workers were left without the organization capacities to push for a social democratic program, including generous and comprehensive social policies. In localities where they did have considerable political clout, American workers tended to gain advantages on ethnic rather than class lines. Only during and after the New Deal was this situation modified, as alliances developed in many places between urban liberal Democrats and industrial unions. Yet the Democrats and the unions never went beyond flexible and ad hoc partnerships. Particular Democratic politicians put together unique constellations of supporters, sometimes including certain unions and sometimes not, while unions retained the option of supporting friendly Republicans as well as Democrats.

Whereas political forces claiming to represent the industrial working class had (in cross-national perspective) relatively little presence in U.S. social politics, national and local groups claiming to speak for the collective interests of women as homemakers were able around the turn of the twentieth century to mount ideologically inspired efforts on behalf of maternalist social policies. Patterns of exclusion from—and tempos of incorporation into—electoral politics shaped the possibilities for women's political consciousness just as they influenced possibilities for working-class conscious-

...ess. But the results for women were quite different.

In major European countries during the nineteenth and early twentieth centuries, either no one except monarchs, bureaucrats, and aristocrats had the right to participate in national politics, or else property ownership, education and other class-based criteria were used to limit electoral participation by categories of men. Thus European women were not the only ones excluded from the suffrage, and, at least at first, economically privileged women did not have to watch lower-class men exercise electoral rights denied to them. Class-defined political cleavages tended to proliferate and persist in Europe, and even politically active women's organizations oriented themselves to class issues. In the United States by contrast, for almost a century the rights and routines of electoral democracy were open to all men (even to the black ex-slaves for some decades after the Civil War), but were denied to all women (Baker 1984).

By virtually universal cultural consensus, woman's "separate sphere" in the nineteenth century was the home, and the place where she sustained the highest moral values in her roles as wife and (especially) mother. Yet this did not mean that American women stayed out of public life. Through reformist and public-regarding voluntary associations, American upper- and middle-class women, joined by some wives of skilled workers, claimed a mission that they felt only their gender could uniquely perform: extending the moral values and social caring of the home into the larger community. In the process, women's groups took a special interest in social policy issues that they felt touched the well-being of other women. By the progressive era, indeed, women's associations had concluded that women should act as "housekeepers for the nation." Promoting such ideas were huge, nation-spanning federations of women's clubs organized at local, state, and national levels. These included the Women's Christian Temperance Union, the National Congress of Mothers, and the General Federation of Women's Clubs—the last of which had by 1911 over one million members in thousands of clubs spread across all states. These women's federations were well-placed to press upon legislators and public opinion across the land the "moral necessity" for new social policies designed to protect women workers and mothers and children (for full details, see Skocpol 1992, part 3).

Although such "maternalist" ideas about social welfare spread across the industrializing world in the late nineteenth and early twentieth centuries, they loomed largest in the United States for both social and political reasons. Socially, American women gained more and better higher education sooner than any other women in the world. This prepared a crucial minority of them for voluntary or irregularly recompensed public leadership, especially since regular elite career opportunities were limited. Widespread education also set the stage for strong alliances between higher-educated professional women and married housewives scattered across the nation, many of whom were relatively well educated and some of whom in every locality had been to college and worked as schoolteachers before marriage.

Politically, meanwhile, American women reacted sharply against their exclusion from a fully democratized male democracy. Throughout the nineteenth century, no major industrializing country differentiated worlds of politics—understood in the broadest sense as patterns of participation in public affairs—so sharply *on strictly gender lines* as did the United States. Given the absence in the United States of bureaucratic and organized working-class initiatives to build a pioneering paternalist welfare state for industrial workers and their families, there was more space left for maternalism in the shaping of fledgling modern social policies. Thus the policies and new public agencies especially for women and children sponsored by American women's associations loomed especially large on the overall agenda of issues that progressive era legislators took seriously.

Using the same perspective that was just applied to understand the possibilities for working-class and women's political consciousness, we can also gain insights about the political outlooks and capacities of U.S. capitalists. To a greater degree than business people in many other capitalist nations, U.S. capitalists (in the apt phrase of David Vogel 1978) "distrust their state." This is, of course, somewhat ironic, given that American capitalists have not had to contend with a highly mobilized, a nationally politically conscious working class and often get their way in governmental affairs. Yet U.S. business owners have had to operate in a long-democratized polity prone to throw up periodic moralistic "reform" movements, including farmers' movements and women's movements inclined to challenge business prerogatives. What is more, the distrust that U.S. capitalists feel toward government reflects the frustrations that they have recurrently experienced in their dealings with a decentralized and fragmented federal state—a state that gives full play to divisions within business along industrial and geographical lines.

Conflicts within the ranks of U.S. business are readily politicized because losers can always "go to court"—or back to the legislatures or to another level in the federal system or to a new bureaucratic agency—for another round of battle in the interminable struggles that never seem to settle most public policy questions. For U.S. capitalists, the state has seemed neither coherent nor reliable. Indeed, the uneven and inconstant effects of U.S. political structures help to explain why—contrary to the expectations of the "welfare capitalism" school—"progressive" corporate leaders have always found it difficult to inspire broad business support for national social policy initiatives, even those that might benefit the economy as a whole on terms favorable to the dominant sectors of business. With a few individual exceptions, American capitalists have never seen government as a positive means to achieve classwide purposes. For the most part, various industries and smaller as well as larger businesses have concentrated on fighting one another through politics. Different sectors of business have come together only episodically and then usually in efforts to block reformers or popularly appealing social movements that want to extend government regulation or taxation and spending for social welfare purposes.

The U.S. federal state with its single-member-district legislatures and its nonprogrammatic political parties allows considerable leverage to interests that can coordinate a policy stance across many legislative districts. What we may call "widespread federated interests" include women's associations such as the General Federation of Women's Clubs, organizations of farmers from the Grange to the American Farm Bureau Federation, business groups such as the Chamber of Commerce, and professional associations such as the National Education Association and the American Medical Association. Such widespread federations of local and state member units are ideal coalition partners for national policy advocacy groups that want to promote, obstruct, or rework social policies—especially as proposals have had to make their way through dozens of state legislatures or through the House of Representatives in Congress.

Occasionally, social groups organized as widespread federations have spurred the enactment of social policies in the United States. Examples of this include support by Union veterans in the Grand Army of the Republic for Civil War benefits during the 1880s and 1890s, support by the General Federation of Women's Clubs and the National Congress of Mothers for mothers' pensions, protective legislation, and Sheppard-Towner programs during the 1910s and 1920s; and support by Townsend Movement, an association of

old people's clubs, for old-age benefits during the 1930s and 1940s. Equally or more often, however, widespread federations of commercial farmers and small businessmen have obstructed or gutted proposed social policies. For example, during the early New Deal from 1933 to 1935, federal agricultural policies had the not fully intended effect on strengthening interest group association among commercial farmers across the disparate crop areas of the South and the Midwest (Finegold and Skocpol 1984). In turn, this meant that the American Farm Bureau Federation was better able to ally with business organizations, including the Chamber of Commerce, to pressure congressional representatives against one liberal New Deal social welfare proposal after another from 1936 onward.

Pinpointing institutional leverage through Congress also helps us to make sense of the special role of "the South" in modern American social policy making, a role that certainly rivals that of either capitalists or the industrial working class. To be sure, the South's role cannot be understood without underlining the class structure of Southern cotton agriculture as a landlord-dominated sharecropper system from the late nineteenth century through the 1930s (Alston and Ferrie 1985). Nor could we possibly ignore the explicit racism that ensured minority white dominance over black majorities in all sectors of economic and social life. Yet the South was militarily defeated in the Civil War, and by the 1930s, this region was not very weighty in the national economy as a whole, nor were its social mores typical of the nation. Thus socioeconomic factors and generalized references to racism will not alone tell us why Southern politicians had so much leverage during and after the New Deal that they could take a leading role in congressional alliances opposed to national welfare standards and any strong federal presence in economic planning.

The influence of Southern agricultural interests in the New Deal depended on the insertion of their class power as landlords and their social power as white racial oligarchs into federal political arrangements that from the 1890s to the 1960s allowed an undemocratized single-party South to coexist with competitive two-party democracy in the rest of the national policy (Key 1949). Above all, Southern leverage was registered through a congressionally centered legislative process in Washington that allowed key committee chairmen from "safe" districts to arbitrate precise legislative details and outcomes. From the New Deal onward, the "national" Democratic Party used congressional committees to broker the internal divisions between its Southern and urban liberal Northern wings (Bensel 1984, chap. 7). This prevented the often contradictory orientations of the two wings from tearing the national party apart but at the price of allowing the enactment of only those social policies that did not bring the national state into direct confrontation with the South's nondemocratic politics and racially embedded systems of repressive labor control.

The U.S. state structure as it had been formed by the 1930s and 1940s, along with the operations of the New Deal party system, magnified the capacities of Southern economic and social elites to affect national policies at the same time that the capacities of other interests, including those sections of organized industrial labor allied with urban Democrats in the North were simultaneously enhanced by the same U.S. state structure and party patterns. Many features of the New Deal Social Security system—and indeed of the entire disjointed configuration of social and economic policies with which the United States emerged from the political watersheds of the New Deal and World War II—can be understood by pinpointing the social interests and the political alliances that were able to gain or retain enhanced leverage through the long-standing federal and congressional institutions of the U.S. state. The New Deal certainly brought social policy innovators to the fore through the newly active federal executive. It also energized urban liberal forces and created new possibilities for political alliances through the electorally strengthened and partially realigned Democratic Party. Nevertheless, in the end, America's federal state and regionally uneven democracy placed severe limits on the political alliances and policies that could prevail as the original foundations were laid for nationwide public social provision in the United States.

Finally, to understand major developments in social policies since the New Deal, it is crucial to remember that the United States was—paradoxically—both the "first" and the "last" to democratize its electorate among the long-standing capitalist democracies. It was the first for white males, who were irreversibly enfranchised by the 1830s, and it became the last for *all* citizens because, except briefly during Reconstruction and its immediate aftermath, most blacks in the United States could not vote until after the migrations from the South after the 1930s and the civil rights upheavals of the 1960s. For all of the twentieth century until the 1960s, the United States was a regionally bifurcated federal polity: a mass two-party democracy in the East, North, and West, coexisting within the same national state with a single-party racial oligarchy in the South.

Only since the 1960s, through major transformations that are far from completed, have American blacks been mobilized into national democracy and has two-party electoral competition made headway in the deep South.

The civil rights revolution of the 1960s began the process of mobilizing blacks into the Southern electorate and on new terms into the national electorate and the Democratic Party. These are processes whose effects have been tumultuous both on agendas of debate over social policy and on political alliances concerned with policy alternatives from the Great Society to the present. Yet the incorporation of blacks into the national polity has not been happening in a social policy vacuum; it is taking place in the context of the configuration of social policies inherited from the New Deal. Within this configuration of policies, "social security" for the stably employed majority of citizens had become by the 1960s institutionally and symbolically bifurcated from "welfare" for the barely deserving poor (Skocpol 1988). For socioeconomic and political reasons alike, working-age blacks were disproportionately clients of the vulnerable welfare components of U.S. social provision.

During the social policy reforms of the 1960s and early 1970s, welfare clients temporarily benefited from the widespread recognition that the New Deal system of social policies had not adequately addressed issues of poverty or responded to the needs of blacks, who could now vote in greater numbers. Liberal Democrats tried to use welfare extensions and new "antipoverty" programs to incorporate blacks into their—otherwise undisturbed—national political coalition. But many social policy reforms of the 1960s and 1970s, soon backfired to disturb rather than reinforce Democratic coalitions. National politics underwent a sea change, and since the 1970s conservative forces hostile to enhanced public social provision have found renewed sources of strength within and beyond the Democratic Party. This has left impoverished people, including many blacks, increasingly isolated in national politics. And it has left welfare programs more vulnerable than ever to attacks by those who question the U.S. federal government's role in providing support for vulnerable citizens.

REFERENCES

Alston, Lee J. and Joseph P. Ferrie. (1985). Labor costs, paternalism, and loyalty in southern agriculture: A constraint on the growth of the welfare state, *Journal of Economic History* 65:95–117.

Amenta, Edwin and Theda Skocpol. (1988). Redefining the New Deal: World War II and the development of social provision in the United States. In *The Politics of Social Policy in the United States*, edited by Margaret Weir, Ann Shola Orloff, and Theda Skocpol. Princeton, NJ: Princeton University Press.

Baker, Paula. (1984). The domestication of politics: Women and American political society, 1780–1920. *American Historical Review* 89:620–47.

Bensel, Richard Franklin. (1984). *Sectionalism and American Political Development, 1880–1980,* Madison: University of Wisconsin Press.

Berkowitz, Edward and Kim McQuaid. (1980). *Creating the Welfare State*. New York: Praeger.

Bjorn, Lars. (1979). Labor parties, economic growth, and redistribution in five capitalist democracies. *Comparative Social Research* 2:93–128.

Bryce, James. (1893). *The American Commonwealth*, volume 1, 3rd ed., rev. New York: Macmillan.

——— (1895). *The American Commonwealth*, vol. 2, 3rd ed., rev. New York: Macmillan.

Castles, Frank. (1978). *The Social Democratic Image of Society*. London: Routledge & Kegan Paul.

Castles, Frank. (1982). The impact of parties on public expenditures. In Frank Castles (ed.), *The Impact of Parties*. Beverly Hills, CA: Sage Publications, 21–96.

Collier, David and Richard Messick. (1975). Prerequisites versus diffusion: Testing alternative explanations of social security adoption, *American Political Science Review* 69: 1299–1315.

Cuff, Robert D. (1973). *The War Industries Board: Business-Government Relations During World War I*. Baltimore, MD: Johns Hopkins University Press.

Cutright, Phillips. (1965). Political structure, economic development, and national social security programs, *American Journal of Sociology* 70: 537–50.

Domhoff, William. (1970). *The Higher Circles*. New York: Random House.

Esping-Andersen, Gösta. (1985). *Politics Against Markets: The Social Democratic Road to Power*. Princeton, NJ: Princeton University Press.

Ferguson, Thomas. (1984). From normalcy to New Deal: Industrial structure, party competition, and American public policy in the great depression, *International Organization* 38, 41–93.

Finegold, Kenneth and Theda Skocpol. (1984). State, party, and industry: from business recovery to the Wagner Act in America's New Deal. In Charles Bright and Susan F. Harding (eds.) *Statemaking and Social Movements: Essays in History and Theory* (pp. 159–92). Ann Arbor, MI: University of Michigan Press.

Fiorina, Morris P. (1977). *Congress: Keystone of the Washington Establishment*. New Haven, CT: Yale University Press.

Flora, Peter and Jens Alber. (1981). Modernization, democratization, and the development of welfare states in Western Europe. In Peter J. Flora and Arnold Heidenheimer (eds.), *The Development of Welfare States in Europe and America* (pp. 37–80). New Brunswick, NJ: Transaction Books.

Grodzins, Morton. (1960). American political parties and the American system. *Western Political Quarterly* 13: 974–98.

Gronbjerg, Kristen, David Street, and Gerald D. Suttles. (1978). *Poverty and Social Change*. Chicago, IL: University of Chicago Press.

Heidenheimer, Arnold J. (1981). Education and social security entitlements in Europe and America. In Peter J. Flora and Arnold Heidenheimer (eds.), *The Development of Welfare States in Europe and America*. (pp. 269–304). New Brunswick, NJ: Transaction Books.

Huntington Samuel P. (1968). *Political Order in Changing Societies*. New Haven, CT: Yale University Press.

Huntington, Samuel P. (1973). Congressional responses to the twentieth century. In *Congress and the American Future*, 2nd edition, the American Assembly, Columbia University. (pp. 6–38). Englewood Cliffs, NJ: Prentice-Hall.

Kaim-Caudle, P. (1973). *Comparative Social Policy and Social Security*. London: Martin Robertson.

Katznelson, Ira. (1981). *City Trenches: Urban Politics and the Patterning of Class in the United States*. New York: Pantheon.

Katznelson, Ira. (1985). Working-class formation and the state: nineteenth-century England in American perspective. In Peter B. Evans, Dietrich Rueschemeyer, and Theda Skocpol (eds.), *Bringing the State Back In*. (pp. 257–84). Cambridge and New York: Cambridge University Press.

Katznelson, Ira, and Margaret Weir. (1985). *Schooling for All: Class, Race, and the Decline of the Democratic Ideal*. New York: Basic Books.

Keller, Morton. (1977). *Affairs of State: Public Life in Late Nineteenth Century America*. Cambridge, MA: Harvard University Press.

Key, V. O. (1949). *Southern Politics in State and Nation*. New York: Alfred A. Knopf.

King, Anthony. (1973). Ideas, institutions and the policies of governments: A comparative analysis, parts I and II, *British Journal of Political Science* 3, 291–313, 409–423.

Korpi, Walter. (1983). *The Democratic Class Struggle*. Boston, MA: Routledge and Kegan Paul.

Leman, Christopher. (1977). Patterns of policy development: Social security in the United States and Canada, *Public Policy* 25, 26–291.

Mayhew, David R. (1986). *Placing Parties in American Politics*. Princeton, NJ: Princeton University Press.

McCormick, Richard L. (1979). The party period and public policy: An exploratory hypothesis, *Journal of American History* 66, 279–98.

McCormick, Richard L. (1986). *The Party Period and Public Policy*. New York: Oxford University Press.

McMurry, Donald. (1922). The political significance of the pension question, 1885–1897. *Mississippi Valley Historical Review* 9, 19–36.

Myles, John. (1984). *Old Age in the Welfare State*. Boston, MA: Little Brown.

Murrin, John M. (1987). A roof without walls: the dilemmas of American national identity. In Richard Beeman, Stephen Botein, and Edward C. Carter II (eds.), *Beyond Confederation: Origins of the Constitution and American National Identity*. (pp. 333–48). Chapel Hill, NC: University of North Carolina Press.

Orloff, Ann Shola and Theda Skocpol. (1984). Why not equal protection? Explaining the politics of public social spending in Britain, 1900–1911, and the United States, 1880s–1920, *American Sociological Review* 49, 6, 726–50.

Patterson, James T. (1967). *Congressional Conservatism and the New Deal*. Lexington, KY: University of Kentucky Press.

Pollard, A. F. (1925). *Factors in American History*. New York: Macmillan.

Quadagno, Jill. (1984). Welfare capitalism and the Social Security Act of 1935, *American Sociological Review* 49, 632–47.

Rimlinger, Gaston. (1971). *Welfare Policy and Industrialization in Europe in America*. New York: Wiley.

Rubinson, Richard. (1986). Class formation, politics, and institutions: Schooling in the United States. *American Journal of Sociology* 92, 519–48.

Sanders, Heywood T. (1980). Paying for the "bloody shirt": The politics of Civil War pensions. In Barry Rundquist (ed.), *Political Benefits*. (pp. 137–60). Lexington, MA: Lexington Books, D.C. Heath.

Scheiber, Harry N. (1978). Federalism and the constitution: The original understanding. In Lawrence M. Friedman and Harry M. Scheiber (eds.), *American Law and the Constitutional Order: Historical Perspectives*. (pp. 85–98). Cambridge, MA: Harvard University Press.

Shalev, Michael. (1983). The social democratic model and beyond: Two generations of comparative research on the welfare state, *Comparative Social Research* 6, 315–51.

Shefter, Martin. (1978). Party, bureaucracy, and political change in the United States. In Louis Maisel and Joseph Cooper (eds.), *Political Parties: Development and Decay*. (pp. 211–65) Beverly Hills, CA: Sage Publications.

Shefter, Martin. (1986). Trade unions and political machines: The organization and disorganization of the American working class in the late nineteenth century. In Ira Katznelson and Aristide Zolberg (eds.), *Working-Class Formation: Nineteenth Century Patterns in Europe and the United States*. (pp. 197–276). Princeton, NJ: Princeton University Press.

Skocpol, Theda. (1988). The limits of the New Deal system and the roots of contemporary welfare dilemmas. In Margaret Weir, Ann Shola Orloff, and Theda Skocpol (eds.), *The Politics of Social Policy in the United States*. (pp. 293–311). Princeton, NJ: Princeton University Press.

Skocpol, Theda. (1991). Targeting within universalism: Politically viable policies to combat poverty in the United States. In Christopher Jencks and Paul E. Peterson (eds.), *The Urban Underclass*. (pp. 411–36). Washington, DC: The Brookings Institution.

Skocpol, Theda. (1992). *Protecting Soldiers and Mothers: The Politics of Social Provision in the United States, 1870s–1920s*. Cambridge, MA: The Belknap Press of Harvard University Press

Skocpol, Theda, and Edwin Amenta. (1985). Did capitalists shape Social Security? *American Sociological Review* 50, 4, 572–75.

Skocpol, Theda, and Gretchen Ritter. (1991). Gender and the origins of modern social policies in Britain and the United States. *Studies in American Political Development* 5, 36–93.

Skowronek, Stephen. (1982). *Building a New American State: The Expansion of National Administrative Capacities, 1877–1920*. Cambridge and New York: Cambridge University Press.

Stephens, John. (1979). *The Transition from Capitalism to Socialism*. London: Macmillan.

Tocqueville, Alexis de. (1969; originally 1850). *Democracy in America*, 13th edition, translated by George Lawrence and edited by J. P. Mayer. Garden City, NY: Anchor Books.

Vatter, Harold G. (1985). *The U.S. Economy in World War II*. New York: Columbia University Press.

Vogel, David. (1978). Why businessmen distrust their state: The political consciousness of American corporate executives, *British Journal of Political Science* 8, 45–78.

Wallace, Michael. (1968). Changing concepts of party in the United States: New York, 1815–1828, *American Historical Review* 74, 453–91.

Wilensky, Harold. (1975). *The Welfare State and Equality.* Berkeley: University of California Press.

Wilensky, Harold, and Charles Lebeaux. (1965). *Industrial Society and Social Welfare.* New York: Free Press.

CHAPTER 10

CONTEMPORARY POLITICS AND POLICY CHOICES

Can America develop public policies that address pressing social and economic problems, while appealing to broad political coalitions that cross racial lines? Should the United States use government regulation or spending to reform its health care system? Can America respond to intensified economic competition from Japan, Europe, and developing nations by devising governmentally led industrial policies? These are among the public policy issues that are on the agenda for national political debate in the 1990s.

Each of these issues—race and public policies, health care reform, and the management of the national economy in a changing world—arises from problems that were inadequately addressed, or perhaps even made worse, during earlier rounds of politics and policy making. Furthermore, each issue raises questions about the capacities and limits of historically formed U.S. governmental institutions and electoral politics. Can Americans use existing representative and electoral arrangements to debate wise, democratic solutions to fundamental social and economic problems? Can the institutions of the U.S. government enact and effectively implement sound public policies to address problems of racial inequality and conflict, insufficient and expensive health care, and economic dislocations in a changing world economy?

The authors of the readings presented in this chapter tackle questions about contemporary policy choices from perspectives that are informed by a sense of U.S. political history and the workings of American government. They draw upon the kinds of comparative, institutional, and historical insights about patterns of U.S. policy making developed in earlier parts of this Reader, and brought together in the readings by Steinmo and Skocpol in Chapter 9.

Each author also writes from a clear partisan and value perspective, which he makes explicit. People who write about contemporary politics and public policy *need* to make their values and partisan commitments clear; otherwise they cannot offer pointed arguments or clear analyses of prospects for the future. Of course, many readers of this volume will not agree with the values and partisan choices that these authors voice. That is fine. Any reader who disagrees with Wilson, Peterson, or Cohen and Zysman should take their arguments as a challenge to rethink the prospects for U.S. public policies from another point of view.

In Reading 30, "Race-Neutral Programs and the Democratic Coalition," William Julius Wilson considers ways in which new public programs in the United States might address the needs of the poor, many of whom are blacks, but without further exacerbating the racial divisions that currently mar American society and politics. Wilson's analysis is informed by a sense of what went wrong for the Democratic party in the wake of the war on poverty and the great society reforms of the 1960s and early 1970s (see the readings in Chapter 7). At that time, federal social programs and affirmative action regulations came to be understood by many white middle-class Americans as designed solely to benefit the very poor and blacks. Thus, Wilson argues, these programs and regulations became subject to conservative political backlash. The Democratic party suffered, especially in presidential elections, and electoral shifts were set in motion that led to the election of a very conservative president, Ronald Reagan, in 1980.

According to Wilson—and also in the view of many advisors to President Bill Clinton—the Democratic party needs to bring together a broad coalition of white, black, and brown middle- and working-class people if it is to win elections and sustain support for government programs to help the majority of American families. Wilson argues that African-Americans, above all others, have a strong stake in the success of broad, cross-racial, and cross-class coalitions (for a similar argument, see Skocpol, 1990). Wilson argues that advocacy for, and enactment of, such "race-neutral" policies as job training, universal health care, and child care programs can help to build broad electoral support for the Democratic party and Democratic presidents. Clearly, many of Wilson's ideas are embodied in the rhetorical themes and policy proposals of the Clinton presidency.

One of the race-neutral policies advocated by Wilson is health insurance coverage for everyone. Part of the reason poor single mothers (about half of whom are black) now cling to Aid to Families with Dependent Children is that this welfare program makes them and their children eligible for Medicaid, the health insurance program for the very poor. If low-wage workers also had access to health insurance, it would be easier for families to move off welfare. But in the United States as of the early 1990s, many small businesses and other employers of low-wage or part-time workers cannot afford to purchase health insurance for such employees.

Nor are low-wage workers the only ones who would benefit from guaranteed access to health insurance. Until the 1960s, most big employers in America were glad to offer generous health insurance to both unionized and non-unionized employees. But since the 1970s, the escalating cost of health care and intensified economic competition have combined to cause employers to cut back on, or even eliminate, health benefits for many workers. Not surprisingly, many middle-class Americans have become worried about health insurance for themselves and their families (Starr, 1991). Consequently, opinion polls show that substantial majorities of Americans want the federal government to take action to ensure universal access to health insurance and to control the spiraling costs of medical care.

Mark Peterson, in Reading 31, tells us that the United States finally may be able to enact health care coverage for all Americans during the 1990s. Historically, reformers attempting to establish public health insurance in America have been defeated again and again—in the 1910s, the 1930s, the 1940s, the 1960s, and the 1970s (Starr, 1982). The regularity of such defeats has caused some to assume that U.S. governmental institutions and patterns of interest-group representation make it inherently impossible ever to have governmentally funded or regulated health insurance in America. But Mark Peterson does not agree. Institutions and patterns of group representation can change, he argues, and that is exactly what has happened in the health policy arena during the past few decades. At one time, big business, insurance companies, and the American Medical Association were jointly dominant and opposed to publicly sponsored health insurance. Now these major interests are at odds with one another, and many community and public interest groups have become active in health policy debates. There have also been institutional shifts in the Congress that give greater scope to representatives and senators who want fundamental reform. With the election of Bill Clinton in 1992, there is at last a president who is willing to provide leadership toward some sort of comprehensive health care reform.

Experts, scholars, and politicians should not underestimate the real possibilities for fundamental change during the 1990s, Peterson argues. The U.S. federal government may well be able to take on a very strong role in creating cost controls and universal citizen access to health care—as the Canadian federal government did in the 1970s. If Peterson is right, then U.S. social policy really might undergo a fundamental transformation in the near future. America would still be different in many ways from European welfare states. The dilemmas of unemployment, low-wage jobs, and single mothers would remain (see Jencks, 1992). But all these policy dilemmas would become somewhat more tractable, if all American citizens were given access to basic health care, regardless of employment or family situation.

Since the mid-1970s, the U.S. national economy has had to confront a variety of serious new problems, including inflation, historically low rates of growth and productivity, high levels of unemployment, and more intense competition from manufacturers in other countries. In Reading 32, Stephen Cohen and John Zysman review these problems. They not only note that countries whose governments have adopted more interventionist policies have often coped most effectively with these difficulties, but also that in the new international economy these same countries pose the greatest threats to the United States. One of the best known examples of a "developmental state" is Japan, where the Ministry of International Trade and Industry (MITI) has long provided tariff protection, subsidies, technology research and development assistance, and other forms of aid to selected industries and firms—often with great success. As a result, Japanese automobiles, electronics, and computer firms, among others, have cut deeply over the past twenty years into world markets that once were virtually monopolized by American firms.

The key motto among Bill Clinton's presidential campaign staff in 1992 was simple: "The Economy, Stupid!" The point was that they should never forget, nor let American voters forget, that the economy was "in a mess" after twelve years of conservative Republican economic policy. Indeed, the Reagan and Bush administrations of 1980 to 1992 had engineered a "conservative revolution," cutting taxes, reducing spending for civilian purposes, scaling back regulation, and, in general, trying to reduce the role of government in the economy (Berman, 1990; Palmer & Sawhill, 1984). According to critics, the results were disastrous, as the program caused a deep recession and a stock market crash, increased the numbers of poor and homeless people, and contributed to mounting deficits and debt (Harrison & Bluestone, 1988). Even some conservatives agreed that things had not worked out as planned (Phillips, 1991).

What is often overlooked in current debates about the Reagan–Bush policies, however, is that by international standards the United States has pursued a limited approach to economic policy throughout the postwar era. Since the 1930s, U.S. economic policy in general has primarily involved the use of macroeconomic measures based on tax adjustments to smooth out the economy's ups and downs with a minimum of government direction, along with reliance on income maintenance programs, such as unemployment insurance and food stamps, that are designed to sustain the unemployed until they can find new jobs. In contrast, many western European governments have routinely used much more direct and selective interventions that involve spending money to retrain unemployed workers and shift them to different sectors of the economy, and to help develop industries that might provide large-scale employment in the future. The European approach is often designed to make structural changes in the economy, not just to help individuals in need or to correct fluctuations in the business cycle (Shonfield, 1965; Katzenstein, 1978; Zysman, 1983).

Periodically, American policy-makers have envisioned more activist unemployment policies. For example, a full employment bill was proposed during the 1940s that would have encouraged government spending to reduce unemployment. However, in the 1940s, and again in the 1960s, when such policies were contemplated, coalitions of political and economic interests, often cutting across party lines, blocked their adoption (see Weir, 1992, for a full discussion). A fragmented and decentralized state and the absence of programmatic political parties prevented advocates of these more active economic policies from overcoming the opposition. Indeed, the full employment bill was defeated in 1945 by a bloc of conservative Democrats and

Republicans in Congress that had joined agricultural and economic interests, represented by such organizations as the American Farm Bureau Federation and the Chamber of Commerce, in order to oppose any government action that might increase the cost of labor.

The conservative prescription for solving America's economic problems has been simple: minimize government intervention and let the economy take care of itself (see Friedman, 1962, for a classic statement of this position). The assumption is that if the state does not interfere, the most efficient firms will survive and prosper, the inefficient ones will fall by the wayside, productivity will rise, unemployment will decline, and things will be fine. Government should only intervene in the economy to correct "market failures." Versions of such prescriptions were adopted by both the Reagan and Bush administrations.

However, as unemployment, budget deficits, and other economic problems persisted or got worse during the 1980s, people began to question the wisdom of the conservative approach and to look for alternative policies (Block, 1990; Cohen & Zysman, 1988; Harrison & Bluestone, 1988; Kuttner, 1992). Economic experts and officials around and in the Clinton administration believe that the United States should try to emulate some of the things the Europeans and Japanese have been doing for years. Government should, they believe, reorganize the health care system to reduce costs and increase the availability of health care to citizens; and it should improve the education and job training available to American workers of the future. Still more daring ideas are also being contemplated (see Kuttner, 1992). Perhaps Washington should create a civilian technology policy, similar to that the Pentagon has had for development of military technology since World War II. Perhaps tax money should be spent to improve the national infrastructure, including the educational system. And perhaps government programs should be created to encourage technological innovation and the creation of new jobs in industries that are likely to do best in international trade.

Obviously, many of these ideas call for the U.S. state to reorganize the fundamentals of the economy, not just to temper the business cycle or correct market failures in the least intrusive way. As we have seen throughout this Reader, the U.S. federal government and national political system have not, in the past, been capable of enacting or successfully implementing such sweeping social and economic policies. Perhaps there will be major political and institutional shifts in the 1990s, responding to unprecedented international pressures and domestic problems. Perhaps the Clinton administration, or its successors, will be both willing and able to carry through the kinds of ideas advocated by William Julius Wilson, Mark Peterson, and Stephen Cohen and John Zysman, avoiding the political and institutional obstacles of the past. Or perhaps there will be a revival of conservative ideas for social and economic policies. Only time will tell.

REFERENCES

Berman, Larry. 1990. *Looking Back on the Reagan Presidency.* Baltimore, Md.: Johns Hopkins Press.

Block, Fred. 1990. *Postindustrial Possibilities: A Critique of Economic Discourse.* Berkeley: University of California Press.

Cohen, Stephen S., and John Zysman. 1988. *Manufacturing Matters.* New York: Basic Books.

Friedman, Milton. 1962. *Capitalism and Freedom.* Chicago: University of Chicago Press.

Harrison, Bennett, and Barry Bluestone. 1988. *The Great U-Turn: Corporate Restructuring and the Polarizing of America.* New York: Basic Books.

Jencks, Christopher. 1992. *Rethinking Social Policy: Race, Poverty, and the Underclass.* Cambridge, Mass.: Harvard University Press.

Katzenstein, Peter J. 1978. *Between Power and Plenty.* Madison: University of Wisconsin Press.

Kuttner, Robert. 1992. "Is There a Democratic Economics?" *The American Prospect* no. 8 (Winter): 25–37.

Palmer, John, and Isabell Sawhill. 1984. *The Reagan Record.* Cambridge, Mass.: Ballinger.

Phillips, Kevin. 1991. *The Politics of Rich and Poor: Wealth and the American Electorate in the Reagan Aftermath.* New York: Harper Collins.

Shonfield, Andrew. 1965. *Modern Capitalism: The Changing Balance of Public and Private Power.* New York: Oxford University Press.

Skocpol, Theda. 1990. "Sustainable Social Policy: Fighting Poverty Without Poverty Programs," *The American Prospect* no. 2 (Summer): 58–70.

Starr, Paul. 1982. *The Social Transformation of American Medicine.* New York: Basic Books.

Starr, Paul. 1991. "The Middle Class and National Health Reform." *The American Prospect* no. 6 (Summer): 7–12.

Weir, Margaret. 1992. *Politics and Jobs: The Boundaries of Employment Policy in the United States.* Princeton, N.J.: Princeton University Press.

Zysman, John. 1983. *Governments, Markets, and Growth.* Ithaca, N.Y.: Cornell University Press.

READING 30

RACE-NEUTRAL PROGRAMS AND THE DEMOCRATIC COALITION

William Julius Wilson

The election of Ron Brown as the first black chairman of the Democratic National Committee triggered a new round of soul-searching among Democrats. Was the party committing political suicide by becoming too strongly identified with the aspirations of minority voters? Had America become so mired in racism that whites would desert the Democrats because blacks seemed to be running things?

My answer to these questions is an emphatic "No." Many white Americans have turned, not against blacks, but against a strategy that emphasizes programs perceived to benefit only racial minorities. In the 1990s the party needs to promote new policies to fight inequality that differ from court-ordered busing, affirmative action programs, and anti-discrimination lawsuits of the recent past. By stressing coalition politics and race-neutral programs such as full employment strategies, job skills training, comprehensive health care, reforms in the public schools, child care legislation, and prevention of crime and drug abuse, the Democrats can significantly strengthen their position. As Chairman Brown himself has emphasized, reinforcing Democratic loyalty among minorities and reaching out to reclaim white support are not mutually exclusive.

Such a change of emphasis is overdue. In the 1960s efforts to raise the public's awareness and conscience about the plight of black Americans helped to enact civil rights legislation and affirmative action programs. However, by the 1980s the civil rights strategy of dramatizing black disadvantage was backfiring. The "myth of black progress" theme, frequently invoked to reinforce arguments for stronger race-specific programs, played easily into the hands of conservative critics of antibias policies. The strategy reinforced the erroneous impression that federal antidiscrimination efforts had largely failed, and it overlooked the significance of complex racial changes since the mid-1960s. It also

aroused concern that Democratic politicians' sensitivity to black complaints had come at the expense of the white majority.

The tortuous struggles of the 1960s produced real gains. To deny those achievements only invites demoralization among both black and white advocates of racial justice. Yet the movement for racial equality needs a new political strategy for the 1990s that appeals to a broader coalition and addresses many problems afflicting minorities that originated in racist practices but will not be solved by race-specific remedies.

DIFFERENTIAL RATES OF BLACK PROGRESS

As we entered the 1980s, the accomplishments of the civil rights struggle were clearly registered in the rising number of blacks in professional, technical, managerial, and administrative positions. Progress was evident also in the increasing enrollment of blacks in colleges and universities and the growing number of black homeowners. These increases were proportionately greater than those for whites. On the other hand, among the disadvantaged segments of the black population, especially the ghetto underclass, many dire problems—poverty, joblessness, family breakup, educational retardation in inner-city public schools, increased welfare dependence, and drug addiction—were getting even worse.

The differential rates of progress in the black community persisted through the 1980s. Family incomes among the poorest of the poor reveal the pattern. From 1978 to 1987, the number of blacks with incomes under half the poverty line (below $4,528 for a three-person family in 1987, adjusting for inflation) increased by 69 percent. In 1978 only one of every three poor blacks fell below half the poverty line, but by 1987 the proportion rose to 45 percent. The average poor black family in 1986 and 1987 slipped further below the poverty level than in any year since the Census Bureau started collecting such data in 1967. While the average income of the lowest fifth of black families in the United States was dropping 24 percent, the average income of the highest fifth of black families was climbing by more than $3,000 and that of the top five percent by almost $9,000. Upper-income whites are considerably wealthier than upper-income blacks, but in 1987 the highest fifth of black families secured a record 47.4 percent of the total black income, compared to the 42.9 percent share of total white family income received by the highest fifth of white families.

From *The American Prospect* 1(Spring) 1990: 74–81. Copyright © 1990 by New Prospect, Inc. Reprinted with the permission of the publishers.

So while income inequality widened generally in America during the 1980s, it widened even more dramatically among black Americans. If we are to fashion remedies for black poverty, we need to understand the origins and dynamics of inequality in the black community. Without disavowing the accomplishments of the civil rights movement, black leaders and liberal policy makers now need to focus on remedies that will make a difference to the poor.

PROGRESS AND PROTEST

Before the emergence of activist black protest, the professionals of the National Association for the Advancement of Colored People (NAACP), working mainly through the courts, achieved important victories in the drive for civil rights. Prior to 1960, the NAACP publicly defined the racial problem as a legal segregation in the South and set as its major goal the end of all state-enforced segregation—as the civil rights slogan then had it, "free by 1963." In landmark Supreme Court decisions, the NAACP won legal mandates to improve the conditions of black Americans. Most important, of course, was the 1954 Supreme Court ruling against mandatory school segregation, which overturned the "separate but equal" doctrine and authoritatively defined blacks as first-class citizens.

Important and necessary as these victories were, it soon became apparent that they were not sufficient. Jim Crow regimes in the South ingeniously circumvented the new rulings and made it apparent to black leaders that they had defined both the problem and the goal too narrowly. The problem, as they now saw it, was token compliance with the newly created mandates; the goal they now set was the end of both *de jure* and *de facto* segregation.

Despite Southern white resistance, black expectations of continued racial progress continued rising. Not only had the Supreme Court ruled in favor of desegregation; the federal government was growing more sensitive to the condition of black America for two reasons.

The first was international. When the new African regimes broke up the old colonial empires, both the West and the Soviet block began competing for influence in the new states. Racial violence and animosities in the United States were now more embarrassing to federal officials than in the past. As a result, Southerners, who had enjoyed significant autonomy in handling racial matters prior to World War II, came under closer national scrutiny.

The increased voting power of blacks in national elections was also a factor. Since the elections of the

1920s, civil rights advocates had monitored the voting records of congressmen and policies of presidents. The lure of the black vote sometimes prompted politicians to support racial equality as did the Democratic and Progressive candidates of 1928. At other times, politicians granted token concessions in the hope of preserving or gaining black support, as did President Franklin D. Roosevelt in 1940 when he increased black participation in the Armed Forces, though still within segregated units.

As early as the forties, the black vote was substantial enough in pivotal Northern states to decide close national elections. In 1948 President Truman recognized that to defeat his favored Republican opponent, Thomas E. Dewey, he needed strong black support. For the first time since Reconstruction, the status of blacks emerged as a central presidential campaign issue. Much to the chagrin of its Southern members, the Democratic Party adopted a civil rights plank as part of its 1948 platform. That same year, satisfying a demand black leaders introduced eight years earlier, President Truman issued an executive order banning racial segregation in the armed forces. Despite a Dixiecrat walkout from the party, the strategy worked: black voters helped Truman narrowly defeat Dewey. The black vote also provided the margin of victory for Kennedy in 1960, and it almost defeated Nixon again in 1968.

In the 1960s, as blacks increased their political resources, white resistance to complete desegregation intensified and black support for protest action mushroomed. For a brief period, the nonviolent resistant strategy proved highly effective, particularly in forcing local governments and private agencies to integrate facilities in Southern cities and towns. The nonviolent demonstrations also pressed the federal government into passage of civil rights legislations in 1964 and voting rights legislation in 1965.

Nonviolent protest was successful for several reasons. The demands accompanying the protests—for example, "end discrimination in voting"—tended to be fairly specific and hard to oppose in principle. The remedies were also relatively straightforward and did not require immediate sacrifices by most whites, which reduced white political backlash in areas outside the South. Federal officials were receptive not only because they saw the international attention these developments were receiving. They recognized the political resources blacks had developed, including the growing army of Northern whites sympathetic to the civil rights movement and to direct action protests.

The demands of the civil rights movement reflected

a general assumption by black leaders in the 1960s that the government could best protect the rights of minority groups not by formally bestowing rewards and punishments based on group membership, but by using antidiscrimination measures to enhance individual freedom. The movement was particularly concerned about access to education, employment, voting, and public accommodations. So from the 1950s to 1970, the emphasis was on freedom of choice; the role of the state was to prevent the formal categorization of people on the basis of race. Antibias legislation was designed to eliminate racial discrimination without considering the proportion of minorities in certain positions. The underlying principle was that individual merit should be the sole determining factor in choosing among candidates for positions. Because civil rights protests clearly upheld this basic American principle, they carried a degree of moral authority that leaders such as Martin Luther King, Jr. repeatedly and effectively invoked.

It would have been ideal if programs based on the principle of freedom of individual opportunity were sufficient to remedy racial inequality. Long periods of racial oppression can result, however, in a system of inequality that lingers even after racial barriers come down. The most disadvantaged minority individuals, crippled by the cumulative effects of both race and class subjugation, disproportionately lack the resources to compete effectively in a free and open market. Conversely, the members of a minority group who stand to benefit most from the removal of racial barriers are the ones who least need extra help.

Eliminating racial barriers creates the greatest opportunities for the better trained, talented, and educated members of minority groups because they possess the most resources to compete. Those resources reflect a variety of advantages—family stability, financial means, peer groups, and schooling—provided or made possible by their parents.

By the late 1960s a number of black leaders began to recognize this dilemma. In November, 1967, for example, Kenneth B. Clark said, "The masses of Negroes are now starkly aware of the fact that recent civil rights victories benefited a very small percentage of middle-class Negroes while their predicament remained the same or worsened," Simply eliminating racial barriers was not going to be enough. As the late black economist Vivian Henderson put it in the NAACP journal *The Crisis*, "If all racial prejudice and discrimination and all racism were erased today, all the ills brought by the process of economic class distinction

and economic depression of the masses of black people would remain."

Accordingly, black leaders and liberal policy makers began to emphasize the need not only to eliminate active discrimination, but also to counteract the effects of past racial oppression. Instead of seeking remedies only for individual complaints of discrimination, they sought government-mandated affirmative action programs to ensure adequate minority representation in employment, education, and public programs.

However, as the political scientist James Fishkin has argued, if the more advantaged members of minority groups benefit disproportionately from policies that embody the principle of equality of individual opportunity, they also profit disproportionately from policies of preferential treatment based solely on their racial group membership. Why? Again simply because minority individuals from the most advantaged families tend to be disproportionately represented among those of their racial group most qualified for preferred status, such as college admissions, higher-paying jobs, and promotions. Thus policies of preferential treatment are likely to improve further the socioeconomic positions of the more advantaged without adequately remedying the problems of the disadvantaged.

To be sure, affirmative action was not intended solely to benefit the more advantaged minority individuals. As William L. Taylor, the former director of the U.S. Civil Rights Commission, has stated, "The focus of much of the [affirmative action] effort has been not just on white collar jobs, but also on law enforcement, construction work, and craft and production in large companies—all areas in which the extension of new opportunities has provided upward mobility for less advantaged minority workers." Taylor also notes that studies show that many minority students entering medical schools during the 1970s were from families of low income.

Affirmative action policies, however, did not really open up broad avenues of upward mobility for the masses of disadvantaged blacks. Like other forms of "creaming," they provided opportunities for those individuals from low socioeconomic background with the greatest educational and social resources. Recent data on income, employment opportunities, and educational attainment confirm that relatively few individuals who reside in the inner-city ghettos have benefited from affirmative action.

During the past two decades, as I have argued previously in *The Truly Disadvantaged* (1987), urban minorities have been highly vulnerable to structural changes in the economy, such as the shift from goods-producing to service-producing industries, the increasing polarization of the labor market into low-wage and high-wage sectors, innovations in technology, and the relocation of manufacturing industries out of the central city. These shifts have led to sharp increases in joblessness and the related problems of highly concentrated poverty, welfare dependency, and family breakup, despite the passage of antidiscrimination legislation and the creation of affirmative action programs. In 1974, for example, 47 percent of all employed black males ages 20 to 24 held blue-collar, semiskilled operative and skilled-craft positions, which typically earned wages adequate to support a family. By 1986 that figure plummeted to 25 percent. A survey I have directed, randomly sampling residents from poor Chicago neighborhoods, revealed that Puerto Rican men up to age 45 and black men under age 36 have borne the blunt of job losses due to deindustrialization.

However, I do not advance the foregoing arguments to suggest that race-specific programs were inefficacious. They clearly helped to bring about a sharp increase in the number of blacks entering higher education and gaining professional and managerial positions. But neither policies based on the principle of equality of individual opportunity, nor policies that call for preferential group treatment, such as affirmative action, will do much for less advantaged blacks because of the combined effects of past discrimination and current structural changes in the economy. Now more than ever, we need broader solutions than those we have employed in the past.

TOWARD A NEW POLITICAL STRATEGY

Full employment policies, job skills training, comprehensive health care legislation, educational reforms in the public schools, child care legislation, and crime and drug abuse prevention programs—these are the race-neutral policies likely to begin making a difference for the poor, black and white.

When presenting this argument to academic audiences, I am frequently told that such programs would face general opposition not only because of their cost, but also because many whites have become disenchanted with the black movement and its calls for intensified affirmative action.

These programs should be presented, however, not as ways to address the plight of poor minorities (though they would greatly benefit from them), but as strategies to help all groups, regardless of race or economic class.

After all, Americans across racial and class lines continue to be concerned about unemployment and job security, declining real wages, escalating medical costs, the sharp decline in the quality of public education, the lack of good child care, and crime and drug trafficking in their neighborhoods.

Public opinion surveys reflect these concerns. For the last several years national opinion polls consistently reveal strong public backing for government labor market strategies, including training efforts to enhance employment. A 1988 Harris poll indicated that almost three-quarters of the respondents would support a tax increase to pay for child care. A 1989 Harris poll reports that almost nine out of ten Americans would like to see fundamental change in the U.S. health care system. And recent surveys conducted by the National Opinion Research Center at the University of Chicago reveal that a substantial majority of Americans want more money spent to improve the nation's schools and to halt rising crime and drug addiction.

Programs that expand employment opportunities and job skills training, improve public education, provide adequate child and health care, and reduce neighborhood crime and drug abuse could alleviate many problems of poor minorities that cannot be successfully attacked by race-specific measures alone. In the 1990s the best political strategy for those committed to racial justice is to promote these programs for all groups in America, not just minorities.

RACE-NEUTRAL PROGRAMS AND COALITION POLITICS

"The economic future of blacks in the United States," Vivian Henderson argued in 1975, "is bound up with that of the rest of the nation. Policies, programs, and politics designed in the future to cope with the problems of the poor and victimized will also yield benefits to blacks. In contrast, any efforts to treat blacks separately from the rest of the nation are likely to lead to frustration, heightened racial animosities, and a waste of the country's resources and the precious resources of black people."

Henderson's warning seems to be especially appropriate in periods of economic stagnation, when public support of programs targeted for minorities—or associated with real or imagined material sacrifice on the part of whites—seems to wane. The economy was strong when affirmative action programs were introduced during the Johnson administration. When the economy turned down in the 1970s, the public's view of affirmative action turned increasingly sour.

Furthermore, as Joseph A. Califano, Johnson's staff assistant for domestic affairs, observed in 1988, such programs were generally acceptable to whites "only as a temporary expedient to speed blacks' entry into the social and economic mainstream." But as years passed, many whites "saw continuing such preferences as an unjust insistence by Democrats that they do penance for an era of slavery and discrimination they had nothing to do with." They also associated the decline in public schools, not with broader changes in society, but with "forced integration."

The Democrats also came under fire for their support of Great Society programs that increasingly and incorrectly acquired the stigma of being intended for poor blacks alone. Virtually separate medical and legal systems developed in many cities. Public services became identified mainly with blacks, private services mainly with whites. In an era of ostensible racial justice, many public programs ironically seemed to develop into a new and costlier form of segregation. White taxpayers saw themselves as being forced to pay for medical and legal services for minorities that many of them could not afford to purchase for their own families.

From the New Deal to the 1960s, the Democrats were able to link Keynesian economics and middle-class prosperity with programs for integrating racial minorities and the poor into the American mainstream. "In periods of great economic progress when [the incomes of the middle classes] are rising rapidly," argues Lester Thurow, "they are willing to share some of their income and jobs with those less fortunate than themselves, but they are not willing to reduce their real standard of living to help either minorities or the poor."

As the economic situation worsened, Ronald Reagan was able to convince many working- and middle-class Americans that the decline in their living standards was attributable to expensive and wasteful programs for the poor (and implicitly for minorities). When Reagan was elected to office in 1980, the New Deal coalition collapsed; the principal groups supporting the Democratic ticket with wide majorities were blacks, Hispanics, and the poor, who represent only a quarter of the American population.

What are the implications for the Democratic party? After losing three straight presidential elections, the Democrats are reexamining their programs and approaches to voters, partly in the hope of recapturing support from disaffected whites who voted for Reagan and Bush. Those steps ought to involve the development of race-neutral programs. Consider, for example, one issue likely to be at the core of new domestic programs—the future of the American workforce.

Social scientists, corporate leaders, and government officials have all expressed concerns about the potential weakening of America's competitive position if we fail to confront the growing shortage of skilled workers. These concerns have led to a heightened awareness of the consequences of poverty, poor education, and joblessness. Many of the new jobs will require higher levels of training and education at the very time when our public schools are graduating too many students who can barely read or write. The 1987 U.S. Department of Labor Study, "Workforce 2000," pointed out that for demographic reasons members of minority groups will necessarily fill a majority of the new jobs in the next decade.

A major policy initiative to improve the quality of the workforce would open up opportunities for the minorities who are heavily represented among the educational have-nots. But such an initiative would also open opportunities for others, and it should draw general support because of concerns over the devastating effects a poorly trained workforce will have on the entire economy.

NON-RACIAL AFFIRMATIVE ACTION

However, even if minorities would benefit disproportionately from new race-neutral initiatives to combat the problems and consequences of social inequality, are there not severe problems in the inner-city ghetto that can only be effectively addressed by creative programs targeted on the basis of race? For example, Roger Wilkins has argued persuasively that the cumulative effects of racial isolation and subjugation have made the plight of the black poor unique. Many inner-city children have a solo parent and lack educational support and stability in their home; Wilkins contends that they need assistance to enable them to become capable adults who can provide their children with emotional and educational support. Accordingly, he maintains that special social service programs are needed for inner-city (presumably, minority) schools.

No serious initiative to improve the quality of the workforce could ignore problems such as poverty, social isolation, and family instability, which impede the formal education of children and ultimately affect their job performance. Service programs to meet these needs could easily fit into an overall race-neutral initiative to improve America's workforce. To be sure, this component of the larger initiative would be introduced only in the most disadvantaged neighborhoods, but the neighborhoods would not have to be racially defined. Poor minorities need not be treated separately from the rest of the nation in a national effort to enhance the skill levels of the labor force.

It is particularly important for blacks and other minorities to recognize that they have a stake in the formation of a Democratic coalition that would develop race-neutral initiatives. Only with multiracial support could programs of social and economic reform get approved in Congress. Black voters who are dubious about this approach ought to be reminded of the success of the Jesse Jackson presidential campaign. By highlighting problems plaguing all groups in America, the Jackson campaign drew far more support from white working- and middle-class voters than most political observers thought possible.

THE POSITIVE EFFECTS OF RACE-NEUTRAL POLICIES

My emphasis on race-neutral programs should be clearly distinguished from the neo-conservative critique of affirmative action that attacks both racial preference and activist social welfare policies. The former is said to be antidemocratic, the latter economically counterproductive to minorities. My approach, in contrast, supports the alliance between activist government and racial justice in three key respects—as guarantor of civil rights, as custodian of coalition politics, and as sponsor of race-neutral strategies that advance the well-being of America's neediest along with that of America as a whole. For those who came of age in the 1970s, it seems paradoxical that this goal is now best achieved via race-neutral approaches. Yet, a society without racial preference has, of course, always been the long-term goal of the civil rights movement.

An emphasis on coalition politics that features progressive, race-neutral policies could have two positive effects. It could help the Democratic Party regain lost political support, and it could lead to programs that would especially benefit the more disadvantaged members of minority groups—without being minority policies.

READING 31

INSTITUTIONAL CHANGE AND THE HEALTH POLITICS OF THE 1990s

Mark A. Peterson

In the 1970s, Canada implemented its new health care financing system while the United States considered reform but failed to act. Reform debate in the 1990s must be informed by the correct lessons of the 1970s and an understanding of the subsequent changes in American government. The different Canadian and U.S. experiences had more to do with prevailing institutional arrangements than enduring societal characteristics. Since then, U.S. institutions—reflecting the way private power is represented and public authority is organized—have been dramatically transformed. These changes, along with the election of a president committed to reform, create a policy environment more conducive to health care reform than was true in the 1970s. The medical, insurance, and business alliance opposed to reform has been disrupted and lacks the means to prevail. Achieving reform remains a major challenge, but there is now an opportunity for bold policy action.

Institutions matter. Institutions change, and that also matters. These are simple declarative statements. No doubt they both are universally obvious. For all of their transparency, however, it is sometimes remarkable how steadfastly observers of the political process—indeed, even participants in government itself—either hold to erroneous conclusions about the impact of institutions or fail to appreciate the ways in which institutional

From *American Behavioral Scientist*, 36(6), 1993: 782–801. Reprinted with the permission of Sage Publications, Inc.
Author's Note: This article derives from a health care policy-making project made possible by the generous support of many institutions and individuals. My appreciation is extended to the American Political Science Association Congressional Fellowship Program; Senator Tom Daschle, as well as Rima Cohen and Peter Rouse on his staff; Thomas Mann and the Governmental Studies Program at the Brookings Institution where I was a guest scholar; the Faculty Aide Program, Milton Fund, and Center for American Political Studies at Harvard University; and Susan Carls, Hanley Chew, Roger Kitterman, Adi Krause, Bryan Matthey, Judy Shih, David Wang, Will West, and Leon Yen for their assistance on the project.

change can dramatically alter the dynamics of political relationships. In the 1990s, for anyone interested in the prospects of comprehensive health care reform in the United States, this kind of interpretive inertia has far greater moment than simply frustrating the isolated political scientist seeking an enhanced understanding of state and society. It has practical consequences for how health policy reformers of every stripe approach one another, assess the intersection of substantive policy and political reality, and set the course for restructuring one of the largest economies in the world: the American health care financing and delivery system.[1]

My argument is quite direct. Too much of the contemporary health care reform debate has been conducted—even by Democratic leaders in the U.S. House and Senate, as well as by some members of President Clinton's health policy team—on the at least implicit assumption that there are unyielding institutional characteristics of American government and politics that simultaneously make the reform enterprise itself extraordinarily precarious and constrict sharply the domain of viable policy options even if reform in some sense moves forward. This assumption follows, it is reasoned, from the failure of any of the competing reform plans to be enacted during the 1970s, when the hopes and opportunities for revamping health care financing were at their then 20th-century zenith. But the 1990s are not the 1970s: Not only have the problems of diminished access, rising cost, and threatened quality been aggravated since then (Aaron, 1991; Marmor, Mashaw, & Harvey, 1990, chap. 6; Reagan, 1992); not only is the general public more ready than ever to ratify, even promote, significant intervention by the government as either the designer or steward of a new system, whatever its final characteristics (Blendon & Donelan, 1991); and not only is the middle class, suffering for the first time setbacks in its health care security, a fresh entrant in the clamor for change (Brown, 1992; Priest & Goldstein, 1992; Starr, 1991). The very institutional setting in which health care reform must be deliberated, crafted, enacted, and implemented has witnessed unprecedented changes since the era of Nixon, Ford, and Carter, when last the reform movement enjoyed such political currency. Change has reoriented both the private institutions—the array of organized interests that coalesce and collide on this issue—and the public institutions—particularly the national legislature—from whose interactions the rules for the nation's 21st-century health care system will emerge (Peterson, in press). In this new institutional environment, effecting fundamental policy change remains a decidedly chal-

lenging proposition, but the presumed lessons of the 1970s are likely to be self-defeating rather than enlightening. The current circumstances, including the return of unified government under the leadership of an activist president committed to reform, suggest that federal policymakers could be poised—if they choose to be—for bold action, rather than primed for "déjà vu all over again," to quote Yogi Berra.

I offer here an institutionalist assessment of the health care reform politics of the 1990s. I begin with a reinterpretation of the lessons of the 1970s (as well as the 1960s), using a brief comparison of the U.S. and Canadian experiences to examine the central role of divergent institutional arrangements in explaining differing policy responses to similar substantive situations (there was a serious struggle over reform in both countries, but Canada acted, whereas the United States did not—institutions, perhaps more than anything else, mattered). Given these cross-national differences, however, I ask how the United States could now nonetheless proceed successfully with the reform agenda. The answer is to be found in major shifts in the interest group community and in the organization of Congress (institutions change, and that matters).

WHAT SHOULD WE LEARN FROM THE 1960s AND 1970s?

After several years of cumulative policy enactments and implementation, Canada consolidated its disparate streams of health care financing reform in 1971, establishing a national "single-payer," provincially administered, publicly financed system with partial subsidy from the federal government (Taylor, 1987). By the end of the same decade, in the United States the heated debate over a similar national health insurance scheme and an employment-based alternative ended with reform advocates soundly defeated and the status quo firmly in place. From these contrary outcomes many drew the conclusion that nations like Canada—portrayed as smaller and less diverse than the United States, more enamored with the communitarian spirit, and constituted under the Westminster parliamentary rules of responsible party government—could adopt such sweeping interjections of the public sector in what had been a significant part of the private economy. The United States, on the other hand—with a population that values individualism and private enterprise, and fragmented governing institutions highly permeable to the influence of concentrated private interests—cannot enact any policy reform predicated on major public sector involvement, be it regulatory or fiscal. The origins, terms, means, and context of the debate were simply different in the two societies.

Scholars attuned to the nuances of each country's health care experiences, populations, and political systems, however, have found that many of these distinctions are more myth than fact (Evans, 1984; Kudrle & Marmor, 1981; Marmor et al., 1990, chap. 6). The U.S. and Canadian health care systems—from financing to delivery—were remarkably similar prior to the implementation of Canada's new financing system. Although the population of Canada is indeed smaller (one tenth of its southern neighbor's), the values and perspectives of its citizens are not all that different (Taylor & Reinhardt, 1991). What pushed Canada over the reform threshold, however, was greater previous experience with meaningful subnational experimentation in financing health care (something the United States has now begun), and, perhaps most important, a parliamentary system's capacity to enact controversial legislation once it has been adopted by the majority party in government (Kudrle & Marmor, 1981).

Where does this disparity leave the United States? Lowering the institutional threshold for reform could theoretically occur in one of three ways. First, the achievement of comprehensive reform could await the substantial restructuring of governing institutions. Quite a few scholars and practitioners have sounded a general alarm about the prosperity of the American constitutional system, with its separation of powers born of an earlier age, to generate stalemate rather than action in any number of policy areas. Some of these critics have promoted the cause of constitutional revisions that would engender more coordinated executive-legislative functions along the lines of parliamentary democracy (Cutler, 1980; Mezey, 1989; Sundquist, 1986). Few individuals in the academy, government, or politics, though, grant that such wholesale changes represent a plausible course of action (see Peterson, 1990, chap. 8).

A second option is to wait for a pressing crisis to envelop the health care system. Even as sluggish a policy-making apparatus as the United States political system can and has responded to the threat or actual advent of disaster. There are those who may wish to argue that the health care system is well on its way to such a calamity. If current trends in medical care inflation should continue, for example, in the lifetimes of the youngest Americans, health care expenditures will absorb 100% of the nation's gross domestic product (GDP) and all of its federal budget! But that nightmare is still some time off. As disconcerting as it may be to have witnessed a near doubling of health care costs as a percentage of national income from 1970 to 1992 (7.5% to 14.2%, see Pear, 1993) while perhaps 70 million citizens either possess no or insufficient insurance coverage, a foreboding sense of crisis is not yet so pronounced as to overcome the kind of institutional rigidities that proved so frustrating by the end of the 1970s.

A third possibility, however, is that U.S. politics and government writ large are not static phenomena, even in the essential character of the institutions by which we are represented and governed. Access, influence, and decision making depend not only on the constitutional outlines of the political system but also on the evolving details of how private power and public authority are manifest in each policy domain. In these respects, there have been some profound institutional changes over the past 20 to 30 years of considerable relevance to health care—in the way in which private groups are mobilized and allied, in the nature of their relationships with elected officials, and even in the structure of Congress itself. The exact institutional rigidities of the 1970s simply no longer exist.

There is little question that a valuable opportunity to secure substantial employment-based reform of the U.S. health care system was lost in the 1970s, when lead activists pressed for a Canadian-style policy that could not survive the political and institutional gauntlet that existed in the United States at that time (see Starr, 1982). Today's policymakers, one hopes, are better readers of the tea leaves. But they have to be the right leaves. The real comparative lessons of the 1960s and 1970s, I would suggest, are twofold. First, the divergence in policy outcomes between Canada and the United States derived more from differences in state than society—in the *prevailing* structure of governance, not medical experience or social values. Second, although the core character of post-World War II American constitutional government has not been directly assaulted, there have been institutional changes in the ensuing years that make for a qualitatively different setting in which to consider comprehensive health care reform in the 1990s. These transformations in private power and public authority and their potential consequences invite closer examination.

WHITHER THE ANTIREFORM ALLIANCE?

Writing about the health care reform conflicts of the 1940s, Monte Poen (1979) entitled his book *Harry S*

Truman Versus the Medical Lobby. It is an apt title. Truman, with his plan for compulsory medical insurance, was the first president to put health care reform formally on the nation's agenda. Although the effort had the support of organized labor and allied associations, Truman found himself relatively alone among elected officials challenging the central precepts of American medicine. The American Medical Association (AMA), which invested vast organizational and financial resources, took the lead in deflecting the president's initiative by working with a receptive Congress (particularly when under Republican control from 1947 to 1948) and playing to the public's neo-Cold War fears of "socialism" (Campion, 1984). The medical interests were so effective at thwarting comprehensive reform efforts that reform proponents shifted the strategy to one of first enacting a considerably more limited program of coverage for the elderly, finally achieved after much delay in 1965 (Marmor, 1973). As Franklin Roosevelt had always feared, the AMA and its allies demonstrated that they could dominate this aspect of U.S. policy-making.

The 1970s may originally have appeared to present a different situation. Medical inflation had changed the dynamics of the debate so much that even a Republican president, Richard Nixon, was promoting a version of national health care financing, albeit more dependent on a mix of private and public insurance mechanisms. The organized advocates of reform also had developed so much political presence that they were cocky enough to reject Nixon's employment-based plan and later compel President Carter to adopt, although reluctantly, the mantle of national health insurance. What they lacked, however, was the capacity to win (see Starr, 1982).

Organized medicine had not lost much political influence since the 1940s. Its alliance with private insurance carriers and the business community had been strengthened. Since the last full-scale reform debate, the United States had experienced a dramatic increase in the percentage of the population covered by private health insurance. This expansion of protection derived largely from businesses picking up the health care bill. World War II wage and price controls and recent government protection of labor organizing made nonwage compensation, like health benefits, appealing to both employers and employees. They became a focus of collective bargaining. The protection health benefits received in the tax code continued their attractiveness once regulations restricting cash wages were lifted and as long as health care costs remained relatively stable. Although the rising costs of medical care in the 1970s

worried most business leaders, they shared the desire of the medical providers and insurance companies to find private solutions and to prevent the government from imposing alternatives. Together they had the clout to forestall any major public sector interventions, especially when reform proponents grew more confident about their own influence than wisdom may have dictated.

To borrow from a medical technology firm's recent series of television commercials, "That was then, this is now." The reform coalition may be weakened somewhat by the decline of organized labor over the past 20 years (Goldfield, 1987), but the previous antireform alliance of medicine, insurance, and business faces a far more significant internal threat. Even physicians alone are no longer speaking with a unified voice. Both the American College of Physicians and the American Academy of Family Physicians, not to mention more activist organizations like Physicians for a National Health Plan, have outpaced the AMA in their willingness to accept restructuring of the health care system (see Ginsburg & Prout, 1990). The AMA itself no longer can nor wishes to sustain the status quo and has joined the call for reform, albeit with the hopes of defining policy changes that serve its own interests. Doctors in particular have also suffered under recent insurance practices, including intrusive case-by-case utilization review that interferes in their clinical decision making. The burdens of collecting fees from patients, processing the variegated paperwork of hundreds of insurance companies, and undergoing utilization review have transformed physicians into business managers and pulled them increasingly away from the practice of medicine. Given the past policy positions of the AMA opposing government programs, it is ironic that doctors in Canada and Germany, countries with universal social insurance systems of health care financing, enjoy the very clinical autonomy that American doctors desire but find rapidly disappearing in our predominantly private system. Despite incomes that remain the highest among providers in the world, the life of the U.S. physician has lost much of its luster. It is little wonder that doctors in Canada and Germany are far more likely than their U.S. counterparts to encourage students to enter the field of medicine. Under these circumstances, it will be hard for doctors to marshall the will or the resources to stand unified in the way of policy change.

The approach of insurance carriers to cost containment erodes the cooperation they previously enjoyed with health care providers. The insurance industry itself, however, is also deeply divided, a schism that has festered under the surface among members of the Health Insurance Association of America (HIAA), the industry's primary trade association. In the past year, the rifts have become more pronounced and public. Whereas the business of small insurance companies is seriously threatened by anything but the most incremental reforms of the health insurance market, larger carriers can adapt more readily to significant market restructuring (assuming they are not cast entirely from the health insurance domain). Larger companies that have moved primarily into managed care, however, have quite different views about acceptable reform strategies than do the companies still concentrating on indemnity plans, which led them to dissent sharply from the HIAA's recent unprecedented acceptance of reform proposals that would standardize reimbursement rates (Pear, 1992).

Despite the over 20 years of unmitigated medical care inflation, many businesses large and small remain philosophically opposed to government intervention in the health care economy. But quite a few others, watching their competitive position in domestic and international markets weaken as a result of untamed health care costs, no longer fear, and in some cases actually invite, government efforts of some kind to rationalize health care financing and contain costs. Even a few CEOs of *Fortune* 500 companies, like retiring Lee Iaccoca of Chrysler Corporation, have either accepted or promoted the idea of a publicly financed system, in part or in total. During the 1970s it would have been inconceivable for the leaders of major business enterprises to stride so boldly into the domain of what was so pejoratively (and erroneously) called "socialized" medicine. Business at the time maintained a commitment to private, competitive solutions to control provider costs, only to find them wanting. In the meantime, the heightened use by private insurance carriers of experiential instead of community rating of premiums, preexisting condition exclusions and medical underwriting, and the "skimming" of business clients with the youngest and healthiest employees left many businesses that were previously dedicated to private health coverage unable to provide for their own employees (see Stone, 1990). Given the economics of the 1990s, it is increasingly difficult for business to argue that it should play the primary role of organizing and paying for the health care of U.S. workers, or, through cost shifting, the costs of care for the uninsured (see Bergthold, 1990; Martin, 1992).

The 1990s have also seen the culmination of a process of institutional change that has transformed the

ways in which all kinds of interests are mobilized and represented in the national policy-making process. Mancur Olson (1965), examining the issue of collective action, provides the theoretical groundwork for understanding why occupationally based, particularly profit-sector interests—such as trade associations—have had an enormous advantage when it comes to organizing for political purposes (see also Walker, 1991). They have fewer potential "members," and the political economics of organizing—the benefits over costs—provide a rational basis for even one member to subsidize substantially the organizational effort.

Other groups, with large *potential* memberships, confront the "free rider" problem. They have difficulty organizing, especially if their political objectives are to secure policy outcomes (e.g., consumer protection, environmental quality, and universal health care) that can be enjoyed by all individuals even if they have not contributed to the collective action. Medical, insurance, and business interests previously had this edge in organizing collectively. Only labor unions, with the assistance of "closed shop" laws that compel membership or contributions, could maintain a sustained organizational presence as advocates of reform.

Since particularly the late 1960s, however, cause-oriented citizen groups, the type of membership associations most threatened by the Olsonian logic of organizing, have benefited from the emergence of new resources that aid in solving the collective action problem. First, the citizenry has become more educated, attuned to politics, and finds greater personal reward from the actual participation in political and social action, thus diminishing free rider inclinations (Walker, 1991; Wilson, 1973). Second, according to Jack Walker (1991), "patrons of political action"— including foundations, government agencies, unions, churches, and wealthy individuals—have become much more significant sources of revenue for citizen groups, permitting these organizations to form without having to depend so extensively on unpredictable membership dues and contributions. In 1985, for example, voluntary associations that were organized around occupations or industries in the profit-making sector of the economy received almost 90% of their revenues from routine membership contributions, whereas less than half of the citizen group budgets came from such sources (Walker, 1991, p. 82).

These trends in the interest group community have affected the health policy domain. Citizen groups, a substantial majority of which oppose the past positions of the medical, insurance, and business interests and favor expanded federal involvement in health and human services, now account for almost 38% of the national membership associations expressing intense interest in these issues. Four in 10 began operations between 1970 and 1985. Another 38% of the groups very interested in health and human services represent individuals and institutions in the nonprofit sector, a healthy majority of which also support greater government commitment in this area (Peterson, in press).

The world of private power organized in the health care policy arena is markedly different today from what was experienced in the 1970s. Where once medical providers, insurance carriers, and business leaders had compatible interests that nurtured their alliance against government-mandated comprehensive reform of the health care system, in the 1990s many of these interests are increasingly in conflict with one another and even prone to internal fissures. No one believes that they, in any numbers, will join a reform crusade, but they are hardly the concerted barrier to reform that they once represented even as late as the 1970s. At the same time, those organizations within the old alliance that continue to adhere to the antireform theme are confronted by a much expanded collection of citizen groups assisted by the changed institutional dynamics of mobilizing and financing organized interests in America.[2]

Many of these changes would be easy to miss if one were not resident "inside the beltway" or were not well versed in the media coverage of how special interests apparently swagger through the halls of Congress. There is no question, for example, that campaign contributions from political action committees (PACs) are staggering in absolute terms and increased in the 1992 election cycle. The efforts of PACs representing the interests of medical providers, medical equipment manufacturers, pharmaceutics, and insurance are particularly impressive ("Campaign Contributions," 1992; Neuffer, 1993a, 1993b). From personal experience as a congressional fellow serving as a legislative assistant on health policy in the U.S. Senate, I can attest that the lobbyists for these interests appear to be as intelligent, informed, with as much previous Capitol Hill experience, and as handsomely compensated as ever.

These legitimate surface impressions, though, fail to recognize much of what has happened to transform group politics in general and health care politics in particular. First, with the increasing number and new diversity of interests resplendent in Washington, DC, it is more difficult for any one group or even block of groups to wield the kind of influence that they might have had in the past, unless an extraordinarily harmo-

nious coalition can be held together (see Salisbury, 1990). I believe that the former medical, insurance, and business alliance is failing that test. Second, the social science research on the terribly complex question of whether campaign financing affects congressional behavior has produced somewhat ambiguous results, with little support for the conventional notion that these dollars translate into actions by legislators that they otherwise would not have taken. It does seem fairly certain, however, that PAC money has far less significance as a source of political influence on those high visibility policy issues that are especially salient to the public (Grenzke, 1989). The debate over health care reform is anything but a back room affair. Finally, the impact of organized interests depends to some extent on the nature of the institution they are attempting to manipulate. How public authority itself is organized affects the pathways of influence. With Congress at the center of these institutional concerns, it is the subject of the next section.

A NEW CONGRESS?

Back when President Truman was fighting the American Medical Association, it did not help his cause that Congress had long since become an oligarchical institution, dominated by either a Republican majority or the conservative coalition of Republicans and southern Democrats. Even when the president's party nominally held most of the seats in the House and Senate, the three-decades-old seniority system left many committee chairmanships—then the core of legislative power—in the hands of the southern Democrats who were opposed to federal policy interventions like compulsory health insurance. It is the oligarchical nature of Congress in the 1940s and 1950s, in combination with closely allied, industry-based interest groups, that lent empirical credence to the widely accepted model of policy-making captured by the term "iron triangle." Government action, from this perspective, was the product of (or held captive to) the relatively low visibility and commonly consensual decisions reached by bureau-level executive branch officials, congressional committee leaders, and like-minded representatives of organized interests (see Gais, Peterson, & Walker, 1984). Given the way that public authority was organized at the time, it was fairly easy for the medical lobby to control the outcome of any health care reform debate.

When Richard Nixon took the oath of office in 1969, little had changed in the structure of Congress, other than the elevated restiveness of less senior members frustrated by the oligarchy of committee chairmen. Any major reform initiative, for example, would have to pass through the House Committee on Ways and Means, whose legislative domain included all revenue issues, social security, and the new Medicare and Medicaid programs. Ways and Means was still chaired by Representative Wilbur Mills (D-AR), one of the most influential members of Congress in the 20th century. He ran his committee without subcommittees, so that all legislature work had to be accomplished under his direct guidance, and with all staff resources firmly in his command. The Democrats on the committee also functioned as the party's "committee on committees," responsible for making all Democratic committee assignments. This duty gave these senior Democrats and their chairman tremendous influence over the rank and file of their party in the House. If Wilbur Mills did not want something, and it was within the jurisdiction of Ways and Means, it is fair to say that it did not happen (Manley, 1970).

By the mid-1970s, however, Congress had become quite a different institution after the implementation of a long series of structural reforms. The restive rank and file had finally accumulated enough strength in the House Democratic caucus to challenge that chamber's committee "barons." Three particularly intractable committee chairmen were actually deposed, but the major strategy employed for overcoming the dominance of committee chairs was to redistribute *institutional*, not personal, power. Ultimately, all committees were required to have subcommittees of standing jurisdiction; no member could chair more than a single subcommittee, and each would be selected by the Democratic members of the committee (usually according to seniority as a norm, not a rule); each of the subcommittees was to have its own independent professional staff; at the full- and subcommittee levels staff resources would have to be shared with the minority party; and the committee chair could no longer single-handedly dominate the meeting times and agendas of the committee. Ways and Means was also stripped of its committee-on-committees responsibilities, and Chairman Mills soon stepped down from his post in the wake of a personal scandal. Although the Senate was already a more decentralized body, somewhat similar changes took place on that side of the Capitol as well (Smith & Deering, 1984).

Enter the health care reform debate of the 1970s. It started with a Congress organizationally hostile to comprehensive reform proponents and ended with a chaotic Congress largely institutionally unsettled after its major internal battles over the distribution of power and its intense clashes with President Nixon over the Vietnam war, the president's impoundments of congressionally appropriated funds, and the Watergate scandal. Wilbur Mills had possessed the power to block but also to broker, as he did with Medicare and Medicaid in 1965. No one in the new Congress remained, or no one any longer had the position, to broker a legislative solution, if one was to be achieved. The Ways and Means Committee itself was under the new and less experienced leadership of Oregon's Al Ullman, who would be defeated in the 1980 election. The Health Subcommittee had just been organized. The full committee also was increased from 25 members to a more cumbersome 37. A decentralized Congress remaining in a state of flux was far more beneficial to the still relatively cohesive antireform alliance of medicine, insurance, and business than to the maturing reform coalition, if only because in this type of setting stymieing action is easier than guiding it through multiple veto points. In addition, having just overwhelmed the old guard, and having acquired some institutional authority of their own, the congressional advocates of policy reform may have been blinded to just how precarious, ironically, their policy agendas would be. President Carter, the health care reform movement's next best hope, also ended up partially a victim of the changed institutional ways of Congress (Jones, 1988; Peterson, 1990). By the end of the 1970s, Washington had become a far less predictable arena for the game of politics, including in the realm of health policy (Peterson, in press).

On first appraisal, the current situation in Congress may appear no better than the chaos of the late 1970s. The legislature remains a decidedly decentralized, if not fragmented, institution. Reelection incentives tend to direct members all too frequently toward parochial (constituency-specific) considerations and short-term policy fixes (Fiorina, 1989; see Arnold, 1990). The laws passed in the 1970s intended to reform campaign finance have instead institutionalized "special" interest giving by promoting the creation of thousands of political action committees (Sabato, 1985). There has been a hue and cry from all quarters about the problems of stalemate and gridlock, a charge laid mostly at the door of Congress. Various think tanks like the Brookings Institution are pondering possible reforms for making the legislative process more responsive and efficient, and even leaders in Congress have organized an internal review of House and Senate procedures and committee systems (see Hook, 1992). Few, therefore, would anticipate a sudden ability on the part of Congress to set a course and take bold action. Nevertheless, it is worth repeating that the Congress of the 1990s is interacting with a universe of organized interests that *is* quite different from 20 years ago, and that fact, in and of itself, is significant. Providers, insurance companies, and business have lost much of their organizational advantage, and by 1985, groups of all kinds, including citizens associations, were reporting equivalent levels of cooperative interactions with congressional committees and subcommittees (Peterson, in press).

There is more to the story of institutional change, however, some elements of which may even inspire restrained optimism. First, during the 1980s more of the legislative action in the House was moving from the committees to the floor, and the House leadership demonstrated greater effectiveness at managing the floor agenda (Smith, 1989). Some power has actually flowed back to the formal leadership (Davidson, 1988). Second, never before have so many party, committee, and subcommittee leaders been as committed to health care reform, and been as experienced in developing the necessary legislation (Peterson, in press). Third, a significant number of rank and file members of both the House and Senate have become health care reform policy entrepreneurs in their own right, crafting and promoting their own comprehensive plans for restructuring the financing of medical services (Kosterlitz, 1991; Peterson, 1992a). A few, like Senator Robert Kerrey of Nebraska, do not even serve on committees of jurisdiction. Although there is the danger that such expansive entrepreneurship could fragment the reform effort if members become overly dedicated to their own plans with their individual nuances, the activities of these policy entrepreneurs to date have elevated the overall knowledge base in Congress about the intricacies of the health care system. Never before have so many members of Congress been as well versed in the problems and the possible policy alternatives (Peterson, 1992a, 1992b, in press). Fourth, although it is too early to judge their impact, the 1992 election cycle has brought 110 new representatives and a dozen first-time senators to the 103rd Congress, reflecting the largest change in the membership of Congress since 1948. They are younger and more diverse than their more senior colleagues, and they all directly or indirectly ran on the campaign theme of breaking the gridlock—with health care reform as one of the central issues of concern.

Finally, Congress now has a capacity for sophisticated policy analysis that may even surpass that of the president of the United States (Peterson, 1992c). As part of the institutional reforms of the 1970s, Congress established the Congressional Budget Office (CBO) and the Office of Technology Assessment (OTA), as well as enhancing the program analysis capabilities of the General Accounting Office (GAO) and the Congressional Research Service (CRS). In conjunction with reforms of Medicare's procedures for reimbursing doctors and hospitals, it created the Physician Payment Review Commission (PPRC) and the Prospective Payment Assessment Commission (ProPAC). These agencies, required to satisfy a bipartisan, multicommittee environment, have in the past two decades fully established their empirical and analytical credibility, with only scattered charges of partisanship (Peterson, 1992c; see Bimber, 1992). Together with the significantly expanded professional committee, subcommittee, and personal office staffs and the information available from executive branch officials and the diverse community of interest group lobbyists, Congress has an unprecedented potential to evaluate rather complex social policy initiatives (Peterson, 1992c).

JUDGING THE OPPORTUNITIES FOR POLICY CHANGE

Social scientists have long been interested in understanding the processes by which issues draw the attention of both electorates and political leaders, and, in some cases, initiate particularly striking shifts in the status quo. Recent research has shown that these processes may have little to do with simplistic notions about the emergence of problems and identification of solutions. Instead, policy change depends on fairly momentary "policy windows" engendered by a confluence of problem awareness, events, public mood, electoral outcomes, and policy entrepreneurship (Kingdon, 1984).

What happens once these windows of opportunity open, however tentatively? Major shifts in policy probably depend on the results of what John Campbell (1992) calls "political" decision making, when ideas and people with influence are both energetically in contention:

> Participants have different goals or preferences; the process is some sort of fight or bargaining; the result is determined by each participant's relative power, or by the amount of energy each is able and willing to expend on that issue and how skillfully resources are deployed.

The ideas, participants, their resources, and the institutional setting in which they "fight" or "bargain," however, are not static phenomena. They are all influenced, to some extent, by what has been wrought before—what policies have been deliberated, enacted, or rejected; how previous programs and the government authorities established to administer them have transformed substantive understanding as well as the political resources of groups; and the degree to which forces either endogenous or exogenous to the immediate issue at hand have reshaped the institutions through which power is applied and by which decisions are made. These attributes define the character of a "polity" at the time of any given policy discourse and set the parameters of what is possible and what is done (see Skocpol, 1992).

From this perspective, policymakers, reform advocates, and scholars watching the current health care reform debate must strike a careful balance in assessing the reform opportunities of the 1990s. On the one hand, for reformers to assume that the circumstances are the same as the 1970s, and thus a time to accept the very compromise that they perhaps carelessly rejected at the time, is to both misinterpret the comparative U.S. and Canadian experiences of that era and ignore a sea change that has occurred in U.S. national institutions (not to mention in the dimensions of the health care problem itself). With the advent of an activist president, the first in more than a generation genuinely committed by principle and campaign promise to serious health care reform, the current institutional setting affords the best chance in this century for fulfilling the most ambitious reform objectives. On the other hand, while avoiding the propensity to seek too little, reformers are also cautioned by the 1970s episode to assess carefully the fluctuating politics of medical care reform and know when to strike a deal—when to fight *and* when to bargain—rather than seek too much and once again watch the opportunity slip away.

Experience has taught us that the costs of timidity are great. President Johnson and the designers of the Medicare program were convinced that the medical lobby retained so much clout that passage of the program required accommodating their interests. As a result, Medicare began by paying doctors fee-for-service reimbursements based on "customary, prevailing, and reasonable" (CPR) rates and hospitals on the principle of cost-based reimbursements (Califano, 1993). In effect, doctors and hospitals set their own incomes, courtesy of the U.S. Treasury, and in the process helped fuel the subsequent inflation in medical costs. Theodore Marmor (1973) and others suggest that Johnson underestimated the leverage he had gained from the pre-

vailing public mood, his own electoral landslide in 1964, and the extraordinary influx of liberal Democrats into the 89th Congress. With health care costs out of control, the access problem worsening, and the quality of services under threat, a similar miscalculation today—giving away too much to the interests with a stake in the status quo—could have devastating consequences. For the same reasons, however, failure to enact any kind of reasonable plan for restructuring the financing of U.S. health care by missing the opportune bargain would leave the economy vulnerable and seriously impair any effort to bring fiscal discipline to federal and state government budgets. As then president-elect Clinton stated with some exasperation at the economic conference in Little Rock, "We are kidding each other . . . if we think we can fiddle around with the entitlements and all this other stuff and get control of this budget, if you don't do something on health care. . . . It's going to bankrupt the country" (quoted in Rovner, 1993, p. 28).

Throughout this article, my argument has been about the prospects, given the institutional setting of the 1990s, of achieving the kind of generic comprehensive reform that would address the problems articulated by President Clinton initially in Little Rock and again in his first State of the Union address. This analysis, however, also offers a framework in which to consider the merits and prospects of specific reform plans. Although there are many who sincerely advocate, for example, employment-based "play-or-pay" initiatives or the various versions of managed competition predicated on the perceived substantive merits of these approaches, much of the support that these plans have received—from health policy specialists, the Democratic leadership in the House and Senate, organized labor, and even the Clinton administration—undoubtedly derives from the belief that they represent the most politically viable, even if not the best, ways in which to reform American health care (see Peterson, 1992a). The Jackson Hole Group (JHG), the originators of the most "free market" version of managed competition, tout the political sensibility of their plan:

> For many years in this country we have had an employment-based system of health care coverage. Seeking politically feasible incremental change, the JHG proposes to build on that system and correct its deficiencies rather than to replace it radically. (Ellwood, Enthoven, & Etheredge, 1992, p. 160)

Political viability demands constant reassessment, however, as the character of the polity changes. I would suggest that these arguments in favor of employment-based approaches alone are suited more to the distribution of private power and structure of public authority present in the 1970s than to what we find today.

That is not to say that the U.S. political system and its governing institutions are now primed to adopt a single-payer Canadian model or its conceptual equivalent with sudden ease and happy flourish. Rather, if the U.S.-Canadian comparison of the 1960s and 1970s has been misinterpreted, and if the institutional changes in the United States since the 1970s have been as pronounced as I have suggested, and if presidential commitment and unified party government can make a difference, then reform plans that involve extensive government involvement and public financing are not as politically vulnerable as some experienced participants and pundits would have us believe (see Feder, 1993).

Given the problems facing the U.S. health care system, and the remarkable changes in the institutional setting in which reform is being debated, all issues and approaches should be on the table (see Marmor & Boyum, 1992). The 1990s are so different from the 1970s—indeed, 1993 is so different from 1990-1992—we should all relinquish the particular reform labels to which we have become attached and think anew about how to craft effective and politically sustainable restructuring of the system for financing, and delivering, health care services. Pay or play, managed competition, and single-payer standing alone do not get us very far in the current climate. Conceptual fusion may be the key. What is important about single-payer approaches is not the explicit channeling of funds through public coffers but, rather, the commitment to ensuring universal access to a comprehensive package of benefits, portability of coverage, clinical autonomy for providers, efficiency of financing, and budgetary control over health care expenditures. From play-or-pay designs we are reminded of the effective role that employers have played and can play in directing information to beneficiaries and acting as collection agents for health care premiums. Managed competition, whatever its form, highlights the importance of finding ways to rationalize the delivery of health care services.

The trick of the 1990s is to identify the sensible way to weave the themes together (see Marmor & Boyum, 1992; Starr, 1992). Because in some senses *everything* is possible today in a way that was never before true, we should regard *anything* as possible and strive to construct a new health care system that serves both the policy and political interests of the current American polity.

NOTES

1. At $838 billion in 1992, the U.S. health care system is about the size of Great Britain's entire economy, and with annual increases on the order of 10% to 12%, it is growing quite a bit faster (Pear, 1993).
2. The ramifications of these changes are possibly susceptible to sophisticated procedures for estimating the likelihoods of different policy outcomes. Stanley Feder, in a 1993 draft paper, illustrates how an empirical analytic technique developed for predicting policy outcomes in foreign nations can be adapted to the domestic debate over health care reform. Called "Factions," this model forces the analyst to consider the full range of participants, their policy positions and the salience of the issue to them, and their political clout.

REFERENCES

Aaron, H. J. (1991). *Serious and unstable condition: Financing America's health care.* Washington, DC: Brookings Institution.

Arnold, R. D. (1990). *The logic of congressional action.* New Haven, CT: Yale University Press.

Bergthold, L. A. (1990). *Purchasing power in health: Business, the state, and health care politics.* New Brunswick, NJ: Rutgers University Press.

Bimber, B. (1992). *Institutions and ideas: The politics of expertise in Congress.* Unpublished doctoral dissertation, Massachusetts Institute of Technology.

Blendon, R. J., & Donelan, K. (1991, Fall). Public opinion and efforts to reform the U.S. health care system: Continuing issues of cost-containment and access to care. *Stanford Law & Policy Review,* pp. 146–154.

Brown, L. D. (1992). Getting there: The political context for implementing health care reform. In C. Brecher (Ed.), *Implementation issues and national health care reform* (pp. 13–46). Washington, DC: Josiah Macy, Jr. Foundation.

Califano, J. A., Jr. (1993, January 28). Break the billion-dollar congress. *The New York Times,* p. A21.

Campaign contributions to those making health policy: Big givers and big takers. (1992, November 15). *The New York Times,* p. E5.

Campbell, J. C. (1992). *How policies change: The Japanese government and the aging society.* Princeton, NJ: Princeton University Press.

Campion, F. D. (1984). *The AMA and U.S. health policy since 1940.* Chicago: Chicago Review Press.

Cutler, L. N. (1980). To form a government. *Foreign Affairs, 59*(4), 126–143.

Davidson, R. H. (1988, Summer). The new centralization on Capitol Hill. *Review of Politics*, pp. 345–364.

Ellwood, P. M., Enthoven, A. C., & Etheredge, L. (1992). The Jackson Hole initiatives for a twenty-first century American health care system. *Health Economics, 1,* 149–168.

Evans, R. G. (1984). *Strained mercy: The economics of Canadian health care.* Toronto: Buttersworth.

Feder, S. A. (1993). *Forecasting health policy decisions.* Paper presented at the Health Policy Workshop, School of Organization and Management, Yale University.

Fiorina, M. P. (1989). *Congress: Keystone of the Washington establishment* (2nd ed.). New Haven, CT: Yale University Press.

Gais, T. L., Peterson, M. A., & Walker, J. L. (1984). Interest groups, iron triangles, and representative institutions in American national government. *British Journal of Political Science, 14*(2), 161–185.

Ginsburg, J. A., & Prout, D. M. (1990). Access to health care. *Annals of Internal Medicine, 112,* 641–661.

Goldfield, M. (1987). *The decline of organized labor in the United States.* Chicago: University of Chicago Press.

Grenzke, J. M. (1989). Shopping in the congressional supermarket: The currency is complex. *American Journal of Political Science, 33*(1), 1–24.

Hook, J. (1992, June 6). Extensive reform proposals cook on the front burner. *Congressional Quarterly Weekly Report*, pp. 1579–1585.

Jones, C. O. (1988). *The trusteeship presidency: Jimmy Carter and the United States Congress.* Baton Rouge: Louisiana State University Press.

Kingdon, J. W. (1984). *Agendas, alternatives, and public policies.* Boston: Little, Brown.

Kosterlitz, J. (1991, April 27). Radical surgeons. *National Journal*, pp. 993–997.

Kudrle, R. T., & Marmor, T. R. (1981). The development of welfare states in North America. In P. Flora & A. J. Heidenheimer (Eds.), *The development of welfare states in Europe and America* (pp. 81–121). New Brunswick, NJ: Transaction Books.

Manley, J. (1970). *The politics of finance.* Boston: Little, Brown.

Marmor, T. R. (1973). *The politics of Medicare.* Chicago: Aldine.

Marmor, T. R., & Boyum, D. (1992, Fall). American medical care reform: Are we doomed to fail? *Daedalus*, pp. 175–194.

Marmor, T. R., Mashaw, J. L., & Harvey, P. L. (1990). *America's misunderstood welfare state: Persistent myths, enduring realities.* New York: Basic Books.

Martin, C. J. (1992, September). *Together again: Business, government, and the quest for cost containment.* Paper presented at the annual meeting of the American Polital Science Association, Chicago.

Mezey, M. L. (1989). *Congress, the president, and public policy.* Boulder, CO: Westview.

Neuffer, E. (1993a, February 14). Funds flowing to guide health reform's course. *The Boston Globe*, p. 1.

Neuffer, E. (1993b, February 14). Members of key health panels benefit from PAC largess. *The Boston Globe*, p. 24.

Olson, M. (1965). *The logic of collective action.* Cambridge, MA: Harvard University Press.

Pear, R. (1992, December 3). In shift, insurers ask U.S. to require coverage for all. *The New York Times*, pp. A1, A22.

Pear, R. (1993, January 5). Health care costs up sharply again, posing new threat. *The New York Times*, pp. A1, A10.

Peterson, M. A. (1990). *Legislating together: The White House and Capitol Hill from Eisenhower to Reagan.* Cambridge, MA: Harvard University Press.

Peterson, M. A. (1992a). Report from Congress: Momentum toward health care reform in the U.S. Senate. *Journal of Health Politics, Policy and Law, 17*(3), 553–573.

Peterson, M. A. (1992b, September). *Leading our way to health: Entrepreneurship and leadership in the health care reform debate* (Center for American Political Studies Occasional Paper No. 97–6). Paper presented at the annual meeting of the American Political Science Association, Chicago.

Peterson, M. A. (1992c). *Health policy making in the information age: Is Congress better informed than the president?* (Center for American Political Studies Occasional Paper No. 92–7). Paper presented at the conference on "Governance in an Era of Skepticism: Administrators and Politicians," sponsored by the International Political Science Association Research Committee on the Structure and Organization of Government, Stockholm, Sweden.

Peterson, M. A. (in press). Political influence in the 1990s: From iron triangles to policy networks. *Journal of Health Policy, Politics and Law.*

Poen, M. M. (1979). *Harry S Truman versus the medical lobby.* Columbia: University of Missouri Press.

Priest, D., & Goldstein, A. (1992, December 22). Middle-class uninsured up by 1 million. *Washington Post*, pp. A1, A4.

Reagan, M. D. (1992). *Curing the crisis: Options for America's health care.* Boulder, CO: Westview.

Rovner, J. (1993, January 2). A job for the deficit bomb squad . . . defusing exploding health-care costs. *Congressional Quarterly Weekly Report*, pp. 28–29.

Sabato, L. J. (1985). *PAC power: Inside the world of political action committees.* New York: Norton.

Salisbury, R. H. (1990). The paradox of interest groups in Washington—More groups, less clout. In A. King (Ed.), *The new American political system* (2nd ed., pp. 203–230). Washington, DC: American Enterprise Institute.

Skocpol, T. (1992). *Protecting soldiers and mothers: The political origins of social policy in the United States.* Cambridge, MA: Harvard University Press.

Smith, S. S. (1989). *Call to order: Floor politics in the House and Senate.* Washington, DC: Brookings Institution.

Smith, S. S., & Deering, C. J. (1984). *Committees in congress.* Washington, DC: Congressional Quarterly Press.

Starr, P. (1982). *The social transformation of American medicine.* New York: Basic Books.

Starr, P. (1991). The middle class and national health reform. *American Prospect, 2,* 7–12.

Starr, P. (1992). *The logic of health care reform.* Knoxville, TN: Whittle Communications.

Stone, D. A. (1990). AIDS and the moral economy of insurance. *American Prospect, 1,* 62–73.

Sundquist, J. L. (1986). *Constitutional reform and effective government.* Washington, DC: Brookings Institution.

Taylor, H., & Reinhardt, U. E. (1991). Does the system fit? *Health Management Quarterly, 13*(3), 2–10.

Taylor, M. G. (1987). *Health insurance and Canadian public policy: The seven decisions that created the Canadian health insurance system and their outcomes.* Toronto: McGill-Queen's University Press.

Walker, J. L., Jr. (1991). *Mobilizing interest groups in America: Patrons, professions, and social movements.* Ann Arbor: University of Michigan Press.

Wilson, J. Q. (1973). *Political organizations.* New York: Basic Books.

READING 32

CAN AMERICA COMPETE?

Stephen S. Cohen and John Zysman

Adjusting to shifting markets and changing technologies depends on how we use knowledge. That means investing broadly in human resources and in our communities, not just narrowly in engineers and scientists.

We contend that production is changing in such profound ways and at such rapid rates as to seriously threaten our nation's place—and the places of most other nations—in the international economic hierarchy. We are, in brief, in the midst of a major industrial transition.

Transition is a word that triggers a reaction—usually bored annoyance. After all, nothing is more permanent than transition, especially in economics. A healthy economy is always in a state of transition. Indeed, as that oldest of professorial remarks has it, it was Father Adam who turned to Eve on the way out of Eden and announced, "I guess we are entering a period of transition." Technology is always changing: think of the railway, the motorcar, the electric grid, saran wrap. And competitors are constantly struggling for a new product, a new process, and a new kind of efficiency. That's what makes the game so constructive; it keeps us on our toes and busy citing Schumpeter. We argue that the present industrial transition is real and colossally consequential.

INTERNATIONAL COMPETITION

Two principal forces—(1) changes in international competition and (2) changes in production technol-

From *Challenge* 29(2) 1986: 56–64. Reprinted with the permission of the publisher, M. E. Sharpe, Inc., 80 Business Park Drive, Armonk, NY 10504 USA.

Stephen S. Cohen and John Zysman are professors at the University of California. Berkeley, and directors of the Berkeley Roundtable on the International Economy (BRIE). Major portions of this paper, which was delivered at the Symposium on the Fortieth Anniversary of the Joint Economic Committee of the Congress of the United States, will appear in Stephen Cohen and John Zysman, *Manufacturing Matters* (forthcoming). Research for the larger work from which this paper was drawn was supported by special grants from the Carnegie Forum on Education and the Economy, and the Office of Technology Assessment. U.S. Congress, to the Berkeley Roundtable on the International Economy.

ogy—are driving the changes in the world's economies. The first motor force is the relatively rapid and massive exposure of major segments of American manufacturing and services to international competition that is different in extent and in kind from anything we have previously experienced. Over the past generation America preached, to itself and to others, a doctrine of interdependence. But it was the other nations that were interdependent, on each other and on the United States. We were independent. As late as 1970 imports into the United States totaled only $40 billion; by 1980 they had climbed to $245 billion; by 1984, to almost $350 billion. Until only yesterday imports in manufacturing averaged around 4 to 5 percent of sales and were easily balanced by exports; now they are about 25 percent of sales, and some 70 percent of U.S. industries are subject to foreign competition. The abrupt change in scale was matched by a change in kind. Old competitors, located mostly in Western Europe, caught up from an unnatural lag in the kind of production that created the wealth and power of the United States—complex manufacturing in such industries as autos, chemicals, and aircraft. They accumulated, or dug up, capital. And they have never been behind in the fundamentals, education and the ability to create technology.

But more important, new competitors have come on line, most prominently across the Pacific. To speed their development, many of the most successful of these new competitors have shaped economic structures, institutions, and policies that are marginally, but crucially, different from ours. We call these economies *developmental states.* Japan is the most successful and the biggest, but it is not the only one. Japanese competition in all lines of production—ranging from the most advanced high-technology products such as very large scale integration (VLSI) semiconductors and optoelectronics through products of complex manufacturing such as automobiles and consumer electronics to such advanced services as banking and process engineering—has, more than any other factor, been responsible for the current debate on American competitiveness.

THE DEVELOPMENTAL STATE—JAPAN

Since we cannot review here a long series of country and sector stories, let us at least briefly consider some fundamentals of the Japanese case. The Japanese government exerted influence on the country's economy during its boom years of the 1950s and 1960s in two important ways. First, it was a gatekeeper controlling the links between the domestic and the international economy. The Japanese government was, in T. J. Pempel's terms, an "official doorman determining what and under what conditions capital, technology, and manufacturing products enter and leave Japan." [See T. J. Pempel, *Policy and Politics in Japan: Creating Conservatism*, Temple University Press, 1982, p. 139.] The discretion to decide what to let in and, at the extreme, out of Japan permitted the doorman to break up the packages of technology, capital, and control that the multinational corporations represent. In almost all cases, neither money nor technology could in itself allow outsiders to buy or bull their way into a permanent position in the Japanese market. This closed market then gave Japanese firms a stable base of demand which permitted rapid expansion of production and innovation in manufacturing.

Second, government agencies—most notoriously, the Ministry of International Trade and Industry (MITI)—sought to orient the development of the domestic economy. Although government bureaucrats have not dictated to an administered market, they have consciously contributed to the development of particular sectors. MITI is not so much a strict director as a player with its own purposes and its own means of interfering in the market to reach its goals. Government industrial strategy assumes that the market pressures of competition can serve as an instrument of policy. It is not simply that the government makes use of competitive forces that arise naturally in the market, but rather that it often induces the very competition it directs. This intense, but controlled, domestic competition substituted for the pressures of the international market to force development. The competition is real, but the government and private sector work together to avoid "disruptive" or "evasive" competition. We do not need to select between cartoon images of Japan, Inc., or a land of unfettered competition. It is the particular interaction of state and market in Japan that is interesting.

Seen from the perspective of the firm, government policy helped provide cash for investment, tax breaks to sustain liquidity, research and development support, and aid to promote exports. These public policies—the web of policies rather than any individual elements of it—changed the options of companies. Without protected markets, the initial investment could not in many cases have been justified by private companies. Without external debt finance, the funds to expand production rapidly would not have been available to the firms. Within a protected market, the easy availability of capital and imported technology was bound to attract entrants to favored sectors.

However, MITI viewed the stampede for entry, which it had encouraged, and the resulting battle for market share, which limited profits, as excessive competition that had to be controlled. The intensive domestic competition was controlled by a variety of mechanisms that included expansion plans agreed to jointly by government and industry, debt financing of rapid expansion that made the bankruptcy of major firms a threat to the entire economy and hence unthinkable, and the oft-cited recession cartels. The dual facts of purposive government influence on economic outcomes and real market competition are reconciled by seeing the system as one of controlled or limited competition.

The very success of Japanese industrial development—combined with intensifying pressures from Japan's trading partners—has begun to loosen the network of relations that characterized the developmental state and on which the strategy of creating advantage in world markets rested. Many formal restrictions on entry to the Japanese market have been lifted. Serious trade problems still remain, however. As long as Japan had to borrow generic technologies on which to build its growth and possessed undeveloped potential markets that could be seized by domestic or foreign producers, formal closure of markets was essential to a system of orchestrated development. Now less formal obstacles to entry may matter as crucially to competition in advanced technology as formal restrictions did a generation earlier.

Japan's imports of manufactured goods remain dramatically below those of the other advanced countries, not having increased as a portion of the national economy since the early 1970s. Japan's unique trade characteristic is the tendency, relative to its trade partners, not to import manufactures in sectors in which it exports. The system of administrative guidance that affects government programs of finance and procurement, the Byzantine distribution systems, and the habits of private coordination amid competition all evolved slowly. Indeed, the Japanese state still exercises a leadership role and exerts substantial influence in high-technology industries, on the one hand, and in declining or mature industries faced with oversupply on the other.

There is a crucial interplay between these two sets of interventionist policies that is likely to continue to spark problems in international markets and enduring tensions between Japan and its trading partners. Promotional policies in which the risks of domestic oversupply are at least in part insured against or underwritten, depending on how one chooses to char-

acterize the particulars of Japanese policies, encourage bursts of investment for domestic demand that translate directly into export drives. Now that Japanese producers tie domestic investment decisions directly to world market strategies, the relationship between strategies in the Japanese market and their impact in the American market is immediate. There is a pattern of aggressive promotion of advancing sectors and of determined insulation and cushioning of mature sectors. This pattern amounts to confining open international competition in the domestic market to sectors in which major Japanese firms are dominant worldwide (or at least able to withstand foreign entry into the home market) and to sectors from which Japanese firms are absent. It implies sustaining closure in those sectors that are under pressure from abroad.

The Japanese system may slowly open and become fully integrated with its advanced-country trading partners. But other would-be Japans stand in line. The challenge of the developmental state will not pass from the contemporary scene.

TECHNOLOGICAL REVOLUTION

The second major force is a technological revolution in production that is spreading across major segments of manufacturing and services. It is built on the advent of mass application of microelectronics-based telecommunications and automatic control technologies. Its emblematics are the semiconductor, the computer, and the robot; potent combinations of these technologies are computer-aided design (CAD), computer-aided manufacturing (CAM), and computer-integrated manufacturing (CIM). Their buzzword translations into business strategy, economic policy debates, and social anxiety include computerization, flexible production, de-skilling, re-skilling, and dislocation—a second industrial revolution.

These two forces—technological change and the new scale and nature of international competition—interrelate and compound: competition drives the development of the technologies, the rates of their diffusion, and, just as important, the ways they are used. In turn, the use of these technologies is a major component of the new strategies throughout the economy for responding to foreign competition. Their combined effect is to propel America smack into the middle of an industrial transition we didn't ask for and may not be prepared to cope with terribly well.

THE ERODING COMPETITIVENESS OF AMERICAN INDUSTRY

In this era of fundamental industrial transition, American producers are not doing very well. Precisely because the changes are basic and likely to prove enduring, the outcomes of industrial competition today will matter powerfully tomorrow. The trade conflicts that have pushed their way onto the front page are not ordinary trade frictions about cars or blouses or semiconductors. They involve serious, long-term conflicts about shifting national positions in the world economy. The wealth and power of nations are the stakes. Once American firms dominated world markets; now they must adjust to them. A mere twenty years ago Europeans wrote books about the American Challenge and the Secrets of the Giant American Firms while they fretted about technology gaps and undoubted American advantages in product, production process, marketing strategy, and management techniques. Now we read about the East Asian Edge, Japan as Number One, and flexible production in Italy, while we worry about innovations in production and management coming from abroad. Unfortunately, the evidence is substantial that the American position has eroded dramatically.

Measured each of seven different ways—by unprecedented trade deficits in manufactured goods; by declining shares of world markets for exports; by lagging rates of productivity increases, eroding profit margins, and declining real wages; by the increasing price elasticities of imports; and by its eroding position in world high-technology markets—American industry confronts a severe problem of competitiveness such as it has never known before. Each measure has its limitations and can, perhaps, be explained away, but, taken together, they defy easy dismissal and portray a serious, long-term problem.

It is misleading to conclude, as many do, that America's comparative advantage in high-technology goods translates into a secure position in international trade in high technology, let alone in manufactures in general. Comparative advantage means, in the end, the thing you do less worse than you do others—not the thing at which you are better than your foreign competitors. It is misleading to conclude that, since there is no rapid "deindustrialization," the path along which American manufacturing is evolving is healthy or secure. American adjustment to the new world economy is quite troubled. Not only do statistical indi-

cators tell the story; there is something going on underneath. Japanese producers, for example, have established real competitive advantages in a range of complex manufactured products. These advantages rest on a wider diffusion of advanced technology, as in steel; on greater investment in automated production technologies, as in segments of the electronics industry; and on an approach to mass production which uses fewer labor hours per unit than American companies in a broad range of consumer durables from machine tools through automobiles.

Though symmetry is the organizing principle of economic theory, as many students learned practicing origami in Economics 101, it is not the organizing principle of international competition. Temporary disequilibria, brought about by superficial causes—as the overvaluation of the dollar is generally treated—can have profound and enduring consequences. Foreign companies that establish sales, distribution networks, and even brand recognition in the U.S. market will tend to hold them as the dollar declines. The superprofits garnered by foreign industries as a result of the dollar's high have in many cases been used for reinvestment in more efficient production that will generate a competitive edge in the years to come. It is perhaps worth noting that, when the dollar rose by almost 50 percent between 1980 and 1984, the prices of imported goods declined by only 2 percent. That means—despite what we are regularly told—it is not so much the U.S. consumer who has benefited from the high dollar as much as foreign producers, middlemen, and retailers [*New York Times*, December 9, 1985].

Similarly, U.S. corporations that moved production to offshore factories during a period of a high dollar will not necessarily move their facilities home when the dollar falls. Indeed, as we argue below, the move abroad to find cheap labor may preclude a strategy of sustained production innovation at home. The moves made during the era of the superdollar may thus have more than long-term locational consequences. They adversely affect the strategic choices of firms as well. Such traditional notions as symmetrical effects and rubber-band responses, in which the system goes back to the predisturbance equilibrium, are inappropriate organizing principles. Strategic choices made in response to one set of factors—often relatively small factors—can have consequences that are not likely to be reversible and that are far greater in scale than what caused them.

AMERICAN ADJUSTMENTS TO CHANGE

The key to American adjustment to a transforming world economy and an evolving technology may prove to be the capacity to remain, or, better still, become once again, competitive in manufacturing processes. This can be seen clearly by considering the international market pressures to which firms and industries must respond and the technologies to which they must adapt. First, the low-cost labor of the newly industrializing countries has permitted firms in those nations to penetrate the markets of the advanced countries. In labor-intensive goods that are sold on the basis of low cost, advanced-country producers cannot compete without protection or basic strategic shifts. They must either reorganize production, making labor-intensive production into a game of automation, or alter their mix of products and, with it, marketing and corporate strategies.

Second, in consumer-durables industries such as autos and televisions, competitive advantage rests on the mastery of complex manufacturing processes, as well as on distinct product and marketing strategies. Those processes are being revolutionized by microelectronics. Finally, in advanced-technology sectors, the ability to implement new engineering and scientific knowledge in products and production is critical. The basic science and much of the generic engineering concepts used in these industries are in the public domain. The ability to commercialize these ideas successfully and to produce the products competitively is the basis of advantage.

American producers over recent years have moved their production offshore, not simply to be closer to their foreign markets, but to find inexpensive labor and components to reduce the cost of products they sell in the United States. Offshore production has been spawned both by the pressure of imports and by competition among American firms. It has been sustained by policy both in the United States and in the countries where export platforms have been located. Recently, some American firms have found another reason to move production abroad. They have sought to escape some of the consequences of the high value of the U.S. dollar.

The move abroad is cumulative; that is, it builds on itself in two ways. First, an offshore production network that is a real alternative to a domestic net has been built up. When the first producers went abroad they had to supply many of the component parts and production

services from an American base. Their suppliers often moved offshore with them, to be closer to the point of final production and to capture some of the same advantages of aid and low-cost labor. Foreign component makers also began to supply American offshore producers. For example, the American semiconductor industry has found that, when their clients move offshore, they begin to buy components from offshore sources as well. In some cases American firms have subcontracted their production abroad, transferring the product and production know-how. This has often speeded the emergence of their own competitors. In fact, once component sources are offshore there is often a temptation to move product assembly offshore; as product assembly moves, additional moves offshore of component suppliers are again encouraged. Once the bulk of production is offshore, there comes a moment when it is seriously tempting to move product engineering abroad. This is not fanciful. We have heard such discussions in American firms. Let us be clear, though—the move offshore gives a one time labor-cost advantage. Production innovation and investment in capital offshore is required to sustain that advantage.

Second, after years of moving abroad to find cheap labor to produce existing products at lower costs, American firms build up an expertise in the management of offshore production. They do not build up an expertise in managing the implementation of the most advanced production technologies or in designing or redesigning a product to facilitate automated production in the United States. Over time, the perception that foreign competition could be met by offshore production took form and force. Even a few years ago, when it was already evident that the Japanese had massively invested in production, some in the semiconductor industry were still calling for more offshore locations as an effective response. Some major corporations have built formal models to set a framework for these choices, but the models (in our view) are built on quite incorrect assumptions about exchange rates and learning curves that serve simply to justify their biases.

We do not intend to exaggerate. There are many goods or pieces of production processes which cannot be effectively automated, which absorb enormous amounts of labor, and which have limited transportation costs. Those are clear candidates for offshore production or assembly. But as programmable automation emerges, the mix of activities which can be carried out in the United States will expand. We suggest simply that earlier moves offshore were often taken without clear attention to the possibilities of traditional automation and that the earlier moves offshore may blind firms to the possibilities and needs of automating at home.

America cannot maintain its wealth or high-wage economy by playing only the role of laboratory for the world, producing the ideas and prototypes and handling distribution, advertising, and sales in our own market, while others make the products. If we can't make the products, our technology edge will erode. After several rounds of product innovation, the innovative initiative will pass to the firms that make the products. These firms end up understanding the market and the product in a way that permits them to become the technology leader. Experience in steel, consumer electronics, and autos alone ought to convince us of this.

The proposition is simple. Lose control of the manufacturing or production process of your product and you risk losing control of both the technology and the final markets. A firm's or a nation's industry cannot survive at a substantial production disadvantage to its major competitors.

Common to these three categories of competition is the importance of manufacturing processes in retaining industrial competitiveness. The revolution in manufacturing is as important as the more often noted acceleration in the pace of product innovation. When pressed by low-cost producers, American companies can sometimes transform a labor-intensive production process into one that is technology-intensive. This, of course, involves substantial displacement of labor, a reorganization of the labor which remains, and changes in corporate habits. Sharp dislocations of workers and communities have generally produced political trouble that disrupts the adjustment process. Competitive position over time, in a broad range of products such as consumer durables, rests squarely on the ability to master the most advanced manufacturing techniques. Even in the so-called haven of high technology, the long-run competitiveness of firms and the national economy rests on translating product advantage into an enduring market position through manufacturing expertise. Manufacturing expertise is critical in this period of fundamental change in production processes. The central capacity required to remain competitive will prove to be dynamic flexibility—the capacity to adjust rapidly to new market and production conditions. That flexibility will turn on corporate strategies and structures, the capacities of the people throughout the production system, and the national technological infrastructure

that will develop and diffuse new production technologies and approaches.

STATIC AND DYNAMIC FLEXIBILITY

The distinction between *static* and *dynamic* flexibility is to us critical, not the differences in techniques used to promote flexibility. *Static flexibility* means the ability of a firm to adjust its operations at any moment to shifting conditions in the market, to the rise and fall of demand, or to the changes in the mix of products the market is asking for. It implies adjustment within a fixed product and production structure. Flexibility has come to mean a whole variety of ways of adjusting company operations to the shifting conditions of the market. The term is used to refer to the ability of a firm efficiently to vary its strategic direction, level of production, composition of goods, length of the workday or week, level of wages, organization of work, or any of a variety of other elements of operations.

The techniques needed to achieve flexibility can thus be technological or organizational. Firms may employ new programmable machine tools to increase the efficiency of batch production, or they may reach an agreement with unions to reduce the number of job categories. The reduction in the number of job categories in the New United Motors (the GM-Toyota venture in Fremont, California) permits easier changes on the shop floor. American Airlines announces it is reducing the number of full-time employees in many airports, by shifting to part-time personnel in order to increase its operational flexibility. A worker buy-out of a steel plant in Weirton, West Virginia, permits a wage reduction, with the workers accepting "wage flexibility" because they have a stake in the company profits. In static terms—that is, at any given moment—increased flexibility means greater capacity to adjust to short-term market changes. Static flexibility consequently decreases risk that the firm won't be able to adapt to changes in the market; it increases the ability to adapt quickly to changed conditions.

Dynamic flexibility, by contrast, means the ability to increase productivity steadily through improvements in production processes and innovation in product. Burton Klein presents the notion well. He argues that Japanese firms, and auto firms originally, "have evolved a practice that can be described as dynamic flexibility . . . ; contrasted with static flexibility, dynamic flexibility is not concerned with producing more than one product (e.g., cars and light trucks) on single production lines—

although the Japanese do this too. Rather it is concerned with designing production lines in a way that they can quickly evolve in response to changes in either the product or production technology. In other words, the central pre-occupation is to get ideas into action quickly . . . [In practice in Japan] the main purpose of dynamic flexibility is to make rapid changes in production technology for the purpose of lowering costs and thereby improving productivity." We agree with Klein that "continuing productivity gains presuppose advances in relevant technologies and a keen desire to make good use of this progress." All studies of postwar economic growth in the advanced countries highlight the fact that technological advance, not the simple increase in the number of machines or the amount of capital or labor employed, is at the core of sustained increases in productivity and economic development. Indeed, productivity advances have waned in the years after drops in research and development expenditures. Increased productivity permits lowered costs or, depending on the response of competitors, higher wages and profits.

Dynamic flexibility is the corporate capacity to develop and introduce these technological advances. A commitment to such flexibility in Japan is reflected in the structure of the market for computer-controlled manufacturing equipment. In Japan many firms internally develop their own production equipment. Almost every Japanese auto company has a large machine tool operation in which 200 to 400 people do nothing but create new tools, which are quickly introduced into the production process. When successful, these machines are often sold on the market. In Japan as a consequence the machine tool market is highly fragmented, that is, it is shared among many producers who are developing equipment for their own internal purposes and then selling it on the open market. In the United States, where less development of production equipment occurs internally, the market for programmable machine tools is highly concentrated, that is, shared among a few big producers. The result, which we return to, is that American firms tend to introduce production innovations periodically, moving from one plateau of best practice to another. The Japanese, studies suggest, move through continuous and iterative production innovation, steadily improving the production process. In fact, the Japanese system, with greater flexibility, has achieved greater productivity gains over the last years than the more rigid American one.

Technological advance inherently involves risk; new ideas may not work in practice or may not work as well as hoped. Consequently, dynamic flexibility involves a management of levels of risk sufficient to match what competitors are doing. Levels of risk, Klein argues, vary from industry to industry. A norm emerges within a given sector. In part, this is a product of the possibilities inherent in the technologies of the moment. If the potential returns are very high and the risk relatively low, one or another firm in a sector may take the risk of product development. In addition, the risk norm, the propensity to engage in risk, depends on the intensity of competition in the industry. In the United States, in our view, firms in many oligopolistic sectors had established a low norm of technological risk that was part of a competitive truce or at least a corporate Geneva convention about the terms of civilized combat that reduced the need to take risks. American firms in a variety of sectors suddenly confronted competitors from foreign sectors where the norms of risk—partly a reflection of the pace of development—were higher. American firms were caught off balance, and the results are evident.

Static and dynamic flexibility are inextricably linked. Static flexibility to short-term shifts in market conditions can be achieved in a variety of ways; how it is achieved will affect the long-term capacity of the firm to introduce the evolving technology on which its product and production position depend. A decision to move production offshore may be taken because it will allow lower wages and/or because it will make it easier to shut plants during downturns. The move offshore, it seems to us, makes it harder to improve steadily the production process itself. When managers decide to reduce skill levels in domestic plants, aimed at reducing skilled-worker resistance to technological development, they may eliminate the very skilled workers required to implement effectively new production technologies. In a similar vein, firms may have to choose between short-term economies of scale, which involve large fixed costs in the form of investment in equipment, and the long-term necessity of responding to evolving technologies, which may involve smaller and less efficient plants. Japanese and American firms have made different choices. Japanese plants for producing cars are only about one-third as large as comparable American plants, ostensibly to permit greater dynamic flexibility.

A period of economic transition is a time when "dynamic flexibility" is of predominant importance. Our contention is that the crucial change now is the

540   *Part Four / The Politics of Public Policy-Making*

transformation of manufacturing, not the replacement of industry by service. The transformation of manufacturing does not simply mean that a few "sunrise" manufacturing sectors, such as personal computers, are assuming the importance once held by certain traditional manufacturing sectors, such as automobiles. Rather, as we shall see in a moment, computers have begun to alter the production process throughout industry. The transformation is occurring because the new high-technology sectors are agents of change, sources of innovation, within the traditional sectors. Much of "high technology" really consists of producer goods—goods used to make other products. As individuals we do not buy a bag of silicon chips—we buy the products that incorporate semiconductors, or we buy products that incorporate semiconductors that have been made by machines that also incorporate those omnipresent chips. We do not buy high-speed computers or mainframe computers—we buy products that are developed or processed on those machines. It is for aircraft design and now automobile design that supercomputers are purchased, while the insurance industry long ago became a dominant buyer of mainframe computers and even minicomputers. The proper object of our concern should be how the new technologies spread throughout the economy as a part of a national response to changing competition. We must have a national economy that can absorb and apply the new technologies.

POLICY CHOICE FOR CHANGE

America has a choice. Our economic and indeed our technological future will be a product of political decisions. It is not simply a choice of whether we do well or badly, but of the kind of society that the economy we create can support.

The need for choice is urgent, for America is not adjusting well to the changing world economy. The evidence is overwhelming that our competitive position in international markets has eroded. We are displaying rigidity where flexibility is required. Even the credibility of the counterarguments that the problem is centrally one of exchange rates or that it can be managed by increasing service exports is crumbling. Furthermore, many of the debates are simply formulated poorly. It is not a matter of deindustrialization, of whether American industry disappears or not. It is a matter of the composition of the manufacturing base. For example, we have been happy exporting capital

goods to developing nations and importing the finished product made with those machines on the grounds (correct, we believe) that America should position itself in the segments of industry that can sustain high wages. Should we be equally content with the fact that America now imports the high value-added textile and apparel machinery built in Europe and Japan with high-wage labor to produce low value-added textiles and apparel produced with low-wage labor? And how should we feel about imports now taking more than 50 percent of our market for advanced machine tools—far more than that if we omit protected sales to defense contractors.

The task is to assure a dynamic adjustment to shifting market and technological conditions that will sustain our high-wage economy. We must sustain the ability to generate and apply product and process innovation. It is not just a matter of innovation, but of the ability to exploit innovation in the market. Technology diffuses quickly, capturing few rents when sold to licensees. The lessons of the last few years make that very clear. Using technological innovation to create and hold market positions for entire industries requires a deep and broad effort. Technology spreads quickly, leaving few advantages through the simple creation of scientific or technological knowledge or investment in simple machines. Thus, all depends on how knowledge is used throughout the economy. And this use rests in the end on investment in people, or human capital, not narrowly, in engineers or scientists—though certainly they are needed—but broadly, in the community as a whole.

Our policy problem is not a matter of capturing gains from others, but of assuring our own abilities to participate fully in the possibilities of the new economy that is emerging. Policy can expand our capacity to make the multiplicity of adjustments that will be required. It can help to upgrade a nation's position in international competition in a substantial and enduring way. Like much in economic reality, but little in economic theory, the relationship is not symmetrical. Policy, all by itself, can hold back an economy that has almost everything going for it; Argentina is a recurring reminder. But policy, however enlightened and astute, can (by itself) only contribute to the upgrading process. It can't do it alone. But the contribution can be very important.

The thing policy is least able to do is to have *no* impact on a nation's competitive position. And that, of course, is what conventional economics sternly prescribes for it. That policy cannot simply go away, or be "held-harmless" in its impacts on the economy, is true not only for America, but for any complex modern society. Like it or not, government affects the economy—both as a direct economic actor (taxing, spending, and, often, doing) and as a set of all-pervasive and ever-changing rules. That truth is compounded by the fact that economic reality today consists of several large and complex economies that are all heavily policy-impacted. One nation's policies affect another nation's position. Were it achievable, policy neutrality in all nations might well be the best rule for the system as a whole (though not necessarily for any one nation in that system). In the absence of such universality, policy neutrality loses any claim for being the best rule for any particular nation.

WHAT ABOUT COMPARATIVE ADVANTAGE?

These thoughts take us right into another core notion that has shaped our policy debate, the forbidding doctrine of comparative advantage, remembered by the millions who once took Economics 101, in rather the same way Latin declensions are remembered by their parents. Revealed comparative advantage, to give it its full name, is the economic doctrine that addresses foreign trade. It tells a nation what its economy will specialize in: the British (because they wrote the text) in manufacturing textiles; the Iberians (because they believed it and lost) in port wine. A nation should, and will, find itself specializing in those activities in which it is the most efficient (or least inefficient) compared to all the others. Having a comparative advantage in something (say, machinery, or, better yet, complex manufacturing) does not mean that you are a world-class winner at it, or even better than the other guy. It means that you are just less worse at it than you are at other things. Your wage level tells you how good you are.

The American policy debate on trade is formulated by the prevalent view of comparative advantage in American economics. Our policy choices are framed by the notion that comparative advantage is revealed, not created. A nation finds its comparative advantage by looking backward in the trade statistics. It does not choose it by looking forward in its policy councils. Policy should not try to create comparative advantage. We are constantly told that nations who subsidize exports are only deluding themselves and, at the same time, subsidizing their consumers. Pull away the sub-

sidy and things will rubber-band back to "normal." Enduring comparative advantage cannot be created by policy.

It is of course true that in a strict, definitional sense comparative advantage cannot be created. But saying that is a little like saying, as the economists do, that foreign trade will always balance out. Prices simply need time and freedom to adjust. That is true, but nugatory. If, for example, we were to let the price of the dollar adjust to the point where one dollar equaled one yen, we could sell the entire economics building at the University of Chicago, brick by brick, to the Japanese to use as disco space. The trick is not to balance trade; it is to balance trade at a high wage level. Similarly, we always have a comparative advantage in something. That is the way the thing is defined. The interesting question is, in what? Can we keep our comparative advantage in activities that pay a high wage? Government policy, we argue, can to a significant degree move the list of favorable activities upward (or downward).

THE ECONOMIC FUTURE

In brief, the outcome of America's passage through the industrial transition need not be exclusively the affair of impersonal and imperturbable technological and economic forces. There is room for choice and action. That is the good news. The bad news is contained in that same sentence: there is room—and need—for choice. Just because we have a choice about our future does not mean that we will take advantage of that opportunity, use it well, and even enjoy the freedom and responsibility choice provides. We have a political system we cherish, one that is artfully constructed to avoid clear choices. And we have an economic ideology, based on a notion of choice, that minimizes the opportunity and desirability of making important, strategic choices.

There is a spectrum of possible economic futures open to us. At one end lies an internationally competitive U.S. economy in which highly productive, educated workers use new technologies flexibly to produce a broad range of high value-added goods and services. They thereby earn the high wages necessary to sustain both the standard of living to which many Americans have grown accustomed and to which most aspire, and the open society that has been so closely linked with a strong and open economy. At the other end of the spectrum lies the real danger of a competitively weakened economy in which a small minority of high-skilled jobs coexists with a majority of low-skilled, low-wage jobs and massive unemployment. Living standards—perhaps along with social equality and political democracy—would deteriorate rapidly as, in order to compete, manufacturing and services move more and more value-added operations offshore and automation strips the labor content from the remaining U.S. facilities and processes.

The industrial and trade transition sets an agenda of certain change, but there is nothing inevitable about the outcome.